GREAT AMERICAN
FAVORITE
BRAND NAME
COOKBOOK

Collector's Edition

PUBLICATIONS INTERNATIONAL, LTD.

Cover photography by Sacco Productions Limited/Chicago.

ISBN: 1-56173-798-4

Library of Congress Catalog Card Number: 92-61806

Pictured on the front cover (clockwise from bottom left): Sour Cherry Pie
(*page 467*), Almond Macaroon Brownies (*page 438*), Chocolate Cherry Cookies
(*page 408*), Linzer Hearts (*page 419*), Triple Chocolate Fantasy (*page 505*), Moroccan
Tomato Dip with Pita Chips (*page 9*), Spinach Salad with Raspberry Dressing (*page 94*),
Holiday Beef Steaks with Vegetable Saute and Hot Mustard Sauce (*page 152*), Seafood
Primavera (*page 314*) and Cornish Hens with Almond Brown Rice Stuffing (*page 344*).

Pictured on the back cover (clockwise from top left): Rio Grande Quesadillas
(*page 224*), Sesame Pork with Broccoli (*page 178*) and Patriotic Pie (*page 462*).

8   7   6   5   4   3   2   1

Manufactured in U.S.A.

Microwave ovens vary in wattage and power output; cooking times given with microwave
directions in this book may need to be adjusted. Consult manufacturer's instructions for
suitable microwave-safe cooking dishes.

CONTENTS

Your Guide to Great Cooking

GREAT AMERICAN FAVORITE BRAND NAME COOKBOOK: COLLECTOR'S EDITION is just that—the largest collection of America's brand name recipes in one convenient source. Clipping recipes from food labels has become an American tradition and now you can collect all your favorites in this marvelous compilation of over 1600 outstanding recipes—without your scissors.

The kitchen, once again, is becoming the heart of the home—a place to gather with family and friends for fabulous meals. With this trend comes the desire for the wholesome goodness of home-cooked meals. But with busy life-styles, cooks today want easy-to-follow recipes suitable for everyday or for entertaining. The GREAT AMERICAN FAVORITE BRAND NAME COOKBOOK: COLLECTOR'S EDITION will bring fresh ideas into your kitchen with little effort for the cook.

With the busy cook in mind, we've selected recipes that you can count on. Every recipe has been tested by expert home economists to assure delicious, successful results with an added bonus—the convenience of your favorite brand-name products. As you page through the book you'll see a wide variety of recipes for every occasion. We've included appetizers, beverages, soups, salads, entrées and breads. We've also devoted five chapters to tempting desserts.

For starters, you'll find tantalizing appetizers and thirst-quenching beverages including flavorful finger foods, creamy dips and spreads, sensational snacks and fruit-filled punches. We've selected exceptional soups—from elegant bisques to hearty stews—and refreshing salads—from crispy vegetable to magnificent pasta—for first courses or substantial suppers.

In addition to recipes for meat, poultry and seafood entrées, you'll find special chapters on easy one-dish meals and popular pasta with quick sauces. To begin your day on the right foot, look to the eggs, cheese and brunch or breads, muffins and coffeecakes sections for inventive morning meals. Or turn to the Pizza & Sandwiches chapter for simple lunches and midnight snacks.

And for grand finales, you won't be able to resist the incredible assortment of decadent desserts. From scrumptious cookies and candies, unbeatable pies and pastries, and delectable cakes and cheesecakes, you'll find dozens of ways to satisfy even the sweetest sweet tooth.

Just by looking at the hundreds of full-color photographs throughout the book, meal planning will be a snap. And with a collection of recipes this comprehensive, you'll always have creative ideas for all your culinary needs. So grab your apron and start cooking—and savoring—the extraordinary results!

APPETIZERS

Start every celebration off right with a wide array of tempting appetizers. You'll find creamy dips and spreads to welcome impromptu guests, fantastic finger foods for a dazzling buffet, fast-fixin' snacks for a carefree bash and impressive first-course starters for an elegant gathering. Discover dozens of ways to make any occasion a smashing success.

Layered Taco Dip

1 pound lean ground beef
1 (4-ounce) can chopped green chilies, undrained
2 teaspoons WYLER'S® or STEERO® Beef-Flavor Instant Bouillon
1 (15- or 16-ounce) can refried beans
1 (16-ounce) container BORDEN® or MEADOW GOLD® Sour Cream
1 (1.7-ounce) package taco seasoning mix
Guacamole
Garnishes: Shredded Cheddar or Monterey Jack cheese, chopped tomatoes, sliced green onions and sliced ripe olives
LA FAMOUS® Tortilla Chips

In large skillet, brown beef; pour off fat. Add chilies and bouillon; cook and stir until bouillon dissolves. Cool. Stir in refried beans. In small bowl, combine sour cream and taco seasoning; set aside. In 7- or 8-inch springform pan or on large plate, spread beef mixture. Top with sour cream mixture and guacamole. Cover; chill several hours. Just before serving, remove side of springform pan. Garnish with cheese, tomatoes, green onions and olives. Serve with tortilla chips. Refrigerate leftovers.
Makes 12 to 15 servings

GUACAMOLE: In small bowl, mash 3 ripe avocados, pitted and peeled. Add ¾ cup chopped fresh tomato, 2 tablespoons REALIME® Lime Juice from Concentrate or REALEMON® Lemon Juice from Concentrate, ½ teaspoon seasoned salt and ⅛ teaspoon garlic salt; mix well.

Spicy Dijon Dip

1 (8-ounce) package cream cheese, softened
¼ cup GREY POUPON® Dijon or Country Dijon Mustard
¼ cup dairy sour cream
1 tablespoon finely chopped scallions
1 (4¼-ounce) can tiny shrimp, drained, or ½ cup cooked shrimp, chopped
Sliced scallions, for garnish
Assorted cut-up vegetables

In small bowl, with electric mixer at medium speed, blend cream cheese, mustard, sour cream and chopped scallions; stir in shrimp. Cover; chill at least 2 hours. Garnish with sliced scallions; serve as a dip with vegetables. *Makes 1½ cups*

Guacamole Dip

½ cup MIRACLE WHIP® Salad Dressing
1 large ripe avocado, peeled, mashed
1 tomato, seeded, chopped
2 tablespoons each: chopped onion, chopped green chilies
1 teaspoon lemon or lime juice

• Mix ingredients until well blended; refrigerate. Serve with tortilla chips. *Makes 2 cups*

Prep time: 15 minutes plus refrigerating

Spicy Dijon Dip

Left to right: Spinach Dip, Cucumber Dill Dip and French Onion Dip

French Onion Dip

2 cups sour cream
½ cup HELLMANN'S® or BEST FOODS® Real, Light or Cholesterol Free Reduced Calorie Mayonnaise
1 package (1.9 ounces) KNORR® French Onion Soup and Recipe Mix

In medium bowl combine sour cream, mayonnaise and soup mix. Cover; chill. Serve with fresh vegetables or potato chips. Garnish as desired.

Makes about 2½ cups

Spinach Dip in Bread Bowl

1 cup MIRACLE WHIP® Salad Dressing
1 cup sour cream
1 package (1.4 ounces) GOOD SEASONS® Ranch Salad Dressing Mix
1 package (10 ounces) BIRDS EYE® Chopped Spinach, thawed, well drained
1 can (8 ounces) water chestnuts, drained, chopped
½ cup chopped red bell pepper
1 loaf (1½ pounds) round sourdough bread

• Mix salad dressing, sour cream and salad dressing mix until well blended. Add spinach, water chestnuts and pepper; mix well. Refrigerate.

• Cut slice from top of bread loaf; remove center leaving 1-inch-thick shell. Cut removed bread into bite-size pieces.

• Spoon spinach dip into bread loaf just before serving. Serve with bread pieces.

Makes 3¼ cups

Prep time: 15 minutes plus refrigerating

Spinach Dip

1 package (10 ounces) frozen chopped spinach, thawed and drained
1½ cups sour cream
1 cup HELLMANN'S® or BEST FOODS® Real, Light or Cholesterol Free Reduced Calorie Mayonnaise
1 package (1.4 ounces) KNORR® Vegetable Soup and Recipe Mix
1 can (8 ounces) water chestnuts, drained and chopped (optional)
3 green onions, chopped

In medium bowl combine spinach, sour cream, mayonnaise, soup mix, water chestnuts and green onions. Cover; chill. Serve with fresh vegetables, crackers or chips. Garnish as desired.

Makes about 3 cups

Cucumber Dill Dip

1 package (8 ounces) light cream cheese, softened
1 cup HELLMANN'S® or BEST FOODS® Real, Light or Cholesterol Free Reduced Calorie Mayonnaise
2 medium cucumbers, peeled, seeded and chopped
2 tablespoons sliced green onions
1 tablespoon lemon juice
2 teaspoons snipped fresh dill *or* ½ teaspoon dried dill weed
½ teaspoon hot pepper sauce

In medium bowl beat cream cheese until smooth. Stir in mayonnaise, cucumbers, green onions, lemon juice, dill and hot pepper sauce. Cover; chill. Serve with fresh vegetables, crackers or chips. Garnish as desired.

Makes about 2½ cups

Moroccan Tomato Dip

- 1 cup (8-ounce can) CONTADINA® Tomato Sauce
- ¾ cup low-sodium garbanzo beans, rinsed and drained
- ½ cup (4 ounces) nonfat plain yogurt
- 2 tablespoons minced green onion
- 1 tablespoon finely chopped parsley
- 1½ teaspoons garlic powder
- 1 teaspoon prepared horseradish
- 1 teaspoon ground cumin
- 1 teaspoon curry powder
- ½ teaspoon paprika
  Pita Chips (recipe follows)

In blender container, process tomato sauce, garbanzo beans, and yogurt until smooth and creamy. Pour into small bowl. Stir in onion, parsley, garlic powder, horseradish, cumin, curry powder, and paprika. Cover and refrigerate 8 to 24 hours to allow flavors to blend. Serve with Pita Chips or crisp vegetable dippers.

Makes 2 cups

PITA CHIPS: Cut pita bread into wedges; separate each wedge into 2 pieces. Place on cookie sheet and brush with fresh lemon juice. Sprinkle with salt-free herb mixture of your choice. Bake in preheated 375°F oven for 7 to 9 minutes or until crisp.

Creamy Slaw Dip

- 1½ cups BORDEN® or MEADOW GOLD® Sour Cream
- 1 cup finely shredded cabbage
- 1 (8-ounce) can water chestnuts, drained and finely chopped
- ⅓ cup prepared slaw dressing
- ¼ cup sliced green onions
- 2 teaspoons WYLER'S® or STEERO® Beef-Flavor Instant Bouillon
- ¼ teaspoon garlic powder

In medium bowl, combine ingredients; mix well. Cover; chill to blend flavors. Garnish as desired. Serve with Krunchers!® Potato Chips or assorted fresh vegetables if desired. Refrigerate leftovers.

Makes about 1½ cups

Taco Dip

Taco Dip

- 12 ounces cream cheese, softened
- ½ cup dairy sour cream
- 2 teaspoons chili powder
- 1½ teaspoons ground cumin
- ⅛ teaspoon ground red pepper
- ½ cup salsa
- 2 cups shredded lettuce or lettuce leaves
- 1 cup (4 ounces) shredded Wisconsin Cheddar cheese
- 1 cup (4 ounces) shredded Wisconsin Monterey Jack cheese
- ½ cup diced plum tomatoes
- ⅓ cup sliced green onions
- ¼ cup sliced ripe olives
- ¼ cup pimiento-stuffed green olives
  Tortilla and blue corn chips

Combine cream cheese, sour cream, chili powder, cumin and red pepper in large bowl; mix until well blended. Stir in salsa. Spread onto 10-inch serving platter lined with lettuce. Top with cheeses, tomatoes, green onions and olives. Serve with chips.

Makes 10 appetizer servings

Favorite recipe from Wisconsin Milk Marketing Board © 1993

Moroccan Tomato Dip

Velveeta® Salsa Dip

1 pound VELVEETA®
Pasteurized Process
Cheese Spread, cubed
1 jar (8 ounces) salsa
2 tablespoons chopped
cilantro

• In saucepan, stir VELVEETA® Pasteurized Process Cheese Spread and salsa over low heat until VELVEETA® Pasteurized Process Cheese Spread is melted. Stir in cilantro.

• Serve hot with tortilla chips or broiled green, red or yellow bell pepper wedges, if desired.

Makes 3 cups

Prep time: 10 minutes
Cooking time: 10 minutes
Microwave cooking time:
5 minutes

Microwave: • Microwave process cheese spread and salsa in 1½-quart microwave-safe bowl on HIGH 5 minutes or until VELVEETA® Pasteurized Process Cheese Spread is melted, stirring after 3 minutes. Stir in cilantro. • Serve as directed.

Variations: Substitute 1 can (14½ ounces) tomatoes, chopped, drained, for salsa.

Substitute 1 can (10 ounces) tomatoes and green chilies, chopped, drained, for salsa.

Substitute VELVEETA® Mexican Pasteurized Process Cheese Spread with Jalapeño Pepper, cubed, for VELVEETA® Pasteurized Process Cheese Spread.

Lawry's® Fiesta Dip

1 package (1.25 ounces)
LAWRY'S® Taco Spices &
Seasonings
1 pint (16 ounces) dairy sour
cream

In medium bowl, combine ingredients. Blend well. Refrigerate until ready to serve. Serve in medium-size bowls with tortilla chips and fresh cut vegetables such as carrots, broccoli, cauliflower or zucchini sticks.

Makes 2 cups

Salsa Pronto

1 can (14½ ounces)
DEL MONTE® Mexican
Style Stewed Tomatoes
¼ cup finely chopped onion
2 tablespoons chopped fresh
cilantro
2 teaspoons lemon juice
1 small clove garlic, minced
⅛ teaspoon hot pepper
sauce*
Tortilla chips

Place tomatoes in blender container. Cover and process on low 2 seconds to chop tomatoes. Combine with onion, cilantro, lemon juice, garlic and pepper sauce. Add additional pepper sauce, if desired. Serve with tortilla chips.   *Makes 2 cups*

*Substitute minced jalapeño to taste for hot pepper sauce.

Zesty Shrimp Dip

¼ cup mayonnaise or salad
dressing
1 (8-ounce) container
BORDEN® or MEADOW
GOLD® Sour Cream
¼ cup BENNETT'S® Cocktail
Sauce
1 (4¼-ounce) can ORLEANS®
Shrimp, drained and
soaked as label directs
2 tablespoons sliced green
onion
1 teaspoon REALEMON®
Lemon Juice from
Concentrate

In small bowl, combine ingredients; mix well. Chill. Serve with assorted fresh vegetables or potato chips. Refrigerate leftovers.

Makes about 2 cups dip

Velveeta® Salsa Dip

Clockwise from top left: Zesty Shrimp Dip, Layered Crab Spread (page 24) and Deviled Clam Mushrooms (page 26)

Black Bean Dip

1 can (15 ounces) black
    beans, rinsed, drained
½ cup MIRACLE WHIP®
    FREE® Dressing
½ cup reduced calorie sour
    cream
1 can (4 ounces) chopped
    green chilies, drained
2 tablespoons chopped
    cilantro
1 teaspoon chili powder
½ teaspoon garlic powder
    Few drops of hot pepper
    sauce

• Mash beans with fork. Stir in remaining ingredients until well blended; refrigerate. Serve with tortilla chips.

Makes 2¼ cups

Prep time: 10 minutes plus refrigerating

Dijon Pesto & Cheese

½ cup chopped parsley
⅓ cup GREY POUPON® Dijon
    or Country Dijon Mustard
¼ cup walnuts, chopped
¼ cup grated Parmesan
    cheese
2 teaspoons dried basil
    leaves
2 cloves garlic, crushed
3 (3-ounce) packages cream
    cheese, well chilled
    Assorted NABISCO®
    Crackers
    Roasted red peppers and
    basil leaves, for garnish

In electric blender container, blend parsley, mustard, walnuts, Parmesan cheese, basil and garlic; set aside.

Roll each square of cream cheese between 2 sheets of waxed paper to an 8×4-inch rectangle. Place 1 cheese rectangle in plastic wrap-lined 8½×4½×2½-inch loaf pan; top with half the parsley mixture. Repeat layers, ending with remaining cheese rectangle. Chill at least 2 hours. Remove from pan; slice and serve on crackers garnished with peppers and basil if desired.

Makes 32 servings

Cucumber Canapés

1 cup cooked rice, cooled to
    room temperature
1 large fresh tomato, peeled
    and diced
½ cup chopped fresh parsley
⅓ cup sliced green onions
¼ cup chopped fresh mint
2 cloves garlic, minced
3 tablespoons plain nonfat
    yogurt*
1 tablespoon lemon juice
1 tablespoon olive oil
¼ teaspoon ground white
    pepper
2 to 3 large cucumbers,
    peeled

Combine rice, tomato, parsley, onions, mint, garlic, yogurt, lemon juice, oil, and pepper in large bowl. Cover and chill. Cut each cucumber crosswise into ½-inch slices; hollow out center of each slice, leaving bottom intact. Fill each cucumber slice with scant tablespoon rice mixture.

Makes about 3 dozen canapés

*Substitute low-fat sour cream for yogurt, if desired.

Favorite recipe from **USA Rice Council**

Horseradish Sauce

½ cup MIRACLE WHIP® Salad
    Dressing
2 tablespoons chili sauce
1 tablespoon KRAFT®
    Prepared Horseradish

• Mix ingredients until well blended; refrigerate. Serve with chilled cooked shrimp.

Makes ¾ cup

Prep time: 5 minutes plus refrigerating

Horseradish Sauce

Cracked Black Pepper and Herb Spread

1 package (8 ounces) cream cheese, softened
6 ounces goat cheese (Montrachet, Chèvre or feta)
¼ cup WISH-BONE® Italian Dressing
½ cup chopped red onion
1 teaspoon fresh chopped thyme leaves*
1 teaspoon fresh chopped sage leaves**
1 teaspoon cracked black pepper

In food processor or blender, process all ingredients until blended; cover and chill. Garnish, if desired, with additional cracked black pepper and serve with assorted fresh vegetables, crackers and breads.
Makes about 2 cups spread.
  Substitution: Use ½ teaspoon dried thyme leaves.
  ****Substitution:*** Use ½ teaspoon dried sage leaves.
  Note: Also terrific with Wish-Bone® Robusto Italian, Blended Italian, Lite Italian or Lite Classic Dijon Vinaigrette Dressing.

Quick Paté Mold

½ pound liverwurst, cut into small pieces
1 (8-ounce) package cream cheese, softened
2 tablespoons finely chopped onion
1 teaspoon WYLER'S® or STEERO® Chicken-Flavor Instant Bouillon
Parsley, optional
Melba rounds

In small mixer bowl, combine liverwurst, cheese, onion and bouillon; beat until smooth. Turn into well-oiled 2-cup mold. Chill. Unmold; garnish with parsley if desired. Serve with Melba rounds. Refrigerate leftovers.
Makes 1 appetizer mold.

Guacamole

3 ripe medium avocados, seeded and peeled
2 tablespoons REALIME® Lime Juice from Concentrate *or* REALEMON® Lemon Juice from Concentrate
½ teaspoon garlic salt
½ teaspoon sugar
¼ teaspoon pepper

In blender container or food processor, mash avocados. Add remaining ingredients; mix well. Chill to blend flavors. Garnish as desired. Serve with WISE® BRAVOS® or LA FAMOUS® Tortilla Chips or fresh vegetables. Refrigerate leftovers.
Makes about 2 cups.
  Variations: Add 1 or more of the following: sour cream, cooked crumbled bacon, chopped water chestnuts, chopped fresh tomato, chopped chilies.

Hot Artichoke Dip

1 package (9 ounces) frozen artichoke hearts, thawed
½ pint (8 ounces) sour cream
¼ cup grated Parmesan cheese
1 envelope LIPTON® Recipe Secrets Golden Onion Recipe Soup Mix
Buttered bread crumbs
Suggested Dippers*

Preheat oven to 350°.
  In food processor or blender, puree artichokes. Add sour cream and cheese; process until smooth. Stir in golden onion recipe soup mix. Turn into 2½-cup casserole, then top with bread crumbs. Bake uncovered 30 minutes or until heated through. Serve with Suggested Dippers.
Makes about 2¼ cups dip.
  Suggested Dippers: Use carrot or celery sticks, whole mushrooms or sliced zucchini.
  Microwave Directions: Omit bread crumbs. Prepare mixture as above. Microwave at HIGH (Full Power), turning casserole occasionally, 8 minutes or until heated through. Let stand covered 5 minutes. Serve as above.

Nutty Blue Cheese Vegetable Dip

1 cup mayonnaise or salad dressing
1 (8-ounce) container BORDEN® or MEADOW GOLD® Sour Cream
¼ cup (1 ounce) crumbled blue cheese
1 tablespoon finely chopped onion
2 teaspoons WYLER'S® or STEERO® Beef-Flavor Instant Bouillon
½ to ¾ cup coarsely chopped walnuts
Assorted fresh vegetables

In medium bowl, combine mayonnaise, sour cream, blue cheese, onion and bouillon; mix well. Stir in nuts; cover and chill. Stir before serving. Garnish as desired. Serve with vegetables. Refrigerate leftovers.
Makes about 2 cups.

Colorful Carrot Dip

1 8-ounce package Light PHILADELPHIA BRAND® Neufchatel Cheese, softened
½ cup finely shredded carrot
1 teaspoon parsley flakes
⅛ teaspoon salt
Dash of pepper

Combine Neufchatel cheese, carrots and seasonings, mixing until well blended. Chill. Serve with vegetable dippers.
1 cup.
  Variations: Substitute freeze-dried chopped chives for parsley flakes.
  Substitute ½ teaspoon dried basil leaves, crushed, for parsley flakes.
  Substitute ¼ teaspoon dill weed or lemon pepper for parsley flakes.

Colorful Carrot Dip

Garden Vegetable Spread

1 8-ounce container Soft
   PHILADELPHIA BRAND®
   Cream Cheese
1/2 cup shredded carrot
1/2 cup shredded zucchini
1 tablespoon chopped parsley
1/4 teaspoon garlic salt
   Dash of pepper

Combine ingredients; mix well. Chill. Serve with party rye or pumpernickel bread slices or assorted crackers. *1 1/3 cups.*

Variation: Serve with LENDER'S® Pre-Sliced Frozen Plain Bagelettes, toasted.

Florentine Dip

1 8-ounce package Light
   PHILADELPHIA BRAND®
   Neufchatel Cheese, softened
1/2 cup plain yogurt
2 tablespoons milk
1 10-ounce package frozen
   spinach, thawed, well-
   drained, chopped
2 hard-cooked eggs, finely
   chopped
1/4 teaspoon pepper
1/4 teaspoon salt

Combine Neufchatel cheese, yogurt and milk, mixing until well blended. Stir in remaining ingredients. Serve with vegetable dippers. *2 1/2 cups.*

Hot Crabmeat Appetizer

1 8-ounce package
   PHILADELPHIA BRAND®
   Cream Cheese, softened
1 7 1/2-ounce can crabmeat,
   drained, flaked
2 tablespoons finely chopped
   onion
2 tablespoons milk
1/2 teaspoon KRAFT® Cream Style
   Horseradish
1/4 teaspoon salt
   Dash of pepper
1/3 cup sliced almonds, toasted

Combine all ingredients except almonds, mixing until well blended. Spoon mixture into 9-inch pie plate; sprinkle with almonds. Bake at 375°, 15 minutes. Serve with crackers. *Approximately 1 1/2 cups.*

Variations: Substitute 8-ounce can minced clams, drained, for crabmeat.

Omit almonds; sprinkle with dill weed.

Warm Herb Cheese Spread

3 (8-ounce) packages cream
   cheese, softened
1/4 cup BORDEN® or MEADOW
   GOLD® Milk
1/4 cup REALEMON® Lemon Juice
   from Concentrate
1/2 teaspoon *each* basil, oregano,
   marjoram and thyme leaves
1/4 teaspoon garlic powder
1/2 pound cooked shrimp,
   chopped (1 1/2 cups), optional

Preheat oven to 350°. In large mixer bowl, beat cheese until smooth. Gradually beat in milk then ReaLemon® brand. Stir in remaining ingredients. Pour into 9-inch quiche dish or pie plate. Cover; bake 15 minutes or until hot. Garnish as desired. Serve warm with crackers or fresh vegetables. Refrigerate leftovers.
Makes about 4 cups.

Microwave: In 9-inch pie plate, prepare cheese spread as above. Cook on 50% power (medium) 5 to 6 minutes or until hot. Stir before serving.

Hot Beef Dip

1/4 cup chopped onion
1 tablespoon PARKAY®
   Margarine
1 cup milk
1 8-ounce package
   PHILADELPHIA BRAND®
   Cream Cheese, cubed
1 3-ounce package smoked
   sliced beef, chopped
1 4-ounce can mushrooms,
   drained
1/4 cup (1 ounce) KRAFT® 100%
   Grated Parmesan Cheese
2 tablespoons chopped parsley

Saute onions in margarine. Add milk and cream cheese; stir over low heat until cream cheese is melted. Add remaining ingredients; heat thoroughly, stirring occasionally. Serve hot with French bread slices, if desired.
2 1/2 cups.

Variation: Substitute 2 1/2-ounce package smoked sliced turkey for 3-ounce package smoked sliced beef.

Serving Suggestion: For a colorful variety, serve with French, whole-wheat or rye bread cubes.

Florentine Dip

Savory Cheddar Spread

**1 8-ounce package
PHILADELPHIA BRAND®
Cream Cheese, softened**
**½ cup MIRACLE WHIP® Salad
Dressing**
**1 cup (4 ounces) 100% Natural
KRAFT® Shredded Mild
Cheddar Cheese**
**2 tablespoons green onion
slices**
**8 crisply cooked bacon slices,
crumbled**
½ cup crushed buttery crackers

Combine cream cheese and salad dressing, mixing until well blended. Add cheddar cheese and onions; mix well. Spoon into 9-inch pie plate; sprinkle with combined bacon and crumbs. Bake at 350°, 15 minutes. Serve with additional crackers.
2 cups.

Variation: Substitute ¼ cup bacon flavored bits for crumbled bacon.

Microwave: Microwave cream cheese on Medium (50%) 30 seconds. Assemble recipe as directed except for sprinkling with bacon and crumbs. Microwave on High 4 minutes or until thoroughly heated, turning dish every 2 minutes. Sprinkle with combined bacon and crumbs. Serve as directed.

Refreshing Cucumber Dip

**1 8-ounce package
PHILADELPHIA BRAND®
Cream Cheese, softened**
½ cup sour cream
1 tablespoon milk
1 teaspoon grated onion
**¼ teaspoon worcestershire
sauce**
⅓ cup finely chopped cucumber

Combine all ingredients except cucumbers, mixing until well blended. Stir in cucumbers. Chill several hours or overnight. Serve with chips or vegetable dippers.
1⅔ cups.

Pineapple-Almond Cheese Spread

**2 cans (8 ounces each) DOLE®
Crushed Pineapple in Juice**
**1 package (8 ounces) cream
cheese, softened**
**4 cups shredded sharp Cheddar
cheese**
½ cup mayonnaise
1 tablespoon soy sauce
**1 cup DOLE® Chopped Natural
Almonds, toasted**
**½ cup finely chopped DOLE®
Green Bell Pepper**
**¼ cup minced green onion or
chives**
**DOLE® Celery stalks or
assorted breads**

Drain pineapple. In large bowl, beat cream cheese until smooth; beat in Cheddar cheese, mayonnaise and soy sauce until smooth. Stir in pineapple, almonds, green pepper and onion. Refrigerate, covered. Use to stuff celery stalks or serve as dip with assorted breads. Serve at room temperature.
Makes 4 cups.

Hawaiian Coconut Spread

**1 8-ounce container Soft
PHILADELPHIA BRAND®
Cream Cheese**
**2 tablespoons KRAFT® Apricot,
Pineapple or Peach
Preserves**
⅓ cup flaked coconut

Combine cream cheese and preserves, mixing until well blended. Add coconut; mix well. Chill. Serve with nut bread slices.
1⅓ cups.

Variations: Add ⅛ teaspoon anise seed.

Substitute ¼ cup whole berry cranberry sauce for KRAFT® Preserves.

Zucchini Chive Dip

**1 8-ounce container Soft
PHILADELPHIA BRAND®
Cream Cheese**
3 tablespoons milk
1 small zucchini, shredded
3 tablespoons chopped chives
⅛ teaspoon salt

Combine cream cheese and milk, mixing until well blended. Add remaining ingredients; mix well. Chill. Serve with vegetable dippers or chips.
1 cup.

Quick Mexican Spread

**1 8-ounce package Light
PHILADELPHIA BRAND®
Neufchatel Cheese, softened**
**1 4-ounce can chopped green
chilies, drained**

Combine Neufchatel cheese and chilies, mixing until well blended. Chill. Serve with tortilla chips or spread over warm tortillas or corn bread.
1 cup.

Piña Pepper Spread

**1 can (8 ounces) DOLE®
Crushed Pineapple in Juice,
drained**
½ cup bottled taco sauce
**1 package (8 ounces) cream
cheese, softened**
Taco chips or crackers

Combine pineapple and taco sauce in small bowl. Place cream cheese on serving plate in block or cut into individual servings. Spoon pineapple mixture over top. Serve with taco chips or crackers.
Makes 4 servings.

Piña Pepper Spread

Mustard Sauce

2 tablespoons CRISCO® Oil
2 tablespoons all-purpose flour
2 tablespoons dry mustard
½ teaspoon salt
1 cup milk

Blend Crisco® Oil, flour, mustard and salt in small saucepan. Cook over medium-high heat 1 minute. Stir in milk. Cook, stirring constantly, until sauce thickens and bubbles.
About 1 cup.

Salmon Mousse

2 envelopes KNOX® Unflavored Gelatine
1 can (15½ ounces) salmon, drained (reserve liquid)*
1 stalk celery, cut into 3-inch pieces
1 small onion, quartered
½ medium cucumber, peeled, seeded and quartered
1 cup (½ pint) whipping or heavy cream
¾ cup mayonnaise
¼ cup lemon juice
1 teaspoon dried dill weed
½ teaspoon salt (optional)

In medium saucepan, sprinkle unflavored gelatine over reserved salmon liquid blended with enough water to equal 1 cup; let stand 1 minute. Stir over low heat until gelatine is completely dissolved, about 5 minutes.

In blender or food processor, process gelatine mixture, vegetables, cream, mayonnaise and lemon juice until blended. Add salmon, dill and salt; process until blended. Pour into 6-cup mold or bowl; chill until firm, about 3 hours. Unmold and serve with assorted crackers.
Makes about 5½ cups spread.
   *Substitution: Use 2 cans (6½ ounces each) tuna, drained (reserve liquid).

Roasted Red Pepper Mousse Spread

1 envelope KNOX® Unflavored Gelatine
½ cup cold water
2 cups (1 pint) whipping or heavy cream
1 jar (8 ounces) roasted red peppers, drained and coarsely chopped
½ cup mayonnaise
1 cup loosely packed basil leaves*
¼ cup grated Parmesan cheese
1 small clove garlic, finely chopped
½ teaspoon salt
⅛ teaspoon pepper

In small saucepan, sprinkle unflavored gelatine over cold water; let stand 1 minute. Stir over low heat until gelatine is completely dissolved, about 3 minutes. Remove from heat and let stand until lukewarm, about 2 minutes.

In large bowl, with electric mixer, beat cream until soft peaks form. Gradually add red peppers, mayonnaise, basil, cheese, garlic, salt and pepper. While beating, gradually add lukewarm gelatine mixture and beat until blended. Pour into 7-cup mold or bowl; chill until firm, about 3 hours. Unmold and serve, if desired, with sliced Italian bread, toasted.
Makes about 6 cups spread.
   *Substitution: Use 1 cup chopped fresh parsley plus 1 teaspoon dried basil leaves.

Shrimp Spread

2 (8-ounce) packages cream cheese, softened
½ cup REALEMON® Lemon Juice from Concentrate
2 (4¼-ounce) cans ORLEANS® Shrimp, drained and soaked as label directs
1 to 2 tablespoons finely chopped green onion
1 tablespoon prepared horseradish
1 teaspoon Worcestershire sauce
¼ teaspoon pepper
⅛ teaspoon garlic powder

In small mixer bowl, beat cheese until fluffy; gradually beat in ReaLemon® brand. Stir in remaining ingredients. Chill to blend flavors. Garnish as desired. Serve with crackers or fresh vegetables. Refrigerate leftovers.
Makes about 3 cups.

Shrimp Spread

Spicy Appetizer Dip

**1 (8-ounce) can crushed
     pineapple in its own juice
1 cup COLLEGE INN® Chicken or
     Beef Broth
3 tablespoons cornstarch
2 tablespoons soy sauce
2 tablespoons white wine
     vinegar
2 tablespoons firmly packed
     light brown sugar
¼ teaspoon crushed red pepper
     Cocktail franks, ham cubes or
     fresh vegetables**

Drain pineapple, reserving juice. In small saucepan, blend reserved juice, broth, cornstarch, soy sauce, vinegar, brown sugar and red pepper. Cook and stir until mixture thickens and boils. Stir in pineapple. Serve hot or cold with cocktail franks, ham cubes or vegetables.
Makes 2 cups.

Mini Monte Cristo Sandwiches

**2 tablespoons butter or
     margarine, softened
2 tablespoons prepared mustard
8 slices white bread
4 slices fontina or Swiss cheese
     (about 4 ounces)
4 slices cooked ham (about
     4 ounces)
3 eggs
½ cup milk
1 envelope LIPTON® Recipe
     Secrets Golden Onion
     Recipe Soup Mix
¼ cup butter or margarine**

Blend 2 tablespoons butter with mustard; evenly spread on each bread slice. Equally top 4 bread slices with cheese and ham; top with remaining bread, buttered side down. Cut each sandwich into 4 triangles.

Beat eggs, milk and golden onion recipe soup mix until well blended. Dip sandwiches in egg mixture, coating well.

In large skillet, melt ¼ cup butter and cook sandwiches over medium heat, turning once, until golden.
Makes about 16 mini sandwiches.

Spicy Appetizer Dip

Rumaki

**16 slices bacon
1 pound chicken livers, cut into
     quarters
1 can (8 ounces) sliced water
     chestnuts, drained
⅓ cup soy sauce
2 tablespoons packed brown
     sugar
1 tablespoon Dijon-style
     mustard**

Cut bacon slices in half crosswise. Wrap ½ slice bacon around piece of chicken liver and water chestnut slice. Secure with wooden pick. (Reserve any remaining water chestnut slices for another use.) Arrange on broiler pan. Combine soy sauce, brown sugar and mustard in small bowl. Brush over bacon rolls. Broil, 6 inches from heat, 15 to 20 minutes or until bacon is crisp and chicken livers are done, turning and brushing with soy sauce mixture occasionally.
Makes about 32 appetizers.

*Favorite recipe from **National Pork Producers Council***

Baked Cream Cheese Appetizer

**1 4-ounce package refrigerated
    crescent dinner rolls
1 8-ounce package
    PHILADELPHIA BRAND®
    Cream Cheese
½ teaspoon dill weed
1 egg yolk, beaten**

Unroll dough on lightly floured surface; press together seams to form
12×4-inch rectangle. Sprinkle top of
cream cheese with half of dill; lightly
press dill into cream cheese. Place
cream cheese, dill-side down, in center
of dough. Sprinkle cream cheese with
remaining dill. Enclose cream cheese
in dough by bringing sides of dough
together, pressing edges to seal. Place
on lightly greased cookie sheet; brush
with egg yolk. Bake at 350°, 15 to 18
minutes or until lightly browned.
Serve with assorted crackers and apple slices.
8 servings.
    Variations: Substitute combined ½
teaspoon dried rosemary leaves,
crushed, and ½ teaspoon paprika for
dill weed.
    Substitute Light PHILADELPHIA
BRAND® Neufchatel Cheese for
cream cheese.

Baked Cream Cheese Appetizer

Blue Cheese Walnut Spread

**1 envelope KNOX® Unflavored
    Gelatine
¾ cup cold water
½ cup sour cream
⅓ cup milk
1 tablespoon lemon juice
1 teaspoon Worcestershire
    sauce
4 ounces blue cheese, crumbled
1 package (8 ounces) cream
    cheese, softened
½ cup walnuts**

In small saucepan, sprinkle unflavored gelatine over ¼ cup cold water;
let stand 1 minute. Stir over low heat
until gelatine is completely dissolved,
about 3 minutes.
    In blender, process sour cream, re-
maining ½ cup water, milk, lemon
juice, Worcestershire sauce and
cheeses until blended. While processing, through feed cap, gradually add
gelatine mixture, then walnuts; process until blended. Pour into

7½×3¾×2¼-inch loaf pan or 4-cup
bowl; chill until firm, about 3 hours.
Unmold onto lettuce-lined platter and
serve, if desired, with crackers, party-
size breads and fruits.
Makes about 3¾ cups spread.

Eggplant Caviar

**1 large eggplant, unpeeled
¼ cup chopped onion
2 tablespoons lemon juice
1 tablespoon olive or vegetable
    oil
1 small clove garlic
½ teaspoon salt
¼ teaspoon TABASCO® pepper
    sauce
    Sieved egg white (optional)
    Lemon slice (optional)**

Preheat oven to 350°F. Place eggplant
in shallow baking dish. Bake 1 hour
or until soft, turning once. Trim off
ends; slice eggplant in half lengthwise. Place cut-side-down in colander
and let drain 10 minutes. Scoop out

pulp; reserve pulp and peel. In
blender or food processor combine
eggplant peel, onion, lemon juice, oil,
garlic, salt and Tabasco® sauce. Cover;
process until peel is finely chopped.
Add eggplant pulp. Cover; process just
until chopped. Place in serving dish.
Garnish with egg white and lemon
slice, if desired. Serve with toast
points.
Makes about 1½ cups.

Garlic Spread

**1 8-ounce package
    PHILADELPHIA BRAND®
    Cream Cheese, softened
½ cup PARKAY® Margarine,
    softened
2 tablespoons chopped parsley
2 tablespoons chopped onion
1 garlic clove, minced**

Combine cream cheese and margarine, mixing until well blended. Add
remaining ingredients; mix well.
Chill.
Approximately 1⅔ cups.

Chili con Queso

2 tablespoons CRISCO® Oil
¼ cup minced onion
1 can (7½ ounces) whole tomatoes, drained and finely chopped
1 can (4 ounces) chopped green chilies, undrained
¼ teaspoon salt
2 cups shredded Cheddar or Monterey Jack cheese (about 8 ounces)
⅓ cup whipping cream
Nacho chips

Heat Crisco® Oil in 1-quart saucepan. Add onion. Cook over medium-high heat, stirring occasionally, until onion is tender. Add tomatoes, chilies and salt. Stir to blend and break apart tomatoes. Heat to boiling. Reduce heat to medium-low. Cook, stirring occasionally, 15 minutes. Remove from heat. Stir in cheese and cream. Cook over low heat, stirring constantly, until cheese melts. Serve with nacho chips.
About 1¾ cups.
Variation: Hot Chili con Queso. Follow recipe above, substituting jalapeño peppers (drained) for green chilies.

Toasted Sesame Cheese Spread

2 tablespoons KIKKOMAN® Soy Sauce
1 package (3 oz.) cream cheese
4 teaspoons sesame seed, toasted
Assorted crackers

Pour soy sauce over cream cheese block in small dish, turning over several times to coat all sides. Cover; refrigerate 2 hours, turning cheese block over often. Remove cheese block from soy sauce and roll in sesame seed. Refrigerate until ready to serve with crackers.
Makes 4 to 6 appetizer servings.

Vegetable Dip Verde

1 cup cottage cheese
1 cup firmly packed parsley sprigs
½ cup chopped green onions
⅓ cup capers, drained
2 hard-cooked eggs, peeled, quartered
2 cloves garlic
1 tablespoon lemon juice
¼ teaspoon salt
¼ teaspoon TABASCO® pepper sauce

In container of blender or food processor combine all ingredients. Cover; process until smooth. Remove to serving bowl. Cover; refrigerate at least 1 hour. Serve with cut-up fresh vegetables.
Makes about 1½ cups.

Manhattan Clam Dip

1 (3-ounce) package cream cheese, softened
¼ cup mayonnaise or salad dressing
1 (8-ounce) container BORDEN® or MEADOW GOLD® Sour Cream
½ cup BENNETT'S® Cocktail Sauce
1 or 2 (6½-ounce) cans SNOW'S® or DOXSEE® Minced Clams, drained
2 tablespoons chopped green onion
1 teaspoon REALEMON® Lemon Juice from Concentrate

In small mixer bowl, beat cheese and mayonnaise until smooth. Stir in remaining ingredients. Chill. Garnish as desired. Serve with assorted fresh vegetables or WISE® COTTAGE FRIES® Potato Chips. Refrigerate leftovers.
Makes about 2 cups.

Tropical Fruit Dip

½ cup mayonnaise
¼ cup sour cream
3 tablespoons lime juice
1 teaspoon honey
½ teaspoon ground cumin
¼ teaspoon TABASCO® pepper sauce
½ cup shredded coconut

In medium bowl combine mayonnaise, sour cream, lime juice, honey, cumin and Tabasco® sauce; mix well. Stir in coconut. Cover, refrigerate at least 1 hour. Serve with cut-up fresh fruit.
Makes about 1 cup.

Cool and Creamy Cucumber Spread

3 medium cucumbers
1 (8-ounce) *plus* 1 (3-ounce) package cream cheese, softened
½ cup sour cream
¼ cup snipped fresh dill*
1½ teaspoons lemon juice
1 envelope LIPTON® Recipe Secrets Vegetable Recipe Soup Mix

Thinly slice 1 cucumber and arrange in bottom of lightly oiled 4-cup ring mold; set aside.
Peel, seed and coarsely chop remaining cucumbers. With food processor or electric mixer, combine cream cheese, 1 cup chopped cucumber, sour cream, dill, lemon juice and vegetable recipe soup mix until smooth. Stir in remaining chopped cucumber. Turn into prepared mold; chill until firm, at least 3 hours. To serve, unmold onto serving platter and fill center, if desired, with cherry tomatoes and leaf lettuce. Serve with assorted crackers.
Makes about 3½ cups spread.
*Substitution: Use 2 tablespoons dried dill weed.

Manhattan Clam Dip

Bacon and Two Onion Cheesecake (left) and Savory Pepper-Herb Cheesecake (right)

salt. Pour into crust; bake at 350°F 30 to 35 minutes or until center is just set. Remove to wire cooling rack; cool to room temperature.

Makes 10 appetizer servings

Bacon and Two Onion Cheesecake

6 slices bacon, diced
1 large sweet onion, chopped
1 clove garlic, minced
1 container (15 oz.) SARGENTO® Light Ricotta Cheese
½ cup half-and-half
2 tablespoons flour
½ teaspoon salt
¼ teaspoon cayenne pepper
2 eggs
½ cup thinly sliced green onions

In 10-inch skillet, cook bacon until crisp; remove to paper towels with slotted spoon. Cook chopped onion and garlic in drippings until tender, about 6 minutes. Drain in strainer; discard bacon drippings. In bowl of electric mixer, combine ricotta cheese, half-and-half, flour, salt and pepper; blend until smooth. Add eggs, one at a time; blend until smooth. Reserve 3 tablespoons of the bacon for garnish. Stir remaining bacon, cooked onion mixture and green onions into ricotta mixture. Lightly grease side of 8- or 9-inch springform pan; pour batter into pan. Bake at 350°F 40 minutes or until center is just set. Remove to wire cooling rack; cool to room temperature. Garnish with reserved bacon; serve with assorted crackers.

Makes 10 appetizer servings

Savory Pepper-Herb Cheesecake

Crust:
1¼ cups fresh dark rye or pumpernickel breadcrumbs (about 2 slices, processed in blender or food processor)
3 tablespoons melted margarine

Filling:
1 container (15 oz.) SARGENTO® Light Ricotta Cheese
½ cup half-and-half
2 tablespoons flour
2 eggs
⅓ cup chopped mixed fresh herbs (such as parsley, basil, mint, tarragon, rosemary, thyme and oregano)
¼ cup chopped fresh chives or green onion tops
1½ teaspoons finely grated lemon peel
½ teaspoon cracked black pepper
¾ teaspoon salt

Lightly grease side of 8- or 9-inch springform pan. Combine crust ingredients; press evenly onto bottom of pan. Chill while preparing filling. In bowl of electric mixer, combine ricotta cheese, half-and-half and flour; blend until smooth. Add eggs, one at a time; blend until smooth. Blend in fresh herbs, chives, lemon peel, pepper and

Salmon Cucumber Mousse

2 envelopes unflavored gelatin
1 cup cold water
2 tablespoons lemon juice
2 containers (8 ounces each) PHILADELPHIA BRAND® Soft Cream Cheese with Smoked Salmon
1 small cucumber, peeled, finely chopped

• Soften gelatin in water; stir over low heat until dissolved. Stir in lemon juice.

• Stir cream cheese, gelatin mixture and cucumber in small bowl until well blended. Pour into 1-quart mold.

• Refrigerate until firm. Unmold onto serving platter. Serve with melba toast rounds.

Makes 3 cups

Prep time: 15 minutes plus refrigerating

Salmon Cucumber Mousse

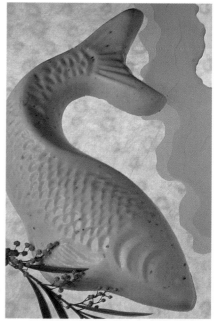

Baked Brie Wrapped in Pastry

¾ cup all-purpose flour
¼ cup LAND O LAKES® Butter, softened
1 package (3 ounces) cream cheese, softened
1 round (8 ounces) Brie cheese (4¼-inch diameter)
1 egg
1 teaspoon water
Apple slices
Crackers

In large mixer bowl combine flour, butter and cream cheese. Beat at low speed, scraping bowl often, until mixture forms a dough, 2 to 3 minutes; shape into ball. Wrap tightly in plastic wrap; refrigerate, 30 to 60 minutes.

Heat oven to 400°. Divide pastry in half. On lightly floured surface, roll out *each* half of dough to ⅛-inch thickness. Cut a 7-inch circle from *each* half. Place one circle on cookie sheet. Place Brie cheese on center of pastry circle and top with other pastry circle. Pinch edges of pastry to seal. Flute edges as desired. Decorate top with small pastry cut-outs. In small bowl beat egg with water; brush over top and sides of pastry. Bake for 15 to 20 minutes or until golden brown. Remove from cookie sheet immediately. Let stand 30 minutes to allow cheese to set. Cut into small wedges and serve with apple slices and crackers.

Makes 8 servings

Baked Brie Wrapped in Pastry

Seafood Cocktails with Watercress Sauce

Seafood Cocktails with Watercress Sauce

    1 large bunch watercress, stems
        removed (about 2 cups
        loosely packed)*
    1 small bunch parsley, stems
        removed (about 1 cup
        loosely packed)*
    1 medium clove garlic, finely
        chopped
    1 envelope LIPTON® Recipe
        Secrets Golden Onion
        Recipe Soup Mix
    ½ pint (8 ounces) sour cream
    ¼ cup mayonnaise
    ⅛ teaspoon pepper
        Suggested Seafood**

In food processor or blender, combine
watercress, parsley and garlic until
blended. Add golden onion recipe soup
mix, sour cream, mayonnaise and
pepper; process until smooth. Chill at
least 2 hours. Serve with Suggested
Seafood. Garnish as desired.
*Makes about 2 cups sauce or about 8
appetizer servings.*
   *Variation: Omit watercress. Use 2
small bunches parsley, stems removed
(about 2 cups loosely packed).

   **Suggested Seafood: Use about 2
pounds cooked and chilled butterflied
shrimp, scallops, crab claws and legs,
lobster meat or clams.

Marinated Mushrooms

    ½ cup WISH-BONE® Italian
        Dressing
    2 pounds fresh mushrooms
    2 teaspoons lemon juice

In large saucepan, heat Italian dressing and cook mushrooms over medium heat, stirring occasionally, 5
minutes. Add lemon juice. Remove
mushrooms with dressing to large
shallow baking dish. Cover and marinate in refrigerator, stirring occasionally, 4 hours or overnight.
Makes about 4 cups mushrooms.
   Note: Also terrific with Wish-
Bone® Robusto Italian or Lite Italian
Dressing.

Beer-Batter Shrimp

    1 cup flour
    1 tablespoon paprika
    ½ teaspoon salt
    1 (12-ounce) can or bottle beer
    ½ teaspoon Worcestershire
        sauce
    ¼ teaspoon TABASCO® pepper
        sauce
        Vegetable oil
    2 pounds shrimp, peeled,
        deveined
        Flour for dredging
        Creole Tartar Sauce (recipe
        follows)

In medium bowl combine 1 cup flour,
paprika and salt. Whisk in beer,
Worcestershire sauce and Tabasco®
sauce. Cover; let stand at room temperature at least 1 hour. In large
heavy saucepot or deep-fat fryer, heat
about 3 inches oil over medium-high
heat to 375°F. Dredge shrimp in flour,
then dip in batter. Fry shrimp, a few
at a time, 2 to 3 minutes or until
golden. Drain on paper towels. Serve
immediately with Creole Tartar
Sauce.
Makes 8 servings.

Creole Tartar Sauce

    ¼ cup finely chopped green
        onions
    ¼ cup finely chopped celery
    ¼ cup finely chopped parsley
    3 tablespoons tomato paste
    2 tablespoons Dijon-style
        mustard
    2 tablespoons olive or vegetable
        oil
    1 tablespoon white wine vinegar
    ¾ teaspoon TABASCO® pepper
        sauce
    ½ teaspoon paprika

In small bowl combine all ingredients
until well blended.
Makes about 1 cup.

Sausage Antipasto Platter

Pesto Spread (recipe follows)
1 large tomato
6 ounces thinly sliced Genoa
   salami
6 ounces thinly sliced ham
   cappicola
6 ounces thinly sliced pepperoni
1 loaf (8 ounces) French bread,
   cut into ¼-inch slices
1 pound unpared cooked new
   potatoes, cut into ¼-inch
   slices
4 ounces pea pods, trimmed,
   strings removed
1 red bell pepper, cut into strips
1 small zucchini, cut diagonally
   into ¼-inch slices
4 ounces mushrooms, sliced
½ cup dry cured olives (optional)

Prepare Pesto Spread. Cut ½-inch slice from top of tomato; zigzag edge. Scoop out pulp. Fill tomato with Pesto Spread; place in center of large serving platter. Arrange remaining ingredients around tomato. To serve, spread slices of bread or potatoes with Pesto Spread and top with sliced meat and vegetables.
Makes 8 servings.

PESTO SPREAD: Combine ¾ cup tightly packed fresh basil leaves, 2 teaspoons crushed fresh rosemary or ¾ teaspoon dried rosemary, crushed, ¼ cup tightly packed Italian parsley and 2 quartered garlic cloves in food processor. Cover and process until blended. Add ⅓ cup French bread crumbs, ¼ cup grated Parmesan cheese, 1 teaspoon lemon juice, ½ teaspoon salt, and dash pepper. With motor running, slowly pour in ⅓ cup light cream and ¼ cup olive oil through feed tube. Process until blended. Pour into small bowl. Refrigerate, covered, 1½ to 2 hours to blend flavors.
Makes about 1 cup.

Favorite recipe from **National Live Stock and Meat Board**

Sausage Antipasto Platter

Party Quiche Squares

1 (11-ounce) package pie crust
   mix
1 (10-ounce) package frozen
   chopped broccoli, thawed
   and well drained
1½ cups shredded Swiss cheese
   (6 ounces)
2 tablespoons all-purpose flour
1 cup COLLEGE INN® Chicken
   Broth
¾ cup heavy cream
5 eggs
2 tablespoons GREY POUPON®
   Dijon Mustard

Prepare pie crust mix according to package directions; roll out on floured surface to 16×11-inch rectangle. Arrange on bottom of ungreased 15½×10½×1-inch baking pan, trimming to fit.

Combine broccoli, cheese and flour; arrange evenly over pastry. Blend chicken broth, cream, eggs and mustard; pour evenly over broccoli mixture. Bake at 350°F for 35 to 40 minutes or until knife inserted in center comes out clean. Cool slightly. To serve, cut into squares. Garnish as desired.
Makes 60 appetizers.

Herbed Cheese Spread

- 1 container (8 ounces) PHILADELPHIA BRAND® Light Pasteurized Process Cream Cheese Product
- ½ cup MIRACLE WHIP® FREE® Dressing
- 2 tablespoons <u>each</u>: chopped fresh parsley, finely chopped green onion
- 1 tablespoon <u>each</u>: chopped fresh oregano, chopped fresh basil and chopped fresh chives
- 1 garlic clove, minced
- 1 teaspoon anchovy paste (optional)
- ¼ teaspoon pepper

• Mix ingredients until well blended. Pipe mixture with pastry tube fitted with star tip into Belgian endive leaves, hollowed out cherry tomatoes and hollowed out summer squash slices.   *Makes 1¼ cups*

Variation: Substitute 1 teaspoon dried oregano leaves, crushed, and 1 teaspoon dried basil leaves, crushed, for 2 tablespoons fresh oregano and basil.

Prep time: 20 minutes

Swiss Cheese Spread

- 2 cups (8 ounces) SARGENTO® Fancy Supreme™ Shredded Swiss Cheese
- 3 tablespoons sour cream
- 2 tablespoons minced onion
- 4 slices crisply cooked bacon, crumbled
- ½ teaspoon salt
- ½ teaspoon garlic powder

Combine all ingredients; beat until smooth and of a spreading consistency. Chill.
Makes about 2 cups

Hot Artichoke Spread

- 1 cup MIRACLE WHIP® Salad Dressing
- 1 cup (4 ounces) KRAFT® 100% Grated Parmesan Cheese
- 1 can (14 ounces) artichoke hearts, drained, chopped
- 1 can (4 ounces) chopped green chilies, drained
- 1 garlic clove, minced
- 2 tablespoons sliced green onions
- 2 tablespoons seeded, chopped tomato

• Heat oven to 350°F.

• Mix all ingredients except onions and tomatoes until well blended.

• Spoon into shallow ovenproof dish or 9-inch pie plate.

• Bake 20 to 25 minutes or until lightly browned. Sprinkle with onions and tomatoes. Serve with toasted bread cutouts.
Makes 2 cups

Prep time: 10 minutes
Cooking time: 25 minutes

Microwave: • Mix all ingredients except onions and tomatoes until well blended.
• Spoon into 9-inch pie plate. • Microwave at MEDIUM (50%) 7 to 9 minutes or until mixture is warm, stirring every 4 minutes. Stir before serving. Sprinkle with onions and tomatoes. Serve with toasted bread cutouts.

Layered Crab Spread

- 2 (8-ounce) packages cream cheese, softened
- 2 tablespoons REALEMON® Lemon Juice from Concentrate
- 1 teaspoon Worcestershire sauce
- ¼ teaspoon garlic powder
- 2 tablespoons finely chopped green onion
- ¾ cup BENNETT'S® Chili Sauce
- 1 (16-ounce) can HARRIS® or ORLEANS® Crab Meat, drained

In large mixer bowl, beat cheese, ReaLemon® brand, Worcestershire and garlic powder until fluffy; stir in onion. On serving plate, spread cheese mixture into 6-inch circle. Top with chili sauce then crabmeat. Cover; chill. Serve with crackers. Refrigerate leftovers.
Makes 12 appetizer servings

Hot Artichoke Spread

Seafood Ravioli with Fresh Tomato Sauce

1 container (8 ounces)
    PHILADELPHIA BRAND®
    Soft Cream Cheese with
    Herb & Garlic
¾ cup chopped LOUIS KEMP®
    CRAB DELIGHTS
    Chunks, rinsed
36 wonton wrappers
    Cold water
    Fresh Tomato Sauce

• Stir cream cheese and crab flavored surimi seafood in medium bowl until well blended.

• For each ravioli, place 1 tablespoonful cream cheese mixture in center of one wonton wrapper. Brush edges with water. Place second wonton wrapper on top. Press edges together to seal, taking care to press out air. Repeat with remaining cream cheese mixture and wonton wrappers.

• For square-shaped ravioli, cut edges of wonton wrappers with pastry trimmer to form square. For round-shaped ravioli, place 3-inch round biscuit cutter on ravioli, making sure center of each cutter contains filling. Press down firmly, cutting through both wrappers, to trim edges. Repeat with remaining ravioli.

• Bring 1½ quarts water to boil in large saucepan. Cook ravioli, a few at a time, 2 to 3 minutes or until they rise to surface. Remove with slotted spoon. Serve hot with Fresh Tomato Sauce. *Makes 18*

Prep time: 25 minutes
Cooking time: 3 minutes per batch

Seafood Ravioli with Fresh Tomato Sauce

Fresh Tomato Sauce

2 garlic cloves, minced
2 tablespoons olive oil
6 plum tomatoes, diced
1 tablespoon red wine vinegar
1 tablespoon chopped parsley

• Cook and stir garlic in oil in medium saucepan 1 minute. Add remaining ingredients.

• Cook over low heat 2 to 3 minutes or until thoroughly heated, stirring occasionally. Cool to room temperature.

Variation: For triangle-shaped ravioli, place 2 teaspoonfuls cream cheese mixture in center of each wonton wrapper; brush edges with water. Fold in half to form triangle. Press edges together to seal, taking care to press out air. Trim edges of wonton wrapper with pastry trimmer, if desired. *Makes 36*

Scandinavian Smörgåsbord

Scandinavian Smörgåsbord

**36 slices party bread, crackers
   or flat bread
   Reduced-calorie
   mayonnaise or salad
   dressing
   Mustard
36 small lettuce leaves or
   Belgian endive leaves
1 can (9¼ ounces)
   STARKIST® Tuna,
   drained and flaked or
   broken into chunks
2 hard-cooked eggs, sliced
¼ pound frozen cooked bay
   shrimp, thawed
½ medium cucumber, thinly
   sliced
36 pieces steamed asparagus
   tips or pea pods
   Capers, plain yogurt, dill
   sprigs, pimento strips,
   red or black caviar, sliced
   green onion for garnish**

Arrange party bread on a tray;
spread each with 1 teaspoon
mayonnaise and/or mustard. Top
with a small lettuce leaf. Top
with tuna, egg slices, shrimp,
cucumber or steamed vegetables.
Garnish as desired.

Makes 36 appetizers

Appetizer Crab Balls

**½ pound crab meat, cartilage
   removed
1½ cups soft bread crumbs
1 egg, slightly beaten
2 tablespoons HEINZ®
   Seafood Cocktail Sauce
2 tablespoons mayonnaise or
   salad dressing
2 tablespoons minced green
   onion
1 tablespoon chopped fresh
   parsley
½ teaspoon dry mustard
   Dash ground red pepper
   Dash black pepper
1 cup crushed potato chips
   HEINZ® Seafood Cocktail
   Sauce**

In large bowl, combine crab
meat, bread crumbs, egg, cocktail
sauce, mayonnaise, green onion,
parsley, mustard, red pepper and
black pepper. Cover; chill at least
1 hour. Form mixture into 36
balls, using a rounded teaspoon
for each. Roll in crushed chips;
place on baking sheet. Bake in
preheated 425°F oven, 10 to 12
minutes or until hot and golden
brown. Serve with additional
cocktail sauce for dipping.

Makes 36 appetizers

Deviled Clam Mushrooms

**12 large mushrooms
   Melted margarine or butter
1 clove garlic, minced
2 tablespoons margarine or
   butter
1 tablespoon flour
1 (6½-ounce) can SNOW'S®
   or DOXSEE® Minced
   Clams, drained,
   reserving 2 tablespoons
   liquid
1 cup fresh bread crumbs
   (2 slices)
1 tablespoon chopped
   parsley
2 teaspoons Worcestershire
   sauce
½ teaspoon dry mustard**

Preheat oven to 400°. Remove
and finely chop mushroom stems;
set aside. Brush caps with
melted margarine. In medium
skillet, cook garlic in *2
tablespoons* margarine until
tender. Stir in flour. Add chopped
mushroom stems and remaining
ingredients except mushroom
caps; mix well. Mound into
mushroom caps; place in shallow
baking pan. Bake 8 to 10
minutes or until hot. Refrigerate
leftovers.

Makes 12 appetizers

Microwave: Prepare
mushrooms as directed above. In
1-quart glass measure with
handle, combine garlic and
margarine. Cook on 100% power
(high) 1 to 1½ minutes or until
garlic is tender. Stir in flour then
chopped mushroom stems and
remaining ingredients except
mushroom caps; mix well. Mound
into mushroom caps; arrange on
microwave-safe plate. Cook on
100% power (high) 5 to 6
minutes, rotating plate once.

Homemade Shrimp Butter

½ cup **LAND O LAKES®**
    Butter, softened
¼ cup mayonnaise
1 package (8 ounces) cream
    cheese, softened
3 tablespoons finely chopped
    onion
1 can (4¼ ounces) broken
    shrimp, rinsed, drained
1 tablespoon lemon juice
    Assorted crackers

In small mixer bowl combine
butter, mayonnaise and cream
cheese. Beat at medium speed,
scraping bowl often, until light
and fluffy, 2 to 3 minutes. Add
onion, shrimp and lemon juice;
continue beating until well
mixed, 1 to 2 minutes. Serve
with crackers. Store refrigerated.
Makes 2 cups

South-of-the-Border Meatballs

1¼ pounds ground beef
1 package (1.25 ounces)
    LAWRY'S® Taco Spices &
    Seasonings
¼ cup unseasoned dry bread
    crumbs
¼ cup finely chopped onion
¼ cup finely chopped green
    bell pepper
1 egg, beaten
1½ cups chunky salsa

In large bowl, combine all
ingredients except salsa; blend
well. Form into 1-inch balls. In
large skillet, brown meatballs on
all sides; drain fat. Add salsa to
skillet. Bring to a boil; reduce
heat and simmer, uncovered, 10
minutes.   *Makes 6 servings*

Presentation: Serve with your
favorite Mexican beer or sangria.

Chicken Nuggets

4 boneless, skinless chicken
    breast halves
    Vegetable oil
1 egg
½ cup water
¾ cup all-purpose flour
1 teaspoon salt
¼ teaspoon pepper
    Apricot Sauce, Dill
    Mayonnaise and Cocktail
    Sauce (recipes follow)
    Red onion rings, for
    garnish

Cut chicken into 1-inch pieces.
Heat 3 inches oil in large heavy
saucepan over medium-high heat
until oil reaches 375°F; adjust
heat to maintain temperature.
Meanwhile, beat egg and water
in large bowl until well mixed.
Add flour, salt and pepper
stirring to form smooth batter.
Dip chicken pieces into batter,
draining off excess. Fry chicken,
a few pieces at a time, in hot oil
about 4 minutes or until golden
brown. Drain on paper towels.
Serve with Apricot Sauce, Dill
Mayonnaise and Cocktail Sauce;
garnish with onion rings.
            Makes 8 servings

APRICOT SAUCE: Mix 1 jar (12
ounces) apricot preserves, 3
tablespoons Dijon mustard and 2
tablespoons prepared horseradish
in small microwave-safe bowl;
blend well. Microwave at HIGH
(100%) 1 to 1½ minutes or until
heated through.

DILL MAYONNAISE:
Combine 1 cup mayonnaise, 2
garlic cloves, minced, and 1½
teaspoons dill weed in small
bowl. Cover; refrigerate 1 hour.

COCKTAIL SAUCE: Combine ¾
cup catsup, 2 tablespoons tomato
paste, 1 tablespoon prepared
horseradish, 4 tablespoons lemon
juice and hot pepper sauce to
taste in small bowl; blend well.

Chicken Nuggets

Nutty Chicken Wings

18 broiler-fryer chicken wings, disjointed, tips discarded
2 eggs
1 tablespoon vegetable oil
1 teaspoon salt
¼ teaspoon pepper
1 cup fine, dry bread crumbs
1 cup finely chopped walnuts
Honey Mustard Dip (recipe follows)

In shallow bowl, beat together eggs, oil, salt and pepper. In second shallow container, place bread crumbs and nuts; mix well. Dip wing pieces in egg mixture, then in crumb mixture, 2 or 3 at a time, turning to coat on all sides. Place wings in greased shallow baking pan. Bake in 400°F oven 30 minutes or until brown and fork tender.

Makes 36 appetizers

HONEY MUSTARD DIP: In small bowl, mix together 1 cup mayonnaise, 2 tablespoons honey, 1 tablespoon prepared mustard, ½ teaspoon coriander and ⅛ teaspoon ground red pepper.

*Favorite recipe from **Delmarva Poultry Industry***

Hot 'n' Honeyed Chicken Wings

3 pounds chicken wings
¾ cup PACE® Picante Sauce
⅔ cup honey
⅓ cup soy sauce
¼ cup Dijon-style mustard
3 tablespoons vegetable oil
2 tablespoons grated fresh ginger
½ teaspoon grated orange peel
Additional PACE® Picante Sauce

Cut off and discard wing tips; cut each wing in half at joint. Place in 13×9-inch baking dish. Combine ¾ cup picante sauce, honey, soy sauce, mustard, oil, ginger and orange peel in small bowl; mix well. Pour over chicken wings. Cover and refrigerate at least 6 hours or overnight.

Preheat oven to 400°F. Place chicken wings and sauce in single layer on foil-lined 15×10-inch jelly-roll pan. Bake 40 to 45 minutes or until brown. Serve warm with additional picante sauce. Garnish as desired.

Makes about 34 appetizers

Deep-Fried Eggplant Sticks

3 tablespoons Chef Paul Prudhomme's VEGETABLE MAGIC®
1 large eggplant, peeled and cut into sticks measuring about 3 inches×½ inch
1½ cups all-purpose flour
1 large egg
1 cup evaporated milk
3½ cups vegetable oil
3 cups unseasoned bread crumbs
Powdered sugar

Evenly sprinkle 1 tablespoon Vegetable Magic over eggplant sticks. Set aside.

Add remaining 2 tablespoons Vegetable Magic to flour and mix well. Set aside.

Beat egg with evaporated milk. Set aside.

Pour oil into 12-inch heavy skillet. Heat over high heat until oil reaches 350°. When oil reaches 250°, dredge eggplant sticks through seasoned flour and drop into egg-milk mixture. Then dredge through bread crumbs, making sure the pieces are separate and well coated. Fry in 350° oil, one batch at a time, 2 to 3 minutes or until golden brown and crisp. (Make sure to turn the pieces early in the cooking process so they cook evenly.) Drain on paper towels, and, while still warm, dust with powdered sugar.

Makes 10 servings

Sweet and Sour Meatballs

1½ pounds lean ground beef
1 cup fresh bread crumbs (2 slices)
1 egg, slightly beaten
4 teaspoons WYLER'S® or STEERO® Beef-Flavor Instant Bouillon
1⅓ cups BAMA® Apricot Preserves
2 tablespoons REALEMON® Lemon Juice from Concentrate

In large bowl, combine beef, crumbs, egg and *2 teaspoons* bouillon; mix well. Shape into 1¼-inch balls. In large skillet, brown meatballs. Remove from pan; pour off fat. In same skillet, combine preserves, ReaLemon® brand and remaining *2 teaspoons* bouillon. Over low heat, cook and stir 10 minutes. Add meatballs; simmer uncovered 10 minutes. Garnish with parsley if desired. Refrigerate leftovers.

Makes about 4 dozen

New England Maple Ribs

2 pounds spareribs, pre-cooked
¾ cup CARY'S®, MAPLE ORCHARDS® or MACDONALD'S™ Pure Maple Syrup
¼ cup BENNETT'S® Chili Sauce
¼ cup chopped onion
1 tablespoon *each* vinegar and Worcestershire sauce
1 teaspoon dry mustard
1 clove garlic, finely chopped

Combine all ingredients except ribs; pour over ribs. Refrigerate at least 4 hours, turning occasionally. Grill or broil ribs as desired, basting frequently with sauce. Refrigerate leftovers.

Makes 4 servings

Hot 'n' Honeyed Chicken Wings

Cajun-Style Chicken Nuggets

1 envelope LIPTON® Recipe
   Secrets Onion or Onion-
   Mushroom Recipe Soup Mix
½ cup plain dry bread crumbs
1½ teaspoons chili powder
1 teaspoon ground cumin
1 teaspoon thyme leaves
¼ teaspoon red pepper
2 pounds boneless chicken
   breasts, cut into 1-inch
   pieces
   Oil

In large bowl, combine onion recipe soup mix, bread crumbs, chili powder, cumin, thyme and pepper. Dip chicken in bread crumb mixture, coating well.

In large skillet, heat ½ inch oil and cook chicken over medium heat, turning once, until done; drain on paper towels. Serve warm and, if desired, with assorted mustards.
Makes about 5 dozen nuggets.
Microwave Directions: Prepare chicken as above. In 13×9-inch baking dish, arrange chicken, then drizzle with 2 to 3 tablespoons oil. Microwave uncovered at HIGH (Full Power) 6 minutes or until chicken is done, rearranging chicken once; drain on paper towels. Serve as above.

Curried Chicken Puffs

½ cup water
⅓ cup PARKAY® Margarine
⅔ cup flour
   Dash of salt
2 eggs
1 8-ounce package
   PHILADELPHIA BRAND®
   Cream Cheese, softened
¼ cup milk
¼ teaspoon salt
   Dash of curry powder
   Dash of pepper
1½ cups chopped cooked chicken
⅓ cup slivered almonds, toasted
2 tablespoons green onion
   slices

Bring water and margarine to boil. Add flour and salt; stir vigorously over low heat until mixture forms ball. Remove from heat; add eggs, one at a time, beating until smooth after each addition. Place level measuring

Curried Chicken Puffs

tablespoonfuls of batter on ungreased cookie sheet. Bake at 400°, 25 minutes. Cool.

Combine cream cheese, milk, salt, curry powder and pepper, mixing until well blended. Add chicken, almonds and onions; mix lightly. Cut tops from cream puffs; fill with chicken mixture. Replace tops. Place puffs on cookie sheet. Bake at 375°, 5 minutes or until warm.
Approximately 1½ dozen.

Note: Unfilled cream puffs can be prepared several weeks in advance and frozen. Place puffs on a jelly roll pan and wrap securely in plastic wrap.

Empress Chicken Wings

1½ pounds chicken wings (about
   8 wings)
3 tablespoons KIKKOMAN® Soy
   Sauce
1 tablespoon dry sherry
1 tablespoon minced fresh
   ginger root
1 clove garlic, minced
2 tablespoons vegetable oil
¼ to ⅓ cup cornstarch
⅔ cup water
2 green onions and tops, cut
   diagonally into thin slices
1 teaspoon slivered fresh ginger
   root

Disjoint chicken wings; discard tips (or save for stock). Combine soy sauce, sherry, minced ginger and garlic in large bowl; stir in chicken. Cover and refrigerate 1 hour, stirring occasionally. Remove chicken; reserve marinade. Heat oil in large skillet over medium heat. Lightly coat chicken pieces with cornstarch; add to skillet and brown slowly on all sides. Remove chicken; drain off fat. Stir water and reserved marinade into same skillet. Add chicken; sprinkle green onions and slivered ginger evenly over chicken. Cover and simmer 5 minutes, or until chicken is tender.
Makes 4 to 6 appetizer servings.

Mini Cocktail Meatballs

1 envelope LIPTON® Recipe
   Secrets Onion, Onion-
   Mushroom, Beefy Mushroom
   or Beefy Onion Recipe
   Soup Mix
1 pound ground beef
½ cup plain dry bread crumbs
¼ cup dry red wine or water
2 eggs, slightly beaten

Preheat oven to 375°.

In medium bowl, combine all ingredients; shape into 1-inch meatballs.

In shallow baking pan, arrange meatballs and bake 18 minutes or until done. Serve, if desired, with assorted mustards or tomato sauce.
Makes about 4 dozen meatballs.

Flaky Ham Puffs

    1 recipe Mustard Sauce (page 16)
Pastry:
  1²/₃ cups all-purpose flour
  ¹/₃ cup yellow cornmeal
  ¹/₄ cup grated Parmesan cheese
  ¹/₄ teaspoon salt
  ¹/₂ cup CRISCO® Oil
    3 tablespoons ice water
Filling:
  ³/₄ cup ground fully cooked ham
      (about 4 ounces)
  ¹/₄ cup dairy sour cream
  ¹/₂ teaspoon prepared mustard
  ¹/₈ teaspoon onion powder
  ¹/₈ teaspoon pepper

Prepare Mustard Sauce as directed. Cover and refrigerate.

For pastry, combine flour, cornmeal, Parmesan cheese and salt in medium mixing bowl. Add Crisco® Oil. Stir with fork until moistened. Add water. Mix well. Divide dough in half. Form each half into a ball. Place 1 ball between 2 large sheets waxed paper. Roll dough ¹/₈ inch thick. Remove top sheet waxed paper. Cut dough into 2-inch circles. Repeat with remaining dough.

For filling, mix all ingredients in small mixing bowl. Preheat oven to 375°F.

To assemble puffs, place one pastry circle on ungreased baking sheet. Place 1 scant teaspoon filling in center of circle. Top with another pastry circle. Press edges of circles together with fork. Repeat with remaining pastry circles and filling.

Bake puffs at 375°F, 10 to 15 minutes, or until light golden brown. Remove to wire rack. Serve hot with Mustard Sauce.

About 2¹/₂ dozen appetizers.

Variation: Flaky Crab Puffs. Follow recipe above, substituting crab filling for ham filling. For crab filling, mix 1 can (6 to 6¹/₂ ounces) crab meat (rinsed and drained), 2 tablespoons grated Parmesan cheese, 1 tablespoon mayonnaise or salad dressing, 1 tablespoon minced green onion and ¹/₈ teaspoon hot pepper sauce in small mixing bowl.

Crispy Wontons

  ³/₄ pound ground pork
    8 water chestnuts, finely
      chopped
  ¹/₄ cup finely chopped green
      onions and tops
    1 tablespoon KIKKOMAN® Soy
      Sauce
  ¹/₂ teaspoon salt
    1 teaspoon cornstarch
  ¹/₂ teaspoon grated fresh ginger
      root
    1 package (1 lb.) wonton skins
      Vegetable oil for frying
      Tomato catsup and hot
      mustard *or* KIKKOMAN®
      Sweet & Sour Sauce

Combine pork, water chestnuts, green onions, soy sauce, salt, cornstarch and ginger in medium bowl; mix well. Place ¹/₂ teaspoonful pork mixture in center of each wonton skin. Fold wonton skin over filling to form a triangle. Turn top of triangle down to meet fold. Turn over; moisten 1 corner with water. Overlap opposite corner over moistened corner; press firmly. Heat oil in wok or large saucepan over medium-high heat to 375°F. Deep fry wontons, a few at a time, 2 to 3 minutes, or until brown and crispy. Drain on paper towels. Serve warm with catsup and mustard or sweet & sour sauce, as desired.

Makes 10 appetizer servings.

Salmon Canapes

    1 (6¹/₂-ounce) can salmon,
      drained and flaked
    1 tablespoon low-calorie
      mayonnaise
    1 tablespoon REALEMON®
      Lemon Juice from
      Concentrate
  ¹/₈ teaspoon dill weed
   24 Melba rounds
    6 slices LITE-LINE® Process
      Cheese Product,* any flavor,
      quartered
   24 thin slices cucumber
      Parsley

In small bowl, combine salmon, mayonnaise, ReaLemon® brand and dill; mix well. On each Melba round, place a Lite-line piece, cucumber slice, 2 teaspoons salmon mixture and parsley. Serve immediately. Refrigerate leftovers.

Makes 24 appetizers; 36 calories per appetizer.

*"¹/₂ the calories"—8% milk fat version.

Calories by product analyses and recipe calculation.

Crispy Wontons

Herbed Cheese Pinwheel Canapes

1 8-ounce package
   PHILADELPHIA BRAND®
   Cream Cheese, softened
2 tablespoons chopped parsley
2 teaspoons lemon juice
½ teaspoon dried basil leaves,
   crushed
⅛ teaspoon pepper
⅛ teaspoon garlic powder
1 1-pound unsliced whole-wheat
   bread loaf, crusts trimmed
   Soft PARKAY® Margarine
¼ cup finely chopped pecans
¼ cup sesame seed
1 tablespoon worcestershire
   sauce

Combine cream cheese, parsley, juice and seasonings, mixing until well blended. Slice bread lengthwise into ½-inch slices. Roll each slice to ¼-inch thickness. Evenly spread each bread slice with cream cheese mixture; roll up, starting at narrow end. Spread bread rolls with margarine, excluding ends. In small skillet, combine remaining ingredients; cook 3 minutes or until worcestershire sauce evaporates. Cool. Coat bread rolls with pecan mixture. Cover; chill at least 30 minutes. Cut each bread roll crosswise into ½-inch slices.
Approximately 2½ dozen.

Herbed Cheese Pinwheel Canapes

Cheese & Nut Stuffed Bread Slices

1 loaf Italian or French bread
   (about 16 inches long)
1 (8-ounce) *plus* 1 (3-ounce)
   package cream cheese,
   softened
4 tablespoons butter or
   margarine, softened
1 cup shredded Cheddar cheese
   (about 4 ounces)
1 envelope LIPTON® Recipe
   Secrets Vegetable Recipe
   Soup Mix
½ cup chopped walnuts

Trim ends of bread, then cut bread crosswise into 4 pieces. Hollow out center of each piece, leaving ½-inch shell; reserve shells (save bread for fresh bread crumbs).

With food processor or electric mixer, combine cream cheese with butter until smooth. Add Cheddar cheese, vegetable recipe soup mix and walnuts; process until blended. Pack into reserved shells. Wrap in plastic wrap or wax paper, then chill at least 4 hours. To serve, cut into ½-inch slices.
Makes about 2 dozen slices.
   Note: Store any remaining cheese mixture, covered, in refrigerator and serve as a spread with crackers.

Mexican Shrimp Cocktail

½ cup WISH-BONE® Italian
   Dressing
½ cup chopped tomato
1 can (4 ounces) chopped green
   chilies, undrained
¼ cup chopped green onions
1½ teaspoons honey
¼ teaspoon hot pepper sauce
1 pound medium shrimp,
   cleaned and cooked
2 teaspoons finely chopped
   coriander (cilantro) or
   parsley

In medium bowl, combine Italian dressing, tomato, chilies, green onions, honey and hot pepper sauce. Stir in shrimp. Cover and marinate in refrigerator, stirring occasionally, at least 2 hours. Just before serving, stir in coriander.
Makes about 6 servings.
   Note: Also terrific with Wish-Bone® Robusto Italian, Lite Italian or Blended Italian Dressing.

Cheese Stuffed Tomatoes

1 cup BORDEN® or MEADOW
   GOLD® Cottage Cheese
¼ cup (1 ounce) crumbled blue
   cheese
1 teaspoon celery seed
1 teaspoon prepared mustard
¼ teaspoon onion powder
30 cherry tomatoes, tops
   removed and seeded

In medium bowl, combine cheeses and seasonings; mix well. Spoon cheese mixture into tomatoes; cover and chill. Refrigerate leftovers.
Makes 30 appetizers.

Cheesy Potato Skins

    4 large baking potatoes, baked
        Oil
    ¼ lb. VELVEETA® Pasteurized
        Process Cheese Spread,
        cubed
    2 tablespoons chopped red or
        green pepper
    2 crisply cooked bacon slices,
        crumbled
    1 tablespoon green onion slices
        Sour cream

Cut potatoes in half lengthwise; scoop out centers, leaving ¼-inch shell. Fry shells, a few at a time, in deep hot oil, 375°, 2 to 3 minutes or until golden brown; drain. Place on cookie sheet. Top with process cheese spread; broil until process cheese spread begins to melt. Top with remaining ingredients.
8 appetizers.

Preparation time: 60 minutes
Cooking time: 10 minutes

Beer Batter Fried Veggies 'n Things

        Oil
    1 envelope LIPTON® Recipe
        Secrets Golden Onion
        Recipe Soup Mix
    1 cup all-purpose flour
    1 teaspoon baking powder
    2 eggs
    ½ cup beer
    1 tablespoon prepared mustard
        Suggested Veggies 'n Things*

In deep-fat fryer, heat oil to 375°.
Meanwhile, in large bowl, beat golden onion recipe soup mix, flour, baking powder, eggs, beer and mustard until smooth and well blended. Let batter stand 10 minutes. Dip Suggested Veggies 'n Things into batter, then carefully drop into hot oil. Fry, turning once, until golden brown; drain on paper towels. Serve warm.
Makes about 4 cups veggies 'n things.
Suggested Veggies 'n Things:
Use any of the following to equal 4 to 5 cups—broccoli florets, cauliflowerets, sliced mushrooms or zucchini, or chilled mozzarella sticks.

Herb Appetizer Cheesecake

    1 cup dry bread crumbs
    ¼ cup PARKAY® Margarine,
        melted
    ¼ cup olive oil
    2 cups fresh basil leaves
    ½ teaspoon salt
    1 garlic clove, cut in half
    2 8-ounce packages
        PHILADELPHIA BRAND®
        Cream Cheese, softened
    1 cup ricotta cheese
    3 eggs
    ½ cup (2 ounces) KRAFT® 100%
        Grated Parmesan Cheese
    ½ cup pine nuts

Combine crumbs and margarine; press onto bottom of 9-inch springform pan. Bake at 350°, 10 minutes.
Place oil, basil, salt and garlic in blender container. Cover; process on high speed until smooth. Combine basil mixture, cream cheese and ricotta cheese, mixing at medium speed on electric mixer until well blended. Add eggs, one at a time, mixing well after each addition. Blend in parmesan cheese; pour over crust. Top with pine nuts. Bake at 325°, 1 hour and 15 minutes. Loosen cake from rim of pan; cool before removing rim of pan. Serve warm or at room temperature.

Garnish with tomato rose and fresh basil, if desired. Chill any remaining cheesecake.
16 servings.
Variation: Substitute 1 cup chopped parsley and 1 tablespoon dried basil leaves for fresh basil leaves.

Beef Kushisashi

    ½ cup KIKKOMAN® Soy Sauce
    ¼ cup chopped green onions
        and tops
    2 tablespoons sugar
    1 tablespoon vegetable oil
    1½ teaspoons cornstarch
    1 clove garlic, pressed
    1 teaspoon grated fresh ginger
        root
    2½ pounds boneless beef sirloin
        steak

Blend soy sauce, green onions, sugar, oil, cornstarch, garlic and ginger in small saucepan. Simmer, stirring constantly, until thickened, about 1 minute; cool. Cover and set aside. Slice beef into ⅛-inch-thick strips about 4 inches long and 1 inch wide. Thread onto bamboo or metal skewers keeping meat as flat as possible; brush both sides of beef with sauce. Place skewers on rack of broiler pan; broil to desired degree of doneness.
Makes 10 to 12 appetizer servings.

Beef Kushisashi

Skewered Pork

Skewered Pork

**½ cup unsweetened
    pineapple juice**
**3 tablespoons HEINZ®
    Worcestershire Sauce**
1 teaspoon ground coriander
1 teaspoon minced garlic
**¼ teaspoon crushed red
    pepper**
⅛ teaspoon black pepper
**1 pound boneless pork loin,
    cut into ⅛-inch slices**

For marinade, in small bowl,
combine pineapple juice,
Worcestershire sauce, coriander,
garlic, red pepper and black
pepper. Place pork in deep bowl;
pour marinade over pork. Cover;
marinate in refrigerator about
1 hour. Meanwhile, soak thin
bamboo skewers in water. Weave
skewers through pork strips so
meat lies flat. Broil, 4 to 5 inches
from heat source, 2 minutes;
turn. Brush with marinade; broil
an additional 2 minutes or until
pork is just cooked.

Makes 20 to 22 appetizers

Antipasto-on-a-Stick

**8 slices cooked lean beef
    (about 12 ounces), cut
    into 1-inch strips**
16 pitted ripe olives
8 small cherry tomatoes
**8 cubes provolone cheese
    (¾ inch)**
**8 marinated artichoke heart
    quarters, drained**
½ cup Italian salad dressing
**2 cups torn Bibb or Romaine
    lettuce (optional)**

Roll up beef strips pinwheel
fashion. Alternately arrange beef
pinwheels, olives, cherry
tomatoes, cheese cubes and
artichoke hearts on eight 9-inch
skewers. Place kabobs in shallow
container; pour dressing over
kabobs. Refrigerate several
hours or overnight. To serve,
arrange skewers on top of
lettuce, if desired. Pour
remaining dressing over all.

Makes 8 appetizers

Preparation Time: 10 minutes

*Favorite recipe from **National Live
Stock & Meat Board***

Prosciutto Fruit Bundles in Endive

**2 tablespoons rice or white
    wine vinegar**
1 tablespoon vegetable oil
1 tablespoon light soy sauce
1 green onion, sliced
1 (4-inch) rib celery, sliced
½ teaspoon sugar
½ teaspoon grated lime rind
¼ teaspoon ground ginger
**4 slices (3×½ inch) *each:*
    cantaloupe, pineapple,
    honeydew melon**
**8 julienne strips (2×¼ inch)
    each: celery, green and
    red bell pepper**
**3 ounces thinly sliced
    domestic prosciutto ham**
24 Belgian endive leaves

For dressing, combine first 8
ingredients in blender or food
processor; cover and blend until
fairly smooth. Place fruits and
vegetables in plastic bag. Add
dressing; turn to coat. Close bag
securely and marinate in
refrigerator 30 minutes.
Meanwhile, trim excess fat from
ham and discard; cut ham
lengthwise into ½-inch-wide
strips. Remove fruits and
vegetables from dressing. Wrap
ham strips around following
combinations: cantaloupe/2 strips
celery; pineapple/2 strips green
pepper; honeydew melon/2 strips
red pepper. Place each bundle on
endive leaf. Cover with plastic
wrap and refrigerate until
serving.

Makes 24 appetizers

*Favorite recipe from **National Live
Stock & Meat Board***

Chili Go Rounds

**1 cup finely chopped fully-
    cooked smoked sausage**
**2 tablespoons HEINZ® Chili
    Sauce**
**1 tablespoon grated
    Parmesan cheese**
¼ teaspoon ground cinnamon
**¼ teaspoon dried thyme
    leaves, crushed**
**1 package (8 ounces)
    refrigerated crescent
    dinner rolls**

In small bowl, combine sausage,
chili sauce, Parmesan cheese,
cinnamon and thyme. Remove
half of dough from container;
unroll. Place dough between 2
pieces of waxed paper and roll
into 13×5×⅛-inch rectangle.
Spread ½ of sausage mixture
over dough. Roll, jelly-roll
fashion, starting at longest side.
Cut into ½-inch slices with sharp
knife; place cut-side down on
baking sheet. Repeat with
remaining dough and sausage
mixture. Bake in preheated
375°F oven, 12 to 14 minutes or
until golden brown.

Makes about 4 dozen appetizers

Country Style Paté in French Bread

1 loaf (12 inches) French bread
1 package (8 ounces) OSCAR MAYER® Braunschweiger Liver Sausage
½ cup MIRACLE WHIP® Salad Dressing
⅓ cup finely chopped pistachio nuts or walnuts
1 tablespoon each: chopped onion, chopped fresh parsley
½ teaspoon dry mustard

• Slice off both ends of bread loaf. Cut loaf into fourths. Remove bread from inside of each fourth leaving ½-inch shell. Tear removed bread into small pieces.

• Mix torn bread with remaining ingredients until well blended.

• Lightly pack about ⅓ cup sausage mixture into each bread piece.

• Wrap securely in plastic wrap; refrigerate several hours or overnight. To serve, cut into ½-inch slices.

Makes 4 to 6 servings

Prep time: 25 minutes plus refrigerating

Chorizo Cheese Tarts

2 packages KEEBLER® Graham Cracker Ready-Crust® Tarts (12 tarts)
2 egg yolks, beaten
1 (12-ounce) package Mexican chorizo sausage
¼ cup minced onion
1 (16-ounce) jar or can chunky salsa
2 eggs, beaten
¾ cup (6 ounces) Mexican chihuahua or Monterey Jack cheese, grated
¼ teaspoon dried oregano

Heat oven to 350°. Brush tarts with a small amount of beaten egg yolks and bake 3 minutes. Remove from oven and prepare the filling.

Remove sausage from casing. Brown in skillet. Add onion and saute until onion is soft and sausage is well done. Mix salsa with remaining egg yolks and eggs. Spoon sausage and onion mixture into tart shells. Pour salsa-egg mixture over sausage; top with grated cheese. Sprinkle with oregano. Bake at 350° for 20 to 25 minutes or until filling is set and cheese is melted.

Makes 12 servings

Reuben Rolls

Reuben Rolls

⅓ cup HELLMANN'S® or BEST FOODS® Real, Light or Cholesterol Free Reduced Calorie Mayonnaise
1 tablespoon Dijon-style mustard
½ teaspoon caraway seeds
1 cup (4 ounces) cooked corned beef, finely chopped
1 cup (4 ounces) shredded Swiss cheese
1 cup sauerkraut, rinsed, drained and patted dry with paper towels
1 package (10 ounces) refrigerated pizza crust dough

In medium bowl combine mayonnaise, mustard and caraway seeds. Add corned beef, cheese and sauerkraut; toss to blend well. Unroll dough onto large ungreased cookie sheet. Gently stretch to 14×12-inch rectangle. Cut dough lengthwise in half. Spoon half of the filling onto each piece, spreading to within 1 inch of edges. From long side, roll each jelly-roll style; pinch to seal edges. Arrange rolls, seam-side down, 3 inches apart. Bake in 425°F oven 10 minutes or until golden brown. Let stand 5 minutes. Cut into 1-inch slices.

Makes about 30 appetizers

Country Style Paté in French Bread

Garlic Spinach Turnovers

Pastry
  1½ **cups all-purpose flour**
  ¼ **teaspoon salt**
  ½ **cup LAND O LAKES®**
      Butter
  1 **egg, slightly beaten**
  3 **tablespoons milk**

Filling
  1 **tablespoon**
      LAND O LAKES® Butter
  ½ **teaspoon minced fresh**
      garlic
  2 **cups torn fresh spinach**
      leaves
  1 **cup fresh mushroom slices**
      (¼ inch)
  ½ **cup coarsely chopped red**
      pepper (1 medium)
  ½ **cup coarsely chopped**
      onion (1 medium)
  2 **tablespoons freshly grated**
      Parmesan cheese
  ¼ **teaspoon coarsely ground**
      pepper
  ⅛ **teaspoon salt**
      Dash ground red pepper
  1 **egg, slightly beaten**
  1 **tablespoon milk**

For pastry, in medium bowl combine flour and ¼ teaspoon salt; cut in ½ cup butter until crumbly. In small bowl stir together 1 egg and 3 tablespoons milk. Add egg mixture to flour mixture; stir until dough leaves side of bowl. Shape into ball. Wrap in plastic wrap; refrigerate while preparing filling.

For filling, in 10-inch skillet cook 1 tablespoon butter until sizzling; stir in garlic. Cook over medium heat, stirring occasionally, until garlic is tender, 1 to 2 minutes. Add spinach leaves, mushrooms, chopped red pepper and onion. Continue cooking, stirring occasionally, until vegetables are tender crisp, 3 to 4 minutes. Stir in Parmesan cheese, pepper, ⅛ teaspoon salt and ground red pepper. Set aside. Cut pastry dough in half.

Heat oven to 400°. On lightly floured surface, roll out half of dough to 12×9-inch rectangle. Cut *each* rectangle into 12 (3-inch) squares. Place *about 1 teaspoon* filling on one half of *each* square; fold other half over, forming triangle. Press edges with fork to seal. Place on ungreased cookie sheets; with knife cut 2 diagonal slits in *each* turnover. Repeat with remaining pastry dough and filling. In small bowl stir together 1 egg and 1 tablespoon milk; brush over turnovers. Bake for 8 to 12 minutes or until lightly browned.
Makes 2 dozen turnovers

Bacon Appetizer Crescents

  1 **package (8 ounces)**
      PHILADELPHIA BRAND®
      Cream Cheese, softened
  8 **slices OSCAR MAYER®**
      Bacon, crisply cooked,
      crumbled
  ⅓ **cup (1½ ounces) KRAFT®**
      100% Grated Parmesan
      Cheese
  ¼ **cup finely chopped onion**
  2 **tablespoons chopped fresh**
      parsley
  1 **tablespoon milk**
  2 **cans (8 ounces each)**
      refrigerated crescent
      dinner rolls
  1 **egg, beaten**
  1 **teaspoon cold water**

• Heat oven to 375°F.

• Beat cream cheese, bacon, Parmesan cheese, onion, parsley and milk in small mixing bowl at medium speed with electric mixer until well blended.

• Separate dough into eight rectangles; firmly press perforations together to seal. Spread each rectangle with 2 rounded measuring tablespoonfuls cream cheese mixture.

• Cut each rectangle in half diagonally; repeat with opposite corners. Cut in half crosswise to form six triangles. Roll up triangles, starting at short ends.

• Place on greased cookie sheet; brush with combined egg and water. Sprinkle with poppy seed, if desired.

• Bake 12 to 15 minutes or until golden brown. Serve immediately.
Makes about 4 dozen

Prep time: 30 minutes
Cooking time: 15 minutes

Bacon Appetizer Crescents

Polenta Strips with Creamy Salsa Spread

Polenta Strips with Creamy Salsa Spread

- **1 package (8 ounces) cream cheese, softened**
- **2 tablespoons chili sauce**
- **2 tablespoons dairy sour cream**
- **1 tablespoon diced green chiles**
- **½ teaspoon LAWRY'S® Seasoned Pepper**
- **3 cups water**
- **1 teaspoon LAWRY'S® Seasoned Salt**
- **¾ cup instant polenta, uncooked**
- **¼ cup chopped fresh cilantro**
- **¼ cup grated Parmesan cheese**
- **½ cup vegetable oil**

For Creamy Salsa Spread, in small bowl, blend together cream cheese, chili sauce, sour cream, green chiles and Seasoned Pepper; chill. In medium saucepan, bring water and Seasoned Salt to a boil. Add polenta in a slow stream, stirring constantly. Reduce heat; simmer, uncovered, 20 minutes or until mixture pulls away from side of pan. Stir in cilantro. Pour mixture into lightly greased 8×4×3-inch loaf pan. Let cool at least 30 minutes to set. Remove from pan. Cut loaf into very thin slices; sprinkle both sides with cheese. Broil 3 inches from heat 5 minutes or until slightly golden brown. In large skillet, heat oil and fry slices until brown and crisp. Place on paper towels to drain. Serve with Creamy Salsa Spread.

Makes 3 dozen strips

Presentation: Great with grilled beef, pork or chicken entrées.

Hint: To prepare in advance, prepare recipe up to loaf stage, then refrigerate (up to 2 weeks) until ready to fry.

Spinach-Cheese Boreks

- **1 container (8 ounces) PHILADELPHIA BRAND® Soft Cream Cheese with Chives & Onion**
- **1 package (10 ounces) BIRDS EYE® Chopped Spinach, thawed, well drained**
- **⅓ cup chopped roasted red bell peppers, drained**
- **⅛ teaspoon pepper**
- **9 frozen phyllo sheets, thawed**
- **6 tablespoons PARKAY® Margarine, melted**

• Heat oven to 375°F.

• Stir cream cheese, spinach, red bell peppers and pepper in medium bowl until well blended.

• Lay one sheet phyllo dough on flat surface. Brush with margarine; cut lengthwise into four 18×3⅓-inch strips.

• For each appetizer, spoon about 1 tablespoon filling about 1 inch from one end of each strip. Fold the end over filling at 45-degree angle. Continue folding as you would a flag to form a triangle that encloses filling.

• Repeat with remaining phyllo and filling.

• Place triangles on cookie sheet. Brush with margarine.

• Bake 12 to 15 minutes or until golden brown.   *Makes 36*

Prep time: 30 minutes
Cooking time: 15 minutes

Notes: Thaw phyllo sheets in refrigerator 8 to 12 hours before using. Because phyllo sheets dry out very quickly, have filling prepared before removing sheets from refrigerator. For best results, work quickly and keep phyllo sheets covered with damp cloth to prevent sheets from drying out.

Before making final folds of triangle, place small herb sprig on phyllo. Fold dough over herb (herb will be on top of appetizer). Bake as directed.

Spinach-Cheese Boreks

Mini Quiches

    1 package (15 ounces)
      refrigerated pie crusts
      (2 crusts)
    ½ cup (2 ounces) KRAFT®
      Natural Gourmet
      Shredded Swiss Cheese
    ⅓ cup MIRACLE WHIP® Salad
      Dressing
    2 tablespoons half and half
    2 eggs, beaten
    2 tablespoons chopped
      green onion
    ½ teaspoon dry mustard
    ¼ cup chopped OSCAR
      MAYER® Ham

• Heat oven to 425°F.

• On lightly floured surface, roll each pie crust to 12-inch circle. Cut each pie crust into twelve circles using 2½-inch biscuit cutter; place in lightly greased cups of miniature muffin pans. Prick bottoms and sides with fork.

• Bake 10 minutes. Remove from oven. Reduce oven temperature to 350°F.

• Mix all remaining ingredients except ham until well blended. Spoon 1 tablespoon cheese mixture into each pastry-lined muffin cup; top evenly with ham.

• Bake 25 to 30 minutes or until golden brown. Immediately remove from pan.   *Makes 24*

Prep time: 20 minutes
Cooking time: 30 minutes

Cocktail Party Tray

    1 pound large raw shrimp,
      peeled and deveined
    1 pound chicken wing
      drumettes
    1 pound skinned boneless
      chicken breasts, cut into
      strips
    1½ cups BENNETT'S® Chili or
      Hot Seafood Sauce
    1 (12-ounce) jar BENNETT'S®
      Cocktail Sauce

In 3 separate plastic bags, combine shrimp, chicken wings and chicken strips each with ½ cup chili or hot seafood sauce. Marinate in refrigerator a few hours or overnight. Remove from sauce. Broil or grill until done, turning frequently. Serve with cocktail sauce. Refrigerate leftovers.   *Makes 12 servings*

Tip: Shrimp can be arranged on skewers with water chestnuts or tomatillo wedges before broiling.

Southwestern Potato Skins

    6 large russet potatoes
    ¾ pound ground beef
    1 package (1.25 ounces)
      LAWRY'S® Taco Spices &
      Seasonings
    ¾ cup water
    ¾ cup sliced green onions
    1 medium tomato, chopped
    1 can (2¼ ounces) sliced ripe
      olives, drained
    1 cup (4 ounces) grated
      Cheddar cheese
    1 recipe Lawry's® Fiesta Dip
      (page 10)

Pierce potatoes with fork. Microwave on HIGH 30 minutes; let cool. Cut in half and scoop out potatoes leaving ¼-inch shell. In medium skillet, brown ground beef until crumbly; drain fat. Stir in Taco Spices & Seasonings and water. Bring to a boil; reduce heat and simmer, uncovered, 15 minutes. Stir in green onions. Spoon meat mixture into potato shells. Top with tomato, olives and cheese. Place on baking sheet and heat under broiler to melt cheese. Spoon dollops of Lawry's® Fiesta Dip on each shell.
      Makes 1 dozen appetizers

Presentation: Sprinkle with additional sliced green onions. Serve with salsa.

Deluxe Fajita Nachos

    2½ cups shredded, cooked
      chicken
    1 package (1.27 ounces)
      LAWRY'S® Spices &
      Seasonings for Fajitas
    ⅓ cup water
    8 ounces tortilla chips
    1¼ cups (5 ounces) grated
      Cheddar cheese
    1 cup (4 ounces) grated
      Monterey Jack cheese
    1 large tomato, chopped
    1 can (2¼ ounces) sliced ripe
      olives, drained
    ¼ cup sliced green onions
      Salsa

In medium skillet, combine chicken, Spices & Seasonings for Fajitas and water; blend well. Bring to a boil; reduce heat and simmer 3 minutes. In large shallow ovenproof platter, arrange chips. Top with chicken and cheeses. Place under broiler to melt cheese. Top with tomato, olives, green onions and desired amount of salsa.
      *Makes 4 appetizer
      or 2 main-dish servings*

Presentation: Serve with guacamole and sour cream.

Substitution: 1¼ pounds cooked ground beef can be used in place of shredded chicken.

Hint: For a spicier version, add sliced jalapeños.

Deviled Deviled Eggs

    6 hard-cooked eggs
    ⅓ cup MIRACLE WHIP® Salad
      Dressing
    2 tablespoons finely chopped
      green onion
    1 teaspoon KRAFT® Pure
      Prepared Mustard
    ½ teaspoon hot pepper sauce
    ⅛ teaspoon salt

• Cut eggs in half. Remove yolks; mash. Blend in remaining ingredients. Refill whites.
      Makes 12

Prep time: 25 minutes

Deluxe Fajita Nachos

Golden Mini Quiches

1 envelope LIPTON® Recipe
    Secrets Golden Onion
    Recipe Soup Mix
1½ cups light cream or half and
    half
3 eggs, beaten
    Pastry for double-crust pie*
1 cup shredded Swiss cheese
    (about 4 ounces)

Preheat oven to 400°.

In medium bowl, thoroughly blend golden onion recipe soup mix, cream and eggs; set aside.

On lightly floured board, roll pastry ⅛ inch thick; cut into 36 (2½-inch) circles. Press into 7½×9¾-inch muffin pans. Evenly fill prepared pans with cheese, then egg mixture. Bake 25 minutes or until knife inserted in center comes out clean and pastry is golden. Serve warm.

Makes 3 dozen mini quiches.

Variation: For one 9-inch quiche, bake one 9-inch unbaked pastry shell at 375°, 10 minutes. Fill pastry shell with cheese, then egg mixture. Bake 40 minutes or until quiche tests done and pastry is golden.

Makes about 7 servings.

Freezing/Reheating Directions: Mini quiches can be baked, then frozen. Simply wrap in heavy-duty aluminum foil; freeze. To reheat, unwrap and bake at 350°, 15 minutes or until heated through. **OR,** place 12 quiches on plate and microwave at HIGH (Full Power) 4 minutes or until heated through, turning plate once.

Crispy Fried Mushrooms

½ cup all-purpose flour
½ teaspoon salt
¼ teaspoon dry mustard
¼ teaspoon paprika
    Dash pepper
½ cup buttermilk
8 ounces whole fresh
    mushrooms
    CRISCO® Oil for frying

Mix flour, salt, mustard, paprika and pepper in large plastic food storage bag. Set aside. Place buttermilk in small bowl. Dip a few mushrooms at a time in buttermilk. Place in bag with flour mixture. Shake to coat.

Heat 2 to 3 inches Crisco® Oil in deep-fryer or heavy saucepan to 375°F. Fry a few mushrooms at a time, 2 to 3 minutes, or until deep golden brown, turning over several times. Drain on paper towels. Serve hot with *catsup,* if desired.

4 to 6 servings.

Grilled Cheese

1 piece raclette cheese*
    (12 to 16 ounces)
1 tablespoon olive or vegetable
    oil
½ teaspoon ground oregano
    Sliced crusty French bread or
    large crackers

Place cheese in 10-inch iron skillet; brush with oil. Sprinkle oregano on top. Place bread slices around cheese in skillet.

Grill cheese, on covered grill, over medium-hot **KINGSFORD® Charcoal Briquets** 10 minutes or until cheese is very soft. Remove to table; spread cheese on bread slices.

Makes 6 servings.

*Raclette cheese is available at specialty cheese shops. You can try another soft cheese, such as Swiss, but cooking time may vary.

Miniature Teriyaki Pork Kabobs

1 pound boneless pork, cut into
    4×1×½-inch strips
1 can (11 ounces) mandarin
    oranges
1 small green bell pepper, cut
    into 1× ×¼×¼-inch strips
¼ cup teriyaki sauce
1 tablespoon honey
1 tablespoon vinegar
⅛ teaspoon garlic powder

Soak 24 (8-inch) bamboo skewers in water 10 minutes. Thread pork strips accordion style with mandarin oranges on skewers. Place 1 pepper strip on end of each skewer. Arrange on broiler pan.

For sauce, combine teriyaki sauce, honey, vinegar and garlic powder in small bowl; mix well. Brush sauce over kabobs. Broil, 6 inches from heat, about 15 minutes or until pork is done, turning and basting with sauce occasionally.

Makes about 24 appetizers.

Favorite recipe from **National Pork Producers Council**

Crispy Fried Mushrooms

Spring Rolls

    ½ pound ground pork
    1 teaspoon KIKKOMAN® Soy
        Sauce
    1 teaspoon dry sherry
    ½ teaspoon garlic salt
    2 tablespoons vegetable oil
    3 cups fresh bean sprouts
    ½ cup sliced onion
    1 tablespoon KIKKOMAN® Soy
        Sauce
    1 tablespoon cornstarch
    ¾ cup water, divided
    8 sheets egg roll skins
    ½ cup prepared biscuit mix
    1 egg, beaten
        Vegetable oil for frying
        Hot mustard, tomato catsup
        and KIKKOMAN® Soy Sauce

Combine pork, 1 teaspoon soy sauce, sherry and garlic salt; mix well. Let stand 15 minutes. Heat 2 tablespoons oil in hot wok or large skillet over medium-high heat; brown pork mixture in hot oil. Add bean sprouts, onion and 1 tablespoon soy sauce. Stir-fry until vegetables are tender-crisp; drain and cool. Dissolve cornstarch in ¼ cup water. Place about ⅓ cupful pork mixture on lower half of egg roll skin. Moisten left and right edges with cornstarch mixture. Fold bottom edge up to just cover filling. Fold left and right edges ½ inch over; roll up jelly-roll fashion. Moisten top edge with cornstarch mixture and seal. Complete all rolls. Combine biscuit mix, egg and remaining ½ cup water in small bowl; dip each roll in batter. Heat oil for frying in wok or large saucepan over medium-high heat to 370°F. Deep fry rolls, a few at a time, in hot oil 5 to 7 minutes, or until golden brown, turning often. Drain on paper towels. Slice each roll into 4 pieces. Serve with mustard, catsup and soy sauce as desired.
Makes 8 appetizer servings.

Grilled Oysters

    12 to 16 fresh oysters in shells
    ½ cup butter or margarine
    2 tablespoons lemon juice
    2 tablespoons chopped parsley

Thoroughly scrub oysters. Arrange oysters on grill grid; do not open shells. Grill oysters, on uncovered grill, over medium-hot **KINGS-FORD® Charcoal Briquets** 12 to 15

Philly® Cream Cheese Stuffed Mushrooms

minutes or until shells steam open. (Discard any oysters that do not open.)

Meanwhile, in saucepan, combine butter, lemon juice and parsley. Heat butter mixture on edge of grill until butter is melted, stirring frequently.

Carefully remove cooked oysters from grill and serve hot with lemon-butter mixture spooned over.
Makes 4 appetizer servings.

Cantonese Meatballs

    1 can (20 oz.) pineapple chunks
        in syrup
    3 tablespoons brown sugar,
        packed
    5 tablespoons KIKKOMAN®
        Teriyaki Sauce, divided
    1 tablespoon vinegar
    1 tablespoon tomato catsup
    1 pound lean ground beef
    2 tablespoons instant minced
        onion
    2 tablespoons cornstarch
    ¼ cup water

Drain pineapple; reserve syrup. Combine syrup, brown sugar, 3 tablespoons teriyaki sauce, vinegar and catsup; set aside. Mix beef with remaining 2 tablespoons teriyaki sauce and onion; shape into 20 meatballs. Brown meatballs in large skillet;

drain off excess fat. Pour syrup mixture over meatballs; simmer 10 minutes, stirring occasionally. Dissolve cornstarch in water; stir into skillet with pineapple. Cook and stir until sauce thickens and pineapple is heated through.
Makes 6 to 8 appetizer servings.

Philly® Cream Cheese Stuffed Mushrooms

    2 pounds medium mushrooms
    6 tablespoons PARKAY®
        Margarine
    1 8-ounce package
        PHILADELPHIA BRAND®
        Cream Cheese, softened
    ½ cup (2 ounces) crumbled
        KRAFT® Natural Blue
        Cheese
    2 tablespoons chopped onion

Remove mushroom stems; chop enough stems to measure ½ cup. Cook half of mushroom caps in 3 tablespoons margarine over medium heat 5 minutes; drain. Repeat with remaining mushroom caps and margarine. Combine cream cheese and blue cheese, mixing until well blended. Stir in chopped stems and onions; fill mushroom caps. Place on cookie sheet; broil until golden brown.
Approximately 2½ dozen.

Baked Stuffed Shrimp

Baked Stuffed Shrimp

**1 pound jumbo raw shrimp
   (about 12 to 16), peeled,
   leaving tails on
1 cup chopped mushrooms
1/3 cup chopped onion
1 clove garlic, finely chopped
1 teaspoon WYLER'S® or
   STEERO® Chicken-Flavor
   Instant Bouillon
1/4 cup margarine or butter
1 1/2 cups soft bread crumbs
   (3 slices bread)
1 tablespoon chopped pimiento
   Melted margarine or butter
   Chopped parsley, optional**

Preheat oven to 400°. In large skillet,
cook mushrooms, onion, garlic and
bouillon in margarine until tender.
Remove from heat; stir in crumbs and
pimiento. Cut a slit along underside of
each shrimp; do not cut through. Remove vein; brush entire shrimp with
margarine. Mound stuffing mixture
in hollow of each shrimp. Place in
greased shallow baking dish. Bake 10
to 12 minutes or until hot. Garnish
with parsley if desired. Refrigerate
leftovers.
Makes 6 to 8 servings.
   Microwave: In 1-quart glass measure, microwave margarine on full
power (high) 45 seconds or until
melted. Add mushrooms, onion, garlic
and bouillon. Microwave on full power
(high) 3 minutes or until onion is tender. Stir in crumbs and pimiento. Prepare shrimp as above. Place in 2

greased 12×7-inch shallow baking
dishes or 1 (12-inch) round glass platter. Microwave on full power (high) 3
minutes or until hot. Proceed as
above.

Baked Stuffed Clams

**12 clams, well scrubbed*
   Water
1 envelope LIPTON® Recipe
   Secrets Vegetable Recipe
   Soup Mix
2 cups fresh bread crumbs
1 teaspoon oregano
1/8 teaspoon pepper
2 tablespoons oil
2 tablespoons grated Parmesan
   cheese**

In large skillet, arrange clams, then
add 1/2 inch water. Cook covered over
medium-high heat 5 minutes or until
clams open. Remove clams, reserving
3/4 cup liquid; strain liquid. (Discard
any unopened clams.) Remove clams
from shells, then chop clams; reserve
12 shell halves.
   Preheat oven to 350°. In small bowl,
combine vegetable recipe soup mix,
bread crumbs, oregano and pepper.
Stir in clams and reserved liquid.
Stuff reserved shells with clam mix-

ture. Arrange on baking sheet; drizzle
with oil, then sprinkle with cheese.
Bake 15 minutes or until golden.
Makes 12 stuffed clams.
   ***Substitution:** Use 2 cans (6 1/2
ounces each) minced or chopped
clams, drained (reserve 1/4 cup liquid).
Mix reserved liquid with 1/2 cup water.
Shells can be purchased separately.
   Microwave Directions: Omit oil.
Cook and stuff clams as above. On
plate, arrange clams and microwave
uncovered at HIGH (Full Power) 5
minutes or until heated through, rearranging clams once.

Baked Artichoke Squares

**3 tablespoons CRISCO® Oil
1 cup chopped fresh
   mushrooms
1/4 cup thinly sliced celery
1 clove garlic, minced
1 can (14 ounces) artichoke
   hearts, drained and chopped
1/3 cup chopped green onion
1/2 teaspoon dried marjoram
   leaves
1/4 teaspoon dried oregano leaves
1/4 teaspoon cayenne
1 cup shredded Cheddar cheese
   (about 4 ounces)
1 cup shredded Monterey Jack
   cheese (about 4 ounces)
2 eggs, slightly beaten**
Pastry:
**1 1/2 cups all-purpose flour
1/2 teaspoon salt
1/2 cup CRISCO® Oil
1/4 cup milk**

Preheat oven to 350°F. Heat Crisco®
Oil in medium skillet. Add mushrooms, celery and garlic. Sauté until
celery is tender. Remove from heat.
Stir in artichoke hearts, onion, marjoram, oregano and cayenne. Add Cheddar cheese, Monterey Jack cheese and
eggs. Mix well. Set aside.
   For pastry, combine flour and salt in
medium mixing bowl. Blend Crisco®
Oil and milk in small mixing bowl.
Add to flour mixture. Stir with fork
until mixture forms a ball. Press
dough in bottom and 1 1/2 inches up
sides of 13×9-inch pan. Bake at 350°F,
10 minutes.
   Spread cheese mixture on baked
crust. Bake at 350°F, about 20 minutes, or until center is set. Cool
slightly. Cut into 24 squares. Serve
warm.
2 dozen appetizers.

Appetizer Ham Logs

- **2 cups ground ham**
- **1 egg, beaten**
- **¼ teaspoon pepper**
- **¼ cup seasoned fine dry bread crumbs**
- **½ cup horseradish sauce**
- **1 tablespoon prepared mustard**
- **⅛ teaspoon celery salt**
  Vegetable oil for frying
  Pimiento strips

Combine ham, egg and pepper in medium bowl; mix well. Shape into 1-inch logs or balls. Roll in bread crumbs. Refrigerate, covered, 1 hour.

To make mustard sauce, combine horseradish sauce, mustard and celery salt in small bowl until well blended. Refrigerate, covered, until serving time.

Heat 3 inches oil in heavy, large saucepan over medium-high heat until oil is 365°F; adjust heat to maintain temperature. Fry ham logs, a few at a time, 2 to 3 minutes or until golden. Drain on paper towels. Garnish with pimiento strips. Serve with mustard sauce.

Makes about 24 appetizers.

*Favorite recipe from **National Pork Producers Council***

Ham-Wrapped Oysters

- **3 tablespoons prepared horseradish**
- **½ pound ham, cut into 3×1×¼-inch strips**
- **2 dozen fresh oysters, shucked**
- **3 tablespoons butter or margarine, melted**
- **1 tablespoon lemon juice**
- **¼ teaspoon garlic powder**

Spread horseradish on 1 side of each ham strip. Place 1 oyster on each ham strip; roll up and secure with wooden pick. Arrange on broiler pan. Combine butter, lemon juice and garlic powder in small cup. Brush each ham roll with some of the lemon-butter. Broil, 5 inches from heat, 10 to 15 minutes or until edges of oysters curl, brushing occasionally with the remaining lemon-butter.

Makes 24 appetizers.

*Favorite recipe from **National Pork Producers Council***

Top: Appetizer Ham Logs and Miniature Teriyaki Pork Kabobs (page 40); bottom: Ham-Wrapped Oysters and Rumaki (page 17)

Broiled Cheese Triangles

4 pocket pita breads (5- to 6-inch diameter)
Melted butter or margarine
1½ cups shredded process American cheese
¼ cup HEINZ® Tomato Ketchup
2 tablespoons finely chopped green bell pepper
2 tablespoons finely chopped ripe olives
2 tablespoons mayonnaise or salad dressing

Split each pita in half horizontally; brush split sides with butter. Cut each pita half into 6 triangles. Place on baking sheet; bake in preheated 350°F oven, 6 to 8 minutes or until crisp and golden brown. Meanwhile, in medium bowl, combine cheese, ketchup, green pepper, olives and mayonnaise. Spread cheese mixture on pita triangles; place on baking sheet. Broil, 5 to 6 inches from heat source, 2 to 3 minutes or until cheese is melted.
Makes 48 appetizers

Note: Pita toast may be prepared in advance. Cool and store in airtight container for up to 7 days.

Crispy Tortellini Bites

⅓ cup grated Parmesan cheese
1 teaspoon dried basil, crushed
½ teaspoon LAWRY'S® Seasoned Pepper
⅛ teaspoon cayenne pepper
1 package (8 or 9 ounces) cheese tortellini
⅓ cup vegetable oil
1 cup dairy sour cream
¾ to 1 teaspoon LAWRY'S® Garlic Powder with Parsley

In medium bowl, combine cheese, basil, Seasoned Pepper and cayenne; set aside. Cook tortellini according to package directions, omitting salt. Run cold water over tortellini; drain. In large skillet, heat oil. Fry cooled tortellini in oil until golden-crisp; drain. Toss cooked tortellini in cheese-spice mixture. In small bowl, blend sour cream and Garlic Powder with Parsley. Serve tortellini with sour cream mixture for dipping.   *Makes 6 servings*

Presentation: Serve with frill toothpicks or mini-skewers.

Hint: Can also be served with prepared LAWRY'S® Extra Rich & Thick Spaghetti Sauce.

Candied Walnuts

2 cups sugar
½ cup water
1 teaspoon vanilla
4 cups walnut halves and pieces

Bring sugar and water to a rolling boil. Boil 1 minute. Stir in vanilla and walnuts; stir until coating sets. Spread on cookie sheet to cool.   *Makes 1 pound*

Orange Candied Walnuts: Use ½ cup orange juice in place of water and 1 teaspoon orange extract in place of vanilla. Cook as directed.

Spiced Walnuts: Add 1 teaspoon *each* ground cinnamon and nutmeg to sugar mixture. Cook as directed.

Sour Cream Walnuts: Substitute ½ cup sour cream or plain yogurt for water. Cook as directed.

Favorite recipe from **Walnut Marketing Board**

Taco Snack Mix

4 cups SPOON SIZE® Shredded Wheat
4 cups pretzel sticks
4 cups tortilla chips
1 (1¼-ounce) package ORTEGA® Taco Seasoning Mix
¼ cup BLUE BONNET® Margarine, melted

In large bowl, combine cereal, pretzels, tortilla chips and taco seasoning mix. Drizzle with margarine, tossing to coat well. Store in airtight container.
Makes 12 cups

Taco Snack Mix

Cheesy Sun Crisps

**2 cups (8 ounces) shredded
   Cheddar cheese
½ cup grated Parmesan
   cheese
½ cup sunflower oil
   margarine, softened
3 tablespoons water
1 cup all-purpose flour
¼ teaspoon salt (optional)
1 cup uncooked quick oats
⅔ cup roasted, salted
   sunflower kernels**

Beat cheeses, margarine and water in large bowl until well blended. Add flour and salt; mix well. Stir in oats and sunflower kernels; mix until well combined. Shape dough into 12-inch long roll; wrap securely. Refrigerate about 4 hours (dough may be stored up to 1 week in refrigerator).

Preheat oven to 400°F. Lightly grease cookie sheets. Cut roll into ⅛- to ¼-inch slices; flatten each slice slightly. Place on prepared cookie sheets. Bake 8 to 10 minutes until edges are light golden brown. Remove immediately; cool on wire rack.

Makes 4 to 5 dozen crackers

*Favorite recipe from the **National Sunflower Association***

Holiday Trail Mix

**1 box (8 ounces) DOLE®
   Whole or Chopped Dates
1 cup DOLE® Whole
   Almonds, toasted
1 cup DOLE® Raisins
1 cup dried banana chips
1 cup dried apricots
½ cup sunflower seed nuts**

• Combine all ingredients in large bowl. Holiday Trail Mix will keep up to 2 weeks in a closed container in the refrigerator.

Makes 11 servings

Preparation Time: 5 minutes

Zesty Snack Mix

Crispy Bagel Chips

**1 envelope LIPTON® Recipe
   Secrets Golden Onion
   Recipe Soup Mix
½ cup butter or margarine,
   melted
1 teaspoon basil leaves
½ teaspoon oregano leaves
¼ teaspoon garlic powder
4 to 5 plain bagels, cut into
   ⅛-inch slices**

Preheat oven to 250°F. In small bowl, thoroughly blend all ingredients except bagels; generously brush on both sides of bagel slices. On two ungreased baking sheets, arrange bagel slices and bake 50 minutes or until crisp and golden. Store in airtight container up to 1 week.

Makes about 28 chips

Zesty Snack Mix

**8 cups prepared popcorn
1½ cups dry roasted unsalted
   mixed nuts
3 tablespoons BLUE
   BONNET® Margarine,
   melted
2 tablespoons GREY
   POUPON® Dijon Mustard
1 (0.7-ounce) package Italian
   salad dressing mix
1 cup seedless raisins**

In large bowl, combine popcorn and nuts; set aside. In small bowl combine margarine, mustard and salad dressing mix. Pour over popcorn mixture, tossing to coat well. Spread in 15½×10½×1-inch baking pan. Bake at 325°F for 15 minutes, stirring after 10 minutes. Remove from oven; stir in raisins. Spread on paper towels to cool. Store in airtight container.

Makes about 6 cups

Cheese Popcorn

**2 quarts popped popcorn
⅓ cup butter or margarine
½ cup SARGENTO® Grated
   Parmesan, Parmesan and
   Romano or Italian-Style
   Cheese**

Spread freshly popped popcorn in flat pan; keep hot and crisp in 200°F oven. Melt butter; add grated cheese. Pour mixture over popcorn. Stir until evenly coated with cheese mixture.

Makes 2 quarts

BEVERAGES

Quench your thirst on a hot summer day with refreshing fruity coolers. Or warm up a nippy winter night with hot cocoas and ciders. Refreshing punches, frosty milk shakes, festive party drinks and comforting hot toddies make celebrations— whether large or small— extra special.

Sparkling White Sangria

- 1 cup KARO® Light Corn Syrup
- 1 orange, sliced
- 1 lemon, sliced
- 1 lime, sliced
- ½ cup orange-flavored liqueur
- 1 bottle (750 ml) dry white wine
- 2 tablespoons lemon juice
- 1 bottle (12 ounces) club soda or seltzer, chilled
- Additional fresh fruit (optional)

In large pitcher combine corn syrup, orange, lemon and lime slices and liqueur. Let stand 20 to 30 minutes, stirring occasionally. Stir in wine and lemon juice. Refrigerate. Just before serving, add soda and ice cubes. If desired, garnish with additional fruit.
Makes about 6 (8-ounce) servings

Preparation Time: 15 minutes, plus standing and chilling

Sangria

- ¾ cup sugar
- ¾ cup orange juice
- ⅓ cup REALEMON® Lemon Juice from Concentrate
- ⅓ cup REALIME® Lime Juice from Concentrate
- 2 (750 ml) bottles medium-dry red wine, chilled
- Orange, peach or plum slices
- Ice

In pitcher, combine sugar and juices; stir until sugar dissolves. Cover; chill. Just before serving, add wine and fruit. Serve over ice.   *Makes about 2 quarts*

Sangria Slush: Omit fruit and ice. Combine sugar, juices and wine; pour into freezer-proof container. Cover; freeze 8 hours or overnight.

Sangria Blush

- 1 cup orange juice
- ½ cup sugar
- 1 bottle (1.5 liters) white Zinfandel wine
- ¼ cup lime or lemon juice
- 1 orange, thinly sliced and seeded
- 1 lime, thinly sliced and seeded
- 16 to 20 ice cubes

Combine orange juice and sugar in small pan. Cook over medium heat, stirring occasionally, until sugar is dissolved. Pour into 2-quart container with tight-fitting lid. Add wine, lime juice and sliced fruits. Cover; refrigerate 2 hours for flavors to blend. Place ice cubes in small punch bowl or large pitcher. Pour wine mixture over ice.   *Makes 8 servings*

Sparkling White Sangria

Sangrita

Bloody Mary Mix

1 quart vegetable juice cocktail
2 tablespoons HEINZ® Worcestershire Sauce
1 tablespoon fresh lime or lemon juice
¼ teaspoon granulated sugar
¼ teaspoon pepper
¼ teaspoon hot pepper sauce
⅛ teaspoon garlic powder

In pitcher, thoroughly combine vegetable juice, Worcestershire sauce, lime juice, sugar, pepper, hot pepper sauce and garlic powder; cover and chill. Serve over ice. Garnish with celery stalks and lime wedges, if desired.   *Makes 1 quart*

Note: To prepare Bloody Mary Cocktail, add 3 or 4 parts Bloody Mary Mix to 1 part vodka.

Purple Passion

1 (6-ounce) can frozen grape juice concentrate, thawed
3 juice cans cold water
1 juice can vodka
½ cup REALEMON® Lemon Juice from Concentrate
¼ cup sugar
Ice
Purple grapes and mint leaves, optional

In pitcher, combine all ingredients except ice, grapes and mint; stir until sugar dissolves. Cover; chill. Serve over ice; garnish with grapes and mint if desired.

Makes about 1 quart

Sugar-Peach Champagne Cocktail

2 fresh California peaches, sliced
¼ cup sugar
1 bottle (750 ml) pink Champagne

Roll peach slices in sugar and place 2 or 3 slices in each of 4 glasses. Fill with Champagne.
Makes 4 servings

Tip: Turn this into a fruit starter for Sunday brunch by filling a Champagne glass with fruit slices. Top with Champagne.

Favorite recipe from **California Tree Fruit Agreement**

Pacific Sunset

1 can (6 ounces) or ¾ cup DOLE® Pineapple Juice, chilled
⅓ cup orange juice, chilled
Ice cubes
1 tablespoon grenadine syrup
Lime wedge for garnish

• Combine juices in tall glass. Add ice. Slowly add grenadine. Garnish with lime wedge.
Makes 1 serving

Wahiawa Refresher

1 bottle (40 ounces) DOLE® Pure & Light Mandarin Tangerine Juice, chilled
5 cups DOLE® Pineapple Juice, chilled
1 bottle (25.4 ounces) sparkling cider, chilled
1 can (15 ounces) real cream of coconut
1 DOLE® Orange, thinly sliced for garnish
DOLE® Fresh or frozen Strawberries for garnish

• Combine all ingredients in punch bowl.
Makes 20 servings

Sangrita

1 can (12 ounces) tomato juice
1½ cups orange juice
¼ cup lime or lemon juice
1 tablespoon finely minced onion
⅛ teaspoon salt
¼ teaspoon hot pepper sauce
Ice cubes
4 small celery stalks with leafy tops

Combine juices, onion, salt and hot pepper sauce in 1-quart container with tight-fitting lid. Cover; refrigerate 2 hours for flavors to blend. Pour into ice-filled tumblers. Add celery stalk to each glass for stirrer.
Makes 4 servings

Kokomo Quencher

**2 bottles (32 ounces each)
  lemon-lime soda, chilled
1 bottle (40 ounces) DOLE®
  Pure & Light Orchard
  Peach Juice, chilled
5 cups DOLE® Pineapple
  Juice, chilled
2 cups fresh or frozen
  blackberries
1 can (15 ounces) real cream
  of coconut
1 lime, thinly sliced for
  garnish**

• Combine all ingredients in
large punch bowl.

Makes 28 servings

Sunlight Sipper

**1½ cups DOLE® Pine-Passion-
  Banana Juice, chilled
1 tablespoon peach
  schnapps
1 tablespoon light rum
1 tablespoon orange liqueur
  Cracked ice**

• Pour juice, schnapps, rum and
orange liqueur in 2 glasses. Add
ice. Garnish as desired

Makes 2 servings

**Clockwise from top: Raspberry
Mint Cooler, Kokomo Quencher
and Sunlight Sipper**

Raspberry Mint Cooler

**1 to 2 cups fresh mint leaves
5 cups DOLE® Pineapple
  Juice, chilled
2 cups DOLE® Fresh or
  frozen Raspberries
1 can (6 ounces) frozen
  limeade concentrate,
  thawed
1 bottle (32 ounces) lemon-
  lime soda, chilled
1 lime, thinly sliced for
  garnish, optional**

• Rub mint leaves around sides
of punch bowl, then drop the
bruised leaves in bottom of bowl.

• Combine remaining ingredients
in punch bowl.

Makes 15 servings

ReaLemonade

**½ cup sugar
½ cup REALEMON® Lemon
  Juice from Concentrate
3¼ cups cold water
  Ice**

In pitcher, dissolve sugar in
ReaLemon® brand; add water.
Cover; chill. Serve over ice.

Makes about 1 quart

Variations

ReaLimeade: Substitute
REALIME® Lime Juice from
Concentrate for ReaLemon®
brand.

Sparkling: Substitute club soda
for cold water.

Slushy: Reduce water to ½ cup.
In blender container, combine
sugar, ReaLemon® brand and ½
cup water. Gradually add 4 cups
ice cubes, blending until smooth.
Serve immediately.

Pink: Stir in 1 to 2 teaspoons
grenadine syrup *or* 1 to 2 drops
red food coloring.

Minted: Stir in 2 to 3 drops
peppermint extract.

Southern Sunshine

Southern Sunshine

**2 cups orange juice
½ cup REALEMON® Lemon
  Juice from Concentrate
¼ cup sugar
1 (32-ounce) bottle lemon-
  lime carbonated
  beverage, chilled
¾ cup Southern Comfort®
  liqueur,* optional
  Ice**

In pitcher, combine juices and
sugar; stir until sugar dissolves.
Cover; chill. Just before serving,
add carbonated beverage and
liqueur if desired. Serve over ice.

Makes about 7 cups

Tip: Recipe can be doubled.

*Southern Comfort is a registered trademark of
the Southern Comfort Corporation.

Pineapple Passion

**2 cups DOLE® Pineapple Juice
8 pineapple juice cubes**

Combine pineapple juice and juice cubes in blender; blend until slushy. Garnish as desired.
Makes 2 servings.
PINEAPPLE JUICE CUBES: Pour unsweetened, canned pineapple juice into your ice cube trays. Freeze and use just like regular ice cubes. Juice cubes add an intriguing tart-sweet flavor to iced tea, mineral water, lemonade, wine coolers (especially sangria), fruit juices and punch.

Pineapple Mint Tulip

**1 cup DOLE® Pineapple Juice
2 tablespoons powdered sugar
1 tablespoon grenadine syrup
1 sprig fresh mint
Ice cubes or pineapple juice cubes (see recipe above)**

In 1-quart measure, combine pineapple juice, sugar and grenadine; stir well. Rub mint sprig around inside of tall glass. Partially fill glass with ice cubes; pour in juice mixture.
Makes 1 serving.

Checkmate

**3 cups DOLE® Pineapple Juice
1½ cups carrot pieces
1½ teaspoons minced fresh ginger root
6 pineapple juice cubes (see recipe above) or ice cubes
1 tablespoon frozen orange juice concentrate**

Puree pineapple juice, carrots and ginger in blender. Strain through a sieve. Pour strained juice back into blender; add juice cubes and juice concentrate. Blend until smooth.
Makes 4 servings.

Left to right: Checkmate, Pineapple Passion and Pineapple Mint Tulip

Island Fruit Cooler

**¾ cup DOLE® Pineapple Juice
½ cup guava, papaya or mango nectar
¼ cup lemon-lime soda
Ice cubes
Fresh fruit for garnish**

In pitcher, combine pineapple and guava juices and soda. Pour over ice cubes in glass. Garnish with fresh fruit.
Makes 2 servings.

Lemon Tea Sparkler

**2 cups brewed tea
½ cup REALEMON® Lemon Juice from Concentrate
½ cup sugar
1 (32-ounce) bottle ginger ale, chilled
Ice**

In pitcher, combine tea, ReaLemon® brand and sugar; stir until sugar dissolves. Just before serving, add ginger ale. Serve over ice.
Makes about 7 cups.

Low Calorie Lemonade

3¼ cups cold water
½ cup REALEMON® Lemon Juice
    from Concentrate
4 to 8 envelopes sugar
    substitute or 1½ teaspoons
    liquid sugar substitute

Combine ingredients; mix well. Serve over ice. Garnish as desired.
Makes about 1 quart.
    To make 1 serving: Combine ¾ cup cold water, 2 tablespoons ReaLemon® brand and 1 to 2 envelopes sugar substitute or ½ teaspoon liquid sugar substitute.

Lemonade Syrup Base

2 cups sugar
½ cup water
2 cups REALEMON® Lemon
    Juice from Concentrate

In medium saucepan, combine sugar and water. Over low heat, cook until sugar dissolves, stirring occasionally; add ReaLemon® brand. Cool. Store covered in refrigerator.
Makes about 3⅔ cups.
    For 1 (8-ounce) serving: Pour ⅓ cup lemonade syrup into glass; add ⅔ cup cold water. Stir; add ice.
    For 1 quart: In pitcher, combine 1⅓ cups lemonade syrup and 2⅔ cups cold water; stir. Add ice.

Hot Tomato Sipper

1 tablespoon WYLER's® or
    STEERO® Beef-Flavor
    Instant Bouillon *or* 3 Beef-
    Flavor Bouillon Cubes
1 (46-ounce) can tomato juice
2 teaspoons prepared
    horseradish
4 drops hot pepper sauce

In large saucepan, combine all ingredients; over low heat, simmer 10 minutes or until bouillon dissolves. Serve hot.
Makes about 1½ quarts.
Microwave: In 2-quart glass measure, combine ingredients. Microwave on full power (high) 12 to 14 minutes or until hot and bouillon dissolves, stirring after 6 minutes.

City Slicker

¾ cup DOLE® Pineapple Juice
    Pineapple juice cubes (see
    page 50) *or* ice cubes
    Ginger ale
    Dash ground ginger
    Cucumber slice, cherry tomato
    and lemon slice for garnish

Pour pineapple juice over juice cubes in glass. Fill with ginger ale. Add ginger and stir. Garnish with cucumber slice, cherry tomato and lemon slice.
Makes 1 serving.

Beefy Mary

2 (10-ounce) cans tomato and
    chile cocktail
1 (13¾-fluid ounce) can
    COLLEGE INN® Beef Broth
¼ cup lemon juice
    Ice
    Celery or cucumber sticks

Combine tomato and chile cocktail, beef broth and lemon juice. Serve over ice; garnish with celery or cucumber sticks.
Makes 6 servings.

Bourbon Slush

2 cups brewed tea
1 (6-ounce) can frozen orange
    juice concentrate, thawed
⅓ cup sugar
2 cups cold water
1 cup bourbon
⅓ cup REALEMON® Lemon Juice
    from Concentrate

In large bowl, combine tea, juice concentrate and sugar; stir until sugar dissolves. Add remaining ingredients. Freeze. About 1 hour before serving, remove from freezer; when mixture is slushy, spoon into cocktail glasses. Garnish as desired.
Makes about 6 cups.

Quick Wink Breakfast Drink

1 ripe, medium DOLE® Banana,
    frozen*
¾ cup milk
1 tablespoon wheat germ
2 teaspoons honey
¼ teaspoon ground cinnamon

Slice banana; puree with remaining ingredients in blender.
Makes 1 to 2 servings.
    *Peel banana and freeze overnight in airtight plastic bag.

Quick Banana Malt

1 ripe, medium DOLE® Banana,
    frozen*
¾ cup milk
3 tablespoons chocolate malted
    milk powder

Slice banana; puree with remaining ingredients in blender.
Makes 1 serving.
    *Peel banana and freeze overnight in airtight plastic bag.

Quick Banana Malt

Brewed Iced Tea

2 quarts cold water
6 individual tea bags

In large saucepan, bring water to a boil. Pour into heat-proof pitcher or bowl; add tea bags. Cover; steep 4 minutes. Remove tea bags. Cool. Serve over Lemon Ice Cubes if desired.

Makes about 2 quarts

Lemon Ice Cubes

1 quart cold water
½ cup REALEMON® Lemon Juice from Concentrate
Mint leaves or fruit pieces, optional

Combine water and ReaLemon® brand. Pour into ice cube trays. Place mint leaf or fruit piece in each cube if desired; freeze. Serve with iced tea, lemonade or carbonated beverages.

Makes about 2 dozen

Lemony Light Cooler

3 cups white grape juice *or* 1 (750 ml) bottle dry white wine, chilled
½ to ¾ cup sugar
½ cup REALEMON® Lemon Juice from Concentrate
1 (32-ounce) bottle club soda, chilled
Strawberries, plum, peach or orange slices or other fresh fruit
Ice

In pitcher, combine grape juice, sugar and ReaLemon® brand; stir until sugar dissolves. Cover; chill. Just before serving, add club soda and fruit. Serve over ice. *Makes about 7 cups*

Tip: Recipe can be doubled.

Kahlúa® Toasted Almond

8 ounces (1 cup) KAHLÚA®
4 ounces (½ cup) amaretto liqueur
Cream or milk

For each serving, pour 1 ounce Kahlúa® and ½ ounce amaretto liqueur over ice in tall glass. Fill with cream; stir.

Makes 8 servings

Apple Cinnamon Cream Liqueur

1 (14-ounce) can EAGLE® Brand Sweetened Condensed Milk (NOT evaporated milk)
1 cup apple schnapps
2 cups (1 pint) BORDEN® or MEADOW GOLD® Whipping Cream *or* Half-and-Half
½ teaspoon ground cinnamon
Ice

In blender container, combine all ingredients except ice; blend until smooth. Serve over ice.

Store tightly covered in refrigerator. Stir before serving.
Makes about 1 quart

FUZZY NAVEL CREAM LIQUEUR: Omit apple schnapps and cinnamon. Add 1 cup peach schnapps and ¼ cup frozen orange juice concentrate, thawed. Proceed as above.

Peppermint Stick Punch

1½ cups sugar
1½ cups REALIME® Lime Juice from Concentrate
1 cup vodka or water
2 tablespoons white creme de menthe *or* ⅛ teaspoon peppermint extract
2 (32-ounce) bottles club soda, chilled
Candy canes

In punch bowl, combine all ingredients except club soda and candy canes; stir until sugar dissolves. Just before serving, add club soda. Hang candy canes on edge of punch bowl or place in each punch cup for stirrer.

Makes about 2½ quarts

Brewed Iced Tea

Fruit Medley Punch

DELLA ROBBIA ICE RING:
Combine 2 (12-ounce) cans ginger ale (1½ cups) and ½ cup ReaLemon® brand. Pour 2½ cups mixture into 1-quart ring mold; freeze. Arrange apricot halves, green grapes, strawberries, orange peel strips or other fruits and mint on top of ice. Slowly pour remaining ReaLemon® brand mixture over fruit; freeze.

Zesty Punch Sipper

> **2 bottles (32 ounces each) ginger ale, chilled**
> **6 cups DOLE® Pineapple Orange Juice, chilled**
> **1 can (6 ounces) frozen lemonade concentrate, thawed**
> **1 DOLE® Orange, thinly sliced for garnish, optional**
> **1 lime, thinly sliced for garnish, optional**

• Combine all ingredients in large punch bowl or two large pitchers.   *Makes 20 servings*

Pineapple Raspberry Punch

> **5 cups DOLE® Pineapple Juice**
> **1 quart raspberry cranberry drink**
> **1 pint fresh raspberries or frozen raspberries**
> **1 lemon, thinly sliced**
> **Ice**

Chill ingredients. Combine in punch bowl.
Makes 12 servings

Chi Chi Punch

> **6 cups DOLE® Pineapple Orange Juice, chilled**
> **1 can (15 ounces) cream of coconut**
> **3 cups vodka**
> **1 quart lemon-lime soda**
> **Cracked ice**
> **1 orange, thinly sliced**
> **Mint sprigs**

• Blend 1 cup pineapple orange juice and cream of coconut in blender. Add to punch bowl with remaining pineapple orange juice. Stir in vodka.

• Just before serving, add lemon-lime soda and ice. Garnish with orange slices and mint sprigs.
Makes 30 (4-ounce) servings

Preparation Time: 10 minutes

Fruit Medley Punch

> **Della Robbia Ice Ring or ice**
> **2 (10-ounce) packages frozen strawberries in syrup, thawed**
> **3 cups apricot nectar, chilled**
> **3 cups cold water**
> **1 cup REALEMON® Lemon Juice from Concentrate**
> **1 cup sugar**
> **1 (6-ounce) can frozen orange juice concentrate, thawed**
> **3 (12-ounce) cans ginger ale, chilled**

Prepare ice ring in advance if desired. In blender container, purée strawberries. In large punch bowl, combine puréed strawberries and remaining ingredients except ginger ale and ice ring; stir until sugar dissolves. Just before serving, add ginger ale and ice ring.
Makes about 3½ quarts

Zesty Punch Sipper

Clockwise from left: Cherry Punch, Meridian Cooler and
Piña Colada Mocktail

Piña Colada Mocktail

**1½ cups DOLE® Pineapple
    Juice, chilled
⅓ cup canned real cream of
    coconut
1½ teaspoons rum extract
    Crushed ice**

• Place all ingredients in
blender. Process until smooth.
                        Makes 4 servings

Piña Colada Smoothie

**½ cup Piña Colada Smoothie
    Base (recipe follows)
1 small ripe banana
1 cup pineapple juice
4 cups ice cubes
¾ cup rum (optional)
    Fresh fruit (optional)**

Prepare Piña Colada Smoothie
Base. In blender combine ½ cup
Smoothie Base with banana and
pineapple juice; process until
smooth. With blender running,
add ice cubes, several at a time,
then rum. Process until thick
and smooth. If desired, garnish
with fresh fruit.
                *Makes about 6
            (6-ounce) servings*

Piña Colada Smoothie Base

**1 cup KARO® Light Corn
    Syrup
1 can (8 ounces) crushed
    pineapple in
    unsweetened juice,
    undrained
1 can (15 ounces) cream of
    coconut
¼ cup lime juice**

In blender combine ingredients;
process until smooth. Store
covered in refrigerator up to 1
week.   *Makes 3½ cups base*

Preparation Time: 10 minutes

Meridian Cooler

**5 cups DOLE® Pine-Orange-
    Guava Juice, chilled
1 bottle (25.4 ounces)
    sparkling cider, chilled
2 cups DOLE® Fresh or
    frozen Raspberries
1 DOLE® Orange, thinly
    sliced for garnish**

• Combine all ingredients in
large punch bowl.
        Makes 10 to 12 servings

Cherry Punch

**1 can (6 ounces) frozen
    lemonade concentrate
5 cups DOLE® Pure & Light
    Mountain Cherry Juice,
    chilled
1 bottle (28 ounces) mineral
    water, chilled
    DOLE® Lemon slices for
    garnish
    Mint sprigs for garnish**

• Thaw and reconstitute
lemonade in large punch bowl
according to label directions.
Add remaining ingredients.
            Makes 16 servings

Daiquiri in Paradise

**2 ripe, medium DOLE®
    Bananas, peeled
2 cups crushed ice
⅔ cup frozen DOLE® Pine-
    Passion-Banana Juice
    concentrate, thawed
½ cup water
¼ cup dark or light rum
¼ cup orange liqueur**

• Combine all ingredients in
blender; puree until slushy.
Serve in stemmed glasses.
Garnish as desired.
            Makes 6 servings

Mai Tai Slush

**1½ cups DOLE® Pineapple
    Juice
1 pint lemon or lime sherbet
1 cup crushed ice
¼ cup rum
2 tablespoons orange liqueur
    Lime slices**

• Combine all ingredients, except
lime slices, in blender. Process
until well blended. Pour into
glasses. Garnish with lime slices.
            Makes 4 to 6 servings

Frozen Margaritas

½ cup tequila
⅓ cup REALIME® Lime Juice
   from Concentrate
¼ cup triple sec or other
   orange-flavored liqueur
1 cup confectioners' sugar
4 cups ice cubes

In blender container, combine all ingredients except ice; blend well. Gradually add ice, blending until smooth. Serve immediately.
Makes about 1 quart

Strawberry Margaritas

1 (10-ounce) package frozen
   strawberries in syrup,
   partially thawed
¼ cup REALIME® Lime Juice
   from Concentrate
¼ cup tequila
¼ cup confectioners' sugar
2 tablespoons triple sec or
   other orange-flavored
   liqueur
3 cups ice cubes

In blender container, combine all ingredients except ice; blend well. Gradually add ice, blending until smooth. Serve immediately.
Makes about 1 quart

Strawberry Margarita (top) and Frozen Margarita (bottom)

Banana Shake

2 ripe bananas, cut up (about
   2 cups)
1 (14-ounce) can EAGLE®
   Brand Sweetened
   Condensed Milk
   (NOT evaporated milk)
1 cup cold water
⅓ cup REALEMON® Lemon
   Juice from Concentrate
2 cups ice cubes

In blender container, combine all ingredients except ice; blend well. Gradually add ice, blending until smooth. Garnish as desired. Refrigerate leftovers. (Mixture stays thick and creamy in refrigerator.)
Makes about 5 cups

Variations

Strawberry-Banana: Reduce bananas to ½ cup; add 1½ cups fresh strawberries, cleaned and hulled *or* 1 cup frozen unsweetened strawberries, partially thawed. Proceed as above.

Mixer Method: Omit ice cubes. In large mixer bowl, mash fruit; gradually beat in ReaLemon® brand, sweetened condensed milk and 2½ cups cold water. Chill before serving.

Santa's Special Malted Cocoa

2½ cups chocolate ice cream
1½ cups milk
6 tablespoons sugar
3 tablespoons NESTLÉ®
   Cocoa
3 tablespoons CARNATION®
   Original Malted Milk
   Powder

In blender container, place all ingredients. Cover; blend until smooth. Serve immediately.
Makes about 4 cups

Easy Pudding Milk Shake

Easy Pudding Milk Shakes

3 cups cold milk
1 package (4-serving size)
   JELL-O® Instant Pudding
   and Pie Filling, any flavor
1½ cups ice cream, any flavor

POUR milk into blender. Add pudding mix and ice cream; cover. Blend at high speed 30 seconds or until smooth. Pour into glasses. Serve immediately. (Mixture thickens as it stands. Thin with additional milk, if desired.)
*Makes about 5 cups or
4 to 6 servings*

Spiced Tea

6 cups water
1 cup firmly packed light brown sugar
6 cinnamon sticks
8 whole cloves
8 tea bags
1 cup orange juice
1/2 cup REALEMON® Lemon Juice from Concentrate

In large saucepan, combine water, sugar, cinnamon and cloves; bring to a boil. Reduce heat; simmer uncovered 10 minutes. Remove spices. Pour over tea bags; steep 5 minutes. Remove tea bags; add fruit juices. Serve hot or cold.
Makes about 1 1/2 quarts.

Hot Spiced Lemonade

3 cups water
2/3 cup firmly packed light brown sugar
1/2 cup REALEMON® Lemon Juice from Concentrate
8 whole cloves
2 cinnamon sticks
Additional cinnamon sticks for garnish, optional

In medium saucepan, combine all ingredients except garnish. Simmer uncovered 20 minutes to blend flavors; remove spices. Serve hot in mugs with cinnamon sticks if desired.
Makes about 4 cups.

   Microwave: In 1-quart glass measure, combine ingredients as above. Microwave on full power (high) 4 to 5 minutes or until heated through. Serve as above.

Hot Cranberry Cider

1 quart apple cider or apple juice
1 (32-ounce) bottle cranberry juice cocktail
1/2 cup REALEMON® Lemon Juice from Concentrate
1/3 cup firmly packed light brown sugar
8 whole cloves
2 cinnamon sticks

In large saucepan, combine ingredients; bring to a boil. Reduce heat; simmer uncovered 10 minutes. Remove spices. Serve warm.
Makes about 2 quarts.

Hot Buttered Pineapple Smoothie

5 1/2 cups DOLE® Pineapple Juice
1/4 cup brown sugar, packed
2 tablespoons margarine
10 whole cloves
3 cinnamon sticks
1 DOLE® Lemon, sliced

In large saucepan, combine pineapple juice, brown sugar, margarine, cloves and cinnamon sticks. Bring to a boil; simmer 5 minutes. Add lemon slices. Serve hot in mugs.
Makes 1 1/2 quarts.

Piña Colada

1/2 cup DOLE® Pineapple Juice
3 ounces rum
1/4 cup canned cream of coconut
2 cups crushed ice

Combine pineapple juice, rum and cream of coconut in blender. Add ice; blend until slushy.
Makes 2 servings.

Party Mai Tais

3 cups pineapple juice, chilled
1 cup light rum
1 (6-ounce) can frozen orange juice concentrate, thawed
1/2 cup REALEMON® Lemon Juice from Concentrate
Ice
Orange slices and maraschino cherries for garnish, optional

In pitcher, combine all ingredients except ice and garnish; stir to dissolve orange juice concentrate. Serve over ice; garnish with orange and cherries if desired.
Makes about 5 cups.

Piña Colada

Pineapple Margarita

2/3 cup DOLE® Pineapple Juice
1 1/2 ounces tequila
1 ounce triple sec
Juice of 1 lemon
Crushed ice

Combine pineapple juice, tequila, triple sec and lemon juice in blender. Add ice; blend until slushy. Serve in frosted glasses. (Do not put salt on rim.)
Makes 2 servings.

Devilish Daiquiri

2 ripe, medium DOLE® Bananas*
   Grated peel and juice from 1
   lemon
⅓ cup light rum
¼ cup creme de banana liqueur
2 tablespoons powdered sugar
2 cups crushed ice

Slice bananas; combine bananas, lemon peel and juice, rum, liqueur and sugar in blender. Add ice; blend until slushy.
Makes 2 to 4 servings.
   *Frozen bananas can be used. Peel bananas and freeze overnight in air-tight plastic bag.

Melon Citrus Cooler

2 cups orange juice, chilled
½ cup REALEMON® Lemon Juice
   from Concentrate
⅓ cup sugar
2 cups fresh or frozen melon
   balls
½ to 1 cup vodka, optional
2 (12-ounce) cans lemon-lime
   carbonated beverage, chilled
   Ice

In pitcher, combine orange juice, ReaLemon® brand and sugar; stir until sugar dissolves. Just before serving, add melon balls, vodka if desired and lemon-lime carbonated beverage. Serve over ice.
Makes about 2 quarts.

The Death Mix

Fresh lime wedge
Celery salt (optional)
Ice
6 ounces tomato juice
1¼ ounces vodka
2 tablespoons lemon juice
½ beef bouillon cube, crushed
½ teaspoon horseradish
10 drops TABASCO® pepper
   sauce
4 drops Worcestershire sauce
   Pinch each of salt, pepper,
   celery salt
Lemon slice (optional)

Wet rim of 12-ounce glass with lime wedge; dip into celery salt. Fill glass with ice. Add remaining ingredients except garnish; stir. Garnish with lemon slice, if desired.
Makes 1 serving.

Seaside Mary

2 cups tomato juice, chilled
1 (8-ounce) bottle DOXSEE® or
   SNOW'S® Clam Juice, chilled
⅓ cup vodka, optional
1 tablespoon REALEMON®
   Lemon Juice from
   Concentrate
1 teaspoon Worcestershire
   sauce
¼ teaspoon celery salt
8 drops hot pepper sauce

In small pitcher, combine ingredients; stir. Serve over ice. Garnish as desired. Refrigerate leftovers.
Makes about 3½ cups.

Bloody Mary

3 cups tomato juice, chilled
¾ cup vodka
4 teaspoons REALEMON®
   Lemon Juice from
   Concentrate
2 teaspoons Worcestershire
   sauce
½ teaspoon celery salt
⅛ teaspoon hot pepper sauce
   Dash pepper

In pitcher, combine ingredients; stir. Serve over ice; garnish as desired.
Makes about 1 quart.
   Tip: For non-alcoholic Bloody Mary, omit vodka. Proceed as above.
BLOODY MARY GARNISHES
   Onion & Olive Pick: Dip cocktail onions in chopped parsley; alternate on toothpick with pimiento-stuffed olives.
   Green Onion Firecracker: With small scissors or very sharp knife, cut tips of green onion to end of dark green onion portion. Chill in ice water until curled.

Bloody Mary

Frosty Chocolate Shake

1 teaspoon KNOX® Unflavored Gelatine
½ cup skim milk
2 tablespoons chocolate syrup
2 packets aspartame sweetener
¼ teaspoon vanilla extract
1 cup ice cubes (6 to 8)

In small saucepan, sprinkle unflavored gelatine over ¼ cup milk; let stand 1 minute. Stir over low heat until gelatine is completely dissolved, about 5 minutes.

In blender, process remaining ¼ cup milk, syrup, sweetener and vanilla until blended. While processing, through feed cap, gradually add gelatine mixture and process until blended. Add ice cubes, 1 at a time; process at high speed until ice is melted.
Makes 2 servings; 77 calories per serving.

Pineapple Orange Slush

3 cups DOLE® Pineapple Orange Juice, chilled
1 pint orange sherbet
1 cup crushed ice

Combine pineapple orange juice and sherbet in blender. Add ice; blend until slushy.
Makes 6 servings.

Sparkling Harvest Cider

2 quarts apple cider, chilled
1 cup REALEMON® Lemon Juice from Concentrate
½ cup sugar
1 (32-ounce) bottle ginger ale, chilled
Apple slices or cinnamon sticks, optional
Ice

In punch bowl, combine apple cider, ReaLemon® brand and sugar; stir until sugar dissolves. Just before serving, add ginger ale. Garnish with apple and cinnamon sticks if desired. Serve over ice.
Makes about 3 quarts.

Christmas Carol Punch

Christmas Carol Punch

2 medium red apples
2 quarts clear apple cider
8 cinnamon sticks
2 teaspoons whole cloves
½ cup SUN-MAID® Raisins
Orange slices
Lemon slices
¼ cup lemon juice

Core apples; slice into ½-inch rings. In Dutch oven, combine cider, cinnamon, cloves, apple rings and raisins. Bring to boil over high heat; reduce heat to low and simmer 5 to 8 minutes or until apples are just tender. Remove cloves; add orange and lemon slices and lemon juice. Pour into punch bowl. Ladle into large mugs, including an apple ring, some raisins and citrus slices in each serving. Serve with spoons.
Makes about 2 quarts.

Fruit Punch

5½ cups DOLE® Pineapple Juice, chilled
1 quart apple juice, chilled
1 package (10 ounces) frozen strawberries, thawed
1 quart ginger ale, chilled
Fresh strawberry slices, lime slices and fresh mint for garnish

In punch bowl, combine pineapple and apple juices. Puree undrained strawberries in blender; stir pureed strawberries into pineapple juice mixture. Pour in ginger ale. Garnish with strawberry slices, lime slices and fresh mint.
Makes 3 quarts.

Orange Tea Punch

4 cups brewed tea
2 cups orange juice, chilled
1 cup REALEMON® Lemon Juice from Concentrate
1 cup sugar
1 quart orange sherbet
1 (32-ounce) bottle ginger ale, chilled

In pitcher, combine tea, orange juice, ReaLemon® brand and sugar; stir until sugar dissolves. Chill. Just before serving, pour tea mixture into large punch bowl; add scoops of sherbet and ginger ale.
Makes about 4 quarts.

Tropical Cream Punch

> **1 (14-ounce) can EAGLE® Brand Sweetened Condensed Milk (NOT evaporated milk)**
> **1 (6-ounce) can frozen orange juice concentrate, thawed**
> **1 (6-ounce) can frozen pineapple juice concentrate, thawed**
> **2 (32-ounce) bottles club soda, chilled**
> **Orange slices**

In punch bowl, combine sweetened condensed milk and juice concentrates; mix well. Gradually add club soda; stir. Garnish with orange slices. Serve over ice.
Makes about 3 quarts.

Tip: Omit orange juice concentrate and pineapple juice concentrate. Add 1 (12-ounce) can frozen pineapple orange juice drink concentrate, thawed. Proceed as above.

Microwave Hot Cocoa

> **5 tablespoons sugar**
> **3 tablespoons HERSHEY'S Cocoa**
> **Dash salt**
> **3 tablespoons hot water**
> **2 cups milk**
> **¼ teaspoon vanilla extract**
> **Sweetened whipped cream (optional)**

In 1-quart microwave-safe bowl, stir together sugar, cocoa, salt and hot water. Microwave at HIGH (100%) 1 to 1½ minutes or until boiling; stir in milk. Microwave at HIGH 1½ to 2 minutes, or until hot. Stir in vanilla; blend well. Serve hot, topped with sweetened whipped cream, if desired.
Makes about four 6-ounce servings.

Single serving: In microwave-safe cup or mug, stir together 1 heaping teaspoon HERSHEY'S Cocoa, 2 heaping teaspoons sugar and dash salt. Add 2 teaspoons cold milk; stir until smooth. Fill cup with milk. Microwave at HIGH (100%) 1 to 1½ minutes or until hot. Stir to blend; serve.

Hot Cocoa Mix

> **1 cup CREMORA® Non-Dairy Creamer***
> **1 cup nonfat dry milk**
> **¾ to 1 cup sugar**
> **½ cup unsweetened cocoa**

In medium bowl, combine ingredients; mix well. Store in airtight container. To serve, spoon 3 heaping tablespoons mix into mug; add ¾ cup boiling water. Stir.
Makes about 3 cups.

Mocha: Add ¼ cup instant coffee.
Mexican: Add 1 teaspoon ground cinnamon.
Low-calorie: Omit sugar. Add 15 envelopes low-calorie sweetener with NUTRASWEET® *or* 2 teaspoons (5 envelopes) low-calorie granulated sugar substitute. To serve, spoon 2 heaping tablespoons into mug; add ¾ cup boiling water. Stir.

*Cremora® non-dairy creamer is a coffee whitener and should not be used as a milk replacement.

Creamy Hot Chocolate

> **1 (14-ounce) can EAGLE® Brand Sweetened Condensed Milk (NOT evaporated milk)**
> **½ cup unsweetened cocoa**
> **1½ teaspoons vanilla extract**
> **⅛ teaspoon salt**
> **6½ cups hot water**
> **CAMPFIRE® Marshmallows, optional**

In large saucepan, combine sweetened condensed milk, cocoa, vanilla and salt; mix well. Over medium heat, slowly stir in water; heat through, stirring occasionally. Top with marshmallows if desired.
Makes about 2 quarts.

Tip: Chocolate can be stored in refrigerator up to 5 days. Mix well and reheat before serving.

Microwave: In 2-quart glass measure, combine all ingredients except marshmallows. Microwave on full power (high) 8 to 10 minutes, stirring every 3 minutes. Top with marshmallows if desired.

Hot Mulled Pineapple Juice

> **5½ cups DOLE® Pineapple Juice**
> **1 apple, cored and cubed**
> **½ cup DOLE® Raisins**
> **½ cup brown sugar, packed**
> **2 cinnamon sticks, broken**
> **1 tablespoon grated orange peel**
> **½ teaspoon whole cloves**
> **Quartered orange slices for garnish**

In saucepan, combine all ingredients; simmer 15 minutes. Strain before serving. Garnish with quartered orange slices.
Makes 6 servings.

Volcano Punch

> **3 quarts DOLE® Pineapple Juice**
> **2 cans (6 ounces each) frozen limeade concentrate**
> **2 quarts ginger ale**
> **2 pints orange or lemon sherbet**
> **Fresh fruit for garnish**

In punch bowl, combine pineapple juice and limeade concentrate. Just before serving, stir in ginger ale and add scoops of sherbet. Garnish with fresh fruit.
Makes about 6 quarts.

Hot Mulled Pineapple Juice

Champagne Sherbet Punch

Champagne Sherbet Punch

3 cups pineapple juice, chilled
¼ cup REALEMON® Lemon Juice from Concentrate
1 quart BORDEN® or MEADOW GOLD® Pineapple Sherbet
1 (750 mL) bottle champagne, chilled

In punch bowl, combine pineapple juice and ReaLemon® brand. Just before serving, scoop sherbet into punch bowl; add champagne. Stir gently. *Makes about 2½ quarts.*
   Tip: For rosy champagne punch, use raspberry sherbet and pink champagne.

Planter's Punch

4 cups orange juice, chilled
4 cups pineapple juice, chilled
¾ cup REALIME® Lime Juice from Concentrate
½ cup grenadine syrup
1½ cups dark rum
Ice

In punch bowl or large pitcher, combine all ingredients except ice; stir. Serve over ice. *Makes about 2½ quarts.*

White Sangria

½ to ¾ cup sugar
½ cup REALEMON® Lemon Juice from Concentrate, chilled
¼ cup REALIME® Lime Juice from Concentrate, chilled
1 (750 mL) bottle sauterne, chilled
¼ cup orange-flavored liqueur
1 (32-ounce) bottle club soda, chilled
Orange, plum or nectarine slices, green grapes or other fresh fruit
Ice

In pitcher, combine sugar and juices; stir until sugar dissolves. Add sauterne and orange-flavored liqueur. Just before serving, add club soda, fruit and ice. *Makes about 2 quarts.*

Pina Colada Punch

Ice Ring, optional, or block of ice
1 (20-ounce) can crushed pineapple, undrained
2 (15-ounce) cans COCO LOPEZ® Cream of Coconut
1 (46-ounce) can pineapple juice, chilled
2 cups light rum, optional
1 (32-ounce) bottle club soda, chilled

Prepare ice ring in advance. In blender container, combine crushed pineapple and cream of coconut; blend until smooth. In large punch bowl, combine pineapple mixture, pineapple juice and rum if desired. Just before serving, add club soda and ice. *Makes about 4 quarts.*
ICE RING: Fill ring mold with water to within 1 inch of top rim; freeze. Arrange pineapple chunks and maraschino cherries on top of ice. Carefully pour small amount of cold water over fruits; freeze.

Rosé Wine Cooler

Berry Mint Ice Ring, optional, or block of ice
1½ cups sugar
1 cup REALEMON® Lemon Juice from Concentrate
2 (750 mL) bottles rosé wine, chilled
1 (32-ounce) bottle club soda, chilled

Prepare ice ring in advance. In large punch bowl, combine sugar and ReaLemon® brand; stir until sugar dissolves. Just before serving, add wine, club soda and ice. *Makes about 3½ quarts.*
BERRY MINT ICE RING: Combine 3 cups water, 1 cup ReaLemon® brand and ¾ cup sugar; stir until sugar dissolves. Pour 3 cups mixture into 6-cup ring mold; freeze. Arrange strawberries and mint leaves on top of ice. Slowly pour remaining ReaLemon® brand mixture over fruit; freeze.

Spirited Egg Nog

1 (32-ounce) can BORDEN® Egg Nog, chilled
½ cup rum, brandy *or* bourbon Whipped cream Ground nutmeg

In pitcher, combine egg nog and liquor. Garnish with whipped cream and nutmeg. Refrigerate leftovers.
Makes about 1 quart.

Syllabub

1 quart BORDEN® or MEADOW GOLD® Half-and-Half
½ cup sugar
⅓ cup REALEMON® Lemon Juice from Concentrate
⅓ cup brandy
3 tablespoons dry or cocktail sherry
Candy lemon sticks, optional

In large mixer bowl, on low speed, beat half-and-half until frothy; gradually beat in sugar then ReaLemon® brand, brandy and sherry. Chill; stir before serving. Garnish with lemon sticks if desired.
Makes about 5 cups.

Lemon Toddy

⅓ cup water
¼ cup REALEMON® Lemon Juice from Concentrate
3 tablespoons honey
3 tablespoons whiskey

In small saucepan, combine ingredients. Over low heat, simmer to blend flavors, stirring occasionally to dissolve honey. Serve hot.
Makes 1 serving.
Microwave: In 2 cup glass measure, combine ingredients. Heat on 100% power (high) for 1 to 1½ minutes or until hot.

Hot Maple Toddy

1 to 1¼ cups whiskey
1 (8-ounce) bottle CARY'S® Pure Maple Syrup
¾ cup REALEMON® Lemon Juice from Concentrate
Butter and cinnamon sticks, optional

In medium saucepan, combine all ingredients except butter and cinnamon sticks. Over low heat, simmer uncovered 10 minutes. Serve hot with butter and cinnamon sticks if desired.
Makes about 3 cups.
Microwave: In 1-quart glass measure, combine ingredients as above. Heat on 100% power (high) 4 to 5 minutes or until heated through. Serve as above.

Simmered Sherry Bouillon

8 cups water
3 tablespoons WYLER'S® or STEERO® Beef-Flavor Instant Bouillon *or* 9 Beef-Flavor Bouillon Cubes
⅓ cup dry or cocktail sherry Lemon slices, optional

In large saucepan, bring water and bouillon to a boil; stir until bouillon dissolves. Remove from heat; stir in sherry. Serve hot. Garnish with lemon slices if desired.
Makes about 2 quarts.
Microwave: In 2-quart glass measure, heat water and bouillon on 100% power (high) 10 to 14 minutes or until boiling. Stir until bouillon dissolves. Proceed as above.

Mulled Cider

2 quarts apple cider
¾ to 1 cup REALEMON® Lemon Juice from Concentrate
1 cup firmly packed light brown sugar
8 whole cloves
2 cinnamon sticks
¾ cup rum, optional Additional cinnamon sticks, optional

In large saucepan, combine all ingredients except rum and additional cinnamon sticks; bring to a boil. Reduce heat; simmer uncovered 10 minutes. Remove spices; add rum just before serving if desired. Serve hot with cinnamon sticks if desired.
Makes about 2 quarts.
Tip: Can be served cold.
Microwave: In deep 3-quart round baking dish, combine ingredients as above. Heat on 100% power (high) 13 to 14 minutes or until hot. Serve as above.

Spirited Coffee Lopez

4 cups hot coffee
½ cup COCO LOPEZ® Cream of Coconut
½ cup Irish whiskey
1 teaspoon vanilla extract Whipped cream

In heatproof pitcher, combine all ingredients except whipped cream; mix well. Pour into mugs; top with whipped cream. Serve immediately.
Makes 5 cups.

Spirited Coffee Lopez

Homemade Hot Cocoa

**½ cup sugar
⅓ cup NESTLÉ® Cocoa
4 cups milk, divided**

In large saucepan, stir sugar and cocoa until smooth. Gradually add about ⅓ cup milk, stirring constantly until smooth paste forms. Gradually stir in remaining milk. Cook over medium heat, stirring frequently, until hot. *Do not boil.* Pour into 4 heat-proof mugs.

Makes four 1-cup servings

Hot "White Chocolate"

**One 6-oz. pkg. (3 foil-wrapped
    bars) NESTLÉ® Premier
    White baking bars,
    divided
½ cup heavy or whipping
    cream
1 quart milk
¼ cup almond flavored
    liqueur**

Coarsely grate ½ foil-wrapped bar (1 oz.) Premier White baking bar; set aside for garnish.

In small mixer bowl, beat heavy cream until stiff peaks form; set aside. In medium saucepan, combine remaining 2½ foil-wrapped bars (5 oz.) Premier White baking bars, broken up, and milk. Cook over medium heat, stirring constantly, until Premier White baking bars are melted. Remove from heat; stir in liqueur.

Pour into five heat-proof mugs; top with whipped cream. Garnish with grated Premier White baking bar.

Makes five 1-cup servings

Mexican Coffee Olé

**¾ cup firmly packed brown
    sugar
¼ cup unsweetened cocoa
2 teaspoons ground
    cinnamon
4 cups freshly brewed coffee
Whipped cream**

Stir brown sugar, cocoa and cinnamon into hot coffee; blend well to dissolve. Pour into individual mugs and top with whipped cream.

Makes 4 cups

*Favorite recipe from **Lawry's**® **Foods, Inc.***

Moroccan Pineapple Tea

**6 cups DOLE® Pineapple
    Juice
    Peel from 1 DOLE® Orange*
1 cup fresh mint leaves
½ cup sugar
2 teaspoons rose water****

• Combine all ingredients in Dutch oven. Heat just to a boil.

• Steep 15 minutes. Strain before serving.   *Makes 8 servings*

*Spiral cut peel from orange using vegetable peeler.

**Available at liquor or drug stores.

Moroccan Pineapple Tea

Wisconsin Spicy Apple Eggnog

   2 beaten eggs
   3 cups milk
   **2 cups light cream or
       half-and-half**
   ⅓ cup sugar
   **½ teaspoon ground cinnamon
       Dash salt**
   **¾ cup apple brandy
       Ground nutmeg**

In a large saucepan, combine beaten eggs, milk, light cream or half-and-half, sugar, cinnamon and salt. Cook and stir over medium heat until mixture is slightly thickened and heated through, but *do not boil.* Remove from heat; stir in apple brandy. To serve, ladle mixture into 12 heat-proof glasses or cups. Sprinkle each serving with nutmeg. Serve warm.
   Makes 12 (4-ounce) servings

Favorite recipe from **Wisconsin Milk Marketing Board** *© 1993*

Hot Buttered Rum

   1 cup granulated sugar
   **1 cup firmly packed brown
       sugar**
   **1 cup LAND O LAKES®
       Butter**
   **2 cups vanilla ice cream,
       softened**
   Rum *or* rum extract
   Boiling water
   Ground nutmeg

In 2-quart saucepan combine granulated sugar, brown sugar and butter. Cook over low heat, stirring occasionally, until butter is melted and sugar is dissolved, 6 to 8 minutes. In large mixer bowl combine cooked mixture with ice cream; beat at medium speed, scraping bowl often, until smooth, 1 to 2 minutes. Store refrigerated up to 2 weeks. For *each* serving, fill mug with *¼ cup* mixture, *1 ounce* rum or *¼ teaspoon* rum extract and *¾ cup* boiling water; sprinkle with nutmeg.
   Makes 16 servings (4 cups)

Hot Spiced Cider

Hot Spiced Cider

   2 quarts apple cider
   **⅔ cup KARO® Light or Dark
       Corn Syrup**
   3 cinnamon sticks
   ½ teaspoon whole cloves
   1 lemon, sliced
   **Cinnamon sticks and
       lemon slices (optional)**

In medium saucepan stir cider, corn syrup, cinnamon sticks, cloves and lemon slices. Bring to boil over medium-high heat. Reduce heat; simmer 15 minutes. Remove spices. If desired, garnish each serving with a cinnamon stick and lemon slice.
   Makes about 10 servings

Preparation Time: 20 minutes

Hawaiian Tea

   **3 cups DOLE® Pineapple
       Orange Juice**
   1 cinnamon stick
   **2 tablespoons chopped
       crystallized ginger**
   ¼ teaspoon anise seed
   ¼ teaspoon whole cloves
   1 orange tea bag
   **1 peppermint tea bag
       Brown sugar, optional**

• Combine juice and spices in saucepan. Bring to a boil. Reduce heat; simmer 1 minute.

• Add tea bags. Cover and steep 5 to 7 minutes. Sweeten with brown sugar, if desired.
   Makes 3 servings

SOUPS

What better way to comfort yourself on a chilly day than with the wonderful aroma of soup simmering on the stove. Try a satisfying chicken noodle soup, a spicy seafood gumbo, a robust turkey stew or a flavorful beef chili. From hearty vegetable soups to creamy, elegant bisques to refreshing chilled soups, you'll find soups for starters, intimate gatherings and informal lunches and suppers.

Swiss Broccoli Soup

 2 tablespoons minced onion
 1 tablespoon butter
 1 jar (12 ounces) HEINZ®
  HomeStyle Chicken
  Gravy
 1¼ cups milk
 1 package (10 ounces) frozen
  chopped broccoli,
  cooked, drained
 1 cup shredded Swiss cheese
  Dash salt and pepper

In 2-quart saucepan, sauté onion in butter until tender. Stir in gravy, milk and broccoli; heat slowly, stirring occasionally. Add cheese, salt and pepper; heat until cheese is melted, stirring frequently.

Makes 4 servings (about 4 cups)

Creamy Tomato Bisque

 2 cups water
 1 (14½-ounce) can whole
  tomatoes, undrained
 ½ cup chopped celery
 2 tablespoons chopped
  onion
 5 teaspoons WYLER'S® or
  STEERO® Chicken-Flavor
  Instant Bouillon *or*
  5 Chicken-Flavor
  Bouillon Cubes
 2 medium fresh tomatoes,
  pared and diced
 ¼ cup margarine or butter
 3 tablespoons flour
 2 cups (1 pint) BORDEN® or
  MEADOW GOLD® Coffee
  Cream *or* Half-and-Half
 1 tablespoon sugar

In large kettle or Dutch oven, combine water, canned tomatoes, celery, onion and bouillon; cover and simmer 20 minutes. In blender or food processor, purée tomato mixture. In same pan,

cook fresh tomatoes in *2 tablespoons* margarine about 5 minutes; remove from pan. In same pan, melt remaining *2 tablespoons* margarine; stir in flour. Add cream; over low heat, cook and stir until thickened. Stir in bouillon mixture, tomatoes and sugar; heat through (*do not boil*). Garnish as desired. Refrigerate leftovers.

Makes about 1½ quarts

Quick Garden Cheese Soup

 1 cup sliced celery
 1 cup chopped onion
 2 tablespoons margarine
 ⅔ cup unsifted flour
 4 cups water
 2 tablespoons WYLER'S® or
  STEERO® Chicken-Flavor
  Instant Bouillon *or*
  6 Chicken-Flavor
  Bouillon Cubes
 ¼ teaspoon pepper
 2 cups frozen broccoli,
  cauliflower and carrot
  combination
 1 cup frozen hash browns
  potatoes
 3 cups BORDEN® or
  MEADOW GOLD® Milk *or*
  Half-and-Half
 2½ cups (10 ounces) shredded
  Cheddar cheese

In large kettle or Dutch oven, cook celery and onion in margarine until tender; stir in flour until smooth. Gradually add water then bouillon, pepper and vegetables; bring to a boil. Reduce heat; cover and simmer 15 minutes. Add milk and cheese. Cook and stir until cheese melts and soup is hot (*do not boil*). Garnish as desired. Refrigerate leftovers.

Makes about 2 quarts

Swiss Broccoli Soup

Dogwood Blossom Soup

- **½ cup (1 stick) unsalted butter**
- **4 cups minced cauliflower (about 1 pound)**
- **2 cups chopped onions**
- **1 tablespoon Chef Paul Prudhomme's VEGETABLE MAGIC®**
- **4 cups chicken broth or water, in all**
- **6 ounces cooked ham, minced**
- **2 bay leaves**
- **¼ teaspoon ground nutmeg**
- **4 cups heavy cream, in all**
- **6 cups very small cauliflowerets (no larger than ½ inch)**

In 5-quart saucepan over medium-high heat, melt butter. When butter comes to a hard sizzle, stir in minced cauliflower and onions. Reduce heat to medium. Cook about 14 minutes, stirring occasionally. Let mixture stick slightly but not brown. Stir in Vegetable Magic and cook 13 minutes more, stirring occasionally and more frequently toward end of cooking time, again taking care not to let mixture brown. Stir in 2 cups broth and cook about 10 minutes, stirring occasionally. Add ham, bay leaves and nutmeg. Stir well and cook about 5 minutes. Add remaining broth, stir well and cook 7 minutes more or until mixture comes to a rolling boil. Whisk in 2 cups cream and cook, whisking occasionally, about 8 minutes or until cream has reduced and thickened somewhat. Whisk in the remaining cream and cook, whisking frequently, about 12 minutes or until soup has reduced and thickened enough to coat a spoon. Add cauliflowerets and cook, whisking frequently, 10 minutes or until soup comes to a boil. Reduce heat to low and cook, whisking occasionally, 10 minutes or until cauliflowerets are tender yet still firm.

Let soup set 10 to 15 minutes before serving for flavors to blend. Remove bay leaves before serving.

Makes about 10 cups

Dogwood Blossom Soup

Corn & Red Pepper Soup

- **2 tablespoons butter or margarine**
- **2 cups seeded and coarsely chopped red bell peppers**
- **1 medium onion, thinly sliced**
- **1 can (14½ ounces) ready-to-serve chicken broth**
- **1 package (10 ounces) frozen whole kernel corn or fresh kernels cut from 4 large ears**
- **½ teaspoon ground cumin**
- **½ cup sour cream**
- **Salt**
- **White pepper**
- **Sunflower seeds for garnish**

Melt butter in 3-quart saucepan over medium heat. Add bell peppers and onion; cook until tender. Add chicken broth, corn and cumin. Bring to a boil. Cover; reduce heat and simmer 20 minutes or until corn is tender. Pour into blender or food processor; process until smooth. Pour into sieve set over bowl; press mixture with rubber spatula to extract all liquid. Discard pulp. Return liquid to pan; whisk in sour cream until evenly blended. Add salt and pepper to taste. Reheat but do not boil. Serve in individual bowls. Garnish with sunflower seeds.   *Makes 4 servings*

Chilly Cucumber Soup

- **2 tablespoons butter or margarine**
- **2 tablespoons all-purpose flour**
- **4 large cucumbers, peeled, seeded and finely chopped (about 3½ cups)**
- **¼ cup finely chopped parsley**
- **¼ cup finely chopped celery leaves**
- **1 envelope LIPTON® Recipe Secrets Golden Onion Recipe Soup Mix**
- **2 cups water**
- **2 cups (1 pint) light cream or half-and-half**

In large saucepan, melt butter and cook flour over medium heat, stirring constantly, 3 minutes. Add cucumbers, parsley and celery leaves. Reduce heat to low and cook 8 minutes or until vegetables are tender. Stir in golden onion recipe soup mix thoroughly blended with water. Bring to a boil, then simmer covered 15 minutes. Remove from heat, then cool.

In food processor or blender, puree soup mixture. Stir in cream; chill. Serve cold and garnish, if desired, with cucumber slices and lemon peel.

Makes about 6 (1-cup) servings

Chilled Avocado Soup

3 small onion slices, each ¼ inch thick, divided
1 can (14½ ounces) ready-to-serve chicken broth
½ cup plain yogurt
1½ tablespoons lemon juice
1 large ripe avocado, halved and pitted
3 to 5 drops hot pepper sauce
Salt
White pepper
¼ cup finely chopped tomato
¼ cup finely chopped cucumber
Cilantro sprigs for garnish
Additional chopped tomatoes and cucumbers for garnish

Place 1 onion slice, chicken broth, yogurt and lemon juice in blender or food processor; process until well blended. Remove pulp from avocado, spoon into blender. Process until smooth. Pour into medium container with tight-fitting lid. Add hot pepper sauce and salt and pepper to taste. Finely chop the remaining 2 onion slices; add to soup. Stir in tomato and cucumber. Cover and refrigerate 2 hours or up to 24 hours. Serve in individual bowls. Garnish with cilantro and additional chopped tomato and cucumber, if desired.

Makes 6 servings

Chilled Avocado Soup (top) and Corn & Red Pepper Soup (bottom)

Gazpacho

1½ pounds fresh tomatoes, seeded and chopped
1½ cups tomato juice
1 medium cucumber, peeled, seeded and chopped
¼ cup finely chopped green bell pepper
¼ cup finely chopped onion
2 tablespoons olive or vegetable oil
2 tablespoons white wine vinegar
1½ teaspoons LAWRY'S® Garlic Salt
¼ teaspoon dried oregano, crushed
LAWRY'S® Seasoned Pepper

In large bowl, combine all ingredients except Seasoned Pepper; blend well. Refrigerate until chilled. Add a sprinkle of Seasoned Pepper to each serving.

Makes 5 to 6 servings

Presentation: Serve in individual chilled bowls.

Hint: For more spice, stir in ¼ teaspoon hot pepper sauce before chilling.

Sausage and Lentil Soup

1 package (10 ounces)
ECKRICH® SMOK-Y-LINKS®
Sausages, cut into ½-inch
slices
½ cup chopped onion
½ cup sliced carrot
½ cup sliced celery
1 clove garlic, minced
2 tablespoons vegetable oil
1 cup lentils, sorted, rinsed
6 cups water
3 teaspoons beef bouillon
granules
1 can (14½ ounces) whole
tomatoes, undrained, cut up
Dash ground black pepper
2 teaspoons lemon juice

Cook onion, carrot, celery and garlic in oil in Dutch oven over medium heat 5 minutes. Add lentils, water and bouillon granules. Bring to a boil over high heat. Reduce heat to low; cover and simmer 30 minutes or until lentils are tender. Add sausage, tomatoes with juice and pepper to lentil mixture. Simmer 10 minutes. Stir in lemon juice.
Makes 6 to 8 servings.

Chili Soup Jarlsberg

1 pound beef round steak, diced
2 tablespoons vegetable oil
2 cans (14½ ounces each)
ready-to-serve beef broth
1 can (15 ounces) dark red
kidney beans
1 can (14½ ounces) tomatoes,
chopped, undrained
1 medium green bell pepper,
chopped
1 medium red bell pepper,
chopped
1 large onion, chopped
1 large clove garlic, minced
3¼ teaspoons chili powder,
divided
¼ teaspoon ground cumin
1½ cups (6 ounces) shredded
NOKKELOST® (or Jarlsberg)
cheese, divided
¼ cup butter or margarine,
softened
1 small clove garlic, minced
12 KAVLI® Norwegian Thick-Style
Crispbreads

Brown beef in hot oil in large, deep saucepan over medium-high heat. Add broth. Bring to a boil over high heat. Reduce heat to low. Cover and simmer 1 hour. Add beans, tomatoes, peppers, onion, large garlic clove, 3 teaspoons of the chili powder and the cumin. Simmer, covered, 30 minutes. Gradually blend in ½ cup of the cheese. Heat just until cheese melts.

Blend butter, small garlic clove and remaining ¼ teaspoon chili powder in small bowl. Spread on crispbreads; arrange on cookie sheet. Bake in preheated 375°F oven several minutes or until butter is melted. Sprinkle with ½ cup of the cheese. Bake just until cheese is melted.

Ladle soup into bowls. Garnish with remaining ½ cup cheese. Serve with crispbreads.
Makes 6 servings.

Chunky Beef Barley Soup

1½ pounds beef stew meat, cut
into ½-inch cubes
2 tablespoons all-purpose flour
2 cloves garlic, minced
¼ cup vegetable oil
2 quarts water
1 can (14½ ounces) tomatoes,
coarsely chopped,
undrained
1 cup coarsely chopped onion
½ cup QUAKER® Scotch® Brand
Pearled Barley*
1 tablespoon salt (optional)
1 teaspoon dried basil, crushed
⅛ teaspoon pepper
1 package (16 ounces) frozen
vegetable medley

Dredge meat in flour. Brown meat with garlic in hot oil in 4-quart Dutch oven over medium-high heat. Add water, tomatoes, onion, barley, salt, basil and pepper. Bring to a boil over high heat. Reduce heat to low. Cover and simmer 1 hour or until meat and barley are tender. Add frozen vegetables. Return to a boil over high heat. Reduce heat to low. Simmer 5 minutes or until vegetables are tender. Additional water may be added if soup becomes too thick upon standing.
Makes about 12 servings.

Substitution: Use ¾ cup Quaker® Scotch® Quick Barley for the pearled barley. Add quick barley with frozen vegetables. Return to a boil; cover and simmer 10 to 12 minutes or until barley is tender.

Chili Soup Jarlsberg

Octoberfest Sausage Soup

- **½ pound ECKRICH® Smoked Sausage**
- **1 cup beef broth**
- **1 cup chicken broth**
- **¼ cup coarsely chopped celery**
- **¼ cup coarsely chopped onion**
- **¼ cup coarsely chopped green bell pepper**
- **2 tablespoons cornstarch, dissolved in 2 tablespoons water**
- **1 cup (4 ounces) shredded Swiss cheese**
- **1 can (8 ounces) sauerkraut, drained**
- **2 cups half and half**
- **¼ teaspoon ground white pepper**
- **2 green onions, sliced**

Combine broths, celery, onion, green pepper and potato in large saucepan; bring to a boil over high heat. Reduce heat to low; simmer until vegetables are crisp-tender, about 15 minutes. Add dissolved cornstarch; cook and stir until soup thickens. Cut sausage into quarters lengthwise, then cut crosswise into ¼-inch pieces. Add sausage, cheese, sauerkraut, half and half and white pepper. Stir. Continue heating until mixture is hot. DO NOT BOIL. Serve immediately. Garnish with green onions.
Makes 4 to 6 servings.

Creamy Clam Bisque

- **¼ cup chopped onion**
- **2 tablespoons margarine or butter**
- **3 tablespoons flour**
  Dash pepper
- **½ cup dry white wine**
- **2 (6½-ounce) cans SNOW'S® or DOXSEE® Chopped Clams, drained, reserving liquid**
- **2 cups (1 pint) BORDEN® or MEADOW GOLD® Half-and-Half**
- **1 egg yolk**
  Paprika, optional

Hearty Vegetable Soup

In medium saucepan, cook onion in margarine until tender. Gradually stir in flour and pepper; add wine and reserved clam liquid. Cook and stir until thickened; remove from heat. Blend half-and-half with egg yolk; stir into wine mixture along with clams. Heat through *(do not boil)*. Garnish with paprika if desired. Refrigerate leftovers.
Makes about 1 quart.

Sausage Corn Chowder

- **1 package (8 ounces) SWIFT PREMIUM® BROWN 'N SERVE™ Microwave Sausage Links, thawed, cut into ½-inch slices**
- **2 cups cubed potatoes**
- **¾ cup chopped onion**
- **½ cup chopped celery**
- **¼ cup water**
- **1 can (12 ounces) corn with red and green bell peppers**
- **1 can (17 ounces) cream-style corn**
- **2 cups milk**
- **1 teaspoon salt**
- **⅛ teaspoon ground thyme**
  Dash ground white pepper

Microwave Directions: Place potatoes, onion, celery and water in 2-quart microwave-safe bowl. Cover with vented plastic wrap and *microwave* on High (100%) 9 to 10 minutes or until vegetables are tender, stirring twice. Stir in sausage, corn, cream-style corn, milk, salt, thyme and pepper. Cover and *microwave* on High 7 to 8 minutes or until hot, stirring twice.
Makes 6 servings.

Hearty Vegetable Soup

- **3 pounds beef shanks, cracked**
- **8 cups water**
- **3 tablespoons WYLER'S® or STEERO® Beef-Flavor Instant Bouillon *or* 9 Beef-Flavor Bouillon Cubes**
- **2 bay leaves**
- **1 (28-ounce) can whole tomatoes, undrained**
- **1 cup pared, sliced carrots**
- **½ cup chopped celery**
- **½ cup chopped onion**
- **1 teaspoon thyme leaves**
- **1 cup uncooked CREAMETTES® Elbow Macaroni**
- **2 cups sliced zucchini (2 small)**

In large kettle or Dutch oven, combine shanks, water, bouillon and bay leaves. Bring to a boil; simmer covered 1½ hours or until meat is tender. Remove shanks and bay leaves; cut meat into cubes. Discard bones. Cool stock; skim fat from surface. Add meat, tomatoes, carrots, celery, onion and thyme; simmer covered 20 minutes. Add macaroni and zucchini. Cook 10 minutes longer or until tender. Refrigerate leftovers.
Makes about 3 quarts.

Turkey-Barley Soup

- **2 quarts chicken or turkey stock**
- **2 medium onions, chopped**
- **½ cup sliced carrots**
- **½ cup sliced celery**
- **⅓ cup uncooked barley, rinsed**
- **4 sprigs parsley**
- **1 bay leaf**
- **1 teaspoon salt**
- **½ teaspoon poultry seasoning**
- **1 can (16 ounces) tomatoes, undrained, chopped**
- **2 cups cubed cooked turkey**
- **¼ teaspoon TABASCO® pepper sauce**
- **2 tablespoons chopped parsley (optional)**

In large saucepot combine chicken stock, onions, carrots, celery, barley, parsley sprigs, bay leaf, salt and poultry seasoning. Cover; bring to a boil. Reduce heat; simmer 45 minutes or until barley is tender. Add tomatoes, turkey and Tabasco® sauce. Cook until heated through. Remove bay leaf. Garnish with chopped parsley, if desired.
Makes 8 servings.

Norwegian Pea Soup

- **3½ quarts water, divided**
- **1 package (1 pound) whole dry yellow peas or split yellow peas, rinsed**
- **1½ cups finely chopped carrots**
- **1½ cups finely chopped onions**
- **¼ teaspoon ground cumin**
- **2½ pound shank end fully cooked ham**
- **KAVLI® Croutons (recipe follows)**
- **1 cup thinly sliced celery**
- **2 tablespoons olive oil**

Place 7 cups of the water and the peas in heavy, large saucepan. Bring to a boil over high heat; boil 2 minutes. Remove from heat. Cover and let soak 1 hour. Drain peas; discard water. (If using split peas, omit this step.)

Return peas to heavy, large saucepan. Add remaining 7 cups water, the carrots, onions and cumin. Bring to a boil over high heat. Reduce heat to low. Cover and simmer 1 hour, stirring occasionally. Add ham; cook 1 hour more, stirring occasionally. Meanwhile, prepare Kavli Croutons. Add celery to soup mixture and cook until peas mash easily, stirring occasionally. Remove ham; cut into cubes. Brown ham in hot oil in large skillet over medium-high heat. Return to soup; heat through. Serve topped with Kavli Croutons.
Makes about 6 servings.

KAVLI® CROUTONS: Melt ⅓ cup butter or margarine in large skillet over medium heat. Add 1 small garlic clove. Cook and stir several minutes. Add 1½ cups coarsely broken KAVLI® Norwegian Thick-Style Crispbreads. Cook and stir until croutons are lightly browned. Stir in 2 tablespoons chopped parsley.

Italian Vegetable Soup

- **1 pound bulk Italian sausage**
- **2 cups chopped onion**
- **2 cloves garlic, finely chopped**
- **7 cups water**
- **4 medium carrots, pared and sliced**
- **1 (28-ounce) can tomatoes, undrained and broken up**
- **2 tablespoons WYLER'S® or STEERO® Beef-Flavor Instant Bouillon or 6 Beef-Flavor Bouillon Cubes**
- **1 teaspoon Italian seasoning**
- **¼ teaspoon pepper**
- **1½ cups coarsely chopped zucchini**
- **1 (15-ounce) can garbanzo beans, drained**
- **1 cup uncooked CREAMETTE® Rotini or Elbow Macaroni**

In large kettle or Dutch oven, brown sausage, onion and garlic; pour off fat. Add water, carrots, tomatoes, bouillon, Italian seasoning and pepper; bring to a boil. Reduce heat; cover and simmer 30 minutes. Add zucchini, beans and rotini. Cover; cook 15 to 20 minutes or until rotini is tender. Garnish as desired. Refrigerate leftovers.
Makes about 2½ quarts.

Broccoli Cheese Soup

- **½ cup chopped onion**
- **¼ cup margarine or butter**
- **¼ cup unsifted flour**
- **3 cups water**
- **2 (10-ounce) packages frozen chopped broccoli, thawed and well drained**
- **4 teaspoons WYLER'S® or STEERO® Chicken-Flavor Instant Bouillon or 4 Chicken-Flavor Bouillon Cubes**
- **1 teaspoon Worcestershire sauce**
- **3 cups (12 ounces) shredded Cheddar cheese**
- **2 cups (1 pint) BORDEN® or MEADOW GOLD® Coffee Cream or Half-and-Half**

In large saucepan or Dutch oven, cook onion in margarine until tender; stir in flour. Gradually stir in water then broccoli, bouillon and Worcestershire. Over medium heat, cook and stir until thickened and broccoli is tender, about 10 minutes. Add cheese and cream. Cook and stir until cheese melts and soup is hot *(do not boil)*. Garnish as desired. Refrigerate leftovers.
Makes about 2 quarts.

Broccoli Cheese Soup (left) and Italian Vegetable Soup (right)

Tortilla Soup

    1 (4-ounce) jar sliced or diced
        pimientos
    ½ cup chopped onion
    ½ teaspoon ground cumin
    1 tablespoon BLUE BONNET®
        Margarine
    2 (13¾-fluid ounce) cans
        COLLEGE INN® Chicken or
        Beef Broth
    1 (8¾-ounce) can whole kernel
        sweet corn, undrained
    2 tablespoons chopped parsley
    2 cups coarsely broken tortilla
        chips
    1 cup shredded Monterey Jack,
        Cheddar or Monterey Jack
        with jalapeño pepper cheese
        (4 ounces)

Drain pimientos, reserving liquid. In medium saucepan, over medium-high heat, cook onion and cumin in margarine for 2 to 3 minutes, stirring occasionally. Stir in reserved pimiento liquid, broth, corn and parsley. Heat to a boil; reduce heat. Cover; simmer 10 minutes.

Meanwhile, arrange tortilla chips, cheese and pimientos in individual serving bowls. Ladle hot soup into bowls. Serve immediately.
Makes 6 to 8 servings.

Borscht

Minestrone

    3 medium carrots
    3 stalks celery
    2 medium onions
    1 large potato
    ¼ pound green beans
    2 medium zucchini
    ½ pound cabbage
    1 medium clove garlic
    ⅓ cup olive oil
    3 tablespoons butter
    3½ cups beef broth
    1½ cups water
    1 can (28 ounces) Italian plum
        tomatoes
    ½ teaspoon salt
    ½ teaspoon dried basil,
        crumbled
    ¼ teaspoon dried rosemary,
        crumbled
    ¼ teaspoon pepper
    1 bay leaf
    1 can (1 pound) cannellini beans

1. Pare carrots; chop coarsely. Chop celery coarsely. Chop onions. Pare potato; cut into ¾-inch cubes. Trim green beans; cut into 1-inch pieces. Trim zucchini; cut into ½-inch cubes. Coarsely shred cabbage. Mince garlic.
2. Heat oil and butter in 5-quart Dutch oven over medium heat. Add onions; sauté, stirring occasionally, until soft and golden but not brown, 6 to 8 minutes. Stir in carrots and potato; sauté 5 minutes. Stir in celery and green beans; sauté 5 minutes. Stir in zucchini; sauté 3 minutes. Stir in cabbage and garlic; cook 1 minute.
3. Add broth, water and liquid from tomatoes to pan. Chop tomatoes coarsely; add to pan. Stir in salt, basil, rosemary, pepper and bay leaf. Heat to boiling; reduce heat to low. Simmer, covered, stirring occasionally, 1½ hours.
4. Rinse and drain cannellini beans; add beans to soup. Cook, uncovered, over medium-low heat, stirring occasionally, until soup is thick, 30 to 40 minutes longer. Remove bay leaf.
Makes about 12 cups; 8 to 10 servings.
Note: Serve sprinkled with grated Parmesan cheese, if desired.

Borscht

    3 cups chopped cabbage
    ¼ cup BLUE BONNET® Margarine
    1 (16-ounce) can sliced beets
    1 (46-fluid ounce) can COLLEGE
        INN® Beef Broth
    2 tablespoons lemon juice
    ½ teaspoon ground black pepper
    1 cup dairy sour cream

In large saucepan, over medium-high heat, cook cabbage in margarine until tender. Drain beets, reserving liquid; chop beets. Stir in beef broth, beets with liquid, lemon juice and pepper. Heat to a boil; reduce heat. Simmer 15 minutes. Serve with dollop of sour cream.
Makes 8 servings.

Spinach-Rice Soup

- 1 can (13¾ oz.) ready-to-serve chicken broth
- 1 package (9.5 oz.) BIRDS EYE® Creamed Spinach, thawed
- ½ cup Original MINUTE® Rice
  Dash of pepper
  Dash of nutmeg

Bring broth and spinach to a full boil in medium saucepan. Stir in rice. Cover; remove from heat. Let stand 5 minutes. Season with pepper and nutmeg.
Makes 3 servings.
  Note: Recipe may be doubled.

Black Bean Soup with Rice and Sherry

- 1 cup dry black beans, rinsed
- 4 cups beef broth
- 4 cups chicken broth
- ½ pound smoked ham hock
- 1 large yellow onion, sliced
- 1 carrot, sliced
- 4 sprigs parsley
- 2 cloves garlic
- 1 teaspoon ground thyme
  Salt
  Pepper
- 3 cups hot cooked rice
- ½ cup dry sherry
- 1 small red onion, chopped

Place beans in large bowl. Cover with water; soak overnight. Drain beans; discard water. Place beans in large stockpot. Add broths, ham hock, yellow onion, carrot, parsley, garlic and thyme. Bring to a boil over high heat. Reduce heat to low. Cover and simmer 6 to 8 hours, stirring occasionally. Strain soup into large saucepan, reserving bean mixture and discarding ham hock. Puree bean mixture, in batches, in blender or food processor. Stir bean mixture into broth. Cook over low heat 2 hours more, stirring occasionally. Season to taste with salt and pepper. Ladle soup into bowls. Top with rice, sherry and red onion.
Makes 6 servings.

Favorite recipe from **USA Rice Council**

Blushing Onion Soup

- 4 cups thinly sliced onions
- 1 clove garlic, finely chopped
- ¼ cup margarine or butter
- 1 (46-ounce) can tomato juice
- 1 cup water
- 2 teaspoons WYLER'S® or STEERO® Beef-Flavor Instant Bouillon *or* 2 Beef-Flavor Bouillon Cubes
- 2 teaspoons parsley flakes
- 8 slices French bread, toasted
- 2 cups (8 ounces) shredded Mozzarella cheese

In large kettle or Dutch oven, cook onions and garlic in margarine until tender. Stir in tomato juice, water, bouillon and parsley. Bring to a boil; reduce heat. Simmer uncovered 20 to 30 minutes, stirring occasionally. Ladle into 8 ovenproof soup bowls. Top with bread slices and sprinkle generously with cheese. Broil 2 to 3 minutes or until cheese melts. Serve immediately.
Makes 8 servings.
  Microwave: In 2-quart glass measure, melt margarine on 100% power (high) 1 minute. Add onions and garlic; cook covered on 100% power (high) 5 to 6 minutes or until onions are tender. Add tomato juice, water, *instant* bouillon and parsley. Cook covered on 100% power (high) 15 to 17 minutes or until boiling. Proceed as above.

Creamed Corn Chowder

- 6 slices bacon, cut in ½-inch pieces
- ½ cup chopped onion
- ⅓ cup chopped green pepper
- 2 (17-ounce) cans cream style sweet corn
- 2 (13¾-fluid ounce) cans COLLEGE INN® Chicken Broth
- ⅛ teaspoon ground black pepper

In large saucepan, over medium-high heat, cook bacon until crisp; remove and crumble bacon. Pour off all but 2 tablespoons drippings. Cook onion and green pepper in reserved drippings 2 to 3 minutes. Add corn, chicken broth and pepper. Heat to a boil; reduce heat. Cover and simmer 15 minutes. Serve garnished with bacon.
Makes 6 servings.

Lentil and Brown Rice Soup

- 1 envelope LIPTON® Recipe Secrets Onion, Beefy Onion or Beefy Mushroom Recipe Soup Mix
- 4 cups water
- ¾ cup lentils, rinsed and drained
- ½ cup uncooked brown or regular rice
- 1 can (14½ ounces) whole peeled tomatoes, undrained and coarsely chopped
- 1 medium carrot, coarsely chopped
- 1 large stalk celery, coarsely chopped
- ½ teaspoon basil leaves
- ½ teaspoon oregano
- ¼ teaspoon thyme leaves (optional)
- 1 tablespoon finely chopped parsley
- 1 tablespoon apple cider vinegar
- ¼ teaspoon pepper

In large saucepan or stockpot, combine onion recipe soup mix, water, lentils, uncooked rice, tomatoes, carrot, celery, basil, oregano and thyme. Bring to a boil, then simmer covered, stirring occasionally, 45 minutes or until lentils and rice are tender. Stir in remaining ingredients.
Makes about 3 (2-cup) servings.
  Microwave Directions: In 3-quart casserole, combine onion recipe soup mix, water, tomatoes, carrot, celery, basil, oregano and thyme. Microwave covered at HIGH (Full Power) 12 minutes or until boiling. Stir in lentils and uncooked brown rice* and microwave covered at MEDIUM (50% Full Power), stirring occasionally, 60 minutes or until lentils and rice are tender. Stir in remaining ingredients. Let stand covered 5 minutes.
  *If using uncooked regular rice, decrease 60-minute cooking time to 30 minutes.

Lentil and Brown Rice Soup

Quick Beef Soup

Beef Barley Vegetable Soup

- **1 pound beef shanks, cracked**
- **7 cups water**
- **1 (14½-ounce) can stewed tomatoes**
- **¾ cup chopped onion**
- **2 tablespoons WYLER'S® or STEERO® Beef-Flavor Instant Bouillon or 6 Beef-Flavor Bouillon Cubes**
- **½ teaspoon basil leaves**
- **1 bay leaf**
- **½ cup regular barley**
- **3 medium carrots, pared and chopped**
- **1½ cups chopped celery**

In large kettle or Dutch oven, combine shanks, water, tomatoes, onion, bouillon, basil and bay leaf. Bring to a boil. Reduce heat; cover and simmer 1 hour. Remove shanks from stock; cut meat into ½-inch pieces. Skim off fat. Add meat and barley; bring to a boil. Reduce heat; cover and simmer 30 minutes. Add carrots and celery; cook 30 minutes longer. Remove bay leaf. Refrigerate leftovers.

Makes about 2½ quarts

Quick Beef Soup

- **1½ pounds lean ground beef**
- **1 cup chopped onion**
- **2 cloves garlic, finely chopped**
- **1 can (28 ounces) tomatoes, undrained**
- **6 cups water**
- **6 beef bouillon cubes**
- **¼ teaspoon pepper**
- **½ cup uncooked orzo**
- **1½ cups frozen peas, carrots and corn vegetable blend**
- **French bread (optional)**

Cook beef, onion and garlic in large saucepan over medium-high heat until beef is brown, stirring to separate meat; drain fat.

Purée tomatoes with juice in covered blender or food processor. Add tomatoes, water, bouillon cubes and pepper to meat mixture. Bring to a boil; reduce heat to low. Simmer, uncovered, 20 minutes. Add orzo and vegetables. Simmer 15 minutes more. Serve with French bread.

Makes 6 servings

*Favorite recipe from **North Dakota Beef Commission***

Turkey Wild Rice Pumpkin Soup

- **2 tablespoons margarine or butter**
- **½ cup chopped onions**
- **½ cup sliced celery**
- **4 cups chicken or turkey broth**
- **1 can (16 ounces) solid-pack pumpkin**
- **2 cups (10 ounces) cubed cooked BUTTERBALL® Turkey**
- **2 cups cooked wild rice**
- **1 cup half and half**
- **1 teaspoon seasoned salt**
- **½ teaspoon ground cinnamon**

Cook and stir margarine, onions and celery in Dutch oven over medium heat until vegetables are crisp-tender, about 5 minutes. Add broth and pumpkin. Bring to a boil; reduce heat and simmer 5 minutes. Stir in turkey, rice, half and half, salt and cinnamon. Heat to serving temperature; do not boil.

Makes 8 servings

Wild Rice Soup

    2 cups water
    ½ cup uncooked wild rice
    ½ teaspoon salt
    3 tablespoons BUTTER FLAVOR CRISCO®
    ½ cup chopped green bell pepper
    ½ cup chopped celery
    ⅓ cup chopped onion
    1 clove garlic, minced
    2 tablespoons all-purpose flour
 1½ teaspoons instant chicken bouillon granules
    ½ teaspoon salt
    ⅛ teaspoon pepper
    ⅛ teaspoon bouquet garni seasoning
    ¾ cup cubed fully cooked ham
    1 medium carrot, grated
    2 tablespoons snipped fresh parsley
    2 cups milk
    2 cups half-and-half

In 2-quart saucepan combine water, wild rice and salt. Heat to boiling. Reduce heat; cover and simmer 30 minutes or until tender. Drain in colander. Set aside. In 2-quart saucepan melt Butter Flavor Crisco®. Add green pepper, celery, onion and garlic. Cook and stir over medium heat about 7 minutes or until tender. Stir in flour, bouillon granules, salt, pepper and bouquet garni. Add cooked rice, ham, carrot, parsley, milk and half-and-half. Cook over medium heat 15 to 20 minutes or until very hot, stirring occasionally. Serve hot. Refrigerate leftover soup.

Makes 4 to 6 servings

Albondigas Soup

    1 pound ground beef
    ¼ cup long-grain rice
    1 egg
    1 tablespoon chopped fresh cilantro
    1 teaspoon LAWRY'S® Seasoned Salt
    ¼ cup ice water
    2 cans (14½ ounces each) chicken broth
    1 can (14½ ounces) whole peeled tomatoes, undrained and cut up
    ¼ cup chopped onion
    1 stalk celery, diced
    1 large carrot, diced
    1 medium potato, diced
    ¼ teaspoon LAWRY'S® Garlic Powder with Parsley

In medium bowl, combine ground beef, rice, egg, cilantro, Seasoned Salt and ice water; form into small meatballs. In large saucepan, combine broth with vegetables and Garlic Powder with Parsley. Bring to a boil; add meatballs. Reduce heat, cover and simmer 30 to 40 minutes, stirring occasionally.

Makes 6 to 8 servings

Presentation: Serve with lemon wedges and warm tortillas.

Hint: For a lower salt version, use homemade chicken broth or low-sodium chicken broth.

Albondigas Soup

Hot and Sour Soup

Sopa de Sonora

7½ cups water, divided
1 cup dry pinto beans, rinsed
1 pound boneless lean pork shoulder, trimmed, cut into 1-inch cubes
1 tablespoon vegetable oil
1 can (14½ ounces) ready-to-serve beef broth
1½ tablespoons LAWRY'S® Minced Onion with Green Onion Flakes
¼ teaspoon LAWRY'S® Garlic Powder with Parsley
1 package (1⅝ ounces) LAWRY'S® Chili Seasoning Mix
2 cups thinly sliced carrots LAWRY'S® Seasoned Salt Condiments*

Place 3 cups of the water and the beans in 3-quart saucepan. Bring to a boil over high heat; boil 2 minutes. Remove from heat. Cover and let soak 1 hour. Drain beans; discard water. Brown pork in hot oil in Dutch oven over medium-high heat. Add beans, remaining 4½ cups water, the broth, minced onion, garlic powder and chili seasoning mix. Bring to a boil over high heat. Reduce heat to low. Cover and simmer 1½ hours. Add carrots; simmer, covered, about 30 minutes or until carrots are tender. Season to taste with seasoned salt. Ladle into bowls. Serve with condiments.
Makes 6 to 8 servings.
Condiments: Cherry tomato quarters, sliced green onions, chopped cilantro, lime wedges, sour cream or LAWRY'S® Chunky Taco Sauce.

Frank and Vegetable Soup

1 package (16 ounces) ECKRICH® Franks, cut into ¼-inch slices
1½ cups chopped onions
1 cup sliced carrots
½ cup sliced celery
1 tablespoon butter or margarine
1 can (14½ ounces) whole tomatoes, undrained
1 package (10 ounces) frozen cut green beans, thawed
5 cups beef broth or bouillon Grated Parmesan cheese

Saute onions, carrots and celery in butter in large saucepan over medium heat 5 minutes. Add tomatoes with juice; break up tomatoes. Mix in beans and broth. Bring to a boil over high heat. Reduce heat to low; simmer 15 minutes. Add franks and simmer 5 minutes more. Top each serving with cheese.
Makes 8 servings.

Hot and Sour Soup

1 ounce dried Oriental mushrooms
2 cans (13¾ ounces each) chicken broth or 3⅓ cups chicken stock
2 cups orange juice
¾ pound boneless pork, cut into julienne strips
1 cup carrots, cut into julienne strips
1 can (8 ounces) sliced water chestnuts, drained
1 tablespoon soy sauce
¼ teaspoon salt
½ pound tofu, drained and cut into ½-inch cubes
3 tablespoons white wine vinegar
¾ teaspoon TABASCO® pepper sauce
¼ cup cornstarch
⅓ cup water

In small bowl pour enough boiling water over mushrooms to cover. Let stand 30 minutes; drain. In large saucepot combine mushrooms, broth, orange juice, pork, carrots, water chestnuts, soy sauce and salt. Bring to a boil. Reduce heat; simmer 3 minutes or until pork is cooked. Add tofu, vinegar and Tabasco® sauce. Combine cornstarch and water until smooth; add to soup. Stir constantly, bring to a boil over medium heat and boil for 1 minute.
Makes 8 servings.

Corned Beef & Cabbage Chowder

2 tablespoons butter or margarine
½ cup thinly sliced celery
½ cup finely chopped onion
2 cups water
2 cups coarsely shredded cabbage
1 cup thinly sliced carrots
1 envelope LIPTON® Recipe Secrets Noodle Soup Mix with Real Chicken Broth
1 teaspoon dry mustard
1½ tablespoons all-purpose flour
2 cups milk
¼ pound thinly sliced cooked corned beef, cut into thin strips

In large saucepan or stockpot, melt butter and cook celery and onion over medium heat until tender. Stir in water, cabbage and carrots. Bring to a boil, then simmer covered, stirring occasionally, 15 minutes or until vegetables are almost tender. Stir in noodle soup mix, then mustard and flour blended with milk. Bring just to the boiling point, then simmer, stirring constantly, until chowder is thickened, about 5 minutes. Stir in corned beef and heat through, but do not boil.

Makes about 3 (1³/₄-cup) servings.

Microwave Directions: In 3-quart casserole, microwave butter at HIGH (Full Power) 1 minute. Add celery and onion and microwave 5 minutes or until vegetables are tender, stirring once. Add water, cabbage and carrots. Microwave covered, stirring occasionally, 15 minutes or until vegetables are tender. Stir in noodle soup mix, then mustard and flour blended with milk. Microwave covered, stirring occasionally, 7 minutes or until chowder is thickened. Stir in corned beef. Let stand covered 5 minutes.

Albondingas Soup

1 pound ground beef
¼ cup seasoned dry bread
    crumbs
2 tablespoons minced onion
2 tablespoons water
1 egg
½ teaspoon salt
³/₄ teaspoon TABASCO® pepper
    sauce, divided
1 large green pepper
2 tablespoons olive or vegetable
    oil
1 medium onion, chopped
1 clove garlic, minced
4 cups beef broth
1 can (16 ounces) tomatoes,
    undrained
¼ teaspoon saffron threads,
    crumbled

In medium bowl combine beef, crumbs, minced onion, water, egg, salt and ¼ teaspoon Tabasco® sauce; mix well. Shape into 1-inch meatballs. Cover; refrigerate. Coarsely chop enough green pepper to yield ½ cup; cut remainder into thin strips for garnish.

In large saucepot heat oil; cook ½ cup chopped green pepper, chopped onion and garlic 3 minutes or until tender. Stir in broth, tomatoes, saffron and remaining ½ teaspoon Tabasco® sauce. Bring to a boil, reduce heat and simmer uncovered 30 minutes; stir occasionally. Add meatballs;

simmer covered 20 minutes longer or until meatballs are cooked. Garnish with green pepper strips.

Makes 6 servings.

Microwave Directions: Prepare meatballs as directed above. Chop and cut green pepper as directed above. In 3-quart microwave-safe casserole place *1 tablespoon* oil, chopped green pepper, chopped onion and garlic. Cover loosely with plastic wrap; cook on High 2 to 4 minutes or until vegetables are softened. Stir in broth, *drained* canned tomatoes, saffron and remaining ½ teaspoon Tabasco® sauce. Cook uncovered on High 10 minutes. Add meatballs and continue to cook uncovered on High 15 to 18 minutes or until meatballs are cooked; stir twice during cooking. Garnish with green pepper strips.

Beefy Vegetable Soup

1 tablespoon vegetable oil
2 pounds boneless beef chuck,
    cut into 1-inch cubes
2 medium onions, chopped
1 can (16 ounces) tomatoes,
    undrained
½ cup uncooked barley, rinsed

10 cups water
¹/₃ cup soy sauce
2 teaspoons dried thyme leaves
½ teaspoon salt
¼ pound fresh spinach leaves
4 large carrots, shredded
2 medium potatoes, pared,
    cubed
2 large celery stalks, sliced
¼ pound green beans, cut into
    pieces
½ teaspoon TABASCO® pepper
    sauce

In large heavy saucepot or Dutch oven heat oil over medium-high heat; add beef and brown on all sides. Remove and set aside. In same pot over medium heat, cook onions 3 minutes or until tender. Return meat to pot; add tomatoes, barley, water, soy sauce, thyme and salt. Cover. Bring to a boil. Reduce heat; simmer 1 hour. Add spinach, carrots, potatoes, celery, beans and Tabasco® sauce. Simmer covered 45 minutes longer or until meat and vegetables are tender.

Makes 10 to 12 servings.

Albondingas Soup

Hearty Meatball Soup

½ pound ground beef
½ pound bulk pork sausage
1 egg
½ teaspoon salt (optional)
⅛ teaspoon pepper (optional)
4 cups water
1 envelope (4-serving size) onion soup mix
1 can (16 ounces) stewed tomatoes
1 can (15¼ ounces) red kidney beans, drained
1 cup diced carrots
1 cup Original MINUTE® Rice
2 tablespoons chopped parsley

Mix ground beef, sausage, egg, salt and pepper thoroughly in medium bowl. Shape into tiny balls. (Brown meatballs in skillet, if desired.)

Bring water to boil in large saucepan; stir in soup mix. Reduce heat; cover and simmer 10 minutes. Add meatballs, tomatoes, kidney beans and carrots; simmer 15 minutes longer. Stir in rice. Cover; remove from heat. Let stand 5 minutes. Add parsley.

Makes 8 to 10 servings

Hearty Chicken and Rice Soup

10 cups chicken broth
1 medium onion, chopped
1 cup sliced celery
1 cup sliced carrots
¼ cup snipped parsley
½ teaspoon cracked black pepper
½ teaspoon dried thyme leaves
1 bay leaf
1½ cups chicken cubes (about ¾ pound)
2 cups cooked rice
2 tablespoons fresh lime juice
Lime slices for garnish

Combine broth, onion, celery, carrots, parsley, pepper, thyme, and bay leaf in Dutch oven. Bring to a boil; stir once or twice. Reduce heat; simmer, uncovered, 10 to 15 minutes. Add chicken; simmer, uncovered, 5 to 10 minutes or until chicken is cooked. Remove and discard bay leaf. Stir in rice and lime juice just before serving. Garnish with lime slices.

Makes 8 servings

Favorite recipe from **USA Rice Council**

Chicken Cilantro Bisque

6 ounces boneless, skinless chicken breasts, cut into chunks
2½ cups low-sodium chicken broth
½ cup cilantro leaves
½ cup sliced green onions
¼ cup sliced celery
1 large clove garlic, minced
½ teaspoon ground cumin
⅓ cup all-purpose flour
1½ cups (12-ounce can) *undiluted* CARNATION® Evaporated Skimmed Milk
Fresh ground pepper, to taste

In large saucepan, combine chicken, broth, cilantro, green onions, celery, garlic and cumin. Heat to boiling; reduce heat and boil gently, covered, for 15 minutes. Pour soup into blender container. Add flour. Cover and blend, starting at low speed, until smooth. Pour mixture back into saucepan. Cook over medium heat, stirring constantly, until mixture comes to a boil and thickens. Remove from heat. Gradually stir in milk. Reheat just to serving temperature. Do not boil. Season with pepper to taste. Garnish as desired.

Makes about 4 servings

Bean Soup Santa Fe

1¼ cups dry black beans
½ cup dry pinto beans
6 cups water
1 can (14½ ounces) beef broth
1 can (14½ ounces) stewed tomatoes, undrained
1½ cups water
1 package (1.27 ounces) LAWRY'S® Spices & Seasonings for Fajitas
2 tablespoons LAWRY'S® Minced Onion with Green Onion Flakes
1 teaspoon dry parsley flakes

In Dutch oven, soak black beans and pinto beans in 6 cups water for 1 hour. Bring to a boil; reduce heat, cover and simmer 1 hour. Drain beans and rinse. Return to Dutch oven; add remaining ingredients. Bring to a boil; reduce heat, cover and simmer 1 hour. *Makes 4 servings*

Tomato, Chicken and Mushroom Soup

¼ pound fresh mushrooms, sliced
1 tablespoon margarine or butter
2 cans (13¾ ounces each) chicken broth
2 cups diced cooked chicken
1 can (14½ ounces) whole tomatoes, cut up
1 can (8 ounces) tomato sauce
1 carrot, thinly sliced
1 envelope GOOD SEASONS® Italian Salad Dressing Mix
¾ cup Original MINUTE® Rice

Cook and stir mushrooms in hot margarine in large saucepan. Add broth, chicken, tomatoes, tomato sauce, carrot and salad dressing mix; stir well. Bring to boil. Reduce heat; cover and simmer 10 minutes. Stir in rice. Cover; remove from heat. Let stand 5 minutes.

Makes 8 servings

Hearty Chicken and Rice Soup

Gazpacho

- 1 (14½-ounce) can stewed tomatoes
- 1 (13¾-fluid ounce) can COLLEGE INN® Chicken or Beef Broth
- 1 medium cucumber, coarsely chopped
- ½ cup sliced scallions
- ¼ cup red wine vinegar
- ¼ teaspoon liquid hot pepper seasoning

Drain tomatoes, reserving liquid; coarsely chop tomatoes. In medium bowl, combine chopped tomatoes, reserved liquid, broth, cucumber, scallions, vinegar and liquid hot pepper seasoning. Refrigerate 2 to 3 hours. Serve cold.
Makes 4 servings.

Wisconsin Cheese 'n Beer Soup

- 2 tablespoons butter or margarine
- 2 tablespoons all-purpose flour
- 1 envelope LIPTON® Recipe Secrets Golden Onion Recipe Soup Mix
- 3 cups milk
- 1 teaspoon Worcestershire sauce
- 1 cup shredded Cheddar cheese (about 4 ounces)
- ½ cup beer
- 1 teaspoon prepared mustard

In medium saucepan, melt butter and cook flour over medium heat, stirring constantly, 3 minutes or until bubbling. Stir in golden onion recipe soup mix thoroughly blended with milk and Worcestershire sauce. Bring just to the boiling point, then simmer, stirring occasionally, 10 minutes. Stir in remaining ingredients and simmer, stirring constantly, 5 minutes or until cheese is melted. Garnish, if desired, with additional cheese, chopped red pepper and parsley.
Makes about 4 (1-cup) servings.

Tortellini Soup

Chicken & Rice Gumbo

- 1 (46-fluid ounce) can COLLEGE INN® Chicken Broth
- 1 pound boneless chicken, cut in bite-size pieces
- 1 (17-ounce) can whole kernel sweet corn, drained
- 1 (14½-ounce) can stewed tomatoes, undrained and chopped
- 1 (10-ounce) package frozen okra, thawed and chopped
- ½ cup uncooked rice
- 1 teaspoon ground black pepper

In large saucepan, over medium-high heat, heat chicken broth, chicken, corn, tomatoes, okra, rice and pepper to a boil. Reduce heat; simmer, uncovered, 20 minutes or until rice is cooked.
Makes 10 servings.

Tortellini Soup

- 2 cloves garlic, crushed
- 1 tablespoon BLUE BONNET® Margarine
- 2 (13¾-fluid ounce) cans COLLEGE INN® Chicken or Beef Broth
- 8 ounces frozen or fresh cheese tortellini
- 1 (15-ounce) can chopped spinach, undrained
- 1 (14½-ounce) can stewed tomatoes, undrained and cut up
- Grated Parmesan cheese

In large saucepan, over medium-high heat, cook garlic in margarine for 2 to 3 minutes. Add broth and tortellini. Heat to a boil; reduce heat; simmer 10 minutes. Add spinach and tomatoes; simmer 5 minutes more. Serve with cheese.
Makes 6 servings.

Chicken and Pasta Soup

1 (2½-pound) chicken, cut up
1 (46-fluid ounce) can COLLEGE INN® Chicken Broth
1 (16-ounce) can cut green beans
1 (6-ounce) can tomato paste
1 cup uncooked small shell macaroni
1 teaspoon dried basil leaves

In large saucepan, over medium-high heat, heat chicken and chicken broth to a boil; reduce heat. Cover; simmer 25 minutes or until chicken is tender. Remove chicken; cool slightly. Add remaining ingredients to broth. Heat to a boil; reduce heat. Cover; simmer 20 minutes or until macaroni is cooked. Meanwhile, remove chicken from bones and cut into bite-size pieces. Add to soup; cook 5 minutes more.
Makes 6 servings.

Quick Deli Turkey Soup

½ pound BUTTERBALL® Deli Turkey Breast, cubed
1 can (13¾ ounces) ready-to-serve chicken broth
1 can (14½ ounces) stewed tomatoes, undrained
1 small zucchini, cut up (about 1 cup)
¼ teaspoon dried basil leaves
½ cup cooked chili-mac pasta or macaroni

Combine broth, tomatoes with juice, zucchini and basil in large saucepan. Bring to a boil over high heat. Reduce heat to medium; simmer 10 minutes or until zucchini is tender. Stir in turkey and pasta. Continue heating until turkey is hot.
Makes 4 servings.

New England Style Turkey Chowder

2 cups diced cooked BUTTERBALL® turkey (¾ pound)
2 cans (17 ounces each) cream-style corn
2½ cups milk
1 cup chicken broth
1 cup diced potato
½ cup finely shredded carrot

½ cup finely chopped onion
1 teaspoon salt
¼ teaspoon ground black pepper

Combine all ingredients in large saucepan. Bring to boil over high heat; reduce heat to low. Cover and simmer 20 minutes, stirring occasionally.
Yield: 6 to 8 servings (9 cups).

Turkey Vegetable Soup

BUTTERBALL® turkey carcass
1 large onion, sliced
3 ribs celery, coarsely chopped
2 teaspoons salt
1 teaspoon dried rosemary leaves
½ teaspoon ground white pepper
2 bay leaves
6 sprigs fresh parsley
12 cups water
3 cubes chicken bouillon
2 cups sliced carrots
½ cup uncooked rice
1 package (10 ounces) frozen peas

Place turkey carcass, onion, celery, salt, rosemary, pepper, bay leaves and parsley in water in Dutch oven. Bring to boil over high heat; reduce heat to low. Cover and simmer 2 hours. Remove carcass. Strip turkey from bones; reserve turkey. Discard carcass. Strain broth and discard vegetables. Bring broth to boil over high heat; add bouillon cubes, carrots and rice. Reduce heat to low; simmer 10 to 12 minutes. Add peas and reserved turkey. Continue to cook 5 to 10 minutes or until vegetables and rice are tender, stirring occasionally.
Yield: 6 to 8 servings (10 cups).

Chicken Noodle Soup

1 (46-fluid ounce) can COLLEGE INN® Chicken Broth
½ pound boneless chicken, cut in bite-size pieces
1½ cups uncooked medium egg noodles
1 cup sliced carrots
½ cup chopped onion
⅓ cup sliced celery
1 teaspoon dried dill weed
¼ teaspoon ground black pepper

In large saucepan, over medium-high heat, heat chicken broth, chicken, noodles, carrots, onion, celery, dill and pepper to a boil. Reduce heat; simmer 20 minutes or until chicken and noodles are cooked.
Makes 8 servings.

Chicken Noodle Soup

Hasty Bouillabaisse

5 green onions, thinly sliced
½ cup chopped green pepper
1 clove garlic, minced
2 tablespoons minced parsley
2 tablespoons olive or vegetable oil
1 can (14½ ounces) stewed or whole tomatoes
1 cup red wine
¾ teaspoon dried thyme leaves
¼ teaspoon dried rosemary, crushed
¼ teaspoon TABASCO® sauce
1 can (16 ounces) mixed vegetables or peas and carrots *or* 2 cans (8 ounces each) other vegetables (beans, corn, carrots, peas, etc.)
1 can (7 ounces) tuna, drained and flaked
1 can (6 ounces) crabmeat, flaked and cartilage removed
1 can (6 ounces) minced clams, drained
1 can (4¼ ounces) shrimp, rinsed and drained

In large saucepan, cook onions, green pepper, garlic and parsley in oil over medium heat until tender. Add tomatoes, wine and seasonings. Simmer 10 minutes. Add vegetables and seafood. Simmer 10 minutes more or until heated through.

Makes 6 to 8 servings

Favorite recipe from **Canned Food Information Council**

Boston Fish Chowder

4 slices bacon
½ cup chopped celery
½ cup chopped onion
1 clove garlic, finely chopped
¼ cup unsifted flour
4 cups water
2 tablespoons WYLER'S® or STEERO® Chicken-Flavor Instant Bouillon *or* 6 Chicken-Flavor Bouillon Cubes
1½ cups pared, cubed potatoes
1 pound fish fillets, fresh or frozen, thawed, cut into bite-size pieces
2 cups (1 pint) BORDEN® or MEADOW GOLD® Coffee Cream *or* Half-and-Half
2 tablespoons chopped pimiento

In large kettle or Dutch oven, cook bacon until crisp; remove and crumble. In drippings, cook celery, onion and garlic until tender; stir in flour. Gradually add water and bouillon, stirring until smooth and well blended; bring to a boil. Add potatoes. Reduce heat and cook 10 minutes. Stir in fish; cook 15 minutes. Add cream and pimiento; heat through (*do not boil*). Garnish with bacon. Refrigerate leftovers.

Makes about 2 quarts

Seafood Gumbo

½ cup chopped onion
½ cup chopped green pepper
½ cup (about 2 ounces) sliced fresh mushrooms
1 clove garlic, minced
2 tablespoons margarine
1 can (28 ounces) whole tomatoes, undrained
2 cups chicken broth
½ to ¾ teaspoon ground red pepper
½ teaspoon dried thyme leaves
½ teaspoon dried basil leaves
1 package (10 ounces) frozen cut okra, thawed
¾ pound white fish, cut into 1-inch pieces
½ pound peeled, deveined shrimp
3 cups hot cooked rice

Cook onion, green pepper, mushrooms, and garlic in margarine in large saucepan or Dutch oven over medium-high heat until tender crisp. Stir in tomatoes and juice, broth, red pepper, thyme, and basil. Bring to a boil. Reduce heat; simmer, uncovered, 10 to 15 minutes. Stir in okra, fish, and shrimp; simmer until fish flakes with fork, 5 to 8 minutes. Serve rice on top of gumbo. *Makes 6 servings*

To microwave: Combine onion, green pepper, mushrooms, garlic, and margarine in deep 2- to 3-quart microproof baking dish. Cover and cook on HIGH 4 minutes; stir after 2 minutes. Stir in tomatoes and juice, broth, red pepper, thyme, and basil. Cover and cook on HIGH 10 minutes; stir. Reduce setting to MEDIUM (50% power) and cook, covered, 10 to 12 minutes. Stir in okra, fish, and shrimp; cook, covered, on HIGH 5 minutes. Let stand 5 minutes. Serve rice on top of gumbo.

Favorite recipe from **USA Rice Council**

Seafood Gumbo

Asparagus and Surimi Seafood Soup

**3 cans (10½ ounces *each*)
    low-sodium chicken
    broth (about 4 cups)**
2 thin slices fresh ginger
**2 cups diagonally sliced
    (½-inch-long) asparagus
    pieces (about ¾ pound)**
¼ cup sliced green onions
**3 tablespoons rice vinegar or
    white wine vinegar**
**¼ teaspoon crushed red
    pepper**
**8 to 12 ounces Surimi
    Seafood, crab flavored,
    chunk style or leg style,
    cut diagonally**

Bring chicken broth and ginger to a boil in a large saucepan. Add asparagus, green onions, vinegar and crushed pepper. Simmer 5 minutes or until the asparagus is crisp tender. Add Surimi Seafood and simmer 5 minutes or until seafood is hot. Remove and discard ginger. Serve hot.

Makes 4 servings

*Favorite recipe from **National Fisheries Institute***

"Dearhearts" Seafood Bisque

"Dearhearts" Seafood Bisque

2 tablespoons olive oil
1 onion, finely chopped
**3 pounds fresh baby
    artichokes, outer leaves
    removed, leaf tips
    trimmed and hearts cut
    into quarters**
2 cups chicken broth
½ cup white wine
**1 pound mixed shellfish
    (shrimp, crab, scallops),
    cleaned and shells
    removed**
1 cup heavy cream
**2 tablespoons chopped
    parsley**
1 teaspoon salt
½ teaspoon ground nutmeg
¼ teaspoon white pepper

Heat oil in large saucepan; add onion and cook gently for 5 minutes or until softened. Add artichokes, broth and wine. Cover and simmer 20 to 30 minutes or until artichokes are tender and a leaf pulls away easily. Process mixture in food processor or blender until smooth. Return soup to saucepan. Stir in shellfish, cream, parsley, salt, nutmeg and pepper. Simmer very gently, uncovered, over low heat 5 to 10 minutes. *Do not boil* or shellfish will become tough.

Makes 6 servings

*Favorite recipe from **Castroville Artichoke Festival***

Arizona Turkey Stew

- 5 medium carrots, cut into thick slices
- 1 large onion, cut into ½-inch pieces
- 3 tablespoons olive or vegetable oil
- 1 pound sliced turkey breast, cut into 1-inch strips
- 1 teaspoon LAWRY'S® Garlic Powder with Parsley
- 3 tablespoons all-purpose flour
- 8 small red potatoes, cut into ½-inch cubes
- 1 package (10 ounces) frozen peas, thawed
- 8 ounces sliced fresh mushrooms
- 1 package (1.62 ounces) LAWRY'S® Spices & Seasonings for Chili
- 1 cup beef broth
- 1 can (8 ounces) tomato sauce

In large skillet, sauté carrots and onion in oil until tender. Stir in turkey strips and Garlic Powder with Parsley; cook 3 minutes or until turkey is just browned. Stir in flour. Pour mixture into 3-quart casserole dish. Stir in remaining ingredients. Bake, covered, in 450°F oven 40 to 45 minutes or until potatoes are tender. Let stand 5 minutes before serving.

Makes 8 to 10 servings

Presentation: Perfect with a crisp green salad.

Hint: Spoon dollops of prepared dumpling mix on top of casserole during the last 15 minutes of baking.

Stove Top Directions: Prepare as above in Dutch oven. Bring mixture to a boil; reduce heat, cover and simmer 40 to 45 minutes or until potatoes are tender. Let stand 5 minutes before serving.

Bistro Burgundy Stew

- 1 pound sirloin beef, cut into 1½-inch pieces
- 3 tablespoons all-purpose flour
- 6 slices bacon, cut into 1-inch pieces (about ¼ pound)
- 2 cloves garlic, pressed
- 3 carrots, peeled and cut into 1-inch pieces (about 1½ cups)
- ¾ cup Burgundy or other dry red wine
- ½ cup GREY POUPON® Dijon Mustard or GREY POUPON® Country Dijon Mustard
- 12 small mushrooms
- 1½ cups scallions, cut into 1½-inch pieces

Coat beef with flour; set aside. In large skillet, over medium heat, cook bacon until just done; pour off excess fat. Add beef and garlic; cook until browned. Add carrots, wine and mustard; cover. Simmer 30 minutes or until carrots are tender, stirring occasionally. Stir in mushrooms and scallions; cook 10 minutes more, stirring occasionally. Garnish as desired.

Makes 6 servings

Santa Fe Stew Olé

- 1 tablespoon vegetable oil
- 1½ pounds beef stew meat, cut into small bite-size pieces
- 1 can (28 ounces) stewed tomatoes, undrained
- 2 medium carrots, sliced into ¼-inch pieces
- 1 medium onion, chopped
- 1 package (1.25 ounces) LAWRY'S® Taco Spices & Seasonings
- 2 tablespoons diced green chiles
- ½ teaspoon LAWRY'S® Seasoned Salt
- ¼ cup water
- 2 tablespoons all-purpose flour
- 1 can (15 ounces) pinto beans, drained

In Dutch oven, heat oil; brown stew meat. Add tomatoes, carrots, onion, Taco Spices & Seasonings, green chiles and Seasoned Salt; blend well. Bring to a boil; reduce heat, cover and simmer 40 minutes. In small bowl, combine water and flour; blend well. Add to stew mixture. Add pinto beans and simmer an additional 15 minutes.

Makes 4 servings

Santa Fe Stew Olé

Bunkhouse Chili

2 pounds lean beef for stew, cut into ½-inch cubes
2 tablespoons vegetable oil
1 medium green bell pepper, chopped
1 medium onion, chopped
1 cup chopped celery
2 cloves garlic, minced
1 can (16 ounces) whole peeled tomatoes, cut into bite-size pieces
1½ cups (12 ounces) beer
1 cup HEINZ® Thick and Rich Original Recipe or Old Fashioned Barbecue Sauce
1 to 2 tablespoons chili powder
1 teaspoon dried oregano leaves, crushed
1 teaspoon salt
¼ teaspoon pepper
2 cans (15 to 17 ounces each) red kidney or pinto beans, drained
Shredded Cheddar cheese
Sliced green onions

In Dutch oven or large saucepot, brown beef, one layer at a time, in oil. Add green pepper, onion, celery and garlic; sauté until tender-crisp. Stir in tomatoes, beer, barbecue sauce, chili powder, oregano, salt and pepper. Cover; simmer 1 hour, stirring occasionally. Add kidney beans; simmer, uncovered, 45 minutes, stirring occasionally. Sprinkle with cheese and green onions just before serving.

Makes 6 to 8 servings
(about 8 cups)

Italian-Style Chili

1 pound lean ground beef
¾ cup chopped onion
1 (26-ounce) jar CLASSICO® Di Napoli (Tomato & Basil) Pasta Sauce
1½ cups water
1 (14½-ounce) can whole tomatoes, undrained and broken up
1 (4-ounce) can sliced mushrooms, drained
2 ounces sliced pepperoni
1 tablespoon WYLER'S® or STEERO® Beef-Flavor Instant Bouillon *or* 3 Beef-Flavor Bouillon Cubes
1 tablespoon chili powder
2 teaspoons sugar

In large kettle or Dutch oven, brown meat with onion; pour off fat. Add remaining ingredients; bring to a boil. Reduce heat; simmer uncovered 30 minutes, stirring occasionally. Garnish as desired. Refrigerate leftovers.

Makes about 2 quarts

Tex-Mex Two Bean Chili

2 tablespoons olive oil
1 cup chopped onion
1 cup chopped green pepper
2 large garlic cloves, pressed
1 pound lean stew meat, cut into ½-inch cubes
½ pound bulk hot Italian sausage*
1¾ cups (15-ounce can) CONTADINA® Tomato Puree
1¾ cups (14.5-ounce can) beef broth
1¼ cups water
⅔ cup (6-ounce can) CONTADINA® Tomato Paste
½ cup (4-ounce can) diced green chiles
3 tablespoons chili powder
1½ teaspoons ground cumin
1 teaspoon salt
1 teaspoon sugar
1 teaspoon dried oregano leaves, crushed
⅛ teaspoon cayenne pepper (optional)
1½ cups (15-ounce can) pinto beans, rinsed and drained
1½ cups (15-ounce can) kidney beans, rinsed and drained

In 6-quart saucepan, heat oil; sauté onion, green pepper and garlic 3 to 4 minutes, or until tender. Add stew meat and sausage, stirring to crumble sausage; cook 5 to 6 minutes. Blend in tomato puree, broth, water, tomato paste, green chiles, chili powder, cumin, salt, sugar, oregano and cayenne pepper, if desired. Bring to a boil. Reduce heat; simmer uncovered 1½ hours, stirring occasionally. Mix in beans. Cover and simmer additional 30 minutes.

Makes 6 servings

Note: If link sausage is used, remove casings before sautéing.

From top to bottom: Italian-Style Chili and Quick Garden Cheese Soup (page 64)

Tex-Mex Two Bean Chili

In Dutch oven, sauté onions, green pepper and garlic in oil. Add turkey and cook until lightly browned. Add tomatoes, chili sauce, chili powder, lemon pepper, basil, thyme and hot pepper sauce. Cover; simmer 45 minutes. Add kidney beans; simmer an additional 20 minutes. Serve topped with green onions, cheese and sour cream. *Makes 8 servings*

Texas Fajita Chili

1¼ cups chopped onion
  1 cup chopped green bell pepper
  1 tablespoon vegetable oil
  2 cans (15¼ ounces each) kidney beans, drained
  1 pound shredded, cooked pork or beef
  1 can (14½ ounces) whole peeled tomatoes, undrained and cut up
  1 cup LAWRY'S® Fajitas Skillet Sauce
  1 can (7 ounces) whole kernel corn, drained
  ½ cup tomato juice or beer
1½ teaspoons chili powder

In large skillet, sauté onion and bell pepper in oil 10 minutes or until tender. Stir in kidney beans, shredded meat, tomatoes, Fajitas Skillet Sauce, corn, tomato juice and chili powder. Bring mixture to a boil; reduce heat, cover and simmer 20 minutes.

Makes 6 servings

Presentation: Serve in individual bowls topped with grated Monterey Jack cheese or sour cream. If desired, serve with dash of hot pepper sauce.

Hearty Turkey Chili

1 cup chopped onions
1 cup chopped green pepper
2 cloves garlic, minced
1 tablespoon vegetable oil
2 pounds ground raw turkey
2 cans (14½ ounces each) tomatoes, cut into bite-size pieces
1 bottle (12 ounces) HEINZ® Chili Sauce
1 tablespoon chili powder
1 teaspoon lemon pepper seasoning
1 teaspoon dried basil leaves, crushed
½ teaspoon dried thyme leaves, crushed
⅛ to ¼ teaspoon hot pepper sauce
2 cans (15½ ounces each) kidney beans, drained
Sliced green onions
Shredded Cheddar cheese
Dairy sour cream or plain yogurt

Hearty Meatless Chili

1 envelope LIPTON® Recipe Secrets Onion, Onion-Mushroom or Beefy Mushroom Recipe Soup Mix
4 cups water
1 can (16 ounces) chick peas or garbanzo beans, rinsed and drained
1 can (16 ounces) red kidney beans, rinsed and drained
1 can (14½ ounces) whole peeled tomatoes, drained and chopped (reserve liquid)
1 cup uncooked lentils, rinsed
1 large stalk celery, coarsely chopped
1 tablespoon chili powder
2 teaspoons ground cumin
1 medium clove garlic, finely chopped
¼ teaspoon crushed red pepper
Hot cooked brown or regular rice
Shredded Cheddar cheese

In large saucepan or stockpot, combine all ingredients except rice and cheese. Bring to a boil, then simmer covered for 20 minutes or until lentils are almost tender. Remove cover and simmer, stirring occasionally, an additional 30 minutes or until liquid is almost absorbed and lentils are tender. Serve, if desired, over rice and top with shredded cheese.

Makes 6 to 8 servings

SALADS

Salads are not only refreshing and healthy, but easy to prepare and delicious! Sample an unbeatable variety of crisp vegetable salads, tossed green salads, creamy salad dressings, molded gelatin salads, ever-popular pasta salads, delightful fruit salads and main-dish meat, poultry and seafood salads. Whether you're looking for a simple side dish, a light lunch or a substantial supper, you'll find it here.

Ensalada Simplese

- **5 cups torn lettuce (combination of romaine and iceberg)**
- **½ cup chopped zucchini**
- **1 can (7 ounces) whole kernel corn, drained**
- **½ cup diced red bell pepper**
- **¼ cup sliced green onions**
- **⅓ cup dairy sour cream**
- **2 tablespoons mayonnaise**
- **1 teaspoon lemon juice**
- **¾ teaspoon dry mustard**
- **½ teaspoon LAWRY'S® Seasoned Salt**
- **½ teaspoon LAWRY'S® Garlic Powder with Parsley**

In large bowl, combine lettuce, zucchini, corn, bell pepper and green onions. Refrigerate. In separate small bowl, combine remaining ingredients. Refrigerate. To serve, gently toss greens and dressing.

Makes 4 to 6 servings

Hint: Adding shredded, cooked chicken or cooked shrimp turns this salad into a main dish.

Dilly Cucumber Salad

- **1 (8-ounce) container BORDEN® or MEADOW GOLD® Sour Cream**
- **¼ cup REALEMON® Lemon Juice from Concentrate**
- **2 to 3 tablespoons sugar**
- **1 teaspoon salt**
- **½ teaspoon dill weed**
- **1 medium cucumber, seeded and sliced**
- **1 medium sweet white onion, sliced and separated into rings**

In medium bowl, combine sour cream, ReaLemon® brand, sugar, salt and dill weed; mix well. Add cucumber and onion. Cover; chill. Refrigerate leftovers.

Makes about 3 cups

Tip: Recipe can be doubled.

Avocado Raspberry Spice Salad

- **¼ cup seedless raspberry jam**
- **3 tablespoons vegetable oil**
- **2½ tablespoons white wine vinegar**
- **¾ teaspoon LAWRY'S® Lemon Pepper Seasoning**
- **¾ teaspoon LAWRY'S® Seasoned Salt**
- **2½ cups shredded napa cabbage**
- **1½ cups shredded red cabbage**
- **2 medium tomatoes, cut into wedges**
- **1 avocado, cubed**
- **½ medium cucumber, thinly sliced**
- **2 tablespoons chopped green onion**

In container with stopper or lid, combine raspberry jam, oil, vinegar, Lemon Pepper Seasoning and Seasoned Salt; blend well. On 4 individual serving plates, arrange napa and red cabbage. Decoratively arrange tomatoes, avocado and cucumber on top. Sprinkle with green onion. Drizzle dressing over each serving.

Makes 4 servings

Presentation: Serve with a light French bread or croissants.

Ensalada Simplese

Herbed Tomato Cucumber Salad

Mustard Tarragon Marinade

**3 tablespoons red wine
    vinegar
1 tablespoon Dijon mustard
1½ teaspoons dried tarragon
2 tablespoons olive oil**

Combine first three ingredients. Slowly whisk oil into mixture until slightly thickened.

Walnut Dressing

**½ cup walnuts
¼ cup olive or vegetable oil
2 tablespoons REALEMON®
    Lemon Juice from
    Concentrate
½ clove garlic**

In blender or food processor, combine ingredients; blend until nuts are finely chopped. Cover; chill. Serve with fruit or green salads. Refrigerate leftovers.
Makes about ½ cup

Tip: Recipe can be doubled.

Dill Onion Vinaigrette

**½ cup vegetable oil
⅓ cup HEINZ® Apple Cider
    Vinegar
2 tablespoons chopped
    green onions
1 teaspoon dried dill weed
½ teaspoon salt
½ teaspoon dry mustard**

In jar, combine all ingredients; cover and shake vigorously. Chill to blend flavors. Shake again before serving with mixed garden salads.
Makes about 1 cup

Herbed Tomato Cucumber Salad

**½ cup MIRACLE WHIP®
    FREE® Dressing
1 cucumber, peeled, seeded,
    chopped
⅓ cup each: finely chopped
    red onion, finely chopped
    fresh basil
¼ teaspoon salt
3 tomatoes, sliced**

• Mix all ingredients except tomatoes until well blended; refrigerate. Spoon over tomatoes.
Makes 6 servings

Prep time: 10 minutes plus refrigerating

Marinated Vegetable Spinach Salad

**Mustard Tarragon Marinade
    (recipe follows)
8 ounces fresh mushrooms,
    quartered
2 slices purple onion,
    separated into rings
16 cherry tomatoes, halved
4 cups fresh spinach leaves,
    washed and stems
    removed
3 slices (3 oz.) SARGENTO®
    Preferred Light™ Sliced
    Mozzarella Cheese, cut
    into julienne strips
Fresh ground black pepper**

Prepare marinade. Place mushrooms, onion and tomatoes in bowl. Toss with marinade and let stand 15 minutes. Meanwhile, wash and dry spinach leaves. Arrange on 4 individual serving plates. Divide marinated vegetables between plates and top each salad with ¼ of the cheese. Serve with fresh ground pepper, if desired.
Makes 4 servings

Italian Herb Dressing

⅔ cup vegetable oil
⅓ cup HEINZ® Gourmet Wine Vinegar
1 clove garlic, split
1 teaspoon dry mustard
½ teaspoon salt
½ teaspoon dried basil leaves, crushed
½ teaspoon dried oregano leaves, crushed
¼ teaspoon crushed red pepper

In jar, combine all ingredients; cover and shake vigorously. Chill to blend flavors. Remove garlic; shake again before serving over tossed green salads.

Makes 1 cup

Thousand Island Dressing

⅔ cup PET® Light Evaporated Skimmed Milk
⅔ cup bottled chili sauce
⅔ cup HOLLYWOOD® Safflower Oil
¼ cup sweet pickle relish
1 tablespoon lemon juice
1 tablespoon sugar
1 teaspoon salt
⅛ teaspoon ground black pepper

Using a wire whisk combine all ingredients in a small bowl. Refrigerate until well chilled. Serve over tossed green salad.

Makes about 2 cups

Rosy Cucumber Dressing

½ cup HEINZ® Chili Sauce
½ cup mayonnaise or salad dressing
½ cup coarsely shredded unpeeled cucumber, drained
1 tablespoon grated onion

In small bowl, combine chili sauce, mayonnaise, cucumber and onion. Cover; chill several hours to blend flavors. Serve over mixed salad greens.

Makes about 1½ cups

Buttermilk Pepper Dressing

1 cup buttermilk
½ cup MIRACLE WHIP® Salad Dressing
2 tablespoons KRAFT® 100% Grated Parmesan Cheese
1 teaspoon coarse grind pepper
1 garlic clove, minced

• Mix ingredients until well blended; refrigerate. Serve with mixed salad greens.

Makes 1 cup

Prep time: 5 minutes plus refrigerating

Family French Dressing

½ cup HEINZ® Tomato Ketchup
½ cup vegetable oil
¼ cup HEINZ® Apple Cider Vinegar
1 tablespoon confectioners sugar
1 clove garlic, split
¼ teaspoon salt
Dash pepper

In jar, combine all ingredients; cover and shake vigorously. Chill to blend flavors. Remove garlic; shake again before serving over tossed green salads.

Makes 1¼ cups

Buttermilk Pepper Dressing

Fresh Vegetable Salad

½ cup WISH-BONE® Italian
    Dressing
1 tablespoon chopped fresh
    tarragon leaves*
1 teaspoon lemon juice
¼ teaspoon pepper
    Assorted Fresh Vegetables**
½ cup sliced green onions
    Salt to taste

In large salad bowl, blend Italian
dressing, tarragon, lemon juice and
pepper. Toss with Assorted Fresh Vegetables and green onions; add salt.
Cover and marinate in refrigerator,
stirring occasionally, 3 hours.
Makes about 6 side-dish servings.
    Substitution: Use 1 teaspoon
dried tarragon leaves.
    ****Assorted Fresh Vegetables:*** Use
any combination of the following to
equal 6 cups—broccoli florets, cauliflowerets, sliced red, green or yellow
pepper, carrots, yellow squash, zucchini or snow peas.
    Hint: For crisp-tender vegetables,
cook vegetables in boiling water
about 1 minute, then immediately
drain and rinse with very cold water
until completely cool.
    Note: Also terrific with Wish-
Bone® Robusto Italian or Blended
Italian Dressing.

Lynn's Salad

1 head DOLE® Cauliflower, cut
    into florettes
1 bunch DOLE® Broccoli, cut
    into florettes
1 jar (6 ounces) marinated
    artichoke hearts, drained
8 ounces mozzarella cheese,
    cubed
2 cups pitted ripe olives
    Dash garlic salt
1 bottle (8 ounces) Italian salad
    dressing

In large bowl, combine cauliflower,
broccoli, artichokes, cheese, olives and
garlic salt. Pour salad dressing over
vegetable mixture. Refrigerate, covered, overnight. Drain salad dressing
(save for another use, if desired).
Makes 6 servings.

Marinated Tomatoes & Cucumbers

Marinated Tomatoes & Cucumbers

2 large tomatoes, sliced
1 small cucumber, sliced
1 small onion, sliced
⅓ cup vegetable oil
⅓ cup REALEMON® Lemon Juice
    from Concentrate
1 tablespoon sugar
¼ teaspoon basil leaves
½ teaspoon salt
1 clove garlic, finely chopped
    Lettuce leaves
    Imitation bacon or cooked
    crumbled bacon

In 2-quart shallow baking dish, arrange tomatoes, cucumber and onion.
In small bowl, combine remaining ingredients except lettuce and imitation
bacon; pour over tomatoes. Chill several hours. Line platter with lettuce;
arrange tomatoes, cucumbers and onion on top and sprinkle with imitation
bacon.
Makes 4 to 6 servings.

Tomato and Onion Salad

6 tablespoons vegetable oil
3 tablespoons tarragon or cider
    vinegar
1 clove garlic, halved
1 tablespoon chopped parsley
¼ teaspoon dry mustard
¼ teaspoon dried oregano leaves
¼ teaspoon salt
¼ teaspoon TABASCO® pepper
    sauce
3 tomatoes, sliced
1 large onion, sliced

In small bowl combine oil, vinegar,
garlic, parsley, mustard, oregano, salt
and Tabasco® sauce; mix well. Cover;
let stand at least 30 minutes. Remove
garlic. Arrange tomato slices alternately with onion rings on serving
platter. Top with salad dressing.
Makes 6 servings.

Bean Sprout & Spinach Salad

Boiling water
1 pound fresh spinach, washed
½ pound fresh bean sprouts
1 tablespoon sugar
4 teaspoons distilled white vinegar
1 tablespoon KIKKOMAN® Soy Sauce
1 teaspoon sesame seed, toasted

Pour boiling water over spinach in colander; rinse immediately with cold water. Drain thoroughly and place in medium serving bowl. Repeat procedure with bean sprouts and place in same bowl. Combine sugar, vinegar, soy sauce and sesame seed; pour over vegetables and toss to combine. Cover and refrigerate at least 1 hour before serving.
Makes 4 servings.

Simple Salad Élégante

¼ cup WISH-BONE® Italian or Lite Italian Dressing
10 small snow peas (about 1½ ounces)
½ cup sliced mushrooms
½ small red pepper, cut into rings
2 cups mixed salad greens

In small bowl, combine all ingredients except salad greens. Cover and marinate in refrigerator, stirring occasionally, 4 hours or overnight. To serve, arrange marinated vegetables on salad greens.
Makes about 2 side-dish servings.

Sunflower Seed Cole Slaw

1 can (20 ounces) DOLE® Pineapple Tidbits
½ pound DOLE® Carrots, shredded
¼ pound DOLE® Green Cabbage, shredded
¼ pound DOLE® Red Cabbage, shredded
½ cup sunflower seeds, lightly toasted
½ cup mayonnaise

2 tablespoons DOLE® Frozen Pineapple-Orange Juice Concentrate
¼ teaspoon salt
Pinch white pepper

Drain pineapple; reserve 2 tablespoons juice. In bowl, combine pineapple, carrots, green and red cabbage and sunflower seeds. To make dressing, in 1-quart measure, combine mayonnaise, juice concentrate, reserved pineapple juice, salt and pepper. Pour over salad mixture and toss. Refrigerate, covered, until ready to serve.
Makes 8 servings.

Dilly Bean Salad

1 envelope LIPTON® Recipe Secrets Onion Recipe Soup Mix
¾ cup water
¼ cup red wine vinegar
¼ cup oil
¼ cup snipped fresh dill*
1 tablespoon finely chopped parsley
1 small clove garlic, finely chopped
1 pound green beans, cooked**
1 can (16 ounces) chick peas (garbanzos) or red kidney beans, rinsed and drained (optional)
2 cups fresh or canned sliced mushrooms

In medium bowl, blend onion recipe soup mix, water and vinegar. Stir in oil, dill, parsley and garlic. Toss with remaining ingredients; chill.
Makes about 6 cups salad.

Substitution: Use 1 tablespoon dried dill weed.

**Substitution:* Use 2 cans (16 ounces each) cut green beans, drained.

Dole's Summer Vegetable Salad

1 head DOLE® Iceberg Lettuce
2 DOLE® Tomatoes
1 cucumber
½ DOLE® Red Bell Pepper
¼ red onion
1 cup sliced DOLE® Celery
1 cup snow peas, ends and strings removed
1 cup sliced DOLE® Cauliflower
Dill Dressing (recipe follows)

Tear lettuce into bite-size pieces. Cut tomatoes into wedges. Slice cucumber, red pepper and red onion. Place all vegetables in salad bowl; toss with Dill Dressing.
Makes 4 servings.
DILL DRESSING: In 1-quart measure, combine ½ cup *each* dairy sour cream and mayonnaise, 1 tablespoon vinegar, 1 teaspoon *each* dried dill weed and onion powder, 1 teaspoon Dijon mustard, ¾ teaspoon garlic salt and cracked pepper to taste. Refrigerate, covered, until ready to serve.

Corn Relish Salad

¾ cup sugar
½ cup CRISCO® Oil
¼ cup white vinegar
½ teaspoon celery seed
¼ teaspoon whole mustard seed
1 can (17 ounces) whole kernel corn, drained
1 can (16 ounces) sauerkraut, pressed to remove excess liquid
½ cup chopped green pepper
⅓ cup chopped onion
1 jar (2 ounces) diced pimiento, drained

Combine sugar, Crisco® Oil, vinegar, celery seed and mustard seed in medium serving bowl. Stir until sugar dissolves. Add remaining ingredients. Mix well. Cover and refrigerate at least 8 hours or overnight. Drain and stir before serving.
6 to 8 servings.

Corn Relish Salad

Spinach Salad with Raspberry Dressing (top) and Citrus, Avocado & Bacon Salad (bottom)

Spinach Salad with Raspberry Dressing

½ cup plain nonfat yogurt
¼ cup fresh or frozen red raspberries, thawed if frozen
1 tablespoon skim milk
1½ teaspoons chopped fresh mint *or* ½ teaspoon dried mint, crushed
4 to 6 cups fresh spinach, washed, drained and trimmed
2 large fresh mushrooms, sliced
1 tablespoon sesame seeds, toasted
4 to 6 red onion rings
6 slices ARMOUR® Lower Salt Bacon, cooked crisp and crumbled

Carefully combine yogurt, raspberries, milk and mint in small bowl; set aside. Combine spinach, mushrooms and sesame seeds in medium bowl; mix well. Arrange spinach mixture evenly on 2 individual salad plates; top with red onion rings. Drizzle yogurt dressing over salads; sprinkle with bacon. Garnish with fresh raspberries and mint sprig, if desired. *Makes 2 servings.*

Nutrition Information Per Serving: 200 calories, 15.8 g protein, 10.1 g fat, 14.1 g carbohydrates, 19.1 mg cholesterol, 556 mg sodium.

Citrus, Avocado & Bacon Salad

3 tablespoons orange juice concentrate, thawed
2 tablespoons vegetable oil
1 tablespoon lime juice
1 tablespoon honey
1 tablespoon white vinegar
3 cups mixed salad greens, washed and drained
½ avocado, peeled, pitted and sliced
6 slices ARMOUR® Lower Salt Bacon, cut in half and cooked crisp
1 (11-ounce) can mandarin oranges, drained

Combine orange juice concentrate, oil, lime juice, honey and vinegar in small bowl; set aside. Divide mixed salad greens evenly between 2 individual

salad plates. Arrange avocado and bacon spoke-fashion over greens. Arrange mandarin oranges on top of greens. Drizzle with dressing. Garnish with chopped unsalted peanuts, if desired.
Makes 2 servings.

Nutrition Information Per Serving: 496 calories, 9.4 g protein, 30.6 g fat, 51.5 g carbohydrates, 18 mg cholesterol, 398 mg sodium.

Eggplant Salad

⅓ cup CRISCO® Oil
1 tablespoon lemon juice
½ teaspoon dried oregano leaves
2 cloves garlic, minced
1 medium eggplant (about 1 pound), peeled and cut into ½-inch cubes
1 medium onion, thinly sliced and separated into rings
1 medium zucchini, halved lengthwise and thinly sliced
1 cup sliced fresh mushrooms
1 medium tomato, peeled, seeded and chopped
¼ teaspoon salt

Combine Crisco® Oil, lemon juice, oregano and garlic in large skillet. Cook over moderate heat, stirring occasionally, until garlic is lightly browned. Add eggplant and onion. Stir to coat. Cook, stirring occasionally, about 10 minutes, or until eggplant is tender. Remove from heat. Transfer to medium serving bowl. Stir in zucchini, mushrooms, tomato and salt. Cover and refrigerate at least 8 hours or overnight. Stir before serving. Sprinkle with *grated Parmesan cheese,* if desired.
6 to 8 servings.

Eggplant Salad

Italian-Style Cauliflower Salad

1 head DOLE® Cauliflower, cut into florettes
½ cup olive or vegetable oil
¼ cup vinegar
1 clove garlic, pressed
½ teaspoon salt
½ teaspoon cracked black pepper
¼ teaspoon dried basil, crumbled
1 cup sliced DOLE® Green or Red Bell Pepper
1 cup sliced DOLE® Celery
1 cup sliced DOLE® Carrots
½ cup sliced pimento-stuffed olives
¼ cup chopped parsley

In large saucepan, cook cauliflower in steamer basket over boiling water 8 minutes or until tender-crisp. Drain; transfer to large bowl. To make dressing, in 1-quart measure, combine oil, vinegar, garlic, salt, pepper and basil. Pour dressing over warm cauliflower. Add remaining ingredients; toss to coat. Refrigerate, covered, overnight.
Makes 6 servings.

Watercress-Carrot Salad

2 medium bunches watercress
6 medium carrots
¾ cup CRISCO® Oil
¼ cup lemon juice
1 tablespoon sugar
¾ teaspoon salt
¼ teaspoon paprika
¼ teaspoon dry mustard
⅛ teaspoon pepper

Remove and discard tough ends and bruised leaves from watercress. Tear remaining watercress into bite-size pieces. Cut carrots in half lengthwise and crosswise. With a vegetable peeler, cut carrot pieces into ribbon-like strips. Combine watercress and carrots in salad bowl.
Blend remaining ingredients in small mixing bowl. Pour over vegetables. Toss to coat. Serve immediately.
6 to 8 servings.

Sprout-Green Bean Salad

3 packages (9 ounces each) frozen French-cut green beans
½ cup CRISCO® Oil
¼ cup white vinegar
2 teaspoons sugar
½ teaspoon salt
¼ teaspoon pepper
1 can (16 ounces) bean sprouts, rinsed and drained
1 cup thinly sliced celery
¾ cup chopped green onion
1 jar (2 ounces) diced pimiento, drained

Cook beans in 3-quart saucepan according to package directions. Drain and cool. Blend Crisco® Oil, vinegar, sugar, salt and pepper in small mixing bowl. Set aside.
Mix green beans, bean sprouts, celery, onion and pimiento in large serving bowl. Stir dressing. Pour over bean mixture. Toss to coat. Cover and refrigerate at least 3 hours. Stir before serving. Garnish with *cherry tomatoes,* if desired.
10 to 12 servings.

Zesty Mushroom Salad

1 cup vegetable oil
⅓ cup wine vinegar
1 tablespoon lemon juice
1 tablespoon chopped chives
½ teaspoon salt
¼ teaspoon TABASCO® pepper sauce
1 small clove garlic, minced
6 cups torn iceberg lettuce
2 cups torn spinach leaves
¼ pound mushrooms, sliced
⅓ cup sliced pitted ripe olives

In jar with tightly fitting lid combine oil, vinegar, lemon juice, chives, salt, Tabasco® sauce and garlic; shake well. In large bowl combine lettuce, spinach, mushrooms and olives. Add ¾ cup dressing and toss lightly to mix well. Refrigerate remaining dressing in covered jar for later use.
Makes 8 servings.

Spinach Salad

¼ **pound sliced bacon**
½ **cup sliced scallions**
2 **tablespoons all-purpose flour**
1 **cup COLLEGE INN® Beef or Chicken Broth**
⅓ **cup red wine vinegar**
8 **cups spinach leaves, torn**
2 **cups sliced fresh mushrooms**

In large skillet, over medium-high heat, cook bacon until crisp. Drain, reserving ¼ cup drippings. Crumble bacon; set aside. In reserved drippings, over medium heat, cook scallions until tender. Stir in flour; cook 1 minute. Stir in broth and vinegar; heat to a boil. Reduce heat; cook until slightly thickened.

In large bowl, mix spinach leaves and mushrooms. Pour hot dressing over salad, tossing to coat well. Sprinkle with reserved bacon pieces. Serve immediately.
Makes 8 servings.

Spinach Salad

Mexican Tossed Salad

3 **large ripe avocados, seeded, peeled and sliced**
½ **cup BORDEN® or MEADOW GOLD® Sour Cream**
¼ **cup REALEMON® Lemon Juice from Concentrate**
1 **tablespoon finely chopped onion**
1 **tablespoon water**
¼ **teaspoon salt**
¼ **teaspoon hot pepper sauce**
6 **cups torn mixed salad greens**
1 **large tomato, seeded and chopped**
1 **cup (4 ounces) shredded mild Cheddar or Monterey Jack cheese**
½ **cup sliced pitted ripe olives**
1 **cup coarsely crushed tortilla chips**

In medium bowl, mash *1 avocado;* stir in sour cream, *3 tablespoons* of the ReaLemon® brand, onion, water, salt and hot pepper sauce. Chill to blend flavors. In large salad bowl, sprinkle remaining *2 avocados* with remaining *1 tablespoon* ReaLemon® brand. Top with salad greens, tomato, cheese and olives; chill. Just before serving, toss with avocado dressing and tortilla chips.
Makes 8 servings.

Cheese and Red Bean Salad

1 **(16-ounce) container BORDEN® or MEADOW GOLD® Cottage Cheese**
1 **(15½-ounce) can kidney beans, drained**
½ **cup chopped green pepper**
½ **cup sliced pimiento-stuffed olives**
½ **cup chopped onion**
¼ **teaspoon seasoned pepper**
Lettuce leaves

In large bowl, combine all ingredients except lettuce; mix well. Chill. Serve on lettuce. Refrigerate leftovers.
Makes 6 to 8 servings.

Country Pineapple Slaw

1 **can (20 ounces) DOLE® Pineapple Chunks in Juice**
1 **package (16 ounces) DOLE® Cole Slaw Mix**
½ **cup sunflower seeds**
Zesty Dressing (recipe follows)

Drain pineapple. In large bowl, combine pineapple with cole slaw mix and sunflower seeds. Toss with Zesty Dressing. Refrigerate, covered, until ready to serve.
Makes 6 servings.
ZESTY DRESSING: In 1-quart measure, combine ½ cup *each* mayonnaise and dairy sour cream, 2 tablespoons lemon juice, 1 tablespoon Dijon mustard and ½ teaspoon caraway seeds. Blend well.

Piñata Salad

- 1 head DOLE® Iceberg Lettuce, torn
- 1 avocado, diced
- 1 can (16 ounces) garbanzo beans, drained
- 1 cup diced DOLE® Tomatoes
- 1 cup ripe olives, cut into wedges or sliced
- 1 cup sliced DOLE® Celery
- 1 cup sliced jicama or radishes
- 4 ounces sharp Cheddar cheese, shredded
  Gazpacho Dressing (recipe follows)
  Chile Dressing (recipe follows)

Place lettuce in salad bowl. Place avocado, garbanzo beans, tomatoes, olives, celery, jicama and cheese in individual bowls for a choice of toppings. Serve with either Gazpacho or Chile Dressing.
Makes 6 to 8 servings.

GAZPACHO DRESSING: In screw-top jar, combine ½ cup olive or vegetable oil, ¼ cup vinegar, 3 sliced green onions, ¾ cup diced tomato, ¼ cup diced green bell pepper, 1 pressed garlic clove, 3 tablespoons chopped cilantro or parsley, 1 teaspoon salt and 6 drops liquid hot pepper seasoning. Shake well to combine.

CHILE DRESSING: Puree 7 ounces (1 can) diced green chiles, 1 cup mayonnaise and ¼ cup dairy sour cream in blender. Refrigerate, covered, until ready to serve.

Cucumber Salad

- 3 medium cucumbers, scored lengthwise with tines of fork and thinly sliced
- ¾ teaspoon salt, divided
- ⅓ cup chopped onion
- ⅓ cup cider vinegar
- 3 tablespoons CRISCO® Oil
- 2 tablespoons sugar
- 1½ teaspoons caraway seeds
- ½ teaspoon paprika
- ⅛ teaspoon pepper

Place cucumbers in medium mixing bowl. Sprinkle with ¼ teaspoon salt. Let stand about 1 hour. Drain.

Blend remaining ingredients and remaining ½ teaspoon salt in small mixing bowl. Pour over cucumbers. Toss to coat. Cover and refrigerate at least 3 hours. Stir before serving.
6 to 8 servings.

Marinated Vegetables

- 4 cups assorted fresh vegetables*
- ¼ cup REALEMON® Lemon Juice from Concentrate
- ¼ cup vegetable oil
- 1 tablespoon sugar
- 1 teaspoon salt
- ½ teaspoon oregano or thyme leaves
- ⅛ teaspoon pepper

Place vegetables in 1½-quart shallow baking dish. In small bowl or jar, combine remaining ingredients; mix well. Pour over vegetables. Cover; refrigerate 6 hours or overnight, stirring occasionally. Serve as appetizer or on lettuce leaves as salad.
Makes 4 cups.

Suggested Vegetables: Cauliflowerets, carrots, mushrooms, cherry tomatoes, broccoli flowerets, zucchini, onion or cucumber.

Tip: Recipe can be doubled.

Tangy Coleslaw

- 1 tablespoon BLUE BONNET® Margarine
- 2 tablespoons all-purpose flour
- 2 tablespoons sugar
- ¼ teaspoon ground black pepper
- 2 tablespoons GREY POUPON® Dijon Mustard
- 1½ cups COLLEGE INN® Chicken Broth
- ⅓ cup white wine vinegar
- 8 cups shredded red or green cabbage
- ½ cup chopped red onion

In medium saucepan, over medium heat, melt margarine. Blend in flour; cook 1 minute. Add sugar, pepper, mustard and chicken broth; cook until mixture thickens and boils. Stir in vinegar. Cover; refrigerate 1 hour.

In large bowl, mix together cabbage and onion. Pour dressing over salad, tossing to coat well. Refrigerate at least 1 hour to blend flavors.
Makes about 9 cups.

Tangy Coleslaw

Yogurt Dressing

**2 cups plain lowfat yogurt
4 teaspoons chopped fresh
   mint or ¼ teaspoon dried
   dill weed
⅛ teaspoon TABASCO®
   pepper sauce**

In small bowl combine yogurt, mint and Tabasco® pepper sauce; mix well. Cover; refrigerate.
Makes 2 cups

Creamy Warm Bacon Dressing

**4 slices OSCAR MAYER®
   Bacon, chopped
1 garlic clove, minced
1 cup MIRACLE WHIP® Salad
   Dressing
½ cup milk**

• Cook bacon until crisp. Drain, reserving 1 tablespoon drippings.

• Heat reserved drippings, bacon and garlic over low heat 1 minute.

• Stir in salad dressing and milk. Continue cooking, stirring occasionally, until thoroughly heated. Serve with spinach salad.
Makes 1½ cups

Prep time: 10 minutes
Cooking time: 10 minutes

Celery Seed Dressing

**½ cup sugar
¼ cup REALEMON® Lemon
   Juice from Concentrate
2 teaspoons cider vinegar
1 teaspoon dry mustard
½ teaspoon salt
½ cup vegetable oil
1 teaspoon celery seed or
   poppy seed**

In blender or food processor, combine all ingredients except oil and celery seed; blend until smooth. On low speed, continue blending, slowly adding oil. Stir in celery seed. Cover; chill. Serve with salad of lettuce and sliced sweet onion if desired. Refrigerate leftovers.   *Makes about 1 cup*

Celery Seed Dressing

Marinated Confetti Coleslaw

**5 cups coarsely shredded
   cabbage (about 1 pound)
1 large fresh tomato, seeded
   and diced
½ cup chopped green bell
   pepper
⅓ cup sliced green onions
½ cup REALEMON® Lemon
   Juice from Concentrate
⅓ cup sugar
⅓ cup vegetable oil
1 teaspoon salt
½ teaspoon dry mustard**

In medium bowl, combine cabbage, tomato, green pepper and green onions. In small saucepan, combine remaining ingredients; bring to a boil. Pour over vegetables. Cover; chill 4 hours or overnight to blend flavors. Refrigerate leftovers.
Makes 6 to 8 servings

Creamy Warm Bacon Dressing

Pineapple-Chili-Cheese Slaw

**1 can (20 ounces) DOLE®
   Pineapple Chunks in
   Juice
6 cups shredded DOLE®
   Green Cabbage
1 cup shredded red cabbage
1 can (15¼ ounces) dark red
   kidney beans, drained
1 can (4 ounces) diced green
   chiles
1 can (4 ounces) sliced ripe
   olives
1½ cups (6 ounces) shredded
   Cheddar cheese**

Cumin-Garlic Dressing
**½ cup reserved pineapple
   juice
¼ cup white vinegar
1 teaspoon ground cumin
½ teaspoon salt
1 clove garlic, pressed**

• Drain pineapple; reserve ½ cup juice for dressing.

• Combine all salad ingredients in bowl. Pour Cumin-Garlic Dressing over salad; toss to coat.
Makes 4 to 6 servings

Cumin-Garlic Dressing: Combine all dressing ingredients in screw-top jar; shake well.

Preparation Time: 20 minutes

Cashew Pea Salad

**½ cup MIRACLE WHIP®
   FREE® Dressing
2 tablespoons lemon juice
½ teaspoon dill weed
1 package (10 ounces) BIRDS
   EYE® Peas, thawed,
   drained
2 cups cauliflowerets
1 can (8 ounces) sliced water
   chestnuts, drained
¼ cup chopped red onion
¼ cup cashews**

Santa Fe Potato Salad

• Mix salad dressing, juice and dill until well blended. Add all remaining ingredients except cashews; mix well. Refrigerate. Sprinkle with cashews just before serving.
Makes 6 cups

Prep time: 15 minutes plus refrigerating

Santa Fe Potato Salad

**6 medium white potatoes
½ cup vegetable oil
½ cup red wine vinegar
1 package (1.25 ounces)
   LAWRY'S® Taco Spices &
   Seasonings
1 can (7 ounces) whole
   kernel corn, drained
⅔ cup sliced celery
⅔ cup shredded carrot
⅔ cup chopped red or green
   bell pepper
2 cans (2¼ ounces each)
   sliced ripe olives, drained
½ cup chopped red onion
2 tomatoes, wedged, halved**

In large saucepan, cook potatoes in boiling water to cover until tender, about 40 minutes; drain. Cool slightly; cut into cubes. In small bowl, combine oil, vinegar and Taco Spices & Seasonings. Add to warm potatoes and toss gently to coat. Cover; refrigerate at least 1 hour. Gently fold in remaining ingredients. Refrigerate until thoroughly chilled. *Makes 10 servings*

Presentation: Serve in lettuce-lined bowl with hamburgers or deli sandwiches.

Creamier Version: Prepare potatoes as above. Replace the vinegar and oil with ½ cup *each* mayonnaise, dairy sour cream and salsa. Mix with Taco Spices & Seasonings and continue as above.

Mai Tai Compote

Mai Tai Compote

- 1 medium DOLE® Fresh Pineapple
- 1 DOLE® Orange, peeled and sliced
- 1 kiwifruit, peeled and sliced
- 1 cup halved DOLE® Strawberries
- 1/2 cup DOLE® Seedless Red Grapes
- 1/4 cup fresh lime juice
- 3 tablespoons honey
- 1 tablespoon light rum
- 1 tablespoon orange-flavored liqueur
- 1/2 teaspoon grated lime peel
- 1 firm DOLE® Banana

Cut pineapple in half lengthwise through crown. Remove fruit with curved knife, leaving shells intact. Trim off core and cut fruit into chunks. In large bowl, combine pineapple, orange, kiwi, strawberries and grapes. To make dressing, in 1-quart measure, combine remaining ingredients, except banana. Pour dressing over fruit. Toss gently to coat. Refrigerate, covered, 1 hour. Just before serving, slice banana into fruit salad. Toss gently. Spoon salad into pineapple shells and serve.
Makes 6 to 8 servings.

Indian Fruit Salad

- 1 DOLE® Fresh Pineapple
- 2 firm DOLE® Bananas
- 1 head DOLE® Iceberg Lettuce, torn
- 1 DOLE® Orange, peeled and sliced

- 2 cups melon balls or diced melon
- 1/2 cup cashew nuts
- 1 cup mayonnaise
- 1/4 cup dairy sour cream
- 1 tablespoon fresh lime juice
- 1 tablespoon sugar
- 1 teaspoon curry powder
- 1/2 teaspoon grated lime peel
- 1/2 teaspoon salt

Twist crown from pineapple. Cut pineapple lengthwise into quarters. Remove fruit from shells with curved knife. Trim off core and dice fruit. Slice bananas into large bowl. Add 2½ cups pineapple (reserve remaining pineapple for another use), lettuce, orange, melon and nuts. To make dressing, in 1-quart measure, combine remaining ingredients; refrigerate, covered, until ready to serve. Pour dressing over salad and toss.
Makes 6 to 8 servings.

Fruit Salad with Poppy Seed Dressing

- 1 pear, cored and sliced
- 1 apple, cored and sliced
- 1 banana, peeled and sliced
- 1 orange, peeled and sectioned
- 1/3 cup CRISCO® Oil
- 2 tablespoons lime juice
- 2 tablespoons honey
- 1/2 teaspoon soy sauce
- 1/2 teaspoon poppy seed
- 1/4 teaspoon ground ginger
- 1/4 teaspoon dry mustard
  Dash salt

Combine pear, apple, banana and orange in medium serving bowl. Blend remaining ingredients in small mixing bowl. Pour over fruit. Toss to coat. Serve immediately.

Tip: Toss your own combination of fresh fruits with poppy seed dressing. Create a refreshing summertime salad with seasonal fruits like grapes, strawberries, peaches and melon. Add variety to this tangy salad with any of your favorites.
4 to 6 servings.

Luau Fruit Salad

- 1 can (20 ounces) DOLE® Pineapple Chunks in Juice
- 3 DOLE® Oranges, peeled and sectioned
- 2 apples, cored and chopped

- 1 papaya, peeled, seeded and cut into chunks
- 1 teaspoon cornstarch
- 1/4 cup vegetable oil
- 2 tablespoons sugar
- 2 tablespoons white vinegar
- 1 tablespoon poppy seeds
- 1 teaspoon grated orange peel
- 1/2 teaspoon paprika
- 1/4 teaspoon salt
- 5 quarts torn DOLE® Romaine Lettuce
- 1/2 cup DOLE® Blanched Slivered Almonds, toasted

Drain pineapple; reserve juice. In large bowl, combine pineapple, oranges, apples and papaya. For dressing, in saucepan, combine reserved pineapple juice and cornstarch. Cook, stirring, until mixture boils and thickens. Cool. Combine pineapple mixture with oil, sugar, vinegar, poppy seeds, orange peel, paprika and salt in blender. Blend until smooth. Pour dressing over fruit and toss; refrigerate, covered. Just before serving, toss with lettuce and sprinkle with almonds.
Makes 12 servings.

Fruit Salad with Orange Almond Dressing

- 1 head DOLE® Leaf Lettuce
- 1 DOLE® Orange, peeled and sectioned
- 1 peach, sliced
- 1/2 cantaloupe, cut into chunks
- 2 cups DOLE® Fresh Pineapple chunks
- 1 cup sliced DOLE® Strawberries
- 1 cup DOLE® Grapes
- 1/2 cup DOLE® Whole Natural Almonds, toasted
  Orange Almond Dressing (recipe follows)

Line large salad bowl with lettuce leaves. Arrange fruit on top; sprinkle with almonds. Serve with Orange Almond Dressing.
Makes 6 to 8 servings.
ORANGE ALMOND DRESSING: In 1-quart measure, combine 1 cup dairy sour cream, 1/2 cup mayonnaise, 1/4 cup toasted DOLE® Chopped Natural Almonds, 2 tablespoons lemon juice and 2 teaspoons grated orange peel. Refrigerate, covered, until ready to serve.

Hot Potato Salad

7 to 8 SIZZLEAN® Breakfast Strips, cut into ½-inch pieces
2 medium onions, chopped fine
1 tablespoon all-purpose flour
4 teaspoons sugar
1½ teaspoons salt
1 teaspoon paprika
½ cup vinegar
1 cup water
6 medium potatoes, pared, cooked, sliced thin

Cook Sizzlean® pieces in medium skillet over medium-low heat until they begin to look crisp. Add onions; cook and stir until tender. Combine flour, sugar, salt and paprika in small cup. Add to Sizzlean® pieces, mixing well. Pour in vinegar and water. Cook and stir until mixture thickens. Add potatoes; reduce heat to low. Heat 10 to 15 minutes or until hot.
Makes 6 servings.

Marinated Potato and Mushroom Salad

1½ pounds new potatoes, cooked and cubed (about 4 cups)
1 cup sliced fresh mushrooms (about 4 ounces)
⅓ cup sliced celery
¼ cup sliced green onions
⅓ cup vegetable oil
¼ cup REALEMON® Lemon Juice from Concentrate
1½ teaspoons Dijon-style mustard
1 teaspoon sugar
1 teaspoon WYLER'S® or STEERO® Chicken-Flavor Instant Bouillon
Cracked black pepper, optional

In shallow baking dish, combine potatoes, mushrooms, celery and onions. In 1-pint jar with tight-fitting lid or cruet, combine remaining ingredients, except pepper; shake well. Pour over potato mixture; mix well. Cover; chill 3 to 4 hours to blend flavors. Serve with pepper if desired. Refrigerate leftovers.
Makes 6 to 8 servings.

Creamy Red Potato Salad

½ cup WISH-BONE® Italian Dressing
¾ cup mayonnaise
½ cup sliced green onions
2 tablespoons snipped fresh dill*
1 teaspoon Dijon-style mustard
1 teaspoon lemon juice
⅛ teaspoon pepper
3 pounds red bliss or new potatoes, cooked and cut into large chunks

In large salad bowl, thoroughly combine all ingredients except potatoes. Toss with warm potatoes; cover and chill.
Makes about 10 side-dish servings.
*Substitution: Use 1 teaspoon dried dill weed.
Notes: Recipe can be halved.
Also terrific with Wish-Bone® Robusto Italian or Blended Italian Dressing.

Fresh and Creamy Potato Salad

4 cups cubed cooked potato
½ cup celery slices
¼ cup chopped green pepper
2 tablespoons green onion slices
1 teaspoon salt
1 8-ounce package PHILADELPHIA BRAND® Cream Cheese, softened
½ cup sour cream
2 tablespoons milk

Combine potatoes, celery, green peppers, onions and salt; mix lightly. Combine cream cheese, sour cream and milk, mixing until well blended. Add to potato mixture; mix lightly. Chill.
6 to 8 servings.

Bacon & Egg Potato Salad

5 cups cooked, peeled and cubed potatoes (about 2 pounds)
¼ cup chopped green onions
⅓ cup REALEMON® Lemon Juice from Concentrate
⅓ cup water
¼ cup vegetable oil
1½ teaspoons celery salt
1 teaspoon Worcestershire sauce
½ teaspoon dry mustard
¼ teaspoon pepper
4 slices bacon, cooked and crumbled
3 hard-cooked eggs, chopped
¼ cup grated Parmesan cheese
3 tablespoons chopped parsley

In large bowl, combine potatoes and onions. In small saucepan, combine ReaLemon® brand, water, oil, celery salt, Worcestershire, mustard and pepper; bring to a boil. Pour over potato mixture; mix well. Cover; chill overnight to blend flavors. Remove from refrigerator 30 minutes before serving; stir in bacon, eggs, Parmesan cheese and parsley. Refrigerate leftovers.
Makes 10 to 12 servings.

Marinated Potato and Mushroom Salad

Green Bean, New Potato & Ham Salad

3 pounds new potatoes, quartered
⅔ cup cold water
1 pound green beans, cut in half
¾ cup MIRACLE WHIP® FREE® Dressing
⅓ cup stone ground mustard
2 tablespoons red wine vinegar
2 cups cubed OSCAR MAYER® Ham
½ cup chopped green onions

• Place potatoes and ⅓ cup water in 3-quart microwave-safe casserole; cover.

• Microwave on HIGH 13 minutes. Stir in beans. Microwave 7 to 13 minutes or until tender; drain.

• Mix salad dressing, mustard and vinegar in large bowl until well blended. Add potatoes, beans and remaining ingredients; mix lightly. Refrigerate.   *Makes 12 cups*

Prep time: 15 minutes plus refrigerating
Microwave cooking time: 26 minutes

Bacon Ranch Potato Salad

3 pounds new potatoes, cut into ¼-inch slices
⅓ cup cold water
½ cup MIRACLE WHIP® Salad Dressing
¼ cup RANCHER'S CHOICE® Creamy Dressing
¼ teaspoon each: salt, pepper
⅛ teaspoon garlic powder
6 slices OSCAR MAYER® Bacon, crisply cooked, crumbled
½ cup each: celery slices, thin red bell pepper strips, sliced green onions

• Place potatoes and water in 3-quart microwave-safe casserole; cover.

• Microwave on HIGH 14 to 16 minutes or until tender, stirring after 8 minutes. Drain.

• Mix dressings and seasonings in large bowl until well blended. Add potatoes and remaining ingredients; mix well. Serve immediately or refrigerate.
Makes 8 cups

Prep time: 15 minutes
Microwave cooking time: 16 minutes

Microwave Potato Salad

7 cups (2½ pounds) cubed red potatoes
⅓ cup cold water
¾ cup MIRACLE WHIP® Salad Dressing
¼ cup milk
¾ cup (3 ounces) KRAFT® Natural Shredded Cheddar Cheese
¾ cup (3 ounces) KRAFT® Natural Shredded Swiss Cheese
½ cup sliced green onions
2 hard-cooked eggs, chopped
½ teaspoon each: salt, pepper

• Place potatoes and water in 3-quart microwave-safe casserole; cover.

• Microwave on HIGH 16 to 18 minutes or until tender, stirring after 9 minutes. Drain.

• Add remaining ingredients; mix well. Refrigerate.
Makes 7 cups

Prep time: 20 minutes plus refrigerating
Microwave cooking time: 18 minutes

Seafood Pea-Ista Salad

½ cup mayonnaise or salad dressing
¼ cup zesty Italian salad dressing
2 tablespoons grated Parmesan cheese
2 cups canned green or yellow black-eyed peas, rinsed
8 ounces corkscrew pasta, cooked, rinsed and drained
1½ cups chopped imitation crabmeat (about 8 ounces)
1 cup broccoli flowerets, partially cooked
½ cup chopped green pepper
½ cup chopped tomato
¼ cup sliced green onions

Combine mayonnaise, Italian salad dressing and cheese in large bowl; blend well. Add peas, pasta, imitation crabmeat, broccoli, pepper, tomato and onions; toss gently to mix. Cover; refrigerate at least 2 hours.
Makes 4 to 6 servings

*Favorite recipe from the **Black-Eyed Pea Jamboree—Athens, Texas***

Lanai Pasta Salad

1 can (20 ounces) DOLE® Pineapple Chunks in Juice
3 cups cooked spiral pasta
2 cups DOLE® Sugar Peas
1 cup sliced DOLE® Carrots
1 cup sliced cucumbers
½ cup bottled reduced-calorie Italian salad dressing
¼ cup chopped cilantro or parsley

• Drain pineapple; reserve ¼ cup juice. Combine pineapple, reserved juice and remaining ingredients in large bowl; toss to coat.   *Makes 6 to 8 servings*

Preparation Time: 15 minutes

Seafood Pea-Ista Salad

Pasta Salad in Artichoke Cups

Ham Tortellini Salad

1 (7- to 8-ounce) package
    cheese-filled spinach
    tortellini
3 cups (12 ounces)
    ARMOUR® Lower Salt
    Ham, cut into ¾-inch
    cubes
½ cup sliced green onions
10 cherry tomatoes, cut in half
1 cup bottled low sodium
    creamy buttermilk *or*
    reduced calorie zesty
    Italian salad dressing
    Leaf lettuce or butterhead
    lettuce, washed and
    drained
¼ cup finely chopped red
    pepper

Cook tortellini according to
package directions omitting salt;
drain and run under cold water
to cool. Combine all ingredients
except leaf lettuce and red pepper
in large bowl. Toss until well
blended. Serve on lettuce-lined
salad plates. Sprinkle with red
pepper. Serve immediately.

Makes 6 servings

Pasta Salad in Artichoke Cups

5 cloves garlic
½ cup white wine
6 medium artichokes for
    cups
1 lemon, cut into halves
1 tablespoon *plus* 1 teaspoon
    olive oil, divided
    Chicken broth
    Basil Vinaigrette Dressing
    (recipe follows)
8 ounces uncooked
    corkscrew pasta or pasta
    twists, cooked, rinsed
    and drained
½ teaspoon dried basil
    leaves, crushed
2 cups sliced cooked
    artichoke hearts (not
    marinated)

Simmer garlic and wine in small
saucepan 10 minutes.
Meanwhile, cut bottoms of
artichokes flat and remove outer
leaves. Cut 1 inch from tops; snip
tips from remaining leaves and
rub ends with lemon. Add
artichokes, wine-garlic mixture
and 1 tablespoon oil to 2 inches
boiling chicken broth in large
saucepan. Cover; simmer 25 to
30 minutes or until leaves pull
easily from base. Drain.

Prepare Basil Vinaigrette
Dressing. Sprinkle pasta with
remaining 1 teaspoon oil and
basil.

Combine pasta, sliced artichoke
hearts and 1 cup dressing in
large bowl; toss gently to coat.
Carefully spread outer leaves of
whole artichokes; remove the
small heart leaves and scoop out
the fuzzy choke. Fill with pasta
mixture. Cover; refrigerate until
serving time. Serve with
remaining dressing. Garnish as
desired.   *Makes 6 servings*

**BASIL VINAIGRETTE
DRESSING:** Combine ⅓ cup
wine vinegar, 2 tablespoons
Dijon mustard and 3 minced
garlic cloves in blender or food
processor. Cover; pulse until well
mixed. Add ¾ cup coarsely cut
fresh basil leaves; pulse to blend.
With motor running, slowly pour
in 1 cup olive oil. Add salt and
pepper to taste.

*Favorite recipe from **Castroville
Artichoke Festival***

Ham Tortellini Salad

Beef & Pasta Salad

**3 cups CREAMETTE® Rotini,
   cooked as package
   directs and drained
1 pound boneless stir-fry
   beef strips
2 teaspoons WYLER'S® or
   STEERO® Beef-Flavor
   Instant Bouillon
2 tablespoons vegetable or
   olive oil
1 cup bottled Italian salad
   dressing
6 ounces Provolone cheese,
   cut into cubes
1 large green bell pepper, cut
   into strips
1 cup cherry tomato halves
½ cup sliced pitted ripe olives
   Grated Parmesan cheese,
   optional**

In large skillet, brown meat and
1 teaspoon bouillon in oil; remove
from skillet. In large bowl,
combine meat, rotini, salad
dressing and remaining
1 teaspoon bouillon; let stand 15
minutes. Add remaining
ingredients except Parmesan
cheese; mix well. Cover; chill.
Serve with Parmesan cheese if
desired. Refrigerate leftovers.
Makes 4 servings

Rainbow Pasta Salad

**8 ounces uncooked tricolor
   corkscrew pasta, cooked,
   rinsed, drained and
   cooled
2 cans (4½ ounces each)
   medium shrimp, drained
   or ½ pound cooked fresh
   shrimp, peeled
½ cup chopped walnuts
   (optional)
¼ cup French salad dressing
¼ cup mayonnaise
2 tablespoons sliced
   pimiento-stuffed green
   olives
1 teaspoon finely chopped
   onion
   Lettuce leaves
   Grape clusters (optional)
   Lemon peel strips
   (optional)**

Combine pasta, shrimp, walnuts,
salad dressing, mayonnaise,
olives and onion in large bowl;
toss gently to coat. Cover;
refrigerate at least 2 hours.
Serve over lettuce. Garnish with
grapes and lemon peel.
Makes 4 servings

Favorite recipe from **North Dakota
Wheat Commission**

Creamy Pesto Pasta Salad

**1 package (7 ounces)
   refrigerated prepared
   pesto
½ cup MIRACLE WHIP® Salad
   Dressing
3 cups (8 ounces) rotini,
   cooked, drained
½ cup pitted ripe olive slices
3 tablespoons chopped sun-
   dried tomatoes in oil,
   drained
½ teaspoon pepper**

• Mix pesto and salad dressing
until well blended. Add
remaining ingredients; mix well.
Refrigerate.   *Makes 4 cups*

Prep time: 15 minutes plus
refrigerating

The Best Macaroni Salad

**5 cups (16 ounces) elbow
   macaroni, cooked,
   drained
1 cup MIRACLE WHIP® Salad
   Dressing
1 cup each: chopped red bell
   pepper, chopped
   cucumber
1 package (8 ounces)
   KRAFT® Natural Cheddar
   Cheese, cubed
½ cup chopped green onions
½ teaspoon each: salt, coarse
   grind pepper**

• Mix ingredients until well
blended; refrigerate.
Makes 8¼ cups

Prep time: 15 minutes plus
refrigerating

Rainbow Pasta Salad

Thai Chicken Fettuccine Salad

 1 cup PACE® Picante Sauce
 ¼ cup chunky peanut butter
 2 tablespoons honey
 2 tablespoons orange juice
 1 teaspoon soy sauce
 ½ teaspoon ground ginger
 6 ounces uncooked
   fettuccine, hot cooked
   and drained
 3 chicken breast halves
   (about 12 ounces),
   boned, skinned and cut
   into 1-inch pieces
 2 tablespoons vegetable oil
   Lettuce or savoy cabbage
   leaves (optional)
 ¼ cup coarsely chopped
   cilantro
 ¼ cup peanut halves
 ¼ cup thin red pepper strips,
   cut into halves
   Additional PACE® Picante
   Sauce (optional)

Combine picante sauce, peanut butter, honey, orange juice, soy sauce and ginger in small saucepan. Cook and stir over low heat until blended and smooth. Reserve ¼ cup picante sauce mixture. Place fettuccine in large bowl. Pour remaining picante sauce mixture over fettuccine; toss gently to coat.

Cook chicken in oil in large skillet over medium-high heat until browned and cooked, about 5 minutes. Add reserved picante sauce mixture; mix well. Arrange fettuccine over lettuce-lined platter. Top with chicken mixture. Sprinkle cilantro, peanut halves and pepper strips over top. Refrigerate to cool to room temperature. Serve with additional picante sauce. Garnish as desired.

Makes 4 servings

Chicken Salad Deluxe

 1¼ cups prepared buttermilk
   salad dressing
 ½ cup mayonnaise
 3 tablespoons half-and-half
 1¾ teaspoons Beau Monde
   seasoning
 1 teaspoon salt
 ½ teaspoon pepper
 5 whole chicken breasts
   (about 2 pounds),
   skinned, cooked and
   cubed
 10 ounces uncooked 100%
   semolina medium shell
   macaroni, cooked,
   rinsed, drained and
   cooled
 3 cups diced celery
 2½ cups seedless green
   grapes, cut lengthwise
   into halves
 1 package (12 ounces)
   slivered almonds,
   reserve 1 tablespoon for
   garnish
 2 cans (2.25 ounces each)
   sliced water chestnuts,
   drained
 ½ cup chopped onion
   Lettuce leaves
   Parsley (optional)
   Sliced star fruit (optional)
   Cantelope slices

Combine salad dressing, mayonnaise, half-and-half, seasoning, salt and pepper in small bowl; blend well. Cover; refrigerate overnight to blend flavors.

Combine chicken, shells, celery, grapes, almonds, water chestnuts and onion in large bowl. Pour dressing over salad; toss gently to coat. Serve on lettuce. Garnish with reserved almonds, parsley and star fruit. Serve with cantelope slices.

Makes 20 servings

*Favorite recipe from **North Dakota Wheat Commission***

Thai Chicken Fettuccine Salad

Chicken Salad Deluxe

Party Pasta Salad

1 package (12 ounces)
    corkscrew pasta
1 can (20 ounces) DOLE®
    Pineapple Chunks in
    Juice
1 cup vegetable oil
½ cup distilled white vinegar
1 tablespoon Dijon mustard
1 tablespoon Worcestershire
    sauce
1 clove garlic, pressed
    Salt and pepper to taste
3 cups DOLE® Cauliflower
    florettes
3 cups DOLE® Broccoli
    florettes
1 DOLE® Red Bell Pepper,
    seeded, chunked
1 cup DOLE® Whole Natural
    Almonds, toasted

• Cook noodles according to package directions.

• Drain pineapple; reserve 3 tablespoons juice for dressing.

• For dressing, combine reserved juice, oil, vinegar, mustard, Worcestershire sauce, garlic, salt and pepper in a screw-top jar; shake well.

• Combine noodles and cauliflower in large bowl. Pour dressing over salad; toss to coat.

• Cover and marinate in refrigerator overnight.

• Add broccoli, red pepper and almonds; toss to coat.
        Makes 12 to 15 servings

Preparation Time: 20 minutes
Cook Time: 10 minutes
Marinate Time: overnight

Black Bean and Rice Salad

2 cups cooked rice, cooled to
    room temperature
1 cup cooked black beans*
1 medium tomato, seeded
    and chopped
½ cup (2 ounces) shredded
    Cheddar cheese
    (optional)
1 tablespoon snipped parsley
¼ cup prepared light Italian
    dressing
1 tablespoon lime juice
    Lettuce leaves

Combine rice, beans, tomato, cheese and parsley in large bowl. Pour dressing and lime juice over rice mixture; toss lightly. Serve on lettuce leaves.
        Makes 4 servings

*Substitute canned black beans, drained, for the cooked beans, if desired.

*Favorite recipe from **USA Rice Council***

Party Pasta Salad

Wild Rice Salad

Rice Pilaf Salad

1 package (6 ounces) ECKRICH®
   Ham, cut into thin strips
1 package (9 ounces) rice pilaf
   mix
3 tablespoons vegetable oil
1 tablespoon vinegar
1 cup chopped zucchini
½ cup cooked peas
¼ cup chopped fresh parsley
½ cup cherry tomato halves
6 lemon wedges
⅓ cup plain yogurt

Cook rice pilaf according to package
directions, omitting butter. Combine
oil and vinegar; pour over warm rice
pilaf in large bowl. Mix in ham, zucchini, peas and parsley. Cool to room
temperature. Garnish each serving
with tomatoes and lemon wedges; top
with about 1 tablespoon yogurt.
Makes 6 servings.

Potluck Pasta Salad

8 ounces spiral pasta
½ cup vegetable oil
¼ cup white vinegar
1 large clove garlic, pressed or
   minced
2 tablespoons lemon juice
2 teaspoons prepared mustard
2 teaspoons Worcestershire
   sauce
1 teaspoon salt
   Dash pepper
¼ pound snow peas, ends and
   strings removed
2 cups DOLE® Broccoli florettes
2 cups sliced fresh mushrooms
1 cup DOLE® Cauliflower
   florettes
1 cup halved cherry tomatoes

Cook pasta according to package directions. Drain. Meanwhile, in screw-
top jar, combine oil, vinegar, garlic,
lemon juice, mustard, Worcestershire,
salt and pepper. Shake well. In large
bowl, combine hot pasta with dressing. Mix well. Add vegetables; toss to
coat. Refrigerate, covered.
Makes 8 servings.

Wild Rice Salad

1 (13¾-fluid ounce) can
   COLLEGE INN® Beef or
   Chicken Broth
1 (6-ounce) package long-grain
   and wild rice
1 (11-ounce) can mandarin
   oranges, drained
1 (8-ounce) can CHUN KING®
   Sliced Water Chestnuts,
   drained
¼ cup sliced scallions
⅓ cup mayonnaise
   Lettuce leaves

Reserve 2 tablespoons broth. Add
enough water to remaining broth to
substitute for water in rice package
directions. Cook rice according to directions omitting butter or margarine; cool. Stir in oranges, water
chestnuts and scallions. Blend reserved broth and mayonnaise; stir
into rice mixture. Cover and refrigerate 2 to 3 hours. Serve on lettuce
leaves.
Makes 6 to 8 servings.

Tabbouleh

¾ cup bulgur, rinsed and drained
   Boiling water
2 cups seeded, chopped
   cucumber
1 large tomato, seeded and
   chopped
1 cup snipped fresh parsley
⅓ cup CRISCO® Oil
⅓ cup chopped green onion
2 tablespoons lemon juice
1 teaspoon dried mint leaves
2 cloves garlic, minced
½ teaspoon salt
⅛ teaspoon white pepper
⅛ teaspoon cayenne

Place bulgur in medium mixing bowl.
Add enough boiling water to just
cover bulgur. Let stand about 1 hour,
or until bulgur is rehydrated. Drain.
   Combine bulgur, cucumber, tomato
and parsley in large serving bowl. Set
aside. Blend remaining ingredients in
small mixing bowl. Pour over bulgur
mixture. Toss to coat. Cover and refrigerate at least 3 hours. Stir before
serving.
10 to 12 servings.

Chilled Rigatoni Salad

1 clove garlic, halved
1½ to 2 cups cooked rigatoni
1 can (14 ounces) artichoke hearts, drained and cut into bite-size pieces
½ cup chopped sweet red pepper or green pepper
½ cup bite-size cubes mozzarella cheese
1 medium carrot, cut into julienne strips
¼ cup sliced pitted black olives
2 ounces salami, cut into thin strips
¼ cup CRISCO® Oil
2 tablespoons white wine vinegar
1 tablespoon olive oil
½ teaspoon salt
½ teaspoon sugar
½ teaspoon dry mustard
¼ to ½ teaspoon dried oregano leaves
¼ to ½ teaspoon dried basil leaves

Rub inside of medium serving bowl with cut sides of garlic. Discard garlic. Mix rigatoni, artichoke hearts, red pepper, mozzarella cheese, carrot, olives and salami in prepared bowl.

Blend remaining ingredients in small bowl. Pour over rigatoni mixture. Toss to coat. Cover and refrigerate 2 to 3 hours. Stir before serving.
4 to 6 servings.

Chicken Salad Supreme

1 cup mayonnaise or salad dressing
¼ cup REALIME® Lime Juice from Concentrate
1 teaspoon salt
¼ teaspoon ground nutmeg
4 cups cubed cooked chicken or turkey
1 (11-ounce) can mandarin orange segments, drained
1 cup seedless green grape halves
¾ cup chopped celery
½ cup slivered almonds, toasted

In large bowl, combine mayonnaise, ReaLime® brand, salt and nutmeg. Add remaining ingredients; mix well. Chill. Serve on lettuce. Refrigerate leftovers.
Makes 4 to 6 servings.

Hot Chicken Salad

2 cups cubed cooked chicken or turkey
1 cup chopped celery
1 (8-ounce) can water chestnuts, drained and coarsely chopped
2 tablespoons finely chopped onion
1 cup mayonnaise or salad dressing
3 tablespoons REALEMON® Lemon Juice from Concentrate
1 teaspoon WYLER'S® or STEERO® Chicken-Flavor Instant Bouillon
2 tablespoons sliced almonds, toasted
2 tablespoons chopped parsley

Preheat oven to 350°. In large bowl, combine all ingredients except almonds and parsley. Turn into 1½-quart baking dish; top with almonds. Bake 20 minutes or until hot. Garnish with parsley. Refrigerate leftovers.
Makes 4 to 6 servings.
   Microwave: Prepare salad as above in 1½-quart baking dish. Microwave on full power (high) 5 to 6 minutes or until hot. Stir before serving. Garnish with parsley.

Cobb Salad

½ cup vegetable oil
¼ cup REALEMON® Lemon Juice from Concentrate
1 tablespoon red wine vinegar
2 teaspoons sugar
½ teaspoon dry mustard
½ teaspoon salt
½ teaspoon Worcestershire sauce
¼ teaspoon garlic powder
¼ teaspoon pepper
6 cups finely shredded lettuce
2 cups finely chopped cooked chicken
3 hard-cooked eggs, finely chopped
2 medium tomatoes, seeded and chopped
1 ripe avocado, seeded, peeled and chopped
¼ cup (1 ounce) blue cheese, crumbled
¼ cup imitation bacon or cooked crumbled bacon

In 1-pint jar with tight-fitting lid or cruet, combine oil, ReaLemon® brand, vinegar, sugar and seasonings; shake well. Chill to blend flavors. In large salad bowl, arrange remaining ingredients; chill. Just before serving, toss with dressing. Refrigerate leftovers.
Makes 4 servings.

Cobb Salad

Cobb Salad

• Mix salad dressing, soy sauce and ginger until well blended.

• Add chicken, pea pods, carrots, onions and sesame seeds; mix well. Refrigerate. Serve on lettuce-covered platter.

Makes 4 servings

Variation: Substitute 3 cups chopped cooked chicken for fried chicken.

Prep time: 20 minutes plus refrigerating

Cobb Salad

    4 skinless boneless chicken breast halves, cooked, cooled
  ⅔ cup vegetable oil
  ⅓ cup HEINZ® Distilled White or Apple Cider Vinegar
    1 clove garlic, minced
    2 teaspoons dried dill weed
  1½ teaspoons granulated sugar
  ½ teaspoon salt
  ¼ teaspoon pepper
    8 cups torn salad greens, chilled
    1 large tomato, diced
    1 medium green bell pepper, diced
    1 small red onion, chopped
  ¾ cup crumbled blue cheese
    6 slices bacon, cooked, crumbled
    1 hard-cooked egg, chopped

Shred chicken into bite-size pieces. For dressing, in jar, combine oil, vinegar, garlic, dill, sugar, salt and pepper; cover and shake vigorously. Pour ½ cup dressing over chicken; toss well to coat. Toss greens with remaining dressing. Line each of 4 large individual salad bowls with greens; mound chicken mixture in center. Arrange mounds of tomato, green pepper, onion, cheese, bacon and egg around chicken.

Makes 4 servings

Spicy Cajun Rice Salad

    2 cups Original MINUTE® Rice
  ½ cup prepared GOOD SEASONS® Italian or Zesty Italian Salad Dressing
  1½ teaspoons hot pepper sauce
    2 teaspoons prepared hot spicy mustard
    2 hard-cooked eggs, chopped
  ½ cup diced celery
  ½ cup toasted chopped pecans
  ¼ cup sliced scallions
  ¼ cup sliced stuffed green olives
  ¼ cup chopped parsley
  ¼ cup sweet pickle relish
    1 tablespoon diced dill pickle

Prepare rice according to package directions.

Combine salad dressing, pepper sauce and mustard in small bowl; blend well. Combine rice with remaining ingredients in large bowl. Spoon dressing mixture over salad, tossing to coat. Cover and chill.

Makes 6 servings

Chinese Chicken Salad

  ½ cup MIRACLE WHIP® Salad Dressing
    1 tablespoon soy sauce
  ½ teaspoon ground ginger
    4 large pieces carry-out fried chicken, chilled, coarsely chopped (about 3 cups)
    1 cup Chinese pea pods, sliced lengthwise
  ½ cup shredded carrot
  ¼ cup chopped green onions
    1 tablespoon sesame seeds, toasted
    3 cups shredded lettuce

Grilled Chicken Salad

¾ pound boned and skinned chicken breast
½ teaspoon salt
½ teaspoon ground black pepper
1½ cups diagonally sliced small zucchini
3 cups cooked rice, cooled to room temperature
1 can (14 ounces) artichoke hearts, drained
¾ cup fresh snow peas, blanched*
½ medium-sized red pepper, cut into 1-inch cubes
⅓ cup light Italian salad dressing
1 teaspoon chopped fresh basil leaves
Lettuce leaves

Season chicken with salt and black pepper. Grill or broil chicken breast. Add zucchini during last 5 minutes of grilling or broiling. Cover and chill chicken and zucchini; cut chicken into ¾-inch cubes. Combine rice, chicken, zucchini, artichokes, snow peas, and red pepper in large bowl. Blend dressing and basil in small bowl. Pour over salad; toss lightly. Serve on lettuce leaves.

Makes 4 servings

*Substitute frozen snow peas, thawed, for fresh snow peas, if desired.

Favorite recipe from **USA Rice Council**

Grilled Chicken Salad

California Chicken Salad

Lemon-Mustard Dressing
⅔ cup olive or vegetable oil
⅓ cup lemon juice
1½ teaspoons dry mustard
Salt and pepper, to taste
Salad
1 package (6 ounces) long-grain and wild rice blend
2¾ cups chicken broth, divided
2 whole chicken breasts, split, boned and skinned
2 stalks celery, thinly sliced
1 green bell pepper, chopped
½ cup chopped red onion
16 lettuce leaves
3 fresh California peaches, sliced

In small bowl, combine all dressing ingredients; set aside. In medium, covered saucepan, cook rice and seasoning packet in 1¾ cups broth 30 minutes. Cool. Meanwhile, in large, covered skillet, poach chicken breasts in remaining 1 cup broth 15 to 20 minutes or until cooked through. Cool; shred chicken. Combine rice with celery, bell pepper and onion. Line serving platter or individual salad plates with lettuce leaves. Arrange ⅔ cup rice, chicken and peach slices on lettuce. Serve Lemon-Mustard Dressing separately.

Makes 4 servings

Favorite recipe from **California Tree Fruit Agreement**

Tropical Chicken Salad

4 cups cubed cooked chicken or turkey
2 large oranges, peeled, sectioned and drained
1½ cups cut-up fresh pineapple, drained
1 cup seedless green grape halves
1 cup sliced celery
¾ cup mayonnaise or salad dressing
3 to 4 tablespoons REALEMON® Lemon Juice from Concentrate
½ teaspoon ground ginger
½ teaspoon salt
½ to ¾ cup nuts

In large bowl, combine chicken, fruit and celery; mix well. Cover; chill. In small bowl, combine remaining ingredients except nuts. Cover; chill. Just before serving, combine chicken mixture, dressing and nuts. Serve in hollowed-out pineapple shells or on lettuce leaves if desired. Refrigerate leftovers.
Makes 4 to 6 servings

Oriental Chicken Salad

4 skinned boneless chicken breast halves (about 1½ pounds)
½ cup water
⅓ cup cider vinegar
3 tablespoons vegetable oil
2 tablespoons brown sugar
1 tablespoon soy sauce
2 teaspoons WYLER'S® or STEERO® Chicken-Flavor Instant Bouillon or 2 Chicken-Flavor Bouillon Cubes
Napa (Chinese cabbage)
Alfalfa sprouts, fresh mushrooms, carrot curls and pea pods

Arrange chicken in shallow baking dish. In small saucepan, combine water, vinegar, *1 tablespoon* oil, sugar, soy sauce and bouillon; cook and stir until bouillon dissolves. Cool. Reserving *½ cup* dressing, pour remainder over chicken. Cover; marinate in refrigerator 30 minutes. Remove chicken from marinade. In skillet, cook chicken in remaining *2 tablespoons* oil until tender. Cut into thin slices. Line plates with napa. Top with chicken, sprouts, mushrooms, carrots and pea pods. Serve with reserved dressing. Refrigerate leftovers.
Makes 4 servings

Mexican Chicken Salad

1 pound skinned boneless chicken breasts, cut into strips
2 tablespoons margarine or butter
½ cup water
2 teaspoons WYLER'S® or STEERO® Chicken-Flavor Instant Bouillon or 2 Chicken-Flavor Bouillon Cubes
1 teaspoon chili powder
½ teaspoon ground cumin
½ teaspoon garlic powder
1½ cups BORDEN® or MEADOW GOLD® Sour Cream, at room temperature
4 tortillas or tostada shells, fried or warmed
Shredded lettuce
Garnishes: chopped tomato, sliced green onions and pitted ripe olives

In large skillet, brown chicken in margarine. Add water, bouillon, chili powder, cumin and garlic powder. Cover; simmer 5 to 10 minutes or until chicken is tender. Stir in sour cream; heat through (*do not boil*). Top each tortilla with lettuce then chicken mixture. Garnish as desired. Refrigerate leftovers.
Makes 4 servings

Turkey Ensalada con Queso

2 cups cooked rice, cooled to room temperature
1½ cups cooked turkey breast cubes
½ cup (2 ounces) jalapeño Monterey Jack cheese, cut into ½-inch cubes
1 can (4 ounces) diced green chiles, undrained
2 tablespoons snipped parsley
¼ cup cholesterol free, reduced calorie mayonnaise
¼ cup plain nonfat yogurt
Lettuce leaves
Tomato wedges for garnish

Combine rice, turkey, cheese, chiles, and parsley in large bowl. Blend mayonnaise and yogurt; add to rice mixture and toss lightly. Serve on lettuce leaves; garnish with tomato wedges.
Makes 4 servings

Favorite recipe from **USA Rice Council**

Oriental Chicken Salad

Smoked Turkey & Artichoke Salad with Hearts of Palm

- ½ cup MIRACLE WHIP® Salad Dressing
- ⅓ cup KRAFT® House Italian Dressing
- ½ teaspoon coarse grind pepper
- ¼ teaspoon dried tarragon leaves, crushed
- 3 cups cubed LOUIS RICH® Hickory Smoked Breast of Turkey
- 1 can (14 ounces) artichoke hearts, drained, quartered
- ⅓ cup each: chopped green, red and yellow bell peppers
- 1 can (14 ounces) hearts of palm, drained
- 1 pint cherry tomatoes

• Mix dressings and seasonings until well blended.

• Stir in turkey, artichokes and peppers; refrigerate. Serve with hearts of palm and tomatoes.

Makes 6 cups

Prep time: 20 minutes plus refrigerating

Turkey Waldorf Salad

- ⅔ cups HELLMANN'S® or BEST FOODS® Real, Light or Cholesterol Free Reduced Calorie Mayonnaise
- 2 tablespoons lemon juice
- ½ teaspoon salt
- ¼ teaspoon freshly ground pepper
- 2 cups diced cooked turkey or chicken
- 2 red apples, cored and diced
- ⅔ cup sliced celery
- ½ cup chopped walnuts

In large bowl combine mayonnaise, lemon juice, salt and pepper. Add turkey, apples and celery; toss to coat well. Cover; chill. Just before serving, sprinkle with walnuts.

Makes about 4 to 6 servings

Tucson Turkey Salad

- 1 (8-ounce) container BORDEN® or MEADOW GOLD® Sour Cream
- 1 tablespoon REALIME® Lime Juice from Concentrate
- 2 teaspoons WYLER'S® or STEERO® Chicken-Flavor Instant Bouillon
- ½ teaspoon ground cumin Dash hot pepper sauce
- ½ pound smoked cooked turkey breast, thinly sliced
- ½ pound Cheddar cheese, thinly sliced
- 1 medium apple, cored and sliced
- 1 cup sliced celery
- ½ cup thin strips pared jicama Lettuce leaves
- ½ cup chopped walnuts, toasted

In medium bowl, combine sour cream, ReaLime® brand, bouillon, cumin and hot pepper sauce. Cover; chill 1 hour. Arrange turkey, cheese, apple, celery and jicama on lettuce. Top with walnuts. Serve with dressing.* Refrigerate leftovers.

Makes 4 servings

*For thinner dressing, add milk to desired consistency.

Smoked Turkey & Artichoke Salad with Hearts of Palm

Layered Turkey Salad

1½ cups salad dressing or
    mayonnaise
1 hard-cooked egg, pressed
    through a sieve or finely
    chopped
2 tablespoons chopped fresh
    parsley
2 tablespoons REALEMON®
    Lemon Juice from
    Concentrate
1 tablespoon finely chopped
    onion
2 teaspoons WYLER'S® or
    STEERO® Chicken-Flavor
    Instant Bouillon
8 cups torn mixed salad
    greens
2 cups cubed cooked turkey
    or chicken
2 cups shredded carrots
1 ounce alfalfa sprouts
    (about 2 cups)
1 (8-ounce) can sliced water
    chestnuts, drained
1½ cups (6 ounces) shredded
    Swiss cheese
4 ounces fresh pea pods *or*
    1 (6-ounce) package
    frozen pea pods, thawed
½ cup coarsely chopped
    cashews

In small bowl, combine salad dressing, egg, parsley, ReaLemon® brand, onion and bouillon. Cover; chill. In large serving bowl, layer greens, turkey, carrots, sprouts, water chestnuts, cheese and pea pods. Stir dressing and pour over salad; sprinkle with cashews. Refrigerate leftovers.

Makes 8 to 10 servings

From top to bottom: Layered Turkey Salad, Tropical Chicken Salad (page 112) and Tucson Turkey Salad

Oriental Shrimp Salad with Puff Bowl

1 pound small raw shrimp,
    peeled, deveined and
    cooked
4 ounces fresh pea pods *or*
    1 (6-ounce) package
    frozen pea pods, thawed
1 (8-ounce) can sliced water
    chestnuts, drained
1 cup sliced fresh
    mushrooms (about
    4 ounces)
1 cup diagonally sliced
    celery
2 ounces fresh bean sprouts
    (about 1 cup)
¼ cup sliced green onions
¾ cup mayonnaise or salad
    dressing
¼ cup REALEMON® Lemon
    Juice from Concentrate
1 tablespoon prepared
    horseradish
¼ to ½ teaspoon garlic salt
    Puff Bowl, optional

In large bowl, combine all ingredients except Puff Bowl; mix well. Cover; chill. Just before serving, spoon into Puff Bowl or onto lettuce. Refrigerate leftovers.

Makes 4 to 6 servings

Puff Bowl

2 eggs
½ cup unsifted flour
½ cup BORDEN® or MEADOW
    GOLD® Milk
¼ teaspoon salt
2 tablespoons margarine or
    butter, melted

Preheat oven to 425°. In small mixer bowl, beat eggs until frothy. Gradually beat in flour; beat until smooth. Add remaining ingredients; mix well. Pour into well-greased 9-inch pie plate. Bake 15 minutes. *Reduce oven temperature to 350°;* continue baking 10 to 15 minutes or until browned. Cool.

Stay Slim Salad

- **2 cups shredded DOLE® Iceberg Lettuce**
- **¼ cup chopped green onion**
- **½ pound sliced cooked chicken**
- **2 small DOLE® Bananas, sliced**
- **1 large DOLE® Pink Grapefruit, peeled and sectioned**
- **1 cup halved cherry tomatoes**
- **½ cup sliced DOLE® Celery Low-Calorie Dressing (recipe follows)**

In medium bowl, combine lettuce and onion. Arrange on 2 salad plates. Arrange chicken in center of each. Arrange bananas, grapefruit, tomatoes and celery around chicken. Serve with Low-Calorie Dressing.
Makes 2 servings.
LOW-CALORIE DRESSING: In screw-top jar, combine ¼ cup lime juice, 2 tablespoons vegetable oil, 2 teaspoons sugar, ½ teaspoon paprika and ¼ teaspoon *each* salt and dry mustard. Shake until well blended.

Festive Chicken Salad

- **1 8¼-ounce can crushed pineapple, undrained**
- **1 8-ounce container Soft PHILADELPHIA BRAND® Cream Cheese**
- **2 cups chopped cooked chicken**
- **1 8-ounce can water chestnuts, drained, sliced**
- **½ cup celery slices**
- **½ cup slivered almonds, toasted**
- **¼ cup green onion slices**
- **¼ teaspoon salt**
  Dash of pepper
- **4 medium tomatoes**
  Lettuce

Drain pineapple, reserving ¼ cup liquid. Combine reserved liquid and cream cheese, mixing until well blended. Add pineapple, chicken, water chestnuts, celery, ¼ cup almonds, onions, salt and pepper; mix lightly. Chill. Cut each tomato into six wedges, almost to stem end. Fill with chicken mixture. Sprinkle with remaining almonds. Serve on lettuce-lined plates.
4 servings.

Variations: Omit tomatoes; serve salad over honeydew or cantaloupe wedges or in lettuce cups.

Substitute chopped pecans for almonds.

Waldorf Chicken Salad

- **1 cup uncooked CREAMETTE® Medium Macaroni Shells, cooked as package directs, rinsed and drained**
- **2 cups cubed cooked chicken or turkey**
- **2 cups coarsely chopped apple**
- **1 cup (4 ounces) cubed mild Cheddar cheese**
- **¾ cup sliced celery**
- **½ cup mayonnaise or salad dressing**
- **¼ cup applesauce**
- **2 teaspoons WYLER'S® or STEERO® Chicken-Flavor Instant Bouillon**
- **½ cup chopped pecans**

In large bowl, combine ingredients; mix well. Chill thoroughly. Garnish as desired. Refrigerate leftovers.
Makes about 7½ cups.

Deluxe Chicken Walnut Salad

- **½ cup WISH-BONE® Chunky Blue Cheese or Lite Chunky Blue Cheese Dressing**
- **2 cups cut-up cooked chicken (about 12 ounces)**
- **½ cup green or red seedless grapes**
- **½ cup chopped walnuts**
- **2 tablespoons sliced green onion**

In medium bowl, combine all ingredients and toss well; cover and chill. Serve, if desired, on croissants.
Makes about 2 main-dish servings.

Turkey Pineapple Salad

- **1½ cups (½ pound) cubed BUTTERBALL® SLICE 'N SERVE® Oven Prepared Breast of Turkey**
- **1½ cups (½ pound) thin strips BUTTERBALL® SLICE 'N SERVE® Turkey Ham**
- **2 cups fresh or canned pineapple chunks**
- **1 cup diced unpared red apple**
- **½ cup sliced celery**
- **¾ cup pecan halves**
- **¼ cup sour cream**
- **¼ cup mayonnaise**
- **½ teaspoon sugar**
- **¼ teaspoon ground ginger**
- **¾ teaspoon prepared mustard**
  Lettuce leaves or pineapple shells

Combine turkey breast, turkey ham, pineapple, apple, celery and pecans in medium bowl. Stir together sour cream, mayonnaise, sugar, ginger and mustard in small bowl. Spoon dressing over salad and toss to blend. Serve immediately on lettuce leaves or pineapple shells.
Makes 6 servings.

To Make Pineapple Shells: Cut pineapple lengthwise into quarters keeping top attached. Core and remove fruit from each quarter.

Turkey Pineapple Salad

Rainbow Fruit Salad

2 peaches, peeled, pitted and sliced
2 DOLE® Oranges, peeled and sliced
2 cups DOLE® Strawberries, hulled and sliced
1 cup DOLE® Seedless Grapes
1 cup melon balls
Pineapple Lime Dressing (recipe follows)

In large bowl, combine fruit. Add Pineapple Lime Dressing; stir gently to coat.
Makes 8 servings.
PINEAPPLE LIME DRESSING: In small bowl, combine ½ cup Dole® Pineapple Juice, ½ teaspoon grated lime peel, 3 tablespoons *each* lime juice and honey and 1 tablespoon chopped crystallized ginger. Whisk until blended.

Ambrosia

1 can (20 ounces) DOLE® Pineapple Chunks in Juice
1 can (11 ounces) DOLE® Mandarin Orange Segments in Syrup
1 firm, large DOLE® Banana, sliced, optional
1½ cups DOLE® Seedless Grapes
1 cup miniature marshmallows
1 cup flaked coconut
½ cup pecan halves or coarsely chopped nuts
1 cup dairy sour cream or plain yogurt
1 tablespoon brown sugar

Drain pineapple and orange segments. In large bowl, combine pineapple, mandarin oranges, banana, grapes, marshmallows, coconut and nuts. In 1-quart measure, combine sour cream and brown sugar. Stir into fruit mixture. Refrigerate, covered, 1 hour or overnight.
Makes 6 servings.

Carrot Pineapple Salad

1 DOLE® Fresh Pineapple
1 honeydew melon
3 large DOLE® Carrots, thinly sliced
½ cup thinly sliced DOLE® Pitted Dates
Honey-Lime Vinaigrette (recipe follows)

Twist crown from pineapple. Cut pineapple lengthwise into quarters. Remove fruit from shells with curved knife. Trim off core and cut fruit into chunks. Cut melon in half; scoop out seeds and cut fruit into 1-inch pieces. In salad bowl, combine pineapple, melon, carrots and dates. Toss with Honey-Lime Vinaigrette; garnish with lime slices, if desired.
Makes 6 servings.
HONEY-LIME VINAIGRETTE: In small bowl, combine ¼ cup honey, 2 tablespoons *each* white wine vinegar and lime juice, 1 tablespoon vegetable oil, and 2 teaspoons grated lime peel. Whisk until blended.

Minted Fruit Salad

½ cup sugar
⅓ cup orange juice
⅓ cup REALEMON® Lemon Juice from Concentrate
⅓ cup water
¼ teaspoon peppermint extract
8 cups assorted fresh fruits
Sherbet

In medium bowl, combine sugar, orange juice, ReaLemon® brand, water and peppermint extract; stir until sugar dissolves. Place fruit in 3-quart shallow baking dish; pour juice mixture over. Cover; chill 3 to 4 hours to blend flavors. Arrange drained fruit on platter; top with sherbet and garnish as desired.
Makes 4 servings.

Creamy Topped Fruit Salad

1 8-ounce package Light PHILADELPHIA BRAND® Neufchatel Cheese, softened
2 tablespoons lemon juice
1 teaspoon grated lemon peel
½ cup whipping cream
¼ cup powdered sugar
2 cups peach slices
2 cups blueberries
2 cups strawberry slices
2 cups grapes

Combine Neufchatel cheese, juice and peel, mixing until well blended. Beat whipping cream until soft peaks form; gradually add sugar, beating until stiff peaks form. Fold into Neufchatel cheese mixture; chill. Layer fruit in 2½-quart glass serving bowl. Top with Neufchatel cheese mixture. Sprinkle with nuts, if desired. Chill. *8 servings.*
   Variation: Substitute PHILADELPHIA BRAND® Cream Cheese for Neufchatel Cheese.

Creamy Topped Fruit Salad

Salmon Salad Provençal

Combine hot rice and peas in large bowl; toss lightly. Add tuna, celery, onions, and capers. Combine lemon juice, oil, curry powder, and pepper sauce in small jar with lid. Pour over rice mixture; toss lightly. Cover and chill 30 minutes. Serve on shredded lettuce and garnish with tomato wedges.

Makes 6 servings

Favorite recipe from **USA Rice Council**

Paella Salad

1 can (13¾ ounces) chicken broth (1¾ cups)
⅔ cup cold water
2¼ cups MINUTE® Premium Long Grain Rice, uncooked
¼ teaspoon saffron threads, crushed
3 cups chopped cooked chicken
2 packages (6 ounces each) frozen cooked tiny shrimp, thawed
1 pound smoked sausage, sliced, halved, browned
2 cups coarsely chopped tomato
1 package (10 ounces) BIRDS EYE® Peas, thawed, drained
⅔ cup MIRACLE WHIP® Salad Dressing
¼ cup finely chopped red onion
½ teaspoon minced garlic
Salt and pepper

• Bring broth and water to boil; stir in rice and saffron. Cover; remove from heat. Let stand 5 minutes or until liquid is absorbed. Cool.

• Mix remaining ingredients until well blended. Stir in rice mixture.   *Makes 8 servings*

Prep time: 25 minutes
Cooking time: 5 minutes plus standing

Salmon Salad Provençal

⅓ cup REALEMON® Lemon Juice from Concentrate
⅓ cup olive or vegetable oil
1 teaspoon sugar
½ teaspoon dry mustard
½ teaspoon salt
¼ teaspoon basil leaves
¼ teaspoon oregano leaves
1 pound fresh or frozen salmon, poached *or* 1 (15½-ounce) can salmon, drained and flaked
¾ pound small new potatoes, cooked and quartered
½ pound fresh green beans, *or* 1 (9-ounce) package frozen cut green beans, cooked and chilled
Lettuce leaves
Tomatoes, hard-cooked eggs and ripe olives

In large shallow dish, combine ReaLemon® brand, oil, sugar, mustard, salt, basil and oregano;

add salmon and potatoes. Cover; chill. Arrange salmon, potatoes and green beans on lettuce; garnish with tomatoes, eggs and olives. Spoon remaining dressing over salad. Refrigerate leftovers.

Makes 4 servings

Curried Tuna Salad

3 cups hot cooked rice
½ cup frozen peas
1 to 2 cans (6½ ounces each) tuna, packed in water, drained and flaked
¾ cup chopped celery
¼ cup sliced green onions
1 tablespoon drained capers (optional)
¼ cup lemon juice
2 tablespoons olive oil
¼ teaspoon curry powder
¼ teaspoon hot pepper sauce
Shredded romaine lettuce
2 medium tomatoes, cut into wedges, for garnish

Tuna & Fresh Fruit Salad

Tuna & Fresh Fruit Salad

Lettuce leaves (optional)
1 can (12½ ounces) STARKIST® Tuna, drained and broken into chunks
4 cups slices or wedges fresh fruit*
¼ cup silvered almonds (optional)

Fruit Dressing
1 container (8 ounces) lemon, mandarin orange or vanilla low-fat yogurt
2 tablespoons orange juice
¼ teaspoon ground cinnamon

Line a large platter or 4 individual plates with lettuce leaves, if desired. Arrange tuna and desired fruit in a decorative design over lettuce. Sprinkle almonds over salad, if desired.

For Fruit Dressing: In a small bowl stir together yogurt, orange juice and cinnamon until well blended. Serve dressing with salad.　　*Makes 4 servings*

*Suggested fresh fruit: Apples, bananas, berries, citrus fruit, kiwifruit, melon, papaya, peaches or pears.

Shrimp Antipasto

1 cup vegetable oil
⅔ cup REALEMON® Lemon Juice from Concentrate
2 tablespoons Dijon-style mustard
2 teaspoons sugar
1½ teaspoons thyme leaves
1 teaspoon salt
1½ pounds raw medium shrimp, peeled, deveined and cooked
6 ounces Provolone cheese, cut into cubes
1 (6-ounce) can pitted ripe olives, drained
4 ounces Genoa salami, cut into cubes
1 large red bell pepper, cut into squares

In large shallow dish or plastic bag, combine oil, ReaLemon® brand, mustard, sugar, thyme and salt; add shrimp, cheese and olives. Cover; marinate in refrigerator 6 hours or overnight, stirring occasionally. Add salami and red pepper; toss. Drain; garnish as desired. Refrigerate leftovers.

Makes about 8 cups

Tip: Cooked scallops can be substituted for all or part of the shrimp.

Salsa Shrimp in Papaya

Lemon juice
12 ounces cooked bay shrimp, rinsed and drained
¾ cup chunky salsa
½ teaspoon LAWRY'S® Lemon Pepper Seasoning
¼ teaspoon LAWRY'S® Garlic Powder with Parsley
3 ripe papayas, halved, peeled and seeds removed

In medium bowl, sprinkle lemon juice over shrimp. Add salsa, Lemon Pepper Seasoning and Garlic Powder with Parsley; cover and marinate in refrigerator 1 hour or overnight. Fill each papaya half with marinated shrimp.

Makes 6 servings

Presentation: Arrange papaya halves on lettuce leaves. Garnish each with chopped parsley and lemon slices.

Salsa Shrimp in Papaya

Garden Patch Salad

6 ounces SWIFT PREMIUM® Deli Hard Salami, cut into julienne strips
1/3 cup olive oil
2 tablespoons fresh lemon juice
1 tablespoon minced fresh parsley
1 tablespoon grated Parmesan cheese
1 clove garlic, minced
6 ounces mozzarella cheese, cubed
1 pint cherry tomatoes, cut into halves
1 medium zucchini, cut lengthwise into halves, sliced thin
1 small onion, cut into quarters, sliced thin

Place oil, lemon juice, parsley, Parmesan cheese and garlic in jar with tight-fitting lid. Shake ingredients together and let stand 1 hour for flavors to blend. Combine salami, mozzarella cheese, tomatoes, zucchini and onion in salad bowl. Pour dressing over salad and toss to blend before serving. *Makes 6 servings.*

Salad Taverna

Chef's Salad

6 cups torn lettuce
6 ounces spinach, rinsed, drained, trimmed and torn into bite-size pieces
8 ounces cooked turkey, cut into thin strips
8 ounces fully cooked ham, cut into thin strips
6 ounces Swiss cheese, cut into thin strips
1 cup broken melba cracker rounds
8 cherry tomatoes, halved
8 pitted black or green olives, halved
3 green onions, chopped

Combine all ingredients in large salad bowl or divide ingredients among individual salad bowls. Garnish with *hard-cooked egg slices,* if desired. Serve with desired dressing. *6 to 8 servings.*

*Favorite recipe from **CRISCO® Oil/Procter & Gamble Company***

Salada di Antipasto

2 quarts mixed salad greens
1/2 pound salami, cut into strips
1 package (8 ounces) mozzarella cheese, cut into strips
1 package (10 ounces) frozen artichoke hearts, cooked and drained
1 cup pitted ripe olives
1 medium tomato, cut into wedges
1/3 cup roasted red peppers, cut into strips
1 cup (8 ounces) WISH-BONE® Robusto Italian Dressing

In large salad bowl, arrange all ingredients except robusto Italian dressing; cover and chill. Just before serving, toss with dressing. Serve, if desired, with Italian bread.
Makes about 4 main-dish servings.
   Note: Also terrific with Wish-Bone® Italian or Lite Italian Dressing.

Salad Taverna

1/3 cup olive or vegetable oil
3 tablespoons lemon juice
1 clove garlic, minced
1/2 teaspoon TABASCO® pepper sauce
1/2 teaspoon anise seed
1/4 teaspoon salt
8 ounces spinach egg noodles, cooked, drained
1/2 pound feta cheese, crumbled or 1 cup ricotta or cottage cheese
2 tomatoes, coarsely chopped
1/2 cup sliced pitted ripe olives
1/4 cup chopped parsley (optional)
1/4 cup pine nuts (optional)

In large bowl combine oil, lemon juice, garlic, Tabasco® sauce, anise seed and salt; mix well. Add noodles, cheese, tomatoes, olives, parsley and pine nuts; toss to coat evenly. Cover; refrigerate at least 1 hour. Serve with additional Tabasco® sauce, if desired.
Makes 4 to 6 servings.

Wild Rice and Seafood Salad

- ½ cup WISH-BONE® Lite Creamy Italian Dressing
- 1 pound medium shrimp, cleaned, cooked and coarsely chopped*
- 2 cups cooked wild or regular white rice
- 1 small red or green pepper, chopped
- ½ cup halved seedless grapes
- ¼ cup sliced almonds, toasted
- 1 teaspoon lemon juice
- 3 dashes hot pepper sauce
  Lettuce leaves

In large bowl, combine all ingredients except lettuce; cover and chill. To serve, line bowl or individual serving dishes with lettuce; fill with shrimp mixture. Garnish, if desired, with lemon slices.
Makes about 6 main-dish servings.
Substitution: Use 2 packages (6 ounces each) frozen crabmeat, thawed and drained. Increase dressing to ¾ cup.
Note: Also terrific with Wish-Bone® Lite Creamy Italian Dressing.

Potato-Tuna Salad

- ½ cup olive or vegetable oil
- ¼ cup white wine vinegar
- 2 tablespoons lemon juice
- 1 clove garlic, minced
- ¾ teaspoon TABASCO® pepper sauce
- ¼ teaspoon salt
- 2 pounds cooked small red potatoes, cubed
- 2 cans (6½ or 7 ounces each) tuna, drained, separated into large chunks
- 1 cup sliced celery
- ⅓ cup sliced green onions
  Fresh spinach leaves (optional)

In large bowl combine oil, vinegar, lemon juice, garlic, Tabasco® sauce and salt; mix well. Add potatoes, tuna, celery and green onions; toss lightly. Cover; refrigerate at least 1 hour. Serve over fresh spinach leaves, if desired.
Makes 6 to 8 servings.

Sea Salad

- 1 bunch DOLE® Broccoli, cut into florettes (2 cups)
- 4 ounces snow peas, ends and strings removed
- 8 ounces shell-shaped pasta
- 2 cups sliced DOLE® Celery
- 2 cups sliced fresh mushrooms
- ½ cup sliced DOLE® Red Bell Pepper
- 8 ounces cooked, shelled shrimp
  Lemon-Mustard Dressing (recipe follows)

To blanch vegetables, cover broccoli and snow peas with boiling water. Let stand 5 minutes. Rinse under cold water to stop cooking; drain. Cook pasta according to package directions; drain. In large bowl, combine vegetables, pasta and shrimp; toss with Lemon-Mustard Dressing. Refrigerate, covered, at least 2 hours before serving.
Makes 4 servings.
LEMON-MUSTARD DRESSING: In 1-quart measure, combine ½ cup olive or vegetable oil, 3 tablespoons lemon juice, 1 tablespoon wine vinegar, 2 teaspoons Dijon mustard, 1 teaspoon dried dill weed, ¼ teaspoon pepper and salt to taste. Blend well.

Curried Pineapple Pasta Salad

- 1 can (20 ounces) DOLE® Pineapple Chunks in Juice
- 2 cups cooked, shredded chicken
- 8 ounces macaroni or other small pasta, cooked
- 2 cups sliced DOLE® Celery
- ½ cup sliced green onion
- ½ cup julienne-cut DOLE® Red Bell Pepper
- ½ cup sliced ripe olives
- ¾ cup mayonnaise
- ⅓ cup chopped chutney
- ¼ cup dairy sour cream
- 2 teaspoons curry powder
- 1 teaspoon salt

Drain pineapple. In salad bowl, combine pineapple, chicken, pasta, celery, onion, red pepper and olives. To make dressing, in 1-quart measure, combine remaining ingredients; toss with salad. Refrigerate, covered, until ready to serve.
Makes 8 servings.

Potato-Tuna Salad

Individual Taco Salads

Steak Salad in Red-Wine Dressing

- ½ cup **WISH-BONE®** Italian Dressing
- ½ cup dry red wine
- 1 tablespoon Worcestershire sauce
- 1 tablespoon rosemary leaves
- 2 teaspoons Dijon-style mustard
- ½ pound beef flank or round steak, thinly sliced
- 1 medium red onion, sliced
- 1 large tomato, coarsely chopped
- 1 cup sliced carrots
- 1 cup sliced zucchini

In large shallow baking dish, thoroughly blend Italian dressing, wine, Worcestershire sauce, rosemary and mustard. Add beef and red onion; turn to coat. Cover and marinate in refrigerator, stirring occasionally, at least 3 hours.

Remove beef, onion and marinade to large shallow heavy-duty aluminum-foil-lined baking pan or broiler rack. Broil beef with marinade, turning occasionally, 3 minutes or until done; cover and chill. To serve, toss beef mixture with tomato, then arrange on serving platter with carrots, zucchini and, if desired, watercress.
Makes about 4 main-dish servings.
Note: Also terrific with Wish-Bone® Robusto Italian, Blended Italian or Lite Italian Dressing.

Individual Taco Salads

- ⅓ cup French Dressing (page 123) **CRISCO®** Oil for frying
- 4 to 6 eight-inch flour tortillas
- 1 pound ground beef
- ¼ cup chopped onion
- 1 can (15½ ounces) kidney beans, rinsed and drained
- 1½ teaspoons chili powder
- 1 teaspoon cumin
- ½ teaspoon salt
- ⅛ teaspoon pepper
- 4 to 6 cups shredded lettuce
- 1 cup shredded Cheddar cheese (about 4 ounces)

Prepare French Dressing as directed. Cover and refrigerate.

Heat 3 inches Crisco® Oil in deep-fryer or heavy saucepan to 375°F.

Place 1 tortilla in oil. Let float 5 to 10 seconds. Press center of tortilla into oil with metal ladle (tortilla will form a bowl shape). While pressing with metal ladle, fry 1 to 2 minutes longer, or until golden brown. Drain on paper towels. Repeat with remaining tortillas.

Combine ground beef and onion in large skillet. Brown over medium-high heat. Drain. Add beans, chili powder, cumin, salt and pepper. Cook over moderate heat, stirring constantly, for 5 minutes, or until flavors are blended. Stir in ⅓ cup French Dressing.

Divide shredded lettuce equally among fried tortillas. Top with meat mixture. Sprinkle with Cheddar cheese. Serve with *dairy sour cream, chopped tomato, chopped black olives* or *taco sauce,* if desired.
4 to 6 servings.

Shaved Ham Salad

- 8 ounces shaved fully cooked ham, coarsely chopped
- 1½ cups coarsely chopped fresh mushrooms
- ¾ cup bite-size cubes mozzarella cheese
- ½ cup quartered pimiento-stuffed olives
- ⅓ cup chopped green onion
- 1 medium tomato, seeded and chopped
- ⅓ cup **CRISCO®** Oil
- 2 tablespoons red wine vinegar
- ¼ teaspoon pepper

Mix ham, mushrooms, mozzarella cheese, olives, onion and tomato in medium serving bowl. Blend remaining ingredients in small mixing bowl. Pour over ham mixture. Toss to coat. Serve immediately, or refrigerate and stir before serving.
6 to 8 servings.

Layered Salad Extraordinaire

1 8-ounce package Light
    PHILADELPHIA BRAND®
    Neufchatel Cheese, softened
3/4 cup (3 ounces) crumbled
    KRAFT® Natural Blue
    Cheese
1/4 cup KRAFT® Light Reduced
    Calorie Mayonnaise
1/4 cup milk
2 tablespoons lemon juice
1 tablespoon chopped chives
2 quarts torn assorted greens
1 cup shredded carrot
2 1/2 cups ham cubes
1 cup chopped green pepper
2 cups chopped tomato

Combine Neufchatel cheese and blue cheese, mixing until well blended. Add mayonnaise, milk, juice and chives; mix well.

Combine greens and carrots. Combine meat and green peppers. In 3-quart bowl, layer greens mixture, tomatoes and meat mixture. Spread Neufchatel cheese mixture over meat mixture to seal. Cover; chill several hours.
8 servings.

Summer Kielbasa Salad

1/2 pound ECKRICH® Polska
    Kielbasa, cut into 1/8-inch
    slices
1 cup shredded red cabbage
1 medium cucumber, sliced thin
4 red radishes, sliced thin
1/2 cup mayonnaise
1/2 cup sour cream
2 tablespoons Dijon mustard
1 tablespoon prepared
    horseradish
1/2 teaspoon dried dill weed
1/2 teaspoon garlic salt
1/4 cup crumbled feta cheese
1 teaspoon chopped fresh
    parsley

Saute kielbasa in 10-inch skillet over medium heat until lightly browned. Drain on paper towels. Cool. Place kielbasa, cabbage, cucumber and radishes in large bowl. Combine mayonnaise, sour cream, mustard, horseradish, dill weed and garlic salt in small bowl. Whisk to blend; stir in cheese. Pour dressing over kielbasa and vegetables. Cover and refrigerate 20 minutes. Sprinkle with parsley and serve.
Makes 4 to 6 servings.

Marinated Oriental Beef Salad

1 (1- to 1 1/4-pound) flank steak
1/3 cup REALEMON® Lemon Juice
    from Concentrate
1/4 cup catsup
1/4 cup vegetable oil
1 tablespoon brown sugar
1/4 teaspoon garlic powder
1/4 teaspoon ground ginger
1/4 teaspoon pepper
8 ounces fresh mushrooms,
    sliced (about 2 cups)
1 (8-ounce) can sliced water
    chestnuts, drained
1 medium sweet onion, sliced
    and separated into rings
1 (6-ounce) package frozen pea
    pods, thawed, or 4 ounces
    fresh pea pods
Lettuce leaves
Tomato wedges

Broil meat 5 minutes on each side or until desired doneness; slice diagonally into thin strips. Meanwhile, in large bowl, combine ReaLemon® brand, catsup, oil, sugar, garlic powder, ginger and pepper; mix well. Add sliced meat, mushrooms, water chestnuts and onion; mix well. Cover; refrigerate 8 hours or overnight, stirring occasionally. Before serving, add pea pods. Serve on lettuce; garnish with tomato. Refrigerate leftovers.
Makes 4 servings.

French Dressing

2/3 cup CRISCO® Oil
1/2 cup catsup
2 tablespoons white wine
    vinegar
1 tablespoon sugar
1 teaspoon paprika
1/2 teaspoon dry mustard

Combine all ingredients in blender pitcher. Blend at medium to high speed until smooth (at least 2 minutes), stopping to scrape pitcher, if necessary.

Cover and store in refrigerator. Stir before serving.
1 1/4 cups.

Marinated Oriental Beef Salad

Beef Asparagus Salad

½ cup MIRACLE WHIP®
    FREE® Dressing
⅓ cup each: finely chopped
    green, red and yellow bell
    peppers
2 tablespoons skim milk
2 tablespoons finely
    chopped fresh basil or
    2 teaspoons dried basil
    leaves, crushed
2 tablespoons chopped
    green onions
¼ teaspoon each: salt,
    pepper
1 pound each: roast beef
    slices, asparagus spears,
    cooked
3 tomatoes, sliced
1 cucumber, sliced
1 summer squash, sliced

• Mix salad dressing, bell
peppers, milk, basil, onions, salt
and pepper until well blended;
refrigerate.

• Arrange remaining ingredients
on serving platter. Serve with
salad dressing mixture.

Makes 8 servings

Prep time: 20 minutes plus
refrigerating

Beef Asparagus Salad

Western Steak Salad

⅔ cup vegetable oil
¼ cup lime juice
2 tablespoons HEINZ® 57
    Sauce
2 tablespoons HEINZ®
    Gourmet Wine Vinegar
½ teaspoon salt
¼ cup HEINZ® 57 Sauce
1 tablespoon lime juice
1 tablespoon vegetable oil
½ teaspoon hot pepper sauce
1 pound boneless beef
    sirloin steak
6 cups torn romaine lettuce
8 cherry tomatoes, halved
1 small avocado, peeled, cut
    into chunks
1 small red onion, halved,
    sliced

For dressing, in jar combine
⅔ cup oil, ¼ cup lime juice, 2
tablespoons 57 Sauce, vinegar
and salt. Cover and shake
vigorously; chill to blend flavors.
In small bowl, combine ¼ cup
57 Sauce, 1 tablespoon lime
juice, 1 tablespoon oil and hot
pepper sauce. Brush on both
sides of steak; let stand 30
minutes. Broil steak, 3 to 4
inches from heat source, to
desired doneness, turning and
brushing once with marinade.
Let steak stand while preparing
salad mixture. In large bowl,
combine romaine, tomatoes,
avocado and onion; toss with ½
cup dressing and divide among 4
salad bowls. Thinly slice steak
across grain; arrange on top of
salad mixture. Serve salad with
remaining dressing, if desired.

Makes 4 servings
(about 1¼ cups dressing)

Sesame Pork Salad

3 cups cooked rice
1½ cups slivered cooked pork*
¼ pound fresh snow peas,
julienned
1 medium cucumber, peeled,
seeded and julienned
1 medium red pepper,
julienned
½ cup sliced green onions
2 tablespoons sesame seeds,
toasted (optional)

Combine all ingredients in large
bowl; stir well. Pour Sesame
Dressing over rice mixture; toss
lightly. Serve at room
temperature or slightly chilled.
Makes 6 servings

Sesame Dressing

¼ cup chicken broth
3 tablespoons rice or white
wine vinegar
3 tablespoons soy sauce
1 tablespoon peanut oil
1 teaspoon sesame oil

Combine all ingredients in small
jar with lid; shake vigorously.
Makes about ¾ cup

*Substitute 1½ cups slivered
cooked chicken for pork, if
desired.

Favorite recipe from **USA Rice
Council**

Stir-Fry Beef Salad

Sesame Pork Salad

Stir-Fry Beef Salad

1 pound boneless beef
sirloin steak
2 tablespoons olive oil,
divided
1 tablespoon grated fresh
ginger root
1 clove garlic, minced
1 small red onion, chopped
1 cup (about 4 ounces) fresh
mushrooms, quartered
3 tablespoons cider vinegar
1 tablespoon soy sauce
1 tablespoon honey
3 cups hot cooked rice
½ pound fresh spinach, torn
into bite-size pieces
1 medium tomato, seeded
and coarsely chopped

Partially freeze steak; slice
across the grain into ⅛-inch
strips. Set aside. Heat 1
tablespoon oil, ginger root, and
garlic in large skillet or wok over
high heat until hot. Stir-fry beef
(half at a time) 1 to 2 minutes.
Remove beef; keep warm. Add
remaining 1 tablespoon oil; heat
until hot. Add onion and
mushrooms; cook 1 to 2 minutes.
Stir in vinegar, soy sauce, and
honey. Bring mixture to a boil.
Add beef and rice; toss lightly.
Serve over spinach. Top with
tomato; serve immediately.
Makes 6 servings

Favorite recipe from **USA Rice
Council**

Hearty Roast Beef, Pear and Pea Pod Salad

Salad
 1 head lettuce
 10 ounces sliced rare roast beef, cut into strips
 2 carrots, peeled, cut into matchstick pieces
 3 fresh California Bartlett pears, cored and sliced
 1 small red onion, halved and thinly sliced
 10 ounces fresh Chinese pea pods (about 1¼ cups), trimmed
 ¼ cup pitted ripe or cured black olives (optional garnish)

Mustard Vinaigrette
 1 bottle (8 ounces) Italian salad dressing
 2 teaspoons Dijon-style mustard

On serving platter or individual plates, arrange lettuce leaves. Place remaining salad ingredients on top. In small bowl, combine vinaigrette ingredients and drizzle over salad.   *Makes 4 servings*

Tip: To keep fruit colors bright, dip pear slices in Mustard Vinaigrette as you cut them, or cut pears just before serving.

*Favorite recipe from **California Tree Fruit Agreement***

Fandangled Fajitas Salad

 1 pound boneless, skinless chicken breasts, thinly sliced
 1 tablespoon vegetable oil
 1 package (1.27 ounces) LAWRY'S® Spices & Seasonings for Fajitas
 ¼ cup water
 4 cups shredded lettuce
 1 can (15 ounces) pinto beans, drained and rinsed
 1 medium onion, slivered
 1 medium green or red bell pepper, slivered
 1 medium tomato, thinly sliced
 1 avocado, thinly sliced
   Fandangled Dressing (recipe follows)

In large skillet, brown chicken pieces in oil; drain fat. Add Spices & Seasonings for Fajitas and water; blend well. Bring to a boil; reduce heat and simmer, uncovered, 3 to 5 minutes. On individual serving plates, arrange lettuce and layer beans, onion, bell pepper, tomato and avocado. Top with equal portions of prepared fajitas mixture. Serve Fandangled Dressing on the side.   *Makes 4 servings*

Presentation: Serve with tortilla chips.

Hint: Ground beef or steak strips can be used in place of chicken.

Fandangled Dressing

 1⅓ cups chunky salsa
 ¼ cup vegetable oil
 2 tablespoons red wine vinegar
 2 tablespoons lime juice

In container with stopper or lid, combine all ingredients; blend well.   *Makes about 1½ cups*

Aztec Chili Salad

 1 pound ground beef
 1 package (1.62 ounces) LAWRY'S® Spices & Seasonings for Chili
 ½ cup water
 1 can (15¼ ounces) kidney beans, undrained
 1 can (14½ ounces) whole peeled tomatoes, undrained and cut up
 ½ cup dairy sour cream
 3 tablespoons mayonnaise
 1 fresh medium tomato, diced
 ¼ cup chopped fresh cilantro
 ½ teaspoon LAWRY'S® Seasoned Pepper
 1 head lettuce
 1 red bell pepper, sliced
 ¼ cup sliced green onions
 1½ cups (6 ounces) grated Cheddar cheese
 ¼ cup sliced ripe olives

In large skillet, brown ground beef until crumbly; drain fat. Stir in Spices & Seasonings for Chili, water, beans and canned tomatoes; blend well. Bring to a boil; reduce heat and simmer, uncovered, 10 minutes. For dressing, in blender or food processor, blend sour cream, mayonnaise, fresh tomato, cilantro and Seasoned Pepper. Refrigerate until chilled. On 6 individual plates, layer lettuce, chili meat, bell pepper, green onions, cheese and olives. Drizzle with chilled dressing.
        Makes 6 servings

Presentation: Serve with jicama wedges arranged around salad plates.

Hint: Ground turkey or shredded chicken can be used in place of ground beef in chili mixture.

Aztec Chili Salad

Summer Fruit Salad

Kona Ham Hawaiian

**1 can (20 ounces) DOLE®
  Pineapple Chunks in
  Syrup***
½ pound ham, cut into strips
½ cup sliced DOLE® Celery
**1 firm, medium DOLE®
  Banana, peeled, sliced**
**1 cup halved DOLE®
  Strawberries**
**½ cup cholesterol-free,
  reduced-calorie
  mayonnaise**
**¼ teaspoon dry mustard
  DOLE® Salad Greens**

• Drain pineapple; reserve 1 tablespoon syrup.

• Combine pineapple, ham, celery, banana and strawberries in bowl.

• Combine mayonnaise, mustard and reserved syrup in small bowl. Pour over salad; toss to coat.

• Serve in salad bowl lined with salad greens.

Makes 4 servings

*Use pineapple packed in juice, if desired.

Preparation Time: 20 minutes

Summer Fruit Salad

**2 cups cooked rice, cooled to
  room temperature**
½ cup quartered strawberries
½ cup grape halves
**2 kiwifruit, sliced into
  quarters**
½ cup pineapple tidbits
½ cup banana slices
¼ cup pineapple juice
**2 tablespoons plain nonfat
  yogurt**
**1 tablespoon honey
  Lettuce leaves**

Combine rice and fruit in large bowl. Blend pineapple juice, yogurt, and honey in small bowl. Pour over rice mixture; toss lightly. Serve on lettuce leaves.
Makes 4 servings

Favorite recipe from **USA Rice Council**

Jicama Orange Burst Salad

¼ cup vegetable oil
**1 tablespoon red wine
  vinegar**
1 tablespoon sugar
2 teaspoons fresh lime juice
**½ teaspoon LAWRY'S®
  Seasoned Salt**
**½ teaspoon LAWRY'S®
  Seasoned Pepper**
**¼ teaspoon dry mustard
  Lettuce**
**3 medium navel oranges,
  peeled and sectioned**
**1 small jicama, peeled and
  julienne-cut into 1-inch
  pieces**
½ cup sliced green onions
¼ cup diced red onion

In medium bowl, combine oil, vinegar, sugar, lime juice, Seasoned Salt, Seasoned Pepper and mustard; blend well. Refrigerate. On bed of lettuce, arrange orange sections, jicama and green and red onions. Drizzle dressing over salad.
Makes 1¼ cups

Poppy Seed Fruit Sauce

**½ cup MIRACLE WHIP®
  FREE® Dressing**
**1 container (8 ounces)
  lemon-flavored lowfat
  yogurt**
2 tablespoons skim milk
**1 tablespoon each: packed
  brown sugar, poppy
  seeds**

• Mix ingredients until well blended; refrigerate. Serve over fresh fruit. *Makes 1⅔ cups*

Prep Time: 5 minutes plus refrigerating

Poolside Fruit Salad Platter with Honey-Lemon Yogurt Dip

Fruit
 2 kiwifruit, peeled and sliced
 2 fresh plums, sliced
 1 fresh California nectarine, sliced
 1 fresh California peach, sliced
 1 fresh California Bartlett pear, cored and sliced
 ⅓ cup fresh blueberries (optional)

Honey-Lemon Yogurt Dip
 1 cup nonfat lemon yogurt
 1 tablespoon honey
 1 strip lemon peel (optional garnish)

Line serving platter with kiwifruit. Top with remaining fruit. In small bowl, combine yogurt and honey. Spoon over fruit. Garnish with lemon peel, if desired. *Makes 6 servings*

*Favorite recipe from **California Tree Fruit Agreement***

California Salad

 2 cups assorted DOLE® fresh fruit
 3 ounces Brie or Camembert cheese
 3 ounces cooked baby shrimp
  Crisp DOLE® Salad Greens

Paradise Dressing
 ¼ cup frozen DOLE® Pine-Orange-Guava Juice concentrate,* thawed
 3 tablespoons honey
 2 teaspoons lime juice
 1 teaspoon lime zest

• Arrange fruit, cheese and shrimp on 2 salad plates lined with salad greens. Serve with Paradise Dressing.
 Makes 2 servings

PARADISE DRESSING: Combine all ingredients in screw-top jar; shake well. Serve over fruit.
 Makes ½ cup

*Do not reconstitute.

Preparation Time: 20 minutes

Ribbon Squares

 1 package (4-serving size) JELL-O® Brand Gelatin, Lemon Flavor
 1 package (4-serving size) JELL-O® Brand Gelatin, Cherry, Raspberry or Strawberry Flavor
 1 package (4-serving size) JELL-O® Brand Gelatin, Lime Flavor
 3 cups boiling water
 1 package (8 ounces) PHILADELPHIA BRAND® Cream Cheese, softened
 1 can (8¼ ounces) crushed pineapple in syrup, undrained
 1 cup thawed COOL WHIP® Whipped Topping
 ½ cup MIRACLE WHIP® Salad Dressing
 1½ cups cold water
  Canned pineapple slices, drained (optional)
  Celery leaves (optional)

DISSOLVE each flavor of gelatin in separate bowls, using 1 cup of the boiling water for each.

BLEND lemon gelatin into cream cheese, beating until smooth. Add pineapple with syrup. Chill until slightly thickened. Stir in whipped topping and salad dressing. Chill until thickened. Stir ¾ cup of the cold water into cherry gelatin; pour into 9-inch square pan. Chill until set but not firm. Stir remaining ¾ cup cold water into lime gelatin; chill until slightly thickened. Spoon lemon gelatin mixture over cherry gelatin layer in pan. Chill until set but not firm. Top with lime gelatin. Chill until firm, about 4 hours or overnight. Unmold; cut into squares. Garnish with pineapple slices and celery leaves, if desired. *Makes 12 servings*

Prep time: 1 hour
Chill time: 6 hours

Poppy Seed Fruit Sauce

Under-the-Sea Salad

- **1 can (16 ounces) pear halves in syrup, undrained**
- **1 package (4-serving size) JELL-O® Brand Gelatin, Lime Flavor**
- **1 cup boiling water**
- **¼ cup cold water**
- **1 tablespoon lemon juice**
- **1 package (8 ounces) PHILADELPHIA BRAND® Cream Cheese, softened**
- **⅛ teaspoon ground ginger**
  Salad greens (optional)
  Seedless red grapes (optional)

DRAIN pears, reserving ½ cup syrup. Dice pears; set aside. Dissolve gelatin in boiling water. Add reserved syrup, cold water and lemon juice. Measure 1¼ cups gelatin into 8×4-inch loaf pan. Chill until set but not firm. Place cream cheese in blender; cover. Blend at low speed until smooth and creamy. Very slowly add remaining gelatin and ginger. Blend at low speed until smooth, about 15 seconds. Chill until thickened. Fold in pears. Spoon over gelatin in pan. Chill until firm, about 2 hours. Unmold. Garnish with crisp salad greens, additional pears and grapes, if desired.

Makes 8 servings

Light Under-the-Sea Salad:
Prepare Under-the-Sea Salad as directed, using pear halves in juice or light syrup, Jell-O® Brand Sugar Free Gelatin and Light Philadelphia Brand® Cream Cheese.

Prep time: 20 minutes
Chill time: 3 hours

Muffin Pan Snacks

Under-the-Sea Salad

Muffin Pan Snacks

- **1 package (4-serving size) JELL-O® Brand Gelatin, any flavor**
- **¾ cup boiling water**
- **½ cup cold water**
  Ice cubes
- **1½ cups diced fresh fruit or vegetables**

DISSOLVE gelatin in boiling water. Combine cold water and ice cubes to make 1 cup. Add to gelatin, stirring until slightly thickened. Remove any unmelted ice. Add fruit. Chill until thickened, about 10 minutes.

PLACE foil baking cups in muffin pans, or use small individual molds. Spoon gelatin mixture into cups or molds, filling each about ⅔ full. Chill until firm, about 2 hours.

PEEL away foil cups carefully or dip molds in warm water for about 5 seconds to unmold.

Makes 6 servings

Prep time: 15 minutes
Chill time: 2 hours

Spiced Cranberry-Orange Mold

1 bag (12 ounces) cranberries*
½ cup sugar*
2 packages (4-serving size each) or 1 package (8-serving size) JELL-O® Brand Gelatin, Orange or Lemon Flavor
1½ cups boiling water
1 cup cold water*
1 tablespoon lemon juice
¼ teaspoon ground cinnamon
⅛ teaspoon ground cloves
1 orange, sectioned and diced
½ cup chopped walnuts
Orange slices (optional)
White kale or curly leaf lettuce (optional)

PLACE cranberries in food processor; cover. Process until finely chopped. Mix with sugar; set aside.

DISSOLVE gelatin in boiling water. Add cold water, lemon juice and spices. Chill until thickened. Fold in cranberry mixture, oranges and walnuts. Spoon into 5-cup mold. Chill until firm, about 4 hours. Unmold. Garnish with orange slices and kale, if desired.

Makes 10 servings

*1 can (16 ounces) whole berry cranberry sauce may be substituted for fresh cranberries. Omit sugar and reduce cold water to ½ cup.

Prep time: 20 minutes
Chill time: 4 hours

Waldorf Salad

2 packages (4-serving size each) or 1 package (8-serving size) JELL-O® Brand Gelatin, Lemon Flavor
1½ cups boiling water
1 tablespoon lemon juice
1 cup cold water
Ice cubes
½ cup MIRACLE WHIP® Salad Dressing
1½ cups diced apples
¾ cup diced celery
¼ cup chopped walnuts

DISSOLVE gelatin in boiling water. Add lemon juice. Combine cold water and ice cubes to make 2 cups. Add to gelatin, stirring until slightly thickened. Remove any unmelted ice. Stir in salad dressing with wire wisk; chill until thickened.

FOLD apples, celery and walnuts into gelatin mixture. Pour into 5-cup mold. Chill until firm, about 3 hours. Unmold. Serve with crisp salad greens and additional salad dressing, if desired. *Makes 10 servings*

Prep time: 20 minutes
Chill time: 3 hours

Strawberry Miracle Mold

2 packages (4-serving size) JELL-O® Brand Gelatin, Strawberry Flavor
1½ cups boiling water
1¾ cups cold water
½ cup MIRACLE WHIP® Salad Dressing
Assorted Fruit

• Dissolve gelatin in boiling water; add cold water. Gradually add to salad dressing, mixing until blended.

• Pour into lightly oiled 1-quart mold or glass serving bowl; chill until firm. Unmold onto serving plate; serve with fruit.
Makes 4 to 6 servings

Prep time: 10 minutes plus chilling

Strawberry Miracle Mold

Snack Cups

1 package (4-serving size)
   JELL-O® Brand Orange,
   Lemon or Lime Flavor Sugar
   Free Gelatin
¾ cup boiling water
½ cup cold water
   Ice cubes
1 tablespoon lemon juice
   (optional)
½ cup each sliced celery,
   chopped cabbage and
   shredded carrot *

Completely dissolve gelatin in boiling water. Combine cold water and ice cubes to make 1¼ cups. Add to gelatin with lemon juice, stirring until slightly thickened. Remove any unmelted ice. Fold in vegetables; spoon into individual glasses. Chill until set, about 30 minutes. Garnish with parsley, if desired.
Makes about 3 cups or 6 servings.

Additional Vegetable Combinations: Use sliced celery with grated carrots and golden raisins.

Use sliced celery with chopped cabbage, chopped apple or sliced ripe or green pitted olives.

Use sliced celery with chopped cucumber and chopped pimiento.

Use sliced celery with drained mandarin orange sections and chopped green pepper.

Snack Cups

Winter Fruit Bowl

2 packages (4-serving size) or
   1 package (8-serving size)
   JELL-O® Brand Lemon
   Flavor Gelatin
1½ cups boiling water
1 can (12 fluid ounces) lemon-
   lime carbonated beverage,
   chilled
   Ice cubes
3 cups diced or sliced fresh
   fruits* (bananas, oranges,
   apples, pears, grapes)

Dissolve gelatin in boiling water. Combine beverage and ice cubes to make 2½ cups. Add to gelatin, stirring until slightly thickened. Remove any unmelted ice. Chill until thickened, about 10 minutes. Fold in fruits. Pour into 8-cup serving bowl. Chill until set, about 3 hours. Garnish with whipped topping and orange sections, if desired.
Makes about 6½ cups or 12 servings.

*Do not use fresh pineapple, kiwifruit, mango, papaya or figs.

Creamy Nectarine Mold with Strawberry Sauce

1 envelope unflavored gelatin
½ cup cold water
1 8-ounce package
   PHILADELPHIA BRAND®
   Cream Cheese, softened
½ cup sugar
½ cup milk
2 tablespoons orange flavored
   liqueur
1 cup whipping cream, whipped
1 nectarine, sliced
1 pint strawberries, sliced
¼ cup sugar
1 tablespoon orange flavored
   liqueur

Soften gelatin in water; stir over low heat until dissolved. Combine cream cheese and sugar, mixing until well blended. Gradually add gelatin, milk and liqueur, mixing until blended. Fold in whipped cream. Spoon ¼ cup cream cheese mixture into lightly oiled 1-quart mold. Arrange nectarines on cream cheese mixture; top with remaining cream cheese mixture. Chill until firm. Unmold onto serving plate.

Combine strawberries, sugar and liqueur; let stand 10 minutes. Serve with mold.
6 to 8 servings.
Variation: Substitute orange juice for orange flavored liqueur. Add 1 teaspoon grated orange peel to cream cheese mixture.

Golden Salad

1 package (4-serving size)
   JELL-O® Brand Lemon or
   Orange Flavor Gelatin
½ teaspoon salt
1¼ cups boiling water
1 can (8¼ ounces) crushed
   pineapple in juice
1 tablespoon lemon juice or
   vinegar
1½ cups shredded carrots
⅓ cup chopped pecans

Dissolve gelatin and salt in boiling water. Stir in undrained pineapple and lemon juice. Chill until thickened. Stir in carrots and nuts and pour into individual molds. Chill until firm, about 3 hours. Unmold. Serve with crisp salad greens and mayonnaise, if desired.
Makes about 3 cups or 6 servings.

Cherry Waldorf Gelatin

2 cups boiling water
1 (6-ounce) package cherry
   flavor gelatin
1 cup cold water
¼ cup REALEMON® Lemon Juice
   from Concentrate
1½ cups chopped apples
1 cup chopped celery
½ cup chopped walnuts or
   pecans
   Lettuce leaves
   Apple slices and celery leaves,
   optional

In medium bowl, pour boiling water over gelatin; stir until dissolved. Add cold water and ReaLemon® brand; chill until partially set. Fold in apples, celery and nuts. Pour into lightly oiled 6-cup mold or 9-inch square baking pan. Chill until set, 4 to 6 hours or overnight. Serve on lettuce. Garnish with celery leaves and apple if desired.
Makes 8 to 10 servings.

Buffet Slaw

2 cans (8¼ ounces each)
     crushed pineapple in juice
2 packages (4-serving size) or
     1 package (8-serving size)
     JELL-O® Brand Lemon
     Flavor Gelatin
1½ cups boiling water
     Ice cubes
3 tablespoons vinegar
½ teaspoon celery salt
1 cup each finely shredded
     green and red cabbage
¼ cup chopped parsley
1 tablespoon finely chopped
     onion

Drain pineapple, reserving juice. Add water to juice to make 1 cup; set aside. Completely dissolve gelatin in boiling water. Combine measured liquid and ice cubes to make 2½ cups. Add to gelatin with vinegar and celery salt, stirring until slightly thickened. Remove any unmelted ice. Chill until thickened, about 10 minutes. Fold in pineapple, cabbage, parsley and onion. Pour into 8-cup bowl. Chill until set, about 3 hours. Garnish with cabbage leaves, parsley and onion rings, if desired.
Makes 6 cups or 12 servings.

Melon Wedges

1 cantaloupe or honeydew
     melon
1 package (4-serving size)
     JELL-O® Brand Apricot or
     Orange Flavor Sugar Free
     Gelatin
1 cup boiling water
¾ cup cold water
1 banana, sliced, ½ cup sliced
     strawberries or 1 can
     (8¼ ounces) crushed
     pineapple in juice, well
     drained

Cut melon in half lengthwise; scoop out seeds and drain well. Dissolve gelatin in boiling water. Add cold water. Chill until slightly thickened. Stir in fruit. Pour into melon halves. Chill until firm, about 3 hours. Cut in wedges. Serve with additional fresh fruit, cottage cheese and crisp greens, if desired.
Makes 6 servings.
   Note: Chill any excess fruited gelatin in dessert dishes.

Ginger Pineapple Mold

Layered Peach Salad

1 can (8 ounces) sliced peaches,
     drained
¼ cup sliced celery
¾ cup boiling water
1 package (4-serving size)
     JELL-O® Brand Gelatin, any
     red flavor
½ cup cold water
     Ice cubes

Arrange peach slices and celery in 8×4-inch loaf pan. Pour boiling water into blender. Add gelatin. Cover and blend at low speed until gelatin is completely dissolved, about 30 seconds. Combine cold water and ice cubes to make 1 cup. Add to gelatin and stir until ice is partially melted; then blend at high speed for 30 seconds. Pour into pan. Chill until firm, about 3 hours. Salad layers as it chills. Unmold. Garnish with celery leaves and additional peach slices, if desired.
Makes about 4 cups or 8 servings.
   Layered Carrot-Pineapple Salad: Prepare Layered Peach Salad as directed, substituting 1 can (8¼ ounces) pineapple slices, drained and cut in half, ¼ cup shredded carrot and orange flavor gelatin for the peaches, celery and red flavor gelatin. Garnish with chicory and carrot curls, if desired.

Ginger Pineapple Mold

1 can (20 ounces) pineapple
     slices in juice
2 packages (4-serving size) or
     1 package (8-serving size)
     JELL-O® Brand Lime or
     Apricot Flavor Gelatin
1½ cups boiling water
1 cup ginger ale or cold water
¼ teaspoon ginger

Drain pineapple, reserving juice. Cut 4 pineapple slices in half; set aside. Cut remaining pineapple slices into chunks. Dissolve gelatin in boiling water. Add reserved juice, ginger ale and ginger. Chill until slightly thickened. Measure 1 cup of the gelatin. Arrange some of the pineapple chunks in 6-cup ring mold; top with measured gelatin. Chill until set but not firm, about 10 minutes. Fold remaining pineapple chunks into remaining gelatin; spoon over gelatin in mold. Chill until firm, about 4 hours. Unmold. Garnish with halved pineapple slices, halved cherry tomatoes and crisp greens, if desired.
Makes 5 cups or 10 servings.

Sparkling Berry Salad

tomato juice. Chill until partially set, about 45 minutes; stir in drained clams. Meanwhile, in small saucepan, heat reserved clam liquid; add lemon gelatin, stirring until dissolved. Remove from heat; add cheese and remaining *2 tablespoons* onions. Chill until partially set, about 30 minutes; stir. In lightly oiled 9×5-inch loaf pan, spoon half the tomato mixture; spread cheese mixture evenly over tomato layer. Top with remaining tomato mixture. Chill 6 hours or until set. Unmold onto lettuce. Garnish as desired. Refrigerate leftovers.
Makes 10 to 12 servings.

Sparkling Berry Salad

- **2 envelopes KNOX® Unflavored Gelatine**
- **2 cups cranberry-raspberry juice***
- **1/3 cup sugar**
- **1 cup club soda**
- **1/4 cup creme de cassis (black currant) liqueur (optional)**
- **1 teaspoon lemon juice**
- **1 teaspoon fresh grated orange peel (optional)**
- **3 cups assorted blueberries, raspberries or strawberries**

In medium saucepan, sprinkle unflavored gelatine over 1 cup cranberry-raspberry juice; let stand 1 minute. Stir over low heat until gelatin is completely dissolved, about 5 minutes. Stir in sugar until dissolved.

In large bowl, blend remaining 1 cup cranberry-raspberry juice, soda, gelatine mixture, liqueur, lemon juice and orange peel. Chill, stirring occasionally, until mixture is consistency of unbeaten egg whites, about 60 minutes. Fold in berries. Pour into 6-cup mold or bowl; chill until firm, about 3 hours. Unmold and serve, if desired, with sour cream.
Makes about 8 servings.
   *Substitution: Use 2 cups cranberry juice cocktail and increase sugar to 1/2 cup.

Clam & Tomato Molded Salad

- **4 envelopes unflavored gelatine**
- **4 cups tomato juice**
- **1/2 cup chopped celery**
- **1/4 cup chopped green onions**
- **2 (6½-ounce) cans SNOW'S® or DOXSEE® Minced Clams, drained, reserving 1/2 cup liquid**
- **1 (4-serving size) package lemon flavor gelatin**
- **1 (16-ounce) container BORDEN® or MEADOW GOLD® Cottage Cheese**
  Lettuce leaves

In medium saucepan, sprinkle unflavored gelatine over *1½ cups* tomato juice; let stand 1 minute. Over low heat, stir until gelatine dissolves. Remove from heat; add celery, *2 tablespoons* onions and remaining *2½ cups*

Mediterranean Orange and Red Onion Salad

- **2 envelopes KNOX® Unflavored Gelatine**
- **1 cup cold water**
- **2½ cups orange juice**
- **2 tablespoons sugar**
- **1 tablespoon lemon juice**
- **2 teaspoons red wine vinegar**
- **4 medium oranges, peeled, sectioned and chopped (about 1 cup)**
- **1/2 cup finely chopped celery**
- **1/4 cup finely chopped red onion**

In medium saucepan, sprinkle unflavored gelatine over cold water; let stand 1 minute. Stir over low heat until gelatine is completely dissolved, about 5 minutes.

In large bowl, blend gelatine mixture, orange juice, sugar, lemon juice and vinegar. Chill, stirring occasionally, until mixture is consistency of unbeaten egg whites, about 40 minutes. Fold in remaining ingredients. Pour into 6-cup ring mold or bowl; chill until firm, about 4 hours. Unmold and garnish, if desired, with celery leaves.
Makes about 8 servings.

Autumn Pear 'n Apple Salad

2 envelopes KNOX® Unflavored Gelatine
2¹/₂ cups apple juice
¹/₄ cup light brown sugar
1¹/₄ cups pear nectar
¹/₄ teaspoon ground cinnamon
¹/₈ teaspoon ground nutmeg
1 small pear, chopped
1 small apple, chopped
6 dried Calimyrna figs, quartered
¹/₄ cup chopped pecans or walnuts (optional)

In medium saucepan, sprinkle unflavored gelatine over 1 cup apple juice; let stand 1 minute. Stir over low heat until gelatine is completely dissolved, about 5 minutes. Stir in sugar until dissolved.

In large bowl, blend remaining 1¹/₂ cups apple juice, pear nectar, gelatine mixture, cinnamon and nutmeg. Chill, stirring occasionally, until mixture is consistency of unbeaten egg whites, about 60 minutes. Fold in remaining ingredients. Pour into 6-cup mold; chill until firm, about 3 hours. Unmold onto serving platter.
Makes about 12 servings.

Classic Tomato Aspic

3 envelopes KNOX® Unflavored Gelatine
3 cups cold tomato juice
2 cups tomato juice, heated to boiling
¹/₄ cup lemon juice
2 tablespoons sugar
1¹/₂ teaspoons Worcestershire sauce
4 to 6 dashes hot pepper sauce

In large bowl, sprinkle unflavored gelatine over 1 cup cold juice; let stand 1 minute. Add hot juice and stir until gelatine is completely dissolved, about 5 minutes. Stir in remaining 2 cups cold juice, lemon juice, sugar, Worcestershire sauce and hot pepper sauce. Pour into 5¹/₂-cup ring mold or bowl; chill until firm, about 4 hours. To serve, unmold and fill, if desired, with salad greens and your favorite cut-up fresh vegetables.
Makes about 10 servings.

Holiday Fruit Salad

3 packages (3 ounces each) strawberry flavor gelatin
3 cups boiling water
2 ripe DOLE® Bananas
1 package (16 ounces) frozen strawberries
1 can (20 ounces) DOLE® Crushed Pineapple in Juice
1 package (8 ounces) cream cheese, softened
1 cup dairy sour cream or plain yogurt
¹/₄ cup sugar
Crisp lettuce leaves

In large bowl, dissolve gelatin in boiling water. Slice bananas into gelatin mixture. Add frozen strawberries and undrained pineapple. Pour half the mixture into 13×9-inch pan. Refrigerate 1 hour or until firm. In mixer bowl, beat cream cheese with sour cream and sugar; spread over chilled layer. Gently spoon remaining gelatin mixture on top. Refrigerate until firm, about 2 hours. Cut into squares; serve on lettuce-lined salad plates. Garnish with additional pineapple, if desired.
Makes 12 servings.

Creamy Garden Salad

2 envelopes unflavored gelatine
1¹/₂ cups water, divided
2 cups mayonnaise
¹/₃ cup lemon juice
³/₄ teaspoon TABASCO® pepper sauce
1¹/₂ cups diced cucumber
1 cup shredded carrot
¹/₂ cup thinly sliced radishes
¹/₂ cup thinly sliced green onions

In medium saucepan sprinkle gelatine over 1 cup water; let stand 1 minute. Stir over low heat until gelatine is completely dissolved. Add remaining ¹/₂ cup water, mayonnaise, lemon juice and Tabasco® sauce; mix well. Chill until slightly thickened. Stir in cucumber, carrot, radishes and green onions. Turn into 6-cup mold. Cover; refrigerate 3 hours or until firm. Unmold onto serving plate.
Makes 6 to 8 servings.

Holiday Fruit Salad

Minted Melon Mold

1¹/₂ cups boiling water
1 (3-ounce) package lemon flavor gelatin
1 (3-ounce) package lime flavor gelatin
³/₄ cup REALIME® Lime Juice from Concentrate
¹/₂ cup cold water
¹/₈ teaspoon peppermint extract
2 cups melon balls (cantaloupe, honeydew, etc.)
Lettuce leaves
Coconut Cream Dressing
Mint leaves and additional melon balls, optional

In medium bowl, pour boiling water over gelatins; stir until dissolved. Add ReaLime® brand, cold water and extract; chill until partially set. Fold in melon. Pour into lightly oiled 5-cup ring mold. Chill until set, about 3 hours or overnight. Unmold onto lettuce. Serve with Coconut Cream Dressing; garnish with mint and melon balls if desired.
Makes 8 to 10 servings.

Coconut Cream Dressing

¹/₂ cup BORDEN® or MEADOW GOLD® Sour Cream
3 tablespoons flaked coconut
1 tablespoon honey
1 tablespoon REALIME® Lime Juice from Concentrate

In small bowl, combine all ingredients; mix well. Chill before serving. Refrigerate leftovers.
Makes about ¹/₂ cup.

MEATS

Today's meat is leaner than ever before! So serve hearty main dishes of beef, pork, veal or lamb for fast family meals or sophisticated entrées for memorable evenings. With dozens of new ideas for grilling, roasting and stir-frying, you can sample sizzling steaks and flavorful kabobs, succulent pork chops and tasty pork tenderloin plus savory international specialties such as Mexican Beef and Rice and Hunan Pork Stir-Fry.

Fast Beef Roast with Mushroom Sauce

- 1 **boneless beef rib eye roast (about 2 pounds)**
- 2 **tablespoons vegetable oil**
- 4 **cups water**
- 1 **can (10¾ ounces) condensed beef broth**
- 1 **cup dry red wine**
- 2 **cloves garlic, minced**
- 1 **teaspoon dried marjoram leaves**
- 4 **black peppercorns**
- 3 **whole cloves**
  Mushroom Sauce (recipe follows)

Tie roast with heavy string at 2-inch intervals. Heat oil in Dutch oven over medium-high heat. Cook roast until evenly browned. Pour off drippings. Add water, broth, wine, garlic, marjoram, peppercorns and cloves; bring to boil. Reduce heat to medium-low; cover and simmer 15 minutes per pound. Check temperature with instant-read thermometer; temperature should be 130°F for rare. *Do not overcook.* Remove roast to serving platter; reserve cooking liquid. Cover roast tightly with plastic wrap or foil; allow to stand 10 minutes before carving (temperature will continue to rise to 140°F for rare). Prepare Mushroom Sauce. Remove strings from roast. Carve into thin slices and top with Mushroom Sauce. Serve with assorted vegetables, if desired.

Makes 6 to 8 servings

Note: A boneless beef rib eye roast will yield three to four 3-ounce cooked servings per pound.

Mushroom Sauce

- 1 **tablespoon butter**
- 1 **cup sliced fresh mushrooms**
- 1 **cup beef cooking liquid, strained**
- 1½ **teaspoons cornstarch**
- ¼ **teaspoon salt**
- 2 **dashes pepper**
- 1 **tablespoon thinly sliced green onion tops**

Melt butter in medium saucepan over medium-high heat. Add mushrooms; cook and stir 5 minutes. Remove; reserve. Add liquid, cornstarch, salt and pepper to pan. Bring to a boil; cook and stir until thickened, 1 to 2 minutes. Remove from heat. Stir in mushrooms and onion.

*Favorite recipe from **National Live Stock and Meat Board***

Marinated Flank Steak

- 1 **(1- to 1½-pound) flank steak**
- ½ **cup REALEMON® Lemon Juice from Concentrate**
- ¼ **cup vegetable oil**
- 2 **teaspoons WYLER'S® or STEERO® Beef-Flavor Instant Bouillon**
- 2 **cloves garlic, finely chopped**
- 1 **teaspoon ground ginger**

Place meat in shallow dish or plastic bag. In small bowl, combine remaining ingredients. Pour over meat. Cover; marinate in refrigerator 4 to 6 hours, turning occasionally. Remove meat from marinade; grill or broil as desired, basting frequently with marinade. Refrigerate leftovers.

Makes 4 to 6 servings

Fast Beef Roast with Mushroom Sauce

Southwest Pot Roast

- ¼ cup all-purpose flour
- 2 teaspoons garlic salt
- ½ teaspoon ground red pepper
- 4 to 5 pounds boneless beef rump roast
- 1 tablespoon vegetable oil
- 1 (13¾-ounce) can COLLEGE INN® Beef Broth
- 2 tablespoons WRIGHT'S® Natural Hickory Seasoning
- 2 cups green or red bell pepper slices
- 2 cups onion wedges
- 3 ears corn-on-the-cob, cut into 1-inch chunks

In shallow bowl, combine flour, garlic salt and ground red pepper. Coat beef with flour mixture. In 8-quart saucepan, brown beef in oil. Add beef broth and hickory seasoning. Bring to a boil; reduce heat. Cover tightly and simmer 2 hours. Add peppers, onions and corn. Cover; simmer 45 minutes longer or until vegetables and beef are fork-tender. To serve, thinly slice beef and serve with vegetables and sauce.   *Makes 6 servings*

Beef Tenderloin en Croute

- 1 beef tenderloin (3 to 4 pounds)
- 1 package (17¼ ounces) frozen ready-to-bake puff pastry sheets
- ½ pound mushrooms, finely chopped
- 2 tablespoons PARKAY® Margarine
- 1 container (8 ounces) PHILADELPHIA BRAND® Soft Cream Cheese with Herb & Garlic
- ¼ cup seasoned dry bread crumbs
- 2 tablespoons Madeira wine
- 1 tablespoon chopped fresh chives
- ¼ teaspoon salt
- 1 egg, beaten
- 1 tablespoon cold water

- Heat oven to 425°F.

- Tie meat with string at 1-inch intervals, if necessary. Place meat on rack in baking pan.

- Roast 45 to 50 minutes or until meat thermometer registers 135°F. Remove from oven; cool 30 minutes in refrigerator. Remove string.

- Thaw puff pastry sheets according to package directions.

- Cook and stir mushrooms in margarine in large skillet 10 minutes or until liquid evaporates.

- Add cream cheese, bread crumbs, wine, chives and salt; mix well. Cool.

- On lightly floured surface, overlap pastry sheets ½ inch to form 14×12-inch rectangle; press edges firmly together to seal. Trim length of pastry 2½ inches longer than length of meat.

- Spread mushroom mixture over top and sides of meat. Place meat in center of pastry.

- Fold pastry over meat; press edges together to seal. Decorate top with pastry trimmings, if desired.

- Brush pastry with combined egg and water. Place meat in greased 15×10×1-inch jelly roll pan.

- Bake 20 to 25 minutes or until pastry is golden brown. Let stand 10 minutes before slicing.
    Makes 8 to 10 servings

Prep time: 25 minutes plus refrigerating
Cooking time: 1 hour and 15 minutes

Beef Tenderloin en Croute

Versatile Barbecue Sauce

¼ **cup chopped onion**
1 **clove garlic, finely chopped**
2 **tablespoons margarine or butter**
1 **cup ketchup**
⅓ **cup firmly packed brown sugar**
¼ **cup REALEMON® Lemon Juice from Concentrate**
1 **tablespoon Worcestershire sauce**
2 **teaspoons WYLER'S® or STEERO® Beef- or Chicken-Flavor Instant Bouillon *or* 2 Beef- or Chicken-Flavored Bouillon Cubes**
1 **teaspoon prepared mustard**

In small saucepan, cook onion and garlic in margarine until tender. Add remaining ingredients; bring to a boil. Reduce heat; simmer uncovered 20 minutes, stirring occasionally. Use as a basting sauce for grilled beef, chicken or pork. Refrigerate leftovers.

Makes about 1½ cups

Microwave: In 1-quart glass measure with handle, melt margarine on 100% power (high) 30 to 45 seconds. Add onion and garlic; cook on 100% power (high) 1½ to 2 minutes or until tender. Add remaining ingredients. Cook loosely covered on 100% power (high) 3 to 5 minutes or until mixture boils; stir. Reduce heat to 50% power (medium); cook covered 4 to 5 minutes to blend flavors.

Soy Marinated London Broil

Herb-Marinated Chuck Steak

1 **pound boneless beef chuck shoulder steak, cut 1 inch thick**
¼ **cup chopped onion**
2 **tablespoons *each* chopped parsley and white vinegar**
1 **tablespoon vegetable oil**
2 **teaspoons Dijon-style mustard**
1 **clove garlic, minced**
½ **teaspoon dried thyme leaves**

Combine onion, parsley, vinegar, oil, mustard, garlic and thyme. Place beef chuck shoulder steak in plastic bag; add onion mixture, spreading evenly over both sides. Close bag securely; marinate in refrigerator 6 to 8 hours (or overnight, if desired), turning at least once. Pour off marinade; discard. Place steak on rack in broiler pan so surface of meat is 3 to 5 inches from heat source. Broil about 16 minutes for rare (18 minutes for medium), turning once. Carve steak diagonally across the grain into thin slices. Garnish as desired.

Makes 4 servings

*Favorite recipe from **National Live Stock and Meat Board***

Soy Marinade

½ **cup REALEMON® Lemon Juice from Concentrate**
½ **cup soy sauce**
½ **cup vegetable oil**
3 **tablespoons ketchup**
3 **to 4 cloves garlic, finely chopped**
¼ **teaspoon pepper**

In large shallow dish or plastic bag, combine ingredients; add beef, pork or chicken. Cover; marinate in refrigerator 4 hours or overnight, turning occasionally. Remove meat from marinade; grill or broil as desired, basting frequently with additional ReaLemon® brand. Refrigerate leftover meat.

Makes about 1½ cups

Mongolian Beef

- ³/₄ **pound boneless tender beef steak (sirloin, rib eye or top loin)**
- 3 **tablespoons cornstarch, divided**
- 4 **tablespoons KIKKOMAN® Teriyaki Sauce, divided**
- 1 **tablespoon dry sherry**
- 1 **clove garlic, minced**
- 1 **cup water**
- 1 **teaspoon distilled white vinegar**
- ¹/₄ to ¹/₂ **teaspoon crushed red pepper**
- 2 **tablespoons vegetable oil, divided**
- 2 **carrots, cut diagonally into thin slices**
- 1 **onion, chunked and separated**
- 1 **green pepper, chunked**

Cut beef across grain into strips, then into 1¹/₂-inch squares. Combine 2 tablespoons cornstarch, 1 tablespoon teriyaki sauce, sherry and garlic in medium bowl; stir in beef. Let stand 30 minutes. Meanwhile, combine water, remaining 1 tablespoon cornstarch, 3 tablespoons teriyaki sauce, vinegar and red pepper; set aside. Heat 1 tablespoon oil in hot wok or large skillet over high heat. Add beef and stir-fry 1 minute; remove. Heat remaining 1 tablespoon oil in same pan. Add carrots, onion and green pepper; stir-fry 4 minutes. Add beef and teriyaki sauce mixture; cook and stir until sauce boils and thickens. *Makes 4 servings.*

Grilled Tenderloin with Cognac

- 1 **beef tenderloin roast (2 pounds)**
- ¹/₄ **cup whole green, white or black peppercorns**
  Garlic Mushrooms (recipe follows)
- ¹/₃ **cup cognac or other brandy**
- 1 **cup whipping cream**
- 2 **tablespoons Dijon-style mustard**
- 1 **tablespoon Worcestershire sauce**
- 2 **teaspoons lemon juice**

Trim excess fat from roast. Crack peppercorns coarsely with mortar and pestle; sprinkle on roast and press into surface.

In grill, arrange medium-hot **KINGSFORD® Charcoal Briquets** around drip pan. Place roast over drip pan. Cover grill and cook, turning once, until meat thermometer registers 140°F for rare (about 45 minutes), 150°F for medium-rare (about 55 minutes), or 170°F for well-done (about 60 minutes). While roast is cooking, prepare Garlic Mushrooms. About 15 minutes before meat is done, place mushrooms next to meat.

When roast is grilled to desired doneness, warm cognac in skillet on range-top. Remove from heat. Place roast in heated skillet. Carefully ignite cognac with match; allow flames to subside, carefully spooning cognac over meat. Remove roast to serving platter; reserve juices.

In saucepan, combine cream, mustard and Worcestershire sauce. Bring to boil. Cook and stir, over medium-low heat, 3 minutes or until slightly thickened. Remove from heat; stir in lemon juice and reserved cognac juices. Carve roast and arrange with Garlic Mushrooms. Pour cream sauce over sliced roast and mushrooms. *Makes 8 servings.*

Garlic Mushrooms

- 32 **large fresh mushrooms**
- ¹/₂ **cup olive or vegetable oil**
- 2 **cloves garlic, minced**

Remove stems from mushrooms; reserve caps. In bowl, combine oil and garlic; add mushroom caps. Gently toss to coat. Remove mushrooms with slotted spoon; place mushroom caps on piece of heavy-duty foil. Seal edges tightly. Grill at side of roast over medium-hot **KINGSFORD® Charcoal Briquets** 10 to 15 minutes or until tender. *Makes 8 servings.*

Stuffed Flank Steak

- 1 **(1¹/₂-pound) flank steak, pounded**
- 2 **cups herb-seasoned stuffing mix**
- 2 **teaspoons WYLER'S® or STEERO® Beef-Flavor Instant Bouillon *or* 2 Beef-Flavor Bouillon Cubes**
  Flour
- 3 **tablespoons vegetable oil**
- 1 **cup chopped onion**
- 1 **clove garlic, chopped**
- 2 **(10³/₄-ounce) cans condensed tomato soup**
- ¹/₂ **teaspoon basil leaves**
  Hot cooked noodles
  Parsley

Preheat oven to 350°. Prepare stuffing mix according to package directions, dissolving bouillon in liquid. Spread stuffing evenly on top of steak to within 1 inch of edges. Roll up, tucking in ends; tie with string. Coat roll with flour. In large skillet, brown in oil. Place in shallow baking dish. In same skillet, cook onion and garlic until tender. Add soup and basil; cook and stir until smooth. Pour over meat. Cover; bake 1 hour, basting occasionally. Serve with noodles; garnish with parsley. Refrigerate leftovers. *Makes 6 servings.*

Stuffed Flank Steak

Grilled Flank Steak Sangrita

- **1 beef flank steak (2½ to 3 pounds)**
- **1 teaspoon salt**
- **¼ teaspoon pepper**
- **1 teaspoon dried thyme, crushed**
- **¼ cup orange juice concentrate, thawed and undiluted**
- **3 tablespoons vegetable oil Fruity Wine Sauce (recipe follows)**

Lightly score steak and rub with salt, pepper and thyme. In shallow glass dish, combine orange juice concentrate and oil. Add steak; turn to coat with marinade. Cover and refrigerate at least 30 minutes. Drain meat; reserve marinade. Grill steak, on covered grill, over medium-hot **KINGSFORD® Charcoal Briquets** 8 to 10 minutes on each side, turning once and basting often with marinade, until done. Cut meat across grain into diagonal slices. Serve with Fruity Wine Sauce.
Makes 6 servings.

Fruity Wine Sauce

- **1½ cups red wine**
- **1 orange, thinly sliced**
- **1 lime, thinly sliced**
- **1 apple, thinly sliced**
- **¾ cup chopped green onion with tops**
- **½ cup butter or margarine**
- **2 tablespoons chopped parsley**

In small saucepan, combine red wine, fruit and green onion; bring to boil. Stir in butter and parsley; cook and stir until butter is melted and sauce is hot.
Makes about 2 cups.

Steak with Hearty Mustard Marinade

- **½ cup Dijon-style mustard**
- **3 tablespoons soy sauce**
- **3 tablespoons dry sherry wine**
- **2 tablespoons brown sugar**
- **1 tablespoon vegetable oil**
- **1 clove garlic, minced**
- **½ teaspoon TABASCO® pepper sauce**
- **2 pounds round steak, 1½ inches thick**

Steak with Hearty Mustard Marinade

In medium bowl combine mustard, soy sauce, wine, sugar, oil, garlic and Tabasco® sauce; mix well. Place steak in large shallow dish or plastic bag; add marinade. Cover; refrigerate at least 5 hours; turn meat occasionally.

Remove meat from marinade; place on grill about 5 inches from source of heat. Brush with marinade. Grill 15 minutes; turn meat and brush with marinade. Grill 10 minutes longer or until desired doneness.
Makes 8 servings.

Peppery Rib Steaks

- **⅓ cup lemon juice**
- **2 tablespoons vegetable oil**
- **1 clove garlic, crushed**
- **1 teaspoon chili powder**
- **1 teaspoon seasoned salt**
- **½ teaspoon seasoned or cracked pepper**
- **4 beef rib eye steaks, cut ¾ to 1 inch thick (about 6 ounces each)**

In shallow glass dish, combine all ingredients except steaks. Add steaks; turn to coat with marinade. Cover and refrigerate at least 2 hours or overnight. Drain steaks; reserve marinade. Grill steaks, on uncovered grill, over medium-hot **MATCH LIGHT® Charcoal Briquets** about 15 minutes or until cooked, turning and basting often with marinade.
Makes 4 servings.

Pepper-Stuffed Flank Steak

- **2 beef flank steaks (about 1 pound each)**
- **1¼ teaspoons garlic powder**
- **¼ teaspoon black pepper**
- **1 green pepper, cut into strips**
- **1 red pepper, cut into strips**
- **1 onion, cut into thin slices**
- **1 can (15 ounces) tomato sauce**
- **½ cup finely chopped onion**
- **¼ cup soy sauce**
- **1 tablespoon sugar**
- **1 teaspoon dry mustard**
- **⅛ teaspoon cayenne pepper**
- **¼ cup vegetable oil**

With meat mallet, pound each steak to ¼-inch thickness. Sprinkle steaks with ¼ teaspoon of the garlic powder and the pepper. Arrange green and red pepper strips horizontally on steaks. Cover with onion slices. Starting at narrow end of each steak, roll up jelly-roll fashion; tie with kitchen twine. Set aside. In large jar with screw-top lid, combine remaining ingredients except oil. Shake to blend. Brush outsides of beef rolls with oil. Lightly oil grid. Grill steaks, on covered grill, over hot **KINGSFORD® Charcoal Briquets** about 30 minutes, turning often, until done. Brush steaks with tomato-soy mixture during last 10 minutes of grilling.
Makes 6 to 8 servings.

Grilled Steak with Mushroom-Wine Sauce

4 beef loin T-bone, porterhouse or filet mignon steaks, cut 1 inch thick (8 ounces each)
3 tablespoons butter or margarine
½ pound mushrooms, sliced (about 2 cups)
¼ cup white wine
2 tablespoons minced parsley
½ teaspoon dried tarragon, crushed
1 teaspoon instant beef bouillon granules

Slash any fat around edge of steaks every 4 inches. Lightly oil grid. Grill steaks on covered grill, over medium-hot **KINGSFORD® with Mesquite Charcoal Briquets** 8 to 10 minutes on each side for medium-rare, or to desired doneness. While steak is grilling, heat butter in large skillet until hot. Add mushrooms and saute 1 minute or until tender. Add wine, parsley, tarragon and beef bouillon granules; simmer 4 minutes, stirring often. Serve sauce over steak.
Makes 4 servings.

Rouladen

6 slices bacon, partially cooked, reserving 2 tablespoons drippings
4 cups sliced onions
6 beef tip steaks (about ¼ pound each), pounded
Dijon-style mustard
6 dill pickle spears
Flour
2 tablespoons vegetable oil
1⅓ cups plus 2 tablespoons water
2 teaspoons WYLER'S® or STEERO® Beef-Flavor Instant Bouillon *or* 2 Beef-Flavor Bouillon Cubes
1 teaspoon thyme leaves
1 bay leaf
1 tablespoon flour
Hot cooked noodles

In large skillet, cook onions in reserved drippings until tender. Remove onions from skillet. On each steak, spread mustard; top with 1 slice bacon, about ½ cup onions and 1 pickle spear. Roll up. Secure with wooden picks. Coat with flour. In same skillet, brown meat in oil. Add 1⅓ cups water, bouillon, thyme and bay leaf; bring to a boil. Cover and simmer 30 minutes or until tender. Remove meat from skillet; remove bay leaf. Mix remaining *2 tablespoons* water and *1 tablespoon* flour; stir into liquid in skillet. Cook and stir until slightly thickened. Remove picks; serve meat with noodles. Garnish as desired. Refrigerate leftovers.
Makes 6 servings.

Flank Steak Bearnaise

1 8-ounce package PHILADELPHIA BRAND® Cream Cheese, cubed
¼ cup milk
1 tablespoon green onion slices
½ teaspoon dried tarragon leaves, crushed
2 egg yolks, beaten
2 tablespoons dry white wine
1 tablespoon lemon juice
1 1½-pound beef flank steak

In saucepan, combine cream cheese, milk, green onions and tarragon; stir over low heat until cream cheese is melted. Stir small amount of hot cream cheese mixture into egg yolks; return to hot mixture. Stir in wine and juice. Cook, stirring constantly, over low heat 1 minute or until thickened. Score steak on both sides. Place on rack of broiler pan. Broil on both sides to desired doneness. With knife slanted, carve steak across grain into thin slices. Serve with cream cheese mixture.
6 servings.

Beef Tenderloin Dijon

1 beef tenderloin roast (about 2 pounds)
1½ teaspoons salt, divided
¾ teaspoon pepper, divided
2 tablespoons olive oil
2 cloves garlic, minced
4 cups water
2 cans (10¾ ounces each) condensed beef broth
1 bay leaf
½ teaspoon dried thyme leaves
2 whole cloves
1 tablespoon *each* cornstarch and Dijon-style mustard

Tie beef tenderloin roast with heavy string at 2-inch intervals. Combine 1 teaspoon of the salt and ½ teaspoon of the pepper; rub on surface of roast. Heat oil in Dutch oven over medium-high heat. Add roast and garlic; cook until evenly browned, about 6 minutes. Remove roast from pan; pour off drippings. Add water, broth, bay leaf, thyme and cloves; bring to a boil. Add roast; reduce heat to medium-low. Cover and simmer about 20 minutes. Check temperature with instant-read thermometer; temperature should register 130°F for rare. Do not overcook. Remove roast to serving platter. Cover tightly with plastic wrap or foil and allow to stand 10 minutes before carving. (Roast will continue to rise about 10°F in temperature to 140°F for rare.)

Strain cooking liquid; reserve 2 cups. Remove Dutch oven from heat; add cornstarch and mustard, mixing to form a thick paste. Gradually add reserved cooking liquid, stirring constantly. Place Dutch oven over medium heat; add remaining ½ teaspoon salt and ¼ teaspoon pepper. Cook until slightly thickened, about 7 minutes. Remove strings from roast. Carve into thin slices. Serve with sauce and steamed vegetables, if desired.

Note: A beef tenderloin roast will yield four 3-ounce cooked servings per pound.

Nutrient data per 3-ounce cooked, trimmed serving: 213 calories; 11 g fat; 70 mg cholesterol; 841 mg sodium; 3.4 mg iron.

Favorite recipe from **National Live Stock and Meat Board**

Beef Tenderloin Dijon

German Beef Roulade

1½ pounds flank steak
4 teaspoons GREY POUPON®
    Dijon Mustard
6 slices bacon, diced
¾ cup chopped onion
⅓ cup chopped dill pickle
¼ cup all-purpose flour
1 (13¾-fluid ounce) can
    COLLEGE INN® Beef Broth

With meat mallet or rolling pin, flatten meat to approximately a 10×8-inch rectangle. Spread mustard over meat.

In large skillet, over medium-high heat, cook bacon and onion until bacon is crisp; pour off fat, reserving ¼ cup. Spread bacon mixture over meat; sprinkle with pickle. Roll up meat from short end; secure with string.

In large skillet, over medium-high heat, brown beef roll in reserved fat; place in 13×9×2-inch baking dish. Stir flour into fat in skillet until smooth; gradually stir in beef broth. Cook and stir over medium heat until thickened. Pour sauce over beef roll. Cover; bake at 325°F for 1½ hours or until done. Let stand 10 minutes before slicing. Skim fat from sauce; strain and serve with meat.
Makes 6 servings.

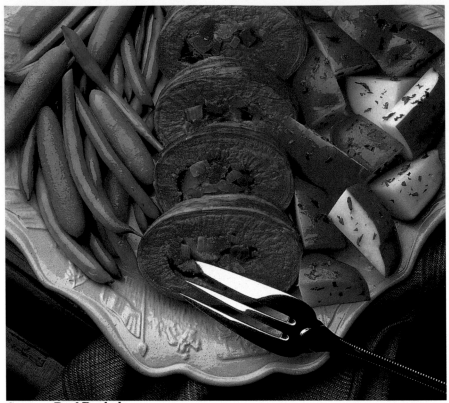

German Beef Roulade

Old-Fashioned Pot Roast

3- to 3½-pound boneless pot
    roast (rump, chuck or round)
1 envelope LIPTON® Recipe
    Secrets Onion, Beefy Onion,
    Beefy Mushroom or Onion-
    Mushroom Recipe Soup Mix
2¼ cups water

In Dutch oven, brown roast over medium heat. Add onion recipe soup mix blended with water. Simmer covered, turning occasionally, 2½ hours or until tender. If desired, thicken gravy.
Makes about 6 servings.

Try some of these delicious international variations!

French-Style Pot Roast: Decrease water to 1¼ cups. Add 1 cup dry red wine and 1 teaspoon thyme leaves.

German-Style Pot Roast: Decrease water to ¾ cup. Add 1½ cups beer, 1 teaspoon brown sugar and ½ teaspoon caraway seeds.

Italian-Style Pot Roast: Decrease water to 1 cup. Add 1 can (14½ ounces) whole peeled tomatoes, un-

drained and chopped, 1 teaspoon basil leaves and 1 bay leaf. (Remove bay leaf before serving.)

Microwave Directions: Decrease water to 1¼ cups. In 3-quart casserole, blend onion recipe soup mix with water and heat at HIGH (Full Power) 5 minutes. Add roast and heat uncovered 10 minutes, turning once. Heat covered at DEFROST (30% Full Power), turning occasionally, 50 minutes or until tender. Let stand covered 10 minutes.

Islander's Beef Barbecue

1 boneless beef chuck roast
    (3 to 3½ pounds)
¾ cup apricot-pineapple jam
2 tablespoons soy sauce
1 teaspoon ground ginger
1 teaspoon grated lemon peel

Slice roast across grain into ¼-inch-thick slices. In bowl, combine remaining ingredients. Grill beef slices, on uncovered grill, over medium-hot **KINGSFORD® Charcoal Briquets** 8 to 10 minutes. Turn and baste often with jam mixture.
Makes 4 to 6 servings.

Eight Flavors Pot Roast

1 can (20 ounces) DOLE®
    Pineapple Chunks in Juice
2½ pounds boneless beef chuck
1 tablespoon vegetable oil
1 small yellow onion, chopped
2 cloves garlic, pressed
1½ cups water
½ cup soy sauce
¼ cup dry sherry
2½ tablespoons brown sugar
2 cinnamon sticks
1 tablespoon minced fresh
    ginger root
1 teaspoon allspice
1 head Chinese cabbage, cut
    into quarters*
4 teaspoons cornstarch
2 tablespoons water

Drain pineapple; reserve juice. Trim excess fat from beef. Heat large pot until hot. Add oil, swirling to coat sides. Cook onion and garlic in hot oil, stirring, 1 minute. Add beef; brown 2 minutes on each side.

In medium bowl, combine reserved pineapple juice, 1½ cups water, soy sauce, sherry, sugar, cinnamon, ginger and allspice; pour over beef. Bring to boil; reduce heat and simmer, covered, turning meat occasionally, 1¼ hours. Add cabbage; cook 30 minutes longer, adding pineapple last 5 minutes.

Remove meat, cabbage and pineapple from pot. Slice meat and arrange on serving platter with cabbage and pineapple. Strain remaining broth. Pour 1 cup into saucepan. Dissolve cornstarch in 2 tablespoons water; add to broth. Cook, stirring, until sauce boils and thickens. Pour over beef to serve.
Makes 6 servings.

*Or use green cabbage (about 2 pounds).

Standing Rib Roast with Madeira Sauce

    2 large cloves garlic, finely
        chopped
    1 teaspoon marjoram leaves
        (optional)
    1 teaspoon thyme leaves
    1 teaspoon salt
    ¼ teaspoon pepper
    5-pound standing rib roast
        (about 3 ribs)
    ¼ cup butter or margarine
    2 cups thinly sliced mushrooms
    ¼ cup Madeira or dry red wine
    1 tablespoon tomato paste
    1 envelope LIPTON® Recipe
        Secrets Onion, Onion-
        Mushroom or Beefy
        Mushroom Recipe Soup Mix
    1 tablespoon all-purpose flour
    1½ cups water
    1 tablespoon finely chopped
        parsley
        Pepper to taste

Preheat oven to 500°. In small bowl, combine garlic, marjoram, thyme, salt and pepper; set aside.

Trim fat from roast. In roasting pan, on rack, place roast; rub with garlic mixture. Roast 10 minutes, then decrease heat to 350° and continue roasting 1½ hours or until meat thermometer reaches 130° (rare) or 150° (medium).

Remove roast to serving platter and keep warm. Skim fat from pan drippings. In medium saucepan, combine pan juices with butter; stir in mushrooms. Cook 5 minutes or until mushrooms are tender. Stir in wine and tomato paste, then onion recipe soup mix and flour blended with water. Bring to a boil, then simmer, stirring frequently, 5 minutes or until sauce is thickened. Stir in parsley and pepper. Serve sauce with roast.
Makes about 6 servings.

Chuckwagon Roast and Vegetables

    1 (3-pound) boneless beef chuck
        roast
    3 tablespoons vegetable oil
    3 tablespoons flour
    1 cup BORDEN® or MEADOW
        GOLD® Buttermilk
    1 cup water
    4 teaspoons WYLER'S® or
        STEERO® Beef-Flavor
        Instant Bouillon *or* 4 Beef-
        Flavor Bouillon Cubes
    ½ teaspoon thyme leaves
    ¼ teaspoon pepper
    4 medium carrots, cut into 1-
        inch pieces
    2 medium onions, cut into
        wedges
    1 (10-ounce) package frozen
        broccoli spears, thawed and
        cut into pieces
    1 (10-ounce) package frozen
        cauliflower, thawed

Preheat oven to 350°. In large skillet, brown roast in oil. Place in 3-quart roasting or baking pan. Add flour to drippings in skillet; cook and stir until browned. Add buttermilk, water, bouillon, thyme and pepper. Cook and stir until bouillon dissolves and mixture thickens slightly, about 10 minutes. Place carrots and onions around meat; spoon sauce over meat. Cover; bake 1 hour and 45 minutes or until meat is tender. Add remaining vegetables; bake 10 minutes longer or until tender. Refrigerate leftovers.
Makes 6 to 8 servings.

Chuckwagon Roast and Vegetables

Barbecued Sausage Kabobs

    1 pound ECKRICH® Smoked
        Sausage, cut into 1-inch
        pieces
    1 cup dried apricots
    1 can (12 ounces) beer
    ½ red bell pepper
    ½ green bell pepper
    1 Spanish onion, cut into
        wedges
    ¼ pound fresh medium
        mushrooms, sliced
    ¾ cup apricot preserves
    1 tablespoon prepared mustard
    2 tablespoons chili sauce
    1 teaspoon Worcestershire
        sauce

Simmer sausage and apricots in beer in large saucepan over low heat 10 minutes. Cut peppers into 1¼-inch squares. Add peppers to sausage mixture; let stand off heat 10 minutes. Assemble kabobs on skewers, alternately threading sausage with onion, red and green peppers, mushrooms and apricots. Combine apricot preserves, mustard, chili sauce and Worcestershire sauce in small saucepan. Heat over medium heat, stirring until blended. Brush kabobs with sauce. Grill or broil, 4 inches from heat, 10 minutes, turning and brushing with more sauce after 5 minutes. Brush with remaining sauce and serve.
Makes 4 servings.

Burgundy Beef Stroganoff

- **2 pounds round steak, cut into ¼-inch strips**
- **2 tablespoons BLUE BONNET® Margarine**
- **4 medium onions, sliced (about 3 cups)**
- **¼ cup all-purpose flour**
- **1 cup COLLEGE INN® Beef Broth**
- **½ cup Burgundy or other dry red wine**
- **3 tablespoons tomato paste**
- **½ teaspoon ground thyme**
- **¾ cup dairy sour cream**
  Hot buttered noodles

In large skillet, over medium heat, brown meat in margarine. Stir in onions and cook for 3 minutes; remove from heat. Sprinkle flour over meat and stir until well combined. Stir in beef broth, Burgundy, tomato paste and thyme until smooth. Cook and stir over medium heat until sauce is thickened and begins to boil. Cover; cook over low heat for 40 to 45 minutes or until tender. Stir sour cream into sauce. (Do not boil.) Serve over hot buttered noodles.
Makes 6 to 8 servings.

Microwave: In 3-quart microwave-proof bowl, place margarine. Microwave, uncovered, on HIGH (100% power) for 1 minute until margarine melts. Toss beef strips with flour; add to margarine. Microwave, uncovered, on HIGH for 6 to 7 minutes, stirring every 2 minutes. Add onions. Microwave, uncovered, on HIGH for 2 to 3 minutes.

Stir in broth, Burgundy, tomato paste and thyme. Cover with plastic wrap; vent. Microwave on HIGH 10 to 12 minutes until sauce is thickened and bubbling. Stir in sour cream. Microwave, uncovered, on HIGH for 1 minute. Let stand 5 minutes before serving. Serve over noodles.

Burgundy Beef Stroganoff

Marinated Flank Steak

- **1 envelope LIPTON® Recipe Secrets Onion or Onion-Mushroom Recipe Soup Mix**
- **½ cup water**
- **½ cup dry red wine**
- **¼ cup olive or vegetable oil**
- **1 tablespoon finely chopped parsley**
- **1 teaspoon oregano**
- **⅛ teaspoon pepper**
- **2- pound beef flank steak**

In large shallow baking dish, thoroughly blend all ingredients except steak; add steak and turn to coat. Cover and marinate in refrigerator, turning steak and piercing with fork occasionally, at least 4 hours. Remove steak, reserving marinade.

Grill or broil steak, turning once. until done. Meanwhile, in small saucepan, bring remaining marinade to a boil, then simmer 5 minutes. if necessary, skim fat from marinade. Serve hot marinade with steak.
Makes about 8 servings.

Sauerbraten

- 1 cup cider vinegar
- ½ cup dry red wine or beef broth
- ½ cup water
- 2 medium onions, thinly sliced
- 1 carrot, sliced
- 1 stalk celery, chopped
- 1 tablespoon salt
- 12 whole peppercorns
- 4 whole cloves
- 2 whole allspice
- 4-pound boneless beef rump roast
- 4 tablespoons all-purpose flour, divided
- ¼ cup CRISCO® OIL
- ⅓ cup cold water
- 1 tablespoon sugar
- ½ cup crushed gingersnap cookies

Mix vinegar, wine, ½ cup water, onions, carrot, celery, salt, peppercorns, cloves and allspice in large bowl or large plastic food storage bag. Add roast. Cover bowl or seal bag. Refrigerate 2 to 3 days, turning roast over each day.

Remove roast from marinade, reserving marinade. Pat roast dry with paper towels. Coat with 2 tablespoons flour. Heat Crisco Oil in Dutch oven. Add roast. Brown over medium-high heat. Pour reserved marinade over roast. Cover. Reduce heat. Simmer 2½ to 3 hours, or until meat is tender turning roast over after half the time. Transfer roast to serving platter; reserving liquid and vegetables in Dutch oven.

Strain vegetables and liquid through wire sieve into large bowl, pressing vegetables to remove liquid. Discard vegetables. Skim and discard fat from liquid. Pour 3 cups liquid into saucepan. Discard remaining liquid. Heat liquid to boiling. Meanwhile, place ⅓ cup cold water in small bowl. Blend in sugar and rmaining 2 tablespoons flour. Add to boiling liquid. Cook, stirring constantly, until mixture is thickened. Stir in gingersnaps. Cook 1 to 2 minutes longer, or until heated through. Serve with roast.
8 to 10 servings.

Beef Goulash

- ¼ cup vegetable oil, divided
- 2 pounds boneless rump or chuck, cut into 1-inch cubes
- 3 medium onions, sliced
- 2 cloves garlic, minced
- 1 can (16 ounces) tomatoes, undrained, cut into pieces
- 4 teaspoons paprika
- 2 beef bouillon cubes
- 1 teaspoon dried marjoram leaves
- 1 teaspoon dried thyme leaves
- ¼ teaspoon TABASCO® pepper sauce
- 1 bay leaf

In large heavy saucepot or Dutch oven heat 2 tablespoons oil; brown meat in 2 batches. Remove; reserve. In same pot heat remaining 2 tablespoons oil; cook onions and garlic 5 minutes or until lightly browned. Stir in tomatoes, paprika, bouillon cubes, marjoram, thyme, Tabasco® sauce and bay leaf. Return meat to pot. Cover; simmer 1½ to 2 hours or until meat is tender; stir occasionally. Remove bay leaf. Serve over noodles, spaetzle, mashed potatoes or rice.
Makes 8 servings.

Brazilian Beans and Rice

- 3 green-tip, medium DOLE® Bananas
- 1 large onion, chopped
- 1 large clove garlic, pressed
- 2 tablespoons minced fresh ginger root
- 1 tablespoon vegetable oil
- ½ pound ground beef
- ½ pound bulk pork sausage
- 1 teaspoon ground cumin
- ¼ teaspoon cayenne pepper
- 1 can (15¼ ounces) kidney beans
- 1 can (11 ounces) black bean soup
- 1 can (8 ounces) stewed tomatoes
- 2 teaspoons minced cilantro or parsley
- 4 to 6 cups shredded lettuce
- 3 to 4 cups hot cooked rice

Cut bananas in half crosswise, then lengthwise. In large skillet, saute onion, garlic and ginger in oil; push to side of skillet. Add bananas; saute 30 to 45 seconds. Remove bananas to plate. Add beef, sausage, cumin and cayenne; brown, stirring in onion mixture. Add undrained beans, soup and tomatoes. Cover; simmer 30 minutes, stirring occasionally. Remove from heat. Stir in cilantro. Place bananas on top. Cover; cook 1 minute. Mound 1 cup lettuce on each plate. Top with ½ cup rice, then bean mixture, spooning bananas to side.
Makes 4 to 6 servings.

Sauerbraten

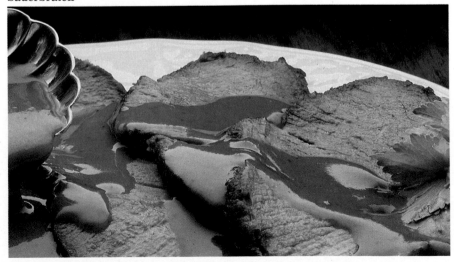

Oven-Baked Bourguignonne

- 2 pounds boneless beef chuck, cut into 1-inch cubes
- ¼ cup all-purpose flour
- 1⅓ cups sliced carrots
- 1 can (14½ ounces) whole peeled tomatoes, undrained and chopped
- 1 bay leaf
- 1 envelope LIPTON® Recipe Secrets Beefy Onion or Onion Recipe Soup Mix
- ½ cup dry red wine
- 1 cup fresh or canned sliced mushrooms
- 1 package (8 ounces) medium or broad egg noodles

Preheat oven to 400°.

In 2-quart casserole, toss beef with flour, then bake uncovered 20 minutes. Add carrots, tomatoes and bay leaf, then beefy onion recipe soup mix blended with wine. Bake covered 1½ hours or until beef is tender. Add mushrooms and bake covered an additional 10 minutes. Remove bay leaf.

Meanwhile, cook noodles according to package directions. To serve, arrange bourguignonne over noodles. *Makes about 8 servings.*

Microwave Directions: Toss beef with flour; set aside. In 2-quart casserole, combine tomatoes, bay leaf and beefy onion recipe soup mix blended with wine. Microwave covered at HIGH (Full Power) 7 minutes, stirring once. Add beef and carrots. Microwave covered at DEFROST (30% Full Power), stirring occasionally, 1¼ hours. Add mushrooms and microwave covered at DEFROST 30 minutes or until beef is tender. Remove bay leaf. Let stand covered 5 minutes. Cook noodles and serve as above.

Freezing/Reheating Directions: Bourguignonne can be baked, then frozen. Simply wrap covered casserole in heavy-duty aluminum foil; freeze. To reheat, unwrap and bake covered at 400°, stirring occasionally to separate beef and vegetables, 1 hour. **OR,** microwave at HIGH (Full Power), stirring occasionally, 20 minutes or until heated through. Let stand covered 5 minutes.

Mexican Beef Stew

- 2 tablespoons CRISCO® Oil
- 2 pounds beef stew meat, cut into 1-inch cubes
- 1 medium onion, chopped
- 1 clove garlic, minced
- 1 can (16 ounces) whole tomatoes, undrained, cut up
- 1 jar (4 ounces) pimiento, drained and mashed
- ½ to 1 teaspoon ground cumin
- ½ teaspoon salt
- ¼ teaspoon pepper

Heat Crisco® Oil in large skillet. Add beef. Brown over medium-high heat. Remove beef with slotted spoon; set aside. Add onion and garlic to skillet. Sauté over moderate heat until onion is tender. Stir in beef and remaining ingredients. Heat to boiling. Cover. Reduce heat. Simmer, stirring occasionally, about 2 hours, or until beef is tender. Add water during cooking, if necessary.
6 to 8 servings.

Mexican Beef Stew

Country French Beef Stew

- 2 pounds boneless beef, cut into 1-inch cubes
- ¼ cup all-purpose flour
- 2 slices bacon, cut into 1-inch pieces
- 3 tablespoons oil
- ¼ cup Cognac (optional)
- 1 envelope LIPTON® Recipe Secrets Onion, Beefy Onion, Onion-Mushroom or Beefy Mushroom Recipe Soup Mix
- 2 cups water
- ½ cup dry red wine
- 2 tablespoons Dijon-style prepared mustard
- 3 carrots, thinly sliced
- ½ pound mushrooms, halved
- 1 package (8 ounces) broad egg noodles

Lightly toss beef with flour; set aside. In Dutch oven, cook bacon until crisp; remove. Reserve drippings. Heat oil with reserved drippings and brown beef, in three batches, over medium-high heat; remove beef and set aside. Into Dutch oven, add Cognac and cook 1 minute or until only a thin glaze of liquid remains. Stir in onion recipe soup mix blended with water, wine and mustard; bring to a boil. Add beef and bacon and simmer covered, stirring occasionally, 1½ hours or until beef is almost tender. Stir in carrots and simmer covered 25 minutes. Add mushrooms and simmer covered an additional 5 minutes or until beef and vegetables are tender.

Meanwhile, cook noodles according to package directions. To serve, arrange stew over noodles. Garnish, if desired, with chopped parsley.
Makes about 8 servings.

Wine-Simmered Beef and Vegetables

Beef Burgundy

- ½ cup all-purpose flour
- ¾ teaspoon salt
- ¼ teaspoon pepper
- 1½ pounds beef round steak, cut into 1-inch pieces
- 5 tablespoons CRISCO® Oil, divided
- 1½ cups water
- 1 cup Burgundy wine
- 1 medium onion, thinly sliced
- ½ cup snipped fresh parsley
- 2 cloves garlic, halved
- 2 bay leaves
- 1½ teaspoons instant beef bouillon granules
- 1 teaspoon dried thyme leaves
- 8 ounces fresh mushrooms, sliced
- ¼ cup sliced almonds
  Hot cooked rice or noodles

Mix flour, salt and pepper in large plastic food storage bag. Add beef. Shake to coat. Heat 4 tablespoons Crisco® Oil in Dutch oven. Add beef and any remaining flour mixture. Brown over medium-high heat. Stir in water, wine, onion, parsley, garlic, bay leaves, bouillon granules and thyme. Heat to boiling. Cover. Reduce heat. Simmer 1½ to 2 hours, or until beef is tender, stirring occasionally. Stir in mushrooms; re-cover. Simmer 20 to 30 minutes longer, or until mushrooms are tender. Remove and discard garlic cloves and bay leaves.

Meanwhile, heat remaining 1 tablespoon Crisco® Oil in small skillet. Add almonds. Cook over moderate heat, stirring constantly, until almonds are lightly browned. Stir into beef mixture just before serving. Serve with rice or noodles.
4 to 6 servings.

Wine-Simmered Beef and Vegetables

- 1½ to 2 pounds beef round steak
- 6 tablespoons all-purpose flour, divided
- ½ teaspoon salt
- ¼ teaspoon pepper
- 3 tablespoons CRISCO® Oil
- 1 medium onion, thinly sliced and separated into rings
- 1 medium green pepper, cored, seeded and sliced into rings
- ⅔ cup julienne carrot strips
- ½ teaspoon dried basil leaves
- ½ teaspoon dried marjoram leaves
- ⅔ cup dry white wine
- ⅔ cup cold water
- ½ teaspoon instant beef bouillon granules

Trim bone and fat from beef. Pound trimmed beef with meat mallet. Cut into serving-size pieces. Set aside. Mix 4 tablespoons flour, salt and pepper in large plastic food storage bag. Add beef. Shake to coat.

Heat Crisco® Oil in large skillet. Add beef and any remaining flour mixture. Brown over medium-high heat. Layer onion, green pepper and carrots over beef. Sprinkle with basil and marjoram. Add wine. Heat to boiling. Cover. Reduce heat. Simmer about 1 hour, or until beef is tender. Transfer beef and vegetables to serving platter, reserving drippings in skillet.

Place cold water in 1-cup measure or small bowl. Blend in remaining 2 tablespoons flour. Stir flour mixture into drippings in skillet. Stir in bouillon granules. Cook over medium-high heat, stirring constantly, until thickened and bubbly. Serve with meat and vegetables.
4 to 6 servings.

Variation: Simmered Beef and Vegetables. Follow recipe above, substituting ⅔ cup water and ¾ teaspoon instant beef bouillon granules for wine.

Stroganoff Superb

- 1 pound beef sirloin steak, cut into thin strips
- 3 tablespoons PARKAY® Margarine
- ½ cup chopped onion
- 1 4-ounce can mushrooms, drained
- ½ teaspoon salt
- ¼ teaspoon dry mustard
- ¼ teaspoon pepper
- 1 8-ounce package PHILADELPHIA BRAND® Cream Cheese, cubed
- ¾ cup milk
  Hot parsleyed noodles

Brown steak in margarine in large skillet. Add onions, mushrooms and seasonings; cook until vegetables are tender. Add cream cheese and milk; stir over low heat until cream cheese is melted. Serve over noodles.
4 to 6 servings.

Carne Asada

> 1 (1¼-pound) top sirloin
> steak
> 2 tablespoons vegetable oil
> ½ cup LAWRY'S® Fajitas
> Skillet Sauce
> ¼ cup orange juice
> ½ teaspoon dried oregano,
> crushed
> Salsa

Pierce steak with fork on both sides and coat with oil; place in large resealable plastic bag. In measuring cup, combine Fajitas Skillet Sauce, orange juice and oregano; pour over steak. Marinate in refrigerator 1 to 2 hours, turning steak occasionally. Remove steak; reserve marinade. Broil steak 4 to 5 minutes on each side until cooked to desired doneness, basting often with reserved marinade. Serve with salsa.
Makes 4 servings

Presentation: Thinly slice steak for taco or burrito filling, or serve with refried beans and Mexican rice for a hearty meal.

Sombrero Taco Cups

> 1 pound ground beef or pork
> 1 package (1.25 ounces)
> LAWRY'S® Taco Spices &
> Seasonings
> ¾ cup water
> ¼ cup salsa
> 2 packages (8 ounces each)
> refrigerator biscuits
> ½ cup (2 ounces) grated
> Cheddar cheese

In medium skillet, brown ground beef until crumbly; drain fat. Add Taco Spices & Seasonings and water; blend well. Bring to a boil; reduce heat and simmer, uncovered, 10 minutes. Stir in salsa. Separate biscuits and press each biscuit into an ungreased muffin cup. Spoon equal amounts of meat mixture into each muffin cup; sprinkle each with cheese. Bake, uncovered, in 350°F oven 12 minutes or until biscuit cups are browned and cheese melts.
Makes 12 pastries

Presentation: Serve as a main dish or as a snack.

Hint: For an extra treat, flatten any leftover biscuit dough into disks; sprinkle with cinnamon-sugar mixture and bake in 350°F oven 5 to 7 minutes or until golden.

Spicy Burrito Bonanza

> ½ pound ground beef
> ½ pound spicy pork sausage
> 1 medium tomato, chopped
> ¼ cup thinly sliced green
> onions
> 1½ teaspoons chili powder
> ½ teaspoon LAWRY'S® Garlic
> Powder with Parsley
> 1 can (8¼ ounces) refried
> beans
> 6 large flour tortillas, warmed
> 1½ cups (6 ounces) grated
> Monterey Jack cheese
> Shredded lettuce

In large skillet, brown ground beef and sausage; drain fat. Add tomato, green onions, chili powder and Garlic Powder with Parsley; blend well. Bring to a boil; reduce heat and simmer, uncovered, 10 minutes. Add refried beans; heat 5 minutes. Spread ½ cup meat mixture on each warm tortilla. Top with a sprinkling of cheese and lettuce. Fold in sides and roll to enclose filling.   *Makes 6 servings*

Presentation: Serve topped with sour cream and avocado slices.

Beef Fajitas

> ½ cup REALEMON® Lemon
> Juice from Concentrate
> *or* REALIME® Lime Juice
> from Concentrate
> ¼ cup vegetable oil
> 2 cloves garlic, finely
> chopped
> 2 teaspoons WYLER'S® or
> STEERO® Beef-Flavor
> Instant Bouillon
> 1 (1- to 1½-pound) top round
> steak
> 10 (6-inch) flour tortillas,
> warmed as package
> directs
> Garnishes: Picante sauce,
> shredded lettuce,
> shredded Cheddar
> cheese and sliced green
> onions

In large shallow dish or plastic bag, combine ReaLemon® brand, oil, garlic and bouillon; add steak. Cover; marinate in refrigerator 6 hours or overnight. Remove steak from marinade; grill or broil 8 to 10 minutes on each side or until steak is cooked to desired doneness, basting frequently with marinade. Slice steak diagonally into thin strips; place on tortillas. Top with one or more garnishes; fold tortillas. Serve immediately. Refrigerate leftovers.   *Makes 10 fajitas*

Carne Asada

Holiday Beef Steaks with Vegetable Saute and Hot Mustard Sauce

      Boneless beef top loin
         steaks, cut 1 inch thick
   ½ cup plain yogurt
    1 teaspoon cornstarch
   ¼ cup condensed beef broth
    2 teaspoons coarse-grained
         mustard
    1 teaspoon *each* prepared
         grated horseradish and
         Dijon-style mustard
   ¼ teaspoon sugar
   ½ teaspoon lemon pepper
    1 package (16 ounces) frozen
         whole green beans
    1 cup quartered large
         mushrooms
    1 tablespoon butter
   ¼ cup water

Place yogurt and cornstarch in medium saucepan and stir until blended. Stir in beef broth, coarse-grained mustard, horseradish, Dijon-style mustard and sugar; reserve. Press lemon pepper into surface of boneless beef top loin steaks. Place steaks on rack in broiler pan so surfaces are 3 to 4 inches from heat. Broil steaks about 15 minutes for rare (20 minutes for medium), turning once. Meanwhile cook beans and mushrooms in butter in large frying pan over medium heat 6 minutes, stirring occasionally. Add water; cover and continue cooking 6 to 8 minutes, stirring occasionally until beans are tender. Cook reserved sauce over medium-low heat 5 minutes, stirring until sauce is slightly thickened. Serve steaks and vegetables with sauce.   *Makes 6 servings*

Preparation Time: 15 minutes
Cooking Time: 15 minutes

Note: A boneless beef top loin steak will yield four 3-ounce cooked servings per pound.

Favorite recipe from **National Live Stock and Meat Board**

Flank Steak with Pineapple Chili Sauce

    1 can (8 ounces) DOLE®
         Crushed Pineapple in
         Juice
    1 beef flank steak
         (1½ pounds)
      Salt and pepper to taste
   ¾ cup chili sauce
   ¼ teaspoon garlic powder
    1 to 2 drops hot pepper
         sauce

• Drain pineapple well; save juice for a beverage.

• Season steak with salt and pepper. Broil 4 inches from heat 5 to 7 minutes on each side for medium-rare.

• Combine drained pineapple, chili sauce, garlic powder and hot pepper sauce in saucepan. Cook over medium heat until heated through.

• Slice steak across the grain into thin slices. Top with chili sauce.
    Makes 4 to 6 servings

Preparation Time: 10 minutes
Cook Time: 15 minutes

Steak Mardi Gras

    1 beef flank steak (1 pound)
    1 tablespoon vegetable oil
    1 jar (12 ounces) HEINZ®
         HomeStyle Mushroom or
         Brown Gravy
    1 can (8 ounces) stewed
         tomatoes
    3 tablespoons chopped fresh
         parsley
    1 teaspoon HEINZ® Gourmet
         Wine Vinegar
   ½ teaspoon granulated sugar
   ⅛ to ¼ teaspoon hot pepper
         sauce

In large skillet, cook steak in oil to desired doneness, turning once; remove and keep warm. In same skillet, stir in remaining ingredients; heat until bubbly. Thinly slice steak diagonally across the grain; spoon sauce over. Serve with rice, if desired.
    Makes 4 servings

Holiday Beef Steaks with Vegetable Saute and Hot Mustard Sauce

Saucy Beef and Vegetable Stir-Fry

Saucy Beef and Vegetable Stir-Fry

1 beef flank steak (1 pound), cut into ¼-inch strips
1 teaspoon minced fresh gingerroot
2 tablespoons vegetable oil
1½ cups broccoli flowerets
1 cup julienne-cut zucchini
1 cup sliced fresh mushrooms
½ cup red or green bell pepper chunks
1 jar (12 ounces) HEINZ® HomeStyle Brown with Onions Gravy
2 tablespoons soy sauce
Dash pepper
Chow mein noodles or hot cooked rice

In preheated large skillet or wok, stir-fry steak and gingerroot in oil; remove. Stir-fry broccoli, zucchini, mushrooms and red pepper 2 to 3 minutes or until tender-crisp, adding more oil if necessary. Stir in gravy, soy sauce and pepper. Return steak to skillet; heat 1 to 2 minutes or until hot. Serve with chow mein noodles. Garnish with sesame seeds, if desired.

Makes 4 servings
(about 4½ cups)

Mandarin Beef

1 pound beef flank steak
3 tablespoons lite soy sauce, divided
6 teaspoons vegetable oil, divided
1 tablespoon cornstarch
3 teaspoons brown sugar, divided
¼ pound green beans, cut diagonally into 2-inch pieces
1 package (10 ounces) frozen asparagus,* thawed and cut diagonally into 2-inch pieces
¼ pound mushrooms, sliced
2 tablespoons dry sherry
6 green onions, cut into 2-inch slivers
½ teaspoon Oriental dark roasted sesame oil**

Cut beef flank steak lengthwise in half. Cut steak across the grain into ⅛-inch-thick strips. Combine 1 tablespoon of the soy sauce, 1 teaspoon of the oil, the cornstarch and 1 teaspoon of the brown sugar; pour over beef strips and marinate 30 minutes.

Heat nonstick frying pan over medium heat; add remaining 5 teaspoons oil. Stir-fry green beans 3 to 4 minutes in oil; add asparagus and mushrooms and cook 2 minutes. Remove vegetables; keep warm. Combine sherry, remaining 2 tablespoons soy sauce and 2 teaspoons brown sugar; reserve. Stir-fry beef (⅓ at a time) 2 to 3 minutes; reserve. Return beef, vegetables and sherry mixture to frying pan and heat through. Stir in green onions. Add sesame oil and stir. Serve immediately.

Makes 4 servings

Preparation Time: 15 minutes
Marinating Time: 30 minutes
Cooking Time: 15 minutes

*Twelve ounces fresh asparagus may be substituted. Cut into 2-inch diagonal pieces; blanch 2 minutes before stir-frying.

**Dark roasted sesame oil may be found in the imported (oriental) section of the supermarket.

*Favorite recipe from **National Live Stock and Meat Board***

Beef Stew with Dumplings

         4 pounds lean boneless beef
              chuck, cut into 2-inch cubes
     ¼ cup plus 2 tablespoons
              FILIPPO BERIO® Olive Oil,
              divided
     2½ teaspoons salt, divided
     ¼ teaspoon pepper
         3 cups dry red wine
         2 cups water
         2 tablespoons tomato paste
         1 large clove garlic, minced
     ½ teaspoon dried thyme,
              crushed
     12 small white onions
         4 carrots, cut into quarters
         4 ribs celery, cut into 2-inch
              pieces
         3 white turnips, cut into
              quarters
     ¼ pound small mushrooms
     ¼ cup chopped parsley
         1 cup all-purpose flour
         2 teaspoons baking powder
     ½ teaspoon sugar
         1 egg, well beaten
     ½ cup milk

Brown beef in ¼ cup of the oil in Dutch oven over medium-high heat. Season with 2 teaspoons of the salt and the pepper. Add wine, water, tomato paste, garlic and thyme. Bring to a boil over high heat. Reduce heat to low. Cover and simmer 1 hour, stirring occasionally. Add onions, carrots, celery, turnips, mushrooms and parsley. Simmer, covered, 20 minutes more.*

Meanwhile, prepare dumplings. Combine flour, baking powder, remaining ½ teaspoon salt and the sugar in small bowl. Add egg, milk and remaining 2 tablespoons oil. Stir to blend. Drop dumplings by tablespoonfuls onto hot stew. Cook, uncovered, 10 minutes.
Makes 8 servings.

*If stew is too thin, thicken sauce before cooking dumplings. To thicken, blend 3 tablespoons all-purpose flour and ½ cup water in small bowl until smooth. Gradually stir mixture into stew. Continue cooking until thickened and smooth, stirring constantly.

Classic Chinese Pepper Steak

Italian-Style Salisbury Steaks

         1 pound ground beef
     ¼ cup seasoned dry bread
              crumbs
     ¼ cup water
         1 egg, slightly beaten
     ½ teaspoon salt
     ¼ teaspoon pepper
     ¼ cup WISH-BONE® Italian or
              Robusto Italian Dressing
         2 cups thinly sliced onions
         2 cups thinly sliced mushrooms
         1 can (8 ounces) tomato sauce
     ½ teaspoon basil leaves

Preheat oven to 350°.

In medium bowl, thoroughly combine ground beef, bread crumbs, water, egg, salt and pepper. Shape into 4 oval patties, then place in 1½-quart oblong baking pan; set aside.

In medium skillet, heat Italian dressing and cook onions with mushrooms over medium heat, stirring occasionally, 5 minutes or until tender. Stir in tomato sauce and basil. Spoon tomato mixture over patties and bake 30 minutes or until done.
Makes 4 servings.

Classic Chinese Pepper Steak

         1 pound boneless beef sirloin
              steak
         1 tablespoon KIKKOMAN® Stir-
              Fry Sauce
         2 tablespoons vegetable oil,
              divided
         2 medium-size green, red or
              yellow bell peppers, cut into
              1-inch squares
         2 medium onions, cut into 1-inch
              squares
     ¼ cup KIKKOMAN® Stir-Fry
              Sauce
         Hot cooked rice (optional)

Cut beef across grain into thin strips, then into 1-inch squares; coat with 1 tablespoon stir-fry sauce. Heat 1 tablespoon oil in hot wok or large skillet over high heat. Add beef and stir-fry 1 minute; remove. Heat remaining 1 tablespoon oil in same pan. Add peppers and onions; stir-fry 5 minutes. Stir in beef and ¼ cup stir-fry sauce; cook and stir just until beef and vegetables are coated with sauce. Serve immediately with rice.
Makes 4 servings.

Orange-Flavored Grilled Beef

         1 orange
         3 tablespoons soy sauce
         2 tablespoons brown sugar
         2 tablespoons cider vinegar
     ½ teaspoon pepper
     ½ teaspoon chili powder
         1 clove garlic, minced
         1 teaspoon grated fresh ginger
         2 pounds beef round tip roast,
              cut into 3-inch cubes

Grate peel from orange to equal 1 tablespoon. Squeeze juice from orange into large bowl. Stir in remaining ingredients except beef. Add beef cubes; toss to coat with marinade. Cover and refrigerate 8 hours or overnight. Drain meat cubes; reserve marinade. Grill beef cubes, on covered grill, over medium-hot **KINGSFORD® Charcoal Briquets** 3 minutes. Turn beef cubes, brush with marinade and cook 5 minutes longer or until done.
Makes 4 servings.

Chinese-Style Beef & Vegetables

⅓ cup WISH-BONE® Italian
   Dressing
1 tablespoon soy sauce
¼ teaspoon ground ginger
1 cup thinly sliced carrots
1 cup sliced mushrooms
1 cup sliced zucchini
1 (1½-pound) boneless sirloin
   steak, cut into thin strips
4 cups hot cooked buttered rice

In small bowl, blend Italian dressing, soy sauce and ginger; reserve 2 tablespoons. In large skillet, heat remaining dressing mixture and cook carrots, covered, over medium heat, stirring occasionally, 10 minutes. Add mushrooms and zucchini and cook covered an additional 5 minutes. Remove vegetables and keep warm. Add reserved dressing mixture to skillet, then add beef. Cook uncovered over high heat, stirring constantly, 5 minutes or until beef is done. Return vegetables to skillet and heat through. To serve, arrange beef and vegetables over hot rice.
Makes about 6 servings.

Note: Also terrific with Wish-Bone® Robusto Italian, Lite Italian or Lite Classic Dijon Vinaigrette Dressing.

Broccoli & Beef Stir-Fry

½ pound boneless tender beef
   steak (sirloin, rib eye or top
   loin)
1 tablespoon cornstarch
4 tablespoons KIKKOMAN® Soy
   Sauce, divided
1 teaspoon sugar
1 teaspoon minced fresh ginger
   root
1 clove garlic, minced
1 pound fresh broccoli
1¼ cups water
4 teaspoons cornstarch
3 tablespoons vegetable oil,
   divided
1 onion, chunked
   Hot cooked rice

Cut beef across grain into thin slices. Combine 1 tablespoon *each* cornstarch and soy sauce with sugar, ginger and garlic in small bowl; stir in beef. Let stand 15 minutes. Meanwhile, remove flowerets from broccoli; cut in half lengthwise. Peel stalks; cut crosswise into ⅛-inch slices. Combine water, 4 teaspoons cornstarch and remaining 3 tablespoons soy sauce; set aside. Heat 1 tablespoon oil in hot wok or large skillet over high heat. Add beef and stir-fry 1 minute; remove. Heat remaining 2 tablespoons oil in same pan. Add broccoli and onion; stir-fry 4 minutes. Stir in beef and soy sauce mixture. Cook and stir until mixture boils and thickens. Serve immediately over rice.
Makes 2 to 3 servings.

Oriental Steak Kabobs

1 cup (8 ounces) WISH-BONE®
   Italian Dressing
¼ cup soy sauce
2 tablespoons brown sugar
½ teaspoon ground ginger
1 green onion, thinly sliced
1 pound boneless beef round,
   cut into 1-inch pieces
12 large mushrooms
2 cups broccoli florets
1 medium red pepper, cut into
   chunks

In large shallow baking dish, combine Italian dressing, soy sauce, brown sugar, ginger and onion. Add beef and vegetables; turn to coat. Cover and marinate in refrigerator, stirring occasionally, 4 hours or overnight. Remove beef and vegetables, reserving marinade.

Onto large skewers, alternately thread beef with vegetables. Grill or broil, turning and basting frequently with reserved marinade, 10 minutes or until beef is done.
Makes about 4 servings.

Note: Also terrific with Wish-Bone® Robusto Italian or Lite Italian Dressing.

Red-Cooked Short Ribs

3 pounds beef short ribs
⅓ to ½ cup all-purpose flour
2 tablespoons vegetable oil
1¾ cups water, divided
½ cup KIKKOMAN® Teriyaki
   Sauce
1 clove garlic, pressed
½ teaspoon ground ginger
⅛ teaspoon ground cloves

Coat ribs thoroughly with flour; reserve ¼ cup excess flour. Heat oil in Dutch oven or large saucepan over medium heat. Add ribs and brown slowly on all sides; drain off excess oil. Combine 1¼ cups water, teriyaki sauce, garlic, ginger and cloves; pour over ribs. Cover; simmer 2 hours, or until ribs are tender. Meanwhile, blend reserved flour and remaining ½ cup water. Remove ribs to serving platter; keep warm. Pour pan drippings into large measuring cup; skim off fat. Add enough water to measure 2½ cups; return to pan and bring to boil. Gradually stir in flour mixture. Cook and stir until thickened; serve with ribs.
Makes 4 servings.

Chinese-Style Beef & Vegetables

Lime Kabobs Polynesian

- ½ cup REALIME® Lime Juice from Concentrate
- ½ cup vegetable oil
- 3 tablespoons sugar
- 1 tablespoon BENNETT'S® Chili Sauce
- ½ to 1 teaspoon curry powder
- ¼ teaspoon garlic powder
- 1 (1½-pound) sirloin steak (about 1 inch thick), cut into cubes
- 1 (8-ounce) can pineapple chunks, drained
- 1 large green pepper, cut into squares
- 2 medium onions, quartered
- 8 ounces fresh whole mushrooms (about 2 cups)
- ½ pint cherry tomatoes

In small bowl, combine ReaLime® brand, oil, sugar, chili sauce and seasonings; pour over meat. Cover; refrigerate 6 hours or overnight, stirring occasionally. Skewer meat with pineapple and vegetables. Grill or broil as desired, turning and basting frequently with marinade. Serve with rice if desired. Refrigerate leftovers.
Makes 6 servings.

Honey-Mustard Beef Ribs

- 1 cup butter or margarine
- 1 bunch green onions with tops, finely chopped
- 1 small yellow onion, finely chopped
- 4 cloves garlic, minced
- 4 tablespoons prepared mustard
- 4 tablespoons honey
- ½ teaspoon liquid smoke, optional
- 1 teaspoon lemon pepper
- 1 teaspoon brown sugar
- 5 pounds beef back ribs

In saucepan, combine butter, green onions, yellow onion and garlic. Cook over low heat 15 minutes or until onions are tender. Remove from heat and add remaining ingredients except ribs. Grill ribs, on covered grill, over medium-hot **KINGSFORD® Charcoal Briquets** 30 to 35 minutes, brushing ribs generously with mustard-honey mixture, until meat is tender.
Makes 4 servings.

Beef with Leafy Greens

- ¾ pound romaine lettuce
- ½ pound boneless tender beef steak (sirloin, rib eye or top loin)
- 4 tablespoons KIKKOMAN® Stir-Fry Sauce, divided
- 1 clove garlic, minced
- 2 tablespoons vegetable oil, divided
- 1 medium onion, chunked
- 1 teaspoon minced fresh ginger root
- 8 cherry tomatoes, halved *or* 1 medium tomato, chunked
- 2 tablespoons chopped unsalted peanuts

Separate and rinse lettuce; pat dry. Cut leaves crosswise into 1-inch strips; set aside. Cut beef across grain into thin slices. Combine 1 tablespoon stir-fry sauce and garlic in small bowl; stir in beef to coat. Heat 1 tablespoon oil in hot wok or large skillet over high heat. Add beef and stir-fry 1 minute; remove. Heat remaining 1 tablespoon oil in same pan. Add onion and ginger; stir-fry 2 minutes. Add lettuce; stir-fry 2 minutes longer. Add beef, tomatoes and remaining 3 tablespoons stir-fry sauce; cook and stir until vegetables are coated with sauce and tomatoes are just heated through. Serve immediately with peanuts.
Makes 2 to 3 servings.

Beef with Leafy Greens

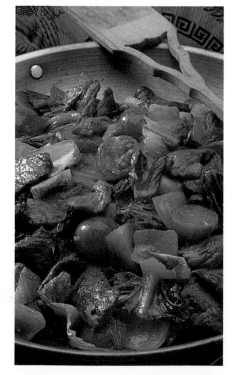

Fiery Beef Stir-Fry

- ½ pound boneless tender beef steak (sirloin, rib eye or top loin)
- 1 tablespoon cornstarch
- 4 tablespoons KIKKOMAN® Soy Sauce, divided
- ½ teaspoon sugar
- 1 clove garlic, minced
- 1¼ cups water
- 4 teaspoons cornstarch
- 1½ teaspoons distilled white vinegar
- ⅛ to ¼ teaspoon ground red pepper (cayenne)
- 3 tablespoons vegetable oil, divided
- 3 cups bite-size cauliflowerets Salt
- 1 onion, chunked and separated
- 1 green pepper, chunked

Cut beef across grain into thin strips. Combine 1 tablespoon *each* cornstarch and soy sauce with sugar and garlic in small bowl; stir in beef. Let stand 15 minutes. Meanwhile, combine water, remaining 3 tablespoons soy sauce, 4 teaspoons cornstarch, vinegar and red pepper; set aside. Heat 1 tablespoon oil in hot wok or large skillet over high heat. Add beef and stir-fry 1 minute; remove. Heat remaining 2 tablespoons oil in same pan. Add cauliflowerets; lightly sprinkle with salt and stir-fry 2 minutes. Add onion and green pepper; stir-fry 4 minutes. Stir in beef and soy sauce mixture; cook and stir until sauce boils and thickens.
Makes 2 to 3 servings.

Beef and Bean Sprout Stir-Fry

- 1 egg white, slightly beaten
- 5 teaspoons soy sauce, divided
- 3 teaspoons cornstarch, divided
- 1/8 teaspoon ground ginger
- 1/8 teaspoon garlic powder
- 1/8 teaspoon salt
  Dash white pepper
- 3/4 to 1 pound boneless beef sirloin, cut into thin strips
- 1/2 cup cold water
- 1 tablespoon oyster sauce (optional)*
- 1/2 teaspoon instant chicken bouillon granules
- 4 tablespoons CRISCO® Oil, divided
- 1 cup sliced fresh mushrooms
- 1/2 cup green onion slices (1-inch slices)
- 1 can (14 ounces) bean sprouts, drained
- 1/2 cup sliced water chestnuts

Blend egg white, 2 teaspoons soy sauce, 1 teaspoon cornstarch, ginger, garlic powder, salt and pepper in medium mixing bowl. Add beef. Stir to coat. Cover; refrigerate 30 minutes.

Combine cold water, oyster sauce (optional), remaining 3 teaspoons soy sauce, remaining 2 teaspoons cornstarch and bouillon granules in small mixing bowl. Mix well. Set aside.

Heat 2 tablespoons Crisco® Oil in large skillet or wok. Add beef mixture. Stir-fry over medium-high heat until beef is browned. Remove mixture from skillet; set aside. Heat remaining 2 tablespoons Crisco® Oil in large skillet. Add mushrooms and onion. Stir-fry over medium-high heat 1 minute. Add bean sprouts and water chestnuts. Stir-fry 1 minute. Add cornstarch mixture and beef. Cook until thickened and bubbly. Serve with *rice* and additional *soy sauce*, if desired. *4 to 6 servings.*

*Available in Oriental foods section of supermarket.

Szechuan Beef & Snow Peas

Szechuan Beef & Snow Peas

- 1/2 pound boneless tender beef steak (sirloin, rib eye or top loin)
- 2 tablespoons cornstarch, divided
- 3 tablespoons KIKKOMAN® Soy Sauce, divided
- 1 tablespoon dry sherry
- 1 clove garlic, minced
- 3/4 cup water
- 1/4 to 1/2 teaspoon crushed red pepper
- 2 tablespoons vegetable oil, divided
- 6 ounces fresh snow peas, trimmed
- 1 medium onion, chunked
  Salt
- 1 medium tomato, chunked
  Hot cooked rice

Slice beef across grain into thin strips. Combine 1 tablespoon *each* cornstarch and soy sauce with sherry and garlic in small bowl; stir in beef. Let stand 15 minutes. Meanwhile, combine water, remaining 1 tablespoon cornstarch, 2 tablespoons soy sauce and red pepper; set aside. Heat 1 tablespoon oil in hot wok or large skillet over high heat. Add beef and stir-fry 1 minute; remove. Heat remaining 1 tablespoon oil in same pan. Add snow peas and onion; lightly sprinkle with salt and stir-fry 3 minutes. Add beef, soy sauce mixture and tomato. Cook and stir until sauce boils and thickens and tomato is heated through. Serve immediately with rice. *Makes 2 to 3 servings.*

Savory Beef Rolls

**1 medium green bell pepper,
    cut into chunks
1 medium onion, sliced
1 clove garlic, minced
1 tablespoon vegetable oil
1 cup prepared stuffing
¼ cup grated Parmesan
    cheese
4 beef cubed steaks
    (6 ounces each)
1 cup water
¾ cup HEINZ® Chili Sauce
1 teaspoon instant beef
    bouillon granules or
    1 bouillon cube**

In large skillet, sauté green
pepper, onion and garlic in oil
until tender-crisp; remove. In
small bowl, combine stuffing and
Parmesan cheese. Place ¼ cup
stuffing mixture on each steak;
roll, jelly-roll fashion, and secure
with toothpicks. In skillet, brown
steak rolls, adding more oil if
necessary. In medium bowl,
combine water, chili sauce,
bouillon and sautéed vegetables;
pour over beef rolls. Cover;
simmer 30 minutes, basting
occasionally. Remove toothpicks;
spoon sauce over rolls.

*Makes 4 servings
(about 2⅓ cups sauce)*

Fruited Beef Kabobs

**1 small green bell pepper, cut
    into 1-inch pieces
1 can (8 ounces) pineapple
    chunks in juice
¾ pound sirloin steak, cut
    into 1-inch cubes
1 can (10½ ounces) mandarin
    oranges, drained
1 onion, cut into wedges
1 package (1.27 ounces)
    LAWRY'S® Spices &
    Seasonings for Fajitas
½ cup undiluted orange juice
    concentrate
½ teaspoon freshly grated
    orange peel**

In medium microwave-safe bowl,
place bell pepper. Cover and
microwave on HIGH 3 minutes.
Let cool. Drain pineapple;
reserve juice. Alternately thread
bell pepper, beef cubes, orange
segments, pineapple and onion
on wooden skewers. Place kabobs
in 13×9×2-inch glass baking
pan. Combine Spices &
Seasonings for Fajitas, orange
juice concentrate, reserved
pineapple juice and orange peel;
pour over kabobs. Cover and
marinate in refrigerator 2 hours
or overnight. Bake, covered, in
350°F oven 15 to 20 minutes or
until beef is to desired doneness.
Uncover, baste with marinade
and place under broiler. Broil 1
to 2 minutes to brown.

Makes 6 servings

Presentation: Serve with crisp
green salad and a rice side dish.

Hint: If desired, you may omit
cooking bell pepper in microwave
oven.

Zesty Beef Stroganoff

**1 (1- to 1¼-pound) sirloin
    steak, cut into ⅛-inch
    strips
¼ cup margarine or butter
8 ounces fresh mushrooms,
    sliced (about 2 cups)
½ cup sliced onion
1 clove garlic, finely chopped
2 tablespoons flour
1 cup water
3 tablespoons REALEMON®
    Lemon Juice from
    Concentrate
3 tablespoons dry red wine
2 teaspoons WYLER'S® or
    STEERO® Beef-Flavor
    Instant Bouillon
¼ teaspoon pepper
1 (8-ounce) container
    BORDEN® or MEADOW
    GOLD® Sour Cream, at
    room temperature
CREAMETTE® Egg
    Noodles, cooked as
    package directs
Chopped parsley**

In large skillet, over medium-
high heat, brown sirloin in
margarine; remove from pan. In
same skillet, cook and stir
mushrooms, onion and garlic
until tender; stir in flour. Add
water, ReaLemon® brand, wine,
bouillon and pepper; cook and
stir until slightly thickened. Stir
in sour cream then meat; heat
through. *Do not boil.* Serve on
noodles; garnish with parsley.
Refrigerate leftovers.

Makes 4 servings

Sherried Beef

**¾ pound beef top round steak
1 cup water
¼ cup dry sherry
3 tablespoons soy sauce
2 large carrots, cut into
    diagonal slices
1 large green pepper, cut into
    strips
1 medium onion, cut into
    chunks
2 tablespoons vegetable oil,
    divided
1 tablespoon cornstarch
2 cups hot cooked rice**

Partially freeze steak; slice
across the grain into ⅛-inch
strips. Combine water, sherry,
and soy sauce. Pour over beef in
dish; marinate 1 hour. Stir-fry
vegetables in 1 tablespoon oil in
large skillet over medium-high
heat. Remove from skillet; set
aside. Drain beef; reserve
marinade. Brown beef in
remaining 1 tablespoon oil.
Combine cornstarch with
reserved marinade in bowl. Add
vegetables and marinade to beef.
Cook, stirring, until sauce is
thickened; cook 1 minute longer.
Serve over rice.

Makes 4 servings

Favorite recipe from **USA Rice
Council**

Sherried Beef

Mexican Beef Stir-Fry

**1 pound beef flank steak
2 tablespoons vegetable oil
1 teaspoon ground cumin
1 teaspoon garlic salt
1 teaspoon dried oregano
     leaves
1 red bell pepper, cut into
     thin strips
1 medium onion, chopped
1 to 2 jalapeño peppers,
     seeded and cut into
     slivers***

Cut beef flank steak diagonally across the grain into 1/8-inch-thick slices. Combine oil, cumin, garlic salt and oregano. Heat 1 tablespoon of the oil mixture in large nonstick frying pan until hot. Add red pepper, onion and jalapeño peppers; stir-fry over medium-high heat 2 to 3 minutes or until tender-crisp. Remove from pan; reserve. Stir-fry beef strips (1/2 at a time) in remaining oil mixture 1 to 2 minutes. Return vegetables to frying pan and heat through.

Makes 4 servings

Serving Suggestions: Mexican Beef Stir-Fry may be served on a lettuce raft, in taco shells or on tostada shells. Top with guacamole, if desired.

Preparation Time: 15 minutes
Cooking Time: 10 minutes

*Wear rubber gloves when working with jalapeño peppers and wash hands with warm soapy water. Avoid touching face or eyes.

*Favorite recipe from **National Live Stock and Meat Board***

Santa Fe Burrito Bake

Mexican Beef Stir-Fry

Santa Fe Burrito Bake

**1½ pounds ground beef
  1 cup water
  1 can (4 ounces) chopped
       green chiles, undrained
  1 package (1.25 ounces) taco
       seasoning mix, dry
  2 cups Wheat CHEX® brand
       cereal, crushed to ¾ cup
  1 loaf frozen bread dough,
       thawed
  1 cup (4 ounces) shredded
       Cheddar cheese
  1 teaspoon margarine or
       butter, melted
     Chili powder
     Salsa, sour cream and
       shredded lettuce**

Preheat oven to 350°F. In large skillet over medium heat cook meat 5 minutes or until no longer pink; drain. Stir in water, chiles and seasoning mix. Add cereal, stirring until well combined; set aside. Roll bread dough into a 15×10-inch rectangle. Spread 2 cups reserved meat mixture in a 4-inch-wide strip lengthwise down center of bread. Top with cheese. Cover with remaining 2 cups meat mixture. Bring sides of dough up over filling. Seal top and sides well. Place seam side down on ungreased baking sheet. Brush with margarine. Sprinkle with chili powder. Bake 30 to 35 minutes or until golden brown. Slice and serve with salsa, sour cream and lettuce.

Makes 6 servings

To decorate top: Cut 1-inch-wide strip from a short side of dough; reserve. Decorate loaf with reserved dough before brushing with margarine.

Mexican Beef and Rice

- **1 pound ground beef**
- **8 scallions thinly sliced***
- **1 can (16 ounces) tomato sauce**
- **1 cup water**
- **¼ cup sliced pitted ripe olives or stuffed green olives**
- **1 tablespoon chili powder**
- **1½ cups Original MINUTE® Rice**
- **Tortilla chips (optional)**

Brown beef with scallions in large skillet, breaking beef into small pieces. Stir in tomato sauce, water, olives and chili powder. Bring to full boil. Stir in rice. Cover; remove from heat. Let stand 5 minutes. Fluff with fork. Serve with tortilla chips.

Makes 4 servings

Microwave Directions: Combine all ingredients except tortilla chips in microwavable dish. Cover and cook on HIGH 10 minutes, stirring halfway through cooking time. Let stand 5 minutes. Fluff with fork. Serve with tortilla chips.

Makes 4 servings

*You may use 1 cup chopped onion for the scallions.

Mexican Beef and Rice

Thai Beef

- **1 pound ground round**
- **1 teaspoon crushed red pepper**
- **1 medium red onion, sliced**
- **1 medium green bell pepper, chopped**
- **¼ cup REALEMON® Lemon Juice from Concentrate**
- **2 teaspoons finely chopped fresh mint leaves *or* ½ teaspoon dried mint leaves**
- **1 teaspoon WYLER'S® or STEERO® Beef-Flavor Instant Bouillon**
- **2 cups hot cooked rice**
- **⅔ cup seeded, chopped cucumber**
- **12 lettuce leaves**

In large skillet, brown meat and red pepper; pour off fat. Add onion, green pepper, ReaLemon® brand, mint and bouillon; mix well. Simmer uncovered until vegetables are tender. Meanwhile, combine rice and cucumber; keep warm. Place about ¼ cup rice mixture and ⅓ cup meat mixture on each lettuce leaf; roll up. Serve immediately. Refrigerate leftovers.

Makes 4 to 6 servings

Meatballs in Sour Cream Sauce

1 pound lean ground beef
1 cup soft bread crumbs
1 egg, slightly beaten
¼ cup grated Parmesan cheese
¼ cup milk
½ teaspoon onion powder
½ teaspoon garlic salt
⅛ teaspoon pepper
1 tablespoon vegetable oil
1 tablespoon paprika
1 medium onion, halved, sliced
1 jar (12 ounces) HEINZ® Mushroom or Brown Gravy
½ cup dairy sour cream
Hot cooked noodles

In large bowl, combine beef, bread crumbs, egg, Parmesan cheese, milk, onion powder, garlic salt and pepper. Form into 20 meatballs, using a rounded tablespoon for each. In large skillet, brown meatballs in oil; drain excess fat. Sprinkle meatballs with paprika; add onion. Cover; cook over low heat 10 minutes. In medium bowl, combine gravy and sour cream; pour over meatballs. Heat slowly, basting meatballs frequently. *Do not boil.* Serve over noodles. Garnish with chopped parsley, if desired.

Makes 4 servings

Saucy Meatballs

1 pound lean ground beef
⅔ cup grated Parmesan cheese
½ cup seasoned dry bread crumbs
½ cup milk
1 egg, slightly beaten
2 tablespoons vegetable oil
1 tablespoon all-purpose flour
1 can (28 ounces) whole peeled tomatoes, cut into bite-size pieces
⅓ to ½ cup HEINZ® 57 Sauce
½ teaspoon salt
Hot buttered noodles

In large bowl, combine beef, Parmesan cheese, bread crumbs, milk and egg. Form into 20 meatballs using a rounded tablespoon for each. In large skillet, brown meatballs in oil; drain excess fat. Sprinkle flour over meatballs, stirring gently to coat. In medium bowl, combine tomatoes, 57 Sauce and salt; pour over meatballs. Simmer, uncovered, 25 minutes or until sauce is desired consistency, stirring occasionally. Serve meatballs and sauce over noodles.

Makes 5 servings (about 3 cups sauce)

Sweet & Sour Meatballs

1½ pounds lean ground beef
1 (8-ounce) can water chestnuts, drained and chopped
2 eggs, slightly beaten
⅓ cup plain dry bread crumbs
4 teaspoons WYLER'S® or STEERO® Beef-Flavor Instant Bouillon
1 tablespoon Worcestershire sauce
1 cup water
½ cup firmly packed light brown sugar
½ cup REALEMON® Lemon Juice from Concentrate
¼ cup ketchup
2 tablespoons cornstarch
¼ teaspoon salt
1 cup diced red and green bell peppers
Hot cooked rice

In large bowl, combine meat, water chestnuts, eggs, crumbs, bouillon and Worcestershire; mix well. Shape into 1¼-inch meatballs. In large skillet, brown meatballs. Remove from pan; pour off fat. In same skillet, combine remaining ingredients except peppers and rice; mix well. Over medium heat, cook and stir until sauce thickens. Reduce heat. Add meatballs; simmer uncovered 10 minutes. Add peppers; heat through. Serve with rice. Garnish with parsley if desired. Refrigerate leftovers.

Makes 6 to 8 servings

Meatballs in Sour Cream Sauce

Saucy Veal and Vegetables

Saucy Veal and Vegetables

2 cups quartered fresh
    mushrooms
1 cup julienne-cut carrots
1 small zucchini, halved
    lengthwise, cut into
    ¼-inch slices
4 green onions, sliced
½ teaspoon dried basil
    leaves, crushed
½ teaspoon salt
¼ teaspoon pepper
¼ teaspoon dried oregano
    leaves, crushed
2 tablespoons vegetable oil,
    divided
1 pound boneless veal
    cutlets, cut into thin
    strips
2 tablespoons dry white wine
1 jar (12 ounces) HEINZ®
    HomeStyle Chicken
    Gravy
¼ cup dairy sour cream
    Hot cooked spaghetti or
    linguine

In large skillet, sauté
mushrooms, carrots, zucchini,
green onions, basil, salt, pepper
and oregano in 1 tablespoon oil;
remove. Add remaining 1
tablespoon oil. Quickly brown
veal in 2 batches; remove. Add
wine; heat. Stir in gravy and
sour cream. Return veal and
vegetables to skillet; heat slowly.
Do not boil. Serve over hot
spaghetti.

Makes 4 servings (about 4 cups)

Glazed Meat Loaf

½ cup ketchup
⅓ cup firmly packed light
    brown sugar
¼ cup REALEMON® Lemon
    Juice from Concentrate
1 teaspoon dry mustard
1½ pounds lean ground beef
1½ cups fresh bread crumbs
    (3 slices)
¼ cup finely chopped onion
1 egg, slightly beaten
1 teaspoon WYLER'S® or
    STEERO® Beef-Flavor
    Instant Bouillon

Preheat oven to 350°. In small
bowl, combine ketchup, sugar,
1 tablespoon ReaLemon® brand
and mustard. In large bowl,
combine remaining ingredients
and ⅓ cup ketchup mixture; mix
well. In shallow baking dish,
shape into loaf. Bake 1 hour;
pour off fat. Pour remaining
ketchup mixture over loaf; bake
10 minutes longer. Garnish as
desired. Refrigerate leftovers.

Makes 4 to 6 servings

Easy Cheesy Meat Loaf

1½ pounds lean ground beef
2 cups fresh bread crumbs
    (4 slices)
1 cup tomato juice
½ cup chopped onion
2 eggs, slightly beaten
2 teaspoons WYLER'S® or
    STEERO® Beef-Flavor
    Instant Bouillon
¼ teaspoon pepper
6 slices BORDEN® Singles
    Process American
    Cheese Food

Preheat oven to 350°. In bowl,
combine all ingredients except
cheese food. In shallow baking
dish, shape half the mixture into
loaf. Cut *4 slices* cheese food into
strips; arrange on meat. Top with
remaining meat; press edges
together to seal. Bake for 1 hour.
Top with remaining cheese food
slices. Refrigerate leftovers.

Makes 4 to 6 servings

Country-Style Veal

- ¼ cup all-purpose flour
- 3 tablespoons water
- 2 tablespoons dry white wine
- 1½ teaspoons instant beef bouillon granules
- ½ teaspoon dried basil leaves
- ½ teaspoon dried thyme leaves
- ¼ teaspoon dried marjoram leaves
- ¼ teaspoon salt
- ⅛ teaspoon pepper
- ⅛ teaspoon garlic powder
- 3 tablespoons CRISCO® Oil
- 1 to 1½ pounds veal round steak, cut into serving-size pieces
- 1 medium onion, halved and thinly sliced
- 8 ounces whole fresh mushrooms
- 2 tomatoes, peeled, seeded and cut into chunks
- 2 slices lemon
- 1 bay leaf

Mix flour, water, wine, bouillon granules, basil, thyme, marjoram, salt, pepper and garlic powder in small mixing bowl. Set aside. Heat Crisco® Oil in large skillet. Add veal. Fry over medium-high heat until no longer pink. Remove veal from skillet; set aside.

Add onion to drippings in skillet. Sauté over moderate heat until tender. Reduce heat to low. Stir in remaining ingredients and the veal. Add flour mixture. Stir. Cover. Simmer, stirring once, 25 to 30 minutes, or until mushrooms are tender. Remove and discard bay leaf.

4 to 6 servings.

Veal Scallopini with Brandy Cream Sauce

- 1 pound veal scallopini, pounded ¼ inch thick (about 4 cutlets)
- ¼ cup all-purpose flour
- 3 tablespoons butter or margarine
- 1 medium apple, thinly sliced
- 1 envelope LIPTON® Recipe Secrets Golden Onion Recipe Soup Mix
- 1½ cups water
- 2 tablespoons brandy
- ½ cup light cream or half and half
- 1 tablespoon light brown sugar

Lightly coat veal with flour.

In large skillet, melt butter and cook veal over medium heat until tender. Remove veal to serving platter and keep warm. Reserve 1 tablespoon drippings. Add apple, then golden onion recipe soup mix thoroughly blended with water and brandy to reserved drippings. Bring to a boil, then simmer, stirring occasionally, 10 minutes. Stir in cream and sugar and heat through. Serve sauce over veal.

Makes about 4 servings.

Stuffed Veal Cutlets

- 1 package (3 ounces) cream cheese, softened
- 2 teaspoons grated Parmesan cheese
- 1 teaspoon Dijon mustard
- ½ teaspoon dried parsley flakes
- ⅛ teaspoon garlic powder
- ½ cup all-purpose flour
- ¼ teaspoon salt
- ⅛ teaspoon pepper
- 1 cup seasoned dry bread crumbs
- 2 eggs
- 8 thin slices fully cooked ham
- 8 veal cutlets, pounded thin
- 8 thin slices Swiss cheese (each about 4 inches square), halved
- CRISCO® Oil for frying

Combine cream cheese, Parmesan cheese, mustard, parsley flakes and garlic powder in small mixing bowl. Mix well. Set aside. Mix flour, salt and pepper in shallow dish. Place bread crumbs on sheet of waxed paper. Beat eggs slightly in another shallow dish. Set aside.

Place ham slice on top of each cutlet. Trim ham to within ½ inch of cutlet edge. Spread each ham slice with one-eighth of cream cheese mixture (a scant tablespoon). Top each with 2 pieces Swiss cheese. Brush top edges of cutlets with egg. Fold in half. Press and pound edges of cutlets together with meat mallet to seal. Carefully coat both sides with flour mixture. Dip stuffed cutlets in egg, and then in bread crumbs, pressing to coat thoroughly. Cover and refrigerate about 1 hour.

Heat 2 inches Crisco® Oil in deep-fryer or large saucepan to 350°F. Fry 1 stuffed cutlet at a time, about 2½ minutes, or until deep golden brown, turning over once. Drain on paper towels.

4 to 8 servings.

Country-Style Veal

Veal Chops Stuffed with Fontina

- 4 loin veal chops, 1 inch thick (about 3 pounds)
- 2 ounces thinly sliced fontina or Swiss cheese
- 2 ounces thinly sliced prosciutto or ham
- 4 tablespoons all-purpose flour
- ½ cup WISH-BONE® Italian or Robusto Italian Dressing
- ½ cup finely chopped onion
- ¾ cup water
- ¾ cup beef broth
- ¼ cup Marsala wine
- 1 tablespoon fresh or dried rosemary leaves, crumbled
- ⅛ teaspoon pepper
- ¼ cup whipping or heavy cream

With knife parallel to cutting board, make a 2-inch-wide by 2-inch-deep cut in meaty side of each chop. Evenly stuff each cut with cheese and prosciutto; secure, if desired, with skewers. Lightly coat chops with 2 tablespoons flour, then dip in ¼ cup Italian dressing. On aluminum-foil-lined broiler rack or in large shallow baking pan, arrange chops and broil, turning once, 10 minutes or until done. Remove to serving platter and keep warm.

Meanwhile, in medium skillet, heat remaining ¼ cup Italian dressing and cook onion over medium heat, stirring occasionally, 5 minutes or until tender. Add water, broth and wine thoroughly blended with rosemary, pepper and remaining 2 tablespoons flour. Bring to a boil, then simmer, stirring occasionally, 3 minutes or until thickened. Stir in cream; heat through. Serve over chops.
Makes about 4 servings.

Lamb Chops with Lemony Apple Glaze

- ½ cup BAMA® Apple Jelly
- ¼ cup REALEMON® Lemon Juice from Concentrate
- ¼ cup steak sauce
- 8 loin lamb chops, 1 inch thick

In small saucepan, melt jelly; stir in ReaLemon® brand and steak sauce. Heat through. Grill or broil chops as desired, basting frequently with sauce. Refrigerate leftovers.
Makes 4 servings.

Veal Parmesan

- 2 tablespoons CRISCO® Oil
- 1 small onion, thinly sliced and separated into rings
- ½ cup chopped green pepper
- 1 clove garlic, minced
- 1 can (15 ounces) tomato sauce
- 2 tablespoons dry white wine
- ¾ teaspoon dried basil leaves
- ½ teaspoon sugar
- ¼ teaspoon fennel seed
- ¼ teaspoon salt
- ⅛ teaspoon pepper
- 1 cup seasoned dry bread crumbs
- ¾ cup grated Parmesan cheese, divided
- ¼ teaspoon pepper
- 2 eggs
- 1 pound veal cutlets, ¼ inch thick
- CRISCO® Oil for frying

For sauce, heat 2 tablespoons Crisco® Oil in medium saucepan. Add onion, green pepper and garlic. Sauté over moderate heat until tender. Stir in tomato sauce, wine, basil, sugar, fennel, salt and ⅛ teaspoon pepper. Heat to boiling. Reduce heat. Simmer, uncovered, for 30 minutes, or until sauce is thickened.

Mix bread crumbs, ¼ cup Parmesan cheese and ¼ teaspoon pepper in shallow dish. Beat eggs slightly in another shallow dish. Dip veal into eggs, then in bread crumb mixture to coat.

Preheat oven to 350°F. Heat ¼ inch Crisco® Oil in large skillet. Add veal. Fry over moderate heat, 3 to 4 minutes, or until golden brown, turning over once. Drain on paper towels. Arrange cutlets in 13×9-inch baking dish. Pour sauce over veal. Sprinkle with remaining ½ cup Parmesan cheese. Bake at 350°F, 15 to 20 minutes or until cheese melts.
4 to 6 servings.

Veal Marengo

Veal Marengo

- 1 tablespoon olive or vegetable oil
- 1½ pounds veal for stew, cut into 1½-inch cubes
- ½ pound small mushrooms
- 2 medium onions, chopped
- 2 cloves garlic, minced
- 2 tablespoons flour
- 1 cup dry white wine
- ½ cup orange juice
- ¼ cup tomato paste
- ½ teaspoon dried basil leaves
- ½ teaspoon dried thyme leaves
- ¼ teaspoon TABASCO® pepper sauce
- 1 chicken bouillon cube
- Hot cooked rice or noodles

In large heavy saucepot or Dutch oven, heat oil; brown meat in 2 batches. Remove; reserve. In same pot cook mushrooms, onions and garlic 5 minutes or until tender. Return meat to pot; sprinkle with flour. Stir constantly; cook 3 minutes. Stir in wine, orange juice, tomato paste, basil, thyme, Tabasco® sauce and bouillon cube. Cover; simmer 1 hour or until meat is tender; stir occasionally. Serve over rice or noodles.
Makes 6 servings.

Basque Lamb

- ¾ cup fresh lemon juice
- 1 cup dry sherry
- ½ cup olive or vegetable oil
- 1 clove garlic, crushed
- 1 boneless lamb shoulder (3 pounds), left untied
- 1 bunch chives, chopped
- 1 clove garlic, chopped
- 1 bunch parsley, chopped
  Salt and pepper

In small bowl, combine lemon juice, sherry, oil and crushed garlic. Let stand 1 hour. Sprinkle inside of roast with an even layer of chives, chopped garlic and parsley. Season with salt and pepper to taste. Roll up meat and tie securely with kitchen twine. In grill, arrange medium-hot **KINGS-FORD® Charcoal Briquets** around drip pan. Fill pan with water. Add hickory chips to coals, if desired. Place roast over drip pan. Cover grill and cook 45 to 60 minutes or until medium-rare, basting often with lemon juice mixture. Remove roast from grill; let stand 15 minutes. Carve into 1-inch-thick slices.
Makes 4 to 6 servings.

Lamb Curry

- 1 cup diced onions
- 1 large tart cooking apple, cored and diced
- 2 to 3 teaspoons curry powder
- ¼ teaspoon ground ginger
- ¼ teaspoon ground black pepper
- 3 tablespoons BLUE BONNET® Margarine
- 3 tablespoons all-purpose flour
- 1 (13¾-fluid ounce) can COLLEGE INN® Chicken Broth
- ¼ cup heavy cream
- 3½ cups diced cooked lamb or other cooked meat
  Curry Accompaniments*

In large saucepan, over medium heat, cook onions, apple, curry powder, ginger and pepper in margarine until tender, about 5 minutes. Blend in flour; gradually stir in chicken broth until smooth. Cook and stir until sauce is thickened and begins to boil. Stir in cream and lamb; cook until heated through. (Do not boil.) Serve with Curry Accompaniments. Garnish as desired.
Makes 6 servings.

Curry Accompaniments: If desired, this curry can be served over hot cooked rice with a selection of the following: chutney, raisins, flaked coconut, salted peanuts, crumbled cooked bacon, hard-cooked eggs, sliced avocado and grated orange peel.

Microwave: In 2-quart microwave-proof bowl, combine onions, apple, curry powder, ginger, pepper and margarine. Microwave, uncovered, on HIGH (100% power) for 4 to 5 minutes, stirring every 2 minutes. Blend in flour; gradually stir in broth until smooth. Microwave, uncovered, on HIGH for 6 to 7 minutes until thickened and bubbling, stirring every 2 minutes. Stir in cream and meat. Microwave on MEDIUM (50% power) for 6 to 7 minutes until heated through, stirring after 3 minutes. Let stand 5 minutes before serving. Serve as above.

Aegean Lamb Stew

- 1 tablespoon vegetable oil
- 2 pounds lamb with bones for stew, cut into large pieces
- 1 large onion, sliced
- 2 cloves garlic, minced
- 1 can (28 ounces) tomatoes, undrained
- ½ teaspoon ground cinnamon
- ½ teaspoon turmeric
- ½ teaspoon TABASCO® pepper sauce
- ¼ teaspoon salt
  Pinch ground cloves
- 6 new potatoes, cut into chunks
- 1 small eggplant, cut into 1-inch pieces
- 1 zucchini, cut into ¾-inch pieces

Preheat oven to 350°F. In large skillet heat oil over medium-high heat. Add lamb, a few pieces at a time; brown on all sides. Arrange lamb in 3-quart casserole. Drain off all but 1 tablespoon fat from skillet; cook onion and garlic 5 minutes or until tender. Add tomatoes; stir up bits from bottom of skillet. Stir in cinnamon, turmeric, Tabasco® sauce, salt and cloves. Pour mixture over lamb. Stir in potatoes. Cover; bake 30 minutes. Stir in eggplant and zucchini. Cover; cook 45 minutes longer or until meat and vegetables are tender.
Makes 6 servings.

Apple and Veal Scallop

- 2 large all-purpose apples, peeled, cored and sliced
- ¼ cup REALEMON® Lemon Juice from Concentrate
- ½ cup unsifted flour
- 1 teaspoon salt
  Fresh ground pepper
- 8 veal scallops (about 12 ounces)
- ¼ cup margarine or butter
- ½ cup apple cider or apple juice
- 1 cup (½ pint) BORDEN® or MEADOW GOLD® whipping cream, unwhipped

In medium bowl, combine apples and ReaLemon® brand; set aside. In paper or plastic bag, combine flour, salt and pepper. Add veal, a few pieces at a time; shake to coat. In large skillet, brown veal on both sides in margarine; remove from skillet and set aside. Stir in apple mixture and cider, scraping bottom of skillet. Cook 3 to 5 minutes. Slowly add cream, stirring constantly. Simmer 5 to 10 minutes or until slightly thickened. Add veal; heat through. Refrigerate leftovers.
Makes 4 servings.

Lamb Curry

Pork Steaks with Peppers

- 2 tablespoons olive or vegetable oil
- 1½ pounds pork blade steaks, ½ inch thick (about 4 to 5)
- 3 medium red, green or yellow peppers, cut into thin strips
- 1 clove garlic, finely chopped
- 1 medium tomato, coarsely chopped
- 1 envelope LIPTON® Recipe Secrets Onion, Onion-Mushroom or Beefy Mushroom Recipe Soup Mix
- 1 cup water
- ½ teaspoon thyme leaves
- ⅛ teaspoon pepper

In large skillet, heat oil and brown steaks over medium-high heat. Remove steaks. Reduce heat to medium; into skillet, add peppers and garlic and cook 5 minutes or until peppers are crisp-tender. Stir in tomato, then onion recipe soup mix blended with water, thyme and pepper; bring to a boil. Return steaks to skillet and simmer uncovered, stirring sauce occasionally, 25 minutes or until steaks and vegetables are tender.
Makes about 4 servings.

Pork Steaks with Peppers

Roasted Leg of Lamb with Lemon-Rosemary Glaze

- 5- to 6-pound leg of lamb
- 6 large cloves garlic, halved
- 4 large sprigs fresh rosemary, torn into pieces*
- ½ teaspoon pepper
- ¼ cup butter or margarine, melted
- 1 can (6 ounces) frozen lemonade concentrate, partially thawed and undiluted
- 1 envelope LIPTON® Recipe Secrets Onion or Onion-Mushroom Recipe Soup Mix

Preheat oven to 325°.

In roasting pan, place lamb fat side up. With knife, make several 1-inch-deep cuts in lamb; stuff cuts with garlic and ½ of the rosemary. Sprinkle with pepper, then drizzle with butter. Roast 1 hour or until meat thermometer reaches 140°.

Meanwhile, in small bowl, blend lemonade concentrate, onion recipe soup mix and remaining rosemary. Pour over lamb, then continue roasting, basting occasionally, 30 minutes or until thermometer reaches 145°.

Remove lamb to serving platter and keep warm. Skim fat from pan drippings and serve pan juices with lamb. Garnish, if desired, with additional rosemary and lemon slices.
Makes about 10 servings.

*Substitution: Use 1 tablespoon dried rosemary leaves.

Grilled Smoked Sausage

- 1 cup apricot or pineapple preserves
- 1 tablespoon lemon juice
- 1½ pounds smoked sausage

In small suacepan, heat preserves. Strain; reserve fruit pieces. Combine strained preserve liquid with lemon juice. Grill whole sausage, on uncovered grill, over low **KINGSFORD® Charcoal Briquets** 5 minutes. Brush with glaze; grill sausage about 5 minutes longer, turning and brushing with glaze occasionally. Garnish with fruit pieces.
Makes 6 servings.

Apricot-Stuffed Lamb Chops

- 4 double loin lamb chops, 2 inches thick (about 2 pounds)
- 4 dried apricots, halved
- 1 envelope LIPTON® Recipe Secrets Onion or Onion-Mushroom Recipe Soup Mix
- 1 cup water
- ¼ cup olive or vegetable oil
- ¼ cup honey
- 2 tablespoons Dijon-style prepared mustard
- 2 teaspoons rosemary leaves
- ½ teaspoon ground ginger

With knife parallel to cutting board, make a 1-inch-wide by 1-inch-deep cut in meaty side of each chop. Stuff each cut with 2 apricot halves; press firmly to close.

In shallow glass baking dish, combine remaining ingredients; add chops and turn to coat. Cover and marinate in refrigerator, turning occasionally, at least 2 hours.

Preheat oven to 425°. Bake chops with marinade, basting and turning chops occasionally, 35 minutes or until meat thermometer reaches 145° (rare), 155° (medium) or 165° (well done).
Makes about 4 servings.

Tasty Pork Ragout

Greek Lamb Sauté with Mostaccioli

½ (1-pound) package
   CREAMETTE®
   Mostaccioli, uncooked
1 medium green bell pepper,
   chopped
1 medium onion, chopped
1 medium eggplant, peeled,
   seeded and cut into
   1-inch cubes
2 cloves garlic, finely
   chopped
1 tablespoon olive or
   vegetable oil
½ pound lean boneless lamb,
   cut into ¾-inch cubes
2 fresh tomatoes, pared,
   seeded and chopped
¼ teaspoon ground nutmeg
¼ cup grated Parmesan
   cheese

Prepare mostaccioli as package directs; drain. In large skillet, cook and stir green pepper, onion, eggplant and garlic in oil until tender-crisp. Add lamb; cook until tender. Stir in tomatoes and nutmeg; heat through. Toss meat mixture with hot cooked mostaccioli and Parmesan cheese. Serve immediately. Refrigerate leftovers.   *Makes 8 servings*

Lime-Basted Lamb Kabobs

Lime-Herb Marinade
¾ cup lime juice
   (about 6 limes)
¼ cup olive or vegetable oil
⅓ cup sugar
1 teaspoon dried cilantro
   leaves
1 teaspoon fresh or dried
   rosemary
1 clove garlic, minced
½ teaspoon black pepper

Lamb Kabobs
1½ to 2 pounds trimmed lamb,
   cut into 1¼-inch cubes
1 package (10 ounces) pearl
   onions, blanched and
   peeled
4 fresh California peaches,
   halved, pitted
½ cup nonfat plain yogurt
   (optional)

In large zip-top plastic bag, combine marinade ingredients. Reserve 3 tablespoons marinade. Add lamb and pearl onions; close bag securely. Refrigerate 30 minutes, turning bag every 10 minutes. Remove lamb and onions, reserving marinade for basting. Thread lamb and onions alternately onto 4 to 6 skewers.

Cook kabobs on uncovered grill over medium, direct heat, turning frequently and brushing with marinade, about 16 minutes for medium rare, 20 minutes for medium and 24 minutes for well done. Brush peaches with marinade and place directly on grill during last 8 minutes, turning after 4 minutes.

Combine reserved 3 tablespoons marinade with yogurt, if desired. Serve as a sauce with lamb and peaches.
                    Makes 4 to 6 servings

Tips: To blanch onions, place whole onions in boiling water. Return to a boil and simmer about 6 minutes; drain and let stand until cool enough to handle. Trim stem end and skin will slip off easily.

If using wooden skewers, soak in water 20 minutes before grilling.

*Favorite recipe from **California Tree Fruit Agreement***

Tasty Pork Ragout

½ pound pork loin, cubed
1 small onion, cut into
   wedges
1 large clove garlic, pressed
½ teaspoon dried rosemary,
   crumbled
2 tablespoons margarine
   Salt and pepper to taste
1 chicken bouillon cube
½ cup boiling water
2 cups DOLE® Cauliflower
   florettes
1 cup sliced DOLE® Carrots
1 cup hot cooked rice

- In 10-inch skillet, sauté pork, onion, garlic and rosemary in margarine over medium-high heat until pork is browned; turn once. Sprinkle with salt and pepper to taste.

- Dissolve bouillon in water in cup; stir into pork mixture. Reduce heat. Cover; simmer 20 minutes.

- Add cauliflower and carrots. Cover; simmer 5 minutes longer or until tender-crisp. Serve over rice. *Makes 2 servings*

Preparation Time: 10 minutes
Cook Time: 30 minutes

Pork 'n' Spicy Apples

- ¼ cup **HEINZ®** 57 Sauce
- ¼ cup **apple jelly**
- ¼ cup **apple juice**
- 1 teaspoon **cornstarch**
- ⅛ teaspoon **ground cinnamon**
  Dash **ground allspice**
- 1 pound **boneless pork loin**
- ¼ cup **all-purpose flour**
- ¼ teaspoon **salt**
- ⅛ teaspoon **pepper**
- 1 tablespoon **vegetable oil**
- 2 large **Granny Smith or Golden Delicious apples, peeled, quartered, sliced ½ inch thick**
- 1 tablespoon **butter or margarine**

In small bowl, combine 57 Sauce, jelly, apple juice, cornstarch, cinnamon and allspice; set aside. Cut pork into 4 slices; flatten each slice to ¼-inch thickness. In small bowl, combine flour, salt and pepper. Dust pork lightly with flour mixture. In large skillet, sauté pork in oil until cooked, about 3 minutes on each side; remove and keep warm. In same skillet, sauté apples in butter 2 to 3 minutes; remove. Pour 57 Sauce mixture into skillet; heat, stirring constantly, until jelly is melted and sauce is thickened. Return apples to skillet; heat through. Spoon apples and sauce over pork.
Makes 4 servings

Pork Loin Roulade

- 4 **boneless center pork loin slices, about 1 pound**
- ½ **red bell pepper, cut into strips**
- ½ **green bell pepper, cut into strips**
- 1 teaspoon **vegetable oil**
- ⅔ cup **orange juice**
- ⅔ cup **bottled barbecue sauce**
- 1 tablespoon **prepared Dijon-style mustard**

Place pork slices between 2 pieces of plastic wrap. Pound with mallet to about ¼-inch thickness.

Place several red and green pepper strips crosswise on each pork portion; roll up jelly-roll style. Secure rolls with wooden toothpicks.

In nonstick skillet, brown pork rolls in vegetable oil. Drain fat from pan. Combine orange juice, barbecue sauce and mustard; add to skillet. Bring mixture to boiling; reduce heat. Cover and simmer 10 to 12 minutes or until pork is tender. Remove toothpicks to serve.
Makes 4 servings

Preparation Time: 20 minutes
Cooking Time: 12 minutes

Favorite recipe from **National Pork Producers Council**

Pork Loin Roulade

Citrus & Spice Pork Loin Roast

- **1 package (1.25 ounces) LAWRY'S® Taco Spices & Seasonings**
- **¾ cup orange marmalade**
- **½ teaspoon LAWRY'S® Garlic Powder with Parsley**
- **1 (3-pound) boneless pork loin roast**

In small bowl, combine Taco Spices & Seasonings, orange marmalade and Garlic Powder with Parsley; blend well. Score pork roast with sharp knife. Place pork roast in large resealable plastic bag and cover with marmalade mixture. Marinate in refrigerator 45 minutes. Remove pork; wrap in foil and place in baking dish. Bake in 350°F oven 1 hour. Open and fold back foil; bake 30 minutes longer or until roast is glazed and internal temperature reaches 170°F on a meat thermometer. Cool 10 minutes before slicing.

Makes 6 servings

Presentation: Slice pork thinly and serve drippings that remain in foil as a flavorful gravy. Garnish with parsley and orange peel, if desired.

Honey Mustard Pork Tenderloin

- **¼ cup vegetable oil**
- **2 tablespoons brown sugar**
- **2 tablespoons honey**
- **2 tablespoons REALEMON® Lemon Juice from Concentrate**
- **1 tablespoon Dijon-style mustard**
- **2 teaspoons WYLER'S® or STEERO® Beef-Flavor or Chicken-Flavor Instant Bouillon**
- **1 (¾- to 1-pound) pork tenderloin**

In large shallow dish or plastic bag, combine all ingredients except tenderloin. Add tenderloin. Cover; marinate in refrigerator 6 hours or overnight. Remove tenderloin from marinade. Grill or broil 30 to 35 minutes or until meat thermometer inserted in center reaches 160°, basting frequently with heated marinade. Refrigerate leftovers.

Makes 2 to 4 servings

Dilled Pork Scallopini

- **1 pound pork tenderloin All-purpose flour**
- **1 egg, slightly beaten**
- **1 tablespoon water**
- **½ cup seasoned dry bread crumbs**
- **2 tablespoons butter or margarine**
- **1 medium carrot, cut into julienne strips**
- **1 jar (12 ounces) HEINZ® HomeStyle Brown Gravy**
- **3 tablespoons half-and-half or milk**
- **1 teaspoon lemon juice**
- **½ teaspoon dried dill weed**
- **1 tablespoon dairy sour cream**

Cut pork crosswise into 12 slices; flatten to ¼-inch thickness. Dust pork lightly with flour. In shallow dish, combine egg and water. Dip pork into egg mixture, then coat with crumbs. In large skillet, sauté pork in butter, a few pieces at a time, about 3 minutes on each side or until golden brown, adding more butter if necessary. Keep pork warm while preparing sauce. For sauce, sauté carrot in same skillet until tender-crisp, 1 to 2 minutes. Stir in gravy, half-and-half, lemon juice and dill; heat through. Stir sour cream into sauce just before serving. Spoon sauce over pork.

Makes 4 servings (about 1¾ cups sauce)

Pork Tenderloin Waldorf

- **2 pork tenderloins (about 1½ pounds)**
- **¾ cup BAMA® Apple Jelly**
- **¼ cup REALEMON® Lemon Juice from Concentrate**
- **¼ cup soy sauce**
- **¼ cup vegetable oil**
- **1 tablespoon finely chopped fresh ginger root**
- **1 cup chopped apple**
- **1 cup fresh bread crumbs (2 slices)**
- **¼ cup finely chopped celery**
- **¼ cup chopped pecans**

Partially slit tenderloins lengthwise, being careful not to cut all the way through; arrange in shallow dish. In small saucepan, combine jelly, ReaLemon® brand, soy sauce, oil and ginger; cook and stir until jelly melts. Reserving *3 tablespoons* jelly mixture, pour remainder over meat. Cover; marinate in refrigerator 4 hours or overnight. Place meat in shallow baking pan. Combine apple, crumbs, celery, nuts and reserved jelly mixture. Spread slits open; fill with apple mixture. Bake 30 minutes in preheated 375° oven. Loosely cover meat, bake 10 minutes longer or until meat thermometer reaches 160°. Refrigerate leftovers.

Makes 4 to 6 servings

From top to bottom: Sweet & Sour Meatballs (page 162) and Pork Tenderloin Waldorf

Pork Roast with Corn Bread & Oyster Stuffing

1 (5- to 7-pound) pork loin roast*
2 tablespoons butter or margarine
1/2 cup chopped onion
1/2 cup chopped celery
2 cloves garlic, minced
1/2 teaspoon fennel seeds, crushed
1 teaspoon TABASCO® pepper sauce
1/2 teaspoon salt
2 cups packaged corn bread stuffing mix
1 can (8 ounces) oysters, undrained, chopped

Preheat oven to 325°F. Make a deep slit in back of each chop on pork loin. In large saucepan melt butter; add onion, celery, garlic and fennel. Cook 5 minutes or until vegetables are tender; stir in Tabasco® sauce and salt. Add corn bread, oysters and oyster liquid; toss to mix well.

Stuff corn bread mixture into slits in pork. (Any leftover stuffing may be baked in covered baking dish during last 30 minutes of roasting.) Place meat in shallow roasting pan. Cook 30 to 35 minutes per pound or until meat thermometer inserted into meat registers 170°F. Remove to heated serving platter. Allow meat to stand 15 minutes before serving.
Makes 10 to 12 servings.

*Have butcher crack backbone of pork loin roast.

Cider-Glazed Pork Roast

1/2 cup apple cider
1/4 cup Dijon-style mustard
1/4 cup vegetable oil
1/4 cup soy sauce
1 boneless pork loin roast (4 to 5 pounds), tied

In small bowl, combine apple cider, mustard, oil and soy sauce. Insert meat thermometer in center of thickest part of roast. Arrange medium-hot **KINGSFORD® Charcoal Briquets** around drip pan. Place roast over drip pan. Cover grill and cook 2½ to 3 hours or until meat thermometer registers 170°F, adding more briquets as necessary. Brush roast with cider mixture 3 or 4 times during last 30 minutes of cooking.
Makes 6 servings.

Glazed Pork Roast

1 (3-pound) boneless pork shoulder roast (Boston Butt)
1 cup KIKKOMAN® Teriyaki Sauce
3 tablespoons brown sugar, packed
3 tablespoons dry sherry
1 teaspoon minced fresh ginger root
1 clove garlic, minced
1/4 cup water
2 tablespoons sugar
1 tablespoon cornstarch

Microwave Directions: Pierce meaty parts of roast with fork; place in large plastic bag. Combine teriyaki sauce, brown sugar, sherry, ginger and garlic; pour over roast. Press air out of bag; tie top securely. Refrigerate 8 hours or overnight, turning bag over occasionally. Reserving marinade, remove roast and place, fat side down, in 8×8-inch shallow microwave-safe dish. Brush thoroughly with reserved marinade. Cover roast loosely with waxed paper. Microwave on Medium-high (70%) 30 minutes, or until meat thermometer inserted into thickest part registers 165°F., rotating dish once and brushing with marinade. Remove roast; let stand 10 minutes before slicing. Meanwhile, combine reserved marinade, water, sugar and cornstarch in 2-cup microwave-safe measuring cup. Microwave on High 3 minutes, until mixture boils and thickens, stirring occasionally. Serve teriyaki glaze with roast.
Makes 6 servings.

Herb-Marinated Pork Roast

3½- to 4-pound bone-in pork loin roast
1 small onion, chopped
1/2 cup CRISCO® Oil
3 tablespoons cider vinegar
1 tablespoon lemon juice
1 teaspoon dried oregano leaves
2 cloves garlic, minced
1/2 teaspoon dried rosemary leaves
1/4 teaspoon dried dill weed
1/4 teaspoon salt
1/4 teaspoon pepper

Place roast in large bowl or large heavy plastic food storage bag. Blend remaining ingredients. Pour over roast. Cover dish or seal bag. Refrigerate 8 hours or overnight, turning roast over occasionally.

Preheat oven to 325°F. Remove roast from marinade. Discard marinade. Place roast in roasting pan. Roast at 325°F, 2 to 3 hours, or until internal temperature registers 170°F. Let stand 15 minutes before carving.
6 to 8 servings.

Pork Roast with Corn Bread & Oyster Stuffing

Pork Roast with Sausage & Spinach Stuffing

Cranberry Glazed Pork Roast

1 (3½- to 4-pound) boneless pork loin roast
Salt and pepper
1 (16-ounce) can whole berry cranberry sauce
¼ cup REALEMON® Lemon Juice from Concentrate
3 tablespoons brown sugar
1 teaspoon cornstarch

Preheat oven to 450°. Place meat in shallow baking dish; season with salt and pepper. Roast 20 minutes. Reduce oven temperature to 325°; continue roasting. Meanwhile, in small saucepan, combine remaining ingredients. Over medium heat, cook and stir until slightly thickened, about 5 minutes. After meat has cooked 1 hour, drain off fat; spoon half of the sauce over meat. Continue roasting 1 to 1½ hours or until meat thermometer reaches 170°, basting occasionally. Spoon remaining sauce over meat; return to oven 10 to 15 minutes. Let stand 10 minutes before slicing. Refrigerate leftovers.
To Make Gravy: In small saucepan, combine meat drippings and 2 tablespoons cornstarch. Over medium heat, cook and stir until thickened. *Makes about 2 cups.*

Pork Roast with Sausage & Spinach Stuffing

1 envelope LIPTON® Recipe Secrets Onion, Onion-Mushroom or Beefy Mushroom Recipe Soup Mix
1 package (10 ounces) frozen chopped spinach, cooked and drained
½ pound sweet Italian sausage links, removed from casing
½ cup fresh bread crumbs
½ cup slivered almonds, toasted
2 eggs, slightly beaten
2 tablespoons finely chopped parsley
2 teaspoons thyme leaves
1 teaspoon finely chopped garlic (about 1 medium clove)
⅛ teaspoon pepper
2½- pound boneless center cut pork loin roast
1 to 2 tablespoons oil

Preheat oven to 350°.

In large bowl, thoroughly combine onion recipe soup mix, spinach, sausage, bread crumbs, almonds, eggs, parsley, 1 teaspoon thyme, ½ teaspoon garlic and pepper; set aside.

Butterfly roast as directed. Spread spinach mixture evenly on cut side of roast. Roll, starting at long end, jelly-roll style; tie securely with string. In roasting pan, on rack, place pork seam side down. Rub roast with oil, then top with remaining garlic and thyme. Roast for 1½ hours or until meat thermometer reaches 165° (medium) or 180° (well done).
Makes about 8 servings.

How to Butterfly a Pork Loin Roast:
1. Place the boneless roast fat side down. Starting at the thickest edge, slice horizontally through the meat, stopping 1 inch from the opposite edge so that the roast can open like a book.
2. Lightly pound the opened roast and remove any fat thicker than ¼ inch.

Satay Pork

½ cup peanut or vegetable oil
¼ cup soy sauce
2 tablespoons chopped peanuts
1 tablespoon Worcestershire sauce
1 tablespoon chopped onion
2 cloves garlic, crushed
2 teaspoons brown sugar
¼ teaspoon curry powder
⅛ teaspoon coriander
3 pounds boneless pork, cut into ½-inch cubes

In shallow glass dish, combine all ingredients except pork. Add pork, turning to coat with marinade. Cover and refrigerate 1 to 2 hours, stirring occasionally. Drain pork; reserve marinade. Thread pork on skewers. Grill kabobs, on uncovered grill, over hot **KINGSFORD® Charcoal Briquets** 5 to 6 minutes or until cooked through, turning often and basting with marinade.
Makes 4 to 6 servings.

Tofu & Vegetable Stir-Fry

Crispy Fried Pork and Apples

6 butterflied pork chops, ½ inch thick
1 large apple, peeled and cored
2 eggs
2 tablespoons half-and-half
1 cup unseasoned dry bread crumbs
1 teaspoon ground ginger
¾ teaspoon salt
½ teaspoon ground coriander (optional)
¼ teaspoon ground allspice
CRISCO® Oil for frying

Pound each chop with meat mallet. Slice apple into 6 rings. Blend eggs and half-and-half in small mixing bowl. Mix bread crumbs, ginger, salt, coriander (optional) and allspice in shallow dish or on sheet of waxed paper. Set aside.

Heat 2 to 3 inches Crisco® Oil in deep-fryer or large saucepan to 350°F. Dip pork and apple rings in egg mixture, then in bread crumb mixture to coat. Fry 2 pieces of pork at a time, 5 to 7 minutes, or until crust is deep golden brown and pork is no longer pink in center. Drain on paper towels. Fry apple rings 2 to 3 minutes, or until deep golden brown. Drain on paper towels.
6 servings.

Tofu & Vegetable Stir-Fry

½ block tofu
1 pound napa (Chinese cabbage) or romaine lettuce*
½ cup water
2 tablespoons cornstarch, divided
4 tablespoons KIKKOMAN® Soy Sauce, divided
¼ pound boneless lean pork
2 teaspoons minced fresh ginger root
1 clove garlic, minced
½ teaspoon sugar
2 tablespoons vegetable oil, divided
1 medium onion, chunked
2 medium tomatoes, chunked

Cut tofu into ½-inch cubes; drain well on several layers of paper towels. Separate and rinse cabbage; pat dry. Cut leaves crosswise into 1-inch strips; set aside. Blend water, 1 tablespoon cornstarch and 3 tablespoons soy sauce; set aside. Cut pork into thin slices, then into thin strips. Combine remaining 1 tablespoon cornstarch and 1 tablespoon soy sauce, ginger, garlic and sugar in small bowl; stir in pork. Heat 1 tablespoon oil in hot wok or large skillet over high heat. Add pork and stir-fry 2 minutes; remove. Heat remaining 1 tablespoon oil in same pan. Add onion; stir-fry 2 minutes. Add cabbage; stir-fry 1 minute. Add tomatoes, pork and soy sauce mixture. Cook and stir gently until sauce boils and thickens. Gently fold in tofu; heat through.
Makes 4 servings.
*If using romaine, increase water to ⅔ cup.

Pineapple Citrus Glazed Pork Roast

1 boneless pork loin roast (3 to 4 pounds)
Garlic salt
Pepper
1 can (20 ounces) DOLE® Crushed Pineapple in Juice
1 cup orange juice
½ cup lemon juice
¼ cup sugar
2 tablespoons cornstarch
1 tablespoon grated orange peel
1 tablespoon grated lemon peel
2 teaspoons dried mint, crushed

Preheat oven to 400°F. Place pork on rack in shallow roasting pan, fat side up. Sprinkle pork with garlic salt and pepper to taste. Insert meat thermometer. Roast in preheated oven, uncovered, 30 minutes. Reduce oven to 325°F and roast 30 minutes longer.

In saucepan, combine undrained pineapple, orange and lemon juices, sugar and cornstarch. Cook, stirring, until mixture boils and thickens. Stir in orange peel, lemon peel and mint. Spread half of glaze over pork after 1 hour of roasting. Continue roasting and baste with glaze every 30 minutes until thermometer reaches 170°F (about 2 hours total cooking time). Remove pork to serving platter. Let stand 15 minutes before slicing. Serve with remaining glaze.
Makes 8 servings.

Hunan Pork Stir-Fry

½ pound boneless lean pork
2 teaspoons cornstarch
6 teaspoons KIKKOMAN® Lite Soy Sauce, divided
2 cloves garlic, minced and divided
¾ cup water
1 tablespoon cornstarch
⅛ to ¼ teaspoon crushed red pepper
3 tablespoons vegetable oil, divided
3 cups bite-size cauliflowerets
1 medium-size green pepper, chunked
2 medium tomatoes, cut into eighths
Hot cooked rice

Cut pork across grain into thin slices, then into strips. Combine 2 teaspoons *each* cornstarch and lite soy sauce with ½ of the garlic in small bowl; stir in pork. Let stand 30 minutes. Meanwhile, combine water, 1 tablespoon cornstarch, remaining 4 teaspoons lite soy sauce and red pepper; set aside. Heat 1 tablespoon oil in hot wok or large skillet over high heat. Add pork and stir-fry 2 minutes; remove. Heat remaining 2 tablespoons oil in same pan over medium-high heat. Add cauliflowerets and remaining garlic; stir-fry 2 minutes. Add green pepper; stir-fry 3 minutes. Stir in tomatoes, pork and soy sauce mixture. Cook and stir gently until sauce boils and thickens. Serve with rice.
Makes 2 to 3 servings.

Crown Roast of Pork with Cognac Glaze

1 cup orange juice
1 jar (12 ounces) red currant or grape jelly
1 envelope LIPTON® Recipe Secrets Onion or Onion-Mushroom Recipe Soup Mix
½ cup Cognac or brandy
½ teaspoon ground ginger
8- to 9-pound crown roast of pork (about 22 ribs)
Warm Dried Fruit Compote (recipe follows)

Preheat oven to 200°.

In medium saucepan, heat orange juice, jelly, onion recipe soup mix, Cognac and ginger over low heat, stirring occasionally, 5 minutes or until jelly is melted.

In roasting pan, place crown roast; brush with jelly glaze, then pour remaining glaze over roast. Loosely cover with heavy-duty aluminum foil; roast 2 hours. Increase heat to 350° and continue roasting, basting occasionally, an additional 1½ hours or until meat thermometer reaches 175°. Remove foil and continue roasting, basting occasionally and adding water if needed, 20 minutes or until thermometer reaches 180°.

Remove roast to serving platter and keep warm. Skim fat from pan drippings and serve pan juices with roast. Spoon Warm Dried Fruit Compote into center cavity and around roast.
Makes about 12 servings.

WARM DRIED FRUIT COMPOTE: In large saucepan, combine 2 cups dried apricots, 2 cups pitted dried prunes, 12 dried figs, halved,* 2 cups orange juice, 2 tablespoons fresh squeezed lemon juice, 3 cinnamon sticks and 1 teaspoon whole cloves. Bring to a boil, then simmer 5 minutes. Stir in 1 cup green or red seedless grapes and simmer 2 minutes or until heated through. Remove cinnamon.
Makes about 8 cups.

***Substitution:** Use 2 packages (11 ounces each) pitted mixed dried fruit instead of apricots, prunes and figs.

Make-Ahead Directions for Compote: Compote can be prepared up to 2 days ahead. Simply combine as above; bring to a boil, then simmer 5 minutes. Cover and refrigerate. Just before serving, heat through; stir in grapes, then continue as above.

Colorful Stir-Fried Pork

⅓ cup KIKKOMAN® Stir-Fry Sauce
1 teaspoon distilled white vinegar
¼ to ½ teaspoon crushed red pepper
¾ pound boneless lean pork
1 tablespoon KIKKOMAN® Stir-Fry Sauce
3 tablespoons vegetable oil, divided
2 medium carrots, cut into julienne strips
1 medium onion, halved and sliced
¼ pound fresh snow peas, trimmed and cut lengthwise in half

Combine ⅓ cup stir-fry sauce, vinegar and red pepper; set aside. Cut pork across grain into thin slices, then into strips; coat with 1 tablespoon stir-fry sauce. Heat 1 tablespoon oil in hot wok or large skillet over high heat. Add pork and stir-fry 2 minutes; remove. Heat remaining 2 tablespoons oil in same pan. Add carrots, onion and snow peas; stir-fry 4 minutes. Stir in pork and stir-fry sauce mixture. Cook and stir just until pork and vegetables are coated with sauce. Serve immediately.
Makes 4 servings.

Hawaiian Roast Pork

1 (3-pound) boneless pork shoulder roast (Boston butt)
½ cup KIKKOMAN® Soy Sauce
1½ teaspoons liquid smoke seasoning

Cut pork in half lengthwise. Place halves in large plastic bag. Combine soy sauce and liquid smoke; pour over pork. Press air out of bag; tie top securely. Turn over several times to coat pieces well. Refrigerate 8 hours or overnight, turning bag over occasionally. Remove pork from marinade and place in shallow baking pan; cover with aluminum foil. Bake at 350°F. 30 minutes. Discard foil; turn pieces over. Bake 1 hour longer, or until meat thermometer inserted into thickest part registers 170°F. To serve, cut across grain into thin slices.
Makes 6 servings.

Colorful Stir-Fried Pork

Saucy Pork and Peppers

2 fresh limes
¼ cup 62%-less-sodium soy
    sauce
1 teaspoon oregano leaves
½ teaspoon thyme leaves
    Dash cayenne pepper
4 cloves garlic, crushed
2 to 3 fresh parsley sprigs
1 bay leaf
1 pound pork tenderloin,
    trimmed and cut into
    1-inch cubes
1 tablespoon olive oil
1 teaspoon brown sugar
2 medium onions, each cut
    into 8 pieces
2 medium tomatoes, each cut
    into 8 pieces and seeded
1 large red bell pepper, cut
    into 8 pieces
1 large green bell pepper, cut
    into 8 pieces

Squeeze juice from limes,
reserving peel. In small bowl,
combine lime juice, lime peel, soy
sauce, oregano, thyme, cayenne
pepper, garlic, parsley and bay
leaf; blend well. Place pork cubes
in plastic bag or non-metal bowl.
Pour lime mixture over pork,

Saucy Pork and Peppers

turning to coat. Seal bag or cover
dish; marinate at least 2 hours or
overnight in refrigerator,
turning pork several times.

Remove lime peel, parsley sprigs
and bay leaf from marinade;
discard. Remove pork from
marinade, reserving marinade.
Drain pork well. Heat oil in
large skillet over high heat. Add
brown sugar; stir until sugar is
dissolved. Add pork cubes; cook
and stir about 5 minutes or until
pork is browned. Reduce heat to
low. Add onions, tomatoes, bell
peppers and reserved marinade;
simmer 10 to 15 minutes or until
pork is tender.
                    Makes 4 servings

*Favorite recipe from **National Pork
Producers Council***

Pork Valenciana

1½ pounds boneless pork loin,
    cut into ¾-inch cubes
2 tablespoons olive oil,
    divided
2 yellow onions, peeled and
    chopped
1 green pepper, seeded and
    chopped
2 cloves garlic, minced
1 8-ounce can whole
    tomatoes, undrained
½ teaspoon salt
1 bay leaf
¼ teaspoon pepper
4 cups water
2 cups uncooked rice
2 chicken bouillon cubes
½ cup sherry (optional)
⅛ teaspoon saffron threads
1 cup peas
1 small jar pimientos, drained
12 green olives

Brown pork in 1 tablespoon of
the oil over medium-high heat;
remove. Add onions, green
pepper, garlic and remaining 1
tablespoon oil. Continue cooking
until slightly brown, about 5
minutes. Return pork to pan and
stir in tomatoes, salt, bay leaf
and pepper. Add water, rice,
bouillon and sherry. Dissolve
saffron in small amount of water

and add to pan. Bring to boil;
cover and simmer over low heat
15 minutes. Remove bay leaf.
Garnish with peas, pimientos
and olives.   *Makes 8 servings*

Preparation Time: 15 minutes
Cooking Time: 20 minutes

*Favorite recipe from **National Pork
Producers Council***

Spicy-Sweet Pineapple Pork

1 pound pork loin, cut into
    ½-inch strips or cubes
¾ cup LAWRY'S® Fajitas
    Skillet Sauce
1 tablespoon finely chopped
    fresh ginger
2 tablespoons vegetable oil
1 green bell pepper, cut into
    chunks
3 green onions, diagonally
    sliced into 1-inch pieces
1 cup hot salsa
3 tablespoons brown sugar
2 tablespoons cornstarch
2 cans (8 ounces each)
    pineapple chunks in juice
½ cup whole cashews

Place pork in large resealable
plastic bag. Combine Fajitas
Skillet Sauce and ginger; add to
pork and marinate in
refrigerator 1 hour. In large
skillet or wok, heat 1 tablespoon
oil. Add bell pepper and green
onions and stir-fry 3 minutes;
remove and set aside. Add pork
and remaining 1 tablespoon oil to
skillet; stir-fry 5 minutes or until
just browned. Return bell pepper
and green onions to skillet. In
small bowl, combine salsa, brown
sugar, cornstarch and juice from
one can pineapple. Add to skillet;
cook until thickened, stirring
constantly. Drain remaining can
pineapple. Add all pineapple
chunks and cashews; simmer 5
minutes.   *Makes 6 servings*

Presentation: Serve over hot
fluffy rice.

Pork Satay

- **1 pound boneless stir-fry pork strips**
- **3 tablespoons REALEMON® Lemon Juice from Concentrate**
- **2 tablespoons peanut butter**
- **2 tablespoons soy sauce**
- **1 tablespoon brown sugar**
- **1 tablespoon vegetable oil**
- **2 cloves garlic, finely chopped**
- **¼ teaspoon crushed red pepper**
- **Peanut Dipping Sauce**

Arrange meat in shallow dish. In small bowl, combine ReaLemon® brand, peanut butter, soy sauce, sugar, oil, garlic and red pepper; mix well. Pour over meat. Cover; marinate in refrigerator 4 hours or overnight, turning occasionally. Thread meat on skewers. Grill or broil as desired, brushing frequently with marinade. Serve with warm Peanut Dipping Sauce. Refrigerate leftovers.

Makes 4 servings

PEANUT DIPPING SAUCE: In small saucepan, combine ½ cup COCO LOPEZ® Cream of Coconut, 3 tablespoons peanut butter, 2 tablespoons ReaLemon® Lemon Juice from Concentrate, 2 tablespoons soy sauce and ¼ teaspoon crushed red pepper; mix well. Cook and stir until peanut butter melts and mixture boils. Reduce heat; simmer uncovered 5 minutes, stirring occasionally.

Makes about ¾ cup

Mu Shu-Style Fajitas

Mu Shu-Style Fajitas

- **1 tablespoon IMPERIAL® Margarine**
- **2 eggs, beaten**
- **¼ teaspoon LAWRY'S® Garlic Powder with Parsley**
- **1 medium carrot, diagonally cut into thin slices**
- **2 tablespoons vegetable oil**
- **1 pound boneless pork, cut into thin strips**
- **1 cup LAWRY'S® Fajitas Skillet Sauce**
- **2 cups shredded cabbage**
- **1 cup sliced fresh mushrooms**
- **1 can (8 ounces) sliced bamboo shoots, drained**
- **6 medium green onions, diagonally cut into 1-inch pieces**
- **1 teaspoon lemon juice**
- **8 medium flour tortillas, warmed**

In large skillet, melt margarine and scramble eggs with Garlic Powder with Parsley; remove and set aside. In same skillet, sauté carrot in 1 tablespoon oil until crisp-tender; remove and set aside. In same skillet, brown pork in remaining 1 tablespoon oil; drain fat. Add Fajitas Skillet Sauce; blend well. Bring to a boil; reduce heat and simmer, uncovered, 3 to 5 minutes. Add eggs, carrots and remaining ingredients except tortillas; heat 2 minutes until vegetables are crisp-tender. Serve piping hot mixture wrapped in warm flour tortillas. *Makes 8 servings*

Presentation: Serve with plum sauce, if desired.

Hint: Also works well with boneless, skinless chicken breast strips.

Sesame Pork with Broccoli

1 can (14½ ounces) chicken broth
2 tablespoons cornstarch
1 tablespoon soy sauce
4 green onions and tops, finely diced
1 pound pork tenderloin, trimmed
1 tablespoon vegetable oil
1 clove garlic, minced
1½ pounds fresh broccoli, cut into bite-size pieces (about 7 cups)
2 tablespoons sliced pimiento, drained
2 tablespoons sesame seed, lightly toasted

In small bowl, combine chicken broth, cornstarch and soy sauce; blend well. Stir in green onions; set aside. Cut pork tenderloin lengthwise into quarters; cut each quarter into bite-size pieces. Heat oil in wok or heavy skillet over medium-high heat. Add pork and garlic; stir-fry 3 to 4 minutes or until pork is tender. Remove pork; keep warm. Add broccoli and broth mixture to wok. Cover and simmer over low heat 8 minutes. Add cooked pork and pimiento; cook just until mixture is hot, stirring frequently. Sprinkle with sesame seed. Serve immediately.
Makes 6 servings

*Favorite recipe from **National Pork Producers Council***

Oriental Fried Rice

3 cups cooked brown rice, cold
½ cup slivered cooked roast pork
½ cup finely chopped celery
½ cup bean sprouts*
⅓ cup sliced green onions
1 egg, beaten
Vegetable cooking spray
¼ teaspoon black pepper
2 tablespoons soy sauce

Combine rice, pork, celery, bean sprouts, onions, and egg in large skillet coated with cooking spray. Cook, stirring, 3 minutes over high heat. Add pepper and soy sauce. Cook, stirring, 1 minute longer.   *Makes 6 servings*

To microwave: Combine rice, pork, celery, bean sprouts, and onions in shallow 2-quart microproof baking dish coated with cooking spray. Cook on HIGH 2 to 3 minutes. Add egg, pepper, and soy sauce. Cook on HIGH 1 to 2 minutes or until egg is set, stirring to separate grains.

*Substitute canned bean sprouts, rinsed and drained, for the fresh bean sprouts, if desired.

Tip: When preparing fried rice always begin with cold rice. The grains separate better if cold and it's a great way to use leftover rice.

*Favorite recipe from **USA Rice Council***

Gingered Beef

1 pound boneless beef sirloin steak, cut ½ inch thick
⅓ cup diagonally sliced celery
1 small red bell pepper, cut into strips
1 to 2 teaspoons grated fresh gingerroot
2 tablespoons vegetable oil, divided
1 cup sliced fresh mushrooms
1 cup snow pea pods
1 jar (12 ounces) HEINZ® HomeStyle Brown Gravy
⅓ cup sliced water chestnuts
4 green onions, cut into ½-inch lengths
1 tablespoon soy sauce
Hot cooked rice

Cut steak across the grain into ⅛-inch strips; set aside. In preheated large skillet or wok, stir-fry celery, red pepper and gingerroot in 1 tablespoon oil 1 minute. Add mushrooms and snow peas and stir-fry 1 to 2 minutes longer or until vegetables are tender-crisp; remove. Stir-fry beef in remaining 1 tablespoon oil. Add gravy, water chestnuts, green onions and soy sauce. Return vegetables to skillet; heat through. Serve over rice.
Makes 4 servings (about 5 cups)

Chop Suey

¼ cup flour
2 teaspoons salt
½ pound cubed veal
½ pound cubed pork
⅓ cup CRISCO® Shortening
1 cup chopped onion
1 cup celery, cut into 1-inch pieces
1 cup beef stock or bouillon
½ cup soy sauce
2 tablespoons molasses
1 can (16 ounces) bean sprouts, drained
Hot cooked rice

Combine flour and salt in large plastic food storage bag; add meat cubes and toss lightly to coat. Brown in hot Crisco® in Dutch oven; add onion and continue browning. Stir in celery, beef stock, soy sauce and molasses. Cover and cook over low heat for 25 minutes. Add bean sprouts; cook 15 minutes more. Thicken with additional flour, if necessary. Serve over hot cooked rice. Refrigerate leftovers.
Makes 4 to 6 servings

Sesame Pork with Broccoli

Stuffed Pork Chops

Stuffed Pork Chops

**4 rib pork chops, cut
1¼ inches thick, slit for
stuffing
1½ cups prepared stuffing
1 tablespoon vegetable oil
Salt and pepper
1 bottle (12 ounces) HEINZ®
Chili Sauce**

Trim excess fat from chops. Place stuffing in pockets of chops; secure with wooden toothpicks or string. In large skillet, brown chops in oil; season with salt and pepper. Place chops in 2-quart oblong baking dish. Pour chili sauce over chops. Cover with foil; bake in 350°F oven, 30 minutes. Stir sauce; turn and baste chops. Cover; bake an additional 30 to 40 minutes or until chops are cooked. Remove toothpicks. Skim excess fat. Spoon sauce over chops.   *Makes 4 servings*

California Pork Cutlets

**2 firm, medium DOLE®
Bananas, peeled
2 teaspoons vegetable oil
4 pork cutlets, ¼ inch thick
½ teaspoon dried rosemary,
crumbled
Salt and pepper to taste
½ cup orange juice
½ teaspoon cornstarch
¼ cup DOLE® Raisins**

• Cut bananas in half crosswise, then lengthwise to make 8 slices. In 12-inch nonstick skillet, sauté bananas in hot oil over medium-high heat until lightly browned; turn once. Remove bananas.

Pork Strips Florentine

**1 pound boneless pork strips
1 package (6 ounces)
seasoned long grain and
wild rice mix, uncooked
1⅔ cups hot water
1 can (2.8 ounces) DURKEE®
French Fried Onions
¼ teaspoon DURKEE® Garlic
Powder
1 package (10 ounces) frozen
chopped spinach, thawed
and well drained
2 tablespoons diced
pimiento (optional)
½ cup (2 ounces) shredded
Swiss cheese**

Preheat oven to 375°F. In 8×12-inch baking dish, combine pork strips, rice, contents of rice seasoning packet, hot water, *½ can* Durkee® French Fried Onions and garlic powder. Bake, covered, for 30 minutes. Stir spinach and pimiento into meat mixture. Bake, covered, 10 minutes or until pork and rice are done. Top with cheese and remaining onions; bake, uncovered, 3 minutes or until onions are golden brown.
Makes 4 servings

- Sprinkle pork with rosemary, salt and pepper. In same skillet, sauté pork, 1 to 2 minutes on each side.

- Blend orange juice and cornstarch in cup. Stir into skillet. Add raisins. Heat to a boil. Reduce heat. Cover; simmer 5 minutes.

- Arrange bananas and 2 cutlets on 2 plates. Spoon sauce over top. *Makes 2 servings*

Preparation Time: 5 minutes
Cook Time: 10 minutes

Island Pork Chops

   1 can (8 ounces) pineapple
      chunks
   1 tablespoon cornstarch
   ⅔ cup HEINZ® Chili Sauce
   ⅓ cup raisins
   1 tablespoon brown sugar
   ⅛ teaspoon ground cinnamon
   4 boneless pork loin chops
      (½ inch thick, about
      5 ounces each)
   1 tablespoon vegetable oil
      Hot cooked couscous or
      rice

Drain pineapple, reserving juice. In medium bowl, blend juice with cornstarch; stir in pineapple, chili sauce, raisins, sugar and cinnamon and set aside. In large skillet, lightly brown pork in oil; drain excess fat. Pour pineapple mixture over pork. Cover; simmer 10 minutes or until pork is cooked. Serve pork and sauce with couscous.

Makes 4 servings
(about 2 cups sauce)

Pork Cutlets with Garden Vegetables

   1½ pounds pork cutlets
     2 teaspoons vegetable oil
   2½ cups peeled, chopped fresh
        tomatoes
     1 can (8 ounces) tomato
        sauce
   ½ cup chopped onion
   ¼ cup chopped fresh chiles
        or 4-ounce can diced
        green chiles
     1 clove garlic, minced
     2 tablespoons fresh lime
        juice
   ½ teaspoon salt
   ¼ teaspoon ground cumin
     1 cup julienne-cut carrots
     1 cup julienne-cut zucchini
   ¼ cup raisins
   ¼ cup slivered almonds

Heat oil in nonstick frying pan. Brown pork cutlets over medium-high heat. Stir in tomatoes, tomato sauce, onion, chiles, garlic, lime juice, salt and cumin. Cover; simmer 20 minutes. Stir in carrots, zucchini and raisins. Cover; simmer 10 minutes longer or until vegetables are tender. Stir in almonds. *Makes 6 servings*

Preparation Time: 15 minutes
Cooking Time: 30 minutes

*Favorite recipe from **National Pork Producers Council***

Island Pork Chops

Mandarin Pork Chops

Mandarin Pork Chops

    4 center-cut pork chops (about
      1 pound)
    1 tablespoon vegetable oil
    ½ cup orange juice
    ¼ cup water
    3 tablespoons brown sugar
    2 tablespoons REALEMON®
      Lemon Juice from
      Concentrate
    1 tablespoon cornstarch
    2 teaspoons WYLER'S® or
      STEERO® Chicken-Flavor
      Instant Bouillon
    1 (11-ounce) can mandarin
      orange segments, drained
    1 medium green pepper, sliced

In large skillet, brown chops in oil on
both sides; remove from pan. In skillet, add remaining ingredients except
orange segments and green pepper;
cook and stir until slightly thickened.
Add pork chops; cover and simmer 20
minutes or until tender. Add orange
segments and green pepper; heat
through. Garnish as desired. Refrigerate leftovers.
Makes 4 servings.

Sweet and Sour Pork Chops

    6 center-cut pork chops (about
      1¾ pounds)
      Vegetable oil
    ½ cup REALEMON® Lemon Juice
      from Concentrate
    3 tablespoons cornstarch
    ½ cup firmly packed brown sugar
    ¼ cup chopped onion
    1 tablespoon soy sauce
    1 teaspoon WYLER'S® or
      STEERO® Chicken-Flavor
      Instant Bouillon *or* 1
      Chicken-Flavor Bouillon
      Cube
    1 (20-ounce) can pineapple
      chunks in heavy syrup,
      drained, reserving syrup
    1 cup thinly sliced carrots
      Green pepper rings

Preheat oven to 350°. In large ovenproof skillet, brown chops in oil. Remove chops from skillet; pour off fat.
In skillet, combine ReaLemon® brand
and cornstarch; mix well. Add sugar,
onion, soy sauce, bouillon and reserved syrup; cook and stir until
slightly thickened and bouillon is dissolved. Add pork chops and carrots.
Cover; bake 1 hour or until tender.
Add pineapple; cover and bake 10
minutes longer. Garnish with green
pepper; serve with rice if desired. Refrigerate leftovers.
Makes 6 servings.

Pork Chops with Sweet Red Peppers

    1 cup dry red wine
    ¼ cup orange juice
    1 clove garlic, minced
    1 bay leaf, crumbled
    1 teaspoon dried savory leaves
    1 teaspoon dried marjoram
      leaves
    ½ teaspoon salt
    ½ teaspoon TABASCO® pepper
      sauce
    4 pork chops, about ¾ inch
      thick
    2 tablespoons vegetable oil
    2 medium red peppers, cut into
      strips
    ½ cup orange sections

In large shallow dish combine wine,
orange juice, garlic, bay leaf, savory,
marjoram, salt and Tabasco® sauce.
Add pork chops. Cover; refrigerate 1½
hours; turn occasionally. Remove
chops and pat dry; reserve marinade.
    In large skillet heat oil over me-
dium heat. Add chops and brown well
on both sides; remove from skillet.
Add peppers to skillet; cook 5 minutes
or until tender. Return chops to skillet. Add reserved marinade and bring
to a boil. Cover. Reduce heat; simmer
20 to 25 minutes or until chops are
done. Remove chops and peppers to
serving dish. Increase heat to high;
boil sauce about 3 minutes or until
slightly thickened. Pour sauce over
chops; garnish with orange sections.
Makes 4 servings.

Dijon Breaded Pork Chops

    ¾ cup finely crushed saltine
      crackers
    ½ teaspoon salt
    ½ teaspoon ground thyme
    ¼ teaspoon pepper
    ⅛ to ¼ teaspoon ground sage
    1 egg
    1 tablespoon Dijon mustard
    4 pork chops, ½ inch thick
    ¼ cup CRISCO® Oil

Mix cracker crumbs, salt, thyme, pepper and sage in shallow dish or on
sheet of waxed paper. Set aside. Blend
egg and mustard in shallow dish. Dip
each chop in egg mixture, then in
cracker mixture to coat.
    Heat Crisco® Oil in large skillet.
Add chops. Fry over moderate heat 16
to 20 minutes, or until pork is no
longer pink, turning over once.
2 to 4 servings.

Mushroom & Pepper Stuffed Chops

2 tablespoons butter or margarine
½ pound mushrooms, sliced
1 small red or green pepper, chopped
½ cup sliced almonds
1 envelope LIPTON® Recipe Secrets Onion or Onion-Mushroom Recipe Soup Mix
1 cup fresh bread crumbs
⅛ teaspoon pepper
4 double loin pork or veal chops, 2 inches thick (about 2½ pounds)

Preheat oven to 350°.

In medium skillet, heat butter and cook mushrooms, red pepper and almonds over medium-high heat 5 minutes or until vegetables are tender. Remove from heat, then stir in onion recipe soup mix combined with bread crumbs and pepper; set aside.

With knife parallel to cutting board, make a deep cut in meaty side of each chop. Evenly stuff each cut with mushroom mixture; secure, if desired, with skewers.

In shallow baking pan, arrange chops and bake 1 hour or until done.
Makes about 4 servings.

Oriental Pork Chops

2 tablespoons vegetable oil
1 clove garlic, minced
4 teaspoons minced ginger root
½ cup dry sherry wine
½ cup soy sauce
¼ cup honey
1 tablespoon grated orange peel
1 tablespoon sesame seeds
¾ teaspoon TABASCO® pepper sauce
4 pork chops, 1 inch thick
1 teaspoon cornstarch
2 tablespoons water
Orange slices, cut into quarters

In medium saucepan heat oil. Add garlic and ginger; cook 1 minute. Remove from heat; add sherry, soy sauce, honey, orange peel, sesame seeds and Tabasco® sauce. Place chops in large shallow dish or plastic bag; add marinade. Cover; refrigerate 1 hour; turn chops occasionally.

Remove chops from marinade; pour marinade into small saucepan. Place chops on grill about 5 inches from source of heat. Grill 10 minutes on each side. Meanwhile, in small bowl combine cornstarch and water; stir into marinade. Stir constantly, bring to a boil over medium heat and boil 1 minute. Brush chops with marinade. Grill 5 to 10 minutes longer or until chops are done; turn and brush frequently with marinade. Serve remaining marinade with chops. Garnish with orange slices.
Makes 4 servings.

Barbecued Pork Leg

1 boneless pork leg roast, rolled and tied (8 to 10 pounds)
Sam's Mop Sauce (recipe follows)
K.C. MASTERPIECE® Hickory Barbecue Sauce

In grill, arrange medium-hot **KINGSFORD® Charcoal Briquets** around drip pan. Place prepared pork leg over drip pan; cover grill and cook pork 4 to 4½ hours (adding additional briquets as necessary) or until meat thermometer inserted in thickest portion registers 170°F. Baste pork with Sam's Mop Sauce every 30 minutes, patting a thin coating of sauce on meat with cotton swab mop or pastry brush. Let stand, covered with foil, 10 minutes before serving.

Meanwhile, in saucepan, combine remaining Mop Sauce with an equal amount of barbecue sauce; bring to boil. Slice pork and serve with sauce mixture.
Makes about 20 servings.

Sam's Mop Sauce

1 lemon
1 cup water
1 cup cider vinegar
1 tablespoon butter or margarine
1 tablespoon olive or vegetable oil
½ teaspoon cayenne pepper
1½ to 3 teaspoons hot pepper sauce
1½ to 3 teaspoons Worcestershire sauce
1½ teaspoons black pepper

With vegetable peeler, remove peel from lemon; squeeze juice from lemon. In heavy saucepan, combine lemon peel, juice and remaining ingredients. Bring to boil. Place saucepan on grill to keep warm, if space permits.
Makes 2¼ cups.

Oriental Pork Chops

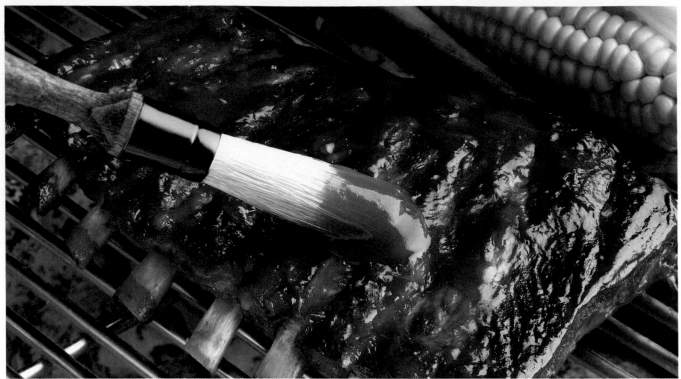

Zesty Barbecued Ribs

Glazed Pork Tenderloin

2 pork tenderloins, about
¾ pound each
½ cup KIKKOMAN® Teriyaki
Baste & Glaze
¼ teaspoon anise seed, crushed
¼ teaspoon pepper
⅛ teaspoon ground cloves
Mustard-Soy Dipping Sauce
(recipe follows)

Place tenderloins on rack in shallow foil-lined baking pan; tuck under thin ends of each tenderloin. Combine teriyaki baste & glaze, anise, pepper and cloves; brush each tenderloin thoroughly with baste & glaze mixture. Bake in 325°F. oven 1 hour, or until meat thermometer inserted into thickest part registers 170°F. Brush occasionally with baste & glaze mixture during baking. Remove from oven and let stand 15 minutes. Cut across grain into thin slices and serve with Mustard-Soy Dipping Sauce.
Makes 4 to 6 servings.
MUSTARD-SOY DIPPING SAUCE: Blend *2 tablespoons dry mustard* with *1 teaspoon each distilled white vinegar* and *water* to make a smooth paste. Cover and let stand 10 minutes. Thin with enough *KIKKOMAN® Soy Sauce* to dipping consistency.

Zesty Barbecued Ribs

6 pounds spareribs
Water
2 cups catsup
½ cup REALEMON® Lemon Juice
from Concentrate
½ cup firmly packed brown sugar
1 tablespoon prepared mustard
½ cup finely chopped onion
¼ cup margarine or butter
¼ cup Worcestershire sauce
1 clove garlic, finely chopped
¼ teaspoon salt
⅛ teaspoon hot pepper sauce

In large pan, cook ribs in boiling water 45 to 60 minutes or until tender. Meanwhile, in medium saucepan, combine remaining ingredients; simmer uncovered 20 minutes, stirring occasionally. Grill or broil ribs as desired, turning and basting frequently with sauce. Refrigerate leftovers.
Makes 6 to 8 servings.
Microwave: To pre-cook ribs, place 1½ pounds ribs in 12×7-inch shallow baking dish. Add ¼ cup water; cover with vented plastic wrap. Microwave on full power (high) 5 minutes. Reduce to ½ power (medium); continue cooking 7 minutes. Turn ribs over; cook covered on ½ power (medium) 7 minutes longer. Repeat with remaining ribs. Proceed as above.

Spicy Country Ribs

1 medium onion, finely chopped
3 cloves garlic, crushed
2 tablespoons vegetable oil
1 can (15 ounces) tomato sauce
½ cup red wine
¼ cup packed brown sugar
¾ teaspoon salt
½ teaspoon dry mustard
½ teaspoon chili powder
½ teaspoon hot pepper sauce
⅛ teaspoon pepper
5 pounds country-style
spareribs

In medium skillet, saute onion and garlic in oil until onion is soft but not brown. Stir in remaining ingredients except spareribs. Bring to boil; reduce heat and simmer, covered, 20 minutes. Trim any excess fat from ribs. Arrange ribs in shallow glass dish. Cover with plastic wrap, vented. Microwave at 50% power 20 minutes, rearranging ribs once. Remove from oven. Brush ribs with sauce. Lightly oil grid. Grill ribs, on covered grill, over medium-hot **KINGSFORD® Charcoal Briquets** 30 minutes or until cooked through, turning often and basting with sauce.
Makes 6 servings.

Chinese-Style Spareribs

- ½ cup butter or margarine
- 1 medium clove garlic, finely chopped
- 1 envelope LIPTON® Recipe Secrets Onion, Onion-Mushroom, Beefy Mushroom or Beefy Onion Recipe Soup Mix
- 1 can (16 ounces) tomato puree
- ½ cup brown sugar
- ¼ cup soy sauce
- ¼ cup white vinegar
- ¼ cup chili sauce
- 5 pounds spareribs, country-style ribs or baby back ribs

Preheat oven to 375°.

In large saucepan, melt butter and cook garlic with onion recipe soup mix over medium heat until garlic is golden. Stir in tomato puree, sugar, soy sauce, vinegar and chili sauce. Bring to a boil, then simmer, stirring occasionally, 15 minutes.

Meanwhile, in large aluminum-foil-lined baking pan or on broiler rack, arrange spareribs meaty side up and bake 20 minutes. Brush spareribs generously with sauce, then continue baking, meaty side up, brushing occasionally with remaining sauce, 50 minutes or until spareribs are done.
Makes about 7 main-dish or 12 appetizer servings.

Bake & Glaze Teri Ribs

- 3 pounds pork spareribs
- ½ teaspoon garlic powder
- ½ teaspoon pepper
- ⅔ cup KIKKOMAN® Teriyaki Baste & Glaze
- ½ teaspoon grated lemon peel

Cut ribs into serving pieces; place, meaty side up, in shallow foil-lined baking pan. Sprinkle garlic powder and pepper evenly over ribs; cover pan loosely with foil. Bake in 350°F. oven 45 minutes. Meanwhile, combine teriyaki baste & glaze and lemon peel. Remove foil and brush both sides of ribs with baste & glaze mixture. Cover and bake 40 minutes longer, or until ribs are tender, brushing with baste & glaze mixture occasionally.
Makes 4 servings.

Roast Loin of Pork Oriental-Style

- ½ cup WISH-BONE® Italian or Robusto Italian Dressing
- ½ cup honey
- 1 tablespoon finely chopped fresh ginger*
- 1 tablespoon hoisin sauce (optional)
- 2 teaspoons soy sauce
- 1 teaspoon Dijon-style mustard
- 1 (3- to 3½-pound) boneless pork loin roast, tied for roasting

Preheat oven to 375°.

In small bowl, combine all ingredients except pork. In roasting pan, on rack, place pork and roast 45 minutes. Brush pork with ½ of the dressing mixture, then continue roasting, basting occasionally, 35 minutes or until meat thermometer reaches 165° (medium) or 180° (well done). Heat remaining dressing mixture and serve with pork.
Makes about 10 servings.

Substitution: Use 1 teaspoon ground ginger.

Kamaaina Spareribs

- 4 pounds lean pork spareribs Salt and pepper
- 1 can (20 ounces) DOLE® Crushed Pineapple, drained
- 1 cup catsup
- ½ cup brown sugar, packed
- ⅓ cup red wine vinegar
- ¼ cup soy sauce
- 1 teaspoon ground ginger
- ½ teaspoon dry mustard
- ¼ teaspoon garlic powder

Have butcher cut across rib bones to make strips 1½ inches wide. Preheat oven to 350°F. Place ribs close together in single layer in baking pan. Sprinkle with salt and pepper to taste. Cover tightly with aluminum foil. Bake in preheated oven 1 hour. Uncover; pour off and discard drippings. In bowl, combine remaining ingredients. Spoon sauce over ribs. Grill over hot coals 15 minutes or bake, uncovered, 30 minutes longer or until ribs are tender and glazed.
Makes 6 servings.

Sweet & Sour Pork Loin

- ½ cup chicken broth or water
- ½ cup catsup
- 2 tablespoons brown sugar
- 2 tablespoons cider vinegar
- 2 tablespoons Worcestershire sauce
- 1 clove garlic, crushed
- ½ teaspoon salt
- ¼ teaspoon black pepper
- ⅛ teaspoon cayenne pepper
- 1 boneless pork loin roast (2 pounds), tied

In saucepan, combine all ingredients except roast. Heat to boiling. Cut roast crosswise into 4 pieces; arrange in shallow glass dish. Pour sweet and sour mixture over pork. Cover and refrigerate overnight. Drain pork; reserve sweet and sour mixture. Grill pork, on uncovered grill, over medium-hot **MATCH LIGHT® Charcoal Briquets** 20 to 25 minutes or until pork is cooked through, turning 3 to 4 times and basting often with sweet and sour mixture.
Makes 4 servings.

Chinese-Style Spareribs

Pineapple Sweet-Sour Spareribs

- 1 can (8¼ ounces) DOLE®
     Pineapple Chunks in
     Syrup*
- ¼ cup soy sauce, divided
- 3 tablespoons cornstarch
- 3 to 4 pounds lean spareribs
- 2 to 3 tablespoons
     vegetable oil
- 1 cup cider vinegar
- ¾ cup brown sugar, packed
- ⅓ cup water
- 2 cloves garlic, pressed
- 1 piece (2 inches) ginger
     root, peeled, minced

- Drain pineapple; reserve syrup.

- Combine 2 tablespoons soy sauce and cornstarch in small bowl. Rub soy sauce mixture onto ribs.

- In 12-inch skillet, sauté ribs, in batches, in oil over medium-high heat until browned.

- Combine reserved syrup, remaining 2 tablespoons soy sauce, vinegar, brown sugar, water, garlic and ginger root in Dutch oven. Add ribs. Heat to a boil. Reduce heat. Cover; simmer 1 hour, stirring occasionally.

- Spoon off fat. Stir in pineapple; heat through.

Makes 3 to 4 servings

*Use pineapple packed in juice, if desired.

Preparation Time: 5 minutes
Cook Time: 1 hour 15 minutes

Oven Barbecued Spareribs

- 3 to 4 pounds pork spareribs
     HEINZ® Thick and Rich
     Hickory Smoke or Old
     Fashioned Barbecue
     Sauce*

Cut spareribs into sections of 2 ribs each. Arrange ribs, rounded side down, on rack in shallow baking pan or on broiler pan. Bake in 350°F oven, 30 minutes. Turn; bake an additional 30 minutes. Drain excess fat, if necessary. Turn ribs; brush generously with barbecue sauce. Bake 10 minutes. Turn; brush generously with barbecue sauce. Bake an additional 10 minutes.

Makes 3 to 4 servings

*For Honey 'n' Spice Oven Barbecued Ribs, substitute mixture of ½ cup Heinz® 57 Sauce and ¼ cup honey for barbecue sauce. Brush on ribs as directed above.

Steak Supreme Tacos

- 1 pound sirloin steak or pork
     butt, cooked and
     shredded or chopped
- 1 package (1.25 ounces)
     LAWRY'S® Taco Spices &
     Seasonings
- ¾ cup water
- 1 can (15 ounces) pinto
     beans, drained
- ½ cup sliced green onions
- ½ cup chopped tomato
- 1 package (10 count)
     LAWRY'S® Taco Shells
     Shredded lettuce
     Avocado chunks
- 2 cups (8 ounces) grated
     Monterey Jack cheese

In large skillet, combine meat, Taco Spices & Seasonings and water. Bring to a boil; reduce heat and simmer, uncovered, 7 minutes. Stir in beans, green onions and tomato. Heat Taco Shells in 350°F oven 5 minutes. Spoon warm meat mixture into shells. Top with lettuce, avocado and cheese. *Makes 10 tacos*

Presentation: Serve with Lawry's® Fiesta Dip (page 10) or a mixture of sour cream and salsa.

Hint: Double recipe for a larger fiesta!

Ham with Fruited Mustard Sauce

Honey Glazed Ham

Ham with Fruited Mustard Sauce

- **1 fully cooked ham slice (1 to 1¼ pounds), cut ½ inch thick***
- **1 tablespoon butter or margarine**
- **1 can (8 ounces) pineapple slices**
- **¼ cup HEINZ® 57 Sauce**
- **2 tablespoons honey**
- **1 tablespoon prepared mustard**
- **1½ teaspoons cornstarch Dash ground allspice**

Cut ham into 4 serving portions. In large skillet, sauté ham in butter about 3 to 4 minutes on each side or until heated through. Meanwhile, drain pineapple, reserving juice. In small bowl, combine juice, 57 Sauce, honey, mustard, cornstarch and allspice. Remove ham from skillet; keep warm.

Pour 57 Sauce mixture into skillet and cook until thickened. Return ham to skillet. Top each ham portion with pineapple slice and spoon sauce over; heat through.   *Makes 4 servings (about ⅔ cup sauce)*

*A 1-pound piece of Canadian bacon, cut into 4 slices, may be substituted.

Honey Glazed Ham

- **¼ cup MAPLE ORCHARDS® Pure Honey**
- **3 tablespoons light brown sugar**
- **2 teaspoons prepared mustard**

Combine ingredients. Use to baste ham frequently during last hour of baking.
Makes enough to glaze a 4-pound ham

Ham Glaze

- **1 cup KARO® Light or Dark Corn Syrup**
- **½ cup packed brown sugar**
- **3 tablespoons prepared mustard**
- **½ teaspoon ground ginger Dash ground cloves**

In medium saucepan combine corn syrup, brown sugar, mustard, ginger and cloves. Bring to boil over medium heat; boil 5 minutes, stirring constantly. Brush on ham frequently during last 30 minutes of baking.
Makes about 1 cup

Preparation Time: 10 minutes

Microwave Directions: In 1½-quart microwavable bowl combine all ingredients. Microwave on HIGH (100%), 6 minutes. Glaze ham as above.

Golden Glazed Ham Loaf

1 pound lean ground ham
1 pound ground pork
1 cup soft bread crumbs
    (2 slices bread)
⅓ cup chopped onion
¼ cup BORDEN® or MEADOW
    GOLD® Milk
1 egg
    Dash pepper
1 cup BAMA® Peach Preserves
    or Orange Marmalade
2 tablespoons REALEMON®
    Lemon Juice from
    Concentrate
1 tablespoon prepared mustard

Preheat oven to 350°. In large bowl, combine all ingredients except preserves, ReaLemon® brand and mustard; mix well. In shallow baking dish, shape into loaf. Bake 1½ hours. Meanwhile, stir together preserves, ReaLemon® brand and mustard. Use ⅓ to ½ cup sauce to glaze loaf during last 30 minutes of baking. Heat remaining glaze and serve with loaf. Garnish as desired. Refrigerate leftovers.
Makes 8 servings.
   Microwave: Prepare loaf as above. Cover loosely; microwave on full power (high) 5 minutes. Rotate dish; microwave on ½ power (medium) 20 to 23 minutes or until center is set. Spread with glaze as above; microwave uncovered on ½ power (medium) 3 to 5 minutes. Let stand 5 minutes before serving. Meanwhile, microwave remaining glaze on full power (high) 1 to 2 minutes or until hot, stirring after 1 minute. Serve as above.

Pineapple-Orange Glazed Ham

1 ARMOUR® Lower Salt Ham
    Nugget (about 1¾ pounds)
⅔ cup orange marmalade
1 (8-ounce) can pineapple
    chunks, drained and juice
    reserved

Preheat oven to 350°F. Spray roasting pan with nonstick cooking spray; place ham in pan. Combine orange marmalade, 2 tablespoons reserved pineapple juice and pineapple chunks in small bowl. Spoon a third over ham; brush to cover entire surface.

Pineapple-Orange Glazed Ham

Bake, uncovered, for 1 hour and 10 minutes, or until ham reaches an internal temperature of 145°F. Baste with pineapple-marmalade sauce every 10 minutes. Serve with remaining sauce. Garnish with fresh mint leaves or parsley, if desired.
Makes 8 to 10 servings.
   Note: Try apricot-pineapple jam in place of orange marmalade for a different flavor combination.

Nutrition Information Per Serving: 185 calories, 14.1 g protein, 3.9 g fat, 17.2 carbohydrates, 39.2 mg cholesterol, 672 mg sodium.

Holiday Baked Ham

1 bone-in smoked ham
    (8½ pounds)
1 can (20 ounces) DOLE® Sliced
    Pineapple in Syrup or Juice
1 cup apricot preserves
1 teaspoon dry mustard
½ teaspoon ground allspice
    Whole cloves
    Maraschino cherries

Preheat oven to 325°F. Remove rind from ham. Place ham on rack in open roasting pan, fat side up. Insert meat thermometer with bulb in thickest part away from fat or bone. Roast ham in preheated oven about 3 hours.
   Drain pineapple; reserve syrup. In small saucepan, combine syrup, preserves, mustard and allspice. Bring to boil; boil, stirring occasionally, 10 minutes. Remove ham from oven, but keep oven hot. Stud ham with cloves; brush with glaze. Using wooden picks, secure pineapple and cherries to ham. Brush again with glaze. Return ham to oven. Roast 30 minutes longer or until thermometer registers 160°F (about 25 minutes per pound total cooking time). Brush with glaze 15 minutes before done. Let ham stand 20 minutes before slicing.
Makes 8 to 10 servings.

Baked Ham with Glazed Vegetables

- **1 cup apricot nectar**
- **1 cup dried apricot halves**
- **1 cup (8 ounces) WISH-BONE® Deluxe French Dressing**
- **¼ cup honey**
- **¼ teaspoon ground cinnamon**
- **⅛ teaspoon ground nutmeg**
- **½ cup sliced almonds (optional)**
- **1 (5- to 6-pound) fully cooked ham butt end with bone**
- **2 pounds sweet potatoes or yams, peeled and cut into large chunks**
- **1 pound pearl onions, peeled**

Preheat oven to 375°.

In medium saucepan, bring nectar to a boil. Add apricots, then remove from heat. Let stand 10 minutes. Stir in deluxe French dressing, honey, cinnamon, nutmeg, then almonds.

On aluminum-foil-lined roasting pan, place ham. With knife, score (lightly cut) fat in diamond pattern. Arrange potatoes and onions around ham. Spoon dressing mixture over ham and vegetables. Loosely cover with heavy-duty aluminum foil and bake, turning vegetables and basting occasionally, 1 hour or until ham is golden and vegetables are tender.
Makes about 10 servings.

Note: Also terrific with Wish-Bone® Lite French Style, Sweet 'n Spicy French or Lite Sweet 'n Spicy French Dressing.

Baked Ham with Wine & Onion Glaze

- **1 envelope LIPTON® Recipe Secrets Onion or Onion-Mushroom Recipe Soup Mix**
- **1 cup water**
- **⅓ cup brown sugar**
- **¼ cup Madeira wine or sherry**
- **2 tablespoons butter or margarine, melted**
- **1 tablespoon finely chopped parsley**
- **5- to 6-pound fully cooked ham butt end**
- **1 pound shallots or small onions, peeled and quartered**

Preheat oven to 375°.

In small bowl, blend onion recipe soup mix, water, sugar, wine, butter and parsley; set aside.

In roasting pan, place ham. With knife, score (lightly cut) fat in diamond pattern; top with soup mixture. Arrange shallots around ham. Bake, stirring shallots and basting ham occasionally, 60 minutes or until golden brown.
Makes about 8 servings.

Baked Ham with Glazed Vegetables

Ham-Stuffed Peppers

- **1½ cups cooked unsalted regular rice (½ cup uncooked)**
- **1 cup (5 ounces) diced cooked ham**
- **1 can (16 ounces) whole kernel corn, drained**
- **1 jar (15½ ounces) spaghetti sauce**
- **1 cup (4 ounces) shredded Cheddar cheese**
- **1 can (2.8 ounces) DURKEE® French Fried Onions**
- **¼ teaspoon DURKEE® Seasoned Salt**
- **¼ teaspoon DURKEE® Ground Black Pepper**
- **4 medium green peppers, cut into halves lengthwise and seeded**
- **¼ cup water**

Preheat oven to 350°. To hot rice in saucepan, add ham, corn, *1 cup* spaghetti sauce, *½ cup* cheese, *½ can* French Fried Onions and the seasonings; stir well. Spoon rice filling into green pepper halves. Arrange stuffed peppers in 8×12-inch baking dish. In small bowl, combine remaining spaghetti sauce and the water; pour over peppers. Bake, covered, at 350° for 30 minutes or until peppers are done. Top with remaining cheese and onions; bake, uncovered, 5 minutes or until onions are golden brown.
Makes 4 servings.

Glazed Ham Steak

- **1 (8-ounce) can crushed pineapple, well drained**
- **½ cup BAMA® Peach or Apricot Preserves**
- **2 tablespoons REALEMON® Lemon Juice from Concentrate**
- **1 teaspoon cornstarch**
- **1 (1- to 1½-pound) center cut ham slice**

In small saucepan, combine pineapple, preserves, ReaLemon® brand and cornstarch; mix well and bring to a boil. Reduce heat; simmer uncovered 10 to 15 minutes to blend flavors. Broil ham to desired doneness on both sides. Spoon pineapple mixture on top; heat until hot and bubbly. Refrigerate leftovers.
Makes 4 servings.

POULTRY

Looking for new ways to prepare economical, low-fat poultry? From classics such as Chicken Fricassee and Chicken Cordon Bleu to foreign fare such as Polynesian Chicken and Rio Grande Quesadillas, you won't need to look any further. Discover how versatile and easy poultry can be with new ideas for baking, stir-frying and grilling. And with ground turkey and turkey cutlets so readily available, this bird is no longer just for the holidays.

Chicken Cordon Bleu

4 large skinless boneless chicken breast halves (about 1¼ pounds)
4 slices lean baked ham
4 ounces Swiss cheese, cut into 4 sticks
2 tablespoons butter or margarine
1 cup sliced fresh mushrooms
¼ teaspoon dried thyme leaves, crushed
⅛ teaspoon ground nutmeg
⅛ teaspoon pepper
2 tablespoons dry white wine
1 jar (12 ounces) HEINZ® HomeStyle Chicken Gravy

Place chicken between waxed paper or plastic wrap and flatten to ¼-inch thickness. Place 1 ham slice and 1 cheese stick on each breast half. Roll chicken, jelly-roll fashion, tucking ends in; secure with wooden toothpicks. In large skillet, brown chicken on all sides in butter; remove. In same skillet, sauté mushrooms, thyme, nutmeg and pepper until mushrooms are tender. Stir in wine, then add gravy. Return chicken to skillet. Cook over low heat, covered, 10 minutes or until chicken is cooked, turning once. Remove toothpicks before serving. *Makes 4 servings (about 1⅔ cups sauce)*

Special Lemony Chicken

¼ cup unsifted flour
1 teaspoon salt
¼ teaspoon pepper
6 skinned boneless chicken breast halves (about 1½ pounds)
¼ cup margarine or butter
¼ cup REALEMON® Lemon Juice from Concentrate
8 ounces fresh mushrooms, sliced (about 2 cups)
Hot cooked rice

In plastic bag, combine flour, salt and pepper. Add chicken, a few pieces at a time; shake to coat. In large skillet, brown chicken in margarine. Add ReaLemon® brand and mushrooms. Reduce heat; cover and simmer 15 minutes or until mushrooms are tender and chicken is cooked through. Serve with rice; garnish with parsley if desired. Refrigerate leftovers.
Makes 6 servings

Easy Peach Glaze

1 (10-ounce) jar BAMA® Peach or Apricot Preserves (1 cup)
2 tablespoons REALEMON® Lemon Juice from Concentrate
1 tablespoon margarine or butter

In small saucepan, combine ingredients; bring to a boil. Reduce heat; simmer uncovered 10 to 15 minutes. Use to glaze chicken, ham loaf, ham, pork, carrots or sweet potatoes.
Makes about 1 cup

Chicken Cordon Bleu

Sierra Chicken Bundles

Classic Savory Chicken Divan

- **¾ pound boneless skinless chicken breasts, cut into strips**
- **2 teaspoons oil**
- **1 cup water**
- **1 tablespoon dry sherry**
- **1 package (10 ounces) BIRDS EYE® Broccoli Spears or Deluxe Broccoli Florets, thawed**
- **1 can (10¾ ounces) condensed cream of chicken soup**
- **1½ cups Original MINUTE® Rice**
- **½ cup shredded Cheddar cheese**

Cook and stir chicken in hot oil in large skillet until lightly browned. Add water, sherry, broccoli and soup. Bring to full boil, separating broccoli spears. Stir in rice. Cover; remove from heat. Let stand 5 minutes. Fluff with fork. Arrange on platter. Sprinkle with cheese.

Makes 4 servings

Microwave Directions: Place chicken and oil in 2-quart microwavable dish. Cook at HIGH 3 minutes, stirring once. Add water, sherry, broccoli, soup and rice. Cover and cook at HIGH 6 minutes longer. Let stand 5 minutes. Arrange on platter. Sprinkle with cheese.

Makes 4 servings

Sierra Chicken Bundles

- **2 cups prepared Mexican or Spanish-style rice mix**
- **¼ cup thinly sliced green onions**
- **½ teaspoon LAWRY'S® Seasoned Pepper**
- **4 whole boneless, skinless chicken breasts**
- **½ cup unseasoned dry bread crumbs**
- **¼ cup grated Parmesan cheese**
- **½ teaspoon chili powder**
- **½ teaspoon LAWRY'S® Garlic Salt**
- **¼ teaspoon ground cumin**
- **¼ cup IMPERIAL® Margarine, melted**

In medium bowl, combine prepared rice, green onions and Seasoned Pepper. Pound chicken breasts between 2 sheets of waxed paper to ¼-inch thickness. Place about ⅓ cup rice mixture in center of each chicken breast; roll and tuck ends under and secure with wooden skewers. In pie plate, combine remaining ingredients except margarine; blend well. Roll chicken bundles in margarine, then in crumb mixture. Place seam-side down in 12×8×2-inch baking dish. Bake, uncovered, in 400°F oven 15 to 20 minutes or until chicken is cooked through. Remove skewers before serving.

Makes 4 servings

Presentation: Serve with assorted steamed vegetables and corn bread.

Chicken Fricassee

- **¼ cup all-purpose flour**
- **½ teaspoon salt**
- **½ teaspoon paprika**
- **⅛ teaspoon pepper**
- **2½ to 3 pounds broiler-fryer chicken pieces**
- **2 tablespoons vegetable oil**
- **1 jar (12 ounces) HEINZ® HomeStyle Chicken or Turkey Gravy**
- **¼ teaspoon ground nutmeg**

In small bowl, combine flour, salt, paprika and pepper. Coat chicken with flour mixture. In large skillet, brown chicken in oil; drain excess fat. In medium bowl, combine gravy and nutmeg with any remaining flour mixture; pour over chicken. Cover; simmer 50 to 60 minutes or until chicken is tender, basting occasionally.

*Makes 5 to 6 servings
(about 1½ cups gravy)*

Chicken Parisian

- ¼ cup unsifted flour
- ¼ teaspoon paprika
- ¼ teaspoon pepper
- 6 skinned boneless chicken breast halves (about 2 pounds)
- 3 tablespoons margarine or butter
- 8 ounces fresh mushrooms, sliced (about 2 cups)
- ½ cup water
- ¼ cup dry white wine
- 2 teaspoons WYLER'S® or STEERO® Chicken-Flavor Instant Bouillon *or* 2 Chicken-Flavor Bouillon Cubes
- 2 teaspoons chopped parsley
- ¼ teaspoon thyme leaves

In plastic bag, combine flour, paprika and pepper. Add chicken, a few pieces at a time; shake to coat. In skillet, brown chicken in margarine; remove from pan. In same skillet, add remaining ingredients; simmer 3 minutes. Add chicken; simmer covered 20 minutes or until tender. Refrigerate leftovers.

Makes 6 servings

Stuffed Chicken Breasts

- 4 skinless, boneless chicken breast halves (about 1 pound), pounded to ¼-inch thickness
- ½ teaspoon ground black pepper, divided
- ¼ teaspoon salt
- 1 cup cooked brown rice (cooked in chicken broth)
- ¼ cup minced tomato
- ¼ cup (about 1 ounce) finely shredded mozzarella cheese
- 3 tablespoons toasted rice bran* (optional)
- 1 tablespoon chopped fresh basil
  Vegetable cooking spray

Season insides of chicken breasts with ¼ teaspoon pepper and salt. Combine rice, tomato, cheese, bran, basil, and remaining ¼ teaspoon pepper. Spoon rice mixture on top of pounded chicken breasts; fold over and secure sides with wooden toothpicks soaked in water. Wipe off outsides of chicken breasts with paper towel. Coat a large skillet with cooking spray and place over medium-high heat until hot. Cook stuffed chicken breasts 1 minute on each side or just until golden brown. Transfer chicken to shallow baking pan. Bake at 350°F. for 8 to 10 minutes. *Makes 4 servings*

*To toast rice bran, spread on baking sheet and bake at 325°F. for 7 to 8 minutes.

Favorite recipe from **USA Rice Council**

Stuffed Chicken Breasts

Mexican Chicken with Spicy Bacon

2 serrano chili peppers
2 cloves garlic
  Dash ground cloves
  Dash ground cinnamon
4 slices bacon, partially cooked
1 whole roasting chicken (3½ to 4 pounds)

Remove stems from peppers. Slit open; remove seeds and ribs. Finely chop peppers and garlic. Place in small bowl. Stir in cloves and cinnamon. Cut bacon into 1-inch pieces.

Lift skin layer of chicken at neck cavity. Insert hand, lifting skin from meat along breast, thigh and drumstick. Using small metal spatula, spread pepper mixture evenly over meat under skin. Place layer of bacon pieces over pepper mixture. Skewer neck skin to back. Tie legs securely to tail with kitchen twine; twist wing tips under back of chicken. Insert meat thermometer in center of thigh muscle, not touching bone.

Arrange medium-hot **KINGS-FORD® Charcoal Briquets** around drip pan. Place chicken, breast-side up, over drip pan. Cover grill and cook about 1 hour or until meat thermometer registers 185°F. Garnish with grilled cherry tomatoes and additional serrano chili peppers, if desired.

Makes 4 servings.

Roasted Dill Chicken

½ cup WISH-BONE® Italian Dressing
1 cup loosely packed snipped fresh dill*
½ cup coarsely chopped shallots or onions
½ teaspoon salt
¼ teaspoon pepper
1 (5- to 5½-pound) roasting chicken
2 pounds all-purpose potatoes, cut into chunks

Preheat oven to 375°.

In food processor or blender, process Italian dressing, dill, shallots, salt and pepper until blended.

In roasting pan, on rack, place chicken; spread dill mixture inside cavity, then under and over skin. Close cavity with skewers or wooden toothpicks; tie legs together with string. Arrange potatoes around chicken. Loosely cover with heavy-duty aluminum foil, then roast 1½ hours, turning potatoes occasionally. Remove foil and continue roasting 15 minutes or until meat thermometer reaches 185° and potatoes are done.

Makes about 4 servings.

***Substitution:** Use 2 tablespoons dried dill weed.*

Note: Also terrific with Wish-Bone® Robusto Italian, Blended Italian or Lite Italian Dressing.

Spinach & Pesto Stuffed Chicken Breasts

¼ cup *plus* 2 tablespoons WISH-BONE® Italian Dressing
¼ cup chopped fresh basil leaves*
¼ cup grated Parmesan cheese
⅛ teaspoon pepper
1 package (10 ounces) frozen chopped spinach, cooked and squeezed dry**
1 cup fresh bread crumbs
4 whole boneless chicken breasts (about 2 pounds), halved

In food processor or blender, process ¼ cup Italian dressing with basil, cheese and pepper until blended. In medium bowl, thoroughly combine dressing mixture, spinach and bread crumbs.

With knife parallel to cutting board, make deep, 3-inch-long cut in center of each chicken breast half to form pocket. Evenly stuff pockets with spinach mixture.

In aluminum-foil-lined large shallow baking pan or on broiler rack, arrange chicken, then brush with remaining 2 tablespoons dressing. Broil, turning once, 7 minutes or until chicken is done.

Makes about 8 servings.

***Substitution:** Use 1 tablespoon dried basil leaves.*

****Substitution:** Use 1 pound fresh spinach leaves, cooked, squeezed dry and chopped (about 1½ cups).*

Note: Also terrific with Wish-Bone® Robusto Italian, Blended Italian or Lite Italian Dressing.

Herb-Roasted Chicken

2½- to 3-pound broiler-fryer chicken
2 cloves garlic, quartered
¼ cup CRISCO® Oil
1 tablespoon lime juice
1 teaspoon dried tarragon leaves
1 teaspoon dried chervil leaves
½ teaspoon dried thyme leaves
  Pepper

Preheat oven to 375°F. Lift skin from chicken breast and place 6 pieces garlic between skin and meat. Cut small slit in each drumstick. Insert a piece of garlic into each slit.

Blend Crisco® Oil and lime juice in small bowl. Brush on chicken. Mix tarragon, chervil and thyme in another small bowl. Rub onto chicken. Sprinkle chicken with pepper.

Place chicken, breast-side up, in roasting pan. Bake at 375°F, 1¼ to 1½ hours, or until juices run clear and meat near bone is no longer pink, brushing with lime juice mixture several times during roasting. Let stand 10 minutes before carving.

4 servings.

Spinach & Pesto Stuffed Chicken Breasts

Apple-Raisin Stuffed Chicken Breasts

1 (13¾-fluid ounce) can
    COLLEGE INN® Chicken
    Broth
⅓ cup BLUE BONNET® Margarine
1 cup herb-seasoned stuffing
    mix
⅓ cup chopped apple
¼ cup seedless raisins
2 whole boneless chicken
    breasts, split and pounded
    (1 pound)
3 tablespoons all-purpose flour
1 teaspoon dried tarragon
    leaves

In saucepan, over medium-high heat, heat ⅓ cup chicken broth and 2 tablespoons margarine until margarine melts. Stir in stuffing mix, apple and raisins. Divide mixture evenly among 4 chicken pieces. Roll up; secure with toothpicks.

In skillet, over medium-high heat, melt remaining margarine. Brown chicken on all sides; remove. Blend flour and tarragon into margarine in skillet. Gradually add remaining broth, stirring constantly until mixture thickens and boils. Return chicken to skillet; reduce heat. Cover; simmer 20 minutes or until done. Garnish as desired.
Makes 4 servings.

Microwave: In 1-quart microwave-proof bowl, place ⅓ cup broth and 2 tablespoons margarine. Microwave, uncovered, on HIGH (100% power) for 1 to 2 minutes until margarine melts. Stir in stuffing mix, apple and raisins. Stuff chicken breasts as above.

In 9-inch microwave-proof pie plate, place remaining margarine. Microwave on HIGH for 35 to 40 seconds until melted. Stir in flour and tarragon. Gradually add remaining broth. Microwave, uncovered, on HIGH for 4 to 5 minutes until mixture thickens and boils, stirring every 2 minutes. Place stuffed chicken in pie plate, turning to coat with sauce; cover with waxed paper. Microwave on HIGH for 8 to 9 minutes until done, rotating dish ¼ turn after 4 minutes. Let stand, covered, 5 minutes.

Apple-Raisin Stuffed Chicken Breasts

Quick Chicken Curry

3 cups cubed cooked chicken *or*
    turkey
1 cup chopped onion
1 clove garlic, finely chopped
¼ cup margarine or butter
¼ cup unsifted flour
2½ cups BORDEN® or MEADOW
    GOLD® Milk
¾ cup COCO LOPEZ® Cream of
    Coconut
1 tablespoon curry powder
1 tablespoon WYLER'S® or
    STEERO® Chicken-Flavor
    Instant Bouillon *or* 3
    Chicken-Flavor Bouillon
    Cubes
¼ cup REALEMON® Lemon Juice
    from Concentrate
Hot cooked rice
Condiments

In large skillet, cook onion and garlic in margarine until tender; stir in flour. Gradually add milk; stir until smooth. Add cream of coconut, curry and bouillon. Over medium heat, cook and stir until thickened. Add ReaLemon® brand; reduce heat and simmer 10 minutes. Add chicken. Cook 10 minutes longer. Serve over rice with condiments. Refrigerate leftovers.
Makes 6 servings.

Suggested condiments: Toasted flaked coconut, cashews, pecans or peanuts, chopped green onion, chopped hard-cooked eggs, chutney, crumbled bacon, raisins or sunflower meats.

Chicken l'Orange

**4 skinless boneless chicken
    breast halves
    (about 1 pound)
2 tablespoons butter or
    margarine
    Salt and pepper
2 teaspoons cornstarch
⅔ cup orange juice
⅓ cup HEINZ® 57 Sauce
¼ cup orange marmalade
    Toasted slivered almonds***

Lightly flatten chicken breasts. In large skillet, sauté chicken in butter until cooked, about 8 to 10 minutes; season with salt and pepper. Remove chicken; set aside. In small bowl, dissolve cornstarch in orange juice; stir in 57 Sauce and marmalade. Pour into skillet. Heat, stirring constantly, until mixture is hot and thickened. Return chicken to skillet; heat through. Spoon sauce over chicken; garnish with almonds.   *Makes 4 servings (about 1 cup sauce)*

*To toast almonds, spread almonds in shallow baking pan; bake in preheated 350°F oven, 8 to 10 minutes or until lightly browned.

Chicken with Peach-Champagne Sauce

**Chicken
    1 whole chicken breast, split,
        boned and skinned
    2 teaspoons lemon juice
        Pepper, to taste
    1 fresh California peach,
        sliced**

**Peach-Champagne Sauce
    1 tablespoon margarine or
        butter
    1 tablespoon minced red
        onion
    1 tablespoon all-purpose
        flour
    ¼ cup Champagne or white
        wine**

**   Spinach noodles, cooked
        (optional)**

For Chicken, in small microwave-safe baking dish, arrange chicken with thicker parts to the outside. Sprinkle with lemon juice and pepper. Cover with waxed paper and microwave on HIGH 5 minutes or until no longer pink and cooked through. Add peach slices to chicken and cook on HIGH 1 to 2 minutes longer; reserve cooking liquid.

For Sauce, in 4-cup glass measure, combine margarine and onion. Cook on HIGH 1 minute. Stir in flour and 3 tablespoons cooking liquid. Stir in Champagne. Cook on HIGH 3 minutes until thickened, stirring after 1½ minutes. Serve chicken and peaches on noodles. Spoon sauce over chicken.
    Makes 2 servings

*Favorite recipe from **California Tree Fruit Agreement***

Chicken with Peach-Champagne Sauce

Creamy Chicken and Mushrooms

1 cup chicken broth
⅓ cup HEINZ® 57 Sauce
1 tablespoon cornstarch
1 teaspoon lemon juice
⅛ teaspoon pepper
1 pound skinless boneless chicken breasts, cut into 1-inch pieces
2 tablespoons vegetable oil, divided
1 cup sliced fresh mushrooms
1 medium onion, sliced
⅓ cup dairy sour cream
½ cup coarsely chopped unsalted peanuts (optional)
Hot cooked noodles
Chopped fresh parsley

For sauce, in medium bowl, combine broth, 57 Sauce, cornstarch, lemon juice and pepper; set aside. In large skillet, sauté chicken in 1 tablespoon oil until cooked, about 5 minutes; remove. Sauté mushrooms and onion in same skillet in remaining 1 tablespoon oil until onion is tender. Stir in sauce mixture; cook until thickened. Gradually stir in sour cream. Return chicken to skillet; heat slowly. *Do not boil.* Stir in peanuts. Serve chicken over noodles; garnish with parsley.

Makes 4 servings (about 4 cups)

Dressed Chicken Breasts with Angel Hair Pasta

Dressed Chicken Breasts with Angel Hair Pasta

1 cup prepared HIDDEN VALLEY RANCH® Original Ranch® Salad Dressing
⅓ cup Dijon-style mustard
4 whole chicken breasts, halved, skinned, boned and pounded thin
½ cup butter or margarine
⅓ cup dry white wine
10 ounces angel hair pasta, cooked and drained
Chopped parsley

In small bowl, whisk together salad dressing and mustard; set aside. In medium skillet, saute chicken in butter until browned; transfer to dish. Keep warm. Pour wine into skillet; cook over medium-high heat, scraping up any browned bits from bottom of skillet, about 5 minutes. Whisk in dressing mixture; blend well. Serve chicken with sauce over pasta; sprinkle with parsley.

Makes 8 servings

Quick Chicken Cacciatore

Quick Chicken Cacciatore

**4 skinned boneless chicken
    breast halves (about
    1 pound), lightly
    seasoned with salt and
    pepper
Flour
2 cloves garlic, finely
    chopped
4 tablespoons olive oil
1 (26-ounce) jar CLASSICO®
    Di Napoli (Tomato &
    Basil) or Di Sicila (Ripe
    Olives & Mushrooms)
    Pasta Sauce
1 small green bell pepper, cut
    into strips
1 small red bell pepper, cut
    into strips
2 slices Provolone cheese,
    cut in half
1 (7-ounce) package of
    2 cups uncooked
    CREAMETTES® Elbow
    Macaroni, cooked as
    package directs and
    drained
Chopped parsley**

Coat chicken with flour. In large
skillet, brown chicken and garlic
in *3 tablespoons* oil; remove
chicken from pan. Add pasta
sauce then chicken. Bring to a
boil; reduce heat. Cover and
simmer 20 minutes, adding
peppers during last 5 minutes.
Uncover; top each chicken breast
with half cheese slice. Toss hot
cooked macaroni with remaining
1 tablespoon oil and parsley.
Serve with chicken and sauce.
Refrigerate leftovers.

Makes 4 servings

Chicken Florentine

**¾ pound boneless skinless
    chicken breasts, cut into
    strips
1 small onion, chopped
2 tablespoons margarine or
    butter
1 garlic clove, minced
1 package (10 ounces) BIRDS
    EYE® Chopped Spinach,
    thawed
1 cup chicken broth
½ cup water
1 cup Original MINUTE® Rice
⅓ cup grated Parmesan
    cheese**

Cook and stir chicken and onion
in hot margarine in large skillet
until chicken is lightly browned.
Add garlic and cook 30 seconds.
Add spinach, broth and water.
Bring to boil. Reduce heat;
simmer 3 minutes. Stir in rice
and cheese. Cover; remove from
heat. Let stand 5 minutes. Fluff
with fork.   *Makes 3 servings*

Microwave Directions: Thaw
and drain spinach, reduce broth
to ¾ cup and omit margarine.
Mix together chicken, onion and
garlic in microwavable dish.
Cover and cook at HIGH 3
minutes. Stir in spinach, broth,
water and rice. Cover and cook
at HIGH 6 minutes longer. Stir
in cheese.   *Makes 3 servings*

Cheesy Chicken Tetrazzini

2 whole skinless boneless chicken breasts, cut into 1-inch pieces (about 1½ pounds)
2 tablespoons butter or margarine
1½ cups sliced mushrooms
1 small red pepper, cut into julienne strips
½ cup sliced green onions
¼ cup all-purpose flour
1¾ cups chicken broth
1 cup light cream or half-and-half
2 tablespoons dry sherry
½ teaspoon salt
¼ teaspoon pepper
¼ teaspoon dried thyme, crushed
1 package (8 ounces) tri-color rotelle pasta, cooked until just tender and drained
¼ cup grated Parmesan cheese
2 tablespoons chopped parsley
1 cup shredded NOKKELOST® Jarlsberg or Jarlsberg Lite Cheese

In skillet, brown chicken in butter. Add mushrooms; cook until brown. Add pepper and green onions; cook several minutes, stirring occasionally. Stir in flour and cook several minutes until blended. Gradually blend in chicken broth, cream and sherry. Cook, stirring, until thickened and smooth. Add salt, pepper and thyme. Toss with pasta, Parmesan cheese and parsley. Spoon into 1½-quart lightly greased baking dish. Bake at 350°F 30 minutes. Top with Jarlsberg cheese. Bake until cheese is melted.
Makes 6 servings

Apple Curry Chicken

Apple Curry Chicken

2 whole chicken breasts, split, skinned and boned
1 cup apple juice, divided
¼ teaspoon salt
Dash of pepper
1½ cups plain croutons
1 medium-size apple, chopped
½ cup finely chopped onion
¼ cup raisins
2 teaspoons brown sugar
1 teaspoon curry powder
¾ teaspoon poultry seasoning
⅛ teaspoon garlic powder

Preheat oven to 350°F. Lightly grease shallow baking dish. Arrange chicken breasts in a single layer in prepared pan. Combine ¼ cup apple juice, salt and pepper in small bowl. Brush all of mixture over chicken. Combine croutons, apple, onion, raisins, sugar, curry powder, poultry seasoning and garlic powder in large bowl. Stir in remaining ¾ cup apple juice; spread over chicken. Cover; bake about 45 minutes or until chicken is tender. Garnish as desired.   *Makes 4 servings*

*Favorite recipe from **Delmarva Poultry Industry, Inc.***

Chicken Apple Sauté

4 skinned boneless chicken breast halves (about 1½ pounds)
1 tablespoon margarine or butter
1 medium all-purpose apple, cored and sliced
1 cup apple juice
1 tablespoon brown sugar, optional
1 tablespoon cornstarch
2 teaspoons WYLER'S® or STEERO® Chicken-Flavor Instant Bouillon
⅛ teaspoon *each* ground cinnamon and nutmeg
½ cup chopped walnuts, toasted

Preheat oven to 350°. In large skillet, brown chicken in margarine; pour off fat. Add apple slices. Combine apple juice, sugar, cornstarch, bouillon and spices. Pour over chicken and apple slices; bring to a boil. Reduce heat; cover and simmer 10 minutes. Cook uncovered 5 minutes or until tender. Garnish with walnuts. Refrigerate leftovers.
Makes 4 servings

Forty-Clove Chicken Filice

1 (3-pound) frying chicken, cut into serving pieces
40 cloves fresh garlic, peeled and left whole
½ cup dry white wine
¼ cup dry vermouth
¼ cup olive oil
4 ribs celery, thickly sliced
2 tablespoons finely chopped parsley
2 teaspoons dried basil
1 teaspoon dried oregano
Pinch of crushed red pepper
1 lemon
Salt and black pepper to taste

Preheat oven to 375°F. Place chicken pieces, skin-side up, in a single layer in shallow baking pan. Combine garlic, wine, vermouth, oil, celery, parsley, basil, oregano and red pepper in medium-sized bowl; mix thoroughly. Sprinkle garlic mixture over chicken pieces. Remove peel from lemon in thin strips; place peel throughout pan. Squeeze juice from lemon and pour over the top. Season with salt and black pepper. Cover pan with aluminum foil. Bake 40 minutes. Remove foil and bake another 15 minutes. Garnish as desired.

Makes 4 to 6 servings

Favorite recipe from **The Fresh Garlic Association**

Forty-Clove Chicken Filice

Broiled Lemon Chicken

4 skinless boneless chicken breast halves (about 1 pound)
¼ cup HEINZ® Worcestershire Sauce
2 tablespoons lemon juice
1 teaspoon minced garlic
½ teaspoon pepper
½ teaspoon grated lemon peel
Vegetable oil

Lightly flatten chicken breasts to uniform thickness. For marinade, in small bowl, combine Worcestershire sauce, lemon juice, garlic, pepper and lemon peel. Place chicken in shallow dish; pour marinade over chicken. Cover; chill 30 minutes, turning once. Place chicken on broiler pan; brush with oil. Broil, 4 to 5 inches from heat source, 3 to 4 minutes; turn. Brush with marinade, then with oil; broil an additional 3 to 4 minutes or until cooked.

Makes 4 servings

Crispy Chicken Parmesan

2 broiler-fryer chickens, cut up, skinned (2½ to 3 pounds each)
1¼ cups MIRACLE WHIP® Salad Dressing
2 cups corn flake crumbs
1 cup (4 ounces) KRAFT® 100% Grated Parmesan Cheese
¼ teaspoon pepper

• Heat oven to 350°F.

• Brush chicken with salad dressing.

• Mix crumbs, cheese and pepper; coat chicken. Place on rack of broiler pan.

• Bake 1 hour or until tender.

Makes 6 to 8 servings

Prep time: 15 minutes
Cooking time: 1 hour

Reuben Chicken

**THOUSAND ISLAND
DRESSING:** In small bowl, combine 1 cup mayonnaise, ¼ cup ketchup, ¼ cup sweet pickle relish, 1 tablespoon chopped onion, ¼ teaspoon salt and ⅛ teaspoon pepper; blend well. Refrigerate leftover dressing for another use.

Makes 1½ cups

Tangy Chicken and Herbs

- 1 medium onion, sliced
- 2 cloves garlic, minced
- ½ teaspoon dried rosemary leaves
- ½ teaspoon dried basil leaves
- ½ teaspoon dried thyme leaves
- 1 tablespoon vegetable oil
- 1 can (16 ounces) whole peeled tomatoes, drained, cut into bite-size pieces
- ½ cup HEINZ® Tomato Ketchup
- ¼ cup HEINZ® Apple Cider Vinegar
- ½ teaspoon salt
- ⅛ teaspoon pepper
- 2½ to 3 pounds broiler-fryer chicken pieces, skinned
  Cornstarch-water mixture
  Hot cooked noodles

In Dutch oven or large skillet, sauté onion, garlic, rosemary, basil and thyme in oil until onion is tender-crisp. Stir in tomatoes, ketchup, vinegar, salt and pepper. Add chicken. Bring to a boil. Reduce heat; cover and simmer, 35 to 40 minutes or until chicken is tender. Thicken sauce with mixture of equal parts cornstarch and water. Serve chicken and sauce with noodles.

*Makes 5 to 6 servings
(about 2½ cups sauce)*

Reuben Chicken

- 4 boneless, skinless chicken breast halves
- ¼ teaspoon salt
- ⅛ teaspoon pepper
- 1 can (8 ounces) Bavarian-style sauerkraut, well drained
- 4 thin corned beef slices
- 4 slices Swiss cheese
- 1 cup Thousand Island Dressing (recipe follows)

Preheat oven to 325°F. Place chicken in a single layer in greased baking pan. Sprinkle with salt and pepper. Press excess liquid from sauerkraut; spoon over chicken. Arrange corned beef and cheese slices over sauerkraut. Pour dressing evenly over the top. Cover pan with aluminum foil. Bake about 1½ hours or until chicken is tender. *Makes 4 servings*

Elegant Chicken Piccata

- ⅓ cup plus 1 tablespoon unsifted flour
- ½ teaspoon paprika
- 4 skinned chicken breast halves
- 3 tablespoons margarine or butter
- ¼ cup water
- 2 cups (1 pint) BORDEN® or MEADOW GOLD® Coffee Cream or Half-and-Half
- 1 tablespoon WYLER'S® or STEERO® Chicken-Flavor Instant Bouillon *or* 3 Chicken-Flavor Bouillon Cubes
- 2 tablespoons dry sherry
- 2 tablespoons REALEMON® Lemon Juice from Concentrate
- ½ to ¾ cup shredded Swiss cheese
  Hot cooked rice

Preheat oven to 350°. In paper or plastic bag, combine *⅓ cup* flour and paprika. Add chicken, a few pieces at a time; shake to coat. In large skillet, over medium heat, brown chicken in margarine on both sides until golden brown. Add water; cover and simmer 20 minutes. Remove chicken; arrange in 12×7-inch baking dish. Stir remaining *1 tablespoon* flour into drippings. Gradually add cream and bouillon. Over low heat, cook and stir until slightly thickened and bouillon is dissolved, about 5 to 10 minutes. Add sherry and ReaLemon® brand; pour over chicken. Bake covered 20 minutes. Uncover; top with cheese. Bake 5 minutes longer. Serve with rice. Refrigerate leftovers.
Makes 4 servings.

Chicken with Potatoes & Peppers

- ¼ cup WISH-BONE® Italian Dressing
- 1 (2½- to 3-pound) chicken, cut into serving pieces
- 1 can (28 ounces) whole peeled tomatoes, undrained and chopped
- 1 pound all-purpose potatoes, cut into chunks
- 2 medium onions, cut into quarters
- 2 medium red, green or yellow peppers, cut into thin strips
- 1 tablespoon fresh rosemary leaves*
- 1 teaspoon thyme leaves
- 1 teaspoon salt
- ¼ teaspoon pepper

Preheat oven to 375°.
In large skillet, heat Italian dressing and brown chicken over medium-high heat; set aside.
In 13×9-inch baking pan, combine remaining ingredients; add chicken and turn to coat. Bake uncovered, stirring occasionally, 50 minutes or until chicken is done and vegetables are tender. Serve, if desired, with French or Italian bread.
Makes about 4 servings.
*Substitution: Use 1 teaspoon dried rosemary leaves.
Note: Also terrific with Wish-Bone® Robusto Italian, Lite Italian or Lite Classic Dijon Vinaigrette Dressing.

Chicken Breasts in Wine Sauce

- ⅓ cup plus 2 tablespoons all-purpose flour, divided
- ½ teaspoon onion salt
- ¼ teaspoon pepper
- 2 whole chicken breasts, skinned and halved lengthwise
- 3 tablespoons CRISCO® Oil
- 2 small onions, cut into thirds
- ⅔ cup dry white wine
- 1 teaspoon instant chicken bouillon granules
- ½ teaspoon dried tarragon leaves
- ¾ cup half-and-half

Mix ⅓ cup flour, onion salt and pepper in large plastic food storage bag. Add chicken. Shake to coat.
Heat Crisco® Oil in large skillet. Add chicken. Brown over medium-high heat. Add onion, wine, bouillon granules and tarragon. Heat to boiling. Cover. Reduce heat. Simmer about 20 minutes, or until juices run clear and meat near bone is no longer pink. Transfer chicken to serving platter. Cover to keep warm. Remove and discard onion.
Place half-and-half in small bowl. Blend in remaining 2 tablespoons flour. Stir into drippings in large skillet. Cook over medium-low heat, stirring constantly, until thickened and bubbly. Serve with chicken.
4 servings.

Chicken with Potatoes & Peppers

Brunswick Stew

    1 (14½-ounce) can peeled
        tomatoes
    1 (17-ounce) can green lima
        beans
    1 (2½-pound) chicken, cut up
    1 (13¾-fluid ounce) can
        COLLEGE INN® Chicken
        Broth
    2 (6-ounce) cans tomato paste
    2 tablespoons red wine vinegar
    2 tablespoons Worcestershire
        sauce
    ¼ teaspoon ground red pepper
    2 cups cubed cooked pork

Drain tomatoes and lima beans, reserving liquid; coarsely chop tomatoes. In large heavy pot, over medium-high heat, combine chicken, chicken broth, tomato paste, tomato liquid, lima bean liquid, red wine vinegar, Worcestershire sauce and pepper; heat to a boil. Reduce heat; cover and simmer 20 minutes. Add tomatoes, lima beans and pork; cover. Simmer 20 to 25 minutes more or until chicken is done.
Makes 6 servings.
Microwave: In 5-quart microwave-proof casserole, combine first 8 ingredients as above. Cover with waxed paper. Microwave on MEDIUM (50% power) for 28 to 30 minutes, stirring twice during cooking time. Add tomatoes, lima beans and pork; cover. Microwave on LOW (30% power) for 18 to 20 minutes. Let stand, covered, 10 minutes before serving.

Brunswick Stew

Chicken Kyoto

    1 cup apple cider
    ½ cup soy sauce
    ½ cup vegetable oil
    ¼ cup sugar
    2 teaspoons ground ginger
    1 broiler-fryer chicken (2 to
        3 pounds), quartered

In small saucepan, combine all ingredients except chicken. Simmer over medium heat 5 to 8 minutes or until sugar is dissolved. Place chicken in shallow glass dish. Pour marinade over chicken; cover and refrigerate about 6 hours. Drain chicken; reserve marinade. Grill chicken, on uncovered grill, over medium-hot **KINGSFORD® Charcoal Briquets**, about 25 minutes on each side or until fork-tender, basting often with marinade.
Makes 4 servings.

Lemon Herbed Chicken

    ½ cup butter or margarine
    ½ cup vegetable oil
    ⅓ cup lemon juice
    2 tablespoons finely chopped
        parsley
    2 tablespoons garlic salt
    1 teaspoon dried rosemary,
        crushed
    1 teaspoon dried summer
        savory, crushed
    ½ teaspoon dried thyme,
        crushed
    ¼ teaspoon coarsely cracked
        black pepper
    6 chicken breast quarters with
        wings attached

In saucepan, combine all ingredients except chicken. Heat until butter melts. Place chicken in shallow glass dish and brush with sauce; let stand 10 to 15 minutes before cooking. Lightly oil grid. Grill chicken, skin-side up, on uncovered grill, over medium-hot **KINGSFORD® Charcoal Briquets** 30 to 45 minutes or until fork-tender, turning and basting with sauce every 10 minutes.
Makes 6 servings.

Country Chicken and Peppers

- 1 (2½- to 3-pound) chicken, cut up
- 1 pound hot Italian sausage, cut in 1-inch pieces
- 4 medium potatoes, unpared, cut in bite-size pieces
- 4 red or green peppers, cut in bite-size pieces
- 4 medium onions, quartered
- 1 (13¾-fluid ounce) can COLLEGE INN® Chicken Broth
- ¼ cup red wine vinegar with garlic
- 2 teaspoons Italian seasoning
- 3 tablespoons cornstarch

Cut each chicken breast into 2 pieces. In large roasting pan, combine chicken, sausage and potatoes. Bake at 425°F for 20 minutes; stir in peppers and onions. In small bowl, combine 1 cup chicken broth, vinegar and Italian seasoning; pour over meat and vegetables in pan. Cover; bake for 40 to 45 minutes more or until chicken is done, stirring occasionally.

Spoon meat and vegetables into serving dish. In 1-quart measuring cup, combine cornstarch with remaining broth until smooth; add enough pan liquid to equal 3 cups. Discard any remaining pan liquid. Return cornstarch mixture to roasting pan; cook and stir over medium heat until mixture thickens and boils. Pour over meat and vegetables.
Makes 6 servings.

Country Chicken and Peppers

Creamy Chicken Tarragon

- 2 tablespoons oil
- 2½- to 3-pound chicken, cut into serving pieces
- 1 envelope LIPTON® Recipe Secrets Onion, Onion-Mushroom or Golden Onion Recipe Soup Mix
- ½ teaspoon tarragon leaves
- 1 cup water
- ½ cup dry white wine
- 2 tablespoons all-purpose flour
- ½ cup whipping or heavy cream

In large skillet, heat oil and brown chicken over medium-high heat; drain. Add onion recipe soup mix and tarragon blended with water and wine. Simmer covered 45 minutes or until chicken is done. Remove chicken to serving platter and keep warm. Into skillet, stir in flour blended with cream. Bring just to the boiling point, then simmer, stirring constantly, until sauce is thickened, about 5 minutes. Serve sauce over chicken.
Makes about 4 servings.

Microwave Directions: Omit oil. In 3-quart casserole, microwave chicken, uncovered, at HIGH (Full Power) 12 minutes, rearranging chicken once; drain. Add onion recipe soup mix and tarragon blended with water and wine. Microwave covered 14 minutes or until chicken is done, rearranging chicken once. Remove chicken to serving platter and keep warm. Into casserole, stir flour blended with cream and microwave uncovered 4 minutes or until sauce is thickened, stirring once. Serve as above.

Baked Apricot Chicken

- 1 (10-ounce) jar BAMA® Apricot or Peach Preserves (1 cup)
- ¼ cup REALEMON® Lemon Juice from Concentrate
- 2 teaspoons soy sauce
- ½ teaspoon salt
- 1 (2½- to 3-pound) broiler-fryer chicken, cut up
- 1 cup dry bread crumbs
- ¼ cup margarine or butter, melted

Preheat oven to 350°. In shallow dish, combine preserves, ReaLemon® brand, soy sauce and salt. Coat chicken with apricot mixture; roll in bread crumbs. Set aside remaining apricot mixture. In greased 13×9-inch baking dish, arrange chicken; drizzle with margarine. Bake uncovered 1 hour or until tender. Heat remaining apricot mixture; serve with chicken. Refrigerate leftovers.
Makes 4 to 6 servings.

Chicken Cacciatore

1/3 cup all-purpose flour
2 1/2- to 3-pound broiler-fryer
    chicken, cut up
1/4 cup CRISCO® Oil
1 medium onion, thinly sliced
    and separated into rings
1/2 cup chopped green pepper
2 cloves garlic, minced
1 can (16 ounces) whole
    tomatoes, undrained
1 can (8 ounces) tomato sauce
1 can (4 ounces) sliced
    mushrooms, drained
3/4 teaspoon salt
1/2 teaspoon dried oregano leaves
    Hot cooked noodles

Place flour in large plastic food storage bag. Add a few chicken pieces. Shake to coat. Remove chicken from bag. Repeat with remaining chicken. Heat Crisco® Oil in large skillet. Add chicken. Brown over medium-high heat. Remove chicken from skillet; set aside. Add onion, green pepper and garlic to skillet. Sauté over moderate heat until tender. Add tomatoes, tomato sauce, mushrooms, salt and oregano, stirring to break apart tomatoes. Place chicken pieces on top of tomato mixture. Cover. Reduce heat. Simmer 30 to 40 minutes, or until chicken is tender and meat near bone is no longer pink. Serve with noodles.
4 servings.

Dan D's Chicken BBQ

1/3 cup white Zinfandel wine
1/3 cup olive or vegetable oil
1 tablespoon Dijon-style
    mustard
1 teaspoon dried rosemary,
    crushed
1 clove garlic, minced
    Salt and pepper
1 broiler-fryer chicken (2 to
    3 pounds), quartered

In shallow glass dish, combine all ingredients except chicken. Add chicken; turn to coat with marinade. Cover and refrigerate several hours or overnight, basting occasionally. Drain chicken; reserve marinade. Grill chicken, on covered grill, over medium-hot **KINGSFORD® Charcoal Briquets** about 15 minutes on each side or until fork-tender, basting often with marinade.
Makes 4 servings.

Chicken Livers in Wine Sauce

1/4 cup CRISCO® Oil
1 medium onion, cut into
    8 pieces
1/2 cup chopped celery
1/4 cup snipped fresh parsley
1 clove garlic, minced
1/3 cup all-purpose flour
3/4 teaspoon salt
1/4 teaspoon pepper
1 pound chicken livers, drained
1/2 cup water
1/2 cup milk
3 tablespoons dry white wine
3/4 teaspoon instant chicken
    bouillon granules
1/2 teaspoon dried rosemary
    leaves
    Hot cooked egg noodles

Heat Crisco® Oil in large skillet. Add onion, celery, parsley and garlic. Sauté over moderate heat until onion is tender. Set aside.

Mix flour, salt and pepper in large plastic food storage bag. Add livers. Shake to coat. Add livers and any remaining flour mixture to onion mixture. Brown livers over medium-high heat, stirring occasionally. Stir in water, milk, wine, bouillon granules and rosemary. Heat to boiling, stirring constantly. Cover. Reduce heat. Simmer, stirring occasionally, 7 to 10 minutes, or until livers are no longer pink. Serve with noodles.
4 to 6 servings.

Spicy Orange Chicken

Grilled Curried Chicken

1 cup (8 ounces) WISH-BONE®
    Creamy Italian Dressing
1/2 cup finely ground unsalted
    peanuts
1/2 cup orange marmalade
2 teaspoons curry powder
1/2 teaspoon tarragon leaves
2 whole chicken breasts (about
    1 pound each), split and
    skinned

In large shallow baking dish, thoroughly blend all ingredients except chicken. Add chicken and turn to coat. Cover and marinate in refrigerator, turning occasionally, 4 hours or overnight. Remove chicken, reserving marinade.

Grill or broil chicken, turning and basting frequently with reserved marinade, until done. If chicken browns too quickly, loosely cover with aluminum foil.
Makes about 4 servings.
    Note: Also terrific with Wish-Bone® Lite Creamy Italian Dressing.

Spicy Orange Chicken

1 cup water
1 medium onion, chopped
1 can (6 ounces) frozen orange
    juice concentrate, thawed,
    undiluted
1/4 cup catsup
3 medium cloves garlic, minced
1 teaspoon ground cinnamon
1 teaspoon TABASCO® pepper
    sauce
1/4 teaspoon salt
2 (2 1/2- to 3-pound) broiler-fryer
    chickens, cut up

In medium bowl combine water, onion, orange concentrate, catsup, garlic, cinnamon, Tabasco® sauce and salt; mix well. Place chicken in large shallow dish or plastic bag; add marinade. Cover; refrigerate at least 4 to 6 hours; turn chicken occasionally.

Remove chicken from marinade; place on grill 4 to 5 inches from source of heat. Grill 25 to 30 minutes or until done; turn frequently and brush each time with marinade. Heat any remaining marinade to a boil and serve with chicken.
Makes 8 servings.

Chicken Breasts with Chunky Salsa

Chicken Breasts with Chunky Salsa

½ cup **MIRACLE WHIP**® Salad
  Dressing
½ cup **RANCHER'S CHOICE**®
  Creamy Dressing
½ teaspoon ground red
  pepper
4 boneless skinless chicken
  breast halves
  (about 1¼ pounds)
  Chunky Salsa

• Mix dressings and red pepper
until well blended.

• Place chicken on grill over
medium-hot coals (coals will
have slight glow) or rack of
broiler pan. Grill, covered, **or**
broil 8 to 10 minutes on each
side or until tender, brushing
frequently with dressing
mixture. Serve with Chunky
Salsa.   *Makes 4 servings*

Note: For more flavor, marinate
chicken in dressing mixture 20
minutes or more before cooking.

Chunky Salsa

1 cup prepared salsa
½ cup finely chopped tomato
¼ cup finely chopped green
  bell pepper
2 tablespoons chopped
  cilantro

• Stir ingredients until well
blended.

Prep time: 15 minutes
Cooking time: 20 minutes

Southern Barbecued Chicken

⅔ cup **HEINZ**® Tomato
  Ketchup
1 tablespoon honey
2 teaspoons lemon juice
  Dash hot pepper sauce
2 to 2½ pounds broiler-fryer
  chicken pieces

In small bowl, combine all
ingredients except chicken. Broil
or grill chicken 25 to 30 minutes,
turning once. Brush ketchup
mixture on chicken; cook an
additional 5 to 10 minutes or
until chicken is tender, turning
and brushing with ketchup
mixture.

Makes 4 to 5 servings
(about ¾ cup sauce)

Herb-Marinated Chicken Breasts

¾ cup **MIRACLE WHIP**® Salad
  Dressing
¼ cup dry white wine
2 cloves garlic, minced
2 tablespoons finely
  chopped green onion
2 teaspoons dried basil
  leaves, crushed
1 teaspoon dried thyme
  leaves, crushed
6 boneless skinless chicken
  breast halves
  (about 1¾ pounds)

Mix dressing, wine, garlic, onion
and seasonings until well
blended. Pour dressing mixture
over chicken. Cover; marinate in
refrigerator several hours or
overnight. Drain. Place chicken
on greased rack of broiler pan.
Broil 4 to 6 minutes on each side
or until tender.

Makes 6 servings

Variation: For outdoor grilling:
Place chicken on greased grill
over low coals (coals will be ash
gray). Grill, uncovered, 4 to 6
minutes on each side or until
tender.

Southern Fried Chicken Strips

¾ cup **BORDEN**® or **MEADOW
  GOLD**® Buttermilk
1 tablespoon **WYLER'S**® or
  STEERO® Chicken-Flavor
  Instant Bouillon
½ teaspoon oregano leaves
1 pound skinned boneless
  chicken breasts, cut into
  strips
1¼ cups unsifted flour
1 to 2 teaspoons paprika
  Vegetable oil
  Peach Dipping Sauce

In large bowl, combine buttermilk, bouillon and oregano; let stand 10 minutes. Stir in chicken. Let stand 30 minutes to blend flavors. In plastic bag, combine flour and paprika. Add chicken, a few pieces at a time; shake to coat. Dip in buttermilk mixture again; coat with flour again. In large skillet, fry chicken strips in hot oil until golden on both sides. Drain on paper towels. Serve with Peach Dipping Sauce. Refrigerate leftovers.

Makes 4 servings

PEACH DIPPING SAUCE: In blender container, combine 1 (16-ounce) jar BAMA® Peach or Apricot Preserves (1½ cups), ¼ cup Dijon-style mustard and 2 tablespoons REALEMON® Lemon Juice from Concentrate; blend until smooth.

Makes about 2 cups

Versatile Chicken

- ¾ cup BORDEN® or MEADOW GOLD® Buttermilk
- 1 tablespoon WYLER'S® or STEERO® Chicken-Flavor Instant Bouillon
- ½ teaspoon oregano leaves, optional
- 3 pounds chicken pieces
- 1 cup unsifted flour
- 1 teaspoon paprika
- ¼ cup margarine or butter, melted

In large bowl, combine buttermilk, bouillon and oregano if desired; let stand 10 minutes. Add chicken, stirring to coat. Let stand 30 minutes to blend flavors. In plastic bag, combine flour and paprika. Add chicken, a few pieces at a time; shake to coat. Arrange chicken in 13×9-inch baking dish. Drizzle with margarine. Bake at 350° for 1 hour or until golden. Refrigerate leftovers.

Makes 4 to 6 servings

Tip: To fry chicken, omit melted margarine; fry in vegetable oil.

Oven Barbecued Chicken

- 1 cup unsifted flour
- 1 teaspoon salt
- 3 pounds chicken pieces
- ¼ cup plus 2 tablespoons margarine or butter, melted
- ¼ cup chopped onion
- 1 clove garlic, finely chopped
- 1 cup ketchup
- ¼ cup firmly packed brown sugar
- ¼ cup REALEMON® Lemon Juice from Concentrate
- ¼ cup water
- 2 tablespoons Worcestershire sauce

Preheat oven to 350°. In plastic bag, combine flour and salt. Add chicken, a few pieces at a time; shake to coat. Place in greased 13×9-inch baking dish; drizzle with ¼ cup margarine. Bake uncovered 30 minutes. Meanwhile, in small saucepan, cook onion and garlic in remaining *2 tablespoons* margarine until tender. Add remaining ingredients; simmer uncovered 10 minutes. Pour over chicken; bake uncovered 30 minutes longer or until tender. Refrigerate leftovers.

Makes 4 to 6 servings

Versatile Chicken

Grilled Chicken Fajitas

1 cup MIRACLE WHIP® Salad Dressing
¼ cup lime juice
3 garlic cloves, minced
1 teaspoon <u>each</u>: dried oregano leaves, crushed, ground cumin
4 boneless skinless chicken breast halves (about 1¼ pounds)
1 <u>each</u>: green, red and yellow bell pepper, quartered
1 onion, cut into 6 wedges
4 flour tortillas (8 inch), warmed
Sour cream
Salsa

• Mix salad dressing, juice, garlic and seasonings until well blended. Pour over chicken. Marinate in refrigerator at least 20 minutes; drain.

• Place chicken on grill over medium-hot coals (coals will have slight glow) or rack of broiler pan. Grill, covered, **or** broil 10 minutes.

• Place vegetables on grill or broiler pan. Continue cooking chicken and vegetables 10 minutes or until tender, turning chicken and vegetables occasionally.

• Slice chicken and bell peppers into strips. Fill tortillas with chicken and vegetables. Top with sour cream and salsa; roll up.

Makes 6 servings

Prep time: 15 minutes plus marinating
Grilling time: 20 minutes

Grilled Greek Chicken

1 cup MIRACLE WHIP® Salad Dressing
½ cup chopped fresh parsley
¼ cup dry white wine or chicken broth
1 lemon, sliced, cut in half
2 tablespoons dried oregano leaves, crushed
1 tablespoon <u>each</u>: garlic powder, pepper
2 broiler-fryer chickens, cut up (2½ to 3 pounds each)

• Mix all ingredients except chicken until well blended. Pour over chicken. Marinate in refrigerator at least 20 minutes; drain.

• Place chicken on grill over medium-hot coals (coals will have slight glow). Grill, covered, 20 to 25 minutes on each side or until tender.

Makes 8 servings

Prep time: 10 minutes plus marinating
Grilling time: 50 minutes

Mediterranean Marinade

⅓ cup olive or vegetable oil
¼ cup REALEMON® Lemon Juice from Concentrate
3 tablespoons dry sherry or water
2 teaspoons rosemary leaves, crushed
2 cloves garlic, finely chopped
1½ teaspoons WYLER'S® or STEERO® Chicken- or Beef-Flavor Instant Bouillon

In large shallow dish or plastic bag, combine ingredients; add chicken, beef or pork. Cover; marinate in refrigerator 4 hours or overnight, turning occasionally. Remove meat from marinade; grill or broil as desired, basting frequently with heated marinade. Refrigerate leftover meat.

Makes about 1 cup

Spicy Microwave Grilled Chicken

1 cup MIRACLE WHIP® Salad Dressing
1 package (1.25 ounces) taco seasoning mix
2 broiler-fryer chickens, cut up (2½ to 3 pounds each)

• Mix salad dressing and taco seasoning mix until well blended.

• Arrange chicken in 13×9-inch microwave-safe baking dish. Brush with salad dressing mixture. Cover with plastic wrap; vent.

• Microwave on HIGH 15 minutes, turning dish after 8 minutes.

• Place chicken on grill over medium-hot coals (coals will have slight glow). Grill, covered, 5 to 10 minutes on each side or until tender and browned.

Makes 6 to 8 servings

Prep time: 5 minutes
Cooking time: 20 minutes
Microwave cooking time: 15 minutes

Spicy Microwave Grilled Chicken

Sweet and Spicy Chicken Barbecue

Grilled Capon

   1 capon or whole roasting chicken (6 to 7 pounds)
   Salt
  ¼ teaspoon poultry seasoning
 1½ medium onions, quartered
   1 tablespoon rubbed sage
   2 stalks celery with leaves, cut into 1-inch pieces
   2 medium carrots, cut into ½-inch pieces
   2 tablespoons butter or margarine, melted
   K.C. MASTERPIECE® Barbecue Sauce

Wash capon thoroughly under cold running water; pat dry with paper toweling. Rub cavity lightly with salt and poultry seasoning. Insert a few onion quarters in neck and fold neck skin over onion. Fold wings across back with tips touching to secure neck skin. Sprinkle 1 teaspoon of the sage in body cavity and stuff with remaining onion quarters, the celery and carrots. Tie legs and tail together with kitchen twine. Insert meat thermometer in center of thigh muscle, not touching bone. Brush skin with melted butter. Rub with remaining 2 teaspoons sage.

Arrange medium-hot **KINGS-FORD® Charcoal Briquets** around drip pan. Place capon, breast-side up, over drip pan; cover grill and cook 1½ to 2 hours or until thermometer registers 185°F. Tent with heavy-duty foil to prevent overbrowning, if necessary. Brush capon with barbecue sauce during last 10 minutes of cooking. Garnish with parsley; serve with additional heated barbecue sauce, if desired.

Makes 6 servings.

Sweet and Spicy Chicken Barbecue

 1½ cups DOLE® Pineapple Orange Juice
   1 cup orange marmelade
  ⅔ cup teriyaki sauce
  ½ cup brown sugar, packed
  ½ teaspoon ground cloves
  ½ teaspoon ground ginger
   4 frying chickens (about 2 pounds each), halved or quartered
   Salt and pepper
   DOLE® Pineapple slices
   4 teaspoons cornstarch

In saucepan, combine juice, marmalade, teriyaki sauce, brown sugar, cloves and ginger. Heat until sugar dissolves; let cool. Sprinkle chicken with salt and pepper to taste. Place in glass baking pan. Pour juice mixture over chicken; turn to coat all sides. Marinate, covered, 2 hours in refrigerator, turning often.

Preheat oven to 350°F. Light charcoal grill. Drain chicken; reserve marinade. Bake chicken in preheated oven 20 minutes. Arrange chicken on lightly greased grill 4 to 6 inches above glowing coals. Grill, turning and basting often with reserved marinade, 20 to 25 minutes or until meat near bone is no longer pink. Grill pineapple slices 3 minutes or until heated through.

In small saucepan, dissolve cornstarch in remaining marinade. Cook over medium heat until sauce boils and thickens. Spoon over chicken.

Makes 8 servings.

Roasted Duckling with Orange & Plum Sauce

- 1 (3-pound) duckling
- 1 medium orange, halved
- 1 medium onion, halved
- ½ cup WISH-BONE® Deluxe French or Lite French Style Dressing
- ½ cup orange juice
- 2 tablespoons brown sugar
- 1 teaspoon grated orange peel (optional)
- ¼ teaspoon ground cinnamon
- ⅛ teaspoon ground cloves
- ⅛ teaspoon ground nutmeg
- 1 tablespoon butter or margarine
- ½ cup chopped onion
- 1 teaspoon finely chopped garlic
- 2 tablespoons brandy
- 2 medium plums, pitted and cut into wedges
- 2 small oranges, peeled, sectioned and seeded

Preheat oven to 400°.

Stuff duckling with orange and onion halves. Close cavity with skewers or wooden toothpicks; tie legs together with string. With pin or fork, pierce skin. In roasting pan, on rack, arrange duckling breast side up. Roast 40 minutes, turning duckling every 10 minutes.

Meanwhile, in small bowl, blend deluxe French dressing, orange juice, sugar, orange peel, cinnamon, cloves and nutmeg. Pour ½ of the dressing mixture over duckling; loosely cover with heavy-duty aluminum foil. Continue roasting, basting occasionally, 30 minutes or until meat thermometer reaches 185°. Remove to serving platter and keep warm.

Meanwhile, in medium saucepan, melt butter and cook onion with garlic over medium heat, stirring occasionally, 5 minutes or until onion is tender. Add brandy, the plums and orange sections and cook, stirring occasionally, 5 minutes. Stir in remaining dressing mixture and heat through. Serve with duckling.
Makes about 2 servings.

Thai Hens

- 3 fresh or thawed Rock Cornish hens (1¼ to 1½ pounds each)
- ½ cup KIKKOMAN® Teriyaki Sauce
- 1 tablespoon grated lemon peel
- 1 tablespoon lemon juice
- 2 cloves garlic, pressed
- ¼ to ½ teaspoon ground red pepper (cayenne)
- 1 tablespoon minced fresh cilantro

Remove and discard giblets and necks from hens. Split hens lengthwise. Rinse halves under cold running water; drain well and pat dry with paper towels. Place in large plastic bag. Combine teriyaki sauce, lemon peel and juice, garlic and red pepper; pour over hens. Press air out of bag; tie top securely. Turn bag over several times to coat halves. Refrigerate 8 hours or overnight, turning bag over occasionally. Reserving marinade, remove hens and place on rack of broiler pan. Broil about 7 inches from heat source 45 to 50 minutes, or until tender, turning over frequently and brushing with reserved marinade. Remove to serving platter and immediately sprinkle cilantro over hens.
Makes 4 to 6 servings.

Lemon Herb Cornish Hens

Lemon Herb Cornish Hens

- 2 (1½-pound) Rock Cornish hens, split in half lengthwise
- Salt and pepper
- 2 tablespoons finely chopped onion
- 1 clove garlic, finely chopped
- ¼ cup vegetable oil
- ¼ cup REALEMON® Lemon Juice from Concentrate
- 2 teaspoons WYLER'S® or STEERO® Chicken-Flavor Instant Bouillon *or* 2 Chicken-Flavor Bouillon Cubes
- 1 teaspoon chopped parsley
- 1 teaspoon rosemary leaves, crushed

Season hens lightly with salt and pepper. In small saucepan, cook onion and garlic in oil until tender. Add remaining ingredients; simmer 10 minutes. Grill hens until tender and crisp, about 1 hour, turning and basting frequently with sauce. Refrigerate leftovers.
Makes 4 servings.

Oven Method: Place hens on rack in roasting pan. Bake at 375° for 1 hour and 15 minutes, basting frequently.

Chicken and Broccoli

1 pound skinned boneless
  chicken breasts, cut into
  bite-size pieces
3 cups broccoli flowerets,
  cooked
1 egg white, beaten
5 teaspoons soy sauce
2 teaspoons cornstarch
¼ cup vegetable oil
8 ounces fresh mushrooms,
  sliced (about 2 cups)
2 tablespoons REALEMON®
  Lemon Juice from
  Concentrate
2 tablespoons dry sherry
1 tablespoon chopped pimiento
  Hot cooked rice

In medium bowl, combine egg white, *3
teaspoons* soy sauce and cornstarch;
mix well. Add chicken; stir to coat. Refrigerate 1 hour. In large skillet, over
high heat, brown chicken in oil; remove. Add mushrooms; cook and stir
until tender. Add chicken, broccoli
and remaining ingredients except
rice; heat through. Serve with rice.
Refrigerate leftovers.
Makes 4 to 6 servings.

Oriental Game Hens

4 Cornish game hens (1 to
  1½ pounds each)
  Salt
½ cup peanut or vegetable oil
½ cup soy sauce
2 tablespoons brown sugar
1 tablespoon wine vinegar
½ teaspoon grated fresh ginger
  Dash ground cloves

Remove giblets from hens. Remove
fatty portion from neck and tail area
of hens. Rinse hens under cold running water. Pat hens dry with paper
toweling. Sprinkle cavities with salt.
Close neck and body openings with
skewers. Tie legs together; tuck wings
under back and tie with kitchen
twine. Arrange hens in shallow micro-
waveable dish and cover with vented
plastic wrap. Microwave at 50% power
10 minutes. For basting sauce, in
small bowl, combine remaining ingredients. Lightly oil grid. Grill hens, on
uncovered grill, over medium-hot
KINGSFORD® Charcoal Briquets
20 minutes or until thigh moves easily and juices run clear, basting often
with sauce.
Makes 4 servings.

Chicken and Broccoli

Chicken Breasts with Artichoke-Cheese Stuffing

4 whole boneless chicken
  breasts, skinned and halved
  lengthwise
1½ cups shredded Monterey Jack
  cheese (about 6 ounces)
¼ cup mayonnaise
1 tablespoon finely chopped
  onion
1 tablespoon dried parsley
  flakes
1 teaspoon Dijon mustard
1 jar (6 ounces) marinated
  artichoke hearts, drained
⅓ cup all-purpose flour
¼ teaspoon salt
⅛ teaspoon pepper
1 egg
2 tablespoons water
1 cup seasoned dry bread
  crumbs
⅓ cup CRISCO® Oil

Pound chicken breasts to ¼-inch
thickness. Set aside. Mix cheese, mayonnaise, onion, parsley flakes and
mustard in small mixing bowl. Cut
artichoke hearts into bite-size pieces.

Stir into cheese mixture. Spread
about ¼ cup cheese mixture down
center of each piece of chicken. Roll
up and secure ends with wooden
picks. Mix flour, salt and pepper in
shallow dish. Dip rolled chicken in
flour mixture to coat. Set aside.

Mix egg and water in shallow dish.
Place bread crumbs in another shallow dish or on sheet of waxed paper.
Dip rolled chicken in egg mixture
then in bread crumbs, pressing to coat
thoroughly. Cover and refrigerate
coated chicken about 1 hour.

Preheat oven to 350°F. Place
Crisco® Oil in 13×9-inch baking pan.
Place in oven 10 minutes. Remove
from oven. Using tongs, roll coated
chicken in hot Crisco Oil. Arrange
chicken in pan. Bake at 350°F, 35
minutes, or until golden brown.
8 servings.

Chicken Cordon Bleu with Golden Cream Sauce

3 whole boneless chicken
  breasts (about 2½ pounds),
  halved and lightly pounded
6 slices Swiss cheese
6 slices cooked ham
2 tablespoons butter or
  margarine
¼ teaspoon ground nutmeg
⅛ teaspoon pepper
1 envelope LIPTON® Recipe
  Secrets Golden Onion
  Recipe Soup Mix
2 cups (1 pint) light cream or
  half and half
¼ cup water
  Hot cooked noodles

Top each chicken breast half with
slice of cheese and ham; roll up and
secure with wooden toothpicks.

In large skillet, melt butter and
brown chicken over medium heat;
drain. Add nutmeg and pepper, then
golden onion recipe soup mix blended
with cream and water. Bring just to
the boiling point, then simmer covered, basting occasionally, 20 minutes
or until chicken is done. To serve, arrange chicken and sauce over hot noodles.
Makes about 6 servings.

Orange-Cashew Chicken

- **1 pound boneless chicken breasts**
- **½ cup KIKKOMAN® Teriyaki Baste & Glaze**
- **2 tablespoons orange juice**
- **2 tablespoons dry white wine**
- **2 tablespoons vegetable oil**
- **1 green pepper, cut into thin strips**
- **½ cup diagonally sliced celery**
- **1 can (11 oz.) mandarin orange segments, drained**
- **½ cup roasted cashews**

Cut chicken into thin slices. Combine teriyaki baste & glaze, orange juice and wine; set aside. Heat oil in hot wok or large skillet over medium heat. Add chicken, green pepper and celery; stir-fry 3 to 4 minutes. Pour in baste & glaze mixture; cook and stir until chicken and vegetables are coated with sauce. Remove from heat; stir in orange segments and cashews. Serve immediately.
Makes 4 servings.

Chicken 'n Vegetable Stir Fry

- **3 tablespoons oil**
- **1 pound boneless chicken breasts, cut into thin strips**
- **½ cup broccoli florets**
- **2 ounces snow peas (about ½ cup)**
- **1 medium carrot, thinly sliced**
- **½ medium red or green pepper, cut into thin strips**
- **1 envelope LIPTON® Recipe Secrets Golden Onion Recipe Soup Mix**
- **1 teaspoon cornstarch**
- **½ teaspoon ground ginger**
- **1½ cups water**
- **2 teaspoons soy sauce**
- **1 teaspoon white or rice vinegar Hot cooked rice**

In large skillet, heat oil and cook chicken with vegetables over medium-high heat, stirring constantly, 10 minutes or until chicken is golden and vegetables are crisp-tender. Thoroughly blend golden onion recipe soup mix, cornstarch, ginger, water, soy sauce and vinegar; stir into chicken mixture. Bring to a boil, then simmer uncovered 5 minutes or until sauce is thickened. Serve

Chicken 'n Vegetable Stir Fry

over hot rice and garnish, if desired, with sliced green onion and toasted sesame seeds.
Makes about 4 servings.

Microwave Directions: Omit oil and decrease ginger to ¼ teaspoon. In 2-quart casserole, microwave chicken, uncovered, at HIGH (Full Power) 4 minutes or until almost done; remove chicken and drain. Add vegetables to casserole and microwave uncovered 5 minutes. Thoroughly blend golden onion recipe soup mix, cornstarch, ginger, water, soy sauce and vinegar; stir into vegetables. Microwave uncovered 5 minutes or until sauce is thickened, stirring once. Return chicken to casserole and heat 1 minute or until heated through. Let stand covered 5 minutes. Serve and garnish as above.

Spicy Smoked Duck

- **1 (4- to 5-pound) frozen duckling, thawed**
- **¼ cup KIKKOMAN® Lite Soy Sauce**
- **1 teaspoon liquid smoke seasoning**
- **½ teaspoon fennel seed, well crushed**
- **¼ teaspoon pepper**
- **⅛ teaspoon ground cloves**

Remove and discard giblets and neck from duckling cavity. Wash duckling; drain and gently pat dry with paper towels. Combine lite soy sauce, liquid

smoke, fennel, pepper and cloves. Brush body cavity with sauce mixture. Place duckling, breast side up, on rack in roasting pan. Roast at 425°F. 1 hour. *Reduce oven temperature to 350°F.* Continue roasting 45 minutes, or until tender. Brush skin of duckling several times with sauce mixture during last 30 minutes of cooking time. Let stand 15 minutes before carving.
Makes 4 servings.

Grilled Game Hens, Texas-Style

- **1 can (8 ounces) tomato sauce**
- **¼ cup vegetable oil**
- **1½ teaspoons chili powder**
- **1 teaspoon paprika**
- **¼ teaspoon garlic powder**
- **¼ teaspoon cayenne pepper**
- **4 Cornish game hens (1 to 1½ pounds each), cut into halves**

In small bowl, combine all ingredients except game hens. Brush hens generously with tomato mixture. Grill hens, on covered grill, over medium-hot **KINGSFORD® with Mesquite Charcoal Briquets** 45 to 50 minutes or until fork-tender, brushing frequently with tomato mixture.
Makes 4 servings.

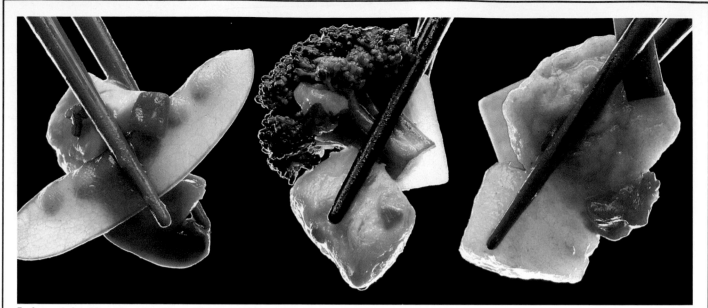

Left to right: Moo Goo Gai Pan, Chicken Walnut Stir-Fry and Sweet-and-Sour Chicken

Chicken Walnut Stir-Fry

5 tablespoons CRISCO® Oil, divided
5 teaspoons soy sauce, divided
3 teaspoons cornstarch, divided
2 whole boneless chicken breasts, skinned, cut into 1-inch pieces
1/2 cup chicken broth
1/2 teaspoon ground ginger
1/2 teaspoon dried crushed red pepper
1 medium onion, cut into 1-inch pieces
1 clove garlic, minced
1/2 pound fresh broccoli, cut into 1-inch pieces
1/2 cup coarsely chopped walnuts
Hot cooked rice

Mix 1 tablespoon Crisco® Oil, 2 teaspoons soy sauce and 1 teaspoon cornstarch in small mixing bowl. Add chicken. Stir to coat. Cover and refrigerate about 30 minutes.

Mix chicken broth, ginger, remaining 3 teaspoons soy sauce and remaining 2 teaspoons cornstarch in small bowl. Set aside.

Heat remaining 4 tablespoons Crisco® Oil in large skillet or wok. Add refrigerated chicken mixture and red pepper. Stir-fry over medium-high heat until chicken is no longer pink. Remove chicken from skillet; set aside. Add onion and garlic to skillet. Stir-fry over medium-high heat until onion is tender. Add broccoli. Stir-fry until tender. Add chicken and chicken broth mixture. Cook, stirring constantly, until thickened. Stir in walnuts. Serve with rice.
4 servings.

Jade & Ruby Stir-Fry

1 whole chicken breast, skinned and boned
1 pound fresh broccoli
2 tablespoons vegetable oil
1 medium onion, chunked
2 tablespoons water
2 medium-size red bell peppers, chunked
1/2 pound fresh mushrooms, quartered
1/3 cup KIKKOMAN® Stir-Fry Sauce
1/4 teaspoon crushed red pepper

Cut chicken into 1-inch square pieces. Remove flowerets from broccoli; cut into bite-size pieces. Peel stalks; cut into thin slices. Heat oil in hot wok or large skillet over high heat. Add chicken; stir-fry 1 minute. Add broccoli and onion; stir-fry 1 minute. Add water; cover and cook 2 minutes, stirring once. Add bell peppers and mushrooms; stir-fry 2 minutes. Stir in stir-fry sauce and crushed red pepper. Cook and stir until chicken and vegetables are coated with sauce. Serve immediately.
Makes 4 servings.

Moo Goo Gai Pan

2 tablespoons cornstarch
2 tablespoons water
3 whole boneless chicken breasts, skinned, cut into 1-inch pieces
1/2 teaspoon salt
1/8 teaspoon pepper
1/4 cup CRISCO® Oil
1/4 cup chopped green onion
2 cups sliced fresh mushrooms
1 jar (2 ounces) sliced pimiento, drained
1 teaspoon ground ginger
1 can (14 1/2 ounces) chicken broth
2 packages (6 to 7 ounces each) frozen pea pods
Hot cooked rice

Blend cornstarch and water in small bowl until smooth. Set aside.

Sprinkle chicken with salt and pepper. Heat Crisco® Oil in large skillet or wok. Add chicken. Stir-fry over medium-high heat until no longer pink. Remove chicken from skillet. Add onion to skillet. Stir-fry over medium-high heat 1 minute. Stir in mushrooms, pimiento and ginger. Cook, stirring constantly, 2 to 3 minutes, or until mushrooms are tender. Add chicken broth and pea pods. Heat to boiling, stirring to break apart pea pods. Add cornstarch mixture. Heat to boiling, stirring constantly. Boil 1 minute. Remove from heat. Stir in chicken. Serve with rice. Sprinkle with *toasted almonds* and serve with *soy sauce*, if desired.
6 to 8 servings.

Sweet-and-Sour Chicken

1 can (16 ounces) whole tomatoes
½ cup plum jelly
¼ cup cider vinegar
1 tablespoon sugar
1 tablespoon cornstarch
1 tablespoon soy sauce
1 teaspoon instant chicken bouillon granules
Batter:
½ cup water
⅓ cup all-purpose flour
⅓ cup cornstarch
1 teaspoon salt
⅛ teaspoon garlic powder
⅛ teaspoon pepper

1 whole boneless chicken breast, skinned, cut into 1- to 1½-inch pieces
CRISCO® Oil for frying
1 large green pepper, cored, seeded and cut into 1-inch pieces
4 green onions, cut into 1-inch pieces
1 can (8 ounces) pineapple chunks, drained
Hot cooked rice

Drain tomatoes, reserving ¼ cup juice. Cut up tomatoes and set aside. Blend reserved juice, plum jelly, vinegar, sugar, 1 tablespoon cornstarch, soy sauce and bouillon granules in small mixing bowl. Set aside.

For batter, blend all ingredients in small mixing bowl. Add chicken. Stir to coat. Heat 2 to 3 inches Crisco® Oil in large saucepan to 350°F. Remove several chicken pieces from batter with slotted spoon. Fry in hot Crisco® Oil 3 to 4 minutes, or until light golden brown. Drain on paper towels. Repeat with remaining chicken.

Discard Crisco® Oil, reserving 2 tablespoons in saucepan. Add green pepper and onions. Stir-fry over medium-high heat about 3 minutes, or until tender. Stir in tomato juice mixture. Heat to boiling, stirring constantly. Continue to boil 1 minute, stirring constantly. Stir in pineapple chunks, chicken and tomatoes. Cook 1 to 2 minutes longer. Serve with rice.
2 to 4 servings.

Mongolian Pot

2 whole chicken breasts, skinned and boned
4 tablespoons KIKKOMAN® Soy Sauce, divided
2 teaspoons minced fresh ginger root
½ teaspoon sugar
2 cans (10¼ oz. each) condensed chicken broth
4 soup cans water
1 large clove garlic, minced
½ pound cabbage, cut into ¾-inch chunks (about 4 cups)
¾ pound fresh spinach, trimmed, washed and drained
3 green onions and tops, cut into 1-inch lengths and slivered
4 ounces vermicelli or thin spaghetti, cooked and drained
¼ pound fresh mushrooms, sliced

Cut chicken into thin strips. Combine 2 tablespoons soy sauce, ginger and sugar in medium dish; stir in chicken. Let stand 15 minutes. Meanwhile, combine chicken broth, water, remaining 2 tablespoons soy sauce and garlic in deep electric skillet or electric wok; bring to boil. Reduce heat; keep broth mixture hot. Arrange cabbage, spinach, green onions, vermicelli and mushrooms on platter. Using chopsticks or tongs, let individuals select and add chicken, vegetables and vermicelli to hot broth. Cook chicken until tender, vegetables to desired

doneness and vermicelli until heated through. Serve in individual bowls with additional soy sauce, as desired. When all foods are cooked, serve broth as soup.
Makes 4 to 6 servings.

Colorful Dragon Stir-Fry

1 whole chicken breast, skinned and boned
1 pound fresh broccoli
5 tablespoons KIKKOMAN® Stir-Fry Sauce, divided
3 tablespoons vegetable oil, divided
1 medium onion, cut into thin wedges
1 medium carrot, cut diagonally into thin slices
2 tablespoons water

Cut chicken into ½-inch strips. Remove flowerets from broccoli; set aside. Peel stalks; cut into thin slices. Coat chicken with 1 tablespoon stir-fry sauce. Heat 1 tablespoon oil in hot wok or large skillet over high heat. Add chicken and stir-fry 3 minutes; remove. Heat remaining 2 tablespoons oil in same pan. Add onion; stir-fry 1 minute. Add broccoli and carrot; stir-fry 2 minutes longer. Pour water into pan. Reduce heat and simmer, covered, 3 minutes; stir once. Add remaining 4 tablespoons stir-fry sauce and chicken. Cook and stir just until chicken and vegetables are coated. Serve immediately.
Makes 4 servings.

Colorful Dragon Stir-Fry

Kung Pao Chicken

**5 teaspoons soy sauce,
    divided**
**5 teaspoons dry sherry,
    divided**
**3½ teaspoons cornstarch,
    divided**
¼ teaspoon salt
**3 skinless boneless chicken
    breast halves, cut into
    bite-size pieces**
**2 tablespoons chicken broth
    or water**
**1 tablespoon red wine
    vinegar**
1½ teaspoons sugar
**3 tablespoons vegetable oil,
    divided**
⅓ cup salted peanuts
**6 to 8 small dried hot chili
    peppers**
**1½ teaspoons minced fresh
    ginger**
**2 green onions, cut into
    1½-inch pieces**

For marinade, combine 2 teaspoons soy sauce, 2 teaspoons sherry, 2 teaspoons cornstarch and salt in large bowl; mix well. Add chicken; stir to coat well. Let stand 30 minutes. Combine remaining 3 teaspoons soy sauce, 3 teaspoons sherry, chicken broth, vinegar, sugar and remaining 1½ teaspoons cornstarch in small bowl; mix well and set aside. Heat 1 tablespoon oil in wok or large skillet over medium heat. Add peanuts and cook until golden. Remove peanuts and set aside. Heat remaining 2 tablespoons oil in wok over medium heat. Add chili peppers and stir-fry until peppers just begin to darken, about 1 minute. Increase heat to high. Add chicken and stir-fry 2 minutes. Add ginger; stir-fry until chicken is cooked through, about 1 minute more. Add onions and peanuts to wok. Stir cornstarch mixture and add to pan; cook and stir until sauce boils and thickens.

Makes 3 servings

Crispy Chicken Stir-Fry

**1 DOLE® Fresh Pineapple
    Vegetable oil**
½ cup peanuts
**1 egg
    Cornstarch
    Soy sauce**
**1 pound boneless, skinless
    chicken breasts, chunked**
1 onion, sliced
2 large cloves garlic, pressed
**1 tablespoon chopped
    ginger root**
1 cup water
¼ cup pale dry sherry
¼ teaspoon ground cloves
¼ teaspoon ground cinnamon
**1 bunch DOLE® Broccoli, cut
    into florettes**
**1 DOLE® Red Bell Pepper,
    seeded, chunked**

• Twist crown from pineapple. Cut pineapple in half lengthwise, then cut pineapple in half again. Cut fruit from shells with knife. Trim off core and cut fruit into bite-size chunks. Measure 2 cups pineapple; refrigerate remainder for another use.

• In 10-inch skillet, heat about ½ inch oil over medium-high heat. Brown peanuts. Remove with slotted spoon to paper towels.

• Combine egg, ⅓ cup cornstarch and 2 teaspoons soy sauce in shallow dish. Coat chicken with batter. In same skillet, sauté chicken in hot oil over medium-high heat until browned. Remove with slotted spoon; drain on paper towels.

• Drain oil, reserving 2 tablespoons in skillet. Stir-fry onion, garlic and ginger root 1 minute. Combine water, ¼ cup soy sauce, 2 teaspoons cornstarch, sherry and spices in small bowl. Stir into skillet; add broccoli and pepper.

• Reduce heat. Cover; simmer 1 to 2 minutes until broccoli is tender-crisp and sauce boils and thickens. Stir in pineapple, peanuts and chicken; heat through.   *Makes 4 servings*

Preparation Time: 15 minutes
Cook Time: 15 minutes

Kung Pao Chicken

Chicken Cashew

1½ pounds skinned boneless chicken breasts, cut into bite-size pieces
2 teaspoons WYLER'S® or STEERO® Chicken-Flavor Instant Bouillon *or*
2 Chicken-Flavor Bouillon Cubes
1¼ cups boiling water
2 tablespoons soy sauce
1 tablespoon cornstarch
2 teaspoons brown sugar
½ teaspoon ground ginger
2 tablespoons vegetable oil
8 ounces fresh mushrooms, sliced (about 2 cups)
½ cup sliced green onions
1 small green bell pepper, sliced
1 (8-ounce) can sliced water chestnuts, drained
½ cup cashews
Hot cooked rice

In small saucepan, dissolve bouillon in water. Combine soy sauce, cornstarch, sugar and ginger; stir into bouillon mixture. In large skillet, brown chicken in oil. Add bouillon mixture; cook and stir until slightly thickened. Add mushrooms, onions, green pepper and water chestnuts; simmer uncovered 5 to 8 minutes, stirring occasionally. Remove from heat; add ¼ cup cashews. Serve with rice. Garnish with remaining ¼ cup cashews. Refrigerate leftovers.

Makes 4 servings

Chicken Cashew

Ginger-Spiced Chicken

1 pound boneless skinless chicken breasts, cut into strips
2 tablespoons oil
1 medium red pepper, cut into thin strips
1 medium green pepper, cut into thin strips
1 cup sliced mushrooms
1 cup chicken broth
3 tablespoons soy sauce
4 teaspoons cornstarch
1 teaspoon garlic powder
1 teaspoon ground ginger
Original MINUTE® Rice
⅓ cup cashews or peanuts (optional)

Stir-fry chicken in hot oil in large skillet until browned. Add peppers and mushrooms; stir-fry until peppers are crisp-tender.

Mix broth, soy sauce, cornstarch, garlic powder and ginger; add to skillet. Bring to boil; boil 1 minute.

Meanwhile, prepare 4 servings rice as directed on package, omitting margarine and salt. Serve chicken and vegetables over rice. Sprinkle with cashews.

Makes 4 servings

Sweet Sour Chicken Sauté

1 can (8 ounces) pineapple chunks
1 tablespoon cornstarch
⅓ cup HEINZ® Apple Cider Vinegar
¼ cup firmly packed brown sugar
⅛ teaspoon black pepper
Vegetable cooking spray
1 small red bell pepper, cut into thin strips
1 small green bell pepper, cut into thin strips
1 medium onion, thinly sliced
1 pound skinless boneless chicken breasts, cut into ½-inch strips

Drain pineapple; reserve juice. Combine juice with cornstarch, vinegar, sugar and black pepper; set aside. Spray large skillet with cooking spray. Sauté bell peppers and onion until tender-crisp; remove. Spray skillet again; sauté chicken 2 to 3 minutes or until chicken changes color. Stir in reserved vinegar mixture; cook 2 to 3 minutes or until chicken is cooked and sauce is thickened. Add vegetables and pineapple; heat, stirring occasionally. Serve with rice if desired.   *Makes 4 servings*

Polynesian Chicken

2½ pounds frying chicken pieces
½ cup seasoned all-purpose flour
¼ cup margarine or butter
1 can (8¼ ounces) pineapple chunks in syrup
2 tablespoons brown sugar
1 tablespoon vinegar
1¼ cups water
½ teaspoon salt
1½ cups Original MINUTE® Rice
1 scallion, sliced

Coat chicken with seasoned flour. Brown chicken well in hot margarine in large skillet. Drain pineapple, reserving ¼ cup syrup. Combine reserved syrup, brown sugar and vinegar in small bowl; pour over chicken. Turn chicken, skin side down. Reduce heat; cover and simmer until fork tender, about 20 minutes or until heated through. Move chicken to side of skillet.

Add pineapple, water and salt. Bring to full boil. Stir in rice. Cover; remove from heat. Let stand 5 minutes. Fluff with fork. Garnish with scallion.
Makes 4 servings

Note: Flour may be seasoned with ¼ teaspoon each pepper and ground nutmeg, or ½ teaspoon paprika and ¼ teaspoon ground ginger.

Chicken-Rice Amandine

¾ pound boneless skinless chicken breasts, cut into strips
1 tablespoon oil
2 cups water
1 tablespoon cornstarch
2 cups (½ package) BIRDS EYE® FARM FRESH Broccoli, Green Beans, Pearl Onions and Red Peppers
¼ teaspoon salt
¼ teaspoon pepper
¼ teaspoon dried tarragon
1 chicken bouillon cube
1½ cups Original MINUTE® Rice
3 tablespoons sliced almonds

Cook and stir chicken in hot oil in large skillet until lightly browned. Mix water and cornstarch in bowl; stir into chicken. Add vegetables, seasonings and bouillon cube. Cook and stir until mixture thickens and comes to full boil. Stir in rice. Cover; remove from heat. Let stand 5 minutes. Fluff with fork and sprinkle with almonds.   *Makes 4 servings*

Microwave Directions: Omit oil. Combine all ingredients except almonds in microwavable dish. Cover and cook at HIGH 6 minutes. Stir cover and cook 6 to 7 minutes longer, or until heated through. Let stand 5 minutes. Fluff with fork and sprinkle with almonds.
Makes 4 servings

Chicken Broccoli Stir-Fry

1 pound skinned boneless chicken breasts, cut into bite-size pieces
1 egg white, beaten
5 teaspoons soy sauce
2 teaspoons cornstarch
¼ cup vegetable oil
8 ounces fresh mushrooms, sliced (about 2 cups)
3 cups broccoli flowerets, steamed
2 tablespoons REALEMON® Lemon Juice from Concentrate
2 tablespoons dry sherry, optional
1 tablespoon chopped pimiento, optional
Hot cooked rice

In medium bowl, combine egg white, *3 teaspoons* soy sauce and cornstarch; add chicken. Cover; refrigerate 1 hour. In large skillet, over high heat, brown chicken in oil; remove. Add mushrooms; cook and stir until tender-crisp. Add chicken and remaining ingredients except rice; heat through. Serve with rice. Refrigerate leftovers.
Makes 4 servings

Polynesian Chicken

Chicken with Pineapple Salsa

Chicken with Pineapple Salsa

1 can (20 ounces) DOLE®
  Crushed Pineapple in
  Juice
4 boneless, skinless chicken
  breast halves
1 large clove garlic, pressed
1 teaspoon ground cumin
  Salt and pepper to taste
1 tablespoon vegetable oil
½ cup minced DOLE® Red
  Bell Pepper
¼ cup minced DOLE® Green
  Bell Pepper
1 tablespoon minced DOLE®
  Green Onion
2 teaspoons minced cilantro
2 teaspoons minced fresh or
  canned jalapeño chiles
1 teaspoon lime zest

• Drain pineapple; reserve juice.

• Rub chicken with garlic;
sprinkle with cumin, salt and
pepper. In 12-inch skillet, sauté
chicken in hot oil over medium-
high heat until browned; turn
once. Add ½ cup pineapple juice
to chicken. Reduce heat. Cover;
simmer 7 to 10 minutes.

• For salsa, combine pineapple,
remaining reserved juice
and remaining ingredients in
bowl.

• Cut each breast into slices.
Serve chicken with pineapple
salsa.   *Makes 4 servings*

Preparation Time: 5 minutes
Cook Time: 15 minutes

Sautéed Pineapple Chicken Amandine

1 DOLE® Fresh Pineapple
2 boneless, skinless chicken
  breast halves
½ teaspoon dried thyme,
  crumbled
¼ teaspoon rubbed sage
⅛ teaspoon ground red
  pepper
1 clove garlic, pressed
1 egg white, lightly beaten
3 tablespoons DOLE®
  Chopped Almonds
2 teaspoons vegetable oil,
  divided
  Zest from 1 DOLE® Orange

• Twist crown from pineapple.
Cut pineapple in half lengthwise.
Refrigerate half for later use,
such as a snack. Cut fruit
from shell with knife. Cut fruit
crosswise into thin slices.

• Pound chicken to ½-inch
thickness. Combine thyme, sage
and red pepper in cup.

• Rub chicken with garlic;
sprinkle with herb mixture. Dip
chicken in egg white, then coat
with almonds.

• In 8-inch nonstick skillet, sauté
pineapple in 1 teaspoon hot
oil over medium-high heat.
Remove from skillet.

• Add remaining 1 teaspoon oil to
skillet. In covered skillet, sauté
chicken over medium-high heat
until browned; turn once.
Sprinkle orange zest over
pineapple. Serve chicken
with pineapple.
          Makes 2 servings

Preparation Time: 15 minutes
Cook Time: 15 minutes

Caribbean Pineapple Chicken

1 DOLE® Fresh Pineapple
1 tablespoon vegetable oil
2 boneless, skinless chicken
  breast halves
1 clove garlic, pressed
2 teaspoons all-purpose flour
¼ cup water
2 to 3 tablespoons honey
1 to 2 tablespoons soy sauce
  Zest and juice from 1 lime
¼ teaspoon coconut extract
  Pinch ground red pepper
1 tablespoon flaked coconut,
  optional
1 to 2 teaspoons minced
  cilantro, optional

• Twist crown from pineapple.
Cut pineapple in half lengthwise.
Refrigerate half for another use.
Cut fruit from shell with
knife. Cut fruit crosswise into 6
slices.

• In 8-inch nonstick skillet, sauté
pineapple in oil over medium-
high heat until slightly browned.
Remove to plates.

• Rub chicken with garlic;
sprinkle with flour. In same
skillet, sauté chicken, covered, in
pan juices over medium-high
heat until browned; turn once.

• Mix water, honey, soy sauce,
lime juice, coconut extract and
red pepper in cup; pour into
skillet. Cover; simmer 12 to 15
minutes. Remove chicken to
serving plates.

• Arrange chicken on plates.
Spoon sauce over top. Sprinkle
with coconut, lime zest and
cilantro.   *Makes 2 servings*

Preparation Time: 10 minutes
Cook Time: 20 minutes

Chicken with Pineapple Mustard Glaze

- **1 can (20 ounces) DOLE® Pineapple Chunks in Syrup***
- **2 chickens (2 pounds each), split in half**
- **4 large cloves garlic**
- **¼ cup margarine, melted**
- **¼ cup chopped parsley**
- **1 teaspoon dried thyme, crumbled**
- **⅓ cup honey**
- **¼ cup Dijon mustard**
- **1 tablespoon cornstarch**

• Drain pineapple; reserve syrup. Arrange chicken, skin side up, on rack in roasting pan. Split each garlic clove lengthwise into 3 or 4 pieces and insert under skin of chicken.

• Combine margarine, parsley and thyme in a cup. Brush generously over chicken. Roast in 400°F oven 30 minutes.

• Combine honey, mustard, ¼ cup reserved pineapple syrup and any remaining margarine mixture in small bowl. Mix well. Brush generously onto chicken. Roast 10 minutes longer.

• Combine pineapple, remaining reserved pineapple syrup and cornstarch with honey sauce in saucepan. Cook, stirring, until sauce boils and thickens. Serve over chicken.

Makes 4 servings

*Use pineapple packed in juice, if desired.

Preparation Time: 10 minutes
Cook Time: 40 minutes

Chicken Sensation

- **1 green-tip DOLE® Banana, peeled**
- **1 tablespoon olive oil**
- **2 boneless, skinless chicken breast halves**
- **2 cloves garlic, pressed**
- **1 teaspoon dried rosemary, crumbled**
- **Salt and pepper to taste**
- **½ cup pitted ripe olives**
- **½ cup cooked pearl onions***
- **Zest and juice from 1 DOLE® Orange**
- **½ cup DOLE® Chopped Dates**
- **1 teaspoon DOLE® Lemon zest**
- **½ teaspoon cornstarch**

• Cut banana in half crosswise, then lengthwise to make 4 pieces.

• In 8-inch nonstick skillet, sauté banana in oil over medium-high heat until slightly browned.

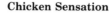

• Rub chicken with garlic and rosemary; sprinkle with salt and pepper. In same skillet, sauté chicken, covered, over medium-high heat until browned; turn once. Add olives and onions.

• Blend orange zest, orange juice, dates, lemon zest and cornstarch in small bowl. Stir into skillet. Cook, stirring, until sauce boils and thickens, 1 to 2 minutes.

Makes 2 servings

*Use cocktail or canned boiled pearl onions, if desired.

Preparation Time: 5 minutes
Cook Time: 15 minutes

Chicken Sensation

Cancun Chicken

1 DOLE® Fresh Pineapple
2 boneless, skinless chicken
   breast halves
   Salt and pepper to taste
½ teaspoon ground cumin
¼ teaspoon dried oregano,
   crumbled
⅛ teaspoon ground cloves
1 tablespoon olive oil
¾ cup DOLE® Pineapple
   Juice
1 tablespoon lime juice
1 teaspoon cornstarch
1 teaspoon minced cilantro

• Twist crown from pineapple. Cut pineapple in half lengthwise. Refrigerate half for another use, such as pasta salad. Cut fruit from shell with a knife. Cut fruit crosswise into 6 slices.

• Pound chicken to ½-inch thickness. Sprinkle with salt and pepper. Combine cumin, oregano and cloves in cup. Sprinkle over chicken.

• In 8-inch skillet, sauté pineapple in hot oil over medium-high heat about 1 minute. Remove from skillet.

• In same skillet, sauté chicken in pan juices. Reduce heat. Cover; simmer 1 to 2 minutes. Remove to plate.

• Blend pineapple juice, lime juice and cornstarch in cup. Pour into skillet. Cook, stirring, until sauce boils and thickens. Stir in cilantro. Serve sauce over chicken and pineapple.

Makes 2 servings

Preparation Time: 15 minutes
Cook Time: 10 minutes

Skewered Chicken with Hawaiian Relish

1 medium DOLE® Fresh
   Pineapple
1 cup peeled papaya or
   DOLE® Orange chunks
½ cup minced DOLE® Red
   Bell Pepper or pimento
2 tablespoons diced green
   chiles
1 teaspoon minced cilantro
   Zest and juice from 1 lime
3 boneless, skinless chicken
   breast halves
1 tablespoon honey

• Soak 4 bamboo skewers in water 5 minutes.

• Twist crown from pineapple. Cut pineapple in half lengthwise. Refrigerate half for another use, such as fruit salad. Cut fruit from shell with knife. Cut fruit into tidbits.

• Combine pineapple, papaya, bell pepper, chiles and cilantro in bowl.

• Sprinkle half of lime juice over relish; set aside.

• Cut each chicken breast into 6 to 8 chunks; skewer on bamboo skewers. Combine remaining half of lime juice and honey in small bowl. Spoon 1 tablespoon honey mixture over chicken.

• Place skewers on broiler rack or pan. Broil 6 inches from heat 4 minutes; turn over. Spoon remaining sauce over chicken. Broil 4 to 5 minutes longer.

• Remove to plate. Cover for 1 minute to complete cooking, if necessary. Serve with relish. Garnish with lime zest.

Makes 2 servings

Preparation Time: 20 minutes
Cook Time: 10 minutes

Cancun Chicken

Honey 'n' Spice Chicken Kabobs

Honey 'n' Spice Chicken Kabobs

- **1 medium green bell pepper, cut into 1-inch squares**
- **4 skinless boneless chicken breast halves (about 1 pound)**
- **1 can (8 ounces) pineapple chunks, drained**
- **½ cup HEINZ® 57 Sauce**
- **¼ cup honey**
- **Melted butter or margarine**

In small saucepan, blanch green pepper in boiling water 1 minute; drain. Cut each chicken breast half into 4 pieces. Alternately thread chicken, green pepper and pineapple onto skewers. In small bowl, combine 57 Sauce and honey. Brush kabobs with butter, then 57 Sauce mixture. Broil, about 6 inches from heat source, 12 to 14 minutes or until chicken is cooked, turning and brushing with 57 Sauce mixture once.

Makes 4 servings

Herb Marinated Chicken Kabobs

- **4 skinless boneless chicken breast halves (about 1 pound)**
- **2 small zucchini, cut into ½-inch slices**
- **1 large red bell pepper, cut into 1-inch squares**
- **½ cup HEINZ® Gourmet Wine Vinegar**
- **½ cup tomato juice**
- **2 tablespoons vegetable oil**
- **1 tablespoon chopped onion**
- **1 tablespoon brown sugar**
- **2 cloves garlic, minced**
- **½ teaspoon dried oregano leaves, crushed**
- **½ teaspoon pepper**

Lightly flatten chicken breasts; cut each breast lengthwise into 3 strips. In large bowl, combine chicken, zucchini and red pepper. For marinade, in jar, combine remaining ingredients; cover and shake vigorously. Pour marinade over chicken and vegetables. Cover; marinate in refrigerator about 1 hour. Drain chicken and vegetables, reserving marinade. Alternately thread chicken and vegetables onto skewers; brush with marinade. Broil, 3 to 5 inches from heat source, 8 to 10 minutes or until chicken is cooked, turning and brushing occasionally with marinade.

Makes 4 servings

Rio Grande Quesadillas

- 2 cups shredded, cooked chicken
- 1 package (1.25 ounces) LAWRY'S® Taco Spices & Seasonings
- ¾ cup water
- 1 can (16 ounces) refried beans
- 6 large flour tortillas
- 1½ cups (6 ounces) grated Monterey Jack cheese
- ¼ cup chopped pimiento
- ¼ cup chopped green onions
- ¼ cup chopped fresh cilantro Vegetable oil

In medium skillet, combine chicken, Taco Spices & Seasonings and water. Bring to a boil; reduce heat and simmer, uncovered, 15 minutes. Stir in refried beans. On ½ side of each tortilla, spread approximately ⅓ cup of chicken-bean mixture. Layer cheese, pimiento, green onions and cilantro on top of each tortilla. Fold each in half. In large skillet, heat a small amount of oil and quickly fry folded tortilla on each side until slightly crisp. Repeat with each folded tortilla.

Makes 6 servings

Presentation: Cut each quesadilla in quarters and serve with chunky salsa and guacamole.

Rio Grande Quesadillas

Green Chile Chicken

- 1 pound skinless boneless chicken breasts, cut into thin strips
- 1 medium onion, sliced
- 1 clove garlic, pressed
- 2 tablespoons vegetable oil
- 1 (12-ounce) jar ORTEGA® Mild Thick and Chunky Salsa
- 1 (4-ounce) can ORTEGA® Diced Green Chiles
- ½ teaspoon dried oregano leaves
  Hot cooked rice or flour tortillas
  Dairy sour cream, optional

In medium skillet, over medium-high heat, cook chicken, onion and garlic in oil until chicken is no longer pink. Add salsa, chiles and oregano. Simmer, uncovered, 10 minutes. Serve over rice or in tortillas. Top with sour cream, if desired.   *Makes 6 servings*

Tortilla Stack Tampico

- 1¼ cups shredded, cooked chicken
- 1 package (1.25 ounces) LAWRY'S® Taco Spices & Seasonings
- 1 cup water
- 1 can (8 ounces) tomato sauce
- 8 medium corn tortillas
- 2 cups (8 ounces) grated Monterey Jack or Cheddar cheese
- 1 can (4 ounces) whole green chiles, rinsed and seeds removed
- 1 can (4¼ ounces) chopped ripe olives
- ½ cup salsa
  Sliced green onions

In large skillet, combine chicken, Taco Spices & Seasonings, water and tomato sauce. Bring to a boil; reduce heat and simmer, uncovered, 10 minutes. Lightly grease 12×8×2-inch baking dish. Dip tortillas in chicken mixture. Place 2 tortillas in bottom of baking dish. Top with ½ of chicken mixture. Sprinkle with ⅔ cup cheese and top with 2 more tortillas. Layer chiles on top of tortillas. Sprinkle with ½ of olives, reserving half, about 2 tablespoons for garnish. Sprinkle ⅔ cup cheese over olives. Top with 2 more tortillas and remaining chicken mixture. Top with remaining 2 tortillas. Pour salsa over tortillas. Garnish with remaining ⅔ cup cheese, reserved 2 tablespoons olives and green onions. Bake, uncovered, in 350°F oven 15 to 20 minutes or until heated through and cheese melts. Cut each stack into quarters to serve.

Makes 8 servings

Presentation: Serve with dollops of sour cream and wedges of fresh pineapple and watermelon, if desired.

Hints: If made in advance, cover tightly with foil or plastic wrap to prevent tortillas from drying out. One can (4 ounces) diced green chiles can be used in place of whole chiles.

Arroz con Pollo Burritos

Arroz con Pollo Burritos

2½ cups shredded, cooked chicken
1 package (1.25 ounces) LAWRY'S® Taco Spices & Seasonings
3¼ cups water
2 tablespoons vegetable oil
1 cup long-grain rice
1 can (8 ounces) tomato sauce
1 teaspoon LAWRY'S® Lemon Pepper Seasoning
1 large tomato, chopped
¼ cup chopped green onions
8 medium flour tortillas, warmed
Grated Cheddar cheese

In large deep skillet, combine chicken, Taco Spices & Seasonings and ¾ cup water. Bring to a boil; reduce heat and simmer, uncovered, 10 minutes. Remove and set aside. In same skillet, heat oil. Add rice; sauté until golden. Add remaining 2½ cups water, tomato sauce and Lemon Pepper Seasoning. Bring to a boil; reduce heat, cover and simmer 20 minutes. Stir in chicken mixture, tomato and green onions; blend well. Heat 5 minutes. Place a heaping ½ cup filling on each tortilla. Fold in sides and roll to enclose filling. Place filled burritos seam-side down on baking sheet. Sprinkle with cheese. Heat in 350°F oven 5 minutes to melt cheese.

Makes 8 servings

Presentation: Garnish with salsa and guacamole.

Turkey Fajitas

⅓ cup REALEMON® Lemon Juice from Concentrate *or* REALIME® Lime Juice from Concentrate
2 tablespoons vegetable oil
1 tablespoon WYLER'S® or STEERO® Chicken-Flavor Instant Bouillon
3 cloves garlic, finely chopped
2 (½-pound) fresh turkey breast tenderloins, pierced with fork
8 (8-inch) flour tortillas, warmed as package directs
   Garnishes: Shredded lettuce and cheese, sliced ripe olives and green onions, salsa, guacamole and sour cream

In large shallow dish or plastic bag, combine ReaLemon® brand, oil, bouillon and garlic; add turkey. Cover; marinate in refrigerator 4 hours or overnight, turning occasionally. Remove turkey from marinade. Grill or broil 10 minutes on each side or until no longer pink, basting frequently with additional ReaLemon® brand. Let stand 10 minutes. Cut turkey into thin slices; place on tortillas. Top with one or more garnishes; fold tortillas. Serve immediately. Refrigerate leftovers.   *Makes 4 servings*

Spicy Pineapple-Cranberry Sauce & Turkey

1 can (20 ounces) DOLE® Pineapple Tidbits in Juice
1 can (16 ounces) jellied cranberry sauce
½ cup frozen orange juice concentrate, thawed*
¼ teaspoon ground allspice
   Zest from 1 DOLE® Orange
6 fresh turkey breast slices (1½ pounds)
1 teaspoon garlic salt
¼ teaspoon pepper
¼ cup all-purpose flour
1 teaspoon rubbed sage
2 tablespoons margarine

• Drain pineapple; save juice for beverage.

• Combine cranberry sauce and orange juice concentrate in saucepan. Heat over medium heat until blended. Add pineapple, allspice and orange zest.

• Sprinkle turkey with garlic salt and pepper. Combine flour and sage in shallow dish. Coat turkey with flour mixture.

• In 12-inch skillet, sauté turkey in margarine over medium-high heat 2 to 2½ minutes on each side. Serve with sauce.
     Makes 6 servings

*Do not reconstitute.

Preparation Time: 15 minutes
Cook Time: 10 minutes

Turkey Fajitas

Sweet & Sour Meatballs with Vegetables

1 pound ground turkey
2 cups Multi-Bran CHEX®
   brand cereal, crushed to
   ¾ cup
¼ cup chopped onion
¼ cup cholesterol-free egg
   product *or* **1 egg, beaten**
2 tablespoons chopped fresh
   parsley
1 clove garlic, minced
1 teaspoon lite soy sauce
¼ teaspoon ground ginger
¼ cup water
16 ounces frozen Oriental *or*
   mixed vegetables,
   prepared according to
   package directions,
   drained
1 cup prepared sweet and
   sour sauce
   Hot cooked rice (optional)

In medium bowl combine turkey, cereal, onion, egg, parsley, garlic, soy sauce and ginger. Mix well. Using 1 rounded tablespoon meat mixture for each, shape into 2-inch balls. Brown meatballs in lightly greased skillet over medium heat, turning often. Add water; cover and cook over low heat 8 to 10 minutes or until no longer pink, stirring occasionally. Drain. Add vegetables and sweet and sour sauce; cook over low heat, stirring gently until meatballs are coated and sauce and vegetables are warm. Serve over rice, if desired.

Makes 6 servings

Toluca Taters

Toluca Taters

1 package (1.62 ounces)
   LAWRY'S® Spices &
   Seasonings for Chili
1 pound ground turkey
1 can (15¼ ounces) kidney
   beans, undrained
1 can (14½ ounces) whole
   peeled tomatoes,
   undrained and cut up
½ cup water
8 medium russet potatoes,
   washed and pierced with
   fork
1 cup (4 ounces) grated
   Cheddar cheese
½ cup thinly sliced green
   onions

In large glass bowl, prepare Spices & Seasonings for Chili with ground turkey, kidney beans, tomatoes and water according to package microwave directions; keep warm. Microwave potatoes on HIGH 25 minutes, turning over after 12 minutes. Slit potatoes lengthwise and pull back skin. Fluff with fork. Top each potato with ½ to ¾ cup prepared chili, 2 tablespoons cheese and 1 tablespoon green onions.

Makes 8 servings

Honey Mustard Turkey Loaf

1½ pounds ground fresh
   turkey
1 cup fresh bread crumbs
   (2 slices)
½ cup BORDEN® or MEADOW
   GOLD® Milk
¼ cup chopped onion
1 egg, beaten
2 teaspoons WYLER'S® or
   STEERO® Chicken-Flavor
   Instant Bouillon
2½ teaspoons prepared
   mustard
1 teaspoon poultry
   seasoning
2 tablespoons honey
1 tablespoon brown sugar

Preheat oven to 350°. Combine turkey, crumbs, milk, onion, egg, bouillon, *1 teaspoon* mustard and poultry seasoning; mix well. In shallow baking dish, shape into loaf. Bake 40 minutes. Combine remaining *1½ teaspoons* mustard, honey and brown sugar. Spoon over loaf; bake 10 minutes longer or until no longer pink. Refrigerate leftovers.

Makes 4 to 6 servings

Turkey a la King

⅓ cup BUTTER FLAVOR
    CRISCO®
⅓ cup chopped green pepper
2 tablespoons chopped
    green onion
5 tablespoons all-purpose
    flour
1 teaspoon seasoned salt
⅛ teaspoon pepper
1½ cups milk
¾ cup water
1 teaspoon instant chicken
    bouillon granules
2 cups cubed cooked turkey
    or chicken
1 can (8 ounces) mushroom
    stems and pieces,
    drained
1 cup frozen peas
1 jar (2 ounces) sliced
    pimiento, drained
    Toast points or patty shells
¼ cup sliced or slivered
    almonds, optional

In 3-quart saucepan melt Butter Flavor Crisco®. Add green pepper and onion. Cook and stir over medium heat until tender. Stir in flour, seasoned salt and pepper. Blend in milk, water and bouillon granules. Cook and stir over medium heat for about 10 minutes, or until mixture thickens and bubbles. Stir in turkey, mushrooms, peas and pimiento. Continue cooking for about 5 minutes, or until hot and peas are tender. Serve over toast points or in patty shells. Top with almonds, if desired. Refrigerate leftovers.

Makes 4 to 6 servings

Country-Style Turkey

1 pound boneless skinless
    turkey or chicken, cut
    into strips
1 small onion, chopped
2 tablespoons margarine or
    butter
2 cups milk
1 package (10 ounces) BIRDS
    EYE® Mixed Vegetables
1 teaspoon salt
¾ teaspoon poultry
    seasoning
1½ cups Original MINUTE®
    Rice

Cook and stir turkey and onion in hot margarine in large skillet until lightly browned. Add milk, vegetables, salt and poultry seasoning. Bring to full boil. Stir in rice. Cover; remove from heat. Let stand 5 minutes. Fluff with fork.   *Makes 4 servings*

Microwave Directions: Omit margarine and reduce milk to 1¾ cups. Mix turkey and onion in 2½-quart microwavable dish. Cover and cook at HIGH 3 minutes. Add remaining ingredients. Cover and cook at HIGH 7 minutes. Stir, cover and cook at HIGH 5 minutes longer or until liquid is absorbed. Fluff with fork.   *Makes 4 servings*

Turkey Mushroom Piccata

½ cup unsifted flour
½ teaspoon basil leaves
½ teaspoon paprika
1 pound fresh turkey breast
    slices
¼ cup plus 2 tablespoons
    REALEMON® Lemon
    Juice from Concentrate
¼ cup margarine or butter
1 cup sliced fresh
    mushrooms
½ cup water
1 teaspoon WYLER'S® or
    STEERO® Chicken-Flavor
    Instant Bouillon

Combine flour, basil and paprika. Dip turkey slices in *¼ cup* ReaLemon® brand, then flour mixture. In large skillet, brown turkey in margarine 2 minutes on each side or until no longer pink. Remove from skillet; keep warm. Add mushrooms, water, bouillon and remaining *2 tablespoons* ReaLemon® brand; cook until mushrooms are tender. Pour over turkey slices. Garnish with parsley. Refrigerate leftovers.

Makes 4 servings

Turkey Vegetable Roll-Ups

½ cup *each* thin strips
    carrots, red bell pepper,
    summer squash and
    zucchini
1 pound fresh turkey breast
    slices
¼ cup unsifted flour
¼ teaspoon paprika
2 tablespoons vegetable oil
⅓ cup water
¼ cup REALEMON® Lemon
    Juice from Concentrate
2 tablespoons dry sherry,
    optional
1 tablespoons WYLER'S® or
    STEERO® Chicken-Flavor
    Instant Bouillon
½ teaspoon thyme leaves

Place equal amounts of vegetables on center of turkey slices; roll up from narrow edge. Combine flour and paprika; coat roll-ups. In large skillet, brown in oil. Add remaining ingredients; cover and simmer 10 minutes or until turkey is no longer pink. Refrigerate leftovers.

Makes 4 to 6 servings

Top to bottom: Turkey Vegetable Roll-Ups and Chicken Parisian (page 193)

Turkey Paprikash

Turkey Paprikash

3-pound BUTTERBALL®
Boneless Breast of Turkey
Vegetable oil
5 teaspoons paprika, divided
Dash salt and ground black
pepper
2 tablespoons butter or
margarine
3/4 cup chopped onion
1 tablespoon all-purpose flour
1 cube chicken bouillon
dissolved in 1 cup hot water
1 cup sour cream
Hot cooked spaetzle or
noodles

Brush turkey with oil. Combine 1 teaspoon paprika, salt and pepper in cup; sprinkle on turkey. Roast turkey according to package directions. Remove from pan. Wrap in foil and let stand 10 to 15 minutes. Melt butter in medium saucepan over medium heat. Add onion; cook and stir until tender. Stir in flour. Gradually add remaining 4 teaspoons paprika and bouillon. Bring to boil over high heat. Reduce heat to low; simmer and stir 3 minutes. Blend small amount of hot mixture into sour cream, then add to sauce. Heat gently over low heat to serving temperature. Do not boil. Remove netting from turkey. Slice turkey; serve with sauce and spaetzle.
Yield: 8 servings.

Turkey Parmigiana

4 to 6 slices (3/8 inch thick)
cooked BUTTERBALL®
turkey (1 pound)
2 eggs, slightly beaten
1 tablespoon water
2 teaspoons vegetable oil
1/2 cup seasoned dried bread
crumbs
3/4 cup grated Parmesan cheese,
divided
Vegetable oil
2 1/2 cups spaghetti or marinara
sauce
2 teaspoons dried oregano
leaves, crushed
3/4 cup (3 ounces) shredded
mozzarella cheese

Preheat oven to 350°F. Combine eggs, water and 2 teaspoons oil in shallow dish; set aside. Combine bread crumbs and 1/2 cup Parmesan cheese in another shallow dish. Dip turkey slices into egg mixture, then coat with bread crumb mixture. Heat oil in heavy skillet over medium heat. Brown turkey slices 2 to 4 minutes per side. Layer turkey in 11×7-inch baking dish. Combine spaghetti sauce and oregano; pour over turkey. Top each turkey slice with mozzarella cheese and remaining 1/4 cup Parmesan cheese. Bake in oven 20 to 25 minutes or until cheese melts.
Yield: 4 servings.

Turkey with Wine-Glazed Vegetables

3-pound BUTTERBALL®
Boneless Breast of Turkey or
Boneless Turkey, thawed if
frozen
Vegetable oil
1 teaspoon dried rosemary
leaves, divided
1 teaspoon dried thyme leaves,
divided
8 carrots, cut into 1/2-inch slices
8 small red potatoes, unpared,
cut into quarters
4 small onions, cut into halves
1 cup chicken broth
1/3 cup white wine
1 medium clove garlic, minced
2 bay leaves
4 ribs celery, cut into 1-inch
pieces
4 teaspoons cornstarch,
dissolved in 1 tablespoon
white wine

Brush turkey with oil; sprinkle with 1/2 teaspoon of the rosemary and 1/4 teaspoon of the thyme. Roast according to package directions.

Meanwhile, place carrots, potatoes and onions in 2-quart casserole. Combine broth, 1/3 cup wine, garlic, bay leaves, remaining 1/2 teaspoon rosemary and remaining 3/4 teaspoon thyme in small saucepan. Bring to a boil over high heat. Reduce heat to low; simmer 3 minutes. Pour over vegetables; cover. Bake alongside turkey during last hour of roasting time. After 45 minutes, add celery.

When done, remove turkey from oven, wrap in foil and let stand 15 minutes before removing netting. Remove vegetables from oven and discard bay leaves. Drain broth into small saucepan. Add turkey pan drippings. Gradually stir dissolved cornstarch into broth mixture. Cook and stir over medium heat until clear and thickened. Pour over hot vegetables and serve with sliced turkey.
Makes 8 servings.

Turkey Parmesan

- 1 teaspoon diet margarine
- 1 (2-ounce) slice raw turkey breast
- 3 tablespoons prepared spaghetti sauce
- 1 teaspoon grated Parmesan cheese
- 1 slice LITE-LINE® Mozzarella Flavor Process Cheese Product*

In small skillet, over medium heat, melt margarine. Add turkey breast slice. Cook 2 minutes; turn. Reduce heat to low; top turkey with remaining ingredients. Cover; cook 2 to 3 minutes longer. Garnish as desired.
Makes 1 serving; 198 calories.
*"½ the calories"—8% milkfat product. Caloric values by product analyses and recipe calculation.

Shanghai Turkey Stir-Fry

- 1 small turkey thigh, skinned and boned
- 3 tablespoons cornstarch, divided
- 4 tablespoons KIKKOMAN® Soy Sauce, divided
- 1 tablespoon dry sherry
- 1 tablespoon minced fresh ginger root
- 1 clove garlic, minced
- 1 cup water
- 3 tablespoons vegetable oil, divided
- 1 large carrot, cut into julienne strips
- 1 onion, sliced
- 1 package (10 oz.) frozen French-style green beans, thawed and drained

Cut turkey into thin, narrow strips; set aside. Combine 2 tablespoons *each* cornstarch and soy sauce with sherry, ginger and garlic in medium bowl; stir in turkey. Let stand 30 minutes. Meanwhile, combine water, remaining 1 tablespoon cornstarch and 2 tablespoons soy sauce; set aside. Heat 2 tablespoons oil in hot wok or large skillet over high heat. Add turkey and stir-fry 3 minutes, or until tender; remove. Heat remaining 1 tablespoon oil in same pan. Add carrot and onion; stir-fry 2 minutes. Add green beans;

stir-fry 1 minute longer. Stir in turkey and soy sauce mixture. Cook and stir until mixture boils and thickens. Serve immediately.
Makes 6 servings.

Turkey Fillets in Spicy Cilantro Marinade

- 1 cup chopped onion
- 1 large tomato, quartered
- ⅓ cup soy sauce
- ¼ cup chopped green pepper
- 3 tablespoons vegetable oil
- 3 tablespoons lime juice
- 2 tablespoons minced cilantro or parsley
- 2 cloves garlic, minced
- ¾ teaspoon pepper
- 4 turkey breast fillets (about ½ pound each)

Place all ingredients, except turkey, in blender; blend 30 seconds. Place turkey fillets in large plastic bag; place bag in bowl. Pour marinade over turkey in bag. Close bag securely; refrigerate 4 hours, turning occasionally. Drain turkey fillets; reserve marinade. Grill turkey, on uncovered grill, over hot KINGSFORD® Charcoal Briquets 5 minutes on each side or until tender, brushing often with marinade.
Makes 4 servings.

Glazed Turkey Kabobs

Glazed Turkey Kabobs

- 16 cubes (1 inch each) cooked BUTTERBALL® turkey (1 pound)
  Water
- 1 can (20 ounces) pineapple chunks, drained; reserve juice
- ½ cup packed brown sugar
- 2 tablespoons soy sauce
- 16 slices bacon, cut into halves
- 2 large red bell peppers, cut into 24 (1½-inch) triangles
- 3 large green bell peppers, cut into 32 (1½-inch) triangles
  Hot cooked rice

Preheat broiler. Add water to pineapple juice to make 1 cup. Combine juice, brown sugar and soy sauce in small saucepan. Bring to boil over high heat. Reduce heat to low; simmer 2 to 3 minutes. Set glaze aside. Cook bacon in large skillet over medium-high heat until done, but not crisp. Dip turkey and pineapple into glaze. Assemble each kabob as follows: red pepper, green pepper, pineapple, bacon piece folded in half, turkey, bacon piece folded in half, pineapple and green pepper. Repeat. Complete kabob with additional red pepper. Brush kabobs with glaze. Broil 4 to 5 inches from heat 4 to 5 minutes. Turn kabobs, brush with glaze and broil 4 to 5 minutes more or until heated through. Serve kabobs on rice.
Yield: 4 servings, 2 kabobs each.

Turkey Schnitzel

- 4 slices (¼ inch thick) cooked BUTTERBALL® turkey (¾ pound)
- ¼ cup lemon juice
- 1 egg
- 2 teaspoons milk
- ¾ cup seasoned dried bread crumbs
  Butter or margarine
  Hot cooked noodles
  Lemon wedges

Marinate turkey slices in lemon juice in plastic bag in refrigerator 1 hour; drain. Blend egg and milk in shallow dish. Dip turkey slices into egg mixture; coat with bread crumbs. Brown turkey in butter in large skillet over medium heat 2 to 4 minutes per side. Serve with noodles and lemon wedges.
Yield: 4 servings.

Raisin-Stuffed Cornish Game Hens with Apples

- 1 envelope LIPTON® Recipe Secrets Onion Recipe Soup Mix
- 1¼ cups apple cider or juice
- 2 cups unseasoned cube stuffing mix
- ⅓ cup raisins
- ⅓ cup coarsely chopped walnuts
- 4 Cornish hens (1 to 1½ pounds each)
- 2 large apples, cored and halved
- ¼ cup brown sugar
- ½ teaspoon ground cinnamon

Preheat oven to 375°.

In medium bowl, blend onion recipe soup mix with cider. Pour ½ mixture into medium bowl; stir in stuffing mix, raisins and walnuts. Stuff hens with raisin mixture; secure cavities with poultry pins or skewers. In shallow baking pan, arrange hens and apples.

To remaining cider mixture, blend in sugar and cinnamon; brush hens and apples with ½ mixture. Bake, brushing occasionally with remaining glaze mixture, 1 hour or until hens are done. To serve, on large platter, arrange hens and apples, sliced.
Makes 4 servings.

Microwave Directions: Prepare hens and glaze mixture as above. Slice apples in quarters. In 3-quart oblong baking dish, arrange hens and apples; brush with ½ glaze. Microwave at HIGH (Full Power), brushing occa-sionally with remaining glaze and turning dish occasionally, 45 minutes or until hens are done. Let stand covered 5 minutes. Serve as above.

Grilled Cornish Game Hens

- 2 Cornish game hens (1 to 1½ pounds each)
- 3 tablespoons olive or vegetable oil
- ⅓ cup lemon juice
- 1 tablespoon black peppercorns, coarsely crushed
- ½ teaspoon salt
  Sprig fresh rosemary

Split hens lengthwise. Rinse under cold running water; pat dry with paper toweling. Place hens in large plastic bag; set in bowl. In small bowl, combine oil, lemon juice, peppercorns and salt. Pour marinade over hens in bag. Close bag securely and refrigerate several hours or overnight, turning hens occasionally to coat with marinade.

Arrange medium-hot **KINGS-FORD® Charcoal Briquets** around drip pan. Just before grilling, add rosemary sprig to coals. Drain hens; reserve marinade. Place hens, skin-side up, over drip pan. Cover grill and cook 45 minutes or until thigh moves easily and juices run clear. Baste with marinade occasionally. Garnish with fresh rosemary, if desired.
Makes 4 servings.

Turkey with Garlic and Chili Pepper Stuffing

- 14- to 16-pound BUTTERBALL® Turkey, thawed if frozen
- 2 medium red bell peppers, chopped
- ½ cup chopped onion
- 4 to 5 large cloves garlic, minced
- ⅓ cup butter or margarine
- 2 cans (4 ounces each) diced green chili peppers, drained
- ¼ cup chopped fresh parsley
- ¼ teaspoon salt
- ¼ teaspoon ground red pepper
- 8 cups unseasoned dried whole wheat or white bread cubes
- 1½ cups (6 ounces) shredded Cheddar cheese
- ¾ to 1 cup chicken broth

Preheat oven to 325°F. To make stuffing, saute red bell peppers, onion and garlic in butter in medium saucepan over medium-high heat until crisp-tender. Stir in chili peppers, parsley, salt and ground red pepper. Combine bread cubes, cheese and vegetable mixture in large bowl. Add enough broth to moisten. Toss to mix.

Prepare turkey for roasting, stuffing neck and body cavities lightly. Roast immediately according to package directions, or roast turkey unstuffed and place stuffing in greased 2½-quart casserole. Cover casserole and bake alongside turkey 1 hour or until hot.
12 to 14 servings (10 cups stuffing).

Turkey with Garlic and Chili Pepper Stuffing

Turkey Florentine

- 6- to 8-pound BUTTERBALL® Breast of Turkey
- 1 package (6 ounces) long grain and wild rice mix
- 1 package (10 ounces) frozen chopped spinach, thawed, drained
- ¾ cup diced fully cooked ham

Roast turkey according to package directions. Prepare rice according to package directions. Stir in spinach and ham. Place in buttered 1½-quart casserole. Bake alongside turkey last 45 minutes of roasting time. Slice turkey and serve with Florentine rice.
Yield: 8 servings.

Turkey Oscar

**4 slices cooked BUTTERBALL®
    turkey (1 pound)
2 tablespoons butter or
    margarine
1 can (6 ounces) crab meat,
    drained, warmed
8 hot cooked asparagus spears
    Bearnaise Sauce (recipe
    follows)
    Toast points, optional**

Heat turkey slices in butter in medium skillet over medium heat. Place
slices on individual plates. Top each
slice with crab meat, asparagus
spears and Bearnaise Sauce. Serve
with toast points.
Yield: 4 servings.

Bearnaise Sauce

**2 tablespoons tarragon vinegar
1 tablespoon dried tarragon
    leaves, crushed
2 tablespoons finely chopped
    shallots or green onions
    Dash freshly ground black
    pepper
2 egg yolks
2 tablespoons water
1 stick (1/2 cup) butter, melted
    and cooled to room
    temperature**

Combine vinegar, tarragon, shallots
and pepper in small saucepan. Over
medium heat, cook and stir until vinegar evaporates and shallots soften.
Blend yolks and water in cup; add to
shallots, stirring constantly over *low*
heat until mixture thickens. Remove
from heat. Add butter gradually, stirring briskly after each addition until
blended.
Yield: 3/4 cup.

Turkey à la Cordon Bleu

**6- to 8-pound BUTTERBALL®
    Breast of Turkey
    Cordon Bleu Rice (recipe
    follows)
    Cordon Bleu Sauce (recipe
    follows)**

Roast turkey according to package di-
rections. Meanwhile, prepare Cordon
Bleu Rice and Cordon Bleu Sauce.
Slice turkey and serve with rice and
sauce.
Yield: 8 to 10 servings.

Turkey Oscar

Cordon Bleu Rice

**3 cups cooked rice
2 cups diced fully cooked ham
    or Canadian-style bacon
1 1/2 cups (6 ounces) shredded
    aged Swiss cheese
3 tablespoons chopped fresh
    parsley
3 tablespoons butter or
    margarine, melted**

Combine rice, ham, cheese, parsley
and butter in medium bowl. Spoon
into 2-quart casserole. Cover and bake
alongside turkey last 40 minutes of
roasting time.
Yield: 5 cups.

Cordon Bleu Sauce

**1/2 stick (1/4 cup) butter or
    margarine
1/4 cup all-purpose flour
1/2 teaspoon salt
2 1/2 cups milk
1 package (3 ounces) cream
    cheese, cut into small
    pieces
1 1/2 cups (6 ounces) shredded
    aged Swiss cheese**

Melt butter in medium saucepan over
medium heat. Blend in flour and salt.
Gradually add milk. Bring to boil,
stirring constantly. Cook and stir 1
minute more. Reduce heat to low. Add
cream cheese and Swiss cheese; stir
until melted.
Yield: 3 1/3 cups.

Turkey Curry

**3 cups cubed cooked
    BUTTERBALL® turkey
    (1 pound)
1/2 cup finely chopped onion
2 tablespoons butter or
    margarine
1 tablespoon curry powder
1 gravy packet (8 ounces)
    included with turkey
2/3 cup water
1/2 cup whipping cream or half
    and half
1 1/2 teaspoons honey
1/2 teaspoon salt
1/4 teaspoon ground black pepper
    Hot cooked rice
    Toasted almonds, shredded
    coconut and/or chopped
    dried fruit, optional**

Cook and stir onion in butter in medium saucepan over low heat 5 minutes or until tender. Add curry powder
and cook 2 minutes, stirring occasionally. Stir in contents of gravy packet
and water. Bring to boil over high
heat, stirring constantly. Reduce heat
to low; simmer 3 to 5 minutes, stirring occasionally. Blend in cream,
honey, salt and pepper. Stir turkey
into sauce and heat 3 to 5 minutes or
until heated through. Serve over rice
with almonds, coconut and/or dried
fruit as a garnish or accompaniment.
Yield: 4 servings.

Turkey Vegetable Medley

Turkey Vegetable Medley

**4 fresh turkey breast slices
 or 4 skinned boneless
 chicken breast halves
1 tablespoon vegetable oil
½ cup water
2 teaspoons WYLER'S® or
 STEERO® Chicken-Flavor
 Instant Bouillon *or*
 2 Chicken-Flavor
 Bouillon Cubes
½ teaspoon thyme leaves or
 tarragon
¼ teaspoon onion powder
1 cup thin strips carrots
1 cup *each* thin strips red
 and green bell peppers**

In large skillet, brown turkey in oil. Add water, bouillon, thyme, onion powder and carrots. Cover; simmer 10 minutes. Add peppers; cover and cook 5 minutes longer or until tender. Refrigerate leftovers.   *Makes 4 servings*

Poached Turkey Tenderloins with Tarragon Sauce

**1 to 1½ pounds turkey
 tenderloins
¾ cup white wine
½ cup chopped celery
¼ cup sliced green onions
3 tablespoons chopped fresh
 tarragon *or* 1 teaspoon
 dry crushed tarragon
½ teaspoon salt
¼ teaspoon white pepper
 Water
 Steamed spinach
 Tarragon Sauce
 (recipe follows)**

In a large skillet, arrange tenderloins in a single layer. Add wine, celery, onions, tarragon, salt, pepper and enough water to cover tenderloins. Cover skillet and poach over low heat about 40 minutes or until no longer pink in center. Remove tenderloins, reserving poaching liquid for Tarragon Sauce.* Slice tenderloins into ½-inch medallions. To serve, arrange medallions on steamed spinach. Drizzle with Tarragon Sauce. Garnish with strips of lemon peel, if desired.
    Makes 4 servings

Note: Recipe may be prepared to this point, cooled, covered and refrigerated for up to two days.

Tarragon Sauce

**Reserved poaching liquid
3 tablespoons cold water
2 tablespoons cornstarch
2 tablespoons chopped fresh
 tarragon *or* ½ teaspoon
 dry crushed tarragon
½ cup plain low-fat yogurt
1 tablespoon chopped
 parsley
1 tablespoon lemon juice**

In a saucepan over high heat, bring reserved poaching liquid to boil for 5 to 10 minutes to reduce liquid; strain. Measure 2 cups liquid and return to saucepan. Bring to boil. Combine cold water and cornstarch. Stir into boiling liquid. Reduce heat and add tarragon. Over low heat, cook sauce until slightly thickened. Stir in yogurt, parsley and lemon juice.

*Favorite recipe from **National Turkey Federation***

Apple & Herb Stuffing

**2 cups sliced celery
1½ cups chopped onion
½ cup margarine or butter
1¾ cups hot water
1 tablespoon WYLER'S® or
 STEERO® Chicken-Flavor
 Instant Bouillon *or*
 3 Chicken-Flavor
 Bouillon Cubes
12 cups dry bread cubes
 (about 16 slices bread)
3 cups coarsely chopped
 apple
1 cup toasted slivered
 almonds
1 tablespoon chopped
 parsley
2 teaspoons poultry
 seasoning
¼ teaspoon rubbed sage
 Rich Turkey Gravy**

In large skillet, cook celery and onion in margarine until tender. Add water and bouillon; cook until bouillon dissolves. In large bowl, combine remaining ingredients except Rich Turkey Gravy; add bouillon mixture. Mix well. Loosely stuff turkey just before roasting. Place remaining stuffing in greased baking dish. Bake at 350° for 30 minutes or until hot. Serve with Rich Turkey Gravy, if desired. Refrigerate leftovers.
    Makes about 2½ quarts

RICH TURKEY GRAVY: In medium skillet, stir ¼ to ⅓ cup flour into ¼ cup pan drippings; cook and stir until dark brown. Stir in 2 cups hot water and 2 teaspoons Wyler's® or Steero® Chicken-Flavor Instant Bouillon *or* 2 Chicken-Flavor Bouillon Cubes; cook and stir until thickened and bouillon is dissolved. Refrigerate leftovers.
Makes about 1½ cups

Turkey Breast with Southwestern Corn Bread Dressing

    5 cups corn bread, coarsely
        crumbled
    4 English muffins, coarsely
        crumbled
    3 mild green chilies, roasted,
        peeled, seeded and
        chopped
    1 red bell pepper, roasted,
        peeled, seeded and
        chopped
    ¾ cup pine nuts, toasted
    1 tablespoon fresh cilantro,
        chopped
    1 tablespoon fresh parsley,
        chopped
    1½ teaspoons *each* fresh basil,
        thyme and oregano,
        chopped, *or* 1 teaspoon
        each dried basil, thyme
        and oregano
    1 pound bulk turkey sausage
    3 cups chopped celery
    1 cup chopped onions
    2 to 4 tablespoons turkey
        broth or water
    1 bone-in turkey breast
        (5 to 6 pounds)
    2 tablespoons chopped
        garlic
    ½ cup fresh cilantro, chopped

1. Preheat oven to 325°F.

2. In large bowl combine corn bread, muffins, chilies, red pepper, pine nuts, 1 tablespoon cilantro, parsley, basil, thyme and oregano.

3. In large skillet, over medium-high heat, sauté sausage, celery and onions 8 to 10 minutes or until sausage is no longer pink and vegetables are tender. Combine with corn bread mixture. Add broth if mixture is dry. Set aside.

4. Loosen skin on both sides of turkey breast, being careful not to tear skin and leaving it connected at breast bone. Spread 1 tablespoon garlic under loosened skin over each breast half. Repeat procedure with ¼ cup cilantro on each side.

5. In lightly greased 13×9×2-inch roasting pan, place turkey breast. Spoon half of stuffing mixture under breast cavity. Spoon remaining stuffing into a lightly greased 2-quart casserole; refrigerate. Roast turkey breast, uncovered, 2 to 2½ hours or until meat thermometer registers 170°F in deepest portion of breast. Bake remaining stuffing, uncovered, along with turkey breast during last 45 minutes.
Makes 12 servings

Favorite recipe from **National Turkey Federation**

Turkey Breast with Southwestern Corn Bread Dressing

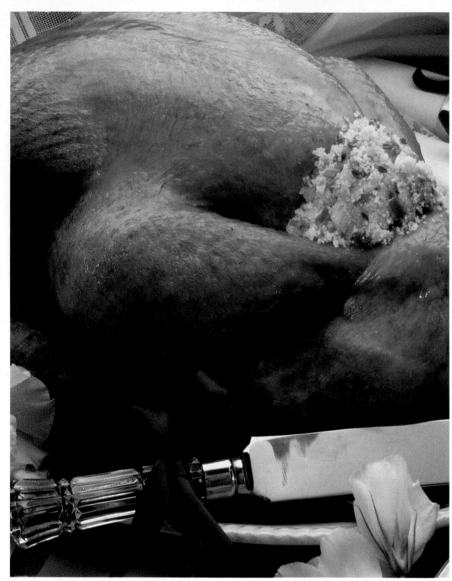

Turkey with Sausage and Orange Corn Bread Stuffing

ORANGE CORN BREAD: Preheat oven to 400°F. Combine 1½ cups yellow cornmeal, ½ cup all-purpose flour, 2 tablespoons sugar, 4 teaspoons baking powder and ½ teaspoon salt in medium bowl. Stir in 1 cup milk, 1 beaten egg, ⅓ cup vegetable oil and 2 teaspoons finely shredded orange peel (zest) until just blended. (Do not overmix.) Pour into greased 9×9×2-inch baking pan. Bake 20 to 25 minutes or until wooden pick inserted near center comes out clean.
Makes 9 servings.

Traditional Gravy

   Drippings
   Fat
   Turkey, chicken or giblet broth
½ **cup all-purpose flour**
   Salt and ground black pepper, to taste
   Cooked giblets, chopped fine, optional

Conventional Directions: Pour drippings from roasting pan into large measuring cup. Place ¼ cup fat from drippings into medium saucepan or roasting pan. Discard any remaining fat from drippings. To drippings, add enough broth to make 4 cups. Stir flour into fat in saucepan. Gradually blend in drippings. Bring to boil over medium-high heat, stirring constantly. Reduce heat to low; continue cooking 3 to 5 minutes. Season with salt and pepper. Add cooked giblets, if desired.
Yield: 4 cups.

Microwave Directions: Pour drippings from roasting pan into large measuring cup. Place ¼ cup fat from drippings into medium microwave-safe bowl. Discard any remaining fat from drippings. To drippings, add enough broth to make 4 cups. Stir flour into fat in bowl. Gradually blend in drippings. Microwave, uncovered, on HIGH 7 to 10 minutes or until mixture comes to boil and thickens, stirring every 2 minutes. Season with salt and pepper. Add cooked giblets, if desired.

Gravy Additions: Add 1 or 2 of the following: 2 tablespoons chopped fresh parsley, 2 tablespoons sherry, ½ cup sour cream or 1 jar (2½ ounces) sliced mushrooms, drained.

Favorite recipe from **Armour Swift-Eckrich**

Turkey with Sausage and Orange Corn Bread Stuffing

½ **roll (8 ounces) ECKRICH® Country Sausage**
12- **to 14-pound BUTTERBALL® Turkey, thawed if frozen**
   Orange Corn Bread (recipe follows)
1 **cup chopped onion**
½ **cup chopped green bell pepper**
½ **cup chopped celery**
2 **eggs, beaten**
1 **teaspoon dried thyme leaves**
½ **teaspoon salt**
1 **to 1¼ cups turkey or chicken broth**

Prepare Orange Corn Bread. Cool and crumble; set aside. Preheat oven to 325°F. To make stuffing, cook sausage, onion, green pepper and celery in large skillet until meat is browned and vegetables are tender. Drain thoroughly. Combine sausage mixture, eggs, thyme and salt in large bowl. Add corn bread; toss to mix. Add enough broth to moisten; toss. Prepare turkey for roasting; stuff neck and body cavities lightly. Roast immediately according to package directions, or roast turkey unstuffed and place stuffing in greased 2½-quart casserole. Cover casserole and bake alongside turkey 1 hour or until hot.
Makes 10 to 12 servings (8 cups stuffing).

Harvest Sausage Stuffing

- 1 pound bulk sausage
- 2 cups chopped celery
- 8 ounces fresh mushrooms, sliced (about 2 cups)
- 1½ cups chopped onion
- 4 teaspoons WYLER'S® or STEERO® Chicken-Flavor Instant Bouillon *or* 4 Chicken-Flavor Bouillon Cubes
- 1 to 1½ cups boiling water
- 2 (7-ounce) packages herb-seasoned stuffing mix
- 1⅓ cups (one-half jar) NONE SUCH® Ready-to-Use Mincemeat
- 1 (8-ounce) can sliced water chestnuts, coarsely chopped
- 2 teaspoons poultry seasoning

In large skillet, brown sausage; pour off fat. Add celery, mushrooms and onion; cook until onion is tender. Add bouillon and water to sausage mixture; bring to a boil. In large bowl, combine remaining ingredients with sausage mixture; mix well. Use to loosely stuff turkey just before roasting; place remaining stuffing in 2-quart greased baking dish; cover. Bake at 350° for 45 minutes or until hot. Refrigerate leftovers.
Makes about 3 quarts.

Turkey with American Stuffing

- 6- to 8-pound BUTTERBALL® Breast of Turkey
- 3 cups dried bread cubes
- 1 cup (4 ounces) crumbled fully cooked sausage
- ¾ cup diced red apple, unpared
- ½ cup chopped onion
- ½ cup chopped walnuts
- 1 teaspoon dried rosemary leaves, crushed
- ½ teaspoon rubbed sage
- ¾ cup water
- ⅓ cup butter or margarine

Roast turkey according to package directions. Meanwhile, prepare stuffing. Combine bread cubes, sausage, apple, onion, walnuts and seasonings in medium bowl. Heat water and butter in small saucepan over medium heat until butter melts. Toss with bread mixture. Spoon into 2-quart casserole.

Cover and bake alongside turkey last 45 minutes of roasting time. Slice turkey and serve with stuffing.
Yield: 8 servings.

Savory Corn Bread Stuffing

- 1 pound fresh mushrooms, sliced (about 4 cups)
- 1 cup chopped celery
- ¾ cup chopped onion
- ½ cup margarine or butter
- 4 teaspoons WYLER'S® or STEERO® Chicken-Flavor Instant Bouillon *or* 4 Chicken-Flavor Bouillon Cubes
- 1⅔ cups boiling water
- 1 pound bulk sausage, browned and drained
- 1 (16-ounce) package corn bread stuffing mix
- 1½ teaspoons poultry seasoning

In large skillet, cook mushrooms, celery and onion in margarine until tender. In large bowl, dissolve bouillon in water. Add sausage, mushroom mixture and remaining ingredients; mix well. Loosely stuff turkey just before roasting. Place remaining stuffing in greased baking dish; bake at 350° for 30 minutes or until hot. Refrigerate leftovers.
Makes about 3 quarts.

Old-Fashioned Bread Stuffing

- 1½ cups chopped onion
- 1½ cups diced celery
- 1 stick (½ cup) butter or margarine
- 1 teaspoon poultry seasoning
- 1 teaspoon rubbed sage
- 1 teaspoon salt
  Dash ground black pepper
- ½ cup water or chicken broth
- 8 cups dried bread cubes (10 to 12 bread slices, cubed and dried overnight)

Cook and stir onion and celery in butter in medium skillet over medium heat until tender. Stir in seasonings. Add onion mixture and water to bread cubes in large bowl. Toss to mix. Stuff neck and body cavities of turkey. Roast immediately.
Yield: 8 cups (enough for 12- to 14-pound turkey).

Cranberry-Sausage: Cut 1 cup fresh cranberries into halves. Cut 1 package (8 ounces) fully cooked sausage links into pieces. Add to bread cubes.

Bacon and Green Pepper: Substitute 1½ cups chopped green bell pepper for celery. Substitute 1 teaspoon dried thyme leaves, crushed, for poultry seasoning and sage. Reduce salt to ½ teaspoon. Add 12 slices cooked diced bacon to bread cubes.

Favorite recipe from **Armour Swift-Eckrich**

Harvest Sausage Stuffing

SEAFOOD

Seafood is finding its way onto more dinner tables than ever before—and for good reason. It's delicious, nutritious and cooks quickly. Serve salmon with a creamy chive sauce, red snapper with a mushroom-rice stuffing or a seafood stir-fry sure to impress friends and family. From spicy Cajun Shrimp to succulent Scallop Kabobs, you'll discover innovative ways to add fish and shellfish to your menus.

Lemon Broiled Fish

½ cup margarine or butter, melted
¼ cup REALEMON® Lemon Juice from Concentrate
2 cups fresh bread crumbs (4 slices)
1 tablespoon chopped parsley
½ teaspoon paprika
1 pound fish fillets, fresh or frozen, thawed

In small bowl, combine margarine and ReaLemon® brand. In medium bowl, combine crumbs, parsley and ¼ cup margarine mixture. Add paprika to remaining margarine mixture; dip fish into mixture. Broil until fish flakes with fork; top with crumb mixture. Return to broiler; heat through. Refrigerate leftovers.

Makes 4 servings

Tangy Cocktail Sauce

¾ cup BENETT'S® Chili Sauce
3 tablespoons REALEMON® Lemon Juice from Concentrate
½ teaspoon prepared horseradish
½ teaspoon Worcestershire sauce

In small bowl, combine all ingredients. Cover; chill. Serve with fish or seafood. Refrigerate leftovers. *Makes about 1 cup*

Quick Tartar Sauce

¾ cup mayonnaise or salad dressing
2 tablespoons pickle relish, drained
1 tablespoon chopped green onion
1 tablespoon REALEMON® Lemon Juice from Concentrate

In small bowl, combine all ingredients. Cover; chill. Serve with fish or seafood. Refrigerate leftovers. *Makes about 1 cup*

Lemon Butter Sauce

½ cup margarine or butter
3 tablespoons REALEMON® Lemon Juice from Concentrate
⅛ teaspoon salt, optional

In small saucepan, melt margarine; stir in ReaLemon® brand and salt if desired. Serve with fish, seafood or vegetables. Refrigerate leftovers.
Makes about ⅔ cup

Parsley Lemon: Add 1 tablespoon chopped parsley.

Herb Lemon: Add 1 teaspoon oregano leaves or dill weed.

Almond Lemon: Add ¼ cup sliced toasted almonds.

Clockwise from top: Lemon Broiled Fish, Lemon Butter Sauce, Tangy Cocktail Sauce and Quick Tartar Sauce

Almondine Fish

• Arrange fish fillets in 12×8-inch microwave dish with thickest parts to outside edges of dish. Drizzle with margarine, then sprinkle with bread crumbs and paprika. Cover with waxed paper. Microwave on HIGH 5 to 9 minutes, rotating dish after 3 minutes. Fish is done when thin areas flake easily with a fork and thick areas are fork tender. Let fish stand 2 to 3 minutes; serve with pineapple sauce.

Makes 4 servings

Preparation Time: 10 minutes
Cook Time: 15 minutes

Almondine Fish

½ **cup margarine or butter, melted**
3 **tablespoons REALEMON® Lemon Juice from Concentrate**
3 **tablespoons sliced almonds, toasted**
1 **pound fish fillets, fresh or frozen, thawed**

Combine margarine and ReaLemon® brand; reserve ¼ cup. Add almonds to remaining margarine mixture; set aside. Broil or grill fish as desired, basting frequently with reserved ¼ cup margarine mixture. Serve with almond sauce. Refrigerate leftovers. *Makes 4 servings*

Herb Fish: Omit almonds. Add 1 teaspoon dill weed.

Garlic Fish: Omit almonds. Add ½ teaspoon garlic powder.

Saucy Fish Fillets

1 **can (8 ounces) DOLE® Pineapple Tidbits in Juice**
1 **tablespoon sugar**
1 **tablespoon cider vinegar**
1½ **teaspoons cornstarch**
½ **teaspoon instant chicken bouillon granules**
¼ **teaspoon ground ginger Pinch ground red pepper**
¼ **cup sliced DOLE® Green Onions**
¼ **cup sliced water chestnuts**
4 **white fish fillets, ½ inch thick**
2 **tablespoons margarine, melted**
½ **cup bread crumbs Paprika**

• **To microwave:** Drain pineapple; reserve juice. For sauce, add enough water to juice to make ⅔ cup liquid. In microwave bowl, whisk together juice mixture, sugar, vinegar, cornstarch, bouillon, ginger and red pepper. Microwave on HIGH 4 to 5 minutes, until sauce boils and thickens, whisking after 2 minutes to prevent lumps. Stir in green onions, water chestnuts and pineapple; set aside.

Crispy Oven Fish

2½ **cups finely crushed KRUNCHERS!® Potato Chips**
½ **cup grated Parmesan cheese**
2 **tablespoons chopped parsley**
½ **cup mayonnaise or salad dressing**
¼ **cup REALEMON® Lemon Juice from Concentrate**
1 **pound fish fillets, fresh or frozen, thawed**

Preheat oven to 400°. Combine chips, cheese and parsley. In small bowl, combine mayonnaise and *2 tablespoons* ReaLemon® brand. Dip fish in remaining *2 tablespoons* ReaLemon® brand, then mayonnaise mixture, then chip mixture. Arrange in greased baking dish. Bake 5 to 10 minutes or until fish flakes with fork. Refrigerate leftovers.

Makes 4 servings

Baja Fish and Rice Bake

3 tablespoons vegetable oil
¾ cup chopped onion
½ cup chopped celery
1 clove garlic, minced
½ cup rice
3½ cups (two 14.5-ounce cans)
    CONTADINA® Stewed
    Tomatoes, cut-up
1 teaspoon lemon pepper
½ teaspoon salt
⅛ teaspoon cayenne pepper
1 pound fish fillets (any firm,
    white fish)
¼ cup finely chopped fresh
    parsley
Lemon slices (optional)

Preheat oven to 400°F. In large skillet, heat oil; sauté onion, celery and garlic. Stir in rice; sauté about 5 minutes, or until rice browns slightly. Add tomatoes with juice, lemon pepper, salt and cayenne pepper. Place fish in 12×7½×2-inch baking dish. Spoon rice mixture over fish. Cover with foil; bake 45 to 50 minutes or until rice is tender. Allow to stand 5 minutes before serving. Sprinkle with parsley. Garnish with lemon slices, if desired.

Makes 6 servings

Baja Fish and Rice Bake

Crispy Oven Fish

Lemon Fish Roll-Ups

1 cup cooked rice
1 (10-ounce) package frozen
    chopped broccoli,
    thawed and well drained
1 cup (4 ounces) shredded
    Cheddar cheese
⅓ cup margarine or butter,
    melted
⅓ cup REALEMON® Lemon
    Juice from Concentrate
½ teaspoon salt
¼ teaspoon pepper
8 fish fillets, fresh or frozen,
    thawed (about 2 pounds)

Preheat oven to 375°. In medium bowl, combine rice, broccoli and cheese. In small bowl, combine margarine, ReaLemon® brand, salt and pepper; add ¼ *cup* to broccoli mixture. Place equal amounts of broccoli mixture on fillets; roll up. Place seam-side down in shallow baking dish; pour remaining margarine mixture over roll-ups. Bake 20 minutes or until fish flakes with fork. Garnish with paprika if desired. Refrigerate leftovers.

Makes 8 servings

Microwave: Prepare fish as above. Arrange in shallow baking dish. Cook tightly covered on 100% power (high) 10 to 12 minutes or until fish flakes with fork, rotating dish once. Serve as above.

Fish Rolls Primavera

1 cup shredded carrots
1 cup shredded zucchini
2 tablespoons finely chopped onion
½ cup fresh bread crumbs (1 slice)
⅛ teaspoon thyme leaves
¼ cup margarine or butter, melted
¼ cup REALEMON® Lemon Juice from Concentrate
4 fish fillets, fresh or frozen, thawed (about 1 pound)

Preheat oven to 375°. In medium bowl, combine vegetables, crumbs and thyme. In small bowl, combine margarine and ReaLemon® brand; add ¼ cup to vegetable mixture. Place equal amounts of vegetable mixture on fillets; roll up. Place seam-side down in shallow baking dish; pour remaining margarine mixture over fish rolls. Bake 15 minutes or until fish flakes with fork. Refrigerate leftovers.

Makes 4 servings

Rice-Stuffed Fish Fillets with Mushroom Sauce

3 cups cooked rice
¼ cup diced pimientos
2 tablespoons snipped parsley
1 teaspoon grated lemon peel
¼ teaspoon salt
¼ teaspoon ground white pepper
1 pound white fish fillets*
Vegetable cooking spray
2 teaspoons margarine, melted
½ teaspoon seasoned salt
¼ teaspoon paprika
Mushroom Sauce (recipe follows)
Lemon slices for garnish

Combine rice, pimientos, parsley, lemon peel, salt, and pepper in large bowl. Place fillets in shallow baking dish coated with cooking spray. Spoon rice mixture on lower portion of each fillet. Fold over to enclose rice mixture; fasten with wooden toothpicks soaked in water. Brush fillets with margarine; sprinkle with seasoned salt and paprika. Bake at 400°F. for 10 to 15 minutes or until fish flakes easily with fork. Prepare Mushroom Sauce while fillets are baking. Transfer fillets to serving platter; garnish platter with lemon slices. Serve fillets with Mushroom Sauce.

Makes 4 servings

*Haddock, orange roughy, sole, or turbot may be used.

Mushroom Sauce

2 cups (about 8 ounces) sliced fresh mushrooms
½ cup sliced green onions
1 teaspoon margarine
½ cup water
⅓ cup white wine
1 tablespoon white wine Worcestershire sauce
½ cup cholesterol free, reduced calorie mayonnaise

Cook mushrooms and onions in margarine in large skillet until tender. Add water, wine, and Worcestershire sauce; bring to a boil. Reduce sauce slightly. Stir in mayonnaise; keep warm.

*Favorite recipe from **USA Rice Council***

Spicy Island Fish Sauté

2 white fish fillets (orange roughy or sole), ½ pound
Juice from 1 lime
1 clove garlic, pressed
2 teaspoons minced ginger root
1 teaspoon minced cilantro
⅛ to ¼ teaspoon ground red pepper
2 firm, medium DOLE® Bananas, peeled
2 tablespoons margarine

Fish Rolls Primavera

- Arrange fish in shallow glass casserole dish.
- Combine lime juice, garlic, ginger, cilantro and red pepper in small bowl. Pour over fish. Cover and marinate in refrigerator 15 minutes or overnight.
- Cut bananas in half crosswise, then lengthwise to make 8 pieces.
- In 12-inch nonstick skillet, sauté bananas in margarine over medium-high heat until lightly browned. Remove bananas to plate.
- Remove fish from marinade. In same skillet, cook fish, covered, over medium-high heat 7 to 10 minutes or until fish flakes easy when tested with a fork, turning fish once.
- Remove fish to plate. Arrange bananas on plate with fish.

Makes 2 servings

Preparation Time: 5 minutes
Marinate Time: 15 minutes or overnight
Cook Time: 15 minutes

Orange Roughy with Cucumber Relish

Lemon Rice Stuffed Sole

      Vegetable cooking spray
 ½ cup thinly sliced celery
 ¼ cup chopped onion
 3 cups cooked brown rice
 2 teaspoons grated lemon
      peel
 ¼ teaspoon salt
 ¼ teaspoon dried thyme
      leaves
 ⅛ teaspoon ground black
      pepper
 2 tablespoons lemon juice
 1 pound fresh or frozen sole
      fillets*
 2 teaspoons margarine,
      melted
 1 tablespoon snipped
      parsley
 ¼ teaspoon seasoned salt

*Substitute any white-fleshed fish such as haddock, turbot, or white fish for the sole, if desired.

Coat large skillet with cooking spray and place over medium-high heat until hot. Add celery and onion; cook 2 to 3 minutes or until tender. Stir in rice, lemon peel, salt, thyme, pepper, and lemon juice. Spoon rice mixture on lower portion of each fillet. Fold over to enclose rice mixture; fasten with wooden toothpicks soaked in water. Place remaining rice mixture in bottom of shallow baking dish coated with cooking spray. Place fillets on top of rice. Brush fish with margarine. Sprinkle with parsley and seasoned salt. Bake, uncovered, at 400°F. for 10 to 15 minutes or until fish flakes easily with fork.

Makes 4 servings

Favorite recipe from **USA Rice Council**

Orange Roughy with Cucumber Relish

 1 can (11 ounces) mandarin
      orange segments,
      drained
 1 small cucumber, peeled,
      seeded, finely chopped
 ⅓ cup HEINZ® Distilled White
      Vinegar
 1 green onion, minced
 1 tablespoon snipped fresh
      dill*
      Nonstick cooking spray
 4 orange roughy fillets
      (about 5 ounces each)
      Dill sprigs (optional)

Reserve 8 orange segments for garnish; coarsely chop remaining segments. In medium bowl, combine chopped oranges, cucumber, vinegar, green onion and dill. Spray broiler pan with cooking spray; place fish on pan. Spoon 1 tablespoon liquid from cucumber mixture over each fillet. Broil, 3 to 4 inches from heat source, 8 to 10 minutes or until fish turns opaque and just flakes when tested with fork. To serve, spoon cucumber relish on top of fish. Garnish with reserved orange segments and dill sprigs.   *Makes 4 servings*

*1 teaspoon dried dill weed may be substituted.

Baked Stuffed Snapper

Clean and butterfly fish. Combine rice, mushrooms, water chestnuts, onions, pimiento, parsley, lemon peel, salt, and pepper; toss lightly. Fill cavity of fish with rice mixture; enclose filling with wooden toothpicks soaked in water. Place fish in 13×9×2-inch baking dish coated with cooking spray; brush fish with margarine. Bake fish at 400°F. for 18 to 20 minutes or until fish flakes easily with fork. Wrap remaining rice in foil and bake in oven with fish.

Makes 4 servings

Tip: One lemon will yield about 1 tablespoon grated lemon peel.

Favorite recipe from **USA Rice Council**

Saucy Topped Flounder

- **1 pound flounder fillets**
  Butter or margarine
  Salt and pepper
- **½ cup HEINZ® Tartar Sauce**
  Paprika

Divide fish into 4 portions; arrange in 2-quart oblong baking dish. Dot fish with about 1 teaspoon butter; season with salt and pepper. Bake in preheated 375°F oven, 10 to 12 minutes or until fish is almost cooked. Remove from oven; carefully spoon off liquid. Spread tartar sauce on each portion of fish; sprinkle with paprika. Return to oven; bake 5 minutes or until fish just turns opaque and just flakes when tested with fork.

Makes 4 servings

Baked Stuffed Snapper

- **1 red snapper (1½ pounds)**
- **2 cups hot cooked rice**
- **1 can (4 ounces) sliced mushrooms, drained**
- **½ cup diced water chestnuts**
- **¼ cup thinly sliced green onions**
- **¼ cup diced pimiento**
- **2 tablespoons chopped parsley**
- **1 tablespoon grated lemon peel**
- **½ teaspoon salt**
- **⅛ teaspoon ground black pepper**
  Vegetable cooking spray
- **1 tablespoon margarine, melted**

Pescado Borracho
(Drunken Fish)

- **1½ pounds red snapper fillets**
  All-purpose flour
- **4 tablespoons vegetable oil**
- **1 small onion, chopped**
- **1 can (14½ ounces) whole peeled tomatoes, undrained and cut up**
- **1 package (1.25 ounces) LAWRY'S® Taco Spices & Seasonings**
- **2 tablespoons diced green chiles**
- **½ cup dry red wine**

Dip fish in flour to coat. In large skillet, brown fish in 2 tablespoons oil. In 2-quart oblong baking dish, place browned fish; set aside. Add remaining 2 tablespoons oil and onion to skillet; sauté onion about 5 minutes or until soft. Add remaining ingredients except wine. Bring to a boil, stirring constantly; add wine and blend well. Pour tomato mixture over fish. Bake, uncovered, in 400°F oven 15 to 20 minutes or until fish flakes easily with fork.

Makes 4 to 6 servings

Presentation: Serve each fillet with sauce; garnish with parsley.

Spanish-Style Baked Catfish

1½ pounds catfish fillets
½ cup yellow cornmeal
Paprika
1 medium onion, chopped
1 tablespoon olive or vegetable oil
1 cup chunky salsa
¼ cup sliced ripe olives
1 teaspoon LAWRY'S® Garlic Salt
1 teaspoon freshly grated lemon peel
Chopped fresh parsley

Rinse and cut catfish into serving pieces; dip in cornmeal to coat. Place in lightly greased 12×8×2-inch baking dish. Sprinkle with paprika. Bake in 425°F oven 20 to 25 minutes or until fish flakes easily with fork. In medium skillet, sauté onion in oil 3 minutes or until tender. Stir in salsa, olives, Garlic Salt and lemon peel; heat through. Serve over baked fish. Sprinkle with parsley.   *Makes 6 servings*

Presentation: Serve with lemon wedges.

Hint: Seasoned dry bread crumbs can be used in place of cornmeal.

Salmon with Chive Sauce

½ cup MIRACLE WHIP® Salad Dressing
¼ cup finely chopped fresh chives
2 tablespoons finely chopped fresh thyme leaves or 2 teaspoons dried thyme leaves, crushed
2 tablespoons finely chopped fresh dill or 2 teaspoons dill weed
¼ teaspoon salt
⅛ teaspoon pepper
¼ cup dry white wine or chicken broth
2 salmon steaks (about ¾ pound)

• Mix salad dressing, herbs, salt and pepper until well blended. Reserve ⅓ cup salad dressing mixture to serve later with cooked salmon. Stir wine into remaining salad dressing mixture; brush on salmon.

• Place salmon on grill over hot coals (coals will be glowing) or rack of broiler pan. Grill, covered, **or** broil 5 to 8 minutes on each side or until fish flakes easily with fork. Serve with reserved salad dressing mixture.
Makes 2 servings

Prep time: 10 minutes
Grilling time: 16 minutes

Salmon with Chive Sauce

Dilly Salmon Loaf

1 (15½-ounce) can salmon, drained and flaked
2 cups fresh bread crumbs (4 slices)
2 eggs, beaten
¼ cup finely chopped onion
3 tablespoons margarine or butter, melted
2 tablespoons REALEMON® Lemon Juice from Concentrate
½ teaspoon salt
¼ teaspoon dill weed
Lemony Dill Sauce

Preheat oven to 350°. In large bowl, combine all ingredients except Lemony Dill Sauce; mix well. Shape into loaf; place in greased shallow baking dish. Bake 35 to 40 minutes. Let stand 5 minutes before serving. Serve with Lemony Dill Sauce; garnish as desired. Refrigerate leftovers.

Makes 4 to 6 servings

LEMONY DILL SAUCE: In small saucepan, melt ⅓ cup margarine or butter. Add ¾ cup mayonnaise, 1 egg, ¼ cup ReaLemon® brand, 2 tablespoons water, 1 tablespoon sugar, 1 teaspoon WYLER'S® or STEERO® Chicken-Flavor Instant Bouillon and ¼ teaspoon dill weed; mix well. Over low heat, cook and stir until thickened (*do not boil*). Refrigerate leftovers.

Makes about 1½ cups

Microwave: For Salmon Loaf, combine ingredients as above. Shape into loaf; place in greased 8-inch baking dish. Cook on 70% power (medium-high) 10 to 11 minutes or until center of loaf is firm, rotating ¼ turn after 5 minutes. Cover with foil; let stand 5 minutes. Serve as above.

For Lemony Dill Sauce, in 1-quart glass measure with handle, melt margarine on 100% power (high) 45 seconds to 1 minute. Add remaining ingredients; mix well. Cook on 70% power (medium-high) 2 to 2½ minutes or until thickened, stirring after 1 minute (*do not boil*).

Salmon with Mustard Dill Sauce

¼ cup mayonnaise or salad dressing
¼ cup BORDEN® or MEADOW GOLD® Sour Cream
1 tablespoon sliced green onion
1 teaspoon Dijon-style mustard
⅓ cup plus 1 teaspoon REALEMON® Lemon Juice from Concentrate
1½ teaspoons dill weed
4 (1-inch-thick) salmon steaks (about 1½ pounds)

In small bowl, combine mayonnaise, sour cream, green onion, mustard, *1 teaspoon* ReaLemon® brand and *½ teaspoon* dill weed. Cover; chill. In large shallow dish or plastic bag, combine remaining *⅓ cup* ReaLemon® brand and *1 teaspoon* dill weed; add salmon. Cover; marinate in refrigerator 1 hour. Grill, broil or bake until fish flakes with fork. Serve with dill sauce. Refrigerate leftovers.

Makes 4 servings

Seafood Royale

4 tablespoons butter or margarine, divided
2 tablespoons all-purpose flour
½ teaspoon dried dill weed
¼ teaspoon seasoned salt
1½ cups (12-ounce can) *undiluted* CARNATION® Evaporated Milk
½ cup dry white wine
½ cup shredded Swiss cheese
1½ cups sliced mushrooms
½ cup finely sliced green onions
1 pound salmon, cooked, bones and skin removed
6 rolls or puff pastry shells

In medium saucepan, melt *2 tablespoons* butter. Whisk in flour, dill and salt; heat until bubbling. Add evaporated milk; stir constantly over medium heat until well thickened. Add wine and cheese; stir until blended. Keep warm. In small skillet, sauté mushrooms and green onions in *remaining 2 tablespoons* butter. Combine sauce, mushrooms, onions and salmon over low heat; stir gently. Serve in hollowed out rolls or puff pastry shells.

Makes 6 servings

Baja Fruited Salmon

1 large navel orange, peeled and diced
1 small grapefruit, peeled and diced
1 medium tomato, seeded and diced
¼ cup diced red onion
1 small jalapeño, seeded and finely chopped
2 tablespoons snipped fresh cilantro
2 tablespoons red wine vinegar
1 tablespoon vegetable oil
½ teaspoon LAWRY'S® Seasoned Salt
¼ teaspoon LAWRY'S® Garlic Powder with Parsley
4 (5 ounces each) salmon steaks
Lemon juice

In medium bowl, combine all ingredients except salmon and lemon juice; refrigerate. Brush salmon steaks with lemon juice. Grill or broil 5 inches from heat source 5 to 7 minutes on each side or until fish flakes easily with fork. Spoon chilled fruit salsa over salmon.

Makes 4 servings

Presentation: Serve with pan-fried potatoes. Garnish with parsley and lemon slices.

Baja Fruited Salmon

Grilled Oriental Fish Steaks

Grilled Oriental Fish Steaks

- 4 **fish steaks (halibut, salmon or swordfish), about ³/₄ inch thick**
- ¼ **cup KIKKOMAN® Lite Soy Sauce**
- 3 **tablespoons minced onion**
- 1 **tablespoon chopped fresh ginger root**
- 1 **tablespoon sesame seed, toasted**
- ½ **teaspoon sugar**

Place fish in single layer in shallow baking pan. Measure lite soy sauce, onion, ginger, sesame seed and sugar into blender container; process on low speed 30 seconds, scraping sides down once. Pour sauce over fish; turn over to coat both sides. Marinate 30 minutes, turning fish over occasionally. Remove fish and broil or grill 4 inches from heat source or moderately hot coals 5 minutes on each side, or until fish flakes easily when tested with fork. Garnish as desired.
Makes 4 servings.

Seafood Creole

- 1 **tablespoon vegetable oil**
- 3 **tomatoes, peeled, coarsely chopped**
- 1 **large onion, chopped**
- 1 **green pepper, chopped**
- 1 **celery stalk, chopped**
- 3 **cloves garlic, minced**
- 1½ **cups water**
- ³/₄ **cup uncooked rice**
- 1 **teaspoon ground cumin**
- ½ **teaspoon dried thyme leaves**
- ½ **teaspoon TABASCO® pepper sauce**
- 1 **bay leaf**
- 1½ **pounds red snapper fillets with skin, cut into 2-inch pieces**
- ¼ **cup chopped parsley**

In large skillet heat oil; cook tomatoes, onion, green pepper, celery and garlic until crisp-tender. Add water, rice, cumin, thyme, Tabasco® sauce and bay leaf. Bring to a boil; reduce heat and simmer covered 10 minutes. Add fish and parsley. Cover; simmer 5 to 10 minutes longer or until liquid is absorbed and fish flakes easily when tested with fork. Remove bay leaf.
Makes 4 servings.

Microwave Directions: In 3-quart microwave-safe casserole place oil, onion, green pepper, celery and garlic. Cover loosely with plastic wrap; cook on High 3 to 4 minutes or until vegetables are crisp-tender. Stir in tomatoes, *1 cup* water, rice, cumin, thyme, Tabasco® sauce and bay leaf. Re-cover; cook on High 20 minutes; stir. Add fish and parsley. Re-cover; cook on High 5 to 7 minutes or until fish flakes easily when tested with fork. Let stand covered 10 minutes before serving. Remove bay leaf.

Poached Red Snapper

- 2 **quarts water**
- 1 **cup (8 ounces) WISH-BONE® Italian Dressing**
- 1 **cup dry white wine**
- 2 **medium carrots, finely chopped**
- ½ **cup chopped shallots or onions**
- 1 **tablespoon lemon juice**
- 1 **teaspoon grated lemon peel (optional)**
- 3 **whole cloves**
- 1 **teaspoon salt**
- ¼ **teaspoon pepper**
- 1 **pound new or all-purpose potatoes, cut into large chunks**
- 1 **whole red snapper (about 2½ to 3 pounds)**
- 1 **pound fresh spinach leaves, stems trimmed**

Place 13×9×2½-inch baking pan on 2 stove burners; fill with water, Italian dressing, wine, carrots, shallots, lemon juice, lemon peel, cloves, salt and pepper. Bring to a boil, then simmer uncovered 5 minutes. Add potatoes and simmer, stirring occasionally, 20 minutes. Add snapper and simmer, basting occasionally, 25 minutes or until fish flakes and potatoes are tender. Carefully remove snapper and potatoes to serving platter and keep warm. Add spinach to cooking liquid and simmer 30 seconds; drain. To serve, arrange potatoes and spinach around snapper.
Makes about 4 servings.

Note: Also terrific with Wish-Bone® Robusto Italian, Blended Italian, Lite Italian or Lite Classic Dijon Vinaigrette Dressing.

Grilled Salmon Steaks with Watercress Sauce

- 1 **cup (8 ounces) WISH-BONE® Italian Dressing**
- ½ **cup chopped watercress**
- 4 **salmon, tuna or swordfish steaks, 1 inch thick (about 2 pounds)**
- ½ **cup whipping or heavy cream**
- 2 **tablespoons dry vermouth Pinch of sugar (optional)**

In large shallow baking dish, combine Italian dressing with watercress. Add fish and turn to coat. Cover and marinate in refrigerator, turning fish occasionally, at least 4 hours. Remove fish, reserving marinade. Grill or broil, turning once and basting with reserved marinade, until fish flakes.

Meanwhile, in small saucepan, bring ¼ cup reserved marinade to a boil, then simmer uncovered 5 minutes. Stir in cream, vermouth and sugar. Cook, stirring occasionally, 3 minutes or until slightly thickened. Serve hot sauce over fish.
Makes about 4 servings.

Note: Also terrific with Wish-Bone® Robusto Italian, Lite Italian, Blended Italian or Lite Classic Dijon Vinaigrette Dressing.

Swordfish Steaks with Dill-Mustard Sauce

Swordfish Steaks with Dill-Mustard Sauce

- ⅓ cup WISH-BONE® Italian Dressing
- 2 swordfish or shark steaks, 1 inch thick (about 1 pound)
- ½ cup dry white wine
- ⅛ teaspoon pepper
- 1 tablespoon snipped fresh dill*
- 1 tablespoon Dijon-style mustard
- ½ cup whipping or heavy cream

In large skillet, heat Italian dressing and cook fish over medium heat, turning once, 8 minutes or until fish flakes. Remove to serving platter and keep warm. Into skillet, add wine, then pepper, dill and mustard. Bring to a boil, then simmer, stirring occasionally, 8 minutes. Stir in cream and heat 1 minute or until thickened. Serve over fish. Garnish, if desired, with baby vegetables.
Makes about 2 servings.

*Substitution: Use 1 teaspoon dried dill weed.

Note: Also terrific with Wish-Bone® Robusto Italian or Blended Italian Dressing.

Teriyaki Fish Fillets

- 1 can (20 ounces) DOLE® Pineapple Chunks in Juice
- 1 clove garlic, pressed
- 2 tablespoons slivered fresh ginger root
- 1 tablespoon minced green onion
- 5 teaspoons teriyaki sauce
- 1 teaspoon white vinegar
- 1 pound sole fillets
- 2 teaspoons cornstarch
- 1 teaspoon minced fresh ginger root
- 1 teaspoon sesame oil

Measure 2 tablespoons juice from pineapple can; mix with garlic, slivered ginger, onion, 3 teaspoons teriyaki sauce and vinegar. Arrange fish in shallow dish. Pour marinade over fish. Refrigerate 10 minutes. Arrange fish on greased broiler rack. Brush with marinade. Broil 6 inches from heat 5 to 6 minutes. In saucepan, combine remaining 2 teaspoons teriyaki sauce, undrained pineapple and remaining ingredients. Cook until sauce boils and thickens. Serve with fish.
Makes 4 servings.

Chinese Trout

- 4 medium trout (about 2 pounds), dressed
- ¼ cup KIKKOMAN® Soy Sauce
- 2 tablespoons vegetable oil, divided
- 1 cup water
- 4 teaspoons cornstarch
- 1 tablespoon sugar
- 2 tablespoons tomato catsup
- 1 tablespoon KIKKOMAN® Soy Sauce
- 2½ teaspoons distilled white vinegar
- ⅛ teaspoon crushed red pepper
- ½ cup sliced green onions and tops
- 2 teaspoons finely chopped garlic
- 2 teaspoons finely chopped fresh ginger root

Score both sides of trout with diagonal slashes ¼ inch deep and 1 inch apart; place in large shallow pan. Combine ¼ cup soy sauce and 1 tablespoon oil; pour over trout, turning to coat both sides well. Marinate 45 minutes, turning over once. Reserving marinade, remove trout and place on rack of broiler pan. Broil 3 inches from heat source 5 minutes on each side, or until fish flakes easily when tested with fork; brush occasionally with reserved marinade. Meanwhile, combine water, cornstarch, sugar, catsup, 1 tablespoon soy sauce, vinegar and red pepper; set aside. Heat remaining 1 tablespoon oil in saucepan over medium-high heat. Add green onions, garlic and ginger; stir-fry 2 minutes. Stir in catsup mixture. Cook and stir until sauce boils and thickens. Serve with trout.
Makes 4 servings.

Tuna Veronique

2 leeks or green onions
½ cup thin carrot strips
1 stalk celery, cut diagonally into slices
1 tablespoon vegetable oil
1¾ cups or 1 can (14½ ounces) chicken broth
2 tablespoons cornstarch
⅓ cup dry white wine
1¼ cups seedless red and green grapes, cut into halves
1 can (12½ ounces) STARKIST® Tuna, drained and broken into chunks
1 tablespoon chopped chives
¼ teaspoon white or black pepper
4 to 5 slices bread, toasted and cut into quarters or 8 to 10 slices toasted French bread

If using leeks, wash thoroughly between leaves. Cut off white portion; trim and slice ¼ inch thick. Discard green portion. For green onions, trim and slice ¼ inch thick. In a large nonstick skillet sauté leeks, carrot and celery in oil for 3 minutes. In a small bowl stir together chicken broth and cornstarch until smooth; stir into vegetables. Cook and stir until mixture thickens and bubbles. Stir in wine; simmer for 2 minutes. Stir in grapes, tuna, chives and pepper. Cook for 2 minutes more to heat through. To serve, ladle sauce over toast points.

Makes 4 to 5 servings

Preparation time: 20 minutes

Tuna in Red Pepper Sauce

2 cups chopped red bell peppers (about 2 peppers)
½ cup chopped onion
1 clove garlic, minced
2 tablespoons vegetable oil
¼ cup dry red or white wine
¼ cup chicken broth
2 teaspoons sugar
¼ teaspoon black pepper
1 red bell pepper, slivered and cut into ½-inch pieces
1 yellow or green bell pepper, slivered and cut into ½-inch pieces
½ cup julienne-strip carrots
1 can (9¼ ounces) STARKIST® Tuna, drained and broken into chunks
Hot cooked pasta or rice

In skillet sauté 2 cups chopped bell peppers, onion and garlic in oil for 5 minutes, or until vegetables are very tender. In blender or food processor container place vegetable mixture; cover and process until puréed. Return to pan; stir in wine, chicken broth, sugar and black pepper. Keep warm. In 2-quart saucepan steam bell pepper pieces and carrots over simmering water for 5 minutes. Stir steamed vegetables into sauce with tuna; cook for 2 minutes, or until heated through. Serve tuna mixture over pasta or rice.   *Makes 4 to 5 servings*

Preparation time: 20 minutes

Tuna Veronique

Tuna in Red Pepper Sauce

Heat oil over medium-high heat in large skillet. Sauté trout 1 to 2 minutes on each side or until fish flakes easily; set aside. Melt butter over medium heat. Sauté garlic and green onion, about 1 minute. Add tomato, corn, snow peas, cilantro, jalapeño, lemon juice, salt and pepper. Simmer about 2 to 3 minutes. Stir in cream; gently simmer about 1 minute more. Top trout with sauce. Serve immediately with tortilla chips.

Makes 4 servings

Rainbow Trout Santa Fe

- 2 tablespoons olive oil
- 4 CLEAR SPRINGS® Brand Idaho Rainbow Trout fillets (4 ounces *each*)
- 2 teaspoons butter
- 2 cloves garlic, minced
- ¼ cup chopped green onion
- 1 small tomato, peeled, seeded and diced
- ½ cup fresh or frozen whole corn kernels
- ½ cup snow peas, cut in half diagonally
- 2 tablespoons chopped cilantro or parsley
- 1 to 1½ teaspoons finely chopped jalapeño pepper*
- 1 teaspoon fresh lemon juice
- ¼ teaspoon salt
  Dash white pepper
- ¼ cup heavy cream
  Flour or corn tortilla chips

*Wear rubber gloves when working with jalapeño peppers and wash hands with warm soapy water. Avoid touching face or eyes.

Broiled Rainbow Trout with Herb Mayonnaise

- 6 tablespoons regular or light mayonnaise
- 1 clove garlic, minced
- 1 tablespoon lemon juice
  Herbs to taste
  Dash of pepper
- 4 CLEAR SPRINGS® Brand Idaho Rainbow Trout fillets (4 ounces *each*)

Combine mayonnaise, garlic, lemon juice, herbs and pepper in bowl; mix well. Cover flesh side of each trout fillet with ¼ of mayonnaise mixture. Broil 4 inches from heat source for about 3 to 5 minutes, or until fish flakes with a fork and topping is bubbly.

Makes 2 to 4 servings

"Crab" Cakes

- 2 eggs, beaten
- ½ cup plain dry bread crumbs
- ¼ cup REALEMON® Lemon Juice from Concentrate
- ¼ cup sliced green onions
- ½ teaspoon dry mustard
- ½ pound imitation crab blend, flaked
  Additional dry bread crumbs
  Vegetable oil

In medium bowl, combine eggs, *½ cup* crumbs, ReaLemon® brand, green onions and mustard. Fold in crab blend. Shape into 8 cakes; coat with additional crumbs. In large skillet, brown in hot oil until golden on both sides. Refrigerate leftovers. *Makes 4 servings*

"Crab" Cakes

Poached Sole with Dill Sauce

1 (13¾-fluid ounce) can
   COLLEGE INN® Chicken
   Broth
6 sole or flounder fillets (about
   1½ pounds)
3 tablespoons lemon juice
1 tablespoon cornstarch
3 tablespoons snipped fresh dill
   or 1 tablespoon dried dill
   weed

In skillet, over medium-high heat, heat 1¼ cup chicken broth to a boil; reduce heat. Add fish; cover and simmer 2 to 3 minutes or until fish flakes easily with fork. Carefully remove fish with slotted spoon to heated serving platter.

Meanwhile, in small saucepan, blend remaining broth and lemon juice into cornstarch. Cook over medium-high heat, stirring, until mixture thickens and boils. Boil 1 minute; stir in dill. To serve, spoon sauce over fish. Garnish as desired.
Makes 6 servings.

Microwave: In 2-quart microwave-proof oblong dish, place fish and 1¼ cups broth; cover with plastic wrap. Microwave on HIGH (100% power) for 5 to 6 minutes until fish flakes easily with fork. Remove fish to warm serving platter.

In 1-quart microwave-proof bowl, mix ¼ cup broth, lemon juice and 2 tablespoons cornstarch. Microwave on HIGH for 4 to 5 minutes until mixture thickens and boils; stir in dill. Spoon sauce over fish; serve as above.

Poached Sole with Dill Sauce

Fisherman's Light Fillets

½ cup WISH-BONE® Lite Italian
   or Italian Dressing
1 small green pepper, cut into
   strips
1 small onion, thinly sliced
1 pound fish fillets
1 medium tomato, coarsely
   chopped
   Hot cooked rice

In large skillet, heat lite Italian dressing and cook green pepper and onion over medium heat, stirring occasionally, 5 minutes or until tender. Add fish and tomato, then simmer covered 10 minutes or until fish flakes. Serve over hot rice.
Makes about 4 servings.

Grilled Fish Steaks with Vegetable Butter

1 envelope LIPTON® Recipe
   Secrets Vegetable Recipe
   Soup Mix
½ cup butter or margarine,
   softened
2 tablespoons brandy or sherry
½ teaspoon ground ginger
4 halibut, cod, swordfish,
   salmon or shark steaks
   (about 2 pounds), ½ inch
   thick
½ cup orange juice
¼ cup oil

In medium bowl, with electric mixer or rotary beater, thoroughly blend vegetable recipe soup mix, butter, brandy and ginger. Turn onto wax paper and shape into 8×2-inch log. Wrap in plastic wrap or wax paper, then chill until firm.

Meanwhile, in large baking dish, arrange fish; add orange juice and oil. Cover and marinate in refrigerator, turning occasionally, at least 1 hour. Remove fish from marinade. Grill or broil until fish flakes. To serve, top each steak with ½-inch slice butter mixture.
Makes 4 servings.

Microwave Directions: Prepare butter mixture and marinate fish as above. In 13×9-inch baking dish, arrange fish and microwave uncovered at HIGH (Full Power), rearranging fish occasionally, 9 minutes or until fish flakes. Top with butter as above. Let stand covered 5 minutes.

Festival Shrimp

1 **DOLE® Fresh Pineapple**
1 **large DOLE® Tomato, cut into quarters**
1 **medium onion, cut into quarters**
1 **jar (4 ounces) pimentos**
¼ **cup canned diced green chilies**
2 **tablespoons lime juice**
1½ **teaspoons ground coriander**
1 **teaspoon garlic salt**
1 **teaspoon sugar**
¼ **cup margarine**
1 **pound medium shrimp, cooked and shelled***
1 **tablespoon chopped fresh cilantro or parsley**
  Hot cooked rice

Twist crown from pineapple. Cut pineapple lengthwise into quarters. Remove fruit from shell with curved knife. Trim off core and cut fruit into chunks. Set aside.

In food processor or blender, combine tomato, onion, pimentos, green chilies, lime juice, coriander, garlic salt and sugar. Process until pureed.

In large skillet, melt margarine. Add pureed sauce and simmer 5 minutes. Stir in shrimp, pineapple and cilantro. Cook just until heated through. Serve immediately over hot rice.
Makes 4 servings.

*Cook shrimp in simmering water 2 to 3 minutes or until pink and firm. Drain; set aside until cool enough to handle. Remove shells; cut along curve of body with sharp knife to remove back vein.

Festival Shrimp

Beer-Batter Shrimp

½ **cup beer**
⅓ **cup all-purpose flour**
⅓ **cup cornstarch**
1 **egg**
2 **tablespoons CRISCO® Oil**
⅛ **teaspoon cayenne**
⅛ **teaspoon garlic powder**
  CRISCO® Oil for frying
1 **pound fresh medium shrimp, peeled, deveined and butterflied**

Combine beer, flour, cornstarch, egg, 2 tablespoons Crisco® Oil, cayenne pepper and garlic powder in medium mixing bowl. Mix well. Cover and refrigerate at least 1 hour.

Heat 2 to 3 inches Crisco® Oil in deep-fryer or large saucepan to 375°F. Dip shrimp in batter. Fry a few shrimp at a time, 1 to 1½ minutes, or until golden brown. Drain on paper towels. Serve immediately or keep warm in 175°F oven.
Makes 4 to 6 servings.

Seafood Kabobs

2 **dozen large sea scallops**
1 **dozen medium shrimp, shelled and deveined**
1 **can (8½ ounces) whole small artichoke hearts, drained**
2 **red or yellow peppers, cut into 2-inch pieces**
¼ **cup olive or vegetable oil**
¼ **cup lime juice**

In large bowl, combine all ingredients and toss gently. Thread scallops, shrimp, artichode hears and peppers alternately on skewers; reserve marinade. Lightly oil grid. Grill kabobs, on uncovered grill, over low **KINGS-FORD® Charcoal Briquets** 6 to 8 minutes or until scallops turn opaque and shrimp turn pink. Turn kabobs carefully at least twice during grilling and brush with marinade
Makes 6 servings.

Deep-Fried Clams

2 **cups oyster crackers, finely crushed**
½ **teaspoon poultry seasoning**
¼ **teaspoon salt**
¼ **teaspoon cayenne**
¼ **teaspoon garlic powder**
¼ **teaspoon ground marjoram**
2 **eggs**
1 **can (10 ounces) whole baby clams, drained**
  CRISCO® Oil for frying

Mix cracker crumbs, poultry seasoning, salt, cayenne, garlic powder and marjoram in large plastic food storage bag. Set aside. Beat eggs slightly in small mixing bowl. Gently stir in clams. Remove a few clams with slotted spoon and add to cracker mixture. Shake to coat. Remove clams from cracker mixture; set aside. Repeat with remaining clams.

Heat 2 to 3 inches Crisco® Oil in deep-fryer or large saucepan to 375°F. Fry a few clams at a time, about 30 seconds, or until golden brown. Drain on paper towels. Serve immediately.
2 to 4 servings.

Steamed Trout with Orange & Ginger

½ cup WISH-BONE® Italian or
   Robusto Italian Dressing
1 medium red onion, chopped
¼ cup orange juice
1 tablespoon finely chopped
   fresh ginger*
1 teaspoon grated orange peel
   (optional)
½ teaspoon ground cumin
⅛ teaspoon pepper
2 whole trout or fresh-water fish
   (about 1 pound each), boned
1 cup coarsely chopped green
   onions
1 cup thinly sliced carrots
1 cup thinly sliced yellow
   squash
1 cup thinly sliced snow peas
   (about 4 ounces)

In large shallow oblong baking dish, thoroughly combine Italian dressing, red onion, orange juice, ginger, orange peel, cumin and pepper. Add trout and turn to coat. Cover and marinate in refrigerator, turning occasionally, at least 3 hours. Remove trout, reserving marinade.

Preheat oven to 450°. For each serving, place 1 trout on 1 piece (18×18-inch) parchment paper or heavy-duty aluminum foil; equally top each with reserved marinade, green onions, carrots, squash and snow peas. Wrap parchment or foil loosely around trout and vegetables, sealing edges airtight with double fold. Bake 20 minutes or until trout flakes. Serve, if desired, with hot cooked wild rice.
Makes 2 servings.
   Substitution: Use 1 teaspoon ground ginger.

Steamed Mussels in White Wine

⅓ cup WISH-BONE® Italian
   Dressing
½ cup chopped shallots or
   onions
3 pounds mussels, well
   scrubbed
⅔ cup dry white wine
½ cup chopped parsley
¼ cup water
   Generous dash crushed red
   pepper

In large saucepan or stockpot, heat Italian dressing and cook shallots over medium heat, stirring occasionally, 2 minutes or until tender. Add remaining ingredients. Bring to a boil, then simmer covered 4 minutes or until mussel shells open. (Discard any unopened shells.) Serve, if desired, with Italian or French bread.
Makes about 3 main-dish or 6 appetizer servings.
   Note: Also terrific with Wish-Bone® Robusto Italian or Blended Italian Dressing.

Steamed Mussels in White Wine

Salmon Cheese Puff Pies

1 (15½-ounce) can salmon,
   drained and flaked
1 cup BORDEN® or MEADOW
   GOLD® Cottage Cheese
¼ cup chopped green pepper
¼ cup chopped onion
3 tablespoons REALEMON®
   Lemon Juice from
   Concentrate
1 (2-ounce) jar pimientos,
   drained and chopped
¼ cup dill weed
1 (10-ounce) package frozen puff
   pastry patty shells, thawed
   in refrigerator overnight

Preheat oven to 450°. In large bowl, combine all ingredients except patty shells. On floured surface, roll each shell to an 8-inch circle. Place equal amounts of salmon mixture in center of each circle. Fold over; seal edges with water and press with fork. Place on ungreased baking sheet; cut slit near center of each turnover. Reduce oven temperature to 400°; bake 25 minutes or until golden brown. Refrigerate leftovers.
Makes 6 servings.

Lemon Swordfish

1 tablespoon grated lemon peel
¾ cup fresh lemon juice
¾ cup olive or vegetable oil
¼ to ½ cup parsley, chopped
2 tablespoons prepared
   horseradish
2 cloves garlic, minced
1 teaspoon dried thyme,
   crushed
1 teaspoon salt
¼ teaspoon pepper
1 bay leaf
1½ pounds swordfish steaks

In shallow glass dish, combine all ingredients except fish. Add swordfish; turn to coat with marinade. Cover and refrigerate at least 2 hours, turning fish occasionally. Drain fish; reserve marinade. Grill swordfish, on uncovered grill, over medium-hot **KINGS-FORD® Charcoal Briquets** about 7 minutes, basting lightly with marinade. Carefully turn swordfish and grill 5 to 6 minutes longer or until fish flakes easily when tested with fork, basting lightly with marinade.
Makes 4 servings.

Shanghai Shrimp

- 4 scallions, cut in 1-inch pieces
- 1 teaspoon minced ginger
- 2 tablespoons peanut oil
- 1 pound large shrimp, shelled and deveined
- 1 cup COLLEGE INN® Chicken Broth
- 1 tablespoon cornstarch
- 1 (11-ounce) can mandarin oranges, undrained
- 1 (8-ounce) can CHUN KING® Sliced Water Chestnuts, undrained
- Hot cooked rice

In large skillet, over medium-high heat, cook scallions and ginger in oil for 2 to 3 minutes. Add shrimp; cook for 3 to 4 minutes. Blend chicken broth into cornstarch; stir into skillet with oranges and water chestnuts. Reduce heat; simmer, covered, until slightly thickened and heated through. Serve over rice. Garnish as desired.

Makes 6 servings.

Shanghai Chicken: Substitute 1 pound boneless chicken, cut in 2-inch strips, for shrimp.

Savory Seafood Stew

- 2/3 cup WISH-BONE® Italian Dressing
- 1/2 cup dry white wine
- 1/4 cup sliced onion
- 6 clams, well scrubbed
- 1 lobster, cut into 2-inch pieces (about 1 pound)
- 1/2 pound fish fillets, cut into large pieces
- 1/4 pound scallops
- 1/4 pound uncooked medium shrimp, cleaned

In large saucepan, combine Italian dressing, wine, onion and clams. Bring to a boil, then simmer covered, stirring occasionally, 5 minutes. Add remaining ingredients, then simmer covered, stirring occasionally, 5 minutes or until seafood is done. (Discard any unopened clam shells.) Serve, if desired, with hot cooked rice or crusty French bread.

Makes about 4 servings.

Note: Also terrific with Wish-Bone® Robusto Italian, Blended Italian or Lite Italian Dressing.

Shanghai Shrimp

Shrimp & Vegetable Stir-Fry

- 2 tablespoons cornstarch, divided
- 4 tablespoons KIKKOMAN® Teriyaki Sauce, divided
- 1 tablespoon minced fresh ginger root
- 1/2 pound medium-size raw shrimp, peeled and deveined
- 3/4 cup water
- 2 tablespoons vegetable oil, divided
- 2 stalks celery, cut diagonally into 1/4-inch-thick slices
- 1 medium-size red bell pepper, cut into 1-inch squares
- 1/4 pound green onions and tops, cut into 1-inch lengths, separating whites from tops

Combine 1 tablespoon *each* cornstarch and teriyaki sauce with ginger in small bowl; add shrimp and stir to coat evenly. Let stand 15 minutes. Meanwhile, combine water, remaining 1 tablespoon cornstarch and 3 tablespoons teriyaki sauce; set aside. Heat 1 tablespoon oil in hot wok or large skillet over high heat. Add shrimp and stir-fry 1 minute; remove. Heat remaining 1 tablespoon oil in same pan. Add celery, red pepper and white parts of green onions; stir-fry 2 minutes. Stir in shrimp, teriyaki sauce mixture and green onion tops. Cook and stir until mixture boils and thickens. Serve over rice, if desired.

Makes 4 servings.

Oriental Seafood Stir-Fry

With slotted spoon, remove shrimp from marinade; stir-fry 2 to 3 minutes, or until shrimp turn pink. Add mushrooms; stir-fry 2 to 3 minutes, adding 1 tablespoon water if necessary to prevent sticking. Stir cornstarch and 6 tablespoons water into marinade; add to skillet and cook about 30 seconds, until thickened. Add celery and remaining ingredients and stir-fry 3 to 4 minutes, until bean sprouts are soft, but still crisp. Serve over hot brown rice, if desired.   *Makes 4 servings*

Oriental Seafood Stir-Fry

½ cup water
3 tablespoons REALEMON®
   Lemon Juice from
   Concentrate
3 tablespoons soy sauce
1 tablespoon brown sugar
1 tablespoon cornstarch
2 ounces fresh pea pods
¾ cup sliced fresh
   mushrooms
¾ cup diced red bell pepper
1 medium onion, cut into
   wedges
1 tablespoon vegetable oil
½ pound imitation crab blend,
   flaked
   Shredded napa (Chinese
   cabbage), angel hair
   pasta or rice noodles

In small bowl, combine water, ReaLemon® brand, soy sauce, sugar and cornstarch. In large skillet or wok, over medium-high heat, cook and stir vegetables in oil until tender-crisp; remove. Add soy mixture; over medium heat, cook and stir until slightly thickened. Add vegetables and crab blend; heat through. Serve with napa, pasta or noodles. Refrigerate leftovers.
Makes 4 servings

Oriental Almond Stir-Fry

2 tablespoons dry sherry
1 tablespoon soy sauce
½ teaspoon sugar
¼ teaspoon ground ginger
1 clove garlic, minced
¾ pound shrimp, peeled and
   deveined
1 tablespoon vegetable oil,
   divided
2 cups diagonally sliced
   celery (¼ inch thick)
2 cups fresh mushrooms,
   sliced
1 tablespoon cornstarch
6 tablespoons water
1 package (10 ounces) frozen
   peas (about 2 cups)
1½ cups bean sprouts
¼ cup BLUE DIAMOND®
   Blanched Whole
   Almonds

Make marinade by combining first five ingredients in a medium bowl. Add shrimp and let stand at least 10 minutes, stirring occasionally. Using heavy non-stick skillet or wok, heat 1½ teaspoons oil over medium-high heat. Add celery and stir-fry 1 minute. Remove from pan and set aside. Heat remaining 1½ teaspoons oil.

Sonora Shrimp

2 tablespoons IMPERIAL®
   Margarine
1 medium green bell pepper,
   coarsely chopped
½ cup chopped onion
½ cup chopped celery
1 can (14½ ounces) whole
   peeled tomatoes,
   undrained and cut up
½ cup dry white wine
½ teaspoon LAWRY'S®
   Seasoned Salt
½ teaspoon LAWRY'S®
   Seasoned Pepper
¼ teaspoon LAWRY'S® Garlic
   Powder with Parsley
¼ teaspoon dried thyme,
   crushed
1 pound medium shrimp,
   peeled and deveined
1 can (2¼ ounces) sliced ripe
   olives, drained

In large skillet, melt margarine and sauté bell pepper, onion and celery. Add remaining ingredients except shrimp and olives; blend well. Bring to a boil; reduce heat and simmer, uncovered, 15 minutes, stirring occasionally. Add shrimp and olives; cook 10 minutes or until shrimp turn pink.
Makes 4 to 6 servings

Presentation: Serve over hot fluffy rice.

Sweet & Sour Shrimp

Sweet & Sour Shrimp

- **1 (20-ounce) can juice-pack pineapple chunks, drained, reserving juice**
- **¾ cup cold water**
- **⅓ cup REALEMON® Lemon Juice from Concentrate**
- **⅓ cup firmly packed light brown sugar**
- **3 tablespoons cornstarch**
- **3 tablespoons soy sauce**
- **⅛ teaspoon ground ginger**
- **1 pound medium raw shrimp, peeled and deveined**
- **1 (8-ounce) can sliced water chestnuts, drained**
- **1 green bell pepper, cut into chunks**
- **Hot cooked rice**

In large skillet, combine reserved pineapple juice, water, ReaLemon® brand, sugar, cornstarch, soy sauce and ginger. Over medium heat, cook and stir until thick and clear. Add shrimp; cook 3 minutes. Add remaining ingredients except rice; heat through. Serve with rice. Refrigerate leftovers.
Makes 4 servings

Cajun Shrimp

- **1 cup sliced fresh mushrooms**
- **6 green onions, sliced**
- **2 tablespoons butter or margarine**
- **1 medium tomato, chopped**
- **½ cup HEINZ® Thick and Rich Cajun Style Barbecue Sauce**
- **1 tablespoon lemon juice**
- **¼ teaspoon salt**
- **1 pound raw medium-size shrimp, shelled, deveined**
- **Hot cooked rice**

In large skillet, sauté mushrooms and green onions in butter 1 to 2 minutes. Add tomato, barbecue sauce, lemon juice and salt; heat to boiling. Stir in shrimp. Simmer, uncovered, 4 to 5 minutes or until shrimp turn pink, stirring frequently. Serve over rice.
Makes 4 servings (about 3 cups)

Cajun Shrimp

Seafood Cacciatore

- **1 pound shrimp, cleaned**
- **1 small onion, chopped**
- **2 garlic cloves, minced**
- **2 tablespoons oil**
- **1 can (14½ ounces) whole tomatoes in juice**
- **1 can (8 ounces) tomato sauce**
- **1¼ cups water**
- **1 medium green pepper, cut into thin strips**
- **¾ teaspoon dried basil**
- **½ teaspoon dried oregano**
- **½ teaspoon salt**
- **⅛ teaspoon ground red pepper**
- **1 chicken bouillon cube**
- **1½ cups Original MINUTE® Rice**
- **8 clams, well scrubbed**

Cook and stir shrimp with onion and garlic in hot oil in large skillet until shrimp turn pink. Stir in tomatoes with juice, tomato sauce, water, green pepper, seasonings and bouillon cube. Bring to full boil, breaking up tomatoes with spoon. Stir in rice. Cover; remove from heat. Let stand 5 minutes.

Meanwhile, place clams on rack in pan with water below rack. Bring to boil. Cover and steam 5 to 10 minutes or until clams open. Discard any unopened clams. Fluff rice mixture with fork and serve topped with clams.   *Makes 4 servings*

Scampi-Style Shrimp

- **2 tablespoons sliced green onion**
- **4 cloves garlic, finely chopped**
- **2 tablespoons margarine or butter**
- **2 tablespoons olive or vegetable oil**
- **1 pound medium raw shrimp, peeled and deveined**
- **¼ cup REALMON® Lemon Juice from Concentrate**
- **⅛ teaspoon salt**

In large skillet, over medium-high heat, cook and stir onion and garlic in margarine and oil 1 minute. Add shrimp; cook and stir until shrimp are pink. Add ReaLemon® brand and salt; heat through. Garnish with parsley if desired. Refrigerate leftovers.
Makes 4 servings

Baked Shrimp Feast

- **½ cup margarine, melted**
- **1 clove garlic, pressed**
- **1 tablespoon Italian seasonings**
- **¼ teaspoon black pepper**
- **2 pounds jumbo shrimp (21 to 26 per pound)**
- **1 pound French bread, sliced or torn into bite-size pieces**

• Preheat oven to 350°F. Combine margarine, garlic, seasonings and pepper in shallow 3-quart casserole dish. Add shrimp; toss to coat shrimp. Cover with foil; bake 25 minutes.

• Pour juices from shrimp into serving bowl to use as a dipping herb sauce for French bread.

• To eat, slip shell from shrimp with one pull, holding tail. Dunk bread in dipping herb sauce.
Makes 6 to 8 servings

Preparation Time: 5 minutes
Cook Time: 25 minutes

Favorite recipe from **Dole Food Company, Inc.**

Tex-Mex Stir-Fry

- **2 tablespoons vegetable oil**
- **1½ cups broccoli flowerettes**
- **2 carrots, thinly sliced diagonally**
- **1 red or green bell pepper, thinly sliced**
- **½ cup thinly sliced celery**
- **1 pound medium shrimp, peeled and deveined**
- **⅓ cup LAWRY'S® Fajitas Skillet Sauce**
- **2 tablespoons brown sugar**
- **1 teaspoon ground ginger**
- **1 teaspoon dry mustard**
- **3 cups chilled, cooked rice Sliced almonds, lightly toasted (optional)**

In large skillet or wok, heat 1 tablespoon oil; add broccoli, carrots, bell pepper and celery. Stir-fry 3 minutes. Remove; set aside. Add remaining 1 tablespoon oil and shrimp to same *hot* skillet; stir-fry 3 minutes. Return vegetables to skillet. Pour in Fajitas Skillet Sauce, brown sugar, ginger and mustard. Cook 2 minutes longer, tossing gently to blend. Cover and set aside. In *hot* medium skillet, place chilled rice. Stir-fry over high heat 3 to 5 minutes or until slightly crisp and browned. Serve shrimp and vegetables over rice. Sprinkle with almonds, if desired.   *Makes 6 servings*

Presentation: Accompany with almond or fortune cookies.

Hint: One pound thinly sliced boneless chicken or pork can be used in place of shrimp. Add 2 teaspoons chopped cilantro for extra flavor.

Tex-Mex Stir-Fry

Shrimp Scampi

- 1½ cups Original MINUTE® Rice
- 1 small onion, chopped
- 1 tablespoon oil
- ¾ pound medium shrimp, cleaned
- 2 to 3 garlic cloves, minced
- 1 bottle (8 ounces) clam juice
- 1 tablespoon cornstarch
- 1 tablespoon chopped parsley
- 1 tablespoon lemon juice
  Dash pepper
- 1 red pepper, diced

Prepare rice as directed on package; keep warm.

Cook and stir onion in hot oil in large skillet until tender but not browned. Add shrimp and garlic; cook and stir until shrimp are pink.

Meanwhile, mix clam juice, cornstarch, parsley, lemon juice and pepper. Add to skillet with red pepper. Bring to boil 1 minute. Serve shrimp mixture over rice.   *Makes 4 servings*

Barbecued Shrimp with Spicy Rice

- 1 pound large shrimp, peeled and deveined
- 4 wooden* or metal skewers
  Vegetable cooking spray
- ⅓ cup prepared barbecue sauce
  Spicy Rice (recipe follows)

Thread shrimp on skewers. To broil in oven, place on broiler rack coated with cooking spray. Broil 4 to 5 inches from heat 4 minutes. Brush with barbecue sauce. Turn and brush with remaining barbecue sauce. Broil 2 to 4 minutes longer or until shrimp are done. To cook on outdoor grill, cook skewered shrimp over hot coals 4 minutes. Brush with barbecue sauce. Turn and brush with remaining barbecue sauce. Grill 4 to 5 minutes longer or until shrimp are done. Serve with Spicy Rice.
      Makes 4 servings

*Soak wooden skewers in water before using to prevent burning.

Spicy Rice

- ½ cup sliced green onions
- ½ cup minced carrots
- ½ cup minced red pepper
- 1 jalapeño or serrano pepper, minced
- 1 tablespoon vegetable oil
- 2 cups cooked rice (cooked in chicken broth)
- 2 tablespoons snipped fresh cilantro
- 1 tablespoon lime juice
- 1 teaspoon soy sauce
  Hot pepper sauce to taste

Barbecued Shrimp with Spicy Rice

Spicy Southern Shrimp Kabobs

Cook onions, carrots, red pepper, and jalapeño pepper in oil in large skillet over medium-high heat until tender crisp. Stir in rice, cilantro, lime juice, soy sauce, and pepper sauce; cook until thoroughly heated. Serve with Barbecued Shrimp.

To microwave: Combine onions, carrots, red pepper, jalapeño pepper, and oil in 2-quart microproof baking dish. Cook on HIGH 2 to 3 minutes or until vegetables are tender crisp. Add rice, cilantro, lime juice, soy sauce, and pepper sauce. Cook on HIGH 3 to 4 minutes, stirring after 2 minutes, or until thoroughly heated. Serve with Barbecued Shrimp.

*Favorite recipe from **USA Rice Council***

Spicy Southern Shrimp Kabobs

1 DOLE® Fresh Pineapple
1 pound jumbo shrimp (24 to 26 per pound), peeled, deveined
6 spicy Italian sausages, cut into 1-inch pieces
½ medium DOLE® Red Bell Pepper, seeded, chunked
½ medium DOLE® Green Bell Pepper, seeded, chunked
¼ cup margarine, melted
¾ teaspoon dried oregano, crumbled
¾ teaspoon dried thyme, crumbled
½ teaspoon salt
¼ teaspoon ground red pepper
¼ teaspoon black pepper

• Twist crown from pineapple. Cut pineapple in half lengthwise. Cut fruit from shell with knife. Cut fruit into chunks.

• For each kabob, arrange 2 pineapple chunks, 2 shrimp, 2 sausage chunks and 2 red or green bell pepper chunks on skewers. Or, arrange as desired to increase the number for appetizer portions. Arrange skewers on rack in broiler pan coated with cooking spray or oil. Combine margarine and seasonings in cup; brush over kabobs.

• Broil 6 inches from heat 8 to 10 minutes, basting and turning occasionally, or until shrimp are opaque. Cool slightly before serving.   *Makes 12 kabobs*

Preparation Time: 20 minutes
Cook Time: 10 minutes

Bacon-Wrapped Shrimp

> 1 pound fresh or frozen shrimp, shelled and deveined
> 1 small onion, finely chopped
> ½ cup olive or vegetable oil
> ½ teaspoon sugar
> ½ teaspoon cayenne pepper
> ¼ teaspoon salt
> ¼ teaspoon dried oregano, crushed
> ½ teaspoon garlic powder
> ½ pound bacon
>   Mexican Fried Rice (recipe follows)

Thaw shrimp, if frozen. Place shrimp in plastic bag; set in bowl. For marinade, in small bowl, combine onion, oil, sugar, cayenne pepper, salt, oregano and garlic powder. Pour marinade over shrimp; close bag. Marinate shrimp 3 hours in refrigerator, turning occasionally.

Cut bacon slices into halves lengthwise, then crosswise. In large skillet, partially cook bacon. Drain on paper toweling. Drain shrimp; reserve marinade. Wrap bacon strips around shrimp and secure with wooden picks. Place shrimp in wire grill basket or on 12×9-inch piece of heavy-duty foil. (If using foil, puncture foil in several places.)

Grill shrimp, on uncovered grill, over medium-hot **KINGSFORD® Charcoal Briquets** 6 minutes or until bacon and shrimp are done, turning basket or individual shrimp once and basting with marinade. Serve with Mexican Fried Rice.
Makes 6 servings.

Mexican Fried Rice

> 3 tablespoons vegetable oil
> 1 cup long grain rice
> 2 cups water
> 1 cup chili salsa
> ½ cup chopped green pepper
> 1 small onion, chopped
> 1 clove garlic, minced

In 12-inch skillet, heat oil. Add rice; cook until golden brown, stirring often. Stir in remaining ingredients. Bring mixture to boil; reduce heat. Cover; simmer 15 to 20 minutes or until rice is tender. Season to taste; serve with additional salsa, if desired.
Makes 6 servings.

Shrimp Creole

> ½ cup WISH-BONE® Italian Dressing
> 1 medium green pepper, cut into chunks
> 1 medium onion, sliced
> 1 can (14½ ounces) whole peeled tomatoes, undrained and chopped
> 1 pound uncooked medium shrimp, cleaned
> ⅛ teaspoon crushed red pepper
> 2 cups hot cooked rice

In medium skillet, heat Italian dressing and cook green pepper and onion over medium heat, stirring occasionally, 5 minutes or until tender. Stir in tomatoes and simmer covered 15 minutes. Add shrimp and red pepper and simmer covered an additional 5 minutes or until shrimp turn pink. To serve, arrange shrimp mixture over hot rice.
Makes about 4 servings.

Note: Also terrific with Wish-Bone® Robusto Italian or Lite Italian Dressing.

Scallops with Golden Cream Sauce

> 2 tablespoons butter or margarine
> 1 medium red pepper, cut into thin strips
> 1 cup uncooked regular rice
> 1 envelope LIPTON® Recipe Secrets Golden Onion Recipe Soup Mix
> 2¼ cups water
> 1 tablespoon lime juice
> ¼ cup light cream or half and half
> 1 pound bay scallops
> 2 medium green onions, sliced

In medium skillet, melt butter and cook red pepper over medium heat until crisp-tender. Stir in uncooked rice, then golden onion recipe soup mix thoroughly blended with water and lime juice. Bring to a boil, then simmer covered 30 minutes or until rice is tender. Stir in remaining ingredients and cook covered 5 minutes or until scallops are tender. Serve, if desired, with freshly ground pepper.
Makes about 4 servings.

Shrimp Creole

Saucy Shrimp over Chinese Noodle Cakes

Chinese Noodle Cakes (recipe follows)
1¼ **cups water**
2 **tablespoons cornstarch, divided**
4 **tablespoons KIKKOMAN® Soy Sauce, divided**
1 **teaspoon tomato catsup**
½ **pound medium-size raw shrimp, peeled and deveined**
2 **tablespoons vegetable oil, divided**
1 **clove garlic, minced**
½ **teaspoon minced fresh ginger root**
1 **green pepper, chunked**
1 **medium onion, chunked**
2 **stalks celery, cut diagonally into thin slices**
2 **tomatoes, chunked**

Prepare Chinese Noodle Cakes. Combine water, 1 tablespoon cornstarch and 3 tablespoons soy sauce with catsup; set aside. Blend remaining 1 tablespoon cornstarch and 1 tablespoon soy sauce in small bowl; stir in shrimp until coated. Heat 1 tablespoon oil in hot wok or large skillet over high heat. Add shrimp and stir-fry 1 minute; remove. Heat remaining 1 tablespoon oil in same pan. Add garlic and ginger; stir-fry until fragrant. Add green pepper, onion and celery; stir-fry 4 minutes. Stir in soy sauce mixture, shrimp and tomatoes. Cook and stir until sauce boils and thickens. Cut Chinese Noodle Cakes into squares and serve with shrimp mixture.
Makes 4 servings.
CHINESE NOODLE CAKES: Cook *8 ounces capellini* (angel hair pasta) according to package directions. Drain; rinse under cold water and drain thoroughly. Heat *1 tablespoon vegetable oil* in large, nonstick skillet over medium-high heat. Add half the capellini; slightly spread to fill bottom of skillet to form noodle cake. Without stirring, cook 5 minutes, or until golden on bottom. Lift cake with wide spatula; add *1 tablespoon oil* to skillet and turn cake over. Cook 5 minutes longer, or until golden brown, shaking skillet occasionally to brown evenly; remove to rack and keep warm in 200°F. oven. Repeat with remaining capellini.

Saucy Shrimp over
Chinese Noodle Cakes

Barbecued Shrimp on a Skewer

1 **envelope LIPTON® Recipe Secrets Onion or Onion-Mushroom Recipe Soup Mix**
1 **can (14½ ounces) whole peeled tomatoes, undrained and chopped**
½ **cup vegetable or olive oil**
¼ **cup dry white wine or vermouth**
¼ **cup chopped fresh basil leaves***
1 **tablespoon lemon juice**
1 **teaspoon cracked peppercorns**
2 **pounds uncooked large shrimp, cleaned**
4 **thin slices cooked ham, cut into strips**
1 **tablespoon finely chopped parsley**

In large bowl, combine onion recipe soup mix, tomatoes, oil, wine, basil, lemon juice and peppercorns. Add shrimp. Cover and marinate in refrigerator, stirring occasionally, at least 2 hours. Remove shrimp, reserving marinade.

On skewers, alternately thread shrimp with ham strips, weaving ham around shrimp. Grill or broil, turning and basting frequently with reserved marinade, until shrimp are done. Bring remaining marinade to a boil, then simmer 2 minutes; stir in parsley. Serve as a dipping sauce or, if desired, arrange skewers over hot cooked rice and top with sauce.
Makes about 6 servings.
***Substitution:** Use 1½ teaspoons dried basil leaves.

Shrimp Etouffée

½ **cup butter or margarine**
2 **medium onions, chopped**
1 **cup chopped celery**
1 **cup chopped green onions**
2 **cloves garlic, minced**
½ **cup flour**
4 **cups water**
2 **cans (16 ounces each) tomatoes, drained**
2 **tablespoons lemon juice**
1 **teaspoon salt**
2 **bay leaves**
¼ **teaspoon dried thyme leaves**
2 **pounds shrimp, peeled, deveined**
½ **teaspoon TABASCO® pepper sauce**
Hot cooked rice

In large saucepot or Dutch oven melt butter; add onions, celery, green onions and garlic. Cook 5 minutes or until tender. Add flour; stir until well blended. Stir in water, tomatoes, lemon juice, salt, bay leaves and thyme. Bring to a boil, reduce heat and simmer covered 30 minutes; stir occasionally. Add shrimp and Tabasco® sauce. Simmer 5 minutes longer or until shrimp turn pink. Remove bay leaves. Serve over rice.
Makes 8 servings.

Scallop Kabobs

Scallop Kabobs

¼ cup **REALEMON® Lemon Juice from Concentrate**
2 tablespoons **vegetable oil**
1 teaspoon **oregano leaves**
½ teaspoon **basil leaves**
1 clove **garlic, finely chopped**
⅛ teaspoon **salt**
1 pound **sea scallops**
8 ounces **fresh mushrooms**
2 small **zucchini, cut into chunks**
2 small **onions, cut into wedges**
½ **red, yellow or green bell pepper, cut into bite-size pieces**

In shallow dish, combine ReaLemon® brand, oil and seasonings; add scallops. Cover; marinate in refrigerator 2 hours, stirring occasionally. Skewer scallops alternately with vegetables. Grill or broil as desired, basting frequently with additional ReaLemon® brand. Refrigerate leftovers.

Makes 4 servings

Tropical Kabobs with Peanut Sauce

1 can (20 ounces) **DOLE® Pineapple Chunks in Juice**
1 pound **large shrimp, peeled, deveined**
½ cup **canned real cream of coconut**
1 tablespoon **vegetable oil**
2 teaspoons **soy sauce**
2 cloves **garlic, minced**
¼ teaspoon **crushed red pepper flakes**
2 small **DOLE® Red or Green Bell Peppers, seeded, chunked**

Peanut Sauce
½ cup **canned real cream of coconut**
¼ cup **smooth peanut butter**
2 tablespoons **soy sauce**
1 tablespoon **lemon juice**
¼ teaspoon **crushed red pepper flakes**

• Drain pineapple; reserve juice.

• Place shrimp in shallow dish. Combine reserved juice, cream of coconut, oil, soy sauce, garlic and pepper flakes in small bowl. Pour over shrimp. Cover and marinate in refrigerator 15 minutes or overnight.

• On skewers, arrange shrimp, pineapple chunks and bell peppers.

• Grill or broil 6 inches from heat 8 to 10 minutes or until shrimp turn opaque. Baste frequently with marinade. Serve with Peanut Sauce. Refrigerate leftovers.

Makes 4 to 6 servings

PEANUT SAUCE: Combine all ingredients in small saucepan. Cook, stirring, until peanut butter melts and mixture begins to boil. Reduce heat. Simmer, uncovered, 10 minutes, stirring occasionally. Serve at room temperature.

Preparation Time: 25 minutes
Marinate Time: 15 minutes or overnight
Cook Time: 20 minutes

Curried Scallops in Rice Ring

Vegetable cooking spray
1½ pounds **bay scallops**
1 tablespoon **margarine**
1 medium **onion, chopped**
1 teaspoon **all-purpose flour**
½ teaspoon **salt**
1 bottle (8 ounces) **clam juice**
1 cup **evaporated skim milk**
1 red **apple, cored and chopped**
½ teaspoon **curry powder**
6 cups **hot cooked rice**
1 tablespoon **snipped parsley**
1 tablespoon **diced pimiento Chutney, chopped peanuts, grated coconut, and raisins for condiments (optional)**

Coat large skillet with cooking spray and place over medium heat until hot. Add scallops; cook

until scallops are almost done, 2 to 3 minutes. Remove scallops from skillet; keep warm. Melt margarine in skillet; add onion and cook 1 to 2 minutes or until tender. Stir in flour and salt; cook, stirring, 2 minutes over medium-high heat. Gradually add clam juice and milk, stirring constantly until thickened. Stir in scallops, apple, and curry powder. Keep warm. Combine rice, parsley, and pimiento; pack into 2-quart ring mold coated with cooking spray. Unmold onto serving platter and fill center of ring with curried scallops. Serve with chutney, chopped peanuts, grated coconut, and raisins.
Makes 6 servings

Favorite recipe from **USA Rice Council**

Scallops Primavera

1 pound scallops
¼ cup REALEMON® Lemon Juice from Concentrate
1 cup thinly sliced carrots
3 cloves garlic, finely chopped
⅓ cup margarine or butter
8 ounces fresh mushrooms, sliced (about 2 cups)
¾ teaspoon thyme leaves
2 teaspoons cornstarch
½ teaspoon salt
¼ cup diagonally sliced green onions
4 ounces fresh pea pods *or* 1 (6-ounce) package frozen pea pods, thawed
2 tablespoons dry sherry
Hot cooked rice

In shallow baking dish, combine scallops and ReaLemon® brand. Cover; marinate in refrigerator 30 minutes, stirring occasionally. In large skillet, over high heat, cook and stir carrots and garlic in margarine until tender-crisp, about 3 minutes. Add mushrooms and thyme; cook and stir about 5 minutes. Stir cornstarch and salt into scallop mixture; add to skillet. Cook and stir until scallops are opaque, about 4 minutes. Add onions, pea pods and sherry; heat through. Serve with rice. Refrigerate leftovers.   *Makes 4 servings*

Spiced Broiled Lobster

4 Maine lobsters (1 to 1½ pounds *each*)
Boiling water
½ cup WISH-BONE® Italian or Lite Italian Dressing
½ small onion, halved
1 tablespoon ketchup
1 tablespoon snipped dill*
2 teaspoons Dijon-style mustard
⅛ teaspoon hot pepper sauce

Place each lobster on its stomach. With tip of sharp knife, make 2 deep criss-cross cuts in each lobster head. Immediately plunge into boiling water and boil 30 seconds or until lobster turns red. Remove from water; let cool slightly. Place each lobster on its back, then make lengthwise cut down each lobster tail; set aside. In food processor or blender, process remaining ingredients; set aside.

In large shallow aluminum-foil-lined baking pan or on broiler rack, arrange prepared lobsters stomach side up, then brush tails with ⅓ of the dressing mixture. Broil on lower rack 20 minutes or until lobster meat turns opaque. (If lobsters brown too quickly, loosely cover with aluminum foil.) Serve with remaining dressing mixture for dipping.   *Makes 4 servings*

*Substitution: Use 1 teaspoon dried dill weed.

Scallops Primavera

ONE-DISH MEALS

Having a busy day? Try Quick Tamale Casserole or One Skillet Spicy Chicken 'n Rice. Skillet dinners, casseroles and pot pies not only make great comfort food but save time for the busy cook. Whether you're entertaining a crowd or bringing a dish to a potluck dinner, these one-dish meals are easy-to-serve and make ahead.

Dairyland Confetti Chicken

Casserole
- 1 cup diced carrots
- ¾ cup chopped onion
- ½ cup diced celery
- ¼ cup chicken broth
- 1 can (10½ ounces) cream of chicken soup
- 1 cup dairy sour cream
- 3 cups cubed cooked chicken
- ½ cup (4 ounces) sliced mushrooms
- 1 teaspoon Worcestershire sauce
- 1 teaspoon salt
- ⅛ teaspoon pepper

Confetti Topping
- 1 cup sifted all-purpose flour
- 2 teaspoons baking powder
- ½ teaspoon salt
- 2 eggs, slightly beaten
- ½ cup milk
- 1 tablespoon chopped green pepper
- 1 tablespoon chopped pimiento
- 1¼ cups (5 ounces) shredded Wisconsin Cheddar cheese, divided

For casserole: In saucepan, combine carrots, onion, celery and chicken broth. Simmer 20 minutes. In 3-quart casserole, mix soup, sour cream, chicken cubes, mushrooms, Worcestershire sauce, salt and pepper. Add simmered vegetables and liquid; mix well.

For confetti topping: In mixing bowl, combine flour, baking powder and salt. Add eggs, milk, green pepper, pimiento and 1 cup of the cheese. Mix just until well blended. Drop tablespoons of topping onto casserole and bake in 350°F oven for 40 to 45 minutes or until golden brown. Sprinkle with remaining ¼ cup cheese and return to oven until melted. Garnish as desired.

Makes 6 to 8 servings

*Favorite recipe from **Wisconsin Milk Marketing Board** © 1993*

Ranch-Style Chicken Casserole

- 1 envelope LIPTON® Recipe Secrets Onion Recipe Soup Mix
- 1½ cups buttermilk
- 1 tablespoon all-purpose flour
- 2 cloves garlic, finely chopped
- 1 pound boneless skinless chicken breasts
- 2 cups frozen mixed vegetables
- ¼ cup dry bread crumbs
- 1 tablespoon butter or margarine, melted
- Paprika (optional)

Preheat oven to 350°F.

In small bowl, thoroughly combine onion recipe soup mix, buttermilk, flour and garlic; set aside.

In lightly greased 2-quart shallow casserole, arrange chicken breasts and vegetables; add soup mixture. Bake, covered, 20 minutes. Remove cover and top with bread crumbs combined with butter. Continue baking, uncovered, 25 minutes. Sprinkle, if desired, with paprika.

Makes 4 servings

Dairyland Confetti Chicken

One Skillet Spicy Chicken 'n Rice

Chicken Enchilada Casserole

1 medium onion, chopped
2 tablespoons vegetable oil
4 cups shredded, cooked chicken or turkey
1 can (15 ounces) tomato sauce
1 can (14½ ounces) whole peeled tomatoes, undrained and cut up
1 package (1.25 ounces) LAWRY'S® Taco Spices & Seasonings
½ teaspoon LAWRY'S® Garlic Powder with Parsley
1 dozen medium corn tortillas
2 cans (2¼ ounces each) sliced ripe olives, drained
3 cups (12 ounces) grated Monterey Jack cheese

In large skillet, sauté onion in oil. Add chicken, tomato sauce, tomatoes, Taco Spices & Seasonings and Garlic Powder with Parsley; blend well. Bring to a boil; reduce heat and simmer, uncovered, 15 minutes. In 13×9×2-inch glass baking dish, place 4 corn tortillas. Pour ⅓ of chicken mixture on tortillas, spreading evenly. Layer with ⅓ of olives and ⅓ of cheese. Repeat layers 2 times, ending with cheese. Bake, uncovered, in 350°F oven 30 to 40 minutes or until heated through and cheese melts.

Makes 8 to 10 servings

Presentation: Serve with prepared Mexican rice and a green salad.

Hint: For a crowd-pleasing entrée, simply double the recipe.

One Skillet Spicy Chicken 'n Rice

¼ cup all-purpose flour
1 teaspoon LAWRY'S® Seasoned Salt
6 to 8 chicken pieces, skinned
2 tablespoons vegetable oil
2 cans (14½ ounces each) whole peeled tomatoes, undrained and cut up
1 package (1.25 ounces) LAWRY'S® Taco Spices & Seasonings
1 cup thinly sliced celery
1 cup long-grain rice
½ cup chopped onion

In plastic bag, combine flour and Seasoned Salt. Add chicken; shake to coat well. In large skillet, brown chicken in oil; continue cooking, uncovered, over low heat 15 minutes. Add remaining ingredients; blend well. Bring to a boil; reduce heat, cover and simmer 20 minutes or until liquid is absorbed and chicken is cooked through.

Makes 4 to 6 servings

Presentation: Sprinkle with chopped parsley.

Chicken and Rice Paprikash

3 teaspoons paprika, divided
¾ teaspoon salt
¼ teaspoon pepper
6 medium chicken thighs
1 can (14½ or 16 ounces) whole tomatoes
1 small onion, sliced and separated into rings
1 teaspoon chicken bouillon granules
2 cloves garlic, minced
1 cup UNCLE BEN'S® CONVERTED® Brand Rice, uncooked
1 large green pepper, cut into thin strips
Light sour cream or plain yogurt (optional)

Combine 1½ teaspoons of the paprika, salt and pepper. Rub seasonings onto chicken thighs, coating all surfaces with mixture; set aside. Drain tomatoes, reserving juice. Chop tomatoes; set aside. Add enough water to juice to equal 2 cups. Combine tomato liquid, onion, bouillon granules, garlic and remaining 1½ teaspoons paprika in 12-inch skillet. Bring to a boil. Stir in rice and tomatoes. Arrange chicken thighs on top of rice mixture. Cover tightly and simmer 20 minutes. Add green pepper. Remove from heat. Let stand covered until all liquid is absorbed, about 5 minutes. Serve with light sour cream or plain yogurt, if desired.

Makes 6 servings

Chicken Broccoli Bake

2 cups chopped cooked broccoli
2 cups cubed cooked chicken or turkey
2 cups soft bread cubes
2 cups shredded process sharp American cheese
1 jar (12 ounces) HEINZ® HomeStyle Chicken or Turkey Gravy
½ cup undiluted evaporated milk
Dash pepper

In buttered 9-inch square baking dish, layer broccoli, chicken, bread cubes and cheese. In medium bowl, combine gravy, milk and pepper; pour over chicken-broccoli mixture. Bake in 375°F oven, 40 minutes. Let stand 5 minutes.

Makes 6 servings

Fancy Chicken Puff Pie

4 tablespoons butter or margarine
¼ cup chopped shallots
¼ cup all-purpose flour
1 cup chicken stock or broth
¼ cup sherry
Salt to taste
⅛ teaspoon white pepper
Pinch ground nutmeg
¼ pound ham, cut into 2×¼-inch strips
3 cups cooked PERDUE® chicken, cut into 2×¼-inch strips
1½ cups fresh asparagus pieces *or* 1 (10-ounce) package frozen asparagus pieces
1 cup (½ pint) heavy cream
Chilled pie crust for a 1-crust pie *or* 1 sheet frozen puff pastry
1 egg, beaten

In medium saucepan, over medium-high heat, melt butter; sauté shallots lightly. Stir in flour; cook 3 minutes. Add broth and sherry. Heat to boiling, stirring constantly; season to taste with salt, pepper and nutmeg. Reduce heat to low and simmer 5 minutes. Stir in ham, chicken, asparagus and cream. Pour chicken mixture into ungreased 9-inch pie plate.

Preheat oven to 425°F. Cut 8-inch circle from crust. Cut hearts from extra dough with cookie cutter, if desired. Place circle on cookie sheet moistened with cold water. Pierce with fork, brush with egg and decorate with hearts; brush hearts with egg.

Bake crust and filled pie plate 10 minutes; reduce heat to 350°F and bake additional 10 to 15 minutes, or until pastry is golden brown and filling is hot and set. With a spatula, place pastry over hot filling and serve immediately.

Makes 4 servings

Fancy Chicken Puff Pie

California-Style Chicken

- 1 can (15 ounces) tomato sauce
- 3 tablespoons red wine vinegar
- 1/2 teaspoon DURKEE® Sweet Basil
- 1/4 teaspoon DURKEE® Garlic Powder
- 12 small red potatoes, thinly sliced (about 3 cups)
- 1 can (2.8 ounces) DURKEE® French Fried Onions
- 2 1/2 pounds chicken pieces, fat trimmed, skinned if desired
- 1 package (10 ounces) frozen whole green beans, thawed and drained

Preheat oven to 375°. In small bowl, combine tomato sauce, vinegar and seasonings. Spread *1/2 cup* tomato mixture in bottom of 9×13-inch baking dish; top with potatoes and *1/2 can* French Fried Onions. Arrange chicken over potatoes and onions. Spoon *1 cup* tomato mixture over chicken and potatoes. Bake, covered, at 375° for 35 minutes. Stir green beans into potatoes. Spoon remaining tomato mixture over chicken. Bake, covered, 10 to 15 minutes or until chicken and beans are done. Top chicken with remaining onions; bake, uncovered, 3 minutes or until onions are golden brown.
Makes 4 to 6 servings.

Old-Fashioned Chicken Pot Pie

- 6 tablespoons butter or margarine, divided
- 3 tablespoons flour
- 2 cups chicken broth
- 1 1/4 teaspoons dried rosemary leaves, divided
- 1/4 teaspoon TABASCO® pepper sauce
- 1/2 pound cubed cooked chicken
- 2 medium carrots, sliced and cooked
- 1 cup frozen peas
- 1 1/2 cups packaged dry biscuit mix
- 1/2 cup milk

Preheat oven to 400°F. In large saucepan melt 3 tablespoons butter. Stir in flour; cook 1 minute. Remove from heat. Gradually add broth. Stir constantly, bring to a boil over medium heat and boil 1 minute. Stir in 1/2 teaspoon rosemary, Tabasco® sauce, chicken, carrots and peas. Spoon mixture into greased 2-quart shallow baking dish.

In medium bowl combine biscuit mix and remaining 3/4 teaspoon rosemary. Cut in remaining 3 tablespoons butter until mixture resembles coarse crumbs. Stir in milk. On heavily floured surface pat out biscuit dough 1/2 inch thick. Cut into 10 triangles. Arrange triangles on chicken mixture. Bake 25 minutes or until biscuits are browned.
Makes 4 servings.

Turkey Cottage Pie

- 1/4 cup butter or margarine
- 1/4 cup all-purpose flour
- 1 envelope LIPTON® Recipe Secrets Golden Onion Recipe Soup Mix
- 2 cups water
- 2 cups cut-up cooked turkey or chicken
- 1 package (10 ounces) frozen mixed vegetables, thawed
- 1 1/4 cups shredded Swiss cheese (about 5 ounces)
- 1/8 teaspoon pepper
- 5 cups hot mashed potatoes

Preheat oven to 375°.

In large saucepan, melt butter and cook flour over medium-low heat, stirring constantly, 5 minutes or until golden. Stir in golden onion recipe soup mix thoroughly blended with water. Bring to a boil, then simmer 15 minutes or until thickened. Stir in turkey, vegetables, 1 cup cheese and pepper. Turn into lightly greased 2-quart casserole; top with hot potatoes, then remaining cheese. Bake 30 minutes or until bubbling.
Makes about 8 servings.

Microwave Directions: In 2-quart casserole, microwave butter at HIGH (Full Power) 1 minute. Stir in flour and microwave uncovered, stirring frequently, 2 minutes. Stir in golden onion recipe soup mix thoroughly blended with water. Microwave uncovered, stirring occasionally, 4 minutes or until thickened. Stir in turkey, vegetables, 1 cup cheese and pepper. Top with hot potatoes, then remaining cheese. Microwave uncovered, turning casserole occasionally, 5 minutes or until bubbling. Let stand uncovered 5 minutes. For additional color, sprinkle, if desired, with paprika.

Scalloped Turkey

- 2 cups diced cooked BUTTERBALL® turkey (3/4 pound)
- 1/2 cup chopped celery
- 1/4 cup chopped green bell pepper
- 3 tablespoons butter or margarine, divided
- 2 tablespoons all-purpose flour
- 1/4 teaspoon salt
- 1 1/2 cups milk
- 1 tablespoon chopped pimiento
- 4 cups potato chips, divided

Turkey Cottage Pie

Preheat oven to 350°F. Cook and stir celery and green pepper in 1 tablespoon butter in medium saucepan over medium heat. Remove from pan. Melt remaining 2 tablespoons butter in same saucepan over medium heat. Blend in flour and salt. Remove from heat. Gradually add milk. Cook over medium heat until mixture thickens, stirring constantly. Add turkey, celery, green pepper and pimiento. Crush potato chips lightly to make 2 cups. Put about 1½ cups potato chips in bottom of buttered 1 to 1½-quart baking dish. Add turkey mixture. Sprinkle remaining chips on top. Bake in oven 30 to 40 minutes or until sauce bubbles.
Yield: 4 servings.

Country-Style Chicken Dinner

3 cups frozen hash brown potatoes
1 can (2.8 ounces) DURKEE® French Fried Onions
1 can (10¾ ounces) condensed cream of chicken soup
1 cup milk
6 slices (¾ ounce *each*) processed American cheese
2 to 2½ pounds chicken pieces, fat trimmed, skinned if desired
1 package (10 ounces) frozen mixed vegetables, thawed and drained

Preheat oven to 375°. In 9×13-inch baking dish, combine frozen potatoes and *½ can* French Fried Onions. In small bowl, blend soup and milk; pour *half* over potato mixture. Arrange cheese slices over potato mixture; top with chicken, skin-side down. Pour remaining soup mixture over chicken. Bake, uncovered, at 375° for 35 minutes. Stir vegetables into potatoes and turn chicken pieces over. Bake, uncovered, 20 minutes or until chicken is done. Stir potato mixture and top chicken with remaining onions; bake, uncovered, 3 minutes or until onions are golden brown. Let stand 15 minutes before serving.
Makes 4 to 6 servings.

Deep Dish Turkey Pie

Chicken Puff Bravo

¾ lb. VELVEETA® Mexican Pasteurized Process Cheese Spread with Jalapeño Pepper, cubed
½ cup sour cream
¼ teaspoon garlic salt
2 eggs, separated
2 10-oz. pkgs. frozen chopped spinach, thawed, well-drained
3 cups chopped cooked chicken
¼ cup chopped red or green pepper
1 4-oz. can sliced mushrooms, drained
2 8-oz. cans PILLSBURY® Refrigerated Quick Crescent Dinner Rolls

In 3-quart saucepan, combine VELVEETA® Mexican Pasteurized Process Cheese Spread with Jalapeño Pepper, sour cream and garlic salt; stir over low heat until process cheese spread is melted. Remove from heat. Beat egg yolks thoroughly; reserve 1 tablespoon for glaze. Gradually stir remaining egg yolks into cheese mixture. Cool. Beat egg whites until stiff

peaks form; fold into cheese mixture. Add remaining ingredients except dough; mix lightly. Unroll one can dough; press onto bottom and sides of greased 12-inch ovenproof skillet, pressing perforations together to seal. Spread spinach mixture over dough. Unroll second can dough; separate into eight triangles. Loosely twist each triangle at pointed end. Arrange dough triangles on spinach mixture, pointed ends towards center. Seal outer edges to crust. Brush dough with reserved egg yolk. Bake at 375°, 35 to 40 minutes or until egg mixture is set.
8 servings.

Preparation time: 20 minutes
Baking time: 40 minutes

Variation: Substitute 2-oz. jar sliced pimento, drained, for red or green pepper.
Recipe Tip: Substitute 12-inch deep-dish pizza pan for skillet.

Deep Dish Turkey Pie

3 cups cubed cooked turkey *or* chicken
1 cup sliced cooked carrots
1 cup cubed cooked potatoes
1 cup frozen green peas, thawed
6 tablespoons margarine or butter
⅓ cup unsifted flour
2 tablespoons WYLER'S® or STEERO® Chicken-Flavor Instant Bouillon *or* 6 Chicken-Flavor Bouillon Cubes
¼ teaspoon pepper
4 cups BORDEN® or MEADOW GOLD® Milk
2¼ cups biscuit baking mix

Preheat oven to 375°. In large saucepan, melt margarine; stir in flour, bouillon and pepper. Over medium heat, gradually add milk; cook and stir until mixture thickens. Add remaining ingredients except biscuit mix; mix well. Pour into 2½-quart baking dish. Prepare biscuit mix according to package directions for rolled biscuits. Roll out to cover dish; cut slashes in center of dough. Place on top of dish; crimp edges. Bake 40 minutes or until golden. Refrigerate leftovers.
Makes 6 servings.

Creamy Turkey & Broccoli

Turkey Cassoulet

**3-pound BUTTERBALL®
    Boneless Turkey
2 cans (15½ ounces each) Great
    Northern beans, drained
1 can (15 ounces) tomato sauce
    special
½ pound fully cooked Polish
    smoked sausage, cut into
    ½-inch pieces
6 slices cooked bacon, cut into
    1-inch pieces
¼ cup chopped onion
2 cloves garlic, minced
1 teaspoon fennel seed
¼ teaspoon ground black pepper**

Roast turkey according to package directions. Combine remaining ingredients in 2-quart casserole. Cover and bake alongside turkey last hour of roasting time. Wrap turkey in foil and let stand 10 to 15 minutes. Remove netting from turkey; slice turkey. To serve, arrange turkey on bean mixture, spooning some beans over turkey slices.
Yield: 8 servings.

Creamy Turkey & Broccoli

**1 package (6 ounces) stuffing
    mix,* plus ingredients to
    prepare mix
1 can (2.8 ounces) DURKEE®
    French Fried Onions
1 package (10 ounces) frozen
    broccoli spears, thawed and
    drained
1 package (1⅛ ounces)
    DURKEE® Cheese Sauce Mix
1¼ cups milk
½ cup sour cream
2 cups (10 ounces) cubed
    cooked turkey or chicken**

Preheat oven to 350°. In medium saucepan, prepare stuffing mix according to package directions; stir in ½ can French Fried Onions. Spread stuffing over bottom of greased 9-inch round baking dish. Arrange broccoli spears over stuffing with flowerets around edge of dish. In medium saucepan, prepare cheese sauce mix according to package directions using 1¼ cups milk. Remove from heat; stir in sour cream and turkey. Pour turkey mixture over broccoli *stalks*. Bake, covered, at 350° for 30 minutes or until heated through. Sprinkle remaining onions over turkey; bake, uncovered, 5 minutes or until onions are golden brown.
Makes 4 to 6 servings.

Microwave Directions: In 9-inch microwave-safe dish, prepare stuffing mix according to package microwave directions; stir in *½ can* onions. Arrange stuffing and broccoli spears in dish as above; set aside. In medium microwave-safe bowl, prepare cheese sauce mix according to package microwave directions using 1¼ cups milk. Add turkey and cook, covered, 5 to 6 minutes, stirring turkey halfway through cooking time. Stir in sour cream. Pour turkey mixture over broccoli *stalks*. Cook, covered, 8 to 10 minutes or until heated through. Rotate dish halfway through cooking time. Top turkey with remaining onions; cook, uncovered, 1 minute. Let stand 5 minutes.

*3 cups leftover stuffing may be substituted for stuffing mix. If stuffing is dry, stir in water, 1 tablespoon at a time, until moist but not wet.

Chicken in French Onion Sauce

**1 package (10 ounces) frozen
    baby carrots, thawed and
    drained or 4 medium
    carrots, cut into strips
    (about 2 cups)
2 cups sliced mushrooms
½ cup thinly sliced celery
1 can (2.8 ounces) DURKEE®
    French Fried Onions
4 chicken breast halves, skinned
    and boned
½ cup white wine
¾ cup prepared HERB-OX®
    Chicken Bouillon
½ teaspoon DURKEE® Garlic Salt
¼ teaspoon DURKEE® Ground
    Black Pepper
DURKEE® Paprika**

Preheat oven to 375°. In 8×12-inch baking dish, combine vegetables and ½ can French Fried Onions. Arrange chicken breasts on vegetables. In small bowl, combine wine, bouillon, garlic salt and pepper; pour over chicken and vegetables. Sprinkle chicken with paprika. Bake, covered, at 375° for 35 minutes or until chicken is done. Baste chicken with wine sauce and top with remaining

onions; bake, uncovered, 3 minutes or until onions are golden brown.
Makes 4 servings.

Microwave Directions: In 8×12-inch microwave-safe dish, combine vegetables and *½ can* onions. Arrange chicken breasts, skinned side down, along sides of dish. Prepare wine mixture as above, except reduce bouillon to ⅓ cup; pour over chicken and vegetables. Cook, covered, on HIGH 6 minutes. Turn chicken breasts over and sprinkle with paprika. Stir vegetables and rotate dish. Cook, covered, 7 to 9 minutes or until chicken is done. Baste chicken with wine sauce and top with remaining onions; cook, uncovered, 1 minute. Let stand for 5 minutes.

Turkey Tetrazzini

        6 slices cooked BUTTERBALL®
            turkey (1 pound)
    ⅔ cup sliced onion
    ½ stick (¼ cup) butter or
            margarine
    ¼ cup all-purpose flour
        1 teaspoon salt
    ¼ teaspoon ground white pepper
    ½ teaspoon poultry seasoning
    ¼ teaspoon dry mustard
        2 cups milk
        1 cup (4 ounces) shredded
            sharp Cheddar cheese,
            divided
        2 tablespoons chopped pimiento
        2 tablespoons sherry
        1 can (4 ounces) sliced
            mushrooms, undrained
        1 package (7 ounces) spaghetti,
            cooked, drained

Preheat oven to 400°F. Cook and stir onion in butter in medium saucepan over medium heat until tender. Blend in flour and seasonings. Remove from heat. Gradually add milk. Stirring constantly, cook over medium heat until mixture thickens. Add ⅔ cup cheese and pimiento, stirring until cheese melts. Add sherry and undrained mushrooms to cheese sauce. Place layer of spaghetti in 12×8-inch baking dish. Cover with layer of turkey and layer of sauce. Repeat the layers. Sprinkle remaining ⅓ cup cheese over top. Bake about 25 minutes.
Yield: 6 servings.

Note: Casserole may be assembled in advance and frozen. To serve, heat, covered, in 350°F oven for 1½ hours or until hot.

Sausage-Chicken Creole

Sausage-Chicken Creole

        1 can (14½ ounces) whole
            tomatoes, undrained and cut
            up
    ½ cup uncooked regular rice
    ½ cup hot water
        2 teaspoons DURKEE® RedHot
            Cayenne Pepper Sauce
    ¼ teaspoon DURKEE® Garlic
            Powder
    ¼ teaspoon DURKEE® Leaf
            Oregano
        1 bag (16 ounces) frozen
            vegetable combination
            (broccoli, corn, red pepper),
            thawed and drained
        1 can (2.8 ounces) DURKEE®
            French Fried Onions
        4 chicken thighs, skinned
    ½ pound link Italian sausage,
            quartered and cooked*
        1 can (8 ounces) tomato sauce

Preheat oven to 375°. In 8×12-inch baking dish, combine tomatoes, uncooked rice, hot water, cayenne pepper sauce and seasonings. Bake, covered, at 375° for 10 minutes. Stir vegetables and *½ can* French Fried Onions into rice mixture; top with chicken and cooked sausage. Pour tomato sauce over chicken and sausage. Bake, covered, at 375° for 40 minutes or until chicken is done. Top chicken with remaining onions; bake, uncovered, 3 minutes or until onions are golden brown.
Makes 4 servings.

*To cook sausage, simmer in water to cover until done. Or, place in microwave-safe dish and cook, covered, on HIGH 3 minutes or until done.

Turkey 'n Stuffing Bake

¼ cup (½ stick) butter or margarine
1¼ cups boiling water
3½ cups seasoned stuffing crumbs*
1 can (2.8 ounces) DURKEE® French Fried Onions
1 can (10¾ ounces) condensed cream of celery soup
¾ cup milk
1½ cups (7 ounces) cubed, cooked turkey
1 package (10 ounces) frozen peas, thawed

Combine butter and water; stir until butter melts. Pour over seasoned stuffing crumbs; toss lightly. Stir in *½ can* Durkee® French Fried Onions. Spoon stuffing mixture into 9-inch shallow baking dish. Press stuffing across bottom and up sides of dish to form a shell. Combine soup, milk, turkey and peas; pour into stuffing shell. Bake, covered, at 350°F for 30 minutes. Top with remaining onions and bake, uncovered, 5 minutes longer.
Makes 4 to 6 servings

*Three cups leftover stuffing may be substituted for butter, water and stuffing crumbs. If stuffing is dry, stir in water, 1 tablespoon at a time, until moist but not wet.

Turkey and Wild Rice Bake

1 package (6 ounces) wild and white rice mix, uncooked
2⅓ cups water
2 cups cooked turkey, cubed
1 can (4 ounces) mushrooms, drained
1 can (14 ounces) whole artichoke hearts, drained and quartered
1 jar (2 ounces) chopped pimiento, drained
1 cup shredded Swiss cheese

Preheat oven to 350°F. In 2-quart lightly greased casserole combine rice with seasoning packet, water, turkey, mushrooms, artichokes and pimiento. Cover and bake 1 hour and 15 minutes or until liquid is absorbed.

Top casserole with cheese. Return to oven and bake, uncovered, 5 to 10 minutes or until cheese is melted and golden brown.
Makes 6 servings

Favorite recipe from **National Turkey Federation**

Classy Cassoulet

6 slices bacon
¼ cup seasoned dry bread crumbs
1 pound hot or sweet Italian sausage, cut into 1-inch-thick slices
1 medium onion, cut into 6 wedges
3 cloves garlic, finely chopped
1 can (16 ounces) sliced carrots, drained
1 can (16 ounces) zucchini, drained
1 can (8 ounces) stewed tomatoes
½ cup chopped celery
1 teaspoon beef-flavored instant bouillon granules
1½ teaspoons dried parsley flakes
1 bay leaf
2 cans (15 ounces each) butter beans, 1 can drained, 1 can undrained

Sauté bacon in large skillet, turning until crisp and browned, about 8 minutes. Remove with slotted spoon to paper towels to drain. Set aside skillet with bacon drippings. Combine 2 tablespoons of the bacon drippings with bread crumbs in small bowl. Set aside.

Sauté sausage, onion and garlic in skillet with bacon drippings until sausage is no longer pink, 12 to 15 minutes. Drain off fat, leaving sausage mixture in skillet. Stir carrots, zucchini, tomatoes, celery, bouillon, parsley, bay leaf and 1 can drained butter beans into skillet with sausage. Add can of undrained butter beans. Bring to a boil; lower heat and simmer, uncovered, for 10 minutes or until mixture is heated through and celery is tender. Remove bay leaf.

Place sausage mixture into one 2-quart or 6 individual broiler-proof casseroles. Crumble bacon over top; sprinkle with bread crumb mixture. Broil 5 inches from heat 1 minute or until crumbs are golden; be careful not to burn crumbs. Serve hot with garnish of sliced, canned cranberry sauce.
Makes 6 servings

Favorite recipe from **Canned Food Information Council**

Pork Skillet Normandy

2 large all-purpose apples, cored, pared and sliced
¼ cup REALEMON® Lemon Juice from Concentrate
1 (¾- to 1-pound) pork tenderloin, cut into ¼-inch slices
½ cup unsifted flour
¼ cup margarine or butter
½ cup apple cider or juice
1 cup (½ pint) BORDEN® or MEADOW GOLD® Whipping Cream, unwhipped
1 teaspoon WYLER'S® or STEERO® Chicken-Flavor Instant Bouillon

In medium bowl, combine apples and ReaLemon® brand. Coat meat with flour. In large skillet, brown meat in margarine; remove from skillet. Stir in apple mixture and cider, scraping bottom of skillet. Cook and stir 3 minutes or until apples are tender-crisp. Slowly add cream and bouillon, stirring constantly. Add meat; simmer uncovered 5 to 10 minutes or until tender. Refrigerate leftovers.
Makes 4 servings

Classy Cassoulet

Sausage Skillet Dinner

Sausage Skillet Dinner

12 ounces fully cooked
    smoked pork link
    sausage, cut diagonally
    into 1-inch pieces
2 tablespoons water
1 medium onion
2 small red cooking apples
2 tablespoons butter, divided
12 ounces natural frozen
    potato wedges
¼ cup cider vinegar
3 tablespoons sugar
½ teaspoon caraway seed
2 tablespoons chopped
    parsley

Place sausage and water in large nonstick frying pan; cover tightly and cook over medium heat 8 minutes, stirring occasionally. Meanwhile cut onion into 12 wedges; core and cut each apple into 8 wedges. Remove sausage to warm platter. Pour off drippings. Cook and stir onion and apples in 1 tablespoon of the butter in same frying pan 4 minutes or until apples are just tender. Remove to sausage platter. Heat remaining 1 tablespoon butter; add potatoes and cook, covered, over medium-high heat 5 minutes or until potatoes are tender and golden brown, stirring occasionally. Combine vinegar, sugar and caraway seed. Reduce heat; return sausage, apple mixture and vinegar mixture to frying pan and cook 1 minute, or until heated through, stirring gently. Sprinkle with parsley.

Makes 4 servings

Preparation time: 5 minutes
Cooking time: 18 minutes

*Favorite recipe from **National Live Stock and Meat Board***

Red Beans and Rice

    Vegetable cooking spray
½ cup chopped onion
½ cup chopped celery
½ cup chopped green pepper
2 cloves garlic, minced
2 cans (15 ounces each) red
    beans,* drained
½ pound fully-cooked low-fat
    turkey sausage, cut into
    ¼-inch slices
1 can (8 ounces) tomato
    sauce
1 teaspoon Worcestershire
    sauce
¼ teaspoon ground red
    pepper
¼ teaspoon hot pepper sauce
3 cups hot cooked rice
    Hot pepper sauce
    (optional)

Coat Dutch oven with cooking spray and place over medium-high heat until hot. Add onion, celery, green pepper, and garlic. Cook 2 to 3 minutes. Add beans, sausage, tomato sauce, Worcestershire sauce, red pepper, and ¼ teaspoon pepper sauce. Reduce heat; cover and simmer 15 minutes. Serve beans with rice and additional pepper sauce.

Makes 6 servings

*Substitute your favorite bean for the red beans, if desired.

*Favorite recipe from **USA Rice Council***

Red Beans and Rice

German-Style Potato Supper

- **1 pound link smoked sausage, cut into 1-inch slices**
- **4 cups frozen potatoes O'Brien**
- **1 cup water**
- **2 teaspoons WYLER'S® or STEERO® Beef-Flavor Instant Bouillon**
- **¼ cup REALEMON® Lemon Juice from Concentrate**
- **2 tablespoons sugar**
- **2 teaspoons cornstarch**
- **½ teaspoon dry mustard**

In large skillet, brown sausage. Stir in potatoes, *¾ cup* water and bouillon; bring to a boil. Cover and simmer 10 minutes. In small bowl, combine remaining ingredients; mix well. Pour over meat mixture; simmer uncovered 5 minutes or until thick and bubbly. Serve immediately. Refrigerate leftovers.

Makes 4 servings

Polish Reuben Casserole

- **2 cans (10¾ ounces each) condensed cream of mushroom soup**
- **1⅓ cups milk**
- **½ cup chopped onion**
- **1 tablespoon prepared mustard**
- **2 cans (16 ounces each) sauerkraut, rinsed and drained**
- **1 package (8 ounces) uncooked medium-width noodles**
- **1½ pounds Polish sausage, cut into ½-inch pieces**
- **2 cups (8 ounces) shredded Swiss cheese**
- **¾ cup whole wheat bread crumbs**
- **2 tablespoons butter, melted**

Combine soup, milk, onion and mustard in medium bowl; blend well. Spread sauerkraut in greased 13×9-inch pan. Top with uncooked noodles. Spoon soup

Polish Reuben Casserole

mixture evenly over top. Top with sausage, then cheese. Combine crumbs and butter in small bowl; sprinkle over top. Cover pan tightly with foil. Bake in preheated 350°F. oven 1 hour or until noodles are tender. Garnish as desired.

Makes 8 to 10 servings

Favorite recipe from **North Dakota Wheat Comission**

Swissed Ham and Noodles Casserole

- **2 tablespoons butter**
- **½ cup chopped onion**
- **½ cup chopped green pepper**
- **1 can (10½ ounces) condensed cream of mushroom soup**
- **1 cup dairy sour cream**
- **1 package (8 ounces) medium noodles, cooked and drained**
- **2 cups (8 ounces) shredded Wisconsin Swiss cheese**
- **2 cups cubed cooked ham (about ¾ pound)**

In 1-quart saucepan melt butter; sauté onion and green pepper. Remove from heat; stir in soup and sour cream. In buttered 2-quart casserole layer ⅓ of the noodles, ⅓ of the Swiss cheese, ⅓ of the ham and ½ soup mixture. Repeat layers, ending with final ⅓ layer of noodles, cheese and ham. Bake in preheated 350°F oven 30 to 45 minutes or until heated through.

Makes 6 to 8 servings

Favorite recipe from **Wisconsin Milk Marketing Board** © 1993

Cheese-Stuffed Beef Rolls

- 1 jar (15½ ounces) spaghetti sauce
- 1 egg, slightly beaten
- ¼ teaspoon DURKEE® Leaf Oregano
- ¼ teaspoon DURKEE® Garlic Powder
- 1 container (15 ounces) ricotta cheese
- ¼ cup (1 ounce) grated Parmesan cheese
- 1 cup (4 ounces) shredded mozzarella cheese
- 1 can (2.8 ounces) DURKEE® French Fried Onions
- 6 thin slices deli roast beef (about ½ pound)
- 2 medium zucchini, sliced (about 3 cups)

Preheat oven to 375°. Spread *½ cup* spaghetti sauce in bottom of 8×12-inch baking dish. In large bowl, thoroughly combine egg, seasonings, ricotta cheese, Parmesan cheese, *½ cup* mozzarella cheese and *½ can* French Fried Onions. Spoon equal amounts of cheese mixture on 1 end of each beef slice. Roll up beef slices jelly-roll style and arrange, seam-side down, in baking dish. Place zucchini along both sides of dish. Pour remaining spaghetti sauce over beef rolls and zucchini. Bake, covered, at 375° for 40 minutes or until heated through. Top beef rolls with remaining mozzarella cheese and onions. Bake, uncovered, 3 minutes or until onions are golden brown.
Makes 6 servings.

Microwave Directions: In large microwave-safe bowl, prepare cheese mixture as above. Cook, covered, on HIGH 2 to 4 minutes or until warmed through. Stir cheese mixture halfway through cooking time. Spread *½ cup* spaghetti sauce in bottom of 8×12-inch microwave-safe dish. Prepare beef rolls and place in dish as above. Arrange zucchini along both sides of dish. Pour remaining spaghetti sauce over beef rolls and zucchini. Cook, loosely covered, 14 to 16 minutes or until heated through. Rotate dish halfway through cooking time. Top beef rolls with remaining mozzarella cheese and onions; cook, uncovered, 1 minute or until cheese melts. Let stand 5 minutes.

Smoked Sausage Noodle Bake

- 1 pound ECKRICH® Smoked Sausage
- 8 ounces uncooked medium egg noodles
- 2 tablespoons butter or margarine
- ½ cup chopped onion
- ½ cup chopped celery
- 1 can (17 ounces) cream-style corn
- ½ cup sour cream
- ½ teaspoon salt
  Dash ground black pepper

Preheat oven to 350°F. Cook noodles according to package directions. Melt butter in small saucepan over medium-high heat. Saute onion and celery until crisp-tender. Combine noodles, onion, celery, corn, sour cream, salt and pepper in large bowl. Pour into buttered shallow 2-quart baking dish. Cut sausage into serving-size pieces. Arrange on top of noodles and push down partially into noodles. Bake 40 minutes or until hot.
Makes 4 to 6 servings.

Meat 'n' Tater Pie

- 2 cups KELLOGG'S® CORN FLAKES® cereal, crushed to make 1 cup, divided
- ½ teaspoon salt
- ¼ teaspoon pepper
- 1 tablespoon prepared mustard
- ⅓ cup milk
- 1 pound ground beef
- 2 eggs
- 2 cups stiff mashed potatoes
- ¼ cup chopped onion
- 2 teaspoons parsley flakes
- 2 tablespoons butter or margarine, melted
- ½ cup shredded American cheese
  Paprika

Combine ½ cup of the crushed cereal, the salt, pepper, mustard and milk in large bowl; beat well. Add ground beef, mixing until combined. Gently press meat mixture in bottom and up side of 9-inch pie pan. Beat eggs lightly in small bowl. Add potatoes, onion and parsley. Stir until combined. Spread potato mixture evenly in meat shell. Place pie pan on baking sheet. Bake at 350°F 35 minutes. Meanwhile, combine remaining ½ cup crushed cereal with melted butter in small bowl; set aside. Sprinkle cheese evenly over potato mixture. Top with cereal mixture. Bake 10 minutes more or until cheese melts. Sprinkle with paprika.
Makes 6 servings.

Ham and Cheese Strata

- 12 white bread slices
- 1½ cups (6 ounces) shredded 100% Natural KRAFT® Mild Cheddar Cheese
- 1 10-ounce package frozen chopped broccoli, thawed, well-drained
- 1 cup chopped ham
- 1 8-ounce package PHILADELPHIA BRAND® Cream Cheese, softened
- 3 eggs
- 1 cup milk
- ½ teaspoon dry mustard

Place six bread slices on bottom of 12×8-inch baking dish. Cover with 1 cup cheddar cheese, broccoli, ham and remaining bread slices, cut in half diagonally. Beat cream cheese until light and fluffy. Add eggs, one at a time, mixing well after each addition. Blend in milk and mustard; pour over bread. Top with remaining cheddar cheese. Bake at 350°, 45 to 50 minutes or until set. Let stand 10 minutes before serving.
Makes 6 servings.

Ham and Cheese Strata

Cheesy Pork Chops 'n Potatoes

- **1 jar (8 ounces) pasteurized processed cheese spread**
- **1 tablespoon vegetable oil**
- **6 thin pork chops, 1/4 to 1/2 inch thick**
- **DURKEE® Seasoned Salt**
- **1/2 cup milk**
- **4 cups frozen cottage fries**
- **1 can (2.8 ounces) DURKEE® French Fried Onions**
- **1 package (10 ounces) frozen broccoli spears,* thawed and drained**

Preheat oven to 350°. Spoon cheese spread into 8×12-inch baking dish; place in oven just until cheese melts, 5 minutes. Meanwhile, in large skillet, heat oil. Brown pork chops on both sides; drain. Sprinkle chops with seasoned salt; set aside. Using fork, stir milk into melted cheese until well blended. Stir cottage fries and *1/2 can* French Fried Onions into cheese mixture. Divide broccoli spears into 6 small bunches. Arrange bunches of spears over potato mixture with flowerets around edges of dish. Arrange chops over broccoli *stalks*. Bake, covered, at 350° for 35 to 40 minutes or until pork chops are done. Top chops with remaining onions; bake, uncovered, 5 minutes or until onions are golden brown.
Makes 4 to 6 servings.

Microwave Directions: Omit oil. Reduce milk to 1/4 cup. In 8×12-inch microwave-safe dish, place cheese spread and milk. Cook, covered, on HIGH 3 minutes; stir to blend. Stir in cottage fries and *1/2 can* onions. Cook,

covered, 5 minutes; stir. Top with broccoli spears as above. Arrange *unbrowned* pork chops over broccoli *stalks* with meatiest parts toward edges of dish. Cook, covered, on MEDIUM (50-60%) 24 to 30 minutes or until pork chops are done. Turn chops over, sprinkle with seasoned salt and rotate dish halfway through cooking time. Top with remaining onions; cook, uncovered, on HIGH 1 minute. Let stand 5 minutes.

*1 small head fresh broccoli (about 1/2 pound) may be substituted for frozen spears. Divide into spears and cook 3 to 4 minutes before using.

Tortilla Lasagna

- **1 tablespoon vegetable oil**
- **1 large onion, chopped**
- **1 medium green pepper, chopped**
- **1 large clove garlic, minced**
- **1 pound ground beef**
- **1 teaspoon dried oregano leaves**
- **1 can (16 ounces) tomatoes, drained, chopped**
- **1 can (8 ounces) tomato sauce**
- **1 cup sour cream**
- **3/4 teaspoon TABASCO® pepper sauce**
- **10 corn tortillas, 5 inches in diameter**
- **1 can (16 ounces) pinto beans, drained**
- **2 cups (8 ounces) shredded Cheddar cheese**

Preheat oven to 350°F. In large skillet heat oil; cook onion, green pepper and garlic 3 minutes or until tender. Add ground beef and oregano, breaking up

meat with fork as it cooks; cook until browned. Drain off fat; remove from heat.

In medium bowl combine tomatoes, tomato sauce, sour cream and Tabasco® sauce; mix well. Cut each tortilla in half. Arrange 10 halves in shallow 11×7-inch baking dish. Spread half the meat mixture over tortillas. Top with half the pinto beans, half the tomato mixture and 1 cup shredded cheese. Repeat with remaining ingredients. Bake 30 minutes or until heated through. Let stand 10 minutes before serving.
Makes 4 servings.

Country French Cassoulet

- **1/4 cup WISH-BONE® Italian Dressing**
- **2 medium onions, chopped**
- **2 medium carrots, chopped**
- **1 pound kielbasa (Polish sausage), sliced diagonally**
- **1/4 cup dry white wine**
- **1 cup chicken broth**
- **1 can (8 ounces) tomato puree**
- **1 teaspoon thyme leaves**
- **2 cups cut-up cooked pork or lamb (about 12 ounces)**
- **1 can (16 ounces) cannellini beans, rinsed and drained**
- **1/2 cup fresh bread crumbs**
- **2 tablespoons butter or margarine, melted**
- **2 tablespoons finely chopped parsley**

Preheat oven to 350°.

In large skillet, heat Italian dressing and cook onions, carrots and kielbasa over medium heat, stirring occasionally, 10 minutes or until vegetables are tender and kielbasa is lightly browned. Stir in wine, then broth, tomato puree, thyme and pork.

In lightly greased deep 2-quart casserole, layer 1/2 of the tomato mixture, then 1/2 of the beans; repeat. Top with bread crumbs combined with butter and parsley. Bake 40 minutes or until heated through.
Makes about 8 servings.

Note: Also terrific with Wish-Bone® Robusto Italian, Blended Italian, Lite Italian or Lite Classic Dijon Vinaigrette Dressing.

Cheesy Pork Chops 'n Potatoes

American-Style Cassoulet

4½ quarts water, divided
1 package (1 pound) dry green peas, rinsed
2 large onions, cut into wedges
1 bay leaf
2 pounds boneless lamb, cut into 1½-inch cubes
2 pounds boneless pork loin, partially frozen and cut into ½-inch slices
1 pound garlic-flavored sausage links
½ cup FILIPPO BERIO® Olive Oil, divided
1 cup coarsely chopped carrots
1 cup chopped onion
1 large clove garlic, minced
1½ cups dry white wine
1 can (14½ ounces) tomatoes
¼ cup tomato paste
⅓ cup chopped parsley
½ teaspoon dried thyme, crushed
Salt
Pepper
½ cup coarse fresh bread crumbs

Place 2 quarts of the water, the peas, onion wedges and bay leaf in large, deep saucepan. Bring to a boil over high heat; boil 2 minutes. Remove from heat. Cover and let soak 1 hour. Drain peas; discard water. Place peas and 2 quarts of the water in same saucepan. Bring to a boil over high heat. Reduce heat to low. Cover and simmer 1 hour or until peas are tender, stirring occasionally. Drain, reserving liquid. Discard bay leaf. Set peas aside; keep warm.

Brown meats, in batches, in ¼ cup of the oil in Dutch oven over medium-high heat. Return meats to Dutch oven; add carrots, chopped onion and garlic. Cook and stir several minutes. Add remaining 2 cups water, the wine, tomatoes, tomato paste, parsley and thyme. Bring to a boil. Reduce heat to low. Cover and simmer 30 minutes, stirring occasionally. Season to taste with salt and pepper. Alternately layer peas and meat mixture in large, deep casserole. Pour 1 cup of the reserved liquid over top. Sprinkle with bread crumbs and drizzle with remaining ¼ cup oil. Bake at 375°F 1 hour. Add additional reserved liquid if casserole becomes dry.
Makes 8 to 10 servings.

Chili Beef and Corn Casserole

Chili Beef and Corn Casserole

1 (13¾-fluid ounce) can COLLEGE INN® Beef Broth
1 (6-ounce) can tomato paste
1 (1¼-ounce) package ORTEGA® Taco Seasoning Mix
¾ cup uncooked rice
1 pound ground beef
1 cup chopped onion
1 (17-ounce) can whole kernel sweet corn, drained
Corn chips, optional
Diced fresh tomato, optional

In small bowl, blend 1 cup beef broth, tomato paste and taco seasoning mix; set aside. In saucepan, over high heat, combine remaining broth and enough water to equal 1¾ cups liquid; heat to a boil. Add rice and cook according to package directions.

In large skillet, over medium-high heat, brown beef and cook onion until done; pour off fat. In 2-quart casserole, layer ⅓ each of the rice, corn, meat mixture and reserved sauce; repeat layers twice, combining the last portion of meat and sauce for the top layer. Cover; bake at 375°F for 40 to 45 minutes or until hot. Garnish with corn chips and diced tomato, if desired.
Makes 4 to 6 servings.

Microwave: Combine first 3 ingredients as above. In 1½-quart microwave-proof bowl, combine remaining broth and enough water to equal 1¾ cups liquid. Stir in rice; cover. Microwave on HIGH (100% power) for 15 to 17 minutes, stirring after 7 minutes.

Crumble beef in 1½-quart microwave-proof bowl. Microwave, uncovered, on HIGH for 2 minutes; stir in onion. Microwave, uncovered, on HIGH for 2 to 3 minutes; pour off fat. In 2-quart microwave-proof casserole, layer as above; cover. Microwave on HIGH for 15 to 17 minutes, rotating casserole ½ turn after 7 minutes. Let stand, covered, for 5 minutes before serving.

Deli-in-a-Skillet

Patchwork Casserole

2 pounds ground beef
2 cups chopped green bell pepper
1 cup chopped onion
2 pounds frozen Southern-style hash-brown potatoes, thawed
2 cans (8 ounces each) tomato sauce
1 cup water
1 can (6 ounces) tomato paste
1 teaspoon salt
½ teaspoon dried basil, crumbled
¼ teaspoon ground black pepper
1 pound pasteurized process American cheese, thinly sliced

Cook and stir beef in Dutch oven over medium heat until crumbled and brown, about 10 minutes; drain off fat.

Add green pepper and onion; sauté until tender, about 4 minutes. Stir in all remaining ingredients except cheese.

Spoon ½ of the meat mixture into 13×9×2-inch baking pan or 3-quart baking dish; top with ½ of the cheese. Spoon remaining meat mixture evenly on top of cheese.

Cover pan with aluminum foil. Bake in preheated 350°F oven 45 minutes.

Cut remaining cheese into decorative shapes; place on top of casserole. Let stand, loosely covered, until cheese melts, about 5 minutes.

Makes 8 to 10 servings

Beef 'n' Tater Bake

1½ pounds lean ground beef
1 cup soft bread crumbs
1 egg, slightly beaten
½ cup chopped onion
⅓ cup HEINZ® Tomato Ketchup
½ teaspoon salt
⅛ teaspoon pepper
1 cup shredded process sharp American cheese, divided
3 cups seasoned hot mashed potatoes

Deli-in-a-Skillet

½ pound corned beef, cooked and cut into pieces*
1 can (14 ounces) sauerkraut
1½ cups water
1½ cups Original MINUTE® Rice
½ cup prepared thousand island dressing
3 ounces Swiss cheese, cut into strips

Mix corned beef, sauerkraut and water in large skillet. Bring to full boil. Stir in rice. Pour dressing over rice and top with cheese. Cover; remove from heat. Let stand 5 minutes.

Makes 4 servings

*You may use knockwurst or other luncheon meat cut into pieces in place of the corned beef.

Patchwork Casserole

In large bowl, combine beef, bread crumbs, egg, onion, ketchup, salt and pepper. Pat meat mixture firmly into 8-inch square baking dish. Bake in 350°F oven, 30 minutes. Remove from oven; drain excess fat. In large bowl, combine ¾ cup cheese with potatoes. Spread potatoes evenly over meat; sprinkle with remaining ¼ cup cheese. Return to oven; bake an additional 20 minutes or until meat is cooked through and potatoes are hot.

Makes 6 servings

Santa Fe Casserole Bake

Brown Rice Chicken Bake

- **3 cups cooked brown rice**
- **1 package (10 ounces) frozen green peas**
- **2 cups cooked chicken breast cubes**
- **½ cup cholesterol free, reduced calorie mayonnaise**
- **⅓ cup slivered almonds, toasted (optional)**
- **2 teaspoons soy sauce**
- **¼ teaspoon ground black pepper**
- **¼ teaspoon garlic powder**
- **¼ teaspoon dried tarragon leaves**
- **Vegetable cooking spray**

Combine rice, peas, chicken, mayonnaise, almonds, soy sauce, and seasonings in bowl. Transfer to 3-quart baking dish coated with cooking spray. Cover and bake at 350°F. for 15 to 20 minutes.   *Makes 6 servings*

Favorite recipe from **USA Rice Council**

Santa Fe Casserole Bake

- **1 pound lean ground beef**
- **1 package (1.25 ounces) LAWRY'S® Taco Spices & Seasonings**
- **2 cups chicken broth**
- **¼ cup all-purpose flour**
- **1 cup dairy sour cream**
- **1 can (7 ounces) diced green chiles**
- **1 package (11 ounces) corn or tortilla chips**
- **2 cups (8 ounces) grated Monterey Jack or Cheddar cheese**
- **½ cup sliced green onions with tops**

In medium skillet, brown meat and stir until crumbly; drain fat. Add Taco Spices & Seasonings; blend well. In small bowl, combine broth and flour. Add to meat mixture; bring to a boil to slightly thicken liquid. Stir in sour cream and chiles; blend well. In 13×9×2-inch lightly greased glass baking dish, place ½ of chips. Top with ½ of beef mixture, ½ of sauce, ½ of cheese and ½ of green onions. Layer again with remaining ingredients ending with green onions. Bake, uncovered, in 375°F oven for 20 minutes. Let stand 5 minutes before cutting.

Makes 6 servings

Easy Kids' Taco-Mac

- **1 pound ground turkey**
- **1 package (1.25 ounces) LAWRY'S® Taco Spices & Seasonings**
- **1 can (14½ ounces) whole peeled tomatoes, undrained and cut up**
- **1 cup water**
- **8 ounces dry macaroni or small spiral pasta**
- **½ cup sliced celery**
- **1 package (8½ ounces) corn muffin mix**
- **1 egg**
- **⅓ cup milk**

In medium skillet, brown ground turkey until crumbly. Blend in Taco Spices & Seasonings, tomatoes, water, pasta and celery. Bring to a boil; reduce heat, cover and simmer 20 minutes. In medium bowl, combine corn muffin mix, egg and milk; stir with fork just to mix. Place meat mixture in 2½-quart casserole dish. Spoon dollops of corn muffin mix on top. Bake in 400°F oven 15 to 20 minutes or until golden.

Makes 6 to 8 servings

Presentation: Sprinkle with grated cheese.

Saucy Beef and Zucchini Skillet

- **1 pound lean ground beef**
- **1 medium onion, sliced**
- **1 tablespoon vegetable oil**
- **3 medium zucchini, split lengthwise, cut into ¼-inch-thick slices (about 4 cups)**
- **1 cup HEINZ® Tomato Ketchup**
- **1 medium tomato, coarsely chopped**
- **¼ cup grated Parmesan cheese**
- **2 teaspoons lemon juice**
- **½ teaspoon salt**
- **½ teaspoon dried oregano leaves, crushed**
- **¼ teaspoon dried thyme leaves, crushed**
- **¼ teaspoon pepper**

Brown beef in large skillet; remove and set aside. Drain excess fat. Sauté onion in oil until tender; add zucchini and sauté 2 minutes. Add reserved beef, ketchup and remaining ingredients. Simmer, covered, 10 minutes, stirring occasionally. Serve over hot cooked elbow macaroni, if desired.

Makes 4 servings (about 5½ cups)

Skillet Sauerbraten

- **¾ pound boneless beef sirloin steak**
- **⅔ cup crushed gingersnaps (about 10 cookies)**
- **½ teaspoon salt**
- **1 tablespoon vegetable oil**
- **1 medium onion, sliced into rings**
- **3 ribs celery, sliced**
- **2 carrots, thinly sliced**
- **1½ cups beef broth**
- **⅓ cup cider vinegar**
- **2 tablespoons cornstarch**
- **2 tablespoons water**
- **3 cups hot cooked brown rice**

Partially freeze steak; slice diagonally across grain into ⅛-inch strips. Combine gingersnap crumbs and salt in medium bowl. Dredge steak slices into crumb mixture; set aside. Heat oil in large skillet over medium-high heat until hot. Add half of steak slices, stirring to brown both sides. Cook for 2 minutes or until done. Reserve and keep warm. Repeat with remaining steak slices. Add onion, celery, and carrots to hot skillet; cook for 5 minutes or until tender crisp. Add broth and vinegar; reduce heat and simmer 5 minutes. Combine cornstarch with water. Add to skillet, stirring constantly, until thickened; cook 1 minute longer. Add reserved steak slices; pour mixture over rice.

Makes 6 servings

Favorite recipe from **USA Rice Council**

Quick Tamale Casserole

- **1½ pounds ground beef**
- **¾ cup sliced green onions**
- **1 can (4 ounces) chopped green chilies, drained and divided**
- **1 can (10¾ ounces) tomato soup**
- **¾ cup salsa**
- **1 can (16 ounces) whole kernel corn, drained**
- **1 can (2¼ ounces) chopped pitted ripe olives (optional)**
- **1 tablespoon Worchestershire sauce**
- **1 teaspoon chili powder**
- **¼ teaspoon garlic powder**
- **4 slices (¾ ounce each) American cheese, halved**
- **4 corn muffins, cut into ½-inch cubes**
- **Mexican Sour Cream Topping (optional)**

In medium skillet, brown ground beef with green onions. Reserve 2 tablespoons chilies for Mexican Sour Cream Topping, if desired. Stir in remaining chilies, tomato soup, salsa, corn, olives, Worchestershire sauce, chili powder and garlic powder until well blended. Place in 2-quart casserole. Top with cheese, then evenly spread muffin cubes over cheese. Bake at 350°F for 5 to 10 minutes or until cheese is melted. Serve with Mexican Sour Cream Topping, if desired.

Makes 6 servings

Mexican Sour Cream Topping

- **1 cup sour cream**
- **2 tablespoons chopped green chilies, reserved from above**
- **2 teaspoons chopped jalapeño peppers (optional)**
- **2 teaspoons lime juice**

Combine all ingredients in small bowl; mix until well blended.

Makes about 1 cup

Quick Tamale Casserole

Spanish Rice and Meatballs

- 6 slices bacon
- 1 pound lean ground beef
- ½ cup soft bread crumbs
- 1 egg, slightly beaten
- ½ teaspoon salt
- ⅛ teaspoon pepper
- ½ cup chopped onion
- ½ cup sliced celery
- ⅔ cup uncooked white rice
- 1½ cups water
- 1 can (16 ounces) whole peeled tomatoes, cut into bite-size pieces
- ⅓ cup HEINZ® 57 Sauce
- ¼ teaspoon pepper
- ⅛ teaspoon hot pepper sauce
- 1 green bell pepper, cut into ¾-inch chunks

In large skillet, cook bacon until crisp; remove, coarsely crumble and set aside. Drain drippings, reserving 1 tablespoon. In large bowl, combine beef, bread crumbs, egg, salt and ⅛ teaspoon pepper. Form into 20 meatballs, using a rounded tablespoon for each. In same skillet, brown meatballs in reserved drippings; remove. In same skillet, sauté onion and celery until tender-crisp; drain excess fat. Add rice, water, tomatoes, 57 Sauce, ¼ teaspoon pepper and hot pepper sauce. Cover; simmer 20 minutes. Stir in bacon, meatballs and green pepper. Cover; simmer an additional 10 minutes or until rice is tender and liquid is absorbed, stirring occasionally.

Makes 4 servings
(4 cups rice mixture)

Spanish Rice and Meatballs

Cheeseburger Pie

- 1 (9-inch) unbaked pastry shell, pricked
- 8 slices BORDEN® Singles Process American Cheese Food
- 1 pound lean ground beef
- ½ cup tomato sauce
- ⅓ cup chopped green bell pepper
- ⅓ cup chopped onion
- 1 teaspoon WYLER'S® or STEERO® Beef-Flavor Instant Bouillon *or* 1 Beef-Flavor Bouillon Cube
- 3 eggs, well beaten
- 2 tablespoons flour

Preheat oven to 450°. Bake pastry shell 8 minutes; remove from oven. *Reduce oven temperature to 350°.* Cut *6 slices* cheese food into pieces. In large skillet, brown meat; pour off fat. Add tomato sauce, green pepper, onion and bouillon; cook and stir until bouillon dissolves. Remove from heat; stir in eggs, flour and cheese food pieces. Turn into prepared pastry shell. Bake 20 to 25 minutes or until hot. Arrange remaining *2 slices* cheese food on top. Bake 3 to 5 minutes longer or until cheese food begins to melt. Refrigerate leftovers.

Makes one 9-inch pie

Fiesta Beef Pot Pie

Crust
- 1⅔ cups all-purpose flour
- ⅓ cup yellow cornmeal
- 2 tablespoons toasted wheat germ
- 1 teaspoon salt
- ⅓ cup finely shredded Cheddar cheese
- ¾ cup CRISCO® Shortening
- 5 to 7 tablespoons cold water

Filling
- 1 pound lean boneless beef chuck, cut into ¼- to ½-inch chunks
- 1 tablespoon CRISCO® Shortening
- ½ cup chopped green pepper*
- ½ cup chopped onion*
- 1 can (14½ ounces) Mexican-style stewed tomatoes,* *undrained*
- 1 can (8½ ounces) whole kernel corn, drained
- 1 can (4 ounces) sliced mushrooms, drained
- ½ cup water
- ⅓ cup tomato paste
- 2 teaspoons sugar
- 1 teaspoon chili powder
- ½ teaspoon ground cumin
- ¼ teaspoon salt
- ⅛ teaspoon crushed red pepper (optional)
- ⅓ cup sliced black olives

Glaze and Topping
- 1 egg, beaten
- ¼ teaspoon salt
- ⅓ cup shredded Cheddar cheese

1. **For crust**, combine flour, cornmeal, wheat germ and 1 teaspoon salt in large bowl. Cut in ⅓ cup cheese and ¾ cup

*If Mexican-style tomatoes are unavailable, use plain stewed tomatoes. Increase green pepper and onion to ⅔ cup each. Add 1 tablespoon diced jalapeno pepper and ¼ teaspoon garlic powder.

Crisco® with pastry blender (or 2 knives) until flour is just blended to form pea-sized chunks. Sprinkle with water, 1 tablespoon at a time. Toss lightly with fork until dough forms a ball. Divide dough in half. Press each half to form 5- to 6-inch "pancake." Roll bottom crust into circle; transfer to 9-inch pie plate. Trim edge even with pie plate.

2. **For filling**, brown beef in 1 tablespoon Crisco® in large skillet. Remove beef with slotted spoon. Add green pepper and onion to skillet and cook until tender. Add beef, undrained tomatoes, corn, mushrooms, water, tomato paste, sugar, chili powder, cumin, ¼ teaspoon salt and red pepper, if desired. Cover. Bring to a boil. Reduce heat and simmer 30 minutes, stirring occasionally. Remove from heat. Stir in olives. Spoon hot filling into unbaked pie crust. Moisten pastry edge with water.

3. Heat oven to 425°F. Roll top crust same as bottom; lift top crust onto filled pie. Trim ½ inch beyond edge of pie plate. Fold top edge under bottom crust. Flute. Cut slits in top crust to allow steam to escape.

4. **For glaze and topping**, combine egg and ¼ teaspoon salt. Brush lightly over top crust. Bake at 425°F for 30 to 40 minutes or until crust is golden brown. Sprinkle with ⅓ cup cheese. Serve hot or warm. Refrigerate leftover pie.

One 9-inch Pie

Meat and Potato Pie

Filling

¼ cup CRISCO® Shortening
1 pound sirloin steak, trimmed and cut into ½-inch cubes
½ cup ½-inch diced onion
½ cup ½-inch diced carrots
¼ cup tomato paste
½ teaspoon dried basil leaves
½ teaspoon dried thyme leaves
½ teaspoon garlic powder
1 can (10½ ounces) condensed double strength beef broth
4½ cups peeled, ¾-inch cubed Idaho (russet) potatoes
1 tablespoon cornstarch
2 tablespoons cold water
½ cup frozen green peas, thawed

Crust

9-inch Classic Crisco® Double Crust (page 461)

1. **For filling**, melt Crisco® in large saucepan. Add steak. Brown on medium-high heat. Add onion and carrots. Cook until onion starts to brown, stirring often. Add tomato paste, basil, thyme and garlic powder. Cook 2 or 3 minutes, stirring constantly. Add broth and potatoes. Reduce heat to low; cover and simmer until potatoes are cooked through but still firm.

2. Dissolve cornstarch in water. Add to saucepan. Cook and stir until thickened. Remove from heat. Stir in peas. Cool to room temperature.

3. **For crust**, heat oven to 375°F. Prepare recipe and press bottom crust into 9-inch deep-dish pie plate or casserole. Spoon in filling. Moisten pastry edge with water. Cover pie with top crust. Cut slits in top crust to allow steam to escape. Bake at 375°F for 30 to 35 minutes or until browned. Serve hot. Refrigerate leftover pie. *One 9-inch Pie*

Meat and Potato Pie

Spring Lamb Skillet

        2 teaspoons olive oil
        1 pound boneless lamb, cut
            into 1-inch cubes
        2 cups thinly sliced yellow
            squash
        2 cups (about 8 ounces)
            sliced fresh mushrooms
        2 medium tomatoes, seeded
            and chopped
    ½ cup sliced green onions
        3 cups cooked brown rice
    ½ teaspoon dried rosemary
            leaves
    ½ teaspoon salt
    ½ teaspoon cracked black
            pepper

Heat oil in large skillet over medium heat until hot. Add lamb and cook 3 to 5 minutes or until lamb is browned. Remove from skillet; reserve. Add squash, mushrooms, tomatoes, and onions; cook 2 to 3 minutes or until vegetables are tender. Stir in rice, rosemary, salt, pepper, and reserved lamb. Cook until thoroughly heated.

Makes 6 servings

*Favorite recipe from **USA Rice Council***

Shrimp La Louisiana

        1 tablespoon margarine
    1½ cups uncooked rice*
        1 medium onion, chopped
        1 green pepper, chopped
    2¾ cups beef broth
    ¼ teaspoon salt
    ¼ teaspoon ground black
            pepper
    ¼ teaspoon hot pepper sauce
        1 pound medium shrimp,
            peeled and deveined
        1 can (4 ounces) sliced
            mushrooms, drained
        3 tablespoons snipped
            parsley
    ¼ cup sliced green onions for
            garnish (optional)

*Recipe based on regular-milled long grain white rice.

Melt margarine in 3-quart saucepan. Add rice, onion, and green pepper. Cook 2 to 3 minutes. Add broth, salt, black pepper, and pepper sauce; bring to a boil. Cover and simmer 15 minutes. Add shrimp, mushrooms, and parsley. Cook 5 minutes longer or until shrimp turn pink. Garnish with green onions.

Makes 8 servings

*Favorite recipe from **USA Rice Council***

Paella

        1 tablespoon olive oil
    ½ pound chicken breast
            chunks
        1 cup uncooked rice*
        1 medium onion, chopped
        1 clove garlic, minced
    1½ cups chicken broth*
        1 can (8 ounces) stewed
            tomatoes, chopped,
            reserving liquid
    ½ teaspoon paprika
    ⅛ to ¼ teaspoon ground red
            pepper
    ⅛ teaspoon ground saffron
    ½ pound medium shrimp,
            peeled and deveined
        1 small red pepper cut into
            strips
        1 small green pepper cut into
            strips
    ½ cup frozen green peas

Heat oil in Dutch oven over medium-high heat until hot. Add chicken and stir until browned. Add rice, onion, and garlic. Cook, stirring, until onion is tender and rice is lightly browned. Add broth, tomatoes, tomato liquid, paprika, ground red pepper, and saffron. Bring to a boil; stir. Reduce heat; cover and simmer 10 minutes. Add shrimp, pepper strips, and peas. Cover and simmer 10 minutes or until rice is tender and liquid is absorbed.

Makes 6 servings

*If using medium grain rice, use 1¼ cups of broth; for parboiled rice, use 1¾ cups of broth.

*Favorite recipe from **USA Rice Council***

Cajun Catfish Skillet

        2 cups water
        1 cup uncooked rice*
    ¼ teaspoon salt
    ¼ teaspoon ground red
            pepper
    ¼ teaspoon ground white
            pepper
    ¼ teaspoon ground black
            pepper
    ½ cup minced green onions
    ½ cup minced green pepper
    ½ cup minced celery
        2 cloves garlic, minced
        1 tablespoon margarine
        1 pound catfish nuggets or
            other firm flesh white
            fish**
        1 can (15½ ounces) tomato
            sauce
        1 teaspoon dried oregano
            leaves

Combine water, rice, salt, red pepper, white pepper, and black pepper in 3-quart saucepan. Bring to a boil; stir. Reduce heat; cover and simmer 15 minutes or until rice is tender and liquid is absorbed. Cook onions, green pepper, celery, and garlic in margarine in large skillet over medium-high heat until tender. Stir vegetable mixture, catfish nuggets, tomato sauce, and oregano into hot rice. Cover and cook over medium heat 7 to 8 minutes or until catfish flakes with fork. *Makes 4 servings*

*Recipe based on regular-milled long grain white rice.

**Substitute 1 pound chicken nuggets for fish, if desired.

*Favorite recipe from **USA Rice Council***

Paella

Bayou Jambalaya

1 medium onion, sliced
½ cup chopped green bell
   pepper
1 clove garlic, minced
1 cup uncooked white rice
2 tablespoons butter or
   margarine
1 cup HEINZ® Tomato
   Ketchup
2¼ cups water
1 tablespoon HEINZ® Vinegar
⅛ teaspoon black pepper
⅛ teaspoon ground red
   pepper
1 medium tomato, coarsely
   chopped
1 cup cubed cooked ham
½ pound deveined shelled
   raw medium-size shrimp

In large skillet, sauté onion,
green pepper, garlic and rice in
butter until onion is tender. Stir
in ketchup, water, vinegar, black
pepper, red pepper, tomato and
ham. Cover; simmer 20 to 25
minutes or until rice is tender.
Add shrimp; simmer, uncovered,
3 to 5 minutes or until shrimp
turn pink, stirring occasionally.
*Makes 4 to 6 servings
(about 6 cups)*

Microwave Directions: Place
onion, green pepper, garlic and
butter in 3-quart microwave-safe
casserole. Cover dish with lid or
vented plastic wrap; microwave
at HIGH (100%) 3 to 4 minutes,
stirring once. Stir in rice,
ketchup, water, vinegar, black
pepper, red pepper, tomato and
ham. Cover and microwave at
HIGH 10 to 12 minutes or until
mixture comes to a boil.
Microwave at MEDIUM (50%)
18 to 20 minutes until rice is
cooked, stirring once. Stir in
shrimp; cover and microwave at
HIGH 2 to 3 minutes or until
shrimp turn pink. Let stand,
covered, 5 minutes before
serving.

Old-Fashioned Tuna Noodle Casserole

¼ cup plain dry bread crumbs
3 tablespoons butter or
   margarine, melted and
   divided
1 tablespoon finely chopped
   parsley
½ cup chopped onion
½ cup chopped celery
1 cup water
1 cup milk
1 package LIPTON® Noodles
   & Sauce—Butter
2 cans (6½ ounces each)
   tuna, drained and flaked

In small bowl, thoroughly
combine bread crumbs, 1
tablespoon of the butter and the
parsley; set aside.

In medium saucepan, melt
remaining 2 tablespoons butter
and cook onion with celery over
medium heat, stirring
occasionally, 2 minutes or until
onion is tender. Add water and
milk; bring to a boil. Stir in
noodles & butter sauce. Continue
boiling over medium heat,
stirring occasionally, 8 minutes
or until noodles are tender. Stir
in tuna. Turn into greased 1-
quart casserole, then top with
bread crumb mixture. Broil
until bread crumbs are golden.
Makes about 4 servings

Quick and Easy Tuna Rice with Peas

1 package (10 ounces) BIRDS
   EYE® Green Peas
1¼ cups water
1 can (11 ounces) condensed
   Cheddar cheese soup
1 can (12½ ounces) tuna,
   drained and flaked
1 chicken bouillon cube
¼ teaspoon pepper
1½ cups Original MINUTE®
   Rice

Bayou Jambalaya

Bring peas, water, soup, tuna, bouillon cube and pepper to full boil in large saucepan. Stir in rice. Cover; remove from heat. Let stand 5 minutes. Fluff with fork.   *Makes 4 servings*

Chicken Cheese Puff

1 can (20 ounces) DOLE®
   Crushed Pineapple in
   Juice
8 eggs, lightly beaten
3 cups shredded Monterey
   Jack cheese
2 cups small curd cottage
   cheese
2 cups diced, cooked
   chicken*
1 can (4 ounces) chopped
   green chiles
½ cup all-purpose flour
1 teaspoon baking powder
½ teaspoon salt
2 tablespoons margarine,
   melted
⅓ cup grated Parmesan
   cheese

• Drain pineapple; save juice for a beverage.

• Blend pineapple, eggs, Monterey Jack cheese, cottage cheese, chicken, chiles, flour, baking powder and salt in medium bowl.

• Coat bottom of 13×9-inch baking pan with margarine. Pour chicken mixture into pan. Sprinkle with Parmesan cheese.

• Bake in 350°F oven 40 to 45 minutes or until toothpick inserted near center comes out clean.   *Makes 8 servings*

*Or use roasted chicken from the deli.

Preparation Time: 10 minutes
Bake Time: 45 minutes

Crab and Rice Primavera

Crab and Rice Primavera

1½ cups BIRDS EYE® FARM
   FRESH Broccoli, Green
   Beans, Pearl Onions and
   Red Peppers
¼ cup water
1⅓ cups milk
¾ pound imitation crabmeat
   or crabmeat
2 tablespoons margarine or
   butter
1 teaspoon garlic powder
¾ teaspoon dried basil
1½ cups Original MINUTE®
   Rice
½ cup grated Parmesan
   cheese

Bring vegetables and water to boil in medium saucepan, stirring occasionally. Reduce heat; cover and simmer 3 minutes.

Add milk, imitation crabmeat, margarine, garlic powder and basil. Bring to full boil. Stir in rice and cheese. Cover; remove from heat. Let stand 5 minutes. Fluff with fork.

Makes 4 servings

Jambalaya

- 2 cloves garlic, crushed
- 1 tablespoon BLUE BONNET® Margarine
- 1 (14½-ounce) can stewed tomatoes, undrained and coarsely chopped
- 1½ cups cubed cooked ham
- 1 (13¾-fluid ounce) can COLLEGE INN® Chicken Broth
- 1 cup uncooked rice
- ½ teaspoon dried thyme leaves
- 12 ounces shrimp, shelled and deveined

In skillet, over medium-high heat, cook garlic in margarine for 1 to 2 minutes. Add remaining ingredients except shrimp; heat to a boil; reduce heat. Cover; simmer 25 minutes. Add shrimp; cook, covered, 5 to 10 minutes or until liquid is absorbed. *Makes 6 servings.*

Creole Chicken Jambalaya

- ¼ cup vegetable oil
- 2 medium onions, chopped
- 6 green onions, chopped
- 2 medium green peppers, chopped
- 1 (2½- to 3-pound) broiler-fryer chicken, cut into 8 pieces
- ½ pound cooked ham, cubed
- ½ pound smoked or Polish sausage, cut into ½-inch slices
- 1 can (16 ounces) tomatoes, cut into pieces, undrained
- 1 can (6 ounces) tomato paste
- 1 teaspoon salt
- 1¾ cups uncooked rice
- ½ cup water
- ¾ teaspoon TABASCO® pepper sauce

In large saucepot or Dutch oven heat oil. Add onions, green onions and peppers; cook 10 minutes or until tender. Add chicken and brown on all sides, about 10 minutes. Add ham, sausage, tomatoes, tomato paste and salt. Cover; simmer 10 minutes; stir in rice. Add water. Cover. Simmer 1 hour or until chicken is done; stir frequently. Add additional water if rice begins to stick to bottom of pan. Before serving, stir in Tabasco® sauce. *Makes 8 servings.*

Jambalaya

Layered Seafood Quiche

- ¾ cup finely chopped onion
- 1 can (12½ ounces) STARKIST® Solid White or Solid Light Tuna in Springwater, drained, flaked
- 2 cups (8 ounces) shredded Cheddar cheese
- 3 eggs, lightly beaten
- 1 can (12 ounces) PET® Evaporated or PET® Light Evaporated Skimmed Milk
- ½ teaspoon salt

Cook onion in medium saucepan, covered, over very low heat until soft, adding water if necessary to prevent scorching. Line bottom of 9-inch pie pan with tuna. Sprinkle with cooked onion; top with cheese. Combine eggs, milk and salt in small bowl; mix well. Pour over cheese. Bake in preheated 350°F oven 30 minutes or until set. Let stand at least 10 minutes before cutting. Garnish as desired. *Makes 8 servings.*

So-Easy Fish Divan

1 package (1⅛ ounces)
   DURKEE® Cheese Sauce Mix
1⅓ cups milk
1 bag (16 ounces) frozen
   vegetable combination
   (brussels sprouts, carrots,
   cauliflower), thawed and
   drained
1 can (2.8 ounces) DURKEE®
   French Fried Onions
1 pound unbreaded fish fillets,
   thawed if frozen
½ cup (2 ounces) shredded
   Cheddar cheese

Preheat oven to 375°. In small saucepan, prepare cheese sauce mix according to package directions using 1⅓ cups milk. In 8×12-inch baking dish, combine vegetables and *½ can* French Fried Onions; top with fish fillets. Pour cheese sauce over fish and vegetables. Bake, covered, at 375° for 25 minutes or until fish flakes easily with fork. Top fish with Cheddar cheese and remaining onions; bake, uncovered, 3 minutes or until onions are golden brown.
Makes 3 to 4 servings.

Beef and Wild Rice Casserole

2⅔ cups boiling water
⅔ cup uncooked wild rice, rinsed
   and drained
4 teaspoons WYLER'S® or
   STEERO® Beef-Flavor
   Instant Bouillon *or* 4 Beef-
   Flavor Bouillon Cubes
1½ pounds lean ground beef
1 cup chopped celery
½ cup chopped onion
1 clove garlic, finely chopped
1 (10¾-ounce) can condensed
   cream of mushroom soup
½ cup uncooked long grain rice
⅛ teaspoon pepper

Preheat oven to 350°. In 2-quart baking dish, combine water, wild rice and bouillon; set aside. In large skillet, brown meat; pour off fat. Stir in celery, onion and garlic; cook until tender. Add soup, long grain rice and pepper. Add meat mixture to wild rice mixture; mix well. Cover. Bake 1 hour and 30 minutes. Serve hot. Refrigerate leftovers.
Makes 8 servings.

Clam Noodle Florentine

½ (1-pound) package
   CREAMETTE® Egg Noodles,
   cooked and drained
⅓ cup chopped onion
¼ cup margarine or butter
¼ cup unsifted flour
½ teaspoon salt
¼ teaspoon pepper
2 cups (1 pint) BORDEN® or
   MEADOW GOLD® Half-and-
   Half or Milk
2 (6½-ounce) cans SNOW'S® or
   DOXSEE® Minced or
   Chopped Clams, drained,
   reserving liquid
1 (10-ounce) package frozen
   chopped spinach, thawed
   and well drained
¼ cup grated Parmesan cheese
½ cup buttered bread crumbs

Preheat oven to 350°. In large saucepan, cook onion in margarine until tender. Stir in flour, salt and pepper. Gradually stir in half-and-half and reserved clam liquid. Over medium heat, cook and stir until thickened and bubbly, about 8 minutes. Remove from heat; add noodles, clams, spinach and cheese. Mix well. Turn into greased 2-quart baking dish. Top with crumbs. Bake 25 to 30 minutes or until hot. Refrigerate leftovers.
Makes 6 to 8 servings.

Herb-Baked Fish & Rice

1½ cups hot HERB-OX® Chicken
   Bouillon
½ cup uncooked regular rice
¼ teaspoon DURKEE® Italian
   Seasoning
¼ teaspoon DURKEE® Garlic
   Powder
1 package (10 ounces) frozen
   chopped broccoli, thawed
   and drained
1 can (2.8 ounces) DURKEE®
   French Fried Onions
1 tablespoon grated Parmesan
   cheese
1 pound unbreaded fish fillets,
   thawed if frozen
   DURKEE® Paprika (optional)
½ cup (2 ounces) shredded
   Cheddar cheese

Preheat oven to 375°. In 8×12-inch baking dish, combine hot bouillon, uncooked rice and seasonings. Bake, covered, at 375° for 10 minutes. Top with broccoli, *½ can* French Fried Onions and the Parmesan cheese. Place fish fillets diagonally down center of dish; sprinkle fish lightly with paprika. Bake, covered, at 375° for 20 to 25 minutes or until fish flakes easily with fork. Stir rice. Top fish with Cheddar cheese and remaining onions; bake, uncovered, 3 minutes or until onions are golden brown.
Makes 3 to 4 servings.

Microwave Directions: In 8×12-inch microwave-safe dish, prepare rice mixture as above, except reduce bouillon to 1¼ cups. Cook, covered, on HIGH 5 minutes, stirring halfway through cooking time. Stir in broccoli, *½ can* onions and the Parmesan cheese. Arrange fish fillets in single layer on top of rice mixture; sprinkle fish lightly with paprika. Cook, covered, on MEDIUM (50–60%) 18 to 20 minutes or until fish flakes easily with fork and rice is done. Rotate dish halfway through cooking time. Top fish with Cheddar cheese and remaining onions; cook, uncovered, on HIGH 1 minute or until cheese melts. Let stand 5 minutes.

Herb-Baked Fish & Rice

Superb Fillet of Sole & Vegetables

- 1 can (10¾ ounces) condensed cream of celery soup
- ½ cup milk
- 1 cup (4 ounces) shredded Swiss cheese
- ½ teaspoon DURKEE® Sweet Basil
- ¼ teaspoon DURKEE® Seasoned Salt
- ¼ teaspoon DURKEE® Ground Black Pepper
- 1 package (10 ounces) frozen baby carrots, thawed and drained
- 1 package (10 ounces) frozen asparagus cuts, thawed and drained
- 1 can (2.8 ounces) DURKEE® French Fried Onions
- 1 pound unbreaded sole fillets, thawed if frozen

Preheat oven to 375°. In small bowl, combine soup, milk, ½ cup cheese and the seasonings; set aside. In 8×12-inch baking dish, combine carrots, asparagus and ½ can French Fried Onions. Roll up fish fillets. (If fillets are wide, fold in half lengthwise before rolling.) Place fish rolls upright along center of vegetable mixture. Pour soup mixture over fish and vegetables. Bake, covered, at 375° for 30 minutes or until fish flakes easily with fork. Stir vegetables; top fish with remaining cheese and onions. Bake, uncovered, 3 minutes or until onions are golden brown.
Makes 3 to 4 servings.

Microwave Directions: Prepare soup mixture as above; set aside. In 8×12-inch microwave-safe dish, combine vegetables as above. Roll up fish fillets as above; place upright around edges of dish. Pour soup mixture over fish and vegetables. Cook, covered, on HIGH 14 to 16 minutes or until fish flakes easily with fork. Stir vegetables and rotate dish halfway through cooking time. Top fish with remaining cheese and onions; cook, uncovered, 1 minute or until cheese melts. Let stand 5 minutes.

Hasty Shore Dinner

- 1 cup small shell pasta, cooked in unsalted water and drained
- ½ cup mayonnaise
- ½ cup milk
- 1 can (10¾ ounces) condensed cream of celery soup
- 1 package (8 ounces) frozen imitation crabmeat,* thawed, drained and cut into chunks
- 1 can (4 ounces) shrimp, drained
- 1 cup (4 ounces) shredded Swiss cheese
- 1 can (2.8 ounces) DURKEE® French Fried Onions
- ½ teaspoon DURKEE® Dill Weed
- ¼ teaspoon DURKEE® Seasoned Salt

Preheat oven to 350°. Return hot pasta to saucepan. Stir in mayonnaise, milk, soup, crabmeat, shrimp, ½ cup cheese, ½ can French Fried Onions and the seasonings; mix well. Pour into 1½-quart casserole. Bake, covered, at 350° for 35 minutes or until heated through. Top with remaining cheese and onions; bake, uncovered, 5 minutes or until onions are golden brown.
Makes 4 to 6 servings.

Microwave Directions: Prepare pasta mixture as above; pour into 1½-quart microwave-safe casserole. Cook, covered, on HIGH 12 to 15 minutes or until heated through. Stir casserole halfway through cooking time. Top with remaining cheese and onions; cook, uncovered, 1 minute or until cheese melts. Let stand 5 minutes.

*1 can (6 ounces) crabmeat, drained, may be substituted for imitation crabmeat.

All-in-One Tuna Casserole

- 1 envelope LIPTON® Recipe Secrets Golden Onion Recipe Soup Mix
- 1½ cups milk
- 1 package (10 ounces) frozen peas and carrots, thawed
- 1 package (8 ounces) medium egg noodles, cooked and drained
- 1 can (6½ ounces) tuna, drained and flaked
- ½ cup shredded Cheddar cheese (about 2 ounces)

Preheat oven to 350°.
In large bowl, blend golden onion recipe soup mix with milk; stir in peas and carrots, cooked noodles and tuna. Turn into greased 2-quart oblong baking dish, then top with cheese. Bake 20 minutes or until bubbling.
Makes about 4 servings.

Superb Fillet of Sole & Vegetables

Chicken Enchiladas

- 3 cups finely chopped cooked chicken
- 1 cup chopped onion
- ¼ cup margarine or butter
- ¼ cup unsifted flour
- 2½ cups hot water
- 1 tablespoon WYLER'S® or STEERO® Chicken-Flavor Instant Bouillon *or* 3 Chicken-Flavor Bouillon Cubes
- 1 (8-ounce) container BORDEN® or MEADOW GOLD® Sour Cream, at room temperature
- 2 cups (8 ounces) shredded Cheddar cheese
- 1 (4-ounce) can chopped mild green chilies, drained
- 1 teaspoon ground cumin
- 12 (6-inch) corn tortillas *or* 10 (8-inch) flour tortillas
- Sour cream, chopped green onions and chopped tomato for garnish

Preheat oven to 350°. In medium saucepan, cook onion in margarine until tender. Stir in flour then water and bouillon; cook and stir until thickened and bouillon dissolves. Remove from heat; stir in sour cream. In large bowl, combine *1 cup* sauce, chicken, *1 cup* cheese, chilies and cumin; mix well. Dip each tortilla into remaining hot sauce to soften; fill each with equal portions of chicken mixture. Roll up. Arrange in greased 13×9-inch baking dish. Spoon remaining sauce over. Sprinkle with remaining cheese. Bake 25 minutes or until bubbly. Garnish as desired. Refrigerate leftovers.
Makes 6 to 8 servings.

Microwave: In 2-quart round baking dish, microwave margarine on full power (high) 1 minute or until melted. Add onion; microwave on full power (high) 3 to 5 minutes or until tender. Stir in flour, then water and bouillon; microwave on full power (high) 8 minutes, or until thickened and bouillon dissolves, stirring every 2 minutes. Stir in sour cream. Proceed as above. Arrange rolled tortillas in greased 12×7-inch baking dish. Microwave on ⅔ power (medium-high) 9 minutes or until bubbly. Let stand 5 minutes before serving.

Cheese-Mushroom Strata

Cheese-Mushroom Strata

- 4 eggs, lightly beaten
- 1 (13¾-fluid ounce) can COLLEGE INN® Chicken or Beef Broth
- ½ cup dairy sour cream
- 2 teaspoons GREY POUPON® Dijon Mustard
- 8 slices white bread, cubed (about 4 cups cubes)
- 2 cups shredded Cheddar cheese (8 ounces)
- 1 (4½-ounce) can sliced mushrooms, drained

In large bowl, beat together eggs, broth, sour cream and mustard. Stir in bread cubes, cheese and mushrooms. Pour into greased 2-quart oval or 12×8×2-inch baking dish. Cover; refrigerate overnight.

Uncover; bake at 350°F for 50 to 60 minutes or until set. Let stand 5 to 10 minutes before serving. Garnish as desired.
Makes 6 to 8 servings.

PASTA

Perk up your meals with popular pasta and make any meal a spectacular occasion. Create luscious lasagnas, magnificent manicottis, savory sauces, fabulous fettuccines and much more. Serve Pasta & Vegetable Toss, Spaghetti alla Bolognese or Seafood Primavera and grace your home with the ambience of Italy. Or try other ethnic flavors with Beef Oriental and Tacos in Pasta Shells.

Tortellini Primavera

1 cup sliced mushrooms
½ cup chopped onion
1 garlic clove, minced
2 tablespoons PARKAY® Margarine
1 package (10 ounces) BIRDS EYE® Chopped Spinach, thawed, well drained
1 container (8 ounces) PHILADELPHIA BRAND® Soft Cream Cheese
1 medium tomato, chopped
¼ cup milk
¼ cup (1 ounce) KRAFT® 100% Grated Parmesan Cheese
1 teaspoon Italian seasoning
¼ teaspoon salt
¼ teaspoon pepper
8 to 9 ounces fresh or frozen cheese-filled tortellini, cooked, drained

Cook and stir mushrooms, onion and garlic in margarine in large skillet. Add all remaining ingredients except tortellini; mix well. Cook until mixture just begins to boil, stirring occasionally. Stir in tortellini; cook until thoroughly heated.

Makes 4 servings

Prep time: 10 minutes
Cooking time: 10 minutes

Pasta Primavera

1 medium onion, finely chopped
1 large clove garlic, minced
2 tablespoons butter or margarine
¾ pound asparagus, cut diagonally into 1½-inch pieces
½ pound mushrooms, sliced
1 medium zucchini, sliced
1 carrot, sliced
1 cup half-and-half or light cream
½ cup chicken broth
1 tablespoon flour
2 teaspoons dried basil
1 pound fettucine, uncooked
¾ cup (3 ounces) SARGENTO® Fancy Supreme™ Shredded Parmesan & Romano Cheese

In large skillet, cook onion and garlic in butter over medium heat until onion is tender. Add asparagus, mushrooms, zucchini and carrot; cook, stirring constantly, 2 minutes. Increase heat to high. Combine half-and-half, broth, flour and basil; add to skillet. Allow mixture to boil, stirring occasionally, until thickened. Meanwhile, cook fettucine according to package directions; drain. In serving bowl, combine cooked fettucine with sauce and Parmesan & Romano cheese.

Makes 8 servings

Tortellini Primavera

Pasta & Vegetable Toss

½ cup chopped onion
1 clove garlic, finely chopped
1 teaspoon Italian seasoning
1 tablespoon olive oil
¼ cup water
2 teaspoons WYLER'S® or STEERO® Beef-Flavor Instant Bouillon
2 cups broccoli flowerets
2 cups sliced zucchini
8 ounces fresh mushrooms, sliced (about 2 cups)
1 medium red bell pepper, cut into thin strips
½ (1-pound) package CREAMETTE® Fettuccini, cooked as package directs and drained

In large skillet, cook onion, garlic and Italian seasoning in oil until tender. Add water, bouillon and vegetables. Cover and simmer 5 to 7 minutes until vegetables are tender-crisp. Toss with hot fettuccini. Serve immediately. Refrigerate leftovers. *Makes 4 servings*

Fresh Tomato Pasta Andrew

1 pound fresh tomatoes, cut into wedges
1 cup packed fresh basil leaves
2 cloves garlic, chopped
2 tablespoons olive oil
8 ounces Camenzola cheese *or* 6 ounces ripe Brie plus 2 ounces Stilton cheese, each cut into small pieces
Salt and white pepper to taste
4 ounces uncooked angel hair pasta, vermicelli or other thin pasta, hot cooked and drained
Grated Parmesan cheese

Place tomatoes, basil, garlic and oil in covered food processor or blender; pulse on and off until ingredients are coarsely chopped but not puréed. Combine tomato mixture and Camenzola cheese in large bowl. Season to taste with salt and white pepper. Add pasta; toss gently until cheese melts. Serve with Parmesan cheese. Garnish as desired.
Makes 2 main-dish or 4 appetizer servings

Pasta Delight

Pasta Delight

1 medium zucchini, sliced
1 tablespoon olive oil
2 tablespoons chopped shallots
2 cloves garlic, chopped
1 medium tomato, diced
2 tablespoons chopped fresh basil *or* ½ teaspoon dried basil, crushed
2 tablespoons grated Parmesan cheese
12 ounces uncooked penne pasta, hot cooked and drained

Cook and stir zucchini in hot oil in large skillet over medium-high heat. Reduce heat to medium. Add shallots and garlic; cook 1 minute. Add tomato; cook and stir 45 seconds. Add basil and cheese. Pour vegetable mixture over penne in large bowl; toss gently to mix.
Makes 4 to 6 servings

*Favorite recipe from **National Pasta Association***

Pasta & Vegetable Toss

Penne with Artichokes

1 package (10 ounces) frozen artichokes
1¼ cups water
2 tablespoons lemon juice
5 cloves garlic, minced
2 tablespoons olive oil, divided
2 ounces sun-dried tomatoes in oil, drained
2 small dried hot red peppers, crushed
2 tablespoons chopped parsley
¼ teaspoon salt
¼ teaspoon pepper
¾ cup fresh bread crumbs
1 tablespoon chopped garlic
12 ounces uncooked penne, hot cooked and drained
1 tablespoon grated Romano cheese

Cook artichokes in water and lemon juice in medium saucepan over medium heat until tender. Cool artichokes, then cut into quarters. Reserve artichoke liquid.

Cook and stir the 5 minced cloves garlic in 1½ tablespoons oil in large skillet over medium-high heat until golden. Reduce heat to low. Add artichokes and tomatoes; simmer 1 minute. Stir in artichoke liquid, red peppers, parsley, salt and pepper. Simmer 5 minutes.

Meanwhile, cook and stir bread crumbs and 1 tablespoon chopped garlic in remaining ½ tablespoon oil. Pour artichoke sauce over penne in large bowl; toss gently to coat. Sprinkle with bread crumb mixture and cheese.

Makes 4 to 6 servings

*Favorite recipe from **National Pasta Association***

Fusilli Pizzaiolo

Fusilli Pizzaiolo

8 ounces mushrooms, sliced
1 large red pepper, diced
1 large green pepper, diced
1 large yellow pepper, diced
10 green onions, chopped
1 large onion, diced
8 cloves garlic, coarsely chopped
3 large shallots, chopped
½ cup chopped fresh basil *or* 2 teaspoons dried basil leaves, crushed
2 tablespoons chopped fresh oregano *or* 1 teaspoon dried oregano, crushed
Dash crushed red pepper
¼ cup olive oil
4 cups canned tomatoes, chopped
Salt and pepper to taste
1 package (16 ounces) uncooked fusilli or spaghetti, hot cooked and drained
2 tablespoons chopped parsley (optional)

Cook and stir mushrooms, peppers, onions, garlic, shallots, basil, oregano and crushed red pepper in hot oil in large skillet until lightly browned. Add tomatoes with juice; bring to a boil. Reduce heat to low; simmer 20 minutes. Season to taste with salt and pepper. Place fusilli on plates. Spoon sauce over fusilli. Garnish with parsley.

Makes 6 to 8 servings

*Favorite recipe from **National Pasta Association***

Fettuccine with Roasted Red Pepper Sauce

3 large red peppers*
½ cup whipping or heavy cream
¼ cup WISH-BONE® Italian Dressing
2 tablespoons chopped fresh basil leaves**
Salt and pepper to taste
1 package (12 ounces) fettuccine or medium egg noodles, cooked and drained
Grated Parmesan cheese

In large aluminum-foil-lined baking pan or on broiler rack, place peppers. Broil, turning occasionally, 20 minutes or until peppers turn almost completely black. Immediately place in paper bag; close bag and let cool about 30 minutes. Under cold running water, peel off skin, then remove stems and seeds.

In food processor or blender, process prepared peppers, cream, Italian dressing, basil, salt and pepper until blended. Toss with hot fettuccine and serve with cheese.
Makes about 4 main-dish servings.
   ***Substitution:** Use 2 cups drained roasted red peppers.
   ****Substitution:** Use 2 teaspoons dried basil leaves.
   Note: Also terrific with Wish-Bone® Robusto Italian, Blended Italian or Lite Italian Dressing.

Fettuccine Alfredo

¾ pound uncooked fettuccine
Boiling salted water
6 tablespoons unsalted butter
⅔ cup whipping cream
½ teaspoon salt
Large pinch ground white pepper
Large pinch ground nutmeg
1 cup freshly grated Parmesan cheese (about 3 ounces)
2 tablespoons chopped fresh parsley

1. Cook fettuccine in large pot of boiling salted water just until al dente, 6 to 8 minutes; drain well. Return to dry pot.
2. While fettuccine is cooking, place butter and cream in 10-inch heavy skillet over medium-low heat. Cook, stirring constantly, until blended and mixture bubbles for 2 minutes. Stir in

salt, pepper and nutmeg. Remove from heat. Gradually stir in Parmesan cheese until thoroughly blended and fairly smooth. Return skillet briefly to heat if necessary to completely blend cheese, but don't let sauce bubble or cheese will become lumpy and tough.
3. Pour sauce over fettuccine in pot. Place over low heat. Stir and toss with 2 forks until sauce is slightly thickened and fettuccine evenly coated, 2 to 3 minutes. Sprinkle with parsley. Serve immediately.
Makes 4 servings.

Smoked Sausage Stuffed Pasta Shells

¾ pound ECKRICH® Smoked Sausage, chopped fine
18 large macaroni shells
1 pound ricotta cheese
1 egg, beaten
1½ cups (6 ounces) shredded mozzarella cheese
½ cup chopped fresh parsley
¼ cup grated Parmesan cheese
½ teaspoon dried basil leaves
½ teaspoon dried oregano leaves
1 jar (15 ounces) prepared spaghetti sauce with mushrooms and onions
⅓ cup water

Fettuccine with Roasted Red Pepper Sauce

Prepare shells according to package directions. Preheat oven to 375°F. Combine ricotta cheese and egg in medium bowl. Add mozzarella, parsley, Parmesan cheese, basil and oregano. Stir in sausage. Combine spaghetti sauce and water in small bowl. Put ¾ cup of the sauce in bottom of 13×9×2-inch baking pan. Fill shells with sausage-cheese mixture and place in pan. Pour remaining sauce over top. Bake 35 minutes or until stuffed shells are heated through and cheese melts.
Makes 9 servings (2 shells each).

Linguine with Red Seafood Sauce

3 tablespoons olive or vegetable oil
1 large onion, finely chopped
2 cloves garlic, minced
½ cup dry white wine
2 cups (16 ounces) canned or homemade meatless spaghetti sauce
2 tablespoons chopped parsley
1 bay leaf, crumbled
2 teaspoons dried basil leaves
¾ teaspoon TABASCO® pepper sauce
½ teaspoon salt
¾ pound medium shrimp, peeled, deveined
¾ pound sea scallops, quartered or bay scallops
12 ounces linguine, cooked, drained

In large heavy saucepot or Dutch oven heat oil; cook onion and garlic 5 minutes or until golden. Add wine; simmer until reduced by half. Stir in spaghetti sauce, parsley, bay leaf, basil, Tabasco® sauce and salt. Cover; simmer 10 minutes. Add shrimp and scallops. Cover; simmer 4 to 5 minutes or until seafood is done. Serve with linguine.
Makes 6 servings.
   Microwave Directions: In 3-quart microwave-safe casserole place oil, onion, garlic and white wine. Cook uncovered on High 5 to 7 minutes or until onion is tender. Stir in spaghetti sauce, parsley, bay leaf, basil, Tabasco® sauce and salt. Cook uncovered on High 5 to 8 minutes or until bubbly. Stir in shrimp and scallops. Cook uncovered on High 7 to 9 minutes or until seafood is done. Serve with linguine.

Santa Fe Pasta

- **³/₄ lb. VELVEETA® Pasteurized Process Cheese Spread**
- **2 tablespoons milk**
- **1 8³/₄-oz. can whole kernel corn, drained**
- **1 8-oz. can kidney beans, drained**
- **2 cups (8 ozs.) mostaccioli noodles, cooked, drained**
- **1 4-oz. can chopped green chilies, drained**
- **¹/₂ teaspoon chili powder**
- **1 cup corn chips**

Cube ¹/₂ lb. VELVEETA® Pasteurized Process Cheese Spread. Combine with milk in saucepan; stir over low heat until process cheese spread is melted. Add corn, beans, noodles, chilies and chili powder; mix lightly. Spoon mixture into 1¹/₂-quart casserole. Bake at 350°, 20 minutes. Top with chips and remaining process cheese spread, sliced. Continue baking until process cheese spread begins to melt.
6 servings.

Preparation time: 15 minutes
Baking time: 25 minutes

Microwave: Cube ¹/₂ lb. VEL-VEETA® Pasteurized Process Cheese Spread. Combine with milk in 2-quart microwave-safe bowl. Microwave on High 2 to 3 minutes or until process cheese spread is melted, stirring after 2 minutes. Stir in corn, beans, noodles, chilies and chili powder; microwave on High 5 minutes, stirring every 2 minutes. Top with chips and remaining process cheese spread, sliced. Microwave on High 2 minutes or until process cheese spread begins to melt.

Creamy Fettucini Alfredo

- **1 8-ounce package PHILADELPHIA BRAND® Cream Cheese, cubed**
- **³/₄ cup (3 ounces) KRAFT® 100% Grated Parmesan Cheese**
- **¹/₂ cup PARKAY® Margarine**
- **¹/₂ cup milk**
- **8 ounces fettucini, cooked, drained**

In large saucepan, combine cream cheese, parmesan cheese, margarine and milk; stir over low heat until smooth. Add fettucini; toss lightly.
4 servings.

Creamy Fettucini Alfredo

Pesto

- **¹/₄ cup plus 1 tablespoon olive oil**
- **2 tablespoons pine nuts**
- **1 cup tightly packed, rinsed, drained, stemmed fresh basil leaves (do not use dried basil)**
- **2 medium cloves garlic**
- **¹/₄ teaspoon salt**
- **¹/₄ cup freshly grated Parmesan cheese**
- **1¹/₂ tablespoons freshly grated Romano cheese**

1. Heat 1 tablespoon of the oil in small saucepan or skillet over medium-low heat. Add pine nuts; saute, stirring and shaking pan constantly, until nuts are light brown, 30 to 45 seconds. Transfer nuts immediately to paper-towel-lined plate to drain.

2. Combine pine nuts, basil leaves, garlic, salt and remaining ¹/₄ cup oil in food processor or blender container. Process until mixture is evenly blended and pieces are very finely chopped.

3. Transfer basil mixture to small bowl. Stir in Parmesan and Romano cheeses. Pesto can be refrigerated, covered with thin layer of olive oil, up to 1 week, or pesto can be frozen for several months. Thaw and bring to room temperature before using.
Makes about ³/₄ cup pesto.

Serving Suggestions: Toss pesto with hot cooked buttered fettuccine or linguine; this recipe will dress ¹/₂ to ³/₄ pound pasta. Stir small amount of pesto into broth-based vegetable or meat soups. Whisk small amount of pesto into vinaigrette for tossed salads. Mix pesto with softened butter to be used on steamed vegetables, poached fish or omelets.

Tagliatelle with Creamy Sauce

Souper Quick "Lasagna"

1½ pounds ground beef
1 envelope LIPTON® Recipe Secrets Onion or Onion-Mushroom Recipe Soup Mix
3 cans (8 ounces each) tomato sauce
1 cup water
½ teaspoon oregano (optional)
1 package (8 ounces) broad egg noodles, cooked and drained
1 package (16 ounces) mozzarella cheese, shredded

Preheat oven to 375°.

In large skillet, brown ground beef over medium-high heat; drain. Stir in onion recipe soup mix, tomato sauce, water and oregano. Simmer covered, stirring occasionally, 15 minutes.

In 2-quart oblong baking dish, spoon enough sauce to cover bottom. Alternately layer noodles, ground beef mixture and cheese, ending with cheese. Bake 30 minutes or until bubbling.
Makes about 6 servings.

Microwave Directions: In 2-quart casserole, microwave ground beef, uncovered, at HIGH (Full Power) 7 minutes, stirring once; drain. Stir in onion recipe soup mix, tomato sauce, water and oregano. Microwave at MEDIUM (50% Full Power) 5 minutes, stirring once. In 2-quart oblong baking dish, spoon enough sauce to cover bottom. Alternately layer as above. Microwave covered at MEDIUM, turning dish occasionally, 10 minutes or until bubbling. Let stand covered 5 minutes.

Tagliatelle with Creamy Sauce

7 to 8 ounces tagliatelle pasta, cooked, drained
1 cup GALBANI® Mascarpone cheese
1 package (10 ounces) frozen peas, cooked, drained
2 ounces (½ cup) finely chopped prosciutto
1½ cups (6 ounces) shredded mozzarella cheese
Butter or margarine

Layer ½ of the tagliatelle in buttered 9×9-inch baking dish. Spoon ½ of the Mascarpone onto tagliatelle. Sprinkle with ½ of the peas and ½ of the prosciutto. Top with ½ of the mozzarella. Repeat layers. Dot with butter. Bake in preheated 350°F oven 20 minutes or until heated through.
Makes 4 to 6 servings.

*Favorite recipe from **Bel Paese Sales Co., Inc.***

Neapolitan Sauce

1 can (28 ounces) Italian plum tomatoes
2 tablespoons butter
1 tablespoon olive oil
1 teaspoon dried basil, crumbled
½ teaspoon salt
⅛ teaspoon pepper
3 tablespoons chopped fresh parsley
½ pound spaghetti, cooked
½ cup freshly grated Parmesan cheese, if desired

Press tomatoes and their liquid through sieve into bowl; discard seeds. Heat butter and oil in 2-quart noncorrosive saucepan over medium heat. Stir in sieved tomatoes, basil, salt and pepper. Heat to boiling; reduce heat to medium-low. Cook, uncovered, stirring frequently, until sauce is reduced and measures 2 cups, 30 to 40 minutes. Stir in parsley. Toss with spaghetti. Serve immediately with Parmesan cheese to sprinkle.
Makes 2 to 3 servings.

Lasagna Deliciousa

- ½ of a 1-pound package uncooked CREAMETTE® Lasagna
- 1 pound bulk Italian sausage
- ½ pound ground beef
- 1 cup chopped onion
- 2 cloves garlic, minced
- 1 can (28 ounces) tomatoes, cut up, undrained
- 2 cans (6 ounces each) tomato paste
- 2 teaspoons sugar
- 2½ teaspoons salt, divided
- 1½ teaspoons dried basil, crushed
- ½ teaspoon fennel seeds
- ¼ teaspoon pepper
- 1 container (15 ounces) ricotta cheese
- 1 egg, beaten
- 1 tablespoon parsley flakes
- 1 cup sliced pitted ripe olives
- 4 cups (1 pound) shredded mozzarella cheese
- ¾ cup grated Parmesan cheese

Prepare lasagna according to package directions; drain. Cook sausage, ground beef, onion and garlic in large skillet over medium-high heat until sausage is no longer pink and onion is tender; drain. Stir in tomatoes, tomato paste, sugar, 2 teaspoons of the salt, the basil, fennel seeds and pepper. Bring to a boil over high heat. Reduce heat to low. Simmer, uncovered, 20 minutes.

In small bowl, blend ricotta, egg, parsley and remaining ½ teaspoon salt. Spoon 1½ cups of the meat sauce into 13×9-inch baking dish. Layer ⅓ *each* of the lasagna, remaining meat sauce, ricotta mixture, olives, mozzarella and Parmesan cheese into dish. Repeat layers. Cover with foil. Bake at 375°F 25 minutes. Uncover. Bake about 20 minutes more or until heated through. Let stand 10 minutes before cutting.
Makes 8 to 10 servings.

Lasagna with White and Red Sauces

- Béchamel Sauce (recipe follows)
- ½ medium onion, sliced
- 1 clove garlic, minced
- 2 to 3 tablespoons vegetable oil
- 1 pound lean ground beef
- 1 can (28 ounces) crushed tomatoes or 1 can (28 ounces) whole tomatoes, chopped, undrained
- ½ cup thinly sliced celery
- ½ cup thinly sliced carrot
- 1 teaspoon dried basil, crushed
- 1 package (1 pound) lasagna noodles, cooked, drained
- 6 ounces BEL PAESE® cheese,* thinly sliced
- 6 hard-cooked eggs, sliced (optional)
- 2 tablespoons butter or margarine, cut into small pieces
- 1 cup (about 2 ounces) freshly grated GALBANI® Parmigiano-Reggiano or Grana Padano cheese

Prepare Béchamel Sauce; set aside. Cook and stir onion and garlic in hot oil in Dutch oven over medium-high heat until tender. Add ground beef and cook until no longer pink, stirring occasionally. Add tomatoes, celery, carrot and basil. Reduce heat to low. Cover and simmer 45 minutes. Remove cover and simmer 15 minutes more.

Arrange ⅓ of the lasagna noodles in bottom of buttered 13½×9-inch baking dish. Add ½ of the Bel Paese® and ½ of the eggs. Spread with meat sauce. Repeat layers of noodles, Bel Paese® and eggs. Spread with Béchamel Sauce. Top with layer of noodles. Dot with butter. Sprinkle with Parmigiano-Reggiano. Bake in preheated 350°F oven 30 to 40 minutes or until heated through. Let stand 10 minutes before cutting.
Makes 6 servings.

*Remove wax coating and moist, white crust from cheese.

BÉCHAMEL SAUCE: Melt 2 tablespoons butter or margarine in small saucepan over medium-low heat. Stir in 2 tablespoons all-purpose flour. Gradually blend in ¾ cup milk. Season to taste with white pepper. Cook until thick and bubbly, stirring constantly.
Makes ¾ cup sauce.

Lasagna with White and Red Sauces

Luscious Vegetarian Lasagna

Luscious Vegetarian Lasagna

- 1 can (14½ ounces) tomatoes, undrained
- 1 can (12 ounces) tomato sauce
- 1 teaspoon dried oregano leaves, crushed
- 1 teaspoon dried basil leaves, crushed
  Dash black pepper
- 1 large onion, chopped
- 1½ teaspoons minced garlic
- 2 tablespoons olive oil
- 2 small zucchini, chopped
- 8 ounces mushrooms, sliced
- 1 large carrot, chopped
- 1 green pepper, chopped
- 1 cup (4 ounces) shredded mozzarella cheese
- 2 cups 1% milkfat cottage cheese
- 1 cup grated Parmesan or Romano cheese
- 8 ounces uncooked lasagna noodles, cooked, rinsed and drained
  Parsley sprigs (optional)

Simmer tomatoes with juice, tomato sauce, oregano, basil and black pepper in medium saucepan over low heat. Cook and stir onion and garlic in hot oil in large skillet over medium-high heat until onion is golden. Add zucchini, mushrooms, carrot and green pepper. Cook and stir until vegetables are tender, 5 to 10 minutes. Stir vegetables into tomato mixture; simmer 15 minutes. Combine mozzarella, cottage and Parmesan cheeses in large bowl; blend well.

Spoon about 1 cup sauce in bottom of 12×8-inch pan. Place a layer of noodles over sauce, then ½ of the cheese mixture and ½ of the remaining sauce. Repeat layers of noodles, cheese mixture and sauce. Bake in preheated 350°F. oven 30 to 45 minutes or until bubbly. Let stand 10 minutes. Garnish with parsley.
Makes 6 to 8 servings

Substitution: Other vegetables may be added or substituted for the ones listed above.

*Favorite recipe from **North Dakota Dairy Promotion Commission***

Spinach Pesto

- 1 bunch fresh spinach, washed, dried and chopped
- 1 cup fresh parsley leaves
- ⅔ cup grated Parmesan cheese
- ½ cup walnut pieces
- 6 cloves fresh garlic, crushed
- 4 flat anchovy filets
- 1 tablespoon dried tarragon leaves, crushed
- 1 teaspoon dried basil leaves, crushed
- 1 teaspoon salt
- ½ teaspoon pepper
- ¼ teaspoon anise or fennel seed
- 1 cup olive oil
  Hot cooked pasta twists, spaghetti or shells
  Mixed salad (optional)

Place all ingredients except oil, pasta and salad in covered food processor. Process until mixture is smooth. With motor running, add oil in thin stream. Adjust seasonings, if desired. Pour desired amount over pasta; toss gently to coat. Serve with salad. Garnish as desired.
Makes 2 cups sauce

Note: Sauce will keep about 1 week in a covered container in the refrigerator.

*Favorite recipe from **The Fresh Garlic Association***

Spinach Pesto

Spinach-Garlic Pasta with Garlic-Onion Sauce

Spinach-Garlic Pasta
 1½ cups all-purpose flour, divided
  2 eggs *plus* 4 yolks
  1 tablespoon olive oil
  ½ pound fresh spinach, blanched, squeezed dry and finely chopped
  6 large cloves fresh garlic, crushed and finely chopped
  ½ teaspoon salt

Garlic-Onion Sauce
  ½ cup butter
  1 tablespoon olive oil
  1 pound Vidalia or other sweet onions, sliced
  ⅓ cup chopped fresh garlic (about 12 large cloves)
  1 tablespoon honey (optional)
  ¼ cup Marsala wine
    Grated Parmesan cheese (optional)

For pasta, place 1 cup flour in large bowl. Make well in center; place eggs, yolks and olive oil in well. Add spinach, garlic and salt. Mix, working in more flour as needed. Knead until dough is smooth. Cover with plastic wrap. Let rest 15 to 30 minutes. Roll dough to desired thickness with pasta machine. Cut into desired width. Cook in boiling water about 2 minutes; drain.

For sauce, heat butter and oil in large skillet over medium heat. Add onions and garlic; cover and cook until soft. Add honey; reduce heat to low. Cook, uncovered, 30 minutes, stirring occasionally. Add wine; cook 5 to 10 minutes more. Pour sauce over pasta; toss gently to coat. Serve with cheese. Garnish as desired.

Makes 2 to 4 servings

*Favorite recipe from **The Fresh Garlic Association***

Spinach Stuffed Manicotti

  1 teaspoon dried rosemary leaves, crushed
  1 teaspoon dried sage leaves, crushed
  1 teaspoon dried oregano leaves, crushed
  1 teaspoon dried thyme leaves, crushed
  1 teaspoon chopped fresh garlic
 1½ teaspoons olive oil
 1½ cups canned or fresh tomatoes, chopped
  1 package (10 ounces) frozen spinach, cooked, drained and squeezed dry
  4 ounces ricotta cheese
  1 slice whole wheat bread, torn into coarse crumbs
  2 egg whites, lightly beaten
  8 uncooked manicotti shells, cooked, rinsed and drained
    Yellow pepper rings (optional)
    Sage sprig (optional)

Cook and stir rosemary, sage, oregano, thyme and garlic in oil in small saucepan over medium heat about 1 minute; do not let herbs turn brown. Add tomatoes; reduce heat to low. Simmer 10 minutes, stirring occasionally.

Combine spinach, cheese and bread crumbs in medium bowl. Fold in egg whites. Stuff manicotti with spinach mixture. Place ⅓ of the tomato mixture on bottom of 13×9-inch pan. Arrange manicotti in pan. Pour remaining tomato mixture over manicotti. Cover with foil. Bake in preheated 350°F. oven 30 minutes or until bubbly. Garnish with yellow pepper rings and sage sprig.

Makes 4 servings

*Favorite recipe from **National Pasta Association***

Spinach Stuffed Manicotti

Chicken and Zucchini Lasagne

8 lasagne noodles
3 cups (¼ inch thick) zucchini slices (about 2 medium)
1 tablespoon butter
1 jar (12 ounces) HEINZ® HomeStyle Chicken Gravy
⅔ cup half-and-half or milk
⅓ cup grated Romano or Parmesan cheese
½ teaspoon dried basil leaves, crushed
¼ teaspoon dried thyme leaves, crushed
1½ cups ricotta cheese
1 egg, slightly beaten
3 green onions, sliced
2 tablespoons chopped fresh parsley
2 cups cubed cooked chicken
1 cup shredded mozzarella cheese
¼ cup grated Romano or Parmesan cheese
¼ cup dry bread crumbs
1 tablespoon butter or margarine, melted
Paprika

Cook lasagne noodles following package directions. In large skillet, lightly sauté zucchini in butter. In medium bowl, combine gravy, half-and-half, ⅓ cup Romano cheese, basil and thyme. In another medium bowl, combine ricotta cheese, egg, green onions and parsley. Pour ⅓ of gravy mixture into 3-quart oblong baking dish. Arrange 4 lasagne noodles over gravy. Cover noodles with half of *each*: ricotta mixture, zucchini, chicken, mozzarella cheese. Spoon ⅓ of gravy mixture over cheese; repeat layers, ending with remaining gravy mixture. In small bowl, combine the ¼ cup Romano cheese, bread crumbs and melted butter; sprinkle over top of lasagne and dust with paprika. Bake in 350°F oven, 45 minutes; let stand 10 minutes before serving.
Makes 6 to 8 servings

Rigatoni with Four Cheeses

3 cups milk
1 tablespoon chopped carrot
1 tablespoon chopped celery
1 tablespoon chopped onion
1 tablespoon parsley sprigs
½ bay leaf
¼ teaspoon black peppercorns
¼ teaspoon hot pepper sauce
Dash ground nutmeg
¼ cup butter
¼ cup all-purpose flour
½ cup grated Wisconsin Parmesan cheese
¼ cup grated Wisconsin Romano cheese
12 ounces uncooked rigatoni, cooked and drained
1½ cups (6 ounces) shredded Wisconsin Cheddar cheese
1½ cups (6 ounces) shredded Wisconsin mozzarella cheese
¼ teaspoon chili powder

Combine milk, carrot, celery, onion, parsley, bay leaf, peppercorns, hot pepper sauce and nutmeg in medium saucepan. Bring to a boil. Reduce heat to low; simmer 10 minutes. Strain; reserve milk.

Melt butter in another medium saucepan over medium heat. Stir in flour. Gradually stir in reserved milk. Cook, stirring constantly, until thickened. Remove from heat. Add Parmesan and Romano cheeses, stirring until blended. Combine pasta and sauce in large bowl; toss gently to coat. Combine Cheddar and mozzarella cheeses in medium bowl. Place ½ of the pasta mixture in buttered 2-quart casserole. Sprinkle cheese mixture over top; place remaining pasta mixture on top. Sprinkle with chili powder. Bake in preheated 350°F. oven 25 minutes or until bubbly. Garnish as desired.   *Makes 6 servings*

Favorite recipe from **Wisconsin Milk Marketing Board** © *1993*

Rigatoni with Four Cheeses

Spicy Ravioli and Cheese

**1 medium red bell pepper,
    thinly sliced
1 medium green bell pepper,
    thinly sliced
1 medium yellow bell pepper,
    thinly sliced
1 tablespoon olive or
    vegetable oil
½ teaspoon LAWRY'S®
    Seasoned Salt
¼ teaspoon LAWRY'S® Garlic
    Powder with Parsley
¼ teaspoon sugar
1 package (8 or 9 ounces)
    fresh or frozen ravioli
1½ cups chunky salsa
4 ounces mozzarella cheese,
    thinly sliced
2 green onions, sliced**

Spicy Ravioli and Cheese

Place bell peppers in baking dish; sprinkle with oil, Seasoned Salt, Garlic Powder with Parsley and sugar. Broil 15 minutes or until tender and browned, turning once. Prepare ravioli according to package directions. Pour ½ of salsa in bottom of 8-inch square baking dish. Alternate layers of bell peppers, ravioli, cheese and green onions. Pour remaining salsa over layers. Cover with foil; bake in 350°F oven 15 to 20 minutes or until heated through and cheese melts.   *Makes 4 to 6 servings*

Presentation: Serve as either a side dish or as a main dish.

Hint: You may also prepare this recipe in individual casseroles.

Creamy Fettuccini Toss

**¼ cup margarine or butter
1 tablespoon flour
2 teaspoons WYLER'S® or
    STEERO® Chicken-Flavor
    Instant Bouillon
¾ teaspoon basil leaves
¼ teaspoon garlic powder
⅛ teaspoon pepper
1 cup (½ pint) BORDEN® or
    MEADOW GOLD® Coffee
    Cream *or* Half-and-Half
1 cup BORDEN® or MEADOW
    GOLD® Milk
½ (1-pound) package
    CREAMETTE® Fettuccini
¼ cup grated Parmesan
    cheese**

In medium saucepan, melt margarine; stir in flour, bouillon, basil, garlic powder and pepper. Gradually add cream and milk. Cook and stir until bouillon dissolves and sauce thickens slightly, about 15 minutes. Meanwhile, cook fettuccini as package directs; drain. Remove sauce from heat; add cheese. In large bowl, pour sauce over *hot* fettuccini; stir to coat. Garnish with parsley, walnuts and bacon if desired. Serve immediately. Refrigerate leftovers.
Makes 6 to 8 servings

Pasta and Broccoli

**1 bunch broccoli, steamed
1 clove garlic, finely chopped
2 tablespoons olive oil
¾ cup (3 ounces) shredded
    American or mozzarella
    cheese
½ cup grated Parmesan
    cheese
¼ cup butter
¼ cup chicken broth
3 tablespoons white wine
1 package (16 ounces)
    uncooked ziti macaroni,
    hot cooked and drained**

Chop broccoli; set aside. Cook and stir garlic in hot oil in large skillet over medium-high heat until lightly browned. Add broccoli; cook and stir 3 to 4 minutes. Add American cheese, Parmesan cheese, butter, broth and wine; stir. Simmer until cheese melts.

Pour sauce over ziti in large bowl; toss gently to coat. Garnish as desired.
Makes 6 to 8 servings

*Favorite recipe from **National Pasta Association***

Ham & Vegetable Primavera

½ pound lean cooked ham, cut into strips
1 medium red bell pepper, cut into strips
3 ounces fresh pea pods (1½ cups)
1 cup sliced fresh mushrooms
⅓ cup sliced green onions
1½ teaspoons Italian seasoning
1 clove garlic, finely chopped
2 tablespoons olive or vegetable oil
1 tablespoon flour
½ cup water
3 tablespoons REALEMON® Lemon Juice from Concentrate
1 teaspoon WYLER'S® or STEERO® Chicken-Flavor Instant Bouillon
½ (1-pound) package CREAMETTE® Spaghetti, cooked as package directs and drained
2 tablespoons grated Parmesan cheese

In large skillet, cook red pepper, pea pods, mushrooms, onions, Italian seasoning and garlic in oil until tender-crisp. Stir in flour then water, ReaLemon® brand and bouillon. Add ham; cook and stir until thickened and bubbly. Toss with hot spaghetti and cheese. Refrigerate leftovers.

Makes 4 servings

Lazy Lasagna

1 pound ground beef
1 jar (32 ounces) spaghetti sauce
1 pound cottage cheese
8 ounces dairy sour cream
8 uncooked lasagna noodles
3 packages (6 ounces each) sliced mozzarella cheese (12 slices)
½ cup grated Parmesan cheese
1 cup water

Cook beef in large skillet over medium-high heat until meat is brown, stirring to separate meat; drain fat. Add spaghetti sauce. Reduce heat to low. Heat through, stirring occasionally; set aside. Combine cottage cheese and sour cream in medium bowl; blend well.

Spoon 1½ cups of the meat sauce in bottom of 13×9-inch pan. Place ½ of the uncooked noodles over sauce, then ½ of the cottage cheese mixture, 4 slices of the mozzarella, ½ of the remaining meat sauce and ¼ cup of the Parmesan cheese. Repeat layers starting with the noodles. Top with remaining 4 slices of mozzarella cheese. Pour water around the sides of the pan. Cover tightly with foil. Bake in preheated 350°F. oven 1 hour. Uncover; bake 20 minutes more or until bubbly. Let stand 15 to 20 minutes. Garnish as desired.

Makes 8 to 10 servings

Favorite recipe from **North Dakota Dairy Promotion Commission**

Tacos in Pasta Shells

1¼ pounds ground beef
1 package (3 ounces) cream cheese with chives, cubed and softened
1 teaspoon salt
1 teaspoon chili powder
18 uncooked jumbo pasta shells, cooked, rinsed and drained
2 tablespoons butter, melted
1 cup prepared taco sauce
1 cup (4 ounces) shredded Cheddar cheese
1 cup (4 ounces) shredded Monterey Jack cheese
1½ cups crushed tortilla chips
1 cup dairy sour cream
3 green onions, chopped
Leaf lettuce (optional)
Small pitted ripe olives (optional)
Cherry tomatoes (optional)

Cook beef in large skillet over medium-high heat until brown, stirring to separate meat; drain fat. Reduce heat to medium-low. Add cream cheese, salt and chili powder; simmer 5 minutes.

Toss shells with butter; fill with beef mixture. Arrange shells in buttered 13×9-inch pan. Pour taco sauce over each shell. Cover with foil. Bake in preheated 350°F. oven 15 minutes. Uncover; top with Cheddar cheese, Monterey Jack cheese and chips. Bake 15 minutes more or until bubbly. Top with sour cream and onions. Garnish with lettuce, olives and tomatoes.

Makes 4 to 6 servings

Favorite recipe from **Southeast United Dairy Industry Association, Inc.**

Tacos in Pasta Shells

Sunday Super Stuffed Shells

Combine spinach, parsley, bread crumbs, eggs, minced garlic and Parmesan in large bowl; blend well. Season to taste with salt. Add cooled meat mixture; blend well. Fill shells with stuffing.

Spread about 1 cup of the spaghetti sauce over bottom of greased 12×8-inch pan. Arrange shells in pan. Pour remaining sauce over shells. Cover with foil. Bake in preheated 375°F. oven 35 to 45 minutes or until bubbly. Serve with zucchini. Garnish as desired.

Makes 9 to 12 servings

Favorite recipe from **The Fresh Garlic Association**

Sunday Super Stuffed Shells

    3 cloves fresh garlic
    2 tablespoons olive oil
    ¾ pound ground veal
    ¾ pound ground pork
    1 package (10 ounces) frozen
        chopped spinach,
        cooked, drained and
        squeezed dry
    1 cup parsley, finely chopped
    1 cup bread crumbs
    2 eggs, beaten
    3 cloves fresh garlic, minced
    3 tablespoons grated
        Parmesan cheese
      Salt to taste
    1 package (12 ounces)
        uncooked jumbo pasta
        shells, cooked, rinsed
        and drained
    3 cups spaghetti sauce
      Sautéed zucchini slices
        (optional)

Cook and stir the 3 whole garlic cloves in hot oil in large skillet over medium heat until garlic is browned. Discard garlic. Add veal and pork; cook until lightly browned, stirring to separate meat; drain fat. Set aside.

Beef Oriental

    1 pound ground beef
    7 green onions, diagonally
        sliced into 2-inch pieces
    3 tablespoons soy sauce
    ¼ teaspoon ground ginger
    2 to 3 ribs celery, diagonally
        sliced into 1-inch pieces
    8 mushrooms, sliced
    1 package (20 ounces) frozen
        pea pods, rinsed under
        hot water and drained
    1 can (8 ounces) tomato
        sauce
    3 cups uncooked corkscrew
        pasta, cooked and
        drained
    3 fresh tomatoes, cut into
        wedges
    1 cup (4 ounces) shredded
        Cheddar cheese, divided
    1 green pepper, cut into thin
        slices

Beef Oriental

Cook beef, onions, soy sauce and ginger in wok over medium-high heat until meat is brown, stirring to separate meat. Push mixture up the side of the wok. Add celery and mushrooms; stir-fry 2 minutes. Push up the side. Add pea pods and tomato sauce; cook 4 to 5 minutes, stirring every minute. Add pasta, tomatoes and ¾ cup of the cheese. Stir gently to combine all ingredients. Cook 1 minute. Add green pepper; sprinkle remaining cheese over top. Reduce heat to low; cook until heated through.

Makes 4 servings

Favorite recipe from **North Dakota Beef Commission**

Spinach Lasagna

Spinach Lasagna

1 pound lean ground beef
2 jars (15½ ounces each) spaghetti sauce
1 can (6 ounces) tomato paste
1 can (4 ounces) mushroom stems and pieces, drained
¼ cup chopped onion
½ teaspoon parsley flakes
½ teaspoon dried oregano leaves, crushed
½ teaspoon dried basil leaves, crushed
¼ teaspoon garlic powder
Seasoned salt and pepper to taste
1 pound dry curd cottage cheese
3 cups (12 ounces) shredded mozzarella cheese, divided
3 ounces grated Romano cheese
1 egg, lightly beaten
1 package (10 ounces) frozen chopped spinach, thawed and squeezed dry
8 ounces uncooked lasagna noodles, cooked, rinsed and drained
3 ounces sliced pepperoni (optional)
½ cup grated Parmesan cheese

Cook beef in large skillet over medium-high heat until brown, stirring to separate meat; drain fat. Add spaghetti sauce, tomato paste, mushrooms, onion and seasonings. Bring to a boil, stirring constantly; set aside.

Combine cottage cheese, 1 cup of the mozzarella cheese, Romano cheese, egg and spinach in medium bowl. Spoon 1½ cups meat sauce in bottom of 13×9-inch pan. Place a layer of noodles over sauce, then ½ of the cheese mixture and pepperoni. Sprinkle with Parmesan cheese. Repeat layers of sauce, noodles and cheese mixture. Sprinkle with remaining mozzarella. Bake in preheated 350°F. oven 30 to 45 minutes or until bubbly. Broil for a few minutes to brown cheese, if desired. Let stand 10 minutes.

Makes 8 to 10 servings

Favorite recipe from **North Dakota Wheat Commission**

Spaghetti alla Bolognese

2 tablespoons olive oil
1 medium onion, chopped
1 pound ground beef
½ small carrot, finely chopped
½ rib celery, finely chopped
1 cup dry white wine
½ cup milk
⅛ teaspoon ground nutmeg
1 can (14½ ounces) whole peeled tomatoes, undrained
1 cup beef broth
3 tablespoons tomato paste
1 teaspoon salt
1 teaspoon dried basil leaves, crushed
½ teaspoon dried thyme leaves, crushed
⅛ teaspoon pepper
1 bay leaf
1 pound uncooked dry spaghetti
1 cup freshly grated Parmesan cheese (about 3 ounces)

1. Heat oil in large skillet over medium heat. Cook and stir onion in hot oil 4 to 5 minutes until soft. Crumble beef into onion mixture. Brown 6 minutes or until meat just loses its pink color.

2. Stir carrot and celery into meat mixture; cook 2 minutes over medium-high heat. Stir in wine; cook 4 to 6 minutes until wine evaporates. Stir in milk and nutmeg; reduce heat to medium and cook 3 to 4 minutes until milk evaporates. Remove from heat.

3. Press tomatoes and juice through sieve into meat mixture; discard seeds.

4. Stir beef broth, tomato paste, salt, basil, thyme, pepper and bay leaf into tomato-meat mixture. Bring to a boil over medium-high heat; reduce heat to low. Simmer, uncovered, 1 to 1½ hours until most of liquid has evaporated and sauce thickens, stirring frequently. Remove and discard bay leaf.

5. To serve, cook spaghetti in large pot of boiling salted water 8 to 12 minutes just until al dente; drain well. Combine hot spaghetti and meat sauce in serving bowl; toss lightly. Sprinkle with cheese.

Makes 4 to 6 servings

Spaghetti & Meatballs

- **1 pound lean ground beef**
- **½ cup finely chopped onion**
- **¾ cup grated Parmesan cheese**
- **½ cup fresh bread crumbs (1 slice)**
- **1 (26-ounce) jar CLASSICO® Pasta Sauce, any flavor**
- **1 egg**
- **2 teaspoons WYLER'S® or STEERO® Beef-Flavor Instant Bouillon**
- **1 teaspoon Italian seasoning**
- **8 ounces fresh mushrooms, sliced (about 2 cups)**
- **1 (1-pound) package CREAMETTE® Spaghetti, cooked as package directs and drained**

In large bowl, combine meat, onion, cheese, crumbs, *½ cup* pasta sauce, egg, bouillon and Italian seasoning; mix well. Shape into meatballs. In large kettle or Dutch oven, brown meatballs; pour off fat. Stir in remaining pasta sauce and mushrooms; simmer uncovered 15 minutes or until hot. Serve over hot cooked spaghetti. Refrigerate leftovers.

Makes 6 to 8 servings

Skillet Pasta Roma

- **½ pound Italian sausage, sliced or crumbled**
- **1 large onion, coarsely chopped**
- **1 large clove garlic, minced**
- **2 cans (14½ ounces each) DEL MONTE® Chunky Pasta Style Stewed Tomatoes**
- **1 can (8 ounces) DEL MONTE® Tomato Sauce**
- **1 cup water**
- **8 ounces uncooked rigatoni or spiral pasta**
- **8 mushrooms, sliced (optional)**
- **Grated Parmesan cheese and parsley (optional)**

In large skillet, brown sausage. Add onion and garlic. Cook until onion is soft; drain. Stir in stewed tomatoes, tomato sauce, water and pasta. Cover and bring to a boil; reduce heat. Simmer, covered, 25 to 30 minutes or until pasta is tender, stirring occasionally. Stir in mushrooms; simmer 5 minutes. Serve in skillet garnished with cheese and parsley, if desired.

Makes 4 servings

Creamy Herbed Chicken

- **1 (9-ounce) package fresh bow tie pasta or fusilli***
- **1 tablespoon vegetable oil**
- **4 boneless, skinless chicken breast halves (about 1 pound), cut into ½-inch strips**
- **1 small red onion, sliced**
- **1 (10-ounce) package frozen green peas, thawed, drained**
- **1 yellow or red pepper, cut into strips**
- **½ cup chicken broth**
- **1 (8-ounce) container soft cream cheese with garlic and herb**

1. Cook pasta in lightly salted boiling water according to package directions (about 5 minutes); drain.

2. Meanwhile, heat oil in large skillet or wok over medium-high heat. Add chicken and onion; stir-fry 3 minutes or until chicken is no longer pink in center.

3. Add peas and yellow pepper; stir-fry 4 minutes. Reduce heat to medium.

4. Stir in broth and cream cheese. Cook, stirring constantly, until cream cheese is melted.

5. Combine pasta and chicken mixture in serving bowl; mix lightly. Season with salt and black pepper to taste. Garnish as desired. *Makes 4 servings*

*Substitute dried bow tie pasta or fusilli for fresh pasta.

Fettuccine with Duckling and Roasted Red Peppers

Fettuccine with Duckling and Roasted Red Peppers

1 frozen duckling (4½ to 5½ pounds), thawed and quartered
Garlic powder
Onion salt
2 tablespoons butter or margarine, melted
1½ tablespoons all-purpose flour
1¼ cups heavy cream
2 tablespoons grated Parmesan cheese
1 pound uncooked fettuccine, hot cooked and drained
½ cup prepared roasted red peppers, drained
¼ cup chopped walnuts
¼ cup sliced pitted ripe olives

Place duckling, skin-side up, on rack in shallow pan. Sprinkle with garlic powder and onion salt. Cook in 350°F. oven about 1½ hours or until internal temperature registers 185°F. when tested with a meat thermometer. Cool; remove bones and skin. Cut duckling into bite-sized pieces; set aside.

Combine butter and flour in medium saucepan; blend well. Cook 1 minute over medium heat. Gradually stir in cream. Stir in cheese. Cook until sauce thickens, stirring constantly.

Place fettuccine in large bowl. Add duckling, peppers, walnuts and olives. Pour sauce over fettuccine; toss gently to coat. Garnish as desired.

Makes 4 main-dish or 8 appetizer servings

Sweet Garlic with Chicken Pasta

Sweet Garlic with Chicken Pasta

8 ounces garlic, minced
5½ tablespoons olive oil
1½ pounds shiitake mushrooms, sliced
2 cups fresh plum tomatoes, diced
1 cup chopped green onions
1 teaspoon crushed red pepper
2 cups chicken broth
1½ pounds chicken breasts, grilled, skinned, boned and diced
1 package (16 ounces) uncooked bow tie noodles, cooked, rinsed and drained
4 ounces cilantro, chopped and divided

Cook and stir garlic in hot oil in large skillet over medium-high heat until lightly browned. Add mushrooms, tomatoes, green onions and crushed red pepper. Cook and stir 2 minutes more. Add broth; simmer mixture to reduce slightly. Add chicken, noodles and ½ of the cilantro; heat through. Garnish with remaining cilantro.

Makes 6 to 8 servings

*Favorite recipe from **National Pasta Association***

Turkey Orzo Italiano

¼ pound sliced mushrooms
½ cup sliced green onions
2 tablespoons margarine
2 cups turkey broth or reduced-sodium chicken bouillon
1 cup orzo pasta, uncooked
½ teaspoon Italian seasoning
½ teaspoon salt
⅛ teaspoon white pepper
2 cups cooked cubed turkey

In large skillet, over medium-high heat, sauté mushrooms and onions in margarine for 1 minute. Add turkey broth and bring to a boil.

Stir in orzo, Italian seasoning, salt and pepper; bring to a boil. Reduce heat and simmer, covered, 15 minutes or until orzo is tender and liquid has been absorbed. Stir in turkey and heat through.

Makes 4 servings

*Favorite recipe from **National Turkey Federation***

An Early Spring Pasta

- 1 cup Oriental Dressing (recipe follows)
- 8 ounces cooked turkey breast, cut into julienne strips
- 4 ounces carrots, cut into julienne strips
- 4 ounces asparagus, diagonally sliced into 1-inch pieces
- 4 ounces spinach, chopped
- 12 ounces uncooked linguine, hot cooked and drained

Heat Oriental Dressing in large saucepan over high heat to a boil. Add turkey, carrots, asparagus and spinach; reduce heat to medium. Cook 2 to 3 minutes. Pour sauce over linguini in large bowl; toss gently to coat.

Makes 4 to 6 servings

Oriental Dressing

- 1 large onion, sliced
- 1 cup water
- ¼ cup *each* soy sauce and rice vinegar
- 1 tablespoon *each* garlic and ginger root, minced
- 1 tablespoon *each* sesame oil and lemon juice
- 1½ teaspoons *each* sugar and pepper
- 1½ teaspoons hot pepper sauce
- 2 tablespoons cornstarch
- ¼ cup water

Spread onion on large baking pan. Heat in preheated 400°F. oven until edges are dark brown, about 15 minutes. Purée onion in covered food processor. Place onion and remaining ingredients except cornstarch and ¼ cup water in medium saucepan. Bring to a boil. Combine cornstarch and ¼ cup water in cup until smooth. Gradually stir into dressing mixture. Heat until mixture boils, stirring constantly. Reduce heat to low; simmer 2 to 3 minutes.

Favorite recipe from **National Pasta Association**

Seafood Primavera

- 1 medium onion, chopped
- 4 green onions, chopped
- ⅓ cup olive oil
- 3 carrots, cut into strips
- 1 zucchini, cut into strips
- 1 *each* small red and yellow pepper, cut into strips
- 3 ounces snow peas
- ⅓ cup sliced mushrooms
- 3 cloves garlic, minced
- ½ pound *each* scallops and shrimp, peeled and deveined
- ⅔ cup clam juice
- ⅓ cup dry white wine
- 1 cup heavy cream
- ½ cup freshly grated Parmesan cheese
- ⅔ cup flaked crabmeat
- 2 tablespoons *each* lemon juice and chopped parsley
- ¼ teaspoon *each* dried basil leaves and dried oregano leaves, crushed
- Freshly ground black pepper to taste
- 1 package (8 ounces) uncooked linguine, hot cooked and drained

Cook and stir onions in hot oil in large skillet over medium-high heat until soft. Add vegetables and garlic; reduce heat to low. Cover; simmer until vegetables are tender. Remove; set aside. Cover and cook scallops and shrimp in same skillet over medium-low heat until opaque. Remove; reserve liquid in pan. Add clam juice; bring to a boil. Add wine; cook over medium-high heat 3 minutes, stirring constantly. Reduce heat to low; add cream, stirring constantly. Add cheese; stir until smooth. Cook until thickened.

Add vegetables, shrimp, scallops and crabmeat to sauce. Heat through. Add remaining ingredients except linguine. Pour over linguine in large bowl; toss gently to coat. Serve with additional grated Parmesan cheese, if desired.

Makes 6 servings

Seafood Lasagna

- 1 large onion, chopped
- 2 tablespoons butter or margarine
- 1½ cups cream-style cottage cheese
- 1 package (8 ounces) cream cheese, cubed, softened
- 2 teaspoons dried basil leaves, crushed
- ½ teaspoon salt
- ⅛ teaspoon pepper
- 1 egg, lightly beaten
- 2 cans (10¾ ounces each) cream of mushroom soup
- ⅓ cup milk
- 1 clove garlic, minced
- ½ cup dry white wine
- ½ pound bay scallops
- ½ pound flounder fillets, cubed
- ½ pound medium shrimp, peeled and deveined
- 1 package (16 ounces) lasagna, cooked, rinsed and drained
- 1 cup (4 ounces) shredded mozzarella cheese
- 2 tablespoons grated Parmesan cheese

Cook onion in hot butter in medium skillet over medium heat until tender, stirring frequently. Stir in cottage cheese, cream cheese, basil, salt and pepper; mix well. Stir in egg; set aside.

Combine soup, milk and garlic in large bowl until well blended. Stir in wine, scallops, flounder and shrimp.

Place a layer of overlapping noodles in greased 13×9-inch pan. Spread ½ of the cheese mixture over noodles. Place a layer of noodles over cheese mixture and top with ½ of the seafood mixture. Repeat layers. Sprinkle with mozzarella and Parmesan cheeses. Bake in preheated 350°F. oven 45 minutes or until bubbly. Let stand 10 minutes.

Makes 8 to 10 servings

Favorite recipe from **New Jersey Department of Agriculture**

Seafood Primavera

Shrimp Noodle Supreme

Shrimp Noodle Supreme

- 1 package (8 ounces) uncooked spinach noodles, hot cooked and drained
- 1 package (3 ounces) cream cheese, cubed and softened
- 1½ pounds medium shrimp, peeled and deveined
- ½ cup butter, softened
  Salt and pepper to taste
- 1 can (10¾ ounces) condensed cream of mushroom soup
- 1 cup dairy sour cream
- ½ cup half-and-half
- ½ cup mayonnaise
- 1 tablespoon chopped chives
- 1 tablespoon chopped parsley
- ½ teaspoon Dijon mustard
- ¾ cup (6 ounces) shredded sharp Cheddar cheese
  Tomato wedges (optional)
  Parsley sprigs (optional)
  Lemon slices (optional)
  Paprika (optional)

Combine noodles and cream cheese in medium bowl. Spread noodle mixture in bottom of greased 13×9-inch glass casserole. Cook shrimp in butter in large skillet over medium-high heat until pink and tender, about 5 minutes. Season to taste with salt and pepper. Spread shrimp over noodles.

Combine soup, sour cream, half-and-half, mayonnaise, chives, chopped parsley and mustard in another medium bowl. Spread over shrimp. Sprinkle Cheddar cheese over top. Bake in preheated 325°F. oven 25 minutes or until hot and cheese melts. Garnish with tomato, parsley sprigs, lemon slices and paprika.   *Makes 6 servings*

*Favorite recipe from **Southeast United Dairy Industry Association, Inc.***

Salmon, Fettuccine & Cabbage

- 1 (9-ounce) package fresh fettuccine
- ¼ cup plus 2 tablespoons seasoned rice vinegar
- 2 tablespoons vegetable oil
- ½ small head of cabbage, shredded (about 7 cups)
- ½ teaspoon fennel seeds
- 1 (15½-ounce) can salmon, drained, flaked, bones removed
  Salt and pepper

1. Cook fettuccine in lightly salted boiling water according to package directions (about 5 minutes); drain.

2. Heat vinegar and oil in large skillet over medium-high heat. Add cabbage; cook 3 minutes or until crisp-tender, stirring occasionally.

3. Stir in fennel seeds. Add fettuccine; toss lightly to coat. Add salmon; mix lightly.

4. Heat thoroughly, stirring occasionally. Season with salt and pepper to taste. Garnish as desired.   *Makes 4 servings*

Garlic Shrimp with Noodles

- **4 tablespoons butter, divided**
- **¼ cup finely chopped onion**
- **2 cups water**
- **1 package LIPTON® Noodles & Sauce — Butter & Herb**
- **2 tablespoons olive oil**
- **1 tablespoon finely chopped garlic**
- **1 pound raw medium shrimp, cleaned**
- **1 can (14 ounces) artichoke hearts, drained and halved**
- **¼ cup finely chopped parsley**
  Pepper to taste

In medium saucepan, melt 2 tablespoons of the butter; add onion and cook until tender. Add water and bring to a boil. Stir in noodles & butter & herb sauce; continue boiling over medium heat, stirring occasionally, 8 minutes or until noodles are tender.

Meanwhile, in large skillet, heat remaining 2 tablespoons butter with olive oil; cook garlic over medium-high heat 30 seconds. Add shrimp and artichokes; cook, stirring occasionally, 3 minutes or until shrimp turn pink. Stir in parsley and pepper. To serve, combine shrimp mixture with hot noodles. Garnish, if desired, with watercress.

Makes about 4 servings

Shrimp in Angel Hair Pasta Casserole

- **1 tablespoon butter**
- **2 eggs**
- **1 cup half-and-half**
- **1 cup plain yogurt**
- **½ cup (4 ounces) shredded Swiss cheese**
- **⅓ cup crumbled feta cheese**
- **⅓ cup chopped parsley**
- **¼ cup chopped fresh basil *or* 1 teaspoon dried basil leaves, crushed**
- **1 teaspoon dried oregano leaves, crushed**
- **1 package (9 ounces) uncooked fresh angel hair pasta**
- **1 jar (16 ounces) mild, thick and chunky salsa**
- **1 pound medium shrimp, peeled and deveined**
- **½ cup (4 ounces) shredded Monterey Jack cheese**
  Snow peas (optional)
  Plum tomatoes stuffed with cottage cheese (optional)

With 1 tablespoon butter, grease 12×8-inch pan. Combine eggs, half-and-half, yogurt, Swiss cheese, feta cheese, parsley, basil and oregano in medium bowl; mix well. Spread ½ of the pasta on bottom of prepared pan. Cover with salsa. Add ½ of the shrimp. Cover with remaining pasta. Spread egg mixture over pasta and top with remaining shrimp. Sprinkle Monterey Jack cheese over top. Bake in preheated 350°F. oven 30 minutes or until bubbly. Let stand 10 minutes. Garnish with snow peas and stuffed plum tomatoes.

Makes 6 servings

*Favorite recipe from **Southeast United Dairy Industry Association, Inc.***

Shrimp in Angel Hair Pasta Casserole

Scallops with Vermicelli

- **1 pound bay scallops**
- **2 tablespoons fresh lemon juice**
- **2 tablespoons chopped parsley**
- **1 onion, chopped**
- **1 clove garlic, minced**
- **2 tablespoons olive oil**
- **2 tablespoons butter, divided**
- **1½ cups canned Italian tomatoes, undrained and cut up**
- **2 tablespoons chopped fresh basil *or* ½ teaspoon dried basil, crushed**
- **¼ teaspoon dried oregano leaves, crushed**
- **¼ teaspoon dried thyme leaves, crushed**
- **2 tablespoons heavy cream**
  Dash ground nutmeg
- **12 ounces uncooked vermicelli, hot cooked and drained**

Rinse scallops. Combine scallops, lemon juice and parsley in glass dish. Cover; marinate in refrigerator while preparing sauce.

Cook and stir onion and garlic in oil and 1 tablespoon of the butter in large skillet over medium-high heat until onion is tender. Add tomatoes with juice, basil, oregano and thyme. Reduce heat to low. Cover; simmer 30 minutes, stirring occasionally.

Drain scallops. Cook and stir scallops in remaining 1 tablespoon butter in another large skillet over medium heat until scallops are opaque, about 2 minutes. Add cream, nutmeg and tomato mixture.

Pour sauce over vermicelli in large bowl; toss gently to coat. Garnish as desired.

Makes 4 servings

*Favorite recipe from **New Jersey Department of Agriculture***

Linguine with Lemon Clam Sauce

- **¼ cup chopped onion**
- **1 clove garlic, finely chopped**
- **2 tablespoons margarine or butter**
- **2 tablespoons olive or vegetable oil**
- **2 (6½-ounce) cans SNOW'S® or DOXSEE® Chopped Clams, drained, reserving ⅔ cup liquid**
- **2 tablespoons REALEMON® Lemon Juice from Concentrate**
- **½ teaspoon cracked black pepper**
- **1 bay leaf**
- **1 tablespoon chopped parsley**
- **¼ to ½ pound CREAMETTE® Linguine, cooked as package directs and drained**
  Grated Parmesan cheese

In medium skillet, cook onion and garlic in margarine and oil until golden. Add reserved clam liquid, ReaLemon® brand, pepper and bay leaf. Bring to a boil; simmer uncovered 5 minutes. Stir in clams and parsley; heat through. Remove bay leaf; serve with hot linguine, cheese and additional pepper. Refrigerate leftovers.

Makes 2 to 3 servings

Scallops with Vermicelli

Tortellini with Three-Cheese Tuna Sauce

1 pound cheese-filled
    spinach and egg tortellini
2 green onions, thinly sliced
1 clove garlic, minced
1 tablespoon butter or
    margarine
1 cup low-fat ricotta cheese
½ cup low-fat milk
1 can (9¼ ounces)
    STARKIST® Tuna,
    drained and broken into
    chunks
½ cup shredded low-fat
    mozzarella cheese
¼ cup grated Parmesan or
    Romano cheese
2 tablespoons chopped fresh
    basil *or* 2 teaspoons
    dried basil, crushed
1 teaspoon grated lemon
    peel
    Fresh tomato wedges for
    garnish (optional)

Tortellini with Three-Cheese Tuna Sauce

Cook tortellini in boiling salted water according to package directions. When tortellini is nearly done, in another saucepan sauté onions and garlic in butter for 2 minutes. Remove from heat. Whisk in ricotta cheese and milk. Add tuna, cheeses, basil and lemon peel. Cook over medium-low heat until mixture is heated and cheeses are melted.

Drain pasta; add to sauce. Toss well to coat; garnish with tomato wedges if desired. Serve immediately.
Makes 4 to 5 servings

Preparation time: 25 minutes

Crabmeat with Herbs and Pasta

1 small onion, minced
1 carrot, shredded
1 clove garlic, minced
⅓ cup olive oil
3 tablespoons butter or
    margarine
6 ounces flaked crabmeat
¼ cup chopped fresh basil *or*
    1 teaspoon dried basil
    leaves, crushed
2 tablespoons chopped
    parsley
1 tablespoon lemon juice
½ cup chopped pine nuts
    (optional)
½ teaspoon salt
½ package (8 ounces)
    vermicelli, hot cooked
    and drained

Cook and stir onion, carrot and garlic in hot oil and butter in large skillet over medium-high heat until vegetables are tender, but not brown. Reduce heat to medium. Stir in crabmeat, basil, parsley and lemon juice. Cook 4 minutes, stirring constantly. Stir in pine nuts and salt. Pour sauce over vermicelli in large bowl; toss gently to coat. Garnish as desired. *Makes 4 servings*

*Favorite recipe from **New Jersey Department of Agriculture***

Creamy Tortellini Primavera

3 tablespoons olive or vegetable oil
1 medium clove garlic, finely chopped
1 envelope LIPTON® Recipe Secrets Vegetable Recipe Soup Mix
2 cups (1 pint) light cream or half and half
1 pound egg or spinach tortellini, cooked and drained
¼ cup grated Parmesan cheese
¼ cup finely chopped parsley
¼ teaspoon pepper

In large skillet, heat oil and cook garlic over medium heat until golden. Stir in vegetable recipe soup mix blended with cream, then hot tortellini. Bring just to the boiling point, then simmer, stirring occasionally, 5 minutes. Stir in remaining ingredients. Garnish, if desired, with additional parsley and cheese.
Makes about 4 appetizer or 2 main-dish servings.

Microwave Directions: In 2-quart casserole, microwave oil with garlic at HIGH (Full Power) 2 minutes. Stir in vegetable recipe soup mix blended with cream and microwave uncovered 4 minutes, stirring twice. Add hot tortellini and microwave uncovered 3 minutes. Stir in remaining ingredients and microwave 1 minute. Garnish and serve as above.

Seafood over Angel Hair Pasta

¼ cup WISH-BONE® Italian Dressing
¼ cup chopped shallots or onions
1 cup thinly sliced carrots
1 cup thinly sliced snow peas (about 4 ounces)
1 cup chicken broth
¼ cup sherry
8 mussels, well scrubbed
½ pound sea scallops
½ pound uncooked medium shrimp, cleaned (keep tails on)
¼ cup whipping or heavy cream
2 tablespoons all-purpose flour
Salt and pepper to taste
8 ounces angel hair pasta or capellini, cooked and drained

Seafood over Angel Hair Pasta

In 12-inch skillet, heat Italian dressing and cook shallots over medium-high heat 2 minutes. Add carrots and snow peas and cook 2 minutes. Add broth, then sherry. Bring to a boil, then add mussels, scallops and shrimp. Simmer uncovered 3 minutes or until seafood is done and mussel shells open. (Discard any unopened shells). Stir in cream blended with flour and cook over medium heat, stirring occasionally, 2 minutes or until sauce is slightly thickened. Stir in salt and pepper. Serve over hot angel hair pasta and, if desired, with freshly ground pepper.
Makes about 4 main-dish servings.
   Note: Also terrific with Wish-Bone® Robusto Italian, Lite Italian, Blended Italian or Lite Classic Dijon Vinaigrette Dressing.

Shrimp Milano

1 lb. frozen cleaned shrimp, cooked, drained
2 cups mushroom slices
1 cup green or red pepper strips
1 garlic clove, minced
¼ cup PARKAY® Margarine
¾ lb. VELVEETA® Pasteurized Process Cheese Spread, cubed
¾ cup whipping cream
½ teaspoon dill weed
⅓ cup (1½ ozs.) KRAFT® 100% Grated Parmesan Cheese
8 ozs. fettucini, cooked, drained

In large skillet, saute shrimp, vegetables and garlic in margarine. Reduce heat to low. Add VELVEETA® Pasteurized Process Cheese Spread, cream and dill. Stir until process cheese spread is melted. Stir in parmesan cheese. Add fettucini; toss lightly.
4 to 6 servings.

Preparation time: 20 minutes
Cooking time: 15 minutes

Spaghetti Mediterranean

1½ **pounds fresh tomatoes (about 4 large)**
12 **pitted green olives**
4 to 6 **flat anchovy fillets**
2 **medium cloves garlic**
½ **pound uncooked spaghetti**
   Boiling salted water
¼ **cup olive oil**
½ **cup chopped fresh parsley**
1 **tablespoon drained capers**
2 **teaspoons chopped fresh basil or ½ teaspoon dried basil, crumbled**
½ **teaspoon dried oregano, crumbled**
½ **teaspoon salt**
¼ **teaspoon dried hot red pepper flakes**

1. Place tomatoes in large saucepan with boiling water to cover 60 seconds to loosen skins. Immediately drain tomatoes and rinse under cold running water. Peel, seed and chop tomatoes coarsely. Slice olives. Chop anchovies. Mince garlic.
2. Cook spaghetti in large kettle of boiling salted water just until al dente, 8 to 12 minutes; drain well.
3. While spaghetti is cooking, heat oil in 10-inch noncorrosive skillet over medium-high heat. Add garlic; cook just until garlic begins to color, 45 to 60 seconds. Stir in tomatoes, parsley, capers, basil, oregano, salt and the pepper flakes.
4. Add olives and anchovies to skillet; cook over medium-high heat, stirring constantly until most of the visible liquid has evaporated and sauce is slightly thickened, about 10 minutes.

Pour sauce over spaghetti in heated serving bowl. Toss lightly and serve immediately.
Makes 3 to 4 servings.

Creamy Spinach Fettucini

1 **small green pepper, chopped**
1 **small red pepper, chopped**
1 **small onion, chopped**
1 **(8-ounce) carton plain nonfat yogurt**
½ **cup canned white sauce**
2 **tablespoons dried Italian seasoning**
1½ **cups (6 ounces) ARMOUR® Lower Salt Ham cut into ½-inch cubes**
12 **ounces uncooked spinach fettucini, cooked according to package directions omitting salt and drained**
6 **slices ARMOUR® Lower Salt Bacon, cooked crisp and crumbled**

Spray large skillet with nonstick cooking spray; place over medium heat. Add vegetables; sauté until tender-crisp. Mix yogurt, white sauce and seasoning in small bowl. Add to vegetables and heat through. Add ham; continue cooking until hot. Spoon over warm fettucini; top with bacon. Garnish with parsley or fresh rosemary, if desired.
Makes 4 to 6 servings.

Nutrition Information Per Serving: 352 calories, 17.7 g protein, 9 g fat, 48 g carbohydrates, 20.6 mg cholesterol, 531 mg sodium.

Summer Spaghetti

1 **pound firm ripe fresh plum tomatoes**
1 **medium onion**
6 **pitted green olives**
2 **medium cloves garlic**
⅓ **cup chopped fresh parsley**
2 **tablespoons finely shredded fresh basil or ¾ teaspoon dried basil, crumbled**
2 **teaspoons drained capers**
½ **teaspoon paprika**
¼ **teaspoon dried oregano, crumbled**
1 **tablespoon red wine vinegar**
½ **cup olive oil**
1 **pound uncooked spaghetti Boiling salted water**

1. Chop tomatoes coarsely. Chop onion and olives. Mince garlic. Combine tomatoes, onion, olives, garlic, parsley, basil, capers, paprika and oregano in medium bowl; toss well. Drizzle vinegar over tomato mixture. Then pour oil over tomato mixture. Stir until thoroughly mixed. Refrigerate, covered, at least 6 hours or overnight.
2. Just before serving, cook spaghetti in large kettle of boiling salted water just until al dente, 8 to 12 minutes; drain well. Immediately toss hot pasta with cold marinated tomato sauce. Serve at once.
Makes 4 to 6 servings.

Spaghetti with Cream Sauce

2 **cups mushroom slices**
1 **cup halved zucchini slices**
1 **garlic clove, minced**
2 **tablespoons PARKAY® Margarine**
⅓ **cup half and half**
½ **lb. VELVEETA® Pasteurized Process Cheese Spread, cubed**
8 **ozs. spaghetti, cooked, drained**

Sauté vegetables and garlic in margarine until zucchini is crisp-tender. Reduce heat to low. Add half and half and VELVEETA® Pasteurized Process Cheese Spread; stir until process cheese spread is melted. Toss with hot spaghetti.
6 servings.

Preparation time: 15 minutes
Cooking time: 10 minutes

Summer Spaghetti

SIDE DISHES

Discover sensational side dishes that will steal the show. Accompany your next meal with crisp vegetables, perfect potatoes and irresistible rice dishes such as Cheddar Sesame Garden Vegetables, Skewered Grilled Potatoes and Spanish Rice au Gratin. You'll find a stuffing for Cornish hens, a mideastern pilaf for kabobs, a colorful vegetable mix to liven up any meat dish, plus much more to enhance all kinds of meals.

Homestyle Zucchini & Tomatoes

2 tablespoons oil
1 medium clove garlic, finely chopped*
3 medium zucchini, thinly sliced (about 4½ cups)
1 can (14½ ounces) whole peeled tomatoes, drained and chopped (reserve liquid)
1 envelope LIPTON® Recipe Secrets Golden Onion or Onion Recipe Soup Mix
½ teaspoon basil leaves

In large skillet, heat oil and cook garlic with zucchini over medium-high heat 3 minutes. Stir in tomatoes, then golden onion recipe soup mix thoroughly blended with reserved liquid and basil. Bring to a boil, then simmer, stirring occasionally, 10 minutes or until zucchini is tender and sauce is slightly thickened.
Makes about 4 servings.
   *Substitution: Use ¼ teaspoon garlic powder.
   Microwave Directions: In 2-quart casserole, combine zucchini with tomatoes. Stir in golden onion recipe soup mix thoroughly blended with reserved liquid, garlic and basil. Microwave covered at HIGH (Full Power) 5 minutes, stirring once. Remove cover and microwave 4 minutes or until zucchini is tender, stirring once. Let stand covered 2 minutes.

Country Bean Barbecue

1 can (16 ounces) lima beans
6 slices bacon, diced
½ cup sliced onion
½ cup diced celery
1 clove garlic, minced
1 cup catsup
1 can (16 ounces) red kidney beans, drained
½ teaspoon TABASCO® pepper sauce

Drain lima beans; reserve ½ cup liquid. In large skillet cook bacon until browned. Drain all but 1 tablespoon bacon fat from skillet. Add onion, celery and garlic; cook 5 minutes or until tender. Stir in catsup, lima beans, reserved lima bean liquid and kidney beans; mix gently. Simmer uncovered 20 minutes; stir occasionally. Stir in Tabasco® sauce.
Makes 6 to 8 servings.

Buffet Bean Bake

6 slices bacon
1 cup packed brown sugar
½ cup vinegar
½ teaspoon salt
1 tablespoon FRENCH'S® America's Favorite Mustard or DURKEE® Famous Sauce
1 can (16 ounces) butter beans, drained
1 can (16 ounces) French-style green beans, drained
1 can (16 ounces) pork and beans, drained
1 can (16 ounces) lima beans, drained
1 can (15½ ounces) yellow wax beans, drained
1 can (15 ounces) kidney beans, drained
1 can (2.8 ounces) DURKEE® French Fried Onions

Preheat oven to 350°. In medium skillet, fry bacon until crisp. Remove from skillet; crumble and set aside. Drain all but about 2 tablespoons drippings from skillet; add sugar, vinegar, salt and mustard. Simmer, uncovered, 10 minutes. In large bowl, combine drained beans, *½ can* French Fried Onions and hot sugar mixture. Spoon bean mixture into 9×13-inch baking dish. Bake, covered, at 350° for 30 minutes or until heated through. Top with crumbled bacon and remaining onions; bake, uncovered, 5 minutes or until onions are golden brown.
Makes 12 to 14 servings.

Homestyle Zucchini & Tomatoes

Broccoli and Pasta

> 1 package (10 ounces) frozen chopped broccoli
> 2 tablespoons CRISCO® Oil
> 2 tablespoons finely chopped onion
> 1 tablespoon snipped fresh parsley
> 1 teaspoon anchovy paste (optional)
> 1 small clove garlic, minced
> ¼ teaspoon salt
> Dash pepper
> 1 cup cooked small shell macaroni
> Grated Parmesan cheese

Cook broccoli according to package directions. Drain and set aside.

Heat Crisco® Oil in medium skillet. Add onion, parsley, anchovy paste (optional) and garlic. Cook over moderate heat, stirring constantly, about 3 minutes, or until onion is tender. Stir in broccoli, salt and pepper. Cook, stirring occasionally, 2 to 3 minutes longer, or until heated through. Remove from heat. Stir in macaroni. Sprinkle with Parmesan cheese. Serve immediately.
4 to 6 servings.

Spiced Red Cabbage

> ¼ cup CRISCO® Oil
> 2-pound head red cabbage, cored and chopped
> 1 small onion, thinly sliced and separated into rings
> 1 small apple, cored and chopped
> ½ cup raisins
> ¼ teaspoon ground cloves
> ⅛ teaspoon ground allspice
> 1 tablespoon white wine vinegar
> 2 teaspoons sugar
> 1 teaspoon salt

Heat Crisco® Oil in Dutch oven or large saucepan. Add cabbage, onion, apple, raisins, cloves and allspice. Stir to coat. Cover. Cook over moderate heat, stirring occasionally, about 1 hour, or until cabbage is tender. Stir in vinegar, sugar and salt.
6 to 8 servings.

Sweet 'n Sour Cabbage

> 1 can (11 ounces) DOLE® Mandarin Orange Segments
> 6 cups DOLE® Shredded Cabbage
> 1 medium onion, chopped
> 1 clove garlic, pressed
> 1 tablespoon vegetable oil
> ¼ cup white wine vinegar
> 1 teaspoon caraway seeds
> 1 teaspoon salt
> 1 cup DOLE® Fresh Pineapple chunks

Drain oranges; reserve ⅓ cup syrup. In large skillet, saute cabbage, onion and garlic in oil until onion is soft. Stir in reserved syrup, vinegar, caraway seeds and salt. Cover and simmer 10 minutes. Stir in pineapple and oranges. Cover; cook 5 minutes longer.
Makes 4 servings.

Carrot Saute

> 1 small clove garlic, pressed
> 2 tablespoons margarine
> 1 tablespoon soy sauce
> 1½ teaspoons water
> ½ teaspoon sugar
> 1 cup sliced DOLE® Carrots
> ½ onion, sliced into chunks
> ½ cup sliced DOLE® Celery
> ¼ cup DOLE® Blanched Slivered Almonds, toasted

In large skillet, saute garlic in margarine. Stir in soy sauce, water and sugar; bring to a boil. Add carrots, onion and celery; saute until tender-crisp. Sprinkle with nuts.
Makes 2 servings.

Brussels Sprouts Amandine

> 1 tablespoon CRISCO® Oil
> ¼ cup sliced almonds
> ¾ cup water
> 1½ teaspoons instant beef bouillon granules
> 1 package (16 ounces) frozen Brussels sprouts
> Dash pepper

Heat Crisco® Oil in medium saucepan. Add almonds. Sauté over moderate heat until light golden brown. Drain on paper towels.

Combine water and bouillon granules in medium saucepan. Heat to boiling. Add Brussels sprouts. Return to boiling. Cover. Reduce heat. Simmer, stirring once to break apart Brussels sprouts, 8 to 12 minutes, or until tender. Drain. Stir in almonds and pepper.
4 to 6 servings.

Broccoli and Pasta

Sesame Broccoli

½ bunch DOLE® Broccoli, cut
    into florettes
1 tablespoon margarine, melted
2 teaspoons sesame seeds,
    toasted
2 teaspoons soy sauce
    Pinch garlic powder
    Pinch ground ginger

In large saucepan, cook broccoli in vegetable steamer basket over boiling water 5 minutes; drain. In small bowl, combine remaining ingredients. In serving bowl, toss broccoli with sesame mixture.
Makes 2 to 3 servings.

Barley with Corn and Red Pepper

½ cup WISH-BONE® Italian
    Dressing
1 medium red pepper, chopped
½ cup chopped onion
1 cup uncooked pearled barley
1¾ cups chicken broth
1¼ cups water
2 tablespoons finely chopped
    coriander (cilantro) or
    parsley
1 tablespoon lime juice
½ teaspoon ground cumin
⅛ teaspoon pepper
1 can (7 ounces) whole kernel
    corn, drained

In large saucepan, heat Italian dressing and cook red pepper with onion over medium heat, stirring occasionally, 5 minutes or until tender. Stir in barley and cook, stirring constantly, 1 minute. Stir in broth, water, coriander, lime juice, cumin and pepper. Simmer covered 50 minutes or until barley is done. (Do not stir while simmering.) Stir in corn.
Makes about 6 servings.

Note: Also terrific with Wish-Bone® Robusto Italian, Lite Italian, Blended Italian or Lite Classic Dijon Vinaigrette Dressing.

Barley with Corn and Red Pepper

Red Cabbage 'n' Apples

¼ cup margarine or butter
⅓ cup REALEMON® Lemon Juice
    from Concentrate
¼ cup firmly packed light brown
    sugar
¼ cup water
½ teaspoon caraway seeds
½ teaspoon salt
4 cups shredded red cabbage
2 medium all-purpose apples,
    cored and coarsely chopped

In large saucepan, melt margarine; stir in ReaLemon® brand, sugar, water, caraway and salt. Add cabbage and apples; bring to a boil. Reduce heat; cover and simmer 25 to 30 minutes.
Makes 6 to 8 servings.

Microwave: In 2-quart round baking dish, melt margarine on 100% power (high) 45 seconds. Stir in ReaLemon® brand, sugar, water, caraway and salt; add cabbage and apples. Cook covered on 100% power (high) 15 to 20 minutes, stirring every 5 minutes. Let stand for 2 minutes before serving.

Vegetable Stir-Fry

1 8-ounce package Light
    PHILADELPHIA BRAND®
    Neufchatel Cheese, cubed
¼ cup sesame seed, toasted
2 cups diagonally cut carrot
    slices
2 cups diagonally cut celery
    slices
¾ cup thin green pepper strips
2 tablespoons PARKAY®
    Margarine
¼ teaspoon salt
    Dash of pepper

Coat Neufchatel cheese cubes with sesame seed; chill. In large skillet or wok, stir-fry vegetables in margarine and seasonings until crisp-tender. Remove from heat. Add Neufchatel cheese to vegetables; mix lightly.
6 to 8 servings.

Variation: Substitute PHILADELPHIA BRAND® Cream Cheese for Neufchatel Cheese.

Tomato-Bread Casserole

½ **pound-loaf French bread, sliced**

3 **tablespoons IMPERIAL® Margarine, softened**

1 **can (14½ ounces) whole peeled tomatoes, cut up**

1½ **pounds fresh tomatoes, thinly sliced**

1 **cup lowfat cottage or ricotta cheese**

¼ **cup olive or vegetable oil**

¾ **teaspoon LAWRY'S® Seasoned Salt**

½ **teaspoon dried oregano, crushed**

½ **teaspoon LAWRY'S® Garlic Powder with Parsley**

½ **cup Parmesan cheese**

Spread bread slices with margarine; cut into large cubes. Arrange on jelly-roll pan. Toast in 350°F oven about 7 minutes. Place ½ of cubes in greased 13×9×2-inch baking dish. Drain canned tomatoes, reserving liquid. Top bread cubes with ½ of fresh tomato slices, ½ reserved tomato liquid, ½ of cottage cheese, ½ of oil, ½ of canned tomatoes, ½ of Seasoned Salt, ½ of oregano and ½ of Garlic Powder with Parsley. Repeat layers. Sprinkle with Parmesan cheese. Bake, covered, in 350°F oven 40 minutes. Uncover and bake 5 minutes longer to brown top.

Makes 8 to 10 servings

Presentation: Sprinkle with parsley. Serve with any grilled or baked meat, fish or poultry entrée.

Simply Green Beans

1 **pound fresh green beans, ends removed and cut in half crosswise**

1 **tablespoon IMPERIAL® Margarine, melted**

3 **tablespoons coarsely grated Romano cheese**

¼ **to ½ teaspoon LAWRY'S® Seasoned Pepper**

¼ **teaspoon LAWRY'S® Garlic Powder with Parsley**

In large saucepan, bring 2 quarts of water to a boil; add beans. After water has returned to a boil, cook beans 4 minutes. Drain; run under cold water. In medium skillet, melt margarine; sauté green beans 3 minutes or until tender. Add remaining ingredients; toss well. Serve hot.

Makes 4 servings

Hint: Great accompaniment to roast chicken or fresh fish fillets.

Microwave Directions: In microwave-safe shallow dish, place green beans and ¼ cup water. Cover with plastic wrap, venting one corner. Microwave on HIGH 14 to 16 minutes, stirring after 7 minutes; drain. Add margarine, Seasoned Pepper and Garlic Powder with Parsley. Stir; let stand covered 1 minute. Sprinkle with cheese.

Cheddar Sesame Garden Vegetables

½ **cup *undiluted* CARNATION® Evaporated Skimmed Milk**

1 **tablespoon plus 2 teaspoons all-purpose flour**

¼ **cup water**

1 **teaspoon country Dijon-style mustard**

½ **cup (2 ounces) shredded reduced-fat Cheddar cheese**

3 **to 4 cups cooked fresh vegetables,* drained**

1 **tablespoons toasted sesame seeds**

In small saucepan, whisk small amount of milk into flour. Stir in remaining milk with water and mustard. Cook over medium heat, stirring constantly, until mixture comes to a boil and thickens. Add cheese; stir until melted. Serve over vegetables. Sprinkle with sesame seeds.

Makes 2 servings

*Your choice of carrots, summer squash, broccoli, cauliflower or asparagus.

Tomato-Bread Casserole

Saltillo Zucchini

Ratatouille

2 cloves garlic, finely
   chopped
¼ cup vegetable oil
1 medium eggplant, pared
   and cut into cubes
   (about 4 to 6 cups)
2 small zucchini, cut into
   ½-inch slices
   (about 2 cups)
1 large sweet onion, thinly
   sliced
1 medium green bell pepper,
   cut into ¼-inch strips
1 (8-ounce) can stewed
   tomatoes
2 tablespoons chopped fresh
   parsley
4 teaspoons WYLER'S® or
   STEERO® Beef-Flavor
   Instant Bouillon *or*
   4 Beef-Flavor Bouillon
   Cubes
1 tablespoon flour
1 teaspoon basil leaves
1 teaspoon oregano leaves

In large saucepan or Dutch oven,
cook garlic in oil until lightly
browned. Add remaining
ingredients; cover and simmer 15
minutes. Uncover and stir; cook
10 minutes longer or until
vegetables are tender.
Refrigerate leftovers.

Makes 6 servings

Squash Olé

6 medium zucchini
1 can (12 ounces) whole
   kernel corn, drained
2 eggs, beaten
¼ cup chopped chives
2 teaspoons LAWRY'S®
   Seasoned Salt
½ cup (2 ounces) grated
   sharp Cheddar cheese
   Paprika

In large saucepan, cook zucchini
in boiling water to cover 5
minutes. Cut in half lengthwise;
remove pulp. Chop pulp into
small pieces, then combine with
corn, eggs, chives and Seasoned
Salt. Pour mixture into zucchini
shells. Place in 2-quart oblong
baking dish. Sprinkle with
cheese and paprika. Bake,
uncovered, in 350°F oven 30
minutes or until cheese melts.

Makes 6 servings

Presentation: Serve with grilled
chicken or fish entrées.

Saltillo Zucchini

½ cup chopped onion
¼ cup sliced celery
2 tablespoons vegetable oil
3½ cups cubed zucchini
1 medium tomato, chopped
¾ teaspoon LAWRY'S® Garlic
   Salt
½ teaspoon LAWRY'S®
   Seasoned Pepper
¼ teaspoon dried oregano,
   crushed

In medium skillet, sauté onion
and celery in oil 5 minutes. Add
remaining ingredients. Bring to
a boil; reduce heat and simmer,
covered, 10 minutes.

Makes 4 servings

Presentation: Serve with any
entrée and fresh bread.

Ratatouille

Pecan-Stuffed Squash

1 (13¾-fluid ounce) can
COLLEGE INN® Beef or
Chicken Broth
2 small acorn squash, halved
and seeded
⅓ cup BLUE BONNET® Margarine
2 cups dry herb-seasoned
stuffing mix
1 (2-ounce) package
PLANTERS® Pecan Pieces
⅓ cup seedless raisins

Reserve ⅔ cup broth; pour remaining broth into shallow baking dish. Place squash cut-side down in broth. Bake at 400°F for 25 to 35 minutes. In medium saucepan, over medium-high heat, heat reserved broth and margarine until margarine melts; stir in stuffing mix, pecans and raisins. Turn squash over, cut-side up; spoon stuffing into squash cavities. Bake 20 minutes more or until squash is done, basting with broth after 10 minutes. *Makes 4 servings.*

Microwave: Reserve ⅔ cup broth. In 2-quart microwave-proof oblong dish, place squash cut-side down in remaining broth. Microwave, uncovered, on HIGH (100% power) for 6 to 7 minutes. In 1-quart microwave-proof bowl, place reserved broth and margarine. Microwave, uncovered, on HIGH for 1 to 2 minutes until margarine melts. Stir in stuffing mix, pecans and raisins. Turn squash over, cut-side up; spoon stuffing into squash cavities. Microwave, uncovered, on HIGH for 5 to 6 minutes until stuffing is heated through and squash is done. Let stand 5 minutes before serving.

Pecan-Stuffed Squash

Golden Squash Bake

8 cups sliced yellow crookneck
squash, cooked and drained
6 slices bacon, cooked and
crumbled
2 eggs
1 cup BORDEN® or MEADOW
GOLD® Cottage Cheese
2 tablespoons flour
2 teaspoons WYLER'S® or
STEERO® Chicken-Flavor
Instant Bouillon
1 cup (4 ounces) shredded
sharp Cheddar cheese

Preheat oven to 350°. In large bowl, combine eggs, cottage cheese, flour and bouillon. Add squash; mix well.

Turn into greased 12×7-inch baking dish. Top with Cheddar cheese and bacon. Bake 20 to 25 minutes. Let stand 5 minutes before serving. Refrigerate leftovers.
Makes 6 to 8 servings.

Southern-Style Squash and Okra

2 small onions, sliced and
separated into rings
3 medium crookneck squash,
cut into ¼-inch slices
1 package (10 ounces) frozen
whole okra, thawed and cut
into bite-size pieces
2 tablespoons butter or
margarine
1 clove garlic, minced
1 teaspoon salt
⅛ teaspoon pepper
½ teaspoon dried thyme,
crushed
1 tablespoon lemon juice
¼ cup grated Cheddar cheese
(1 ounce)

Place onion slices, squash and okra on 24×18-inch piece of heavy-duty foil. Dot with butter. Sprinkle with garlic,

salt, pepper, thyme and lemon juice. Fold and seal foil edges tightly. Grill packet, on covered grill, over medium-hot **KINGSFORD® Charcoal Briquets** 25 to 30 minutes or until tender, turning packet over once. To serve, unwrap foil packet and sprinkle with Cheddar cheese.
Makes 4 to 6 servings.

Creamy Baked Mashed Potatoes

1 envelope LIPTON® Recipe
Secrets Vegetable Recipe
Soup Mix
4 cups hot mashed potatoes*
1 cup shredded Cheddar or
Swiss cheese (about
4 ounces)
½ cup chopped green onions
(optional)
1 egg, slightly beaten
⅛ teaspoon pepper

Preheat oven to 375°.
In lightly greased 1½-quart casserole, thoroughly combine all ingredi-

ents except ¼ cup cheese. Bake 40 minutes. Top with remaining cheese and bake an additional 5 minutes or until cheese is melted.
Makes about 8 servings.

*Do not use salt when preparing hot mashed potatoes.

Microwave Directions: In lightly greased 1½-quart casserole, thoroughly combine all ingredients except ¼ cup cheese. Microwave covered at HIGH (Full Power), turning casserole occasionally, 7 minutes or until heated through. Top with remaining cheese, then let stand covered 5 minutes.

Crisp Onion-Roasted Potatoes

    1 envelope LIPTON® Recipe
      Secrets Onion or Onion-
      Mushroom Recipe Soup Mix
    ½ cup olive or vegetable oil
    ¼ cup butter or margarine,
      melted
    1 teaspoon thyme leaves
      (optional)
    1 teaspoon marjoram leaves
      (optional)
    ¼ teaspoon pepper
    2 pounds all-purpose potatoes,
      cut into quarters

Preheat oven to 450°.
   In shallow baking or roasting pan, thoroughly blend all ingredients except potatoes. Add potatoes and turn to coat thoroughly. Bake, stirring potatoes occasionally, 60 minutes or until potatoes are tender and golden brown. Garnish, if desired, with chopped parsley.
Makes about 8 servings.

Chinese Spinach

    3 tablespoons CRISCO® Oil
    1 tablespoon soy sauce
    1 teaspoon lime juice
    ½ teaspoon sugar
    ⅛ teaspoon pepper
    1 clove garlic, minced
    ½ cup diagonally sliced green
      onion, 1-inch slices
   12 ounces fresh spinach,
      trimmed, washed and torn
      into bite-size pieces
    ¼ cup sliced water chestnuts
    1 jar (2 ounces) sliced pimiento,
      drained

Heat Crisco® Oil, soy sauce, lime juice, sugar and pepper in large skillet. Add garlic. Stir-fry over medium-high heat about 1 minute, or until garlic is light brown. Add onion. Stir-fry 1 minute. Add spinach, water chestnuts and pimiento. Stir-fry 2 to 3 minutes longer, or until spinach is tender.
4 to 6 servings.

Spinach Almond Casserole

    1 recipe Sesame Vegetable
      Topping (page 330)
    2 packages (10 ounces each)
      frozen chopped spinach,
      thawed
    2 tablespoons CRISCO® Oil
    ¼ cup chopped onion
    2 tablespoons chopped celery
    2 tablespoons all-purpose flour
    1 teaspoon salt
    ½ teaspoon dried dill weed
    ⅛ teaspoon pepper
    1 cup half-and-half
    1 egg, slightly beaten
    3 tablespoons chopped almonds

Crisp Onion-Roasted Potatoes

Prepare Sesame Vegetable Topping as directed. Set aside. Preheat oven to 325°F.
   Press excess moisture from spinach. Set aside.
   Heat Crisco® Oil in medium saucepan. Add onion and celery. Sauté over moderate heat until tender. Remove from heat. Stir in flour, salt, dill weed and pepper. Return to heat. Blend in half-and-half. Cook, stirring constantly, until bubbly. Remove from heat. Blend in egg. Stir in spinach and almonds. Transfer to lightly oiled 1-quart casserole. Sprinkle with Sesame Vegetable Topping. Bake at 325°F, 35 to 40 minutes, or until hot and topping is light brown.
6 to 8 servings.

Saucy Garden Patch Vegetables

    1 can (11 ounces) condensed
      Cheddar cheese soup
    ½ cup sour cream
    ¼ cup milk
    ½ teaspoon DURKEE® Seasoned
      Salt
    1 bag (16 ounces) frozen
      vegetable combination
      (broccoli, corn, red pepper),
      thawed and drained
    1 bag (16 ounces) frozen
      vegetable combination
      (brussels sprouts, carrots,
      cauliflower), thawed and
      drained
    1 cup (4 ounces) shredded
      Cheddar cheese
    1 can (2.8 ounces) DURKEE®
      French Fried Onions

Preheat oven to 375°. In large bowl, combine soup, sour cream, milk, seasoned salt, vegetables, ½ cup cheese and ½ can French Fried Onions. Spoon into 8×12-inch baking dish. Bake, covered, at 375° for 40 minutes or until vegetables are done. Top with remaining cheese and onions; bake, uncovered, 3 minutes or until onions are golden brown.
Makes 8 to 10 servings.

Microwave Directions: Prepare vegetable mixture as above; spoon into 8×12-inch microwave-safe dish. Cook, covered, on HIGH 10 to 12 minutes or until vegetables are done. Stir vegetables halfway through cooking time. Top with remaining cheese and onions; cook, uncovered, 1 minute or until cheese melts. Let stand for 5 minutes.

Sweet 'n Sour Stir Fry

Sweet 'n Sour Stir Fry

2 tablespoons oil
1 cup thinly sliced carrots
1 cup snow peas (about
    4 ounces)
1 small green pepper, cut into
    chunks
1 cup sliced water chestnuts
1 medium tomato, cut into
    wedges
½ cup sliced cucumber, halved
¾ cup WISH-BONE® Sweet 'n
    Spicy French Dressing
2 tablespoons brown sugar
2 teaspoons soy sauce

In medium skillet, heat oil and cook carrots, snow peas and green pepper over medium heat, stirring frequently, 5 minutes or until crisp-tender. Add water chestnuts, tomato, cucumber and sweet 'n spicy French dressing blended with brown sugar and soy sauce. Simmer covered 5 minutes or until vegetables are tender. Top, if desired, with sesame seeds. *Makes about 6 servings.*
   Note: Also terrific with Wish-Bone® Lite Sweet 'n Spicy French, Russian or Lite Russian Dressing.

Sesame Vegetable Topping

2 tablespoons CRISCO® Oil
2 tablespoons finely chopped
    onion
2 teaspoons sesame seeds
½ cup buttery round cracker
    crumbs

Heat Crisco® Oil in small skillet. Add onion. Sauté over moderate heat until tender-crisp. Add sesame seeds. Cook, stirring constantly, 1 minute. Remove from heat. Stir in cracker crumbs. Use as a topping for vegetable dishes. *About ½ cup.*

Almondine Butter Sauce

½ cup sliced almonds
⅓ cup butter or margarine
¼ cup REALEMON® Lemon Juice
    from Concentrate

In small skillet, over medium low heat, cook almonds in margarine until golden; remove from heat. Stir in ReaLemon® brand. Serve warm over cooked vegetables or fish. *Makes ⅔ cup.*

Easy "Hollandaise" Sauce

½ lb. VELVEETA® Pasteurized
    Process Cheese Spread,
    cubed
¼ cup milk
¼ teaspoon paprika
1 egg, beaten
2 teaspoons lemon juice

Combine VELVEETA® Pasteurized Process Cheese Spread, milk and paprika in saucepan; stir over low heat until process cheese spread is melted. Stir small amount of hot mixture into egg; return to hot mixture. Cook, stirring constantly, over low heat until thickened. Stir in juice. Serve over hot cooked vegetables or fish. *1¼ cups.*

Preparation time: 5 minutes
Cooking time: 15 minutes

   Microwave: Microwave process cheese spread, milk and paprika in 1-quart microwave-safe bowl. Microwave on High 2½ to 3½ minutes or until process cheese spread is melted, stirring every minute. Stir small amount of hot mixture into egg; return to hot mixture. Microwave on Medium (50%) 1 to 1½ minutes or until thickened, stirring every 30 seconds. Stir in juice. Serve over hot cooked vegetables or fish.

Pronto Zucchini

4 cups mushroom slices
4 cups zucchini slices
¼ cup PARKAY® Margarine
½ cup spaghetti sauce
¼ lb. VELVEETA® Pasteurized
    Process Cheese Spread,
    cubed
2 teaspoons dried oregano
    leaves, crushed

In large skillet, saute vegetables in margarine until crisp-tender. Drain. Reduce heat to low. Add sauce, VELVEETA® Pasteurized Process Cheese Spread and oregano; stir until process cheese spread is melted. *4 to 6 servings.*

Preparation time: 10 minutes
Cooking time: 15 minutes

   Variation: Substitute 2 tablespoons chopped fresh oregano leaves for dried oregano leaves.

Cheese & Bacon Potato Bake

1 (13¾-fluid ounce) can
  COLLEGE INN® Chicken or
  Beef Broth
5 medium potatoes, pared and
  thinly sliced (about 5 cups)
1 large onion, thinly sliced
6 slices bacon
3 tablespoons all-purpose flour
1 cup shredded sharp Cheddar
  cheese (4 ounces)

In medium saucepan, over medium-high heat, heat broth to a boil; reduce heat. Add potatoes and onion; cover and simmer 5 minutes. Drain, reserving 1½ cups broth. In skillet, over medium-high heat, cook bacon until crisp. Remove and crumble bacon; pour off all but 3 tablespoons drippings. Blend flour into reserved drippings. Gradually add reserved broth; cook over medium heat, stirring constantly, until thickened. Stir in cheese until melted. In greased 2-quart baking dish, layer ⅓ each potato-onion mixture, sauce and bacon. Repeat layers twice. Bake at 400°F for 35 minutes or until done.
Makes 6 servings.

Classic Spanish Rice

1½ cups Original MINUTE® Rice
1 onion, cut into thin wedges
1 garlic clove, minced
¼ cup (½ stick) margarine or
  butter
1½ cups water
1 can (8 oz.) tomato sauce
1 small green pepper, diced
1 teaspoon salt
½ teaspoon prepared mustard
  (optional)
  Sliced stuffed green olives

Cook and stir rice, onion and garlic in hot margarine in large skillet over medium heat, stirring frequently until mixture is lightly browned. Stir in remaining ingredients except olives. Bring to a full boil. Cover; remove from heat. Let stand 5 minutes. Fluff with fork. Garnish with olives. Serve with chicken or your favorite main dish.
Makes 4 servings.

Galbani® Fontina Potato Surprise

2½ pounds potatoes
3 tablespoons butter or
  margarine, melted
¼ cup freshly grated imported
  Parmesan cheese
1 egg
1 egg white
⅛ teaspoon salt
⅛ teaspoon ground nutmeg
4 tablespoons fine dry bread
  crumbs, divided
8 ounces GALBANI® Fontina, cut
  into chunks
¼ cup freshly grated sharp
  Provolone cheese
¼ pound prosciutto, cut into
  small pieces
2 tablespoons butter or
  margarine, cut into small
  pieces

Cook potatoes in boiling water in large saucepan over medium-low heat until tender. Drain. Cool slightly; pare. Press potatoes through food mill or mash until smooth. Combine potatoes, melted butter, Parmesan cheese, egg, egg white, salt and nutmeg in large bowl until smooth; set aside.

Sprinkle ½ of the bread crumbs in well-buttered 9-inch round baking dish. Tilt dish to coat. Spread about ½ of the potato mixture on bottom and sides of dish. Combine Fontina, Provolone and prosciutto in small bowl. Sprinkle over potato mixture in dish. Cover with remaining potato mixture; sprinkle with remaining bread crumbs. Dot with pieces of butter. Bake in preheated 350°F oven 40 minutes or until thin crust forms. Let stand 5 minutes. Invert baking dish onto serving plate, tapping gently to remove. Serve immediately.
Makes 4 to 6 servings.

*Favorite recipe from **Bel Paese Sales Co., Inc.***

Cheese & Bacon Potato Bake

Skewered Grilled Potatoes

Skewered Grilled Potatoes

2 pounds red potatoes, quartered
⅓ cup cold water
½ cup MIRACLE WHIP® Salad Dressing
¼ cup dry white wine or chicken broth
2 teaspoons dried rosemary leaves, crushed
1 teaspoon garlic powder

• Place potatoes and water in 2-quart microwave-safe casserole; cover.

• Microwave on HIGH 12 to 15 minutes or until tender, stirring after 8 minutes. Drain.

• Mix remaining ingredients until well blended. Stir in potatoes. Refrigerate 1 hour. Drain, reserving marinade.

• Arrange potatoes on skewers. Place on grill over hot coals (coals will be glowing). Grill, covered, 6 to 8 minutes or until potatoes are tender and golden brown, brushing occasionally with reserved marinade and turning after 4 minutes.
Makes 8 servings

Prep time: 20 minutes plus refrigerating
Grilling time: 8 minutes
Microwave cooking time: 15 minutes

Monterey Potatoes

4 cups peeled and sliced russet potatoes
¾ cup sliced red bell pepper
¼ cup chopped shallots
1 tablespoon all-purpose flour
1 teaspoon LAWRY'S® Garlic Salt
½ teaspoon dried basil, crushed
¼ teaspoon dry mustard
½ cup milk
1 cup (4 ounces) grated Monterey Jack cheese

In lightly greased 8-inch square microwave-safe baking dish, combine potatoes, bell pepper and shallots. Cover with plastic wrap, venting one corner. Microwave on HIGH 10 to 12 minutes, stirring every 4 minutes. Set aside and keep covered. In 2-cup glass measure, combine flour, Garlic Salt, basil and mustard; blend well. Gradually stir in milk. Microwave on HIGH 3 minutes, stirring after 1½ minutes. Add cheese; stir until cheese melts. Pour over potato mixture and toss to coat.
Makes 4 servings

Presentation: Serve as a side dish for most entrées.

Crispened New Potatoes

1½ lbs. very small, scrubbed new potatoes (about 12)
½ cup QUAKER® Oat Bran™ hot cereal, uncooked
2 tablespoons grated Parmesan cheese
1 tablespoon snipped fresh parsley *or* 1 teaspoon dried parsley flakes
½ teaspoon snipped fresh dill *or* ½ teaspoon dried dill weed
½ teaspoon paprika
¼ cup skim milk
1 egg white, slightly beaten
1 tablespoon margarine, melted

Heat oven to 400°F. Lightly spray 11×7-inch dish with no-stick cooking spray or oil lightly. Cook whole potatoes in boiling water 15 minutes. Drain; rinse in cold water.

In shallow dish, combine oat bran, cheese, parsley, dill and paprika. In another shallow dish, combine milk and egg white. Coat each potato in oat bran mixture; shake off excess. Dip into egg mixture, then coat again with oat bran mixture. Place into prepared dish; drizzle with margarine. Cover; bake 10 minutes. Uncover; bake an additional 10 minutes or until potatoes are tender.
Makes 4 servings

Colorful Cauliflower Bake

- 1 cup KELLOGG'S® ALL-BRAN® cereal
- 2 tablespoons margarine, melted
- ¼ teaspoon garlic salt
- ¼ cup flour
- ½ teaspoon salt
- ⅛ teaspoon white pepper
- 1⅓ cups skim milk
- 1 chicken bouillon cube
- 1 package (16 ounces) frozen, cut cauliflower, thawed, well drained
- ½ cup sliced green onions
- 2 tablespoons drained, chopped pimento

1. Combine Kellogg's® All-Bran® cereal, margarine and garlic salt; set aside.

2. In 3-quart saucepan, combine flour, salt and pepper. Gradually add milk, mixing until smooth, using a wire whip if necessary. Add bouillon cube. Cook, stirring constantly, over medium heat until bubbly and thickened. Remove from heat.

3. Add cauliflower, onions and pimento, mixing until combined. Spread evenly in 1½-quart serving dish. Sprinkle with cereal mixture.

4. Bake at 350° about 20 minutes or until thoroughly heated and sauce is bubbly.
Makes 6 servings

Note: 3½ cups fresh cauliflower flowerets, cooked crisp-tender, may be substituted for frozen cauliflower.

Savory Grilled Potatoes in Foil

- ½ cup MIRACLE WHIP® Salad Dressing
- 3 garlic cloves, minced
- ½ teaspoon paprika
- ¼ teaspoon each: salt, pepper
- 3 baking potatoes, cut into ¼-inch slices
- 1 large onion, sliced

• Mix salad dressing and seasonings in large bowl until well blended. Stir in potatoes and onions to coat.

• Divide potato mixture evenly among six 12-inch square pieces of heavy-duty foil. Seal each to form packet.

• Place foil packets on grill over medium-hot coals (coals will have slight glow). Grill, covered, 25 to 30 minutes or until potatoes are tender.
Makes 6 servings

Prep time: 15 minutes
Grilling time: 30 minutes

Dole® Hawaiian Baked Potatoes

- 1 can (8 ounces) DOLE® Crushed Pineapple in Juice
- 2 baking potatoes, baked*
- ½ cup pasteurized process cheese spread or canned cheese soup, heated
- ½ cup chopped ham or 2 slices cooked, chopped bacon
- 2 tablespoons chopped DOLE® Green Bell Pepper
- 2 tablespoons chopped DOLE® Green Onion

• Drain pineapple; save juice for a beverage.

• Split and open baked potatoes.

• Combine remaining ingredients in small bowl. Spoon over potatoes.   *Makes 2 servings*

*Prick potatoes with fork. Microwave on HIGH 10 to 15 minutes until fork inserts easily.

Preparation Time: 5 minutes
Cook Time: 15 minutes

Savory Grilled Potatoes in Foil

Italian-Style Roasted Peppers

Confetti Fried Rice

1 can (20 ounces) DOLE®
   Pineapple Chunks in Juice
3½ teaspoons vegetable oil
1 egg, beaten
1 carrot, shredded
1 clove garlic, pressed
4 cups cooked rice
1 can (8 ounces) water
   chestnuts, chopped
4 ounces cooked ham, julienne-
   cut
½ cup frozen peas, thawed
⅓ cup chopped green onions
¼ cup soy sauce
¼ teaspoon ground ginger

Drain pineapple. Heat ½ teaspoon oil in wok or large skillet over low heat. Add egg and swirl around bottom of wok until egg sets in 6-inch pancake. Remove and cool. Cut into ⅛-inch strips. Heat remaining 3 teaspoons oil in wok over high heat. Stir-fry carrot and garlic about 1 minute or until tender. Add rice, stirring until grains separate. Reduce heat slightly. Stir in pineapple, water chestnuts, ham, peas, onions, soy sauce and ginger; increase heat and heat through. Gently stir in egg strips.
Makes 6 servings.

Potato Pancakes

4 medium white potatoes,
   peeled and coarsely
   shredded
1 small onion, grated
1 egg
⅓ cup all-purpose flour
1½ teaspoons salt
⅛ teaspoon pepper
2 tablespoons CRISCO® Oil

Combine potatoes, onion, egg, flour, salt and pepper in medium mixing bowl. Mix well. Heat Crisco® Oil in large skillet. Spoon ¼ cup potato mixture into skillet for each of 4 pancakes. Flatten with spatula. Cook over moderate heat 10 to 15 minutes, or until golden brown, turning over once. Drain on paper towels. Add additional Crisco® Oil, if necessary. Repeat with remaining potato mixture.
6 to 8 servings.

Note: To keep shredded potatoes from turning brown, place in cold water until ready to use. Drain thoroughly and pat dry between paper towels before using.

Italian-Style Roasted Peppers

6 large red, green or yellow
   peppers
1 cup (8 ounces) WISH-BONE®
   Italian Dressing
½ cup chopped fresh basil
   leaves*
⅛ teaspoon pepper

In large aluminum-foil-lined baking pan or on broiler rack, place red peppers. Broil, turning occasionally, 20 minutes or until peppers turn almost completely black. Immediately place in paper bag; close bag and let cool about 30 minutes. Under cold running water, peel off skin, then remove stems and seeds; slice into long thick strips.

In large bowl, combine peppers with remaining ingredients. Cover and marinate in refrigerator, stirring occasionally, at least 4 hours. For best flavor, serve peppers at room temperature and, if desired, with olives, mozzarella cheese and tomatoes.
Makes about 3 cups roasted peppers.

   Substitution: Use 1 tablespoon dried basil leaves.

   Note: Also terrific with Wish-Bone® Robusto Italian or Lite Italian Dressing.

Homespun Scalloped Potatoes

1 8-ounce package
   PHILADELPHIA BRAND®
   Cream Cheese, cubed
1¼ cups milk
½ teaspoon salt
⅛ teaspoon pepper
4 cups thin potato slices
2 tablespoons chopped chives

In large saucepan, combine cream cheese, milk, salt and pepper; stir over low heat until smooth. Add potatoes and chives; mix lightly. Spoon into 1½-quart casserole; cover. Bake at 350°, 1 hour and 10 minutes or until potatoes are tender. Stir before serving.
6 servings.

   Make Ahead: Prepare as directed except for baking. Cover; refrigerate overnight. When ready to serve, bake as directed.

Garden Medley Rice

**1 can (13¾ oz.) ready-to-serve
   chicken broth**
**2 cups assorted vegetables
   (broccoli florets, sliced
   yellow squash, peas, grated
   carrot)**
1 teaspoon onion flakes
**1 teaspoon snipped fresh
   rosemary or ½ teaspoon
   dried rosemary leaves**
¼ teaspoon garlic powder
**1½ cups Original MINUTE® Rice
   Freshly ground pepper
   (optional)**

Stir together broth, vegetables, onion flakes, rosemary and garlic powder in saucepan and bring to a full boil. Stir in rice. Cover; remove from heat. Let stand 5 minutes. Fluff with fork and sprinkle with pepper. Serve with chicken cutlets or your favorite main dish.
Makes 4 servings.

Microwave Directions: Stir together all ingredients except pepper in microwavable bowl. Cover with plastic wrap and cook at HIGH 4 minutes. Stir; cover and cook at HIGH 3 to 5 minutes longer. Stir again; cover and cook at HIGH 3 minutes. Let stand 5 minutes. Fluff with fork and sprinkle with pepper. Serve with chicken cutlets or your favorite main dish.
Makes 4 servings.

New Year Fried Rice

3 strips bacon, diced
**¾ cup chopped green onions
   and tops**
⅓ cup diced red bell pepper
¼ cup frozen green peas, thawed
1 egg, beaten
4 cups cold, cooked rice
**2 tablespoons KIKKOMAN® Soy
   Sauce**

Cook bacon in wok or large skillet over medium heat until crisp. Add green onions, red pepper and peas; stir-fry 1 minute. Add egg and scramble. Stir in rice and cook until heated, gently separating grains. Add soy sauce; cook and stir until heated through. Serve immediately.
Makes 6 to 8 servings.

Risotto with Vegetables

**2 tablespoons butter or
   margarine**
2 tablespoons vegetable oil
1 medium onion, chopped
1 clove garlic, minced
1 cup sliced mushrooms
**1 cup uncooked Arborio or long
   grain rice***
Pinch saffron (optional)
**2 cups hot chicken broth,
   divided**
**¼ teaspoon TABASCO® pepper
   sauce**
1 to 1½ cups hot water, divided
**1 package (9 ounces) frozen
   artichoke hearts, cooked
   and drained**
**½ cup fresh or canned roasted
   red peppers, coarsely
   chopped****

In medium skillet heat butter and oil; cook onion, garlic and mushrooms 5 minutes or until onions are translucent. Add rice; cook 1 to 2 minutes or until partly translucent. Stir in saffron, if desired.

Add ½ cup hot broth and Tabasco® sauce; stir constantly until rice absorbs broth. Add remaining broth and hot water, ½ cup at a time; stir constantly from bottom and sides of pan and wait until rice just begins to dry out before adding more liquid. Cook and stir until rice is tender but firm to the bite, and is the consistency of creamy rice pudding. (The total amount of liquid used will vary. Watch rice carefully to ensure proper consistency.) Total cooking time is about 30 minutes. Stir in artichokes and roasted peppers. Serve with additional Tabasco® sauce, if desired.
Makes 6 servings.

*Arborio rice gives the best results. Do not use converted rice.

**To roast peppers, hold over source of heat with a fork until skin blisters. Cool slightly; peel and chop.

Citrus Candied Sweet Potatoes

**2 (16- or 18-ounce) cans sweet
   potatoes, drained**
**1¼ cups firmly packed light brown
   sugar**
2 tablespoons cornstarch
¾ cup orange juice
**¼ cup REALEMON® Lemon Juice
   from Concentrate**
**2 tablespoons margarine or
   butter, melted**

Preheat oven to 350°. In 2-quart shallow baking dish, arrange sweet potatoes. In medium bowl, combine sugar and cornstarch; add orange juice, ReaLemon® brand and margarine. Pour over sweet potatoes. Bake 50 to 55 minutes, basting occasionally with sauce.
Makes 6 to 8 servings.

Microwave: Arrange sweet potatoes as above. Increase cornstarch to 3 tablespoons. In 1-quart glass measure, combine sugar and cornstarch. Add orange juice, ReaLemon® brand and margarine. Cook on 100% power (high) 5 to 8 minutes until slightly thickened, stirring every 2 minutes. Pour over sweet potatoes; cook on 100% power (high) 8 minutes, basting after 4 minutes. Let stand 2 minutes before serving.

Garden Medley Rice

Kahlúa® Candied Yams

**4 medium-sized yams,
   cooked* *or* 1 can
   (1 lb. 3 oz.) yams
¼ cup butter
⅓ cup firmly packed brown
   sugar
¼ cup KAHLÚA®**

Cut yams in serving size pieces.
In heavy skillet, melt butter with
sugar. Add Kahlúa®; cook 1
minute. Add yams; turn until
brown on all sides. Cover. Reduce
heat; cook about 15 minutes.
Turn yams once more before
serving.

Makes 4 to 6 servings

*In large saucepan, boil yams
until tender but still firm.
Remove from pan; let cool
slightly. Peel.

Maple Glazed Sweet Potatoes

**1½ pounds sweet potatoes or
   yams, cooked, peeled
   and quartered
½ cup CARY'S®, MAPLE
   ORCHARDS® or
   MACDONALD'S™ Pure
   Maple Syrup
½ cup orange juice
3 tablespoons margarine or
   butter, melted
1 tablespoon cornstarch
1 teaspoon grated orange
   peel**

Preheat oven to 350°F. Arrange
sweet potatoes in 1½-quart
shallow baking dish. Combine
remaining ingredients; pour over
potatoes. Bake 40 minutes or
until hot and sauce is thickened,
basting frequently. Refrigerate
leftovers.

Makes 6 to 8 servings

Confetti Corn

**6 medium tomatoes
2 tablespoons IMPERIAL®
   Margarine
⅓ cup chopped green onions
⅓ cup chopped red bell
   pepper
1 package (10 ounces) frozen
   corn, thawed
2 tablespoons vinegar
2 tablespoons chopped fresh
   cilantro
1 teaspoon LAWRY'S® Garlic
   Salt**

Cut ¼ inch off top of tomatoes.
Hollow out, reserving pulp. Chop
pulp into chunks; set aside. In
medium skillet, melt margarine
and sauté green onions and bell
pepper. Add corn, vinegar,
tomato pulp, cilantro and Garlic
Salt; blend well. Heat 5 minutes
or until flavors are blended.
Place tomato shells on baking
dish and heat in 350°F oven 5
minutes. Spoon tomato-corn
mixture into shells.

Makes 6 servings

Presentation: Serve on a lettuce-
lined platter as a side dish with
grilled chicken, fish or beef
entrées.

Easy Mideastern Pilaf

**1½ cups beef broth
1 medium onion, chopped
¼ cup raisins
2 tablespoons margarine or
   butter
1½ cups Original MINUTE®
   Rice
½ cup sliced almonds
2 tablespoon chopped
   parsley**

Combine broth, onion, raisins
and margarine in medium
saucepan. Bring to full boil. Stir
in rice. Cover; remove from heat.
Let stand 5 minutes. Stir in
almonds and parsley. Serve with
kabobs or your favorite main
dish.   *Makes 4 servings*

Oriental Rice Pilaf

**½ cup chopped onion
1 clove garlic, minced
1 tablespoon sesame oil
1¾ cups beef broth
1 cup uncooked rice*
1 tablespoon reduced-
   sodium soy sauce
⅛ to ¼ teaspoon red pepper
   flakes
⅓ cup thinly sliced green
   onions
⅓ cup diced red pepper
2 tablespoons sesame seeds,
   toasted**

Cook onion and garlic in oil in
2- to 3-quart saucepan over
medium heat until onion is
tender. Add broth, rice, soy
sauce, and pepper flakes. Bring
to a boil; stir once or twice.
Reduce heat; cover and simmer
15 minutes or until rice is tender
and liquid is absorbed. Stir
remaining ingredients into
cooked rice; cover and let stand 5
minutes. Fluff with fork.

Makes 6 servings

To microwave: Combine onion,
garlic, and oil in deep 2- to
3-quart microproof baking dish.
Cover and cook on HIGH 2
minutes. Add broth, rice, soy
sauce, and pepper flakes; stir.
Cover and cook on HIGH 5
minutes. Reduce setting to
MEDIUM (50% power) and cook,
covered, 15 minutes or until rice
is tender and liquid is absorbed.
Stir remaining ingredients into
cooked rice; cover and let stand 5
minutes. Fluff with fork.

*Recipe based on regular-milled
long grain white rice.

Favorite recipe from **USA Rice
Council**

Oriental Rice Pilaf

Bacon Pilaf

- **2 tablespoons unsalted margarine or butter**
- **2 medium tomatoes, coarsely chopped**
- **¼ cup sliced green onions**
- **8 slices ARMOUR® Lower Salt Bacon, cooked crisp and crumbled**
- **1 cup uncooked rice**
- **1 teaspoon no salt added chicken-flavor instant bouillon**

Melt margarine in large skillet or saucepan over medium heat. Add tomatoes and green onions; sauté for 2 minutes. Stir in 2 cups water and remaining ingredients. Heat to boiling; reduce heat and cover. Simmer about 20 to 25 minutes, or until liquid is absorbed. Fluff rice with fork before serving. Garnish with parsley, if desired.

Makes 4 to 6 servings

Spicy Monterey Rice

- **2 cups water**
- **1 cup uncooked long grain rice**
- **1 tablespoon WYLER'S® or STEERO® Chicken-Flavor Instant Bouillon *or* 3 Chicken-Flavor Bouillon Cubes**
- **1 (16-ounce) container BORDEN® or MEADOW GOLD® Sour Cream, at room temperature**
- **1½ cups (6 ounces) shredded Colby cheese**
- **1 cup (4 ounces) shredded Monterey Jack cheese**
- **1 (4-ounce) can chopped green chilies, undrained**
- **½ cup chopped red bell pepper**
- **⅛ teaspoon pepper**

Preheat oven to 350°. In medium saucepan, combine water, rice and bouillon; bring to a boil. Reduce heat; cover and simmer 15 minutes or until rice is tender. In large bowl, combine all ingredients except ½ cup Colby cheese; mix well. Turn into buttered 1½-quart baking dish. Bake 20 to 25 minutes. Top with remaining ½ cup cheese; bake 3 minutes longer or until cheese melts. Let stand 5 minutes. Refrigerate leftovers. Garnish as desired.   *Makes 6 servings*

Spicy Thai Rice

- **2 cups water**
- **1 cup uncooked rice***
- **¼ cup chopped green onions**
- **2 fresh red chiles, seeded and chopped**
- **1 tablespoon snipped cilantro**
- **1 tablespoon margarine**
- **1 teaspoon minced fresh ginger root**
- **¾ teaspoon salt**
- **⅛ teaspoon ground turmeric**
- **1 to 2 teaspoons lime juice**
  Chopped roasted peanuts for garnish (optional)
  Red pepper flakes for garnish (optional)

Combine water, rice, onions, chiles, cilantro, margarine, ginger root, salt, and turmeric in 2- to 3-quart saucepan. Bring to a boil; stir once or twice. Reduce heat; cover and simmer 15 minutes or until rice is tender and liquid is absorbed. Stir in lime juice; fluff with fork. Garnish with peanuts and pepper flakes.

Makes 6 servings

*Recipe based on regular-milled long grain rice. For medium grain rice, use 1½ cups water. For brown rice, cook 45 minutes.

Favorite recipe from **USA Rice Council**

Spicy Thai Rice

Arroz Blanco

1 tablespoon margarine
½ cup chopped onion
2 cloves garlic, minced
1 cup uncooked rice*
2 cups chicken broth

Melt margarine in 2- to 3-quart saucepan over medium heat. Add onion and garlic; cook until onion is tender. Add rice and broth. Bring to a boil; stir. Reduce heat; cover and simmer 15 minutes or until rice is tender and liquid is absorbed. Fluff with fork.   *Makes 6 servings*

To microwave: Combine margarine, onion, and garlic in deep 2- to 3-quart microproof baking dish. Cover and cook on HIGH 2 minutes. Stir in rice and broth; cover and cook on HIGH 5 minutes. Reduce setting to MEDIUM (50% power) and cook 15 minutes or until rice is tender and liquid is absorbed. Let stand 5 minutes. Fluff with fork.

*Recipe based on regular-milled long grain white rice.

Tip: Prepare a double batch of Arroz Blanco to have one batch ready for Rice with Tomato and Chiles or Green Rice (recipes follow) later in the week.

*Favorite recipe from **USA Rice Council***

Clockwise from top: Arroz Blanco, Green Rice and Rice with Tomato and Chiles

Rice with Tomato and Chiles

1 green pepper, diced
½ cup chopped onion
1 jalapeño pepper, chopped
1 tablespoon olive oil
1 recipe Arroz Blanco
1 can (14½ ounces) whole tomatoes, drained and chopped
⅛ teaspoon dried oregano leaves
2 tablespoons snipped cilantro for garnish

Cook green pepper, onion, and jalapeño pepper in oil in large skillet over medium-high heat until tender crisp. Stir in rice mixture, tomatoes, and oregano; cook 5 minutes longer. Garnish with cilantro.

Makes 6 servings

To microwave: Combine green pepper, onion, jalapeño pepper, and oil in 2- to 3-quart microproof baking dish. Cook on HIGH 3 to 4 minutes. Add rice mixture, tomatoes, and oregano; cover with waxed paper and cook on HIGH 3 to 4 minutes, stirring after 2 minutes. Garnish with cilantro.

Tip: To reduce the heat level of jalapeño peppers, scrape and discard the seeds and membranes before chopping.

*Favorite recipe from **USA Rice Council***

Green Rice

2 Anaheim chiles
1 jalapeño pepper
1 tablespoon margarine or olive oil
¼ cup sliced green onions
¼ cup snipped cilantro
1 recipe Arroz Blanco
¼ teaspoon dried oregano leaves

Chop chiles and pepper in food processor or blender until minced but not liquid. Melt margarine in large skillet over low heat. Add chile mixture and cook 1 minute over medium heat. Stir in onions and cilantro; cook 15 to 30 seconds. Add rice mixture and oregano; heat through.

Makes 6 servings

*Favorite recipe from **USA Rice Council***

Pepper Rice

Pepper Rice

    2 teaspoons vegetable oil
    1 teaspoon hot chili oil
    ½ cup diced red pepper
    ½ cup diced yellow pepper
    ½ cup diced green pepper
    2 to 3 cloves fresh garlic,
        minced
    3 cups cooked rice
    ½ teaspoon seasoned salt

Heat oils in large skillet; add peppers and garlic. Cook until tender. Stir in rice and salt. Cook 3 minutes, stirring constantly, until thoroughly heated.

Makes 6 servings

To microwave: Combine oils, peppers, and garlic in 2-quart microproof baking dish. Cook on HIGH 2 to 3 minutes. Add rice and salt; cook on HIGH 2 to 3 minutes or until rice is thoroughly heated.

Tip: Use lemon juice or toothpaste to remove garlic odor from hands after mincing.

Favorite recipe from **USA Rice Council**

Spanish Rice au Gratin

    Vegetable cooking spray
    ½ cup chopped onion
    ½ cup chopped celery
    ⅓ cup chopped green pepper
    1 can (16 ounces) whole
        tomatoes, drained and
        chopped
    1 teaspoon chili powder
    ½ teaspoon Worcestershire
        sauce
    2 cups cooked brown rice
    ½ cup (2 ounces) shredded
        Cheddar cheese

Coat large skillet with cooking spray and place over medium-high heat until hot. Add onion, celery, and green pepper; cook until tender crisp. Add tomatoes, chili powder, and Worcestershire sauce. Stir in rice. Reduce heat; simmer about 5 minutes to blend flavors. Remove from heat. Top with cheese; cover and allow cheese to melt, about 3 minutes.

Makes 4 servings

Tip: Add your favorite canned beans, cooked ground beef, or chicken for a main-dish version.

Favorite recipe from **USA Rice Council**

Antipasto Rice

    1½ cups water
    ½ cup tomato juice
    1 cup uncooked rice*
    1 teaspoon dried basil leaves
    1 teaspoon dried oregano
        leaves
    ½ teaspoon salt (optional)
    1 can (14 ounces) artichoke
        hearts, drained and
        quartered
    1 jar (7 ounces) roasted red
        peppers, drained and
        chopped
    1 can (2¼ ounces) sliced ripe
        olives, drained
    2 tablespoons snipped
        parsley
    2 tablespoons lemon juice
    ½ teaspoon ground black
        pepper
    2 tablespoons grated
        Parmesan cheese

Combine water, tomato juice, rice, basil, oregano, and salt in 2- to 3-quart saucepan. Bring to a boil; stir once or twice. Reduce heat; cover and simmer 15 minutes or until rice is tender and liquid is absorbed. Stir in artichokes, red peppers, olives, parsley, lemon juice, and black pepper. Cook 5 minutes longer or until thoroughly heated. Sprinkle with cheese.

Makes 8 servings

*Recipe based on regular-milled long grain rice. For medium grain rice, use 1¼ cups water and cook for 15 minutes. For parboiled rice, use 1¾ cups water and cook for 20 to 25 minutes. For brown rice, use 1¾ cups water and cook for 45 to 50 minutes.

Favorite recipe from **USA Rice Council**

Antipasto Rice

Spinach Feta Rice

1 cup uncooked rice*
1 cup chicken broth
1 cup water
1 medium onion, chopped
1 cup (about 4 ounces) sliced
    fresh mushrooms
2 cloves garlic, minced
    Vegetable cooking spray
1 tablespoon lemon juice
½ teaspoon dried oregano
    leaves
6 cups shredded fresh
    spinach leaves
    (about ¼ pound)
4 ounces feta cheese,
    crumbled
    Freshly ground black
    pepper
    Chopped pimiento for
    garnish (optional)

Combine rice, broth, and water
in medium saucepan. Bring to a
boil; stir once or twice. Reduce
heat; cover and simmer 15
minutes or until rice is tender
and liquid is absorbed. Cook
onion, mushrooms, and garlic in
large skillet coated with cooking
spray until onion is tender. Stir
in lemon juice and oregano. Add
spinach, cheese, mushroom
mixture, and pepper to rice; toss
lightly until spinach is wilted.
Garnish with pimiento.
Makes 6 servings

*Recipe based on regular-milled
long grain rice.

Favorite recipe from **USA Rice
Council**

Pesto Rice and Vegetables

1½ cups packed basil, arugula,
    watercress, or spinach
    leaves
1 clove garlic
⅓ cup grated Parmesan
    cheese
1 tablespoon olive oil
    Vegetable cooking spray
1½ cups broccoli flowerets
1 cup sliced carrots
3 cups cooked brown or
    white rice

Finely mince basil and garlic in
food processor. Add cheese and
oil; pulse until well combined,
scraping bowl as necessary. Coat
large skillet with cooking spray
and place over medium-high
heat until hot. Cook broccoli and
carrots until tender crisp. Stir in
rice and basil mixture. Serve
immediately.
Makes 6 servings

Favorite recipe from **USA Rice
Council**

Saucy Peas and Rice

1 cup sliced mushrooms
1 tablespoon margarine or
    butter
1 package (10 ounces) BIRDS
    EYE® Green Peas
1 can (10¾ ounces)
    condensed cream of
    mushroom soup
1 cup milk
    Dash of pepper
1½ cups Original MINUTE®
    Rice

Cook and stir mushrooms in hot
margarine in large skillet until
lightly browned. Add peas, soup,
milk and pepper. Bring to boil;
reduce heat, cover and simmer 2
minutes. Stir in rice. Cover;
remove from heat. Let stand 5
minutes. Fluff with fork.
Makes 4 servings

Microwave Directions: Mix
ingredients in microwavable
dish. Cover and cook at HIGH 3
minutes. Stir; cover and cook at
HIGH 6 minutes longer. Fluff
with fork. *Makes 4 servings*

Saucy Peas and Rice

Quick Risotto

2¼ cups chicken broth, divided
1 cup uncooked rice*
  Vegetable cooking spray
½ cup thinly sliced carrots
½ cup thinly sliced yellow squash
½ cup thinly sliced zucchini
¼ cup dry white wine
½ cup grated Parmesan cheese
¼ teaspoon ground white pepper

Combine 1¾ cups broth and rice in 3-quart saucepan. Bring to a boil; stir once or twice. Reduce heat; cover and simmer 15 minutes or until rice is tender and liquid is absorbed. Coat large skillet with cooking spray and place over medium-high heat until hot. Cook carrots, squash, and zucchini 2 to 3 minutes or until tender crisp. Add wine; cook 2 minutes longer. Set aside and keep warm. Add remaining ½ cup broth to hot rice; stir over medium-high heat until broth is absorbed. Stir in cheese, pepper, and reserved vegetables. Serve immediately.
Makes 6 servings

To microwave: Combine rice and 2 cups broth in 2-quart baking dish. Cover and cook on HIGH 5 minutes, then on MEDIUM (50% power) for 15 minutes. Cook carrots, squash, and zucchini in microproof dish coated with cooking spray on HIGH 3 to 4 minutes or until tender crisp; stir after 2 minutes. Combine with remaining ingredients and add to rice. Cook on HIGH 1 to 2 minutes, stirring after 1 minute.

*Recipe based on regular-milled medium grain rice.

Tip: Medium grain rice will yield the best consistency for risottos, but long grain rice can be used.

*Favorite recipe from **USA Rice Council***

Carrots in Orange Rice

1½ cups sliced carrots
½ cup orange juice
⅓ cup raisins (optional)
1 cup Original MINUTE® Rice
½ teaspoon grated orange rind

Cook carrots in medium saucepan with water to cover until tender, about 10 minutes. Drain, reserving ¾ cup cooking liquid. Combine measured liquid, orange juice and raisins in medium saucepan. Bring to boil. Stir in rice and orange rind. Cover; remove from heat. Let stand 5 minutes. Stir in carrots.
Makes 4 servings

Lemon Rice

1 cup uncooked rice*
1 teaspoon margarine (optional)
1 clove garlic, minced
1 teaspoon grated lemon peel
⅛ to ¼ teaspoon ground black pepper
2 cups chicken broth
2 tablespoons snipped fresh parsley

Combine rice, margarine, garlic, lemon peel, pepper, and broth in 2- to 3-quart saucepan. Bring to a boil; stir once or twice. Reduce heat; cover and simmer 15 minutes or until rice is tender and liquid is absorbed. Stir in parsley.   *Makes 6 servings*

To microwave: Combine rice, margarine, garlic, lemon peel, pepper, and broth in deep 2- to 3-quart microproof baking dish. Cover and cook on HIGH 5 minutes. Reduce setting to MEDIUM (50% power) and cook 15 minutes or until rice is tender and liquid is absorbed. Stir in parsley.

*Recipe based on regular-milled long grain white rice.

*Favorite recipe from **USA Rice Council***

Sherried Mushroom Rice

1 garlic clove, minced
1½ tablespoons margarine or butter
2 cups sliced mushrooms
¼ cup chopped red pepper
1 cup chicken broth
¼ cup water
¼ cup dry sherry or chicken broth
2 teaspoons dried minced onion
½ teaspoon salt
1½ cups Original MINUTE® Rice
2 tablespoons grated Parmesan cheese
1 tablespoon chopped parsley

Cook and stir garlic in hot margarine in large skillet 1 minute. Add mushrooms and red pepper; cook, stirring occasionally, 2 minutes.

Add broth, water, sherry, onion flakes and salt. Bring to boil. Stir in rice. Cover; remove from heat. Let stand 5 minutes. Fluff with fork and sprinkle with grated cheese and parsley. Serve with steak or your favorite main dish. Garnish as desired.
Makes 4 servings

Microwave Directions: Cut margarine into pieces. Cook garlic, margarine and mushrooms in microwavable dish at HIGH 2 to 3 minutes. Stir in remaining ingredients except Parmesan cheese and parsley. Cover and cook at HIGH 4 minutes. Fluff with fork and sprinkle with parmesan cheese and parsley. Serve with steak or your favorite main dish.
Makes 4 servings

Lemon Rice

Wild Rice Sauté

- **½ cup sliced, fresh mushrooms**
- **¼ cup chopped green onions**
- **1 clove garlic, minced**
- **2 tablespoons HOLLYWOOD® Safflower Oil**
- **3 cups cooked wild rice**
- **¼ teaspoon salt**
- **¼ teaspoon ground black pepper**
- **¼ teaspoon dried rosemary sprigs**
- **2 tablespoons peach schnapps liqueur**

In a large skillet, sauté mushrooms, onions and garlic in hot oil for 1½ minutes. Add rice, seasonings and peach schnapps; cook 1½ minutes longer, stirring frequently.   *Makes 6 servings*

Almond Brown Rice Stuffing

- **⅓ cup slivered almonds**
- **2 teaspoons margarine**
- **2 medium tart red apples, cored and diced**
- **½ cup chopped onion**
- **½ cup chopped celery**
- **½ teaspoon poultry seasoning**
- **¼ teaspoon dried thyme leaves**
- **¼ teaspoon ground white pepper**
- **3 cups cooked brown rice (cooked in chicken broth)**

Cook almonds in margarine in large skillet over medium-high heat until golden brown. Add apples, onion, celery, poultry seasoning, thyme, and pepper; cook until vegetables are tender crisp. Stir in rice; cook until thoroughly heated. Serve or use as stuffing for poultry or pork roast. Stuffing may be baked in covered baking dish at 375°F. for 15 to 20 minutes.

Makes 6 servings

Variations: For Mushroom Stuffing, add 2 cups (about 8 ounces) sliced mushrooms; cook with apples, onion, celery, and seasonings.

For Raisin Stuffing, add ½ cup raisins; cook with apples, onion, celery, and seasonings.

*Favorite recipe from **USA Rice Council***

Apricot and Walnut Brown Rice Stuffing

- **½ cup chopped onion**
- **½ cup chopped celery**
- **1 teaspoon margarine**
- **3 cups cooked brown rice**
- **⅔ cup coarsely chopped dried apricots**
- **¼ cup coarsely chopped walnuts**
- **¼ cup raisins, plumped***
- **2 tablespoons snipped parsley**
- **½ teaspoon dried thyme leaves**
- **¼ teaspoon salt**
- **¼ teaspoon rubbed sage**
- **¼ teaspoon ground black pepper**
- **½ cup chicken broth**

Cook onion and celery in margarine in large skillet over medium-high heat until tender crisp. Add rice, apricots, walnuts, raisins, parsley, thyme, salt, sage, pepper, and broth; transfer to 2-quart baking dish. Bake in covered baking dish at 375°F. for 15 to 20 minutes. (Stuffing may be baked inside poultry.)
Makes 6 servings

*To plump raisins, cover with 1 cup boiling water. Let stand 1 to 2 minutes; drain.

*Favorite recipe from **USA Rice Council***

Almond Brown Rice Stuffing

Brown Rice Royal

**2 cups (about 8 ounces)
  sliced fresh mushrooms**
**½ cup thinly sliced green
  onions**
1 tablespoon vegetable oil
**3 cups cooked brown rice
  (cooked in beef broth)**

Cook mushrooms and onions in oil in large skillet over medium-high heat until tender. Add rice. Stir until thoroughly heated.
Makes 6 servings

To microwave: Combine mushrooms, onions, and oil in 2-quart microproof baking dish. Cook on HIGH 2 to 3 minutes. Add rice; continue to cook on HIGH 3 to 4 minutes, stirring after 2 minutes, or until thoroughly heated.

Favorite recipe from **USA Rice Council**

Brown Rice Royal

Lemon Vegetable Sauté

**1 cup DOLE® Broccoli
  florettes**
**1 cup DOLE® Cauliflower
  florettes**
**2 tablespoons margarine,
  divided**
1 tablespoon water
2 tablespoons sugar
**1 small DOLE® Lemon, thinly
  sliced**

• In 10-inch skillet, sauté vegetables in 1 tablespoon margarine over medium-high heat. Reduce heat to medium-low. Cover; cook 3 to 4 minutes or until tender-crisp.

• Add remaining 1 tablespoon margarine, water and sugar. Mix until blended and glazed. Stir in lemon until well mixed and heated. Serve with baked pork chops, ham steaks or deli-roasted chicken, if desired.
Makes 2 servings

Preparation Time: 10 minutes
Cook Time: 10 minutes

Home-Style Creamed Corn Casserole

**2 cans (17 ounces each)
  cream-style corn**
1 cup Original MINUTE® Rice
1 egg, slightly beaten
½ teaspoon salt
⅛ teaspoon pepper
**⅛ teaspoon ground nutmeg
  (optional)**

Combine all ingredients in large bowl; mix well. Pour into greased 9-inch square baking dish. Bake at 375° for 25 minutes or until liquid is absorbed. Garnish as desired. *Makes 6 servings*

Microwave Directions:
Combine all ingredients in large bowl; mix well. Pour into greased 9-inch square microwavable dish. Cover and cook at HIGH 15 minutes or until liquid is absorbed. Garnish as desired.
Makes 6 servings

Lemon Garlic Pasta Toss

**3 cloves garlic, finely
  chopped**
¼ cup olive or vegetable oil
**3 tablespoons REALEMON®
  Lemon Juice from
  Concentrate**
**2 teaspoons WYLER'S® or
  STEERO® Chicken-Flavor
  Instant Bouillon**
⅛ teaspoon pepper
**½ (1-pound) package
  CREAMETTE® Spaghetti,
  cooked as package
  directs and drained**
**¼ cup grated Parmesan
  cheese**
¼ cup chopped fresh parsley

In small skillet, cook garlic in oil until golden. Add ReaLemon® brand, bouillon and pepper; cook and stir until bouillon dissolves. In large bowl, toss hot pasta with garlic mixture, cheese and parsley; serve immediately. Refrigerate leftovers.
Makes 4 servings

PIZZA & SANDWICHES

Pizza—one of America's favorite foods—is as much fun to make as it is to eat since you add your favorite tempting toppings. And with increasing popularity comes an array of innovative ingredients from green chilies and shrimp to artichokes and pineapple. And sandwiches are not just for lunch boxes anymore. From grilled sizzling chicken sandwiches to pita pockets filled with spectacular salads to gourmet burgers, sandwiches are also perfect for outdoor dining or casual suppers.

Classic Pizza

½ tablespoon active dry yeast
1 teaspoon sugar
½ cup very warm water (105°F to 115°F)
1¾ cups all-purpose flour
¾ teaspoon salt
2 tablespoons olive oil
1 medium onion, chopped
1 medium clove garlic, minced
1 can (14½ ounces) whole peeled tomatoes, undrained, chopped
2 tablespoons tomato paste
1 teaspoon dried oregano, crumbled
½ teaspoon dried basil, crumbled
⅛ teaspoon black pepper
1¾ cups shredded mozzarella cheese
½ cup grated Parmesan cheese
½ small red bell pepper, chopped
½ small green bell pepper, chopped
⅓ cup pitted ripe olives, cut into halves
4 fresh medium mushrooms, sliced
1 can (2 ounces) flat anchovy fillets, drained

1. Sprinkle yeast and ½ teaspoon of the sugar over warm water in small bowl; stir until yeast is dissolved. Let stand until mixture is bubbly.
2. Place 1½ cups of the flour and ¼ teaspoon of the salt in medium bowl; stir in yeast mixture and 1 tablespoon of the oil, stirring until a smooth, soft dough forms. Knead on floured surface, using as much remaining flour as needed to form stiff elastic dough. Let dough rise, covered, in greased bowl in warm place until doubled in bulk, 30 to 45 minutes.
3. Meanwhile, heat remaining 1 tablespoon oil in medium saucepan over medium heat. Add onion; cook until soft, about 5 minutes. Add garlic; cook 30 seconds. Add tomatoes, tomato paste, oregano, basil, remaining ½ teaspoon sugar, remaining ½ teaspoon salt and the black pepper. Heat to boiling; reduce heat to medium-low.

Simmer, uncovered, stirring occasionally, until sauce is thick, 10 to 15 minutes. Transfer sauce to bowl; let cool.
4. Heat oven to 450°F. Punch dough down. Knead briefly on lightly floured surface to distribute air bubbles; let dough rest 5 minutes. Flatten dough into circle on lightly floured surface. Roll out dough into 10-inch circle. Place circle in greased 12-inch pizza pan; pat dough out to edges of pan. Let stand, covered, 15 minutes.
5. Mix mozzarella and Parmesan cheeses in small bowl. Spread sauce evenly over pizza dough. Sprinkle with two-thirds of the cheeses. Arrange bell peppers, olives, mushrooms and anchovies on top of pizza. Sprinkle remaining cheeses on top of pizza. Bake until crust is golden brown, about 20 minutes. Cut into wedges to serve.
Makes 4 to 6 servings.

Pizza Bread Pronto

½ pound sliced SWIFT PREMIUM® or MARGHERITA® Deli Peperoni
Butter or margarine, softened
4 mini French rolls, 8 inches long, sliced lengthwise
Grated Parmesan cheese
1 can (8 ounces) pizza sauce
Sliced mozzarella cheese
Dried oregano leaves

Spread butter over cut sides of rolls and sprinkle with Parmesan cheese. Broil, 4 inches from heat, until lightly browned. Spread several tablespoons pizza sauce over each. Layer peperoni over sauce. Top with mozzarella cheese and sprinkle with oregano. Broil until cheese melts. Serve hot.
Makes 8 servings.

Classic Pizza

Thick 'n Cheesy Vegetable Pizza

Thick 'n Cheesy Vegetable Pizza

- 2 loaves (1 pound each) frozen bread dough, thawed
- 1 envelope LIPTON® Recipe Secrets Vegetable Recipe Soup Mix
- ¼ cup olive or vegetable oil
- 2 tablespoons chopped fresh basil leaves*
- 1 large clove garlic, finely chopped
- ¼ teaspoon pepper
- 2 cups shredded mozzarella cheese (about 6 ounces)
- 1 cup fresh or canned sliced mushrooms
- 1 medium tomato, coarsely chopped

Preheat oven to 425°.

Into lightly oiled 12-inch pizza pan, press dough to form crust; set aside.

In small bowl, blend vegetable recipe soup mix, oil, basil, garlic and pepper; spread evenly on dough. Top with remaining ingredients. Bake 20 minutes or until cheese is melted and crust is golden brown. To serve, cut into wedges.
Makes about 6 servings.

Substitution: Use 2 teaspoons dried basil leaves.

Pineapple Pizza

- 2 cans (8 ounces each) DOLE® Crushed Pineapple in Juice
- ½ cup bottled pizza sauce
- 1 clove garlic, pressed
- 1 teaspoon dried oregano, crumbled
- ½ loaf frozen bread dough, thawed
- ½ pound Italian sausage, crumbled, cooked
- 1 small DOLE® Green Bell Pepper, seeded and sliced
- ¼ cup chopped green onion
- 2 cups shredded mozzarella cheese
- 2 tablespoons grated Parmesan cheese

Preheat oven to 500°F. Drain pineapple well, pressing out excess juice with back of spoon. In small bowl, combine pizza sauce, garlic and oregano. Roll and stretch thawed dough to fit greased 12-inch pizza pan. Spread dough with pizza sauce mixture. Top with sausage, green pepper, onion, pineapple and cheeses. Bake in preheated oven 12 to 15 minutes or until pizza is bubbly and crust is browned.
Makes 4 servings.

Party Pizza

- ½ pound ECKRICH® Beef Smoked Sausage, cut into ¼-inch slices
- 1 loaf (16 ounces) frozen bread dough, thawed
  Cornmeal
- 2 tablespoons butter or margarine
- 1½ cups green bell pepper strips
- 1½ cups sliced onions
- 8 ounces fresh mushrooms, sliced
- 3 cups (12 ounces) shredded mozzarella cheese, divided
- 1 jar (8 ounces) pizza sauce
- 1 teaspoon dried oregano leaves
- ½ teaspoon dried basil leaves
- ½ teaspoon fennel seeds
- ½ cup grated Parmesan cheese

Let bread dough warm and start to rise. Preheat oven to 425°F. Sprinkle cornmeal in 12-inch circle on buttered pizza pan or baking sheet. Place bread dough on cornmeal; stretch and pull to fit 12-inch circle. Bake 7 minutes. Remove from oven. Melt butter in medium skillet over medium-high heat; add green peppers, onions and mushrooms. Saute until vegetables just begin to lose their crispness. Stir in sausage. Cover bread with ½ of the mozzarella cheese. Combine pizza sauce, oregano, basil and fennel seeds in small bowl; spread over mozzarella cheese. Top with sausage mixture. Return to oven and bake 20 to 25 minutes more or until done. Top with remaining 1½ cups mozzarella cheese; sprinkle with Parmesan cheese. Return to oven and bake until mozzarella melts, about 5 minutes more. To serve, cut into wedges or squares.
Makes 1 pizza, 12-inch diameter.

Arizona's 7-Layer Taco Sandwich

- **1 pound thinly sliced BUTTERBALL® Deli Turkey Breast**
- **½ cup coarsely chopped ripe olives**
- **½ teaspoon chili powder**
- **½ teaspoon ground cumin**
- **¼ teaspoon salt**
- **½ cup mayonnaise**
- **½ cup sour cream**
- **½ cup sliced green onions**
- **4 large oval slices French bread, about ½ inch thick**
- **1 large tomato, sliced**
- **1 ripe avocado, peeled, sliced**
- **¾ cup (3 ounces) shredded Cheddar cheese**
- **¾ cup (3 ounces) shredded Monterey Jack cheese**
- **Lettuce leaves**
- **Salsa**

Preheat oven to 350°F. Combine olives, chili powder, cumin and salt in medium bowl; reserve two tablespoons. Stir mayonnaise, sour cream and onions into remaining olive mixture. Using ½ of the mayonnaise mixture, spread on 1 side of each bread slice. Top with tomato and turkey. Spread remaining mayonnaise mixture on top of turkey. Top with avocado slices. Sprinkle with cheeses. Transfer sandwiches to baking sheet. Bake until hot, about 15 minutes. Top with reserved olive mixture. Serve on lettuce leaves with salsa.
Makes 4 open-faced sandwiches.

Arizona's 7-Layer Taco Sandwich

Garden-Fresh Pitas

- **1½ cups cut-up cooked chicken (about 9 ounces)**
- **⅓ cup WISH-BONE® Creamy Italian or Lite Creamy Italian Dressing**
- **¼ cup finely chopped celery**
- **4 small pita breads, split Lettuce leaves**
- **1 medium tomato, sliced**
- **½ cup thinly sliced cucumber**

In medium bowl, combine chicken, creamy Italian dressing and celery; cover and chill. To serve, line breads with lettuce, tomato and cucumber; spoon in chicken mixture.
Makes about 4 servings.

Turkey Cranberry Croissant

- **Thin-sliced cooked BUTTERBALL® turkey (1 pound)**
- **1 package (8 ounces) cream cheese, softened**
- **¼ cup orange marmalade**
- **½ cup chopped pecans**
- **6 croissants or rolls, split**
- **¾ cup whole berry cranberry sauce**
- **Lettuce leaves**

Combine cream cheese, marmalade and pecans in small bowl. Spread top and bottom halves of croissants with cream cheese mixture. Layer turkey on bottom halves. Spoon 2 tablespoons cranberry sauce over turkey. Add lettuce and croissant top.
Yield: 6 sandwiches.

Lipton® Onion Burgers

- **1 envelope LIPTON® Recipe Secrets Onion, Onion-Mushroom, Beefy Onion or Beefy Mushroom Recipe Soup Mix**
- **2 pounds ground beef**
- **½ cup water**

In large bowl, combine all ingredients; shape into 8 patties. Grill or broil until done. Serve, if desired, on hamburger rolls.
Makes 8 servings.

Microwave Directions: Prepare patties as above. In oblong baking dish, arrange 4 patties and microwave uncovered at HIGH (Full Power) 6 minutes, turning patties once. Repeat with remaining patties. Let stand covered 5 minutes. Serve as above.

Butter Crusted Pan Pizza

Butter Crusted Pan Pizza

Pizza Dough
1 package (¼ ounce) active dry yeast
½ cup warm water (105° to 115°F)
½ cup LAND O LAKES® Butter, melted, cooled (105° to 115°F)
3 to 3½ cups all-purpose flour
¼ cup freshly grated Parmesan cheese
2 teaspoons salt
3 eggs

Topping
¼ cup LAND O LAKES® Butter
3 cups (3 medium) thinly sliced onions
1 teaspoon minced fresh garlic
8 medium Roma (Italian) tomatoes, sliced ⅛ inch thick
1 teaspoon dried basil leaves
½ teaspoon coarsely ground pepper
½ cup freshly grated Parmesan cheese

For pizza dough, in large mixer bowl dissolve yeast in warm water. Add ½ cup cooled butter, *2 cups* flour, ¼ cup Parmesan cheese, salt and eggs. Beat at medium speed, scraping bowl often, until smooth, 1 to 2 minutes. By hand, stir in enough remaining flour to make dough easy to handle. Turn dough onto lightly floured surface; knead until smooth and elastic, 3 to 5 minutes. Place in greased bowl; turn greased side up. Cover; let rise in warm place until double in size, about 1 hour. Dough is ready if indentation remains when touched. Punch down dough; divide in half. Let stand 10 minutes.

Heat oven to 400°. For topping, in 10-inch skillet melt ¼ cup butter until sizzling. Add onions and garlic; cook over medium heat, stirring occasionally, until onions are tender, 6 to 8 minutes. Set aside. Pat one half of dough on bottom of greased 12-inch pizza pan. Repeat for second pizza. Divide sautéed onions between pizzas. On *each* pizza arrange half of tomato slices; sprinkle *each* with ½ teaspoon basil leaves and ¼ teaspoon coarsely ground pepper. Sprinkle *each* with ¼ cup Parmesan cheese. If desired, arrange additional suggested topping ingredients on pizzas. Bake for 16 to 22 minutes or until golden brown.
Makes 2 (12-inch) pizzas

Tip: Additional suggested toppings: sautéed red, yellow *or* green peppers; tiny cooked shrimp; chopped marinated artichokes; sliced green *or* ripe olives; etc.

Hawaiian Pineapple Pizza

1 long loaf (1 pound) French bread
1½ cups pizza sauce
4 ounces Canadian bacon, slivered
1 small DOLE® Green Bell Pepper, sliced
1 can (20 ounces) DOLE® Pineapple Tidbits in Juice, drained
2 cups shredded mozzarella cheese

• Cut bread lengthwise. Spread with pizza sauce.
• Top with remaining ingredients. Broil 4 inches from heat until cheese melts.
Makes 6 to 8 servings

Preparation Time: 15 minutes
Cook Time: 10 minutes

Mexicali Pizza

Vegetable oil
2 large flour tortillas *or* 4 small flour tortillas
1 pound ground beef
1 package (1.25 ounces) LAWRY'S® Taco Spices & Seasonings
¾ cup water
1½ cups (6 ounces) grated Monterey Jack or Cheddar cheese
3 tablespoons diced green chiles
2 medium tomatoes, sliced
1 can (2¼ ounces) sliced ripe olives, drained
½ cup salsa

In large skillet, pour in oil to ¼ inch depth; heat. (For small tortillas, use small skillet.) Fry each flour tortilla about 5 seconds. While still pliable, turn tortilla over. Fry until golden brown. (Edges of tortilla should turn up about ½ inch.) Drain well on paper towels. In medium skillet, brown ground beef until crumbly; drain fat. Add Taco Spices & Seasonings and water; blend well. Bring to a boil; reduce heat and simmer, uncovered, 5 minutes. Place fried tortillas on pizza pan. Layer taco meat, ½ of cheese, chiles, tomatoes, remaining ½ of cheese, olives and salsa on each fried tortilla. Bake, uncovered, in 425°F oven 15 minutes for large pizzas or 7 to 8 minutes for small pizzas. *Makes 4 servings*

Hint: One pound ground turkey or 1½ cups shredded, cooked chicken can be used in place of beef.

Gourmet Olé Burgers

1½ pounds ground beef
1 package (1.25 ounces)
    LAWRY'S® Taco Spices &
    Seasonings
¼ cup ketchup
    Monterey Jack cheese
    slices
    Salsa

In medium bowl, combine ground beef, Taco Spices & Seasonings and ketchup; blend well. Shape into patties. Grill or broil burgers 5 to 7 minutes on each side or to desired doneness. Top each burger with a slice of cheese. Return to grill or broiler until cheese melts. Top with a dollop of salsa.

Makes 6 to 8 servings

Presentation: Serve on lettuce-lined hamburger buns. Garnish with avocado slices, if desired.

Hint: Cut cheese with cookie cutters for interesting shapes.

Party Hero

¾ pound creamy coleslaw
⅓ cup bottled salad dressing
    (Thousand Island,
    creamy Italian or creamy
    blue cheese)
1 (8-inch) round loaf of bread
    (French, Italian, rye or
    sourdough), about
    1½ pounds
    Leaf lettuce
½ pound cooked turkey,
    thinly sliced
½ pound cooked ham, thinly
    sliced
¼ pound Cheddar, Muenster
    or Swiss cheese, sliced

Drain excess liquid from coleslaw; add *2 tablespoons* bottled dressing to coleslaw, mixing well. Cut a thin slice from top of bread; spread cut surface of slice with some of the bottled dressing. Hollow out bread, leaving about ½-inch-thick bread shell. Line bread shell with lettuce; brush with remaining bottled dressing. Press turkey onto bottom; cover with half of coleslaw mixture. Repeat with ham, remaining coleslaw mixture and cheese. Garnish with lettuce; cover with top bread slice. Place 6 to 8 long wooden picks into sandwich to secure. Chill no longer than 4 to 6 hours before serving. To serve, cut between picks to form 6 to 8 wedge-shaped sandwiches.

Makes 6 to 8 sandwiches

Sizzling Chicken Sandwiches

4 boneless, skinless chicken
    breast halves
1 package (1.27 ounces)
    LAWRY'S® Spices &
    Seasonings for Fajitas
1 cup chunky salsa
¼ cup water
    Lettuce
4 large sandwich buns, split
4 slices Monterey Jack
    cheese
    Red onion slices
    Avocado slices
    Chunky salsa

Place chicken in large resealable plastic bag. In small bowl, combine Spices & Seasonings for Fajitas, 1 cup salsa and water; pour over chicken. Marinate in refrigerator 2 hours. Remove chicken; reserve marinade. Grill or broil 5 to 7 minutes on each side, basting frequently with marinade, until chicken is cooked through. Place on lettuce-lined sandwich buns. Top with cheese, onion, avocado and salsa.

Makes 4 servings

Hint: Do not baste chicken with marinade during last 5 minutes of cooking.

Gourmet Olé Burger

Tasty Turkey Burgers

1 pound ground fresh turkey
½ cup BENNETT'S® Chili
**   Sauce**
½ cup plain dry bread crumbs
1 egg, slightly beaten
¼ cup chopped green onions
1 teaspoon WYLER'S® or
**   STEERO® Chicken-Flavor**
**   Instant Bouillon**
**   Hamburger buns, split**

In medium bowl, combine all ingredients except buns. Shape into 4 to 6 patties. Grill, broil or pan-fry as desired. Serve on buns with additional Bennett's® Chili Sauce. Garnish as desired. Refrigerate leftovers.
Makes 4 to 6 sandwiches

Burger Toppers

"Secret Recipe" Sauce

¾ cup MIRACLE WHIP®
**   FREE® Dressing**
3 tablespoons dill pickle
**   relish**
3 tablespoons catsup

• Mix ingredients until well blended; refrigerate.
Makes ¾ cup

Prep time: 5 minutes plus refrigerating

Zippy Mustard Sauce

¾ cup MIRACLE WHIP®
**   FREE® Dressing**
2 tablespoons KRAFT® Pure
**   Prepared Mustard**
2½ teaspoons Worcestershire
**   sauce**

• Mix ingredients until well blended; refrigerate.
Makes ¾ cup

Prep time: 5 minutes plus refrigerating

Cucumber Onion Sauce

½ cup MIRACLE WHIP®
**   FREE® Dressing**
¼ cup seeded chopped
**   cucumber**
1 tablespoon chopped onion

• Mix ingredients until well blended; refrigerate.
Makes ¾ cup

Prep time: 5 minutes plus refrigerating

All-American Cheeseburgers

1 pound lean ground beef
1 tablespoon WYLER'S® or
**   STEERO® Beef-Flavor**
**   Instant Bouillon**
¼ cup chopped onion
4 slices BORDEN® Singles
**   Process American**
**   Cheese Food**
4 hamburger buns, split,
**   buttered and toasted**
**   Lettuce**
4 slices tomato

In medium bowl, combine beef, bouillon and onion; mix well. Shape into 4 patties. Grill or broil to desired doneness. Top with cheese food slices; heat until cheese food begins to melt. Top bottom halves of buns with lettuce, tomato and meat patties. Serve open-face or with bun tops. Refrigerate leftovers.
Makes 4 servings

Variations

Santa Fe Burgers: Add 3 tablespoons salsa or taco sauce to ground beef. On a warm tortilla, spread refried beans; top with shredded lettuce, cooked burger, cheese food slice, salsa and sour cream.

Kansas City Burgers: Add ½ cup thawed frozen hash browns and 2 tablespoons barbecue sauce to ground beef. Place each cooked burger on bun; top with cheese food slice, cooked, crumbled bacon and sliced green onion.

Seasoned Burgers

1 pound lean ground beef
1 teaspoon WYLER'S® or
**   STEERO® Beef-Flavor**
**   Instant Bouillon**

Combine ingredients; shape into patties. Grill or broil 5 to 7 minutes on each side or to desired doneness. Serve as desired.   *Makes 4 servings*

Variations

Italian Burgers: Combine beef mixture with 2 tablespoons grated Parmesan cheese and 1 teaspoon Italian seasoning. Prepare as above. Serve with pizza sauce. Garnish as desired.

Oriental Burgers: Combine beef mixture with 1 (8-ounce) can water chestnuts, drained and chopped, and ¼ cup sliced green onions. Prepare as above. Top with pineapple slice; serve with sweet and sour sauce.

Mexican Burgers: Combine beef mixture with 1 (4-ounce) can chopped green chilies, drained, and ¼ cup chopped onion. Prepare as above. Serve with sour cream and salsa.

Garden Burgers: Combine beef mixture with 1 tablespoon chopped green bell pepper and 2 tablespoons Thousand Island salad dressing. Prepare as above. Serve with coleslaw and chopped tomato.

Mid-West Burgers: Combine beef mixture with ½ cup frozen hash browns potatoes, thawed, and 2 tablespoons barbecue sauce. Prepare as above. Serve with barbecue sauce.

German Burgers: Combine beef mixture with 2 tablespoons chopped dill pickle and 1 teaspoon caraway seed. Prepare as above. Serve with sauerkraut if desired.

Clockwise from top left: Mexican Burger, Oriental Burger, Garden Burger and Italian Burger

Loaf Sandwiches with Bacon & Ham

- ¼ **cup unsalted margarine or butter, melted**
- 1 **to 2 teaspoons garlic powder**
- 1 **large loaf French bread**
- 3 **ounces ARMOUR® Lower Salt Ham, thinly sliced**
- 2 **ounces ARMOUR® Lower Salt Monterey Jack Cheese, thinly sliced**
- 6 **cherry tomato slices**
- 6 **slices ARMOUR® Lower Salt Bacon, cut in half and cooked crisp**
- 12 **(¼-inch) zucchini slices**

Combine margarine and garlic powder in small bowl; set aside. Make 6 diagonal cuts at equal distances along loaf of bread, cutting ¾ of the way through loaf. Spread margarine mixture on cut sides of bread. Evenly distribute ham and cheese among cuts. Place 1 tomato slice, 2 bacon pieces and 2 zucchini slices in each cut. If desired, wrap entire loaf with foil and bake in 375°F. oven about 15 to 20 minutes, or until cheese is melted. Cut into 6 servings.
Makes 6 servings.

Nutritional Information Per Serving: 380 calories, 14.1 protein, 16.3 g fat, 44 g carbohydrates, 23 mg cholesterol, 701 mg sodium.

Loaf Sandwiches with Bacon & Ham

Sloppy Joes

- 2 **pounds ground beef**
- 1 **envelope LIPTON® Recipe Secrets Onion, Onion-Mushroom, Beefy Mushroom or Beefy Onion Recipe Soup Mix**
- 1 **can (15 ounces) tomato sauce**
- ½ **cup sweet pickle relish**

In large skillet, brown ground beef over medium-high heat; drain. Stir in remaining ingredients. Simmer, stirring occasionally, 10 minutes. Serve, if desired, over toasted hamburger rolls.
Makes about 8 servings.

Microwave Directions: In 2-quart casserole, microwave ground beef, uncovered, at HIGH (Full Power) 7 minutes; drain. Stir in remaining ingredients. Microwave covered, stirring occasionally, 4 minutes or until heated through. Let stand covered 5 minutes. Serve as above.

Stuffed Cheese Burgers

- 1½ **cups shredded Monterey Jack cheese (about 8 ounces)**
- 1 **can (2¼ ounces) chopped black olives**
- ⅛ **teaspoon hot pepper sauce**
- 1¾ **pounds ground beef**
- ¼ **cup finely chopped onion**
- 1 **teaspoon salt**
- ½ **teaspoon pepper**
- 6 **hamburger buns**
  Butter or margarine, melted

In large bowl, combine cheese, olives and hot pepper sauce. Divide mixture evenly and shape into 6 balls. Mix ground beef with onion, salt and pepper; shape into 12 thin patties. Place 1 cheese ball in center of each of 6 patties and top each with a second patty. Seal edges to enclose cheese balls. Lightly oil grid. Grill patties, on covered grill, over medium-hot **KINGSFORD® Charcoal Briquets** 5 to 6 minutes on each side or until done.

Split buns, brush with butter and place, cut-side down, on grill to heat through. Serve Cheese Burgers on buns.
Makes 6 servings.

Avocado & Bacon Pitas

- 2 **(6-inch) pita breads, cut in half**
- 4 **leaves leaf lettuce, washed and drained**
- 12 **slices ARMOUR® Lower Salt Bacon, cut in half and cooked crisp**
- 1 **avocado, peeled, pitted and sliced**
- 1 **(15¼-ounce) can pineapple spears, well drained**
- 4 **radishes, thinly sliced**
- 8 **tablespoons bottled low sodium, reduced calorie zesty Italian salad dressing**

Open sliced edges of pita bread halves. Line with leaf lettuce. Divide bacon, avocado, pineapple and radishes evenly among bread pockets. Before serving, spoon 2 tablespoons of the dressing over top of each sandwich.
Makes 4 sandwiches.

Nutrition Information Per Sandwich: 319 calories, 10.1 g protein, 17.2 g fat, 35.2 g carbohydrates, 18 mg cholesterol, 558 mg sodium.

Barbecue Ham Sandwiches

1 cup catsup
3 tablespoons REALEMON®
    Lemon Juice from
    Concentrate
¼ cup chopped onion
¼ cup firmly packed brown sugar
2 tablespoons Worcestershire
    sauce
1 teaspoon prepared mustard
1 pound thinly sliced cooked
    ham
    Buns or hard rolls

In medium saucepan, combine all ingredients except ham and buns. Simmer uncovered 5 minutes. Add ham; heat through. Serve on buns. Refrigerate leftovers.
Makes 6 to 8 sandwiches.

Microwave: In 2-quart round baking dish, combine ingredients as above. Cover with wax paper; microwave on full power (high) 3 minutes. Stir in ham; cover with wax paper and microwave on full power (high) 3 to 4 minutes or until hot. Serve as above.

Barbecue Ham Sandwiches

Texas-Style Steak on Hot Bread

½ cup olive or vegetable oil
¼ cup lime juice
¼ cup red wine vinegar
1 medium onion, finely chopped
1 clove garlic, minced
1 teaspoon chili powder
½ teaspoon salt
¼ teaspoon ground cumin
1 beef skirt or flank steak (about
    1½ pounds)
1 round loaf French or
    sourdough bread
1 cup salsa
1 cup guacamole

In shallow glass dish, combine oil, lime juice, vinegar, onion, garlic, chili powder, salt and cumin. With meat mallet, pound steak to ¼-inch thickness. Place steak in marinade; turn to coat. Cover and refrigerate several hours or overnight, turning several times. Drain steak; discard marinade. Grill steak, on covered grill, over medium-hot **KINGSFORD® Charcoal Briquets** 4 to 8 minutes on each side, or until done. Cut bread into 1-inch slices and toast on grill. Heat salsa. Carve steak into ¾-inch diagonal strips. Arrange steak on toasted bread. Top with hot salsa and guacamole.
Makes 4 to 6 servings.

The California Classic

¼ cup MIRACLE WHIP® Salad
    Dressing
1 teaspoon KRAFT® Pure
    Prepared Mustard
4 rye bread slices
    Alfalfa sprouts
4 cooked turkey slices
¼ lb. VELVEETA® Pasteurized
    Process Cheese Spread,
    sliced
    Thin tomato slices
    Peeled avocado slices

Combine salad dressing and mustard; mix well. Spread bread slices with salad dressing mixture. For each sandwich, top one bread slice with sprouts, turkey, VELVEETA® Pasteurized Process Cheese Spread, tomatoes, avocados and second bread slice.
2 sandwiches.

Preparation time: 10 minutes

Variation: Substitute salami slices or boiled ham slices for turkey.

Quick 'n Easy Tacos

1 pound ground beef
1 can (14½ ounces) whole
    peeled tomatoes, undrained
    and coarsely chopped
1 medium green pepper, finely
    chopped
1 envelope LIPTON® Recipe
    Secrets Onion, Onion-
    Mushroom or Beefy
    Mushroom Recipe Soup Mix
1 tablespoon chili powder
3 drops hot pepper sauce
8 taco shells
    Taco Toppings*

In medium skillet, brown ground beef over medium-high heat; drain. Stir in tomatoes, green pepper, onion recipe soup mix, chili powder and hot pepper sauce. Bring to a boil, then simmer 15 minutes or until slightly thickened. Serve in taco shells with assorted Taco Toppings.
Makes about 4 servings.

***Taco Toppings:** Use shredded Cheddar or Monterey Jack cheese, shredded lettuce, chopped tomatoes, sliced pitted ripe olives, sour cream or taco sauce.

Microwave Directions: In 2-quart casserole, microwave ground beef with green pepper, uncovered, at HIGH (Full Power) 4 minutes, stirring once; drain. Stir in tomatoes, onion recipe soup mix, chili powder and hot pepper sauce. Microwave uncovered, stirring occasionally, 7 minutes or until heated through. Let stand uncovered 5 minutes. Serve as above.

Sesame Chicken in Pitas

Sesame Chicken in Pitas

½ cup MIRACLE WHIP®
    FREE® Dressing
1 tablespoon <u>each</u>: soy
    sauce, toasted sesame
    seeds
1 teaspoon sesame oil
    (optional)
⅛ teaspoon ground ginger
1 cup chopped cooked
    chicken
½ cup <u>each</u>: chopped
    Chinese pea pods,
    chopped red bell pepper
¼ cup cashews
2 whole wheat pita breads,
    cut in half

• Mix dressing, soy sauce, sesame seeds, oil and ginger until well blended.

• Add chicken, vegetables and cashews; mix well. Spoon into pita pockets.

Makes 2 servings

Prep time: 15 minutes

Tuna Cobb Salad Pockets

⅓ cup vegetable oil
¼ cup REALEMON® Lemon
    Juice from Concentrate
2 teaspoons red wine
    vinegar, optional
1 teaspoon sugar
½ teaspoon Worcestershire
    sauce
⅛ teaspoon garlic powder
1 (6½-ounce) can tuna,
    drained and flaked
2 cups shredded lettuce
½ cup diced avocado
½ cup diced tomato
1 hard-cooked egg, chopped
2 tablespoons cooked,
    crumbled bacon
2 tablespoons crumbled blue
    cheese
4 Pita bread rounds, cut in
    half

In medium bowl, combine oil, ReaLemon® brand, vinegar, sugar, Worcestershire and garlic powder; pour over tuna. Cover; marinate in refrigerator 1 hour. Stir in remaining ingredients except Pita bread. Serve in Pita bread. Refrigerate leftovers.

Makes 4 sandwiches

Amigo Pita Pocket Sandwiches

1 pound ground turkey
1 package (1.25 ounces)
    LAWRY'S® Taco Spices &
    Seasonings
1 can (6 ounces) tomato
    paste
½ cup water
½ cup chopped green bell
    pepper
1 can (7 ounces) whole
    kernel corn, drained
8 pita breads
    Curly lettuce leaves
    Grated Cheddar cheese

In large skillet, brown turkey; drain fat. Add remaining ingredients except pita bread, lettuce and cheese; blend well. Bring to a boil; reduce heat and simmer, uncovered, 15 minutes. Cut off top ¼ of pita breads. Open pita breads to form pockets. Line each with lettuce leaves. Spoon ½ cup filling into each pita bread and top with cheese.   *Makes 8 servings*

Presentation: Serve with vegetable sticks and fresh fruit.

Amigo Pita Pocket Sandwiches

Tuna Sandwich Melts

½ cup MIRACLE WHIP® Salad
    Dressing
1 can (6½ ounces) tuna in
    water, drained
½ cup chopped celery
½ cup (¼ pound) cubed
    VELVEETA® Pasteurized
    Process Cheese Spread
¼ cup chopped onion
4 hamburger buns, split

• Mix all ingredients except buns
until well blended. Fill each bun
with ½ cup tuna mixture. Place
two sandwiches on paper towel.

• Microwave on HIGH 1 minute
or until thoroughly heated.
Repeat with remaining
sandwiches.

Makes 4 sandwiches

Prep time: 15 minutes
Microwave cooking time:
    2 minutes

Croissant Sandwich

1 beef flank steak
    (1¼ to 1½ pounds)
    HEINZ® Worcestershire
    Sauce
1 package (3 ounces) cream
    cheese, softened
2 tablespoons minced green
    onions
1 tablespoon HEINZ®
    Worcestershire Sauce
    Generous dash pepper
4 to 6 croissants, split,
    heated
    Spinach, romaine or lettuce
    leaves

Generously sprinkle both sides of
steak with Worcestershire sauce;
broil steak 3 inches from heat
source, 5 to 6 minutes per side.
Cover; chill. In small bowl,
combine cream cheese, green
onions, 1 tablespoon
Worcestershire sauce and pepper.
Thinly slice meat diagonally
across grain. Spread half of each
croissant with cream cheese
mixture; arrange one portion of
meat on top. Cover meat with
spinach; top with remaining
croissant half.

Makes 4 to 6 servings
(½ cup cheese mixture)

Curried Turkey and Ham Croissants

1 pound fresh asparagus *or*
    1 (10-ounce) package
    frozen asparagus spears,
    cooked and drained
12 ounces thinly sliced
    cooked ham
12 ounces thinly sliced
    cooked turkey breast
6 ounces sliced Swiss
    cheese
8 croissants, split
    Curry Sauce

Preheat oven to 350°. Arrange
equal amounts of asparagus,
ham, turkey and cheese on
bottom half of each croissant.
Place top halves of croissants on
cheese. Bake 10 to 15 minutes or
until hot. Meanwhile, make
Curry Sauce; spoon over
croissants. Garnish with paprika
if desired. Refrigerate leftovers.

Makes 8 servings

CURRY SAUCE: In small
saucepan, melt ¼ cup margarine
or butter; stir in 2 tablespoons
flour, ½ teaspoon curry powder
and ¼ teaspoon salt. Gradually
add 1½ cups BORDEN® or
MEADOW GOLD® Coffee Cream
or Half-and-Half; over medium
heat, cook and stir until
thickened, about 5 minutes.
Remove from heat; slowly stir in
¼ cup REALEMON® Lemon
Juice from Concentrate.

Makes about 1½ cups

Curried Turkey and Ham Croissant

EGGS, CHEESE & BRUNCH DISHES

Rise and shine! You'll look forward to your wake-up call with this collection of glorious brunch recipes. Dazzle guests with a breathtaking buffet of frittatas, quiches and pancakes. From Brunch Potato Cassoulet to Scandinavian Salmon-Cheddar Pie, these enticing dishes are great morning, noon and night.

Saucy Mediterranean Frittata

Sauce
- **1 can (8 ounces) tomato sauce**
- **1 teaspoon dried minced onion**
- **¼ teaspoon dried basil leaves, crushed**
- **¼ teaspoon dried oregano leaves, crushed**
- **⅛ teaspoon minced dried garlic**
- **⅛ teaspoon pepper**

Frittata
- **⅓ cup chopped onion**
- **1 tablespoon olive oil**
- **1 medium tomato, chopped**
- **1 tablespoon finely chopped fresh basil *or* 1 teaspoon dried basil leaves, crushed**
- **¼ teaspoon dried oregano leaves, crushed**
- **⅓ cup cooked orzo**
- **⅓ cup chopped pitted ripe olives**
- **8 eggs**
- **½ teaspoon salt**
- **⅛ teaspoon pepper**
- **2 tablespoons butter**
- **½ cup (2 ounces) shredded mozzarella cheese**

For sauce, combine all sauce ingredients in small saucepan. Simmer over medium-low heat 5 minutes, stirring often. Set aside; keep warm.

For frittata, cook and stir onion in hot oil in *ovenproof* 10-inch skillet until tender. Add tomato, basil and oregano; cook and stir 3 minutes. Stir in orzo and olives; set aside. Beat eggs, salt and pepper in medium bowl. Stir in tomato mixture; set aside. Melt butter in same skillet. Add

egg mixture; sprinkle with cheese. Cook over low heat 8 to 10 minutes until bottom and most of middle is set. Broil 1 to 2 minutes or until top is browned. Serve with sauce. Garnish as desired. Cut into wedges to serve. *Makes 4 to 6 servings*

*Favorite recipe from **Kansas Poultry Association***

Italian Baked Frittata

- **1 cup broccoli flowerets**
- **½ cup sliced mushrooms**
- **½ red pepper, cut into rings**
- **2 green onions, sliced into 1-inch pieces**
- **1 tablespoon BLUE BONNET® Margarine**
- **8 eggs**
- **¼ cup GREY POUPON® Dijon Mustard or GREY POUPON® Country Dijon Mustard**
- **¼ cup water**
- **½ teaspoon Italian seasoning**
- **1 cup shredded Swiss cheese (4 ounces)**

In 10-inch ovenproof skillet, over medium-high heat, cook broccoli, mushrooms, red pepper and onions in margarine until tender-crisp, about 5 minutes. Remove from heat.

In small bowl, with electric mixer at medium speed, beat eggs, mustard, water and Italian seasoning until foamy; stir in cheese. Pour mixture into skillet over vegetables. Bake at 375°F for 20 to 25 minutes or until set. Serve immediately.

Makes 4 servings

Italian Baked Frittata

Wisconsin Swiss Linguine Tart

Wisconsin Swiss Linguine Tart

- ½ **cup butter, divided**
- 2 **cloves garlic, minced**
- 30 **thin French bread slices**
- 3 **tablespoons all-purpose flour**
- 1 **teaspoon salt**
- ¼ **teaspoon white pepper Dash ground nutmeg**
- 2½ **cups milk**
- ¼ **cup grated Wisconsin Parmesan cheese**
- 2 **eggs, beaten**
- 8 **ounces fresh linguine, cooked and drained**
- 2 **cups (8 ounces) shredded Wisconsin Swiss cheese, divided**
- ⅓ **cup sliced green onions**
- 2 **tablespoons minced fresh basil *or* 1 teaspoon dried basil leaves, crushed**
- 2 **plum tomatoes, each cut lengthwise into eighths**

Melt ¼ cup butter in small saucepan over medium heat. Add garlic; cook 1 minute. Brush 10-inch pie plate with butter mixture. Line bottom and side of pie plate with bread, allowing 1-inch overhang. Brush bread with remaining butter mixture. Bake in preheated 400°F. oven 5 minutes or until lightly browned.

Melt remaining ¼ cup butter in medium saucepan over low heat. Stir in flour and seasonings. Gradually stir in milk; cook, stirring constantly, until thickened. Add Parmesan cheese. Stir some of the sauce into eggs; stir back into sauce. Set aside. Combine linguine, 1¼ cups Swiss cheese, onions and basil in large bowl. Pour sauce over linguine mixture; toss to coat. Pour into crust. Arrange tomatoes on top; sprinkle with remaining ¾ cup Swiss cheese. Bake in preheated 350°F. oven 25 minutes or until warm; let stand 5 minutes. Garnish as desired.

Makes 8 servings

*Favorite recipe from **Wisconsin Milk Marketing Board** © 1993*

Double Onion Quiche

- 3 **cups thinly sliced yellow onions**
- 3 **tablespoons butter or margarine**
- 1 **cup thinly sliced green onions**
- 3 **eggs**
- 1 **cup heavy cream**
- ½ **cup grated Parmesan cheese**
- ¼ **teaspoon hot pepper sauce**
- 1 **package (1 ounce) HIDDEN VALLEY RANCH® Milk Recipe Original Ranch® Salad Dressing Mix**
- 1 **9-inch deep-dish pastry shell, baked and cooled Sprig fresh oregano**

Preheat oven to 350°F. In medium skillet, sauté yellow onions in butter, stirring occasionally, about 10 minutes. Add green onions and cook 5 minutes longer. Remove from heat and let cool.

In large bowl, whisk eggs until frothy. Whisk in cream, cheese, pepper sauce and salad dressing mix. Stir in onion mixture. Pour egg and onion mixture into baked and cooled pastry shell. Bake until top is browned and knife inserted in center comes out clean, 35 to 40 minutes. Cool on wire rack 10 minutes before slicing. Garnish with oregano.

Makes 8 servings

Spinach & Mushroom Quiche

2 tablespoons margarine
1½ cups sliced fresh
       mushrooms
½ cup shredded carrots
½ cup finely chopped green
       onions
2 garlic cloves, minced
1 package (10 ounces) frozen
       chopped spinach, thawed
       and drained
3 eggs
1 container (15 ounces)
       ricotta cheese
½ teaspoon salt
¼ teaspoon ground nutmeg
1 unbaked 9-inch pie shell

Preheat oven to 425°F. In medium skillet over medium heat, heat margarine until melted and bubbly. In hot margarine, sauté mushrooms, carrots, green onions and garlic, 3 to 5 minutes until tender-crisp. Stir in spinach and cook 1 minute longer; remove from heat.

In medium bowl, beat eggs. Stir in ricotta, salt and nutmeg until well blended. Stir in vegetable mixture; mix well.

Pour mixture into pie shell. Bake 10 minutes. *Reduce oven temperature to 375°F.* Bake 35 minutes longer or until filling is set and crust is golden-brown. Serve hot or refrigerate to serve cold or at room temperature.

Makes 6 servings

Preparation time: 20 minutes
Baking time: 45 minutes

Vegetable & Cheese Pot Pie

2 tablespoons butter or
       margarine
½ cup sliced green onions
1¾ cups water
1 package LIPTON® Noodles
       & Sauce—Chicken Flavor
1 package (16 ounces) frozen
       mixed vegetables,
       partially thawed
1 cup shredded mozzarella
       cheese (4 ounces)
1 teaspoon prepared
       mustard
½ cup milk
1 tablespoon all-purpose
       flour
   Salt and pepper to taste
   Pastry for 9-inch single-
       crust pie
1 egg yolk
1 tablespoon water

Preheat oven to 425°F. In large saucepan, melt butter and cook green onions over medium heat 3 minutes or until tender. Add 1¾ cups water and bring to a boil. Stir in noodles & chicken flavor sauce and vegetables, then continue boiling over medium heat, stirring occasionally, 7 minutes or until noodles are almost tender. Stir in cheese, mustard and milk blended with flour. Cook over medium heat, stirring frequently, 2 minutes or until thickened. Add salt and pepper.

Turn into greased 1-quart round casserole or soufflé dish, then top with pastry. Press pastry around edge of casserole to seal; trim excess pastry, then flute edges. (Use extra pastry to make decorative shapes.) Brush pastry with egg yolk beaten with 1 tablespoon water. With tip of knife, make small slits in pastry. Bake 12 minutes or until crust is golden brown.

Makes 4 servings

Vegetable & Cheese Pot Pie

Quiche Florentine

    1 15-oz. pkg. PILLSBURY® All
      Ready Pie Crust
    2 cups (8 ozs.) VELVEETA®
      Shredded Pasteurized
      Process Cheese Food
    ⅓ cup (1½ ozs.) KRAFT® 100%
      Grated Parmesan Cheese
    1 10-oz. pkg. frozen chopped
      spinach, thawed, well-
      drained
    4 crisply cooked bacon slices,
      crumbled
    ¾ cup milk
    3 eggs, beaten
    ¼ teaspoon pepper

Prepare pie crust according to package directions for filled one-crust pie using 9-inch pie plate. (Refrigerate remaining crust for later use.) In large bowl, combine remaining ingredients; mix well. Pour into unbaked pie crust. Bake at 350°, 35 to 40 minutes or until knife inserted in center comes out clean. Let stand 10 minutes before serving.
6 to 8 servings.

Preparation time: 15 minutes
Baking time: 40 minutes plus standing time

Savory Onion Cheese Tart

    1 envelope LIPTON® Recipe
      Secrets Golden Onion
      Recipe Soup Mix
    1 cup milk
    1 egg, slightly beaten
    ½ teaspoon rosemary leaves
    1 package (8 ounces) mozzarella
      cheese, shredded
    1 package (15 ounces)
      refrigerated pie crusts for
      2 (9-inch) crusts

In small bowl, thoroughly blend golden onion recipe soup mix, milk, egg and rosemary. Stir in cheese. Freeze 1 hour or refrigerate at least 2 hours until mixture is slightly thickened and not runny.

Preheat oven to 375°. On two aluminum-foil-lined baking sheets, unfold pie crusts. Fold crust edges over 1 inch to form rim. Brush, if desired, with 1 egg yolk beaten with 2 tablespoons water. Fill center of each prepared crust with ½ soup mixture; spread evenly to rim. Bake 25 minutes or until crusts are golden brown. To serve, cut into wedges.
Makes 2 tarts.

Freezing/Reheating Directions:
Tarts can be baked, then frozen. Simply wrap in heavy-duty aluminum foil; freeze. To reheat, unwrap and bake at 350° until heated through.

Savory Onion Cheese Tart

Turkey and Caper Quiche

    ¾ cup diced cooked
      BUTTERBALL® turkey
      Pastry for single 9-inch pie
      crust*
    ½ cup (2 ounces) shredded
      Swiss cheese
    ⅓ cup diced tomato
    ¼ cup minced onion
    1 teaspoon capers
    3 eggs, beaten
    1 tablespoon Dijon mustard
    1 teaspoon seasoned salt
    1 cup half and half

Preheat oven to 350°F. Line 9-inch quiche dish or pie pan with pastry. Trim edges and flute. Layer turkey, cheese, tomato, onion and capers in crust. Blend eggs, mustard, salt and half and half in small bowl. Pour mixture into pie crust. Bake in oven 40 to 50 minutes or until knife inserted 1 inch from center comes out clean.
Yield: 4 servings.

*Substitute frozen 9-inch deep dish pie crust, thawed, for pastry. Omit quiche dish; bake directly in foil pan.

Swiss Chicken Quiche

    1 (9-inch) unbaked pastry shell,
      pricked
    2 cups cubed cooked chicken or
      turkey
    1 cup (4 ounces) shredded
      Swiss cheese
    2 tablespoons flour
    1 tablespoon WYLER'S® or
      STEERO® Chicken-Flavor
      Instant Bouillon
    1 cup BORDEN® or MEADOW
      GOLD® Milk
    3 eggs, well beaten
    ¼ cup chopped onion
    2 tablespoons chopped green
      pepper
    2 tablespoons chopped pimiento

Preheat oven to 425°. Bake pastry shell 8 minutes; remove from oven. Reduce oven temperature to 350°. In medium bowl, toss cheese with flour and bouillon; add remaining ingredients. Mix well. Pour into prepared shell. Bake 40 to 45 minutes or until set. Let stand 10 minutes before serving. Garnish as desired. Refrigerate leftovers.
Makes 6 servings.

Gingery Banana Waffles

Serve pancakes hot with pancake syrup and additional cooked Sizzlean® strips, if desired.
Makes 5 servings.

Gingery Banana Waffles

    3 cups flour
    4 teaspoons baking powder
    2 teaspoons ground cinnamon
1½ teaspoons ground ginger
    1 teaspoon salt
    4 eggs
  ⅔ cup brown sugar, packed
    2 extra-ripe, medium DOLE®
      Bananas
1¼ cups milk
  ½ cup molasses
  ½ cup margarine, melted
    4 firm, medium DOLE® Bananas,
      sliced
      Maple syrup

Preheat waffle iron. In large bowl, combine flour, baking powder, cinnamon, ginger and salt. In medium bowl, beat eggs with brown sugar until light and fluffy. Puree extra-ripe bananas in blender (1 cup). Beat pureed bananas, milk, molasses and margarine into egg mixture; add to dry ingredients. Stir until just moistened. For each waffle, cook ¾ cup batter in waffle iron until golden. Serve with sliced bananas and syrup.
Makes 8 servings.

Mandarin Orange French Toast

    1 can (11 ounces) DOLE®
      Mandarin Orange Segments
    1 tablespoon grated orange peel
  ½ cup orange juice
    1 tablespoon brown sugar
    2 teaspoons cornstarch
    1 teaspoon vanilla extract
      Dash ground nutmeg
    2 eggs, lightly beaten
  ½ cup half-and-half
    4 slices (½ inch thick each)
      stale French bread or thick-
      sliced white bread
    2 tablespoons margarine
  ¼ cup DOLE® Sliced Natural
      Almonds, toasted, optional

Drain syrup from oranges into saucepan. Stir in orange peel and juice, brown sugar, cornstarch, vanilla and nutmeg. Cook over low heat, stirring, until sauce thickens slightly and turns clear. Remove from heat; add orange segments.

In pie plate, combine eggs and half-and-half. Dip bread in egg mixture, saturating both sides. Melt margarine in large skillet until hot. Cook soaked bread in skillet until golden brown on each side. Place 2 slices French toast on each plate; top with Mandarin orange sauce. Sprinkle with almonds, if desired.
Makes 2 servings.

Oatmeal Griddlecakes

    8 SIZZLEAN® Breakfast Strips
1½ cups uncooked rolled oats
    2 cups milk
    1 cup all-purpose flour
    2 tablespoons packed dark
      brown sugar
    2 teaspoons baking powder
    1 teaspoon salt
    3 eggs, lightly beaten
  ¼ cup butter or margarine,
      melted, cooled
      Pancake syrup

Cook Sizzlean® strips according to package directions. Dice and set aside. Mix oats and milk in large bowl and set aside until all milk has been absorbed. Combine flour, brown sugar, baking powder and salt in small bowl. Add eggs and diced Sizzlean® pieces to oat mixture; mix well. Stir in flour mixture. Add butter and stir only long enough to blend batter. Do not overmix.

Lightly grease griddle or heavy skillet and heat over medium heat until water drop flicked onto it "dances" and instantly evaporates. Pour or ladle batter into pan to form 3½-inch-diameter pancakes. Cook 2 to 3 minutes until small bubbles form on pancake surface and begin to break.

Flip over and brown other side. Stack cooked pancakes on heated platter and keep warm. Repeat cooking procedure using remaining batter.

Chocolate Waffles

    1 cup all-purpose flour
  ¾ cup sugar
  ½ cup HERSHEY'S Cocoa
  ½ teaspoon baking powder
  ½ teaspoon baking soda
  ¼ teaspoon salt
    1 cup buttermilk or sour milk*
    2 eggs
  ¼ cup butter or margarine, melted

In large bowl, stir together flour, sugar, cocoa, baking powder, baking soda and salt. Add buttermilk and eggs; beat just until blended. Gradually add butter, beating until smooth. Bake in hot waffle iron according to manufacturer's directions. Serve warm with pancake syrup. For dessert, serve with ice cream, fruit-flavored syrups or sweetened whipped cream.
10 to 12 four-inch waffles.
    *To sour milk: use 1 tablespoon vinegar plus milk to equal 1 cup.

Philly® Cream Cheese Brunch Quiche

        Pastry for 1-crust 10-inch pie
    1 **8-ounce package**
         PHILADELPHIA BRAND®
         Cream Cheese, cubed
    1 **cup milk**
    4 **eggs, beaten**
    ¼ **cup chopped onion**
    1 **tablespoon PARKAY®**
         Margarine
    1 **cup finely chopped ham**
    ¼ **cup chopped pimento**
    ¼ **teaspoon dill weed**
         Dash of pepper

On lightly floured surface, roll pastry to 12-inch circle. Place in 10-inch pie plate. Turn under edge; flute. Prick bottom and sides of pastry with fork. Bake at 400°, 12 to 15 minutes or until pastry is lightly browned.

Combine cream cheese and milk in saucepan; stir over low heat until smooth. Gradually add cream cheese mixture to eggs, mixing until well blended. Saute onions in margarine. Add onions and remaining ingredients to cream cheese mixture; mix well. Pour into pastry shell. Bake at 350°, 35 to 40 minutes or until set. Garnish with ham slices and fresh dill, if desired.
8 servings.

Variations: Substitute ¼ cup finely chopped green pepper for dill weed.

Substitute 10-ounce package frozen chopped spinach, cooked, drained, 1 cup (4 ounces) shredded KRAFT® 100% Natural Swiss Cheese and 6 crisply cooked bacon slices, crumbled, for ham, pimento and dill weed.

Substitute 4-ounce package pepperoni slices, chopped, ¼ cup (1 ounce) KRAFT® 100% Grated Parmesan Cheese and ½ teaspoon dried oregano leaves, crushed, for ham, pimento and dill weed. Place pepperoni on bottom of baked pastry shell; continue as directed.

Tempting Cheese Crepes

    ⅔ **cup flour**
    ½ **teaspoon salt**
    3 **eggs, beaten**
    1 **cup milk**
    2 **8-ounce packages Light**
         PHILADELPHIA BRAND®
         Neufchatel Cheese, softened
    ¼ **cup sugar**
    1 **teaspoon vanilla**
         Strawberry-Banana Topping

Combine flour, salt and eggs; beat until smooth. Gradually add milk, mixing until well blended. For each crepe, pour ¼ cup batter into hot, lightly greased 8-inch skillet or crepe pan, tilting skillet to cover bottom. Cook over medium-high heat until lightly browned on both sides, turning once.

Combine Neufchatel cheese, sugar and vanilla, mixing until well blended. Spread approximately ¼ cup Neufchatel cheese mixture onto each crepe. Fold in thirds. Place in 13×9-inch baking dish. Bake at 350°, 15 to 20 minutes or until thoroughly heated. Serve with Strawberry-Banana Topping.
8 servings.

Preparation Tip: Lightly grease and preheat the skillet or crepe pan until a drop of water sizzles when sprinkled on. If the skillet isn't really hot, crepes may be too thick and stick to the pan.

Strawberry-Banana Topping

    1 **10-ounce package frozen**
         strawberries, thawed
    1 **tablespoon cornstarch**
    1 **banana, sliced**

Drain strawberries, reserving liquid. Add enough water to reserved liquid to measure 1¼ cups; gradually add to cornstarch in saucepan, stirring until well blended. Bring to boil over medium heat, stirring constantly. Boil 1 minute. Stir in fruit.
2 cups.

Southwestern Egg Puff

    1 **lb. VELVEETA® Mexican**
         Pasteurized Process Cheese
         Spread with Jalapeño
         Pepper, cubed
    2 **cups cottage cheese**
    6 **eggs, beaten**
    ½ **cup picante sauce**
    ¼ **cup PARKAY® Margarine,**
         melted
    ¼ **cup flour**
    ½ **teaspoon baking powder**
    ½ **teaspoon seasoned salt**
    1 **12-oz. can whole kernel corn**
         with sweet peppers, drained

In large bowl, combine ingredients; mix well. Pour into greased 12×8-inch baking dish. Bake at 350°, 35 to 40 minutes or until golden brown. Top with additional picante sauce, sour cream and avocado slices, if desired.
4 to 6 servings.

Preparation time: 10 minutes
Baking time: 40 minutes

Variation: Substitute VELVEETA® Pasteurized Process Cheese Spread for Process Cheese Spread with Jalapeño Pepper.

Huevos Rancheros

    2 **tablespoons vegetable oil**
    1 **small onion, chopped**
    1 **green pepper, chopped**
    1 **tomato, peeled and chopped**
    1 **can (8 ounces) tomato sauce**
    ½ **cup water**
    1 **clove garlic, minced**
    1 **teaspoon dried oregano leaves**
    ½ **teaspoon salt**
    ½ **to 1 teaspoon TABASCO®**
         pepper sauce
    6 **eggs**
         Tortillas or toasted English
         muffins

In large skillet heat oil; add onion and green pepper. Cook 5 minutes or until tender. Add tomato, tomato sauce, water, garlic, oregano, salt and Tabasco® sauce. Cover; simmer 20 minutes. Break eggs, 1 at a time, into cup and slip into sauce. Cover; simmer over low heat 5 minutes or until eggs are set. Serve over tortillas or English muffins.
Makes 6 servings.

Philly® Cream Cheese Brunch Quiche, spinach variation (top) and Tempting Cheese Crepes (bottom)

Colorful Ham Omelet

3 tablespoons unsalted margarine or butter, divided
¼ cup finely chopped onion
¼ cup *each* finely chopped red and green pepper
½ cup (2 ounces) ARMOUR® Lower Salt Ham cut into ¼-inch cubes
6 eggs
¼ cup (1 ounce) shredded ARMOUR® Lower Salt Cheddar Cheese

Melt 1 tablespoon of the margarine in small skillet or omelet pan over medium heat. Add onion and red and green peppers; sauté about 3 to 5 minutes, or until tender. Add ham cubes; heat thoroughly. Remove and set aside.

Melt 1 tablespoon of the margarine in same pan over medium heat; add 3 well-beaten eggs. Cook eggs, pulling edges toward center, until almost set. Spoon half of the ham mixture over eggs. Cover and continue cooking until set. *Do not overcook.* Fold half of the omelet over other half. Sprinkle half of the cheese over top. Gently slide onto serving plate. Repeat with remaining ingredients. Serve immediately. Garnish with cilantro, if desired.
Makes 2 servings.

Microwave Directions: Place 1 tablespoon of the margarine, onion, red and green peppers, and ham in small microwave-safe dish. Cook on High power for 3 minutes; set aside. Separate eggs; beat egg whites in medium bowl until soft peaks form. Beat egg yolks with 2 tablespoons water in small bowl. Gently fold yolk mixture into whites. Melt remaining 2 tablespoons margarine in microwave-safe 9-inch pie plate; swirl to coat bottom. Carefully pour half of the egg mixture into pie plate. Cook on Medium power (50%) about 7 to 9 minutes or until almost set. Spoon half of the ham mixture and cheese over eggs. Cook on Medium-High power (70%) for 2 more minutes, or until eggs are set. Fold and remove omelet from pie plate as above. Repeat with remaining ingredients. Garnish as above.

Nutrition Information Per Serving: 497 calories, 27 g protein, 42 g fat, 6.4 g carbohydrates, 851 mg cholesterol, 500 mg sodium.

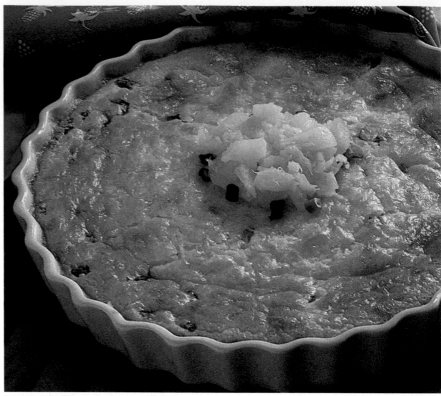

Pineapple Brunch Casserole

Eggs Arnold

¼ cup butter or margarine
2 medium onions, peeled, thinly sliced
8 eggs
½ cup milk
1 teaspoon TABASCO® pepper sauce
¼ teaspoon salt
2 tablespoons chopped parsley
4 English muffins
1 tablespoon spicy brown mustard
3 ounces thinly sliced salami

In medium skillet melt butter; cook onions over low heat about 15 to 20 minutes or until lightly golden. Meanwhile, in large bowl beat together eggs, milk, Tabasco® sauce and salt. When onions are cooked, stir in egg mixture. When edges begin to set, draw cooked portions toward center so uncooked portion flows to bottom. Stir constantly; cook over low heat about 4 to 6 minutes or until eggs are cooked throughout, but still moist. Gently stir in parsley. Split and toast English muffins; spread with mustard. Top with salami slices and egg mixture. Serve with additional Tabasco® sauce, if desired.
Makes 4 servings.

Pineapple Brunch Casserole

1 can (8 ounces) DOLE® Crushed Pineapple in Juice
1 cup biscuit mix
1 cup milk
4 eggs, lightly beaten
6 tablespoons margarine, melted
1 teaspoon Dijon mustard
½ teaspoon onion powder
Pinch ground nutmeg
4 ounces cooked ham, diced
1 cup shredded Monterey Jack or sharp Cheddar cheese
2 green onions, finely chopped

Preheat oven to 350°F. Drain pineapple. Reserve 2 tablespoons pineapple for garnish, if desired. Combine biscuit mix, milk, eggs, margarine, mustard, onion powder and nutmeg in blender or in large mixer bowl until smooth. Stir in ham, cheese, onions and pineapple. Pour into greased 9-inch pie plate. Bake in preheated oven 35 to 40 minutes or until set. Garnish with reserved pineapple, if desired.
Makes 6 servings.

Sausage Omelet

- 1 package (8 ounces) SWIFT PREMIUM® BROWN 'N SERVE™ Sausage Links
- ¼ cup chopped onion
- ¼ cup chopped green bell pepper
- 5 eggs
- ¼ cup milk
- 1 tomato, chopped
- 1½ tablespoons butter or margarine

Heat sausage in heavy 8-inch oven-proof skillet according to package directions. Remove sausage and keep warm. Saute onion and green pepper in same skillet over medium-high heat until vegetables are tender. Combine eggs and milk in medium bowl. Add onion, green pepper and tomato. Melt butter in same skillet over low heat. Add egg mixture and cook until eggs are almost set. Arrange sausage on top of eggs. To finish cooking top of omelet, broil, 4 inches from heat, until center is firm and top is lightly browned. Cut into wedges and serve immediately.
Makes 5 servings.

Cream Cheese Kugel

- 1 8-ounce package PHILADELPHIA BRAND® Cream Cheese, softened
- ¼ cup PARKAY® Margarine, melted
- 4 eggs, beaten
- ½ cup milk
- ¼ cup sugar
- ½ teaspoon salt
- 4 cups (8 ounces) fine noodles, cooked, drained
- ½ cup raisins
- ¼ teaspoon cinnamon

Combine cream cheese and margarine, mixing until well blended. Blend in eggs, milk, sugar and salt. Add noodles and raisins; mix well. Pour mixture into 12×8-inch baking dish. Sprinkle with cinnamon. Bake at 375°, 30 minutes or until set.
6 to 8 servings.

Variation: Substitute 8¼-ounce can crushed pineapple, drained, for raisins.

Microwave: Prepare recipe as directed except for baking. Microwave on High 8 minutes, turning dish after 4 minutes. Microwave on Medium (50%) 9 to 12 minutes or until center is set.

Phyllo Spinach Pie

- 1 container (15 ounces) ricotta cheese
- 1 package (10 ounces) frozen chopped spinach, cooked and squeezed dry
- 2 eggs, slightly beaten
- 2 tablespoons grated Parmesan cheese
- 1 envelope LIPTON® Recipe Secrets Vegetable Recipe Soup Mix
- ¼ teaspoon ground nutmeg
- 2 cups fresh or canned sliced mushrooms
- 15 phyllo strudel sheets
- ½ cup butter or margarine, melted

Preheat oven to 375°.

In large bowl, thoroughly combine ricotta, spinach, eggs, Parmesan cheese, vegetable recipe soup mix and nutmeg; stir in mushrooms and set aside.

Unfold phyllo strudel sheets; cover with wax paper, then damp cloth. Brush 1 sheet at a time with melted butter. Place 6 buttered sheets across 9-inch pie plate, extending sheets over sides; press gently into pie plate. Place an additional 6 buttered sheets in opposite direction across 9-inch pie plate, extending sheets over sides, to form a cross, press gently into pie plate. Turn spinach mixture into prepared pie plate; gently fold sheets over spinach mixture to cover. Form remaining 3 buttered sheets into a ball and place on center of pie; brush with butter. Bake 35 minutes or until golden. Let stand 10 minutes before serving.
Makes about 8 servings.

Freezing Directions: Pie can be frozen up to 1 month. Simply prepare as above, but do not brush with butter or bake. Wrap in heavy-duty aluminum foil; freeze. To serve, unwrap, then brush with butter as above and bake at 375°, 90 minutes or until golden. Let stand as above.

Sausage 'n Egg Brunch Special

- ½ pound ECKRICH® Smoked Sausage
- 12 ounces frozen shredded hash brown potatoes, thawed
- ½ cup sour cream
- ¼ cup milk
- ½ cup (2 ounces) shredded sharp Cheddar cheese
- 1 tablespoon chopped chives
- 4 eggs

Preheat oven to 350°F. Combine potatoes, sour cream, milk, cheese and chives in medium bowl. Spoon into buttered shallow 2-quart rectangular casserole. Bake 40 minutes. Cut sausage into halves lengthwise, then cut crosswise into bite-sized pieces. Arrange down center of casserole. Bake 10 minutes more. Shape a well in each corner of the potato mixture. Break an egg into each well. Bake 10 to 12 minutes more or until eggs reach desired doneness. Serve immediately.
Makes 4 servings.

Sausage Omelet

Scandinavian Salmon-Cheddar Pie

- **3 large eggs**
- **¼ cup milk**
- **3 tablespoons chopped parsley, divided**
- **2 tablespoons butter, melted**
- **2 tablespoons minced green onion**
- **1 tablespoon plus 1 teaspoon lemon juice**
- **1 teaspoon Worcestershire sauce**
- **½ teaspoon dry mustard**
- **2 cups (8 ounces) shredded Wisconsin Cheddar cheese**
- **½ pound fresh cooked, flaked salmon *or* 1 can (6½ ounces) salmon, drained, deboned and flaked**
- **1 (9-inch) pie shell, baked and cooled**
- **¾ cup dairy sour cream**
- **¾ cup finely chopped cucumber**
- **1 teaspoon dill weed**
- **⅛ teaspoon ground white pepper**

Heat oven to 425°F. Beat eggs in large bowl; add milk, 2 tablespoons of the parsley, the butter, green onion, 1 tablespoon lemon juice, Worcestershire sauce and mustard; mix well. Fold in cheese and salmon; pour into cooled pie shell. Bake 20 to 25 minutes or until just set and crust is golden brown. Let stand 10 minutes before serving. Combine sour cream, cucumber, remaining 1 tablespoon parsley, dill, remaining 1 teaspoon lemon juice and pepper; mix well. Dollop each serving with sour cream mixture.

Makes 6 servings

*Favorite recipe from **Wisconsin Milk Marketing Board** © 1993*

Rice Bran Granola Cereal

- **2 cups uncooked old-fashioned rolled oats**
- **1 cup crisp rice cereal**
- **¾ cup rice bran**
- **¾ cup raisins**
- **⅓ cup slivered almonds**
- **1 tablespoon ground cinnamon**
- **⅓ cup honey**
- **1 tablespoon margarine, melted**
- **Vegetable cooking spray**

Combine oats, cereal, bran, raisins, almonds, and cinnamon in large bowl; stir in honey and margarine. Spread mixture on baking sheet coated with cooking spray. Bake in preheated 350°F. oven for 8 to 10 minutes. Let cool. Serve as a topping for yogurt and/or fresh fruit. Store in a tightly covered container.

Makes 10 (½-cup) servings

Tip: Can be served as a cereal (with milk) or as a snack.

*Favorite recipe from **USA Rice Council***

Scandinavian Salmon-Cheddar Pie

Praline Pancakes

- **1½ cups skim milk**
- **2 tablespoons margarine, melted**
- **2 teaspoons brandy**
- **1 teaspoon vanilla extract**
- **1 cup all-purpose flour**
- **2 tablespoons sugar**
- **1 teaspoon baking powder**
- **¼ teaspoon salt**
- **⅛ teaspoon ground cinnamon**
- **1 cup cooked rice, cooled**
- **⅓ cup pecans, coarsely chopped**
- **4 egg whites, stiffly beaten**
- **Vegetable cooking spray**
- **Reduced-calorie syrup (optional)**

Combine milk, margarine, brandy, vanilla, flour, sugar, baking powder, salt, and cinnamon in large bowl; stir until smooth. Stir in rice and pecans. Fold in beaten egg whites. Pour scant ¼ cup batter onto hot griddle coated with cooking spray. Cook over medium heat until bubbles form on top and underside is lightly browned. Turn to brown other side. Serve warm drizzled with syrup.   *Makes 6 servings*

Favorite recipe from **USA Rice Council**

Rice Bran Buttermilk Pancakes

**1 cup rice flour or
   all-purpose flour
¾ cup rice bran
1 tablespoon sugar
1 teaspoon baking powder
½ teaspoon baking soda
1¼ cups low-fat buttermilk
3 egg whites, beaten
   Vegetable cooking spray
   Fresh fruit or reduced-
    calorie syrup (optional)**

Sift together flour, bran, sugar, baking powder, and baking soda into large bowl. Combine buttermilk and egg whites in small bowl; add to flour mixture. Stir until smooth. Pour ¼ cup batter onto hot griddle coated with cooking spray. Cook over medium heat until bubbles form on top and underside is lightly browned. Turn to brown other side. Serve with fresh fruit or syrup.   *Makes about 10 (4-inch) pancakes*

Variation: For Cinnamon Pancakes, add 1 teaspoon ground cinnamon to dry ingredients.

Favorite recipe from **USA Rice Council**

Rice Bran Buttermilk Pancakes

Brunch Rice

Brunch Rice

1 teaspoon margarine
¾ cup shredded carrots
¾ cup diced green pepper
¾ cup (about 3 ounces) sliced fresh mushrooms
6 egg whites, beaten
2 eggs, beaten
½ cup skim milk
½ teaspoon salt
¼ teaspoon black pepper
3 cups cooked brown rice
½ cup (2 ounces) shredded Cheddar cheese
6 corn tortillas, warmed (optional)

Heat margarine in large skillet over medium-high heat until hot. Add carrots, green pepper, and mushrooms; cook 2 minutes. Combine egg whites, eggs, milk, salt, and black pepper in small bowl. Reduce heat to medium and pour egg mixture over vegetables. Continue stirring 1½ to 2 minutes. Add rice and cheese; stir gently to separate grains. Heat 2 minutes. Serve immediately or spoon mixture into warmed corn tortillas.
Makes 6 servings

*Favorite recipe from **USA Rice Council***

Breakfast in a Cup

3 cups cooked rice
1 cup (4 ounces) shredded Cheddar cheese, divided
1 can (4 ounces) diced green chiles
1 jar (2 ounces) diced pimientos, drained
⅓ cup skim milk
2 eggs, beaten
½ teaspoon ground cumin
½ teaspoon salt
½ teaspoon ground black pepper
Vegetable cooking spray

Combine rice, ½ cup cheese, chiles, pimientos, milk, eggs, cumin, salt, and pepper in large bowl. Evenly divide mixture into 12 muffin cups coated with cooking spray. Sprinkle with remaining ½ cup cheese. Bake at 400°F. for 15 minutes or until set.   *Makes 12 servings*

Tip: Breakfast cups may be stored in the freezer in tightly sealed container or freezer bag. To reheat frozen breakfast cups, microwave each cup on HIGH 1 minute.

*Favorite recipe from **USA Rice Council***

Brown Rice, Mushroom, and Ham Hash

1 tablespoon olive oil
2 cups (about 8 ounces) sliced fresh mushrooms
1 small onion, minced
1 clove garlic, minced
3 cups cooked brown rice
1 cup (6 ounces) diced turkey ham
½ cup chopped walnuts (optional)
¼ cup snipped parsley
1 tablespoon white wine vinegar
1 tablespoon Dijon mustard
¼ teaspoon ground black pepper

Heat oil in Dutch oven or large saucepan over medium-low heat until hot. Add mushrooms, onion, and garlic; cook until tender. Stir in rice, ham, walnuts, parsley, vinegar, mustard, and pepper; cook, stirring until thoroughly heated.
Makes 8 servings

*Favorite recipe from **USA Rice Council***

Brunch Potato Cassoulet

Brunch Potato Cassoulet

2 tablespoons unsalted margarine or butter
2 cups (8 ounces) ARMOUR® Lower Salt Ham, cut into ½-inch cubes
2 cups frozen natural potato wedges
1 cup sliced mushrooms
½ cup chopped red onion
½ cup chopped green bell pepper
1 cup frozen speckled butter beans, cooked according to package directions, omitting salt, drained
Lower salt cheese (optional)

Preheat oven to 350°F. Melt margarine in large skillet over medium heat. Add ham, potatoes, mushrooms, onion and green bell pepper; cook over medium heat about 5 to 6 minutes, or until onion is soft. Stir in cooked beans. Transfer to medium earthenware pot or ovenproof Dutch oven. Bake, covered, about 10 to 12 minutes, or until heated through. If desired, sprinkle with lower salt cheese and broil 4 to 6 inches from heat source about 2 to 3 minutes or until cheese is melted and slightly browned.

Makes 4 to 6 servings

Ham Breakfast Sandwich

1 ounce Neufchatel or light cream cheese, softened
2 teaspoons apricot spreadable fruit
2 teaspoons plain nonfat yogurt
6 slices raisin bread
Lettuce leaves
1 package (6 ounces) ECKRICH® Lite Lower Salt Ham
3 Granny Smith apple rings

Combine cheese, spreadable fruit and yogurt in small bowl. Spread on bread slices. To make each sandwich: Place lettuce on 1 slice bread. Top with 2 slices ham, 1 apple ring and another slice of bread.   *Makes 3 sandwiches*

Mushroom Frittata

1 teaspoon butter or margarine
1 medium zucchini, shredded
1 medium tomato, chopped
1 can (4 ounces) sliced mushrooms, drained
6 eggs, beaten
¼ cup milk
2 teaspoons Dijon mustard
½ teaspoon LAWRY'S® Seasoned Salt
½ teaspoon LAWRY'S® Seasoned Pepper
2 cups (8 ounces) grated Swiss cheese

In large, ovenproof skillet, melt butter and sauté zucchini, tomato and mushrooms 1 minute. In large bowl, combine remaining ingredients; blend well. Pour egg mixture into skillet; cook 10 minutes over low heat. To brown top, place skillet under broiler 2 to 3 minutes.

Makes 4 servings

Presentation: Serve directly from skillet or remove frittata to serving dish. Serve with additional Swiss cheese and fresh fruit.

Hint: Try serving frittata with prepared Lawry's® Spaghetti Sauce Seasoning Blend with Imported Mushrooms.

Ham Breakfast Sandwich

BREADS, MUFFINS & COFFEECAKES

Fill your kitchen with the tantalizing aromas of homemade bread fresh from the oven! From quick-to-make muffins to slow-rising yeast breads, you'll create new family favorites. Make breakfast extra special with a heartwarming buttery coffeecake. Enhance a lunch-time salad with aromatic herb popovers. Or round off a hearty meal with wholesome wheat bread.

Apricot Date Mini-Loaves

**1 package DUNCAN HINES®
   Bakery Style Cinnamon
   Swirl Muffin Mix**
½ teaspoon baking powder
2 egg whites
⅔ cup water
½ cup chopped dried apricots
½ cup chopped dates

1. Preheat oven to 350°F. Grease four 5⅜×2⅝×1⅞-inch mini-loaf pans.

2. Combine muffin mix and baking powder in large bowl. Break up any lumps. Add egg whites, water, apricots and dates. Stir until well blended, about 50 strokes.

3. Knead swirl packet from Mix for 10 seconds before opening. Cut off one end of swirl packet. Squeeze contents onto batter. Swirl into batter with knife or spatula, folding from bottom of bowl to get an even swirl. Do not completely mix into batter. Divide evenly into pans. Sprinkle with contents of topping packet from Mix.

4. Bake at 350°F for 30 to 35 minutes or until toothpick inserted in center comes out clean. Cool 15 minutes. Loosen loaves from pans. Lift out with knife. Cool completely. Garnish as desired.   *4 Mini-Loaves*

Tip: This recipe may also be baked in greased 8½×4½×2½-inch loaf pan at 350°F for 55 to 60 minutes or until toothpick inserted in center comes out clean. Cool 10 minutes before removing loaf from pan.

Chocolate Chunk Banana Bread

2 eggs, lightly beaten
**1 cup mashed ripe bananas
   (about 3 medium
   bananas)**
⅓ cup vegetable oil
¼ cup milk
2 cups all-purpose flour
1 cup sugar
**2 teaspoons CALUMET®
   Baking Powder**
¼ teaspoon salt
**1 package (4 ounces)
   BAKER'S® GERMAN'S®
   Sweet Chocolate,
   coarsely chopped**
½ cup chopped nuts

HEAT oven to 350°F.

STIR eggs, bananas, oil and milk until well blended. Add flour, sugar, baking powder and salt; stir until just moistened. Stir in chocolate and nuts. Pour into greased 9×5-inch loaf pan.

BAKE for 55 minutes or until toothpick inserted in center comes out clean. Cool in pan 10 minutes. Remove from pan to cool on wire rack.

Makes 1 loaf

Prep time: 20 minutes
Baking time: 55 minutes

Apricot Date Mini-Loaves

Banana Macadamia Nut Bread

Banana Bran Loaf

- **1 cup mashed ripe bananas (about 2 large)**
- **½ cup sugar**
- **⅓ cup liquid vegetable oil margarine**
- **2 egg whites**
- **⅓ cup skim milk**
- **1¼ cups all-purpose flour**
- **1 cup QUAKER® Oat Bran™ hot cereal, uncooked**
- **2 teaspoons baking powder**
- **½ teaspoon baking soda**

Heat oven to 350°F. Lightly spray 8×4-inch or 9×5-inch loaf pan with no stick cooking spray or oil lightly. Combine bananas, sugar, margarine, egg whites and milk; mix well. Add combined flour, oat bran, baking powder and baking soda, mixing just until moistened. Pour into prepared pan. Bake 55 to 60 minutes or until wooden pick inserted in center comes out clean. Cool 10 minutes in pan; remove to wire rack. Cool completely.

Makes 16 servings

Tips:

To freeze bread slices: Layer waxed paper between each slice of bread. Wrap securely in foil or place in freezer bag. Seal, label and freeze.

To reheat bread slices: Unwrap frozen bread slices; wrap in paper towel. Microwave at HIGH about 30 seconds for each slice, or until warm.

Banana Macadamia Nut Bread

- **2 cups all-purpose flour**
- **¾ cup sugar**
- **½ cup LAND O LAKES® Butter, softened**
- **2 eggs**
- **1 teaspoon baking soda**
- **½ teaspoon salt**
- **1 tablespoon grated orange peel**
- **1 teaspoon vanilla**
- **1 cup mashed ripe bananas (2 medium)**
- **¼ cup orange juice**
- **1 cup flaked coconut**
- **1 jar (3½ ounces) coarsely chopped macadamia nuts *or* walnuts (¾ cup)**

Heat oven to 350°. In large mixer bowl combine flour, sugar, butter, eggs, baking soda, salt, orange peel and vanilla. Beat at low speed, scraping bowl often, until well mixed, 2 to 3 minutes. Add bananas and orange juice. Continue beating, scraping bowl often, until well mixed, 1 minute. By hand, stir in coconut and nuts. (Batter will be thick.) Spread into 1 greased 9×5-inch loaf pan or 3 greased 5½×3-inch mini-loaf pans.

Bake 9×5-inch loaf for 60 to 65 minutes or mini loaves for 35 to 45 minutes, or until wooden pick inserted in center comes out clean. Cool 10 minutes; remove from pan.

Makes 1 (9×5-inch) loaf or 3 mini loaves

Corn Bread

- **¼ cup CRISCO® Shortening**
- **¼ cup sugar**
- **2 egg whites**
- **1 cup all-purpose flour**
- **1 cup yellow cornmeal**
- **4 teaspoons baking powder**
- **½ teaspoon salt (optional)**
- **1¼ cups skim milk**

1. Heat oven to 425°F. Grease 9-inch square pan.

2. Cream Crisco® and sugar with fork in medium bowl until blended. Add egg whites. Beat until fairly smooth.

3. Combine flour, cornmeal, baking powder and salt (if used) in separate bowl. Add to shortening mixture alternately with milk. Stir until dry ingredients are just moistened. Pour into pan.

4. Bake at 425°F for 20 minutes or until light golden brown around edges. Cut in squares. Serve warm.

Makes 9 servings

Pear Nut Bread with Citrus Cream Cheese

Pear Nut Bread
  1 package (14 ounces) nut bread mix
  ⅛ teaspoon ground nutmeg
  1 fresh California Bartlett pear, cored and finely chopped (about 1¼ cups)

Citrus Cream Cheese
  1 package (8 ounces) light cream cheese (Neufchatel), softened
  1 tablespoon finely grated orange peel

Grease and flour 8×4×3-inch loaf pan. Prepare bread mix according to package directions, adding nutmeg and *substituting pear for ½ the liquid required.* Bake according to package directions. In small bowl, combine cream cheese and orange peel. Spread Citrus Cream Cheese on Pear Nut Bread. *Makes 1 loaf*

Favorite recipe from **California Tree Fruit Agreement**

Lemon Blueberry Poppy Seed Bread

Bread
  1 package DUNCAN HINES® Bakery Style Blueberry Muffin Mix
  2 tablespoons poppy seed
  1 egg
  ¾ cup water
  1 tablespoon grated lemon peel

Drizzle
  ½ cup confectioners sugar
  1 tablespoon lemon juice

1. Preheat oven to 350°F. Grease and flour 8½×4½×2½-inch loaf pan.

2. Rinse blueberries from Mix with cold water and drain.

3. **For bread,** combine muffin mix and poppy seed in medium bowl. Break up any lumps. Add egg and water. Stir until moistened, about 50 strokes. Fold in blueberries and lemon peel. Pour into pan. Sprinkle with contents of topping packet from Mix. Bake at 350°F for 1 hour or until toothpick inserted in center comes out clean. Cool in pan 10 minutes. Loosen loaf from pan. Invert onto cooling rack. Turn right-side up. Cool completely.

4. **For drizzle,** combine confectioners sugar and lemon juice in small bowl. Stir until smooth. Drizzle over loaf.

1 Loaf (12 Slices)

Tip: To help keep topping intact when removing loaf from pan, place aluminum foil over top.

Lemon Blueberry Poppy Seed Bread

Favorite Banana Bread

1 8-ounce package
    PHILADELPHIA BRAND®
    Cream Cheese, softened
1 cup sugar
1/4 cup **PARKAY®** Margarine
1 cup mashed ripe banana
2 eggs
2 1/4 cups flour
1 1/2 teaspoons baking powder
1/2 teaspoon baking soda
1 cup chopped nuts

Combine cream cheese, sugar and margarine, mixing until well blended. Blend in banana and eggs. Add combined remaining ingredients, mixing just until moistened. Pour into greased and floured 9×5-inch loaf pan. Bake at 350°, 1 hour and 10 minutes or until wooden pick inserted near center comes out clean. Cool 5 minutes; remove from pan. Serve with additional cream cheese, if desired.
1 loaf.

Pumpkin Nut Bread

3 1/2 cups unsifted flour
2 teaspoons baking soda
1 1/2 teaspoons ground cinnamon
1/2 teaspoon baking powder
2 cups sugar
2/3 cup shortening
4 eggs
1 (16-ounce) can pumpkin (about 2 cups)
1/2 cup water
1 (9-ounce) package NONE SUCH® Condensed Mincemeat, crumbled
1 cup chopped nuts

Preheat oven to 350°. Stir together flour, baking soda, cinnamon and baking powder; set aside. In large mixer bowl, beat sugar and shortening until fluffy. Add eggs, pumpkin and water; mix well. Stir in flour mixture, mincemeat and nuts. Turn into 2 greased 9×5-inch loaf pans. Bake 55 to 60 minutes or until wooden pick inserted near center comes out clean. Cool 10 minutes; remove from pan. Cool completely.
Makes two 9×5-inch loaves.

Louisiana Corn Muffins

1 cup flour
1 cup yellow cornmeal
2 tablespoons sugar
2 1/2 teaspoons baking powder
1/2 teaspoon salt
1 cup milk
1/2 cup vegetable oil
2 eggs, lightly beaten
1/2 teaspoon **TABASCO®** pepper sauce
1 can (8 3/4 ounces) whole kernel corn, drained, or 1 cup fresh or thawed frozen corn kernels

Preheat oven to 400°F. Grease twelve 3×1 1/4-inch muffin cups. In large bowl combine flour, cornmeal, sugar, baking powder and salt. In medium bowl combine milk, oil, eggs and Tabasco® sauce. Make a well in center of dry ingredients; add milk mixture and stir just to combine. Stir in corn. Spoon batter into prepared muffin cups. Bake 15 to 20 minutes or until a cake tester inserted in center comes out clean. Cool 5 minutes on wire rack. Remove from pans. Serve warm.
Makes 12 muffins.

Microwave Directions: Prepare muffin batter as directed above. Spoon approximately 1/3 cup batter into each of 6 paper baking cup–lined 6-ounce custard cups or microwave-safe muffin pan cups. Cook uncovered on High 4 to 5 1/2 minutes or until cake tester inserted in center comes out clean; turn and rearrange cups or turn muffin pan 1/2 turn once during cooking. Cool 5 minutes on wire rack. Remove from pans. Repeat procedure with remaining batter. Serve warm.

Golden Oatmeal Muffins

1 package **DUNCAN HINES®**
    Moist Deluxe Butter Recipe
    Golden Cake Mix
1 cup quick-cooking oats
1/4 teaspoon salt
3/4 cup milk
2 large eggs, slightly beaten
2 tablespoons butter or margarine, melted
Honey or jam

1. Preheat oven to 400°F. Grease 24 muffin cups.
2. Combine dry cake mix, oats and salt in bowl. Beat together milk, eggs and butter. Add to dry ingredients, stirring just until moistened. Spoon into muffin cups, filling two-thirds full.
3. Bake at 400°F for 13 minutes or until golden brown. Serve with honey or your favorite jam.
24 muffins.

Honey-Lemon Muffins

3/4 cup **ROMAN MEAL®** Original Wheat, Rye, Bran, Flax Cereal
1 1/2 cups all-purpose flour
1 tablespoon baking powder
1/2 teaspoon salt
1 egg, slightly beaten
1 cup plain yogurt
1/2 cup vegetable oil
1/2 cup honey
2 teaspoons grated lemon peel
1 to 2 tablespoons lemon juice

In large bowl, combine cereal, flour, baking powder and salt. In small bowl, mix egg, yogurt, oil, honey, lemon peel and juice. Add liquid mixture to flour mixture; stir just until moistened. Batter will be lumpy; do not overmix. Spoon batter evenly into 12 greased 2 1/2-inch muffin cups. Bake in preheated 375° oven 20 to 25 minutes or until golden brown. Remove to wire rack to cool.
Makes 1 dozen muffins.

Golden Oatmeal Muffins

Cranberry Muffins and Creamy Orange Spread

2 cups flour
6 tablespoons sugar
2 teaspoons baking powder
½ teaspoon salt
¾ cup milk
½ cup PARKAY® Margarine, melted
1 egg, beaten
¾ cup coarsely chopped cranberries
Creamy Orange Spread:
1 8-ounce package PHILADELPHIA BRAND® Cream Cheese, softened
1 tablespoon sugar
1 tablespoon orange juice
1 teaspoon grated orange peel

Combine flour, 4 tablespoons sugar, baking powder and salt; mix well. Add combined milk, margarine and egg, mixing just until moistened. Fold in combined remaining sugar and cranberries. Spoon into greased medium-size muffin pan, filling each cup ⅔ full. Bake at 400°, 20 to 25 minutes or until golden brown.

Combine cream cheese, sugar, orange juice and peel, mixing until well blended. Chill. Serve with muffins.
1 dozen.

Variation: Substitute Light PHILA-DELPHIA BRAND® Neufchatel Cheese for Cream Cheese.

Raisin Scones

Walnut Streusel Muffins

3 cups all-purpose flour
1½ cups packed brown sugar
¾ cup butter or margarine
1 cup chopped DIAMOND® Walnuts
2 teaspoons baking powder
1 teaspoon *each* ground nutmeg and ginger
½ teaspoon *each* baking soda and salt
1 cup buttermilk or soured milk
2 eggs, beaten

In medium bowl, combine 2 cups of the flour and the sugar; cut in butter to form fine crumbs. In small bowl, combine ¾ cup of the crumbs and ¼ cup of the walnuts; set aside. Into remaining crumb mixture, stir in remaining 1 cup flour, the baking powder, spices, soda, salt and remaining ¾ cup walnuts. In another small bowl, combine buttermilk and eggs; stir into dry ingredients just to moisten. Spoon into 18 greased or paper-lined 2¾-inch muffin cups, filling about ⅔ full. Top each with a generous spoonful of reserved crumb-nut mixture. Bake in preheated 350°F oven 20 to 25 minutes or until springy to the touch. Cool in pans 10 minutes. Loosen and remove from pans. Serve warm.
Makes 1½ dozen muffins.

Blueberry Muffins

1 package DUNCAN HINES® Moist Deluxe White Cake Mix
2 tablespoons all-purpose flour
1 teaspoon baking powder
⅔ cup milk
3 large eggs
⅓ cup CRISCO® Oil or CRISCO® PURITAN® Oil
1 cup rinsed fresh or well-drained, thawed, frozen blueberries

1. Preheat oven to 375°F. Line 24 muffin cups with paper liners.
2. Combine dry cake mix, flour and baking powder in large bowl. Beat milk, eggs and oil together with fork; add to mixture in bowl and stir just until dry ingredients are moistened. Fold in blueberries.
3. Spoon batter into muffin cups, filling one-third full.
4. Bake at 375°F for 15 to 20 minutes or until golden brown.
24 muffins.

Raisin Scones

2 cups all-purpose flour
2 tablespoons sugar
2 teaspoons baking powder
½ teaspoon baking soda
½ teaspoon salt
½ teaspoon ground nutmeg
½ cup butter or margarine, cut into chunks
1 cup SUN-MAID® Raisins
¾ cup buttermilk
1 egg white, lightly beaten, for glaze
Sugar, for glaze

In large bowl, combine flour, 2 tablespoons sugar, the baking powder, soda, salt and nutmeg. Cut in butter until mixture resembles coarse meal. Mix in raisins, then mix in buttermilk with fork. Gather dough into ball and knead on lightly floured board about 2 minutes. Roll or pat dough out ¾ inch thick. With sharp knife, cut into 3-inch triangles. Space apart on greased baking sheets. Brush tops with egg white; sprinkle with sugar. Bake in preheated 425°F oven for about 15 minutes or until nicely browned. Serve warm with butter or jam.
Makes about 1 dozen scones.

Lemon Tea Muffins

Molasses Muffins

    1²/₃ cups unsifted all-purpose flour
      3 tablespoons sugar
      2 teaspoons baking powder
      1 teaspoon ground ginger
     ¹/₂ teaspoon salt
     ¹/₂ cup dark molasses
      2 eggs, slightly beaten
     ¹/₄ cup CRISCO® Oil
     ¹/₄ cup milk

Preheat oven to 400°F. Place paper liners in 12 muffin cups. Set aside.

Mix flour, sugar, baking powder, ginger and salt in medium mixing bowl. Make a well in center of mixture. Set aside. Blend remaining ingredients in small mixing bowl. Pour into well in dry ingredients. Stir just until ingredients are moistened. Pour into lined muffin cups, filling each about two-thirds full. Bake at 400°F, about 15 minutes, or until centers spring back when touched lightly. *1 dozen muffins.*

Variation: Orange Raisin Muffins. Follow recipe above, omitting ginger. Add ¹/₂ cup raisins and 2 teaspoons grated orange peel to dry ingredients.

Lemon Tea Muffins

      2 cups unsifted flour
      2 teaspoons baking powder
     ¹/₂ teaspoon salt
      1 cup margarine or butter,
          softened
      1 cup granulated sugar
      4 eggs, separated
     ¹/₂ cup REALEMON® Lemon Juice
          from Concentrate
     ¹/₄ cup finely chopped nuts
      2 tablespoons light brown sugar
     ¹/₄ teaspoon ground nutmeg

Preheat oven to 375°. Stir together flour, baking powder and salt; set aside. In large mixer bowl, beat margarine and granulated sugar until fluffy. Add egg yolks; beat until light. Gradually stir in ReaLemon® brand alternately with dry ingredients *(do not overmix).* In small mixer bowl, beat egg whites until stiff but not dry; fold one-third egg whites into lemon mixture. Fold remaining egg whites into lemon mixture. Fill paper-lined or greased muffin cups ³/₄ full. Combine remaining ingredients; sprinkle evenly over muffins. Bake 15 to 20 minutes. Cool 5 minutes; remove from pan. Serve warm.
Makes about 1¹/₂ dozen.

Treasure Bran Muffins

    1¹/₄ cups whole bran cereal
      1 cup milk
     ¹/₄ cup oil
      1 egg, beaten
    1¹/₄ cups flour
     ¹/₂ cup sugar
      1 tablespoon baking powder
     ¹/₂ teaspoon salt
     ¹/₂ cup raisins

                *   *   *

      1 8-ounce package
          PHILADELPHIA BRAND®
          Cream Cheese, softened
     ¹/₄ cup sugar
      1 egg, beaten

Combine cereal and milk; let stand 2 minutes. Add combined oil and egg; mix well. Add combined dry ingredients, mixing just until moistened. Stir in raisins. Spoon into greased and floured medium-size muffin pan, filling each cup ²/₃ full.

Combine cream cheese, sugar and egg, mixing until well blended. Drop rounded measuring tablespoonfuls of cream cheese mixture onto batter. Bake at 375°, 25 minutes.
1 dozen.

Moist Orange Mince Muffins

      2 cups unsifted flour
     ¹/₂ cup sugar
      1 tablespoon baking powder
      1 teaspoon salt
     ¹/₂ teaspoon baking soda
      1 egg, slightly beaten
      1 (8-ounce) container BORDEN®
          LITE-LINE® or VIVA® Orange
          Yogurt
     ¹/₃ cup BORDEN® or MEADOW
          GOLD® Milk
     ¹/₃ cup vegetable oil
      1 (9-ounce) package NONE
          SUCH® Condensed
          Mincemeat, finely crumbled
     ¹/₃ cup BAMA® Orange
          Marmalade, melted, optional

Preheat oven to 400°. In medium bowl, combine dry ingredients; set aside. In medium bowl, combine egg, yogurt, milk, oil and mincemeat; mix well. Stir into flour mixture only until moistened. Fill greased or paper baking cup–lined muffin cups ³/₄ full. Bake 20 to 25 minutes or until golden brown. Immediately turn out of pan. Brush warm muffins with marmalade if desired.
Makes about 1¹/₂ dozen.

Chocolate Chunk Sour Cream Muffins

- 1½ **cups all-purpose flour**
- ½ **cup sugar**
- 1½ **teaspoons CALUMET® Baking Powder**
- ½ **teaspoon cinnamon**
- ¼ **teaspoon salt**
- 2 **eggs, lightly beaten**
- ½ **cup milk**
- ½ **cup sour cream or plain yogurt**
- ¼ **cup (½ stick) margarine, melted**
- 1 **teaspoon vanilla**
- 1 **package (4 ounces) BAKER'S® GERMAN'S® Sweet Chocolate, chopped**

HEAT oven to 375°F.

MIX flour, sugar, baking powder, cinnamon and salt; set aside. Stir eggs, milk, sour cream, margarine and vanilla in large bowl until well blended. Add flour mixture; stir just until moistened. Stir in chocolate.

FILL 12 paper- or foil-lined muffin cups ⅔ full with batter.

BAKE for 30 minutes or until toothpick inserted in center comes out clean. Remove from pan to cool on wire rack.

Makes 12 muffins

Prep time: 15 minutes
Baking time: 30 minutes

Streusel Raspberry Muffins

- **Pecan Streusel Topping (recipe follows)**
- 1½ **cups all-purpose flour**
- ½ **cup sugar**
- 2 **teaspoons baking powder**
- ½ **cup milk**
- ½ **cup butter or margarine, melted**
- 1 **egg, beaten**
- 1 **cup fresh or individually frozen whole unsugared raspberries**

Preheat oven to 375°F. Grease or paper-line 12 (2½-inch) muffin cups. Prepare Pecan Streusel Topping; set aside.

In large bowl, combine flour, sugar and baking powder. In small bowl, combine milk, butter and egg until blended. Stir into flour mixture just until moistened. Spoon ½ of the batter into muffin cups. Divide raspberries among cups, then top with remaining batter. Sprinkle Pecan Streusel Topping over tops. Bake 25 to 30 minutes or until golden and wooden pick inserted in center comes out clean. Remove from pan.

Makes 12 muffins

PECAN STREUSEL TOPPING: In small bowl, combine ¼ cup *each* chopped pecans, firmly packed brown sugar and all-purpose flour. Stir in 2 tablespoons melted butter or margarine until mixture resembles moist crumbs.

Lemon Glazed Zucchini Muffins

- 2 **cups all-purpose flour**
- ⅔ **cup granulated sugar**
- 1 **tablespoon baking powder**
- 1 **teaspoon salt**
- ½ **teaspoon ground nutmeg**
- 2 **teaspoons grated lemon peel**
- ¾ **cup chopped walnuts, pecans or hazelnuts**
- ½ **cup dried fruit bits or golden raisins**
- ½ **cup milk**
- ⅓ **cup vegetable oil**
- 2 **eggs**
- 1 **cup zucchini, shredded, packed into cup, not drained**
- ½ **cup powdered sugar**
- 2 to 3 **teaspoons lemon juice**

Preheat oven to 400°F. Grease well or paper-line 12 (2½-inch) muffin cups. In large bowl, combine flour, granulated sugar, baking powder, salt, nutmeg and lemon peel. Stir in nuts and fruit. In small bowl, combine

Left to right: Chocolate Chunk Sour Cream Muffins and Chocolate Chunk Banana Bread (page 372)

milk, oil and eggs until blended. Pour into flour mixture; add zucchini, stirring just until moistened. Spoon into muffin cups. Bake 20 to 25 minutes or until wooden pick inserted in center comes out clean. Remove from pan. Meanwhile, in small bowl, combine powdered sugar and lemon juice until smooth. Drizzle over warm muffins.

Makes 12 muffins

Cinnamon Spiced Microwave Muffins

1½ cups all-purpose flour
½ cup sugar
2 teaspoons baking powder
½ teaspoon salt
½ teaspoon ground nutmeg
½ teaspoon ground coriander
½ teaspoon ground allspice
½ cup milk
⅓ cup butter or margarine, melted
1 egg
¼ cup sugar
1 teaspoon ground cinnamon
¼ cup butter or margarine, melted

In large bowl, combine flour, ½ cup sugar, baking powder, salt, nutmeg, coriander and allspice. In small bowl, combine milk, ⅓ cup melted butter and egg. Stir into flour mixture just until moistened.

Line 6 microwavable muffin-pan cups with double paper liners. Spoon batter into each cup, filling ½ full. Microwave at HIGH (100%) 2½ to 4½ minutes or until wooden pick inserted in center comes out clean. Rotate dish ½ turn halfway through cooking. Let stand 5 minutes. Remove from pan. Repeat procedure with remaining batter.

Meanwhile, combine remaining ¼ cup sugar and cinnamon in a shallow dish. Roll warm muffins in remaining ¼ cup melted butter, then sugar-cinnamon mixture. Serve warm.

Makes about 12 muffins

Chocolate Cherry Cordial Muffins

Chocolate Cherry Cordial Muffins

2 cups all-purpose flour
¼ cup granulated sugar
¼ cup firmly packed brown sugar
2 teaspoons baking powder
½ teaspoon baking soda
½ teaspoon salt
One 11½-oz. pkg. (2 cups) NESTLÉ® Toll House® Milk Chocolate Morsels, divided
½ cup candied cherries, chopped, or raisins
¾ cup milk
⅓ cup vegetable oil
1 egg

Preheat oven to 375°F. Grease twelve muffin cups or line with cupcake liners. In large bowl, combine flour, granulated sugar, brown sugar, baking powder, baking soda and salt. Stir in 1¾ cups milk chocolate morsels and cherries; set aside.

In small bowl, combine milk, oil and egg. Stir into flour mixture just until moistened. Spoon into prepared muffin cups (muffin cups will be full). Sprinkle with remaining ¼ cup milk chocolate morsels.

Bake 18 to 21 minutes until golden. Cool 5 minutes; remove from pan. *Makes 1 dozen*

Apple-Cranberry Muffins

1¾ cup *plus* 2 tablespoons
    all-purpose flour
½ cup sugar, divided
1½ teaspoons baking powder
½ teaspoon baking soda
½ teaspoon salt
1 egg
¾ cup milk
¾ cup sweetened applesauce
¼ cup butter or margarine,
    melted
1 cup fresh cranberries,
    coarsely chopped
½ teaspoon ground cinnamon

In medium bowl, combine 1¾ cups flour, ¼ cup sugar, baking powder, baking soda and salt. In small bowl, combine egg, milk, applesauce and butter; mix well. Add egg mixture to flour mixture; stir just until moistened. Batter will be lumpy; do not overmix. In small bowl, toss cranberries with remaining 2 tablespoons flour; fold into batter. Spoon batter evenly into 12 greased 2¾-inch muffin cups. In measuring cup, combine remaining ¼ cup sugar and cinnamon. Sprinkle over tops of muffins. Bake in preheated 400°F oven 20 to 25 minutes or until golden brown. Remove to wire rack to cool.

Makes 1 dozen muffins

Favorite recipe from **Western New York Apple Growers Association, Inc.**

Apple-Walnut Muffins

2 cups all-purpose flour
⅔ cup sugar
2¼ teaspoons baking powder
¾ teaspoon salt
¼ teaspoon ground cinnamon
1 egg
⅔ cup milk
3 tablespoons vegetable oil
1 teaspoon grated lemon
    peel
¾ teaspoon vanilla
1 cup chopped DIAMOND®
    Walnuts
¾ cup coarsely grated pared
    apple

In medium bowl, sift flour with sugar, baking powder, salt and cinnamon. In small bowl, beat egg; add milk, oil, lemon peel and vanilla. Stir into dry ingredients, mixing just until flour is moistened. Fold in walnuts and apple. Spoon batter into 12 greased 2½-inch muffin cups. Bake in preheated 400°F oven 20 to 25 minutes or until golden brown and wooden pick inserted in center comes out clean.   *Makes 12 muffins*

Banana Blueberry Muffins

2 extra-ripe, medium DOLE®
    Bananas, peeled
2 eggs
1 cup firmly packed brown
    sugar
½ cup margarine, melted
1 cup blueberries
1 teaspoon vanilla
2¼ cups all-purpose flour
2 teaspoons baking powder
½ teaspoon ground cinnamon
½ teaspoon salt

Purée bananas in blender. In medium bowl, combine 1 cup puréed bananas, eggs, sugar and margarine until well blended. Stir in blueberries and vanilla. In large bowl, combine flour, baking powder, cinnamon and salt. Stir banana mixture into flour mixture until evenly moistened. Spoon batter into well greased 2½-inch muffin cups. Bake in 350°F oven 25 to 30 minutes or until wooden pick inserted in center comes out clean. Serve warm.

Makes 12 muffins

Pecan Peach Muffins

Topping (recipe follows)
1½ cups all-purpose flour
½ cup granulated sugar
2 teaspoons baking powder
1 teaspoon ground cinnamon
¼ teaspoon salt
½ cup butter or margarine,
    melted
¼ cup milk
1 egg
2 medium peaches, peeled,
    diced (about 1 cup)

Preheat oven to 400°F. Paper-line 12 (2½-inch) muffin cups. Prepare Topping; set aside.

In large bowl, combine flour, granulated sugar, baking powder, cinnamon and salt. In small bowl, combine butter, milk and egg until blended. Pour into flour mixture, stirring just until moistened. Fold in peaches. Spoon into muffin cups. Sprinkle Topping over batter. Bake 20 to 25 minutes or until wooden pick inserted in center comes out clean. Remove from pan.

Makes 12 muffins

TOPPING: In small bowl, combine ½ cup chopped pecans, ⅓ cup packed brown sugar, ¼ cup all-purpose flour and 1 teaspoon ground cinnamon. Add 2 tablespoons melted butter or margarine, stirring until mixture is crumbly.

**Clockwise from top right: Apple-Cranberry Muffins, Wholesome Wheat Bread (page 398) and
Nut-Filled Christmas Wreath (page 396)**

Mini Morsel Tea Biscuits

Preheat oven to 400°F. Grease two large cookie sheets. In large bowl, combine flour, sugar, baking powder and salt. With pastry blender or two knives, cut in butter until mixture resembles coarse crumbs. Stir in mini morsels; set aside. In small bowl, beat three eggs with evaporated milk and vanilla extract. Stir into dry ingredients just until soft dough forms.

Turn dough onto well-floured surface. Knead briefly. Pat dough to ¾-inch thickness. Cut with 2½-inch fluted round biscuit cutter. Place on prepared cookie sheets. Beat remaining egg with milk; brush over dough.

Bake 15 to 17 minutes until golden brown. Serve warm.
Makes about 1½ dozen

Peanut Orange Breakfast Puffs

- **2 cups sifted all-purpose flour**
- **1 tablespoon baking powder**
- **1 teaspoon salt**
- **¼ cup sugar**
- **1 egg, beaten**
- **1 cup milk**
- **¼ cup peanut oil**
- **½ cup chopped salted peanuts**

Topping
- **¼ cup sugar**
- **1 teaspoon grated orange peel**
- **¼ cup butter or margarine, melted**

In large bowl, sift together flour, baking powder, salt and ¼ cup sugar. In small bowl, combine egg, milk and peanut oil. Add liquid all at once to flour mixture, stirring only until moistened. Fold in chopped peanuts. Fill greased 2½-inch muffin cups ⅔ full. Bake in preheated 425°F oven 15 to 20 minutes or until tops are lightly browned. Meanwhile, in small bowl, blend ¼ cup sugar and orange peel until crumbly. When muffins are baked, remove from muffin cups and immediately dip tops in melted butter, then in orange-sugar mixture. Serve warm. *Makes 12 muffins*

Favorite recipe from **Oklahoma Peanut Commission**

Mini Morsel Tea Biscuits

- **4 cups all-purpose flour**
- **⅓ cup sugar**
- **2 tablespoons baking powder**
- **½ teaspoon salt**
- **½ cup (1 stick) butter or margarine**
- **1 cup (half of 12-oz. pkg.) NESTLÉ® Toll House® Semi-Sweet Chocolate Mini Morsels**
- **4 eggs, divided**
- **1 cup CARNATION® Evaporated Milk**
- **1½ teaspoons vanilla extract**
- **2 tablespoons milk**

Southern Biscuit Muffins

- **2½ cups all-purpose flour**
- **¼ cup sugar**
- **1½ tablespoons baking powder**
- **¾ cup cold butter or margarine**
- **1 cup cold milk**

Preheat oven to 400°F. Grease 12 (2½-inch) muffin cups. (These muffins brown better on the sides and bottom when baked without paper liners.) In large bowl, combine flour, sugar and baking powder. Cut in butter until mixture resembles coarse crumbs. Stir in milk just until flour mixture is moistened. Spoon into muffin cups. Bake 20 minutes or until golden. Remove from pan. Cool on wire rack. Serve with jelly, jam or honey.
Makes 12 muffins

Southern Biscuit Muffin

Bacon Cheese Muffins

½ **pound bacon**
    (10 to 12 slices)
    Vegetable oil
1 **egg, beaten**
¾ **cup milk**
1¾ **cups all-purpose flour**
¼ **cup sugar**
1 **tablespoon baking powder**
1 **cup (4 ounces) shredded**
    Wisconsin Cheddar
    cheese
½ **cup crunchy nutlike cereal**
    nuggets

Preheat oven to 400°F. In large skillet, cook bacon over medium-high heat until crisp. Drain, reserve drippings. If necessary, add oil to drippings to measure ⅓ cup. In small bowl, combine ⅓ cup drippings, egg and milk; set aside. Crumble bacon; set aside.

In large bowl, combine flour, sugar and baking powder. Make well in center. Add drippings-egg mixture all at once to flour mixture, stirring just until moistened. Batter should be lumpy. Fold in bacon, cheese and cereal. Spoon into buttered or paper-lined 2½-inch muffin cups, filling about ¾ full. Bake 15 to 20 minutes or until golden. Remove from pan. Cool on wire rack.   *Makes 12 muffins*

Favorite recipe from **Wisconsin Milk Marketing Board** © *1993*

Calico Bell Pepper Muffins

¼ **cup** *each* **finely chopped**
    red, yellow and green
    bell pepper
¼ **cup butter or margarine**
2 **cups all-purpose flour**
2 **tablespoons sugar**
1 **tablespoon baking powder**
¾ **teaspoon salt**
½ **teaspoon dried basil leaves**
1 **cup milk**
2 **eggs**

Preheat oven to 400°F. Grease or paper-line 12 (2½-inch) muffin cups. In small skillet, over medium-high heat, cook peppers in butter until color is bright and peppers are tender crisp about 3 minutes. Set aside.

In large bowl, combine flour, sugar, baking powder, salt and basil. In small bowl, combine milk and eggs until blended. Add milk mixture and peppers and any liquid in skillet to flour mixture. Stir just until moistened. Spoon into muffin cups. Bake 15 minutes or until golden and wooden pick inserted in center comes out clean. Remove from pan. Serve warm.
        Makes 12 muffins

Calico Bell Pepper Muffins

French Breakfast Puffs

Paul Bunyan Sticky Buns

1 package (16 ounces) hot roll mix
½ cup butter or margarine, melted
2 tablespoons water
1 cup packed brown sugar
1 cup chopped DIAMOND® Walnuts
¾ cup granulated sugar
1 tablespoon ground cinnamon

Prepare dough as package directs for rolls. Knead gently on lightly floured board 1 minute. Place dough in lightly greased bowl; turn once to grease surface. Cover; let rise in warm place (85°F) until doubled, about 1 hour. To prepare syrup, in small saucepan, combine ¼ cup of the butter, the water and brown sugar. Stir over medium heat until sugar dissolves. Bring to boil; reduce heat to low and simmer gently 1 minute. Pour at once into 11×7-inch baking pan, tilting to spread syrup evenly. Sprinkle ½ cup of the walnuts over syrup layer; set aside. After dough has risen, turn out onto lightly floured board. Let rest 5 minutes, then stretch and roll into 30×5-inch rectangle. Brush with remaining ¼ cup butter. In small bowl, combine granulated sugar and cinnamon; sprinkle over butter. Arrange remaining ½ cup walnuts on top. Starting from 5-inch side, roll up loosely, jelly-roll fashion, pinching edges to seal. Cut roll into 6 equal pieces. Place cut sides up in prepared pan, spreading pinwheels open a little. Cover; let rise in warm place 35 to 45 minutes or until almost doubled. Cover lower shelf of oven with foil. Bake buns on center shelf of preheated 375°F oven 25 to 35 minutes or until golden. Immediately invert onto tray. Cool 5 minutes. Serve warm.
Makes 6 large buns.

Southern Hush Puppies

CRISCO® Oil for frying
¾ cup yellow cornmeal
⅓ cup unsifted all-purpose flour
1½ teaspoons baking powder
½ teaspoon salt
½ cup buttermilk
1 egg
¼ cup finely chopped onion

Heat 2 to 3 inches Crisco® Oil in deep-fryer or large saucepan to 375°F. Mix cornmeal, flour, baking powder and salt in medium mixing bowl. Add remaining ingredients. Mix well. Drop batter by tablespoonfuls into hot Crisco® Oil. Fry a few at a time, 3 to 4 minutes, or until golden brown. Drain on paper towels. Repeat with remaining batter. Serve immediately or keep warm in 175°F oven.
About 1 dozen hush puppies.

Italian Pepperoni Puffs

2¼ to 2¾ cups unsifted all-purpose flour, divided
1 package (¼ ounce) active dry yeast
1 tablespoon sugar
1 teaspoon garlic salt
½ teaspoon Italian seasoning
¼ teaspoon onion powder
¾ cup very warm water (120° to 130°F)
2 tablespoons CRISCO® Oil
1 egg
½ cup grated Parmesan cheese
¼ cup finely chopped pepperoni CRISCO® Oil for frying

Mix 1½ cups flour, yeast, sugar, garlic salt, Italian seasoning and onion powder in large mixing bowl. Add warm water, Crisco® Oil and egg. Beat with electric mixer at low speed until ingredients are moistened, scraping bowl constantly. Beat at medium speed 3 minutes, scraping bowl occasionally. Stir in Parmesan cheese and enough remaining flour to make a slightly stiff dough.

Knead dough on lightly floured surface 5 to 8 minutes, or until smooth and elastic, adding additional flour as necessary. Place in lightly oiled medium mixing bowl. Turn dough over to coat both sides with Crisco® Oil. Cover; let rise in warm place 40 to 50 minutes, or until doubled.

Punch down dough. Place on lightly floured surface. Divide dough in half. Roll each half to ⅛-inch thickness. Cut into 2-inch rounds. Place ½ teaspoon chopped pepperoni in center of half of the rounds. Brush edges with water. Top with remaining rounds. Press edges together with fork to seal. Cover; let rise in warm place about 30 minutes, or until doubled.

Heat 2 to 3 inches Crisco® Oil in deep-fryer or large saucepan to 365°F. Fry 3 or 4 puffs at a time, 3 to 4 minutes, or until golden brown, turning

Raised Doughnuts

over several times. Drain on paper towels. Sprinkle with *grated Parmesan cheese*, if desired. Serve warm. *1½ to 2 dozen puffs.*

French Breakfast Puffs

1½ cups unsifted all-purpose flour
½ cup confectioners sugar
1 teaspoon baking powder
1 teaspoon salt
¾ teaspoon ground nutmeg
½ cup milk
½ cup water
¼ cup CRISCO® Oil
1½ teaspoons grated lemon peel
3 eggs
CRISCO® Oil for frying
Confectioners sugar

Mix flour, ½ cup confectioners sugar, baking powder, salt and nutmeg in small mixing bowl. Set aside. Combine milk, water, Crisco® Oil and lemon peel in medium saucepan. Heat to rolling boil over medium-high heat. Add flour mixture all at once. Beat with wooden spoon until mixture pulls away from sides of pan into a ball. Remove from heat; cool slightly. Add eggs, one at a time, beating after each addition.

Heat 2 to 3 inches Crisco® Oil in deep-fryer or large saucepan to 350°F.

Drop dough by tablespoonfuls into hot Crisco® Oil. Fry 3 or 4 puffs at a time, 4 to 6 minutes, or until golden brown, turning over several times. Drain on paper towels. Sprinkle top of each puff with confectioners sugar. *About 32 puffs.*

Raised Doughnuts

3½ to 4½ cups unsifted all-purpose flour, divided
¾ cup sugar, divided
2 packages (¼ ounce each) active dry yeast
1 teaspoon salt
1 cup milk
¼ cup vegetable shortening
2 eggs, slightly beaten
CRISCO® Oil for frying

Mix 2 cups flour, ¼ cup sugar, yeast and salt in large mixing bowl. Set aside. Combine milk and shortening in small saucepan. Cook over moderate heat until very warm (120° to 130°F). Add to flour mixture. Add eggs. Beat with electric mixer at low speed 1 minute, scraping bowl constantly. Beat at medium speed 3 minutes, scraping bowl occasionally. Stir in enough remaining flour to make a soft dough.

Knead dough on lightly floured surface 5 to 8 minutes, or until smooth and elastic, adding additional flour as necessary (dough will be slightly sticky). Place in lightly oiled medium mixing bowl. Turn dough over to coat both sides with Crisco® Oil. Cover; let rise in warm place 40 to 50 minutes, or until doubled.

Oil baking sheet. Set aside. Punch down dough. Place on lightly floured surface. Divide dough in half. Roll each half to ½-inch thickness. Cut into 2½-inch rounds with doughnut cutter. Place doughnuts and holes on prepared baking sheet. Cover; let rise in warm place about 30 minutes, or until doubled.

Heat 2 to 3 inches Crisco® Oil in deep-fryer or large saucepan to 375°F. Fry 2 or 3 doughnuts at a time, 1 to 1½ minutes, or until golden brown, turning over once. To fry holes, place several at a time in hot Crisco® Oil. Fry 45 to 60 seconds, or until golden brown, turning over occasionally. Drain on paper towels. Place remaining ½ cup sugar in large plastic food storage bag. Add a few doughnuts and holes at a time; shake to coat. *1½ dozen doughnuts and 1½ dozen holes.*

Variation: Glazed Raised Doughnuts. Follow recipe above, except reduce sugar to ¼ cup and do not shake doughnuts in sugar. Before frying doughnuts, combine 1 cup confectioners sugar, 2 tablespoons milk, 1 tablespoon honey and 1 teaspoon grated lemon or orange peel in small mixing bowl. Beat at medium speed with electric mixer until smooth. After frying, dip one side of warm doughnuts in glaze. Cool doughnuts, glazed side up, on wire rack over waxed paper.

Jamaican Sweet Buns

2 cups all-purpose flour
¼ cup sugar
4 teaspoons baking powder
2 teaspoons grated lemon peel
¼ teaspoon salt
½ cup butter or margarine
½ cup milk
2 egg yolks, lightly beaten
¾ cup SUN-MAID® Raisins
¾ cup shredded coconut
1 egg white, beaten, for glaze
Sugar, for glaze

In medium bowl, combine flour, the ¼ cup sugar, the baking powder, peel and salt. Cut in butter until mixture resembles coarse meal. Combine milk and yolks; mix into flour mixture to form soft dough. Mix in raisins and coconut just to blend. Evenly divide dough into six 4-inch greased tart pans; flatten tops. Brush generously with egg white; sprinkle heavily with sugar (about 2 teaspoons on each). Space apart on baking sheet. Bake in preheated 450°F oven about 15 minutes or until springy to the touch and well browned. Cool in pans. Serve with whipped sweet butter. *Makes 6 buns.*

Fresh Sage & Pepper Popovers

Popovers
   3 eggs, room temperature
   1¼ cups milk, room temperature
   1¼ cups all-purpose flour
   1½ teaspoons fresh sage leaves,* rubbed
   ¼ teaspoon coarsely ground pepper
   ¼ teaspoon salt

Sage Butter
   ½ cup LAND O LAKES® Butter, softened
   1½ teaspoons fresh sage leaves,* rubbed
   ¼ teaspoon coarsely ground pepper

Heat oven to 450°. For popovers, in small mixer bowl beat eggs at medium speed, scraping bowl often, until light yellow, 1 to 2 minutes. Add milk; continue beating for 1 minute to incorporate air. By hand, stir in all remaining popover ingredients. Pour batter into greased 6-cup popover pan or 6 custard cups. Bake for 15 minutes; *reduce temperature to 350°. Do not open oven.* Continue baking for 25 to 30 minutes or until golden brown.

For Sage Butter, in small mixer bowl beat all Sage Butter ingredients at low speed, scraping bowl often, until light and fluffy, 1 to 2 minutes; set aside.

Insert knife in popovers to allow steam to escape. Serve immediately with sage butter.
Makes 6 popovers

Tip: Eggs and milk should be at room temperature (72°F) to help ensure successful popovers.

*You may substitute ½ teaspoon dried sage leaves, crumbled, for the 1½ teaspoons fresh sage leaves, rubbed.

Italian Parmesan Twists

   1 cup grated Parmesan cheese
   1½ teaspoons Italian herb seasoning*
   1 loaf frozen bread dough, thawed
   ⅓ cup LAND O LAKES® Butter, melted
   Pizza sauce, warmed

Heat oven to 450°. In 9-inch pie pan combine Parmesan cheese and Italian seasoning. Divide dough into 8 sections; divide *each* section into 4 pieces. (There should be 32 pieces of dough.) Roll *each* piece into 4-inch rope. Dip *each* rope in melted butter; roll in Parmesan mixture. Twist rope 3 times. Place on greased cookie sheets. Bake for 7 to 9 minutes or until golden brown. Serve warm with pizza sauce.
Makes 32 twists

*You may substitute ¼ teaspoon *each* dried oregano leaves, dried marjoram leaves and dried basil leaves and ⅛ teaspoon rubbed sage for the 1½ teaspoons Italian herb seasoning.

Broiled Herb Baguettes

   ¼ cup MIRACLE WHIP® Salad Dressing
   ½ teaspoon each: garlic salt, Italian seasoning
   4 drops hot pepper sauce
   2 tablespoons KRAFT® 100% Grated Parmesan Cheese
   4 French bread rolls, split

• Mix all ingredients except bread until well blended.

• Evenly spread salad dressing mixture onto bread halves. Broil 3 to 4 minutes or until golden brown.   *Makes 4 servings*

Prep time: 5 minutes
Cooking time: 4 minutes

Quicky Sticky Buns

   3 tablespoons packed brown sugar, divided
   ¼ cup KARO® Light or Dark Corn Syrup
   ¼ cup coarsely chopped pecans
   2 tablespoons softened MAZOLA® Margarine, divided
   1 can (8 ounces) refrigerated crescent dinner rolls
   1 teaspoon cinnamon

Preheat oven to 350°F. In small bowl combine 2 tablespoons of the brown sugar, the corn syrup, pecans and 1 tablespoon of the margarine. Spoon about 2 teaspoons mixture into each of 9 (2½-inch) muffin pan cups. Unroll entire crescent roll dough; pinch seams together to form 1 rectangle. Combine remaining 1 tablespoon brown sugar and the cinnamon. Spread dough with remaining 1 tablespoon margarine; sprinkle with cinnamon mixture. Roll up from short end. Cut into 9 slices. Place one slice in each prepared muffin pan cup. Bake 25 minutes or until golden brown. Immediately invert pan onto cookie sheet or tray; cool 10 minutes.
Makes 9 buns

Preparation Time: 15 minutes
Bake Time: 25 minutes, plus cooling

Quicky Sticky Buns

Hot Cross Buns

Buns:
- **2 pkgs. active dry yeast**
- **½ cup warm water (105° to 115°F)**
- **1 cup warm milk (105° to 115°F)**
- **½ cup (1 stick) butter, softened**
- **½ cup granulated sugar**
- **3 eggs**
- **½ teaspoon salt**
- **½ teaspoon vanilla extract**
- **5 to 5½ cups all-purpose flour, divided**
- **1 cup raisins**
- **½ teaspoon cinnamon**
- **One 12-oz.pkg. (2 cups) NESTLÉ® Toll House® Semi-Sweet Chocolate Morsels**

Glaze:
- **1 cup confectioners' sugar**
- **2 tablespoons milk**

Buns: Grease two 13×9-inch baking pans. In small bowl, dissolve yeast in warm water; let stand 10 minutes. In large bowl, combine warm milk, butter, granulated sugar, eggs, salt and vanilla extract. Add yeast mixture. Stir in 2 cups flour, raisins and cinnamon. Gradually stir in enough remaining flour to make a soft dough. Turn dough onto lightly floured surface. Knead 2 minutes. Knead in semi-sweet chocolate morsels; continue kneading 3 minutes or until dough is smooth and elastic.

Place dough in lightly greased bowl; turn over to grease surface. Cover with cloth towel; let rise in warm place (70° to 75°F) until double in bulk, about 1 hour. Punch down dough; cover and let rise 30 minutes longer.

Punch down dough; divide into 24 pieces. Shape each piece into a smooth ball. Place 12 balls in each prepared pan. Cover; let rise in warm place until double in bulk, about 45 minutes.

Preheat oven to 350°F. Bake 20 to 25 minutes until golden brown. Cool 15 minutes.

Glaze: In small bowl, combine confectioners' sugar and milk, stirring until smooth. Drizzle glaze over buns, forming a cross on each. Serve warm or cool completely.   *Makes 24 buns*

Almond Butter Loaves

Crust
- **½ cup firmly packed brown sugar**
- **⅓ cup butter or margarine, softened**
- **1 cup toasted almonds, finely chopped (see Tip)**
- **½ cup all-purpose flour**

Cake
- **1 package DUNCAN HINES® Moist Deluxe Butter Recipe Golden Cake Mix**
- **3 eggs**
- **⅔ cup water**
- **½ cup butter or margarine, softened**

Glaze
- **1 cup confectioners sugar**
- **1 to 2 tablespoons water**
- **¼ teaspoon almond extract**
- **3 tablespoons sliced almonds, for garnish**

1. Preheat oven to 350°F. Grease and flour two 9×5×3-inch loaf pans.

2. **For crust,** combine brown sugar and ⅓ cup butter in large bowl. Beat at medium speed with electric mixer until light and fluffy. Stir in toasted almonds and flour. Blend well. Divide and press evenly into pans.

3. **For cake,** combine cake mix, eggs, ⅔ cup water and ½ cup butter in large bowl. Beat at medium speed with electric mixer for 4 minutes. Pour into pans. Bake at 350°F for 45 to 50 minutes or until toothpick inserted in center comes out clean. Cool in pans 10 minutes. Invert onto cooling racks, crust-side up. Cool completely.

4. **For glaze,** combine confectioners sugar, 1 tablespoon water and almond extract in small bowl. Stir until smooth. Add water, 1 teaspoon at a time, until glaze is desired consistency. Spoon over cooled loaves. Sprinkle sliced almonds over top.
          2 Loaves (16 Slices)

Note: For ease in slicing loaves, use a serrated knife.

Tip: To toast almonds, spread in a single layer on baking sheet. Bake at 325°F for 6 to 8 minutes or until fragrant and light golden brown. Cool before chopping.

Almond Butter Loaf

Cranberry Streusel Coffee Cake

Cake Batter
1½ cups flour
1½ teaspoons baking powder
½ teaspoon salt
6 tablespoons (¾ stick) unsalted butter, softened
¾ cup granulated sugar
2 teaspoons grated orange peel
2 eggs
½ cup milk

Streusel
½ cup light brown sugar
¼ cup flour
½ teaspoon cinnamon
2 tablespoons butter, softened
½ cup chopped walnuts

Cranberry Filling
1½ cups OCEAN SPRAY® fresh or frozen Cranberries
¼ cup granulated sugar
2 tablespoons orange juice

1. Preheat oven to 350°F. Grease and flour 8-inch square cake pan. Stir together flour, baking powder and salt on piece of waxed paper until well mixed.

2. Cream together 6 tablespoons butter, ¾ cup granulated sugar and orange peel in large bowl. Add eggs, one at a time, beating well after each addition. Stir in flour mixture alternately with milk, beginning and ending with flour. Set batter aside.

3. For streusel, combine all streusel ingredients in small bowl. Mix together with fork until crumbly; set aside.

4. For cranberry filling, place filling ingredients in a small saucepan. Cook over medium heat, stirring constantly, until berries start to pop. Remove from heat; cool to room temperature.

5. Spread half of the cake batter over bottom of prepared pan. Sprinkle with half of the streusel; spoon on half of the cranberry filling. Cover with remaining batter; top with remaining filling and streusel.

6. Bake 50 to 60 minutes until toothpick inserted in center comes out clean. Cool on wire rack. Serve warm or cool slightly.

Makes about 9 servings

Sock-It-To-Me Cake

Sock-It-To-Me Cake

Streusel Filling
1 package DUNCAN HINES® Moist Deluxe Butter Recipe Golden Cake Mix, divided
2 tablespoons brown sugar
2 teaspoons ground cinnamon
1 cup finely chopped pecans

Cake
4 eggs
1 cup dairy sour cream
⅓ cup CRISCO® Oil or CRISCO® PURITAN® Oil
¼ cup water
¼ cup granulated sugar

Glaze
1 cup confectioners sugar
1 tablespoon milk

1. Preheat oven to 375°F. Grease and flour 10-inch tube pan.

2. **For streusel filling**, combine 2 tablespoons cake mix, brown sugar and cinnamon in medium bowl. Stir in pecans. Set aside.

3. **For cake**, combine remaining cake mix, eggs, sour cream, oil, water and granulated sugar in large bowl. Beat at medium speed with electric mixer for 2 minutes. Pour two-thirds of batter into pan. Sprinkle with streusel filling. Spoon remaining batter evenly over filling. Bake at 375°F for 45 to 55 minutes or until toothpick inserted in center comes out clean. Cool in pan 25 minutes. Invert onto serving plate. Cool completely.

4. **For glaze,** combine confectioners sugar and milk in small bowl. Stir until smooth. Add more milk to thin glaze as needed. Drizzle over cake.

12 to 16 Servings

Tip: For a quick glaze, heat ½ cup Duncan Hines® Vanilla Frosting in small saucepan over medium heat, stirring constantly, until thin.

Crullers

  1 8-ounce package
    PHILADELPHIA BRAND®
    Cream Cheese, softened
  1/3 cup PARKAY® Margarine
  1 cup flour
    Dash of salt
    Sugar

Combine cream cheese and margarine, mixing until well blended. Add flour and salt; mix well. Shape dough into ball; chill 1 hour. On lightly floured surface, roll dough to 12×6-inch rectangle. Cut dough into twenty-four 1/2-inch strips. Fry in deep hot oil, 375°, 1 to 2 minutes or until golden brown, turning once using tongs. Drain on paper towels. Roll in sugar.
2 dozen.

Easy Apple Kuchen

  2 envelopes active dry yeast
  1/4 cup warm water (about 110°F)
  2 large eggs
  1 package DUNCAN HINES®
    Moist Deluxe Yellow
    Cake Mix
  1 1/4 cups all-purpose flour
  1 1/2 cups sugar
  1 tablespoon ground cinnamon
  1/3 cup butter or margarine
  6 medium apples or 2 cans
    (20 ounces each) pie-sliced
    apples, drained

1. Dissolve yeast in warm water in large mixer bowl. Blend in eggs and half of dry cake mix. Beat for 1 minute at medium speed. Add remaining cake mix and beat for 3 minutes at medium speed. (Batter should be quite stiff but not doughlike.) Let rest 5 minutes.
2. Sprinkle flour on board. Scrape batter out onto prepared board. Knead batter until flour is worked in, about 100 strokes. Place in greased bowl, cover, and let rise in warm, draft-free place for 30 minutes.
3. For topping, mix sugar and cinnamon in bowl; cut in butter with pastry blender or 2 knives.
4. Preheat oven to 350°F. Grease 13×9×2-inch pan and 8×8×2-inch pan. Pare, core and slice apples.
5. Punch down dough with greased fingertips. Spread dough to 1/4- to 1/3-inch thickness on bottom of pans. Arrange apple slices in rows on top. Sprinkle with topping. Let rise in warm place for 30 minutes.

6. Bake at 350°F for 25 to 30 minutes or until toothpick inserted in center comes out clean. Serve warm.
24 servings.

Blueberries 'n Cheese Coffeecake

  1/2 cup PARKAY® Margarine
  1 1/4 cups granulated sugar
  2 eggs
  2 1/4 cups flour
  1 tablespoon baking powder
  1 teaspoon salt
  3/4 cup milk
  1/4 cup water
  2 cups blueberries
  1 8-ounce package
    PHILADELPHIA BRAND®
    Cream Cheese, cubed
  1 teaspoon grated lemon peel
        *   *   *
  1/4 cup granulated sugar
  1/4 cup flour
  1 teaspoon grated lemon peel
  2 tablespoons PARKAY®
    Margarine
    Powdered sugar

Beat margarine and granulated sugar until light and fluffy. Add eggs, one at a time, mixing well after each addition. Add combined 2 cups flour, baking powder and salt alternately with combined milk and water, mixing well after each addition. Toss blueberries with remaining flour; fold into batter with cream cheese and peel. Pour into greased and floured 13×9-inch baking pan.

Combine granulated sugar, flour and peel; cut in margarine until mixture resembles coarse crumbs. Sprinkle over batter. Bake at 375°, 1 hour. Cool. Sprinkle with powdered sugar before serving.
12 servings.

  Variation: Substitute 2 cups frozen blueberries, thawed, well-drained, for fresh blueberries.

Fruity Swirl Coffeecake

  1 8-ounce package
    PHILADELPHIA BRAND®
    Cream Cheese, softened
  1 cup sugar
  1/2 cup PARKAY® Margarine
  2 eggs
  1/2 teaspoon vanilla
  1 3/4 cups flour
  1 teaspoon baking powder
  1/2 teaspoon baking soda
  1/4 teaspoon salt
  1/4 cup milk
  1/2 cup KRAFT® Red Raspberry
    Preserves

Combine cream cheese, sugar and margarine, mixing until well blended. Add eggs, one at a time, mixing well after each addition. Blend in vanilla. Add combined dry ingredients alternately with milk, mixing well after each addition. Pour into greased and floured 13×9-inch baking pan; dot with preserves. Cut through batter with knife several times for marble effect. Bake at 350°, 35 minutes.
12 servings.

Easy Apple Kuchen

Cream Cheese Swirl Coffee Cake

Combine cream cheese, margarine and granulated sugar, mixing at medium speed on electric mixer until well blended. Gradually add milk, mixing well after each addition. Blend in eggs and vanilla. Add combined dry ingredients to cream cheese mixture; mix well. Pour half of batter into greased and floured 13×9-inch baking pan. Dot with preserves; cover with remaining batter. Bake at 350°, 35 to 40 minutes or until wooden pick inserted in center comes out clean.

Combine coconut, brown sugar, cinnamon and margarine; mix well. Spread onto cake; broil 3 to 5 minutes, or until golden brown.
16 servings.

Orange Wake-Up Cake

    1 package DUNCAN HINES®
        Moist Deluxe Butter Recipe
        Golden Cake Mix
 2/3 cup water
    3 large eggs
 1/2 cup (1 stick) butter or
        margarine, softened
    2 tablespoons grated orange
        peel
 1/2 cup chopped pecans
 1/3 cup packed brown sugar
 1/4 cup fine graham cracker
        crumbs
    2 tablespoons butter or
        margarine, melted
1 1/2 teaspoons ground cinnamon
    1 cup confectioners' sugar
    2 tablespoons hot water
 1/4 teaspoon vanilla extract

1. Preheat oven to 375°F. Grease and flour two 9×1 1/2-inch round layer pans.
2. Combine dry cake mix, water, eggs and 1/2 cup butter in large mixer bowl. Mix cake as directed on package. Fold in 1 tablespoon of the orange peel. Divide batter evenly in pans.
3. For topping, combine pecans, brown sugar, graham cracker crumbs, 2 tablespoons butter, remaining orange peel and cinnamon; mix well. Sprinkle evenly over batter in pans.
4. Bake at 375°F for 25 to 30 minutes or until toothpick inserted in center comes out clean.
5. For glaze,* mix confectioners' sugar, hot water and vanilla until smooth. Drizzle over warm cakes. Serve warm or cool in pans.
12 to 16 servings.
   *Or heat 2/3 cup DUNCAN HINES® Vanilla Frosting in a small saucepan over medium heat, stirring constantly, until thin.

Cream Cheese Swirl Coffee Cake

    2 (3-ounce) packages cream
        cheese, softened
    2 tablespoons confectioners'
        sugar
    2 tablespoons REALEMON®
        Lemon Juice from
        Concentrate
    2 cups unsifted flour
    1 teaspoon baking powder
    1 teaspoon baking soda
 1/4 teaspoon salt
    1 cup granulated sugar
 1/2 cup margarine or butter,
        softened
    3 eggs
    1 teaspoon vanilla extract
    1 (8-ounce) container BORDEN®
        or MEADOW GOLD® Sour
        Cream
        Cinnamon-Nut Topping*

Preheat oven to 350°. In small bowl, beat cheese, confectioners' sugar and ReaLemon® brand until smooth; set aside. Stir together flour, baking powder, baking soda and salt; set aside. In large mixer bowl, beat granulated sugar and margarine until fluffy. Add eggs and vanilla; mix well. Add dry ingredients alternately with sour cream; mix well. Pour half of batter into greased and floured 10-inch tube pan. Spoon cheese mixture on top of batter to within 1/2 inch of pan edge. Spoon remaining batter over filling, spreading to pan edge. Sprinkle with Cinnamon-Nut Topping. Bake 40 to 45 minutes or until wooden pick inserted near center comes out clean. Cool 10 minutes; remove from pan. Serve warm.
Makes one 10-inch cake.
   Cinnamon-Nut Topping: Combine 1/4 cup finely chopped nuts, 2 tablespoons granulated sugar and 1/2 teaspoon ground cinnamon.

Apricot Crumble Cake

    1 8-ounce package
        PHILADELPHIA BRAND®
        Cream Cheese, softened
 1/2 cup PARKAY® Margarine
1 1/4 cups granulated sugar
 1/4 cup milk
    2 eggs
    1 teaspoon vanilla
1 3/4 cups flour
    1 teaspoon baking powder
 1/2 teaspoon baking soda
 1/4 teaspoon salt
    1 10-ounce jar KRAFT® Apricot
        or Peach Preserves
    2 cups flaked coconut
 2/3 cup packed brown sugar
    1 teaspoon cinnamon
 1/3 cup PARKAY® Margarine,
        melted

Chocolate Chip Banana Bread

Chocolate Chip Banana Bread

- **2 cups all-purpose flour**
- **1 cup sugar**
- **1 teaspoon baking powder**
- **½ teaspoon baking soda**
- **1 teaspoon salt**
- **1 cup mashed ripe bananas (about 3 small)**
- **½ cup shortening**
- **2 eggs**
- **1 cup HERSHEY'S MINI CHIPS Semi-Sweet Chocolate**
- **½ cup chopped walnuts**

Heat oven to 350°F. Grease bottom only of 9×5-inch loaf pan. In large mixer bowl, combine all ingredients except small chocolate chips and walnuts; blend well on medium speed of electric mixer. Stir in chips and walnuts. Pour batter into prepared pan. Bake 60 to 65 minutes or until wooden pick inserted in center comes out clean. Cool 10 minutes; remove from pan. Cool completely on wire rack.
1 loaf.

Cheese Casserole Bread

- **2 cups warm milk (105° to 115°)**
- **2 packages active dry yeast**
- **3 tablespoons sugar**
- **1 tablespoon butter**
- **½ teaspoon salt**
- **4½ cups all-purpose flour**
- **6 ounces Cheddar cheese, cut into ½-inch cubes**

In large bowl, combine milk and yeast; stir to dissolve yeast. Add sugar, butter and salt; stir until butter is melted. Stir in 3 cups of the flour; beat until smooth. Stir in remaining flour and cheese; mix well. Pour batter into well-buttered 1½-quart round casserole. Cover with waxed paper; let rise in warm place (85°) until doubled, about 1 hour. Remove waxed paper. Bake in preheated 350° oven 50 to 55 minutes or until toothpick inserted into center comes out clean. Let cool in dish on wire rack 10 minutes. Loosen edge; remove from dish. Cool slightly on wire rack; serve warm with butter.
Makes 1 loaf.

*Favorite recipe from **American Dairy Association***

Golden Apple Boston Brown Bread

- **¼ cup butter or margarine, softened**
- **⅓ cup honey**
- **⅓ cup light molasses**
- **1 cup whole wheat flour**
- **1 cup rye flour**
- **1 cup yellow cornmeal**
- **2 teaspoons baking soda**
- **½ teaspoon salt**
- **2 cups buttermilk**
- **2 cups coarsely chopped Washington Golden Delicious apples**

In large bowl, cream butter, honey and molasses. In medium bowl, combine flours, cornmeal, baking soda and salt. Add flour mixture to butter mixture alternately with buttermilk, mixing well after each addition. Stir in apples. Pour batter into 2 greased 8½×4½×2½-inch loaf pans. Bake in preheated 350° oven 1 hour or until toothpick inserted into center comes out clean. Let cool in pans on wire racks 10 minutes. Loosen edges; remove from pans. Cool slightly on wire racks; serve warm.
Makes 2 loaves.

Variation: To steam brown bread, divide batter evenly between 2 greased 1-pound coffee cans. Cover with aluminum foil; tie foil to cans with string. Place rack in large kettle; add boiling water to depth of 1 inch. Place cans on rack; cover. Steam over low heat 3 hours or until toothpick inserted near center comes out clean. If necessary, add more boiling water during steaming. Cool as above.

*Favorite recipe from **Washington Apple Commission***

Cottage Herb Rolls

- **1 package active dry yeast**
- **¼ cup warm water**
- **2½ cups unsifted flour**
- **¼ cup sugar**
- **1 teaspoon oregano leaves**
- **1 teaspoon salt**
- **½ cup cold margarine or butter**
- **1 cup BORDEN® or MEADOW GOLD® Cottage Cheese**
- **1 egg, beaten**
- **Melted margarine or butter**

Dissolve yeast in warm water. In large bowl, combine flour, sugar, oregano and salt; mix well. Cut in cold margarine until mixture resembles coarse cornmeal. Blend in cheese, egg and yeast. Turn onto well-floured surface; knead. Shape into ball; place in well-greased bowl. Brush top with melted margarine. Cover; let rise until doubled. Punch down; shape as desired. Brush with melted margarine; cover. Let rise again until nearly doubled. Bake in preheated 375° oven 12 to 15 minutes. Serve warm.
Makes 1½ to 2 dozen.

Cottage Herb Rolls

Golden Raisin Spice Bread

- **2 cups unsifted flour**
- **2 teaspoons baking powder**
- **1 teaspoon ground cinnamon**
- **½ teaspoon ground nutmeg**
- **½ teaspoon salt**
- **1 cup sugar**
- **½ cup margarine or butter, softened**
- **3 eggs**
- **½ cup milk**
- **½ cup REALEMON® Lemon Juice from Concentrate**
- **1 cup golden seedless raisins**

Preheat oven to 350°. Stir together flour, baking powder, cinnamon, nutmeg and salt; set aside. In large mixer bowl, beat sugar and margarine until fluffy. Add eggs, 1 at a time; beat well. Add milk alternately with dry ingredients; stir well. Stir in ReaLemon® brand and raisins. Turn into greased and floured 9×5-inch loaf pan. Bake 55 to 60 minutes or until wooden pick inserted near center comes out clean. Cool 10 minutes; remove from pan. Cool completely. Store tightly wrapped.
Makes one 9×5-inch loaf.

Cinnamon-Raisin Swirl Loaf

- **2 cups SUN-MAID® Raisins**
  Water
- **6¾ to 7¼ cups all-purpose flour**
- **2 packages active dry yeast**
- **2 cups milk**
- **¾ cup granulated sugar**
- **¼ cup butter or margarine**
- **2 teaspoons salt**
- **3 eggs**
- **2 teaspoons ground cinnamon**
  Powdered Sugar Icing (recipe follows)

Cinnamon-Raisin Swirl Loaf

In small bowl, combine raisins with enough hot tap water to cover. Plump 5 minutes; drain well. Set aside. In large bowl, combine 3 cups of the flour and the yeast. In medium saucepan, heat milk, ¼ cup of the granulated sugar, the butter and salt over low heat just until warm (115° to 120°F) and until butter is almost melted, stirring constantly. Add to flour mixture; add eggs. Beat at low speed of electric mixer for ½ minute, scraping sides of bowl constantly. Beat 3 minutes at high speed, scraping bowl occasionally. Stir in plumped raisins. Stir in as much remaining flour as can be mixed in with a spoon. Turn out onto lightly floured board. Knead in enough remaining flour to make a moderately stiff dough that is smooth and elastic (6 to 8 minutes total). Shape into a ball. Place dough in lightly greased bowl; turn once to grease surface. Cover; let rise in warm place (85°F) until doubled, about 1¼ hours.

Punch dough down; divide in half. Cover; let rest 10 minutes. Roll each half into 15×7-inch rectangle. Brush entire surface lightly with water. Combine remaining ½ cup granulated sugar and the cinnamon; sprinkle ½ of the sugar mixture over each rectangle. Roll up, jelly-roll fashion, starting from a 7-inch side; pinch edges and ends to seal. Place, sealed edges down, in 2 greased 9×5×3-inch loaf pans. Cover; let rise in warm place until nearly doubled, 35 to 45 minutes. Bake in preheated 375°F oven 35 to 40 minutes or until bread sounds hollow when tapped, covering bread with foil the last 15 minutes to prevent overbrowning. Remove bread from pans; cool completely on wire racks. Drizzle with Powdered Sugar Icing.
Makes 2 loaves.
POWDERED SUGAR ICING: In medium bowl, combine 1 cup sifted powdered sugar, ¼ teaspoon vanilla and enough milk (about 1½ tablespoons) to make of drizzling consistency.

Breakfast Raisin Ring

Breakfast Raisin Ring

- **1 package (8 ounces) PHILADELPHIA BRAND® Cream Cheese, cubed**
- **1 cup cold water**
- **1 package (16 ounces) hot roll mix**
- **1 egg**
- **1 teaspoon vanilla**
- **½ cup packed brown sugar**
- **⅓ cup PARKAY® Margarine**
- **¼ cup granulated sugar**
- **1½ teaspoons ground cinnamon**
- **1½ teaspoons vanilla**
- **½ cup golden raisins**
- **Vanilla Drizzle**

• Blend 6 ounces cream cheese and water in small saucepan. Cook over low heat until mixture reaches 115° to 120°F, stirring occasionally.

• Stir hot roll mix and yeast packet in large bowl. Add cream cheese mixture, egg and 1 teaspoon vanilla, mixing until dough pulls away from sides of bowl.

• Knead dough on lightly floured surface 5 minutes or until smooth and elastic. Cover; let rise in warm place 20 minutes.

• Beat remaining cream cheese, brown sugar, margarine, granulated sugar, cinnamon and

1½ teaspoons vanilla in small mixing bowl at medium speed with electric mixer until well blended.

• Roll out dough to 20×12-inch rectangle; spread cream cheese mixture over dough to within 1½ inches from outer edges of dough. Sprinkle with raisins.

• Roll up from long end, sealing edges. Place, seam-side down, on greased cookie sheet; shape into ring, pressing ends together to seal. Make 1 inch cuts through ring from outer edge at 2-inch intervals. Cover; let rise in warm place 30 minutes.

• Heat oven to 350°F.

• Bake 30 to 40 minutes or until golden brown. Cool slightly. Drizzle with Vanilla Drizzle.
Makes 8 to 10 servings

Prep time: 30 minutes plus rising
Cooking time: 40 minutes

Vanilla Drizzle

- **1 cup powdered sugar**
- **1 to 2 tablespoons milk**
- **1 teaspoon vanilla**
- **½ teaspoon ground cinnamon (optional)**

• Mix ingredients in small bowl until smooth.

Nut-Filled Christmas Wreath

- **2 tablespoons warm water (105° to 115°F)**
- **1 package active dry yeast**
- **3 tablespoons sugar, divided**
- **2 eggs**
- **¼ cup butter or margarine, melted, cooled**
- **3 tablespoons milk**
- **¾ teaspoon salt**
- **½ teaspoon ground cardamom**
- **2½ to 3 cups all-purpose flour**
- **Cherry-Nut Filling (recipe follows)**
- **Almond Icing (recipe follows)**

In large bowl, combine water, yeast and 1 tablespoon sugar; stir to dissolve yeast. Let stand until bubbly, about 5 minutes. Add remaining 2 tablespoons sugar, eggs, butter, milk, salt and cardamom; mix well. Stir in 1½ cups flour until smooth. Stir in enough remaining flour to make dough easy to handle. Turn out onto lightly floured surface. Knead 10 minutes or until dough is smooth and elastic, adding as much remaining flour as needed to prevent sticking. Shape dough into ball. Place in large, lightly greased bowl; turn dough once to grease surface. Cover with waxed paper; let rise in warm place (85°F) until doubled, about 1 hour. Meanwhile, prepare Cherry-Nut Filling.

Punch dough down. Roll out dough on floured surface into 24×9-inch rectangle. Sprinkle Cherry-Nut Filling over dough to within 1 inch from edges. Roll up dough, jelly-roll style, beginning on 24-inch side; pinch seam to seal. Using sharp knife; cut roll in half lengthwise; turn each half cut-side up. Carefully twist halves together, keeping cut sides up to expose filling. Place dough on greased cookie sheet; shape into a ring. Pinch ends together to seal. Cover; let stand in warm place until almost doubled, about 45 minutes. Bake in preheated 375°F oven 20 minutes or until evenly browned. Remove bread from cookie sheet to wire rack; cool slightly. Prepare Almond Icing; drizzle over warm bread. Serve warm or at room temperature.

Makes 1 coffee cake

CHERRY-NUT FILLING: In medium bowl, combine ¾ cup chopped nuts (hazelnuts, almonds, walnuts or pecans), ¼ cup *each* all-purpose flour, chopped candied red cherries, chopped candied green cherries, and softened butter or margarine, 2 tablespoons brown sugar and ½ teaspoon almond extract; mix well.

ALMOND ICING: In small bowl, combine 1 cup sifted powdered sugar, 1 to 2 tablespoons milk and ¼ teaspoon almond extract; blend until smooth.

Apricot Cardamom Wreath

Apricot Cardamom Wreath

Bread
- 1 cup granulated sugar
- 1 teaspoon ground cardamom
- ½ cup LAND O LAKES® Butter
- 1 can (12 ounces) evaporated milk
- 2 teaspoons salt
- 2 packages (¼ ounce *each*) active dry yeast
- ¼ cup warm water (105° to 115°F)
- ½ cup dairy sour cream
- 3 eggs
- 6 to 7 cups all-purpose flour

Filling
- 2 to 2½ cups water
- ¼ cup brandy *or* water
- 1 package (6 ounces) dried apricots (2 cups)
- 1 egg, slightly beaten
- 2 tablespoons milk
- Large crystal sugar

For bread, in 2-quart saucepan stir together granulated sugar and cardamom; add butter, evaporated milk and salt. Cook over medium heat, stirring occasionally, until butter is melted, 5 to 8 minutes. Cool to warm (105° to 115°F). In large mixer bowl dissolve yeast in ¼ cup warm water; stir in warm milk mixture, sour cream, 3 eggs and *3 cups* flour. Beat at medium speed, scraping bowl often, until smooth, 1 to 2 minutes. By hand, stir in enough remaining flour to make dough easy to handle. Turn dough onto lightly floured surface; knead until smooth and elastic, about 5 minutes. Place in greased bowl; turn greased side up. Cover; let rise in warm place until double in size, about 1 to 1½ hours. Dough is ready if indentation remains when touched.

For filling, in 2-quart saucepan combine *2 cups* water, brandy and apricots. Cook over low heat, stirring occasionally and adding small amounts of additional water, if necessary, until apricots are tender and mixture is thickened, 40 to 45 minutes; set aside.

Punch down dough; divide in half. Let rest 10 minutes. On lightly floured surface roll one half of dough to 20×9-inch rectangle; cut into 3 (3-inch-wide) strips. Spread *each* strip with *¼ cup* apricot mixture to within ½ inch of edges. Bring 20-inch sides up together; pinch sides and ends tightly to seal well. Gently braid filled strips together. Place on greased large cookie sheet; form into wreath or leave as a braid. Pinch ends to seal well. Repeat with remaining dough and apricot mixture. Cover; let rise in warm place 30 minutes.

Heat oven to 350°. Bake for 25 to 30 minutes or until lightly browned. (Cover with aluminum foil if bread browns too quickly.) In small bowl stir together beaten egg and 2 tablespoons milk. Brush breads with egg mixture; sprinkle with large crystal sugar. Continue baking for 5 to 10 minutes or until golden brown. Remove from cookie sheets; cool on wire racks.

Makes 2 wreaths

Tip: For best results, bake 1 wreath at a time.

Blueberry Sour Cream Tea Ring

Streusel
   ¼ **cup firmly packed brown
      sugar**
   ¼ **cup chopped pecans**
   ½ **teaspoon ground cinnamon**

Cake
   1 **package DUNCAN HINES®
      Blueberry Muffin Mix**
   ½ **cup dairy sour cream**
   1 **egg**
   2 **tablespoons water**

Glaze
   ½ **cup confectioners sugar**
   1 **tablespoon milk**

1. Preheat oven to 350°F. Grease 7-cup tube pan.

2. **For streusel,** combine brown sugar, pecans and cinnamon in small bowl. Set aside.

3. Rinse blueberries from Mix with cold water and drain.

4. **For cake,** empty muffin mix into bowl. Break up any lumps. Add sour cream, egg and water. Stir until blended. Spread ⅔ cup batter in pan. Sprinkle ⅓ cup streusel over batter. Place one half of blueberries over streusel. Repeat layers ending with batter on top. Bake at 350°F for 28 to 32 minutes or until toothpick inserted in center comes out clean. Cool in pan 10 minutes. Invert onto cooling rack. Turn right-side up.

5. **For glaze,** combine confectioners sugar and milk in small bowl. Stir until smooth. Drizzle over warm cake.

12 Servings

Tip: This recipe may be baked in one 8½×4½-inch loaf pan at 350°F for 45 to 50 minutes or until toothpick inserted in center comes out clean.

Touch of Honey Bread

Touch of Honey Bread

   2½ **to 3 cups all-purpose flour**
   1 **cup QUAKER® Oat Bran™
      hot cereal, uncooked**
   1 **package quick-rise yeast**
   ½ **teaspoon salt**
   1¼ **cups water**
   2 **tablespoons honey**
   2 **tablespoons margarine**

In large mixer bowl, combine 1 cup flour, oat bran, yeast and salt. Heat water, honey and margarine until very warm (120° to 130°F). Add to dry ingredients; beat at low speed of electric mixer until moistened. Increase speed to medium; continue beating 3 minutes. Stir in enough remaining flour to form a stiff dough.

Lightly spray bowl with no stick cooking spray or oil lightly. Turn dough out onto lightly floured surface. Knead 8 to 10 minutes or until dough is smooth and elastic. Place into prepared bowl, turning once to coat surface of dough. Cover; let rise in warm place 30 minutes or until doubled in size.

Lightly spray 8×4-inch loaf pan with no stick cooking spray or oil lightly. Punch down dough. Roll into 15×7-inch rectangle. Starting at narrow end, roll up dough tightly. Pinch ends and seam to seal; place seam side down in prepared pan. Cover; let rise in warm place 30 minutes or until doubled in size.

Heat oven to 375°F. Bake 35 to 40 minutes or until golden brown. Remove from pan; cool on wire rack at least 1 hour before slicing. Serve as sandwich bread, toasted or spread with jelly, jam or fruit preserves.

Makes 16 servings

Wholesome Wheat Bread

   5½ **to 6 cups whole wheat flour**
   2 **packages active dry yeast**
   1 **teaspoon salt**
   1 **teaspoon ground cinnamon**
   1 **cup KARO® Dark Corn
      Syrup**
   1 **cup water**
   ½ **cup HELLMANN'S® or
      BEST FOODS® Real
      Mayonnaise**
   2 **eggs**

In large mixer bowl, combine 2 cups of the flour, the yeast, salt and cinnamon. In medium saucepan, combine corn syrup, water and real mayonnaise; heat mixture over medium heat, stirring occasionally, until very warm (120° to 130°F). Pour hot mixture into flour mixture; beat at medium speed 2 minutes. Reduce speed to low; beat in 2 more cups of the flour and the eggs until well mixed. Beat at medium speed 2 minutes. By hand, stir in enough of the remaining flour to make dough easy to handle. Turn out onto lightly floured surface. Knead 10 minutes or until dough is smooth and elastic, adding as much remaining flour as needed to prevent sticking. Shape dough into a ball. Place in large, greased bowl; turn dough once to grease surface. Cover with towel; let rise in warm place (85°F) until doubled, about 1 hour.

Punch dough down; divide in half. Cover; let rest 10 minutes. Shape each half into 8×4-inch oval. Place on large, greased and floured baking sheet. Cut 3 slashes, ¼ inch deep, in top of each loaf. Cover; let rise in warm place until doubled, about 1½ hours. Bake in preheated 350°F oven 30 to 40 minutes or until loaves are browned and sound hollow when tapped. Immediately remove from baking sheet to wire racks to cool.

Makes 2 loaves

Bran Pita Bread

1 package active dry yeast
1¼ cups warm water
    (110° to 115°F)
1½ cups KELLOGG'S®
    ALL-BRAN® cereal
1½ cups all-purpose flour,
    divided
½ teaspoon salt
¼ cup vegetable oil
1 cup whole wheat flour

1. In large bowl of electric mixer, dissolve yeast in warm water, about 5 minutes. Add

Kellogg's® All-Bran® cereal, mixing until combined. On low speed, beat in 1 cup of the all-purpose flour, the salt and oil. Beat on high speed 3 minutes, scraping sides of bowl.

2. Using dough hooks on mixer or by hand, stir in whole wheat flour. Continue kneading with mixer on low speed or by hand 5 minutes longer or until dough is smooth and elastic. Add the remaining ½ cup all-purpose flour, if needed, to make soft dough.

3. Divide dough into 12 portions. Roll each portion between floured hands into a smooth ball. Cover with plastic wrap or a damp cloth; let rest 10 minutes.

4. On a well-floured surface, lightly roll one piece of dough at a time into 6-inch rounds, turning dough over once. Do not stretch, puncture or crease dough. Keep unrolled dough covered while rolling each dough piece. Place 2 rounds of dough at a time on ungreased baking sheet.

5. Bake in 450°F oven about 4 minutes or until dough is puffed and slightly firm. Turn with a spatula; continue baking about 2 minutes or until lightly browned; cool. Repeat with remaining dough. Cut in half and fill with a vegetable or meat filling.

Makes 12 servings

Bran Pita Bread

60-Minute Oatmeal Nut Loaf

3¼ cups all-purpose flour,
    divided
1 cup rolled oats
½ cup pecan pieces
2 teaspoons grated orange
    peel
½ teaspoon salt
1 pkg. FLEISCHMANN'S®
    RapidRise Yeast
1 cup milk
¼ cup water
2 tablespoons honey
1 tablespoon margarine or
    butter
1 egg, beaten
½ cup powdered sugar
1 to 1½ teaspoons milk
    Pecan halves

Set aside 1 cup flour. In large bowl, mix remaining 2¼ cups flour, oats, pecan pieces, orange peel, salt and yeast. In saucepan, over low heat, heat 1 cup milk, water, honey and margarine until very warm (125° to 130°F); stir into dry mixture. Mix in only enough reserved flour to make soft dough. On lightly floured surface, knead 4 minutes.

Roll dough into 13×9-inch rectangle. Roll up from short side, jelly-roll style; seal seam and ends. Place on greased baking sheet; flatten slightly. Cover; let rise in warm (80° to 85°F) draft-free place 20 minutes.

Preheat oven to 375°F. Make 3 diagonal slashes on top of loaf; brush with egg. Bake 20 to 25 minutes or until golden. Remove from baking sheet; cool on wire rack. In small bowl, mix powdered sugar and 1 teaspoon milk. Add additional milk, if necessary, to make desired consistency. Drizzle over loaf; garnish with pecan halves.

Makes 1 loaf

*Favorite recipe from **National Pecan Marketing Council***

COOKIES & CANDIES

Satisfy the cookie monster in your home in dozens of ways. Cookies of every description are filled with chocolate, oats, nuts, fruits and more. From peanut butter bar cookies to festive decorated cut-out cookies to rich, gooey brownies, you'll discover luscious ways to fill your cookie jar. Then tempt your friends and family with mouth-watering truffles, caramels, fudges and more. These candies are perfect for gift-giving and pleasing everyone's sweet tooth.

Chocolate-Dipped Crescents

1½ cups powdered sugar
1 cup LAND O LAKES® Butter, softened
1 egg
1½ teaspoons almond extract
2½ cups all-purpose flour
1 teaspoon cream of tartar
1 teaspoon baking soda
1 package (6 ounces) semisweet chocolate chips (1 cup), melted
Powdered sugar

Heat oven to 375°. In large mixer bowl combine 1½ cups powdered sugar and butter. Beat at medium speed, scraping bowl often, until creamy, 1 to 2 minutes. Add egg and almond extract; continue beating until well mixed, 1 to 2 minutes. Reduce speed to low. Add flour, cream of tartar and baking soda. Continue beating, scraping bowl often, until well mixed, 1 to 2 minutes. Shape into 1-inch balls. Roll balls into 2-inch ropes; shape into crescents. Place 2 inches apart on ungreased cookie sheets. Bake for 8 to 10 minutes or until set. Cookies do not brown. Cool completely. Dip half of *each* cookie into chocolate; sprinkle remaining half with powdered sugar. Refrigerate until set.

Makes about 4½ dozen cookies

Chocolate-Dipped Almond Horns

1 can SOLO® Almond Paste
3 egg whites
½ cup superfine sugar
½ teaspoon almond extract
¼ cup plus 2 tablespoons all-purpose flour
½ cup sliced almonds
5 squares (1 ounce each) semisweet chocolate, melted and cooled

Preheat oven to 350°F. Grease 2 cookie sheets; set aside. Break almond paste into small pieces and place in medium bowl or container of food processor. Add egg whites, sugar and almond extract. Beat with electric mixer or process until mixture is very smooth. Add flour and beat or process until blended.

Spoon almond mixture into pastry bag fitted with ½-inch (#8) plain tip. Pipe mixture into 5- or 6-inch crescent shapes on prepared cookie sheets about 1½ inches apart. Sprinkle with sliced almonds.

Bake 13 to 15 minutes or until edges are golden. Cool cookie sheets on wire racks 2 minutes. Remove from cookie sheets and cool completely on wire racks. Dip ends of cookies in melted chocolate and place on sheet of foil. Let stand until chocolate is set.

Makes about 16 cookies

Chocolate-Dipped Crescents

Clockwise from top left: Hershey's Great American Chocolate Chip Cookies (page 412), Reese's™ Chewy Chocolate Cookies, Chocolate Chip Whole Wheat Cookies and Chocolate Cookie Sandwiches

Chocolate Cookie Sandwiches

- ½ cup shortening
- 1 cup sugar
- 1 egg
- 1 teaspoon vanilla extract
- 1½ cups all-purpose flour
- ⅓ cup HERSHEY'S Cocoa
- ½ teaspoon baking soda
- ½ teaspoon salt
- ¼ cup milk
  Creme Filling (recipe follows)

Heat oven to 350°F. In large mixer bowl, beat shortening, sugar, egg and vanilla until light and fluffy. Stir together flour, cocoa, baking soda and salt; add alternately with milk to shortening mixture, beating until mixture is well blended. Drop dough by teaspoonfuls onto ungreased cookie sheet. Bake 10 to 11 minutes or just until cookies are soft-set (do not overbake). Cool slightly; remove from cookie sheet to wire rack. Cool completely. Spread bottom of one cookie with about 1 tablespoon Creme Filling; cover with another cookie. Repeat with remaining cookies and filling.
About 15 filled cookies.

Creme Filling

- 2 tablespoons butter or margarine, softened
- 2 tablespoons shortening
- ½ cup marshmallow creme
- ⅔ cup powdered sugar
- ¾ teaspoon vanilla extract

In small mixer bowl, beat butter and shortening until blended. Gradually beat in marshmallow creme. Add powdered sugar and vanilla; beat to spreading consistency.

Chocolate Chip Whole Wheat Cookies

- 1 cup whole wheat flour
- ½ teaspoon baking soda
- ½ teaspoon salt
- ¾ cup shortening
- 1½ cups packed light brown sugar
- 1 egg
- ¼ cup water
- 1 teaspoon vanilla extract
- 2 cups quick-cooking oats
- 1 cup raisins or chopped dried apricots
- 1 cup HERSHEY'S MINI CHIPS Semi-Sweet Chocolate

Heat oven to 350°F. Lightly grease cookie sheet. Stir together flour, baking soda and salt. In large mixer bowl, beat shortening and brown sugar until well blended. Add egg, water and vanilla; beat well. Gradually beat mixture into shortening mixture. Stir in remaining ingredients. Drop dough by teaspoonfuls onto prepared cookie sheet; flatten slightly. Bake 10 to 12 minutes or until golden brown. Remove from cookie sheet to wire rack; cool completely.
About 5 dozen cookies.

Reese's™ Chewy Chocolate Cookies

- 2 cups all-purpose flour
- ¾ cup HERSHEY'S Cocoa
- 1 teaspoon baking soda
- ½ teaspoon salt
- 1¼ cups (2½ sticks) butter or margarine, softened
- 2 cups sugar
- 2 eggs
- 2 teaspoons vanilla extract
- 1⅔ cups (10-oz. pkg.) REESE'S Peanut Butter Chips

Gingerbread People

Black-Eyed Susans

Filling:
    1 cup chopped SUN-MAID®
        Muscat Raisins
    ½ cup orange juice
    ½ teaspoon grated orange peel
    ¼ cup sugar
        Dash salt
Dough:
    ½ cup butter or margarine,
        softened
    ½ cup peanut butter
    1 cup sugar
    1 egg
    1 teaspoon vanilla
    1¼ cups all-purpose flour
    ½ teaspoon baking powder
    ¼ teaspoon salt

To prepare Filling: In small saucepan, combine all filling ingredients. Cook over medium heat, stirring frequently, until sugar dissolves and mixture thickens slightly. Cool while preparing dough.

To prepare Dough: In medium bowl, cream butter, peanut butter, sugar, egg and vanilla. In small bowl, sift flour with baking powder and salt; stir into creamed mixture. Cover and chill dough several hours. Roll out dough on lightly floured board to ⅛-inch thickness. Cut into 3-inch rounds with cookie cutter. Place 2 teaspoons of filling in centers of *half* the dough rounds. Cut small circles from centers of remaining dough rounds.* Place on top of raisin-filled rounds. Press edges together lightly to seal. Place on greased baking sheets. Bake in preheated 350°F oven 10 to 12 minutes or until golden brown. Cool on baking sheets a few minutes. Remove to wire rack to cool completely.
Makes about 1½ dozen cookies.

*A doughnut cutter works well. Simply cut ½ of dough with holes and ½ without.

Heat oven to 350°F. In bowl, stir together flour, cocoa, baking soda and salt. In large mixer bowl, beat butter and sugar until light and fluffy. Add eggs and vanilla; beat well. Gradually add flour mixture, beating well. Stir in chips. Drop by rounded teaspoonfuls onto ungreased cookie sheet. Bake 8 to 9 minutes. (Do not overbake; cookies will be soft. They will puff while baking and flatten while cooling.) Cool slightly; remove from cookie sheet to wire rack. Cool completely.
About 4½ dozen cookies.

Pan Recipe: Spread batter in greased 15½×10½×1-inch jelly-roll pan. Bake at 350°F. 20 minutes or until set. Cool completely in pan on wire rack; cut into bars.
About 4 dozen bars.

Gingerbread People

    1 package DUNCAN HINES®
        Moist Deluxe Spice Cake Mix
    2 teaspoons ground ginger
    2 large eggs
    ⅓ cup CRISCO® Oil or CRISCO®
        PURITAN® Oil
    ⅓ cup dark molasses
    ½ cup all-purpose flour
        Dark raisins

1. Combine all ingredients, except raisins, in large bowl; mix well (mixture will be soft). Refrigerate 2 hours.
2. Preheat oven to 375°F. Roll dough to ¼-inch thickness on lightly floured surface. Cut with 6-inch cookie cutter. Place on ungreased cookie sheets. Press raisins in dough for eyes and buttons.
3. Bake at 375°F for 8 to 10 minutes or until edges just start to brown. Cool several minutes on cookie sheet, then remove to racks to finish cooling.
About 14 six-inch cookies.

Double Chocolate Chunk Cookies

Chocolate Chip Lollipops

- **1 package DUNCAN HINES® Chocolate Chip Cookie Mix**
- **1 egg**
- **2 teaspoons water Flat ice cream sticks Assorted decors**

1. Preheat oven to 375°F.

2. Combine cookie mix, contents of buttery flavor packet from Mix, egg and water in large bowl. Stir until thoroughly blended. Shape dough into 24 (1-inch) balls. Place balls 3 inches apart on ungreased baking sheets (see Tip). Push ice cream stick into center of each ball. Flatten dough ball with hand to form round lollipop. Decorate by pressing decors onto dough. Bake at 375°F for 8 to 9 minutes or until light golden brown. Cool 1 minute on baking sheets. Remove to cooling racks. Cool completely. Store in airtight container.   *2 Dozen Cookies*

Tip: For best results, use shiny baking sheets for baking cookies. Dark baking sheets cause cookie bottoms to become too brown.

Double Chocolate Chunk Cookies

- **4 squares BAKER'S® Semi-Sweet Chocolate**
- **½ cup (1 stick) margarine or butter, slightly softened**
- **½ cup granulated sugar**
- **¼ cup firmly packed brown sugar**
- **1 egg**
- **1 teaspoon vanilla**
- **1 cup all-purpose flour**
- **½ teaspoon CALUMET® Baking Powder**
- **¼ teaspoon salt**
- **¾ cup chopped walnuts (optional)**
- **4 squares BAKER'S® Semi-Sweet Chocolate**

MELT 1 square chocolate in small microwavable bowl on HIGH 1 to 2 minutes or until almost melted, stirring after each minute. **Stir until chocolate is completely melted.** Cut 3 squares chocolate into large chunks; set aside.

BEAT margarine, sugars, egg and vanilla until light and fluffy. Stir in 1 square melted chocolate.

Mix in flour, baking powder and salt. Stir in chocolate chunks and walnuts. Refrigerate 30 minutes.

HEAT oven to 375°F. Drop dough by heaping tablespoonfuls, about 2 inches apart, onto greased cookie sheets. Bake for 8 minutes or until lightly browned. Cool 5 minutes on cookie sheets. Remove and finish cooling on wire racks.

MELT 4 squares chocolate in small microwavable bowl on HIGH 1 to 2 minutes or until almost melted, stirring after each minute. **Stir until chocolate is completely melted.** Dip ½ of each cookie into melted chocolate. Let stand on waxed paper until chocolate is firm.
    Makes about 2 dozen cookies

Prep time: 30 minutes
Chill time: 30 minutes
Baking time: 8 minutes

Double Chocolate Chunk Mocha Cookies: Prepare Double Chocolate Chunk Cookies as directed, adding 2 tablespoons instant coffee to the margarine mixture before beating.

Chocolate Chip Lollipops

Pecan Florentines

- ¾ **cup pecan halves, pulverized***
- ½ **cup all-purpose flour**
- ⅓ **cup firmly packed brown sugar**
- ¼ **cup light corn syrup**
- ¼ **cup butter or margarine**
- 2 **tablespoons milk**
- ⅓ **cup semisweet chocolate chips**

Preheat oven to 350°F. Line cookie sheets with foil; lightly grease foil. Combine pecans and flour in small bowl. Combine brown sugar, syrup, butter and milk in medium saucepan. Stir over medium heat until mixture comes to a boil. Remove from heat; stir in flour mixture. Drop batter by teaspoonfuls about 3 inches apart onto prepared cookie sheets.

Bake 10 to 12 minutes or until lacy and golden brown. (Cookies are soft when hot, but become crispy as they cool.) Remove cookies by lifting foil from cookie sheet; set foil on flat, heat-proof surface. Cool cookies completely on foil.

Place chocolate chips in small heavy-duty plastic bag; close securely. Set bag in bowl of hot water until chips are melted, being careful not to let any water into bag. (Knead bag lightly to check that chips are completely melted.) Pat bag dry. With scissors, snip off a small corner from one side of bag. Squeeze melted chocolate over cookies to decorate. Let stand until chocolate is set. Peel foil off cookies.

Makes about 3 dozen cookies

*To pulverize pecans, place in food processor or blender. Process until thoroughly ground with a dry, not pasty, texture.

Original Toll House® Chocolate Chip Cookies

- 2¼ **cups all-purpose flour**
- 1 **teaspoon baking soda**
- 1 **teaspoon salt**
- 1 **cup (2 sticks) butter, softened**
- ¾ **cup granulated sugar**
- ¾ **cup firmly packed brown sugar**
- 1 **teaspoon vanilla extract**
- 2 **eggs**
- One **12-oz.pkg. (2 cups) NESTLE® Toll House® Semi-Sweet Chocolate Morsels**
- 1 **cup nuts, chopped**

Preheat oven to 375°F. In small bowl, combine flour, baking soda and salt; set aside.

In large mixer bowl, beat butter, granulated sugar, brown sugar and vanilla extract until creamy. Beat in eggs. Gradually beat in flour mixture. Stir in semi-sweet chocolate morsels and nuts. Drop by rounded measuring tablespoonfuls onto ungreased cookie sheets.

Bake 9 to 11 minutes until edges are golden brown. Let stand on cookie sheets 2 minutes. Remove from cookie sheets; cool.

Makes about 5 dozen cookies

Chocolate No-Bake Cookies

- 1½ **cups quick-cooking oats**
- ½ **cup flaked coconut**
- ¼ **cup chopped walnuts**
- ¾ **cup sugar**
- ¼ **cup milk**
- ¼ **cup LAND O LAKES® Butter**
- 3 **tablespoons unsweetened cocoa**

In medium bowl combine oats, coconut and walnuts; set aside. In 2-quart saucepan combine sugar, milk, butter and cocoa. Cook over medium heat, stirring occasionally, until mixture comes to a full boil, 3 to 4 minutes. Remove from heat. Stir in oats mixture. Quickly drop mixture by rounded teaspoonfuls onto waxed paper. Cool completely. Store in refrigerator.

Makes about 2 dozen cookies

Microwave Directions: In medium bowl combine oats, coconut and walnuts; set aside. In medium microwave-safe bowl melt butter on HIGH 50 to 60 seconds. Stir in sugar, milk and cocoa. Microwave on HIGH 1 minute; stir. Microwave on HIGH until mixture comes to a full boil, 1 to 2 minutes. Continue as directed.

Double-Dipped Hazelnut Crisps (page 406) and Pecan Florentines

Choco-Caramel Delights

½ cup (1 stick) butter or
    margarine, softened
⅔ cup sugar
1 egg, separated
2 tablespoons milk
1 teaspoon vanilla extract
1 cup all-purpose flour
⅓ cup HERSHEY'S Cocoa
¼ teaspoon salt
1 cup finely chopped pecans
    Caramel Filling
    (recipe follows)
½ cup HERSHEY'S Semi-
    Sweet Chocolate Chips
    or Premium Semi-Sweet
    Chocolate Chunks
1 teaspoon shortening

In small mixer bowl, beat butter, sugar, egg yolk, milk and vanilla until blended. Stir together flour, cocoa and salt; blend into butter mixture. Refrigerate about 1 hour or until firm enough to handle.

Heat oven to 350°F. Lightly grease cookie sheet. Beat egg white slightly. Shape dough into 1-inch balls. Dip each ball into egg white; roll in pecans to coat. Place 1 inch apart on prepared cookie sheet. Press thumb gently in center of each ball.

Bake 10 to 12 minutes or until set. Meanwhile, prepare Caramel Filling. Remove cookies from oven; carefully press center of each cookie again with thumb to make indentation. Immediately spoon about ½ teaspoon Caramel Filling in center of each cookie. Carefully remove from cookie sheet to wire rack. Cool completely.

In small microwave-safe bowl, place chocolate chips and shortening. Microwave at HIGH (100%) 1 minute or until smooth when stirred. Place wax paper under wire rack with cookies. Drizzle chocolate mixture over top of cookies.

Makes about 2 dozen cookies

CARAMEL FILLING: In small saucepan, combine 14 unwrapped light caramels and 3 tablespoons whipping cream. Cook over low heat, stirring frequently, until caramels are melted and mixture is smooth.

Double-Dipped Hazelnut Crisps

¾ cup semisweet chocolate
    chips
1¼ cups all-purpose flour
¾ cup powdered sugar
⅔ cup whole hazelnuts,
    toasted, hulled and
    pulverized*
¼ teaspoon instant espresso
    coffee powder
    Dash salt
½ cup butter or margarine,
    softened
2 teaspoons vanilla
4 squares (1 ounce each)
    bittersweet or semisweet
    chocolate
4 ounces white chocolate
2 teaspoons shortening,
    divided

Preheat oven to 350°F. Lightly grease cookie sheets or line with parchment paper. Melt chocolate chips in top of double boiler over hot, not boiling, water. Remove from heat; cool. Blend flour, sugar, hazelnuts, coffee powder and salt in large bowl. Blend in butter, melted chocolate and vanilla until dough is stiff but smooth. (If dough is too soft to handle, cover and refrigerate until firm.)

Roll out dough, one fourth at a time, to ⅛-inch thickness on lightly floured surface. Cut out with 2-inch scalloped round cutter. Place 2 inches apart on prepared cookie sheets.

Bake 8 minutes or until not quite firm. (Cookies should not brown. They will puff up during baking and then fall again.) Remove to wire racks to cool.

Place bittersweet and white chocolates in separate small bowls. Add 1 teaspoon shortening to each bowl. Place

*To pulverize hazelnuts, place in food processor or blender. Process until thoroughly ground with a dry, not pasty, texture.

Choco-Caramel Delights

bowls over hot water; stir until chocolates are melted and smooth. Dip cookies, one at a time, halfway into bittersweet chocolate. Place on waxed paper; refrigerate until chocolate is set. Dip other halves of cookies into white chocolate; refrigerate until set. Store cookies in airtight container in cool place. (If cookies are frozen, chocolate may discolor.)

Makes about 4 dozen cookies

Chocolate Sugar Cookies

3 squares BAKER'S®
 Unsweetened Chocolate
1 cup (2 sticks) margarine or
 butter
1 cup sugar
1 egg
1 teaspoon vanilla
2 cups all-purpose flour
1 teaspoon baking soda
¼ teaspoon salt
 Additional sugar

MICROWAVE chocolate and margarine in large microwavable bowl on HIGH 2 minutes or until margarine is melted. **Stir until chocolate is completely melted.**

STIR 1 cup sugar into melted chocolate mixture until well blended. Stir in egg and vanilla until completely mixed. Mix in flour, soda and salt. Refrigerate 30 minutes.

HEAT oven to 375°F. Shape dough into 1-inch balls; roll in additional sugar. Place on ungreased cookie sheets. (If a flatter, crisper cookie is desired, flatten ball with bottom of drinking glass.)

BAKE for 8 to 10 minutes or until set. Remove from cookie sheets to cool on wire racks.

Makes about 3½ dozen cookies

Prep time: 15 minutes
Chill time: 30 minutes
Baking time: 8 to 10 minutes

Chocolate Sugar Cookies, Jam-Filled Chocolate Sugar Cookies and Chocolate-Caramel Sugar Cookies

Jam-Filled Chocolate Sugar Cookies: Prepare Chocolate Sugar Cookie dough as directed; roll in finely chopped nuts in place of sugar. Make indentation in each ball; fill center with your favorite jam. Bake as directed.

Chocolate-Caramel Sugar Cookies: Prepare Chocolate Sugar Cookie dough as directed; roll in finely chopped nuts in place of sugar. Make indentation in each ball; bake as directed. Microwave 1 package (14 ounces) KRAFT® Caramels with 2 tablespoons milk in microwavable bowl on HIGH 3 minutes or until melted, stirring after 2 minutes. Fill centers of cookies with caramel mixture. Place 1 square BAKER'S® Semi-Sweet Chocolate in a zipper-style sandwich bag. Close bag tightly. Microwave on HIGH about 1 minute or until chocolate is melted. Fold down top of bag tightly and snip a tiny piece off 1 corner (about ⅛ inch). Holding top of bag tightly, drizzle chocolate through opening over cookies.

Chocolate Pudding Cookies

1 package (4-serving size)
 JELL-O® Instant
 Pudding, Chocolate
 Flavor
1 cup buttermilk baking mix
¼ cup oil
1 egg
 Peanut butter chips or
 other assorted candies

PREHEAT oven to 350°. Put pudding mix and baking mix in bowl. Mix together with wooden spoon. Add oil and egg. Mix together until dough forms a ball.

SHAPE dough into ½-inch balls. Place balls about 2 inches apart on ungreased cookie sheet.

PRESS your thumb into middle of each ball to make a thumbprint. Put peanut butter chips or candies in thumbprint. Bake at 350° for 5 to 8 minutes or until lightly browned. Remove cookies to wire racks; cool.

Makes 36 cookies

Triple Chocolate Pretzels

- **2 squares (1 ounce each) unsweetened chocolate**
- **½ cup butter or margarine, softened**
- **½ cup granulated sugar**
- **1 egg**
- **2 cups cake flour**
- **1 teaspoon vanilla**
- **¼ teaspoon salt**
  Mocha Glaze (recipe follows)
- **2 ounces white chocolate, chopped**

Melt unsweetened chocolate in top of double boiler over hot, not boiling, water. Remove from heat; cool. Cream butter and granulated sugar in large bowl until light. Add egg and melted chocolate; beat until fluffy. Stir in flour, vanilla and salt until well blended. Cover; chill until firm, about 1 hour.

Preheat oven to 400°F. Lightly grease cookie sheets or line with parchment paper. Divide dough into 4 equal parts. Divide each part into 12 pieces. To form pretzels, knead each piece briefly to soften dough. Roll into a rope about 6 inches long. Form each rope on prepared cookie sheets into a pretzel shape. Repeat with all pieces of dough, spacing cookies 2 inches apart.

Bake 7 to 9 minutes or until firm. Remove to wire racks to cool. Prepare Mocha Glaze. Dip pretzel cookies, one at a time, into glaze to coat completely. Place on waxed paper, right side up. Let stand until glaze is set. Melt white chocolate in small bowl over hot water. Squeeze melted chocolate through pastry bag or drizzle over pretzels to decorate. Let stand until chocolate is completely set.

Makes 4 dozen cookies

Mocha Glaze

- **1 cup (6 ounces) semisweet chocolate chips**
- **1 teaspoon light corn syrup**
- **1 teaspoon shortening**
- **1 cup powdered sugar**
- **3 to 5 tablespoons hot coffee or water**

Combine chocolate chips, corn syrup and shortening in small heavy saucepan. Stir over low heat until chocolate is melted. Stir in powdered sugar and enough coffee to make a smooth glaze.

"M&M's"® Chocolate Candies Easy Party Cookies

- **1 cup butter or margarine, softened**
- **1 cup packed light brown sugar**
- **½ cup granulated sugar**
- **2 eggs**
- **2 teaspoons vanilla**
- **2¼ cups all-purpose flour**
- **1 teaspoon salt**
- **1 teaspoon baking soda**
- **1½ cups "M&M's"® Plain Chocolate Candies, divided**

Preheat oven to 375°F. Beat together butter, brown sugar and granulated sugar in large bowl until light and fluffy. Blend in eggs and vanilla. Combine flour, salt and baking soda in small bowl. Add to butter mixture; mix well. Stir in ½ cup of the candies. Drop dough by rounded teaspoonfuls 2 inches apart onto ungreased cookie sheets. Press additional candies into top of each cookie. Bake 10 to 12 minutes or until golden brown. Remove to wire racks to cool completely.

Makes about 6 dozen cookies

Chocolate Cherry Cookies

- **2 squares (1 ounce each) unsweetened chocolate**
- **½ cup butter or margarine, softened**
- **½ cup sugar**
- **1 egg**
- **2 cups cake flour**
- **1 teaspoon vanilla**
- **¼ teaspoon salt**
  Maraschino cherries, well drained (about 48)
- **1 cup (6 ounces) semisweet or milk chocolate chips**

Melt unsweetened chocolate in top of double boiler over hot, not boiling, water. Remove from heat; cool. Cream butter and sugar in large bowl until light. Add egg and melted chocolate; beat until fluffy. Stir in flour, vanilla and salt until well blended. Cover; refrigerate until firm, about 1 hour.

Preheat oven to 400°F. Lightly grease cookie sheets or line with parchment paper. Shape dough into 1-inch balls. Place 2 inches apart on prepared cookie sheets. With knuckle of finger, make a deep indentation in center of each ball. Place a cherry into each indentation.

Bake 8 minutes or just until set. Meanwhile, melt chocolate chips in small bowl over hot water. Stir until melted. Remove cookies to wire racks to cool. Drizzle melted chocolate over tops while still warm. Refrigerate until chocolate is set.

Makes about 4 dozen cookies

Chocolate Cherry Cookies, Chocolate Spritz (page 420) and Triple Chocolate Pretzels

Lacy Chocolate Crisps (top) and Florentines (bottom)

Lacy Chocolate Crisps

- **½ cup light corn syrup**
- **⅓ cup butter or margarine**
- **1 package (4 oz.) BAKER'S® GERMAN'S® Sweet Chocolate**
- **½ cup firmly packed light brown sugar**
- **1 cup flour**
- **⅔ cup BAKER'S® ANGEL FLAKE® Coconut**

Bring corn syrup to a boil. Add butter and chocolate. Cook and stir over low heat until smooth. Remove from heat; stir in sugar, flour and coconut. Drop from tablespoon onto lightly greased baking sheets, leaving 3 inches between. Bake at 300° for 15 minutes, or until wafers bubble vigorously and develop lacy holes. Cool on sheets 2 minutes; lift with spatula and finish cooling on racks. (If wafers harden on sheets, return briefly to oven.) If desired, roll warm wafers over wooden spoon handle; cool. Fill with tinted sweetened whipped cream.
Makes 2½ dozen.

Florentines

- **½ cup flour**
- **¼ teaspoon baking soda**
  Dash of salt
- **¼ cup butter or margarine**
- **⅓ cup firmly packed brown sugar**
- **2 tablespoons light corn syrup**
- **1 egg, well beaten**
- **½ cup BAKER'S® ANGEL FLAKE® Coconut**
- **½ teaspoon vanilla**
- **2 squares BAKER'S® Semi-Sweet Chocolate**
- **1 tablespoon butter or margarine**

Mix flour, soda and salt. Cream ¼ cup butter. Gradually add sugar and beat until light and fluffy. Add corn syrup and egg; blend well. Stir in flour mixture, coconut and vanilla. Drop by half teaspoonfuls onto greased baking sheets, leaving 2 inches between. Bake at 350° about 10 minutes. Cool on baking sheets 1 minute, remove quickly and finish cooling on racks. (If wafers harden on sheets, return briefly to oven.) Melt chocolate and 1 tablespoon butter in saucepan over very low heat, stirring constantly until smooth. Drizzle over wafers.
Makes 4 dozen.

Swiss Cinnamon Cookies

- **3 egg whites**
- **3¼ cups powdered sugar (approximately)**
- **3 cups DIAMOND® Walnuts, finely ground**
- **1 tablespoon ground cinnamon Chopped DIAMOND® Walnuts, colored sugars, candied cherries, dragées, for garnish**

In medium bowl, beat egg whites until foamy. Gradually beat in 2 cups of the sugar. Beat until mixture holds soft peaks, 3 to 4 minutes; remove ¾ cup of the batter, cover and set aside. Mix the 3 cups walnuts, the cinnamon and ¾ cup more of the sugar into larger egg white-sugar portion. Working with a third of the dough at a time, roll out to ⅛-inch thickness on pastry cloth or board heavily dusted with powdered sugar. Cut into desired shapes with cookie cutters. Place on greased or parchment-lined baking sheets. With tip of knife, spread reserved egg white mixture ⅛ inch thick onto top of each cookie, spreading almost to edges. Decorate immediately, as desired, with chopped walnuts, colored sugars, candied cherries and dragées. Bake in preheated 300°F oven 12 to 14 minutes or until cookies are just set and very lightly browned. Remove to wire racks to cool completely. Store in airtight container. Cookies can be securely wrapped and frozen up to 2 months.
Makes about 3 dozen (3-inch) cookies.

Slice 'n' Bake Lemon Cookies

2¼ cups unsifted flour
¼ teaspoon baking soda
½ cup margarine or butter, softened
½ cup shortening
½ cup granulated sugar
½ cup firmly packed light brown sugar
1 egg
3 tablespoons REALEMON® Lemon Juice from Concentrate
Egg white, beaten
Sliced almonds

Stir together flour and baking soda; set aside. In large mixer bowl, beat margarine, shortening and sugars until fluffy. Add egg; mix well. Gradually add dry ingredients and ReaLemon® brand; mix well. Chill 2 hours; form into two 10-inch rolls. Wrap well; freeze until firm. Preheat oven to 350°. Cut rolls into ¼-inch slices; place 1 inch apart on greased baking sheets. Brush with egg white; top with almonds. Bake 10 to 12 minutes or until lightly browned.
Makes about 5 dozen.

Jelly Jewels

1 package DUNCAN HINES® Moist Deluxe Yellow Cake Mix
¾ cup CRISCO® shortening
2 large egg yolks
1 tablespoon milk
2 large egg whites
2 tablespoons water
1¼ cups ground nuts
Red or green jelly

1. Preheat oven to 375°F. Grease cookie sheets.
2. Combine dry cake mix, shortening, egg yolks and milk; mix well. Shape into 1-inch balls.
3. Combine egg whites and water. Beat with fork until blended. Dip balls in egg white mixture, then roll in nuts. Place 2 inches apart on cookie sheets.
4. Bake at 375°F for 12 to 15 minutes or until golden brown. Immediately press thumb or thimble into center of each cookie making a depression. Cool several minutes on cookie sheets, then remove to racks to finish cooling. Before serving, fill depressions with jelly.
About 4 dozen 2-inch cookies.

Almond Shortbread Cookies

2½ cups unsifted flour
1 teaspoon baking soda
1 teaspoon cream of tartar
1 cup margarine or butter, softened
1½ cups confectioners' sugar
1 egg
1 (9-ounce) package NONE SUCH® Condensed Mincemeat, crumbled
½ cup sliced almonds
½ teaspoon almond extract
Almond Frosting
Additional sliced almonds

Preheat oven to 375°. Stir together flour, baking soda and cream of tartar; set aside. In large mixer bowl, beat margarine and sugar until fluffy. Add egg; mix well. Stir in mincemeat, *½ cup* almonds and extract. Add flour mixture; mix well (dough will be stiff). Roll into 1¼-inch balls. Place on ungreased baking sheets; flatten slightly. Bake 10 to 12 minutes or until lightly browned. Cool. Frost with Almond Frosting and garnish with additional almonds if desired.
Makes about 3 dozen.
ALMOND FROSTING: In small mixer bowl, combine 2¼ cups confectioners' sugar, 3 tablespoons margarine or butter, softened, 3 tablespoons water and ½ teaspoon almond extract; beat well.
Makes about 1 cup.

Granola Cookies

1 cup sugar
½ cup CRISCO® Oil
⅓ cup honey
2 eggs
¼ cup water
2 cups unsifted all-purpose flour
1¾ cups quick-cooking rolled oats
1 teaspoon baking soda
1 teaspoon salt
1 teaspoon ground cinnamon
½ cup chopped dried apricots
½ cup raisins
½ cup chopped nuts
½ cup miniature semisweet chocolate chips
½ cup flaked coconut

Preheat oven to 350°F. Grease baking sheet. Set aside.

Mix sugar, Crisco® Oil, honey, eggs and water in large mixing bowl. Add flour, oats, baking soda, salt and cinnamon. Mix well. Stir in remaining ingredients.

Drop by teaspoonfuls about 2 inches apart onto prepared baking sheet. Bake at 350°F, about 8 minutes, or until almost no indentation remains when touched lightly. Cool on wire rack.
4½ to 5 dozen cookies.

Variation: Granola Bars. Follow recipe above, except spread dough in greased and floured 15×10-inch jelly roll pan. Bake at 350°F, about 15 minutes, or until top is light brown. Cool completely on wire rack. Cut into 48 bars.

Jelly Jewels

Lemon Blossom Cookies

2 cups margarine or butter, softened
1½ cups confectioners' sugar
¼ cup REALEMON® Lemon Juice from Concentrate
4 cups unsifted flour
Finely chopped nuts, optional
Assorted fruit preserves and jams or pecan halves

Preheat oven to 350°. In large mixer bowl, beat margarine and sugar until fluffy. Add ReaLemon® brand; beat well. Gradually add flour; mix well. Chill 2 hours. Shape into 1-inch balls; roll in nuts if desired. Place 1 inch apart on greased baking sheets. Press thumb in center of each ball; fill with preserves or pecan. Bake 14 to 16 minutes or until lightly browned. *Makes about 6 dozen.*

Easy Peanut Butter Cookies

1 (14-ounce) can EAGLE® Brand Sweetened Condensed Milk (NOT evaporated milk)
¾ cup peanut butter
2 cups biscuit baking mix
1 teaspoon vanilla extract
Granulated sugar

Preheat oven to 375°. In large mixer bowl, beat sweetened condensed milk and peanut butter until smooth. Add biscuit mix and vanilla; mix well. Shape into 1-inch balls. Roll in sugar. Place 2 inches apart on ungreased baking sheets. Flatten with fork. Bake 6 to 8 minutes or until *lightly* browned (do not overbake). Cool. Store tightly covered at room temperature. *Makes about 5 dozen.*
Peanut Blossoms: Shape as above; *do not flatten.* Bake as above. Press solid milk chocolate candy in center of each ball immediately after baking.
Peanut Butter & Jelly Gems: Press thumb in center of each ball of dough; fill with jelly, jam or preserves. Bake as above.
Any-Way-You-Like'm Cookies: Stir 1 cup semi-sweet chocolate chips *or* chopped peanuts *or* raisins *or* flaked coconut into dough. Proceed as above.

Hershey's Great American Chocolate Chip Cookies

2¼ cups all-purpose flour
1 teaspoon baking soda
½ teaspoon salt
1 cup (2 sticks) butter, softened
¾ cup granulated sugar
¾ cup packed light brown sugar
1 teaspoon vanilla extract
2 eggs
2 cups (12-oz. pkg.) HERSHEY'S Semi-Sweet Chocolate Chips
1 cup chopped nuts (optional)

Heat oven to 375°F. In bowl, stir together flour, baking soda and salt. In large mixer bowl, beat butter, granulated sugar, brown sugar and vanilla until light and fluffy. Add eggs; beat well. Gradually add flour mixture, beating well. Stir in chocolate chips and nuts, if desired. Drop by rounded teaspoonfuls onto ungreased cookie sheet. Bake 9 to 11 minutes or until lightly browned. Cool slightly; remove from cookie sheet to wire rack. Cool completely.
About 6 dozen cookies.
Pan Recipe: Spread in greased 15½×10½×1-inch jelly-roll pan. Bake at 375°F. 20 minutes or until lightly browned. Cool completely; cut into bars.
About 4 dozen bars.

Lemon Blossom Cookies

Chocolate Kahlúa® Bears

¼ cup KAHLÚA®
2 squares (1 ounce each) unsweetened chocolate
⅔ cup shortening
1⅔ cups sugar
2 eggs
2 teaspoons vanilla
2 cups sifted all-purpose flour
2 teaspoons baking powder
¾ teaspoon salt
½ teaspoon ground cinnamon
Chocolate Icing (recipe follows)

To Kahlúa® in measuring cup, add enough water to make ⅓ cup liquid. In small saucepan over low heat, melt chocolate; cool. In large bowl, beat shortening, sugar, eggs and vanilla until light and fluffy. Stir in chocolate. In small bowl, combine flour, baking powder, salt and cinnamon. Add dry ingredients to egg mixture alternately with ⅓ cup liquid. Cover; refrigerate until firm. Roll out dough, one fourth at a time, about ¼ inch thick on well-floured surface. Cut out with bear-shaped or other cookie cutters. Place 2 inches apart on ungreased cookie sheets. Bake in preheated 350° oven 8 to 10 minutes. Remove to wire racks to cool. Spread Chocolate Icing in thin, even layer on cookies. Let stand until set; decorate as desired.
Makes about 2½ dozen cookies.
CHOCOLATE ICING: In medium saucepan, combine 6 squares (1 ounce each) semisweet chocolate, ⅓ cup butter or margarine, ¼ cup Kahlúa® and 1 tablespoon light corn syrup. Cook over low heat until chocolate melts, stirring to blend. Add ¾ cup sifted powdered sugar; beat until smooth. If necessary, beat in additional Kahlúa® to make spreading consistency.

Clockwise from top: Coconut Washboards, Melting Moments, Coconut Macaroons and Coconut Dream Bars (page 430)

Coconut Washboards

2 cups flour
¾ teaspoon CALUMET® Baking Powder
¼ teaspoon cinnamon
¼ teaspoon nutmeg
⅛ teaspoon salt
¾ cup butter
1 cup firmly packed brown sugar
1 egg
1 teaspoon vanilla
½ teaspoon almond extract
1⅓ cups (about) BAKER'S® ANGEL FLAKE® Coconut

Mix flour with baking powder, spices and salt. Cream butter. Gradually add sugar, beating until light and fluffy. Add egg, vanilla and almond extract; beat well. Add flour mixture, blending well. Stir in coconut. Divide dough into 2 parts. Chill, if necessary, until dough is easily handled. Spread or pat each half into a 10×9-inch rectangle. Cut each rectangle into 4 strips lengthwise. Cut each strip into 10 pieces. Place about 2 inches apart on ungreased baking sheets. Using a floured fork, gently press ridges into cookies. Bake at 375° for 8 to 10 minutes, or until golden brown.
Makes about 6½ dozen.

Melting Moments

1 cup flour
2 tablespoons cornstarch
½ cup unsifted confectioners sugar
1 cup butter or margarine, softened
1⅓ cups (about) BAKER'S® ANGEL FLAKE® Coconut

Mix flour with cornstarch and sugar in a bowl. Blend in butter to form a soft dough. Cover and chill, if necessary, until dough is firm enough to handle. Shape into small balls, about ¾ inch in diameter. Roll in coconut and place on ungreased baking sheets, about 1½ inches apart. Flatten with lightly floured fork, if desired. Bake at 300° for 20 to 25 minutes, or until lightly browned.
Makes about 3 dozen.
Almond Melting Moments: Prepare Melting Moments as directed, adding 2 teaspoons almond extract with the butter.

Coconut Macaroons

1⅓ cups (about) BAKER'S® ANGEL FLAKE® Coconut
⅓ cup sugar
3 tablespoons flour
⅛ teaspoon salt
2 egg whites
½ teaspoon almond extract

Combine coconut, sugar, flour and salt in mixing bowl. Stir in egg whites and almond extract; mix well. Drop from teaspoon onto lightly greased baking sheets. Garnish with candied cherry halves, if desired. Bake at 325° for 20 to 25 minutes, or until edges of cookies are golden brown. Remove from baking sheets immediately.
Makes about 18.
Raisin Macaroons: Prepare Coconut Macaroons as directed, adding ⅓ cup raisins before baking.
Chip Macaroons: Prepare Coconut Macaroons as directed, adding ⅓ cup BAKER'S® Semi-Sweet Chocolate Flavored Chips before baking.
Nut Macaroons: Prepare Coconut Macaroons as directed, adding ⅓ cup chopped pecans or almonds before baking.
Fruited Macaroons: Prepare Coconut Macaroons as directed, adding ⅓ cup chopped mixed candied fruit before baking. Garnish with candied cherry halves, maraschino cherries or whole almonds, if desired.

Pinwheels and Checkerboards

2 cups flour
1 teaspoon CALUMET® Baking Powder
½ teaspoon salt
⅔ cup butter or margarine
1 cup sugar
1 egg
1 teaspoon vanilla
2 squares BAKER'S® Unsweetened Chocolate, melted

Mix flour, baking powder and salt. Cream butter. Gradually add sugar and continue beating until light and fluffy. Add egg and vanilla; beat well. Gradually add flour mixture, mixing well after each addition. Divide dough in half; blend chocolate into one half. Use prepared doughs to make Pinwheels or Checkerboards.

Pinwheels: Roll chocolate and vanilla doughs separately between sheets of waxed paper into 12×8-inch rectangles. Remove top sheets of paper and invert vanilla dough onto chocolate dough. Remove remaining papers. Roll up as for jelly roll; then wrap in waxed paper. Chill until firm, at least 3 hours (or freeze 1 hour). Cut into ¼-inch slices and place on baking sheets. Bake at 375° about 10 minutes, or until cookies just begin to brown around edges. Cool on racks.
Makes about 4½ dozen.

Checkerboards: Set out small amount of milk. Roll chocolate and vanilla doughs separately on lightly floured board into 9×4½-inch rectangles. Brush chocolate dough lightly with milk and top with vanilla dough. Using a long sharp knife, cut lengthwise into 3 strips, 1½ inches wide. Stack strips, alternating colors and brushing each layer with milk. Cut lengthwise again into 3 strips, ½ inch wide. Invert middle section so that colors are alternated; brush sides with milk. Press strips together lightly to form a rectangle. Wrap in waxed paper. Chill overnight. Cut into ⅛-inch slices, using a very sharp knife. Place on baking sheets. Bake at 375° for about 8 minutes, or just until white portions begin to brown. Cool on racks.
Makes about 5 dozen.

Wheat Germ Cookies

1 package DUNCAN HINES® Moist Deluxe Yellow Cake Mix
1 large egg
3 tablespoons brown sugar
¼ cup CRISCO® Oil or CRISCO® PURITAN® Oil
2 tablespoons butter or margarine, melted
½ cup wheat germ
2 tablespoons water
½ cup chopped nuts

1. Preheat oven to 375°F.
2. Combine dry cake mix, egg, brown sugar, oil, butter, wheat germ and water in bowl. Mix with spoon. (Dough will be stiff.) Stir in nuts.
3. Drop by teaspoonfuls, 2 inches apart, on ungreased cookie sheets.
4. Bake at 375°F for 10 minutes for chewy cookies, 12 minutes for crispy cookies. Cool 1 minute on cookie sheet, then remove to rack to finish cooling.
About 3 dozen cookies.

Lemon Sugar Cookies

3 cups unsifted flour
2 teaspoons baking powder
½ teaspoon salt
2 cups sugar
1 cup shortening
2 eggs
¼ cup REALEMON® Lemon Juice from Concentrate
Additional sugar

Preheat oven to 350°. Stir together flour, baking powder and salt; set aside. In large mixer bowl, beat sugar and shortening until fluffy; beat in eggs. Stir in dry ingredients, then ReaLemon® brand; mix well. Chill 2 hours. Shape into 1¼-inch balls; roll in additional sugar. Place 2 inches apart on greased baking sheets; flatten. Bake 8 to 10 minutes or until lightly browned.
Makes about 8 dozen.

Thumbprint Cookies

1 package (4-serving size) JELL-O® Instant Pudding and Pie Filling, any flavor
1 package (10 ounces) pie crust mix
2 tablespoons butter or margarine, melted
4 to 5 tablespoons cold water
1 package (4 ounces) BAKER'S® GERMAN'S® Sweet Chocolate, broken into squares
Whole or chopped toasted nuts

Combine pudding mix and pie crust mix in medium bowl; add butter and 4 tablespoons of the water. Mix with fork until soft dough forms. (If dough is too dry, add 1 tablespoon water.) Shape dough into 1-inch balls. Place 1 inch apart on ungreased baking sheets; press thumb deeply into center of each.

Cut each square of chocolate in half. Press 1 half into center of each cookie. Bake in preheated 350° oven for about 15 minutes or until lightly browned. Immediately press nuts lightly into chocolate centers. Remove from baking sheets and cool on wire racks.
Makes 3 dozen.

Coconut Thumbprints: Prepare Thumbprint Cookies as directed, omitting chocolate and nuts. Mix 1⅓ cups (about) BAKER'S® ANGEL FLAKE® Coconut with ½ cup sweetened condensed milk; spoon into centers of cookies before baking.

Jam Thumbprints: Prepare Thumbprint Cookies as directed, omitting chocolate and nuts. Spoon ½ teaspoon jam into center of each cookie after baking.

Cream Cheese and Jelly Thumbprints: Prepare Thumbprint Cookies as directed, omitting chocolate and nuts. Using 1 package (3 ounces) cream cheese, softened, spoon ½ teaspoon cream cheese into center of each cookie before baking and top each with ½ teaspoon jelly after baking.

Wheat Germ Cookies

Double Mint Chocolate Cookies

Apricot-Pecan Tassies

Base
- 1 cup all-purpose flour
- ½ cup butter, cut into pieces
- 6 tablespoons reduced-calorie cream cheese

Filling
- ¾ cup firmly packed light brown sugar
- 1 egg, lightly beaten
- 1 tablespoon butter, softened
- ½ teaspoon vanilla
- ¼ teaspoon salt
- ⅔ cup California dried apricot halves, diced (about 4 ounces)
- ⅓ cup chopped pecans

For base, in food processor, combine flour, ½ cup butter and cream cheese; process until mixture forms large ball. Wrap dough in plastic wrap and chill 15 minutes.

For filling, combine brown sugar, egg, 1 tablespoon butter, vanilla and salt in bowl until smooth. Stir in apricots and nuts.

Preheat oven to 325°F. Shape dough into 2 dozen 1-inch balls and place in paper-lined or greased miniature muffin cups.

Double Mint Chocolate Cookies

Cookies
- 2 cups granulated sugar
- 1 cup unsweetened cocoa
- 1 cup LAND O LAKES® Butter, softened
- 1 cup buttermilk or sour milk
- 1 cup water
- 2 eggs
- 2 teaspoons baking soda
- 1 teaspoon baking powder
- ½ teaspoon salt
- 1 teaspoon vanilla
- 4 cups all-purpose flour

Frosting
- 4 cups powdered sugar
- 1 cup LAND O LAKES® Butter, softened
- 1 teaspoon salt
- 2 tablespoons milk
- 2 teaspoons vanilla
- ½ teaspoon mint extract
- ½ cup crushed starlight peppermint candy

Preheat oven to 400°F. Grease cookie sheets. For cookies, in large bowl, combine granulated sugar, cocoa, 1 cup butter, buttermilk, water, eggs, baking soda, baking powder, ½ teaspoon salt and 1 teaspoon vanilla. Beat at low speed, scraping bowl often, until well mixed, 1 to 2 minutes. Stir in flour until well mixed, 3 to 4 minutes. Drop rounded teaspoonfuls of dough 2 inches apart onto prepared cookie sheets.

Bake 7 to 9 minutes or until top of cookie springs back when touched lightly in center. Remove to wire rack to cool.

For frosting, in small bowl, combine powdered sugar, 1 cup butter, 1 teaspoon salt, milk, 2 teaspoons vanilla and mint extract. Beat at medium speed, scraping bowl often, until light and fluffy, 2 to 3 minutes. Spread ½ tablespoonful of frosting on the top of each cookie. Sprinkle with candy.
Makes about 8 dozen cookies

Apricot-Pecan Tassies

Brandy Lace Cookies

Chocolate Madeleines

 ¾ cup (1½ sticks) butter
 ⅓ cup HERSHEY'S Cocoa
 1¼ cups all-purpose flour
 1 cup sugar
 ⅛ teaspoon salt
 3 eggs
 2 egg yolks
 ½ teaspoon vanilla extract
   Chocolate Frosting
   (recipe follows)

Heat oven to 350°F. Lightly grease indentations of madeleine mold pan (each shell is 3×2 inches). In medium saucepan, melt butter; remove from heat. Stir in cocoa, blending well; cool slightly. In bowl, stir together flour, sugar and salt; gradually blend into butter mixture. In small bowl, lightly beat eggs, egg yolks and vanilla with fork until well blended; stir into chocolate mixture, blending well. Over very low heat, cook, stirring constantly, until mixture is warm; *do not simmer or boil.* Remove from heat. Fill each mold half full with batter (do not overfill).

Bake 8 to 10 minutes or until wooden pick inserted in center comes out clean. Invert onto wire rack; cool completely. Prepare Chocolate Frosting; frost flat sides of cookies. Press frosted sides together, forming shells.
Makes about 1½ dozen filled cookies

CHOCOLATE FROSTING: In small bowl, stir together 1¼ cups powdered sugar and 2 tablespoons HERSHEY'S Cocoa; set aside. In small mixer bowl, beat 2 tablespoons softened butter and ¼ cup cocoa mixture until light and fluffy. Gradually add remaining cocoa mixture alternately with 2 to 2½ tablespoons milk, beating to spreading consistency. Stir in ½ teaspoon vanilla extract.

Press dough on bottom and up side of each cup; fill each with 1 teaspoon apricot-pecan filling. Bake 25 minutes or until golden and filling sets. Cool and remove from cups. Cookies can be wrapped tightly in plastic wrap and frozen up to six weeks.
Makes 2 dozen cookies

Favorite recipe from **California Apricot Advisory Board**

Brandy Lace Cookies

 ¼ cup sugar
 ¼ cup MAZOLA® Margarine
 ¼ cup KARO® Light or Dark
   Corn Syrup
 ½ cup all-purpose flour
 ¼ cup very finely chopped
   pecans or walnuts
 2 tablespoons brandy
   Melted white and/or
   semisweet chocolate
   (optional)

Preheat oven to 350°F. Lightly grease and flour cookie sheets. In small saucepan combine sugar, margarine and corn syrup. Bring to boil over medium heat, stirring constantly. Remove from heat. Stir in flour, pecans and brandy. Drop 12 evenly spaced half teaspoonfuls of batter onto prepared cookie sheets.

Bake 6 minutes or until golden. Cool 1 to 2 minutes or until cookies can be lifted but are still warm and pliable; remove with spatula. Curl around handle of wooden spoon; slide off when crisp. If cookies harden before curling, return to oven to soften. Drizzle with melted chocolate, if desired.
Makes 4 to 5 dozen cookies

Almond Rice Madeleines

Vegetable cooking spray
1 cup whole blanched almonds, lightly toasted
1½ cups sugar
¾ cup flaked coconut
3 cups cooked rice, chilled
3 egg whites
Fresh raspberries (optional)
Frozen nondairy whipped topping, thawed (optional)
Powdered sugar (optional)

Preheat oven to 350°F. Coat madeleine pans* with cooking spray. Place almonds in food processor fitted with knife blade; process until finely ground. Add sugar and coconut to processor; process until coconut is finely minced. Add rice; pulse to blend. Add egg whites; pulse to blend. Spoon mixture evenly into madeleine pans, filling to tops.

Bake 25 to 30 minutes or until lightly browned. Cool completely in pans on wire rack. Cover and refrigerate 2 hours or until serving time. Run a sharp knife around each madeleine shell and gently remove from pan. Invert onto serving plates; serve with raspberries and whipped topping, if desired. Sprinkle with powdered sugar, if desired.

Makes about 3 dozen madeleines

*You may substitute miniature muffin pans for madeleine pans, if desired.

Favorite recipe from **USA Rice Council**

Cherry Surprises

Cherry Surprises

**1 package DUNCAN HINES®
Golden Sugar Cookie Mix**
36 to 40 candied cherries
½ cup semi-sweet chocolate chips
1 teaspoon CRISCO® Shortening

1. Preheat oven to 375°F. Grease baking sheets.

2. Prepare cookie mix following package directions for original recipe. Shape thin layer of dough around each candied cherry. Place 2 inches apart on baking sheets. Bake at 375°F for 8 minutes or until set but not browned. Cool 1 minute on baking sheets. Remove to cooling racks. Cool completely.

3. Combine chocolate chips and shortening in small resealable plastic bag. Place bag in bowl of hot water for several minutes. Dry with paper towel. Knead until blended and chocolate is smooth. Snip pinpoint hole in corner of bag. Drizzle chocolate over cookies. Allow drizzle to set before storing between layers of waxed paper in airtight container.

3 to 3½ Dozen Cookies

Tip: Well-drained maraschino cherries may be substituted for candied cherries.

Almond Rice Madeleines

Linzer Hearts

1 package DUNCAN HINES®
   Golden Sugar Cookie Mix
½ cup all-purpose flour
½ cup finely ground almonds
1 egg
1 tablespoon water
3 tablespoons confectioners
   sugar
½ cup *plus* 1 tablespoon
   seedless red raspberry
   jam, warmed

1. Preheat oven to 375°F.

2. Combine cookie mix, contents of buttery flavor packet from Mix, flour, almonds, egg and water in large bowl. Stir with spoon until blended. Roll dough ⅛ inch thick on lightly floured board. Cut out 3-inch hearts with floured cookie cutter. Cut out centers of half the hearts with smaller heart cookie cutter. Reroll dough as needed. Place 2 inches apart on ungreased baking sheets. Bake whole hearts at 375°F for 8 to 9 minutes and cut-out hearts for 6 to 7 minutes or until edges are lightly browned. Cool 1 minute on baking sheets. Remove to cooling racks. Cool completely.

3. To assemble, dust cut-out hearts with sifted confectioners sugar. Spread warm jam over whole hearts almost to edges; top with cut-out hearts. Press together to make sandwiches. Fill center with ¼ teaspoon jam. Store between layers of waxed paper in airtight container.

22 (3-inch) Sandwich Cookies

Tip: If you like a softer cookie, make these a day ahead.

Bavarian Cookie Wreaths

3½ cups all-purpose flour
1 cup sugar, divided
3 teaspoons grated orange
   peel, divided
¼ teaspoon salt
1⅓ cups butter or margarine
¼ cup Florida orange juice
⅓ cup finely chopped
   blanched almonds
1 egg white *beaten with*
   1 teaspoon water
Tinted Frosting
   (recipe follows)

Preheat oven to 400°F. Lightly grease cookie sheets. In large bowl, mix flour, ¾ cup sugar, 2 teaspoons orange peel and salt. Using pastry blender, cut in butter until mixture resembles coarse crumbs; add orange juice, stirring until mixture holds together. Knead a few times and press into a ball.

Shape dough into ¾-inch balls; lightly roll each on floured surface into 6-inch-long strip. Using two strips, twist together to make a rope. Pinch ends of rope together to make wreath; place on prepared cookie sheet.

In shallow dish, mix almonds, remaining ¼ cup sugar and 1 teaspoon orange peel. Brush top of wreaths with egg white mixture and sprinkle with almond-sugar mixture. Bake 8 to 10 minutes or until lightly browned. Remove to wire racks to cool completely. Frost with Tinted Frosting, if desired.

Makes about 5 dozen cookies

Tinted Frosting

1 cup confectioners' sugar
2 tablespoons butter or
   margarine, softened
1 to 2 teaspoons milk
   Few drops green food color
   Red cinnamon candies

In small bowl, mix sugar, butter, 1 teaspoon milk and few drops green food color. Add more milk if necessary to make frosting spreadable. Fill pastry bag fitted with small leaf tip (#67). Decorate each wreath with 3 or 4 leaves and red cinnamon candies for berries.

Tip: Use various decorations for special holidays—or serve plain.

*Favorite recipe from **Florida Department of Citrus***

Linzer Hearts

Brandied Buttery Wreaths

Cookies
- 2¼ cups all-purpose flour
- ⅓ cup granulated sugar
- ⅔ cup LAND O LAKES®
  Butter, softened
- 1 egg
- 1 teaspoon ground nutmeg
- ¼ teaspoon salt
- 2 tablespoons grated orange
  peel
- 2 tablespoons brandy*
- ⅓ cup chopped maraschino
  cherries, drained

Glaze
- 1¼ cups powdered sugar
- 1 to 2 tablespoons milk
- 1 tablespoon brandy**
- ⅛ teaspoon ground nutmeg
  Red and green maraschino
  cherries, drained, halved

Heat oven to 350°. For cookies, in large mixer bowl combine flour, granulated sugar, butter, egg, 1 teaspoon nutmeg, salt, orange peel and 2 tablespoons brandy. Beat at low speed, scraping bowl often, until well mixed, 1 to 2 minutes. By hand, stir in ⅓ cup chopped cherries. Shape rounded teaspoonfuls of dough into 1-inch balls; form into 5-inch long strips. Shape strips into circles (wreaths), candy canes *or* leave as strips. Place 2 inches apart on greased cookie sheets. Bake for 8 to 12 minutes or until edges are lightly browned.

For glaze, in small bowl stir together all glaze ingredients *except* halved maraschino cherries. Dip or frost warm cookies with glaze. If desired, decorate with maraschino cherries.

Makes about 2 dozen cookies

*You may substitute 1 teaspoon brandy extract *plus* 2 tablespoons water for the 2 tablespoons brandy.

**You may substitute ¼ teaspoon brandy extract *plus* 1 tablespoon water for the 1 tablespoon brandy.

Best Ever Spritz

- ⅔ cup sugar
- 1 cup LAND O LAKES®
  Butter, softened
- 1 egg
- ½ teaspoon salt
- 2 teaspoons vanilla
- 2¼ cups all-purpose flour

Heat oven to 400°. In large mixer bowl combine sugar, butter, egg, salt and vanilla. Beat at medium speed, scraping bowl often, until mixture is light and fluffy, 2 to 3 minutes. Add flour. Beat at low speed, scraping bowl often, until well mixed, 2 to 3 minutes. If desired, add the ingredients from one of the following variations. If dough is too soft, cover; refrigerate until firm enough to form cookies, 30 to 45 minutes. Place dough into cookie press; form desired shapes 1 inch apart on cookie sheets. Bake for 6 to 8 minutes or until edges are lightly browned.

Makes about 5 dozen cookies

Variations:

Lebkuchen Spice Spritz: To Best Ever Spritz dough add *1 teaspoon each ground cinnamon and ground nutmeg, ½ teaspoon ground allspice and ¼ teaspoon ground cloves.* Glaze: In small bowl stir together *1 cup powdered sugar, 2 tablespoons milk* and *½ teaspoon vanilla* until smooth. Drizzle or pipe over warm cookies.

Eggnog Glazed Spritz: To Best Ever Spritz dough add *1 teaspoon ground nutmeg.* Glaze: In small bowl stir together *1 cup powdered sugar; ¼ cup LAND O LAKES® Butter, softened; 2 tablespoons water* and *¼ teaspoon rum extract* until smooth. Drizzle over warm cookies.

Mint Kisses: To Best Ever Spritz dough add *¼ teaspoon mint extract.* Immediately after removing cookies from oven place *1 chocolate candy kiss* on *each* cookie.

Piña Colada Spritz: Omit vanilla in Best Ever Spritz recipe and add *1 tablespoon pineapple juice* and *¼ teaspoon rum extract;* stir in *½ cup finely chopped coconut.* Frosting: In small mixer bowl combine *1 cup powdered sugar; 2 tablespoons LAND O LAKES® Butter, softened; 2 tablespoons pineapple preserves* and *1 tablespoon pineapple juice.* Beat at medium speed, scraping bowl often, until light and fluffy, 2 to 3 minutes. Spread on cooled cookies. If desired, sprinkle with *toasted coconut.*

Chocolate Chip Spritz: To Best Ever Spritz dough add *¼ cup coarsely grated semi-sweet chocolate.*

Chocolate Spritz

- 2 squares (1 ounce each)
  unsweetened chocolate
- 1 cup butter, softened
- ½ cup granulated sugar
- 1 egg
- 1 teaspoon vanilla
- ¼ teaspoon salt
- 2¼ cups all-purpose flour
  Powdered sugar

Preheat oven to 400°F. Line cookie sheets with parchment paper or leave ungreased. Melt chocolate in top of double boiler over hot, not boiling, water. Remove from heat; cool. Cream butter, granulated sugar, egg, vanilla and salt in large bowl until light and fluffy. Blend in melted chocolate and flour until stiff. Fit cookie press with your choice of plate. Load press with dough. Press cookies out 2 inches apart onto prepared cookie sheets.

Bake 5 to 7 minutes or just until very slightly browned around edges. Remove to wire rack to cool. Dust with powdered sugar.

Makes about 5 dozen cookies

Lebkuchen Spice Spritz and Brandied Buttery Wreaths

Snowballs

½ cup DOMINO®
    Confectioners 10-X Sugar
¼ teaspoon salt
1 cup butter or margarine,
    softened
1 teaspoon vanilla extract
2¼ cups all-purpose flour
½ cup chopped pecans
    Additional DOMINO®
    Confectioners 10-X Sugar

In large bowl, combine ½ cup sugar, salt and butter; mix well. Add vanilla. Gradually stir in flour. Work nuts into dough. Cover and chill until firm.

Preheat oven to 400°F. Form dough into 1-inch balls. Place 1 inch apart on ungreased cookie sheets.

Bake 8 to 10 minutes or until set but not brown. Roll in additional sugar immediately. Cool on wire racks. Roll in sugar again. Store in airtight container.
Makes about 5 dozen cookies

Jingle Jumbles

¾ cup butter or margarine,
    softened
1 cup packed brown sugar
¼ cup molasses
1 egg
2¼ cups unsifted all-purpose
    flour
2 teaspoons baking soda
1 teaspoon ground ginger
1 teaspoon ground cinnamon
½ teaspoon salt
½ teaspoon ground cloves
1¼ cups SUN-MAID® Raisins
    Granulated sugar

In large bowl, cream butter and sugar. Add molasses and egg; beat until fluffy. In medium bowl, sift together flour, baking soda, ginger, cinnamon, salt and cloves. Stir into molasses mixture. Stir in raisins. Cover and chill about 30 minutes.

Preheat oven to 375°F. Grease cookie sheets. Form dough into 1½-inch balls; roll in granulated

Peanut Butter Cut-Out Cookies

sugar, coating generously. Place 2 inches apart on prepared cookie sheets.

Bake 12 to 14 minutes or until edges are firm and centers are still slightly soft. Remove to wire rack to cool.
Makes about 2 dozen cookies

Peanut Butter Cut-Out Cookies

½ cup (1 stick) butter or
    margarine
1 cup REESE'S Peanut
    Butter Chips
⅔ cup packed light brown
    sugar
1 egg
¾ teaspoon vanilla extract
1⅓ cups all-purpose flour
¾ teaspoon baking soda
½ cup finely chopped pecans
    Chocolate Chip Glaze
    (recipe follows)

In medium saucepan, combine butter and peanut butter chips; cook over low heat, stirring constantly, until melted. Pour into large mixer bowl; add brown sugar, egg and vanilla, beating until well blended. Stir in flour, baking soda and pecans; blend

well. Refrigerate 15 to 20 minutes or until firm enough to roll.

Heat oven to 350°F. Roll out dough, a small portion at a time, on lightly floured board or between 2 pieces of wax paper to ¼-inch thickness. (Keep remaining dough in refrigerator.) With cookie cutters, cut into desired shapes; place 2 inches apart on ungreased cookie sheet.

Bake 7 to 8 minutes or until almost set (do not overbake). Cool 1 minute; remove from cookie sheet to wire rack. Cool completely. Spread or drizzle a thin coating of Chocolate Chip Glaze onto each cookie; allow to set.
Makes about 3 dozen cookies

CHOCOLATE CHIP GLAZE: In small microwave-safe bowl, place 1 cup HERSHEY'S Semi-Sweet Chocolate Chips and 1 tablespoon shortening. Microwave at HIGH (100%) 1 minute; stir. If necessary, microwave at HIGH an additional 15 seconds at a time, stirring after each heating, just until chips are melted when stirred.

Philly® Cream Cheese Cookie Dough

1 package (8 ounces) PHILADELPHIA BRAND® Cream Cheese, softened
¾ cup butter, softened
1 cup powdered sugar
2¼ cups all-purpose flour
½ teaspoon baking soda

• Beat cream cheese, butter and sugar in large mixing bowl at medium speed with electric mixer until well blended.

• Add flour and soda; mix well.

Makes 3 cups dough

Chocolate Mint Cutouts

• Heat oven to 325°F.

• Add ¼ teaspoon mint extract and few drops green food coloring to 1½ cups Cookie Dough; mix well. Refrigerate 30 minutes.

• On lightly floured surface, roll dough to ⅛-inch thickness; cut with assorted 3-inch cookie cutters. Place on ungreased cookie sheet.

• Bake 10 to 12 minutes or until edges begin to brown. Cool on wire rack.

• Melt ¼ cup mint flavored semi-sweet chocolate chips in small saucepan over low heat, stirring until smooth. Drizzle over cookies.

Makes about 3 dozen cookies

Snowmen

• Heat oven to 325°F.

• Add ¼ teaspoon vanilla to 1½ cups Cookie Dough; mix well. Refrigerate 30 minutes.

• For each snowman, shape dough into two small balls, one slightly larger than the other. Place balls, slightly overlapping, on ungreased cookie sheet; flatten with bottom of glass. Repeat with remaining dough.

• Bake 18 to 20 minutes or until light golden brown. Cool on wire rack.

• Sprinkle each snowman with sifted powdered sugar. Decorate with icing as desired. Cut miniature peanut butter cups in half for hats.

Makes about 2 dozen cookies

Choco-Orange Slices

• Heat oven to 325°F.

• Add 1½ teaspoons grated orange peel to 1½ cups Cookie Dough; mix well. Shape into 8×1½-inch log. Refrigerate 30 minutes.

• Cut log into ¼-inch slices. Place on ungreased cookie sheet.

• Bake 15 to 18 minutes or until edges begin to brown. Cool on wire rack.

• Melt ⅓ cup BAKER'S® Semi-Sweet Real Chocolate Chips with 1 tablespoon orange juice and 1 tablespoon orange flavored liqueur in small saucepan over low heat, stirring until smooth. Dip cookies into chocolate mixture.

Makes about 2½ dozen cookies

Preserve Thumbprints

• Heat oven to 325°F.

• Add ½ cup chopped pecans and ½ teaspoon vanilla to 1½ cups Cookie Dough; mix well. Refrigerate 30 minutes.

• Shape dough into 1-inch balls. Place on ungreased cookie sheet. Indent centers; fill each with 1 teaspoon KRAFT® Preserves.

• Bake 14 to 16 minutes or until light golden brown. Cool on wire rack.

Makes about 3⅓ dozen cookies

Clockwise from top left: Preserve Thumbprints, Snowmen, Choco-Orange Slices and Chocolate Mint Cutouts

Peanut Butter Bears

**1 cup SKIPPY® Creamy
  Peanut Butter**
**1 cup MAZOLA® Margarine,
  softened**
1 cup packed brown sugar
**⅔ cup KARO® Light or Dark
  Corn Syrup**
2 eggs
4 cups flour, divided
1 tablespoon baking powder
1 teaspoon cinnamon
¼ teaspoon salt

In large bowl with mixer at medium speed, beat peanut butter, margarine, brown sugar, corn syrup and eggs until smooth. Reduce speed; beat in 2 cups of the flour, the baking powder, cinnamon and salt. With spoon stir in remaining 2 cups flour. Wrap dough in plastic wrap; refrigerate 2 hours. Preheat oven to 325°F. Divide dough in half; set aside half. On floured surface roll out dough to ⅛-inch thickness. Cut with floured bear cookie cutter. Repeat with remaining dough. Bake on ungreased cookie sheets 10 minutes or until lightly browned. Remove from cookie sheets; cool completely on wire racks. Decorate as desired.

Makes about 3 dozen bears

Prep Time: 35 minutes, plus chilling
Bake Time: 10 minutes, plus cooling

Note: Use dough scraps to make bear faces. Make one small ball of dough for muzzle. Form 3 smaller balls of dough and press gently to create eyes and nose; bake as directed. If desired, use frosting to create paws, ears and bow ties.

Old-Fashioned Molasses Cookies

**4 cups sifted all-purpose
  flour**
**2 teaspoons
  ARM & HAMMER® Pure
  Baking Soda**
1½ teaspoons ground ginger
½ teaspoon ground cinnamon
⅛ teaspoon salt
1½ cups molasses
**½ cup lard or shortening,
  melted**
**¼ cup butter or margarine,
  melted**
⅓ cup boiling water

Sift together flour, baking soda, spices and salt. Combine molasses, lard, butter and water in large bowl. Add dry ingredients to liquid and blend well. Cover and chill several hours or overnight.

Turn onto well-floured board. Using floured rolling pin, roll to ¼-inch thickness. Cut with 3½-inch floured cookie cutter. Sprinkle with sugar and place on ungreased baking sheets. Bake in 375°F oven 12 minutes. Cool on racks.

Makes about 3 dozen cookies

Favorite Butter Cookies

Cookies
2½ cups all-purpose flour
1 cup granulated sugar
**1 cup LAND O LAKES®
  Butter, softened**
1 egg
1 teaspoon baking powder
2 tablespoons orange juice
1 tablespoon vanilla
Frosting
4 cups powdered sugar
**½ cup LAND O LAKES®
  Butter, softened**
3 to 4 tablespoons milk
2 teaspoons vanilla
**Food coloring, colored
  sugars, flaked coconut
  and cinnamon candies
  for decorations**

For cookies, in large mixer bowl combine all cookie ingredients. Beat at low speed, scraping bowl often, until well mixed, 1 to 2 minutes. If desired, divide dough into 3 equal portions; color ⅔ of dough with desired food colorings. Mix until dough is evenly colored. Wrap in plastic food wrap; refrigerate until firm, 2 to 3 hours.

Heat oven to 400°. On lightly floured surface, roll out dough, ⅓ at a time, to ¼-inch thickness. Cut out with cookie cutters. Place 1 inch apart on ungreased cookie sheets. If desired, sprinkle colored sugars on some of the cookies or bake and decorate later. Bake for 6 to 10 minutes or until edges are lightly browned. Remove immediately. Cool completely.

For frosting, in small mixer bowl combine powdered sugar, ½ cup butter, 3 to 4 tablespoons milk and 2 teaspoons vanilla. Beat at low speed, scraping bowl often, until fluffy, 1 to 2 minutes. Frost or decorate cookies.

*Makes about 3 dozen
(3-inch) cookies*

Decorating Ideas:

Wreaths: Cut cookies with 2-inch round cookie cutter; bake as directed. Frost with green colored frosting. Color coconut green; sprinkle frosted cookies with coconut. Place 3 cinnamon candies together to resemble holly.

Christmas Trees: Color dough green; cut with Christmas tree cutter. Sprinkle with colored sugars; bake as directed.

Angels: Cut cookies with angel cookie cutter; bake as directed. Use blue frosting for dress, yellow frosting for hair and white frosting for wings, face and lace on dress.

Peanut Butter Bears

Philly® Cream Cheese Apricot Cookies

1½ cups PARKAY® Margarine
1½ cups granulated sugar
1 8-ounce package
    PHILADELPHIA BRAND®
    Cream Cheese, softened
2 eggs
2 tablespoons lemon juice
1½ teaspoons grated lemon peel
4½ cups flour
1½ teaspoons baking powder
    KRAFT® Apricot Preserves
    Powdered sugar

Combine margarine, granulated sugar and cream cheese, mixing until well blended. Blend in eggs, juice and peel. Add combined flour and baking powder; mix well. Chill several hours. Shape level measuring tablespoonfuls of dough into balls. Place on ungreased cookie sheet; flatten slightly. Indent centers; fill with preserves. Bake at 350°, 15 minutes. Cool; sprinkle with powdered sugar.
Approximately 7 dozen.

Raisin Oatmeal Crispies

1 cup butter or margarine,
    softened
1 cup sugar
3 cups rolled oats, uncooked
¾ cup all-purpose flour
1 teaspoon baking soda
½ teaspoon ground cloves
½ teaspoon ground cinnamon
1 cup SUN-MAID® Raisins
¼ cup milk

In large bowl, blend together butter and sugar; add oats. Sift flour with baking soda, cloves and cinnamon.

Add to oats mixture, blending well. Stir in raisins and milk; mix thoroughly. Roll dough into 1-inch balls. Place 3 inches apart on greased baking sheets. Bake in preheated 350°F oven 12 to 15 minutes or until golden brown.
Makes about 4 dozen cookies.

Walnutty Ribbons

2 cups all-purpose flour
½ teaspoon baking powder
½ cup butter or margarine,
    softened
¾ cup sugar
1 egg
2 teaspoons rum flavoring
1 teaspoon vanilla
1 teaspoon grated lemon peel
1 tablespoon milk
1 cup finely chopped DIAMOND®
    Walnuts
⅓ cup orange marmalade (or
    other jam)

In medium bowl, sift flour with baking powder; set aside. In large bowl, cream butter, sugar, egg, rum, vanilla and peel. Blend in flour mixture and milk to make a stiff dough. Divide into 4 equal portions and shape each into a roll about 12 inches long. Transfer to lightly greased cookie sheets, placing rolls about 3 inches apart. Make a wide depression down center of each roll with handle of knife. In small bowl, mix walnuts with marmalade. Spoon ¼ of the mixture down center of each roll. Bake in preheated 350°F oven 15 to 20 minutes or until edges are lightly browned. Slide rolls off onto wire racks to cool. Cut into 1¼-inch slices to serve.
Makes about 3 dozen cookies.

Chocolate Crackles

⅔ cup butter or margarine
⅓ cup HERSHEY'S Cocoa
2 cups all-purpose flour
1 cup granulated sugar
2 teaspoons baking powder
½ teaspoon salt
2 eggs
1 teaspoon vanilla extract
½ cup chopped nuts
    Powdered sugar

In large microwave-safe bowl, place butter.   Microwave at HIGH (100%) 45 seconds to 1 minute or until melted. Add cocoa; blend well. Beat in flour, granulated sugar, baking powder, salt, eggs and vanilla. Stir in nuts. Refrigerate at least 8 hours or until firm.

Shape dough into 1-inch balls; roll in powdered sugar. On wax paper in bottom of microwave oven, place 8 balls 2 inches apart in circle. Microwave at MEDIUM (50%) 2 to 3 minutes or until surface is dry but cookies are soft when touched. Cool completely on wax paper.
About 4 dozen cookies.

Pecan Tassies

1 8-ounce package
    PHILADELPHIA BRAND®
    Cream Cheese, softened
1 cup PARKAY® Margarine
2 cups flour
2 eggs, beaten
1½ cups packed brown sugar
2 teaspoons vanilla
1½ cups chopped pecans

Combine cream cheese and margarine, mixing until well blended. Add flour; mix well. Chill. Divide dough into quarters; divide each quarter into 12 balls. Press each ball onto bottom and sides of miniature muffin pans. Combine eggs, brown sugar and vanilla; stir in pecans. Spoon into pastry shells, filling each cup. Bake at 325°, 30 minutes or until pastry is golden brown. Cool 5 minutes; remove from pans. Sprinkle with powdered sugar, if desired.
4 dozen.

Philly® Cream Cheese Apricot Cookies

Reese's™ Cookies

2 cups all-purpose flour
1 teaspoon baking soda
1 cup shortening *or* ¾ cup
  (1½ sticks) butter or
  margarine, softened
1 cup granulated sugar
½ cup packed light brown sugar
1 teaspoon vanilla extract
2 eggs
1⅔ cups (10-oz. pkg.) REESE'S
  Peanut Butter Chips
1 cup HERSHEY'S Semi-Sweet
  Chocolate Chips or Milk
  Chocolate Chips

Heat oven to 350°F. Stir together flour and baking soda. In large mixer bowl, beat shortening, granulated sugar, brown sugar and vanilla. Add eggs; beat well. Gradually add flour mixture, beating well. Stir in chips. Drop dough by rounded teaspoonfuls onto ungreased cookie sheet. Bake 8 to 10 minutes or until lightly browned. Cool slightly; remove from cookie sheet to wire rack. Cool completely. *About 5 dozen cookies.*

Macaroon Almond Crumb Bars

1 (18¼- or 18½-ounce) package
  chocolate cake mix
¼ cup vegetable oil
2 eggs
1 (14-ounce) can EAGLE® Brand
  Sweetened Condensed Milk
  (NOT evaporated milk)
½ to 1 teaspoon almond extract
1½ cups coconut macaroon
  crumbs (about 8 macaroons)
1 cup chopped slivered almonds

Preheat oven to 350° (325° for glass dish). In large mixer bowl, combine cake mix, oil and *1 egg.* Beat on medium speed until crumbly. Press firmly on bottom of greased 13×9-inch baking pan. In medium mixing bowl, combine sweetened condensed milk, remaining egg and extract; mix well. Add *1 cup* macaroon crumbs and almonds. Spread evenly over prepared crust. Sprinkle with remaining *½ cup* crumbs. Bake 30 to 35 minutes or until lightly browned. Cool thoroughly. Cut into bars. Store loosely covered at room temperature. *Makes 36 bars.*

Macaroon Almond Crumb Bars (top) and Toffee Bars (bottom)

Rich Lemon Bars

1½ cups plus 3 tablespoons
  unsifted flour
½ cup confectioners' sugar
¾ cup cold margarine or butter
4 eggs, slightly beaten
1½ cups granulated sugar
1 teaspoon baking powder
½ cup REALEMON® Lemon Juice
  from Concentrate
  Additional confectioners'
  sugar

Preheat oven to 350°. In medium bowl, combine *1½ cups* flour and confectioners' sugar; cut in margarine until crumbly. Press onto bottom of lightly greased 13×9-inch baking pan; bake 15 minutes. Meanwhile, in large bowl, combine eggs, granulated sugar, baking powder, ReaLemon® brand and remaining *3 tablespoons* flour; mix well. Pour over baked crust; bake 20 to 25 minutes or until golden brown. Cool. Cut into bars. Sprinkle with additional confectioners' sugar. Store covered in refrigerator; serve at room temperature.
Makes 30 bars.

Lemon Pecan Bars: Omit 3 tablespoons flour in lemon mixture. Sprinkle ¾ cup finely chopped pecans over top of lemon mixture. Bake as above.

Coconut Lemon Bars: Omit 3 tablespoons flour in lemon mixture. Sprinkle ¾ cup flaked coconut over top of lemon mixture. Bake as above.

Toffee Bars

½ cup margarine or butter
1 cup oats
½ cup firmly packed brown sugar
½ cup unsifted flour
½ cup finely chopped walnuts
¼ teaspoon baking soda
1 (14-ounce) can EAGLE® Brand
  Sweetened Condensed Milk
  (NOT evaporated milk)
2 teaspoons vanilla extract
1 (6-ounce) package semi-sweet
  chocolate chips

Preheat oven to 350°. In medium saucepan, melt *6 tablespoons* margarine; stir in oats, sugar, flour, nuts and baking soda. Press firmly on bottom of greased 13×9-inch baking pan; bake 10 to 15 minutes or until lightly browned. Meanwhile, in medium saucepan, combine remaining *2 tablespoons* margarine and sweetened condensed milk. Over medium heat, cook and stir until mixture thickens slightly, about 15 minutes. Remove from heat; stir in vanilla. Pour over crust. Return to oven; bake 10 to 15 minutes longer or until golden brown. Remove from oven; immediately sprinkle chips on top. Let stand 1 minute; spread while still warm. Cool to room temperature; chill thoroughly. Cut into bars. Store tightly covered at room temperature.
Makes 36 bars.

Peanut Butter Bars

**1 package DUNCAN HINES®
    Peanut Butter Cookie Mix
2 egg whites
½ cup chopped peanuts
1 cup confectioners sugar
2 tablespoons water
½ teaspoon vanilla extract**

1. Preheat oven to 350°F.

2. Combine cookie mix, contents of peanut butter packet from Mix and egg whites in large bowl. Stir until thoroughly blended. Press in ungreased 13×9×2-inch pan. Sprinkle peanuts over dough. Press lightly. Bake at 350°F for 16 to 18 minutes or until golden brown. Cool completely.

3. Combine confectioners sugar, water and vanilla extract in small bowl. Stir until blended. Drizzle glaze over top. Cut into bars.   *24 Bars*

Tip: Bar cookies look best when cut neatly into uniform sizes. Measure with ruler using knife to mark surface. Cut with sharp knife.

Linzer Bars

**¾ cup butter or margarine,
    softened
½ cup sugar
1 egg
½ teaspoon grated lemon
    peel
½ teaspoon ground cinnamon
¼ teaspoon salt
⅛ teaspoon ground cloves
2 cups all-purpose flour
1 cup DIAMOND® Walnuts,
    finely chopped or ground
1 cup raspberry or apricot
    jam**

Preheat oven to 325°F. Grease 9-inch square pan. In large bowl, cream butter, sugar, egg, lemon peel, cinnamon, salt and cloves. Blend in flour and walnuts. Set aside about ¼ of the dough for lattice top. Pat remaining dough into bottom and about ½ inch up sides of pan. Spread with jam. Make pencil-shaped strips of remaining dough, rolling against floured board with palms of hands. Arrange in lattice pattern over top, pressing ends against dough on sides.

Bake 45 minutes or until lightly browned. Cool in pan on wire rack. Cut into bars.
                  Makes 2 dozen small bars

Caramel Chocolate Pecan Bars

Caramel Chocolate Pecan Bars

**Crust
    2 cups all-purpose flour
    1 cup firmly packed brown
        sugar
    ½ cup LAND O LAKES®
        Butter, softened
    1 cup pecan halves**

**Filling
    ⅔ cup LAND O LAKES®
        Butter
    ½ cup firmly packed brown
        sugar
    ½ cup butterscotch chips
    ½ cup semi-sweet chocolate
        chips**

Heat oven to 350°. For crust, in large mixer bowl combine flour, 1 cup brown sugar and ½ cup butter. Beat at medium speed, scraping bowl often, until well mixed and particles are fine, 2 to 3 minutes. Press on bottom of ungreased 13×9-inch baking pan. Sprinkle pecans evenly over unbaked crust.

For filling, in 1-quart saucepan combine ⅔ cup butter and ½ cup brown sugar. Cook over medium heat, stirring constantly, until mixture comes to a full boil, 4 to 5 minutes. Boil, stirring constantly, until candy thermometer reaches 242°F or small amount of mixture dropped

Peanut Butter Bars

into ice water forms a firm ball, 1 minute. Pour over pecans and crust. Bake for 18 to 20 minutes or until entire caramel layer is bubbly. Immediately sprinkle with butterscotch and chocolate chips. Allow to melt slightly, 3 to 5 minutes. Swirl chips leaving some whole for a marbled effect. Cool completely; cut into bars.

Makes 3 dozen bars

Blueberry Cheesecake Bars

- 1 package DUNCAN HINES® Bakery Style Blueberry Muffin Mix
- ¼ cup butter or margarine, softened
- ⅓ cup finely chopped pecans
- 1 package (8 ounces) cream cheese, softened
- ½ cup sugar
- 1 egg
- 3 tablespoons lemon juice
- 1 teaspoon grated lemon peel

1. Preheat oven to 350°F. Grease 9-inch square pan.

2. Rinse blueberries from Mix with cold water and drain.

3. Place muffin mix in medium bowl. Cut in butter with pastry blender or two knives. Stir in pecans. Press into bottom of pan. Bake at 350°F for 15 minutes or until set.

4. Combine cream cheese and sugar in medium bowl. Beat until smooth. Add egg, lemon juice and lemon peel. Beat well. Spread over baked crust. Sprinkle with blueberries. Sprinkle contents of topping packet from Mix over blueberries. Return to oven. Bake at 350°F for 35 to 40 minutes or until filling is set. Cool completely. Refrigerate until ready to serve. Cut into bars.   *16 Bars*

Tip: Lower oven temperature by 25°F when using glass baking dishes. Glass heats more quickly and retains heat longer.

Apricot Oatmeal Bars

Crumb Mixture
- 1¼ cups all-purpose flour
- 1¼ cups quick-cooking oats
- ½ cup sugar
- ¾ cup LAND O LAKES® Butter, melted
- ½ teaspoon baking soda
- ¼ teaspoon salt
- 2 teaspoons vanilla

Filling
- 1 jar (10 ounces) apricot preserves
- ½ cup flaked coconut

Heat oven to 350°. For crumb mixture, in large mixer bowl combine all crumb mixture ingredients. Beat at low speed, scraping bowl often, until mixture is crumbly, 1 to 2 minutes. *Reserve 1 cup crumb mixture;* press remaining crumb mixture into greased 13×9-inch baking pan.

For filling, spread apricot preserves to within ½ inch from edge of crumb mixture; sprinkle with reserved crumb mixture and coconut. Bake for 22 to 27 minutes or until edges are lightly browned. Cool completely. Cut into bars.

Makes 3 dozen bars

Old-World Raspberry Bars

Crumb Mixture
- 2¼ cups all-purpose flour
- 1 cup sugar
- 1 cup chopped pecans
- 1 cup LAND O LAKES® Butter, softened
- 1 egg

Filling
- 1 jar (10 ounces) raspberry preserves

Heat oven to 350°. For crumb mixture, in large mixer bowl combine all crumb mixture ingredients. Beat at low speed, scraping bowl often, until mixture is crumbly, 2 to 3 minutes. *Reserve 1½ cups crumb mixture;* press remaining crumb mixture on bottom of greased 8-inch square baking pan. Spread preserves to within ½ inch from edge of unbaked crumb mixture. Crumble remaining crumb mixture over preserves. Bake for 42 to 50 minutes or until lightly browned. Cool completely. Cut into bars.

Makes 2 dozen bars

Top to bottom: Apricot Oatmeal Bars and Old-World Raspberry Bars

Festive Cookie Bars

Bottom Layer:
- **1¼ cups all-purpose flour**
- **1 teaspoon granulated sugar**
- **1 teaspoon baking powder**
  Dash salt
- **⅔ cup butter or margarine**
- **2 tablespoons cold coffee or water**
- **1 egg yolk**
- **1 package (12 ounces) real semisweet chocolate pieces**

Top Layer:
- **½ cup butter or margarine, softened**
- **1 cup granulated sugar**
- **1 tablespoon vanilla**
- **2 eggs plus 1 egg white**
- **1 cup SUN-MAID® Raisins**
- **1 cup DIAMOND® Walnuts**
  Powdered sugar, for garnish

To prepare bottom layer: In large bowl, combine flour, granulated sugar, baking powder and salt. Cut in butter until mixture resembles coarse crumbs. In small bowl, mix coffee and egg yolk to blend; stir into flour mixture to moisten evenly. Form dough into a roll. With floured fingertips, press evenly onto bottom of greased 15×10-inch jelly-roll pan. (Layer will be thin.) Bake in preheated 350°F oven 10 minutes. Sprinkle chocolate pieces evenly over crust; return to oven 2 minutes to melt chocolate. Remove from oven; spread evenly with spatula. Allow to stand several minutes to set.

To prepare top layer: In large bowl, cream butter, granulated sugar and vanilla. Beat in eggs and egg white, one at a time, mixing well after each addition. (Mixture will appear slightly curdled.) Stir in raisins and walnuts. Spread evenly over chocolate layer. Return to oven; bake 20 to 25 minutes or until top is browned. Dust with powdered sugar. Cool in pan; cut into bars.
Makes 3½ to 4 dozen bars.
Note: Cookies freeze well.

Frosted Toffee Bars

- **2 cups QUAKER® Oats (Quick or Old Fashioned), uncooked**
- **½ cup packed brown sugar**
- **½ cup margarine, melted**
- **½ cup semisweet chocolate chips**
- **¼ cup chopped peanuts**

In medium bowl, combine oats, sugar and margarine; mix well. Spread in greased 9-inch square pan. Bake in preheated 350° oven 13 minutes or until light golden brown; cool. In small, heavy saucepan over low heat, melt chips. Spread over oat mixture; sprinkle with nuts. Refrigerate until chocolate is set. Cut into 2×1½-inch bars. Store in tightly covered container in refrigerator.
Makes about 2 dozen bars.

Coconut Dream Bars

- **1 cup flour**
- **¼ cup firmly packed brown sugar**
- **⅓ cup softened butter or margarine**
- **2 eggs**
- **¾ cup firmly packed brown sugar**
- **¼ cup flour**
- **½ teaspoon CALUMET® Baking Powder**
- **1⅓ cups (about) BAKER'S® ANGEL FLAKE® Coconut**
- **1 teaspoon vanilla**
- **1 cup chopped walnuts**

Combine 1 cup flour and ¼ cup brown sugar. Add butter and mix until blended. Press into ungreased 9-inch square pan; bake at 350° for 15 minutes. Meanwhile, beat eggs until thick and light in color. Gradually beat in ¾ cup brown sugar and continue beating until mixture is light and fluffy. Mix ¼ cup flour with the baking powder; fold into egg mixture. Mix in coconut, vanilla and nuts. Spread over baked crust in pan. Bake 20 to 25 minutes longer or until lightly browned. Cool; cut in bars, triangles or squares.
Makes about 2 dozen.

Chocolate 'n' Oat Bars

- **1 cup unsifted flour**
- **1 cup quick-cooking oats**
- **¾ cup firmly packed light brown sugar**
- **½ cup margarine or butter, softened**
- **1 (14-ounce) can EAGLE® Brand Sweetened Condensed Milk (NOT evaporated milk)**
- **1 cup chopped nuts**
- **1 (6-ounce) package semi-sweet chocolate chips**

Preheat oven to 350° (325° for glass dish). In large bowl, combine flour, oats, sugar and margarine; mix well. Reserving ½ cup oat mixture, press remainder on bottom of 13×9-inch baking pan. Bake 10 minutes. Pour sweetened condensed milk evenly over crust. Sprinkle with nuts and chocolate chips. Top with remaining oat mixture; press down firmly. Bake 25 to 30 minutes or until lightly browned. Cool. Cut into bars. Store covered at room temperature.
Makes 36 bars.

Chocolate 'n' Oat Bars

Triple Layer Cookie Bars (left) and Pecan Pie Bars (right)

Triple Layer Cookie Bars

½ cup margarine or butter
1½ cups graham cracker crumbs
1 (7-ounce) package flaked coconut (2⅔ cups)
1 (14-ounce) can EAGLE® Brand Sweetened Condensed Milk (NOT evaporated milk)
1 (12-ounce) package semi-sweet chocolate chips
½ cup creamy peanut butter

Preheat oven to 350° (325° for glass dish). In 13×9-inch baking pan, melt margarine in oven. Sprinkle crumbs evenly over margarine. Top evenly with coconut then sweetened condensed milk. Bake 25 minutes or until lightly browned. In small saucepan, over low heat, melt chips with peanut butter. Spread evenly over hot coconut layer. Cool 30 minutes. Chill thoroughly. Cut into bars. Store loosely covered at room temperature. *Makes 36 bars.*

Pecan Pie Bars

2 cups unsifted flour
½ cup confectioners' sugar
1 cup cold margarine or butter
1 (14-ounce) can EAGLE® Brand Sweetened Condensed Milk (NOT evaporated milk)
1 egg
1 teaspoon vanilla extract
1 (6-ounce) package almond brickle chips
1 cup chopped pecans

Preheat oven to 350° (325° for glass dish). In medium bowl, combine flour and sugar; cut in margarine until crumbly. Press firmly on bottom of 13×9-inch baking pan. Bake 15 minutes. Meanwhile, in medium bowl, beat sweetened condensed milk, egg and vanilla. Stir in chips and pecans. Spread evenly over crust. Bake 25 minutes or until golden brown. Cool. Cut into bars. Store covered in refrigerator. *Makes 36 bars.*

Crunch Bars

5 cups bite-size crispy rice or wheat square cereal
½ cup margarine or butter
1 cup butterscotch *or* peanut butter flavored chips
1 (3½-ounce) can flaked coconut (1⅓ cups)
1 (14-ounce) can EAGLE® Brand Sweetened Condensed Milk (NOT evaporated milk)
1 cup chopped pecans

Preheat oven to 350° (325° for glass dish). Coarsely crush *3 cups* cereal. In 13×9-inch baking pan, melt margarine in oven. Sprinkle crushed cereal over margarine; top evenly with chips, coconut, sweetened condensed milk, nuts and *2 cups* uncrushed cereal. Press down firmly. Bake 25 to 30 minutes or until lightly browned. Cool thoroughly. Cut into bars. Store loosely covered at room temperature. *Makes 36 bars.*

Magic Cookie Bars

½ **cup margarine or butter**
1½ **cups graham cracker *or* other crumbs***
1 **(14-ounce) EAGLE® Brand Sweetened Condensed Milk (NOT evaporated milk)**
1 **cup semi-sweet chocolate chips *or* other toppings****
1 **(3½-ounce) can flaked coconut (1⅓ cups)**
1 **cup chopped nuts*****

Magic Cookie Bars

Preheat oven to 350° (325° for glass dish). In 13×9-inch baking pan, melt margarine in oven. Sprinkle crumbs over margarine; pour sweetened condensed milk evenly over crumbs. Sprinkle with chips then coconut and nuts; press down firmly. Bake 25 to 30 minutes or until lightly browned. Cool. Chill thoroughly if desired. Cut into bars. Store loosely covered at room temperature.
Makes 36 bars.

Crumbs: Vanilla wafer, chocolate wafer, ginger snap cookie, quick-cooking oats, wheat germ.

****Toppings:*** Peanut butter flavored chips, butterscotch flavored chips, plain multi-colored candy-coated chocolate pieces, raisins, chopped dried apricots, almond brickle chips, banana chips, chopped candied cherries, small gumdrop candies, miniature marshmallows.

*****Nuts:*** Walnuts, pecans, almonds, peanuts, cashews, macadamia nuts.

Flavor Variations:

Mint: Combine ½ teaspoon peppermint extract and 4 drops green food coloring if desired with sweetened condensed milk. Proceed as above.

Mocha: Add 1 tablespoon instant coffee and 1 tablespoon chocolate flavored syrup with sweetened condensed milk. Proceed as above.

Peanut Butter: Combine ⅓ cup peanut butter with sweetened condensed milk. Proceed as above.

Maple: Combine ½ to 1 teaspoon maple flavoring with sweetened condensed milk. Proceed as above.

Seven Layer Magic Cookie Bars: Add 1 (6-ounce) package butterscotch flavored chips after chocolate chips.

Apple Raisin Snack Bars

1½ **cups old fashioned or quick oats, uncooked**
¾ **cup flour**
½ **cup packed brown sugar**
¼ **cup granulated sugar**
¾ **cup PARKAY® Margarine**

* * *

2 **8-ounce packages PHILADELPHIA BRAND® Cream Cheese, softened**
2 **eggs**
1 **cup chopped apple**
⅓ **cup raisins**
1 **tablespoon granulated sugar**
½ **teaspoon cinnamon**

Combine oats, flour and sugars; cut in margarine until mixture resembles coarse crumbs. Reserve 1 cup oat mixture; press remaining mixture onto bottom of greased 13×9-inch baking pan. Bake at 350°, 15 minutes.

Combine cream cheese and eggs, mixing until well blended. Pour over crust. Top with combined remaining ingredients; sprinkle with reserved oat mixture. Bake at 350°, 25 minutes. Cool; cut into bars.
Approximately 1½ dozen.

Variation: Substitute Light PHILADELPHIA BRAND® Neufchatel Cheese for Cream Cheese.

Chocolate Streusel Bars

1¾ **cups unsifted flour**
1½ **cups confectioners' sugar**
½ **cup unsweetened cocoa**
1 **cup cold margarine or butter**
1 **(8-ounce) package cream cheese, softened**
1 **(14-ounce) can EAGLE® Brand Sweetened Condensed Milk (NOT evaporated milk)**
1 **egg**
2 **teaspoons vanilla extract**
½ **cup chopped walnuts, optional**

Preheat oven to 350°. In large bowl, combine flour, sugar and cocoa; mix well. Cut in margarine until crumbly (mixture will be dry). Reserving 2 cups crumb mixture, press remainder firmly on bottom of 13×9-inch baking pan. Bake 15 minutes. Meanwhile, in large mixer bowl, beat cheese until fluffy. Gradually beat in sweetened condensed milk until smooth. Add egg and vanilla; mix well. Pour evenly over baked crust. Combine reserved crumb mixture with nuts if desired; sprinkle evenly over cheese mixture. Bake 25 minutes or until bubbly. Cool. Chill. Cut into bars. Store covered in refrigerator.
Makes 24 to 36 bars.

Raspberry Oatmeal Bars

**1 package DUNCAN HINES®
  Moist Deluxe Yellow
  Cake Mix
2½ cups quick-cooking oats
¾ cup (1½ sticks) butter or
  margarine, melted
1 cup (12-ounce jar) raspberry
  preserves or jam*
1 tablespoon water**

1. Preheat oven to 375°F. Grease 13×9×2-inch pan.
2. Combine dry cake mix and oats in large bowl; add melted butter and stir until crumbly. Measure half of crumb mixture (about 3 cups) into pan. Press firmly to cover bottom. Combine preserves and water; stir until blended. Spread over crumb mixture in pan. Sprinkle remaining crumb mixture over preserves; pat firmly to make top even.
3. Bake at 375°F for 18 to 23 minutes or until top is very light brown. Cool in pan on rack; cut into bars. Store in airtight container.
4 dozen bars.
   *Apricot, blackberry or strawberry preserves can be substituted.

Fruit & Nut Snack Bars

**½ cup margarine or butter,
  softened
1¼ cups granulated sugar
3 eggs
1⅓ cups (one-half jar) NONE
  SUCH® Ready-to-Use
  Mincemeat (Regular *or*
  Brandy & Rum)
½ cup chopped pecans
2 (1-ounce) squares
  unsweetened chocolate,
  melted
¼ teaspoon salt
1½ cups unsifted flour
  Confectioners' sugar
  Pecan halves, optional**

Preheat oven to 350°. In large mixer bowl, beat margarine and granulated sugar until fluffy. Add eggs; beat well. Stir in mincemeat, chopped pecans, chocolate and salt; mix well. Stir in flour. Spread evenly into lightly greased 13×9-inch baking pan. Bake 30 minutes or until wooden pick inserted near center comes out clean. Cool. Sprinkle with confectioners' sugar. Cut into bars. Garnish with pecan halves if desired.
Makes 24 to 36 bars.

Lebkuchen Jewels

**¾ cup packed brown sugar
1 egg
1 cup honey
1 tablespoon grated lemon peel
1 teaspoon lemon juice
2¾ cups all-purpose flour
1 teaspoon *each* ground
  nutmeg, cinnamon and
  cloves
½ teaspoon *each* baking soda
  and salt
1 cup SUN-MAID® Golden
  Raisins
½ cup *each* mixed candied fruits
  and citron
1 cup chopped DIAMOND®
  Walnuts
  Lemon Glaze (recipe follows)
  Candied cherries and citron,
  for garnish**

In large bowl, beat sugar and egg until smooth and fluffy. Add honey, lemon peel and juice; beat well. In medium bowl, sift flour with nutmeg, cinnamon, cloves, baking soda and salt; gradually mix into egg-sugar mixture on low speed. Stir in fruits and nuts. Spread batter into greased 15×10-inch jelly-roll pan. Bake in preheated 375°F oven 20 minutes or until lightly browned. Cool slightly in pan; brush with Lemon Glaze. Cool; cut into diamonds. Decorate with candied cherries and slivers of citron, if desired. Store in covered container up to 1 month.
Makes about 4 dozen.
LEMON GLAZE: In small bowl, combine 1 cup sifted powdered sugar with enough lemon juice (1½ to 2 tablespoons) to make a thin glaze.

Jungle Bars

**2 ripe, medium DOLE® Bananas
8 ounces dried figs
8 ounces dried apricots
8 ounces DOLE® Pitted Dates
8 ounces DOLE® Raisins
2 cups granola
8 ounces DOLE® Chopped
  Natural Almonds, toasted
1 cup flaked coconut**

Coarsely chop bananas, figs, apricots, dates, raisins and granola in food processor or run through food grinder. Stir in almonds. Press mixture into greased 13×9-inch baking dish. Sprinkle with coconut. Cover; refrigerate 24 hours to allow flavors to blend. Cut into squares.
Makes 24 bars.

Raspberry Oatmeal Bars

Pumpkin Cheesecake Bars

- 1 (16-ounce) package pound cake mix
- 3 eggs
- 2 tablespoons margarine or butter, melted
- 4 teaspoons pumpkin pie spice
- 1 (8-ounce) package cream cheese, softened
- 1 (14-ounce) can EAGLE® Brand Sweetened Condensed Milk (NOT evaporated milk)
- 1 (16-ounce) can pumpkin (about 2 cups)
- ½ teaspoon salt
- 1 cup chopped nuts

Preheat oven to 350°. In large mixer bowl, on low speed, combine cake mix, *1 egg,* margarine and *2 teaspoons* pumpkin pie spice until crumbly. Press onto bottom of 15×10-inch jellyroll pan. In large mixer bowl, beat cheese until fluffy. Gradually beat in sweetened condensed milk then remaining *2 eggs,* pumpkin, remaining *2 teaspoons* pumpkin pie spice and salt; mix well. Pour over crust; sprinkle with nuts. Bake 30 to 35 minutes or until set. Cool. Chill; cut into bars. Store covered in refrigerator.
Makes 48 bars.

Pumpkin Cheesecake Bars

Pineapple Dream Bars

- ½ cup margarine, softened
- 1 cup dark brown sugar, packed
- 1⅓ cups flour
- 1 can (8¼ ounces) DOLE® Crushed Pineapple in Syrup or Juice
- 2 eggs
- 1 teaspoon baking powder
- 1 teaspoon ground cinnamon
- ¼ teaspoon ground nutmeg
- ¼ teaspoon salt
- 1 teaspoon rum extract
- 1½ cups flaked coconut
- 1 cup chopped walnuts
- ½ cup chopped maraschino cherries

Preheat oven to 350°F. In medium mixer bowl, beat margarine and ⅓ cup brown sugar. Blend in 1 cup flour until mixture is crumbly. Pat into bottom of 13×9-inch baking pan. Bake in preheated oven 10 to 15 minutes or until golden. Keep oven hot, but remove pan to cool.

Drain pineapple well, pressing out excess liquid with back of spoon. In large bowl, beat eggs with remaining ⅔ cup brown sugar until thick. In small bowl, combine remaining ⅓ cup flour, baking powder, cinnamon, nutmeg and salt. Stir dry ingredients and extract into egg mixture. Fold in pine-

apple, coconut, nuts and cherries. Spread over baked crust. Bake 30 minutes longer or until set. Cool slightly on wire rack; cut into bars. *Makes 18 bars.*

Cheesecake Bars

- 2 cups unsifted flour
- 1½ cups firmly packed brown sugar
- 1 cup cold margarine or butter
- 1½ cups quick-cooking oats
- 2 (8-ounce) packages cream cheese, softened
- ½ cup granulated sugar
- 3 eggs
- ¼ cup BORDEN® or MEADOW GOLD® Milk
- 1 teaspoon vanilla extract
- ¼ cup REALEMON® Lemon Juice from Concentrate

Preheat oven to 350°. In bowl, combine flour and brown sugar; cut in margarine until crumbly. Stir in oats. Reserving *1½ cups* mixture, press remainder into 15×10-inch jellyroll pan; bake 10 minutes. Meanwhile, in large mixer bowl, beat cheese and granulated sugar until fluffy. Add eggs; beat well. Add milk and vanilla, then ReaLemon® brand; beat well. Pour over crust; sprinkle with reserved mixture. Bake 25 minutes or until lightly browned. Cool. Refrigerate.
Makes 40 bars.

Chocolate Pecan Bars

- 1¼ cups unsifted flour
- 1 cup confectioners' sugar
- ½ cup unsweetened cocoa
- 1 cup cold margarine or butter
- 1 (14-ounce) can EAGLE® Brand Sweetened Condensed Milk (NOT evaporated milk)
- 1 egg
- 2 teaspoons vanilla extract
- 1½ cups chopped pecans

Preheat oven to 350° (325° for glass dish). In large bowl, combine flour, sugar and cocoa; cut in margarine until crumbly. Press firmly on bottom of 13×9-inch baking pan. Bake 15 minutes. In medium bowl, beat sweetened condensed milk, egg and vanilla. Stir in pecans. Spread evenly over baked crust. Bake 25 minutes or until lightly browned. Cool. Cut into bars. Store covered in refrigerator.
Makes 36 bars.

Marble Squares

½ cup PARKAY® Margarine
¾ cup water
1½ 1-ounce squares unsweetened
     chocolate
2 cups flour
2 cups sugar
1 teaspoon baking soda
½ teaspoon salt
2 eggs, beaten
½ cup sour cream

* * *

1 8-ounce package
     PHILADELPHIA BRAND®
     Cream Cheese, softened
⅓ cup sugar
1 egg
1 6-ounce package semi-sweet
     chocolate pieces

Combine margarine, water and chocolate in saucepan; bring to a boil. Remove from heat. Stir in combined flour, sugar, baking soda and salt. Add eggs and sour cream; mix well. Pour into greased and floured 15×10×1-inch jelly roll pan.

Combine cream cheese and sugar, mixing until well blended. Blend in egg. Spoon over chocolate batter. Cut through batter with knife several times for marble effect. Sprinkle with chocolate pieces. Bake at 375°, 25 to 30 minutes or until wooden pick inserted in center comes out clean.
Approximately 2 dozen.

Marble Squares

Peanutty Chocolate Snack Squares

5 graham crackers, broken into
     squares
½ cup sugar
1 cup light corn syrup
1 cup (6-oz. pkg.) HERSHEY'S
     Semi-Sweet Chocolate Chips
1 cup REESE'S Creamy Peanut
     Butter
1 cup dry roasted peanuts

Line bottom of 8-inch square pan with graham cracker squares, cutting to fit as necessary. In 2-quart microwave-safe bowl, stir together sugar and corn syrup. Microwave at HIGH (100%), stirring every 2 minutes, until mixture boils; boil 3 minutes. Stir in chocolate chips, peanut butter and peanuts. Pour over crackers; spread carefully. Cover; refrigerate until firm. Cut into 2-inch squares. Refrigerate leftovers.
16 servings.

Bonbon Cups

1 package (8 squares) BAKER'S®
     Semi-Sweet Chocolate
1 cup sifted confectioners sugar
1 tablespoon milk
1 tablespoon light corn syrup
½ cup chopped mixed candied
     fruits
1 teaspoon rum extract
     (optional)
2 tablespoons butter or
     margarine

Melt 4 squares of the chocolate in saucepan over very low heat, stirring constantly until smooth. Remove from heat. Add sugar, milk and corn syrup. Stir in fruits and extract. Spoon into 3 dozen paper or aluminum foil bonbon cups; chill.

Melt remaining 4 squares chocolate with the butter in saucepan over very low heat, stirring constantly until smooth. Cool slightly; spoon onto fruit filling in cups, mounding the chocolate. Chill until firm. Store in refrigerator.
Makes 3 dozen.

Minty Chocolate Squares

1 6-ounce package semi-sweet
     chocolate pieces
1 cup PARKAY® Margarine
1¾ cups graham cracker crumbs
1 cup flaked coconut
½ cup chopped nuts
2 8-ounce packages
     PHILADELPHIA BRAND®
     Cream Cheese, softened
1 cup sifted powdered sugar
½ teaspoon mint extract
     Few drops green food coloring
     (optional)

Melt ⅓ cup chocolate pieces with ¾ cup margarine over low heat, stirring until smooth. Add combined crumbs, coconut and nuts; mix well. Press onto bottom of ungreased 13×9-inch baking pan; chill. Combine cream cheese, sugar, extract and food coloring, mixing until well blended. Spread over crust; chill. Melt remaining chocolate pieces with remaining margarine over low heat, stirring until smooth. Spread over cream cheese layer; chill. Cut into squares. Serve chilled.
Approximately 3 dozen.

Best Brownies

½ cup (1 stick) butter or
    margarine, melted
1 cup sugar
1 teaspoon vanilla extract
2 eggs
½ cup all-purpose flour
⅓ cup HERSHEY'S Cocoa
¼ teaspoon baking powder
¼ teaspoon salt
½ cup chopped nuts (optional)
    Creamy Brownie Frosting
    (recipe follows)

Heat oven to 350°F. Grease 9-inch
square baking pan. In medium bowl,
stir together butter, sugar and vanilla. Add eggs; with spoon, beat well.
Stir together flour, cocoa, baking powder and salt; gradually add to egg
mixture, beating until well blended.
Stir in nuts, if desired. Spread batter
evenly into prepared pan. Bake 20 to
25 minutes or until brownie begins to
pull away from sides of pan. Cool completely in pan on wire rack. Frost
with Creamy Brownie Frosting. Cut
into squares.
About 16 brownies.

Creamy Brownie Frosting

3 tablespoons butter or
    margarine, softened
3 tablespoons HERSHEY'S
    Cocoa
1 tablespoon light corn syrup or
    honey
½ teaspoon vanilla extract
1 cup powdered sugar
1 to 2 tablespoons milk

In small mixer bowl, beat butter, cocoa, corn syrup and vanilla until
blended. Add powdered sugar and
milk; beat to spreading consistency.
About 1 cup frosting.

Lemon Iced Ambrosia Bars

1½ cups unsifted flour
⅓ cup confectioners' sugar
¾ cup cold margarine or butter
2 cups firmly packed light brown
    sugar
4 eggs, beaten
1 cup flaked coconut
1 cup finely chopped pecans
3 tablespoons flour
½ teaspoon baking powder
    Lemon Icing*

Preheat oven to 350°. In medium
bowl, combine flour and confectioners' sugar; cut in margarine until
crumbly. Press onto bottom of lightly
greased 13×9-inch baking pan; bake
15 minutes. Meanwhile, in large bowl,
combine remaining ingredients except icing; mix well. Spread evenly
over baked crust; bake 20 to 25 minutes. Cool. Spread with Lemon Icing;
chill. Cut into bars. Store covered in
refrigerator.
Makes 36 bars.
LEMON ICING: Combine 2 cups
confectioners' sugar, 3 tablespoons
REALEMON® Lemon Juice from
Concentrate and 2 tablespoons softened margarine; mix until smooth.
Makes about ⅔ cup.

Double-Deck Brownies

⅔ cup flour
½ teaspoon CALUMET® Baking
    Powder
¼ teaspoon salt
2 eggs
1 cup sugar
½ cup butter or margarine,
    melted and cooled
⅓ cup BAKER'S® ANGEL FLAKE®
    Coconut
¼ teaspoon almond extract
2 squares BAKER'S®
    Unsweetened Chocolate,
    melted
1 square BAKER'S® Semi-Sweet
    Chocolate, melted

Lemon Iced Ambrosia Bars

Mix flour, baking powder and salt.
Beat eggs thoroughly. Gradually add
sugar and continue beating until
light and fluffy. Blend in butter; then
stir in flour mixture. Measure ½ cup
into small bowl. Stir in coconut and
almond extract; set aside. Add unsweetened chocolate to remaining
batter; spread in greased 8-inch
square pan. Drop coconut batter by
teaspoonfuls over chocolate batter.
Then spread carefully to form a thin
layer. Bake at 350° for 30 to 35 minutes or until lightly browned. Cool in
pan. Drizzle with semi-sweet chocolate. Cut into squares or bars.
Makes about 20.

Peanut Butter Paisley Brownies

½ cup (1 stick) butter or
    margarine, softened
¼ cup REESE'S Peanut Butter
1 cup granulated sugar
1 cup packed light brown sugar
3 eggs
1 teaspoon vanilla extract
2 cups all-purpose flour
2 teaspoons baking powder
¼ teaspoon salt
½ cup (5½ oz. can) HERSHEY'S
    Syrup

Heat oven to 350°F. Grease 13×9×2-
inch baking pan. In large mixer bowl,
beat butter and peanut butter. Add
granulated sugar and brown sugar;
beat well. Add eggs, one at a time,
beating well after each addition.
Blend in vanilla. Stir together flour,
baking powder and salt; mix into peanut butter mixture, blending well.

Spread half of batter into prepared
pan. Spoon syrup over top. Carefully
spread with remaining batter. Swirl
with metal spatula or knife for marbled effect. Bake 35 to 40 minutes or
until lightly browned. Cool completely in pan on wire rack. Cut into
squares.
About 36 brownies.

Lemony Raisin-Coconut Squares

Crust:
- ¼ cup butter or margarine, softened
- ½ cup packed light brown sugar
- 1 cup all-purpose flour
- ¼ cup toasted shredded coconut*

Topping:
- 2 eggs
- 1 cup packed light brown sugar
- 1 tablespoon grated lemon peel
- ¼ cup lemon juice
- ¼ teaspoon salt
- 1½ cups SUN-MAID® Raisins
- ¾ cup toasted shredded coconut*
- Powdered sugar, for garnish

To prepare crust: In small bowl, cream butter and the ½ cup brown sugar. Blend in flour and the ¼ cup coconut. Mixture will be dry. Grease 9-inch square cake pan. Line bottom and 2 opposite sides with foil, allowing foil to extend slightly beyond edges; generously grease foil. Press crust mixture evenly into bottom of pan. Bake in preheated 350°F oven about 12 minutes or until edges brown lightly. Remove from oven.

To prepare topping: In medium bowl, beat eggs until foamy with electric mixer. Add the 1 cup brown sugar, the lemon peel and juice, and salt. Beat 2 minutes. Stir in raisins and coconut. Spread topping evenly over crust. Bake 20 to 25 minutes or until top begins to brown. Cool in pan. Loosen edges with sharp knife. Grasp foil edges and lift out of pan. With sharp knife, cut into 16 squares. Dust with powdered sugar, if desired.
Makes 16 squares.

*To toast 1 cup coconut, spread in shallow baking pan. Bake in 350°F oven about 10 minutes or until lightly browned, stirring occasionally. Cool.

Clockwise from top left: Peanut Butter Paisley Brownies, Scrumptious Chocolate Layer Bars and Best Brownies

Scrumptious Chocolate Layer Bars

- 2 cups (12-oz. pkg.) HERSHEY'S Semi-Sweet Chocolate Chips
- 1 package (8 oz.) cream cheese
- ⅔ cup (5-oz. can) evaporated milk
- 1 cup chopped walnuts
- ¼ cup sesame seeds (optional)
- 1 teaspoon almond extract, divided
- 3 cups all-purpose flour
- 1½ cups sugar
- 1 teaspoon baking powder
- ½ teaspoon salt
- 1 cup (2 sticks) butter or regular margarine
- 2 eggs

Heat oven to 375°F. Grease 13×9×2-inch baking pan. In medium saucepan, combine chocolate chips, cream cheese and evaporated milk; cook over low heat, stirring constantly, until chips are melted and mixture is blended. Remove from heat; stir in walnuts, sesame seeds, if desired, and ½ teaspoon almond extract. Blend well; set aside. Stir together remaining ingredients; blend well with electric mixer until mixture resembles coarse crumbs. Press half of crumb mixture into prepared pan; spread with chocolate mixture. Sprinkle remaining crumbs over filling. Bake 35 to 40 minutes or until golden brown. Cool completely in pan on wire rack. Cut into bars.
About 36 bars.

Walnut Crunch Brownies

Brownie Layer:
    4 squares BAKER'S®
        Unsweetened Chocolate
    ¾ cup (1½ sticks) margarine
        or butter
    2 cups granulated sugar
    4 eggs
    1 teaspoon vanilla
    1 cup all-purpose flour

Walnut Topping:
    ¼ cup (½ stick) margarine or
        butter
    ¾ cup firmly packed brown
        sugar
    2 eggs
    2 tablespoons all-purpose
        flour
    1 teaspoon vanilla
    4 cups chopped walnuts

HEAT oven to 350°F.

MICROWAVE chocolate and ¾ cup margarine in large microwavable bowl on HIGH 2 minutes or until margarine is melted. **Stir until chocolate is completely melted.**

STIR granulated sugar into melted chocolate mixture. Mix in 4 eggs and 1 teaspoon vanilla until well blended. Stir in 1 cup flour. Spread in greased 13×9-inch pan.

MICROWAVE ¼ cup margarine and brown sugar in same bowl on HIGH 1 minute or until margarine is melted. Stir in 2 eggs, 2 tablespoons flour and 1 teaspoon vanilla until completely mixed. Stir in walnuts. Spread mixture evenly over brownie batter.

BAKE for 45 minutes or until toothpick inserted into center comes out with fudgy crumbs. **Do not overbake.** Cool in pan; cut into squares.
                    Makes about 24 brownies

Prep time: 20 minutes
Baking time: 45 minutes

Almond Macaroon Brownies

Brownie Layer:
    6 squares BAKER'S®
        Semi-Sweet Chocolate
    ½ cup (1 stick) margarine or
        butter
    ⅔ cup sugar
    2 eggs
    1 teaspoon vanilla
    1 cup all-purpose flour
    ⅔ cup toasted chopped
        almonds

Cream Cheese Topping:
    4 ounces PHILADELPHIA
        BRAND® Cream Cheese,
        softened
    ⅓ cup sugar
    1 egg
    1 tablespoon all-purpose
        flour
    1 cup BAKER'S® ANGEL
        FLAKE® Coconut
    Whole almonds (optional)
    1 square BAKER'S®
        Semi-Sweet Chocolate,
        melted (optional)

HEAT oven to 350°F.

MICROWAVE 6 squares chocolate and margarine in large microwavable bowl on HIGH 2 minutes or until margarine is melted. **Stir until chocolate is completely melted.**

STIR ⅔ cup sugar into melted chocolate mixture. Mix in 2 eggs and vanilla until well blended. Stir in 1 cup flour and ⅓ cup of the almonds. Spread in greased 8-inch square pan.

MIX cream cheese, ⅓ cup sugar, 1 egg and 1 tablespoon flour in same bowl until smooth. Stir in the remaining ⅓ cup almonds and the coconut. Spread over brownie batter. Garnish with whole almonds, if desired.

BAKE for 35 minutes or until toothpick inserted into center comes out with fudgy crumbs. **Do not overbake.** Cool in pan. Drizzle with 1 square melted chocolate, if desired.
                    Makes about 16 brownies

Prep time: 20 minutes
Baking time: 35 minutes

Peanut-Layered Brownies

Brownie Layer:
    4 squares BAKER'S®
        Unsweetened Chocolate
    ¾ cup (1½ sticks) margarine
        or butter
    2 cups granulated sugar
    3 eggs
    1 teaspoon vanilla
    1 cup all-purpose flour
    1 cup chopped peanuts

Peanut Butter Layer:
    1 cup peanut butter
    ½ cup powdered sugar
    1 teaspoon vanilla

Glaze:
    4 squares BAKER'S®
        Semi-Sweet Chocolate
    ¼ cup (½ stick) margarine or
        butter

HEAT oven to 350°F.

MICROWAVE unsweetened chocolate and ¾ cup margarine in large microwavable bowl on HIGH 2 minutes or until margarine is melted. **Stir until chocolate is completely melted.**

STIR granulated sugar into chocolate mixture. Mix in eggs and 1 teaspoon vanilla until well blended. Stir in flour and peanuts. Spread in greased 13×9-inch pan.

BAKE for 30 to 35 minutes or until toothpick inserted into center comes out with fudgy crumbs. **Do not overbake.** Cool in pan.

MIX peanut butter, powdered sugar and 1 teaspoon vanilla in separate bowl until blended and smooth. Spread over brownies.

MICROWAVE semi-sweet chocolate and ¼ cup margarine in small microwavable bowl on HIGH 2 minutes or until margarine is melted. **Stir until chocolate is completely melted.** Spread over peanut butter layer. Cool until set. Cut into squares.
                    Makes about 24 brownies

Prep time: 20 minutes
Baking time: 30 to 35 minutes

Clockwise from top right: Peanut-Layered Brownies, Almond Macaroon Brownies and Walnut Crunch Brownies

Rich 'n' Creamy Brownie Bars

Brownies
  1 package DUNCAN HINES®
      Chocolate Lovers'
      Double Fudge
      Brownie Mix
  2 eggs
  ⅓ cup water
  ¼ cup CRISCO® Oil or
      CRISCO® PURITAN® Oil
  ½ cup chopped pecans

Topping
  1 package (8 ounces) cream
      cheese, softened
  2 eggs
  1 pound (3½ cups)
      confectioners sugar
  1 teaspoon vanilla extract

1. Preheat oven to 350°F. Grease bottom of 13×9×2-inch pan.

2. **For brownies,** combine brownie mix, contents of fudge packet from Mix, eggs, water and oil in large bowl. Stir with spoon until well blended, about 50 strokes. Stir in pecans. Spread evenly in pan.

3. **For topping,** beat cream cheese in large bowl at medium speed with electric mixer until smooth. Beat in eggs, confectioners sugar and vanilla extract until smooth. Spread evenly over brownie mixture. Bake at 350°F for 45 to 50 minutes or until edges and top are golden brown and shiny. Cool completely. Refrigerate until well chilled. Cut into bars.

48 Bars

Tip: Always use the pan size called for in Duncan Hines® recipes. Using a different size pan can give brownies an altogether different texture.

Fudgy Rocky Road Brownies

Heath® Blond Brickle Brownies

1⅓ cups all-purpose flour
  ½ teaspoon baking powder
  ¼ teaspoon salt
  2 eggs, room temperature
  ½ cup granulated sugar
  ½ cup packed brown sugar
  ⅓ cup butter or margarine, melted
  1 teaspoon vanilla
  ¼ teaspoon almond extract
  1 package (6 ounces)
      HEATH® BITS 'O
      BRICKLE®, divided
  ½ cup chopped pecans
      (optional)

Preheat oven to 350°F. Grease 8-inch square baking pan. Combine flour, baking powder and salt; set aside. Beat eggs well. Gradually add granulated and brown sugars; beat until thick and creamy. Add melted butter, vanilla and almond extract. Gently stir in flour mixture until moistened. Fold in ⅔ cup of the Heath® Bits 'O Brickle® and nuts. Pour into prepared pan.

Bake 30 minutes. Remove from oven and immediately sprinkle remaining Heath® Bits 'O Brickle® over top. Cool completely in pan on wire rack before cutting.

Makes 16 generous bars

Rich 'n' Creamy Brownie Bars

Fudgy Rocky Road Brownies

Brownies
  1 cup LAND O LAKES®
    Butter
  4 squares (1 ounce *each*)
    unsweetened chocolate
  2 cups granulated sugar
  1½ cups all-purpose flour
  4 eggs
  2 teaspoons vanilla
  ½ cup chopped salted
    peanuts

Frosting
  ¼ cup LAND O LAKES®
    Butter
  1 package (3 ounces) cream
    cheese
  1 square (1 ounce)
    unsweetened chocolate
  ¼ cup milk
  2¾ cups powdered sugar
  1 teaspoon vanilla
  2 cups miniature
    marshmallows
  1 cup salted peanuts

One Bowl Brownies

Heat oven to 350°. For brownies, in 3-quart saucepan combine 1 cup butter and 4 squares chocolate. Cook over medium heat, stirring constantly, until melted, 5 to 7 minutes. Stir in granulated sugar, flour, eggs and 2 teaspoons vanilla until well mixed. Stir in ½ cup chopped peanuts. Spread into greased 13×9-inch baking pan. Bake for 20 to 25 minutes or until brownies start to pull away from sides of pan.

For frosting, in 2-quart saucepan combine ¼ cup butter, cream cheese, 1 square chocolate and milk. Cook over medium heat, stirring occasionally, until melted, 6 to 8 minutes. Remove from heat; stir in powdered sugar and 1 teaspoon vanilla until smooth. Stir in marshmallows and 1 cup peanuts. Immediately spread over hot brownies. Cool completely; cut into bars. Store refrigerated.

Makes 4 dozen bars

One Bowl Brownies

  4 squares BAKER'S®
    Unsweetened Chocolate
  ¾ cup (1½ sticks) margarine
    or butter
  2 cups sugar
  3 eggs
  1 teaspoon vanilla
  1 cup all-purpose flour
  1 cup chopped nuts
    (optional)

HEAT oven to 350°F.

MICROWAVE chocolate and margarine in large microwavable bowl on HIGH 2 minutes or until margarine is melted. **Stir until chocolate is completely melted.**

STIR sugar into melted chocolate mixture. Mix in eggs and vanilla until well blended. Stir in flour and nuts. Spread in greased 13×9-inch pan.

BAKE for 30 to 35 minutes or until toothpick inserted into center comes out with fudgy crumbs. **Do not overbake.** Cool in pan; cut into squares.
Makes about 24 brownies

Prep time: 10 minutes
Baking time: 30 to 35 minutes

Tips:

• For cakelike brownies, stir in ½ cup milk with eggs and vanilla. Increase flour to 1½ cups.

• When using a glass baking dish, reduce oven temperature to 325°F.

Chocolate Cherry Brownies

- **1 jar (16 ounces) maraschino cherries**
- **⅔ cup (1 stick plus 3 tablespoons) margarine**
- **1 package (6 ounces) semi-sweet chocolate pieces (1 cup), divided**
- **1 cup sugar**
- **1 teaspoon vanilla**
- **2 eggs**
- **1¼ cups all-purpose flour**
- **¾ cup QUAKER® Oats (quick or old fashioned, uncooked)**
- **1 teaspoon baking powder**
- **¼ teaspoon salt (optional)**
- **½ cup chopped nuts (optional)**
- **2 teaspoons vegetable shortening**

Heat oven to 350°F. Lightly grease 13×9-inch baking pan. Drain cherries; reserve 12 and chop remainder. In large saucepan over low heat, melt margarine and ½ cup chocolate pieces, stirring until smooth. Remove from heat; cool slightly. Add sugar and vanilla. Beat in eggs, one at a time. Add combined flour, oats, baking powder and salt. Stir in chopped cherries and nuts. Spread into prepared pan. Bake about 25 minutes or until brownies pull away from sides of pan. Cool completely in pan on wire rack.

Cut reserved cherries in half; place evenly on top of brownies. In saucepan over low heat, melt remaining ½ cup chocolate pieces and vegetable shortening, stirring constantly until smooth.* Drizzle over brownies; cut into about 2½-inch squares. Store tightly covered.

Makes about 2 dozen bars

*Microwave Directions: Place chocolate pieces and shortening in microwavable bowl. Microwave at HIGH 1 to 1½ minutes, stirring after 1 minute.

Cappucino Bon Bons

White Chocolate Brownies

- **1 package DUNCAN HINES® Chocolate Lovers' Milk Chocolate Chunk Brownie Mix**
- **2 eggs**
- **⅓ cup water**
- **⅓ cup CRISCO® Oil or CRISCO® PURITAN® Oil**
- **¾ cup coarsely chopped white chocolate**
- **¼ cup sliced natural almonds**

1. Preheat oven to 350°F. Grease bottom of 13×9×2-inch pan.

2. Combine brownie mix, eggs, water and oil in large bowl. Stir with spoon until well blended, about 50 strokes. Fold in white chocolate. Spread in pan. Sprinkle top with almonds. Bake at 350°F for 25 to 28 minutes or until set. Cool completely. Cut into bars.

48 Small or 24 Large Brownies

Tip: For Decadent Brownies, combine 3 ounces coarsely chopped white chocolate and 2 tablespoons CRISCO® Shortening in small heavy saucepan. Melt over low heat, stirring constantly. Drizzle over cooled brownies.

Cappucino Bon Bons

- **1 package DUNCAN HINES® Fudge Brownie Mix, Family Size**
- **2 eggs**
- **⅓ cup water**
- **⅓ cup CRISCO® Oil or CRISCO® PURITAN® Oil**
- **1½ tablespoons FOLGERS® Coffee Crystals**
- **1 teaspoon ground cinnamon**
  Whipped topping, for garnish
  Ground cinnamon, for garnish

1. Preheat oven to 350°F. Place 40 (2-inch) foil liners on baking sheets.

2. Combine brownie mix, eggs, water, oil, coffee and 1 teaspoon cinnamon in large bowl. Stir with spoon until well blended, about 50 strokes. Fill each liner with 1 measuring tablespoonful batter. Bake at 350°F for 12 to 15 minutes or until toothpick inserted in center comes out clean. Cool completely. Garnish with whipped topping and a dash of cinnamon. Refrigerate until ready to serve.   *40 Bon Bons*

Tip: To make larger Bon Bons, use twelve 2½-inch foil liners and fill with ¼ cup batter. Bake for 28 to 30 minutes.

Brownie Bon Bons

2 jars (10 ounces each) maraschino cherries with stems
Cherry liqueur (optional)*
4 squares BAKER'S® Unsweetened Chocolate
¾ cup (1½ sticks) margarine or butter
2 cups granulated sugar
4 eggs
1 teaspoon vanilla
1 cup all-purpose flour
Chocolate Fudge Filling (recipe follows)
½ cup powdered sugar

HEAT oven to 350°F.

MICROWAVE chocolate and margarine in large microwavable bowl on HIGH 2 minutes or until margarine is melted. **Stir until chocolate is completely melted.**

STIR granulated sugar into melted chocolate mixture. Mix in eggs and vanilla until well blended. Stir in flour. Fill greased 1¾×1-inch miniature muffin cups ⅔ full with batter.

BAKE for 20 minutes or until toothpick inserted into center comes out with fudgy crumbs. **Do not overbake.** Cool slightly in muffin pans; loosen edges with tip of knife. Remove from pans. Turn each brownie onto wax paper-lined tray while warm. Make ½-inch indentation into top of each brownie with end of wooden spoon. Cool completely.

PREPARE Chocolate Fudge Filling. Drain cherries, reserving liquid or liqueur. Let cherries stand on paper towels to dry. Combine powdered sugar with enough reserved liquid to form a thin glaze.

*For liqueur-flavored cherries, drain liquid from cherries. Do not remove cherries from jars. Refill jars with liqueur to completely cover cherries; cover tightly. Let stand at least 24 hours for best flavor.

SPOON or pipe about 1 teaspoon Chocolate Fudge Filling into indentation of each brownie. Gently press cherry into filling. Drizzle with powdered sugar glaze.

Makes about 48 bon bons

Prep time: 1 hour
Baking time: 20 minutes

Chocolate Fudge Filling

3 squares BAKER'S® Unsweetened Chocolate
1 package (3 ounces) PHILADELPHIA BRAND® Cream Cheese, softened
1 teaspoon vanilla
¼ cup corn syrup
1 cup powdered sugar

MELT chocolate in small microwavable bowl on HIGH 1 to 2 minutes or until almost melted, stirring after each minute. **Stir until chocolate is completely melted.** Set aside.

BEAT cream cheese and vanilla in small bowl until smooth. Slowly pour in corn syrup, beating until well blended. Add chocolate; beat until smooth. Gradually add powdered sugar, beating until well blended and smooth. *Makes about 1 cup*

Brownie Candy Cups

1 package DUNCAN HINES® Chocolate Lovers' Double Fudge Brownie Mix
2 eggs
⅓ cup water
¼ cup CRISCO® Oil or CRISCO® PURITAN® Oil
30 miniature peanut butter cup candies, wrappers removed

1. Preheat oven to 350°F. Place 30 (2-inch) foil liners in muffin pans or on baking sheets.

2. Combine brownie mix, contents of fudge packet from Mix, eggs, water and oil in large bowl. Stir with spoon until well blended, about 50 strokes. Fill each liner with 2 measuring tablespoonfuls batter. Bake at 350°F for 10 minutes. Remove from oven. Push 1 peanut butter cup candy in center of each cupcake until even with surface of brownie. Bake 5 to 7 minutes longer. Cool 5 to 10 minutes in pans. Remove to cooling racks. Cool completely.

30 Brownie Cups

Tip: Pack these brownies in your child's lunch bag for a special treat.

Brownie Bon Bons

Holiday Almond Treats

**2½ cups crushed vanilla
   wafers**
**1¾ cups toasted ground
   almonds, divided**
½ cup sifted powdered sugar
½ teaspoon ground cinnamon
**1 cup LIBBY'S® Pumpkin Pie
   Mix**
**⅓ cup almond liqueur or
   apple juice**

In medium bowl, blend vanilla
wafer crumbs, *1 cup* ground
almonds, powdered sugar and
cinnamon. Stir in pumpkin pie
mix and almond liqueur. Form
into 1-inch balls. Roll in
remaining ¾ cup ground
almonds. Refrigerate.

Makes 4 dozen

Rich Chocolate Pumpkin Truffles

**2½ cups crushed vanilla
   wafers**
**1 cup toasted ground
   almonds**
**¾ cup sifted powdered sugar,
   divided**
**2 teaspoons ground
   cinnamon**
**1 cup (6 ounces) chocolate
   pieces, melted**
**½ cup LIBBY'S® Solid Pack
   Pumpkin**
**⅓ cup coffee liqueur or apple
   juice**

In medium bowl, combine vanilla
wafer crumbs, ground almonds,
½ cup powdered sugar and
cinnamon. Blend in melted
chocolate, pumpkin and coffee
liqueur. Form into 1-inch balls.
Refrigerate. Dust with
remaining ¼ cup powdered sugar
just before serving.

Makes 4 dozen candies

Easy Chocolate Truffles

**1½ packages (12 ounces)
   BAKER'S® Semi-Sweet
   Chocolate**
**1 package (8 ounces)
   PHILADELPHIA BRAND®
   Cream Cheese, softened**
3 cups powdered sugar
**1½ teaspoons vanilla
   Ground nuts, unsweetened
   cocoa or BAKER'S®
   ANGEL FLAKE®
   Coconut, toasted**

MELT chocolate in large
microwavable bowl on HIGH 2 to
3 minutes or until almost
melted, stirring after each
minute. **Stir until chocolate is
completely melted.** Set aside.

BEAT cream cheese until
smooth. Gradually add sugar,
beating until well blended. Add
melted chocolate and vanilla;
mix well. Refrigerate about 1
hour. Shape into 1-inch balls.
Roll in nuts, cocoa or coconut.
Store in refrigerator.

Makes about 5 dozen candies

Prep time: 15 minutes
Chill time: 1 hour

Variation: To flavor truffles with
liqueurs, omit vanilla. Divide
truffle mixture into thirds. Add 1
tablespoon liqueur (almond,
coffee or orange) to each third
mixture; mix well.

Milk Chocolate Orange Truffles

**One 11½-oz. pkg. (2 cups)
   NESTLÉ® Toll House®
   Milk Chocolate Morsels**
**One 6-oz. pkg. (1 cup) NESTLÉ®
   Toll House® Semi-Sweet
   Chocolate Morsels**
**¾ cup heavy or whipping
   cream**
**1 teaspoon grated orange
   rind**
**2 tablespoons orange
   flavored liqueur**
**1½ cups toasted walnuts,
   finely chopped**

Line three large cookie sheets
with wax paper. Place milk
chocolate morsels and semi-
sweet chocolate morsels in large
bowl; set aside. In small
saucepan over low heat, bring
heavy cream and orange rind
just to boil; pour over morsels.
Let stand 1 minute; whisk until
smooth. Whisk in liqueur.
Transfer to small mixer bowl;
press plastic wrap directly on
surface. Refrigerate 35 to 45
minutes, *just* until mixture
begins to thicken. Beat 10 to 15
seconds, *just* until chocolate
mixture has lightened in color.
(*Do not overbeat or truffles will
be grainy.*) Shape rounded
teaspoonfuls of chocolate mixture
into balls; place on prepared
cookie sheets. Refrigerate 10 to
15 minutes. Roll in walnuts.
Refrigerate in airtight
containers.

Makes about 6 dozen

Chocolate-Coated Truffles: Omit
walnuts. Line three large cookie
sheets with foil. Prepare
chocolate mixture and shape into
balls as directed. Freeze 30 to 40
minutes until firm. Melt one
11½-oz. pkg. (2 cups) Nestlé®
Toll House® Milk Chocolate
Morsels with 3 tablespoons
vegetable shortening. Drop
frozen truffles, one at a time,
into chocolate mixture. Stir
quickly and gently to coat;
remove with fork, shaking off
excess coating. Return to cookie
sheets. Refrigerate 10 to 15
minutes until firm. Refrigerate
in airtight containers.

Easy Chocolate Truffles and Chocolate-Coated Almond Toffee (page 447)

Creamy Nut Dipped Candies

        5 cups powdered sugar
        ¾ cup flaked coconut
        ⅓ cup LAND O LAKES®
            Butter, softened
        ¼ teaspoon salt
        3 tablespoons milk
        2 teaspoons vanilla
        1 cup mixed nuts
        1 package (10 ounces)
            almond bark, vanilla *or*
            chocolate candy coating

In large mixer bowl combine *4 cups* powdered sugar, coconut, butter, salt, milk and vanilla. Beat at medium speed, scraping bowl often, until light and fluffy, 4 to 5 minutes. By hand, knead in remaining 1 cup powdered sugar. (Dough may be soft.) Form 1 teaspoon of dough around *each* nut; roll into ball. Refrigerate until firm, 2 hours. In 2-quart saucepan over low heat, melt almond bark. Dip chilled balls into melted coating; place on waxed paper. Drizzle with remaining almond bark. Store refrigerated.

Makes about 5½ dozen candies

Buttery Pecan Caramels

        2 cups sugar
        2 cups half-and-half (1 pint)
        ¾ cup light corn syrup
        ½ cup LAND O LAKES®
            Butter
        ½ cup semi-sweet real
            chocolate chips, melted
        64 pecan halves

In 4-quart saucepan combine sugar, *1 cup* half-and-half, corn syrup and butter. Cook over medium heat, stirring occasionally, until mixture comes to a full boil, 7 to 8 minutes. Add remaining 1 cup half-and-half; continue cooking, stirring often, until candy thermometer reaches 245°F or small amount of mixture dropped into ice water forms a firm ball, 35 to 40 minutes. Pour into buttered 8-inch square pan. Cover; refrigerate 1 to 1½ hours to cool. Cut into 64 pieces. Drop ¼ teaspoon melted chocolate on top of *each* caramel; press pecan half into chocolate. Cover; store refrigerated.

Makes 64 caramels

Buttery Peanut Brittle (top) and Buttery Pecan Caramels (bottom)

Buttery Peanut Brittle

        2 cups sugar
        1 cup light corn syrup
        ½ cup water
        1 cup LAND O LAKES®
            Butter, cut into pieces
        2 cups raw Spanish peanuts
        1 teaspoon baking soda

In 3-quart saucepan combine sugar, corn syrup and water. Cook over low heat, stirring occasionally, until sugar is dissolved and mixture comes to a full boil, 20 to 30 minutes. Add butter; continue cooking, stirring occasionally, until candy thermometer reaches 280°F or small amount of mixture dropped into ice water forms a pliable strand, 80 to 90 minutes. Stir in peanuts; continue cooking, stirring constantly, until candy thermometer reaches 305°F or small amount of mixture dropped into ice water forms a brittle strand, 12 to 14 minutes. Remove from heat; stir in baking soda. Pour mixture onto 2 buttered cookie sheets; spread about ¼ inch thick. Cool completely; break into pieces.

Makes 2 pounds

Creamy Nut Dipped Candies

Chocolate-Coated Almond Toffee

- 1 cup (2 sticks) butter or margarine
- 1 cup sugar
- 3 tablespoons water
- 1 tablespoon corn syrup
- ½ cup toasted chopped almonds
- 6 squares BAKER'S® Semi-Sweet Chocolate
- ⅓ cup toasted finely chopped almonds

COOK butter, sugar, water and corn syrup in heavy 2-quart saucepan over medium heat until mixture boils, stirring constantly. Boil gently, stirring frequently, 10 to 12 minutes or until golden brown and very thick. (Or until ½ teaspoon of mixture will form a hard, brittle thread when dropped in 1 cup cold water.)

REMOVE from heat. Stir in ½ cup almonds. Spread evenly onto well-buttered 15½×10½×1-inch baking pan. Let stand until almost cool to the touch.

MELT chocolate in small microwavable bowl on HIGH 2 minutes or until almost melted, stirring after each minute. **Stir until chocolate is completely melted.**

SPREAD melted chocolate over toffee; sprinkle with ⅓ cup almonds. Let stand until chocolate is firm. Break into pieces.

Makes about 1½ pounds candy

Prep time: 30 minutes

Butter Almond Crunch

- 1½ cups HERSHEY'S MINI CHIPS Semi-Sweet Chocolate or HERSHEY'S Semi-Sweet Chocolate Chips, divided
- 1¾ cups chopped almonds, divided
- 1½ cups (3 sticks) butter or margarine
- 1¾ cups sugar
- 3 tablespoons light corn syrup
- 3 tablespoons water

Heat oven to 350°F. Line 13×9×2-inch pan with foil; butter foil. Sprinkle 1 cup chocolate chips into pan; set aside.

In shallow baking pan, spread almonds. Bake 7 minutes or until golden brown; set aside.

In heavy 3-quart saucepan, melt butter; blend in sugar, corn syrup and water. Over medium heat, cook, stirring constantly, to 300°F. on a candy thermometer (hard-crack stage) or until syrup, when dropped into very cold water, separates into threads which are hard and brittle. (Bulb of candy thermometer should not rest on bottom of saucepan.) Remove from heat; stir in 1½ cups toasted almonds. Immediately pour mixture evenly over chocolate chips in prepared pan; *do not disturb chips.* Sprinkle with remaining ¼ cup toasted almonds and remaining ½ cup chocolate chips; cool slightly.

With sharp knife, score into 1½-inch squares, wiping knife blade after drawing through candy. Cool completely; remove from pan. Remove foil; break into pieces. Store in tightly covered container in cool, dry place.

Makes about 2 pounds candy

Butter Almond Crunch

Chocolate Caramel Drops

- 24 KRAFT® Caramels (about 7 ounces)
- 2 tablespoons heavy cream
- 1 cup (about) pecan halves
- 4 squares BAKER'S® Semi-Sweet Chocolate

MICROWAVE caramels and cream in large microwavable bowl on HIGH 1½ minutes; stir. Microwave 1½ minutes longer; stir until caramels are completely melted. Cool.

PLACE pecan halves on lightly greased cookie sheets in clusters of 3. Spoon caramel mixture over nuts, leaving ends showing. Let stand until set, about 30 minutes.

MELT chocolate in small microwavable bowl on HIGH 1 to 2 minutes or until almost melted, stirring after each minute. **Stir until chocolate is completely melted.** Spread melted chocolate over caramel mixture. Let stand until chocolate is set.

Makes about 2 dozen candies

Prep time: 20 minutes
Standing time: 30 minutes

Chocolate-Dipped Morsels

Buckeyes

**2 (3-ounce) packages cream cheese, softened
1 (14-ounce) can EAGLE® Brand Sweetened Condensed Milk (NOT evaporated milk)
2 (12-ounce) packages peanut butter flavored chips
1 cup finely chopped peanuts
1/2 pound chocolate confectioners' coating***

In large mixer bowl, beat cheese until fluffy. Gradually beat in sweetened condensed milk until smooth. In heavy saucepan, over low heat, melt peanut butter chips; stir into cheese mixture. Add nuts. Chill 2 to 3 hours; shape into 1-inch balls. In small heavy saucepan, over low heat, melt confectioners' coating. With wooden pick, dip each peanut ball into melted coating, not covering completely. Place on wax paper-lined baking sheets until firm. Store covered at room temperature or in refrigerator. *Makes about 7 dozen.*

*Chocolate confectioners' coating can be purchased in candy specialty stores.

Chocolate Pecan Critters

**1 (11½-ounce) package milk chocolate chips
1 (6-ounce) package semi-sweet chocolate chips
1/4 cup margarine or butter
1 (14-ounce) can EAGLE® Brand Sweetened Condensed Milk (NOT evaporated milk)
1/8 teaspoon salt
2 cups coarsely chopped pecans
2 teaspoons vanilla extract
Pecan halves**

In heavy saucepan, over medium heat, melt chips and margarine with sweetened condensed milk and salt. Remove from heat; stir in chopped nuts and vanilla. Drop by teaspoonfuls onto wax paper-lined baking sheets. Top with pecan halves. Chill. Store tightly covered. *Makes about 5 dozen.*

Microwave: In 2-quart glass measure, microwave chips, margarine, sweetened condensed milk and salt on full power (high) 3 minutes, stirring after 1½ minutes. Stir to melt chips; stir in chopped nuts and vanilla. Proceed as above.

Chocolate-Dipped Morsels

**4 squares BAKER'S® Semi-Sweet Chocolate
Assorted morsel centers***

Melt chocolate in saucepan over very low heat, stirring constantly until smooth. Insert wooden picks or skewers into fruit and marshmallow centers. Dip quickly, one at a time, into chocolate. (To dip pretzels or nuts, stir into chocolate; then remove with fork.) Let stand or chill on rack or waxed paper until chocolate is firm.

For best eating quality, chill dipped fresh or canned fruits and serve the same day.
Makes 1 to 1½ dozen.

Suggested Morsel Centers.
Fruits: Firm strawberries, ½-inch banana slices, fresh pineapple wedges or drained canned pineapple chunks, peeled orange slices, orange wedges, well-drained stemmed maraschino cherries, dried figs, dried dates or dried apricots.

Unsalted Pretzels and Large Marshmallows.

Nuts: Walnuts or pecan halves or whole almonds or Brazil nuts.

Clockwise from top left: Chocolate Pecan Critters, Fruit Bon Bons, Milk Chocolate Bourbon Balls, Buckeyes, Foolproof Dark Chocolate Fudge (page 451), Peanut Butter Logs and Layered Mint Chocolate Candy

Peanut Butter Logs

- 1 (12-ounce) package peanut butter flavored chips
- 1 (14-ounce) can EAGLE® Brand Sweetened Condensed Milk (NOT evaporated milk)
- 1 cup CAMPFIRE® Miniature Marshmallows
- 1 cup chopped peanuts

In heavy saucepan, over low heat, melt chips with sweetened condensed milk. Add marshmallows; stir until melted. Remove from heat; cool 20 minutes. Divide in half; place each portion on a 20-inch piece of wax paper. Shape each into 12-inch log. Roll in nuts. Wrap tightly; chill 2 hours or until firm. Remove paper; cut into 1/4-inch slices.
Makes two 12-inch logs.

Microwave: In 2-quart glass measure, microwave chips, sweetened condensed milk and marshmallows on full power (high) 4 minutes or until melted, stirring after 2 minutes. Let stand at room temperature 1 hour. Proceed as above.

Peanut Butter Fudge: Stir peanuts into mixture. Spread into wax paper-lined 8- or 9-inch square pan. Chill 2 hours or until firm. Turn fudge onto cutting board; peel off paper and cut into squares.

Layered Mint Chocolate Candy

- 1 (12-ounce) package semi-sweet chocolate chips
- 1 (14-ounce) can EAGLE® Brand Sweetened Condensed Milk (NOT evaporated milk)
- 2 teaspoons vanilla extract
- 6 ounces white confectioners' coating*
- 1 tablespoon peppermint extract Few drops green or red food coloring, optional

In heavy saucepan, over low heat, melt chips with *1 cup* sweetened condensed milk. Stir in vanilla. Spread half the mixture into wax paper-lined 8- or 9-inch square pan; chill 10 minutes or until firm. Hold remaining chocolate mixture at room temperature. In heavy saucepan, over low heat, melt coating with remaining sweetened condensed milk. Stir in peppermint extract and food coloring if desired. Spread on chilled chocolate layer; chill 10 minutes longer or until firm. Spread reserved chocolate mixture on mint layer. Chill 2 hours or until firm. Turn onto cutting board; peel off paper and cut into squares. Store loosely covered at room temperature.
Makes about 1 3/4 pounds.
*White confectioners' coating can be purchased in candy specialty stores.

Milk Chocolate Bourbon Balls

- 1 (12-ounce) package vanilla wafer cookies, finely crushed (about 3 cups crumbs)
- 5 tablespoons bourbon or brandy
- 1 (11 1/2-ounce) package milk chocolate chips
- 1 (14-ounce) can EAGLE® Brand Sweetened Condensed Milk (NOT evaporated milk) Finely chopped nuts

In medium mixing bowl, combine crumbs and bourbon. In heavy saucepan, over low heat, melt chips. Remove from heat; add sweetened condensed milk. Gradually add crumb mixture; mix well. Let stand at room temperature 30 minutes or chill. Shape into 1-inch balls; roll in nuts. Store tightly covered.
Makes about 5 1/2 dozen.

Tip: Flavor of these candies improves after 24 hours. They can be made ahead and stored in freezer. Thaw before serving.

Fruit Bon Bons

- 1 (14-ounce) can EAGLE® Brand Sweetened Condensed Milk (NOT evaporated milk)
- 2 (7-ounce) packages flaked coconut (5 1/3 cups)
- 1 (6-ounce) package fruit flavor gelatin, any flavor
- 1 cup ground blanched almonds
- 1 teaspoon almond extract Food coloring, optional

In large mixing bowl, combine sweetened condensed milk, coconut, 1/3 cup gelatin, almonds, extract and enough food coloring to tint mixture desired shade. Chill 1 hour or until firm enough to handle. Using about 1/2 tablespoon mixture for each, shape into 1-inch balls. Sprinkle remaining gelatin onto wax paper; roll each ball in gelatin to coat. Place on wax paper-lined baking sheets; chill. Store covered at room temperature or in refrigerator.
Makes about 5 dozen.

Crunchy Clusters

- 1 (12-ounce) package semi-sweet chocolate chips *or* 3 (6-ounce) packages butterscotch flavored chips
- 1 (14-ounce) can EAGLE® Brand Sweetened Condensed Milk (NOT evaporated milk)
- 1 (3-ounce) can chow mein noodles *or* 2 cups pretzel sticks, broken into ½-inch pieces
- 1 cup dry roasted peanuts *or* whole roasted almonds

In heavy saucepan, over low heat, melt chips with sweetened condensed milk. Remove from heat. In large mixing bowl, combine noodles and nuts; stir in chocolate mixture. Drop by tablespoonfuls onto wax paper-lined baking sheets; chill 2 hours or until firm. Store loosely covered in cool dry place.
Makes about 3 dozen.

Microwave: In 2-quart glass measure, combine chips and sweetened condensed milk. Microwave on full power (high) 3 minutes, stirring after 1½ minutes. Stir until smooth. Proceed as above.

Caramel Peanut Balls

- 3 cups *finely* chopped dry roasted peanuts
- 1 (14-ounce) can EAGLE® Brand Sweetened Condensed Milk (NOT evaporated milk)
- 1 teaspoon vanilla extract
- ½ pound chocolate confectioners' coating*

In heavy saucepan, combine nuts, sweetened condensed milk and vanilla. Over medium heat, cook and stir 8 to 10 minutes or until mixture forms ball around spoon and pulls away from side of pan. Cool 10 minutes. Chill if desired. Shape into 1-inch balls. In small heavy saucepan, over low heat, melt confectioners' coating. With wooden pick, dip each ball into melted coating, covering half of ball. Place on wax paper-lined baking sheets until firm. Store covered at room temperature or in refrigerator.
Makes about 4½ dozen.

*Chocolate confectioners' coating can be purchased in candy specialty stores.

Top to bottom: **Apricot Almond Chewies, Chipper Peanut Candy, Caramel Peanut Balls, Crunchy Clusters (Butterscotch and Chocolate)**

Chipper Peanut Candy

- 1 (6-ounce) package butterscotch flavored chips
- 1 (14-ounce) can EAGLE® Brand Sweetened Condensed Milk (NOT evaporated milk)
- 1 cup peanut butter
- 2 cups crushed WISE® Potato Chips
- 1 cup coarsely chopped peanuts

In heavy saucepan, melt butterscotch chips with sweetened condensed milk and peanut butter. Over medium heat, cook and stir until well blended. Remove from heat. Add potato chips and nuts; mix well. Press into aluminum foil-lined 8- or 9-inch square pan. Chill. Turn candy onto cutting board; peel off foil and cut into squares. Store loosely covered at room temperature.
Makes about 2 pounds.

Microwave: In 2-quart glass measure, combine sweetened condensed milk, butterscotch chips and peanut butter. Microwave on full power (high) 4 minutes, stirring after 2 minutes. Proceed as above.

Foolproof Dark Chocolate Fudge

**3 (6-ounce) packages semi-
    sweet chocolate chips**
**1 (14-ounce) can EAGLE® Brand
    Sweetened Condensed Milk
    (NOT evaporated milk)**
Dash salt
1/2 to 1 cup chopped nuts
1 1/2 teaspoons vanilla extract

In heavy saucepan, over low heat, melt chips with sweetened condensed milk and salt. Remove from heat; stir in nuts and vanilla. Spread evenly into wax paper-lined 8- or 9-inch square pan. Chill 2 hours or until firm. Turn fudge onto cutting board; peel off paper and cut into squares. Store loosely covered at room temperature.
Makes about 2 pounds.

Microwave: In 1-quart glass measure, combine chips with sweetened condensed milk. Microwave on full power (high) 3 minutes. Stir until chips melt and mixture is smooth. Stir in remaining ingredients. Proceed as above.

Creamy Dark Chocolate Fudge: Melt 2 cups CAMPFIRE® Miniature Marshmallows with chips and sweetened condensed milk. Proceed as above.

Milk Chocolate Fudge: Omit 1 (6-ounce) package semi-sweet chocolate chips. Add 1 cup milk chocolate chips. Proceed as above.

Creamy Milk Chocolate Fudge: Omit 1 (6-ounce) package semi-sweet chocolate chips. Add 1 cup milk chocolate chips and 2 cups CAMPFIRE® Miniature Marshmallows. Proceed as above.

Mexican Chocolate Fudge: Reduce vanilla to 1 teaspoon. Add 1 tablespoon instant coffee and 1 teaspoon ground cinnamon to sweetened condensed milk. Proceed as above.

Butterscotch Fudge: Omit chocolate chips and vanilla. In heavy saucepan, melt 2 (12-ounce) packages butterscotch flavored chips with sweetened condensed milk. Remove from heat; stir in 2 tablespoons white vinegar, 1/8 teaspoon salt, 1/2 teaspoon maple flavoring and 1 cup chopped nuts. Proceed as above.

Foolproof Dark Chocolate Fudge

Easy Rocky Road

**2 cups (12-oz. pkg.) HERSHEY'S
    Semi-Sweet Chocolate Chips**
**1/4 cup (1/2 stick) butter or
    margarine**
2 tablespoons shortening
3 cups miniature marshmallows
1/2 cup chopped nuts

Butter 8-inch square pan. In large microwave-safe bowl, place chocolate chips, butter and shortening. Microwave at HIGH (100%) 1 to 1 1/2 minutes or just until chocolate chips are melted and mixture is smooth when stirred. Add marshmallows and nuts; blend well. Spread evenly in prepared pan. Cover; refrigerate until firm. Cut into 2-inch squares.
16 squares.

Apricot Almond Chewies

**4 cups finely chopped dried
    apricots (about 1 pound)**
**4 cups flaked coconut or
    coconut macaroon crumbs
    (about 21 macaroons)**
**2 cups slivered almonds, toasted
    and finely chopped**
**1 (14-ounce) can EAGLE® Brand
    Sweetened Condensed Milk
    (NOT evaporated milk)**
Whole almonds, optional

In large mixing bowl, combine all ingredients except whole almonds. Chill 2 hours. Shape into 1-inch balls. Top each with whole almond if desired. Store tightly covered in refrigerator.
Makes about 6 1/2 dozen.

Chocolate Creams

**1 package (8 squares) BAKER'S®
    Semi-Sweet Chocolate**
1/2 cup butter or margarine
**1 3/4 cups sifted confectioners
    sugar**
**2 tablespoons light cream or
    half and half**
1 teaspoon vanilla
**1 cup finely chopped nuts or
    grated BAKER'S® Semi-
    Sweet Chocolate**

Melt chocolate with butter in saucepan over very low heat, stirring constantly until smooth. Blend in sugar, cream and vanilla. Chill about 30 minutes. Shape into 1/2-inch balls and roll in nuts. Store in refrigerator.
Makes about 4 1/2 dozen.

Napoleon Crèmes

Crumb Mixture
 ¾ cup LAND O LAKES®
   Butter
 ¼ cup granulated sugar
 ¼ cup unsweetened cocoa
 1 teaspoon vanilla
 2 cups graham cracker
   crumbs

Filling
 2 cups powdered sugar
 ½ cup LAND O LAKES®
   Butter, softened
 1 package (3½ ounces)
   instant vanilla
   pudding mix
 3 tablespoons milk

Frosting
 1 package (6 ounces) semi-
   sweet real chocolate
   chips (1 cup)
 2 tablespoons
   LAND O LAKES® Butter

For crumb mixture, in 2-quart saucepan combine ¾ cup butter, granulated sugar, cocoa and vanilla. Cook over medium heat, stirring occasionally, until butter melts, 5 to 6 minutes. Remove from heat. Stir in crumbs. Press on bottom of buttered 9-inch square pan; cool.

Napoleon Crèmes

For filling, in small mixer bowl combine all filling ingredients. Beat at medium speed, scraping bowl often, until smooth, 1 to 2 minutes. Spread over crust; refrigerate until firm, about 30 minutes.

For frosting, in 1-quart saucepan melt frosting ingredients over low heat; spread over bars. Cover; refrigerate until firm, about 1 hour. Cut into squares; store refrigerated.

Makes 64 candies

Malted Milk Chocolate Balls

**One 11½-oz. pkg. (2 cups)
   NESTLÉ® Toll House®
   Milk Chocolate Morsels,
   divided
 1 tablespoon vegetable oil
 1 cup CARNATION® Original
   Malted Milk Powder
 1 tablespoon vegetable
   shortening**

Line two large cookie sheets with foil. In small saucepan over low heat, melt 1 cup milk chocolate morsels with oil, stirring until smooth. Remove from heat. Stir in malted milk powder. Transfer to small bowl. Refrigerate about 30 minutes until firm. Shape rounded measuring teaspoonfuls of dough mixture into balls; place on prepared cookie sheets. Freeze 20 minutes.

Melt remaining 1 cup milk chocolate morsels and shortening, stirring until smooth. Drop frozen milk balls, one at a time, into chocolate mixture. Stir quickly and gently to coat; remove with fork, shaking off excess coating. Return to cookie sheets. Refrigerate 10 to 15 minutes until firm. Gently loosen from foil with metal spatula. Refrigerate in airtight containers.

Makes about 2 dozen

Left to right: Rocky Road Fudge, Apricot Fudge and Macadamia Nut Fudge

Rich Chocolate Fudge

Fudge
 4 cups sugar
 ½ cup LAND O LAKES®
   Butter
 1 can (12 ounces) evaporated
   milk
 1 package (12 ounces) semi-
   sweet real chocolate
   chips (2 cups)
 3 bars (4 ounces *each*) sweet
   baking chocolate
 1 jar (7 ounces) marshmallow
   cream
 2 teaspoons vanilla

Variations

Macadamia Nut
 1¼ cups coarsely chopped
   macadamia nuts

Rocky Road
 1¼ cups coarsely chopped
   walnuts, toasted
 30 marshmallows (3 cups), cut
   into quarters

Apricot
 1¼ cups coarsely chopped
   dried apricots

In 4-quart saucepan combine sugar, butter and evaporated milk. Cook over medium-high heat, stirring occasionally, until mixture comes to a full boil, 10 to 14 minutes. Reduce heat to medium; boil, stirring constantly, until candy thermometer reaches 228°F or small amount of mixture dropped into ice water forms a 2-inch soft thread, 6 to 7 minutes. Remove from heat; gradually stir in chocolate chips and chocolate until melted. Stir in marshmallow cream and vanilla until well blended.

For Macadamia Nut Fudge, stir in *1 cup* nuts. Spread into buttered 13×9-inch pan. Sprinkle with remaining ¼ cup nuts.

For Rocky Road Fudge, stir in *1 cup* nuts, then stir in marshmallows, leaving marbled effect. Spread into buttered 13×9-inch pan. Sprinkle with remaining ¼ cup nuts.

For Apricot Fudge, stir in apricots. Spread into buttered 13×9-inch pan.

Cool completely at room temperature. Cut into 1-inch squares. Store covered in cool place.
Makes about 9 to 10 dozen pieces

Fantasy Fudge

¾ cup (1½ sticks) margarine or butter
3 cups sugar
⅔ cup evaporated milk
1 package (8 ounces) BAKER'S® Semi-Sweet Chocolate, broken into pieces
1 jar (7 ounces) KRAFT® Marshmallow Creme
1 teaspoon vanilla
1 cup chopped nuts

MICROWAVE margarine in 4-quart microwavable bowl on HIGH 1 minute or until melted. Add sugar and milk; mix well.

MICROWAVE on HIGH 3 minutes; stir. Microwave 2 minutes longer or until mixture begins to boil; mix well. Microwave 3 minutes; stir. Microwave 2½ minutes longer. Let stand 2 minutes.

STIR in chocolate until melted. Add marshmallow creme and vanilla; mix well. Stir in nuts. Pour into greased 13×9-inch pan. Cool at room temperature; cut into squares.
Makes about 4 dozen candies

Prep time: 20 minutes

White Peanut Butter Fudge

Two 6-oz. pkgs. (6 foil-wrapped bars) NESTLÉ® Premier White baking bars, divided
½ cup creamy peanut butter
One 7-oz. jar marshmallow cream
1½ cups sugar
⅔ cup CARNATION® Evaporated Milk
¼ teaspoon salt

Grease 8- or 9-inch square baking pan. Break up 1 foil-wrapped bar (2 oz.) Premier White baking bar; place in small saucepan with peanut butter. Stir over low heat until smooth; set aside. Break up remaining 5 foil-wrapped bars (10 oz.) Premier White baking bars; set aside.

In heavy-gauge medium saucepan, combine marshmallow cream, sugar, evaporated milk and salt. Bring to *full rolling boil* over medium-high heat, stirring constantly. *Boil 5 minutes,* stirring constantly. Remove from heat. Stir in broken Premier White baking bars until smooth; pour into prepared pan. Top with tablespoonfuls peanut butter mixture; swirl with metal spatula to marbleize. Refrigerate until firm. Cut into 1-inch squares.

Makes about 2 pounds or 64 squares

Top to bottom: Fantasy Fudge and Chocolate Caramel Drops (page 447)

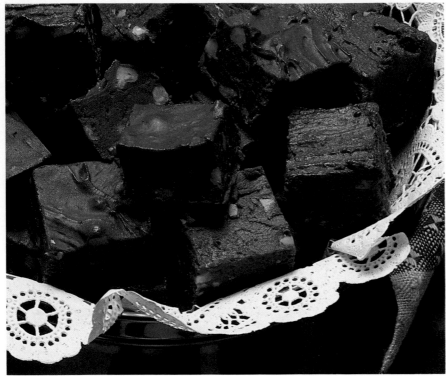

Dorchester Fudge

Dorchester Fudge

- **1 package (8 squares) BAKER'S®**
  Semi-Sweet Chocolate,
  finely chopped
- **1/2 cup marshmallow topping**
- **1/2 cup chopped nuts* (optional)**
- **1/4 cup butter or margarine, at**
  room temperature
- **1/2 teaspoon vanilla**
- **1 1/2 cups sugar**
- **2/3 cup evaporated milk**

Place chocolate in a bowl with marshmallow topping, nuts, butter and vanilla; set aside. Combine sugar and milk in 2-quart saucepan. Cook and stir over medium heat until mixture comes to a *full rolling boil*. Keep at full rolling boil 5 minutes, stirring constantly. Carefully pour boiling sugar syrup over chocolate mixture and stir until chocolate is melted. Pour into buttered 8-inch square pan. Chill until firm, about 1 hour. Cut into squares.
Makes 1 1/2 pounds or about 3 dozen pieces.
  *Or use 1 cup BAKER'S® ANGEL FLAKE® Coconut.
  Mocha Almond Fudge: Prepare Dorchester Fudge as directed, using chopped toasted blanched almonds for the nuts and adding 2 teaspoons MAXWELL HOUSE® or YUBAN® Instant Coffee to milk mixture.
  Peanut Butter Fudge: Prepare Dorchester Fudge as directed, substituting 1/2 cup peanut butter for the nuts and butter.
  Fudge Shapes: Prepare Dorchester Fudge as directed, omitting the nuts; cool slightly and pour fudge mixture onto waxed paper on baking sheet. Top with waxed paper and roll with rolling pin until 1/2 inch thick. Remove top paper; run tines of fork across surface, scoring fudge. Chill until firm; then cut into shapes with small cookie cutters. Garnish with toasted almonds, if desired.

Creamy White Fudge

- **1 1/2 pounds white confectioners'**
  coating*
- **1 (14-ounce) can EAGLE® Brand**
  Sweetened Condensed Milk
  (NOT evaporated milk)
- **1/8 teaspoon salt**
- **3/4 to 1 cup chopped nuts**
- **1 1/2 teaspoons vanilla extract**

In heavy saucepan, over low heat, melt coating with sweetened condensed milk and salt. Remove from heat; stir in nuts and vanilla. Spread evenly into wax paper-lined 8- or 9-inch square pan. Chill 2 hours or until firm. Turn fudge onto cutting board; peel off paper and cut into squares. Store tightly covered at room temperature.
Makes about 2 1/4 pounds.
  Microwave: In 2-quart glass measure, combine coating, sweetened condensed milk and salt. Microwave on full power (high) 3 to 5 minutes or until coating melts, stirring after 3 minutes. Stir in nuts and vanilla. Proceed as above.
  Praline Fudge: Omit vanilla. Add 1 teaspoon maple flavoring and 1 cup chopped pecans. Proceed as above.
  Confetti Fudge: Omit nuts. Add 1 cup chopped mixed candied fruit. Proceed as above.

  Rum Raisin Fudge: Omit vanilla. Add 1 1/2 teaspoons white vinegar, 1 teaspoon rum flavoring and 3/4 cup raisins. Proceed as above.
  Cherry Fudge: Omit nuts. Add 1 cup chopped candied cherries.
  *White confectioners' coating can be purchased in candy specialty stores.

Raspberry Fudge Balls

- **1 8-ounce package**
  PHILADELPHIA BRAND®
  Cream Cheese, softened
- **1 6-ounce package semi-sweet**
  chocolate pieces, melted
- **3/4 cup vanilla wafer crumbs**
- **1/4 cup KRAFT® Raspberry**
  Preserves, strained
  Finely chopped almonds
  Cocoa
  Powdered sugar

Combine cream cheese and chocolate, mixing until well blended. Stir in crumbs and preserves. Chill several hours or overnight. Shape into 1-inch balls; roll in almonds, cocoa or sugar.
Approximately 3 dozen.

Chocolate-Almond Fudge

4 cups sugar
1³/₄ cups (7-oz. jar) marshmallow creme
1¹/₂ cups (12-oz. can) evaporated milk
1 tablespoon butter or margarine
2 cups (12-oz. pkg.) HERSHEY'S Semi-Sweet Chocolate Chips
1 HERSHEY'S Milk Chocolate Bar (7 oz.), broken into pieces
1 teaspoon vanilla extract
³/₄ cup slivered almonds, toasted and coarsely chopped*

Line 9-inch square pan with foil; set aside. In heavy 4-quart saucepan, stir together sugar, marshmallow creme, evaporated milk and butter. Cook over medium heat, stirring constantly, until mixture comes to a full rolling boil; boil, stirring constantly, 7 minutes. Remove from heat; *immediately* add chocolate chips and chocolate bar pieces, stirring until chocolate is melted and mixture is smooth. Stir in vanilla and almonds. Pour into prepared pan; cool until firm. Cut into 1-inch squares. Store in tightly covered container.
About 5 dozen squares or 4 pounds.

*To toast almonds: Heat oven to 350°F. Spread almonds in thin layer in shallow baking pan. Bake 8 to 10 minutes, stirring occasionally, until light golden brown; cool.

Variation: 1 HERSHEY'S Milk Chocolate Bar with Almonds (7 oz.) may be substituted for HERSHEY'S Milk Chocolate Bar.

Chocolate Philly® Cream Cheese Fudge

4 cups sifted powdered sugar
1 8-ounce package PHILADELPHIA BRAND® Cream Cheese, softened
4 1-ounce squares unsweetened chocolate, melted
1 teaspoon vanilla
Dash of salt
¹/₂ cup chopped nuts

Gradually add sugar to cream cheese, mixing well after each addition. Add remaining ingredients; mix well. Spread into greased 8-inch square pan. Chill several hours; cut into squares.
1³/₄ pounds.

Variations: Omit vanilla and nuts; add few drops peppermint extract and ¹/₄ cup crushed peppermint candy. Sprinkle with additional ¹/₄ cup crushed peppermint candy before chilling.

Omit nuts; add 1 cup shredded coconut. Garnish with additional coconut.

Omit nuts; add ¹/₂ cup chopped maraschino cherries, drained. Garnish with whole cherries.

Rich Cocoa Fudge

3 cups sugar
²/₃ cup HERSHEY'S Cocoa or HERSHEY'S Premium European Style Cocoa
¹/₈ teaspoon salt
1¹/₂ cups milk
¹/₄ cup (¹/₂ stick) butter or margarine
1 teaspoon vanilla extract

Line 8- or 9-inch square pan with foil; butter foil. Set aside. In heavy 4-quart saucepan, stir together sugar, cocoa and salt; stir in milk. Cook over medium heat, stirring constantly, until mixture comes to full rolling boil. Boil, without stirring, to 234°F. or until syrup, when dropped into very cold water, forms a soft ball that flattens when removed from water. (Bulb of candy thermometer should not rest on bottom of saucepan). Remove from heat. Add butter and vanilla. *Do not stir.* Cool at room temperature to 110°F. (lukewarm). Beat with wooden spoon until fudge thickens and loses some of its gloss. Quickly spread into prepared pan; cool. Cut into squares.
About 36 pieces or 1³/₄ pounds.

Variations: Nutty Rich Cocoa Fudge: Beat cooked fudge as directed. *Immediately* stir in 1 cup chopped almonds, pecans or walnuts and quickly spread into prepared pan.

Marshmallow-Nut Cocoa Fudge: Increase cocoa to ³/₄ cup. Cook fudge as directed. Add 1 cup marshmallow creme with butter and vanilla. *Do not stir.* Cool to 110°F. (lukewarm). Beat 10 minutes; stir in 1 cup chopped nuts and pour into prepared pan. (Fudge does not set until poured into pan).

Double-Decker Fudge

1 cup REESE'S Peanut Butter Chips
1 cup HERSHEY'S Semi-Sweet Chocolate Chips or HERSHEY'S MINI CHIPS Semi-Sweet Chocolate
2¹/₄ cups sugar
1³/₄ cups (7-oz. jar) marshmallow creme
³/₄ cup evaporated milk
¹/₄ cup (¹/₂ stick) butter or margarine
1 teaspoon vanilla extract

Measure peanut butter chips into one medium bowl and chocolate chips into second medium bowl; set aside. Butter 8-inch square pan; set aside. In heavy 3-quart saucepan, combine sugar, marshmallow creme, evaporated milk and butter. Cook over medium heat, stirring constantly, until mixture boils; continue boiling and stirring for 5 minutes. Remove from heat; stir in vanilla. Immediately stir one-half of hot mixture into peanut butter chips until chips are completely melted; quickly pour into prepared pan. Stir remaining hot mixture into chocolate chips until chips are completely melted. Quickly spread over top of peanut butter layer; cool. Cut into 1-inch squares.
About 5 dozen pieces.

In glass dish: Double-Decker Fudge; on server: Chocolate-Almond Fudge; on counter: Nutty Rich Cocoa Fudge

PIES & PASTRIES

Picture-perfect pies filled with the season's bounty—who can resist them? Choose from an abounding assortment of America's favorites— unbeatable berry, crunchy pecan, light-as-air meringue, scrumptious cherry, luscious chocolate, creamy ice cream, traditional apple plus much more. And for extra-special occasions, try flaky Mini Almond Pastries, homemade Apple Turnovers and fancy Almond Heart Napoleons.

Georgia Peach Pie

Crust
> 10-inch Classic Crisco® Double Crust (see page 461)

Filling
> 1 can (29 ounces) yellow cling peaches in heavy syrup
> 3 tablespoons reserved peach syrup
> 3 tablespoons cornstarch
> 1 cup sugar, divided
> 3 eggs
> ⅓ cup buttermilk
> ½ cup butter or margarine, melted
> 1 teaspoon vanilla

Glaze
> 2 tablespoons butter or margarine, melted
> Sugar

1. **For crust,** prepare recipe and press bottom crust into 10-inch pie plate. Do not bake. Heat oven to 400°F.

2. **For filling,** drain peaches, reserving 3 tablespoons syrup. Set aside. Cut peaches into small pieces. Place in large bowl. Combine cornstarch and 2 to 3 tablespoons sugar. Add 3 tablespoons reserved peach syrup. Add remaining sugar, eggs and buttermilk. Mix well. Stir in ½ cup melted butter and vanilla. Pour over peaches. Stir until peaches are coated. Pour filling into unbaked pie crust. Moisten pastry edge with water.

3. Cover pie with top crust. Cut slits or designs in top crust to allow steam to escape.

4. **For glaze,** brush with 2 tablespoons melted butter. Sprinkle with sugar. Bake at 400°F for 45 minutes or until filling in center is bubbly and crust is golden brown. Cool to room temperature before serving. Refrigerate leftover pie.

One 10-inch Pie

Peach Amaretto Cheese Pie

> 1 (9-inch) unbaked pastry shell
> 1 (8-ounce) package cream cheese, softened
> 1 (14-ounce) can EAGLE® Brand Sweetened Condensed Milk (NOT evaporated milk)
> 2 eggs
> 3 tablespoons amaretto liqueur
> 1½ teaspoons almond extract
> 3 fresh medium peaches, peeled and sliced
> 2 tablespoons BAMA® Peach Preserves

Preheat oven to 375°. Bake pastry shell 15 minutes. In large mixer bowl, beat cheese until fluffy. Gradually beat in sweetened condensed milk until smooth. Add eggs, *2 tablespoons* amaretto and *1 teaspoon* extract; mix well. Pour into pastry shell. Bake 25 minutes or until set. Cool. Arrange peach slices on top. In small saucepan, combine preserves, remaining *1 tablespoon* amaretto and *½ teaspoon* extract. Over low heat, cook and stir until hot. Spoon over top of pie. Chill. Refrigerate leftovers.

Makes one 9-inch pie

Georgia Peach Pie

Mini Fruit Cheese Tarts

Coconut Custard Pie

1 (9-inch) unbaked pastry shell
1 cup flaked coconut
3 eggs
1 (14-ounce) can EAGLE® Brand
 Sweetened Condensed Milk
 (NOT evaporated milk)
1¼ cups hot water
1 teaspoon vanilla extract
¼ teaspoon salt
⅛ teaspoon ground nutmeg

Preheat oven to 425°. Toast ½ cup coconut; set aside. Bake pastry shell 8 minutes; cool slightly. Meanwhile, in medium mixing bowl, beat eggs. Add sweetened condensed milk, water, vanilla, salt and nutmeg; mix well. Stir in remaining ½ cup coconut. Pour into prepared pastry shell. Sprinkle with toasted coconut. Bake 10 minutes. Reduce oven temperature to 350°; continue baking 25 to 30 minutes or until knife inserted near center comes out clean. Cool. Chill if desired. Refrigerate leftovers.
Makes one 9-inch pie.

Raisin Sour Cream Pie

¾ cup sugar
2 tablespoons cornstarch
¼ teaspoon salt
2 eggs, beaten
2 cups dairy sour cream
1 cup SUN-MAID® Raisins
2 tablespoons lemon juice
1 (9-inch) pie shell, baked, or
 crumb crust

In top of double boiler, blend together sugar, cornstarch and salt. In small bowl, combine beaten eggs, 1½ cups of the sour cream, the raisins and lemon juice. Stir into sugar mixture. Set over hot, not boiling, water and cook until thick, stirring frequently. Pour into baked pie shell. When cool, top with remaining ½ cup sour cream. Chill several hours.
Makes one 9-inch pie.

Plum Pudding Pie

⅓ cup plus 2 tablespoons
 KAHLÚA®
½ cup golden raisins
½ cup chopped pitted dates
⅓ cup chopped candied cherries
½ cup chopped walnuts
⅓ cup dark corn syrup
½ teaspoon pumpkin pie spice
¼ cup butter or margarine,
 softened
¼ cup packed brown sugar
2 tablespoons all-purpose flour
¼ teaspoon salt
2 eggs, slightly beaten
1 (9-inch) unbaked pie shell
1 cup whipping cream
 Maraschino cherries (optional)

In medium bowl, combine ⅓ cup of the Kahlúa®, the raisins, dates and cherries; mix well. Cover; let stand 1 to 4 hours. Stir in walnuts, corn syrup and spice. In large bowl, cream butter, sugar, flour and salt. Stir in eggs. Add fruit mixture; blend well. Pour into unbaked pie shell. Bake in preheated 350° oven 35 minutes or until filling is firm and crust is golden. Cool completely on wire rack. When ready to serve, in small bowl, beat whipping cream with remaining 2 tablespoons Kahlúa® just until soft peaks form. Spoon cream into pastry bag fitted with large star tip and pipe decoratively on top. If desired, garnish with maraschino cherries.
Makes 8 servings.

Strawberry Tart Glace

Pastry for 1-crust 9-inch pie
2 8-ounce packages Light
 PHILADELPHIA BRAND®
 Neufchatel Cheese, softened
½ cup sugar
1 tablespoon milk
¼ teaspoon vanilla
1 quart strawberries, hulled
1 tablespoon cornstarch
¼ cup water
 Few drops red food coloring
 (optional)

On lightly floured surface, roll pastry to 12-inch circle. Place in 10-inch quiche dish. Prick bottom and sides of pastry with fork. Bake at 450°, 9 to 11 minutes or until golden brown.
 Combine Neufchatel cheese, ¼ cup sugar, milk and vanilla, mixing at medium speed on electric mixer until well blended. Spread onto bottom of crust. Puree 1 cup strawberries. Top Neufchatel cheese mixture with remaining strawberries. Combine remaining sugar and cornstarch in saucepan; gradually add pureed strawberries and water. Cook, stirring constantly, over medium heat until mixture is clear and thickened. Stir in food coloring. Pour over strawberries; chill.
8 servings.
 Variations: Substitute PHILADELPHIA BRAND® Cream Cheese for Neufchatel Cheese.
 Substitute 9-inch pie plate for 10-inch quiche dish.
 Substitute almond extract for vanilla.

Mini Fruit Cheese Tarts

24 (2- or 3-inch) prepared tart-
 size crusts
1 (8-ounce) package cream
 cheese, softened
1 (14-ounce) can EAGLE® Brand
 Sweetened Condensed Milk
 (NOT evaporated milk)
⅓ cup REALEMON® Lemon Juice
 from Concentrate
1 teaspoon vanilla extract
 Assorted fruit (strawberries,
 blueberries, bananas,
 raspberries, orange
 segments, cherries,
 kiwifruit, grapes, pineapple,
 etc.)
¼ cup BAMA® Apple Jelly,
 melted

Cinnamon Fruit Tart with Sour Cream Filling

In large mixer bowl, beat cheese until fluffy. Gradually beat in sweetened condensed milk until smooth. Stir in ReaLemon® brand and vanilla. Spoon equal portions into crusts. Top with fruit; brush with jelly. Chill 2 hours or until set. Refrigerate leftovers.
Makes 24 tarts.

Cinnamon Fruit Tart with Sour Cream Filling

   1 envelope KNOX® Unflavored
      Gelatine
 ¼ cup cold water
   1 cup (8 ounces) creamed
      cottage cheese
 ¾ cup canned pineapple juice
 ½ cup sour cream
 ½ cup milk
 ¼ cup sugar
   1 teaspoon lemon juice
      Cinnamon Graham Cracker
         Crust (recipe follows)
      Suggested Fresh Fruit*
   2 tablespoons orange or apricot
      marmalade, melted

In small saucepan, sprinkle unflavored gelatine over cold water; let stand 1 minute. Stir over low heat until gelatine is completely dissolved, about 3 minutes.

In blender or food processor, process cottage cheese, pineapple juice, sour cream, milk, sugar and lemon juice until blended. While processing, through feed cap, gradually add gelatine mixture and process until blended. Pour into Cinnamon Graham Cracker Crust; chill until firm, about 3 hours. To serve, top with Suggested Fresh Fruit, then brush with marmalade.
Makes 12 servings, 223 calories per serving.

   Suggested Fresh Fruit: Use any combination of the following to equal 2 cups—sliced strawberries, kiwi or oranges; blueberries or raspberries.
CINNAMON GRAHAM CRACKER CRUST: In small bowl, combine 2 cups graham cracker crumbs, 1 tablespoon sugar, ½ teaspoon ground cinnamon and ¼ cup melted butter. Press into 10-inch tart pan. Bake at 375°, 8 minutes; cool.

Strawberry and Cream Napoleons

   1 package (17¼ ounces) frozen
      puff pastry sheets, thawed
      according to package
      directions
   1 envelope KNOX® Unflavored
      Gelatine
 ¼ cup cold water
   2 cups (1 pint) whipping or
      heavy cream
 ¼ cup raspberry liqueur
 ½ cup confectioners sugar
 ½ cup strawberry preserves,
      heated
   4 cups sliced strawberries
      (about 2 pints)
      Strawberry Glaze (recipe
         follows)

Preheat oven to 425°.

   On lightly floured surface, unfold pastry sheets, then separate, using perforated lines, into 3 rectangles. Cut each rectangle in half crosswise.* Place on ungreased baking sheets and bake 20 minutes or until puffed and golden. On wire rack, cool completely.

   Chill large mixing bowl at least 15 minutes. Meanwhile, in small saucepan, sprinkle unflavored gelatine over cold water; let stand 1 minute. Stir over low heat until gelatine is completely dissolved, about 3 minutes. In chilled bowl, while beating cream on low speed, gradually add gelatine mixture and liqueur, then beat on medium speed until thickened, about 5 minutes. Add sugar, then beat on high speed until soft peaks form, about 2 minutes.

   To serve, with long, serrated knife, cut each pastry rectangle in half horizontally. Reserve the 8 best rectangles for tops. Evenly brush 8 rectangles with ½ preserves, then top with ½ strawberries and ½ cream mixture. Repeat layers, ending with reserved pastry tops. Decoratively drizzle tops with Strawberry Glaze.
Makes 8 large napoleons.

   Hint: For smaller napoleons, cut each pastry rectangle in thirds crosswise and proceed as above.
STRAWBERRY GLAZE: In small bowl, thoroughly blend ½ cup sifted confectioners sugar, 2 teaspoons water and 1 teaspoon strawberry preserves, heated.

Fruit and Cream Cookie Tart

Mom's Summer Fruit Lattice Pie

**1 unbaked double 9-inch pie crust
10 fresh California nectarines or peaches, sliced
½ cup sugar
⅓ cup all-purpose flour
1 teaspoon finely grated lemon peel
Milk and sugar (optional)**

Preheat oven to 425°F. Line 9-inch pie pan with one crust. Cut remaining crust into ½-inch strips. In large bowl, gently toss nectarines with sugar, flour and lemon peel. Spoon into crust. Weave dough strips over top to form lattice crust. Seal and crimp edges. Brush lattice top with milk and sprinkle with sugar, if desired. Place on baking sheet. Bake 10 minutes. Reduce heat to 350°F and bake 45 to 50 minutes or until lattice top is golden brown and fruit is tender. Cool. *Makes 8 servings*

*Favorite recipe from **California Tree Fruit Agreement***

Fruit and Cream Cookie Tart

**Crust
1 package DUNCAN HINES® Golden Sugar Cookie Mix
Filling
1 package (8 ounces) cream cheese, softened
⅓ cup sugar
½ teaspoon vanilla extract
Topping
Peach slices
Banana slices
Fresh blueberries
Grape halves
Kiwifruit slices
Fresh strawberry slices
½ cup apricot preserves, heated and strained**

1. Preheat oven to 350°F.

2. **For crust,** prepare cookie mix following package directions for original recipe. Spread evenly on ungreased 12-inch pizza pan. Bake at 350°F for 14 to 16 minutes or until edges are light brown. Cool completely.

3. **For filling,** combine cream cheese, sugar and vanilla extract in small bowl. Beat at low speed with electric mixer until smooth. Spread on cooled crust. Refrigerate until chilled.

4. **For topping,** dry fruits thoroughly on paper towels. Arrange fruit in circles on chilled crust working from outside edge toward center. Brush fruit with warmed preserves to glaze. Refrigerate until ready to serve.
12 Servings

Tip: To keep bananas and peaches from turning brown, dip slices in lemon juice.

Pastry Chef Tarts

**1 package (10 ounces) pie crust mix
1 egg, beaten
1 to 2 tablespoons cold water
1½ cups cold half and half or milk
1 package (4-serving size) JELL-O® Instant Pudding and Pie Filling, French Vanilla or Vanilla Flavor
Assorted berries or fruit*
Mint leaves (optional)**

PREHEAT oven to 425°. Combine pie crust mix with egg. Add just enough water to form dough. Form 2 to 3 tablespoons dough into a round. Press each round onto bottom and up sides of each 3- to 4-inch tart pan. (Use tart pans with removable bottoms, if possible.) Pierce pastry several times with fork. Place on baking sheet. Bake for 10 minutes or until golden. Cool slightly. Remove tart shells from pans; cool completely on racks.

POUR half and half into small bowl. Add pudding mix. Beat with wire whisk until well blended, 1 to 2 minutes. Spoon into tart shells. Chill until ready to serve.

ARRANGE fruit on pudding. Garnish with mint leaves, if desired. *Makes 10 servings*

*We suggest any variety of berries, mandarin orange sections, melon balls, halved seedless grapes, sliced peaches, kiwifruit or plums.

Note: Individual graham cracker crumb tart shells may be substituted for baked tart shells.

Prep time: 20 minutes
Baking time: 10 minutes

Pastry Chef Tarts

Mixed Berry Pie

Crust
        9-inch Classic Crisco®
        Double Crust
        (recipe follows)

Filling
    2 cups canned or frozen
        blackberries, thawed and
        well drained
    1½ cups canned or frozen
        blueberries, thawed and
        well drained
    ½ cup canned or frozen
        gooseberries, thawed
        and well drained
    ⅛ teaspoon almond extract
    ¼ cup sugar
    3 tablespoons cornstarch

1. **For crust,** prepare recipe and press bottom crust into 9-inch pie plate. Do not bake. Heat oven to 425°F.

2. **For filling,** combine blackberries, blueberries, gooseberries and almond extract in large bowl. Combine sugar and cornstarch. Add to berries. Toss well to mix. Spoon into unbaked pie crust.

3. Cut top crust into leaf shapes and arrange on top of pie *or* cover pie with top crust. Flute edge. Cut slits in top crust, if using, to allow steam to escape.

4. Bake at 425°F for 40 minutes or until filling in center is bubbly and crust is golden brown. Cool until barely warm or to room temperature before serving.   *One 9-inch Pie*

Classic Crisco® Crust

8-, 9- or 10-inch Single Crust
    1⅓ cups all-purpose flour
    ½ teaspoon salt
    ½ cup CRISCO® Shortening
    3 tablespoons cold water

8- or 9-inch Double Crust
    2 cups all-purpose flour
    1 teaspoon salt
    ¾ cup CRISCO® Shortening
    5 tablespoons cold water

10-inch Double Crust
    2⅔ cups all-purpose flour
    1 teaspoon salt
    1 cup CRISCO® Shortening
    7 to 8 tablespoons cold water

1. **For pie dough,** spoon flour into measuring cup and level. Combine flour and salt in medium bowl. Cut in Crisco® using pastry blender (or 2 knives) until all flour is blended to form pea-size chunks. Sprinkle with water, 1 tablespoon at a time. Toss lightly with fork until dough will form a ball.

2. **For single crust,** press dough between hands to form 5- to 6-inch "pancake." Flour lightly on both sides. Roll between sheets of waxed paper on dampened countertop until 1 inch larger than upside-down pie plate. Peel off top sheet. Flip into pie plate. Remove other sheet. Fold dough edge under and flute.

3. For recipes using a **baked** pie crust, heat oven to 425°F. Prick bottom and sides thoroughly with fork (50 times) to prevent shrinkage. Bake 10 to 15 minutes or until lightly browned. (For recipes using an **unbaked** pie crust, follow baking directions given in that recipe.)

4. **For double crust,** divide dough in half. Roll each half separately as described in step 2. Transfer bottom crust to pie plate. Trim edge even with pie plate. Add desired filling to unbaked pie crust. Moisten pastry edge with water. Lift top crust onto filled pie. Trim ½-inch beyond edge of pie plate. Fold top edge under bottom crust. Flute. Cut slits in top crust to allow steam to escape. Bake according to specific recipe directions.

Mixed Berry Pie

Blackberry Ice Cream Pie

Crust
>9-inch Classic Crisco® Single Crust (see page 461)

Filling
>1 package (3 ounces) peach or berry flavor gelatin (not sugar free)
>1 cup boiling water
>1 pint vanilla ice cream, softened
>1¾ cups fresh or frozen dry pack blackberries, partially thawed

1. **For crust,** prepare recipe and bake. Cool.

2. **For filling,** combine gelatin and water in large bowl. Stir until dissolved. Cut ice cream into small chunks. Add to gelatin mixture, a spoonful at a time. Blend with wire whisk after each addition.

3. Dry blackberries between paper towels. Fold into gelatin mixture. Spoon into cooled baked pie crust. Refrigerate or freeze several hours before serving. Refrigerate or freeze leftover pie.
One 9-inch Pie

It's the Berries Pie

>1 quart fresh strawberries, washed and hulled, reserving 8 for garnish
>1 KEEBLER® Ready-Crust Butter Flavored Pie Crust
>1½ cups fresh or frozen raspberries (without sugar)
>2 tablespoons sugar
>1 package (3 ounces) triple berry or raspberry flavored sugar-free gelatin
>1 cup boiling water
>Reduced-calorie whipped topping (optional)

Place whole strawberries, hull side down, in the pie crust. Purée raspberries and sugar in blender or food processor. Press through a sieve to remove seeds. Set raspberry purée aside. Prepare gelatin according to package directions using 1 cup boiling water. Chill until slightly thickened. Stir raspberry purée into gelatin and pour over strawberries. Chill until firm. Garnish with a dollop of whipped topping and a fresh berry, if desired.
Makes 8 servings

Minnesota Blueberry Pie

Crust
>8-inch Classic Crisco® Double Crust (see page 461)

Filling
>⅔ to 1 cup sugar, to taste
>¼ cup all-purpose flour
>½ teaspoon cinnamon
>3 cups fresh blueberries
>1 to 2 tablespoons butter or margarine

1. **For crust,** prepare recipe and press bottom crust into 8-inch pie plate. Do not bake. Heat oven to 375°F.

2. **For filling,** combine sugar, flour and cinnamon. Sprinkle over blueberries in large bowl. Toss lightly to coat well. Spoon into unbaked pie crust. Dot with butter. Moisten pastry edge with water.

3. Cover pie with top crust. Cut slits in top crust to allow steam to escape.

4. Sprinkle lightly with sugar, if desired. Bake at 375°F for 45 to 60 minutes or until filling in center is bubbly and crust is golden brown. Cool until barely warm or to room temperature before serving.
One 8-inch Pie

Patriotic Pie

Crust
>1 package DUNCAN HINES® Blueberry Muffin Mix, separated
>¼ cup butter or margarine, softened

Filling
>1 quart vanilla ice cream, softened (see Tip)
>½ cup crumb mixture, reserved from Crust

Topping
>Can of blueberries from Mix
>1 pint fresh strawberries, rinsed, drained and sliced
>2 tablespoons sugar (optional)

1. Preheat oven to 400°F. Grease 9-inch pie plate.

2. **For crust,** place muffin mix in medium bowl. Cut in butter with pastry blender or 2 knives. Spread evenly in ungreased 9-inch square baking pan. *Do not press.* Bake at 400°F for 10 to 12 minutes. Stir. Reserve ½ cup crumb mixture for filling. Press remaining crumb mixture against bottom and sides of pie plate to form crust. Cool completely.

3. **For filling,** spread ice cream over crust. Sprinkle with reserved crumb mixture. Freeze several hours or until firm.

4. **For topping,** rinse blueberries from Mix with cold water and drain. Combine strawberries and sugar, if desired.

5. To serve, let pie stand 5 minutes at room temperature. Top with blueberries and strawberries. Cut into 8 wedges using sharp knife.
8 Servings

Tip: Ice cream can be softened by allowing to stand at room temperature for 15 minutes or placed in the refrigerator for 30 minutes.

Patriotic Pie

Create-a-Crust Apple Pie

- 2 medium all-purpose apples, pared and sliced (about 2 cups)
- 1 tablespoon REALEMON® Lemon Juice from Concentrate
- ½ cup plus 2 tablespoons biscuit baking mix
- 1 (14-ounce) can EAGLE® Brand Sweetened Condensed Milk (NOT evaporated milk)
- 1½ cups water
- 3 eggs
- ¼ cup margarine or butter, softened
- 1½ teaspoons vanilla extract
- ½ teaspoon ground cinnamon
- ½ teaspoon ground nutmeg

Preheat oven to 350°. In medium bowl, toss apples with ReaLemon® brand, then *2 tablespoons* biscuit mix. Arrange on bottom of buttered 10-inch pie plate. In blender container, combine remaining ingredients. Blend on low speed 3 minutes. Let stand 5 minutes. Pour evenly over apples. Bake 35 to 40 minutes or until golden brown around edge. Cool slightly; serve warm or chilled with vanilla ice cream. Refrigerate leftovers.
Makes one 10-inch pie.

Dutch Apple Raisin Pie

- 1½ cups SUN-MAID® Raisins
- 1 cup water
- ½ cup sugar
- 1 tablespoon all-purpose flour
- ½ teaspoon ground cinnamon
- ¼ teaspoon salt
- 1 tablespoon lemon juice
- 4 cups pared and sliced apples (4 to 6 apples)
- Pastry for double-crust 9-inch pie
- 1 egg, beaten, for glaze
- Sugar, for glaze

In large saucepan over low heat, simmer raisins in water until liquid is almost absorbed, 5 to 7 minutes. Meanwhile, in small bowl, mix sugar, flour, cinnamon and salt. Stir into raisin mixture along with lemon juice and apples. Turn into pastry-lined 9-inch pie plate. Cover with top crust, seal and flute edges. Cut slits for steam to escape. Brush with beaten egg and sprinkle with sugar. Bake in preheated 425°F oven 10 minutes; reduce heat to 350°F and bake 45 to 55 minutes longer or until crust is golden brown. Cool on wire rack. Serve warm or at room temperature.
Makes one 9-inch pie.
   Note: If desired, sprinkle filling with grated Cheddar cheese just before covering with top crust.

Brandied Fruit Pie

- 1 KEEBLER® Ready-Crust® Graham Cracker Pie Crust
- 2 packages (8 ounces each) mixed, pitted dried fruit
- ¾ cup plus 1 tablespoon water
- ¼ cup plus 1 tablespoon brandy
- 5 thin slices lemon
- ¾ cup packed brown sugar
- 1 teaspoon ground cinnamon
- ¼ teaspoon ground nutmeg
- ¼ teaspoon ground cloves
- ¼ teaspoon salt
- ½ cup graham cracker crumbs
- ¼ cup butter or margarine, melted
- Hard sauce or whipped cream (optional)
- Lemon slices for garnish

In medium saucepan, combine dried fruit, ¾ cup of the water, ¼ cup of the brandy and the 5 lemon slices. Simmer over low heat 10 minutes or until liquid is absorbed. Remove and discard lemon slices. Stir in sugar, spices, salt, remaining 1 tablespoon water and remaining 1 tablespoon brandy; pour into pie crust. Sprinkle graham cracker crumbs evenly over top of pie. Drizzle melted butter over crumbs. Bake in preheated 350° oven 30 minutes. Cool on wire rack. Serve warm or at room temperature. If desired, serve with hard sauce or whipped cream and lemon slices.
Makes 8 servings.

Brandied Fruit Pie

Apple Chess Pie

- 1 (9-inch) unbaked pastry shell
- 4 eggs
- 1 (14-ounce) can EAGLE® Brand Sweetened Condensed Milk (NOT evaporated milk)
- 1 cup applesauce
- ½ cup margarine or butter, melted
- ¼ cup REALEMON® Lemon Juice from Concentrate
- 2 tablespoons cornmeal

Preheat oven to 425°. Bake pastry shell 8 minutes; remove from oven. Reduce oven temperature to 350°. In large mixer bowl, beat eggs. Add remaining ingredients except pastry shell; mix well. Pour into prepared pastry shell. Bake 40 to 45 minutes or until knife inserted near center comes out clean. Cool. Serve warm or chilled. Refrigerate leftovers.
Makes one 9-inch pie.

Fresh Strawberry Pie

Microwave Hershey® Bar Pie

Chocolate Crumb Crust
1 HERSHEY'S Milk Chocolate Bar (7 oz.), broken into pieces
¹/₃ cup milk
1¹/₂ cups miniature marshmallows
1 cup (¹/₂ pt.) cold whipping cream
Sweetened whipped cream
Chilled cherry pie filling (optional)

Prepare crumb crust; set aside. In medium microwave-safe bowl, combine chocolate bar pieces, milk and marshmallows. Microwave at HIGH (100%) 1¹/₂ to 2¹/₂ minutes or until chocolate is softened and mixture is melted and smooth when stirred. Cool completely. In small mixer bowl, beat whipping cream until stiff; fold into chocolate mixture. Spoon into crust. Cover; refrigerate several hours or until firm. Garnish with sweetened whipped cream; serve with chilled cherry pie filling, if desired.
8 servings.

Chocolate Crumb Crust

¹/₂ cup butter or margarine
1¹/₂ cups graham cracker crumbs
6 tablespoons HERSHEY'S Cocoa
¹/₃ cup powdered sugar

Grease 9-inch microwave-safe pie plate. In small microwave-safe bowl, microwave butter at HIGH (100%) 1 minute or until melted. Stir in graham cracker crumbs, cocoa and powdered sugar until well blended. Press onto bottom and up side of prepared pie plate. Microwave an additional 1 to 1¹/₂ minutes until bubbly. (Do not overcook.) Cool completely before filling.

Fresh Strawberry Pie

1 (9-inch) baked pastry shell
1¹/₄ cups sugar
1 tablespoon cornstarch
1¹/₂ cups water
3 tablespoons REALEMON® Lemon Juice from Concentrate
1 (4-serving size) package strawberry flavor gelatin
1 quart fresh strawberries, cleaned and hulled

In medium saucepan, combine sugar and cornstarch; add the water and ReaLemon® brand. Over high heat, bring to a boil. Reduce heat; cook and stir until slightly thickened and clear, 4 to 5 minutes. Add gelatin; stir until dissolved. Cool to room temperature. Stir in strawberries; turn into prepared pastry shell. Chill 4 to 6 hours or until set. Refrigerate leftovers.
Makes one 9-inch pie.

Praline Ice Cream Pudding Pie

2 tablespoons light brown sugar
2 tablespoons butter or margarine
¹/₃ cup chopped nuts
1 lightly baked 9-inch pie shell*
1¹/₂ cups cold milk
1 cup (¹/₂ pint) vanilla ice cream, softened
1 package (6-serving size) JELL-O® Butter Pecan Flavor Instant Pudding and Pie Filling

Combine brown sugar, butter and nuts in small saucepan. Heat over medium heat until butter is melted. Pour into pie shell. Bake in preheated 450° oven for 5 minutes or until bubbly. Cool on wire rack.

Combine milk and ice cream in medium bowl until thoroughly blended. Add pie filling mix. With electric mixer at low speed, beat until blended, about 1 minute. Pour immediately over nut mixture in pie shell. Chill until set, about 3 hours. Garnish with whipped topping and pecan halves or chopped nuts, if desired.
Makes one 9-inch pie.

*Decrease recommended baking time by 5 minutes.

Harvest Cherry Pie

Pastry for 2-crust pie
1¹/₃ cups (one-half jar) NONE SUCH® Ready-to-Use Mincemeat (Regular or Brandy & Rum)
³/₄ cup chopped nuts
1 (21-ounce) can cherry pie filling
1 egg yolk plus 2 tablespoons water, optional

Place rack in lower half of oven; preheat oven to 425°. In small bowl, stir together mincemeat and nuts; turn into pastry-lined 9-inch pie plate. Spoon cherry pie filling over mincemeat. Cover with top crust; cut slits near center. Seal and flute. For a more golden crust, mix egg yolk and water; brush over entire surface of pie. Bake 25 to 30 minutes or until golden brown. Serve warm or cool. Garnish as desired.
Makes one 9-inch pie.

Strawberry Cheese Pie

- 1 (9-inch) baked pastry shell or graham cracker crumb crust
- 1 (8-ounce) package cream cheese, softened
- 1 (14-ounce) can EAGLE® Brand Sweetened Condensed Milk (NOT evaporated milk)
- ⅓ cup REALEMON® Lemon Juice from Concentrate
- 1 teaspoon vanilla extract
- 1 quart fresh strawberries, cleaned and hulled (about 1½ pounds)
- 1 (16-ounce) package prepared strawberry glaze, chilled

In large mixer bowl, beat cheese until fluffy. Gradually beat in sweetened condensed milk until smooth. Stir in ReaLemon® brand and vanilla. Pour into prepared pastry shell. Chill 3 hours or until set. Top with strawberries and desired amount of glaze. Refrigerate leftovers.

Makes one 9-inch pie

Raspberry Crumble Tart

- 2 cups all-purpose flour
- ¾ cup granulated sugar
- ¾ cup LAND O LAKES® Butter, softened
- 3 egg yolks
- 1 teaspoon vanilla
- ½ cup coarsely chopped blanched almonds *or* pine nuts
- ½ cup raspberry *or* favorite flavor preserves
- 1 teaspoon grated lemon peel
  Powdered sugar
  Fresh raspberries
  Sweetened whipped cream

Heat oven to 350°. In large mixer bowl combine flour, granulated sugar, butter, egg yolks and vanilla. Beat at low speed, scraping bowl often, until well mixed, 2 to 3 minutes. By hand, stir in almonds. *Reserve 1½ cups mixture;* set aside. Press remaining mixture onto bottom of ungreased 9-inch removable bottom tart pan. Bake 10 minutes. Spread preserves to within ½ inch from edge; sprinkle with lemon peel. Crumble reserved mixture over

preserves. Continue baking for 30 to 35 minutes or until lightly browned. Cool completely; remove from tart pan. Sprinkle with powdered sugar. Serve with fresh raspberries and sweetened whipped cream.

Makes 10 to 12 servings

Cinnamony Apple Pie

Crust
- 9-inch Classic Crisco® Double Crust (see page 461)

Filling
- 1 tablespoon lemon juice
- 1 tablespoon cinnamon candies, crushed
- ⅓ cup honey
- 1 teaspoon cinnamon
- 3 to 4 cups thinly sliced, peeled Gravenstein or other baking apples (about 1½ pounds or 3 to 4 medium)
- 1 tablespoon butter or margarine

Glaze
- 1 teaspoon half-and-half or milk

1. **For crust,** prepare recipe and press bottom crust into 9-inch pie plate. Do not bake. Heat oven to 450°F. Reserve dough scraps for cutouts, if desired.

2. **For filling,** heat lemon juice in small saucepan. Add crushed candies. Stir until dissolved. Stir in honey and cinnamon. Arrange apples in unbaked pie crust. Drizzle with honey mixture. Dot with butter. Moisten pastry edge with water.

3. Cover pie with top crust. Cut slits in top crust to allow steam to escape. Decorate with pastry cutouts, if desired.

4. **For glaze,** brush with half-and-half. Place pie in oven. *Reduce oven temperature to 350°F.* Bake for 1 hour or until filling in center is bubbly and crust is golden brown. Cool until barely warm or to room temperature before serving.

One 9-inch Pie

Cinnamony Apple Pie

Apple Gingerbread Pie

Crust
½ cup CRISCO® Shortening
¼ cup sugar
1¼ cups all-purpose flour
½ cup ground pecans
½ teaspoon ginger

Filling
4½ cups thinly sliced, peeled McIntosh or Granny Smith apples (about 1¾ pounds or 4 to 5 medium)
3 tablespoons honey
2 tablespoons water
⅓ cup golden raisins
⅓ cup currants
½ to 1 teaspoon apple pie spice, to taste

Topping
1 cup whipping cream, whipped
2 tablespoons finely chopped pecans

1. **For crust,** heat oven to 375°F. Cream Crisco® and sugar until light, using spoon. Stir in flour, ground pecans and ginger. Blend until mixture is uniform. Press into 9-inch pie plate. Bake at 375°F for 10 to 12 minutes or until lightly browned. Cool.

2. **For filling,** combine apples, honey and water in large saucepan. Simmer, covered, 20 minutes or until apples are tender. Stir in raisins, currants and apple pie spice. Cool. Spoon into cooled baked pie crust.

3. **For topping,** spread whipped cream over filling. Sprinkle with chopped pecans. Refrigerate until ready to serve. Refrigerate leftover pie.   *One 9-inch Pie*

Sour Cherry Pie

Sour Cherry Pie

Filling
2 cans (16 ounces each) pitted red tart cherries
1 cup reserved cherry liquid
1½ cups sugar, divided
⅓ cup cornstarch
⅛ teaspoon salt
1 tablespoon butter or margarine
¼ teaspoon almond extract
3 to 4 drops red food color

Crust and Glaze
9-inch Classic Crisco® Double Crust (see page 461)
Milk
Sugar

1. **For filling,** drain cherries in large strainer over bowl, reserving 1 cup liquid. Combine ¾ cup sugar, cornstarch and salt in medium saucepan. Stir in reserved 1 cup cherry liquid. Cook and stir on medium heat 3 to 4 minutes or until mixture thickens. Remove from heat. Stir in cherries, remaining ¾ cup sugar, butter, almond extract and food color. Refrigerate 1 hour.

2. **For crust,** heat oven to 400°F. Prepare recipe and press bottom crust into 9-inch pie plate. Spoon in filling. Cover pie with top crust. Cut slits in top crust to allow steam to escape.

3. **For glaze,** brush with milk. Sprinkle with sugar. Bake at 400°F for 10 minutes. *Reduce oven temperature to 350°F.* Bake for 40 to 45 minutes or until filling in center is bubbly and crust is golden brown. Cool until barely warm or to room temperature before serving.
One 9-inch Pie

Sweet Potato Pecan Pie

1 (9-inch) unbaked pastry shell
1 pound (2 medium) yams or sweet potatoes, cooked and peeled
¼ cup margarine or butter
1 (14-ounce) can EAGLE® Brand Sweetened Condensed Milk (NOT evaporated milk)
1 teaspoon grated orange rind
1 teaspoon vanilla extract
1 teaspoon ground cinnamon
½ teaspoon ground nutmeg
¼ teaspoon salt
2 eggs
Pecan Topping

Preheat oven to 350°. In large mixer bowl, beat hot yams with margarine until smooth. Add remaining ingredients except pastry shell and Pecan Topping; mix well. Pour into pastry shell. Bake 30 minutes. Remove from oven; spoon Pecan Topping evenly over top. Return to oven; bake 20 to 25 minutes or until golden brown. Cool. Serve warm or chilled. Refrigerate leftovers.
Makes one 9-inch pie.
PECAN TOPPING: In small mixer bowl, combine 1 egg, 3 tablespoons dark corn syrup, 3 tablespoons firmly packed light brown sugar, 1 tablespoon margarine, melted, and ½ teaspoon maple flavoring; mix well. Stir in 1 cup chopped pecans.

Banana Mocha Ice Cream Pie

1 pint chocolate ice cream, softened
1 pint coffee ice cream, softened
¼ cup coffee-flavored liqueur
1 firm, medium DOLE® Banana, peeled, diced
Chocolate Cookie Crust (recipe follows)

Combine softened ice creams with liqueur. Fold in diced banana. Pour into prepared Chocolate Cookie Crust. Freeze until firm. Garnish with sliced bananas and mocha-flavored candies.
Makes one 8- or 9-inch pie.
CHOCOLATE COOKIE CRUST: Combine 2 cups chocolate wafer crumbs and ½ cup melted margarine. Blend well. Pour into buttered 8- or 9-inch pie pan. Press evenly over bottom and sides of pan. Chill.

Banana Layered Pie

Classic Banana Cream Pie

2 eggs
½ cup plus 2 tablespoons sugar
¼ cup flour
2 cups milk, scalded
½ cup margarine
1 tablespoon vanilla extract
5 firm, medium DOLE® Bananas
1 baked 9-inch pastry shell
1 cup whipping cream

In heavy saucepan, beat eggs, ½ cup sugar and flour until pale lemon color. Gradually beat hot milk into egg mixture. Cook, stirring constantly, over medium heat until sauce thickens, about 5 minutes. Remove from heat. Stir in margarine and vanilla until blended. Place plastic wrap directly on surface of filling to cover. Cool.

To assemble pie, slice bananas; reserve a few slices for garnish, if desired. Fold remaining bananas into filling; spoon into baked pastry shell. Beat cream with remaining 2 tablespoons sugar until soft peaks form. Spread on top of pie.
Makes 8 servings.

Banana Layered Pie

2¼ cups cold milk
1 package (6-serving size) JELL-O® Vanilla Flavor Instant Pudding and Pie Filling
1 baked 9-inch pie shell or prepared graham cracker crumb crust, cooled
2 medium bananas
½ cup thawed COOL WHIP® Non-Dairy Whipped Topping
Lemon juice

Pour cold milk into bowl. Add pie filling mix. With electric mixer at low speed, beat until blended, about 1 minute. Pour ½ cup of the pie filling into pie shell.

Slice 1 banana; arrange slices on filling in shell. Top with ¾ cup of the pie filling.

Blend whipped topping into remaining pie filling. Spread over filling in pie shell. Chill about 3 hours. Slice remaining banana; brush with lemon juice. Arrange banana slices on pie. Garnish with additional whipped topping, if desired.
Makes one 9-inch pie.

Peach Surprise Pie

**2 8-ounce packages Light
 PHILADELPHIA BRAND®
 Neufchatel Cheese, softened
¼ cup sugar
½ teaspoon vanilla
 Pastry for 1-crust 9-inch pie,
 baked
1 16-ounce can peach slices,
 drained
¼ cup KRAFT® Red Raspberry
 Preserves
1 teaspoon lemon juice**

Combine Neufchatel cheese, sugar and vanilla, mixing until well blended. Spread onto bottom of crust; chill several hours or overnight. Top with peaches just before serving. Combine preserves and juice, mixing until well blended. Spoon over peaches. Garnish with fresh mint, if desired.
6 to 8 servings.

Impossible Pie

**1 (14-ounce) can EAGLE® Brand
 Sweetened Condensed Milk
 (NOT evaporated milk)
1½ cups water
½ cup biscuit baking mix
3 eggs
¼ cup margarine or butter,
 softened
1½ teaspoons vanilla extract
1 cup flaked coconut**

Preheat oven to 350°. In blender container, combine all ingredients except coconut. Blend on low speed 3 minutes. Pour mixture into buttered 10-inch pie plate; let stand 5 minutes. Sprinkle coconut over top. Carefully place in oven; bake 35 to 40 minutes or until knife inserted near edge comes out clean. Cool slightly; serve warm or cool. Refrigerate leftovers.
Makes one 10-inch pie.

Tip: Pie can be baked in buttered 9-inch pie plate but it will be extremely full.

Impossible Lemon Pie: Add 3 tablespoons REALEMON® Lemon Juice from Concentrate and 1 tablespoon grated lemon rind to ingredients in blender.

Almond Ginger Ice Cream Pie

**Almond Crust (recipe follows)
1 can (20 ounces) DOLE®
 Crushed Pineapple in Juice
1 quart vanilla ice cream,
 softened
½ cup DOLE® Blanched Slivered
 Almonds, toasted
¼ cup crystallized ginger,
 chopped
3 tablespoons almond-flavored
 liqueur
1 tablespoon grated orange peel**

Prepare Almond Crust. Drain pineapple; reserve all but ½ cup juice. In large bowl, combine pineapple, reserved juice and remaining ingredients. Spoon into prepared crust; freeze overnight or until firm. Let soften slightly before slicing. Garnish as desired.
Makes 8 to 10 servings.
ALMOND CRUST: In bowl, combine 1½ cups vanilla wafer crumbs, ⅔ cup toasted ground Dole® Almonds and ¼ cup melted margarine. Press onto bottom and sides of 9-inch pie plate. Freeze until ready to use.

Peachy Mince Pie with Cheddar Crust

**1 (9-ounce) package pie crust
 mix
1 cup (4 ounces) shredded
 sharp Cheddar cheese
1 jar NONE SUCH® Ready-to-Use
 Mincemeat (Regular *or*
 Brandy & Rum)
1 (16-ounce) can sliced peaches,
 drained
1 egg yolk plus 2 tablespoons
 water, optional**

Place rack in lower half of oven; preheat oven to 425°. Prepare pie crust mix as package directs for 2-crust pie, adding cheese. Turn mincemeat into pastry-lined 9-inch pie plate. Top with peach slices. Cover with top crust; cut slits near center. Seal and flute. For a more golden crust, mix egg yolk and water; brush over entire surface of pie. Bake 20 minutes or until golden. Serve warm or cool. Garnish as desired.
Makes one 9-inch pie.

Peach Surprise Pie

"Door County" Cherry Pie

Crust
> 9-inch Classic Crisco® Single Crust (see page 461)

Filling
> 1 package (8 ounces) cream cheese, softened
> ¾ cup confectioners sugar
> ½ to 1 teaspoon vanilla, to taste
> ½ teaspoon almond extract
> 1 cup whipping cream, whipped
> ⅛ to ¼ cup chopped, slivered almonds, to taste

Topping
> 2½ cups pitted "Door County" (or other variety) cherries (fresh or frozen)
> ½ cup cherry juice*
> 2 tablespoons granulated sugar (tart cherries will require more sugar)
> 1½ tablespoons cornstarch
> 1 tablespoon quick-cooking tapioca
> ½ teaspoon vanilla
> ½ teaspoon almond extract
> 3 or 4 drops red food color
> Whipped cream (optional)

1. **For crust,** prepare recipe and bake. Cool.

2. **For filling,** combine cream cheese and confectioners sugar in large bowl. Beat at medium speed of electric mixer until smooth. Beat in ½ to 1 teaspoon vanilla and ½ teaspoon almond extract. Fold in whipped cream and nuts. Spoon into cooled baked pie crust. Refrigerate until firm.

3. **For topping,** combine cherries, cherry juice, granulated sugar, cornstarch, tapioca, ½ teaspoon vanilla, ½ teaspoon almond extract and food color in medium saucepan. Cook and stir on medium heat until mixture comes to a boil. Boil 6 minutes. Remove from heat. Cool until

Key Lime Pie (left) and Banana Cream Pie (right)

thickened. Spread over filling. Garnish with whipped cream, if desired. Refrigerate leftover pie.

One 9-inch Pie

*Thaw cherries, if frozen. Mash and press additional cherries through large strainer over bowl to obtain ½ cup juice.

Classic Rhubarb Pie

Crust
> 9-inch Classic Crisco® Double Crust (see page 461)

Filling
> 4 cups fresh or thawed frozen rhubarb, cut into ½- to ¾-inch pieces
> 1⅓ to 1½ cups sugar, to taste
> ⅓ cup all-purpose flour
> 2 tablespoons butter or margarine

Glaze
> 1 tablespoon milk
> Sugar

1. **For crust,** prepare recipe and press bottom crust into 9-inch pie plate leaving overhang. Do not bake. Heat oven to 400°F.

2. **For filling,** combine rhubarb and sugar in large bowl. Mix well. Stir in flour. Spoon into unbaked pie crust. Dot with butter. Moisten pastry edge with water.

3. Cover pie with woven lattice top or top crust. Flute edge. Cut slits in top crust, if using, to allow steam to escape.

4. **For glaze,** brush with milk. Sprinkle with sugar. Cover edge with foil to prevent overbrowning. Bake at 400°F for 20 minutes. *Reduce oven temperature to 325°F.* Remove foil. Bake 30 minutes or until filling in center is bubbly and crust is golden brown (if using frozen rhubarb bake 60 to 70 minutes). Cool until barely warm or to room temperature before serving.

One 9-inch Pie

Banana Cream Pie

- 1 (9-inch) baked pastry shell
- 3 tablespoons cornstarch
- 1⅔ cups water
- 1 (14-ounce) can EAGLE® Brand Sweetened Condensed Milk (NOT evaporated milk)
- 3 egg *yolks*, beaten
- 2 tablespoons margarine or butter
- 1 teaspoon vanilla extract
- 3 medium bananas
  REALEMON® Lemon Juice from Concentrate
- 1 cup (½ pint) BORDEN® or MEADOW GOLD® Whipping Cream, stiffly whipped

In heavy saucepan, dissolve cornstarch in water; stir in sweetened condensed milk and egg *yolks*. Cook and stir until thickened and bubbly. Remove from heat; add margarine and vanilla. Cool slightly. Slice *2 bananas*; dip in ReaLemon® brand and drain. Arrange on bottom of prepared pastry shell. Pour filling over bananas; cover. Chill until set. Spread top with whipped cream. Slice remaining banana; dip in ReaLemon® brand, drain and garnish top of pie. Refrigerate leftovers.

Makes one 9-inch pie

Key Lime Pie

- 1 (9- or 10-inch) baked pastry shell *or* graham cracker crumb crust*
- 6 egg *yolks*
- 2 (14-ounce) cans EAGLE® Brand Sweetened Condensed Milk (NOT evaporated milk)
- 1 (8-ounce) bottle REALIME® Lime Juice from Concentrate
  Yellow or green food coloring, optional
  BORDEN® or MEADOW GOLD® Whipping Cream, stiffly whipped *or* whipped topping

Preheat oven to 325°. In large mixer bowl, beat egg *yolks* with sweetened condensed milk. Stir in ReaLime® brand and food coloring if desired. Pour into prepared pastry shell; bake 40 minutes. Cool. Chill. Top with whipped cream. Garnish as desired. Refrigerate leftovers.

Makes one 9- or 10-inch pie

*If using frozen packaged pie shell or 6-ounce packaged graham cracker crumb pie crust, use 1 can Eagle® Brand Sweetened Condensed Milk, 3 egg *yolks* and ½ cup ReaLime® brand. Bake 30 minutes. Proceed as above.

Classic Lemon Meringue Pie

Crust
- 9-inch Classic Crisco® Single Crust (see page 461)

Filling
- 1½ cups sugar
- 3 tablespoons plus 1½ teaspoons cornstarch
- 1½ cups water
- 4 egg yolks, lightly beaten
- ½ cup lemon juice
- 3 tablespoons butter or margarine
- 2 tablespoons grated lemon peel

Meringue
- 4 egg whites
- ¼ teaspoon cream of tartar
- ½ cup sugar
- ½ teaspoon vanilla

1. **For crust,** prepare recipe and bake. Cool. Heat oven to 375°F.

2. **For filling,** combine 1½ cups sugar and cornstarch in medium saucepan. Stir in water gradually. Cook and stir on medium heat until mixture thickens and boils. Add about one-third of hot mixture to egg yolks. Mix well. Return to saucepan. Cook and stir 2 minutes. Stir in lemon juice, butter and lemon peel. Spoon into cooled baked crust.

3. **For meringue,** beat egg whites and cream of tartar at high speed of electric mixer until soft peaks form. Beat in ½ cup sugar, 1 tablespoon at a time, until sugar is dissolved and stiff peaks form. Beat in vanilla. Spread over filling, covering completely and sealing to edge of pie.

4. Bake at 375°F for 10 to 15 minutes or until meringue is lightly browned. Cool to room temperature before serving. Refrigerate leftover pie.

One 9-inch Pie

Classic Lemon Meringue Pie

Cherry Cheese Pie

- 1 (9-inch) graham cracker crumb crust
- 1 (8-ounce) package cream cheese, softened
- 1 (14-ounce) can EAGLE® Brand Sweetened Condensed Milk (NOT evaporated milk)
- 1/3 cup REALEMON® Lemon Juice from Concentrate
- 1 teaspoon vanilla extract
  Canned cherry pie filling, chilled

In large bowl, beat cheese until fluffy. Gradually add sweetened condensed milk; beat until smooth. Stir in ReaLemon® brand and vanilla. Pour into prepared crust. Chill 3 hours or until set. Top with desired amount of pie filling before serving. Refrigerate leftovers.
Makes one 9-inch pie.

Topping Variations:

Ambrosia: In small saucepan, combine 1/2 cup BAMA® Peach or Apricot preserves, 1/4 cup flaked coconut, 2 tablespoons orange-flavored liqueur and 2 teaspoons cornstarch; cook and stir until thickened. Remove from heat. Chill thoroughly. Arrange fresh orange sections (1 or 2 oranges) on top of pie; drizzle with sauce.
Makes about 1/2 cup.

Glazed Strawberry: In saucepan, combine 3 tablespoons BAMA® Apple Jelly and 1 tablespoon ReaLemon® brand. Cook and stir until jelly melts. Combine 1/2 teaspoon cornstarch and 1 tablespoon water; add to jelly mixture. Cook and stir until thickened and clear. Cool 10 minutes. Arrange sliced strawberries over top of pie; spoon glaze over strawberries.

Cranberry Nut: In small bowl, combine 1 cup chilled cranberry-orange relish, 1/2 cup chopped walnuts and 1 teaspoon grated orange rind. Spread over pie. Garnish with orange twists if desired.
Makes about 1 cup.

ReaLemon Meringue Pie

- 1 (9-inch) baked pastry shell
- 1 2/3 cups sugar
- 6 tablespoons cornstarch
- 1/2 cup REALEMON® Lemon Juice from Concentrate
- 4 eggs, separated*
- 1 1/2 cups boiling water
- 2 tablespoons margarine or butter
- 1/4 teaspoon cream of tartar
  Mint leaves, optional

Preheat oven to 350°. In heavy saucepan, combine 1 1/3 cups sugar and cornstarch; add ReaLemon® brand. In small bowl, beat egg yolks; add to lemon mixture. Gradually add water, stirring constantly. Over medium heat, cook and stir until mixture boils and thickens, about 8 to 10 minutes. Remove from heat. Add margarine; stir until melted. Pour into prepared pastry shell. In small mixer bowl, beat egg whites with cream of tartar until soft peaks form; gradually add remaining 1/3 cup sugar, beating until stiff but not dry. Spread on top of pie, sealing carefully to edge of shell. Bake 12 to 15 minutes or until golden brown. Cool. Chill before serving. Garnish with mint if desired. Refrigerate leftovers.
Makes one 9-inch pie.

*Use only Grade A clean, uncracked eggs.

Easy Chocolate Mousse Pie

- Graham Cracker Crust (recipe follows)
- 1 package (8 oz.) cream cheese, softened
- 1/2 cup HERSHEY'S Cocoa
- 1 cup powdered sugar
- 1 1/2 teaspoons vanilla extract
- 2 cups (1 pt.) whipping cream
  Chocolate curls and sweetened whipped cream (optional)

Prepare Graham Cracker Crust; set aside. In large mixer bowl, beat cream cheese and cocoa until fluffy and well blended. Gradually add powdered sugar; blend well. Stir in vanilla. In small mixer bowl, beat whipping cream until stiff; fold into cheese mixture. Pour into cooled crust; refrigerate until firm. Garnish with chocolate curls and sweetened whipped cream, if desired.
8 servings.

Graham Cracker Crust

- 1 1/2 cups graham cracker crumbs
- 1/3 cup butter or margarine, melted
- 3 tablespoons sugar

Heat oven to 350°F. In small bowl, stir together graham cracker crumbs, butter and sugar. Press mixture firmly onto bottom and up side of 9-inch pie pan. Bake 10 minutes; cool.

Eggnog Pie

- 1 cup cold dairy or canned eggnog
- 1 package (6-serving size) JELL-O® Vanilla Flavor Instant Pudding and Pie Filling
- 1 tablespoon rum or 1/4 teaspoon rum extract
- 1/4 teaspoon nutmeg
- 3 1/2 cups (8 ounces) COOL WHIP® Non-Dairy Whipped Topping, thawed
- 1 prepared 8- or 9-inch graham cracker crumb crust, cooled

Pour cold eggnog into bowl. Add pie filling mix, rum and nutmeg. With electric mixer at low speed, beat until blended, about 1 minute. Let stand 5 minutes. Fold in 2 cups of the whipped topping. Spoon into pie crust. Chill until firm, about 2 hours. Garnish with remaining whipped topping. Sprinkle with additional nutmeg, if desired.
Makes one 8- or 9-inch pie.

ReaLemon Meringue Pie

Berry-Bottomed Walnut Pie

Cranberry Filling (recipe
    follows)
2 eggs
¾ cup dark corn syrup
⅓ cup packed brown sugar
3 tablespoons butter or
    margarine, melted
1 teaspoon grated orange peel
2 cups DIAMOND® Walnuts
1 (9-inch) unbaked pie shell
    Sweetened whipped cream, for
    garnish

Prepare Cranberry Filling; cool. In
medium bowl, beat eggs, corn syrup,
sugar, butter and orange peel. Mix in
walnuts. Spread Cranberry Filling
evenly in pie shell. Top with walnut
mixture. Bake in preheated 350°F
oven about 45 minutes or until filling
is set and crust is browned. Cool on
wire rack. Serve at room temperature.
Top with sweetened whipped cream, if
desired.
Makes one 9-inch pie.
CRANBERRY FILLING: In medium
saucepan, combine 1½ cups fresh
cranberries, 6 tablespoons orange
juice and 3 tablespoons granulated
sugar. Bring to boil over high heat.
Reduce heat to medium; cook 3 minutes. In small dish, mix 2 teaspoons
cornstarch with 1 tablespoon water.
Stir into cranberry mixture. Cook and
stir until mixture is the consistency of
thick jam.

Simply Superb Pecan Pie

3 eggs, beaten
1 cup sugar
½ cup dark corn syrup
1 teaspoon vanilla
6 tablespoons butter or
    margarine, melted, cooled
1 cup pecan pieces or halves
1 (9-inch) unbaked pie shell

In large bowl, beat eggs, sugar, corn
syrup, vanilla and butter. Stir in pecans. Pour into unbaked pie shell.
Bake in preheated 350° oven 45 to 60
minutes or until knife inserted halfway between outside and center
comes out clean. Cool on wire rack.
Makes one 9-inch pie.

*Favorite recipe from National Pecan Mar-
keting Council, Inc.*

Fluffy Orange Pie

Chess Pie

½ cup butter or margarine,
    softened
½ cup packed brown sugar
½ cup granulated sugar
4 eggs
½ teaspoon salt
1 teaspoon grated lemon peel
1 teaspoon lemon juice
1 teaspoon vanilla
1 cup finely chopped DIAMOND®
    Walnuts
1 cup finely chopped SUN-
    MAID® Raisins
1 (9-inch) unbaked pie shell
Walnut Cream Topping:
1 cup whipping cream
2 tablespoons powdered sugar
½ cup finely chopped or ground
    DIAMOND® Walnuts

In medium bowl, cream butter and
brown and granulated sugars until
fluffy. Beat in eggs, one at a time, until well blended. Stir in salt, lemon
peel and juice, vanilla, walnuts and
raisins. (Mixture will appear slightly
curdled.) Pour into unbaked pie shell.
Bake, below oven center, in preheated
350°F oven 40 to 45 minutes or until
just barely set in center. Top will be a
deep brown. Cool on wire rack. Serve
with Walnut Cream Topping.
Makes 8 servings.

To prepare Walnut Cream Topping:
In medium bowl, beat cream until soft
peaks form. Fold in powdered sugar
and walnuts.

Fluffy Orange Pie

2 cups vanilla wafer crumbs
    (about 50 wafers)
⅓ cup margarine or butter,
    melted
1 (8-ounce) package cream
    cheese, softened
1 (14-ounce) can EAGLE® Brand
    Sweetened Condensed Milk
    (NOT evaporated milk)
1 (6-ounce) can frozen orange
    juice concentrate, thawed
1 cup (½ pint) BORDEN® or
    MEADOW GOLD® Whipping
    Cream, whipped

Combine crumbs and margarine;
press firmly on bottom and up side of
9-inch pie plate. Chill. Meanwhile, in
large mixer bowl, beat cheese until
fluffy; gradually beat in sweetened
condensed milk then juice concentrate until smooth. Fold in whipped
cream. Pile into crust. Chill 2 hours
or until set. Garnish as desired. Refrigerate leftovers.
Makes one 9-inch pie.

Classic Meringue Pie

- ⅔ **cup sugar**
- ⅓ **cup flour**
- ½ **teaspoon salt**
- 2¾ **cups milk**
- 2 **squares BAKER'S®**
  Unsweetened Chocolate
- 3 **eggs, separated**
- 2 **teaspoons butter or margarine**
- 2 **teaspoons vanilla**
- 1 **baked 9-inch Pie Shell, cooled**
  (recipe follows)
- 6 **tablespoons sugar**

Mix ⅔ cup sugar, the flour and salt in saucepan. Gradually stir in milk; add chocolate. Cook and stir over medium heat until mixture is smooth and thickened; then cook and stir 5 minutes longer. Remove from heat. Beat egg yolks slightly. Stir a small amount of the hot mixture into egg yolks, mixing well. Return to remaining hot mixture in saucepan. Cook 2 minutes longer. Blend in butter and vanilla. Cover surface with plastic wrap and cool 30 minutes without stirring. Pour into pie shell.

Beat egg whites until foamy throughout. Gradually add 6 tablespoons sugar and continue beating until meringue forms stiff peaks. Pile lightly on filling; then spread to edge of pie shell to seal well. Bake at 425° for 8 minutes, or until meringue is lightly browned. Cool to room temperature before serving.
Makes one 9-inch pie.

Pie Shell

- 1¼ **cups flour**
- ½ **teaspoon salt**
- ½ **cup shortening**
- 3 **tablespoons (about) cold water**

Mix flour and salt in bowl. Lightly cut in shortening with a pastry blender until mixture resembles coarse meal. Sprinkle in water, a small amount at a time, mixing lightly with pastry blender or fork until all particles are moistened and cling together when pastry is pressed into a ball. Cover with a damp cloth and let stand a few minutes. Roll pastry thin (less than ⅛ inch) on lightly floured board. Line a 7-, 8- or 9-inch pie pan with pastry. Trim 1 inch larger than pan; fold under to form standing rim; flute edge.

For a baked pie shell, prick pastry thoroughly with fork. Bake at 425° for 12 to 15 minutes or until lightly browned. Cool.

Frozen Peanut Butter Pie

- 3½ **cups (8 ounces) COOL WHIP®**
  Non-Dairy Whipped Topping,
  thawed
- 1 **prepared 9-inch graham**
  cracker crumb crust, cooled
- ⅓ **cup strawberry jam**
- 1 **cup cold milk**
- ½ **cup chunky peanut butter**
- 1 **package (4-serving size)**
  JELL-O® Vanilla Flavor
  Instant Pudding and Pie
  Filling

Spread 1 cup of the whipped topping in bottom of pie crust; freeze for about 10 minutes. Carefully spoon jam over whipped topping.

Gradually add milk to peanut butter in bowl, blending until smooth. Add pie filling mix. With electric mixer at low speed, beat until well blended, 1 to 2 minutes. Fold in remaining whipped topping. Spoon over jam in pie crust. Freeze until firm, about 4 hours. Garnish with additional whipped topping and chopped nuts, if desired.
Makes one 9-inch pie.

Frozen Peach Cream Pies

- 1 **(8-ounce) package cream**
  cheese, softened
- 1 **(14-ounce) can EAGLE® Brand**
  Sweetened Condensed Milk
  (NOT evaporated milk)
- 2 **cups chopped pared fresh,**
  canned or frozen peaches,
  pureed (about 1½ cups)
- 1 **tablespoon REALEMON®**
  Lemon Juice from
  Concentrate
- ¼ **teaspoon almond extract**
  Few drops yellow and red food
  coloring, optional
- 1 **(8-ounce) container frozen**
  non-dairy whipped topping,
  thawed
- 2 **(6-ounce) packaged graham**
  cracker crumb crusts
  Additional peach slices

In large mixer bowl, beat cheese until fluffy. Gradually beat in sweetened condensed milk, then pureed peaches, ReaLemon® brand, extract and food coloring if desired. Fold in whipped topping. Pour equal portions into crusts. Freeze 4 hours or until firm. Remove from freezer 5 minutes before serving. Garnish with additional peaches. Return ungarnished leftovers to freezer.
Makes 2 pies.

Frozen Peach Cream Pies

Fresh Pineapple Pie

    Nut Crust (recipe follows)
    1 large DOLE® Fresh Pineapple
    ½ cup sugar
    2 tablespoons cornstarch
    1 teaspoon grated lemon peel
    ⅛ teaspoon ground nutmeg
    1½ cups water
    3 drops yellow food coloring,
        optional

Prepare Nut Crust. Twist crown from pineapple. Cut pineapple lengthwise into quarters. Remove fruit from shells with curved knife. Trim off core and cut fruit into bite-size chunks. In large saucepan, combine sugar, cornstarch, lemon peel and nutmeg. Stir in water and food coloring. Cook, stirring constantly, until sauce is clear and thickened. Remove from heat. Add pineapple. Cool. Spoon pineapple mixture into prepared crust. Refrigerate, covered, overnight.
Makes 6 to 8 servings.
NUT CRUST: Preheat oven to 400°F. In large bowl, combine 1¾ cups vanilla wafer crumbs, ⅔ cup ground toasted walnuts, 5 tablespoons melted margarine and 1 tablespoon sugar. Press onto bottom and sides of 9-inch pie plate. Bake in preheated oven 8 minutes. Cool.

Margarita Pie

    ½ cup margarine or butter
    1¼ cups finely crushed pretzels
    ¼ cup sugar
    1 (14-ounce) can EAGLE® Brand
        Sweetened Condensed Milk
        (NOT evaporated milk)
    ⅓ cup REALIME® Lime Juice
        from Concentrate
    2 to 4 tablespoons tequila
    2 tablespoons triple sec or other
        orange-flavored liqueur
    1 cup (½ pint) BORDEN® or
        MEADOW GOLD® Whipping
        Cream, whipped
    Additional whipped cream,
        orange twists and mint
        leaves or pretzels for
        garnish, optional

In small saucepan, melt margarine; stir in pretzel crumbs and sugar. Mix well. Press crumbs on bottom and up side of buttered 9-inch pie plate; chill. In large bowl, combine sweetened condensed milk, ReaLime® brand, tequila and triple sec; mix well. Fold in whipped cream. Pour into prepared crust. Freeze or chill until firm, 4 hours in freezer or 2 hours in refrigerator. Garnish as desired. Refrigerate or freeze leftovers.
Makes one 9-inch pie.

Orange 'n Vanilla Mousse Pie

    1 envelope KNOX® Unflavored
        Gelatine
    ¼ cup cold water
    1 cup (½ pint) whipping or
        heavy cream, heated to
        boiling
    1 package (8 ounces) cream
        cheese, softened
    1 can (6 ounces) frozen orange
        juice concentrate, partially
        thawed and undiluted
    ¾ cup confectioners sugar
    1½ teaspoons vanilla extract
    1 (9-inch) graham cracker crust

In blender, sprinkle unflavored gelatine over cold water; let stand 1 minute. Add hot cream and process at low speed until gelatine is completely dissolved, about 2 minutes. Add cream cheese, orange juice concentrate, sugar and vanilla; process until blended. Chill blender container until mixture is slightly thickened, about 15 minutes. Pour into prepared crust; chill until firm, about 3 hours. Garnish, if desired, with whipped cream and orange slices.
Makes about 8 servings.

Cranberry Crumb Pie

    1 (9-inch) unbaked pastry shell
    1 (8-ounce) package cream
        cheese, softened
    1 (14-ounce) can EAGLE® Brand
        Sweetened Condensed Milk
        (NOT evaporated milk)
    ¼ cup REALEMON® Lemon Juice
        from Concentrate
    3 tablespoons light brown sugar
    2 tablespoons cornstarch
    1 (16-ounce) can whole berry
        cranberry sauce
    ¼ cup cold margarine or butter
    ⅓ cup unsifted flour
    ¾ cup chopped walnuts

Preheat oven to 425°. Bake pastry shell 8 minutes; remove from oven. Reduce oven temperature to 375°. In large mixer bowl, beat cheese until fluffy. Gradually beat in sweetened condensed milk until smooth. Stir in ReaLemon® brand. Pour into prepared pastry shell. In small bowl, combine *1 tablespoon* sugar and cornstarch; mix well. Stir in cranberry sauce. Spoon evenly over cheese mixture. In medium mixing bowl, cut margarine into flour and remaining *2 tablespoons* sugar until crumbly. Stir in nuts. Sprinkle evenly over cranberry mixture. Bake 45 to 50 minutes or until bubbly and golden. Cool. Serve at room temperature or chill thoroughly. Refrigerate leftovers.
Makes one 9-inch pie.

Margarita Pie

Traditional Pumpkin Pie with Sour Cream Topping (left) and Streusel Topping (right)

Traditional Pumpkin Pie

- **1 (9-inch) unbaked pastry shell**
- **1 (16-ounce) can pumpkin (about 2 cups)**
- **1 (14-ounce) can EAGLE® Brand Sweetened Condensed Milk (NOT evaporated milk)**
- **2 eggs**
- **1 teaspoon ground cinnamon**
- **½ teaspoon ground ginger**
- **½ teaspoon ground nutmeg**
- **½ teaspoon salt**

Preheat oven to 425°. In large mixer bowl, combine all ingredients except pastry shell; mix well. Pour into prepared pastry shell. Bake 15 minutes. Reduce oven temperature to 350°; continue baking 35 to 40 minutes or until knife inserted 1 inch from edge comes out clean. Cool. Garnish as desired. Refrigerate leftovers.
Makes one 9-inch pie.

Topping Variations:

Sour Cream Topping: In medium mixing bowl, combine 1½ cups BORDEN® or MEADOW GOLD® Sour Cream, 2 tablespoons sugar and 1 teaspoon vanilla extract. After 30 minutes of baking, spread evenly over top of pie; bake 10 minutes longer. Garnish as desired.

Streusel Topping: In medium mixing bowl, combine ½ cup firmly packed light brown sugar and ½ cup unsifted flour; cut in ¼ cup cold margarine or butter until crumbly. Stir in ¼ cup chopped nuts. After 30 minutes of baking, sprinkle on top of pie; bake 10 minutes longer.

No-Bake Pumpkin Pie

- **1 egg**
- **1 (14-ounce) can EAGLE® Brand Sweetened Condensed Milk (NOT evaporated milk)**
- **1 teaspoon ground cinnamon**
- **½ teaspoon *each* ground ginger, nutmeg and salt**
- **1 envelope KNOX® Unflavored Gelatine**
- **2 tablespoons water**
- **1 (16-ounce) can pumpkin (about 2 cups)**
- **1 KEEBLER® Ready-Crust® Graham Cracker Pie Crust**

In medium bowl, beat egg; beat in sweetened condensed milk and spices. In medium saucepan, sprinkle gelatine over water; let stand 1 minute. Over *low* heat, stir until gelatine dissolves. Add sweetened condensed milk mixture; over *low* heat, cook and stir constantly until mixture thickens slightly, 5 to 10 minutes. Remove from heat. Add pumpkin. Pour into crust. Chill 4 hours or until set. Garnish as desired. Refrigerate leftovers.
Makes one pie.

Paradise Pumpkin Pie

- **Pastry for 1-crust 9-inch pie**
- **1 8-ounce package PHILADELPHIA BRAND® Cream Cheese, softened**
- **¼ cup sugar**
- **½ teaspoon vanilla**
- **1 egg**

* * *

- **1¼ cups canned pumpkin**
- **1 cup evaporated milk**
- **½ cup sugar**
- **2 eggs, beaten**
- **1 teaspoon cinnamon**
- **¼ teaspoon ground ginger**
- **¼ teaspoon ground nutmeg**
- **Dash of salt**
- **Maple syrup**
- **Pecan halves**

On lightly floured surface, roll pastry to 12-inch circle. Place in 9-inch pie plate. Turn under edge; flute. Combine cream cheese, sugar and vanilla, mixing at medium speed on electric mixer until well blended. Blend in egg. Spread onto bottom of pastry shell.

Combine all remaining ingredients except syrup and pecans; mix well. Carefully pour over cream cheese mixture. Bake at 350°, 65 minutes. Cool. Brush with syrup; top with pecan halves.
8 servings.

Maple Walnut Cream Pie

Crust
> 9-inch Classic Crisco®
> Single Crust
> (see page 461)

Filling
> 1 cup pure maple syrup or
> maple-flavored pancake
> syrup
> ½ cup milk
> 2 egg yolks, lightly beaten
> 1 envelope (1 tablespoon)
> unflavored gelatin
> ¼ cup water
> 1 teaspoon maple flavor or
> extract
> 1 cup whipping cream,
> whipped
> ¾ cup chopped walnuts
>
> Sweetened whipped cream
> Baked pastry cutouts*
> (optional)

1. **For crust,** prepare recipe and bake. Reserve dough scraps for pastry cutouts, if desired. Cool.

2. **For filling,** combine syrup and milk in small saucepan. Cook on low heat just until hot. *Do not boil.* Stir small amount of hot mixture gradually into egg yolks. Return egg mixture to saucepan. Bring to a boil on medium heat. Simmer 1 minute. Soften gelatin in water. Remove saucepan from heat. Add softened gelatin and maple flavor. Stir until gelatin dissolves. Refrigerate until mixture begins to thicken.

3. Fold whipped cream into maple mixture. Fold in nuts. Spoon into cooled baked pie crust. Refrigerate 2 hours or until firm. Garnish with whipped cream and baked pastry cutouts, if desired. Refrigerate leftover pie.   *One 9-inch Pie*

For baked pastry cutouts, roll dough scraps together. Cut into desired shapes. Brush with beaten egg white, if desired. Bake at 425°F for 5 minutes or until golden brown. Cool.

Deep-Dish Almond Pumpkin Pie

Crust
> 9-inch Classic Crisco®
> Single Crust
> (see page 461)

Almond Layer
> 1 cup finely chopped
> almonds
> ½ cup firmly packed brown
> sugar
> 3 tablespoons butter or
> margarine, softened
> 2 teaspoons all-purpose flour
> ¼ teaspoon almond extract

Pumpkin Filling
> 1¼ cups *granulated* brown
> sugar
> 1 package (3 ounces) cream
> cheese, softened
> 2 eggs
> 1¼ cups cooked or canned
> solid pack pumpkin
> (not pumpkin pie filling)
> ½ cup evaporated milk
> ⅓ cup dairy sour cream
> 1 tablespoon molasses
> 1 teaspoon cinnamon
> ½ teaspoon nutmeg
> ½ teaspoon salt
> ¼ teaspoon ginger
> ⅛ teaspoon ground cloves
> ½ teaspoon almond extract
>
> Baked pastry cutouts
> (optional)

1. **For crust,** prepare recipe and press into 9-inch deep-dish pie plate. Do not bake. Reserve dough scraps for pastry cutouts (see previous recipe), if desired. Heat oven to 425°F.

2. **For almond layer,** combine nuts, brown sugar, butter, flour and ¼ teaspoon almond extract. Toss with fork until well blended. Spoon into unbaked pie crust. Press firmly on bottom and part way up sides. Refrigerate.

Deep-Dish Almond Pumpkin Pie

3. **For pumpkin filling,** combine *granulated* brown sugar and cream cheese in large bowl. Beat at medium speed of electric mixer until well blended. Beat in eggs, pumpkin, evaporated milk, sour cream and molasses at low speed. Add cinnamon, nutmeg, salt, ginger, cloves and ½ teaspoon almond extract. Beat 1 minute. Spoon over almond layer.

4. Bake at 425°F for 15 minutes. *Reduce oven temperature to 350°F.* Bake for 50 to 60 minutes. Cover edge of pie with foil, if necessary, to prevent overbrowning. Cool to room temperature. Decorate with baked pastry cutouts, if desired. Refrigerate leftover pie.

One 9-inch Pie

Honey Crunch Pecan Pie

Honey Crunch Pecan Pie

Crust
>   **9-inch Classic Crisco®**
>   **Single Crust**
>   **(see page 461)**

Filling
- 4 eggs, lightly beaten
- 1 cup light corn syrup
- ¼ cup firmly packed brown sugar
- ¼ cup granulated sugar
- 2 tablespoons butter or margarine, melted
- 1 tablespoon bourbon
- 1 teaspoon vanilla
- ½ teaspoon salt
- 1 cup chopped pecans

Topping
- ⅓ cup firmly packed brown sugar
- 3 tablespoons butter or margarine
- 3 tablespoons honey
- 1½ cups pecan halves

1. **For crust,** prepare recipe and press into 9-inch pie plate. Do not bake. Heat oven to 350°F.

2. **For filling,** combine eggs, corn syrup, sugars, melted butter, bourbon, vanilla and salt in large bowl. Stir in chopped pecans. Mix well. Spoon into unbaked pie crust. Bake at 350°F for 15 minutes. Cover edge with foil to prevent overbrowning. Bake for 20 minutes. Remove from oven. Remove foil and save.

3. **For topping,** combine brown sugar, butter and honey in medium saucepan. Cook about 2 minutes or until sugar dissolves. Add pecan halves. Stir until coated. Spoon over pie. Recover edge with foil. Bake 10 to 20 minutes or until topping is bubbly and crust is golden brown. Cool to room temperature before serving. Refrigerate leftover pie. *One 9-inch Pie*

Chocolate Pecan Pie

- 1 package (4 ounces) BAKER'S® GERMAN'S® Sweet Chocolate
- 2 tablespoons margarine or butter
- 1 cup corn syrup
- ⅓ cup sugar
- 3 eggs
- 1 teaspoon vanilla
- 1½ cups pecan halves
- 1 unbaked 9-inch pie shell COOL WHIP® Whipped Topping, thawed (optional)

HEAT oven to 350°F.

MICROWAVE chocolate and margarine in large microwavable bowl on HIGH 2 minutes or until margarine is melted. **Stir until chocolate is completely melted.**

STIR in corn syrup, sugar, eggs and vanilla until well blended. Stir in pecans, reserving 8 halves for garnish, if desired. Pour filling into pie shell.

BAKE for 55 minutes or until knife inserted 1 inch from center comes out clean. Cool on wire rack. Garnish with whipped topping and chocolate-dipped pecan halves, if desired.

Makes 8 servings

Prep time: 20 minutes
Baking time: 55 minutes

Chocolate Truffle Tart

Chocolate Truffle Tart

Crust:
- ⅔ cup all-purpose flour
- ½ cup sugar
- ½ cup walnuts, ground
- 6 tablespoons (¾ stick) butter or margarine, softened
- ⅓ cup NESTLÉ® Cocoa

Filling:
- 1 cup heavy or whipping cream
- ¼ cup sugar
- One 8-oz. pkg. (4 foil-wrapped bars) NESTLÉ® Semi-Sweet Chocolate baking bars, broken up
- 2 tablespoons seedless raspberry jam

  Additional whipped cream for garnish
  Fresh raspberries for garnish

Crust: Preheat oven to 350°F. In small mixer bowl, beat flour, ½ cup sugar, walnuts, butter and cocoa until soft dough forms. Press dough into 9-inch fluted tart pan with removable bottom.

Bake 12 to 14 minutes until puffed. Cool completely.

Filling: In medium saucepan, bring heavy cream and ¼ cup sugar just to a boil, stirring occasionally. Remove from heat. Stir in semi-sweet chocolate baking bars and jam; cool 5 minutes. Whisk until chocolate is melted and mixture is smooth. Transfer to small mixer bowl. Cover; refrigerate 45 to 60 minutes until mixture is cool and slightly thickened.

Beat Filling just until color lightens slightly. Pour into Crust. Refrigerate. Garnish with whipped cream and raspberries.
Makes 10 to 12 servings

Chocolate Turtle Pie

- ¼ cup caramel or butterscotch flavor dessert topping
- 1 baked 8- or 9-inch pie shell, cooled
- ¾ cup pecan halves
- 1 package (4-serving size) JELL-O® Pudding and Pie Filling, Chocolate Flavor*
- 1¾ cups milk*
- 1¾ cups (4 ounces) COOL WHIP® Whipped Topping, thawed

BRING caramel topping to boil in small saucepan, stirring constantly. Pour into pie shell. Arrange pecans on top; chill.

COMBINE pie filling mix and milk in medium saucepan. Cook and stir over medium heat until mixture comes to full boil. Cool 5 minutes, stirring twice. Pour into pie shell; place plastic wrap on surface of filling. Chill 3 hours. Remove plastic wrap. Cover with whipped topping. Drizzle with additional caramel topping and garnish with additional pecans, if desired.
Makes 8 servings

*1 package (4-serving size) instant pudding may be substituted for 1 package (4-serving size) cooked pudding mix. Prepare as directed on package, using 1½ cups *cold* milk.

Prep time: 15 minutes
Chill time: 3 hours

Chocolate Mudslide Pie

Chocolate Mudslide Pie

One 8-oz. pkg. (4 foil-wrapped bars) NESTLÉ® Semi-Sweet Chocolate baking bars, broken up
1 teaspoon TASTER'S CHOICE® Freeze-Dried Instant Coffee
1 teaspoon water
¾ cup sour cream
½ cup granulated sugar
1 teaspoon vanilla extract
One 9-inch prepared chocolate crumb crust
1 cup confectioners' sugar
¼ cup NESTLÉ® Cocoa
1½ cups heavy or whipping cream
2 tablespoons NESTLÉ® Toll House® Semi-Sweet Chocolate Mini Morsels

In small saucepan over low heat, melt semi-sweet chocolate baking bars; cool 10 minutes. In small bowl, dissolve instant coffee in water. Add sour cream, granulated sugar and vanilla extract; stir until sugar is dissolved. Blend in melted chocolate. Spread in crust; set aside.

In small mixer bowl, beat confectioners' sugar, cocoa and heavy cream until stiff peaks form. Spoon cream mixture into pastry bag fitted with star tip; pipe onto pie. Sprinkle with mini morsels. Cover; refrigerate at least 4 hours until firm.

Makes 8 servings

German Sweet Chocolate Pie

1 package (4 ounces) BAKER'S® GERMAN'S® Sweet Chocolate
⅓ cup milk
1 package (3 ounces) PHILADELPHIA BRAND® Cream Cheese, softened
2 tablespoons sugar (optional)
3½ cups (8 ounces) COOL WHIP® Whipped Topping, thawed
1 (9-inch) prepared crumb crust
Chocolate shavings or curls (optional)

MICROWAVE chocolate and 2 tablespoons of the milk in large microwavable bowl on HIGH 1½ to 2 minutes or until chocolate is almost melted, stirring halfway through heating time. **Stir until chocolate is completely melted.**

BEAT in cream cheese, sugar and the remaining milk until well blended. Refrigerate to cool, about 10 minutes.

STIR in whipped topping gently until smooth. Spoon into crust. Freeze until firm, about 4 hours. Garnish with chocolate shavings or curls, if desired.

Makes 8 servings

Prep time: 20 minutes
Freezing time: 4 hours

Saucepan preparation: Heat chocolate and 2 tablespoons of the milk in saucepan over very low heat until chocolate is melted, stirring constantly. Remove from heat. Continue as above.

German Sweet Chocolate Pie

Ice Cream Shop Pie

**1½ cups cold half and half or
  milk
  1 package (4-serving size)
  JELL-O® Instant Pudding
  and Pie Filling, any flavor
3½ cups (8 ounces) COOL
  WHIP® Whipped Topping,
  thawed
  Ice Cream Shop
  Ingredients*
  1 packaged chocolate,
  graham cracker or vanilla
  crumb crust**

POUR half and half into large
bowl. Add pudding mix. Beat
with wire whisk until well
blended, 1 to 2 minutes. Let
stand 5 minutes or until slightly
thickened.

FOLD whipped topping and Ice
Cream Shop ingredients into
pudding mixture. Spoon into
crust.

FREEZE pie until firm, about 6
hours or overnight. Remove from
freezer. Let stand at room
temperature about 10 minutes
before serving to soften. Store
any leftover pie in freezer.

Makes 8 servings

Rocky Road Pie: Use any
chocolate flavor pudding mix and
chocolate crumb crust. Fold in ½
cup *each* BAKER'S® Semi-Sweet
Real Chocolate Chips, KRAFT®
Miniature Marshmallows and
chopped nuts with whipped
topping. Serve with chocolate
sauce, if desired.

Toffee Bar Crunch Pie: Use
French vanilla or vanilla flavor
pudding mix and graham cracker
crumb crust, spreading ⅓ cup
butterscotch sauce onto bottom of
crust before filling. Fold in 1 cup
chopped chocolate-covered
English toffee bars (about 6 bars)
with whipped topping. Garnish
with additional chopped toffee
bars, if desired.

Strawberry Banana Split Pie:
Use French vanilla or vanilla
flavor pudding mix, reducing
half and half to ¾ cup and

adding ¾ cup pureed BIRDS
EYE® Quick Thaw Strawberries
with the half and half. Use
vanilla crumb crust and line
bottom with banana slices.
Garnish with whipped topping,
maraschino cherries and chopped
nuts. Serve with remaining
strawberries, pureed, if desired.

Chocolate Cookie Pie: Use
French vanilla or vanilla flavor
pudding mix and chocolate
crumb crust. Fold in 1 cup
chopped chocolate sandwich
cookies with whipped topping.

Nutcracker Pie: Use butter
pecan flavor pudding mix and
graham cracker crumb crust.
Fold in 1 cup chopped mixed
nuts with whipped topping.

Peppermint Stick Pie: Use
French vanilla or vanilla flavor
pudding mix and chocolate
crumb crust. Fold in ½ cup
crushed hard peppermint
candies, ½ cup BAKER'S® Semi-
Sweet Real Chocolate Chips and
2 teaspoons peppermint extract
with whipped topping.

Prep time: 15 minutes
Freezing time: 6 hours

Peppermint Parfait Pie

**1 (9-inch) baked pastry shell
1 (1-ounce) square
  unsweetened chocolate
1 (14-ounce) can EAGLE®
  Brand Sweetened
  Condensed Milk
  (NOT evaporated milk)
½ teaspoon vanilla extract
1 (8-ounce) package cream
  cheese, softened
3 tablespoons white creme
  de menthe liqueur
  Red food coloring, optional
1 (8-ounce) container frozen
  non-dairy whipped
  topping, thawed
  (3½ cups)**

In small saucepan, melt
chocolate with ½ cup sweetened
condensed milk; stir in vanilla.
Spread on bottom of prepared
pastry shell. In large mixer bowl,
beat cheese until fluffy.
Gradually beat in remaining
sweetened condensed milk. Stir
in liqueur and food coloring if
desired. Fold in whipped topping.
Pour into prepared pastry shell.
Chill 4 hours or until set.
Garnish as desired. Refrigerate
leftovers.

Makes one 9-inch pie

Fluffy Grasshopper Pie

**2 cups finely crushed creme-
  filled chocolate sandwich
  cookies
  (about 24 cookies)
¼ cup margarine or butter,
  melted
1 (8-ounce) package cream
  cheese, softened
1 (14-ounce) can EAGLE®
  Brand Sweetened
  Condensed Milk
  (NOT evaporated milk)
3 tablespoons REALEMON®
  Lemon Juice from
  Concentrate
¼ cup green creme de
  menthe liqueur
¼ cup white creme de cacao
  liqueur
1 (4-ounce) container frozen
  non-dairy whipped
  topping, thawed
  (1¾ cups)**

Combine crumbs and margarine;
press firmly on bottom and up
side to rim of buttered 9-inch pie
plate. Chill. Meanwhile, in large
mixer bowl, beat cheese until
fluffy. Gradually beat in
sweetened condensed milk until
smooth. Stir in ReaLemon®
brand and liqueurs. Fold in
whipped topping. Chill 20
minutes; pour into crust. Chill or
freeze 4 hours or until set.
Garnish as desired. Refrigerate
or freeze leftovers.

Makes one 9-inch pie

**Top to bottom: Rocky Road Pie, Toffee Bar Crunch Pie and
Strawberry Banana Split Pie**

Almond Heart Napoleons

- 1 package (17¼ ounces) frozen puff pastry sheets
- 1¼ cups cold half and half or milk
- 2 tablespoons almond liqueur*
- 1 package (4-serving size) JELL-O® Instant Pudding and Pie Filling, French Vanilla or Vanilla Flavor
- ½ cup confectioners sugar
- 2 teaspoons (about) hot water
- 1 square BAKER'S® Semi-Sweet Chocolate, melted

THAW puff pastry as directed on package. Preheat oven to 350°. Unfold pastry. Using 2-inch heart-shaped cookie cutter, cut each sheet into 12 hearts. Bake on ungreased baking sheets for 20 minutes or until golden. Remove from baking sheets. Cool on racks. When pastry is completely cooled, split each heart horizontally in half.

POUR half and half and liqueur into small bowl. Add pudding mix. Beat with wire whisk until well blended, 1 to 2 minutes. Chill 10 minutes.

SPREAD about 1 tablespoon of the pudding mixture onto bottom half of each pastry; top with remaining pastry half.

STIR together confectioners sugar and hot water in small bowl to make thin glaze. Spread over hearts. (If glaze becomes too thick, add more hot water until glaze is of desired consistency.) Before glaze dries, drizzle chocolate on top to form thin lines. Draw wooden pick through chocolate to make design. Chill until ready to serve.

Makes 2 dozen pastries

Prep time: 30 minutes
Baking time: 20 minutes

*½ teaspoon almond extract may be substituted for 2 tablespoons almond liqueur.

Slovakian Kolacky

- 2 packages (¼ ounce *each*) active dry yeast
- ¼ cup warm water (105° to 115°F)
- 7 cups all-purpose flour
- 1 teaspoon salt
- 2 cups LAND O LAKES® Butter, softened
- 4 eggs, slightly beaten
- 2 cups whipping cream (1 pint)
- Fruit preserves

In small bowl dissolve yeast in warm water. In large bowl combine flour and salt; cut in butter until crumbly. Stir in yeast, eggs and whipping cream. Turn dough onto lightly floured surface; knead until smooth, 2 to 3 minutes. Place in greased bowl; turn greased side up. Cover; refrigerate until firm, 6 hours or overnight.

Heat oven to 375°. Roll out dough, ½ at a time, on sugared surface to ⅛-inch thickness. Cut into 3-inch squares. Spoon 1 teaspoon preserves in center of *each* square. Bring up two opposite corners to center; pinch together to seal. Fold sealed tip to one side; pinch to seal. Place 1-inch apart on ungreased cookie sheets. Bake for 10 to 15 minutes or until lightly browned.

Makes 5 dozen kolacky

Apple Turnovers

Filling
- 1¾ cups chopped, peeled tart cooking apples (about ⅔ pound or 2 medium)
- ⅓ cup water
- ⅓ cup firmly packed brown sugar
- ¼ teaspoon cinnamon
- ⅛ teaspoon nutmeg
- 1 tablespoon all-purpose flour
- 1 teaspoon granulated sugar
- 1 tablespoon butter or margarine

Pastry
- 9-inch Classic Crisco® Double Crust (see page 461)

Glaze
- ½ cup confectioners sugar
- 1 tablespoon milk
- ¼ teaspoon vanilla

Slovakian Kolacky

1. **For filling,** combine apples and water in small saucepan. Cook and stir on high heat until mixture comes to a boil. Reduce heat to low. Simmer 5 minutes. Stir in brown sugar, cinnamon and nutmeg. Simmer 5 minutes. Stir frequently. Combine flour and granulated sugar. Stir into apple mixture. Bring to a boil. Boil 1 minute. Stir in butter.

2. **For pastry,** heat oven to 425°F. Prepare dough and divide in half. Roll each half to 1/16-inch thickness. Use lid from 3-pound Crisco can as pattern. Cut six 5¼-inch circles from each half. (Reroll as necessary.)

3. Place about 1 tablespoon apple filling on each dough circle. Moisten edges with water. Fold in half over filling. Press with fork to seal. Place on ungreased baking sheet. Prick tops with fork. Bake at 425°F for 20 minutes or until golden brown. Cool 10 minutes on wire rack.

4. **For glaze,** combine confectioners sugar, milk and vanilla in small bowl. Stir well. Drizzle over turnovers. Serve warm or cool.   *12 Turnovers*

Note: Any canned fruit pie filling can be substituted for fresh apple filling.

Mini Almond Pastries

Mini Almond Pastries

¼ cup powdered sugar
¼ cup LAND O LAKES®
    Butter, softened
1 tube (3½ ounces) almond
    paste (⅓ cup)
2 egg yolks
2 teaspoons grated lemon
    peel
½ teaspoon almond extract
¼ cup granulated sugar
1 package (17¼ ounces)
    frozen prerolled sheets
    puff pastry, thawed
    (2 sheets)

In small mixer bowl combine powdered sugar, butter, almond paste, egg yolks, lemon peel and almond extract. Beat at low speed, scraping bowl often, until well mixed, 1 to 2 minutes; set aside. Sprinkle about *1 tablespoon* granulated sugar on surface or pastry cloth. Unfold 1 sheet puff pastry on sugared surface; sprinkle with about

1 tablespoon granulated sugar. Roll out puff pastry sheet into 12-inch square. Cut square into 2 (12×6-inch) rectangles. Spread ¼ of (*about 3 tablespoons*) almond paste mixture on *each* rectangle. Working with 1 (12×6-inch) rectangle at a time, fold ½ inch of both 12-inch sides in toward center of pastry. Continue folding both 12-inch sides, ½ inch at a time, until 12-inch sides meet in center. Fold one 12-inch side on top of other 12-inch side; firmly press layers together. Repeat with remaining 12×6-inch rectangle. Repeat with remaining ingredients. Wrap *each* pastry roll in plastic wrap; refrigerate at least 2 hours.

Heat oven to 400°. Cut pastry rolls into ½-inch slices. Place slices 2 inches apart on greased or parchment-lined cookie sheets. Bake for 7 to 11 minutes or until lightly browned. Remove from pan immediately.

Makes 7 to 8 dozen pastries

Philly® Cream Cheese Cream Puff Ring

Philly® Cream Cheese Cream Puff Ring

- 1 cup water
- ½ cup PARKAY® Margarine
- 1 cup flour
- ¼ teaspoon salt
- 4 eggs
- 2 8-ounce packages PHILADELPHIA BRAND® Cream Cheese, softened
- 1½ cups powdered sugar
- 1 teaspoon vanilla
- 1 cup whipping cream, whipped
- 2 bananas, sliced
- 1 1-ounce square unsweetened chocolate, melted
- 1 tablespoon milk

Bring water and margarine to boil. Add flour and salt; stir vigorously over low heat until mixture forms ball. Remove from heat. Add eggs, one at a time, beating well after each addition. Drop ten ½ cupfuls of dough on lightly greased cookie sheet to form 9-inch ring. Bake at 400°, 50 to 55 minutes or until golden brown. Remove from cookie sheet immediately; cool.

Combine cream cheese, 1 cup sugar and vanilla, mixing until well blended. Reserve ½ cup cream cheese mixture; fold whipped cream and bananas into remaining mixture. Chill. Carefully cut top from ring; fill with whipped cream mixture. Replace top. Add remaining sugar, chocolate and milk to reserved cream cheese mixture; mix well. Spread over ring.
10 servings.

Chocolate-Almond Tarts

- Chocolate Tart Shells (recipe follows)
- ¾ cup sugar
- ¼ cup HERSHEY'S Cocoa
- ¼ cup cornstarch
- ¼ teaspoon salt
- 2 cups milk
- 2 egg yolks, slightly beaten
- 2 tablespoons butter or margarine
- ¼ teaspoon almond extract
- Sliced almonds

Prepare Chocolate Tart Shells; set aside. In saucepan, stir together sugar, cocoa, cornstarch and salt; blend in milk and egg yolks. Cook over medium heat, stirring constantly, until mixture boils; boil and stir 1 minute. Remove from heat; blend in butter and almond extract. Pour into Chocolate Tart Shells; press plastic wrap directly onto surface. Refrigerate. Garnish with almonds.
6 servings.

Chocolate Tart Shells

- 1½ cups vanilla wafer crumbs (about 45 wafers)
- ⅓ cup powdered sugar
- ¼ cup HERSHEY'S Cocoa
- 6 tablespoons butter or margarine, melted

Heat oven to 350°F. In bowl, stir together crumbs, powdered sugar, cocoa and butter until completely blended. Divide mixture among six 4-ounce tart pans with removable bottoms; press mixture firmly onto bottoms and up sides of pans. Bake 5 minutes; cool.

Napoleons

- 1 package (17¼ oz.) frozen puff pastry sheets
- Chocolate Filling (recipe follows)
- Vanilla Frosting (recipe follows)
- Chocolate Glaze (recipe follows)

Thaw folded pastry sheets according to package directions. Heat oven to 350°F. Gently unfold sheets. On lightly floured surface, roll each sheet to a 15×12-inch rectangle; trim to even edges. Place on large ungreased baking sheets; with fork, prick each sheet thoroughly. Bake 18 to 20 minutes or until puffed and golden brown. (If pastry puffs during baking, remove from oven and prick with fork until pastry deflates; finish baking.) Cool completely on baking sheets. Prepare Chocolate Filling. Cut each pastry rectangle lengthwise into 3 equal pieces. Spread one-fourth of the Chocolate Filling on top of each of 4 pieces of pastry; stack to form 2 filled pastries. Top each with remaining piece of pastry. Prepare Vanilla Frosting; spread on top of each pastry. Prepare Chocolate Glaze; drizzle over frosting in decorative design. Refrigerate at least 1 hour or until filling is set. Carefully cut each pastry into 6 pieces. Cover; refrigerate leftovers. *12 servings.*

Chocolate Filling

1 envelope unflavored gelatin
2 tablespoons cold water
¼ cup boiling water
1 cup sugar
½ cup HERSHEY'S Cocoa
2 cups chilled whipping cream
2 teaspoons vanilla extract

In small bowl, sprinkle gelatin over cold water; let stand 1 minute to soften. Add boiling water; stir until gelatin is completely dissolved and mixture is clear. Cool slightly. In large mixer bowl, stir together sugar and cocoa. Add whipping cream and vanilla; at medium speed, beat, scraping bottom of bowl occasionally, until stiff. Pour in gelatin mixture; beat until well blended. Refrigerate to spreading consistency, if necessary. **VANILLA FROSTING:** In small mixer bowl, combine 1½ cups powdered sugar, 1 tablespoon light corn syrup, ¼ teaspoon vanilla extract and 1 to 2 tablespoons hot water; beat to spreading consistency. (Add additional water, ½ teaspoon at a time, if necessary).
CHOCOLATE GLAZE: In small saucepan, melt ¼ cup (½ stick) butter or margarine. Remove from heat; stir in ⅓ cup HERSHEY'S Cocoa until smooth. Cool slightly.

Chocolate-Filled Cream Puffs

Chocolate Cream Filling (recipe follows)
1 cup water
½ cup (1 stick) butter or margarine
¼ teaspoon salt
1 cup all-purpose flour
4 eggs
Powdered sugar

Prepare Chocolate Cream Filling. Heat oven to 400°F. In medium saucepan, heat water, butter and salt to rolling boil. Add flour all at once; stir vigorously over low heat about 1 minute or until mixture leaves side of pan and forms a ball. Remove from heat; add eggs, one at a time, beating well after each addition until smooth and velvety. Drop batter by spoonfuls into 12 balls onto ungreased cookie sheet. Bake 35 to 40 minutes or until puffed and golden brown. While puff is warm, horizontally slice off small portion of top; reserve tops. Remove any soft piece of dough from inside of puff; cool on wire rack. Fill puffs with Chocolate Cream Filling. Replace tops; dust with powdered sugar. Refrigerate until serving time. *About 12 servings.*

Chocolate Cream Filling

1¼ cups sugar
⅓ cup HERSHEY'S Cocoa
⅓ cup cornstarch
¼ teaspoon salt
3 cups milk
3 egg yolks, slightly beaten
2 tablespoons butter or margarine
1½ teaspoons vanilla extract

In medium saucepan, stir together sugar, cocoa, cornstarch and salt; stir in milk. Cook over medium heat, stirring constantly, until mixture boils; boil and stir 1 minute. Remove from heat. Gradually stir small amount of chocolate mixture into egg yolks; blend well. Return egg mixture to chocolate mixture in pan; stir and heat just until boiling. Remove from heat; blend in butter and vanilla. Pour into bowl; press plastic wrap directly onto surface. Refrigerate 1 to 2 hours or until cold. *About 3¾ cups.*

Chocolate-Filled Cream Puffs (top), Chocolate-Almond Tarts (middle) and Napoleons (bottom)

CAKES & CHEESECAKES

What better way to top off any celebration than with a moist, delectable cake! Create a special grand finale with an extravagant multi-tiered torte, cream-filled cake roll or dreamy chocolate layer cake. Delight children—young and old—with colorful shaped cakes for a birthday party or holiday gathering. Or treat your family to a simple shortcake to spruce up a weeknight meal. And when you desire the smooth and creamy decadence of fabulous cheesecake, select from a wide assortment including velvety chocolate, caramel apple, heavenly orange and rocky road.

Ice Cream Cone Cakes

1 package DUNCAN HINES® Moist Deluxe Cake Mix (any flavor)

Frosting
- **1 cup semi-sweet chocolate chips**
- **5 cups confectioners sugar**
- **¾ cup CRISCO® Shortening**
- **½ cup water**
- **⅓ cup non-dairy powdered creamer**
- **2 teaspoons vanilla extract**
- **½ teaspoon salt**
  Chocolate jimmies or sprinkles
  Assorted decors
  Candy gumdrops
- **2 maraschino cherries, for garnish**

1. Preheat oven to 350°F. Grease and flour one 8-inch round cake pan and one 8-inch square pan.

2. Prepare cake following package directions for basic recipe. Pour about 2 cups batter into round pan. Pour about 3 cups batter into square pan. Bake at 350°F for 30 to 35 minutes or until toothpick inserted in center comes out clean. Cool following package directions.

3. **For frosting,** melt chocolate chips in small saucepan over low heat. Set aside. Combine confectioners sugar, shortening, water, non-dairy powdered creamer, vanilla extract and salt in large bowl. Beat at medium speed with electric mixer for 3 minutes. Beat at high speed for 5 minutes. Add confectioners sugar to thicken or water to thin frosting as needed. Divide frosting in half. Blend melted chocolate chips into one half.

4. To assemble, cut cooled cake and arrange as shown (see Tip). Frost cone with chocolate frosting, reserving ½ cup. Place writing tip in pastry bag. Fill with remaining ½ cup chocolate frosting. Pipe waffle pattern onto cones; sprinkle with chocolate jimmies. Spread white frosting on ice cream parts; decorate with assorted decors and gumdrops. Top each with maraschino cherry.   *12 to 16 Servings*

Tip: For ease in handling, freeze cake before cutting into ice cream and cone shapes.

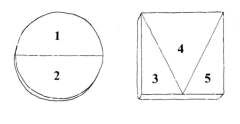

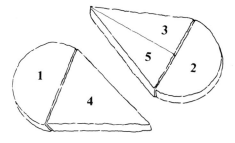

Ice Cream Cone Cakes

Dream Castle Cake

8. Decorate castle and towers as shown, using frosting to attach candies, if needed.

9. Arrange wafer cookies on front of castle for gate.

Makes 24 to 28 servings

Tip: For easier frosting of cones, hold cone over fingers of one hand while frosting with other hand. Place in position, touching up frosting, if needed.

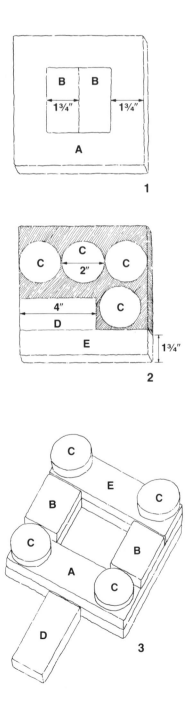

Dream Castle Cake

Cakes & Frostings
   3 (8-inch) square cakes
5¼ cups Buttercream Frosting
      (page 525)*
   2 cups Base Frosting
      (page 525), if desired

Decorations & Equipment
      Assorted colored sugar
   4 sugar ice cream cones
      Small purple and white
         gumdrops
      Pastel candy-coated
         chocolate pieces
   2 pink sugar wafer cookies
   1 (19×13-inch) cake board,
      cut in half crosswise and
      covered

1. Trim tops and edges of cakes. Place one square cake on prepared cake board. Frost top with some of the white frosting.

2. Cut remaining cakes as shown in diagrams 1 and 2.

3. Place piece A over bottom layer. Frost top of piece A with some of the white frosting.

4. Position remaining pieces as shown in diagram 3, connecting with some of the white frosting.

5. Frost entire cake with Base Frosting to seal in crumbs.

6. Frost again with white frosting. Cover piece D (bridge) with colored sugar.

7. Frost cones with blue and yellow frostings. Place as shown in photo.

*Color ½ cup frosting blue and ½ cup yellow; reserve 4¼ cups white frosting.

Speedy Racetrack Cake

Cakes & Frostings
    1 (9-inch) round cake
    1 (13×9-inch) cake
    3½ cups Buttercream Frosting
        (page 525)*
    1½ cups Base Frosting
        (page 525), if desired

Decorations & Equipment
    Green colored sugar
    2 to 3 rolls white donut-
        shaped hard candies, cut
        in half
    ½ (16-ounce) box cinnamon
        graham crackers
    2- to 3-inch race cars
        Flags, if desired
    1 (19×13-inch) cake board,
        cut to fit cake, if desired,
        and covered

*Mix 2 cups frosting with 2 tablespoons unsweetened cocoa powder. Color 1½ cups green.

1. Trim tops and edges of cakes. Cut round cake in half crosswise. Cut 13×9-inch cake as shown in diagram 1.

2. Position pieces on prepared cake board as shown in diagram 2, connecting with some of the green frosting.

3. Frost entire cake with Base Frosting to seal in crumbs.

4. Using wooden pick, draw area for track, about 2 inches wide, as shown in photo. Frost center of cake with green frosting. Sprinkle with colored sugar. Frost track and sides of cake with chocolate frosting.

5. Arrange hard candies, cut-side down, around inside of track. Cut graham crackers about ¼ inch higher than cake. Arrange around edge of cake, attaching with more chocolate frosting, if needed.

6. Let frosting harden before placing cars and flags on track.
Makes 20 to 24 servings

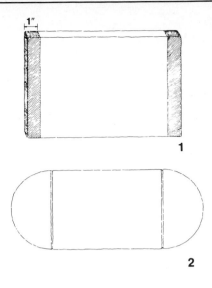

1

2

Drum Layer Cake

    1 package DUNCAN HINES®
        Moist Deluxe Cake Mix
        (any flavor)
    2 containers (16 ounces
        each) DUNCAN HINES®
        Vanilla Layer Cake
        Frosting, divided
    Green food coloring
    Candy-coated chocolate
        pieces
    Thin pretzel sticks
    2 Lollipops

1. Preheat oven to 350°F. Grease and flour two 8-inch round cake pans.

2. Prepare, bake and cool cake following package directions for basic recipe.

3. To assemble, place one cake layer on serving plate. Spread with ¾ cup Vanilla frosting. Top with second cake layer. Tint 1¼ cups frosting with green food coloring. Spread green frosting on sides of cake. Spread ¾ cup Vanilla frosting on top of cake. To decorate drum, place candy pieces around bottom and top edges of cake on green frosting. Arrange pretzel sticks in zig-zag design between candies. Place lollipops on top of cake with sticks crisscrossing for drumsticks.

12 to 16 Servings

Tip: Spread leftover frosting between graham crackers for a delicious snack.

Speedy Racetrack Cake

Candy Cane Cake

**1 package DUNCAN HINES®
Moist Deluxe Cake Mix
(any flavor)**

Frosting
5 cups confectioners sugar
¾ cup CRISCO® Shortening
½ cup water
**⅓ cup non-dairy powdered
creamer**
2 teaspoons vanilla extract
½ teaspoon salt
Red food coloring
**Maraschino cherry halves,
well drained**

1. Preheat oven to 350°F. Grease and flour 13×9×2-inch pan.

2. Prepare, bake and cool cake following package directions for basic recipe. Remove from pan. Freeze cake for ease in handling.

3. **For frosting,** combine confectioners sugar, shortening, water, non-dairy powdered creamer, vanilla extract and salt in large bowl. Beat at medium speed with electric mixer for 3 minutes. Beat at high speed for 5 minutes. Add confectioners sugar to thicken or water to thin

frosting as needed. Reserve 2 cups frosting. Tint remaining frosting with red food coloring.

4. Cut frozen cake and arrange as shown. Spread white frosting on cake. Mark candy cane stripes in frosting with tip of knife. Place star tip in decorating bag and fill with red frosting. To make stripes, arrange maraschino cherry halves and pipe red frosting following lines.
12 to 16 Servings

Tip: For a quick dessert, serve leftover cake pieces with sugared strawberries or dollops of whipped cream.

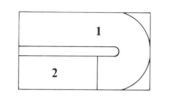

Candy Cane Cake

Tic-Tac-Toe Cake

Tic-Tac-Toe Cake

Cake & Frostings
1 (8-inch) square cake
**2½ cups Buttercream Frosting,
divided (page 525)**
2 tablespoons milk

Decorations & Equipment
4 black licorice twists
3 large red gumdrops
24 small red candies
**1 (19×13-inch) cake board,
cut in half crosswise and
covered, or large plate**

1. Trim top and edges of cake. Place on prepared cake board.

2. Stir milk into 1 cup Buttercream Frosting until well blended. Frost entire cake with thinned frosting to seal in crumbs.

3. Frost again with remaining 1½ cups Buttercream Frosting.

4. Using wooden pick, mark cake into thirds, both horizontally and vertically. Arrange 2 licorice twists over horizontal lines; cut and place remaining licorice twists as shown in photo.

5. Decorate with gumdrops and candies as shown.
Makes 9 to 12 servings

Jet Plane Cake

Cake & Frostings
1 (13×9-inch) cake
3½ cups Buttercream Frosting
(page 525)*
1 cup Base Frosting
(page 525), if desired

Decorations & Equipment
4 pastel miniature
marshmallows
1 small red gumdrop
1 (19×13-inch) cake board,
cut to fit cake, if desired,
and covered
Pastry bag and medium
writing tip

1. Trim top and edges of cake. Cut as shown in diagram 1.

2. Place piece A in center of prepared cake board. Frost top with some of the white frosting, then place piece B over frosting. Starting 3 inches from 1 side make an angled cut in piece B toward the front as shown in diagram 2.

3. Position remaining pieces on prepared cake board as shown in diagram 3, connecting with some of the white frosting. Trim sides to make nose about 1 inch wide. Trim top side edges of piece B to give a rounded appearance as shown in photo.

4. Frost entire cake with Base Frosting to seal in crumbs.

5. Using wooden pick, draw areas for windows as shown. Frost with light gray frosting.

6. Frost remaining cake with white frosting.

7. Using writing tip and blue frosting, pipe outlines for windows and design on wings as shown. Attach flattened marshmallows and gumdrop as shown.
Makes 14 to 16 servings

*Color ½ cup frosting blue and ½ cup light gray; reserve 2½ cups white frosting.

Jet Plane Cake

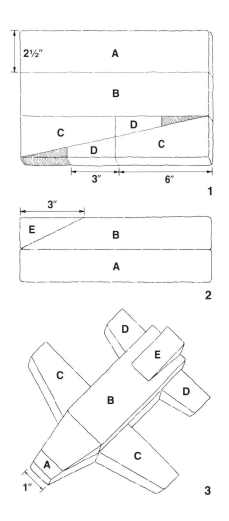

Baseball Cake

1 package DUNCAN HINES®
Moist Deluxe Yellow
Cake Mix
1 container (16 ounces)
DUNCAN HINES® Vanilla
Layer Cake Frosting
Red licorice laces
Green tinted shredded
coconut, optional

1. Preheat oven to 350°F. Grease and flour 2½-quart ovenproof glass bowl with rounded bottom.

2. Prepare cake following package directions for basic recipe; pour into bowl. Bake 55 to 65 minutes or until toothpick inserted in center comes out clean. Cool in bowl on cooling rack 15 minutes. Invert onto cooling rack. Cool completely.

3. To assemble, place cake on serving plate. Frost with Vanilla frosting. Cut 1 licorice lace into 1-inch pieces. Apply licorice laces and pieces on cake to resemble baseball seams. Arrange tinted coconut around base of cake, if desired.
12 to 16 Servings

Easy German Chocolate Cake

1 package DUNCAN HINES®
   Moist Deluxe Swiss
   Chocolate Cake Mix
3 large eggs
½ cup CRISCO® Oil or CRISCO®
   PURITAN® Oil
1¼ cups water
1 cup chopped nuts
⅓ cup butter or regular
   margarine, melted
1 cup packed light brown sugar
1 can (3½ ounces) flaked
   coconut
¼ cup milk

1. Preheat oven to 350°F. Grease and flour 13×9×2-inch pan.
2. Combine dry cake mix, eggs, oil and water in large mixer bowl. Mix cake as directed on package. Stir in ½ cup nuts. Turn batter into pan and spread evenly.
3. Bake at 350°F for 35 to 40 minutes or until toothpick inserted in center comes out clean. Cool in pan on rack.
4. For topping, combine butter, brown sugar, coconut, milk and remaining ½ cup nuts. Spread evenly over cooled cake. Place under broiler and broil 2 to 3 minutes or until bubbly.
12 to 16 servings.

Petits Fours

Lickety-Split Cocoa Cake

1½ cups all-purpose flour
1 cup sugar
¼ cup HERSHEY'S Cocoa
1 teaspoon baking soda
½ teaspoon salt
1 cup water
¼ cup plus 2 tablespoons
   vegetable oil
1 tablespoon white vinegar
1 teaspoon vanilla extract
Lickety-Split Cocoa Frosting
   (page 497)

Heat oven to 350°F. Grease and flour 8-inch square or 9-inch round baking pan. In large bowl, stir together flour, sugar, cocoa, baking soda and salt. Add water, oil, vinegar and vanilla; beat with spoon or wire whisk just until batter is smooth and ingredients are well blended. Pour batter into prepared pan. Bake 35 to 40 minutes or until wooden pick inserted in center comes out clean. Cool in pan; frost with Lickety-Split Cocoa Frosting.
6 to 8 servings.

Petits Fours

1 package DUNCAN HINES®
   Moist Deluxe White
   or Yellow Cake Mix
3 large eggs
⅓ cup CRISCO® Oil or CRISCO®
   PURITAN® Oil
1¼ cups water
3 cups granulated sugar
¼ teaspoon cream of tartar
1½ cups hot water
1 teaspoon vanilla extract
2¼ cups confectioners' sugar
   Food coloring, if desired
   Frosted roses or candy
   decorations, if desired

1. Line 15½×10½×1-inch jelly roll pan with waxed paper. Preheat oven to 350°F.
2. Combine dry cake mix, eggs, oil and 1¼ cups water in large mixer bowl. Mix cake as directed on package. Turn batter into pan and spread evenly.

3. Bake at 350°F for 25 to 30 minutes or until toothpick inserted in center comes out clean. Immediately turn cake out onto towel and peel off paper. Cool.
4. Cut cooled cake into seventy 1½-inch shapes. Place on racks with waxed paper under racks.
5. For frosting, combine granulated sugar, cream of tartar, and 1½ cups hot water in heavy saucepan. Cook over medium heat until syrup reaches 226°F on candy thermometer. Cool until lukewarm (110°F). Stir in vanilla extract. Gradually beat in confectioners' sugar until frosting is of good pouring consistency. Tint frosting with food coloring, if desired.
6. Pour frosting over cakes on racks. After frosting one rack, remove frosting from waxed paper and return to bowl of frosting. If frosting becomes too thick, heat over hot water or add a few drops of hot water. Repeat until all cakes are frosted. Decorate with frosted roses or candy decorations.
70 cakes.

Cocoa Spice Snacking Cake

- ¼ cup (½ stick) butter or margarine, melted
- ¼ cup HERSHEY'S Cocoa
- ¾ cup applesauce
- 1 cup all-purpose flour
- 1 cup sugar
- ¾ teaspoon baking soda
- ½ teaspoon ground cinnamon
- ¼ teaspoon ground nutmeg
- ¼ teaspoon salt
- 1 egg, slightly beaten
- ½ cup chopped nuts
- ½ cup raisins
  Powdered sugar (optional)

Heat oven to 350°F. Grease 9-inch square baking pan. In small bowl, combine butter and cocoa, stirring until smooth; stir in applesauce. Stir together flour, sugar, baking soda, cinnamon, nutmeg and salt. Add cocoa mixture and egg; stir until dry ingredients are moistened. Stir in nuts and raisins. Spread into prepared pan. Bake 28 to 30 minutes or until wooden pick inserted in center comes out clean. Cool in pan on wire rack. Sprinkle powdered sugar over top, if desired.
9 servings.

Cool and Minty Party Cake

- 1 (14-ounce) can EAGLE® Brand Sweetened Condensed Milk (NOT evaporated milk)
- 2 teaspoons peppermint extract
- 8 drops green food coloring
- 2 cups (1 pint) BORDEN® or MEADOW GOLD® Whipping Cream, whipped (do not use non-dairy whipped topping)
- 1 (18¼- or 18½-ounce) package white cake mix
  Green creme de menthe
- 1 (8-ounce) container frozen non-dairy whipped topping, thawed

In large mixing bowl, combine sweetened condensed milk, extract and food coloring. Fold in whipped cream. Pour into aluminum foil-lined 9-inch round layer cake pan; cover. Freeze at least 6 hours or overnight. Meanwhile, prepare and bake cake mix as package directs for two 9-inch round layers. Remove from pans; cool thoroughly. With table fork, poke holes in layers 1 inch apart halfway through each layer. Spoon small amounts of creme de menthe in holes. Place 1 cake layer on serving plate; top with ice cream layer then second cake layer. Trim ice cream layer to fit cake layers. Frost quickly with topping. Return to freezer until ready to serve. Garnish as desired.
Makes one 9-inch cake.

Tip: Cake can be made 1 week ahead and stored in freezer.

Kahlúa® Sweetheart Cake

- ¾ cup unsweetened cocoa
- 1 teaspoon instant coffee crystals
- 1 cup boiling water
- ½ cup plus 2 tablespoons KAHLÚA®
- ½ cup butter or margarine, softened
- ¼ cup shortening
- 1⅓ cups sugar
- 3 eggs
- 1 teaspoon vanilla
- 2 cups sifted all-purpose flour
- 1½ teaspoons baking soda
- ¾ teaspoon salt
- ¼ teaspoon baking powder
  KAHLÚA® Fudge Frosting (recipe follows)

In small heatproof bowl, blend cocoa, coffee and water. Stir in ½ cup Kahlúa®; cool. In large bowl, beat butter, shortening, sugar, eggs and vanilla until light and fluffy. In small bowl, combine four, baking soda, salt and baking powder. Add flour mixture to butter mixture alternately with cocoa mixture, beating well after each addition. Line bottoms of two 9-inch round pans with parchment paper; lightly grease sides of pans. Divide batter evenly between prepared pans. Bake in preheated 350° oven 25 to 30 minutes or just until toothpick inserted into center comes out clean. Do not overbake. Let cool in pans on wire racks 5 minutes. Loosen edges; remove from pans. Peel off parchment paper; cool completely on wire racks. Prepare Kahlúa® Fudge Frosting. Brush bottom of each layer with 1 tablespoon of remaining Kahlúa®. Fill and frost layers with frosting. Decorate as desired. Let frosting set.
Makes 10 to 12 servings.

KAHLÚA® FUDGE FROSTING: In medium saucepan, combine 1 package (6 ounces) semisweet chocolate chips, ¼ cup *each* Kahlúa® and half-and-half and 1 cup butter or margarine. Stir over medium heat until chocolate melts. Remove from heat; blend in 2½ cups powdered sugar. Beat until frosting is cool and holds its shape. (Pan may be placed over ice water to hasten cooling.)

Cool and Minty Party Cake

Strawberries Romanoff on Angel Slices

New Orleans Crumb Cake

- **1 package DUNCAN HINES® Moist Deluxe Devil's Food Cake Mix**
- **3 large eggs**
- **½ cup CRISCO® Oil or CRISCO® PURITAN® Oil**
- **1⅓ cups water**
- **1 cup graham cracker crumbs**
- **3 tablespoons CRISCO® Shortening, melted**
- **1 package (6 ounces) semisweet chocolate pieces (1 cup)**
- **½ cup chopped nuts Sweetened whipped cream, if desired**

1. Preheat oven to 350°F. Grease and flour 13×9×2-inch pan.
2. Combine dry cake mix, eggs, oil and water in large mixer bowl. Mix cake as directed on package. Turn batter into pan and spread evenly.
3. Combine graham cracker crumbs and melted shortening; mix well. Stir in chocolate pieces and nuts. Sprinkle evenly over batter.
4. Bake at 350°F for 40 to 50 minutes or until toothpick inserted in center comes out clean. Cool in pan on rack. Serve with whipped cream.
16 servings.

Birthday Cakelets

- **2 packages DUNCAN HINES® Moist Deluxe Devil's Food Cake Mix**
- **6 large eggs**
- **1 cup CRISCO® Oil or CRISCO® PURITAN® Oil**
- **2⅔ cups water**
- **2 cups light corn syrup**
- **4 large egg whites**
- **⅛ teaspoon salt Red food coloring**
- **½ teaspoon peppermint extract**

1. Preheat oven to 350°F. Grease and flour two 13×9×2-inch pans.
2. Combine dry cake mix, whole eggs, oil and water in large mixer bowl. Mix, bake and cool cakes as directed on package. Freeze cooled cakes at least 2 hours.
3. For frosting, heat syrup to boiling. Beat egg whites in large mixer bowl at medium speed until frothy. Add salt and continue beating until soft peaks form. Turn mixer to high speed and gradually add hot corn syrup,

Strawberries Romanoff on Angel Slices

- **1 package DUNCAN HINES® Angel Food Cake Mix**
- **1⅓ cups water**
- **1½ pints fresh strawberries, hulled and halved lengthwise**
- **⅓ cup orange juice**
- **3 tablespoons orange-flavored liqueur**
- **2 tablespoons sugar**
- **1 cup whipping cream**
- **½ teaspoon vanilla extract**

1. Preheat oven to 375°F.
2. Prepare cake with water as directed on package. Pour batter into ungreased 10-inch tube pan. Cut through batter with knife or spatula to remove large air bubbles.
3. Bake at 375°F for 30 to 40 minutes or until top crust is golden brown, firm and dry. Do not underbake. To cool, hang pan upside down on funnel or bottle at least 1½ hours.
4. Place strawberries in bowl. Combine orange juice, 2 tablespoons of the liqueur and sugar; pour over strawberries. Cover with plastic wrap. Refrigerate, occasionally spooning liquid over strawberries.
5. Beat whipping cream until soft peaks form. Beat in remaining 1 tablespoon liqueur and vanilla extract. Beat until thick. Refrigerate until ready to use.
6. To serve, cut cake into slices. Spoon some strawberries and liquid over cake slices; top with whipped cream.
12 to 16 servings.

beating until soft peaks form. Fold in food coloring to tint delicate pink. Fold in peppermint extract.

4. Draw heart on 3-inch square of cardboard; cut out. Set heart pattern on lower left corner of one cake. Cut around pattern through cake. Cut out 11 more hearts before removing cake pieces. Repeat with remaining cake.

5. Frost sides and tops of each cake heart. Insert pink birthday candle in center of each heart.

24 servings.

Continental Flair Frosting

1 cup sugar
1 cup heavy cream or
evaporated milk
4 squares BAKER'S®
Unsweetened Chocolate
½ cup butter or margarine, at
room temperature
1 teaspoon rum extract or
vanilla

Combine sugar and cream in saucepan. Bring to a boil over medium heat, stirring constantly. Reduce heat and simmer gently for 6 minutes. Remove from heat. Add chocolate and stir until chocolate is melted. Blend

in butter and rum extract. Chill until mixture begins to thicken; then beat until thick, creamy and of spreading consistency.

Makes about 2½ cups, or enough to cover tops and sides of two 8- or 9-inch cake layers, the top and sides of one 9-inch square or 13×9-inch cake, or the tops of 24 cupcakes.

Note: Recipe may be halved.

Royal Glaze

8 bars (8 oz.) HERSHEY'S Semi-
Sweet Baking Chocolate,
broken into pieces
½ cup whipping cream

In small saucepan, combine chocolate pieces and whipping cream. Cook over very low heat, stirring constantly, until chocolate is melted and mixture is smooth; do not boil. Remove from heat. Cool, stirring occasionally, until mixture begins to thicken, 10 to 15 minutes.

About 1 cup.

Birthday Cakelets

Lemon Icing

2 tablespoons margarine or
butter
3 to 4 teaspoons REALEMON®
Lemon Juice from
Concentrate
1 cup confectioners' sugar

In small saucepan, melt margarine with ReaLemon® brand; remove from heat. Stir in sugar; mix well. Drizzle warm icing over 10 inch bundt or tube cake, coffee cake or sweet rolls.

Makes about ½ cup.

Chocolate Butter Frosting

6 tablespoons butter or
margarine
Dash of salt
1 pound (4 cups) confectioners
sugar
2 squares BAKER'S®
Unsweetened Chocolate,
melted and cooled
4 tablespoons (about) milk
1½ teaspoons vanilla

Cream butter with salt. Gradually beat in part of the sugar. Blend in chocolate. Alternately add remaining sugar with milk until of spreading consistency, beating after each addition until smooth. Blend in vanilla.

Makes 3 cups, or enough to cover tops and sides of two 8- or 9-inch layers or the top and sides of one 13×9-inch cake.

Lickety-Split Cocoa Frosting

3 tablespoons butter or
margarine, softened
¼ cup HERSHEY'S Cocoa
1¼ cups powdered sugar
2 to 3 tablespoons milk
½ teaspoon vanilla extract

In small mixer bowl, beat butter until light and fluffy. Add cocoa, powdered sugar, milk and vanilla; beat until smooth and of desired consistency.

About 1 cup frosting.

Fudgey Pecan Cake

**1 cup (2 sticks) butter or
     margarine, melted
1½ cups sugar
1½ teaspoons vanilla extract
  3 eggs, separated
⅔ cup HERSHEY'S Cocoa
½ cup all-purpose flour
  3 tablespoons water
¾ cup finely chopped pecans
⅛ teaspoon cream of tartar
⅛ teaspoon salt
     Royal Glaze (recipe follows)
     Pecan halves**

Heat oven to 350°F. Line bottom of 9-inch springform pan with aluminum foil; butter foil and side of pan. In large mixer bowl, beat butter, sugar and vanilla until light and fluffy. Add egg yolks, one at a time, beating well after each addition. Add cocoa, flour and water; beat well. Stir in pecans. In small mixer bowl, beat egg whites, cream of tartar and salt until stiff peaks form; carefully fold into chocolate mixture. Pour batter into prepared pan. Bake 45 minutes or until top begins to crack slightly. (Cake will not test done in center.) Cool 1 hour. Cover; refrigerate until firm. Remove side of pan.

Prepare Royal Glaze; pour over cake, allowing glaze to run down side. With narrow metal spatula, spread glaze evenly on top and side. Garnish with pecan halves.
10 to 12 servings.

Royal Glaze: In small saucepan, combine 1⅓ cups HERSHEY'S Semi-Sweet Chocolate Chips and ½ cup whipping cream. Cook over very low heat, stirring constantly, until chips are melted and mixture begins to thicken.

Pound Cake

**1 package (2-layer size) yellow
     cake mix or pudding-
     included cake mix
1 package (4-serving size)
     JELL-O® Vanilla,
     Butterscotch, Butter Pecan
     or Lemon Flavor Pudding
     and Pie Filling
1 cup (½ pint) sour cream or
     plain yogurt
⅓ cup vegetable oil
4 eggs
⅛ to ¼ teaspoon mace (optional)**

Combine all ingredients in large bowl. With electric mixer at low speed, blend just to moisten, scraping sides of bowl often. Then beat at medium speed for 4 minutes. Pour batter into 2 greased and floured 9×5-inch loaf pans. Bake in preheated 350° oven for 40 to 45 minutes or until cake tester inserted in center of cake comes out clean and cakes begin to pull away from sides of pans. Cool in pans on wire rack 15 minutes. Remove from pans and finish cooling on wire racks. Sprinkle with confectioners sugar, if desired.
Makes two 9×5-inch loaves.

Mocha Pudding Cake

**1¼ cups granulated sugar, divided
  1 cup all-purpose flour
  2 teaspoons baking powder
¼ teaspoon salt
½ cup (1 stick) butter or
     margarine
  1 bar (1 oz.) HERSHEY'S
     Unsweetened Baking
     Chocolate
½ cup milk
  1 teaspoon vanilla extract
½ cup packed light brown sugar
¼ cup HERSHEY'S Cocoa
  1 cup hot strong coffee
     Ice cream**

Heat oven to 350°F. In bowl, stir together ¾ cup granulated sugar, flour, baking powder and salt. In small saucepan over low heat, melt butter with baking chocolate; add to dry ingredients with milk and vanilla. Beat until smooth. Pour batter into 8- or 9-inch square baking pan.

Stir together remaining ½ cup granulated sugar, brown sugar and cocoa; sprinkle evenly over batter. Pour coffee over top; do not stir. Bake 35 to 40 minutes or until center is almost set. Let stand 15 minutes; spoon into dessert dishes, spooning sauce from bottom of pan over top. Serve with ice cream.
About 8 servings.

Chocolatetown Special Cake

**½ cup HERSHEY'S Cocoa or
     HERSHEY'S Premium
     European Style Cocoa
½ cup boiling water
⅔ cup shortening
1¾ cups sugar
  1 teaspoon vanilla extract
  2 eggs
2¼ cups all-purpose flour
1½ teaspoons baking soda
½ teaspoon salt
1⅓ cups buttermilk or sour milk*
     One-Bowl Buttercream
     Frosting (recipe follows)**

Heat oven to 350°F. Grease and flour two 9-inch round baking pans. In small bowl, stir together cocoa and water until smooth; set aside. In large mixer bowl, beat shortening, sugar and vanilla until light and fluffy. Add eggs; beat well. Stir together flour, baking soda and salt; add to shortening mixture alternately with buttermilk. Blend in cocoa mixture; beat well.

Pour batter into prepared pans. Bake 35 to 40 minutes or until wooden pick inserted in center comes out clean. Cool 10 minutes; remove from pans to wire rack. Cool completely. Frost with One-Bowl Buttercream Frosting.
8 to 10 servings.

*To sour milk: Use 1 tablespoon plus 1 teaspoon white vinegar plus milk to equal 1⅓ cups.

One-Bowl Buttercream Frosting

**6 tablespoons butter or
     margarine, softened
2⅔ cups powdered sugar
½ cup HERSHEY'S Cocoa or
     HERSHEY'S Premium
     European Style Cocoa
⅓ cup milk
  1 teaspoon vanilla extract**

In small mixer bowl, beat butter. Add powdered sugar and cocoa alternately with milk; beat to spreading consistency (additional milk may be needed). Blend in vanilla.
About 2 cups frosting.

Chocolatetown Special Cake

Strawberry Tunnel Cream Cake

1 (10-inch) prepared round angel food cake
2 (3-ounce) packages cream cheese, softened
1 (14-ounce) can EAGLE® Brand Sweetened Condensed Milk (NOT evaporated milk)
1/3 cup REALEMON® Lemon Juice from Concentrate
1 teaspoon almond extract
2 to 4 drops red food coloring, optional
1 cup chopped fresh strawberries
1 (12-ounce) container frozen non-dairy whipped topping, thawed (5 1/4 cups)
Additional fresh strawberries, optional

Invert cake onto serving plate. Cut 1-inch slice crosswise from top of cake; set aside. With sharp knife, cut around cake 1 inch from center hole and 1 inch from outer edge, leaving cake walls 1 inch thick. Remove cake from center, leaving 1-inch-thick base on bottom of cake. Reserve cake pieces. In large mixer bowl, beat cheese until fluffy. Gradually beat in sweetened condensed milk until smooth. Stir in ReaLemon® brand, extract and food coloring if desired. Stir in reserved torn cake pieces and chopped strawberries. Fold in *1 cup* whipped topping. Fill cavity of cake with strawberry mixture; replace top slice of cake. Chill 3 hours or until set. Frost with remaining whipped topping; garnish with strawberries if desired. Store in refrigerator.
Makes one 10-inch cake.

Chocolate Sheet Cake

1 1/4 cups margarine or butter
1/2 cup unsweetened cocoa
1 cup water
2 cups unsifted flour
1 1/2 cups firmly packed brown sugar
1 teaspoon baking soda
1 teaspoon ground cinnamon
1/2 teaspoon salt
1 (14-ounce) can EAGLE® Brand Sweetened Condensed Milk (NOT evaporated milk)
2 eggs
1 teaspoon vanilla extract
1 cup confectioners' sugar
1 cup nuts

Preheat oven to 350°. In small saucepan, melt *1 cup* margarine; stir in *1/4 cup* cocoa, then water. Bring to a boil; remove from heat. In large mixer bowl, combine flour, brown sugar, baking soda, cinnamon and salt. Add cocoa mixture; beat well. Stir in *1/3 cup* sweetened condensed milk, eggs and vanilla. Pour into greased 15×10-inch jellyroll pan. Bake 15 minutes or until cake springs back when lightly touched. In small saucepan, melt remaining *1/4 cup* margarine; add remaining *1/4 cup* cocoa and remaining sweetened condensed milk. Stir in confectioners' sugar and nuts. Spread on *warm* cake.
Makes one 15×10-inch cake.

Banana Mocha Cake

2 extra-ripe, medium DOLE® Bananas
1 teaspoon instant coffee powder
1 1/4 cups flour
2/3 cup sugar
1/4 cup cornstarch
3 tablespoons cocoa
1 teaspoon baking soda
1/2 teaspoon salt
1/3 cup vegetable oil
1 egg, lightly beaten
1 tablespoon vinegar
1 teaspoon vanilla extract
Silky Mocha Frosting (recipe follows)

Preheat oven to 350°F. Puree bananas in blender (1 cup). Stir coffee powder into pureed bananas. In 9-inch square baking pan, combine flour, sugar, cornstarch, cocoa, baking soda and salt. Blend well. Make a well in center of dry ingredients. Add banana mixture, oil, egg, vinegar and vanilla. Stir in dry mixture with fork until well blended. Bake in preheated oven 30 minutes. Cool completely on wire rack. Spread cake with Silky Mocha Frosting.
Makes 12 servings.
SILKY MOCHA FROSTING: In large mixer bowl, combine 3 tablespoons margarine, 1 1/2 cups sifted powdered sugar, 2 tablespoons cocoa and 1 teaspoon instant coffee powder. Add 2 tablespoons milk and 1/2 teaspoon vanilla extract. Beat until smooth.

Strawberry Tunnel Cream Cake

Golden Crunch Cake

2 cups fine vanilla wafer crumbs
1 cup finely chopped pecans
½ cup sugar
**¼ cup (½ stick) butter or
  margarine**
**1 package DUNCAN HINES®
  Moist Deluxe Butter Recipe
  Golden Cake Mix**
3 large eggs
**½ cup (1 stick) butter or
  margarine, softened**
⅔ cup water

1. Preheat oven to 375°F. Grease two 9×5×3-inch pans.
2. Combine wafer crumbs, pecans and sugar in bowl. Add ¼ cup butter and cut in with pastry blender until crumbs are fine. Divide evenly in pans; press on bottom and sides.
3. Combine dry cake mix, eggs, ½ cup butter and water in large mixer bowl. Mix cake as directed on package. Divide batter evenly in pans.
4. Bake at 375°F for 50 to 60 minutes or until toothpick inserted in center comes out clean. Cool in pans on racks 5 minutes. Carefully loosen cake from pans and turn upside down on racks; cool completely.
20 servings.

Choco-Coconut Cake Roll

**4 eggs, separated, at room
  temperature**
**½ cup plus ⅓ cup granulated
  sugar, divided**
1 teaspoon vanilla extract
½ cup all-purpose flour
⅓ cup HERSHEY'S Cocoa
½ teaspoon baking powder
¼ teaspoon baking soda
⅛ teaspoon salt
⅓ cup water
Powdered sugar
**Cherry-Coconut Filling (recipe
  follows)**

Heat oven to 375°F. Line 15½×10½×1-inch jelly roll pan with foil; generously grease foil. Set aside. In large mixer bowl, beat egg whites until soft peaks form. Gradually add ½ cup granulated sugar, beating until stiff peaks form. Set aside.

Choco-Coconut Cake Roll

In small mixer bowl, on medium speed, beat egg yolks and vanilla 3 minutes. Gradually add remaining ⅓ cup granulated sugar; continue beating 2 additional minutes. Stir together flour, cocoa, baking powder, baking soda and salt; beating on low speed of electric mixer, add to egg yolk mixture alternately with water just until batter is smooth. Gradually fold chocolate mixture into beaten egg whites until well blended.

Spread batter evenly in prepared pan. Bake 12 to 15 minutes or until top springs back when touched lightly. Immediately loosen cake from edges of pan; invert onto clean towel sprinkled with powdered sugar. Carefully peel off foil. Immediately roll cake and towel together starting from narrow end; place on wire rack to cool completely.

Prepare Cherry-Coconut Filling. Carefully unroll cake; remove towel. Spread cake with filling; reroll cake. Refrigerate. Sprinkle powdered sugar over top just before serving.
8 to 10 servings.

Cherry-Coconut Filling

**1 cup (½ pt.) cold whipping
  cream**
3 tablespoons powdered sugar
3 drops red food color (optional)
**⅓ cup chopped maraschino
  cherries, well-drained**
½ cup flaked coconut

In small mixer bowl, beat whipping cream, powdered sugar and food color, if desired, until stiff. Fold in cherries and coconut.

Blueberry Angel Food Cake Roll

Cherry Cream Nut Roll

   5 eggs, separated
   ½ cup granulated sugar
   1 teaspoon brandy extract or rum extract
   1 can SOLO® or 1 jar BAKER® Nut Filling
   ½ cup all-purpose flour
   ½ teaspoon baking powder
   ¼ teaspoon salt
      Confectioners sugar

Filling
   2 cups heavy cream
   3 to 4 tablespoons confectioners sugar
   1½ teaspoons brandy extract or rum extract
   1 can SOLO® or 1 jar BAKER® Cherry Filling

Preheat oven to 350°F. Grease 15×10-inch jelly-roll pan. Line pan with waxed paper. Grease paper and set aside.

Beat egg yolks and granulated sugar about 5 minutes in large bowl with electric mixer until thick and pale yellow. Beat in brandy extract and nut filling until well blended.

Beat egg whites in separate bowl with electric mixer until stiff peaks form. Stir 3 heaping tablespoons egg whites into nut mixture to lighten. Fold in remaining egg whites. Sift flour, baking powder and salt over nut mixture and fold in. Spread batter evenly in prepared pan.

Bake 20 to 22 minutes or until center springs back when lightly pressed.

Sprinkle towel with confectioners sugar. Invert cake onto sugared towel and remove pan. Peel off waxed paper and trim off any crusty edges. Roll up cake and towel, jelly-roll style, starting from short side. Place on wire rack and cool completely.

To fill cake, unroll cooled cake on flat surface. Whip cream in large bowl with electric mixer until soft peaks form. Add 3 to 4 tablespoons confectioners sugar and brandy extract and whip until firm. Fold whipped cream into cherry filling. Spread half of cherry cream over cake. Reroll cake without towel and place, seam-side down, on serving plate. Spread remaining cherry cream over side and top of cake. Refrigerate until ready to serve.
Makes 8 to 10 servings

Blueberry Angel Food Cake Rolls

   1 package DUNCAN HINES® Angel Food Cake Mix
      Confectioners sugar
   1 can (21 ounces) blueberry pie filling
      Mint leaves, for garnish (optional)

1. Preheat oven to 350°F. Line two 15½×10½×1-inch jelly-roll pans with aluminum foil.

2. Prepare cake following package directions. Divide into pans. Spread evenly. Cut through batter with knife or spatula to remove large air bubbles. Bake at 350°F for 15 minutes or until set. Invert cakes at once onto clean, lint-free dishtowels dusted with confectioners sugar. Remove foil carefully. Starting at short end, roll up each cake with towel jelly-roll fashion. Cool completely.

3. Unroll cakes. Spread about 1 cup blueberry pie filling to within 1 inch of edges on each cake. Reroll and place seam-side down on serving plate. Dust with confectioners sugar. Garnish with mint leaves, if desired.
16 to 20 Servings

Tip: For a variation in flavor, substitute cherry pie filling for blueberry pie filling.

Fresh Peach Mousse Cake

   ¾ cup whipping cream
   ¼ cup sugar, divided
   ½ teaspoon vanilla extract
   ¼ teaspoon almond extract
   3 egg whites
   1 package (10¾ ounces) frozen pound cake, thawed
   3 fresh California peaches, sliced
      Mint sprigs (optional garnish)

In large chilled bowl, whip cream until stiff, gradually beating in 2 tablespoons sugar and the extracts; set aside. In medium bowl, beat egg whites with remaining 2 tablespoons sugar until stiff. Carefully fold egg whites into whipped cream mixture so as not to reduce volume; refrigerate mousse mixture until chilled. Cut cake horizontally into 3 layers.

Reserve 5 peach slices for garnish. Place one cake layer on serving plate. Spread with ⅓ of mousse and ½ of remaining peach slices. Repeat layering, ending with mousse. Refrigerate until chilled. Garnish with reserved peach slices and mint sprigs, if desired.

Makes 8 servings

Favorite recipe from **California Tree Fruit Agreement**

Mini Morsel Pound Cake

    3 cups all-purpose flour
    2 teaspoons baking powder
    ½ teaspoon salt
    1½ cups (3 sticks) butter or
       margarine, softened
    1½ cups granulated sugar
    4 eggs
    1 teaspoon vanilla extract
    ¼ cup milk
One 12-oz. pkg. (2 cups)
       NESTLÉ® Toll House®
       Semi-Sweet Chocolate
       Mini Morsels
       Confectioners' sugar for
       garnish

Preheat oven to 350°F. Grease and flour 10-inch fluted tube pan or two 9×5-inch loaf pans. In small bowl, combine flour, baking powder and salt; set aside.

In large mixer bowl, beat butter and granulated sugar until creamy. Add eggs, one at a time, beating well after each addition. Blend in vanilla extract. Add flour mixture alternately with milk. Stir in mini morsels. Pour into prepared pan.

Bake 60 to 70 minutes until cake tester inserted into center comes out clean. Cool 15 minutes; remove from pan. Cool completely. Sprinkle with confectioners' sugar.

Makes 16 to 20 servings

Della Robbia Cake

Cake
    1 package DUNCAN HINES®
       Angel Food Cake Mix
    1½ teaspoons grated lemon
       peel

Glaze
    6 tablespoons sugar
    1½ tablespoons cornstarch
    1 cup water
    1 tablespoon lemon juice
    ½ teaspoon vanilla extract
       Few drops red food
       coloring
    6 cling peach slices
    6 medium strawberries,
       sliced

1. Preheat oven to 375°F.

2. **For cake,** prepare following package directions adding lemon peel with Cake Flour Mixture (red "B" packet). Bake and cool following package directions.

3. **For glaze,** combine sugar, cornstarch and water in small saucepan. Cook on medium-high heat until mixture thickens and clears. Remove from heat. Stir in lemon juice, vanilla extract and red food coloring.

4. Alternate peach slices with strawberry slices around top of cooled cake. Pour glaze over fruit and top of cake. Refrigerate leftovers.   *12 to 16 Servings*

Tip: Use only metal or glass mixing bowls when preparing angel food cake mixes. Plastic or ceramic bowls can retain traces of grease which will prevent the egg whites from reaching full volume.

Della Robbia Cake

Holiday Fruitcake

- 1 cup chopped candied fruit
- ⅔ cup pitted dates, chopped
- ½ cup chopped walnuts
- ¼ cup brandy or orange juice
- 1 package (6-serving size) JELL-O® Instant Pudding and Pie Filling, Vanilla Flavor
- 1 package (2-layer size) yellow cake mix
- 4 eggs
- 1 cup (½ pint) sour cream
- ⅓ cup vegetable oil
- 1 tablespoon grated orange rind
- ⅔ cup cold milk
  Marzipan Fruits (recipe follows) (optional)

MIX together candied fruit, dates, walnuts and brandy.

RESERVE ⅓ cup pudding mix; set aside. Combine cake mix, remaining pudding mix, eggs, sour cream, oil and orange rind in large bowl. Beat at low speed of electric mixer just to moisten, scraping sides of bowl often. Beat at medium speed 4 minutes. Stir in fruit mixture.

POUR batter into well-greased and floured 10-inch fluted tube pan. Bake at 350° for 45 minutes or until cake tester inserted in center comes out clean. Cool in pan 15 minutes. Remove from pan; finish cooling on wire rack.

BEAT reserved pudding mix and milk in small bowl until smooth. Spoon over top of cake to glaze. Garnish with Marzipan Fruits, if desired.   *Makes 12 servings*

Prep time: 30 minutes
Baking time: 45 minutes

Marzipan Fruits

- 1¾ cups BAKER'S® ANGEL FLAKE® Coconut, finely chopped
- 1 package (4-serving size) JELL-O® Brand Gelatin, any flavor
- 1 cup ground blanched almonds
- ⅔ cup sweetened condensed milk
- 1½ teaspoons sugar
- 1 teaspoon almond extract
  Food coloring (optional)
  Whole cloves (optional)
  Citron or angelica (optional)

MIX together coconut, gelatin, almonds, milk, sugar and extract. Shape by hand into small fruits, or use small candy molds. If desired, use food coloring to paint details on fruit; add whole cloves and citron for stems and blossom ends. Chill until dry. Store in covered container at room temperature up to 1 week.
  Makes 2 to 3 dozen confections

Prep time: 30 minutes

Top to bottom: Eggnog Cheesecake (page 536), Holiday Fruitcake and Raspberry Gift Box (page 559)

Fudge Ribbon Cake

1 (18¼- or 18½-ounce)
    package chocolate cake
    mix
1 (8-ounce) package cream
    cheese, softened
2 tablespoons margarine or
    butter, softened
1 tablespoon cornstarch
1 (14-ounce) can EAGLE®
    Brand Sweetened
    Condensed Milk
    (NOT evaporated milk)
1 egg
1 teaspoon vanilla extract
    Confectioners' sugar or
    Chocolate Drizzle
    (recipe follows)

Preheat oven to 350°. Prepare cake mix as package directs. Pour batter into *well-greased* and floured 10-inch fluted tube pan. In small mixer bowl, beat cheese, margarine and cornstarch until fluffy. Gradually beat in sweetened condensed milk, then egg and vanilla until smooth. Pour evenly over cake batter. Bake 50 to 55 minutes or until wooden pick inserted near center comes out clean. Cool 15 minutes; remove from pan. Cool. Sprinkle with confectioners' sugar or drizzle with Chocolate Drizzle.

Makes one 10-inch cake

CHOCOLATE DRIZZLE: In small saucepan, over low heat, melt 1 (1-ounce) square unsweetened or semi-sweet chocolate and 1 tablespoon margarine or butter with 2 tablespoons water. Remove from heat. Stir in ¾ cup confectioners' sugar and ½ teaspoon vanilla extract. Stir until smooth.   *Makes ⅓ cup*

Fudge Ribbon Sheet Cake:
Prepare cake mix as package directs. Pour batter into *well-greased* and floured 15×10-inch jellyroll pan. Prepare cream cheese topping as above; spoon evenly over batter. Bake 20 minutes or until wooden pick inserted near center comes out clean. Cool. Frost with 1 (16-ounce) can ready-to-spread chocolate frosting.

Left to right: Lemon Cheesecake with Raspberry Sauce (page 535) and Triple Chocolate Fantasy

Triple Chocolate Fantasy

Cake
1 package DUNCAN HINES®
    Moist Deluxe Devil's
    Food Cake Mix
3 eggs
1⅓ cups water
½ cup CRISCO® Oil or
    CRISCO® PURITAN® Oil
½ cup ground walnuts
    (see Tip)

Chocolate Glaze
1 package (12 ounces) semi-
    sweet chocolate chips
¼ cup *plus* 2 tablespoons
    butter or margarine
¼ cup coarsely chopped
    walnuts, for garnish

White Chocolate Glaze
3 ounces white chocolate,
    coarsely chopped
1 tablespoon CRISCO®
    Shortening

1. Preheat oven to 350°F. Grease and flour 10-inch Bundt® pan.

2. **For cake,** combine cake mix, eggs, water, oil and ground walnuts in large bowl. Beat at medium speed with electric mixer for 2 minutes. Pour into pan. Bake at 350°F for 45 to 55 minutes or until toothpick inserted in center comes out clean. Cool in pan 25 minutes. Invert onto serving plate. Cool completely.

3. **For chocolate glaze,** combine chocolate chips and butter in small heavy saucepan. Heat over low heat until chips are melted. Stir constantly until shiny and smooth. (Glaze will be very thick.) Spread hot glaze over cooled cake. Garnish with coarsely chopped walnuts.

4. **For white chocolate glaze,** combine white chocolate and shortening in small heavy saucepan. Heat on low heat until melted, stirring constantly. Drizzle hot glaze over top of cake.   *12 to 16 Servings*

Tip: To grind walnuts, use a food processor fitted with steel blade. Process until fine.

Easy Pina Colada Cake

- 1 (18¼- to 18½-ounce) package yellow cake mix*
- 1 (4-serving size) package *instant* vanilla flavor pudding and pie filling mix
- 1 (15-ounce) can COCO LOPEZ® Cream of Coconut
- ½ cup plus 2 tablespoons rum
- ⅓ cup vegetable oil
- 4 eggs
- 1 (8-ounce) can crushed pineapple, *well drained*
  Whipped cream, pineapple chunks, maraschino cherries, toasted coconut for garnish

Preheat oven to 350°. In large mixer bowl, combine cake mix, pudding mix, ½ *cup* cream of coconut, ½ *cup* rum, oil and eggs. Beat on medium speed 2 minutes. Stir in pineapple. Pour into well-greased and floured 10-inch bundt or tube pan. Bake 50 to 55 minutes. Cool 10 minutes. Remove from pan. With a table knife or skewer, poke holes about 1 inch apart in cake almost to bottom. Combine remaining cream of coconut and remaining *2 tablespoons* rum; slowly spoon over cake. Chill thoroughly. Garnish as desired. Store in refrigerator.
Makes one 10-inch cake.

*If cake mix with "pudding in" is used, omit pudding mix.

Rum-Nut Pudding Cake

- 1 cup chopped pecans or walnuts
- 1 package (2-layer size) yellow cake mix*
- 1 package (4-serving size) JELL-O® Vanilla or Butter Pecan Flavor Instant Pudding and Pie Filling
- 4 eggs
- ¾ cup water*
- ¼ cup vegetable oil
- ⅔ cup dark rum
- 1 cup sugar
- ½ cup butter or margarine

Sprinkle nuts evenly in bottom of greased and floured 10-inch tube or fluted tube pan. Combine cake mix, pudding mix, eggs, ½ cup of the water, the oil and ⅓ cup of the rum in large bowl. With electric mixer at low speed, blend just to moisten, scraping sides of bowl often. Then beat at medium speed for 4 minutes. Pour batter into pan. Bake in preheated 325° oven for about 1 hour or until cake tester inserted in center comes out clean and cake begins to pull away from sides of pan. Do not underbake. Cool in pan on wire rack 15 minutes.

Meanwhile, combine sugar, butter and remaining ¼ cup water in small saucepan. Cook and stir over medium-high heat until mixture comes to a boil; boil 5 minutes, stirring constantly. Stir in remaining rum and bring just to a boil.

Invert cake onto serving plate and prick with cake tester or wooden pick. Carefully spoon warm syrup over warm cake. Garnish with whipped topping and pecans, if desired.
Makes one 10-inch cake.

**Substitution:* Use pudding-included cake mix, reducing water in batter to ¼ cup.

Kentucky Jam Cake

- 1½ cups flour
- 1 teaspoon baking soda
- ½ teaspoon salt
- 1 teaspoon allspice
- ¼ teaspoon cinnamon
- ¾ cup buttermilk
- 2 tablespoons whiskey, bourbon or fruit juice
- ⅓ cup shortening
- ½ cup granulated sugar
- ½ cup firmly packed brown sugar
- 3 eggs, separated
- ½ cup seedless raspberry or blackberry jam
- 2 squares BAKER'S® Unsweetened Chocolate, melted and cooled
- 1 cup raisins
- ½ cup chopped nuts*

Mix flour, soda, salt and spices. Combine buttermilk and whiskey. Cream shortening. Gradually beat in sugars and continue beating until light and fluffy. Add egg yolks and beat thoroughly. Alternately add flour and buttermilk mixtures, beating after each addition until smooth. Blend in jam and chocolate. Fold in raisins and nuts. Beat egg whites until stiff peaks form; fold into batter.

Pour into well-greased 9-inch tube pan. Bake at 350° for 50 to 55 minutes, or until cake tester inserted in center of cake comes out clean. Cool in pan 15 minutes. Remove sides of pan and finish cooling upright on rack. Loosen from tube and bottom; invert onto rack. Wrap in aluminum foil or plastic wrap. Store in refrigerator at least 2 days to mellow flavors. Serve at room temperature. Sprinkle with confectioners sugar and garnish with raspberries, if desired.
Makes one 9-inch cake.

*Or use 8 squares Baker's® Semi-Sweet Chocolate, cut into large (⅜-inch) chunks.

Easy Pina Colada Cake

Surprise Carrot Cake

1 8-ounce package
  PHILADELPHIA BRAND®
  Cream Cheese, softened
¼ cup sugar
1 egg, beaten

* * *

2 cups flour
1¾ cups sugar
2 teaspoons baking soda
2 teaspoons cinnamon
1 teaspoon salt
1 cup oil
3 eggs, beaten
3 cups shredded carrot
½ cup chopped nuts

Combine cream cheese, sugar and egg, mixing until well blended. Set aside.

Combine dry ingredients. Add combined oil and eggs, mixing just until moistened. Fold in carrots and nuts. Reserve 2 cups batter; pour remaining batter into greased and floured 9-inch bundt pan. Pour cream cheese mixture over batter; carefully spoon reserved batter over cream cheese mixture, spreading to cover. Bake at 350°, 55 minutes or until wooden pick inserted in center comes out clean. Cool 10 minutes; remove from pan. Cool thoroughly. Sprinkle with powdered sugar, if desired.
12 servings.
Variation: Substitute Light PHILADELPHIA BRAND® Neufchatel Cheese for Cream Cheese.

Surprise Carrot Cake

Pudding Poke Cake

1 package (2-layer size) yellow
  cake mix or pudding-
  included cake mix*
  Ingredients for cake mix
2 packages (4-serving size)
  JELL-O® Chocolate Flavor
  Instant Pudding and Pie
  Filling*
1 cup confectioners sugar
4 cups cold milk

Prepare and bake cake as directed on package for 13×9-inch cake. Remove from oven. Poke holes at once down through cake to pan with round handle of wooden spoon. (Or poke holes with plastic drinking straw, using turning motion to make large holes.) Holes should be at 1-inch intervals.

Only after the holes are made, combine pudding mix with sugar in large bowl. Gradually stir in milk. Beat with electric mixer at low speed for not more than 1 minute. Do not overbeat. Quickly, before pudding thickens, pour about half of the thin pudding evenly over warm cake and into holes. (This will make stripes in cake.) Allow remaining pudding to thicken slightly; then spoon over the top, swirling it to "frost" the cake. Chill at least 1 hour. Store cake in refrigerator.
Makes one 13×9-inch cake.

Peanut Butter Poke Cake: Prepare Pudding Poke Cake as directed, using chocolate flavor instant pudding and pie filling. Add ½ cup peanut butter to pudding mix and confectioners sugar with ½ cup of the milk; blend well before adding remaining milk and beating.

*Additional Flavor Combinations: Use yellow cake mix with butterscotch or pistachio flavor pudding mix.

Use chocolate cake mix with chocolate, vanilla, coconut cream, banana cream or pistachio flavor pudding mix.

Use lemon cake mix with lemon flavor pudding mix.

Use white cake mix with butterscotch, chocolate, pistachio or vanilla pudding mix.

Old-Fashioned Lemon Pudding Cake

3 eggs, separated
1 cup sugar
¼ cup unsifted flour
¼ teaspoon salt
1 cup BORDEN® or
  MEADOW GOLD® Milk
¼ cup REALEMON® Lemon Juice
  from Concentrate

Preheat oven to 325°. In small mixer bowl, beat egg whites until stiff but not dry; set aside. In medium bowl, combine sugar, flour and salt. In small bowl, beat egg yolks; stir in milk and ReaLemon® brand. Add to flour mixture; mix well. Fold in egg whites; pour into 1-quart baking dish. Place in larger pan; fill with 1 inch hot water. Bake 50 to 55 minutes or until top is well browned. Cool about 30 minutes before serving. Spoon pudding over cake in serving dishes. Refrigerate leftovers.
Makes 6 to 8 servings.

Individual Servings: Pour mixture into 8 (6-ounce) custard cups; place in shallow pan. Fill with 1 inch hot water. Bake 35 to 40 minutes.

Hot Fudge Sundae Cake

(use all the ice cream). Place top cake layer over ice cream. Cover and freeze.

4. **For fudge sauce,** combine evaporated milk and sugar in medium saucepan. Stir constantly on medium heat until mixture comes to a rolling boil. Boil and stir for 1 minute. Add unsweetened chocolate and stir until melted. Beat over heat until smooth. Remove from heat. Stir in butter, vanilla extract and salt.

5. To serve, cut cake into serving squares. Spoon hot fudge sauce on top of each cake square. Garnish with whipped cream, maraschino cherries and mint leaves, if desired.

12 to 16 Servings

Tip: Fudge sauce may be prepared ahead and refrigerated in tightly sealed jar. Reheat when ready to serve.

Caramel Fudge Cake

- 1 (18¼- or 18½-ounce) package chocolate cake mix
- 1 (14-ounce) package EAGLE™ Brand Caramels, unwrapped
- ½ cup margarine or butter
- 1 (14-ounce) can EAGLE® Brand Sweetened Condensed Milk (NOT evaporated milk)
- 1 cup coarsely chopped pecans

Preheat oven to 350°. Prepare cake mix as package directs. Pour *2 cups* batter into greased 13×9-inch baking pan; bake 15 minutes. Meanwhile, in heavy saucepan, over low heat, melt caramels and margarine. Remove from heat; add sweetened condensed milk. *Mix well.* Spread caramel mixture evenly over cake; spread remaining cake batter over caramel mixture. Top with pecans. Return to oven; bake 30 to 35 minutes longer or until cake springs back when lightly touched. Cool. Garnish as desired.

Makes 10 to 12 servings

Hot Fudge Sundae Cake

- 1 package DUNCAN HINES® Moist Deluxe Dark Dutch Fudge Cake Mix
- ½ gallon brick vanilla ice cream

Fudge Sauce
- 1 can (12 ounces) evaporated milk
- 1¾ cups sugar
- 4 squares (1 ounce each) unsweetened chocolate
- ¼ cup butter or margarine
- 1½ teaspoons vanilla extract
- ¼ teaspoon salt
  Whipped cream, for garnish
  Maraschino cherries, for garnish
  Mint leaves, for garnish (optional)

1. Preheat oven to 350°F. Grease and flour 13×9×2-inch pan.

2. Prepare, bake and cool cake following package directions for basic recipe.

3. Remove cake from pan. Split cake in half horizontally. Place bottom layer back in pan. Cut ice cream into even slices and place evenly over bottom cake layer

Easy Carrot Cake

- 1¼ cups MIRACLE WHIP® Salad Dressing
- 1 package (2-layer size) yellow cake mix
- 4 eggs
- ¼ cup cold water
- 2 teaspoons ground cinnamon
- 2 cups finely shredded carrots
- ½ cup chopped walnuts
- 1 container (16 ounces) ready-to-spread cream cheese frosting

• Heat oven to 350°F.

• Beat salad dressing, cake mix, eggs, water and cinnamon at medium speed with electric mixer until well blended. Stir in carrots and walnuts. Pour into greased 13×9-inch baking pan.

• Bake 30 to 35 minutes or until wooden pick inserted in center comes out clean. Cool completely. Spread cake with frosting.

Makes 12 servings

Prep time: 15 minutes
Cooking time: 35 minutes

Light and Luscious Lemon Cake

**1 package DUNCAN HINES®
Moist Deluxe Lemon
Supreme Cake Mix**

Frosting
**1 can (6 ounces) frozen
lemonade concentrate,
thawed**
**1 can (14 ounces) sweetened
condensed milk**
**1 container (8 ounces) frozen
whipped topping, thawed**
**3 drops yellow food coloring
(optional)
Lemon slices, for garnish
Mint leaves, for garnish**

1. Preheat oven to 350°F. Grease and flour 13×9×2-inch pan.

2. Prepare and bake cake following package directions for basic recipe. Cool in pan 15 minutes. Invert onto cooling rack. Cool completely. Split cake in half horizontally (see Tip).

3. **For frosting,** combine lemonade concentrate and sweetened condensed milk in medium bowl. Fold in whipped topping. Add food coloring, if desired. Blend well. Place bottom cake layer on serving plate. Spread one-third frosting on top. Place top cake layer on frosting. Frost sides and top with remaining frosting. Garnish with lemon slices and mint leaves. Refrigerate until ready to serve.
12 to 16 Servings

Tip: To cut cake evenly, measure cake with ruler. Divide into 2 equal layers. Mark with toothpicks. Cut through layer with large serrated knife using toothpicks as guide.

Dainty Pineapple Upside Down Cakes

**1¼ cups firmly packed brown
sugar**
**⅔ cup butter or margarine,
melted**
**1 can (20 ounces) pineapple
slices, drained**
**15 maraschino cherries,
halved and drained**
**1 package DUNCAN HINES®
Moist Deluxe Pineapple
Supreme Cake Mix**

1. Preheat oven to 350°F.

2. Combine brown sugar and butter in small bowl. Press about 2 teaspoons mixture in each 2½-inch diameter muffin cup. Cut pineapple slices into thirds. Place 1 pineapple section and 1 cherry half in each cup.

3. Prepare cake mix following package directions for basic recipe. Fill muffin cups ¾ full. Bake at 350°F for 15 to 20 minutes or until toothpick inserted in center comes out clean. Loosen cupcakes from sides of pan. Invert onto cooling rack. Cool. *30 Cupcakes*

Tip: For ease in removing cupcakes, bake one muffin pan at a time. If any topping remains in pan, re-melt in warm oven for several minutes and spread on cupcakes.

Light and Luscious Lemon Cake

Fudge 'n' Banana Cupcakes

- **1 package DUNCAN HINES®**
  Moist Deluxe Devil's Food
  Cake Mix
- **3 large eggs**
- **½ cup CRISCO® Oil or CRISCO®**
  PURITAN® Oil
- **1⅓ cups water**
- **½ cup (1 stick) butter or**
  margarine
- **2 ounces (2 squares)**
  unsweetened chocolate
- **1 pound confectioners' sugar**
- **½ cup half-and-half**
- **1 teaspoon vanilla extract**
- **4 medium bananas**
- **2 tablespoons lemon juice**

1. Preheat oven to 350°F. Line 24 muffin cups with paper baking cups.
2. Combine dry cake mix, eggs, oil and water in large mixer bowl. Mix, bake and cool cupcakes as directed on package.
3. For frosting,* melt butter and chocolate in heavy saucepan over low heat. Remove from heat. Add confectioners' sugar alternately with half-and-half, mixing until smooth after each addition. Beat in vanilla extract. Add more confectioners' sugar to thicken or milk to thin as needed.
4. Using small paring knife, remove cone-shaped piece from top center of each cupcake. Dot top of each cone with frosting. Frost top of each cupcake spreading frosting down into cone-shaped hole. Slice bananas and dip in lemon juice. Stand three banana slices in each hole. Set cone-shaped pieces, pointed-side-up, on banana slices.
24 cupcakes.
   *Or use 1 can Duncan Hines® Dark Dutch Fudge or Chocolate Frosting.

Pineapple Upside-Down Cake

- **1 can (20 ounces) DOLE®**
  Pineapple Slices in Juice
- **⅔ cup margarine**
- **⅔ cup brown sugar, packed**
- **10 maraschino cherries**
- **¾ cup granulated sugar**
- **2 eggs, separated**
- **1 teaspoon grated lemon peel**
- **1 teaspoon lemon juice**
- **1 teaspoon vanilla extract**
- **1½ cups flour**
- **1¾ teaspoons baking powder**
- **¼ teaspoon salt**
- **½ cup dairy sour cream**

Preheat oven to 350°F. Drain pineapple; reserve 2 tablespoons liquid. In 9- or 10-inch cast iron skillet, melt ⅓ cup margarine. Remove from heat. Add brown sugar and stir until blended. Arrange pineapple slices in skillet. Place 1 cherry in center of each slice.

In large bowl, beat remaining ⅓ cup margarine with ½ cup granulated sugar until fluffy. Beat in egg yolks, lemon peel and juice, and vanilla. In medium bowl, combine flour, baking powder and salt. Blend dry ingredients into creamed mixture alternately with sour cream and reserved pineapple liquid. In large bowl, beat egg whites until soft peaks form.

Gradually beat in remaining ¼ cup granulated sugar until stiff peaks form. Fold into batter. Spread evenly over pineapple in skillet.

Bake in preheated oven about 35 minutes or until cake springs back when touched. Let stand in skillet on wire rack 10 minutes. Invert onto serving plate. Serve warm or cold. *Makes 8 to 10 servings.*

Bittersweet Glaze

- **2 squares BAKER'S®**
  Unsweetened Chocolate
- **2 tablespoons butter or**
  margarine
- **Dash of salt**
- **1¾ cups confectioners sugar**
- **3 tablespoons (about) hot water**

1. Melt chocolate with butter in saucepan over very low heat, stirring constantly until smooth. Remove from heat and add salt. Alternately add sugar with water until of spreading consistency.
Makes 1 cup, or enough for a 9- or 10-inch tube cake, 9-inch square cake, 10-inch cake roll or about 3½ dozen cookies.

Pineapple Upside-Down Cake

Black Bottom Cupcakes

2 packages (3 ounces each) cream cheese, softened
1⅓ cups sugar
1 egg
1 package (6 ounces) chocolate chips
1½ cups flour
¼ cup unsweetened cocoa
1 teaspoon baking soda
½ teaspoon salt
2 extra-ripe, medium DOLE® Bananas
⅓ cup vegetable oil
1 teaspoon vanilla extract
1 firm, large DOLE® Banana

Preheat oven to 350°F. Line 18 muffin cups with paper liners. In small bowl, beat cream cheese and ⅓ cup sugar until light and fluffy. Add egg; beat until well blended. Stir in chocolate chips. Set aside.

In large bowl, combine remaining 1 cup sugar, flour, cocoa, baking soda and salt; mix well. Puree extra-ripe bananas in blender (1 cup). Combine pureed bananas with oil and vanilla; stir into flour mixture until smooth.

Divide batter evenly among prepared muffin cups. Thinly slice firm banana; place 2 slices in center of batter in each muffin cup. Divide cream cheese mixture evenly over bananas in muffin cups. Bake in preheated oven 30 minutes or until wooden pick inserted in center comes out clean. Cool in pan on wire rack.
Makes 18 cupcakes.

Chocolate Butterscotch Chip Cupcakes

½ cup cake flour
1 package (6 ounces) butterscotch-flavored pieces (1 cup), divided
1 package (6 ounces) semisweet chocolate pieces (1 cup), divided
1 package DUNCAN HINES® Moist Deluxe White Cake Mix
3 egg whites or 3 whole eggs
⅓ cup CRISCO® Oil or CRISCO® PURITAN® Oil
1¼ cups water

1. Preheat oven to 350°F. Line 24 muffin cups with paper baking cups.
2. Combine cake flour, ½ cup butterscotch pieces and ½ cup chocolate pieces in small bowl.

Black Bottom Cupcakes

3. Combine dry cake mix, egg whites or whole eggs, oil and water in large mixer bowl. Mix cake as directed on package. Stir in chocolate-butterscotch mixture. Spoon batter into muffin cups, filling about two-thirds full.
4. Bake at 350°F for 18 to 23 minutes or until toothpick inserted in centers comes out clean. Cool in pans on racks 10 minutes. Remove from pans; cool completely on racks.
5. For chocolate-butterscotch frosting, melt remaining ½ cup butterscotch and ½ cup chocolate pieces in small saucepan over low heat; stir until smooth. Spread over cooled cupcakes.
24 cupcakes.

Creme-Filled Cupcakes

¾ cup shortening
1¼ cups sugar
2 eggs
1 teaspoon vanilla extract
1¾ cups all-purpose flour
½ cup HERSHEY'S Cocoa
1 teaspoon baking soda
½ teaspoon salt
1 cup milk
Vanilla Creme (recipe follows)

Heat oven to 375°F. Paper-line muffin cups (2½ inches in diameter). In large mixer bowl, beat shortening and sugar until light and fluffy. Add eggs and vanilla; blend well. Stir together

flour, cocoa, baking soda and salt; add to shortening mixture alternately with milk. Fill prepared pans ⅔ full with batter. Bake 20 to 25 minutes or until wooden pick inserted in center comes out clean. Remove to wire racks; cool completely. Prepare Vanilla Creme; spoon into pastry tube with open star tip. Insert tip into center of top of cupcake; gently squeeze until cupcake begins to peak. Cover top with swirl of filling.
About 2 dozen cupcakes.

Vanilla Creme

¼ cup all-purpose flour
½ cup milk
¼ cup (½ stick) butter or margarine, softened
¼ cup shortening
2 teaspoons vanilla extract
¼ teaspoon salt
4 cups powdered sugar

In small saucepan, blend flour and milk; cook over low heat, stirring constantly with wire whisk, until mixture thickens and just begins to boil. Remove from heat; refrigerate. In large mixer bowl, beat butter and shortening until creamy; blend in vanilla, salt and refrigerated flour mixture. Gradually beat in powdered sugar to spreading consistency.

Quick Chocolate Frosting

4 bars (4 oz.) HERSHEY'S Unsweetened Baking Chocolate
¼ cup (½ stick) butter or margarine
3 cups powdered sugar
1 teaspoon vanilla extract
⅛ teaspoon salt
⅓ cup milk

In small saucepan over very low heat, melt chocolate and butter; pour into small mixer bowl. Add powdered sugar, vanilla and salt. Blend in milk; beat to spreading consistency. (If frosting is too thick, add additional milk, 1 teaspoonful at a time, until frosting is of desired consistency.)
About 2 cups.

Chocolate Surprise Cupcakes

Filling:
   1 package (8 ounces)
      PHILADELPHIA BRAND®
      Cream Cheese, softened
   ⅓ cup granulated sugar
   1 egg
   ½ cup **BAKER'S®** Semi-Sweet
      Real Chocolate Chips

Cupcakes:
   2 squares **BAKER'S®**
      Unsweetened Chocolate
   ⅓ cup vegetable oil
   1¼ cups all-purpose flour
   1 cup granulated sugar
   ¾ cup water
   1 egg
   1 teaspoon vanilla
   ½ teaspoon baking soda
   ¼ teaspoon salt
      Powdered sugar (optional)

HEAT oven to 350°F.

BEAT cream cheese, ⅓ cup granulated sugar and 1 egg until smooth. Stir in chips; set aside.

MELT chocolate in small microwavable bowl on HIGH 1 to 2 minutes or until almost melted, stirring after each minute. **Stir until chocolate is completely melted.**

BEAT melted chocolate, oil, flour, 1 cup granulated sugar, water, 1 egg, vanilla, baking soda and salt in large bowl with wire whisk or fork until blended and smooth. Spoon ½ the batter evenly into 18 greased or paper-lined muffin cups. Top each with 1 tablespoon of the cream cheese mixture. Spoon the remaining batter evenly over cream cheese mixture.

BAKE for 30 to 35 minutes or until toothpick inserted in center comes out clean. Remove from pans to cool on wire racks. Sprinkle with powdered sugar, if desired.   *Makes 18 cupcakes*

Prep time: 15 minutes
Baking time: 30 to 35 minutes

Glazed Cranberry Mini-Cakes

   ⅓ cup butter or margarine,
      softened
   ⅓ cup granulated sugar
   ⅓ cup packed light brown
      sugar
   1 egg
   1¼ teaspoons vanilla extract
   1⅓ cups all-purpose flour
   ¾ teaspoon baking powder
   ¼ teaspoon baking soda
   ¼ teaspoon salt
   2 tablespoons milk
   1¼ cups coarsely chopped
      fresh cranberries
   ½ cup coarsely chopped
      walnuts
   1⅔ cups (10-oz. pkg.)
      HERSHEY'S Vanilla Milk
      Chips, divided
      Vanilla Glaze
      (recipe follows)

Heat oven to 350°F. Lightly grease or paper-line small muffin cups (1¾ inches in diameter). In small mixer bowl, beat butter, granulated sugar, brown sugar, egg and vanilla until light and fluffy. Stir together flour, baking powder, baking soda and salt; gradually mix into butter mixture. Add milk; stir until blended. Stir in cranberries, walnuts and ½ cup vanilla milk chips (reserve remaining chips for glaze). Fill muffin cups about ⅞ full with batter. Bake 18 to 20 minutes or until wooden pick inserted in center comes out clean. Cool 5 minutes; remove from pans to wire racks. Cool completely. Prepare Vanilla Glaze; drizzle glaze on tops. Place on wax paper-covered tray; refrigerate 10 minutes to set glaze.
Makes about 3 dozen mini-cakes

VANILLA GLAZE: In small microwave-safe bowl, place remaining HERSHEY'S Vanilla Milk Chips; sprinkle 2 tablespoons vegetable oil over chips. Microwave at HIGH (100%) 30 seconds; stir

vigorously. If necessary, microwave at HIGH additional 30 seconds or just until chips are melted when stirred.

Strawberry Shortcake

Cake
   1 package **DUNCAN HINES®**
      Moist Deluxe French
      Vanilla Cake Mix
   3 eggs
   1¼ cups water
   ½ cup butter or margarine,
      softened

Filling and Topping
   2 cups whipping cream,
      chilled
   ⅓ cup sugar
   ½ teaspoon vanilla extract
   1 quart fresh strawberries,
      rinsed, drained and
      sliced
      Mint leaves, for garnish

1. Preheat oven to 350°F. Grease two 9-inch round cake pans with butter or margarine. Sprinkle bottom and sides with granulated sugar.

2. **For cake,** combine cake mix, eggs, water and butter in large bowl. Beat at medium speed with electric mixer for 2 minutes. Pour into pans. Bake at 350°F for 30 to 35 minutes or until toothpick inserted in center comes out clean. Cool in pans 10 minutes. Invert onto cooling rack. Cool completely.

3. **For filling and topping,** beat whipping cream, sugar and vanilla extract until stiff in large bowl. Reserve ⅓ cup for garnish. Place one cake layer on serving plate. Spread with half the remaining whipped cream and sliced strawberries. Repeat with remaining layer and whipped cream. Garnish with reserved whipped cream and mint leaves. Refrigerate until ready to serve.
12 Servings

Tip: Whipping cream doubles in volume when whipped. For best results, chill bowl and beaters.

Strawberry Shortcake

Chocolate Strawberry Shortcake

- 2 pints strawberries, cut in half
- 2 tablespoons sugar
- 1 teaspoon vanilla
- 2 (9-inch) layers One Bowl Chocolate Cake
  Semi-Sweet Chocolate Glaze (page 525)
- 3½ cups (8 ounces) COOL WHIP® Whipped Topping, thawed
  Chocolate-dipped strawberries (optional)

MIX strawberries, sugar and vanilla. Spoon ½ of the strawberries on 1 cake layer. Drizzle with ½ the chocolate glaze; top with ½ the whipped topping. Repeat layers. Garnish with chocolate-dipped strawberries, if desired. Refrigerate.

Makes 12 servings

Prep time: 15 minutes

One Bowl Chocolate Cake

- 6 squares BAKER'S® Semi-Sweet Chocolate
- ¾ cup (1½ sticks) margarine or butter
- 1½ cups sugar
- 3 eggs
- 2 teaspoons vanilla
- 2½ cups all-purpose flour
- 1 teaspoon baking soda
- ¼ teaspoon salt
- 1½ cups water

HEAT oven to 350°F.

MICROWAVE chocolate and margarine in large microwavable bowl on HIGH 2 minutes or until margarine is melted. **Stir until chocolate is completely melted.**

STIR sugar into melted chocolate mixture until well blended. Beat in eggs, one at a time, with electric mixer until completely mixed. Add vanilla. Add ½ cup of the flour, the baking soda and salt; mix well. Beat in the remaining 2 cups flour alternately with water until smooth. Pour into 2 greased and floured 9-inch layer pans.

BAKE for 35 minutes or until toothpick inserted into center comes out clean. Cool in pans 10 minutes. Remove from pans to cool on wire racks. Fill and frost as desired.

Makes 12 servings

Prep time: 15 minutes
Baking time: 35 minutes

Chocolate Toffee Crunch Fantasy

- 1 package DUNCAN HINES® Moist Deluxe Devil's Food Cake Mix
- 12 bars (1.4 ounces each) chocolate covered toffee bars, divided
- 2 cups whipping cream, chilled

1. Preheat oven to 350°F. Grease and flour 10-inch tube pan.

2. Prepare, bake and cool cake following package directions for basic recipe. Split cake horizontally into three layers. Chop 11 candy bars into pea-size pieces (see Tip). Whip cream until stiff peaks form. Fold candy pieces into whipped cream.

3. To assemble, place one split cake layer on serving plate. Spread 1½ cups whipped cream mixture on top. Repeat with remaining layers and whipped cream mixture. Frost sides and top with remaining whipped cream mixture. Chop remaining candy bar coarsely. Sprinkle over top. Refrigerate until ready to serve.   *12 Servings*

Tip: To quickly chop toffee candy bars, place a few bars in food processor fitted with steel blade. Pulse several times until pea-size pieces form. Repeat with remaining candy bars.

Chocolate Strawberry Shortcake

German Sweet Chocolate Cake

- 1 package (4 ounces) BAKER'S® GERMAN'S® Sweet Chocolate
- ½ cup water
- 2 cups all-purpose flour
- 1 teaspoon baking soda
- ¼ teaspoon salt
- 1 cup (2 sticks) margarine or butter, softened
- 2 cups sugar
- 4 egg yolks
- 1 teaspoon vanilla
- 1 cup buttermilk
- 4 egg whites
  Classic Coconut-Pecan Filling and Frosting (page 525)

HEAT oven to 350°F. Line bottoms of three 9-inch layer pans with waxed paper.

MICROWAVE chocolate and water in large microwavable bowl on HIGH 1½ to 2 minutes until chocolate is almost melted. **Stir until chocolate is completely melted.**

MIX flour, baking soda and salt; set aside. Beat margarine and sugar until light and fluffy. Add egg yolks, one at a time, beating well after each addition. Stir in melted chocolate and vanilla. Add flour mixture alternately with buttermilk, beating after each addition until smooth.

BEAT egg whites until they form stiff peaks. Gently stir into batter; pour into prepared pans.

BAKE for 30 minutes or until cake springs back when lightly touched.

REMOVE from oven; immediately run spatula between cake and sides of pans. Cool in pans 15 minutes. Remove from pans; peel off waxed paper. Cool on wire racks.

SPREAD Classic Coconut-Pecan Filling and Frosting between layers and over top of cake.
Makes 12 servings

Prep time: 35 to 40 minutes
Baking time: 30 minutes

Top to bottom: German Sweet Chocolate Cake and Wellesly Fudge Cake with Easy Fudge Frosting (page 525)

Wellesley Fudge Cake

- 4 squares BAKER'S® Unsweetened Chocolate
- 1¾ cups sugar
- ½ cup water
- 1⅔ cups all-purpose flour
- 1 teaspoon baking soda
- ¼ teaspoon salt
- ½ cup (1 stick) margarine or butter, softened
- 3 eggs
- ¾ cup milk
- 1 teaspoon vanilla

HEAT oven to 350°F.

MICROWAVE chocolate, ½ cup of the sugar and the water in large microwavable bowl on HIGH 1 to 2 minutes or until chocolate is almost melted, stirring once. **Stir until chocolate is completely melted.** Cool to lukewarm.

MIX flour, baking soda and salt; set aside. Beat margarine and the remaining 1¼ cups sugar until light and fluffy. Add eggs, one at a time, beating well after each addition. Add flour mixture alternately with milk, beating after each addition until smooth. Stir in chocolate mixture and vanilla. Pour into 2 greased and floured 9-inch layer pans.

BAKE for 30 to 35 minutes or until cake springs back when lightly pressed. Cool in pans 10 minutes. Remove from pans to cool on wire racks. Frost as desired. *Makes 12 servings*

Prep time: 30 minutes
Baking time: 30 to 35 minutes

Cinnamon Ripple Cake

**1 package DUNCAN HINES®
    Angel Food Cake Mix**
1¹/₃ cups water
3¹/₂ teaspoons ground cinnamon
³/₄ cup whipping cream
¹/₂ cup cold milk
¹/₃ cup confectioners' sugar
1 teaspoon vanilla extract

1. Preheat oven to 375°F.
2. Prepare cake with water as directed on package. Spoon one-fourth of batter into ungreased 10-inch tube pan and spread evenly. With small fine sieve, sprinkle one teaspoon cinnamon over batter. Repeat layering two more times, ending with batter.
3. Bake at 375°F for 30 to 40 minutes or until top crust is golden brown, firm and looks very dry. Do not underbake.
4. To cool cake, hang pan upside down on bottle or funnel. When completely cooled, remove from pan.
5. To serve, beat whipping cream and milk in chilled bowl with chilled beaters until thick. Blend in confectioners' sugar, vanilla extract and remaining ¹/₂ teaspoon cinnamon. Cut cake into slices and top with cinnamon cream.
12 to 16 servings.

French Apple Cake

**3 cooking apples, pared, cored
    and sliced (about 3 cups)**
²/₃ cup sugar
1 tablespoon all-purpose flour
¹/₂ teaspoon ground cinnamon
**2 tablespoons butter or
    margarine, melted**
2 tablespoons lemon juice
**1 package DUNCAN HINES®
    Moist Deluxe White Cake Mix**
3 large eggs
**¹/₃ cup CRISCO® Oil or CRISCO®
    PURITAN® Oil**
1¹/₄ cups water

1. Preheat oven to 350°F. Grease 13×9×2-inch pan.
2. Arrange apples in pan. Mix sugar, flour and cinnamon; sprinkle over apples. Combine melted butter and lemon juice; drizzle over apples.
3. Place dry cake mix, eggs, oil and water in large mixer bowl. Mix cake as directed on package. Turn batter into pan over apples and spread evenly.
4. Bake at 350°F for 40 to 50 minutes or until toothpick inserted in center comes out clean. Cool 1 to 2 minutes in pan. Invert on large platter or tray; remove pan after 1 to 2 minutes. Serve warm.
12 to 16 servings.

Marble Chiffon Cake

**2 tablespoons plus 1¹/₂ cups
    sugar, divided**
**2 tablespoons plus ¹/₂ cup
    vegetable oil, divided**
¹/₃ cup HERSHEY'S Cocoa
1 cup cold water, divided
2 cups all-purpose flour
1 tablespoon baking powder
1 teaspoon salt
7 eggs, separated
2 teaspoons vanilla extract
**¹/₂ teaspoon cream of tartar
    Chocolate Glaze**

Heat oven to 325°F. In small bowl, combine 2 tablespoons sugar, 2 tablespoons oil, cocoa and ¹/₄ cup water; stir until smooth. Set aside. In small mixer bowl, stir together flour, remaining 1¹/₂ cups sugar, baking powder and salt; add remaining ¹/₂ cup oil, egg yolks, remaining ³/₄ cup water and vanilla. Beat on low speed of electric mixer until combined; continue beating on high speed 5 minutes. In large mixer bowl, with clean set of beaters, beat egg whites with cream of tartar until stiff peaks form.

Pour batter in thin stream over beaten whites, gently folding with rubber spatula just until blended. Remove one-third of batter to separate bowl; gently fold in chocolate mixture. Pour half of light batter into ungreased 10-inch tube pan; top with half of chocolate batter. Repeat layers. With narrow spatula or knife, swirl gently through batters to marble. Bake 65 to 70 minutes or until top springs back when touched lightly. Invert pan on heat-proof funnel; cool cake completely. Loosen cake from pan; invert onto serving plate. Spread Chocolate Glaze over top of cake, allowing to drizzle down sides.
12 to 16 servings.

Chocolate Glaze

**2 tablespoons butter or
    margarine**
¹/₄ cup HERSHEY'S Cocoa
3 tablespoons water
¹/₂ teaspoon vanilla extract
1¹/₄ cups powdered sugar

In small saucepan over low heat, melt butter. Stir in cocoa and water. Cook, stirring constantly, until mixture thickens. Do not boil. Remove from heat. Stir in vanilla. Gradually add powdered sugar, beating with wire whisk until smooth. Add additional water, ¹/₂ teaspoon at a time, until desired consistency.

Cinnamon Ripple Cake

Carrot Cake (left) and Chocolate Yogurt Cake (right)

Carrot Cake

2¼ cups unsifted all-purpose flour
1½ cups sugar
2 teaspoons baking soda
1½ teaspoons ground cinnamon
½ teaspoon ground nutmeg
½ teaspoon salt
1 cup CRISCO® Oil
3 eggs
½ cup milk
2 cups shredded carrot
1½ cups flaked coconut
¾ cup chopped nuts
½ cup currants or raisins
Frosting:
1 package (3 ounces) cream cheese, softened
2 tablespoons butter or margarine, softened
2 tablespoons milk
¼ teaspoon vanilla
Dash salt
2 to 2¼ cups confectioners sugar

Preheat oven to 325°F. Oil and flour 13×9-inch baking pan. Set aside.

Mix flour, sugar, baking soda, cinnamon, nutmeg and salt in large mixing bowl. Add Crisco® Oil, eggs, milk and carrot. Beat with electric mixer at low speed until ingredients are moistened, scraping bowl constantly. Beat at medium speed 2 minutes, scraping bowl occasionally. Stir in coconut, nuts and currants. Pour into prepared pan. Bake at 325°F, 55 to 60 minutes, or until wooden pick inserted in center comes out clean. Cool completely on wire rack.

For frosting, blend cream cheese and butter in small mixing bowl. Add milk, vanilla and salt. Mix well. Stir in enough confectioners sugar until thick enough to spread. Spread on cooled cake.

One 13×9-inch cake.

Chocolate Yogurt Cake

2 cups unsifted all-purpose flour
1½ cups sugar
½ cup unsweetened cocoa
2 teaspoons baking soda
1 teaspoon salt
1 cup plain yogurt
3 eggs
⅔ cup CRISCO® Oil
1½ teaspoons vanilla
Frosting:
1 package (6 ounces) semisweet chocolate chips
¼ cup butter or margarine
⅔ cup plain yogurt
½ teaspoon vanilla
⅛ teaspoon salt
2½ to 3 cups confectioners sugar

Preheat oven to 350°F. Grease and flour two 9-inch round layer pans. Set aside.

Mix flour, sugar, cocoa, baking soda and salt in large mixing bowl. Add yogurt, eggs, Crisco® Oil and vanilla. Beat with electric mixer at low speed until ingredients are moistened, scraping bowl constantly. Beat at medium speed 2 minutes, scraping bowl occasionally. Pour into prepared pans. Bake at 350°F, 30 to 35 minutes, or until wooden pick inserted in center comes out clean. Cool 10 minutes. Remove from pans. Cool completely on wire rack.

For frosting, combine chocolate chips and butter in small saucepan. Cook over low heat, stirring constantly, until melted. Transfer mixture to medium mixing bowl. Cool slightly. Blend in yogurt, vanilla and salt. Stir in enough confectioners sugar until frosting is thick enough to spread. Fill and frost cooled cake.

One 2-layer cake.

Banana Fudge Marble Cake

Cake
- 1 package DUNCAN HINES® DeLights Fudge Marble Cake Mix
- 2 eggs
- 1 cup ripe mashed banana
- ½ cup water

Frosting
- 1 package (4-serving size) banana instant pudding and pie filling mix
- 2 envelopes whipped topping mix
- 1¼ cups milk
- 1 banana, sliced
- Lemon juice
- ½ cup frozen whipped topping, thawed

1. Preheat oven to 350°F. Grease and flour two 9-inch round cake pans.

2. **For cake,** combine cake mix, eggs, mashed banana and water in large bowl. Beat at medium speed with electric mixer for 2 minutes. Pour into pans. Bake and cool following package directions.

3. **For frosting,** combine pudding mix, whipped topping mix and milk in large bowl. Beat at high speed with electric mixer for 2 to 3 minutes or until light and fluffy. Fill and frost cake. Refrigerate for several hours before serving. Dip banana slices in lemon juice. Blot dry. Garnish with whipped topping and banana slices.   *12 Servings*

Tip: Serve cake slices with 2 tablespoons Fudge Sauce (page 508).

Pecan Pumpkin Torte

Cake
- 2 cups crushed vanilla wafers
- 1 cup chopped pecans
- ¾ cup LAND O LAKES® Butter, softened
- 1 package (18 ounces) spice cake mix
- 1 can (16 ounces) solid-packed pumpkin
- ¼ cup LAND O LAKES® Butter, softened
- 4 eggs

Filling
- 3 cups powdered sugar
- ⅔ cup LAND O LAKES® Butter, softened
- 4 ounces cream cheese, softened
- 2 teaspoons vanilla
- ¼ cup caramel topping
- Pecan halves

Heat oven to 350°. For cake, in large mixer bowl combine wafer crumbs, 1 cup chopped pecans and ¾ cup butter. Beat at medium speed, scraping bowl often, until crumbly, 1 to 2 minutes. Press mixture evenly on bottom of 3 greased and floured 9-inch round cake pans. In same bowl combine cake mix, pumpkin, ¼ cup butter and eggs. Beat at medium speed, scraping bowl often, until well mixed, 2 to 3 minutes. Spread 1¾ cups batter over crumbs in *each* pan. Bake for 20 to 25 minutes or until wooden pick inserted in center comes out clean. Cool 5 minutes; remove from pans. Cool completely.

For filling, in small mixer bowl combine powdered sugar, ⅔ cup butter, cream cheese and vanilla. Beat at medium speed, scraping bowl often, until light and fluffy, 2 to 3 minutes. On serving plate layer 3 cakes, nut side down, with ½ cup filling spread between *each* layer. With remaining filling, frost sides only of cake. Spread caramel topping over top of cake, drizzling some over the frosted sides. Arrange pecan halves in rings on top of cake. Store refrigerated.

Makes 16 servings

Tip: To remove cake easily from pan, place wire rack on top of cake and invert; repeat with remaining layers.

Coconut Lemon Torte

- 1 (14-ounce) can EAGLE® Brand Sweetened Condensed Milk (NOT evaporated milk)
- 2 egg *yolks*
- ½ cup REALEMON® Lemon Juice from Concentrate
- 1 teaspoon grated lemon rind, optional
- Yellow food coloring, optional
- 1 (18¼- or 18½-ounce) package white cake mix
- 1 (4-ounce) container frozen non-dairy whipped topping, thawed (1¾ cups)
- Flaked coconut

Preheat oven to 350°. In medium saucepan, combine sweetened condensed milk, egg *yolks*, ReaLemon® brand, rind and food coloring if desired. Over medium heat, cook and stir until thickened, about 10 minutes. Chill. Meanwhile, prepare cake mix as package directs. Pour batter into two well-greased and floured 8- or 9-inch round layer cake pans. Bake 30 minutes or until lightly browned. Remove from pans; cool thoroughly. With sharp knife, remove crust from top of each cake layer. Split layers in half horizontally. Spread equal portions of lemon mixture between layers and on top to within 1 inch of edge. Frost side and 1-inch rim on top of cake with whipped topping. Coat side of cake with coconut; garnish as desired. Store covered in refrigerator.

Makes one 8- or 9-inch cake

Pecan Pumpkin Torte

Lemon Cream Almond Torte

½ cup sifted cake flour
½ teaspoon baking powder
⅛ teaspoon salt
½ cup butter or margarine, softened
¾ cup granulated sugar
1 cup BLUE DIAMOND® Blanched Almond Paste
3 eggs
1 tablespoon brandy
1 teaspoon vanilla
⅛ teaspoon almond extract
  Lemon Cream (recipe follows)
  Powdered sugar (optional)
  Lemon slices (optional)

In small bowl, combine flour, baking powder and salt. In large bowl, cream butter and granulated sugar. Add almond paste; beat until smooth. Add eggs, 1 at a time, beating well after each addition. Mix in brandy, vanilla and almond extract. Stir in flour mixture. Pour into greased and floured 8×2-inch round pan. Bake in preheated 325° oven 45 minutes or until toothpick inserted into center comes out clean. Let cool in pan on wire rack 15 minutes. Loosen edge; remove from pan. Cool completely on wire rack. Meanwhile, prepare Lemon Cream. Slice cake horizontally in half. Spread Lemon Cream over cut side of bottom layer; top with second layer, cut side down. Refrigerate until serving time. To serve, if desired, place lace doily over top of torte. Sift powdered sugar evenly over top; carefully remove doily. Garnish with lemon slices.
Makes 8 to 10 servings.

Lemon Cream

3 egg yolks
⅓ cup granulated sugar
2 tablespoons all-purpose flour
1 cup milk, scalded
2 teaspoons grated lemon peel
2 tablespoons lemon juice
½ teaspoon vanilla

In medium saucepan, beat egg yolks and sugar until thick and pale yellow. Stir in flour. Gradually pour in hot milk, stirring constantly. Stir in lemon peel. Bring mixture to a boil over medium heat, stirring constantly. Stir and boil 1 minute. Remove from heat; add lemon juice and vanilla. Cool completely, stirring occasionally.

Mexican Cocoa Torte

½ cup HERSHEY'S Cocoa
⅓ cup shortening
1 cup sugar
½ cup strong coffee
¼ teaspoon ground cinnamon
1 package (11 oz.) pie crust mix
2 cups (1 pt.) cold whipping cream
  HERSHEY'S MINI CHIPS Semi-Sweet Chocolate

In small saucepan, combine cocoa, shortening, sugar, coffee and cinnamon. Cook over very low heat, stirring constantly, until smooth and creamy; cool to room temperature. Stir together pie crust mix and ¾ cup of the cocoa mixture; combine thoroughly. Shape into small ball; refrigerate 1 hour.

Heat oven to 350°F. Line two cookie sheets with foil; mark two 8-inch circles on each. Cut pastry ball into 4 pieces. Place dough pieces on foil; press with fingers into marked circles. Bake 10 to 12 minutes; cool on cookie sheets.

In small mixer bowl, combine whipping cream and remaining cocoa mixture; beat until very thick. Place one pastry round on serving plate; spread with one-fourth whipped cream mixture. Repeat, using remaining three rounds, ending with whipped cream mixture on top. Refrigerate several hours; cut into wedges to serve. Garnish with small chocolate chips.
Makes one 8-inch torte.

Elegant Angel Torte

1 package DUNCAN HINES® Angel Food Cake Mix
1⅓ cups water
2 cups whipping cream
¼ cup chocolate syrup
1 tablespoon sugar
⅓ cup orange marmalade
6 red maraschino cherries with stems, if desired
6 pecan halves, if desired
¼ cup chocolate curls, if desired

1. Preheat oven to 375°F.
2. Prepare cake with water as directed on package. Pour batter into ungreased 10-inch tube pan. Cut through batter with knife or spatula to remove large air bubbles.
3. Bake at 375°F for 30 to 40 minutes or until top crust is golden brown, firm and dry. Do not underbake. To cool, hang pan upside down on funnel or bottle at least 1½ hours.
4. Slice cooled cake crosswise into four 1-inch layers.
5. Whip cream until stiff. Beat in chocolate syrup and sugar. Place bottom cake slice on serving plate; spread with ⅓ cup whipped cream. Top with next layer; spread with orange marmalade. Top with next layer; spread with ⅓ cup whipped cream. Add final layer. Frost sides and top with remaining whipped cream. Decorate with cherries, pecans and chocolate curls.
12 to 16 servings.

Elegant Angel Torte

Crème de Cacao Torte

⅔ cup butter or margarine,
   softened
1⅔ cups sugar
   3 eggs
½ teaspoon vanilla extract
2 cups all-purpose flour
⅔ cup HERSHEY'S Cocoa
1¼ teaspoons baking soda
¼ teaspoon baking powder
1⅓ cups milk
   2 tablespoons crème de cacao
      (chocolate-flavored liqueur)
      (optional)
      Crème de Cacao Filling (recipe
      follows)
      Chocolate Ganache Glaze
      (recipe follows)

Heat oven to 350°F. Grease and flour two 9-inch round baking pans. In large mixer bowl, beat butter, sugar, eggs and vanilla until blended. Stir together flour, cocoa, baking soda and baking powder; add to butter mixture alternately with milk, blending just until combined.

Pour batter into prepared pans. Bake 30 to 35 minutes or until wooden pick inserted in center comes out clean. Cool 10 minutes; remove from pans to wire racks. Sprinkle each layer with 1 tablespoon crème de cacao; cool completely.

Meanwhile, prepare Crème de Cacao Filling. Split each cake layer horizontally into 2 layers. Place one layer on serving plate; spread with one-third of filling. Repeat layering with remaining cake and filling, ending with cake layer. Cover tightly; refrigerate at least 8 hours. Prepare Chocolate Ganache Glaze; spoon on top of chilled cake, allowing glaze to drizzle down side of cake. Refrigerate.
10 to 12 servings.
CRÈME DE CACAO FILLING: In small mixer bowl, beat 1 cup (½ pt.) cold whipping cream, 2 tablespoons crème de cacao and 1 tablespoon HERSHEY'S Cocoa until stiff. Cover; refrigerate.
About 2 cups.

Crème de Cacao Torte

Chocolate Ganache Glaze

1 HERSHEY'S SPECIAL DARK
   Mildly Sweet Chocolate Bar
   (7 oz.), broken into pieces
¼ cup whipping cream
1 tablespoon butter
1½ teaspoons crème de cacao
   (chocolate-flavored liqueur)

In medium saucepan, combine chocolate bar pieces, whipping cream and butter; cook over low heat, stirring constantly, until mixture is melted and smooth. Stir in crème de cacao. Cool to lukewarm (glaze will be slightly thickened).
About 1 cup.

Cocoa Cream Cheese Frosting

3 packages (3 oz. each) cream
   cheese, softened
⅓ cup butter or margarine,
   softened
5 cups powdered sugar
1 cup HERSHEY'S Cocoa
5 to 7 tablespoons light cream

In large mixer bowl, beat cream cheese and butter. Stir together powdered sugar and cocoa; add alternately with light cream to cream cheese mixture. Beat to spreading consistency.
About 3½ cups frosting. (Fills and frosts three 8- or 9-inch layers.)

Viennese Cherry Cheese Torte

Festive Cranberry Torte

    1 8-ounce package
        PHILADELPHIA BRAND®
        Cream Cheese, softened
¼ cup sugar
½ cup whipping cream, whipped
    1 10¾-ounce frozen pound
        cake, thawed
    1 14-ounce jar cranberry orange
        sauce

Combine cream cheese and sugar, mixing until well blended. Fold in whipped cream. Split cake horizontally into four layers. Spread bottom layer with ½ cup cranberry orange sauce; top with second layer. Spread second layer with ⅔ cup cream cheese mixture; top with third layer. Spread third layer with ½ cup cranberry orange sauce. Cover with top cake layer. Frost top and sides of torte with remaining cream cheese mixture. Chill several hours or overnight. Top with remaining cranberry orange sauce just before serving. Garnish with whole cranberries and fresh mint, if desired.
10 to 12 servings.
  Variation: Substitute Light PHILADELPHIA BRAND® Neufchatel Cheese for Cream Cheese.

Viennese Cherry Cheese Torte

    1 package DUNCAN HINES®
        Moist Deluxe Butter Recipe
        Golden Cake Mix
    3 large eggs
½ cup (1 stick) butter or
        margarine, softened
⅔ cup water
    1 package (8 ounces) plus
        1 package (3 ounces) cream
        cheese, softened
⅔ cup sugar
¼ teaspoon ground nutmeg
    2 tablespoons milk
    1 can (21 ounces) cherry pie
        filling

1. Preheat oven to 375°F. Grease and flour two 8×1½- or 9×1½-inch round layer pans.
2. Combine dry cake mix, eggs, butter and water in large mixer bowl. Mix, bake and cool as directed on package. Refrigerate layers to make splitting easier. Split each cake into 2 thin layers.
3. For filling, beat cream cheese, sugar, nutmeg and milk until smooth.
4. Place one layer on cake plate. Spread with ½ cup cream cheese filling; top with ½ cup cherry filling. Repeat layers, ending with cake layer.

Spread remaining cream cheese filling over top layer and top with remaining cherry filling. Refrigerate until ready to serve.
12 to 16 servings.

Viennese Chocolate Torte

    1 cup flour
½ teaspoon salt
½ cup ground walnuts
¾ cup unsalted butter
1¼ cups confectioners sugar
    8 egg yolks
    1 package (8 squares) BAKER'S®
        Semi-Sweet Chocolate,
        melted and cooled
    1 teaspoon vanilla
    8 egg whites
    1 cup (10-ounce jar) apricot jam
        Continental Flair Frosting, half
        recipe (page 497)
        Sweetened whipped cream or
        thawed COOL WHIP®
        Whipped Topping

Mix flour, salt and walnuts. Cream butter. Gradually beat in sugar and continue beating until light and fluffy. Add egg yolks, a few at a time, beating thoroughly after each addition. Gradually stir in chocolate. Add flour mixture and vanilla, stirring just to blend. Beat egg whites until soft peaks form. Blend about ¼ cup of the beaten egg whites into the chocolate mixture; gently fold in remaining egg whites.
  Pour into 2 greased and floured 9-inch layer pans. Bake at 350° for 40 to 45 minutes, or until cake tester inserted in centers comes out clean. Cool in pans 10 minutes. Remove from pans and finish cooling on racks.
  Split layers horizontally, making 4 layers. Stir jam in saucepan over low heat until melted. Spread about ⅓ cup over tops of three layers. Stack on a rack placed on a tray; top with fourth layer. Prepare frosting as directed, cooling only slightly. Pour quickly over cake, covering top and sides. Place cake on serving plate. If desired, spoon frosting drippings into plastic-lined decorating bag fitted with writing tip; pipe a name or greeting on cake. Store in refrigerator at least one day to mellow flavors. Serve at room temperature with sweetened whipped cream.
Makes one 9-inch torte.

Open House Ribbon Torte

- **1 package DUNCAN HINES® Moist Deluxe Fudge Marble Cake Mix**
- **3 large eggs**
- **⅓ cup CRISCO® Oil or CRISCO® PURITAN® Oil**
- **1¼ cups water**
- **1 cup whipping cream**
- **1 cup milk**
- **1 package (4-serving-size) chocolate instant pudding and pie filling mix**

1. Preheat oven to 350°F. Grease and flour two 8×1½- or 9×1½-inch round layer pans.
2. Combine dry cake mix, eggs, oil and water in large mixer bowl. Mix as directed on package but do not add contents of small packet. Turn half of batter (about 2½ cups) into one pan. Blend contents of small packet into remaining batter and turn into remaining pan.
3. Bake and cool layers as directed on package. Chill cooled layers to make splitting easier. Split each layer into two thin layers.
4. Whip cream until stiff. Blend in milk and pudding mix. Let set for 1 minute.
5. Place one chocolate layer on plate. Spread one-fourth pudding mixture over layer. Top with remaining layers, alternating light and dark layers and spreading pudding mixture between layers. Frost top layer with pudding mixture. Refrigerate until ready to serve.
12 to 16 servings.

Chocolate Almond Philly® Cream Cheese Torte

- **1 8-ounce package PHILADELPHIA BRAND® Cream Cheese, softened**
- **¼ cup PARKAY® Margarine**
- **1 cup sugar**
- **2 eggs**
- **½ teaspoon vanilla**
- **1½ cups flour**
- **1 teaspoon baking soda**
- **½ teaspoon baking powder**
- **½ cup milk**
- **2 1-ounce squares unsweetened chocolate, melted**
- **Almond and Chocolate Philly® Cream Cheese Cream Frostings**

Combine cream cheese, margarine and sugar, mixing until well blended. Blend in eggs and vanilla. Add combined dry ingredients alternately with milk, mixing well after each addition. Blend in chocolate. Spread batter into wax paper-lined 15×10×1-inch jelly roll pan. Bake at 350°, 12 to 15 minutes or until wooden pick inserted in center comes out clean. Cool thoroughly. Cut crosswise into four equal sections; remove from pan. Spread three sections with almond frosting; chill until frosting is firm. Stack. Top with remaining layer; frost top and sides with chocolate frosting. *12 servings.*

Almond and Chocolate Philly® Cream Cheese Cream Frostings

- **1 8-ounce package PHILADELPHIA BRAND® Cream Cheese, softened**
- **6½ cups sifted powdered sugar**
- **½ cup whipping cream**
- **½ cup chopped almonds, toasted**
- **2 1-ounce squares unsweetened chocolate, melted**

Beat cream cheese at medium speed on electric mixer. Gradually add 5 cups sugar, mixing well after each addition. Add whipping cream, beating at high speed until creamy. Divide mixture in half. Add remaining sugar and almonds to one half, mixing until well blended. Stir chocolate into remaining half. Chill chocolate frosting until thickened for spreading consistency.

Black Forest Torte

- **1 (18¼- or 18½-ounce) package chocolate cake mix**
- **1 (21-ounce) can cherry pie filling, drained and chilled, reserving ½ cup sauce**
- **1 (6-ounce) package semi-sweet chocolate chips**
- **1 (14-ounce) can EAGLE® Brand Sweetened Condensed Milk (NOT evaporated milk)**
- **½ teaspoon almond extract**

Preheat oven to 350°. Prepare and bake cake mix as package directs for two 9-inch round layers. Remove from pans; cool thoroughly. In heavy saucepan, over medium heat, melt chips with sweetened condensed milk. Cook and stir until mixture thickens, about 10 minutes. Cool 20 minutes. Meanwhile, combine cherries, reserved sauce and extract. Place 1 cake layer on serving plate, top side up. With sharp knife, remove crust from top of cake layer to within ½ inch of edge; top with half the chocolate mixture then the cherries. Top with second cake layer and remaining chocolate mixture. Garnish as desired.
Makes one 9-inch cake.

Open House Ribbon Torte

Chocolate Raspberry Torte

  3 eggs, separated
  ⅛ teaspoon cream of tartar
  ⅛ teaspoon salt
1½ cups sugar
  1 cup LAND O LAKES®
      Butter, melted
1½ teaspoons vanilla
  ½ cup all-purpose flour
  ½ cup unsweetened cocoa
  3 tablespoons water
  ¾ cup finely chopped
      almonds
  ⅓ cup raspberry preserves
  1 cup whipping cream,
      whipped, sweetened
      Fresh raspberries

Heat oven to 350°. Grease 9-inch round cake pan. Line with aluminum foil leaving excess foil over edges; grease foil. Set aside. In small mixer bowl combine egg whites, cream of tartar and salt. Beat at high speed, scraping bowl often, until soft peaks form, 1 to 2 minutes; set aside. In large mixer bowl combine egg yolks, sugar, butter and vanilla. Beat at medium speed, scraping bowl often, until well mixed, 1 to 2 minutes. Add flour, cocoa and water. Continue beating, scraping bowl often, until well mixed, 1 to 2 minutes. By hand, stir in chopped almonds. Fold beaten egg whites into chocolate mixture. Spread into prepared pan. Bake for 40 to 55 minutes or until wooden pick inserted in center comes out clean. Cool on wire rack 1 hour; remove from pan by lifting foil. Cover; refrigerate until completely cooled, 2 to 3 hours.

To serve, remove foil; place on serving plate. Spread raspberry preserves on top. Pipe sweetened whipped cream to form a lattice top; garnish with raspberries.

Makes 12 servings

Chocolate Intensity

Chocolate Raspberry Torte

Chocolate Intensity

Cake:
**One 8-oz. pkg. (4 foil-wrapped
      bars) NESTLÉ®
      Unsweetened Chocolate
      baking bars**
  ½ cup (1 stick) butter or
      margarine, softened
1½ cups granulated sugar
  3 whole eggs
  2 teaspoons vanilla extract
  ⅔ cup all-purpose flour

Coffee Crème Anglaise:
  ⅓ cup granulated sugar
  2 teaspoons cornstarch
  1 tablespoon TASTER'S
      CHOICE® Freeze-Dried
      Instant Coffee
1½ cups milk
  4 egg yolks, beaten
  1 teaspoon vanilla extract

      Confectioners' sugar for
          garnish
      Heavy or whipping cream
          for garnish

Cake: Preheat oven to 350°F. Grease 9-inch springform pan. In small saucepan over low heat, melt unsweetened chocolate baking bars; set aside. In small mixer bowl, beat butter, 1½ cups granulated sugar, whole eggs and 2 teaspoons vanilla extract until thick and pale yellow. Blend in melted chocolate. Gradually beat in flour. Spread in prepared pan.

Bake 25 to 28 minutes until cake tester inserted in center comes out clean. Cool 15 minutes; loosen and remove side of pan. Cool completely.

Coffee Crème Anglaise: In medium saucepan, combine ⅓ cup granulated sugar, cornstarch and instant coffee; stir in milk. Cook over medium heat, stirring constantly, until mixture comes to a boil; boil 1 minute. Remove from heat. Whisk small amount of hot milk mixture into yolks; return to saucepan. Cook over low heat, stirring constantly, until mixture thickens and coats back of spoon. Strain through a fine mesh sieve into small bowl. Stir in 1 teaspoon vanilla extract. Press plastic wrap directly on surface; refrigerate.

Sprinkle cake with confectioners' sugar; cut into wedges. Spoon 3 to 4 tablespoons Coffee Crème Anglaise onto each dessert plate. Dot with heavy cream. Pull toothpick through heavy cream to make decorative design. Top with cake.

Makes 10 to 12 servings

Base Frosting

3 cups powdered sugar, sifted
½ cup butter or margarine, softened
¼ cup milk
½ teaspoon vanilla

Combine powdered sugar, butter, milk and vanilla in large bowl. Beat with electric mixer until smooth. Add more milk, 1 teaspoon at a time, if necessary. Frosting should be fairly thin.

Makes about 2 cups

Buttercream Frosting

6 cups powdered sugar, sifted and divided
¾ cup butter or margarine, softened
¼ cup vegetable shortening
6 to 8 tablespoons milk, divided
1 teaspoon vanilla

Combine 3 cups powdered sugar, butter, shortening, 4 tablespoons milk and vanilla in large bowl. Beat with electric mixer until smooth. Add remaining powdered sugar; beat until light and fluffy, adding more milk, 1 tablespoon at a time, as needed for good spreading consistency.

Makes about 3½ cups

Easy Fudge Frosting

4 squares BAKER'S® Unsweetened Chocolate
2 tablespoons margarine or butter
4 cups powdered sugar
½ cup milk
1 teaspoon vanilla

MICROWAVE chocolate and margarine in large microwavable bowl on HIGH 1 minute or until margarine is melted. **Stir until chocolate is completely melted.**

STIR in sugar, milk and vanilla until smooth. Let stand, if necessary, until of spreading consistency, stirring occasionally. Spread quickly. (Add 2 to 3 tablespoons additional milk if frosting becomes too thick.)

Makes about 2½ cups or enough to frost tops and sides of 2 (8- to 9-inch) layer cakes.

Prep time: 10 minutes

Classic Coconut-Pecan Filling and Frosting

1½ cups (12 ounce can) evaporated milk
1½ cups sugar
4 egg yolks
¾ cup (1½ sticks) margarine or butter
1½ teaspoons vanilla
2 cups BAKER'S® ANGEL FLAKE® Coconut
1½ cups chopped pecans

COMBINE milk, sugar, egg yolks, margarine and vanilla in saucepan. Cook over medium heat until mixture thickens and is golden brown, about 12 minutes, stirring constantly. Remove from heat.

STIR in coconut and pecans. Beat until cool and of spreading consistency.

Makes about 4¼ cups or enough to fill and frost top of 1 (3-layer) cake, frost tops of 2 (13×9-inch) cakes or frost 24 cupcakes

Prep time: 20 minutes

Semi-Sweet Chocolate Glaze

3 squares BAKER'S® Semi-Sweet Chocolate
3 tablespoons water
1 tablespoon margarine or butter
1 cup powdered sugar
½ teaspoon vanilla

MICROWAVE chocolate, water and margarine in large microwavable bowl on HIGH 1 to 2 minutes until chocolate is almost melted, stirring once. **Stir until chocolate is completely melted.**

STIR in sugar and vanilla until smooth. For thinner glaze, add ½ to 1 teaspoon additional water.

Makes about ¾ cup

Prep time: 10 minutes

Kahlúa® Marbled Pumpkin Cheesecake

¾ cup gingersnap crumbs
¾ cup graham cracker
  crumbs
¼ cup powdered sugar
¼ cup (4 tablespoons) melted
  unsalted butter
2 (8-ounce) packages cream
  cheese, softened
1 cup granulated sugar
4 eggs
1 (1-pound) can pumpkin
½ teaspoon ground cinnamon
¼ teaspoon ground ginger
¼ teaspoon ground nutmeg
½ cup KAHLÚA®

Heat oven to 350°F. In bowl, combine gingersnap and graham cracker crumbs with powdered sugar and butter. Toss to combine. Press evenly onto bottom of 8-inch springform pan. Bake 5 minutes. Cool.

In mixer bowl, beat cream cheese until smooth. Gradually add granulated sugar and beat until light. Add eggs, one at a time, beating well after each addition. Transfer 1 cup mixture to separate bowl and blend in pumpkin, cinnamon, ginger, nutmeg and Kahlúa®. Pour half of pumpkin mixture into prepared crust. Top with half of cream cheese mixture. Repeat layers using remaining pumpkin and cream cheese mixtures. Using table knife, cut through layers with uplifting motion in four to five places to create marbled effect. Place on baking sheet and bake at 350°F for 45 minutes. Without opening oven door, let cake stand in turned-off oven 1 hour. Remove from oven and cool, then chill. Remove from pan.

Makes about 12 servings

Marble Cheesecake

Crust
1 cup graham cracker
  crumbs
3 tablespoons sugar
3 tablespoons PARKAY®
  Margarine, melted

Filling
3 packages (8 ounces each)
  PHILADELPHIA BRAND®
  Cream Cheese, softened
¾ cup sugar
1 teaspoon vanilla
3 eggs
1 square BAKER'S®
  Unsweetened Chocolate,
  melted

• *Crust:* Heat oven to 350°F.

• Mix crumbs, sugar and margarine; press onto bottom of 9-inch springform pan. Bake 10 minutes.

• *Filling:* Increase oven temperature to 450°F.

• Beat cream cheese, sugar and vanilla at medium speed with electric mixer until well blended. Add eggs, 1 at a time, mixing well after each addition.

• Blend chocolate into 1 cup batter. Spoon plain and chocolate batters alternately over crust; cut through batters with knife several times for marble effect.

• Bake 10 minutes. Reduce oven temperature to 250°F; continue baking 30 minutes. Loosen cake from rim of pan; cool before removing rim of pan. Refrigerate.

Makes 10 to 12 servings

Prep time: 20 minutes plus
  refrigerating
Cooking time: 40 minutes

Triple Chocolate & Vanilla Cheesecake

1½ cups finely crushed
  creme-filled chocolate
  sandwich cookies
  (about 18 cookies)
3 tablespoons margarine or
  butter, melted
4 (8-ounce) packages cream
  cheese, softened
1 (14-ounce) can EAGLE®
  Brand Sweetened
  Condensed Milk
  (NOT evaporated milk)
4 eggs
⅓ cup unsifted flour
1 tablespoon vanilla extract
2 (1-ounce) squares semi-
  sweet chocolate, melted
  Chocolate Glaze

Preheat oven to 350°. Combine crumbs and margarine; press firmly on bottom of 9-inch springform pan. In large mixer bowl, beat cheese until fluffy. Gradually beat in sweetened condensed milk until smooth. Add eggs, flour and vanilla; mix well. Divide batter in half. Add chocolate to one half of batter; mix well. Pour into prepared pan. Top evenly with vanilla batter. Bake 50 to 55 minutes or until center springs back when lightly touched. Cool. Remove side of pan. Top with Chocolate Glaze. Chill. Refrigerate leftovers.

Makes one 9-inch cheesecake

CHOCOLATE GLAZE: In small saucepan, over low heat, melt 2 (1-ounce) squares semi-sweet chocolate with ¼ cup BORDEN® or MEADOW GOLD® Whipping Cream. Cook and stir until thickened and smooth. Remove from heat; spread over cheesecake.

Makes about ⅓ cup

Marble Cheesecake

Chocolate Velvet Cheesecake

Chocolate Velvet Cheesecake

Crust
   1 cup vanilla wafer crumbs
  ½ cup chopped pecans
   3 tablespoons granulated
      sugar
  ¼ cup (½ stick) PARKAY®
      Margarine, melted

Filling
   2 packages (8 ounces each)
      PHILADELPHIA BRAND®
      Cream Cheese, softened
  ½ cup packed brown sugar
   2 eggs
   1 package (6 ounces)
      BAKER'S® Semi-Sweet
      Real Chocolate Chips,
      melted
   3 tablespoons almond-
      flavored liqueur

Topping
   2 cups BREAKSTONE'S®
      Sour Cream
   2 tablespoons granulated
      sugar

• *Crust:* Heat oven to 325°F.

• Mix crumbs, pecans, granulated sugar and margarine; press onto bottom of 9-inch springform pan. Bake 10 minutes.

• *Filling:* Beat cream cheese and brown sugar at medium speed with electric mixer until well blended. Add eggs, 1 at a time, mixing well after each addition. Blend in chocolate and liqueur; pour over crust.

• Bake 35 minutes. Increase oven temperature to 425°F.

• *Topping:* Mix sour cream and granulated sugar; carefully spread over cheesecake. Bake 10 minutes. Loosen cake from rim of pan; cool before removing rim of pan. Refrigerate. Garnish with chocolate leaves, if desired.

Makes 10 to 12 servings

Prep time: 20 minutes plus
  refrigerating
Cooking time: 45 minutes

TO MAKE CHOCOLATE LEAVES: Wash and dry lemon leaves. Brush leaves with melted semi-sweet chocolate chips; refrigerate. Carefully peel back leaves from chocolate.

Boston Cream Cheesecake

Crust
   1 package (one-layer size)
      yellow cake mix

Filling
   2 packages (8 ounces each)
      PHILADELPHIA BRAND®
      Cream Cheese, softened
  ½ cup granulated sugar
   1 teaspoon vanilla
   2 eggs
  ⅓ cup BREAKSTONE'S® Sour
      Cream

Topping
   2 squares BAKER'S®
      Unsweetened Chocolate
   3 tablespoons PARKAY®
      Margarine
   2 tablespoons boiling water
   1 cup powdered sugar
   1 teaspoon vanilla

• *Crust:* Heat oven to 350°F.

• Grease bottom of 9-inch springform pan. Prepare cake mix as directed on package; pour batter evenly into springform pan. Bake 20 minutes.

• *Filling:* Beat cream cheese, granulated sugar and vanilla at medium speed with electric mixer until well blended. Add eggs, 1 at a time, mixing well after each addition. Blend in sour cream; pour over cake layer.

• Bake 35 minutes. Loosen cake from rim of pan; cool before removing rim of pan.

• *Topping:* Melt chocolate and margarine over low heat, stirring until smooth. Remove from heat. Add water and remaining ingredients; mix well. Spread over cheesecake. Refrigerate. Garnish with strawberries and fresh mint, if desired.

Makes 10 to 12 servings

Prep time: 20 minutes plus
  refrigerating
Cooking time: 55 minutes

Chocolate Chip Cheesecake

Chocolate Chip Cheesecake

Crust
> 1 package DUNCAN HINES®
>   Moist Deluxe Devil's
>   Food Cake Mix
> ½ cup CRISCO® Oil or
>   CRISCO® PURITAN® Oil

Filling
> 3 packages (8 ounces each)
>   cream cheese, softened
> 1½ cups sugar
> 1 cup dairy sour cream
> 1½ teaspoons vanilla extract
> 4 eggs, lightly beaten
> ¾ cup mini semi-sweet
>   chocolate chips, divided
> 1 teaspoon all-purpose flour

1. Preheat oven to 350°F. Grease 10-inch springform pan.

2. **For crust,** combine cake mix and oil in large bowl. Mix well. Press into bottom of pan. Bake at 350°F for 22 to 25 minutes. Remove from oven. *Increase oven temperature to 450°F.*

3. **For filling,** place cream cheese in large bowl. Beat at low speed with electric mixer adding sugar gradually. Add sour cream and vanilla extract, mixing until blended. Add eggs, mixing only until incorporated. Toss ½ cup chocolate chips with flour. Fold into cream cheese mixture. Pour filling onto crust. Sprinkle with remaining ¼ cup chocolate chips. Bake at 450°F for 5 to 7 minutes. *Reduce oven temperature to 250°F.* Bake for 60 to 65 minutes longer or until set. Loosen cake from sides of pan with knife or spatula. Cool completely on cooling rack. Refrigerate until ready to serve. Remove sides of pan.   *12 to 16 Servings*

Tip: Place pan of water on bottom shelf of oven during baking to prevent cheesecake from cracking.

Premier White Lemon Cheesecake

Crust:
> 6 tablespoons (¾ stick)
>   butter or margarine,
>   softened
> ¼ cup sugar
> 1 egg yolk
> 1¼ cups all-purpose flour
> ⅛ teaspoon salt

Cheesecake:
> Two 6-oz. pkgs. (6 foil-wrapped
>   bars) NESTLÉ® Premier
>   White baking bars
> ½ cup heavy or whipping
>   cream
> Two 8-oz. pkgs. cream cheese,
>   softened
> 1 tablespoon lemon juice
> ¼ teaspoon salt
> 3 egg whites
> 1 whole egg
>
>   Lemon twist for garnish
>   Fresh mint leaves for
>   garnish
>   Premier White Curls for
>   garnish
>   (directions follow)

Crust: Preheat oven to 350°F. Grease 9-inch springform pan. In small mixer bowl, beat butter and sugar until creamy. Blend in egg yolk. Beat in flour and ⅛ teaspoon salt. Press mixture onto bottom and 1 inch up side of prepared pan. Bake 14 to 16 minutes until crust is set; set aside.

Cheesecake: In small saucepan over low heat, melt Premier White baking bars with heavy cream, stirring constantly until smooth. Set aside.

In large mixer bowl, beat cream cheese, lemon juice and ¼ teaspoon salt until smooth. Blend in Premier White mixture. Beat in egg whites and whole egg. Pour into Crust.

Bake 35 minutes or until edge is lightly browned. Loosen and remove side of pan. Cool completely. Refrigerate. Garnish with lemon, mint and Premier White Curls.

Makes 10 to 12 servings

PREMIER WHITE CURLS: Shave a few "curls" from edge of Nestlé® Premier White baking bar with a vegetable peeler.

Premier White Lemon Cheesecake

Cherry Heart Cheesecake

Crust
   1⅓ cups crushed chocolate
         wafer cookies
   ¼ cup LAND O LAKES®
         Butter, melted
   2 tablespoons sugar

Filling
   4 eggs, separated
   ½ cup LAND O LAKES®
         Butter, softened
   2 packages (8 ounces each)
         cream cheese, softened
   1 cup sugar
   1 tablespoon cornstarch
   1 teaspoon baking powder
   1 tablespoon lemon juice

Topping
   1 carton (8 ounces) dairy
         sour cream (1 cup)
   2 tablespoons sugar
   1 teaspoon vanilla
   1 can (21 ounces) cherry pie
         filling
   3 tablespoons cherry
         flavored liqueur

Heat oven to 325°. For crust, in small bowl stir together all crust ingredients; press mixture on bottom of 9-inch springform pan. Bake 10 minutes; cool.

For filling, in small mixer bowl beat egg whites at high speed, scraping bowl often, until soft peaks form, 1 to 2 minutes; set aside. In large mixer bowl combine ½ cup butter, cream cheese and egg yolks. Beat at medium speed, scraping bowl often, until smooth and creamy, 2 to 3 minutes. Add 1 cup sugar, cornstarch, baking powder and lemon juice. Continue beating, scraping bowl often, until well mixed, 1 to 2 minutes. By hand, fold in beaten egg whites. Spoon filling into prepared pan. Bake for 60 to 80 minutes or until center is set and firm to the touch. (Cheesecake surface will be slightly cracked.) Cool 15 minutes; loosen sides of cheesecake from pan by running knife around inside of pan. Cool completely. (Cheesecake center will dip slightly upon cooling.)

For topping, in small bowl stir together sour cream, 2 tablespoons sugar and vanilla. Spread evenly over top of cheesecake. Spoon out 2 to 3 tablespoons of cherry sauce from pie filling; drop by teaspoonfuls onto sour cream topping. Carefully pull knife or spatula through cherry sauce forming hearts. Cover; refrigerate 4 hours or overnight. In medium bowl stir together remaining pie filling and liqueur. Serve over slices of cheesecake. Store refrigerated.

Makes 10 servings

Creamy Baked Cheesecake

   1¼ cups graham cracker
         crumbs
   ¼ cup sugar
   ⅓ cup margarine or butter,
         melted
   2 (8-ounce) packages cream
         cheese, softened
   1 (14-ounce) can EAGLE®
         Brand Sweetened
         Condensed Milk
         (NOT evaporated milk)
   3 eggs
   ¼ cup REALEMON® Lemon
         Juice from Concentrate
   1 (8-ounce) container
         BORDEN® or MEADOW
         GOLD® Sour Cream, at
         room temperature
         Fresh strawberries, hulled
         and sliced

Preheat oven to 300°. Combine crumbs, sugar and margarine; press firmly on bottom of 9-inch springform pan. In large mixer bowl, beat cheese until fluffy. Gradually beat in sweetened condensed milk until smooth. Add eggs and ReaLemon® brand; mix well. Pour into prepared pan. Bake 50 to 55 minutes or until center is set; top with sour cream. Bake 5 minutes longer. Cool. Chill. Just before serving, remove side of springform pan. Top with strawberries. Refrigerate leftovers.

Makes one 9-inch cheesecake

Caramel-Apple Sundae Cheesecake

Crust
   ⅓ cup PARKAY® Margarine
   ⅓ cup sugar
   1 egg
   1¼ cups flour

Filling
   2 packages (8 ounces each)
         PHILADELPHIA BRAND®
         Cream Cheese, softened
   ⅔ cup sugar, divided
   2 tablespoons flour
   3 eggs
   ½ cup BREAKSTONE'S® Sour
         Cream
   1 cup chopped peeled apple
   ¾ teaspoon ground cinnamon
   ½ cup KRAFT® Caramel
         Topping, divided
   ¼ cup chopped pecans

• *Crust:* Heat oven to 450°F.

• Beat margarine and sugar at medium speed with electric mixer until light and fluffy. Blend in egg. Add flour; mix well. Spread dough onto bottom and sides of 9-inch springform pan. Bake 10 minutes.

• *Filling:* Reduce oven temperature to 350°F.

• Beat cream cheese, ⅓ cup sugar and flour at medium speed with electric mixer until well blended. Add eggs, 1 at a time, mixing well after each addition. Blend in sour cream.

• Toss apples in remaining sugar and cinnamon. Stir into cream cheese mixture. Pour over crust. Swirl ¼ cup caramel topping into cream cheese mixture.

• Bake 1 hour. Loosen cake from rim of pan; cool before removing rim of pan. Refrigerate. Top with remaining caramel topping and pecans.

Makes 10 to 12 servings

Prep time: 25 minutes plus refrigerating
Cooking time: 1 hour

Cherry Heart Cheesecake

Chocolate Caramel Pecan Cheesecake

2 cups vanilla wafer crumbs
6 tablespoons PARKAY®
 Margarine, melted

* * *

1 14-ounce bag KRAFT®
 Caramels
1 5-ounce can evaporated milk
1 cup chopped pecans, toasted
2 8-ounce packages
 PHILADELPHIA BRAND®
 Cream Cheese, softened
½ cup sugar
1 teaspoon vanilla
2 eggs
½ cup semi-sweet chocolate
 pieces, melted

Combine crumbs and margarine; press onto bottom and sides of 9-inch springform pan. Bake at 350°, 10 minutes.

In 1½-quart heavy saucepan, melt caramels with milk over low heat, stirring frequently, until smooth. Pour over crust. Top with pecans. Combine cream cheese, sugar and vanilla, mixing at medium speed on electric mixer until well blended. Add eggs, one at a time, mixing well after each addition. Blend in chocolate; pour over pecans. Bake at 350°, 40 minutes. Loosen cake from rim of pan; cool before removing rim of pan. Chill. Garnish with whipped cream, additional chopped nuts and maraschino cherries, if desired.
10 to 12 servings.

Miniature Cheesecakes

⅓ cup graham cracker crumbs
1 tablespoon sugar
1 tablespoon PARKAY®
 Margarine, melted

* * *

1 8-ounce package
 PHILADELPHIA BRAND®
 Cream Cheese, softened
¼ cup sugar
1½ teaspoons lemon juice
½ teaspoon grated lemon peel
¼ teaspoon vanilla
1 egg
 KRAFT® Strawberry or Apricot
 Preserves

Combine crumbs, sugar and margarine. Press rounded measuring tablespoonful of crumb mixture onto bottom of each of six paper-lined muffin cups. Bake at 325°, 5 minutes.

Combine cream cheese, sugar, juice, peel and vanilla, mixing at medium speed on electric mixer until well blended. Blend in egg; pour over crust, filling each cup ¾ full. Bake at 325°, 25 minutes. Cool before removing from pan. Chill. Top with preserves just before serving.
6 servings.

Variation: Substitute fresh fruit for KRAFT® Preserves.

Make Ahead: Wrap chilled cheesecakes individually in plastic wrap; freeze. Let stand at room temperature 40 minutes before serving.

Northwest Cheesecake Supreme

1 cup graham cracker crumbs
3 tablespoons sugar
3 tablespoons PARKAY®
 Margarine, melted

* * *

4 8-ounce packages
 PHILADELPHIA BRAND®
 Cream Cheese, softened
1 cup sugar
3 tablespoons flour
4 eggs
1 cup sour cream
1 tablespoon vanilla
1 21-ounce can cherry pie filling

Miniature Cheesecakes

Combine crumbs, sugar and margarine; press onto bottom of 9-inch springform pan. Bake at 325°, 10 minutes.

Combine cream cheese, sugar and flour, mixing at medium speed on electric mixer until well blended. Add eggs, one at a time, mixing well after each addition. Blend in sour cream and vanilla; pour over crust. Bake at 450°, 10 minutes. Reduce oven temperature to 250°; continue baking 1 hour. Loosen cake from rim of pan; cool before removing rim of pan. Chill. Top with cherry pie filling just before serving.
10 to 12 servings.

Variation: Substitute 1½ cups finely chopped nuts and 2 tablespoons sugar for graham cracker crumbs and sugar in crust.

Piña Colada Cheesecake

1½ cups vanilla wafer or graham
 cracker crumbs
½ cup flaked coconut, optional
3 tablespoons margarine, melted
1 can (8 ounces) DOLE®
 Crushed Pineapple in Juice
3 packages (8 ounces each)
 cream cheese, softened
3 eggs
1 cup sugar
1 cup dairy sour cream
3 tablespoons dark rum
2 teaspoons coconut extract
 Pineapple Topping (recipe
 follows)

Preheat oven to 350°. In medium bowl, combine cookie crumbs, coconut and margarine. Press onto bottom and sides of 9-inch springform pan. Bake 10 minutes. Cool.

Drain pineapple. In large bowl, beat cream cheese, eggs and sugar. Stir pineapple, sour cream, rum and coconut extract into cream cheese mixture. Pour into prepared crust. Bake in preheated oven 50 to 55 minutes or until set. Cool to room temperature; refrigerate until chilled. Spread Pineapple Topping over cheesecake just before serving.
Makes 16 servings.

PINEAPPLE TOPPING: In saucepan, combine 20 ounces (1 can) undrained Dole® Crushed Pineapple in Juice, ½ cup sugar, 1 tablespoon dark rum and 1 tablespoon cornstarch. Cook, stirring constantly, until thickened and clear. Cool.

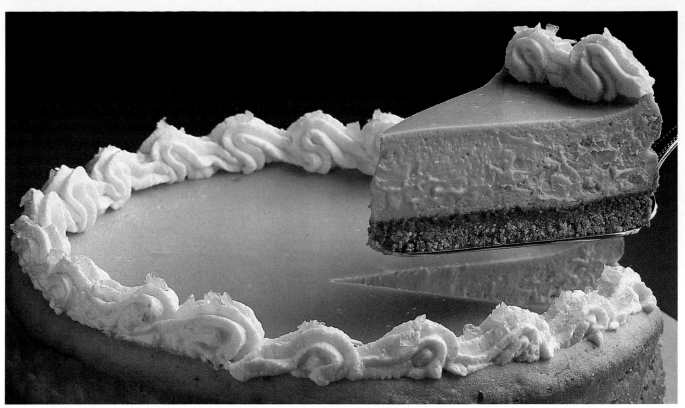

Butterscotch Cheesecake

Butterscotch Cheesecake

- 1/3 **cup margarine or butter, melted**
- 1 1/2 **cups graham cracker crumbs**
- 1/3 **cup firmly packed brown sugar**
- 1 **(14-ounce) can EAGLE® Brand Sweetened Condensed Milk (NOT evaporated milk)**
- 3/4 **cup cold water**
- 1 **(3 5/8-ounce) package butterscotch pudding and pie filling mix**
- 3 **(8-ounce) packages cream cheese, softened**
- 3 **eggs**
- 1 **teaspoon vanilla extract**
  Whipped cream
  Crushed hard butterscotch candy

Preheat oven to 375°. Combine margarine, crumbs and sugar; press firmly on bottom of 9-inch springform pan. In medium saucepan, combine sweetened condensed milk and water; mix well. Stir in pudding mix. Over medium heat, cook and stir until thickened and bubbly. In large mixer bowl, beat cheese until fluffy. Beat in eggs and vanilla then pudding mixture. Pour into prepared pan. Bake 50 minutes or until golden brown around edge (center will be soft). Cool to room temperature. Chill thoroughly. Garnish with whipped cream and crushed candy. Refrigerate leftovers.
Makes one 9-inch cheesecake.

Frozen Mocha Cheesecake

- 1 1/4 **cups chocolate wafer cookie crumbs (about 24 wafers)**
- 1/4 **cup margarine or butter, melted**
- 1/4 **cup sugar**
- 1 **(8-ounce) package cream cheese, softened**
- 1 **(14-ounce) can EAGLE® Brand Sweetened Condensed Milk (NOT evaporated milk)**
- 2/3 **cup chocolate flavored syrup**
- 1 **to 2 tablespoons instant coffee**
- 1 **teaspoon hot water**
- 1 **cup (1/2 pint) BORDEN® or MEADOW GOLD® Whipping Cream, whipped**
  Additional chocolate crumbs, optional

Combine crumbs, margarine and sugar; press firmly on bottom and up side of 8- or 9-inch springform pan or 13×9-inch baking pan. In large mixer bowl, beat cheese until fluffy. Gradually beat in sweetened condensed milk and chocolate syrup until smooth. In small bowl, dissolve coffee in water; add to cheese mixture. Mix well. Fold in whipped cream. Pour into prepared pan; cover. Freeze 6 hours or overnight. Garnish with additional chocolate crumbs if desired. Return leftovers to freezer.
Makes one 8- or 9-inch cheesecake.

Orange-Butterscotch Cheesecake

Crust
- 1¼ cups old fashioned or quick-cooking oats, uncooked
- ¼ cup packed brown sugar
- 2 tablespoons flour
- ¼ cup PARKAY® Squeeze Spread

Filling
- 3 packages (8 ounces each) PHILADELPHIA BRAND® Cream Cheese, softened
- ¾ cup granulated sugar
- 2 teaspoons grated orange peel
- 1 teaspoon vanilla
- 4 eggs

Topping
- ½ cup packed brown sugar
- ⅓ cup light corn syrup
- ¼ cup PARKAY® Squeeze Spread
- 1 teaspoon vanilla

• *Crust:* Heat oven to 350°F.

• Mix oats, brown sugar, flour and spread; press onto bottom of 9-inch springform pan. Bake 15 minutes.

• *Filling:* Reduce oven temperature to 325°F.

• Beat cream cheese, granulated sugar, peel and vanilla at medium speed with electric mixer until well blended. Add eggs, 1 at a time, mixing well after each addition; pour over crust.

• Bake 1 hour and 5 minutes. Loosen cake from rim of pan; cool before removing rim of pan.

• *Topping:* Mix brown sugar, corn syrup and spread in saucepan; bring to boil, stirring constantly. Remove from heat; stir in vanilla. Refrigerate until slightly thickened. Spoon over cheesecake. Garnish with orange slice and fresh mint, if desired.

Makes 10 to 12 servings

Prep time: 35 minutes plus refrigerating
Cooking time: 1 hour 5 minutes

Mini Cheesecakes

Mini Cheesecakes

- 1½ cups graham cracker or chocolate wafer crumbs
- ¼ cup sugar
- ¼ cup margarine or butter, melted
- 3 (8-ounce) packages cream cheese, softened
- 1 (14-ounce) can EAGLE® Brand Sweetened Condensed Milk (NOT evaporated milk)
- 3 eggs
- 2 teaspoons vanilla extract

Preheat oven to 300°. Combine crumbs, sugar and margarine; press equal portions onto bottoms of 24 lightly greased* or paper-lined muffin cups. In large mixer bowl, beat cheese until fluffy. Gradually beat in sweetened condensed milk until smooth. Add eggs and vanilla; mix well. Spoon equal amounts of mixture (about 3 tablespoons) into prepared cups. Bake 20 minutes or until cakes spring back when lightly touched. Cool. Chill. Garnish as desired. Refrigerate leftovers.

Makes about 2 dozen

*If greased muffin cups are used, cool baked cheesecakes. Freeze 15 minutes; remove from pans. Proceed as above.

Orange-Butterscotch Cheesecake

Lemon Cheesecake with Raspberry Sauce

Crust
>1 package DUNCAN HINES®
>   Moist Deluxe Lemon
>   Supreme Cake Mix
>½ cup CRISCO® Oil or
>   CRISCO® PURITAN® Oil
>⅓ cup finely chopped pecans

Filling
>3 packages (8 ounces each)
>   cream cheese, softened
>¾ cup sugar
>2 tablespoons lemon juice
>1 teaspoon grated lemon
>   peel
>3 eggs, lightly beaten

Raspberry Sauce
>1 package (12 ounces) frozen
>   dry pack red raspberries,
>   thawed
>⅓ cup sugar
>Fresh raspberries, for
>   garnish
>Lemon slices, for garnish
>Mint leaves, for garnish

1. Preheat oven to 350°F. Grease 10-inch springform pan.

2. **For crust,** combine cake mix and oil in large bowl. Mix well. Stir in pecans. Press mixture into bottom of pan. Bake at 350°F for about 20 minutes or until light golden brown. Remove from oven. *Increase oven temperature to 450°F.*

3. **For filling,** place cream cheese in large bowl. Beat at low speed with electric mixer, adding ¾ cup sugar gradually. Add lemon juice and lemon peel. Add eggs, mixing only until incorporated. Pour filling onto crust. Bake at 450°F for 5 to 7 minutes. *Reduce oven temperature to 250°F.* Bake 30 minutes longer or until set. Loosen cake from sides of pan with knife or spatula. Cool completely on cooling rack. Refrigerate 2 hours or until ready to serve. Remove sides of pan.

4. **For raspberry sauce,** combine thawed raspberries and ⅓ cup sugar in small saucepan. Bring to a boil. Simmer until

berries are soft. Strain through sieve into small bowl to remove seeds. Cool completely.

5. To serve, garnish cheesecake with raspberries, lemon slices and mint leaves. Cut into slices and serve with raspberry sauce.
12 to 16 Servings

Tip: Overbeating cheesecake batter can incorporate too much air, which may cause the cheesecake to crack during baking.

Heavenly Delight Cheesecake

>1 tablespoon graham cracker
>   crumbs
>1 cup lowfat (1% to 2%)
>   cottage cheese
>2 packages (8 ounces each)
>   Light PHILADELPHIA
>   BRAND® Neufchatel
>   Cheese, softened
>⅔ cup sugar
>2 tablespoons flour
>3 eggs
>2 tablespoons skim milk
>¼ teaspoon almond extract or
>   vanilla

• Heat oven to 325°F.

• Lightly grease bottom of 9-inch springform pan. Sprinkle with crumbs. Dust bottom; remove excess crumbs.

Heavenly Delight Cheesecake

• Place cottage cheese in blender container; cover. Blend at medium speed until smooth.

• Beat cottage cheese, Neufchatel cheese, sugar and flour at medium speed with electric mixer until well blended. Add eggs, 1 at a time, mixing well after each addition. Blend in milk and extract; pour into pan.

• Bake 45 to 50 minutes or until center is almost set. (Center of cheesecake appears soft but firms upon cooling.) Loosen cake from rim of pan; cool before removing rim of pan. Refrigerate. Garnish with raspberries, strawberries or blueberries and fresh mint, if desired.
Makes 10 to 12 servings

Prep time: 15 minutes plus refrigerating
Cooking time: 50 minutes

Variations

Prepare as directed; omit blender method. Place cottage cheese in large bowl of electric mixer; beat at high speed until smooth. Add Neufchatel cheese, sugar and flour, mixing at medium speed until well blended. Continue as directed.

Substitute 1 cup vanilla wafer crumbs and ¼ cup (½ stick) PARKAY® Margarine, melted, for graham cracker crumbs; press onto bottom of ungreased pan.

Heavenly Orange Cheesecake

Heavenly Orange Cheesecake

Crust
  1 cup chocolate wafer
      crumbs
  3 tablespoons PARKAY®
      Margarine, melted

Filling
  1 envelope unflavored gelatin
  ½ cup orange juice
  3 packages (8 ounces each)
      PHILADELPHIA BRAND®
      Cream Cheese, softened
  ¾ cup sugar
  1 cup whipping cream,
      whipped
  2 teaspoons grated orange
      peel

• *Crust:* Heat oven to 350°F.

• Mix crumbs and margarine;
press onto bottom of 9-inch
springform pan. Bake 10
minutes. Cool.

• *Filling:* Soften gelatin in juice;
stir over low heat until
dissolved. Beat cream cheese and
sugar at medium speed with
electric mixer until well blended.
Gradually add gelatin;
refrigerate until slightly
thickened.

• Fold in whipped cream and
peel; pour over crust. Refrigerate
until firm. Garnish with orange
slices and fresh mint, if desired.
Makes 10 to 12 servings

Prep time: 25 minutes plus
  refrigerating

Very Blueberry Cheesecake

Crust
  1½ cups vanilla wafer crumbs
  ¼ cup (½ stick) PARKAY®
      Margarine, melted

Filling
  1 envelope unflavored gelatin
  ¼ cup cold water
  2 packages (8 ounces each)
      PHILADELPHIA BRAND®
      Cream Cheese, softened
  1 tablespoon lemon juice
  1 teaspoon grated lemon
      peel
  1 jar (7 ounces) KRAFT®
      Marshmallow Creme
  3½ cups (8 ounces) COOL
      WHIP® Non-Dairy
      Whipped Topping,
      thawed
  2 cups blueberries, puréed

• *Crust:* Mix crumbs and
margarine; press onto bottom of
9-inch springform pan.
Refrigerate.

• *Filling:* Soften gelatin in water;
stir over low heat until dissolved.
Gradually add gelatin to cream
cheese, mixing at medium speed
with electric mixer until well
blended. Blend in juice and peel.
Beat in marshmallow creme.
Fold in whipped topping and
blueberries; pour over crust.

• Refrigerate until firm. Garnish
with additional whipped topping
and lemon peel, if desired.
Makes 10 to 12 servings

Prep time: 25 minutes plus
  refrigerating

Eggnog Cheesecake

  2 packages (5½ ounces
      each) chocolate-laced
      pirouette cookies
  ⅓ cup graham cracker
      crumbs
  3 tablespoons PARKAY®
      Margarine, melted
  2 packages (8 ounces each)
      PHILADELPHIA BRAND®
      Cream Cheese, softened
  2 cups cold prepared eggnog
  2 cups cold milk
  2 packages (4-serving size
      each) JELL-O® Instant
      Pudding and Pie Filling,
      French Vanilla or Vanilla
      Flavor
  1 tablespoon rum
  ⅛ teaspoon ground nutmeg
      COOL WHIP® Whipped
      Topping, thawed
      (optional)
      Ribbon (optional)

RESERVE 1 cookie for garnish,
if desired. Cut 1-inch piece off
one end of each of the remaining
cookies. Crush 1-inch pieces into
crumbs; set aside remaining
cookies for sides of cake.
Combine cookie crumbs, graham
cracker crumbs and margarine
until well mixed. Press crumb
mixture firmly onto bottom of
9-inch springform pan.

BEAT cream cheese at low speed of electric mixer until smooth. Gradually add 1 cup of the eggnog, blending until mixture is very smooth. Add remaining eggnog, milk, pudding mix, rum and nutmeg. Beat until well blended, about 1 minute. Pour cream cheese mixture carefully into pan. Chill until firm, about 3 hours. Run hot metal spatula or knife around edges of pan before removing sides of pan.

PRESS remaining cookies, cut sides down, into sides of cake. Garnish with whipped topping and reserved cookie, if desired. Tie ribbon around cake, if desired. *Makes 12 servings*

Prep time: 45 minutes
Chill time: 3 hours

Rocky Road Cheesecake

Crust
- 1 cup chocolate wafer crumbs
- 3 tablespoons PARKAY® Margarine, melted

Filling
- 1 envelope unflavored gelatin
- ¼ cup cold water
- 2 containers (8 ounces each) PHILADELPHIA BRAND® Soft Cream Cheese
- ¾ cup sugar
- ⅓ cup cocoa
- ½ teaspoon vanilla
- 2 cups KRAFT® Miniature Marshmallows
- 1 cup whipping cream, whipped
- ½ cup chopped nuts

• *Crust:* Heat oven to 350°F.

• Mix crumbs and margarine; press onto bottom of 9-inch springform pan. Bake 10 minutes. Cool.

• *Filling:* Soften gelatin in water; stir over low heat until dissolved. Beat cream cheese, sugar, cocoa and vanilla at medium speed with electric mixer until well blended. Gradually add gelatin.

• Fold in remaining ingredients; pour over crust. Refrigerate until firm. Garnish with additional miniature marshmallows, if desired.

Makes 10 to 12 servings

Prep time: 25 minutes plus refrigerating

Chilled Raspberry Cheesecake

- 1½ cups vanilla wafer crumbs (about 45 wafers, crushed)
- ⅓ cup HERSHEY'S Cocoa
- ⅓ cup powdered sugar
- ⅓ cup butter or margarine, melted
- 1 package (10 oz.) frozen raspberries, thawed
- 1 envelope unflavored gelatin
- ½ cup cold water
- ½ cup boiling water
- 2 packages (8 oz. each) cream cheese, softened
- ½ cup granulated sugar
- 1 teaspoon vanilla extract
- 3 tablespoons seedless red raspberry preserves
- Chocolate Whipped Cream (recipe follows)

Heat oven to 350°F. In medium bowl, stir together crumbs, cocoa and powdered sugar; stir in melted butter, mixing thoroughly. Press mixture onto bottom and 1½ inches up side of 9-inch springform pan. Bake 10 minutes; cool completely. Puree and strain raspberries; set aside. In small bowl, sprinkle gelatin over cold water; let stand several minutes to soften. Add boiling water; stir until gelatin dissolves completely and mixture is clear. In large mixer bowl, beat cream cheese, granulated sugar and vanilla until smooth. Gradually add raspberry puree and gelatin, mixing thoroughly; pour into prepared crust. Refrigerate several hours or overnight. With narrow knife, loosen cake from side of pan; remove side of pan. Spread raspberry preserves over top. Garnish with Chocolate Whipped Cream. Cover; refrigerate leftovers.

Makes 10 to 12 servings

CHOCOLATE WHIPPED CREAM: In small mixer bowl, stir together ½ cup powdered sugar and ¼ cup HERSHEY'S Cocoa. Add 1 cup (½ pt.) cold whipping cream and 1 teaspoon vanilla extract; beat until stiff.

Chilled Raspberry Cheesecake

DESSERTS

Great meals demand a memorable dessert to conclude the perfect evening. Indulge in exquisite truffle loaves and bavarians, fluffy parfaits and mousses, fruit-filled cobblers and crêpes and inviting ice creams and sauces sure to satisfy every craving. Show off your culinary creativity with these divine desserts and win rave reviews!

Chocolate Hazelnut Truffle Dessert

Truffle Dessert
- **1 cup whipping cream**
- **¼ cup LAND O LAKES® Butter**
- **2 bars (8 ounces *each*) semi-sweet chocolate**
- **4 egg yolks**
- **¾ cup powdered sugar**
- **3 tablespoons rum *or* orange juice**
- **1 cup coarsely chopped hazelnuts *or* filberts, toasted**

Custard
- **1 cup whipping cream**
- **¼ cup granulated sugar**
- **1 teaspoon cornstarch**
- **3 egg yolks**
- **1 teaspoon vanilla**

For truffle dessert, in 2-quart saucepan combine 1 cup whipping cream, butter and chocolate. Cook over medium heat, stirring occasionally, until chocolate is melted, 5 to 7 minutes. Whisk in 4 egg yolks, one at a time. Continue cooking, stirring constantly, until mixture reaches 160°F and thickens slightly, 3 to 4 minutes. Remove from heat; whisk in powdered sugar and rum. Stir in hazelnuts. Line 8×4-inch loaf pan with aluminum foil leaving 1 inch of foil over *each* edge. Pour chocolate mixture into prepared pan. Freeze 8 hours or overnight.

For custard, in 2-quart saucepan cook 1 cup whipping cream over medium heat until it just comes to a boil, 4 to 6 minutes. Remove from heat. Meanwhile, in medium bowl combine granulated sugar and cornstarch. Whisk in 3 egg yolks until mixture is light and creamy, 3 to 4 minutes. Gradually whisk hot cream into beaten egg yolks. Return mixture to saucepan; stir in vanilla. Cook over medium heat, stirring constantly, until custard reaches 160°F and is thick enough to coat back of metal spoon, 4 to 5 minutes. (Do not boil because egg yolks will curdle.) Refrigerate 8 hours or overnight.

To serve, remove truffle dessert from pan using foil to lift out. Remove foil. Slice truffle dessert with hot knife into 16 slices. Spoon about 1 tablespoon custard onto individual dessert plates; place slice of truffle dessert over custard. *Makes 16 servings*

Chocolate Hazelnut Truffle Dessert

Chocolate Truffle Loaf with Sweet Raspberry Sauce

Chocolate Truffle Loaf with Sweet Raspberry Sauce

2 cups heavy cream, divided
3 egg yolks
16 squares (1 ounce *each*) semisweet chocolate
½ cup KARO® Light or Dark corn syrup
½ cup MAZOLA® Margarine
¼ cup confectioners sugar
1 teaspoon vanilla Sweet Raspberry Sauce (recipe follows)

Line 9¼×5¼×2¾-inch loaf pan with plastic wrap. In small bowl mix ½ cup of the cream with the egg yolks. In large saucepan combine chocolate, corn syrup and margarine; stir over medium heat until melted. Add egg mixture. Cook 3 minutes over medium heat, stirring constantly. Cool to room temperature. In small bowl with mixer at medium speed, beat remaining 1½ cups cream, sugar and vanilla until soft peaks form. Gently fold into chocolate mixture just until combined. Pour into prepared pan; cover with plastic wrap.

Refrigerate overnight or chill in freezer 3 hours. Slice and serve with Sweet Raspberry Sauce.
Makes 12 servings

SWEET RASPBERRY SAUCE:
In blender or food processor puree 1 package (10 ounces) frozen raspberries, thawed; strain to remove seeds. Stir in ⅓ cup Karo® Light Corn Syrup.

Preparation Time: 30 minutes, plus chilling

Lemon Strawberry Stars

1 pound cake loaf (about 12 ounces)
1 package (4-serving size) JELL-O® Instant Pudding and Pie Filling, Lemon Flavor
2 cups cold milk Sliced strawberries Strawberry Sauce (recipe follows) (optional)

SLICE pound cake horizontally into 5 layers. Cut each layer into 2 star shapes with large cookie cutter. (Reserve cake scraps for snacking or other use.)

PREPARE pudding mix with milk as directed on package.

TOP ½ of the pound cake stars with ½ of the sliced strawberries and ½ of the pudding. Cover with remaining stars, strawberries and pudding. Serve with Strawberry Sauce, if desired.   *Makes 5 servings*

Prep time: 15 minutes

Strawberry Sauce

2 packages (10 ounces each) BIRDS EYE® Quick Thaw Strawberries, thawed
2 teaspoons cornstarch

PLACE strawberries in food processor or blender; cover. Process until smooth. Combine cornstarch with small amount of the strawberries in medium saucepan; add remaining strawberries. Bring to boil over medium heat, stirring constantly; boil 1 minute. Chill.
Makes 2 cups

Prep time: 30 minutes
Chill time: 3 hours

Lemon Strawberry Stars

Strawberry-White Chocolate Tiramisu

Two 6-oz. pkgs. (6 foil-wrapped bars) NESTLÉ® Premier White baking bars
1½ cups heavy or whipping cream, divided
One 3-oz. pkg. cream cheese, softened
36 ladyfingers, split (three 3-oz. pkgs.)
1¼ cups cooled espresso or strong coffee
2 tablespoons brandy, optional
2 pints strawberries, divided

Melt over hot (not boiling) water, Premier White baking bars with ¼ cup heavy cream, stirring until smooth; cool completely.

In large mixer bowl, beat cream cheese until fluffy. Stir in melted baking bar mixture. In small mixer bowl, beat remaining 1¼ cups cream until stiff peaks form; fold into cream cheese mixture.

Line side of 9×3-inch springform pan with ladyfinger halves, cut sides in. Arrange half of remaining ladyfingers on bottom of pan. In small bowl, combine espresso and brandy; brush half over ladyfingers in bottom of pan. Cover with half the cream cheese filling. Slice 1 pint strawberries; arrange over filling. Repeat ladyfinger, espresso mixture and filling layers. Halve remaining 1 pint strawberries; arrange decoratively on top. Cover; refrigerate until set, 4 hours or overnight. Remove side of pan before serving.

Makes 10 to 12 servings

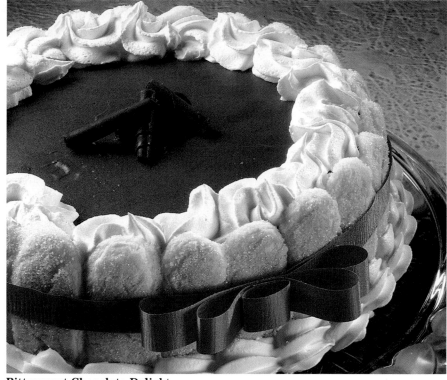
Bittersweet Chocolate Delight

Bittersweet Chocolate Delight

3 egg yolks
½ cup granulated sugar
1 cup milk
2 tablespoons cornstarch
3 foil-wrapped bars (6 oz.) NESTLÉ® Unsweetened Chocolate baking bars, broken up
3 tablespoons almond-flavored liqueur
Two 3-oz. pkgs. ladyfingers (about 48), split
1½ cups heavy or whipping cream
1 cup confectioners' sugar
Whipped cream for garnish
Chocolate Curls for garnish (directions follow)

In medium saucepan, whisk together egg yolks and granulated sugar. Whisk in milk and cornstarch until smooth. Cook over medium heat, stirring constantly with wire whisk, until mixture comes to a boil. Boil 1 minute, whisking constantly; remove from heat. Whisk in chocolate until smooth. Blend in liqueur. Transfer to large bowl; press plastic wrap directly on surface. Cool to room temperature.

Line side of 9-inch springform pan with ladyfinger halves, cut sides in. Arrange half of remaining ladyfingers on bottom of pan; set aside the remaining half.

Stir cooled chocolate mixture until smooth. In small mixer bowl, beat heavy cream with confectioners' sugar until soft peaks form; fold into chocolate mixture. Spoon half of the chocolate mixture into prepared pan; top with remaining ladyfingers and chocolate mixture. Cover; refrigerate overnight. Loosen and remove side of pan. Garnish with whipped cream and Chocolate Curls.

Makes 10 to 12 servings

CHOCOLATE CURLS: Shave a few "curls" from edge of 1 foil-wrapped bar (2 oz.) Nestlé® Semi-Sweet baking bar with vegetable peeler.

Hot Chocolate Soufflé

Hot Chocolate Soufflé

¾ cup HERSHEY'S Cocoa
1 cup sugar, divided
½ cup all-purpose flour
¼ teaspoon salt
2 cups milk
6 egg yolks, well-beaten
2 tablespoons butter or
    margarine
1 teaspoon vanilla extract
8 egg whites
¼ teaspoon cream of tartar
    Sweetened whipped cream

Adjust oven rack to lowest position. Heat oven to 350°F. Lightly butter 2½-quart soufflé dish; sprinkle with sugar. For collar, measure length of heavy-duty aluminum foil to fit around soufflé dish; fold into thirds lengthwise. Lightly butter one side. Attach foil, buttered side in, around outside of dish allowing foil to extend at least 2 inches above dish. Secure foil with tape or string.

In saucepan, stir together cocoa, ¾ cup sugar, flour and salt; gradually stir in milk. Cook over medium heat, stirring constantly with wire whisk, until mixture boils; remove from heat.

Gradually stir small amount of chocolate mixture into beaten egg yolks; blend well. Return egg mixture to pan, blending well. Cook and stir 1 minute. Add butter and vanilla, stirring until blended. Set aside; cool 20 minutes.

In large mixer bowl, beat egg whites with cream of tartar until soft peaks form; gradually add remaining ¼ cup sugar, beating until stiff peaks form. Gently fold about one-third of beaten egg whites into chocolate mixture. Lightly fold chocolate mixture, half at a time, into remaining beaten egg whites just until blended; do not overfold.

Gently pour mixture into prepared dish; smooth top with spatula. Place dish in larger baking pan; pour hot water into pan to depth of 1 inch. Bake 65 to 70 minutes. Carefully remove foil. Serve immediately with sweetened whipped cream.
8 to 10 servings.

Chilly Strawberry Souffles

1 10-ounce package frozen
    strawberries, thawed
2 envelopes unflavored gelatin
2¼ cups cold water
1 8-ounce package Light
    PHILADELPHIA BRAND®
    Neufchatel Cheese, softened
¼ cup sugar
1 tablespoon lemon juice
    Few drops red food coloring
    (optional)
2 cups thawed frozen whipped
    topping

Drain strawberries, reserving liquid. Chop strawberries. Soften gelatin in ½ cup water; stir over low heat until dissolved. Add remaining water. Combine Neufchatel cheese and sugar, mixing until well blended. Gradually add gelatin mixture to Neufchatel cheese mixture, mixing until well blended. Stir in reserved liquid, juice and food coloring. Chill, stirring occasionally, until thickened but not set. Beat with electric mixer or wire whisk until smooth. Fold in strawberries and whipped topping. Wrap 3-inch collar of foil around individual dessert dishes; secure with tape. Pour mixture into dishes; chill until firm. Remove collar before serving.
8 to 10 servings.
  Variations: Substitute PHILADELPHIA BRAND® Cream Cheese for Neufchatel Cheese. Increase sugar to ⅔ cup. Substitute 1 cup whipping cream, whipped, for whipped topping.
  Substitute 1-quart souffle dish for individual dessert dishes.

Individual Fudge Soufflés

½ cup (1 stick) butter or
    margarine, softened
1¼ cups sugar
1 teaspoon vanilla extract
4 eggs
⅔ cup milk
½ teaspoon powdered instant
    coffee
⅔ cup all-purpose flour
⅔ cup HERSHEY'S Cocoa
1½ teaspoons baking powder
1 cup (½ pt.) whipping cream
2 tablespoons powdered sugar

Heat oven to 325°F. Grease and sugar eight 6-ounce ramekins or custard cups; set aside. In large mixer bowl, beat butter, sugar and vanilla until light and fluffy. Add eggs, one at a time, beating well after each addition. Scald milk; remove from heat and add powdered coffee, stirring until dissolved. Stir together flour, cocoa and baking powder; add alternately with milk mixture to butter mixture. Beat 1 minute on medium speed.

Divide batter evenly among prepared ramekins. Place ramekins in two 8-inch square pans; place pans in oven. Pour hot water into pans to depth of ⅛ inch. Bake 45 to 50 minutes or until wooden pick inserted in center comes out clean. Remove pans from oven; allow ramekins to stand in water 5 minutes. Remove ramekins from water; cool slightly. Serve in ramekins or invert onto dessert dishes. In small mixer bowl, beat whipping cream with powdered sugar until stiff; spoon onto warm soufflés. *8 servings.*

Fruited Chocolate Trifle

⅔ cup sugar
2 tablespoons cornstarch
⅛ teaspoon salt
2 eggs, slightly beaten
3 cups milk, scalded
3 squares BAKER'S®
　Unsweetened Chocolate
3 tablespoons almond liqueur*
12 ladyfingers, split
1 pint fresh strawberries, hulled
　and halved
1 can (16 ounces) apricot halves,
　drained

Combine sugar, cornstarch and salt in bowl. Add eggs and mix well. Gradually pour in hot milk, stirring constantly. Return to saucepan. Cook and stir over very low heat until mixture is smooth and thickened. Remove from heat. Add chocolate and liqueur; stir until chocolate is melted. Cool slightly.

Arrange half of the ladyfingers, fruits and chocolate custard in layers in a serving dish; repeat layers with remaining ingredients. Chill at least 2 hours. Before serving, garnish with sweetened whipped cream and additional strawberries, if desired. *Makes 8 to 10 servings.*
　*Or use ½ teaspoon almond extract.

Hawaiian Trifle

2 packages (3⅛ ounces each)
　vanilla flavor pudding and
　pie filling mix (not instant)
2 cups milk
1½ cups DOLE® Pineapple Juice
2 cups whipping cream
1 package (16 ounces) frozen
　pound cake, thawed
½ cup cream sherry
1 cup raspberry jam, melted
1 can (20 ounces) DOLE®
　Crushed Pineapple in Juice
Maraschino cherries, optional

Prepare pudding mix according to package directions, using milk and pineapple juice as liquid. Place saucepan in bowl of ice water to cool pudding; stir often. In medium bowl, beat 1 cup cream until soft peaks form; fold into cooled pudding. Cut pound cake in half lengthwise. Drizzle sherry over cake; cut cake into chunks.

Spoon 1 cup pudding into 2½- to 3-quart glass serving bowl. Top with half the cake and half the jam. Reserve ½ cup undrained pineapple for garnish. Spoon half the remaining pineapple on top of jam in serving bowl. Spoon half the remaining pudding on top. Repeat layering with remaining ingredients, ending with pudding. Refrigerate, covered, overnight.

In medium bowl, beat remaining 1 cup cream until soft peaks form; spread over top of trifle. Drain reserved ½ cup pineapple. Garnish trifle with pineapple and maraschino cherries, if desired.
Makes 8 servings.

Peach Melba Trifle

1 (14-ounce) can EAGLE® Brand
　Sweetened Condensed Milk
　(NOT evaporated milk)
1½ cups cold water
1 (4-serving size) package
　***instant* vanilla flavor pudding**
　and pie filling mix
2 cups (1 pint) BORDEN® or
　MEADOW GOLD® Whipping
　Cream, whipped
¼ cup plus 1 tablespoon dry
　sherry *or* orange juice
6 cups angel food cake cubes
　(about 10 ounces)
1½ pounds fresh peaches, pared
　and sliced *or* 1 (29-ounce)
　can sliced peaches, drained
½ cup red raspberry preserves
　Toasted almonds and
　additional preserves,
　optional

In large bowl, combine sweetened condensed milk and water. Add pudding mix; beat well. Chill 5 minutes. Fold in whipped cream and *1 tablespoon* sherry. Place *3 cups* cake cubes in 3- to 4-quart glass serving bowl. Sprinkle with *2 tablespoons* sherry. Top with half the peach slices, *½ cup* preserves and half the pudding mixture. Repeat layering with remaining cake, sherry, peach slices and pudding. Garnish with almonds and preserves if desired. Chill thoroughly. Refrigerate leftovers.
Makes 10 to 12 servings.

Peach Melba Trifle

Angel Strawberry Bavarian

- **1 package DUNCAN HINES® Angel Food Cake Mix**
- **1 package (10 ounces) sweetened, frozen sliced strawberries, thawed**
- **1 package (4-serving size) strawberry flavored gelatin**
- **1 cup boiling water**
- **2½ cups whipping cream, chilled and divided**
- **2½ tablespoons confectioners sugar**
- **¾ teaspoon vanilla extract**
- **4 fresh strawberries, sliced and fanned, for garnish**
- **Mint leaves, for garnish**

1. Preheat oven to 375°F.

2. Prepare, bake and cool cake following package directions. Cut cooled cake into 1-inch cubes.

3. Drain thawed strawberries, reserving juice.

4. Combine gelatin and boiling water in small bowl. Stir until gelatin is dissolved. Add enough water to strawberry juice to measure 1 cup; stir into gelatin. Refrigerate until gelatin is slightly thickened. Beat gelatin until foamy.

5. Beat 1 cup whipping cream until stiff peaks form in large bowl. Fold into gelatin along with strawberries.

6. Alternate layers of cake cubes and strawberry mixture in 10-inch tube pan. Press lightly. Cover. Refrigerate overnight.

7. Unmold cake onto serving plate. Beat remaining 1½ cups whipping cream, confectioners sugar and vanilla extract until stiff peaks form. Frost sides and top of cake. Refrigerate until ready to serve. Garnish with fresh strawberries and mint leaves.   *12 to 16 Servings*

Tip: For easiest cutting, use a knife with a thin sharp blade.

Old-Fashioned Bread Pudding with Vanilla Sauce

Pudding
- **4 cups cubed white bread**
- **½ cup raisins**
- **2 cups milk**
- **¼ cup LAND O LAKES® Butter**
- **½ cup granulated sugar**
- **2 eggs, slightly beaten**
- **½ teaspoon ground nutmeg**
- **1 teaspoon vanilla**

Vanilla Sauce
- **½ cup granulated sugar**
- **½ cup firmly packed brown sugar**
- **½ cup whipping cream**
- **½ cup LAND O LAKES® Butter**
- **1 teaspoon vanilla**

Heat oven to 350°. For pudding, in large bowl combine bread and raisins. In 1-quart saucepan combine milk and ¼ cup butter. Cook over medium heat until butter is melted, 4 to 7 minutes. Pour milk mixture over bread; let stand 10 minutes. Stir in remaining pudding ingredients. Pour into greased 1½-quart casserole. Bake for 40 to 50 minutes or until set in center.

For Vanilla Sauce, in 1-quart saucepan combine ½ cup granulated sugar, brown sugar, whipping cream and ½ cup butter. Cook over medium heat, stirring occasionally, until mixture thickens and comes to a full boil, 5 to 8 minutes. Stir in 1 teaspoon vanilla. Serve sauce over warm pudding. Store refrigerated.

Makes 6 servings

Angel Strawberry Bavarian

Apple Pumpkin Desserts

1 (21-ounce) can COMSTOCK® Brand Apple Filling or Topping
1 (16-ounce) can COMSTOCK® Brand Pumpkin (about 2 cups)
1 (14-ounce) can EAGLE® Brand Sweetened Condensed Milk (NOT evaporated milk)
2 eggs
1 teaspoon ground cinnamon
½ teaspoon ground nutmeg
½ teaspoon salt
1 cup gingersnap crumbs (about 18 cookies)
2 tablespoons margarine or butter, melted

Heat oven to 400°F. Spoon apple filling into 8 to 10 custard cups. In large mixer bowl, beat pumpkin, sweetened condensed milk, eggs, cinnamon, nutmeg and salt; spoon over apple filling. Combine crumbs and margarine. Sprinkle over pumpkin mixture. Place cups on 15×10-inch baking pan. Bake 10 minutes. *Reduce heat to 350°F;* bake 15 minutes or until set. Cool. Refrigerate leftovers.

Makes 8 to 10 servings

Bavarian Rice Cloud with Bittersweet Chocolate Sauce

Bavarian Rice Cloud with Bittersweet Chocolate Sauce

1 envelope unflavored gelatin
1½ cups skim milk
3 tablespoons sugar
2 cups cooked rice
2 cups frozen light whipped topping, thawed
1 tablespoon almond-flavored liqueur
½ teaspoon vanilla extract
Vegetable cooking spray
Bittersweet Chocolate Sauce (recipe follows)
2 tablespoons sliced almonds, toasted

Sprinkle gelatin over milk in small saucepan; let stand 1 minute or until gelatin is softened. Cook over low heat, stirring constantly until gelatin dissolves. Add sugar and stir until dissolved. Add rice; stir until well blended. Cover and chill until the consistency of unbeaten egg whites. Fold in whipped topping, liqueur, and vanilla. Spoon into 4-cup mold coated with cooking spray. Cover and chill until firm. To serve, unmold onto serving platter. Spoon chocolate sauce over rice dessert. Sprinkle with toasted almonds. *Makes 10 servings*

Bittersweet Chocolate Sauce

3 tablespoons unsweetened cocoa
3 tablespoons sugar
½ cup low-fat buttermilk
1 tablespoon almond-flavored liqueur

Combine cocoa and sugar in small saucepan. Add buttermilk, mixing well. Place over medium heat and cook until sugar dissolves. Stir in liqueur; remove from heat.

Tip: Unmold gelatin desserts onto slightly dampened plate. This will allow you to move the mold and position it where you want it on the plate.

Favorite recipe from **USA Rice Council**

Fruit Glazed Baked Custards

3 eggs
1 (14-ounce) can EAGLE® Brand
Sweetened Condensed Milk
(NOT evaporated milk)
1 cup water
1 teaspoon vanilla extract
½ cup red currant jelly
2 tablespoons orange-flavored
liqueur *or* orange juice
1 tablespoon cornstarch
Few drops red food coloring,
optional
Fresh strawberries or other
fruit

Preheat oven to 350°. In medium mixing bowl, beat eggs; stir in sweetened condensed milk, water and vanilla. Pour equal portions of mixture into six 6-ounce custard cups. Set cups in shallow pan; fill pan with 1 inch hot water. Bake 45 to 50 minutes or until knife inserted in center comes out clean. Cool. In small saucepan, combine jelly, liqueur and cornstarch. Cook and stir until jelly melts and mixture comes to a boil. Stir in food coloring if desired. Cool to room temperature. Invert custards onto serving plates. Top with sauce and strawberries. Refrigerate leftovers.
Makes 6 servings.

Strawberry-Chocolate Bavarian Cream

1 package (10 oz.) frozen sliced
strawberries, thawed*
2 envelopes unflavored gelatin
½ cup sugar
1 cup HERSHEY'S Semi-Sweet
Chocolate Chips
2¼ cups milk, divided
1 teaspoon vanilla extract
1 cup (½ pt.) cold whipping
cream
Strawberry Cream (recipe
follows)

Lightly oil 5- or 6-cup mold. Drain strawberries; reserve syrup. Add water to syrup to equal ¾ cup. Stir gelatin into liquid; set aside. Refrigerate drained berries for use in Strawberry Cream.

In medium saucepan, combine sugar, chocolate chips and ½ cup milk; over low heat, cook, stirring constantly, until mixture is smooth and very hot. Add gelatin mixture, stir-

Quick Chocolate Mousse

ring until gelatin is completely dissolved. Remove from heat; add remaining 1¾ cups milk and vanilla. Pour into bowl; refrigerate, stirring occasionally, until mixture mounds when dropped from a spoon.

Beat whipping cream until stiff; fold into chocolate mixture. Pour into prepared mold; refrigerate until firm. Unmold; garnish with Strawberry Cream.
8 to 10 servings.

*1 cup sweetened sliced fresh strawberries may be substituted for frozen.
STRAWBERRY CREAM: Mash or puree reserved strawberries to equal ½ cup. In small mixer bowl, beat 1 cup (½ pt.) cold whipping cream and 1 teaspoon vanilla extract until stiff. Fold in strawberry puree and 2 or 3 drops red food color.

Creamy Low-Calorie Rice Pudding

1 package (4-serving size)
JELL-O® Sugar Free Vanilla
Pudding and Pie Filling
3 cups skim or low-fat milk
½ cup Original MINUTE® Rice
¼ cup raisins
⅛ teaspoon ground cinnamon

Combine all ingredients in medium saucepan. Bring to a boil over medium heat, stirring constantly. Pour into 1-quart casserole or individual dessert dishes. Place plastic wrap directly on surface of hot pudding. Chill 30 minutes; remove plastic wrap. Sprinkle with additional cinnamon, if desired.
Makes 8 servings.

Quick Chocolate Mousse

1 (14-ounce) can EAGLE® Brand
Sweetened Condensed Milk
(NOT evaporated milk)
1 (4-serving size) package
***instant* chocolate flavor**
pudding and pie filling mix
1 cup cold water
1 cup (½ pint) BORDEN® or
MEADOW GOLD® Whipping
Cream, whipped

In large mixer bowl, beat sweetened condensed milk, pudding mix and water; chill 5 minutes. Fold in whipped cream. Spoon into serving dishes; chill. Garnish as desired.
Makes 8 to 10 servings.

Peanut Butter Shells with Chocolate-Almond Cream

1²/₃ cups (10-oz. pkg.) REESE'S
    Peanut Butter Chips
1 tablespoon plus 2 teaspoons
    vegetable shortening (NOT
    butter, margarine or oil)
    Chocolate-Almond Bar Cream
    Filling

In microwave-safe bowl, place peanut butter chips and shortening. Microwave at HIGH (100%) 1½ minutes or until smooth when stirred. Paper line 15 muffin cups (2³/₄ inches in diameter). With narrow pastry brush, thickly and evenly coat inside pleated surface and bottom of each paper cup with peanut butter mixture. Refrigerate coated cups 10 minutes; recoat any thin spots. (If necessary, microwave peanut butter mixture 30 seconds to thin.) Tightly cover cups; refrigerate until firm.

Remove only a few peanut butter shells from refrigerator at a time; carefully peel paper from each cup. (Will keep weeks in an airtight container in the refrigerator.) Fill each cup with Chocolate-Almond Bar Cream Filling; refrigerate several hours or overnight.
15 cups.

Chocolate-Almond Bar Cream Filling

1 HERSHEY'S Milk Chocolate
    Bar with Almonds (7 oz.)
1½ cups miniature marshmallows
    or 15 large marshmallows
¹/₃ cup milk
1 cup (½ pt.) cold whipping
    cream

With knife, chop chocolate bar into small pieces. In microwave-safe bowl, place chocolate pieces, marshmallows and milk. Microwave at HIGH 1 minute; stir. Microwave 30 seconds; stir until smooth. Cool slightly, about 5 minutes. Meanwhile, in small mixer bowl, beat whipping cream until stiff. Fold whipped cream into melted chocolate mixture.

Creamy Banana Pudding

1 (14-ounce) can EAGLE® Brand
    Sweetened Condensed Milk
    (NOT evaporated milk)
1½ cups cold water
1 (3½-ounce) package instant
    vanilla pudding and pie
    filling mix
2 cups (1 pint) BORDEN® or
    MEADOW GOLD® Whipping
    Cream, whipped
36 vanilla wafers
3 medium bananas, sliced and
    dipped in lemon juice

In large mixing bowl, combine sweetened condensed milk and water. Add pudding mix; beat until well blended. Chill 5 minutes. Fold in whipped cream. Spoon *1 cup* pudding mixture into 2½-quart round glass serving bowl. Top with one-third each of the vanilla wafers, bananas and pudding. Repeat layering twice, ending with pudding mixture. Chill thoroughly. Garnish as desired. Refrigerate leftovers.
Makes 8 to 10 servings.

    Tip: Mixture can be layered in individual serving dishes.

Old-Fashioned Rice Pudding

4 cups cold milk
1 cup Original MINUTE® Rice
1 package (4-serving size)
    JELL-O® Vanilla or Coconut
    Cream Flavor Pudding and
    Pie Filling
¼ cup raisins (optional)
1 egg, well beaten
¼ teaspoon ground cinnamon
¹/₈ teaspoon ground nutmeg

Combine milk, rice, pudding mix, raisins and egg in medium saucepan. Bring to a full boil over medium heat, stirring constantly. Remove from heat. Cool 5 minutes, stirring twice. Pour into individual dessert dishes or serving bowl. Sprinkle with cinnamon and nutmeg; serve warm. (For chilled pudding, place plastic wrap directly on hot pudding. Cool slightly; then chill about 1 hour. Stir before serving; sprinkle with cinnamon and nutmeg.)
Makes 10 servings.

    Old-Fashioned Fruited Rice Pudding: Add 1 can (17½ oz.) drained fruit cocktail to pudding after cooling 5 minutes. Garnish as desired.

Creamy Banana Pudding

Clockwise from top: Pudding Tart-in-a-Dish, Quick Coffee Fluff and Pudding in a Cloud

Pudding Tart-in-a-Dish

- **1 package (4-serving size) JELL-O® Pudding and Pie Filling, any flavor except Lemon**
- **2 cups milk**
- **½ cup graham cracker crumbs or cookie crumbs**
- **2 to 3 teaspoons butter or margarine, melted**

Combine pudding mix and milk in medium saucepan; blend well. Cook and stir over medium heat until mixture comes to a full boil. Cool 5 minutes, stirring twice.

Combine crumbs and butter; mix well. Press mixture on bottom and sides of individual dessert glasses. Spoon pudding into crumb-lined glasses. Chill. Garnish with prepared whipped topping and additional crumbs, if desired.

Makes about 2½ cups or 4 servings.

Pudding in a Cloud

- **1 package (4-serving size) JELL-O® Pudding and Pie Filling, any flavor except Lemon**
- **2 cups milk**
- **2 cups thawed COOL WHIP® Non-Dairy Whipped Topping**

Combine pudding mix and milk in medium saucepan; blend well. Cook and stir over medium heat until mixture comes to a full boil. Pour into bowl; cover surface of pudding with plastic wrap. Chill.

Spoon ⅓ cup of the whipped topping into each of 6 dessert glasses. Using the back of a spoon, make a depression in the center and spread topping up the sides of each glass. Spoon pudding mixture into glasses. Chill.

Makes about 3½ cups or 6 servings.

Quick Coffee Fluff

- **1 tablespoon MAXWELL HOUSE® or YUBAN® Instant Coffee**
- **2¼ cups cold milk**
- **1 envelope DREAM WHIP® Whipped Topping Mix**
- **1 package (6-serving size) JELL-O® Vanilla Flavor Instant Pudding and Pie Filling**
- **½ teaspoon cinnamon (optional)**
- **½ cup chopped nuts (optional)**

Dissolve coffee in milk in bowl. Add whipped topping mix, pudding mix and cinnamon. With electric mixer at low speed, beat until well blended, about 1 minute. Gradually increase beating speed and beat until mixture forms soft peaks, 3 to 6 minutes. Fold in nuts. Spoon into individual dessert glasses. Chill. Garnish with additional whipped topping and pecan halves.

Makes 8 or 9 servings.

Fruit and Juice Pudding

1 can (17 ounces) fruit cocktail
1 package (4-serving size)
JELL-O® Vanilla Flavor
Pudding and Pie Filling
1²/₃ cups milk

Microwave:* Drain fruit cocktail, reserving ¹/₃ cup syrup; set aside. Combine pudding mix and milk in 1¹/₂-quart microwave-safe bowl; blend well. Add reserved syrup. Cook at HIGH 3 minutes. Stir well and cook 2 minutes longer; then stir again and cook 1 minute or until mixture comes to a boil. Cover surface of pudding with plastic wrap. Chill. Fold in fruit. Spoon into individual dessert dishes. *Makes 3 cups or 6 servings.*

*Ovens vary. Cooking time is approximate.

Pudding Tortoni

1¹/₄ cups cold milk
1 package (4-serving size)
JELL-O® Pistachio or Vanilla
Flavor Instant Pudding and
Pie Filling
1³/₄ cups thawed COOL WHIP®
Non-Dairy Whipped Topping
³/₄ cup BAKER'S® ANGEL FLAKE®
Coconut, toasted*
¹/₄ cup chopped drained
maraschino cherries
¹/₂ teaspoon almond extract

Pour cold milk into bowl. Add pudding mix. With electric mixer at low speed, beat until well blended, 1 to 2 minutes. Blend in whipped topping. Fold in coconut, cherries and almond extract. Spoon into muffin pan lined with paper baking cups. Freeze until firm, about 3 hours. *Makes 3¹/₂ cups or 6 servings.*

To toast coconut: Spread coconut in a thin layer in shallow pan. Toast in preheated 350° oven for 7 to 12 minutes or until lightly browned, stirring frequently.

Baked Almond Pudding

¹/₄ cup firmly packed brown sugar
³/₄ cup slivered almonds, toasted
1 (14-ounce) can EAGLE® Brand
Sweetened Condensed Milk
(NOT evaporated milk)
5 eggs
1 cup (¹/₂ pint) BORDEN® or
MEADOW GOLD® Whipping
Cream
¹/₂ teaspoon almond extract
Additional toasted almonds,
optional

Preheat oven to 325°. In 8-inch round layer cake pan, sprinkle sugar; set aside. In blender or food processor container, grind nuts; add sweetened condensed milk, eggs, ¹/₂ cup cream and extract. Blend thoroughly. Pour into prepared pan; set in larger pan. Fill larger pan with 1 inch hot water. Bake 40 to 45 minutes or until knife inserted near center comes out clean. Cool. Chill thoroughly; invert onto serving plate. Beat remaining cream for garnish; top with additional almonds if desired. Refrigerate leftovers.
Makes 8 to 10 servings.

Hot Fudge Sauce (top) and
Coconut Pecan Sauce (bottom)

Hot Fudge Sauce

1 (6-ounce) package semi-sweet
chocolate chips *or*
4 (1-ounce) squares semi-
sweet chocolate
2 tablespoons margarine or
butter
1 (14-ounce) can EAGLE® Brand
Sweetened Condensed Milk
(NOT evaporated milk)
2 tablespoons water
1 teaspoon vanilla extract

In heavy saucepan, over medium heat, melt chips and margarine with sweetened condensed milk, water and vanilla. Cook and stir constantly until thickened, about 5 minutes. Serve warm over ice cream. Refrigerate leftovers.
Makes about 2 cups.

Mocha: Add 1 teaspoon instant coffee. Proceed as above.

Microwave: In 1-quart glass measure, combine ingredients. Cook on 100% power (high) 3 to 3¹/₂ minutes, stirring after each minute.

To Reheat: In small heavy saucepan, combine desired amount of sauce with small amount of water. Over low heat, stir constantly until heated through.

Coconut Pecan Sauce

1 (14-ounce) can EAGLE® Brand
Sweetened Condensed Milk
(NOT evaporated milk)
2 egg yolks, beaten
¹/₄ cup margarine or butter
¹/₂ cup flaked coconut
¹/₂ cup chopped pecans
1 teaspoon vanilla extract

In heavy saucepan, combine sweetened condensed milk, egg yolks and margarine. Over medium heat, cook and stir until thickened and bubbly, about 8 minutes. Stir in remaining ingredients. Serve warm over ice cream or cake.
Makes about 2 cups.

Microwave: In 1-quart glass measure, combine sweetened condensed milk, egg yolks and margarine. Cook on 70% power (medium-high) 4 to 5 minutes, stirring after 3 minutes. Proceed as above.

To Reheat: In small heavy saucepan, combine desired amount of sauce with small amount of water. Over low heat, stir constantly until heated through.

Buried Treasures

**"Treasures," such as:
    broken cookies,
    miniature marshmallows,
    peanut butter, fruit,
    chocolate chips, nuts
2 cups cold milk
1 package (4-serving size)
    JELL-O® Instant Pudding,
    any flavor**

CHOOSE 4 different "treasures" to "bury." You will need about 2 tablespoons of each treasure. Put a treasure on the bottom of each dessert dish. You may put more than one treasure in each dish, if desired.

POUR 2 cups of cold milk into shaker. Add pudding mix. Put lid on shaker very tightly. Shake very hard for at least 45 seconds, holding top and bottom of shaker tightly.

OPEN shaker. Gently spoon or pour pudding from shaker over the treasures. Pudding will thicken quickly and be ready to eat in 5 minutes or put dishes into refrigerator to chill until serving time.

Makes 4 servings

Quick and Easy Raspberry Mousse

**One 3-oz. pkg. raspberry-
    flavored gelatin
½ cup boiling water
One 6-oz. pkg. (1 cup) NESTLÉ®
    Toll House® Semi-Sweet
    Chocolate Morsels
1 cup ice cubes (about 8)
½ cup heavy or whipping
    cream
1 tablespoon sugar, optional
    Fresh raspberries for
    garnish**

In blender container, combine gelatin and boiling water. Cover; remove center of cover. With blender running, gradually add semi-sweet chocolate morsels; blend until chocolate is melted and mixture is smooth. With blender running, add ice, one cube at a time, blending until ice is completely melted and mixture is creamy. Pour into six individual dessert dishes. Refrigerate 2 to 3 hours until set.

In small mixer bowl, beat heavy cream with sugar until soft peaks form. Spoon over desserts. Garnish with raspberries.

Makes 6 servings

Banana Chocolate Chip Parfaits

Chocolate Mousse

**1½ cups cold lowfat milk
1 package (4-serving size)
    JELL-O® Sugar Free
    Instant Pudding and Pie
    Filling, Chocolate Flavor
1 cup thawed COOL WHIP®
    Whipped Topping
    Raspberries (optional)
    Mint leaves (optional)**

POUR milk into small bowl. Add pudding mix. Beat with wire whisk until well blended, 1 to 2 minutes. Fold in whipped topping. Spoon into serving bowl or individual dessert dishes. Chill until ready to serve. Garnish with additional whipped topping, raspberries and mint leaves, if desired.

Makes 5 (½-cup) servings

Prep time: 5 minutes

Buried Treasures

Banana Chocolate Chip Parfaits

**1 package DUNCAN HINES®
Chocolate Chip
Cookie Mix**

Pudding
3 tablespoons cornstarch
¼ teaspoon salt
1⅔ cups water
**1 can (14 ounces) sweetened
condensed milk**
3 egg yolks, beaten
**2 tablespoons butter or
margarine**
1½ teaspoons vanilla extract
**3 ripe bananas, sliced
Whipped topping, for
garnish
Mint leaves, for garnish**

1. Preheat oven to 375°F. Grease 13×9×2-inch pan.

2. Prepare cookie mix following package directions for original recipe. Spread in pan. Bake at 375°F for 15 to 18 minutes or until edges are light golden brown. Cool.

3. **For pudding**, combine cornstarch, salt and water in medium saucepan. Add sweetened condensed milk and egg yolks. Cook over medium heat, stirring constantly, until thickened. Remove from heat. Stir in butter and vanilla extract. Cool.

4. To assemble, cut outer edges from cookie bars. Crumble to make about 1¾ cups crumbs. Layer pudding, banana slices and crumbs in parfait dishes. Repeat layers 1 or 2 more times ending with pudding. Garnish with whipped topping and mint leaves. Refrigerate until ready to serve.   *6 Parfaits*

Tip: Cut remaining cookie bars into 1×2-inch pieces. Serve with parfaits.

Black Forest Parfaits

**1 package (8 ounces)
PHILADELPHIA BRAND®
Cream Cheese, softened**
2 cups cold milk
**1 package (4-serving size)
JELL-O® Instant Pudding
and Pie Filling, Chocolate
Flavor**
**1 can (21 ounces) cherry pie
filling**
1 tablespoon cherry liqueur
**½ cup chocolate wafer
crumbs**

BEAT cream cheese with ½ cup of the milk at low speed of electric mixer until smooth. Add pudding mix and remaining milk. Beat until smooth, 1 to 2 minutes.

MIX together cherry pie filling and liqueur. Reserve a few cherries for garnish, if desired. Spoon ½ of the pudding mixture evenly into individual dessert dishes; sprinkle with wafer crumbs. Cover with pie filling; top with remaining pudding mixture. Chill until ready to serve. Garnish with reserved cherries and additional wafer crumbs, if desired.

Makes 4 to 6 servings

Prep time: 15 minutes

Two Great Tastes Pudding Parfaits

**1 package (4¾ oz.) vanilla
pudding and pie filling**
3½ cups milk
**1 cup REESE'S Peanut
Butter Chips**
**1 cup HERSHEY'S Semi-
Sweet Chocolate Chips
or Premium Semi-Sweet
Chocolate Chunks
Whipped topping (optional)**

In large heavy saucepan, combine pudding mix and 3½ cups milk (rather than amount listed in package directions). Cook over medium heat, stirring constantly, until mixture comes to full boil. Remove from heat; divide hot mixture between 2 heatproof medium bowls. Immediately stir peanut butter chips into mixture in one bowl and chocolate chips into mixture in second bowl. Stir both mixtures until chips are melted and mixture is smooth. Cool slightly, stirring occasionally. In parfait glasses, wine glasses or dessert dishes, alternately layer peanut butter and chocolate mixtures. Place plastic wrap directly onto surface of each dessert; refrigerate several hours or overnight. Garnish with whipped topping, if desired.

Makes about 4 to 6 servings

Two Great Tastes Pudding Parfaits

Double Fudge Brownie Baked Alaska

Brownies
- ¾ cup firmly packed brown sugar
- ½ cup LAND O LAKES® Butter, softened
- ¾ cup all-purpose flour
- 1½ cups semi-sweet miniature real chocolate chips, melted
- 3 eggs

Filling
- ½ gallon chocolate-flavored ice cream, softened

Meringue
- 6 egg whites
- ¼ teaspoon salt
- 1 teaspoon vanilla
- ¾ cup granulated sugar
- ½ cup semi-sweet miniature real chocolate chips

Heat oven to 350°. Grease 9-inch round cake pan. Line with aluminum foil leaving excess foil over edges; grease foil. Set aside.

For brownies, in large mixer bowl combine brown sugar and butter. Beat at medium speed, scraping bowl often, until smooth, 2 to 3 minutes. Add flour, melted chocolate and eggs. Continue beating, scraping bowl often, until well mixed, 2 to 3 minutes. Pour into prepared pan. Bake for 40 to 50 minutes or until wooden pick inserted halfway between edge and center comes out clean. Cool completely; remove from pan by lifting foil.

For filling, line 2½-quart bowl with foil; pack ice cream into bowl. Cover; freeze until firm, 3 to 4 hours.

Heat oven to 450°. For meringue, in large mixer bowl beat egg whites at high speed, scraping bowl often, until soft peaks form, 1 to 2 minutes. Add salt and vanilla. Continue beating, gradually adding granulated sugar, until stiff peaks form, 2 to 3 minutes. Fold in ½ cup chocolate chips.

To assemble, place brownies on ovenproof plate. Invert ice cream onto brownies; remove bowl and foil. Spread meringue evenly over entire surface, covering any holes. Bake for 3 to 5 minutes or until lightly browned. Serve immediately.

Makes 12 servings

Easy Chocolate Berry Charlotte

Cake:
- ½ cup all-purpose flour
- ¼ teaspoon baking powder
- ¼ teaspoon salt
- 3 eggs
- ½ cup granulated sugar
- 1 teaspoon vanilla extract
- 2 tablespoons vegetable oil
  Confectioners' sugar
- 1 cup strawberry jam

Filling:
- 3 foil-wrapped bars (6 oz.) NESTLÉ® Semi-Sweet Chocolate baking bars
- 1 cup heavy or whipping cream
- 4 to 6 cups strawberry ice cream, softened
  Whipped cream for garnish
  Strawberries for garnish

Cake: Preheat oven to 350°F. Grease 15½×10½×1-inch baking pan. Line bottom with wax paper. In small bowl, combine flour, baking powder and salt; set aside. In large mixer bowl, beat eggs, granulated sugar and vanilla extract until thick and pale yellow. Beat in oil and flour mixture. Spread in prepared pan.

Bake 13 to 16 minutes until golden brown. Sprinkle cloth towel with confectioners' sugar. Immediately invert cake onto towel. Gently peel off wax paper. Starting at long side, roll warm cake jelly-roll style with towel inside. Place seam-side down on wire rack; cool. Unroll cake. Spread jam over cake to within ½ inch of edges; roll up cake. Wrap tightly in foil; freeze 2 hours.

Filling: In small saucepan over low heat, melt semi-sweet chocolate baking bars with heavy cream, stirring until smooth. Remove from heat; cool completely.

Slice jelly roll into ½-inch slices. Tightly line bottom and sides of 2½-quart bowl or 6-cup charlotte mold with cake slices. Spoon one third of ice cream into lined mold. Spread half of Filling over ice cream. Repeat layers; top with remaining ice cream. Cover with plastic wrap; freeze until firm or up to 1 week.

To serve, remove plastic wrap; dip mold into bowl of warm water for 15 to 20 seconds. Invert mold onto serving platter; remove mold. Let stand at room temperature 15 minutes until slightly softened. Garnish with whipped cream and strawberries.

Makes 8 to 10 servings

Strawberry Ice

- 1 quart fresh strawberries, cleaned and hulled (about 1½ pounds)
- 1 cup sugar
- ½ cup water
- 3 tablespoons REALEMON® Lemon Juice from Concentrate
  Red food coloring, optional

In blender container, combine sugar, water and ReaLemon® brand; mix well. Gradually add strawberries; blend until smooth, adding food coloring if desired. Pour into 8-inch square pan; freeze about 1½ hours. In small mixer bowl, beat until slushy. Return to freezer. To soften, place in refrigerator 1 hour before serving. Return leftovers to freezer. *Makes 6 servings*

Easy Chocolate Berry Charlotte

Philly® Cream Cheese Fruit Clouds

1 8-ounce package
  PHILADELPHIA BRAND®
  Cream Cheese, softened
½ cup sugar
1 tablespoon lemon juice
2 teaspoons grated lemon peel
1 cup whipping cream, whipped
  Assorted fruit

Combine cream cheese, sugar, juice and peel, mixing until well blended. Fold in whipped cream. With back of spoon, shape on wax paper–lined cookie sheet to form ten shells; freeze. Fill each shell with fruit. Garnish with fresh mint, if desired.
10 servings.

Variations: Prepare cream cheese mixture as directed. Spread into 8-inch square pan; freeze. Cut into squares; top with fruit.

Substitute Light PHILADELPHIA BRAND® Neufchatel Cheese for Cream Cheese.

Fresh Pineapple Melba

2 packages (10 ounces each)
  frozen raspberries, thawed
  Sugar
2 tablespoons cornstarch
3 tablespoons raspberry-
  flavored brandy
1 DOLE® Fresh Pineapple
3 cups (1½ pints) vanilla ice
  cream
  Fresh raspberries for garnish,
  optional

In 2-quart saucepan, combine raspberries and their juice, sugar to taste and cornstarch. Stir until cornstarch is dissolved. Cook over medium heat, stirring constantly, until sauce turns clear and is slightly thickened. Remove from heat. Stir in brandy. Place plastic wrap directly on surface of sauce to cover. Refrigerate.

Twist crown from pineapple. Cut pineapple lengthwise into quarters. Remove fruit from shells with curved knife. Trim off core and cut fruit into chunks. Refrigerate, covered, until serving time.

To serve, spoon pineapple into 6 dessert dishes. Top each with scoop of ice cream. Drizzle with raspberry sauce; garnish with fresh raspberries, if desired.
Makes 6 servings.

Philly® Cream Cheese Fruit Clouds

Peaches in Port

6 to 8 large fresh peaches,
  peeled and cut into sixths
2 teaspoons lemon juice
¼ cup tawny port wine
2 tablespoons butter or
  margarine

Arrange peaches on 24×18-inch piece of heavy-duty foil. Sprinkle with lemon juice and port; dot with butter. Fold foil loosely around fruit and seal edges tightly. Grill packet, on covered grill, over medium-hot **KINGSFORD® Charcoal Briquets** about 15 minutes or until fruit is hot, turning packet once.
Makes 4 to 6 servings.

Fruit Kabobs with Whiskey Baste

2 tablespoons honey
2 tablespoons whiskey
1 tablespoon lemon juice
1 can (8 ounces) pineapple
  chunks, drained
1 large banana, diagonally sliced
  into 1-inch pieces
1 orange, peeled and sectioned
8 maraschino cherries

In large bowl, combine honey, whiskey and lemon juice; add pineapple chunks, banana pieces, orange sections and cherries. Gently toss to coat fruit well. Cover and refrigerate up to 2 hours or until ready to grill.

Remove fruit with slotted spoon, reserving whiskey baste. Alternately thread fruit on skewers. Grill fruit kabobs, on covered grill, over medium-low **KINGSFORD® Charcoal Briquets** 5 to 10 minutes or until fruit is warmed through, basting frequently with whiskey baste.
Makes 4 servings.

Cheddar Cheese Pears

**3 fresh pears, peeled, cored and
  cut into halves *or* 1 can
  (29 ounces) pear halves,
  drained**
2 teaspoons grated lemon peel
2 tablespoons fresh lemon juice
**½ cup shredded Cheddar cheese
  (about 2 ounces)**

Arrange pears on large square of
heavy-duty foil. Sprinkle lemon peel
and juice over pears. Fill pear halves
with cheese. Fold up foil around pears;
seal edges tightly. Grill packet over
medium-hot **KINGSFORD® Charcoal Briquets** 15 minutes or until
pears are hot and cheese is soft.
Makes 6 servings.

Hot Fruit Compote

**1 (20-ounce) can pineapple
  chunks, drained**
**1 (17-ounce) can pitted dark
  sweet cherries, drained**
**1 (16-ounce) can sliced peaches,
  drained**
**1 (16-ounce) can pear halves,
  drained**
**1 (11-ounce) can mandarin
  orange segments, drained**
¼ cup margarine or butter
**½ cup firmly packed light brown
  sugar**
½ cup orange juice
**¼ cup REALEMON® Lemon Juice
  from Concentrate**
**½ teaspoon ground cinnamon
  Sour cream and brown sugar**

Preheat oven to 350°. In 13×9-inch
baking dish, combine fruits. In small
saucepan, melt margarine; add sugar,
orange juice, ReaLemon® brand and
cinnamon. Pour mixture over fruits.
Bake 20 minutes or until hot. Serve
warm with sour cream and brown
sugar.
Makes 8 to 10 servings.

Bananas Foster

4 firm, small DOLE® Bananas
½ cup brown sugar, packed
**¼ cup margarine
  Dash cinnamon**
**⅓ cup light rum
  Coffee or vanilla ice cream**

Cut bananas into halves lengthwise,
then crosswise. In 10-inch skillet,
heat brown sugar and margarine until sugar is melted. Cook and stir 2
minutes or until slightly thickened.
Add bananas; cook slowly 1 to 2 minutes or until bananas are heated and
glazed. Sprinkle lightly with cinnamon. Add rum. Carefully ignite rum
with long match. Spoon liquid over
bananas until flames die out, about 1
minute. Serve warm over ice cream.
Makes 4 servings.

Spiced Lemon Pears

1½ cups water
**1 cup firmly packed light brown
  sugar**
**¼ cup REALEMON® Lemon Juice
  from Concentrate**
2 cinnamon sticks
6 whole cloves
**4 fresh pears, halved, pared and
  core removed**

In large saucepan, combine all ingredients except pears. Bring to a boil;
cook and stir until sugar dissolves.
Add pears; cover and simmer 10 minutes or until pears are tender. Serve
warm or chilled as a dessert, meat accompaniment or salad.
Makes 4 servings.
Microwave: In 2-quart round baking dish, combine all ingredients except pears. Cover with plastic wrap;
microwave on full power (high) 6 minutes or until mixture boils. Stir; add
pears. Cover; microwave 6 minutes or
until tender. Proceed as above.

Snow Topped Apples

2 medium baking apples
2 teaspoons raisins
**2 teaspoons chopped nuts
  Dash of cinnamon**
2 teaspoons PARKAY® Margarine
**2 tablespoons Light
  PHILADELPHIA BRAND®
  Neufchatel Cheese**

Core apples; remove peel around top
of apples. Place each in 10-ounce custard cup. Fill center of apples with
combined raisins, nuts and cinnamon;
dot with margarine. Bake at 375°, 25
to 30 minutes or until soft. Top warm
apples with Neufchatel cheese. Sprinkle with additional chopped nuts, if
desired.
2 servings.
Variation: Substitute Soft PHILADELPHIA BRAND® Cream Cheese
for Neufchatel Cheese.
Microwave: Prepare apples as
directed. Cover custard cups with
plastic wrap vented at one edge. Microwave on High 2½ to 3 minutes or
until apples are soft. Serve as directed.

Bananas Foster

Pears au Chocolat

4 fresh rice pears with stems
½ cup sugar
1 cup water
1 teaspoon vanilla extract
Nut Filling (optional, recipe follows)
Chocolate Sauce (recipe follows)
Sweetened whipped cream

Core pears from bottom but leave stems intact; peel. Slice piece off bottom to make a flat base. In medium saucepan, stir together sugar and water; add pears. Cover; simmer over low heat 10 to 20 minutes (depending on ripeness) or just until pears are soft. Remove from heat; add vanilla. Cool pears in syrup; refrigerate. To serve, drain pears; spoon Nut Filling into cavities. Place pears on dessert plates. Prepare Chocolate Sauce; pour or spoon sauce onto each pear. Garnish with whipped cream. Serve with sauce.
4 servings.
NUT FILLING: In small bowl, stir together 6 tablespoons finely chopped nuts, 2 tablespoons powdered sugar and 1 teaspoon milk.
CHOCOLATE SAUCE: In small saucepan, combine 6 tablespoons water, 6 tablespoons sugar and 1/4 cup butter; heat to boiling. Remove from heat; stir in 1⅓ cups HERSHEY'S MINI CHIPS Semi-Sweet Chocolate. Stir until chocolate has completely melted; beat or whisk until smooth. Cool.

Flaming Pineapple

1 fresh pineapple
½ cup packed light brown sugar
½ teaspoon ground cinnamon
⅛ teaspoon freshly ground nutmeg
¼ cup butter or margarine
½ cup light rum
Ice cream, whipped cream or chilled soft custard (optional)

Cut pineapple in half lengthwise, leaving on green top. Cut each half lengthwise into four sections. Carefully cut pineapple away from peel. Remove core, then cut pineapple into 1-inch chunks; rearrange pineapple chunks on peel. Place in large baking pan or foil pan. Sprinkle with brown sugar, cinnamon and nutmeg; dot with butter. Place pan on edge of grill. Heat pineapple, on covered grill, over medium-hot **KINGSFORD® Charcoal Briquets** 10 minutes; remove pan from grill.

In small saucepan, heat rum on range-top over low heat just until hot. Carefully ignite with match; pour flaming rum over pineapple, stirring sauce and spooning over pineapple. Serve with ice cream.
Makes 8 servings.

Applesauce Yogurt Dessert

1 package (4-serving size) JELL-O® Brand Sugar Free Gelatin, any red flavor
1 cup boiling water
¾ cup chilled unsweetened applesauce
¼ teaspoon cinnamon
½ cup vanilla yogurt

Dissolve gelatin in boiling water. Measure ¾ cup of the gelatin; add applesauce and cinnamon. Pour into individual dessert glasses or serving bowl. Chill until set but not firm.

Chill remaining gelatin until slightly thickened. Blend in yogurt. Spoon over gelatin in glasses. Chill until set, about 2 hours. Garnish with additional yogurt and mint leaves, if desired.
Makes 2 cups or 4 servings.

Fruited Tilt

1 package (4-serving size) JELL-O® Brand Gelatin, any flavor
¾ cup boiling water
½ cup cold water
Ice cubes
1 cup sliced or diced fresh fruit*
1 cup thawed COOL WHIP® Non-Dairy Whipped Topping

Dissolve gelatin in boiling water. Combine cold water and ice cubes to make 1¼ cups. Add to gelatin, stirring until slightly thickened. Remove any unmelted ice. Fold in fruit. Spoon half of the fruited gelatin into individual parfait glasses. Tilt glasses in refrigerator by catching bases between bars of rack and leaning tops against wall; chill until set. Spoon whipped topping into glasses; top with remaining fruited gelatin. Stand glasses upright. Chill about 30 minutes.
Makes 6 to 8 servings.

*Do not use fresh pineapple, kiwifruit, mango, papaya or figs.

Pears au Chocolat

Fruit Whip

**¾ cup boiling water
1 package (4-serving size)
    JELL-O® Brand Gelatin, any
    flavor
½ cup cold water or fruit juice
    Ice cubes
1 cup fresh or canned fruit*
    (optional)**

Pour boiling water into blender. Add gelatin. Cover and blend at low speed until gelatin is completely dissolved, about 30 seconds. Combine cold water and ice cubes to make 1¼ cups. Add to gelatin and stir until ice is partially melted; then blend at high speed for 30 seconds. Pour into dessert glasses or serving bowl. Spoon in fruit. Chill until firm, 20 to 30 minutes. Dessert layers as it chills. Garnish with additional fruit and mint, if desired.
Makes 4½ cups or 6 servings.
    *See note, page 556 (Fruited Tilt).

Molded Strawberries Romanoff

**1 pint strawberries, hulled
2 tablespoons sugar
2 packages (4-serving size) or
    1 package (8-serving size)
    JELL-O® Brand Strawberry
    Flavor Gelatin
2 cups boiling water
2 tablespoons brandy*
1 tablespoon orange liqueur*
1¾ cups thawed COOL WHIP®
    Non-Dairy Whipped Topping**

Slice strawberries, reserving a few whole berries for garnish, if desired. Sprinkle sliced berries with sugar; let stand 15 minutes. Drain, reserving liquid. Add enough cold water to liquid to make 1 cup. Dissolve gelatin in boiling water. Measure ¾ cup of the gelatin and add brandy, orange liqueur and ½ cup of the measured liquid. Chill until slightly thickened. Fold in whipped topping. Pour into 6-cup mold. Chill until set but not firm. Add remaining measured liquid to remaining gelatin. Chill until thickened; fold in sliced berries. Spoon over creamy layer in mold. Chill until firm, about 4 hours. Unmold. Garnish with reserved berries.
Makes 6 cups or 12 servings.
    ***Substitution:** Use ½ teaspoon brandy extract and 3 tablespoons orange juice for the brandy and orange liqueur.

Fruit Whip

Lime Chiffon Squares

**¼ cup margarine or butter,
    melted
1 cup graham cracker crumbs
1 (3-ounce) package lime flavor
    gelatin
1 cup boiling water
1 (14-ounce) can EAGLE® Brand
    Sweetened Condensed Milk
    (NOT evaporated milk)
1 (8-ounce) can crushed
    pineapple, undrained
2 tablespoons REALIME® Lime
    Juice from Concentrate
4 cups CAMPFIRE® Miniature
    Marshmallows
1 cup (½ pint) BORDEN® or
    MEADOW GOLD® Whipping
    Cream, whipped**

Combine margarine and crumbs; press firmly on bottom of 9-inch square *or* 12×7-inch baking dish. In large mixing bowl, dissolve gelatin in water; stir in sweetened condensed milk, pineapple and ReaLime® brand.

Fold in marshmallows and whipped cream. Pour into prepared dish. Chill until set. Refrigerate leftovers.
Makes 10 to 12 servings.

Self-Layering Dessert

**¾ cup boiling water
1 package (4-serving size)
    JELL-O® Brand Gelatin, any
    flavor
½ cup cold water
    Ice cubes
½ cup thawed COOL WHIP® Non-
    Dairy Whipped Topping**

Pour boiling water into blender. Add gelatin. Cover and blend at low speed until gelatin is completely dissolved, about 30 seconds. Combine cold water and ice cubes to make 1¼ cups. Add to gelatin and stir until ice is partially melted. Then add whipped topping; blend at high speed for 30 seconds. Pour into dessert glasses. Chill about 30 minutes. Dessert layers as it chills.
Makes 3 cups or 6 servings.

Fruit Sparkles

DISSOLVE raspberry flavor gelatin in remaining 1 cup boiling water. Spoon in ice cream, stirring until melted and smooth. Pour into serving bowl. Chill until set but not firm.

ARRANGE peach slices and raspberries on ice cream mixture in bowl. Add mint leaves, if desired. Spoon peach gelatin over fruit. Chill until firm, about 3 hours. *Makes 10 servings*

Prep time: 20 minutes
Chill time: 4 hours

Fudgy Chocolate Ice Cream

- **5 (1-ounce) squares unsweetened chocolate, melted**
- **1 (14-ounce) can EAGLE® Brand Sweetened Condensed Milk (NOT evaporated milk)**
- **2 teaspoons vanilla extract**
- **2 cups (1 pint) BORDEN® or MEADOW GOLD® Half-and-Half**
- **2 cups (1 pint) BORDEN® or MEADOW GOLD® Whipping Cream, unwhipped**
- **½ cup chopped nuts, optional**

In large mixer bowl, beat chocolate, sweetened condensed milk and vanilla. Stir in half-and-half, whipping cream and nuts if desired. Pour into ice cream freezer container. Freeze according to manufacturer's instructions. Freeze leftovers. *Makes about 1½ quarts*

Refrigerator-Freezer Method: Omit half-and-half. Reduce chocolate to 3 (1-ounce) squares. Whip whipping cream. In large mixer bowl, beat chocolate, sweetened condensed milk and vanilla; fold in whipped cream and nuts if desired. Pour into 9×5-inch loaf pan or other 2-quart container; cover. Freeze 6 hours or until firm. Return leftovers to freezer.

Fruit Sparkles

- **1 package (4-serving size) JELL-O® Brand Sugar Free Gelatin, any flavor**
- **1 cup boiling water**
- **1 cup chilled fruit flavor seltzer, sparkling water, club soda or other sugar free carbonated beverage**
- **1 cup sliced banana and strawberries***
- **Mint leaves (optional)**

DISSOLVE gelatin in boiling water. Add beverage. Chill until slightly thickened. Add fruit. Pour into individual dessert dishes. Chill until firm, about 1 hour. Garnish with additional fruit and mint leaves, if desired. *Makes 6 (½-cup) servings*

*1 cup drained mandarin orange sections or crushed pineapple may be substituted for bananas and strawberries.

Prep time: 15 minutes
Chill time: 1½ hours

Peach Melba Dessert

- **1 package (4-serving size) JELL-O® Brand Gelatin, Peach Flavor**
- **2 cups boiling water**
- **¾ cup cold water**
- **1 package (4-serving size) JELL-O® Brand Gelatin, Raspberry Flavor**
- **1 pint vanilla ice cream, softened**
- **1 can (8¾ ounces) sliced peaches, drained***
- **½ cup fresh raspberries**
- **Mint leaves (optional)**

DISSOLVE peach flavor gelatin in 1 cup of the boiling water. Add cold water. Chill until slightly thickened.

*1 fresh peach, peeled and sliced, may be substituted for canned peaches.

Fudgy Chocolate Ice Cream

Fresh Fruit Ice Cream

**3 cups (1½ pints) BORDEN®
or MEADOW GOLD®
Half-and-Half
1 (14-ounce) can EAGLE®
Brand Sweetened
Condensed Milk
(NOT evaporated milk)
1 cup puréed or mashed
fresh fruit (bananas,
peaches, raspberries or
strawberries)
1 tablespoon vanilla extract
Food coloring, optional**

In ice cream freezer container, combine all ingredients; mix well. Freeze according to manufacturer's instructions. Freeze leftovers.

Makes about 1½ quarts

Vanilla Ice Cream: Omit fruit and food coloring. Increase half-and-half to 4 cups. Proceed as above.

Refrigerator-Freezer Method:
Omit half-and-half. In large bowl, combine sweetened condensed milk and vanilla; stir in 1 cup puréed or mashed fruit and food coloring if desired. Fold in 2 cups Borden® or Meadow Gold® Whipping Cream, whipped (*do not use non-dairy whipped topping*). Pour into 9×5-inch loaf pan or other 2-quart container; cover. Freeze 6 hours or until firm. Return leftovers to freezer.

Raspberry Gift Box

**2 packages (4-serving size
each) or 1 package
(8-serving size) JELL-O®
Brand Gelatin, Raspberry
Flavor
1½ cups boiling water
¾ cup cran-raspberry juice
Ice cubes
3½ cups (8 ounces) COOL
WHIP® Whipped Topping,
thawed
Raspberry Sauce
(recipe follows)
Gumdrop Ribbon*
(optional)
Frosted Cranberries**
(optional)**

Dissolve gelatin in boiling water. Combine cran-raspberry juice and ice cubes to make 1¾ cups. Add to gelatin, stirring until ice is melted. Chill until slightly thickened. Fold in whipped topping. Pour into 9×5-inch loaf pan. Chill until firm, about 4 hours.

Prepare Raspberry Sauce, Gumdrop Ribbon and Frosted Cranberries, if desired.

Unmold gelatin mixture onto serving plate. Cut Gumdrop Ribbon into 2 (10×1-inch) strips and 1 (5×1-inch) strip. Place strips on raspberry loaf, piecing strips together as necessary, to resemble ribbon. Cut 7 (3×1-inch) strips; form into bow. Place on gumdrop ribbon. Decorate with Frosted Cranberries. Serve with Raspberry Sauce.

Makes 8 servings

Raspberry Sauce

**2 packages (10 ounces each)
BIRDS EYE® Quick Thaw
Red Raspberries, thawed
2 teaspoons cornstarch**

Place raspberries in food processor or blender; cover. Process until smooth; strain to remove seeds. Combine cornstarch with small amount of the raspberries in medium saucepan; add remaining raspberries. Bring to boil over medium heat, stirring constantly; boil 1 minute. Chill.

Makes 2 cups

Prep time: 30 minutes
Chill time: 4 hours

*To make ribbon, place gumdrops on surface sprinkled with sugar. Flatten into strips with rolling pin. Cut with sharp knife into 1-inch-wide strips. Use to decorate as shown on page 326.

**To frost cranberries, dip into beaten egg white. Roll in sugar; let stand until dry.

Fresh Fruit Ice Cream

Frozen Passion

2 (14-ounce) cans EAGLE® Brand Sweetened Condensed Milk (NOT evaporated milk)
1 (2-liter) bottle *or* 5 (12-ounce) cans carbonated beverage, any flavor

In ice cream freezer container, combine ingredients; mix well. Freeze according to manufacturer's instructions. Store leftovers in freezer.
Makes 2 to 3 quarts.

Passion Shakes: In blender container, combine *one-half* can sweetened condensed milk, *1 (12-ounce) can* carbonated beverage and *3 cups* ice. Blend until smooth. Repeat for additional shakes. Store leftovers in freezer.
Makes 1 or 2 quarts.

Pudding Ice Cream

2 cups cold light cream or half and half
1 package (4-serving size) JELL-O® Vanilla or Chocolate Flavor Instant Pudding and Pie Filling
3½ cups (8 ounces) COOL WHIP® Non-Dairy Whipped Topping, thawed

Pour cold cream into bowl. Add pudding mix. With electric mixer at low speed, beat until well blended, 1 to 2 minutes. Let stand 5 minutes. Fold in whipped topping. Pour into 2-quart covered plastic container. Freeze until firm, about 6 hours.
Makes 6 cups or 12 servings.

Toffee Crunch Pudding Ice Cream: Prepare Pudding Ice Cream as directed, using vanilla flavor pudding mix and folding in ⅔ cup crushed chocolate-covered toffee bar with the whipped topping.

Rum Raisin Pudding Ice Cream: Prepare Pudding Ice Cream as directed, using vanilla flavor pudding mix. Soak ½ cup chopped raisins in 2 tablespoons light rum; fold in with the whipped topping.

Rocky Road Pudding Ice Cream: Prepare Pudding Ice Cream as directed, using chocolate flavor pudding mix and folding in 1 cup miniature marshmallows and ½ cup chopped walnuts with the whipped topping.

Cinnamon Walnut Pudding Ice Cream: Prepare Pudding Ice Cream as directed, using vanilla flavor pudding mix and adding 2 tablespoons light brown sugar and ½ teaspoon cinnamon to the pudding mix. Add ½ cup finely chopped walnuts with the whipped topping.

Fruit Pudding Ice Cream: Prepare Pudding Ice Cream as directed, folding in 1 cup pureed fruit (strawberries, peaches or raspberries) with the whipped topping.

Chocolate Chip Pudding Ice Cream: Prepare Pudding Ice Cream as directed, using chocolate flavor pudding mix and folding in ¾ cup BAKER'S® Real Semi-Sweet Chocolate Chips with the whipped topping.

Almond Creme

2 packages (4 ounces each) BAKER'S® GERMAN'S® Sweet Chocolate
¼ cup water
⅔ cup sweetened condensed milk
2 cups heavy cream
½ teaspoon vanilla
½ cup toasted slivered blanched almonds

Melt chocolate in water in saucepan over very low heat, stirring constantly until smooth. Cool. Combine chocolate, condensed milk, cream and vanilla in large bowl of electric mixer. Chill; then whip until soft peaks form. Fold in almonds. Spoon into 9-inch square pan or 1½-quart freezer container. Freeze until firm, about 5 hours. Garnish with additional toasted almonds, if desired.
Makes 8 to 10 servings.

Chocolate Cream Pudding

1 cup sugar
¼ cup HERSHEY'S Cocoa
⅓ cup cornstarch
¼ teaspoon salt
3 cups milk
3 egg yolks, slightly beaten
2 tablespoons butter or margarine
1½ teaspoons vanilla extract

In heavy saucepan, stir together sugar, cocoa, cornstarch and salt; stir in milk and egg yolks. Over medium-high heat, cook, stirring constantly, 1 minute. Remove from heat; blend in butter and vanilla. Pour into bowl or individual serving dishes; press plastic wrap directly onto surface. Cool; refrigerate until set.
6 to 8 servings.

Frozen Passion

Frozen Chocolate Banana Loaf

Banana Bonanza Ice Cream

    2 cups milk
    2 cups whipping cream
    2 eggs, beaten
1¼ cups sugar
    **2 extra-ripe, medium DOLE®
    Bananas**
  ½ teaspoon vanilla extract
  ¼ teaspoon salt
  ⅛ teaspoon ground nutmeg

In large saucepan, combine milk, cream, eggs and sugar. Cook and stir over low heat until mixture thickens slightly and coats metal spoon. Cool to room temperature. Puree bananas in blender (1 cup). In large bowl, combine cooled custard, pureed bananas, vanilla, salt and nutmeg. Pour into ice cream freezer can. Freeze according to manufacturer's directions. *Makes 2 quarts.*

Frozen Chocolate Banana Loaf

**1½ cups chocolate wafer cookie
    crumbs (about 30 wafers)**
  ¼ cup sugar
    **3 tablespoons margarine or
    butter, melted**
    **1 (14-ounce) can EAGLE® Brand
    Sweetened Condensed Milk
    (NOT evaporated milk)**
  ⅔ cup chocolate flavored syrup
    **2 small ripe bananas, mashed
    (¾ cup)**
    **2 cups (1 pint) BORDEN® or
    MEADOW GOLD® Whipping
    Cream, whipped (*do not use
    non-dairy whipped topping*)**

Line 9×5-inch loaf pan with aluminum foil, extending foil above sides of pan; butter foil. Combine crumbs, sugar and margarine; press firmly on bottom and halfway up sides of prepared pan. In large bowl, combine sweetened condensed milk, syrup and bananas; mix well. Fold in whipped cream. Pour into prepared pan; cover. Freeze 6 hours or until firm. To serve, remove from pan; peel off foil. Garnish as desired; slice. Return leftovers to freezer.
Makes 8 to 10 servings.

Raspberry Freeze

  ¼ cup honey
    **1 8-ounce package
    PHILADELPHIA BRAND®
    Cream Cheese, softened**
    **1 10-ounce package frozen
    raspberries, partially
    thawed, undrained**
    1 cup banana slices
    **2 cups KRAFT® Miniature
    Marshmallows**
    1 cup whipping cream, whipped

Gradually add honey to cream cheese, mixing until well blended. Stir in fruit; fold in marshmallows and whipped cream. Pour into lightly oiled 9-inch square pan; freeze. Place in refrigerator 30 minutes before serving. Cut into squares.
9 servings.

    Variations: Prepare mixture as directed. Spoon raspberry mixture into ten 5-ounce paper drinking cups; insert wooden sticks in center. Freeze.
    Prepare mixture as directed. Pour raspberry mixture into lightly oiled 9-inch springform pan with ring insert; freeze. Place in refrigerator 1 hour before serving. Loosen dessert from rim of pan; remove rim of pan.

Bananas Coco Lopez (left) and Coconut Fudge Sauce (right)

Pineapple Orange Dessert Sauce

**1 can (20 ounces) DOLE®
  Pineapple Chunks in Juice,
  undrained
½ cup orange juice
1 tablespoon cornstarch
1 tablespoon sugar
1 teaspoon ground ginger
1 teaspoon grated orange peel
  Vanilla ice cream
  DOLE® Blanched Slivered
  Almonds, toasted**

In saucepan, combine pineapple chunks, orange juice, cornstarch, sugar, ginger and orange peel. Cook and stir until sauce boils and thickens. Cool to room temperature. Spoon sauce over ice cream. Sprinkle with almonds.
Makes 2 cups sauce.

Chocolate Custard Sauce

**1 egg, slightly beaten
¼ cup sugar
¼ teaspoon salt
1½ cups milk
1 square BAKER'S®
  Unsweetened Chocolate,
  melted
½ teaspoon vanilla**

Combine egg, sugar, salt and milk in saucepan. Cook and stir over medium heat until mixture begins to thicken slightly and coats a metal spoon, about 5 minutes. Remove from heat. Stir in chocolate and vanilla. Beat with hand or electric mixer until blended. Cover surface with plastic wrap. Chill. Serve over fruit, desserts or cake. Store any leftover sauce in refrigerator.
Makes 1½ cups.

Melon Sorbet Cooler

**1 envelope KNOX® Unflavored
  Gelatine
½ cup sugar
1 cup water
2½ cups pureed cantaloupe
  (about 1 large)*
⅓ cup rum (optional)
2 tablespoons lemon juice**

In medium saucepan, mix unflavored gelatin with sugar; blend in water. Let stand 1 minute. Stir over low heat until gelatine is completely dissolved, about 5 minutes. Let cool to room temperature; stir in remaining ingredients. Pour into 9-inch square baking pan; freeze 3 hours or until firm.

With electric mixer or food processor, beat mixture until smooth. Return to pan; freeze 2 hours or until firm. To serve, let stand at room tem-perature 15 minutes or until slightly softened. Garnish, if desired, with fresh mint.
Makes about 8 servings.
  ***Variation:** Use 2½ cups pureed honeydew melon (about ½ medium).*

Microwave Classic Chocolate Sauce

**2 bars (2 oz.) HERSHEY'S
  Unsweetened Baking
  Chocolate
2 tablespoons butter or
  margarine
1 cup sugar
¾ cup evaporated milk
¼ teaspoon salt
½ teaspoon vanilla extract**

In medium microwave-safe bowl, place chocolate and butter. Microwave at HIGH (100%) 1 to 1½ minutes or until chocolate is melted and mixture is smooth when stirred. Add sugar, evaporated milk and salt; blend well. Microwave at HIGH 2 to 3 minutes, stirring with wire whisk after each minute, or until mixture is smooth and hot. Stir in vanilla. Serve warm over ice cream or other desserts.
About 1½ cups sauce.

Bananas Coco Lopez

**4 firm medium bananas, peeled
  and sliced
  REALEMON® Lemon Juice
  from Concentrate
1 cup COCO LOPEZ® Cream of
  Coconut
¼ teaspoon ground cinnamon
½ teaspoon vanilla extract**

Dip sliced bananas in ReaLemon® brand. In large skillet or chafing dish, combine cream of coconut and cinna-mon; bring to a boil. Add bananas and vanilla. Over medium heat, cook and stir 2 to 3 minutes. Serve warm over ice cream or cake.
Makes 4 to 6 servings.
  Microwave: Dip sliced bananas in ReaLemon® brand. In 2-quart glass measure, combine cream of coconut and cinnamon. Microwave on full power (high) 2 minutes or until mix-ture boils. Add bananas and vanilla. Microwave on full power (high) 1½ to 2 minutes or until bananas are heated through *(do not overheat).*

Coconut Fudge Sauce

1 (6-ounce) package semi-sweet chocolate chips *or*
  4 (1-ounce) squares semi-sweet chocolate
1 (14-ounce) can EAGLE® Brand Sweetened Condensed Milk (NOT evaporated milk)
1 (15-ounce) can COCO LOPEZ® Cream of Coconut

In heavy saucepan, over medium heat, melt chips with sweetened condensed milk. Cook, stirring constantly, until sauce is slightly thickened, about 5 minutes. Gradually stir in cream of coconut; heat through. Serve warm over ice cream or with fresh fruit. Refrigerate leftovers.
Makes about 3½ cups.

  Microwave: In 1-quart glass measure, combine chips and sweetened condensed milk. Microwave on full power (high) 3 to 3½ minutes, stirring after each minute. Gradually stir in cream of coconut; microwave on full power (high) 2 minutes, stirring after each minute.

Ginger Mandarin Sauce over Vanilla Ice Cream

1 can (20 ounces) lychee fruit
1 can (11 ounces) DOLE® Mandarin Orange Segments
1 tablespoon cornstarch
½ cup orange juice
¼ cup sugar
2 tablespoons margarine
2 tablespoons finely chopped crystallized ginger
1 teaspoon grated orange peel
  Vanilla ice cream

Drain lychees and orange segments; reserve syrup. In saucepan, dissolve cornstarch in orange juice; add reserved syrup and sugar. Cook, stirring, until sauce boils and thickens. Stir in margarine, ginger, orange peel and fruit. Heat through. Serve sauce warm or at room temperature over ice cream. Store leftover sauce in covered container in refrigerator up to 1 week.
Makes 4 cups sauce.

Toasted Almond Souffle

1 8-ounce package PHILADELPHIA BRAND® Cream Cheese, softened
⅓ cup sugar
½ teaspoon almond extract
¼ teaspoon salt
4 eggs, separated
½ cup half and half
2 tablespoons sliced almonds

Combine cream cheese, sugar, extract and salt, mixing until well blended. Lightly beat egg yolks; blend into cream cheese mixture. Gradually add half and half. Beat egg whites until stiff peaks form. Fold into cream cheese mixture; pour into 1½-quart souffle dish. With tip of spoon, make slight indentation or "track" around top of souffle 1 inch from edge to form top hat. Top with almonds. Bake at 325°, 50 minutes or until light golden brown.
6 to 8 servings.

Tropical Crisp

1 DOLE® Fresh Pineapple
4 DOLE® Bananas
1 cup brown sugar, packed
1 cup flour
¾ cup rolled oats
½ cup flaked coconut
½ teaspoon ground nutmeg
½ cup margarine, softened

Preheat oven to 350°F. Twist crown from pineapple. Cut pineapple lengthwise into quarters. Remove fruit from shells with curved knife. Trim off core and cut fruit into chunks. Cut bananas into chunks. In 9-inch baking dish, toss bananas and pineapple with ¼ cup brown sugar. In medium bowl, combine remaining ¾ cup brown sugar, flour, oats, coconut and nutmeg. Cut in margarine until crumbly. Sprinkle over fruit mixture. Bake in preheated oven 45 to 50 minutes or until topping is crisp and juices have begun to bubble around edges.
Makes 8 servings.

Banana Mocha Layered Dessert

1 cup whipping cream
2 tablespoons sugar
1 teaspoon instant coffee powder
½ teaspoon vanilla extract
3 firm, medium DOLE® Bananas
1 package (8½ ounces) chocolate wafer cookies

In large mixer bowl, beat cream, sugar, coffee powder and vanilla until stiff peaks form. Slice bananas. Crumble half the wafers into bottom of 8-inch square pan. Top with half the banana slices. Spread with half the mocha cream. Repeat layers. Refrigerate until ready to serve. Garnish with additional banana slices, if desired.
Makes 8 servings.

Ginger Mandarin Sauce over Vanilla Ice Cream

Lace Cookie Ice Cream Cups

½ cup light corn syrup
½ cup LAND O LAKES®
    Butter
1 cup all-purpose flour
½ cup firmly packed brown
    sugar
1 package (2½ ounces)
    slivered almonds, finely
    chopped (½ cup)
Semi-sweet real chocolate
    chips,* melted
Your favorite ice cream

Heat oven to 300°. In 2-quart saucepan over medium heat bring corn syrup to a full boil, 2 to 3 minutes. Add butter; reduce heat to low. Continue cooking, stirring occasionally, until butter melts, 3 to 5 minutes. Remove from heat. Stir in flour, brown sugar and almonds. Drop tablespoonfuls of dough 4 inches apart onto greased cookie sheets. Bake for 11 to 13 minutes or until cookies bubble and are golden brown. *Cool 1 minute on cookie sheets.* Working quickly, remove and shape cookies over inverted small custard cups to form cups. Cool completely; remove from custard cups.

For *each* cup, spread 1 tablespoon melted chocolate on outside bottom and 1 inch up outside edge of *each* cooled cookie cup. Refrigerate, chocolate side up, until hardened, about 30 minutes. Just before serving, fill *each* cup with large scoop of ice cream. If desired, drizzle with additional melted chocolate.

Makes 2 dozen cookie cups

*A 6-ounce (1 cup) package chocolate chips will coat 8 to 9 cookie cups, using 1 tablespoon chocolate per cup.

Tip: Make desired number of cups. With remaining dough, bake as directed above *except* shape into cones or leave flat. Serve as cookies.

Chocolate Covered Banana Pops

3 firm, large DOLE® Bananas,
    peeled
9 wooden popsicle sticks
2 cups semisweet chocolate
    chips or milk chocolate
    chips
2 tablespoons vegetable
    shortening
1½ cups DOLE® Chopped
    Almonds

• Cut each banana into thirds. Insert wooden stick into each banana piece; place on tray covered with waxed paper. Freeze until firm, about 1 hour.

• In top of double boiler over hot, not boiling water, melt chocolate chips and shortening.

• Remove bananas from freezer just before dipping. Dip each banana into warm chocolate; allow excess to drip off. Immediately roll in almonds. Cover; return to freezer. Serve frozen.   *Makes 9 pops*

Preparation Time: 15 minutes
Freezer Time: 60 minutes

Chocolate Peanut Butter Ice Cream Sauce

One 11½-oz. pkg. (2 cups)
    NESTLÉ® Toll House®
    Milk Chocolate Morsels
¼ cup peanut butter
⅓ cup milk

In small saucepan, combine all ingredients. Cook over very low heat, stirring constantly, until chocolate melts and mixture is smooth. Serve warm over ice cream or other desserts. Refrigerate leftover sauce. Reheat before serving.

Makes about 1½ cups

Quick Butterscotch Sauce

One 12-oz.pkg. (2 cups)
    NESTLÉ® Toll House®
    Butterscotch Flavored
    Morsels
⅔ cup heavy or whipping
    cream
Chopped nuts, optional

In small heavy-gauge saucepan, combine butterscotch morsels and heavy cream. Cook over low heat, stirring constantly, until morsels are melted and mixture is smooth; cool slightly. Serve warm over ice cream or other desserts; top with nuts. Refrigerate leftover sauce. Reheat before serving.

Makes about 1½ cups sauce

Luscious Chocolate Almond Sauce

1 cup (half of 12-oz. pkg.)
    NESTLÉ® Toll House®
    Semi-Sweet Chocolate
    Mini Morsels
¼ cup heavy or whipping
    cream
2 tablespoons (¼ stick)
    butter
⅛ teaspoon salt
¼ cup almonds, chopped
2 tablespoons almond-
    flavored liqueur

In small heavy-gauge saucepan over low heat, combine mini morsels, heavy cream, butter and salt, stirring constantly until smooth; remove from heat. Stir in almonds and liqueur; cool slightly. Serve warm over ice cream or other desserts. Refrigerate leftover sauce. Reheat before serving.

Makes about 1 cup sauce

**Top to bottom: Chocolate Peanut Butter Ice Cream Sauce, Quick Butterscotch Sauce and
Luscious Chocolate Almond Sauce**

Tortoni Squares

1 envelope unflavored gelatin
½ cup cold water
2 8-ounce containers Soft
PHILADELPHIA BRAND®
Cream Cheese
2 tablespoons sugar
1 17-ounce can apricot halves,
drained, chopped
2 tablespoons chopped
almonds, toasted
¼ teaspoon rum flavoring
2 cups thawed frozen whipped
topping
2 cups macaroon cookies,
crumbled

Soften gelatin in water; stir over low heat until dissolved. Cool. Combine cream cheese and sugar, mixing until well blended. Gradually add gelatin, mixing until blended. Stir in apricots, almonds and flavoring. Fold in whipped topping. Place macaroons on bottom of 9-inch square baking pan; top with cream cheese mixture. Chill until set; cut into squares.
9 servings.

Cherry-Topped Icebox Cake

Ice Cream and Orange Dessert

¾ cup boiling water
1 package (4-serving size)
JELL-O® Brand Orange,
Peach or Lemon Flavor
Gelatin
1 cup (½ pint) vanilla ice cream
½ cup crushed ice
1 medium orange, peeled and
cut into bite-size pieces

Pour boiling water into blender. Add gelatin. Cover and blend at low speed until gelatin is completely dissolved, about 30 seconds. Add ice cream and crushed ice. Blend at high speed until ice is melted, about 30 seconds. Pour into bowl. Stir in orange. Chill until firm, about 1 hour. When ready to serve, spoon into flat-bottom ice cream cups or dessert dishes.
Makes about 3 cups or 6 servings.

Cherry-Topped Icebox Cake

20 whole graham crackers
2 cups cold milk
1 package (6-serving size)
JELL-O® Vanilla or Chocolate
Flavor Instant Pudding and
Pie Filling
1¾ cups thawed COOL WHIP®
Non-Dairy Whipped Topping
2 cans (21 ounces each) cherry
pie filling

Line 13×9-inch pan with some of the graham crackers, breaking crackers, if necessary. Pour cold milk into bowl. Add pudding mix. With electric mixer at low speed, beat until well blended, 1 to 2 minutes. Let stand 5 minutes; then blend in whipped topping. Spread half of the pudding mixture over crackers. Add another layer of crackers. Top with remaining pudding mixture and remaining crackers. Spread cherry pie filling over crackers. Chill about 3 hours.
Makes 12 servings.
Chocolate-Frosted Icebox Cake: Prepare Cherry-Topped Icebox Cake as directed, substituting ¾ cup ready-to-spread chocolate fudge frosting for the cherry pie filling. Carefully spread frosting over top layer of graham crackers.

Peach Cream Cake

1 (7-inch) prepared loaf angel
food cake, frozen
1 (14-ounce) can EAGLE® Brand
Sweetened Condensed Milk
(NOT evaporated milk)
1 cup cold water
1 (3½-ounce) package instant
vanilla pudding and pie
filling mix
1 teaspoon almond extract
2 cups (1 pint) whipping cream,
whipped
4 cups sliced, pared fresh
peaches *or* 1 (20-ounce)
package frozen sliced
peaches, thawed

Cut cake into ¼-inch slices; arrange half the slices on bottom of 13×9-inch baking dish. In large mixer bowl, combine sweetened condensed milk and water; mix well. Add pudding mix; beat until well blended. Chill 5 minutes. Stir in extract; fold in whipped cream. Pour half the cream mixture over cake slices; arrange half the peach slices on top. Repeat layering, ending with peach slices. Chill 4 hours or until set. Cut into squares to serve. Refrigerate leftovers.
Makes 10 to 12 servings.

Creamy Lemon Sherbet

- **1 cup sugar**
- **2 cups (1 pint) BORDEN® or MEADOW GOLD® Whipping Cream, unwhipped**
- **½ cup REALEMON® Lemon Juice from Concentrate**
- **Few drops yellow food coloring**

In medium bowl, combine sugar and cream, stirring until sugar is dissolved. Stir in ReaLemon® brand and food coloring. Pour into 8-inch square pan or directly into sherbet dishes. Freeze 3 hours or until firm. Remove from freezer 5 minutes before serving. Return leftovers to freezer.
Makes about 3 cups.

Creamy Lime Sherbet: Substitute REALIME® Lime Juice from Concentrate for ReaLemon® brand and green food coloring for yellow.

Frozen Chocolate Graham Cups

- **1½ cups cold milk**
- **1 package (4-serving size) JELL-O® Chocolate Flavor Instant Pudding and Pie Filling**
- **1 cup thawed COOL WHIP® Non-Dairy Whipped Topping**
- **7 whole graham crackers, broken in pieces**
- **½ cup miniature marshmallows**
- **¼ cup chopped salted peanuts**

Pour cold milk into bowl. Add pudding mix. With electric mixer at low speed, beat until well blended, 1 to 2 minutes. Let stand 5 minutes. Fold in whipped topping, crackers, marshmallows and peanuts. Spoon into muffin pan lined with paper baking cups. Freeze until firm, about 3 hours. Garnish with additional whipped topping, if desired.
Makes about 8 servings.

Frozen Vanilla Graham Cups: Prepare Frozen Chocolate Graham Cups as directed, substituting vanilla flavor instant pudding and pie filling for the chocolate flavor pudding and ¼ cup chopped nuts or slivered almonds and ¼ cup diced maraschino cherries for the marshmallows and peanuts.
Makes 6 servings.

Butterscotch Apple Squares

- **¼ cup margarine or butter**
- **1½ cups graham cracker crumbs**
- **2 small all-purpose apples, pared and chopped (about 1¼ cups)**
- **1 (6-ounce) package butterscotch flavored chips**
- **1 (14-ounce) can EAGLE® Brand Sweetened Condensed Milk (NOT evaporated milk)**
- **1 (3½-ounce) can flaked coconut (1⅓ cups)**
- **1 cup chopped nuts**

Preheat oven to 350° (325° for glass dish). In 3-quart shallow baking pan (13×9-inch), melt margarine in oven. Sprinkle crumbs evenly over margarine; top with apples. In heavy saucepan, over medium heat, melt chips with sweetened condensed milk. Pour butterscotch mixture evenly over apples. Top with coconut and nuts; press down firmly. Bake 25 to 30 minutes or until lightly browned. Cool. Chill thoroughly. Garnish as desired. Refrigerate leftovers.
Makes 12 servings.

Microwave: In 2½-quart shallow baking dish (12×7-inch), microwave margarine on full power (high) 1 minute or until melted. Sprinkle crumbs evenly over margarine; top with apples. In 1-quart glass measure, microwave chips with sweetened condensed milk on ⅔ power (medium-high) 2 to 3 minutes. Mix well. Pour butterscotch mixture evenly over apples. Top with coconut and nuts. Press down firmly. Microwave on full power (high) 8 to 9 minutes. Proceed as above.

Peanut Butter Snacking Cups

- **¾ cup graham cracker crumbs**
- **3 tablespoons butter or margarine, melted**
- **3½ cups (8 ounces) COOL WHIP® Non-Dairy Whipped Topping, thawed**
- **1 cup milk**
- **½ cup chunky peanut butter**
- **1 package (4-serving size) JELL-O® Vanilla Flavor Instant Pudding and Pie Filling**
- **¼ cup strawberry preserves**

Line 12-cup muffin pan with paper baking cups. Combine crumbs and butter; mix well. Press about 1 tablespoon of the crumb mixture into each cup. Top each with about 1 tablespoon of the whipped topping. Gradually blend milk into peanut butter in bowl. Add pudding mix. With electric mixer at low speed, beat until blended, 1 to 2 minutes. Fold in remaining whipped topping. Spoon into crumb-lined cups. Top each cup with 1 teaspoon of the preserves. Freeze about 4 hours; peel off papers.
Makes 12 servings.

Creamy Lemon Sherbet

Sparkling Lemon-Lime Sorbet

1 envelope KNOX® Unflavored
    Gelatine
½ cup sugar
1 cup water
1 cup Champagne, sauterne or
    ginger ale
½ cup fresh lemon juice (about
    3 lemons)
⅓ cup fresh lime juice (about
    3 limes)

In medium saucepan, mix unflavored gelatine with sugar; blend in water. Let stand 1 minute. Stir over low heat until gelatine is completely dissolved, about 5 minutes. Let cool to room temperature; stir in remaining ingredients. Pour into 9-inch square baking pan; freeze 3 hours or until firm.

With electric mixer or food processor, beat mixture until smooth. Return to pan; freeze 2 hours or until firm. To serve, let stand at room temperature 15 minutes or until slightly softened. Spoon into dessert dishes or stemmed glassware. Garnish, if desired, with fresh mint.
Makes 6 servings; 110 calories per serving with Champagne or sauterne; 90 calories per serving with ginger ale.
Variation: For a Sparkling Citrus Mint Sorbet, increase water to 2 cups; omit Champagne. After gelatine is dissolved, add ¼ cup loosely packed mint leaves and simmer over low heat 5 minutes; strain. Let cool to room temperature, then proceed as above.
78 calories per serving.

Mt. Gretna Chocolate Fondue

4 bars (4 oz.) HERSHEY'S
    Unsweetened Baking
    Chocolate, broken into
    pieces
1 cup (½ pt.) light cream
1 cup sugar
¼ cup REESE'S Creamy Peanut
    Butter
1½ teaspoons vanilla extract
    Assorted Fondue Dippers:
    cake pieces, marshmallows,
    cherries, grapes, mandarin
    orange segments, pineapple
    chunks, strawberries, fresh
    fruit slices

In medium saucepan, combine chocolate and light cream. Cook, over low heat, stirring constantly, until chocolate melts and mixture is smooth. Stir in sugar and peanut butter; continue cooking until slightly thickened. Remove from heat; stir in vanilla. Pour into fondue pot or chafing dish; serve warm with Assorted Fondue Dippers.
About 2 cups fondue.

Acapulco Flan

20 KRAFT® Caramels
2 tablespoons water
1 8-ounce package
    PHILADELPHIA BRAND®
    Cream Cheese, softened
½ cup sugar
6 eggs, beaten
1 teaspoon vanilla
2 cups milk

Melt caramels with water over low heat, stirring until smooth. Pour into greased 9-inch layer pan. Combine cream cheese and sugar, mixing until well blended. Blend in eggs and vanilla. Gradually add milk, mixing until well blended. Set layer pan in baking pan on oven rack; slowly pour milk mixture over caramel sauce. Pour boiling water into baking pan to ½-inch depth. Bake at 350°, 45 minutes or until knife inserted 2 inches from edge of pan comes out clean. Remove from water immediately; cool 5 minutes. Invert onto serving dish with rim. Serve warm or chilled.
6 to 8 servings.

Mexicana Bread Pudding

1 cup SUN-MAID® Raisins
1 cup orange juice
¾ cup packed brown sugar
½ teaspoon *each* ground
    cinnamon and grated orange
    peel
¼ teaspoon ground nutmeg
5 cups lightly packed 1-inch
    French bread cubes (about
    6 ounces)
2½ cups shredded Monterey Jack
    cheese
½ cup chopped DIAMOND®
    Walnuts
    Cream, lightly sweetened
    whipped cream or ice cream
    (optional)

In small saucepan, combine raisins, juice, sugar, cinnamon, peel and nutmeg. Bring to boil over medium heat, stirring occasionally. In large bowl, toss bread with raisin mixture. Add 2 cups of the cheese and the walnuts; toss. Turn into buttered 1½-quart baking dish; sprinkle remaining ½ cup cheese on top. Bake in preheated 375°F oven 15 to 20 minutes or until cheese is melted. Serve warm, topped with cream, if desired.
Makes 6 servings.

Fruit Juice Gelatine Cooler

1 envelope KNOX® Unflavored
    Gelatine
2 to 4 tablespoons sugar
2 cups fruit juice, heated to
    boiling*

In medium bowl, mix unflavored gelatine with sugar; add hot juice and stir until gelatine is completely dissolved, about 5 minutes. Pour into 2-cup bowl, mold or dessert dishes; chill until firm, about 3 hours. To serve, unmold onto serving platter.
Makes about 4 servings.
   *Do not use fresh or frozen pineapple juice.

Mt. Gretna Chocolate Fondue

Chocolate Plunge

⅔ cup corn syrup
½ cup heavy cream
1 package (8 ounces)
  BAKER'S® Semi-Sweet
  Chocolate *or* 2 packages
  (4 ounces each)
  BAKER'S® GERMAN'S®
  Sweet Chocolate
Assorted fresh fruit
  (strawberries, sliced
  kiwifruit, pineapple,
  apples or bananas) or
  cake cubes

MICROWAVE corn syrup and cream in large microwavable bowl on HIGH 1½ minutes or until mixture boils. Add chocolate; stir until melted. Serve warm as a dip with fresh fruit or cake cubes.

Makes 1½ cups

Prep time: 10 minutes

Saucepan preparation: Heat corn syrup and cream in 2-quart saucepan until boiling, stirring constantly. Remove from heat. Continue as above.

"All Grown Up" Mint Chocolate Sauce

One 10-oz.pkg. (1½ cups)
  NESTLÉ® Toll House®
  Mint Flavored Semi-
  Sweet Chocolate Morsels
1 cup half and half
1 tablespoon corn syrup
3 tablespoons butter or
  margarine, softened
3 tablespoons mint flavored
  liqueur
1 teaspoon vanilla extract

In medium saucepan, melt mint chocolate morsels with half and half and corn syrup, stirring until smooth. Remove from heat; stir in butter, liqueur and vanilla extract. Transfer to small bowl or decorative glass container; cover with plastic wrap. Cool. Refrigerate up to 1 week. Reheat before serving.

Makes about 2 cups

Lemon Ginger Sauce

Lemon Ginger Sauce

½ cup MIRACLE WHIP®
  FREE® Dressing
2 tablespoons lemon juice
1½ tablespoons packed brown
  sugar
1 teaspoon <u>each</u>: grated
  lemon peel, ground
  ginger

• Mix ingredients until well blended; refrigerate. Serve over fresh fruit. *Makes ½ cup*

Prep time: 5 minutes plus refrigerating

Mint Chocolate Chip Brownie Squares

1 (21.5- or 23.6-ounce)
  package fudge
  brownie mix
¾ cup coarsely chopped
  walnuts
1 (14-ounce) can EAGLE®
  Brand Sweetened
  Condensed Milk
  (NOT evaporated milk)
2 teaspoons peppermint
  extract
  Green food coloring,
  optional
2 cups (1 pint) BORDEN®
  or MEADOW GOLD®
  Whipping Cream,
  whipped
½ cup mini chocolate chips

Chocolate Plunge

Line 13×9-inch baking pan with aluminum foil; grease foil. Prepare brownie mix as package directs; stir in walnuts. Pour into prepared pan. Bake as directed. Cool thoroughly. In large bowl, combine sweetened condensed milk, peppermint extract and food coloring if desired. Fold in whipped cream and chips. Pour over brownie layer. Cover; freeze 6 hours or until firm. To serve, lift brownies from pan using foil; cut into squares. Garnish as desired. Freeze leftovers.

Makes 10 to 12 servings

Strawberry Sundae Dessert (left) and Frozen Lemon Squares (right)

Frozen Lemon Squares

- **1¼ cups graham cracker crumbs**
- **¼ cup sugar**
- **¼ cup margarine or butter, melted**
- **3 egg *yolks***
- **1 (14-ounce) can EAGLE® Brand Sweetened Condensed Milk (NOT evaporated milk)**
- **½ cup REALEMON® Lemon Juice from Concentrate**
  Yellow food coloring, optional
  Whipped topping *or* BORDEN® or MEADOW GOLD® Whipping Cream, whipped

Preheat oven to 325°. Combine crumbs, sugar and margarine; press firmly on bottom of 8- or 9-inch square pan. In small mixer bowl, beat egg *yolks*, sweetened condensed milk, ReaLemon® brand and food coloring if desired. Pour into prepared pan. Bake 30 minutes. Cool. Top with whipped topping. Freeze 4 hours or until firm. Let stand 10 minutes before serving. Garnish as desired. Freeze leftovers.

Makes 6 to 9 servings

Tip: Dessert can be chilled instead of frozen.

Strawberry Sundae Dessert

- **1 (8½-ounce) package chocolate wafers, finely crushed (2½ cups crumbs)**
- **½ cup margarine or butter, melted**
- **1 (14-ounce) can EAGLE® Brand Sweetened Condensed Milk (NOT evaporated milk)**
- **1 tablespoon vanilla extract**
- **2 cups (1 pint) BORDEN® or MEADOW GOLD® Whipping Cream, whipped**
- **2 (10-ounce) packages frozen strawberries in syrup, thawed**
- **¼ cup sugar**
- **1 tablespoon REALEMON® Lemon Juice from Concentrate**
- **2 teaspoons cornstarch**

Combine crumbs and margarine. Press half the crumb mixture on bottom of 9-inch square baking pan. In large bowl, combine sweetened condensed milk and vanilla. Fold in whipped cream. Pour into prepared pan. In blender or food processor, combine strawberries, sugar and ReaLemon® brand; blend until smooth. Spoon ¾ cup strawberry mixture evenly over cream mixture. Top with remaining crumb mixture. Cover; freeze 6 hours or until firm. For sauce, in small saucepan, combine remaining strawberry mixture and cornstarch. Over medium heat, cook and stir until thickened. Cool. Chill. Cut dessert into squares; serve with sauce. Freeze leftover dessert; refrigerate leftover sauce.

Makes 9 to 12 servings

Chocolate-Berry Parfaits

Chocolate Cream Pudding (page 560)
1 package (10 oz.) frozen sliced strawberries, thawed *or*
1 cup sweetened sliced fresh strawberries
1 cup (1/2 pt.) cold whipping cream
1/4 cup powdered sugar
Fresh strawberries (optional)

Prepare Chocolate Cream Pudding; cool completely. Drain strawberries; in blender, puree to equal 1/2 cup. In small mixer bowl, beat whipping cream and powdered sugar until stiff; fold in strawberry puree. In parfait or wine glasses, alternately layer Chocolate Cream Pudding and strawberry cream. Garnish with strawberries.
8 to 10 servings.

Cookies and Cream Parfaits

1 envelope KNOX® Unflavored Gelatine
1/4 cup cold water
2 cups (1 pint) vanilla or chocolate ice cream, softened
1 cup (1/2 pint) whipping or heavy cream
22 chocolate sandwich cookies
1 teaspoon vanilla extract

In small saucepan, sprinkle unflavored gelatine over cold water; let stand 1 minute. Stir over low heat until gelatine is completely dissolved, about 3 minutes. Remove from heat and let stand until lukewarm, about 1 minute.

In blender or food processor, process ice cream, whipping cream, 10 cookies and vanilla until blended. While processing, through feed cap, gradually add lukewarm gelatine mixture and process until blended. Let stand until mixture is slightly thickened, about 5 minutes.

Meanwhile, coarsely crush remaining 12 cookies. In parfait glasses or dessert dishes, alternately layer gelatine mixture with crushed cookies; chill until set, about 2 hours. Garnish, if desired, with whipped cream and additional cookies.
Makes about 6 servings.

Elegant Chocolate Mousse

3 squares BAKER'S® Unsweetened Chocolate
3/4 cup water
3/4 cup sugar
1/8 teaspoon salt
3 egg yolks, slightly beaten
1 1/2 teaspoons vanilla
1 3/4 cups heavy cream*
3 tablespoons sugar*
3/4 teaspoon vanilla*

Melt chocolate in water in saucepan over very low heat, stirring constantly until smooth. Stir in 3/4 cup sugar and the salt. Bring to a boil over medium heat, stirring constantly. Reduce heat and simmer 5 minutes, stirring constantly.

Blend a small amount of the hot mixture into egg yolks; stir into remaining hot mixture. Cook and stir 1 minute longer. Cool to room temperature; then add 1 1/2 teaspoons vanilla. Whip the cream with 3 tablespoons sugar and 3/4 teaspoon vanilla until soft peaks form. Gradually blend in chocolate mixture. Spoon into 9-inch square pan or 1 1/2-quart freezer container. Freeze until firm, at least 6 hours.
Makes 8 servings.

*Or use 3 1/2 cups thawed COOL WHIP® Non-Dairy Whipped Topping.

Chocolate-Berry Parfaits

Hershey® Bar Mousse

1 HERSHEY'S Milk Chocolate Bar (7 oz.), broken into pieces
1/4 cup water
2 eggs, slightly beaten
1 cup (1/2 pt.) cold whipping cream

Line 8-inch square pan with foil. In medium microwave-safe bowl, place chocolate pieces and water. Microwave at HIGH (100%) 1 1/2 minutes or until chocolate is softened. Stir until chocolate is melted and mixture is smooth. (If necessary, microwave at HIGH a few additional seconds to melt chocolate.) Stir in beaten eggs. Microwave at MEDIUM (50%) 1 1/2 to 2 1/2 minutes or until mixture is very hot, but not boiling. Cool to lukewarm. In small mixer bowl, beat whipping cream until stiff; fold into chocolate mixture. Pour into prepared pan. Cover; freeze until firm. Cut into squares; serve frozen.
4 servings.

Very Berry Sorbet

1 envelope KNOX® Unflavored Gelatine
1/2 cup sugar
1 1/2 cups water
2 cups pureed strawberries or raspberries (about 1 1/2 pints)*
1/2 cup creme de cassis (black currant) liqueur or cranberry juice cocktail
2 tablespoons lemon juice

In medium saucepan, mix unflavored gelatine with sugar; blend in water. Let stand 1 minute. Stir over low heat until gelatine is completely dissolved, about 5 minutes. Let cool to room temperature; stir in remaining ingredients. Pour into 9-inch square baking pan; freeze 3 hours or until firm.

With electric mixer or food processor, beat mixture until smooth. Return to pan; freeze 2 hours or until firm. To serve, let stand at room temperature 15 minutes or until slightly softened. Spoon into dessert dishes or stemmed glassware. Garnish, if desired, with fresh fruit.
Makes 8 servings.

Substitution: Use 1 package (10 ounces) frozen strawberries or raspberries, partially thawed and pureed.

Thanksgiving Cranberry Cobbler

**1 package DUNCAN HINES®
   Moist Deluxe Yellow
   Cake Mix**
½ teaspoon ground cinnamon
¼ teaspoon ground nutmeg
**1 cup (2 sticks) butter or
   margarine, softened**
½ cup chopped nuts
**1 can (21 ounces) peach pie
   filling**
**1 can (16 ounces) whole
   cranberry sauce**
   **Vanilla ice cream or sweetened
   whipped cream**

1. Preheat oven to 350°F.
2. Combine dry cake mix, cinnamon and nutmeg in bowl. Cut in butter with pastry blender or two knives until crumbly. Stir in nuts; set aside.
3. Combine peach pie filling and cranberry sauce in ungreased 13×9×2-inch pan; mix well. Sprinkle crumb mixture over fruit.
4. Bake at 350°F for 45 to 50 minutes or until golden brown. Serve warm with ice cream or whipped cream.
16 servings.

Thanksgiving Cranberry Cobbler

Fresh Fruit Parfaits

**1 envelope KNOX® Unflavored
   Gelatine**
1¾ cups cold water
**9 packets aspartame sweetener
   or 3 tablespoons sugar**
**⅓ cup fresh lemon juice (about
   2 lemons)**
**1 medium peach or nectarine,
   sliced**
1 medium banana, sliced
**1½ cups seedless green grapes,
   halved**
1½ cups sliced strawberries

In medium saucepan, sprinkle unflavored gelatine over ½ cup cold water; let stand 1 minute. Stir over low heat until gelatine is completely dissolved, about 3 minutes. Stir in sweetener until dissolved, then add lemon juice and remaining 1¼ cups water.

In large bowl, combine fruit. Into 6 (8 ounce) parfait or dessert glasses, evenly divide fruit. Evenly pour gelatine mixture over fruit to cover; chill until firm, about 3 hours.
Makes 6 servings; 80 calories per serving with aspartame sweetener; 98 calories per serving with sugar.

Delightful Dessert Pancake

**1 8-ounce package Light
   PHILADELPHIA BRAND®
   Neufchatel Cheese, softened**
3 tablespoons honey
1 teaspoon grated lemon peel
1 teaspoon lemon juice

* * *

½ cup milk
½ cup flour
¼ teaspoon salt
2 eggs, beaten
**1 tablespoon PARKAY®
   Margarine**
2 cups assorted fruit
¼ cup toasted flake coconut

Combine Neufchatel cheese, honey, peel and juice, mixing until well blended. Chill.

Gradually add milk to combined flour and salt; beat until smooth. Beat in eggs. Heat heavy 10-inch ovenproof skillet in 450° oven until very hot. Add margarine to coat skillet; pour in batter immediately. Bake on lowest oven rack at 450°, 10 minutes. Reduce oven temperature to 350°; continue baking 10 minutes or until golden brown. Fill with fruit; sprinkle with coconut. Serve immediately with Neufchatel cheese mixture.
6 to 8 servings.

Swedish Apple Cake

1 cup packed brown sugar
2 tablespoons all-purpose flour
¼ teaspoon ground nutmeg
⅛ teaspoon salt
1 cup water
**2 tablespoons butter or
   margarine**
**1 can (20 ounces) apple pie
   filling**
**1 package DUNCAN HINES®
   Moist Deluxe Lemon
   Supreme Cake Mix**
3 large eggs
**⅓ cup CRISCO® Oil or CRISCO®
   PURITAN® Oil**
1¼ cups water

1. For sauce, combine brown sugar, flour, nutmeg and salt in small baking dish. Gradually stir in 1 cup water. Add butter; set aside.
2. Spread apple pie filling in 13×9×2-inch pan.
3. Combine dry cake mix, eggs, oil and 1¼ cups water in large mixer bowl. Mix as directed on package. Spread batter evenly over apples.
4. Preheat oven to 350°F. Bake cake and sauce for 43 to 48 minutes or until toothpick inserted in center comes out clean.
5. To serve, spoon warm cake and apples in serving bowls and top with sauce.
16 to 20 servings.

Apple Lasagna

Apple Lasagna

2 cups (8 ounces) shredded
  Cheddar cheese
1 cup ricotta cheese
1 egg, lightly beaten
¼ cup granulated sugar
1 teaspoon almond extract
2 cans (20 ounces each)
  apple pie filling
8 uncooked lasagna noodles,
  cooked, rinsed and
  drained
6 tablespoons all-purpose
  flour
6 tablespoons packed brown
  sugar
¼ cup quick-cooking oats
½ teaspoon ground cinnamon
  Dash ground nutmeg
3 tablespoons margarine
1 cup dairy sour cream
⅓ cup packed brown sugar

Combine Cheddar cheese, ricotta cheese, egg, granulated sugar and almond extract in medium bowl; blend well. Spread 1 can apple pie filling over bottom of greased 13×9-inch pan. Layer ½ of the noodles over filling, then spread cheese mixture over noodles. Top with remaining noodles, then remaining can of apple pie filling.

Combine flour, 6 tablespoons brown sugar, oats, cinnamon and nutmeg in small bowl. Cut in margarine until crumbly. Sprinkle over apple pie filling. Bake in preheated 350°F. oven 45 minutes. Cool 15 minutes.

Meanwhile, prepare garnish by blending sour cream and ⅓ cup brown sugar in small bowl until smooth. Cover; refrigerate.

To serve, cut lasagna into squares and garnish with sour cream mixture.
Makes 12 to 15 servings

Favorite recipe from **North Dakota Wheat Commission**

Seasonal Fruit Cobbler

Apple
  5 cups sliced, peeled
    cooking apples (about
    1⅔ pounds or 5 medium)
  1 cup sugar
  ⅓ cup water or apple juice
  2 tablespoons butter or
    margarine
  2 tablespoons all-purpose
    flour
  ½ teaspoon cinnamon
  ¼ teaspoon nutmeg

Blueberry
  4 cups blueberries
  ½ cup sugar
  1 tablespoon cornstarch
  1 teaspoon lemon juice
  1 teaspoon grated lemon
    peel

Cherry
  4 cups pitted fresh or thawed
    frozen dry pack red tart
    cherries
  1¼ cups sugar
  3 tablespoons cornstarch
  ¼ teaspoon cinnamon
  ¼ teaspoon almond extract

Peach
  4 cups sliced peaches or
    1 bag (20 ounces) thawed
    frozen dry pack peach
    slices
  ½ cup sugar
  ⅓ cup water
  1 tablespoon cornstarch
  ¼ teaspoon cinnamon
    Dash of nutmeg

Biscuit Topping
  1 cup all-purpose flour
  2 tablespoons sugar
  1½ teaspoons baking powder
  ¼ teaspoon salt
  ¼ cup CRISCO® Shortening
  1 egg, slightly beaten
  ¼ cup milk
  ½ teaspoon vanilla

1. **Select fruit recipe.** Heat oven to 400°F. Combine all ingredients in large saucepan. Cook and stir on medium heat until mixture comes to a boil and thickens. Stir and simmer 1 minute. Pour into 8-inch square glass baking dish or 2-quart baking dish. Place in oven.

2. **For biscuit topping,** combine flour, sugar, baking powder and salt. Cut in Crisco® until coarse crumbs form. Combine egg, milk and vanilla. Add all at once to flour mixture. Stir just until moistened. Remove baking dish from oven.

3. Drop biscuit mixture in 8 mounds on top of hot fruit. Bake at 400°F for 20 minutes or until golden brown. Serve warm with cream or ice cream, if desired.

8 Servings

Blueberry Crisp

Rice Crêpes

1 carton (8 ounces) egg
    substitute*
⅔ cup evaporated skim milk
1 tablespoon margarine,
    melted
½ cup all-purpose flour
1 tablespoon granulated
    sugar
1 cup cooked rice
    Vegetable cooking spray
2½ cups fresh fruit
    (strawberries,
    raspberries, blueberries,
    or other favorite fruit)
    Low-sugar fruit spread
    (optional)
    Light sour cream (optional)
1 tablespoon confectioner's
    sugar for garnish
    (optional)

Rice Crêpe

Combine egg substitute, milk, and margarine in small bowl. Stir in flour and granulated sugar until smooth and well blended. Stir in rice; let stand 5 minutes. Heat 8-inch nonstick skillet or crêpe pan; coat with cooking spray. Spoon ¼ cup batter into pan. Lift pan off heat; quickly tilt pan in rotating motion so that bottom of pan is completely covered with batter. Place pan back on heat and continue cooking until surface is dry, about 45 seconds. Turn crêpe over and cook 15 to 20 seconds; set aside. Continue with remaining crêpe batter. Place waxed paper between crêpes. Spread each crêpe with your favorite filling: strawberries, raspberries, blueberries, fruit spread, or sour cream. Roll up and sprinkle with confectioner's sugar for garnish.

Makes 10 crêpes

*Substitute 8 egg whites or 4 eggs for 1 carton (8 ounces) egg substitute, if desired.

Favorite recipe from **USA Rice Council**

Blueberry Crisp

3 cups cooked brown rice
3 cups fresh blueberries
¼ cup plus 3 tablespoons
    firmly packed brown
    sugar, divided
    Vegetable cooking spray
⅓ cup rice bran
¼ cup whole-wheat flour
¼ cup chopped walnuts
1 teaspoon ground cinnamon
3 tablespoons margarine

Combine rice, blueberries, and 3 tablespoons sugar. Coat 8 individual custard cups or 2-quart baking dish with cooking spray. Place rice mixture in cups or baking dish; set aside. Combine bran, flour, walnuts, remaining ¼ cup sugar, and cinnamon in bowl. Cut in margarine with pastry blender until mixture resembles coarse meal. Sprinkle over rice mixture. Bake at 375°F. for 15 to 20 minutes or until thoroughly heated. Serve warm.

Makes 8 servings

Favorite recipe from **USA Rice Council**

ACKNOWLEDGMENTS

The publishers would like to thank the companies and organizations
listed below for the use of their recipes in this book.

American Dairy Association
Arm & Hammer Division, Church & Dwight Co., Inc.
Armour Swift-Eckrich
Bel Paese Sales Company
Best Foods, a Division of CPC International Inc.
Black-Eyed Pea Jamboree—Athens, Texas
Blue Diamond Growers
Borden Kitchens, Borden, Inc.
California Apricot Advisory Board
California Tree Fruit Agreement
Canned Food Information Council
Carnation, Nestlé Food Company
Castroville Artichoke Festival
Checkerboard Kitchens, Ralston Purina Company
Chef Paul Prudhomme's Magic Seasoning Blends™
Clear Springs Trout Company
Contadina Foods, Inc., Nestlé Food Company
Curtice Burns, Inc.
Delmarva Poultry Industry, Inc.
Del Monte Corporation
Diamond Walnut Growers, Inc.
Dole Food Company, Inc.
Domino Sugar Corporation
Filippo Berio Olive Oil

Florida Department of Citrus
The Fresh Garlic Association
Heinz U.S.A.
Hershey Chocolate U.S.A.
The HVR Company
Kahlúa Liqueur
Kansas Poultry Association
Keebler Company
Kellogg Company
Kikkoman International Inc.
The Kingsford Products Company
Kraft General Foods, Inc.
Land O'Lakes, Inc.
Lawry's® Foods, Inc.
Leaf, Inc.
Libby's, Nestlé Food Company
Thomas J. Lipton Co.
M&M/Mars
McIlhenny Company
Nabisco Foods Group
National Fisheries Institute
National Live Stock & Meat Board
National Pasta Association
National Pecan Marketing Council
National Pork Producers Council
National Sunflower Association
National Turkey Federation
Nestlé Chocolate and Confection Company

New Jersey Department of Agriculture
Norseland Foods, Inc.
North Dakota Beef Commission
North Dakota Dairy Promotion Commission
North Dakota Wheat Commission
Ocean Spray Cranberries, Inc.
Oklahoma Peanut Commission
Pace Foods, Inc.
Perdue Farms
Pet Incorporated
The Procter & Gamble Company, Inc.
The Quaker Oats Company
Reckitt & Colman Inc.
Roman Meal Company
Sargento Cheese Company, Inc.
Sokol and Company
Southeast United Dairy Industry Association, Inc.
StarKist Seafood Company
Sun•Maid Growers of California
Uncle Ben's Rice
USA Rice Council
Walnut Marketing Board
Washington Apple Commission
Western New York Apple Growers Association, Inc.
Wisconsin Milk Marketing Board

PHOTO CREDITS

The publishers would like to thank the companies and organizations
listed below for the use of their photographs in this book.

Armour Swift-Eckrich
Bel Paese Sales Company
Best Foods, a Division of CPC International Inc.
Borden Kitchens, Borden, Inc.
California Apricot Advisory Board
California Tree Fruit Agreement
Canned Food Information Council
Checkerboard Kitchens, Ralston Purina Company
Chef Paul Prudhomme's Magic Seasoning Blends™
Contadina Foods, Inc., Nestlé Food Company

Dole Food Company, Inc.
Heinz U.S.A.
Hershey Chocolate U.S.A.
The HVR Company
Keebler Company
Kellogg Company
Kikkoman International Inc.
Kraft General Foods, Inc.
Lawry's® Foods, Inc.
Thomas J. Lipton Co.
McIlhenny Company
Nabisco Foods Group
National Live Stock & Meat Board
National Pork Producers Council

National Turkey Federation
Nestlé Chocolate and Confection Company
Norseland Foods, Inc.
Perdue Farms
The Procter & Gamble Company, Inc.
The Quaker Oats Company
Reckitt & Colman Inc.
Sargento Cheese Company, Inc.
StarKist Seafood Company
Sun•Maid Growers of California
USA Rice Council
Wisconsin Milk Marketing Board

INDEX

METRIC CONVERSION CHART

VOLUME MEASUREMENT (dry)

⅛ teaspoon = .5 mL
¼ teaspoon = 1 mL
½ teaspoon = 2 mL
¾ teaspoon = 4 mL
1 teaspoon = 5 mL
1 tablespoon = 15 mL
2 tablespoons = 25 mL
¼ cup = 50 mL
⅓ cup = 75 mL
⅔ cup = 150 mL
¾ cup = 175 mL
1 cup = 250 mL
2 cups = 1 pint = 500 mL
3 cups = 750 mL
4 cups = 1 quart = 1 L

VOLUME MEASUREMENT (fluid)

1 fluid ounce (2 tablespoons) = 30 mL
4 fluid ounces (½ cup) = 125 mL
8 fluid ounces (1 cup) = 250 mL
12 fluid ounces (1½ cups) = 375 mL
16 fluid ounces (2 cups) = 500 mL

WEIGHT (MASS)

½ ounce = 15 g
1 ounce = 30 g
3 ounces = 85 g
3.75 ounces = 100 g
4 ounces = 115 g
8 ounces = 225 g
12 ounces = 340 g
16 ounces = 1 pound = 450 g

DIMENSION

1/16 inch = 2 mm
⅛ inch = 3 mm
¼ inch = 6 mm
½ inch = 1.5 cm
¾ inch = 2 cm
1 inch = 2.5 cm

OVEN TEMPERATURES

250°F = 120°C
275°F = 140°C
300°F = 150°C
325°F = 160°C
350°F = 180°C
375°F = 190°C
400°F = 200°C
425°F = 220°C
450°F = 230°C

BAKING PAN SIZES

Utensil	Size in Inches/Quarts	Metric Volume	Size in Centimeters
Baking or	8 × 8 × 2	2 L	20 × 20 × 5
Cake pan	9 × 9 × 2	2.5 L	22 × 22 × 5
(square or	12 × 8 × 2	3 L	30 × 20 × 5
rectangular)	13 × 9 × 2	3.5 L	33 × 23 × 5
Loaf Pan	8 × 4 × 3	1.5 L	20 × 10 × 7
	9 × 5 × 3	2 L	23 × 13 × 7
Round Layer	8 × 1½	1.2 L	20 × 4
Cake Pan	9 × 1½	1.5 L	23 × 4
Pie Plate	8 × 1¼	750 mL	20 × 3
	9 × 1¼	1 L	23 × 3
Baking Dish	1 quart	1 L	
or Casserole	1½ quart	1.5 L	
	2 quart	2 L